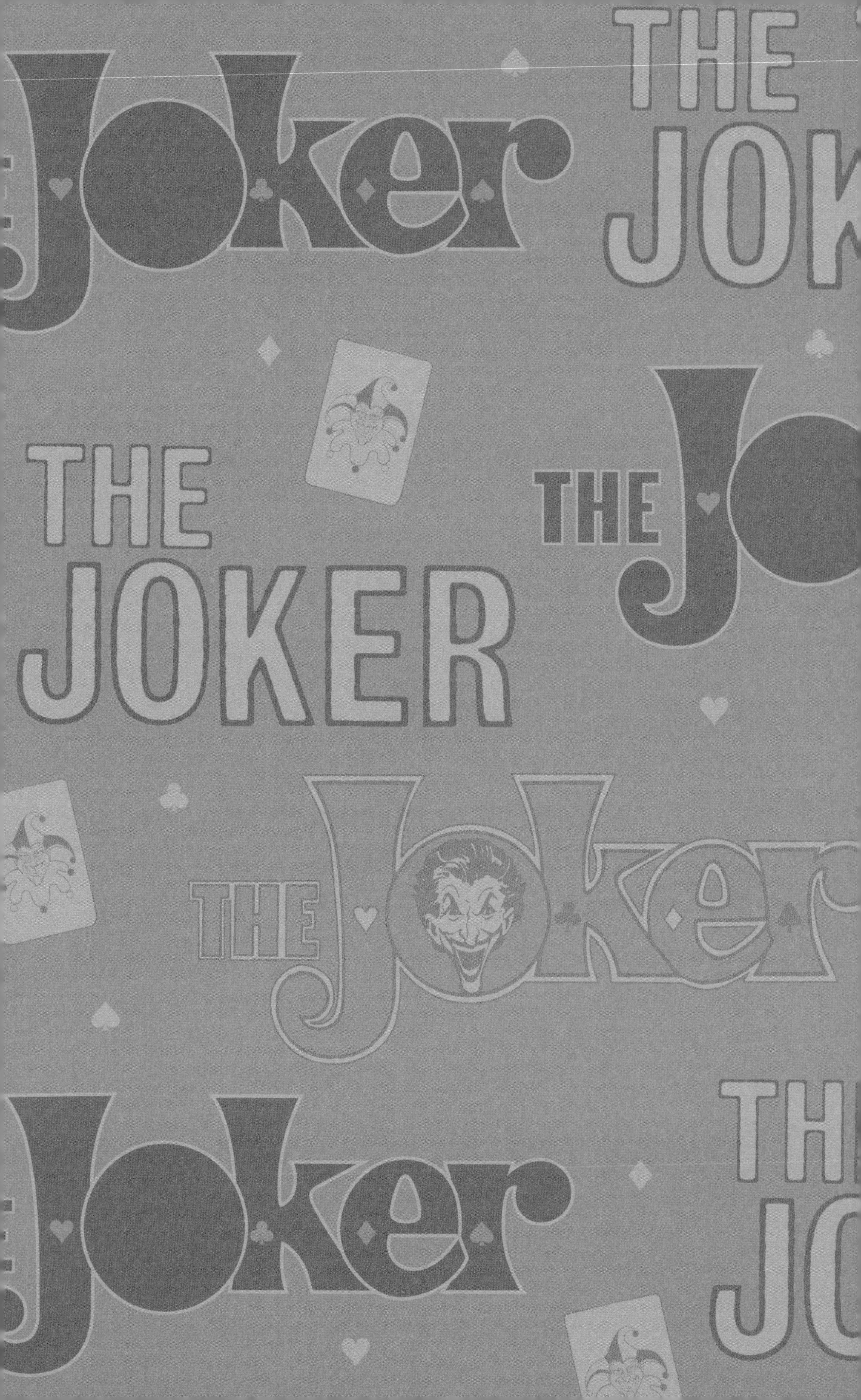
Joker
THE JOKER
THE JOKER
THE Jo
THE Joker
Joker
THE JO

THE Joker

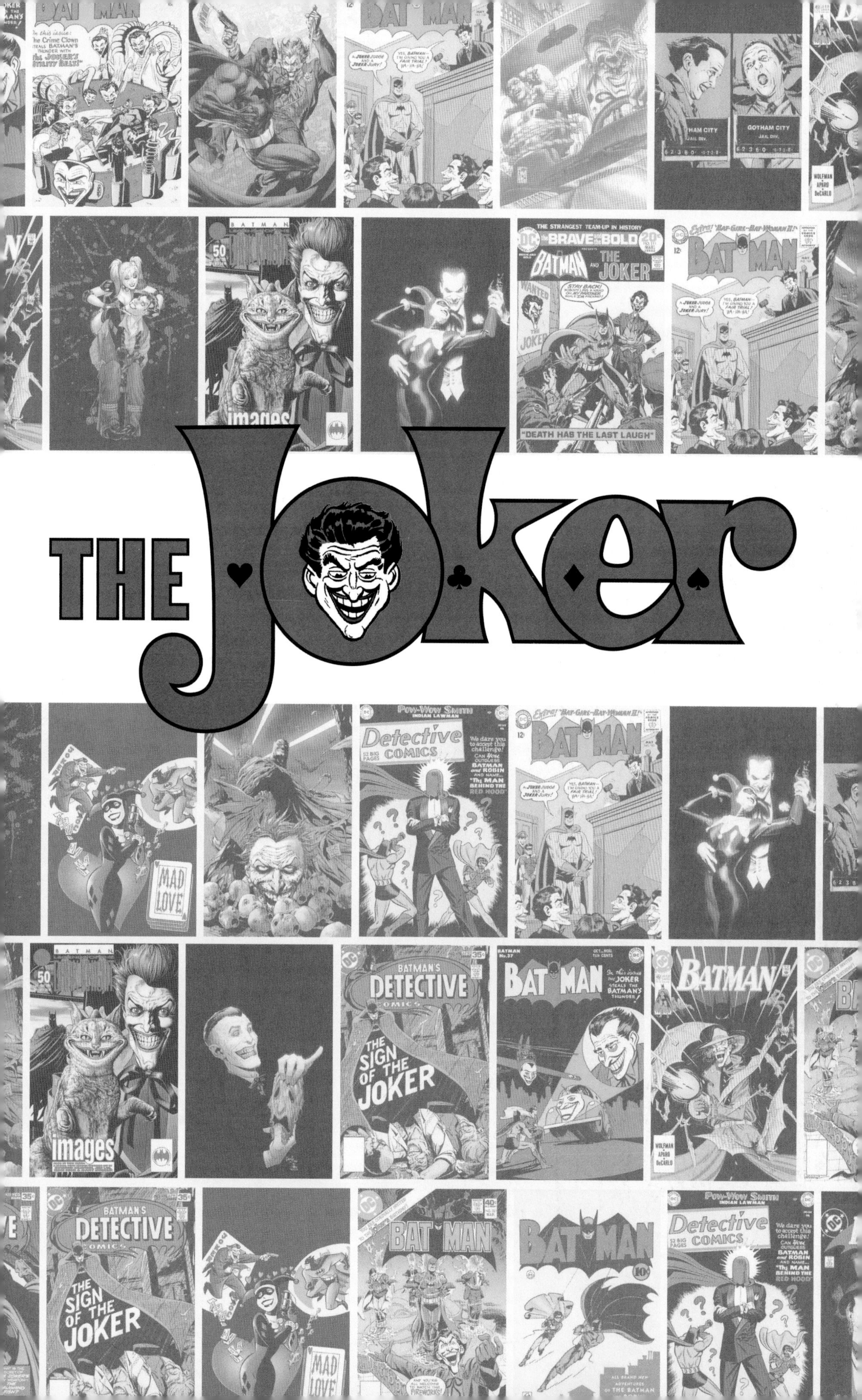

BATMAN
In this issue: The Crime Clown steals Batman's thunder with the Joker's utility belt!
GOTHAM CITY
JAIL DIV.
WOLFMAN
APARO
DeCARLO
THE STRANGEST TEAM-UP IN HISTORY
THE BRAVE AND THE BOLD
BATMAN AND THE JOKER
STAY BACK! NOBODY LAYS A HAND ON MY PRISONER!
WANTED
"DEATH HAS THE LAST LAUGH"
A JOKER JUDGE AND A JOKER JURY!
YES, BATMAN— I'M GIVING YOU A FAIR TRIAL! HA-HA-HA!
images
MAD LOVE
POW-WOW SMITH
INDIAN LAWMAN
Detective COMICS
52 BIG PAGES
We dare you to accept this challenge! Can you outguess Batman and Robin and name... "The Man Behind the Red Hood"
BATMAN'S DETECTIVE COMICS
THE SIGN OF THE JOKER

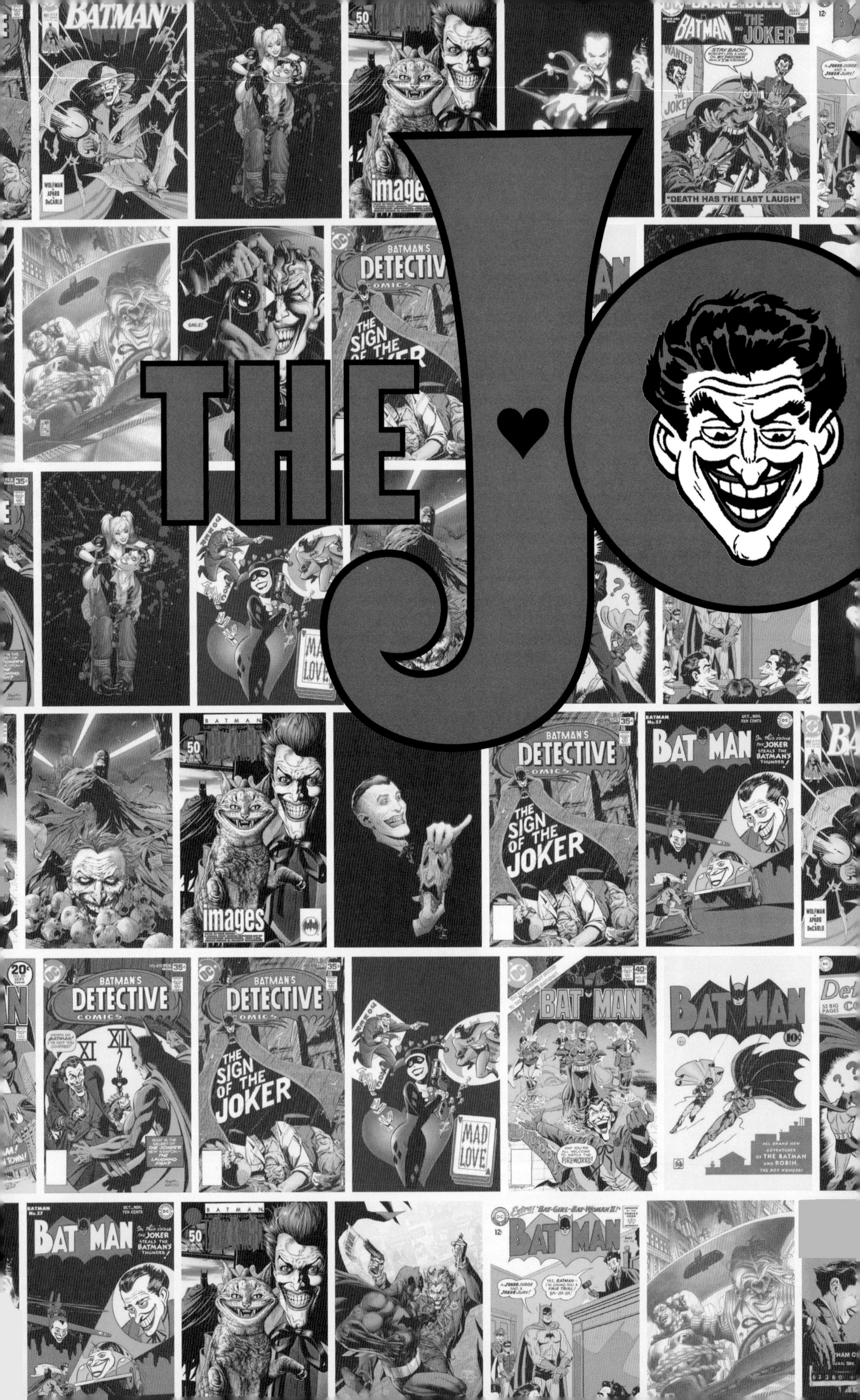
THE J♥
BATMAN
WOLFMAN APARO DeCARLO
images
THE BRAVE AND THE BOLD
BATMAN AND THE JOKER
"DEATH HAS THE LAST LAUGH"
SMILE!
BATMAN'S DETECTIVE COMICS
THE SIGN OF THE JOKER
MAD LOVE
BATMAN No. 37
In this issue THE JOKER STEALS THE BATMAN'S THUNDER!
ALL BRAND NEW ADVENTURES OF THE BATMAN AND ROBIN, THE BOY WONDER!
AND YOU'RE ALL WELCOME TO WATCH THE FIREWORKS!
"BAT-GIRL—BAT-WOMAN II!"
A JOKER JUDGE AND A JOKER JURY!
YES, BATMAN— I'M GIVING YOU A FAIR TRIAL! HA-HA-HA!

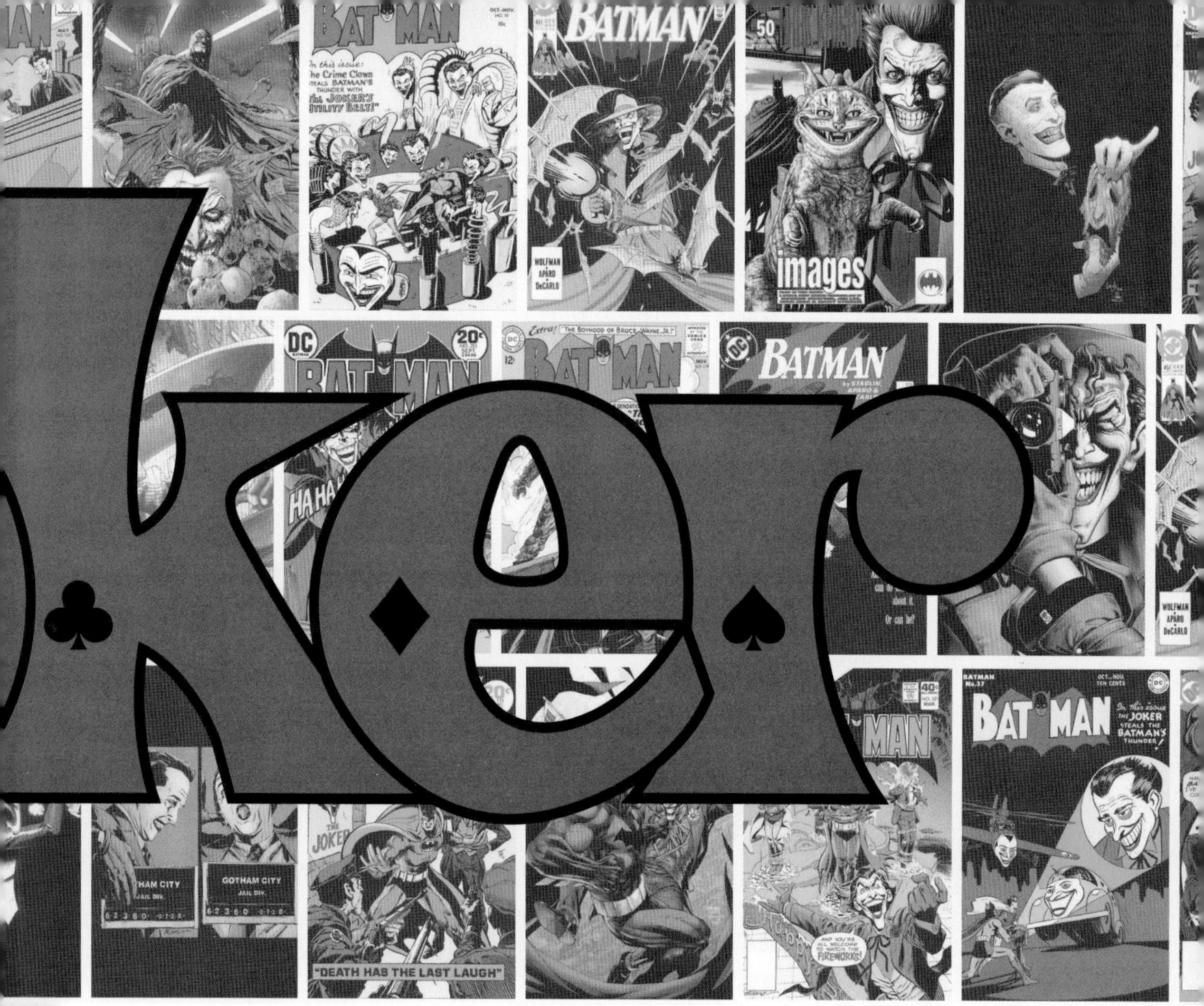
BATMAN
The Crime Clown steals Batman's thunder with The Joker's utility belt!
images
"DEATH HAS THE LAST LAUGH"
GOTHAM CITY JAIL DIV.
AND YOU'RE ALL WELCOME TO WATCH THE FIREWORKS!
In this issue the JOKER steals the BATMAN'S thunder!

80 YEARS of THE CLOWN PRINCE OF CRIME

the DELUXE EDITION

JIM LEE, SCOTT WILLIAMS,
and **ALEX SINCLAIR**
collection cover artists

BATMAN created by **BOB KANE**
with **BILL FINGER**
SUPERMAN created by
JERRY SIEGEL and **JOE SHUSTER**
By special arrangement with the Jerry Siegel family

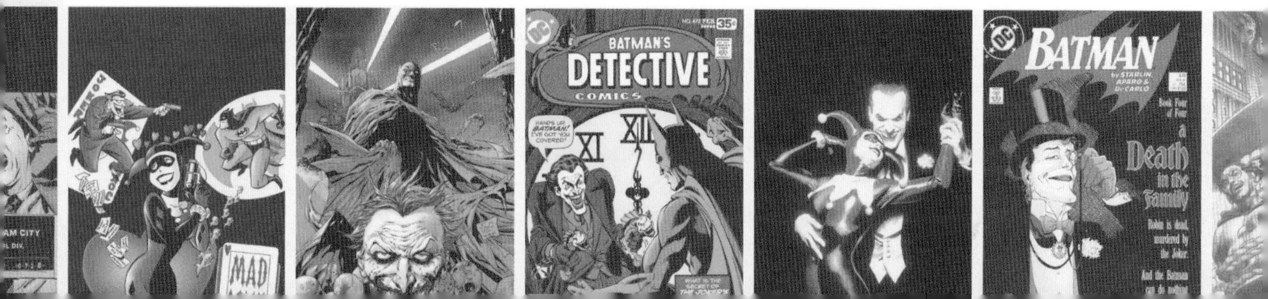
BATMAN'S DETECTIVE COMICS
BATMAN
Death in the Family

50
images
BATMAN'S
DETECTIVE
COMICS
THE SIGN OF THE JOKER
BAT MAN
In this issue THE JOKER STEALS THE BATMAN'S THUNDER!
WOLFMAN
APARO
DeCARLO

WHITNEY ELLSWORTH JACK SCHIFF JULIUS SCHWARTZ PAUL LEVITZ DENNIS O'NEIL ARCHIE GOODWIN SCOTT PETERSON BOB SCHRECK MATT IDELSON PETER J. TOMASI MIKE MARTS	EDITORS – ORIGINAL SERIES
E. NELSON BRIDWELL MICHAEL SIGLAIN JANELLE ASSELIN KATIE KUBERT	ASSOCIATE EDITORS – ORIGINAL SERIES
DAN RASPLER BILL KAPLAN DARREN VINCENZO MORGAN DONTANVILLE NACHIE CASTRO	ASSISTANT EDITORS – ORIGINAL SERIES
JEB WOODARD	GROUP EDITOR – COLLECTED EDITIONS
ERIKA ROTHBERG	EDITOR – COLLECTED EDITION
ALEX GALER	ASSOCIATE EDITOR – COLLECTED EDITION
STEVE COOK	DESIGN DIRECTOR – BOOKS
MEGEN BELLERSEN	PUBLICATION DESIGN
ERIN VANOVER	PUBLICATION PRODUCTION
BOB HARRAS	SENIOR VP – EDITOR-IN-CHIEF, DC COMICS
DAN DIDIO	PUBLISHER
JIM LEE	PUBLISHER & CHIEF CREATIVE OFFICER
BOBBIE CHASE	VP – NEW PUBLISHING INITIATIVES
DON FALLETTI	VP – MANUFACTURING OPERATIONS & WORKFLOW MANAGEMENT
LAWRENCE GANEM	VP – TALENT SERVICES
ALISON GILL	SENIOR VP – MANUFACTURING & OPERATIONS
HANK KANALZ	SENIOR VP – PUBLISHING STRATEGY & SUPPORT SERVICES
DAN MIRON	VP – PUBLISHING OPERATIONS
NICK J. NAPOLITANO	VP – MANUFACTURING ADMINISTRATION & DESIGN
NANCY SPEARS	VP – SALES
JONAH WEILAND	VP – MARKETING & CREATIVE SERVICES
MICHELE R. WELLS	VP & EXECUTIVE EDITOR, YOUNG READER

THE JOKER: 80 YEARS OF THE CLOWN PRINCE OF CRIME: THE DELUXE EDITION

DC Comics, 2900 West Alameda Ave., Burbank, CA 91505
Printed by Transcontinental Interglobe, Beauceville, QC, Canada. 4/10/20. First Printing.
ISBN: 978-1-4012-9993-4

Library of Congress Cataloging-in-Publication Data is available.

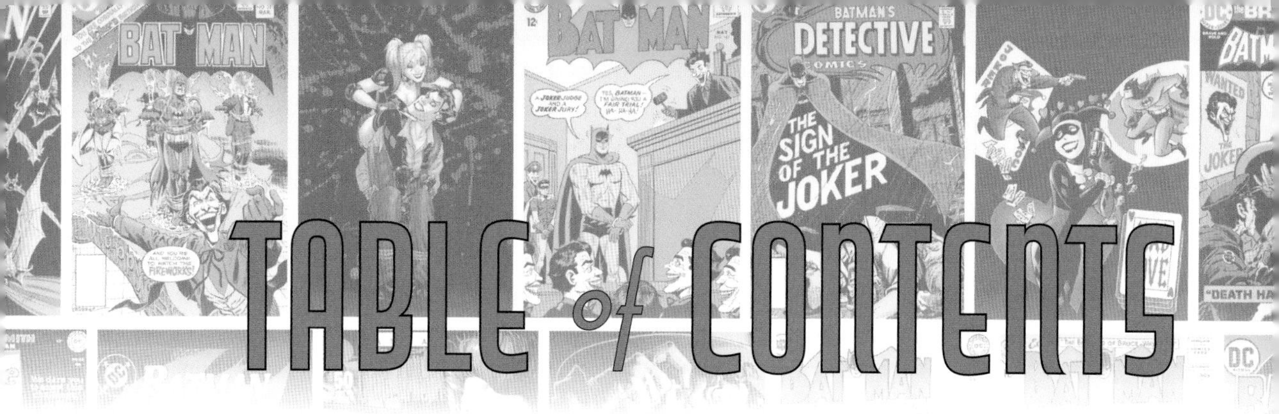
BATMAN
BATMAN'S
DETECTIVE
COMICS
THE SIGN OF THE JOKER

TABLE of CONTENTS

BATMAN
images
BATMAN
THE JOKER
"DEATH HAS THE LAST LAUGH"
BATMAN'S
DETECTIVE

Titles in parentheses were originally untitled and are titled here for reader convenience.

Some comics reprinted in this volume were produced in a time when racism played a larger role in society and popular culture both consciously and unconsciously. They are presented here without alteration for historical reference.

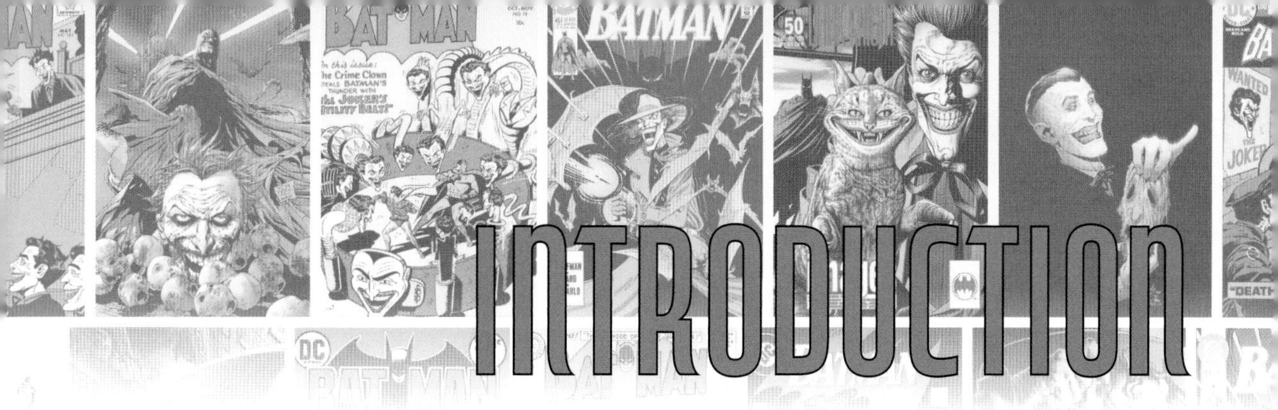

INTRODUCTION

by **DAN DiDIO**

Of all the introductions I've written over the years, this one ranks among the most unusual. Out of context, it might seem strange that we're highlighting the 80-year killing spree of Gotham City's most recognized mass murderer. A despicable character who strikes fear, not inspiration, in everyone he encounters. This is not someone you'd normally celebrate, and yet here we are. I'm talking about, of course, the Joker: Gotham's Clown Prince of Crime. The villainous creature so closely associated with the greatest moments and stories in Batman's history, it's hard to imagine one without the other.

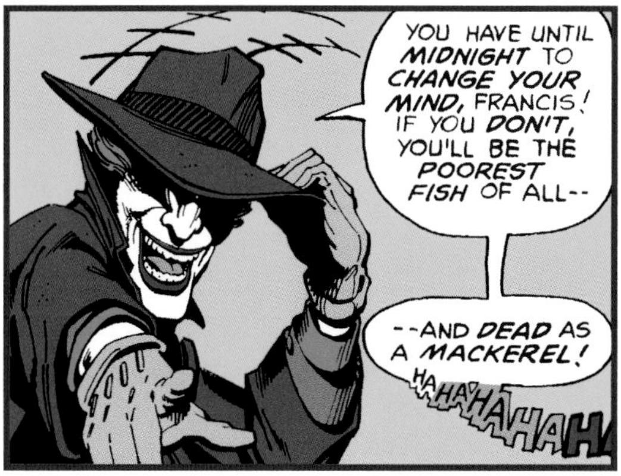
YOU HAVE UNTIL *MIDNIGHT* TO *CHANGE YOUR MIND,* FRANCIS! IF YOU *DON'T,* YOU'LL BE THE *POOREST FISH* OF ALL--
--AND *DEAD* AS A *MACKEREL!*
HAHAHAHAHAH

I'm sure when Bill Finger and Jerry Robinson, working with Bob Kane, created the Joker, they knew they had something special. But how special it wound up being, I have to believe, was something beyond even their wildest dreams. From the moment of his introduction in *Batman* #1, the Joker had a look and style all his own. And while so many villains (and heroes) came with a patented origin story that defined their motivations, the Joker's background was always cloaked in mystery. An agent of chaos, his only true motivation was to challenge the order Batman desperately craved.

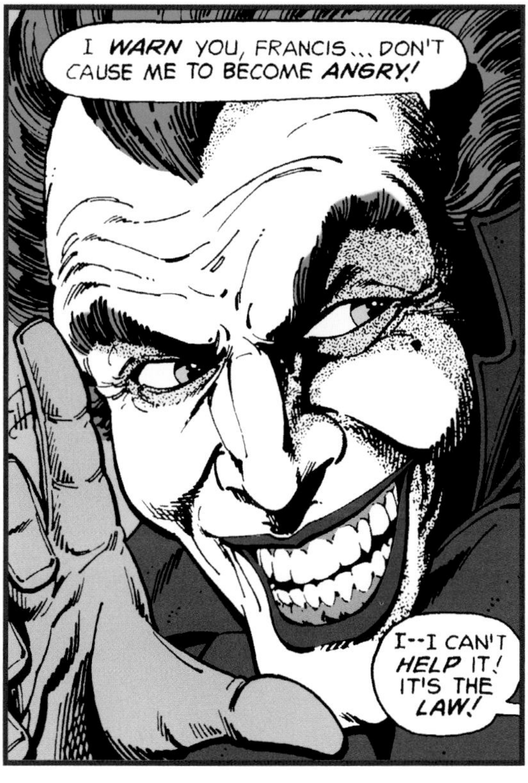
I *WARN* YOU, FRANCIS... DON'T CAUSE ME TO BECOME *ANGRY!*
I--I CAN'T *HELP* IT! IT'S THE *LAW!*

Over the years, there have been several attempts to create a defining origin for the Joker. Yet instead of bringing clarity and enlightening us as to his past, each story led us down shadowed alleys of misdirection designed to conflict and contradict, and to this day, in comics, no one true origin has emerged. If you ask me, I prefer it that way. With the Joker, not knowing is half the fun.

Of course, the other half of the fun is the mayhem he brought to the stories we've told in the form of a murderer's row of comics all-stars. A great character usually attracts great talent, and the list of creators who have plied their craft in telling his stories is a veritable who's who of comics' greatest talents. Now,

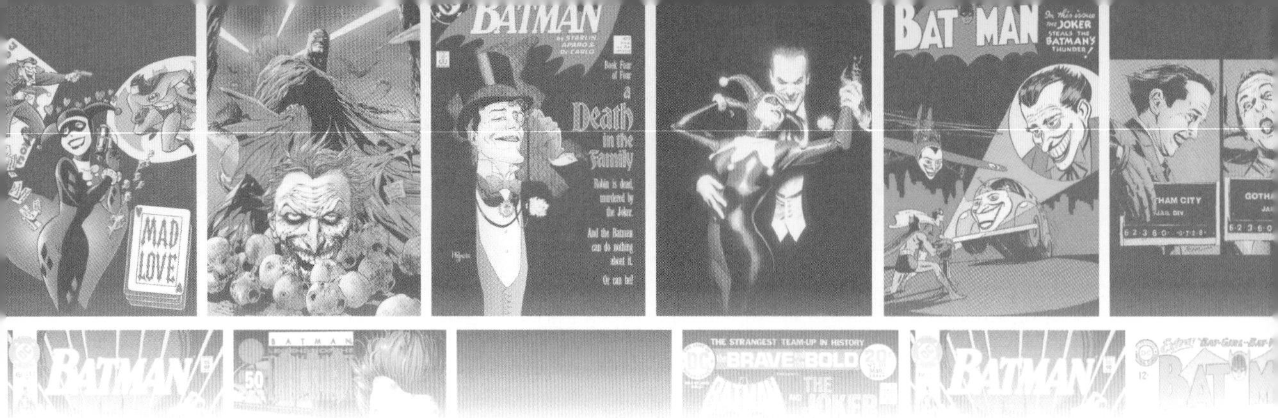
MAD LOVE
BATMAN
Book Four of Four
a Death in the Family
Robin is dead, murdered by the Joker.
And the Batman can do nothing about it.
Or can he?
BAT MAN
In this issue the JOKER steals the BATMAN'S THUNDER!
THE STRANGEST TEAM-UP IN HISTORY
BATMAN

normally I would list out all the folks involved, but in this case I decided to forgo that process for a simple reason: there are just too many amazing talents to name and I'm always nervous about leaving someone out. So look through this book and think of the names that have made an impact in comics over the last 80 years, and you'll probably find a Joker story in their portfolio. And I can tell you, each and every one of those stories has fed into my passion and love of comics. The Joker touches the primal fear in all of us. His battle cry is a siren's call for anarchy driven by an unrelenting urge to push society to the brink of madness, a place where he permanently resides. And we, as the reader, get to enjoy the sheer pleasure these stories bring.

We have the greatest hero in Batman, so it only makes sense that we should have the greatest villain in the Joker.

So sit back and relax, and get swept up in the madness and mayhem that is the Joker.

There's no better ride in comics.

Dan DiDio
DC Comics Co-Publisher
January 2020

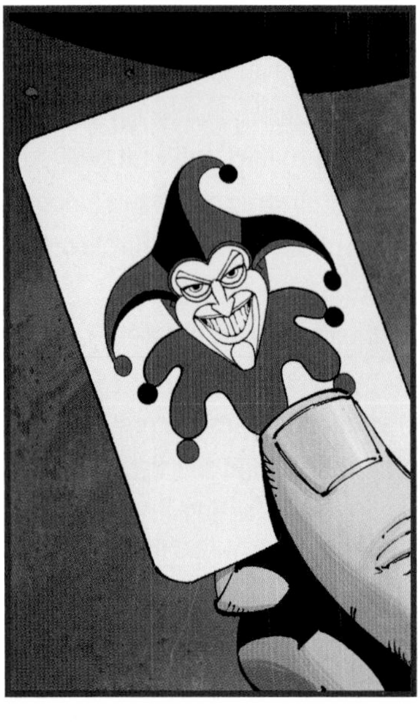

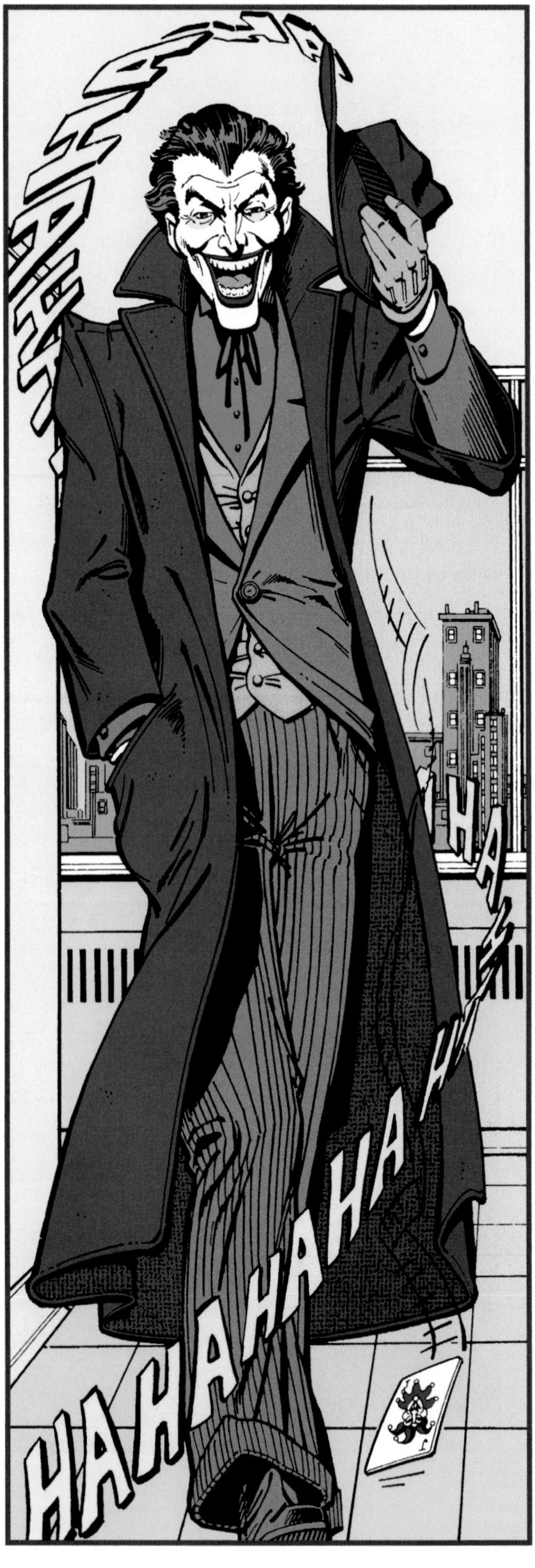
HAHAHAHAHAHA

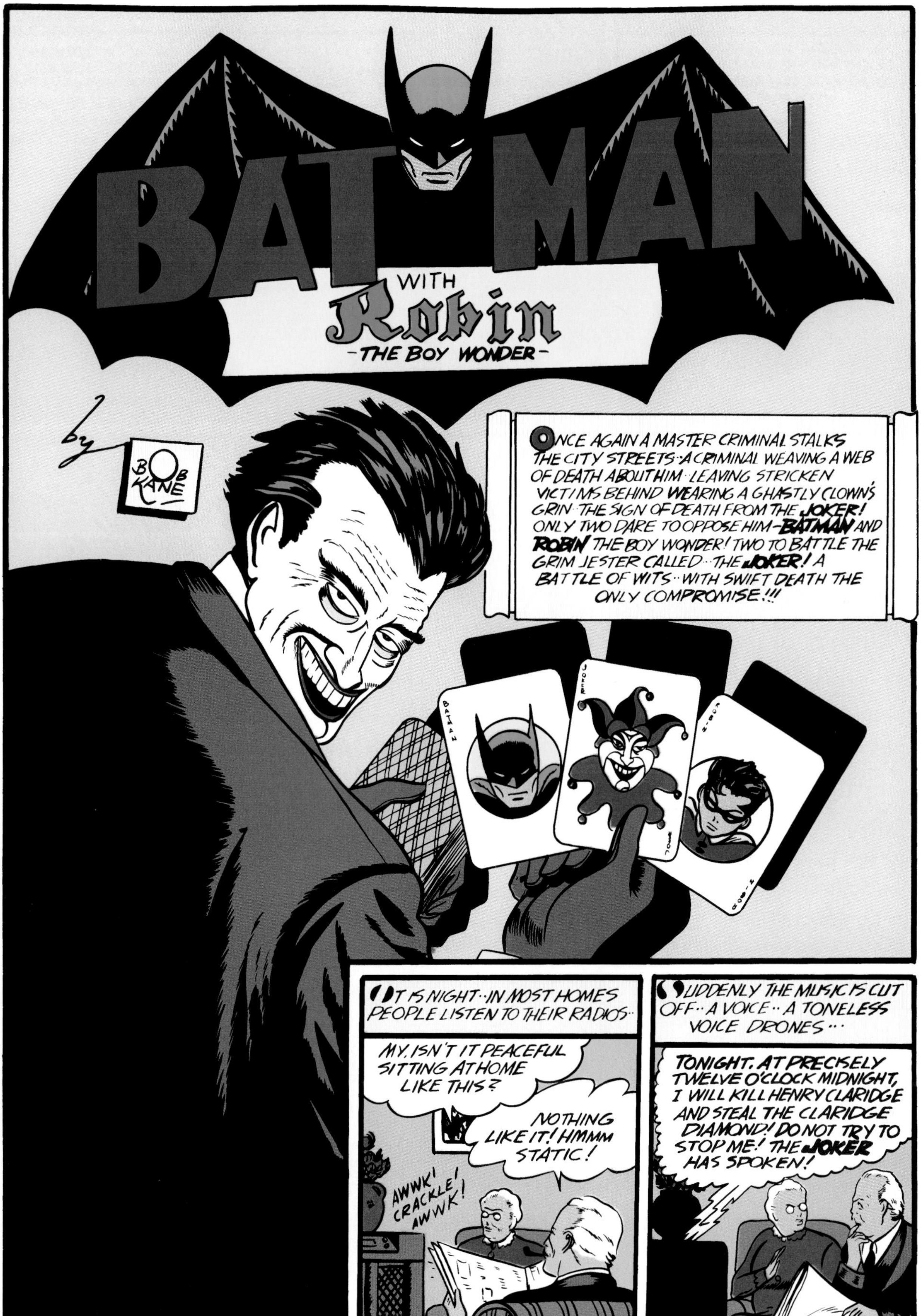
BATMAN
WITH
Robin
-THE BOY WONDER-
by
BOB KANE
ONCE AGAIN A MASTER CRIMINAL STALKS THE CITY STREETS.. A CRIMINAL WEAVING A WEB OF DEATH ABOUT HIM.. LEAVING STRICKEN VICTIMS BEHIND WEARING A GHASTLY CLOWN'S GRIN.. THE SIGN OF DEATH FROM THE JOKER! ONLY TWO DARE TO OPPOSE HIM-BATMAN AND ROBIN THE BOY WONDER! TWO TO BATTLE THE GRIM JESTER CALLED.. THE JOKER! A BATTLE OF WITS.. WITH SWIFT DEATH THE ONLY COMPROMISE!!!
BATMAN
JOKER
ROBIN
IT IS NIGHT.. IN MOST HOMES PEOPLE LISTEN TO THEIR RADIOS..
MY, ISN'T IT PEACEFUL SITTING AT HOME LIKE THIS?
NOTHING LIKE IT! HMMM STATIC!
AWWK! CRACKLE! AWWK!
SUDDENLY THE MUSIC IS CUT OFF.. A VOICE.. A TONELESS VOICE DRONES..
TONIGHT, AT PRECISELY TWELVE O'CLOCK MIDNIGHT, I WILL KILL HENRY CLARIDGE AND STEAL THE CLARIDGE DIAMOND! DO NOT TRY TO STOP ME! THE JOKER HAS SPOKEN!

THEN ONCE AGAIN MUSIC....

HENRY, DID YOU HEAR? HENRY CLARIDGE, THE MILLIONAIRE, TO BE KILLED. THE FAMOUS DIAMOND STOLEN!

HAW! THAT'S JUST A GAG-LIKE THAT FELLOW WHO SCARED EVERYBODY WITH THAT STORY ABOUT MARS THE LAST TIME! HA! HA! PAY NO ATTENTION TO IT, DEAR!

RADIO STATIONS ARE SWAMPED WITH CALLS! OFFICIALS DECLARE THE STRANGE MESSAGE IS *NOT* A PART OF THE PROGRAM. THE "GAG" HAS BECOME A *REALITY!*

HENRY CLARIDGE, FRANTIC WITH FEAR, CALLS THE POLICE

YOU'VE GOT TO PROTECT ME! I'M GOING TO BE *KILLED*...ROBBED!

DON'T WORRY, MR. CLARIDGE. YOU AND THAT DIAMOND OF YOURS WILL BE SAFE ENOUGH! WE'LL ALL STAY IN THE SAME ROOM WHERE THE DIAMOND IS KEPT, AND WATCH YOU.

ELEVEN O'CLOCK! ONE HOUR TO GO!

BONG! BONG!

AN INFLEXIBLE CORDON IS FORMED ABOUT THE DOOMED MAN!

TIME DRAGS ON-SECONDS, MINUTES, THEN THE FATAL HOUR *TWELVE O'CLOCK!*

I'M STILL ALIVE! I'M NOT DEAD! I'M SAFE!...

THE JOKER HAS FULFILLED HIS THREAT. CLARIDGE IS DEAD!!

SLOWLY THE FACIAL MUSCLES PULL THE DEAD MAN'S MOUTH INTO A REPELLANT, GHASTLY GRIN, THE SIGN OF DEATH FROM THE *JOKER!*

IT'S...IT'S HORRIBLE!

GROTESQUE! THE JOKER BRINGS *DEATH* TO HIS VICTIMS WITH A *SMILE!*

THEN WITHOUT WARNING!

...I'M SAAA-- AAGH! AAGH...!

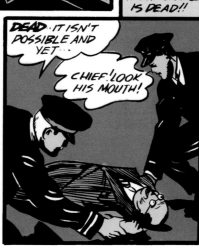

DEAD...IT ISN'T POSSIBLE AND YET...

CHIEF! LOOK HIS MOUTH!

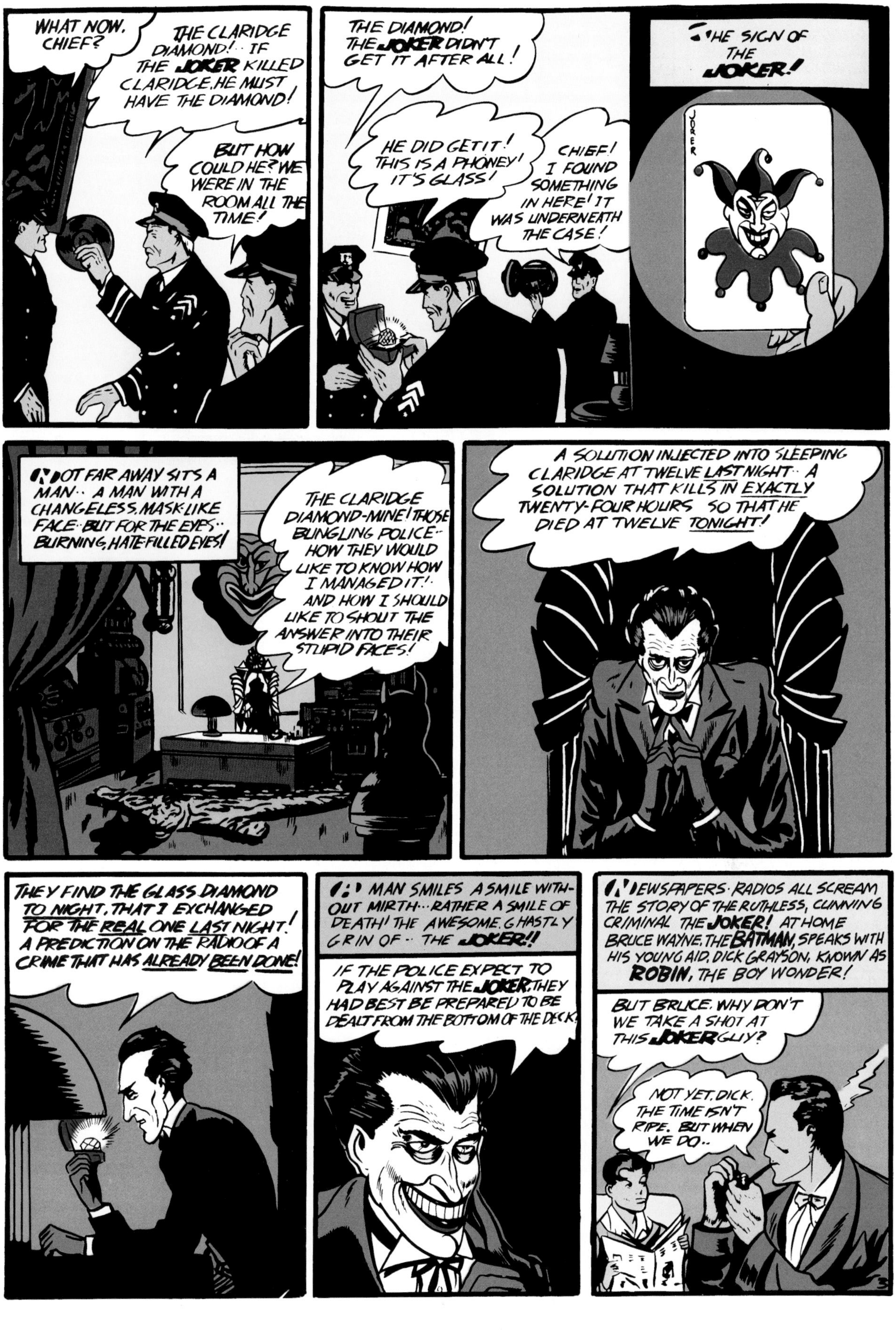
WHAT NOW, CHIEF?
THE CLARIDGE DIAMOND!·· IF THE JOKER KILLED CLARIDGE, HE MUST HAVE THE DIAMOND!
BUT HOW COULD HE? WE WERE IN THE ROOM ALL THE TIME!
THE DIAMOND! THE JOKER DIDN'T GET IT AFTER ALL!
HE DID GET IT! THIS IS A PHONEY! IT'S GLASS!
CHIEF! I FOUND SOMETHING IN HERE! IT WAS UNDERNEATH THE CASE!
THE SIGN OF THE JOKER!
JOKER
NOT FAR AWAY SITS A MAN·· A MAN WITH A CHANGELESS, MASK-LIKE FACE·· BUT FOR THE EYES·· BURNING, HATE-FILLED EYES!
THE CLARIDGE DIAMOND-MINE! THOSE BUNGLING POLICE·· HOW THEY WOULD LIKE TO KNOW HOW I MANAGED IT!·· AND HOW I SHOULD LIKE TO SHOUT THE ANSWER INTO THEIR STUPID FACES!
A SOLUTION INJECTED INTO SLEEPING CLARIDGE AT TWELVE LAST NIGHT·· A SOLUTION THAT KILLS IN EXACTLY TWENTY-FOUR HOURS SO THAT HE DIED AT TWELVE TONIGHT!
THEY FIND THE GLASS DIAMOND TO NIGHT, THAT I EXCHANGED FOR THE REAL ONE LAST NIGHT! A PREDICTION ON THE RADIO OF A CRIME THAT HAS ALREADY BEEN DONE!
A MAN SMILES A SMILE WITHOUT MIRTH··· RATHER A SMILE OF DEATH! THE AWESOME, GHASTLY GRIN OF·· THE JOKER!!
IF THE POLICE EXPECT TO PLAY AGAINST THE JOKER, THEY HAD BEST BE PREPARED TO BE DEALT FROM THE BOTTOM OF THE DECK!
NEWSPAPERS· RADIOS ALL SCREAM THE STORY OF THE RUTHLESS, CUNNING CRIMINAL THE JOKER! AT HOME BRUCE WAYNE, THE BATMAN, SPEAKS WITH HIS YOUNG AID, DICK GRAYSON, KNOWN AS ROBIN, THE BOY WONDER!
BUT BRUCE, WHY DON'T WE TAKE A SHOT AT THIS JOKER GUY?
NOT YET, DICK. THE TIME ISN'T RIPE. BUT WHEN WE DO··
3

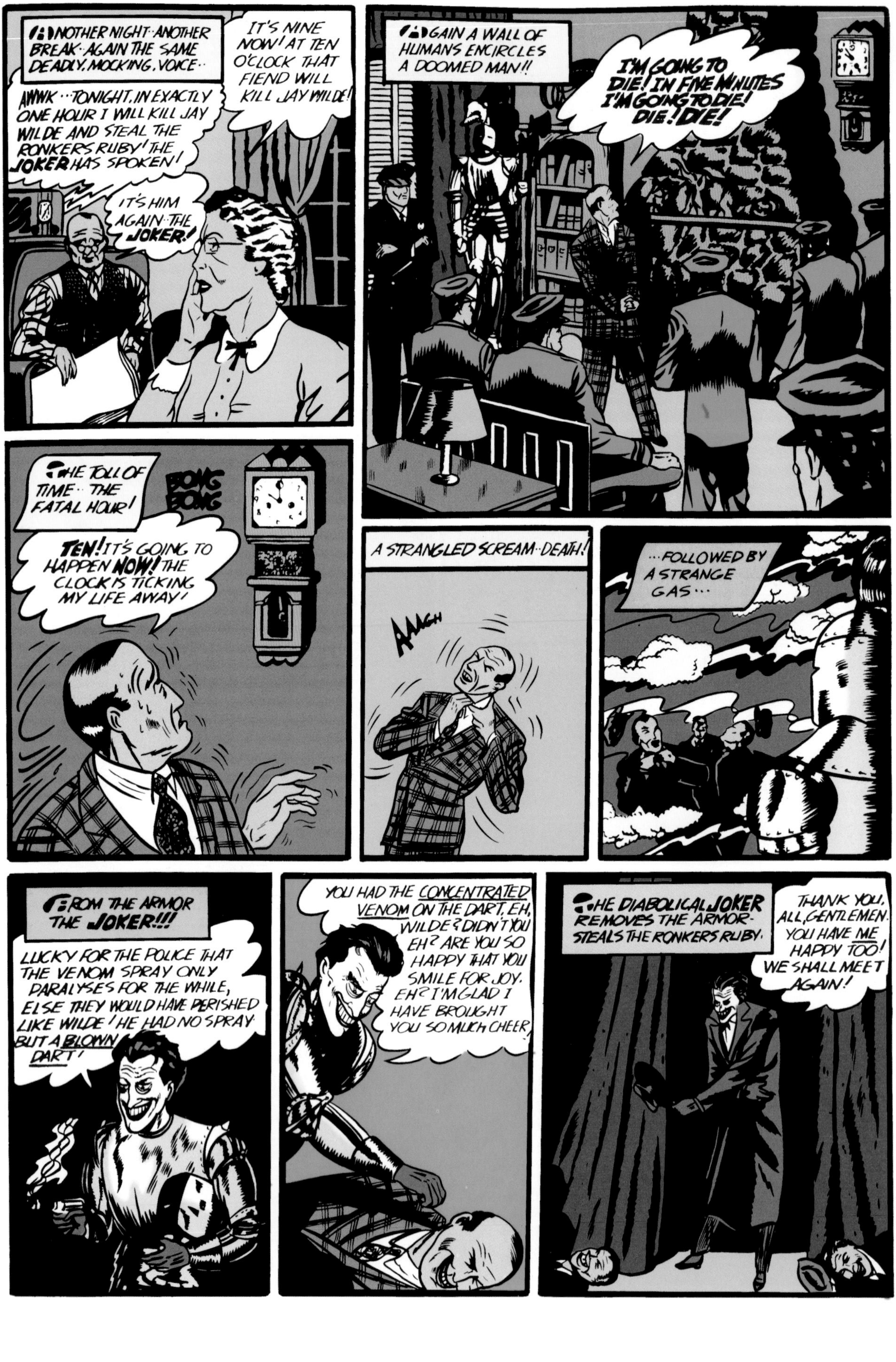
ANOTHER NIGHT · ANOTHER BREAK · AGAIN THE SAME DEADLY, MOCKING, VOICE · ·
IT'S NINE NOW! AT TEN O'CLOCK THAT FIEND WILL KILL JAY WILDE!
AWWK · · · TONIGHT, IN EXACTLY ONE HOUR I WILL KILL JAY WILDE AND STEAL THE RONKERS RUBY! THE JOKER HAS SPOKEN!
IT'S HIM AGAIN · THE JOKER!
AGAIN A WALL OF HUMANS ENCIRCLES A DOOMED MAN!!
I'M GOING TO DIE! IN FIVE MINUTES I'M GOING TO DIE! DIE! DIE!
THE TOLL OF TIME · · THE FATAL HOUR!
BONG BONG
TEN! IT'S GOING TO HAPPEN NOW! THE CLOCK IS TICKING MY LIFE AWAY!
A STRANGLED SCREAM · · DEATH!
AAAGH
· · · FOLLOWED BY A STRANGE GAS · · ·
FROM THE ARMOR THE JOKER!!!
LUCKY FOR THE POLICE THAT THE VENOM SPRAY ONLY PARALYSES FOR THE WHILE, ELSE THEY WOULD HAVE PERISHED LIKE WILDE! HE HAD NO SPRAY · BUT A BLOWN DART!
YOU HAD THE CONCENTRATED VENOM ON THE DART, EH, WILDE? DIDN'T YOU EH? ARE YOU SO HAPPY THAT YOU SMILE FOR JOY, EH? I'M GLAD I HAVE BROUGHT YOU SO MUCH CHEER,
THE DIABOLICAL JOKER REMOVES THE ARMOR · STEALS THE RONKERS RUBY.
THANK YOU, ALL, GENTLEMEN. YOU HAVE ME HAPPY TOO! WE SHALL MEET AGAIN!

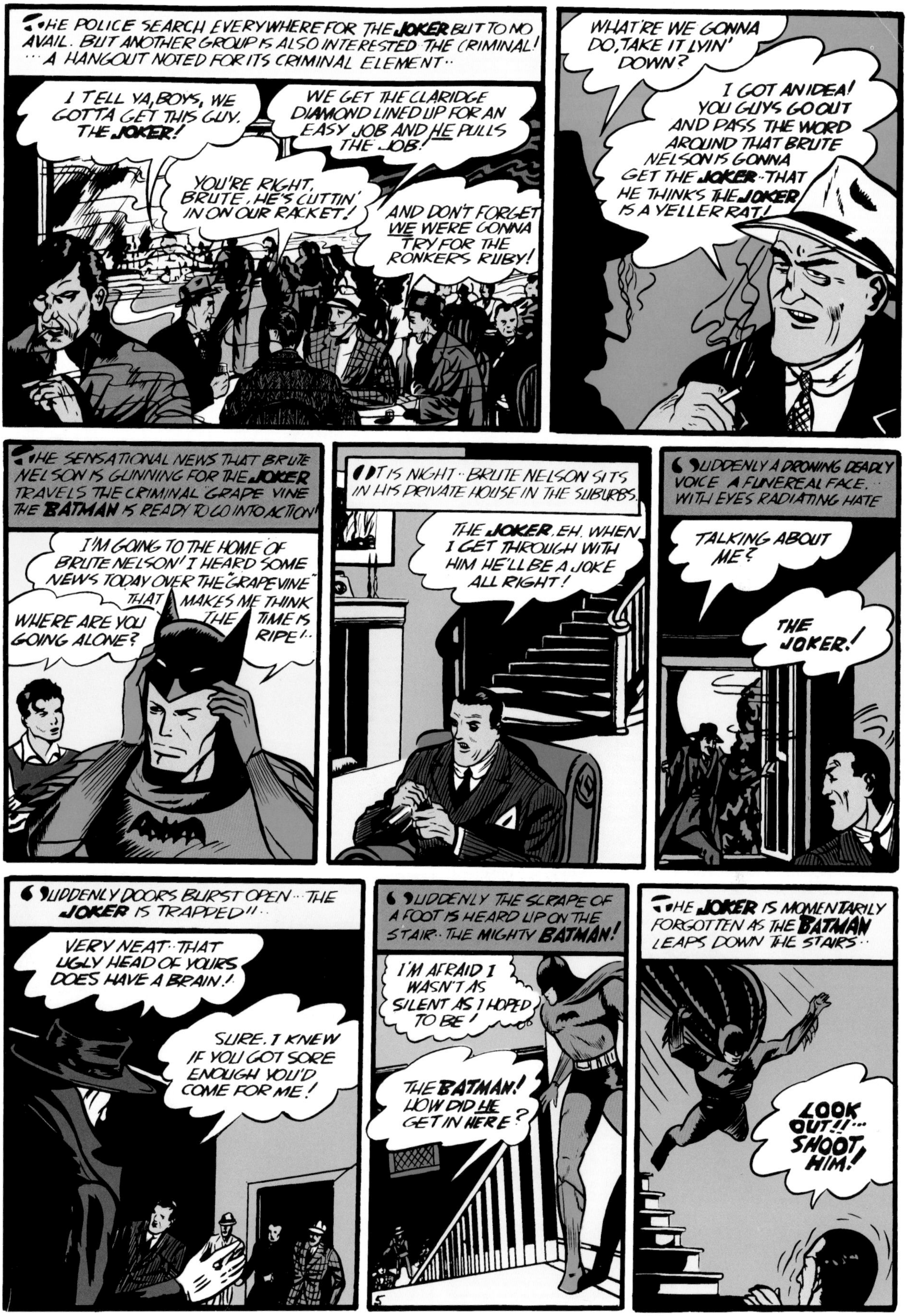
THE POLICE SEARCH EVERYWHERE FOR THE JOKER BUT TO NO AVAIL. BUT ANOTHER GROUP IS ALSO INTERESTED THE CRIMINAL! ... A HANGOUT NOTED FOR ITS CRIMINAL ELEMENT..
I TELL YA, BOYS, WE GOTTA GET THIS GUY, THE JOKER!
WE GET THE CLARIDGE DIAMOND LINED UP FOR AN EASY JOB AND HE PULLS THE JOB!
YOU'RE RIGHT, BRUTE, HE'S CUTTIN' IN ON OUR RACKET!
AND DON'T FORGET WE WERE GONNA TRY FOR THE RONKERS RUBY!
WHAT'RE WE GONNA DO, TAKE IT LYIN' DOWN?
I GOT AN IDEA! YOU GUYS GO OUT AND PASS THE WORD AROUND THAT BRUTE NELSON IS GONNA GET THE JOKER-THAT HE THINKS THE JOKER IS A YELLER RAT!
THE SENSATIONAL NEWS THAT BRUTE NELSON IS GUNNING FOR THE JOKER TRAVELS THE CRIMINAL GRAPE VINE THE BATMAN IS READY TO GO INTO ACTION!
I'M GOING TO THE HOME OF BRUTE NELSON! I HEARD SOME NEWS TODAY OVER THE "GRAPEVINE" THAT MAKES ME THINK THE TIME IS RIPE!..
WHERE ARE YOU GOING ALONE?
IT IS NIGHT.. BRUTE NELSON SITS IN HIS PRIVATE HOUSE IN THE SUBURBS.
THE JOKER, EH. WHEN I GET THROUGH WITH HIM HE'LL BE A JOKE ALL RIGHT!
SUDDENLY A DRONING DEADLY VOICE A FUNEREAL FACE.. WITH EYES RADIATING HATE
TALKING ABOUT ME?
THE JOKER!
SUDDENLY DOORS BURST OPEN.. THE JOKER IS TRAPPED!!..
VERY NEAT.. THAT UGLY HEAD OF YOURS DOES HAVE A BRAIN!
SURE. I KNEW IF YOU GOT SORE ENOUGH YOU'D COME FOR ME!
SUDDENLY THE SCRAPE OF A FOOT IS HEARD UP ON THE STAIR.. THE MIGHTY BATMAN!
I'M AFRAID I WASN'T AS SILENT AS I HOPED TO BE!
THE BATMAN! HOW DID HE GET IN HERE?
THE JOKER IS MOMENTARILY FORGOTTEN AS THE BATMAN LEAPS DOWN THE STAIRS..
LOOK OUT!!... SHOOT HIM!

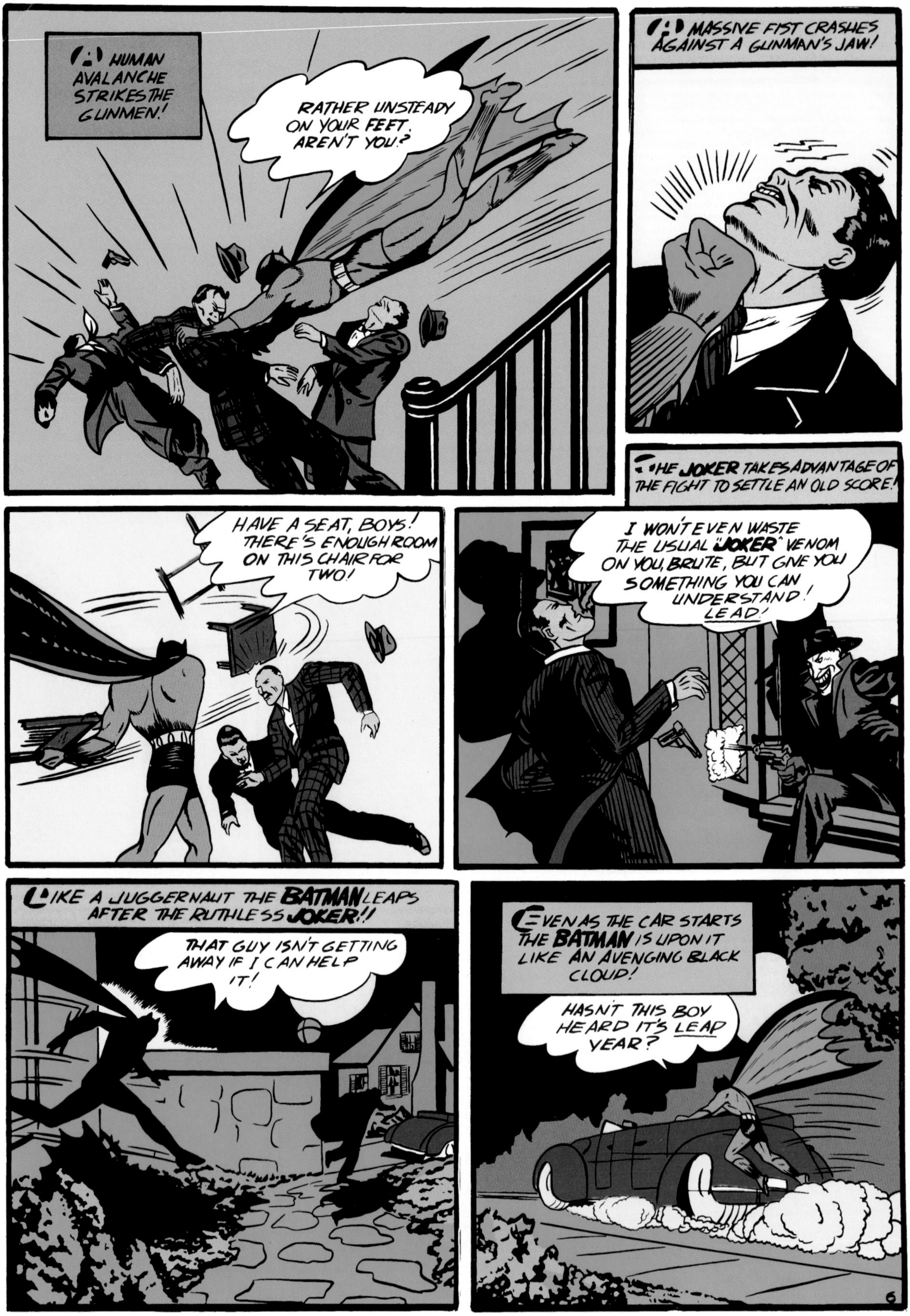
A HUMAN AVALANCHE STRIKES THE GUNMEN!
RATHER UNSTEADY ON YOUR FEET, AREN'T YOU?
A MASSIVE FIST CRASHES AGAINST A GUNMAN'S JAW!
THE JOKER TAKES ADVANTAGE OF THE FIGHT TO SETTLE AN OLD SCORE!
HAVE A SEAT, BOYS! THERE'S ENOUGH ROOM ON THIS CHAIR FOR TWO!
I WON'T EVEN WASTE THE USUAL "JOKER" VENOM ON YOU, BRUTE, BUT GIVE YOU SOMETHING YOU CAN UNDERSTAND! LEAD!
LIKE A JUGGERNAUT THE BATMAN LEAPS AFTER THE RUTHLESS JOKER!!
THAT GUY ISN'T GETTING AWAY IF I CAN HELP IT!
EVEN AS THE CAR STARTS THE BATMAN IS UPON IT LIKE AN AVENGING BLACK CLOUD!
HASN'T THIS BOY HEARD IT'S LEAP YEAR?
6

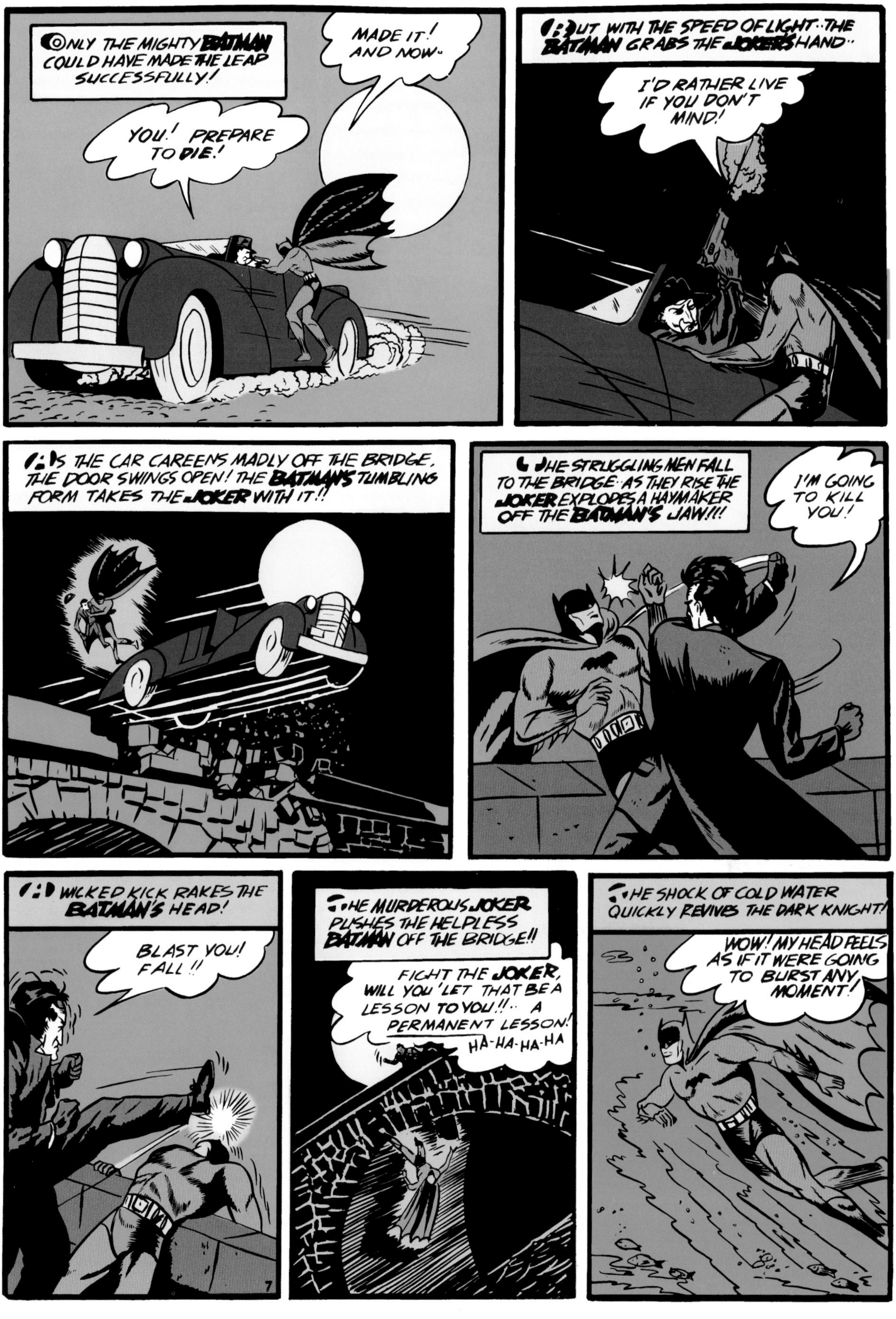
ONLY THE MIGHTY BATMAN COULD HAVE MADE THE LEAP SUCCESSFULLY!
MADE IT! AND NOW..
YOU! PREPARE TO DIE!
BUT WITH THE SPEED OF LIGHT..THE BATMAN GRABS THE JOKER'S HAND..
I'D RATHER LIVE IF YOU DON'T MIND!
AS THE CAR CAREENS MADLY OFF THE BRIDGE, THE DOOR SWINGS OPEN! THE BATMAN'S TUMBLING FORM TAKES THE JOKER WITH IT!!
THE STRUGGLING MEN FALL TO THE BRIDGE..AS THEY RISE THE JOKER EXPLODES A HAYMAKER OFF THE BATMAN'S JAW!!!
I'M GOING TO KILL YOU!
A WICKED KICK RAKES THE BATMAN'S HEAD!
BLAST YOU! FALL!!
THE MURDEROUS JOKER PUSHES THE HELPLESS BATMAN OFF THE BRIDGE!!
FIGHT THE JOKER, WILL YOU! LET THAT BE A LESSON TO YOU!!.. A PERMANENT LESSON!
HA-HA-HA-HA
THE SHOCK OF COLD WATER QUICKLY REVIVES THE DARK KNIGHT!
WOW! MY HEAD FEELS AS IF IT WERE GOING TO BURST ANY MOMENT!

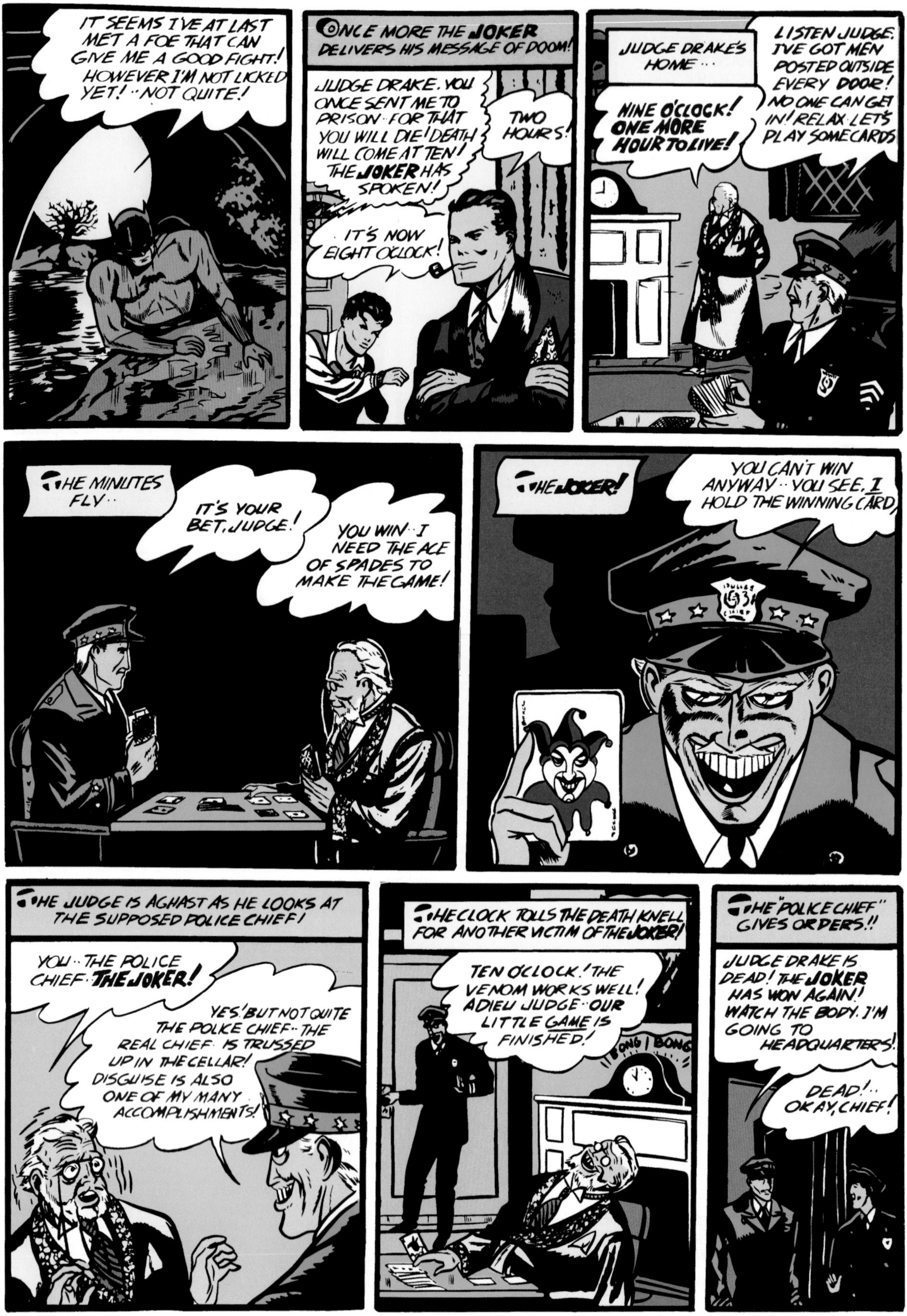

IT SEEMS I'VE AT LAST MET A FOE THAT CAN GIVE ME A GOOD FIGHT! HOWEVER I'M NOT LICKED YET! .. NOT QUITE!
ONCE MORE THE JOKER DELIVERS HIS MESSAGE OF DOOM!
JUDGE DRAKE. YOU ONCE SENT ME TO PRISON .. FOR THAT YOU WILL DIE! DEATH WILL COME AT TEN! THE JOKER HAS SPOKEN!
TWO HOURS!
IT'S NOW EIGHT O'CLOCK!
JUDGE DRAKE'S HOME ...
NINE O'CLOCK! ONE MORE HOUR TO LIVE!
LISTEN JUDGE. I'VE GOT MEN POSTED OUTSIDE EVERY DOOR! NO ONE CAN GET IN! RELAX. LET'S PLAY SOME CARDS
THE MINUTES FLY ..
IT'S YOUR BET, JUDGE!
YOU WIN .. I NEED THE ACE OF SPADES TO MAKE THE GAME!
THE JOKER!
YOU CAN'T WIN ANYWAY .. YOU SEE, I HOLD THE WINNING CARD,
THE JUDGE IS AGHAST AS HE LOOKS AT THE SUPPOSED POLICE CHIEF!
YOU .. THE POLICE CHIEF .. THE JOKER!
YES! BUT NOT QUITE THE POLICE CHIEF .. THE REAL CHIEF IS TRUSSED UP IN THE CELLAR! DISGUISE IS ALSO ONE OF MY MANY ACCOMPLISHMENTS!
THE CLOCK TOLLS THE DEATH KNELL FOR ANOTHER VICTIM OF THE JOKER!
TEN O'CLOCK! THE VENOM WORKS WELL! ADIEU JUDGE .. OUR LITTLE GAME IS FINISHED!
BONG ! BONG
THE "POLICE CHIEF" GIVES ORDERS!!
JUDGE DRAKE IS DEAD! THE JOKER HAS WON AGAIN! WATCH THE BODY. I'M GOING TO HEADQUARTERS!
DEAD! .. OKAY, CHIEF!

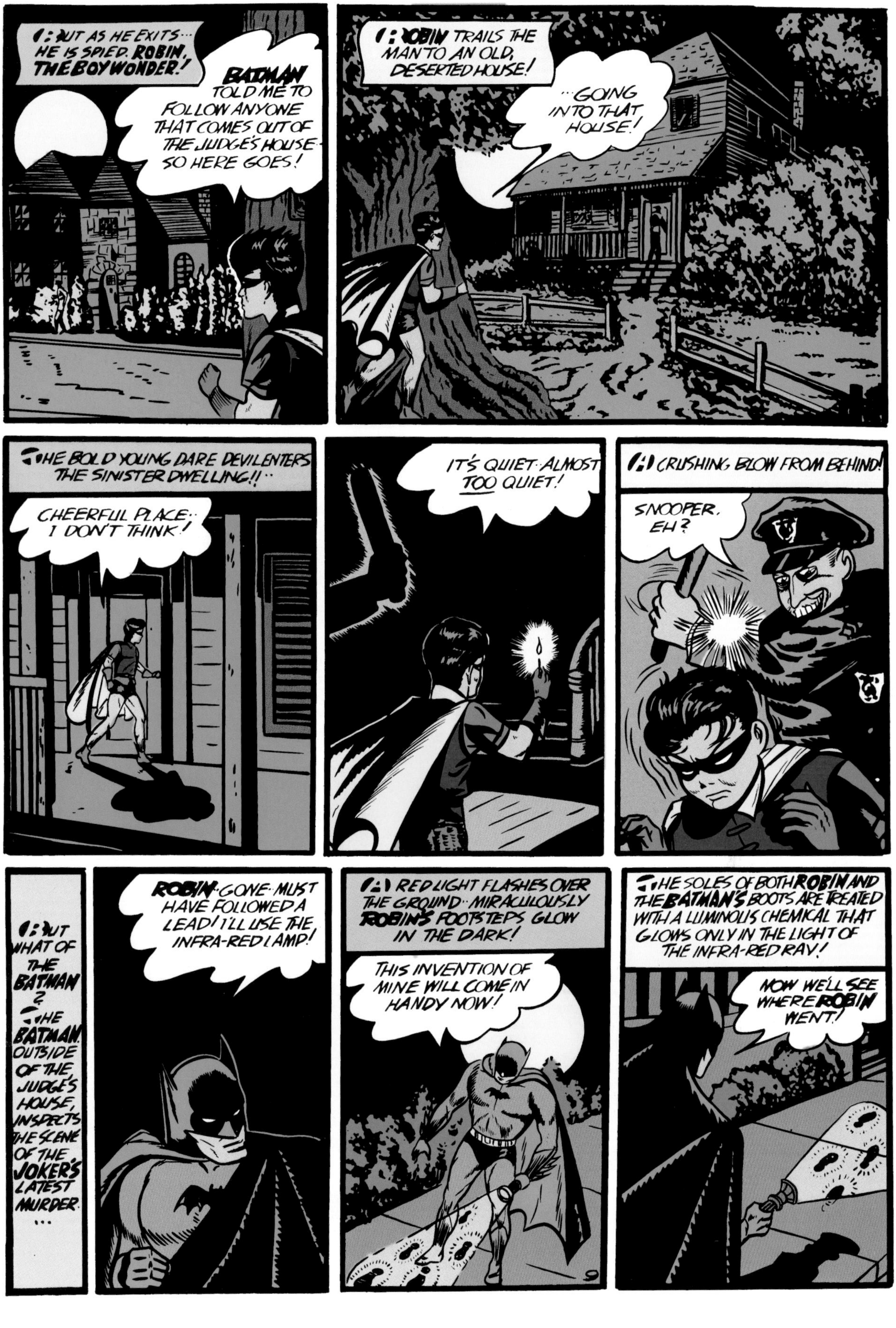
BUT AS HE EXITS... HE IS SPIED. ROBIN, THE BOY WONDER!
BATMAN TOLD ME TO FOLLOW ANYONE THAT COMES OUT OF THE JUDGE'S HOUSE-- SO HERE GOES!
ROBIN TRAILS THE MAN TO AN OLD, DESERTED HOUSE!
...GOING INTO THAT HOUSE!
THE BOLD YOUNG DARE DEVIL ENTERS THE SINISTER DWELLING!!..
CHEERFUL PLACE.. I DON'T THINK!
IT'S QUIET.. ALMOST TOO QUIET!
A CRUSHING BLOW FROM BEHIND!
SNOOPER, EH?
BUT WHAT OF THE BATMAN? THE BATMAN, OUTSIDE OF THE JUDGE'S HOUSE, INSPECTS THE SCENE OF THE JOKER'S LATEST MURDER...
ROBIN GONE.. MUST HAVE FOLLOWED A LEAD! I'LL USE THE INFRA-RED LAMP!
A RED LIGHT FLASHES OVER THE GROUND.. MIRACULOUSLY ROBIN'S FOOTSTEPS GLOW IN THE DARK!
THIS INVENTION OF MINE WILL COME IN HANDY NOW!
THE SOLES OF BOTH ROBIN AND THE BATMAN'S BOOTS ARE TREATED WITH A LUMINOUS CHEMICAL THAT GLOWS ONLY IN THE LIGHT OF THE INFRA-RED RAY!
NOW WE'LL SEE WHERE ROBIN WENT!

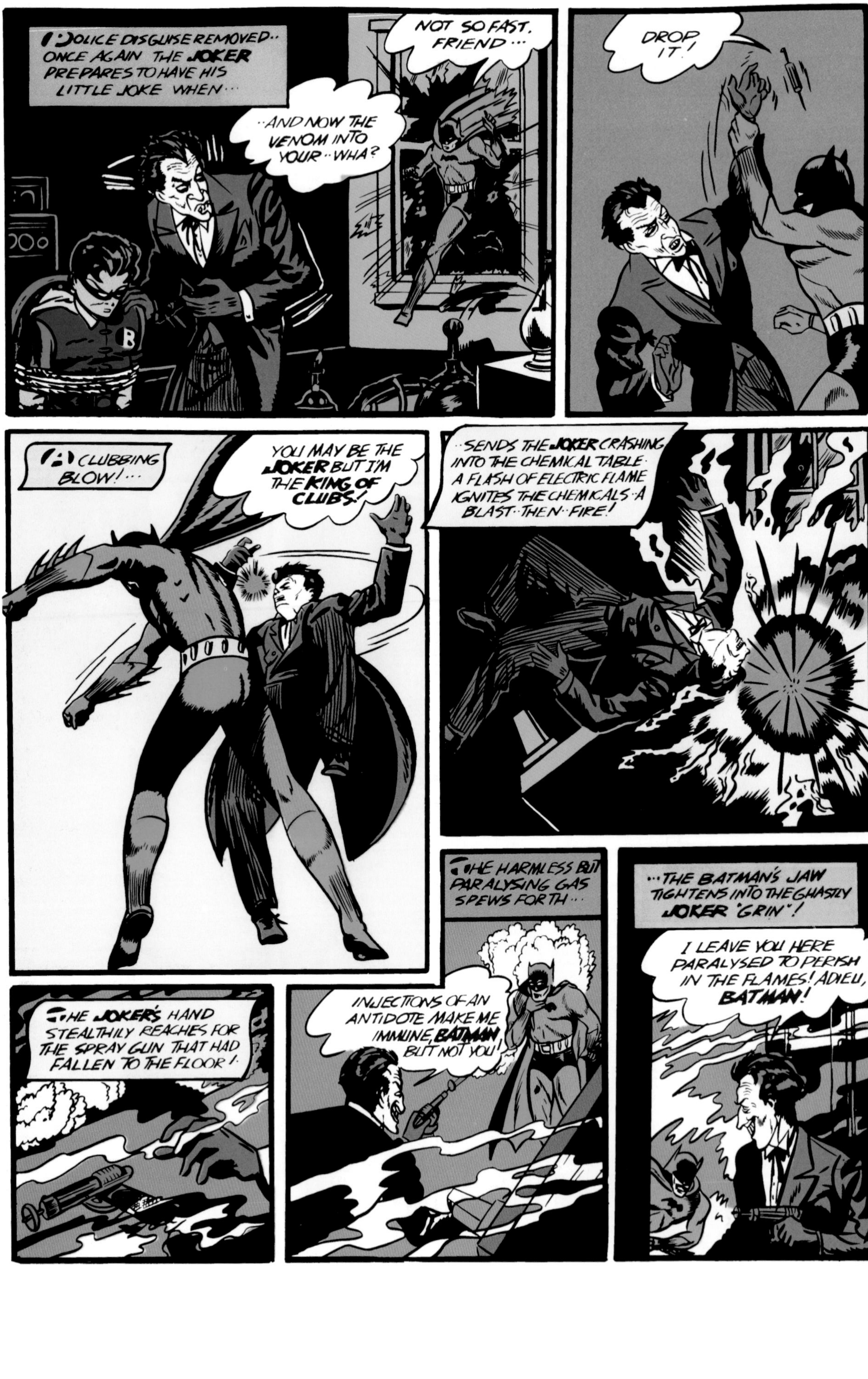
POLICE DISGUISE REMOVED.. ONCE AGAIN THE JOKER PREPARES TO HAVE HIS LITTLE JOKE WHEN...
..AND NOW THE VENOM INTO YOUR..WHA?
NOT SO FAST, FRIEND...
DROP IT!
A CLUBBING BLOW!...
YOU MAY BE THE JOKER BUT I'M THE KING OF CLUBS!
..SENDS THE JOKER CRASHING INTO THE CHEMICAL TABLE. A FLASH OF ELECTRIC FLAME IGNITES THE CHEMICALS..A BLAST..THEN..FIRE!
THE JOKER'S HAND STEALTHILY REACHES FOR THE SPRAY GUN THAT HAD FALLEN TO THE FLOOR!
THE HARMLESS BUT PARALYSING GAS SPEWS FORTH...
INJECTIONS OF AN ANTIDOTE MAKE ME IMMUNE, BATMAN BUT NOT YOU!
...THE BATMAN'S JAW TIGHTENS INTO THE GHASTLY JOKER "GRIN"!
I LEAVE YOU HERE PARALYSED TO PERISH IN THE FLAMES! ADIEU, BATMAN!

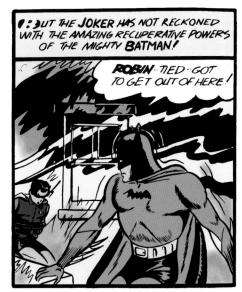

1: BUT THE JOKER HAS NOT RECKONED WITH THE AMAZING RECUPERATIVE POWERS OF THE MIGHTY BATMAN!

ROBIN...TIED...GOT TO GET OUT OF HERE!

AN ESCAPE FROM A FIERY DEATH!

A FEW MOMENTS LATER..

THE JOKER IS GONE! I'D GIVE ANYTHING TO KNOW WHERE!

HE BOASTED INSIDE THAT HE WAS GOING TO GET THE CLEOPATRA NECKLACE NEXT!

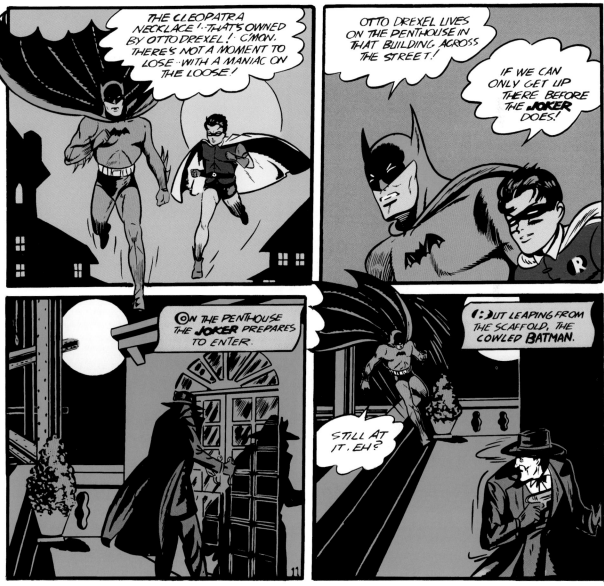

THE CLEOPATRA NECKLACE!...THAT'S OWNED BY OTTO DREXEL! C'MON. THERE'S NOT A MOMENT TO LOSE...WITH A MANIAC ON THE LOOSE!

OTTO DREXEL LIVES ON THE PENTHOUSE IN THAT BUILDING ACROSS THE STREET!

IF WE CAN ONLY GET UP THERE BEFORE THE JOKER DOES!

ON THE PENTHOUSE THE JOKER PREPARES TO ENTER.

1: BUT LEAPING FROM THE SCAFFOLD, THE COWLED BATMAN.

STILL AT IT, EH?

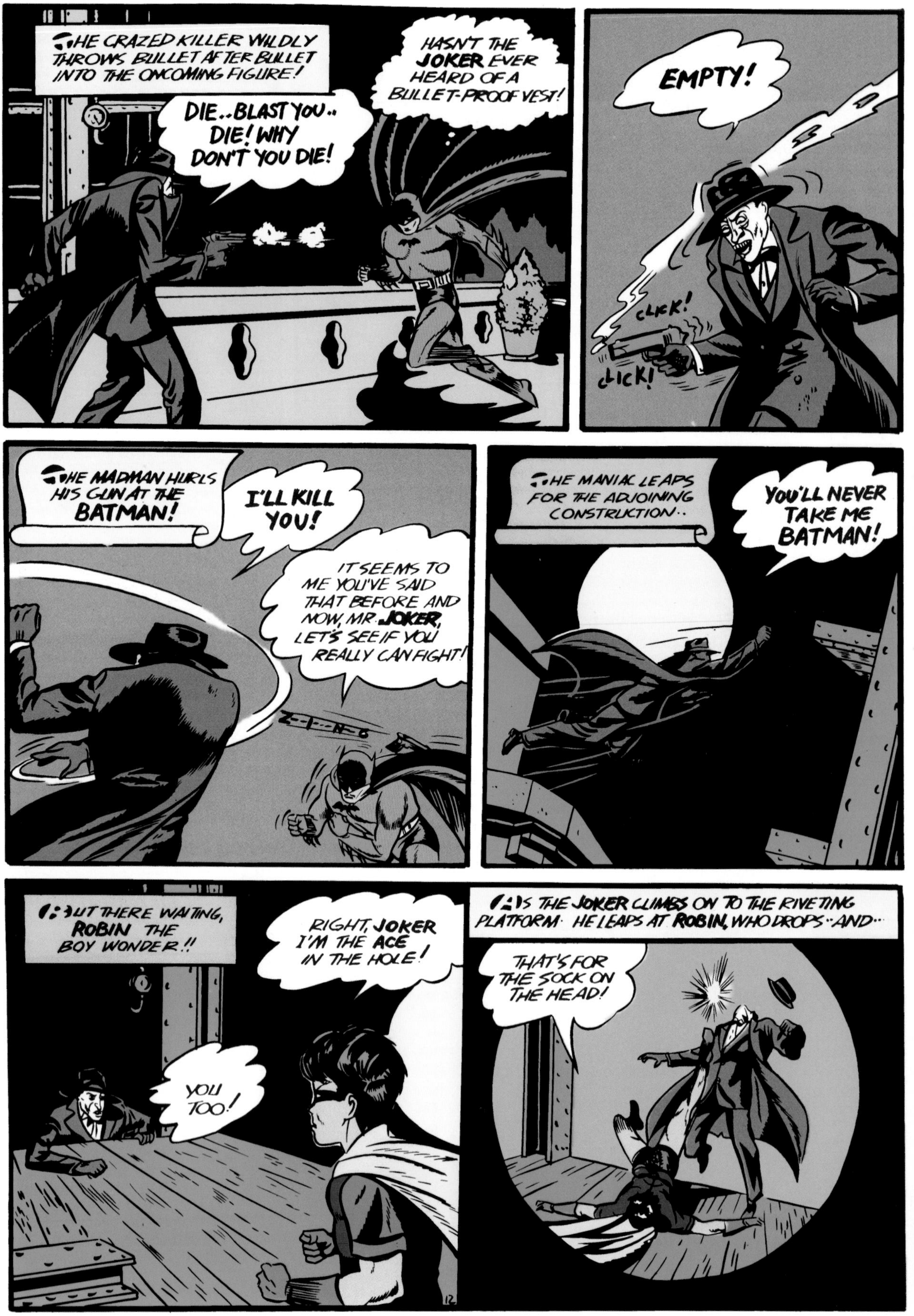
THE CRAZED KILLER WILDLY THROWS BULLET AFTER BULLET INTO THE ONCOMING FIGURE!
HASN'T THE JOKER EVER HEARD OF A BULLET-PROOF VEST!
DIE..BLAST YOU.. DIE! WHY DON'T YOU DIE!
EMPTY!
CLICK!
CLICK!
THE MADMAN HURLS HIS GUN AT THE BATMAN!
I'LL KILL YOU!
IT SEEMS TO ME YOU'VE SAID THAT BEFORE AND NOW, MR. JOKER, LET'S SEE IF YOU REALLY CAN FIGHT!
Z-I-N-G
THE MANIAC LEAPS FOR THE ADJOINING CONSTRUCTION..
YOU'LL NEVER TAKE ME BATMAN!
BUT THERE WAITING, ROBIN THE BOY WONDER!!
RIGHT, JOKER I'M THE ACE IN THE HOLE!
YOU TOO!
12
AS THE JOKER CLIMBS ON TO THE RIVETING PLATFORM HE LEAPS AT ROBIN, WHO DROPS--AND--
THAT'S FOR THE SOCK ON THE HEAD!

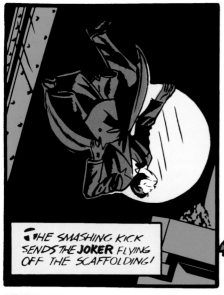

THE SMASHING KICK SENDS THE JOKER FLYING OFF THE SCAFFOLDING!

AS THE FRANTIC MAN FALLS PAST THE PENTHOUSE BALUSTRADE, A HAND REACHES OUT...

AAGH! I'M FALLING!

OH NO YOU'RE NOT!

THE STRONG ARM OF THE BATMAN HAULS HIM BACK TO SAFETY!

YOU'RE TOO VALUABLE A PRIZE TO LOSE!

YOU PLAYED YOUR LAST HAND, JOKER!

FINAL BLOW WITH ALL THE STRENGTH OF THE BATMAN BEHIND IT!!

NEXT DAY

DAILY STAR 2¢

BATMAN CAPTURES JOKER
LEAVES JOKER I FRONT OF POLIC STATION. DRIVES A

BUT WHAT I'D LIKE TO KNOW IS HOW HIS VICTIMS' MOUTHS TURNED UP IN THAT TERRIBLE GRIN!!

SOME SORT OF DRUG THAT PULLED THE MUSCLES OF THE FACE! THE JOKER WAS A CLEVER BUT DIABOLICAL KILLER! TOO CLEVER AND TOO DEADLY TO BE FREE!

BUT EVEN AS BRUCE SPEAKS, AT THE STATE PRISON, THE JOKER IS PLANNING, PLOTTING FOR HIS ESCAPE!

THEY CAN'T KEEP ME HERE! I KNOW OF A WAY OUT—THE JOKER WILL YET HAVE THE LAST LAUGH!

BOB KANE

THE Amazing BATMAN
AMERICA'S MOST FAMOUS ADVENTURE-STRIP CHARACTER... WITH THAT SENSATIONAL NEW DISCOVERY, THAT LAUGHING YOUNG DARE-DEVIL Robin THE BOY WONDER
WILL THRILL YOU EVERY MONTH WITH THEIR ASTOUNDING EXPLOITS IN DETECTIVE COMICS

21

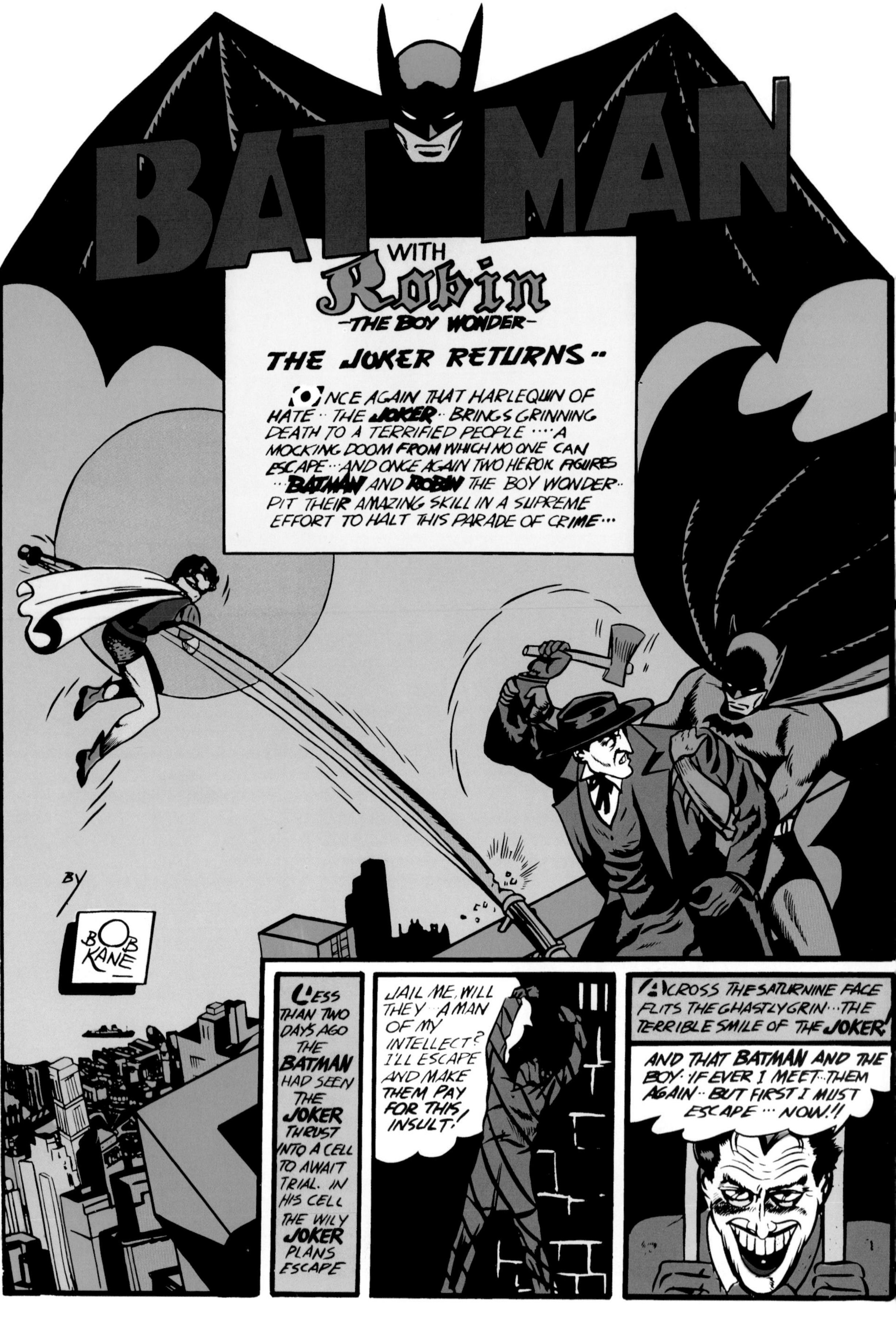
BATMAN
WITH
Robin
-THE BOY WONDER-
THE JOKER RETURNS..
ONCE AGAIN THAT HARLEQUIN OF HATE.. THE JOKER.. BRINGS GRINNING DEATH TO A TERRIFIED PEOPLE .... A MOCKING DOOM FROM WHICH NO ONE CAN ESCAPE... AND ONCE AGAIN TWO HEROIC FIGURES ..BATMAN AND ROBIN THE BOY WONDER.. PIT THEIR AMAZING SKILL IN A SUPREME EFFORT TO HALT THIS PARADE OF CRIME...
BY BOB KANE
LESS THAN TWO DAYS AGO THE BATMAN HAD SEEN THE JOKER THRUST INTO A CELL TO AWAIT TRIAL. IN HIS CELL THE WILY JOKER PLANS ESCAPE
JAIL ME, WILL THEY.. A MAN OF MY INTELLECT? I'LL ESCAPE AND MAKE THEM PAY FOR THIS INSULT!
ACROSS THE SATURNINE FACE FLITS THE GHASTLY GRIN... THE TERRIBLE SMILE OF THE JOKER!
AND THAT BATMAN AND THE BOY.. IF EVER I MEET THEM AGAIN.. BUT FIRST I MUST ESCAPE... NOW!!

FROM THE BACK OF HIS MOUTH THE **JOKER** UNSCREWS TWO FALSE TEETH!

INSIDE EACH TOOTH IS A CHEMICAL, WHICH WHEN MIXED TOGETHER, FORMS A POWERFUL EXPLOSIVE··· MY MEANS OF ESCAPE!

MOMENTS LATER A TERRIFIC EXPLOSION BLOWS A GAPING HOLE IN THE CELL WALL!!

FREEDOM! AU REVOIR GENTLEMEN··· TILL WE MEET AGAIN—HA·HA·HA

"STARTLING NEWS STIRS BRUCE WAYNE AND YOUNG DICK GRAYSON!

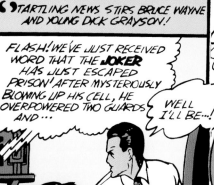

FLASH! WE'VE JUST RECEIVED WORD THAT THE **JOKER** HAS JUST ESCAPED PRISON! AFTER MYSTERIOUSLY BLOWING UP HIS CELL, HE OVERPOWERED TWO GUARDS AND···

WELL I'LL BE···!

THE **JOKER** FREE! I CAN HARDLY BELIEVE IT!

I CAN! HE'S A VERY UNUSUAL MAN! HE'S SHREWD, SUBTLE AND ABOVE ALL RUTHLESS!! MARK MY WORDS, THE JOKER WILL RETURN WITH A VENGEANCE!

AT THAT MOMENT A FIGURE GHOSTS THROUGH THE GLOOM THAT HANGS OVER THE DECAYING GRAVE-STONES OF A DESERTED CEMETERY!

THE PHANTOM LIKE FORM PUSHES AGAINST A CURIOUS GRAVESTONE··· THE GROUND SLIPS AWAY REVEALING A YAWNING GAP AT HIS FEET

THE FIGURE DESCENDS INTO THE CRYPT··· A LIGHT SWITCHES ON··· AND REVEALS **THE JOKER**!!

HERE IN MY LABORATORY I WILL ONCE MORE LET ALL KNOW THAT THE **JOKER** IS STILL IN THE GAME··· AND IS STILL HIGH CARD!!

ONCE AGAIN AS PEOPLE LISTEN AT RADIOS COMES THAT BREAK··· A DEADLY VOICE A MESSAGE OF DOOM!!

AWWK··HEAR ME NOW! TO CHIEF OF POLICE CHALMERS I BRING DEATH··TONIGHT AT TEN O'CLOCK··THE **JOKER** HAS SPOKEN!!

Panel 1: THAT NIGHT...A POLICE CORDON PROTECTS THE MAN MARKED FOR DEATH!

HE WOULDN'T DARE... NOT TO A POLICE CHIEF...**HE WOULDN'T DARE!**...ALMOST TIME... **ALMOST TIME**...

Panel 2: SUDDENLY THE JINGLE OF THE TELEPHONE BELL...

WHAT! I CAN'T HEAR YOU, SPEAK LOUDER!!

WHO? YOU WANT TO SPEAK TO THE CHIEF? JUST A MINUTE, I'LL PUT HIM ON!!

Panel 3: AAAAAAAAAAG!

JOKER

Panel 4: THE CLOCK TOLLS THE HOUR...TEN O'CLOCK...THE **JOKER** HAS STRUCK AGAIN!

LOOK! ON HIS FACE... THAT TERRIBLE GRIN...THE SIGN OF DEATH FROM THE **JOKER!**

DEAD! HE'S DEAD!

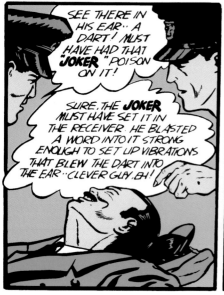

Panel 5: SEE THERE IN HIS EAR...A DART! MUST HAVE HAD THAT "**JOKER**" POISON ON IT!

SURE, THE **JOKER** MUST HAVE SET IT IN THE RECEIVER. HE BLASTED A WORD INTO IT STRONG ENOUGH TO SET UP VIBRATIONS THAT BLEW THE DART INTO THE EAR...CLEVER GUY, EH!

Panel 6: THE FOLLOWING DAY A FAMOUS PAINTING IS STOLEN FROM A GALLERY AND IN ITS PLACE FOR ALL THE WORLD TO SEE....

THE **JOKER** AGAIN!

Panel 7: A RARE GEM IS STOLEN. THE OWNER GRINNING IN DEATH, AS IF HE ENJOYED THE VISIT FROM THE **JOKER!**

3

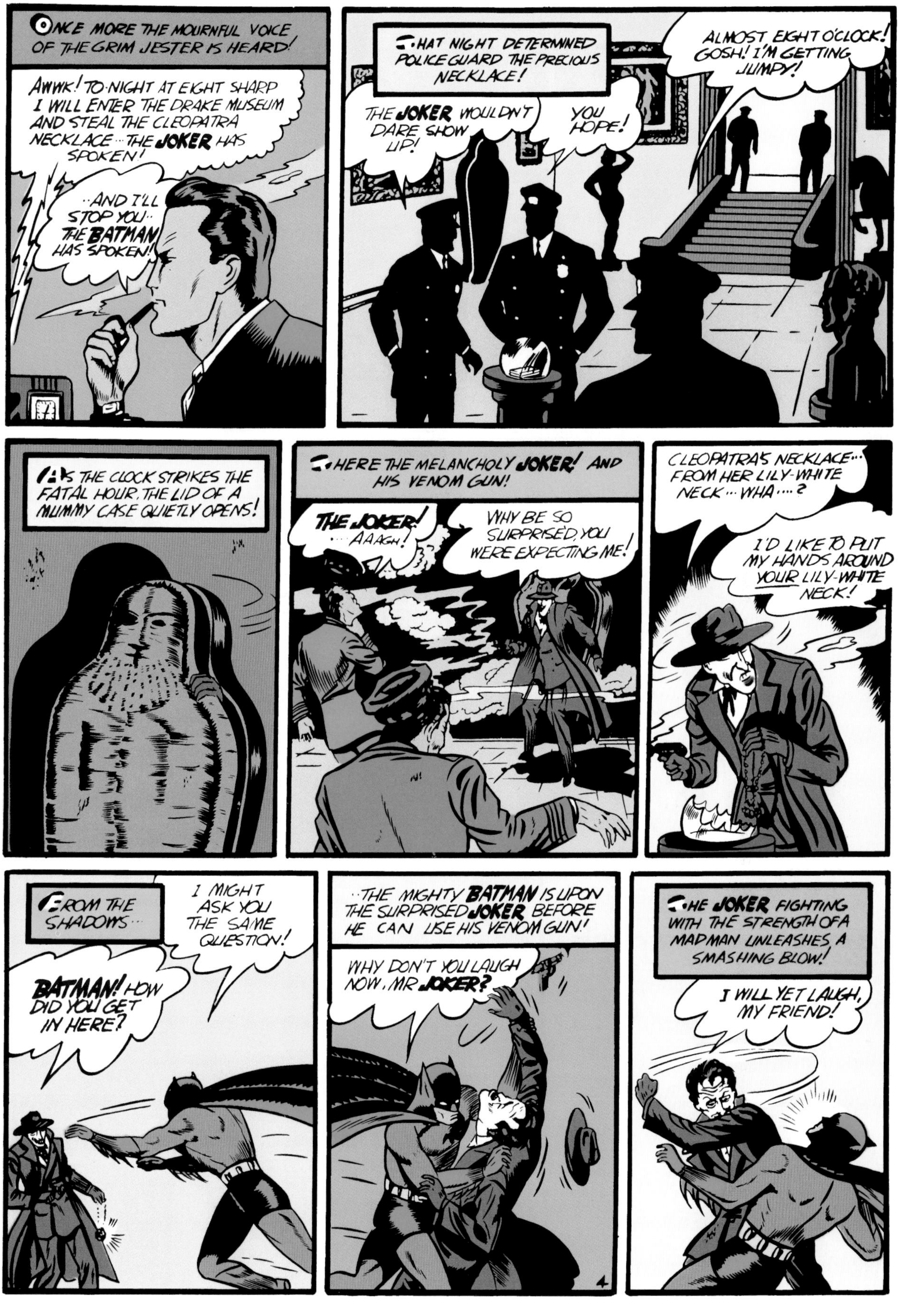
ONCE MORE THE MOURNFUL VOICE OF THE GRIM JESTER IS HEARD!
AWWK! TO-NIGHT AT EIGHT SHARP I WILL ENTER THE DRAKE MUSEUM AND STEAL THE CLEOPATRA NECKLACE... THE JOKER HAS SPOKEN!
..AND I'LL STOP YOU.. THE BATMAN HAS SPOKEN!
THAT NIGHT DETERMINED POLICE GUARD THE PRECIOUS NECKLACE!
THE JOKER WOULDN'T DARE SHOW UP!
YOU HOPE!
ALMOST EIGHT O'CLOCK! GOSH! I'M GETTING JUMPY!
AS THE CLOCK STRIKES THE FATAL HOUR, THE LID OF A MUMMY CASE QUIETLY OPENS!
THERE THE MELANCHOLY JOKER! AND HIS VENOM GUN!
THE JOKER! ... AAAGH!
WHY BE SO SURPRISED, YOU WERE EXPECTING ME!
CLEOPATRA'S NECKLACE... FROM HER LILY-WHITE NECK ... WHA ....?
I'D LIKE TO PUT MY HANDS AROUND YOUR LILY-WHITE NECK!
FROM THE SHADOWS ...
I MIGHT ASK YOU THE SAME QUESTION!
BATMAN! HOW DID YOU GET IN HERE?
..THE MIGHTY BATMAN IS UPON THE SURPRISED JOKER BEFORE HE CAN USE HIS VENOM GUN!
WHY DON'T YOU LAUGH NOW, MR JOKER?
THE JOKER FIGHTING WITH THE STRENGTH OF A MADMAN UNLEASHES A SMASHING BLOW!
I WILL YET LAUGH, MY FRIEND!

THE MADMAN REACHES FOR AN ANCIENT MACE!

I'LL FINISH YOU ONCE AND FOR ALL...MR. BATMAN... HA...HA...HA...HA...

(A) SHEER, DESPERATE TWIST OF THE BATMAN'S BODY AND THE MACE GIVES HIM A GLANCING BLOW ON THE SIDE OF THE HEAD

SUDDENLY THE POUNDING OF RUNNING FEET...RAISED VOICES...

THE POLICE FROM DOWNSTAIRS -- THEY MUSN'T FIND ME!

IT'S AFTER EIGHT!...LETS SEE IF THE BOYS ARE ALL RIGHT!

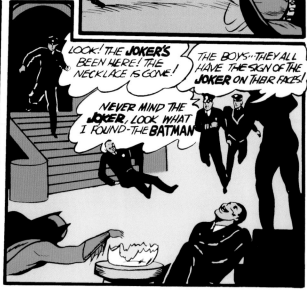

LOOK! THE JOKER'S BEEN HERE! THE NECKLACE IS GONE!

THE BOYS...THEY ALL HAVE THE SIGN OF THE JOKER ON THEIR FACES!

NEVER MIND THE JOKER, LOOK WHAT I FOUND--THE BATMAN!

THE BATMAN! WELL, WE HAVE CAUGHT SOMEBODY! NOW I'M GOING TO DO SOMETHING I'VE WANTED TO DO FOR A LONG TIME...TAKE OFF THE BATMAN'S MASK AND SEE WHO HE REALLY IS!

(A) HAND REACHES OUT TO WRENCH OFF BATMAN'S COWL!

WILL THE COWL BE TAKEN OFF?

IF THE BATMAN IS REVEALED AS BRUCE WAYNE HIS CAREER AS A NEMESIS OF CRIME IS FINISHED!

IS THIS THE END OF THE MIGHTY BATMAN?

5

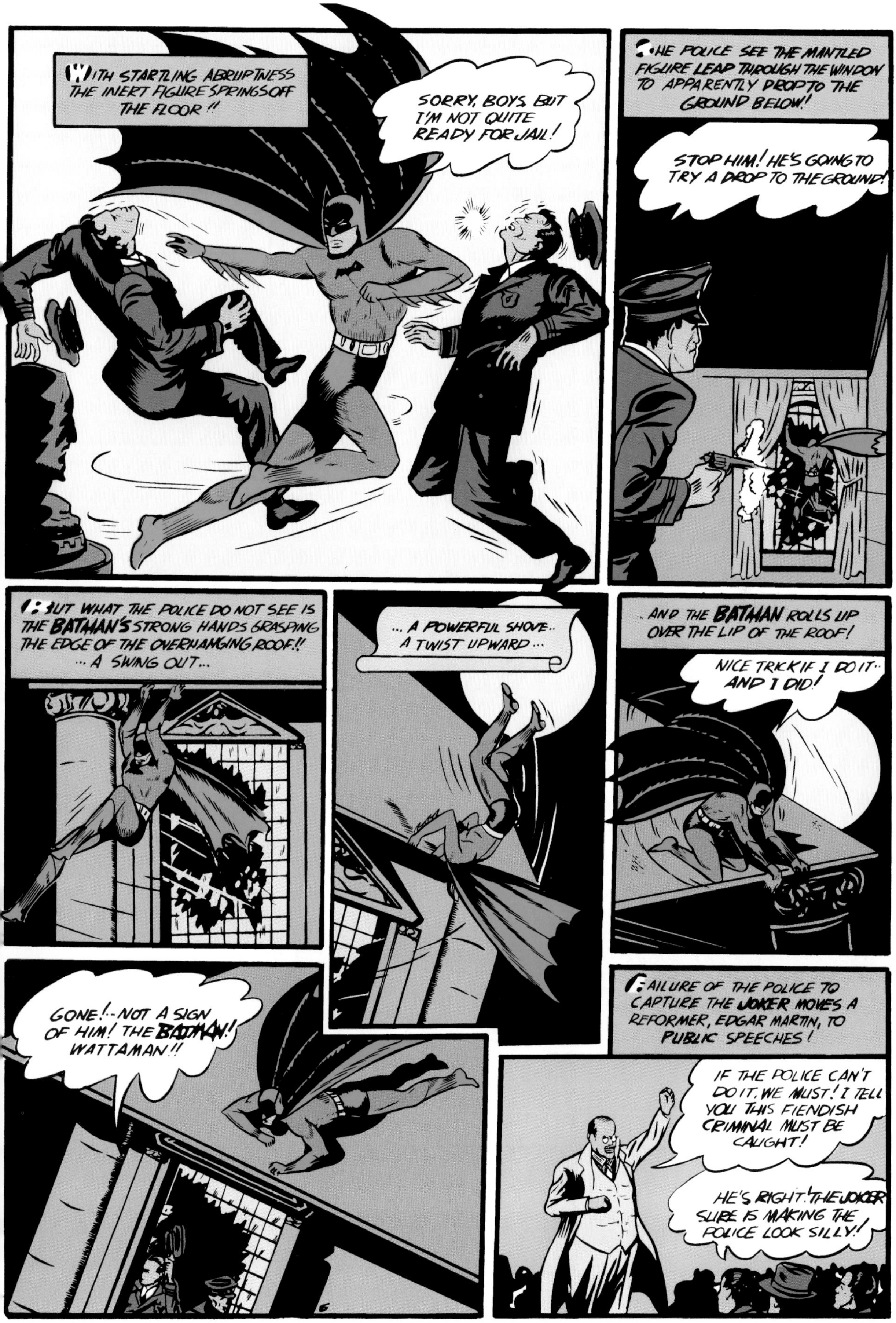
WITH STARTLING ABRUPTNESS THE INERT FIGURE SPRINGS OFF THE FLOOR!!
SORRY, BOYS, BUT I'M NOT QUITE READY FOR JAIL!
THE POLICE SEE THE MANTLED FIGURE LEAP THROUGH THE WINDOW TO APPARENTLY DROP TO THE GROUND BELOW!
STOP HIM! HE'S GOING TO TRY A DROP TO THE GROUND!
BUT WHAT THE POLICE DO NOT SEE IS THE BATMAN'S STRONG HANDS GRASPING THE EDGE OF THE OVERHANGING ROOF!! ... A SWING OUT...
... A POWERFUL SHOVE.. A TWIST UPWARD ...
.. AND THE BATMAN ROLLS UP OVER THE LIP OF THE ROOF!
NICE TRICK IF I DO IT.. AND I DID!
GONE!--NOT A SIGN OF HIM! THE BATMAN! WATTAMAN!!
FAILURE OF THE POLICE TO CAPTURE THE JOKER MOVES A REFORMER, EDGAR MARTIN, TO PUBLIC SPEECHES!
IF THE POLICE CAN'T DO IT, WE MUST! I TELL YOU THIS FIENDISH CRIMINAL MUST BE CAUGHT!
HE'S RIGHT! THE JOKER SURE IS MAKING THE POLICE LOOK SILLY!

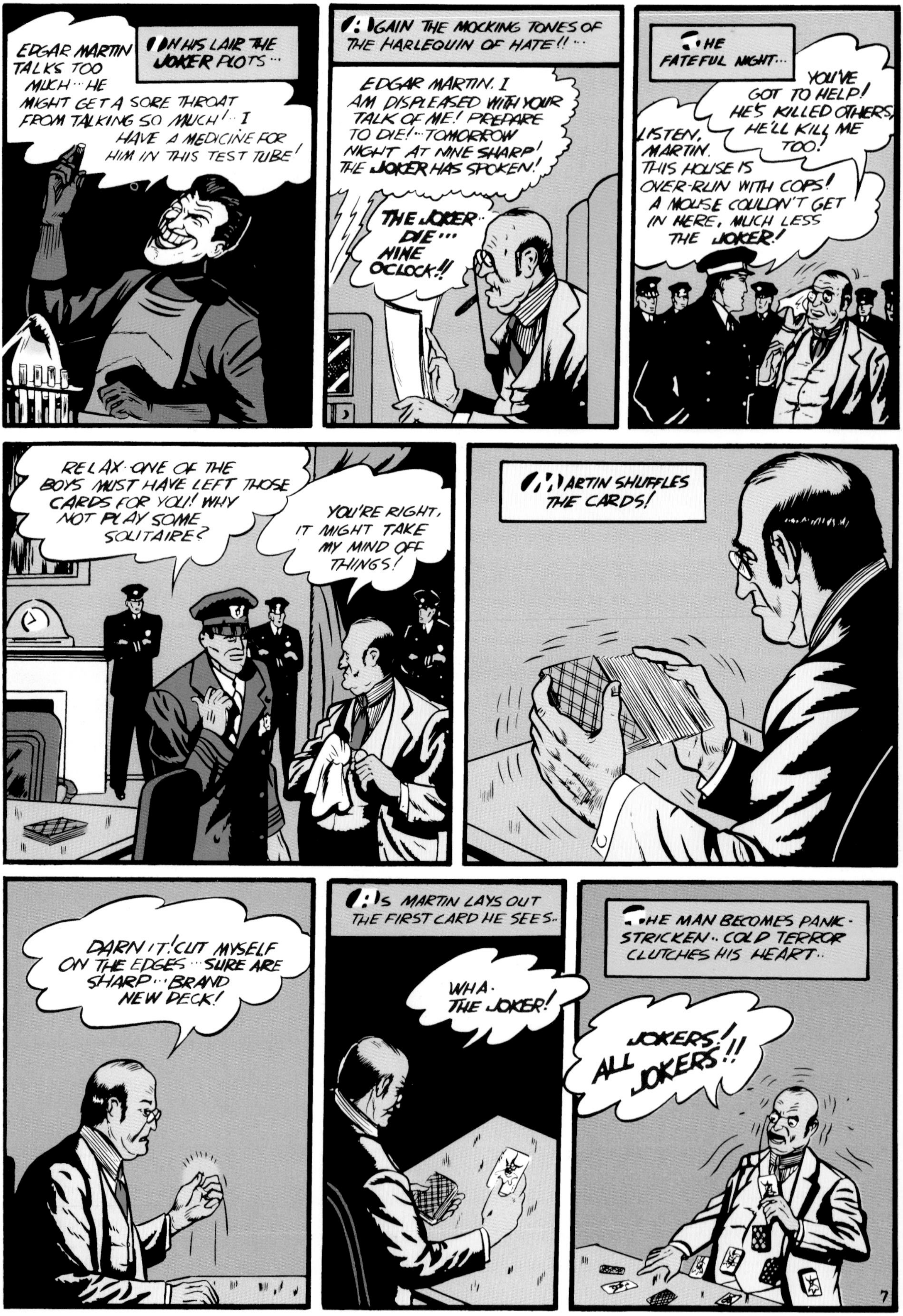
IN HIS LAIR THE JOKER PLOTS...
EDGAR MARTIN TALKS TOO MUCH... HE MIGHT GET A SORE THROAT FROM TALKING SO MUCH!.. I HAVE A MEDICINE FOR HIM IN THIS TEST TUBE!
AGAIN THE MOCKING TONES OF THE HARLEQUIN OF HATE!!...
EDGAR MARTIN, I AM DISPLEASED WITH YOUR TALK OF ME! PREPARE TO DIE!..TOMORROW NIGHT AT NINE SHARP! THE JOKER HAS SPOKEN!
THE JOKER.. DIE... NINE OCLOCK!!
THE FATEFUL NIGHT...
YOU'VE GOT TO HELP! HE'S KILLED OTHERS, HE'LL KILL ME TOO!
LISTEN, MARTIN. THIS HOUSE IS OVER-RUN WITH COPS! A MOUSE COULDN'T GET IN HERE, MUCH LESS THE JOKER!
RELAX. ONE OF THE BOYS MUST HAVE LEFT THOSE CARDS FOR YOU! WHY NOT PLAY SOME SOLITAIRE?
YOU'RE RIGHT, IT MIGHT TAKE MY MIND OFF THINGS!
MARTIN SHUFFLES THE CARDS!
DARN IT! CUT MYSELF ON THE EDGES... SURE ARE SHARP... BRAND NEW DECK!
AS MARTIN LAYS OUT THE FIRST CARD HE SEES..
WHA. THE JOKER!
THE MAN BECOMES PANIC-STRICKEN.. COLD TERROR CLUTCHES HIS HEART..
JOKERS! ALL JOKERS!!
7

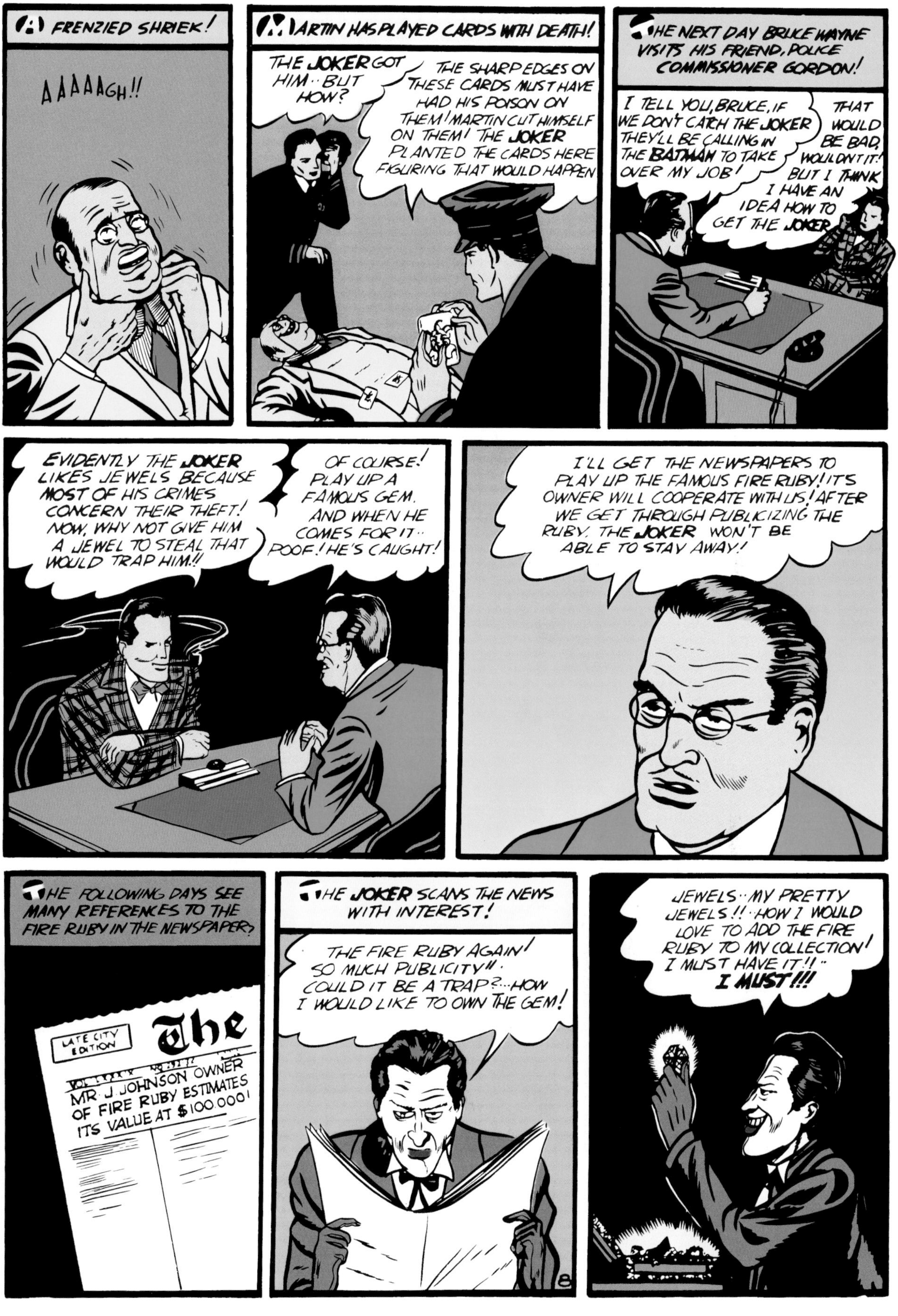
A FRENZIED SHRIEK!
AAAAAGH!!
MARTIN HAS PLAYED CARDS WITH DEATH!
THE JOKER GOT HIM.. BUT HOW?
THE SHARP EDGES ON THESE CARDS MUST HAVE HAD HIS POISON ON THEM! MARTIN CUT HIMSELF ON THEM! THE JOKER PLANTED THE CARDS HERE FIGURING THAT WOULD HAPPEN
THE NEXT DAY BRUCE WAYNE VISITS HIS FRIEND, POLICE COMMISSIONER GORDON!
I TELL YOU, BRUCE, IF WE DON'T CATCH THE JOKER THEY'LL BE CALLING IN THE BATMAN TO TAKE OVER MY JOB!
THAT WOULD BE BAD, WOULDN'T IT! BUT I THINK I HAVE AN IDEA HOW TO GET THE JOKER
EVIDENTLY THE JOKER LIKES JEWELS BECAUSE MOST OF HIS CRIMES CONCERN THEIR THEFT! NOW, WHY NOT GIVE HIM A JEWEL TO STEAL THAT WOULD TRAP HIM!!
OF COURSE! PLAY UP A FAMOUS GEM. AND WHEN HE COMES FOR IT.. POOF! HE'S CAUGHT!
I'LL GET THE NEWSPAPERS TO PLAY UP THE FAMOUS FIRE RUBY! ITS OWNER WILL COOPERATE WITH US! AFTER WE GET THROUGH PUBLICIZING THE RUBY, THE JOKER WON'T BE ABLE TO STAY AWAY!
THE FOLLOWING DAYS SEE MANY REFERENCES TO THE FIRE RUBY IN THE NEWSPAPERS
LATE CITY EDITION
The
MR. J. JOHNSON OWNER OF FIRE RUBY ESTIMATES ITS VALUE AT $100.000!
THE JOKER SCANS THE NEWS WITH INTEREST!
THE FIRE RUBY AGAIN! SO MUCH PUBLICITY!! COULD IT BE A TRAP?... HOW I WOULD LIKE TO OWN THE GEM!
8
JEWELS.. MY PRETTY JEWELS!! HOW I WOULD LOVE TO ADD THE FIRE RUBY TO MY COLLECTION! I MUST HAVE IT!!.. I MUST!!!

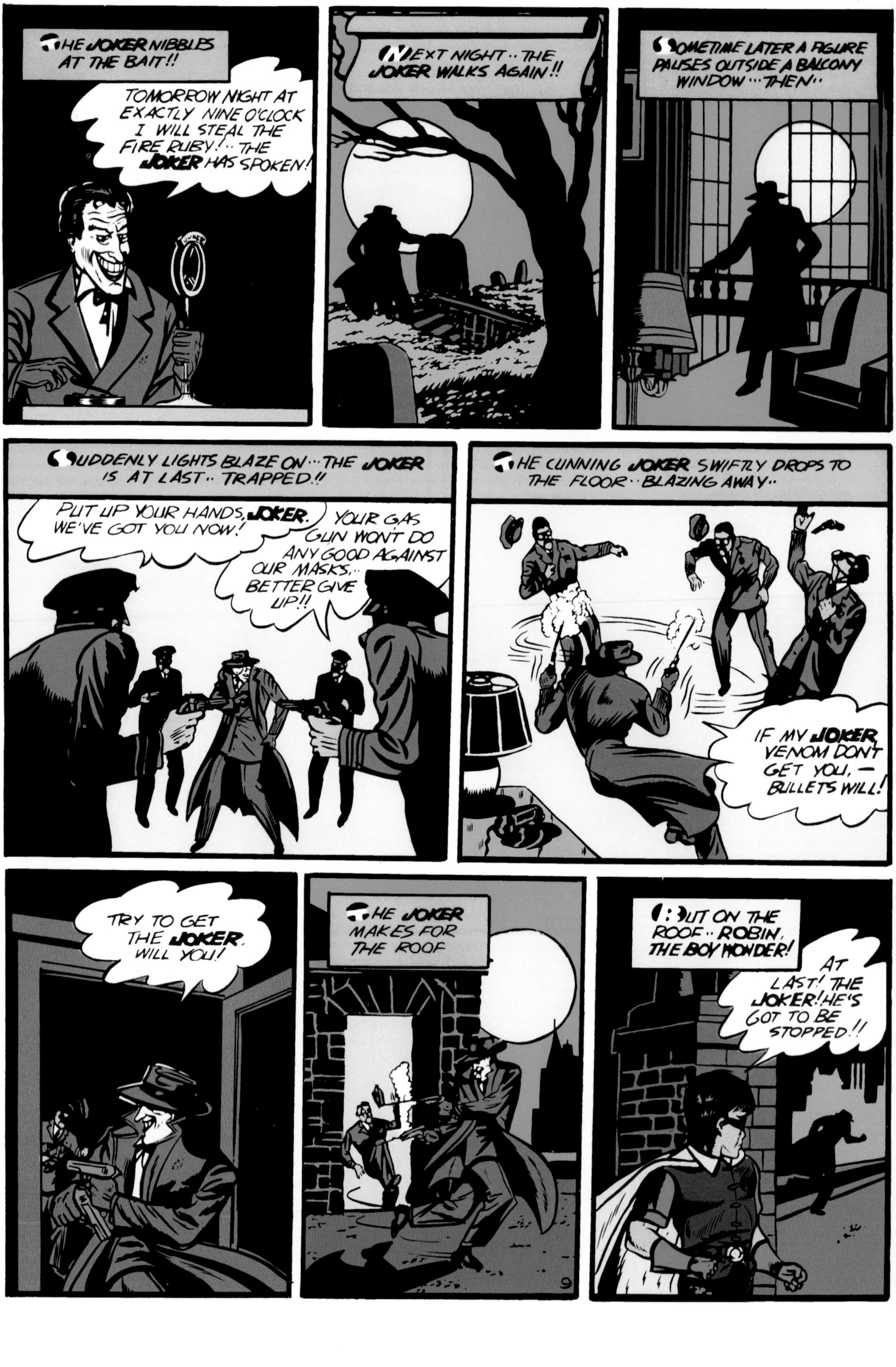
THE JOKER NIBBLES AT THE BAIT!!
TOMORROW NIGHT AT EXACTLY NINE O'CLOCK I WILL STEAL THE FIRE RUBY!.. THE JOKER HAS SPOKEN!
NEXT NIGHT.. THE JOKER WALKS AGAIN!!
SOMETIME LATER A FIGURE PAUSES OUTSIDE A BALCONY WINDOW... THEN..
SUDDENLY LIGHTS BLAZE ON... THE JOKER IS AT LAST.. TRAPPED!!
PUT UP YOUR HANDS, JOKER. WE'VE GOT YOU NOW!
YOUR GAS GUN WON'T DO ANY GOOD AGAINST OUR MASKS,.. BETTER GIVE UP!!
THE CUNNING JOKER SWIFTLY DROPS TO THE FLOOR.. BLAZING AWAY..
IF MY JOKER VENOM DON'T GET YOU, — BULLETS WILL!
TRY TO GET THE JOKER, WILL YOU!
THE JOKER MAKES FOR THE ROOF
BUT ON THE ROOF.. ROBIN, THE BOY WONDER!
AT LAST! THE JOKER! HE'S GOT TO BE STOPPED!!
9

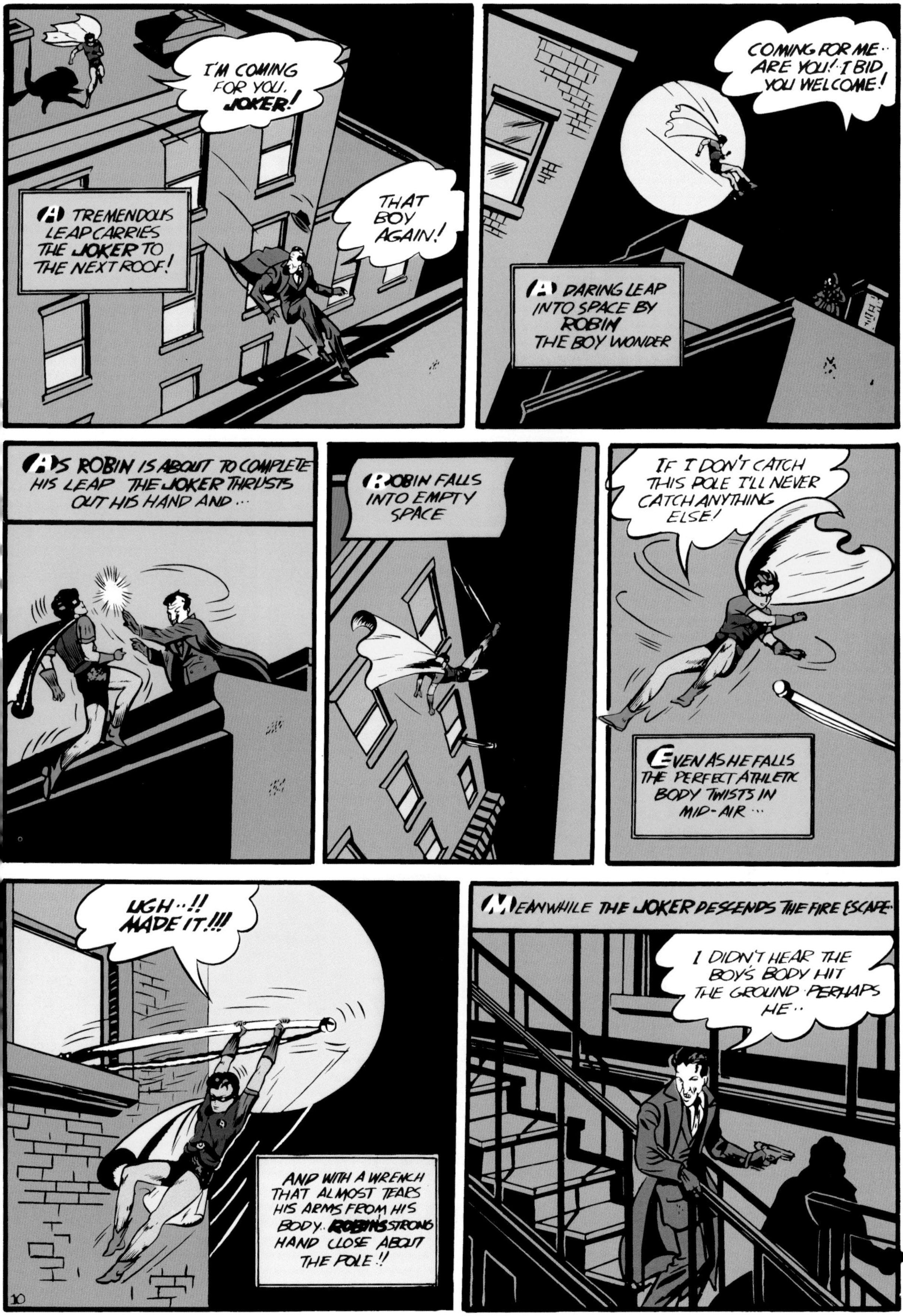
I'M COMING FOR YOU, JOKER!
A TREMENDOUS LEAP CARRIES THE JOKER TO THE NEXT ROOF!
THAT BOY AGAIN!
COMING FOR ME.. ARE YOU!..I BID YOU WELCOME!
A DARING LEAP INTO SPACE BY ROBIN THE BOY WONDER
AS ROBIN IS ABOUT TO COMPLETE HIS LEAP THE JOKER THRUSTS OUT HIS HAND AND...
ROBIN FALLS INTO EMPTY SPACE
IF I DON'T CATCH THIS POLE I'LL NEVER CATCH ANYTHING ELSE!
EVEN AS HE FALLS THE PERFECT ATHLETIC BODY TWISTS IN MID-AIR...
UGH..!! MADE IT!!!
AND WITH A WRENCH THAT ALMOST TEARS HIS ARMS FROM HIS BODY.. ROBIN'S STRONG HAND CLOSE ABOUT THE POLE!!
10
MEANWHILE THE JOKER DESCENDS THE FIRE ESCAPE..
I DIDN'T HEAR THE BOY'S BODY HIT THE GROUND. PERHAPS HE..

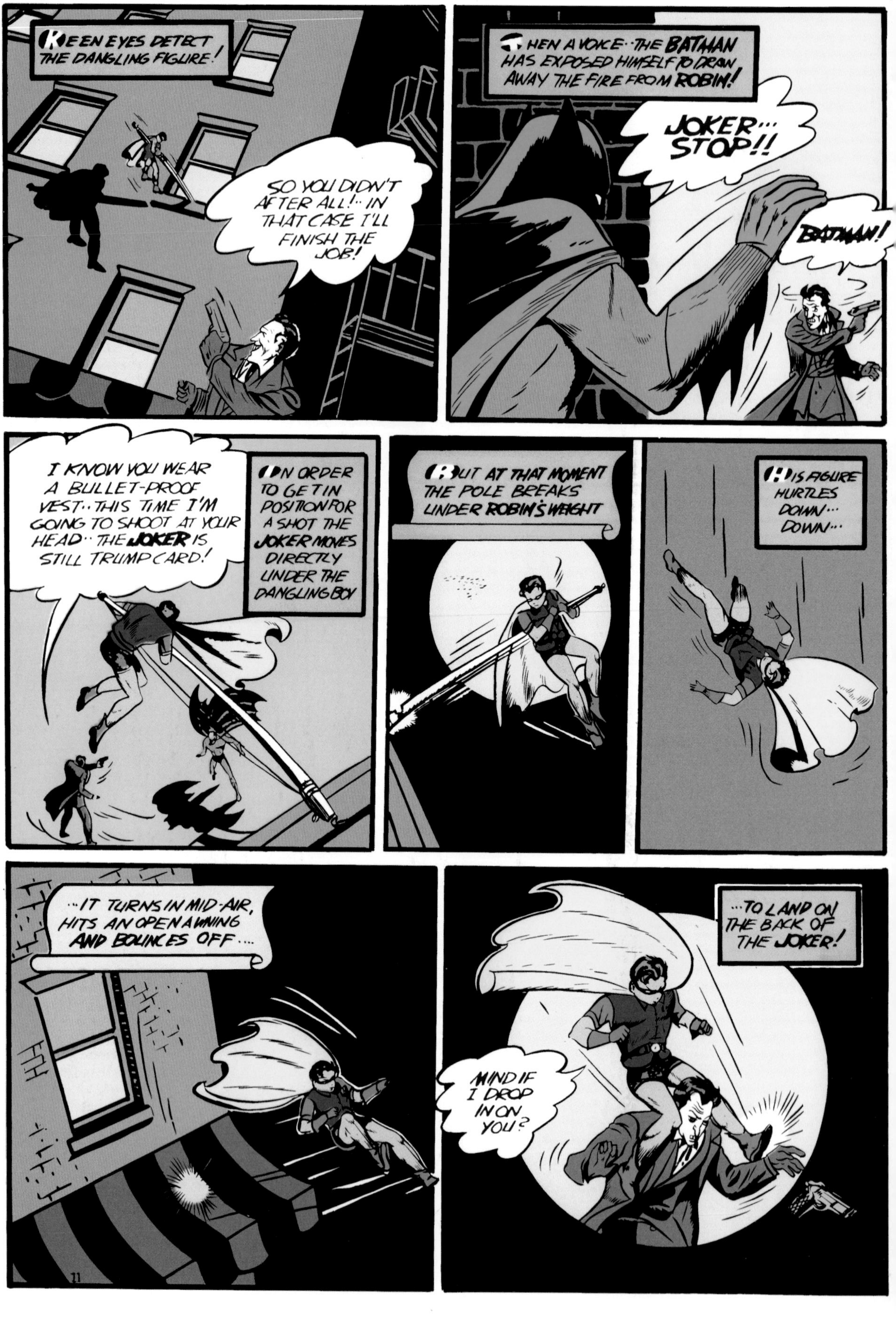
KEEN EYES DETECT THE DANGLING FIGURE!
SO YOU DIDN'T AFTER ALL!.. IN THAT CASE I'LL FINISH THE JOB!
THEN A VOICE.. THE BATMAN HAS EXPOSED HIMSELF TO DRAW AWAY THE FIRE FROM ROBIN!
JOKER... STOP!!
BATMAN!
I KNOW YOU WEAR A BULLET-PROOF VEST.. THIS TIME I'M GOING TO SHOOT AT YOUR HEAD.. THE JOKER IS STILL TRUMP CARD!
IN ORDER TO GET IN POSITION FOR A SHOT THE JOKER MOVES DIRECTLY UNDER THE DANGLING BOY
BUT AT THAT MOMENT THE POLE BREAKS UNDER ROBIN'S WEIGHT
HIS FIGURE HURTLES DOWN... DOWN...
...IT TURNS IN MID-AIR, HITS AN OPEN AWNING AND BOUNCES OFF....
11
...TO LAND ON THE BACK OF THE JOKER!
MIND IF I DROP IN ON YOU?

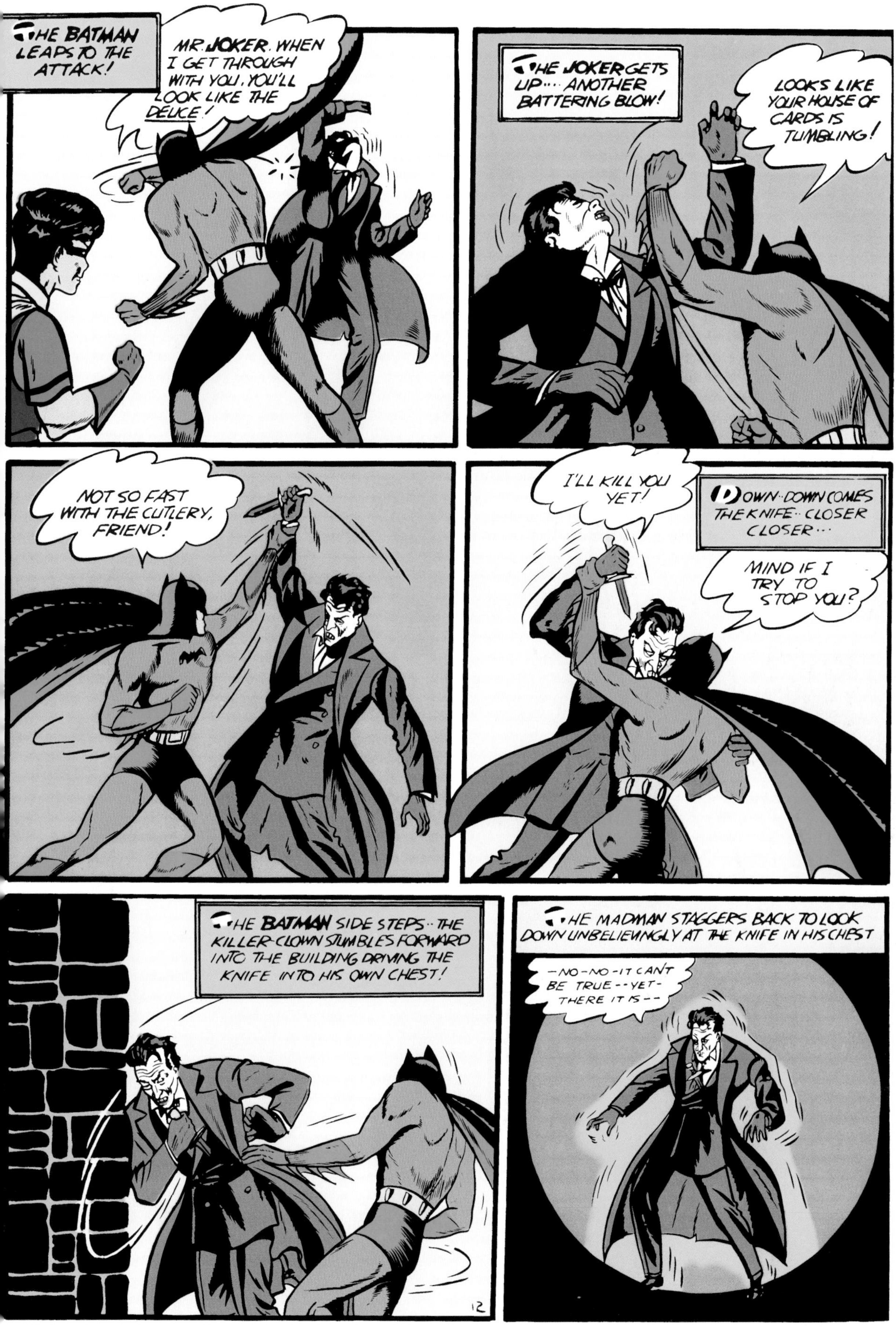
THE BATMAN LEAPS TO THE ATTACK!
MR. JOKER, WHEN I GET THROUGH WITH YOU, YOU'LL LOOK LIKE THE DEUCE!
THE JOKER GETS UP.... ANOTHER BATTERING BLOW!
LOOKS LIKE YOUR HOUSE OF CARDS IS TUMBLING!
NOT SO FAST WITH THE CUTLERY, FRIEND!
I'LL KILL YOU YET!
DOWN.. DOWN COMES THE KNIFE.. CLOSER CLOSER...
MIND IF I TRY TO STOP YOU?
THE BATMAN SIDE STEPS.. THE KILLER-CLOWN STUMBLES FORWARD INTO THE BUILDING DRIVING THE KNIFE INTO HIS OWN CHEST!
12
THE MADMAN STAGGERS BACK TO LOOK DOWN UNBELIEVINGLY AT THE KNIFE IN HIS CHEST
--NO--NO--IT CAN'T BE TRUE--YET-- THERE IT IS--

PEAL AFTER PEAL OF WILD HYSTERICAL LAUGHTER COMES FROM HIS GAPING MOUTH

HA! HA! HA! THE JOKER IS GOING TO DIE HA! HA! THE LAUGH IS ON THE JOKER! HA! HA! LAUGH CLOWN LAUGH! HA! HA! HA! HA-HA-HA-HA

THE **JOKER** HAS PLAYED HIS LAST HAND AND LOST!

JOKER, THIS TIME YOU COULDN'T WIN... THE CARDS WERE STACKED AGAINST YOU!

LOOK - STILL GRINNING IN DEATH!

YES - AND WHEN THE FLESH IS GONE - THE GRINNING SKULL WILL STILL CARRY THE SIGN OF THE **JOKER**... INTO ETERNITY!

THERE'S SOMEONE ON THE GROUND! LOOK, **BATMAN** AND THAT KID, **ROBIN**!

LET'S GO, **ROBIN**... THE POLICE SEEM TO THINK IT'S TIME TO TAKE OVER!

THE ONLY THING TO TAKE OVER IS THE BODY!

WHY, IT'S THE **JOKER**! IT SEEMS THE **BATMAN** HAS SAVED US A LOT OF TROUBLE!--- WE'D BETTER CALL THE AMBULANCE!

BUT IN THE AMBULANCE A STARTLING FACT IS BROUGHT TO LIGHT!!

WHAT'S THE MATTER, DOC, YOU LOOK AS IF YOU HAD SEEN A GHOST!

I MIGHT HAVE... I JUST EXAMINED THIS MAN - HE ISN'T DEAD! - HE'S STILL ALIVE - AND HE'S GOING TO **LIVE**!

BOB KANE

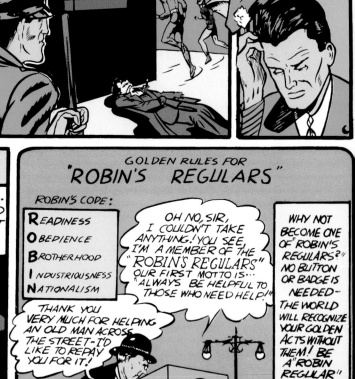

GOLDEN RULES FOR "**ROBIN'S REGULARS**"

ROBIN'S CODE:

R EADINESS
O BEDIENCE
B ROTHERHOOD
I NDUSTRIOUSNESS
N ATIONALISM

OH NO, SIR, I COULDN'T TAKE ANYTHING! YOU SEE, I'M A MEMBER OF THE "ROBIN'S REGULARS" OUR FIRST MOTTO IS... "ALWAYS BE HELPFUL TO THOSE WHO NEED HELP!"

THANK YOU VERY MUCH FOR HELPING AN OLD MAN ACROSS THE STREET - I'D LIKE TO REPAY YOU FOR IT!

WHY NOT BECOME ONE OF "ROBIN'S REGULARS?" NO BUTTON OR BADGE IS NEEDED - THE WORLD WILL RECOGNIZE YOUR GOLDEN ACTS WITHOUT THEM! BE A "ROBIN REGULAR" BY BEING **REGULAR**!

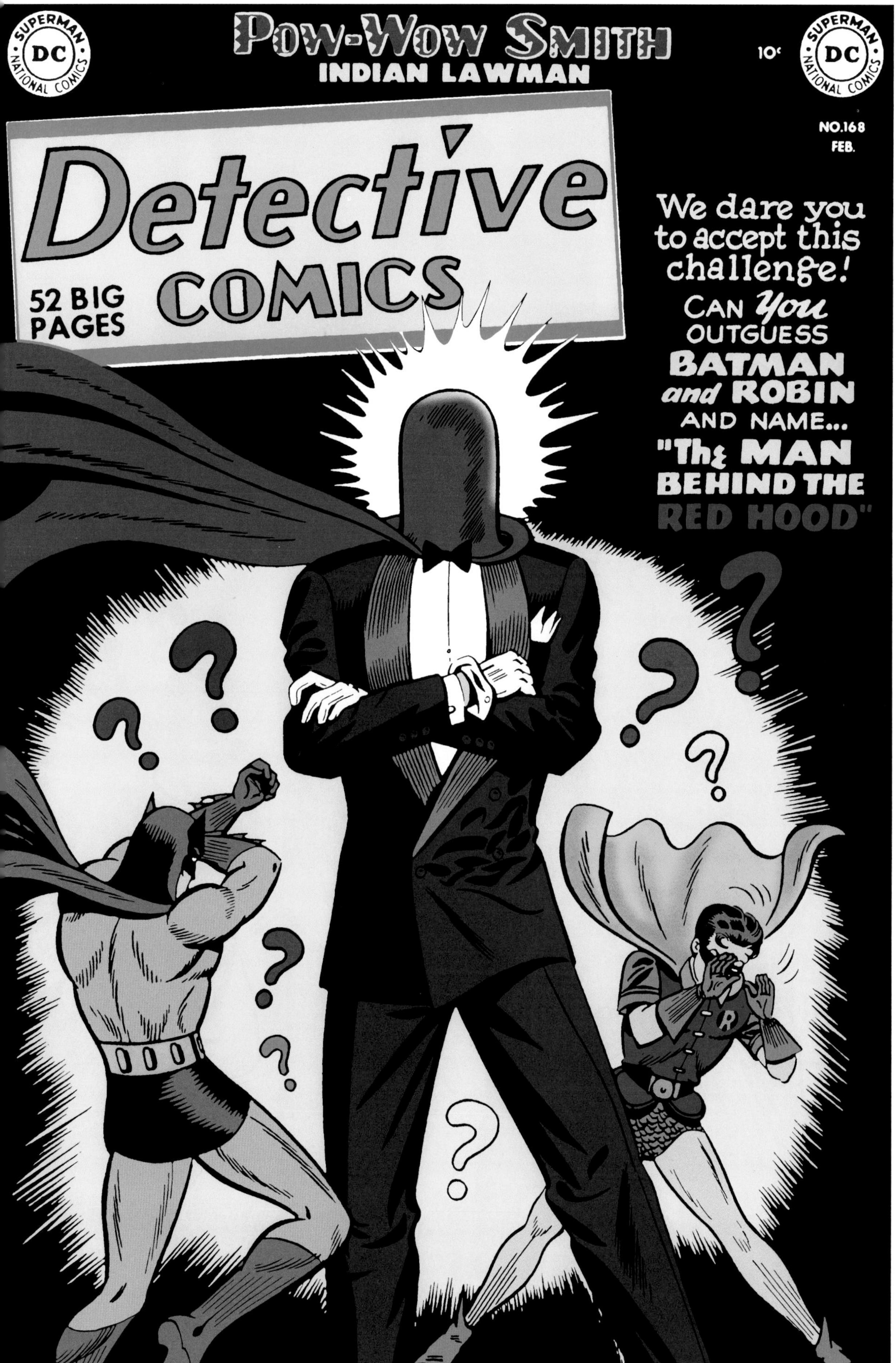
SUPERMAN DC NATIONAL COMICS
POW-WOW SMITH
INDIAN LAWMAN
10¢
SUPERMAN DC NATIONAL COMICS
NO.168
FEB.
Detective COMICS
52 BIG PAGES
We dare you to accept this challenge!
CAN YOU OUTGUESS
BATMAN and ROBIN
AND NAME...
"THE MAN BEHIND THE RED HOOD"

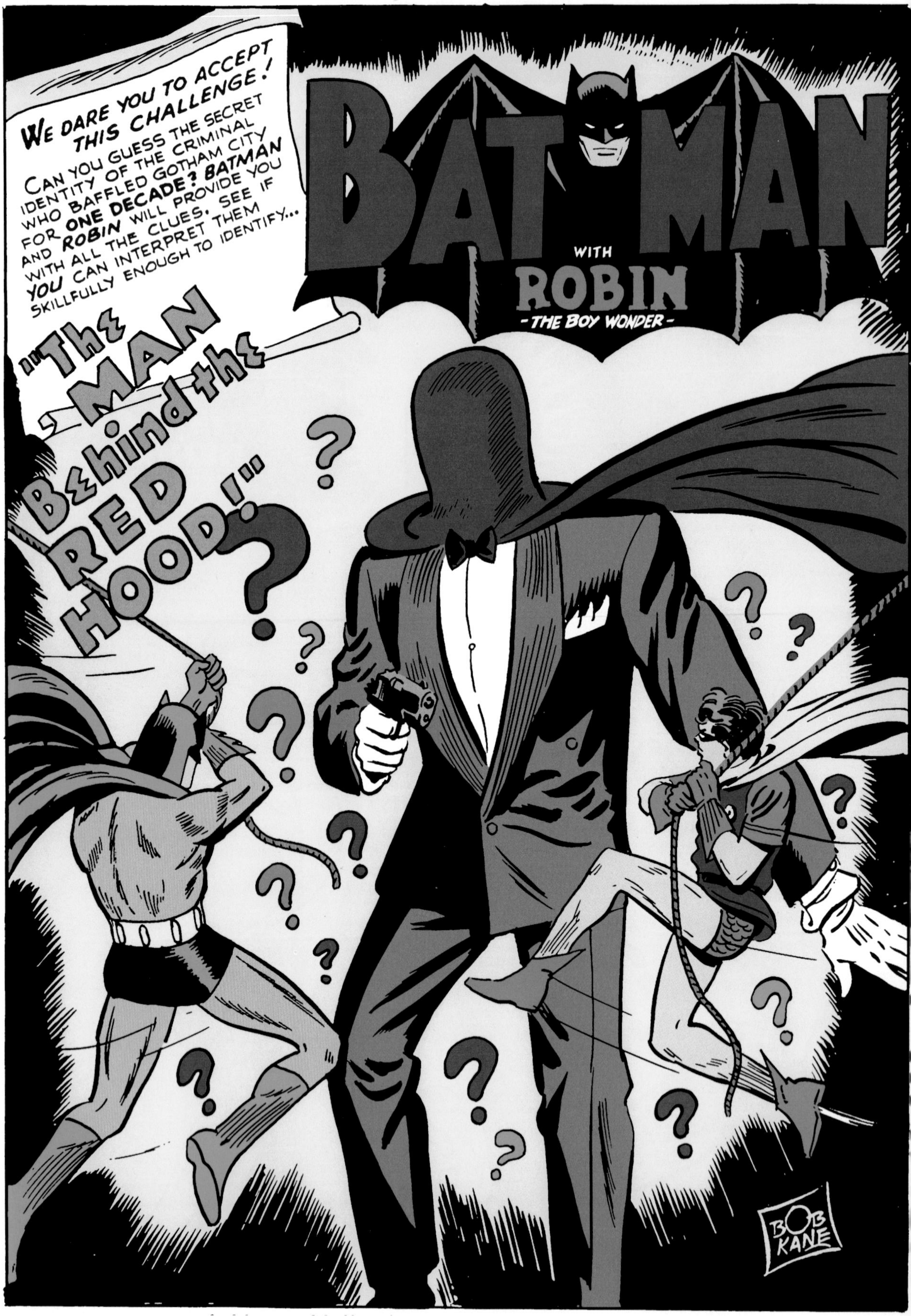
We dare you to accept this challenge!
Can you guess the secret identity of the criminal who baffled Gotham City for one decade? Batman and Robin will provide you with all the clues. See if you can interpret them skillfully enough to identify...
"The Man Behind the Red Hood!"
Batman
with
Robin
-The Boy Wonder-
Bob Kane

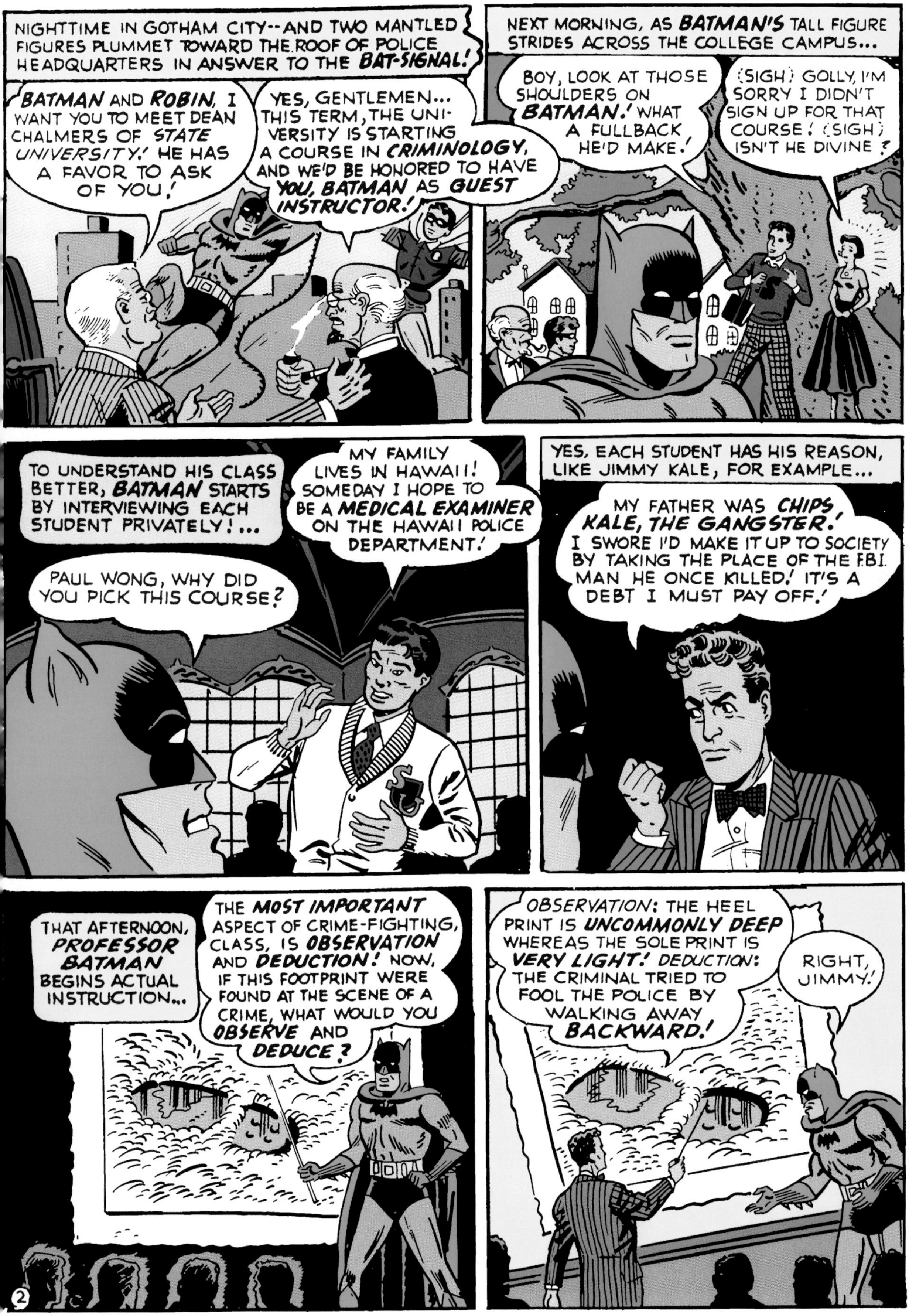
NIGHTTIME IN GOTHAM CITY--AND TWO MANTLED FIGURES PLUMMET TOWARD THE ROOF OF POLICE HEADQUARTERS IN ANSWER TO THE BAT-SIGNAL!
BATMAN AND ROBIN, I WANT YOU TO MEET DEAN CHALMERS OF STATE UNIVERSITY! HE HAS A FAVOR TO ASK OF YOU!
YES, GENTLEMEN... THIS TERM, THE UNIVERSITY IS STARTING A COURSE IN CRIMINOLOGY, AND WE'D BE HONORED TO HAVE YOU, BATMAN AS GUEST INSTRUCTOR!
NEXT MORNING, AS BATMAN'S TALL FIGURE STRIDES ACROSS THE COLLEGE CAMPUS...
BOY, LOOK AT THOSE SHOULDERS ON BATMAN! WHAT A FULLBACK HE'D MAKE!
(SIGH) GOLLY, I'M SORRY I DIDN'T SIGN UP FOR THAT COURSE! (SIGH) ISN'T HE DIVINE?
TO UNDERSTAND HIS CLASS BETTER, BATMAN STARTS BY INTERVIEWING EACH STUDENT PRIVATELY!...
PAUL WONG, WHY DID YOU PICK THIS COURSE?
MY FAMILY LIVES IN HAWAII! SOMEDAY I HOPE TO BE A MEDICAL EXAMINER ON THE HAWAII POLICE DEPARTMENT!
YES, EACH STUDENT HAS HIS REASON, LIKE JIMMY KALE, FOR EXAMPLE...
MY FATHER WAS CHIPS KALE, THE GANGSTER! I SWORE I'D MAKE IT UP TO SOCIETY BY TAKING THE PLACE OF THE F.B.I. MAN HE ONCE KILLED! IT'S A DEBT I MUST PAY OFF!
THAT AFTERNOON, PROFESSOR BATMAN BEGINS ACTUAL INSTRUCTION...
THE MOST IMPORTANT ASPECT OF CRIME-FIGHTING, CLASS, IS OBSERVATION AND DEDUCTION! NOW, IF THIS FOOTPRINT WERE FOUND AT THE SCENE OF A CRIME, WHAT WOULD YOU OBSERVE AND DEDUCE?
2
OBSERVATION: THE HEEL PRINT IS UNCOMMONLY DEEP WHEREAS THE SOLE PRINT IS VERY LIGHT! DEDUCTION: THE CRIMINAL TRIED TO FOOL THE POLICE BY WALKING AWAY BACKWARD!
RIGHT, JIMMY!

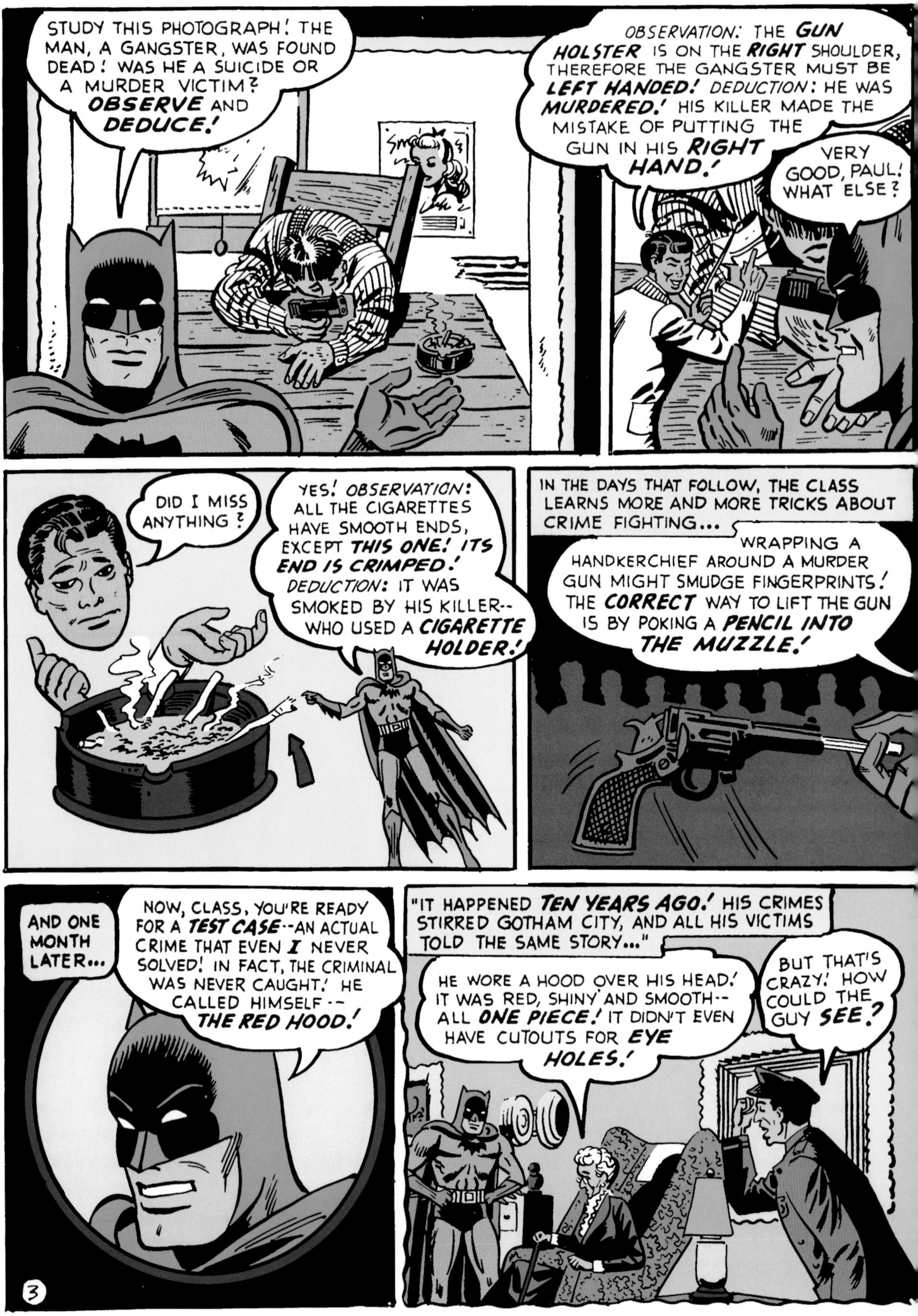
STUDY THIS PHOTOGRAPH! THE MAN, A GANGSTER, WAS FOUND DEAD! WAS HE A SUICIDE OR A MURDER VICTIM? OBSERVE AND DEDUCE!
OBSERVATION: THE GUN HOLSTER IS ON THE RIGHT SHOULDER, THEREFORE THE GANGSTER MUST BE LEFT HANDED! DEDUCTION: HE WAS MURDERED! HIS KILLER MADE THE MISTAKE OF PUTTING THE GUN IN HIS RIGHT HAND!
VERY GOOD, PAUL! WHAT ELSE?
DID I MISS ANYTHING?
YES! OBSERVATION: ALL THE CIGARETTES HAVE SMOOTH ENDS, EXCEPT THIS ONE! ITS END IS CRIMPED! DEDUCTION: IT WAS SMOKED BY HIS KILLER-- WHO USED A CIGARETTE HOLDER!
IN THE DAYS THAT FOLLOW, THE CLASS LEARNS MORE AND MORE TRICKS ABOUT CRIME FIGHTING...
WRAPPING A HANDKERCHIEF AROUND A MURDER GUN MIGHT SMUDGE FINGERPRINTS! THE CORRECT WAY TO LIFT THE GUN IS BY POKING A PENCIL INTO THE MUZZLE!
AND ONE MONTH LATER...
NOW, CLASS, YOU'RE READY FOR A TEST CASE--AN ACTUAL CRIME THAT EVEN I NEVER SOLVED! IN FACT, THE CRIMINAL WAS NEVER CAUGHT! HE CALLED HIMSELF-- THE RED HOOD!
"IT HAPPENED TEN YEARS AGO! HIS CRIMES STIRRED GOTHAM CITY, AND ALL HIS VICTIMS TOLD THE SAME STORY..."
HE WORE A HOOD OVER HIS HEAD! IT WAS RED, SHINY AND SMOOTH-- ALL ONE PIECE! IT DIDN'T EVEN HAVE CUTOUTS FOR EYE HOLES!
BUT THAT'S CRAZY! HOW COULD THE GUY SEE?
3

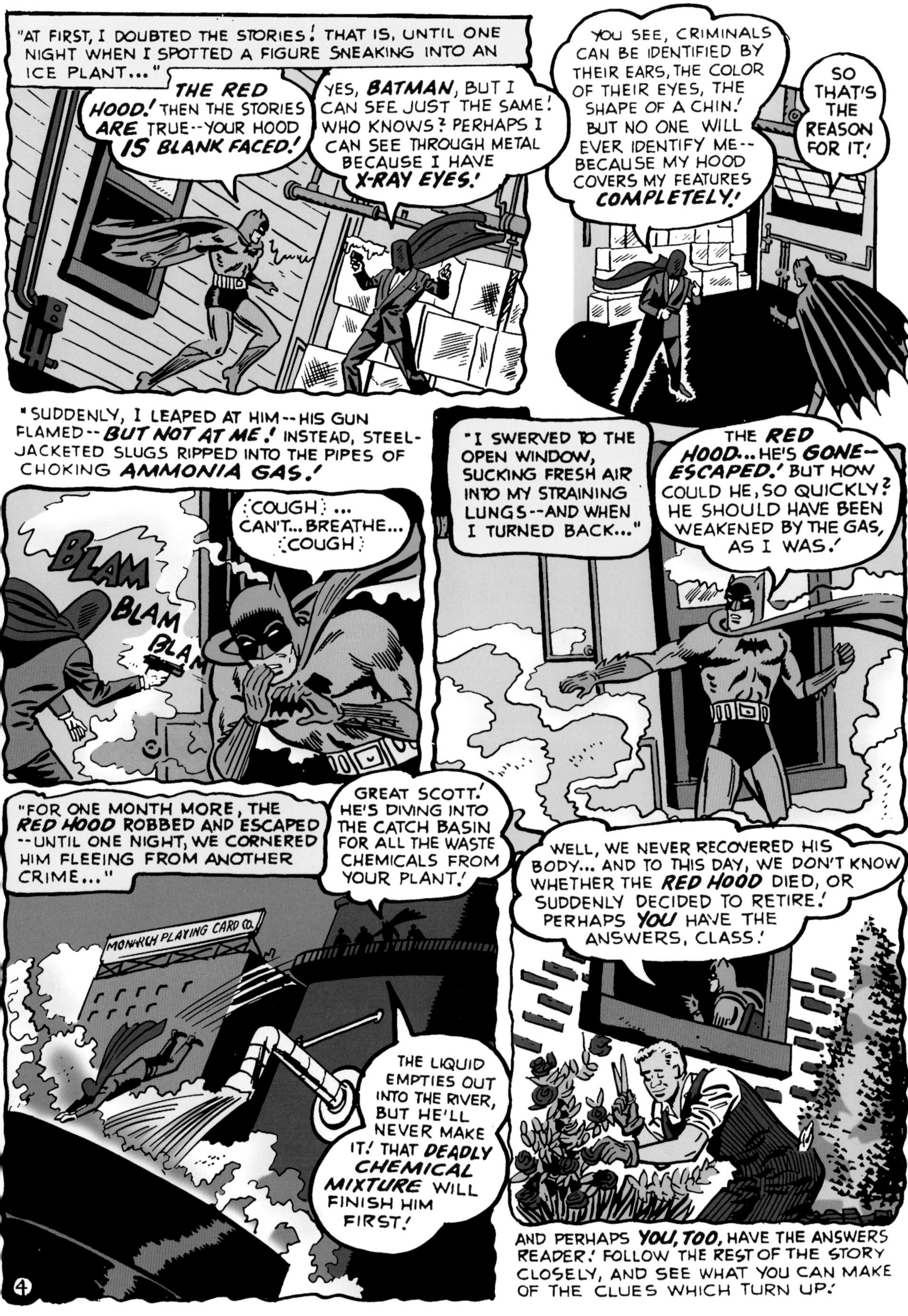

"AT FIRST, I DOUBTED THE STORIES! THAT IS, UNTIL ONE NIGHT WHEN I SPOTTED A FIGURE SNEAKING INTO AN ICE PLANT..."
THE RED HOOD! THEN THE STORIES ARE TRUE--YOUR HOOD IS BLANK FACED!
YES, BATMAN, BUT I CAN SEE JUST THE SAME! WHO KNOWS? PERHAPS I CAN SEE THROUGH METAL BECAUSE I HAVE X-RAY EYES!
YOU SEE, CRIMINALS CAN BE IDENTIFIED BY THEIR EARS, THE COLOR OF THEIR EYES, THE SHAPE OF A CHIN! BUT NO ONE WILL EVER IDENTIFY ME--BECAUSE MY HOOD COVERS MY FEATURES COMPLETELY!
SO THAT'S THE REASON FOR IT!
"SUDDENLY, I LEAPED AT HIM--HIS GUN FLAMED--BUT NOT AT ME! INSTEAD, STEEL-JACKETED SLUGS RIPPED INTO THE PIPES OF CHOKING AMMONIA GAS!
BLAM
BLAM
BLAM
COUGH ... CAN'T...BREATHE... COUGH
"I SWERVED TO THE OPEN WINDOW, SUCKING FRESH AIR INTO MY STRAINING LUNGS--AND WHEN I TURNED BACK..."
THE RED HOOD...HE'S GONE--ESCAPED! BUT HOW COULD HE, SO QUICKLY? HE SHOULD HAVE BEEN WEAKENED BY THE GAS, AS I WAS!
"FOR ONE MONTH MORE, THE RED HOOD ROBBED AND ESCAPED--UNTIL ONE NIGHT, WE CORNERED HIM FLEEING FROM ANOTHER CRIME..."
GREAT SCOTT! HE'S DIVING INTO THE CATCH BASIN FOR ALL THE WASTE CHEMICALS FROM YOUR PLANT!
MONARCH PLAYING CARD CO.
THE LIQUID EMPTIES OUT INTO THE RIVER, BUT HE'LL NEVER MAKE IT! THAT DEADLY CHEMICAL MIXTURE WILL FINISH HIM FIRST!
WELL, WE NEVER RECOVERED HIS BODY... AND TO THIS DAY, WE DON'T KNOW WHETHER THE RED HOOD DIED, OR SUDDENLY DECIDED TO RETIRE! PERHAPS YOU HAVE THE ANSWERS, CLASS!
AND PERHAPS YOU, TOO, HAVE THE ANSWERS READER! FOLLOW THE REST OF THE STORY CLOSELY, AND SEE WHAT YOU CAN MAKE OF THE CLUES WHICH TURN UP!
4

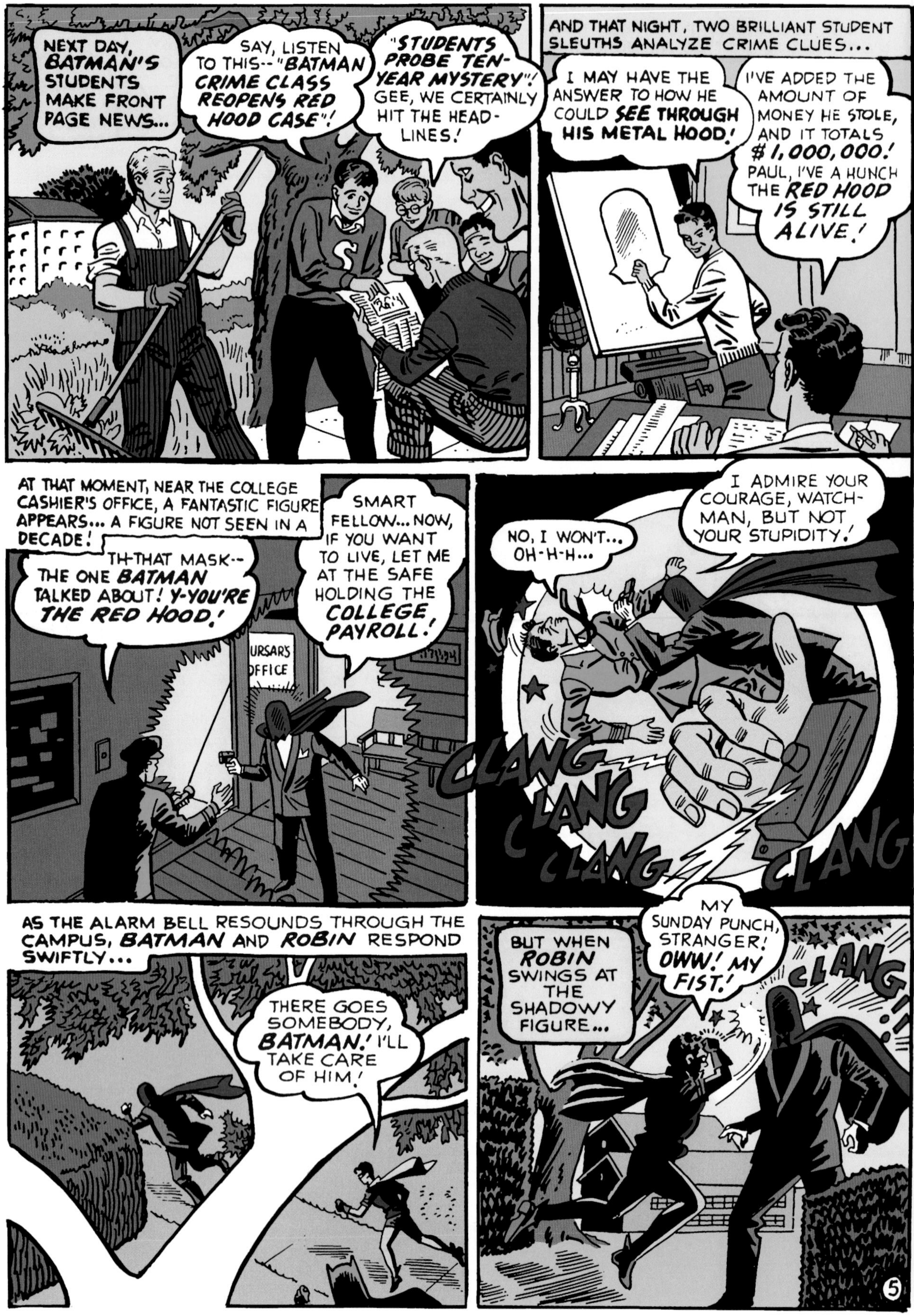
NEXT DAY, BATMAN'S STUDENTS MAKE FRONT PAGE NEWS...
SAY, LISTEN TO THIS--"BATMAN CRIME CLASS REOPENS RED HOOD CASE"!
"STUDENTS PROBE TEN-YEAR MYSTERY"! GEE, WE CERTAINLY HIT THE HEAD-LINES!
AND THAT NIGHT, TWO BRILLIANT STUDENT SLEUTHS ANALYZE CRIME CLUES...
I MAY HAVE THE ANSWER TO HOW HE COULD SEE THROUGH HIS METAL HOOD!
I'VE ADDED THE AMOUNT OF MONEY HE STOLE, AND IT TOTALS $1,000,000! PAUL, I'VE A HUNCH THE RED HOOD IS STILL ALIVE!
AT THAT MOMENT, NEAR THE COLLEGE CASHIER'S OFFICE, A FANTASTIC FIGURE APPEARS... A FIGURE NOT SEEN IN A DECADE!
TH-THAT MASK--THE ONE BATMAN TALKED ABOUT! Y-YOU'RE THE RED HOOD!
SMART FELLOW...NOW, IF YOU WANT TO LIVE, LET ME AT THE SAFE HOLDING THE COLLEGE PAYROLL!
URSAR'S OFFICE
NO, I WON'T... OH-H-H...
I ADMIRE YOUR COURAGE, WATCH-MAN, BUT NOT YOUR STUPIDITY!
CLANG
CLANG
CLANG
CLANG
CLANG
AS THE ALARM BELL RESOUNDS THROUGH THE CAMPUS, BATMAN AND ROBIN RESPOND SWIFTLY...
THERE GOES SOMEBODY, BATMAN! I'LL TAKE CARE OF HIM!
BUT WHEN ROBIN SWINGS AT THE SHADOWY FIGURE...
MY SUNDAY PUNCH, STRANGER! OWW! MY FIST!
CLANG!!
5

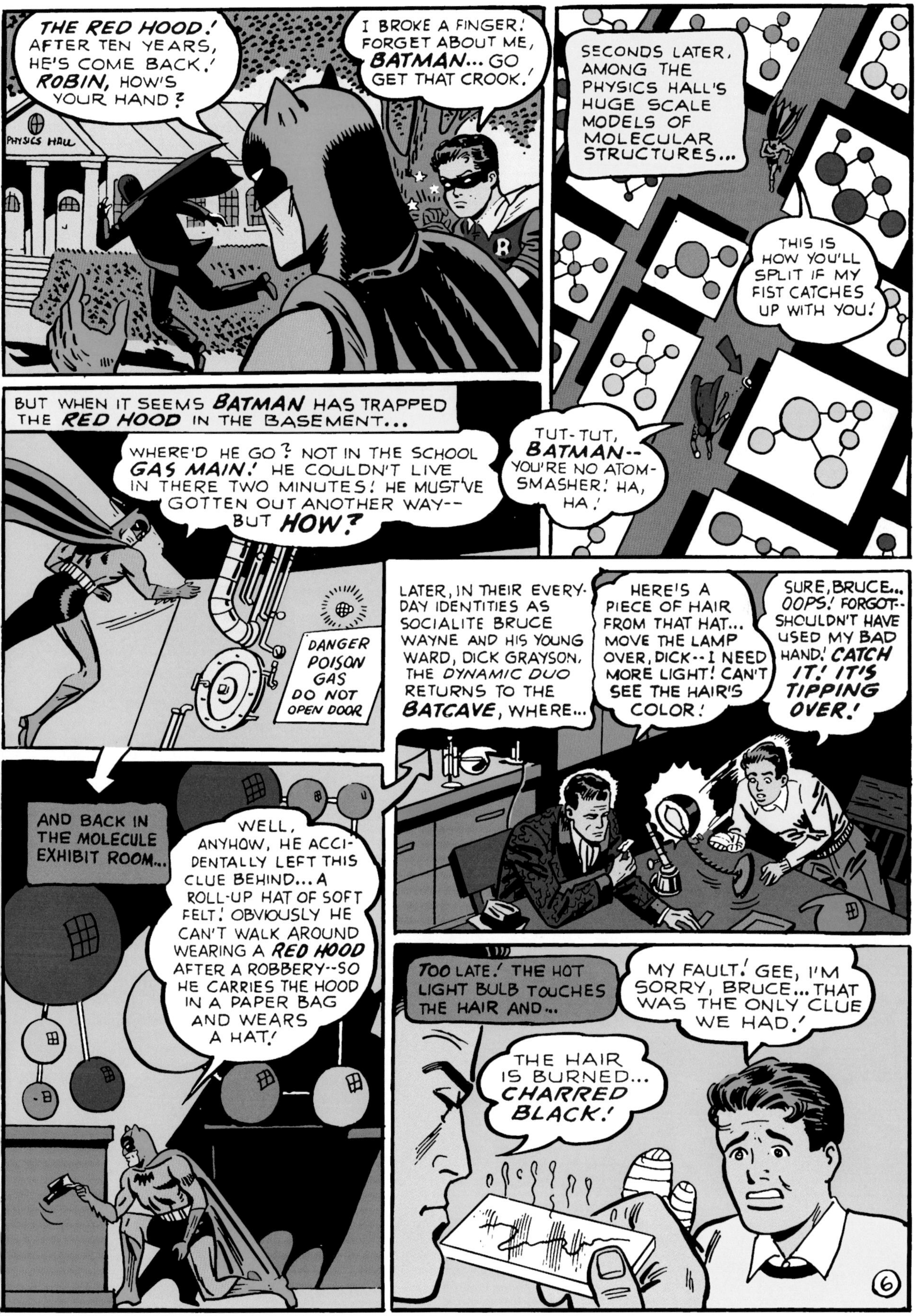
THE RED HOOD! AFTER TEN YEARS, HE'S COME BACK! ROBIN, HOW'S YOUR HAND?
I BROKE A FINGER! FORGET ABOUT ME, BATMAN... GO GET THAT CROOK!
PHYSICS HALL
SECONDS LATER, AMONG THE PHYSICS HALL'S HUGE SCALE MODELS OF MOLECULAR STRUCTURES...
THIS IS HOW YOU'LL SPLIT IF MY FIST CATCHES UP WITH YOU!
TUT-TUT, BATMAN-- YOU'RE NO ATOM-SMASHER! HA, HA!
BUT WHEN IT SEEMS BATMAN HAS TRAPPED THE RED HOOD IN THE BASEMENT...
WHERE'D HE GO? NOT IN THE SCHOOL GAS MAIN! HE COULDN'T LIVE IN THERE TWO MINUTES! HE MUST'VE GOTTEN OUT ANOTHER WAY-- BUT HOW?
DANGER POISON GAS DO NOT OPEN DOOR
LATER, IN THEIR EVERY-DAY IDENTITIES AS SOCIALITE BRUCE WAYNE AND HIS YOUNG WARD, DICK GRAYSON, THE DYNAMIC DUO RETURNS TO THE BATCAVE, WHERE...
HERE'S A PIECE OF HAIR FROM THAT HAT... MOVE THE LAMP OVER, DICK-- I NEED MORE LIGHT! CAN'T SEE THE HAIR'S COLOR!
SURE, BRUCE... OOPS! FORGOT-- SHOULDN'T HAVE USED MY BAD HAND! CATCH IT! IT'S TIPPING OVER!
AND BACK IN THE MOLECULE EXHIBIT ROOM...
WELL, ANYHOW, HE ACCI-DENTALLY LEFT THIS CLUE BEHIND... A ROLL-UP HAT OF SOFT FELT! OBVIOUSLY HE CAN'T WALK AROUND WEARING A RED HOOD AFTER A ROBBERY--SO HE CARRIES THE HOOD IN A PAPER BAG AND WEARS A HAT!
TOO LATE! THE HOT LIGHT BULB TOUCHES THE HAIR AND...
MY FAULT! GEE, I'M SORRY, BRUCE... THAT WAS THE ONLY CLUE WE HAD!
THE HAIR IS BURNED... CHARRED BLACK!
6

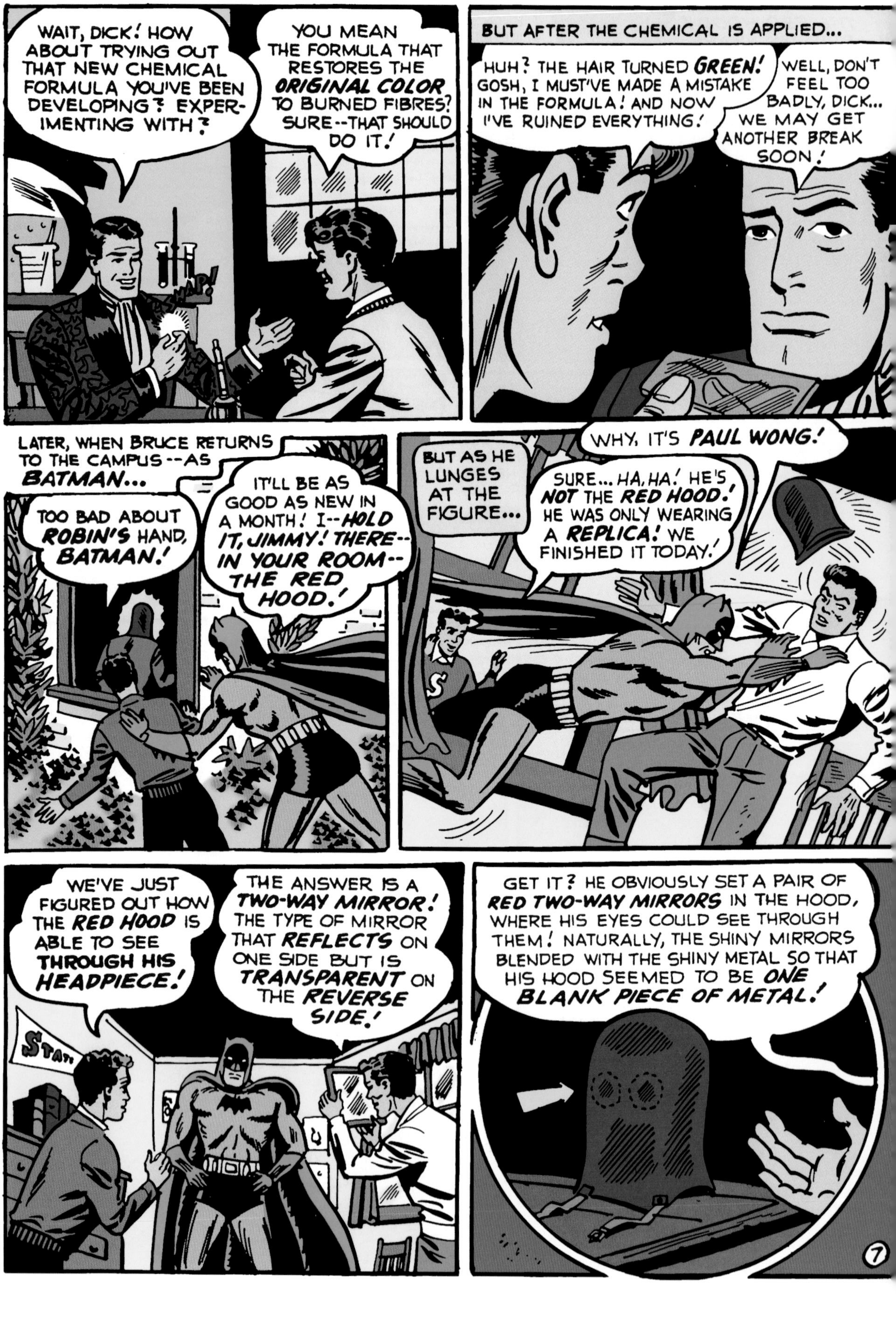
WAIT, DICK! HOW ABOUT TRYING OUT THAT NEW CHEMICAL FORMULA YOU'VE BEEN DEVELOPING? EXPERIMENTING WITH?
YOU MEAN THE FORMULA THAT RESTORES THE ORIGINAL COLOR TO BURNED FIBRES? SURE--THAT SHOULD DO IT!
BUT AFTER THE CHEMICAL IS APPLIED...
HUH? THE HAIR TURNED GREEN! GOSH, I MUST'VE MADE A MISTAKE IN THE FORMULA! AND NOW I'VE RUINED EVERYTHING!
WELL, DON'T FEEL TOO BADLY, DICK... WE MAY GET ANOTHER BREAK SOON!
LATER, WHEN BRUCE RETURNS TO THE CAMPUS--AS BATMAN...
TOO BAD ABOUT ROBIN'S HAND, BATMAN!
IT'LL BE AS GOOD AS NEW IN A MONTH! I--HOLD IT, JIMMY! THERE--IN YOUR ROOM--THE RED HOOD!
BUT AS HE LUNGES AT THE FIGURE...
WHY, IT'S PAUL WONG!
SURE... HA, HA! HE'S NOT THE RED HOOD! HE WAS ONLY WEARING A REPLICA! WE FINISHED IT TODAY!
WE'VE JUST FIGURED OUT HOW THE RED HOOD IS ABLE TO SEE THROUGH HIS HEADPIECE!
THE ANSWER IS A TWO-WAY MIRROR! THE TYPE OF MIRROR THAT REFLECTS ON ONE SIDE BUT IS TRANSPARENT ON THE REVERSE SIDE!
GET IT? HE OBVIOUSLY SET A PAIR OF RED TWO-WAY MIRRORS IN THE HOOD, WHERE HIS EYES COULD SEE THROUGH THEM! NATURALLY, THE SHINY MIRRORS BLENDED WITH THE SHINY METAL SO THAT HIS HOOD SEEMED TO BE ONE BLANK PIECE OF METAL!
7

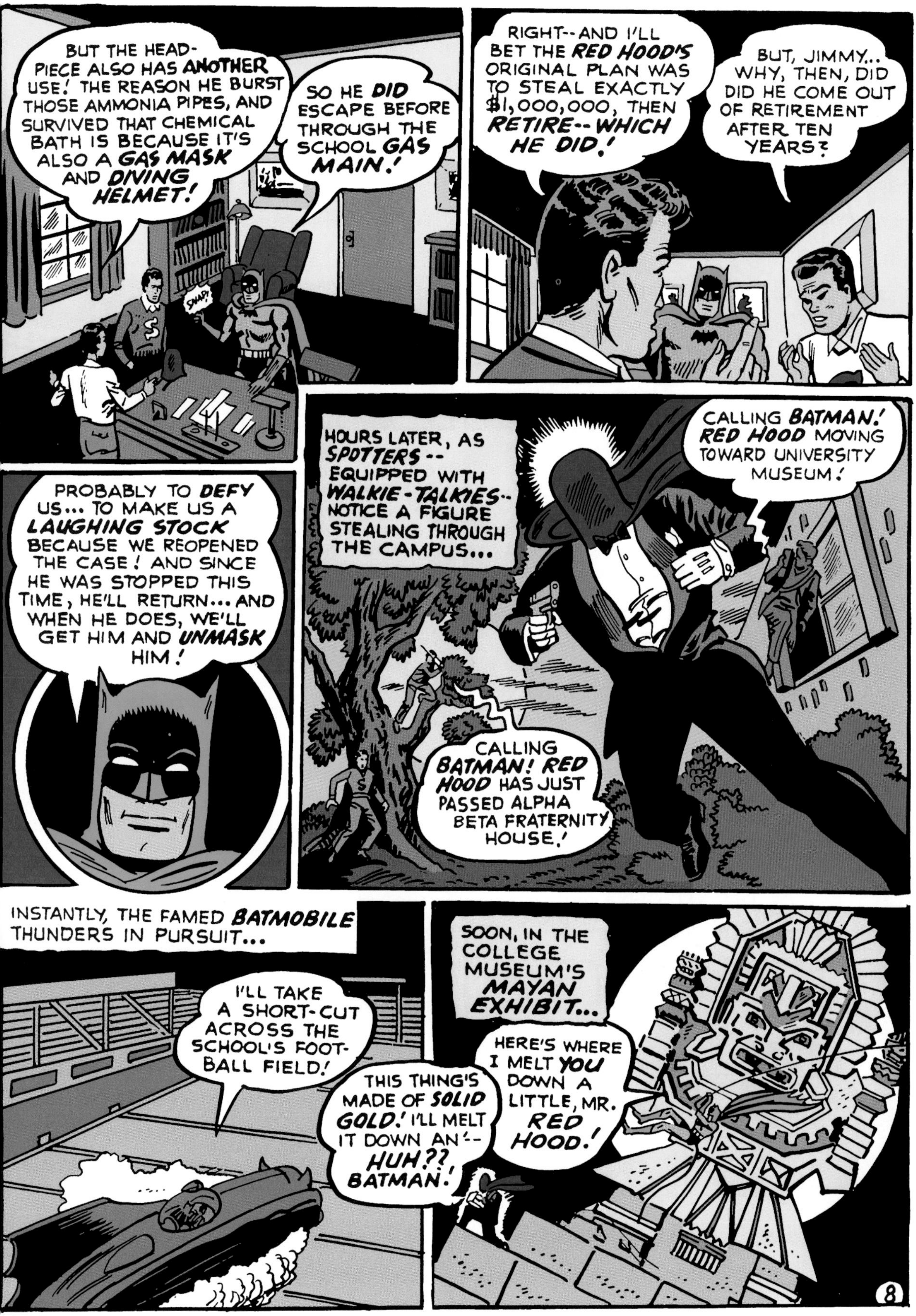
BUT THE HEAD-PIECE ALSO HAS ANOTHER USE! THE REASON HE BURST THOSE AMMONIA PIPES, AND SURVIVED THAT CHEMICAL BATH IS BECAUSE IT'S ALSO A GAS MASK AND DIVING HELMET!
SO HE DID ESCAPE BEFORE THROUGH THE SCHOOL GAS MAIN!
SNAP!
RIGHT--AND I'LL BET THE RED HOOD'S ORIGINAL PLAN WAS TO STEAL EXACTLY $1,000,000, THEN RETIRE--WHICH HE DID!
BUT, JIMMY... WHY, THEN, DID DID HE COME OUT OF RETIREMENT AFTER TEN YEARS?
PROBABLY TO DEFY US... TO MAKE US A LAUGHING STOCK BECAUSE WE REOPENED THE CASE! AND SINCE HE WAS STOPPED THIS TIME, HE'LL RETURN... AND WHEN HE DOES, WE'LL GET HIM AND UNMASK HIM!
HOURS LATER, AS SPOTTERS -- EQUIPPED WITH WALKIE-TALKIES -- NOTICE A FIGURE STEALING THROUGH THE CAMPUS...
CALLING BATMAN! RED HOOD MOVING TOWARD UNIVERSITY MUSEUM!
CALLING BATMAN! RED HOOD HAS JUST PASSED ALPHA BETA FRATERNITY HOUSE!
INSTANTLY, THE FAMED BATMOBILE THUNDERS IN PURSUIT...
I'LL TAKE A SHORT-CUT ACROSS THE SCHOOL'S FOOT-BALL FIELD!
SOON, IN THE COLLEGE MUSEUM'S MAYAN EXHIBIT...
THIS THING'S MADE OF SOLID GOLD! I'LL MELT IT DOWN AN'-- HUH??, BATMAN!
HERE'S WHERE I MELT YOU DOWN A LITTLE, MR. RED HOOD!
8

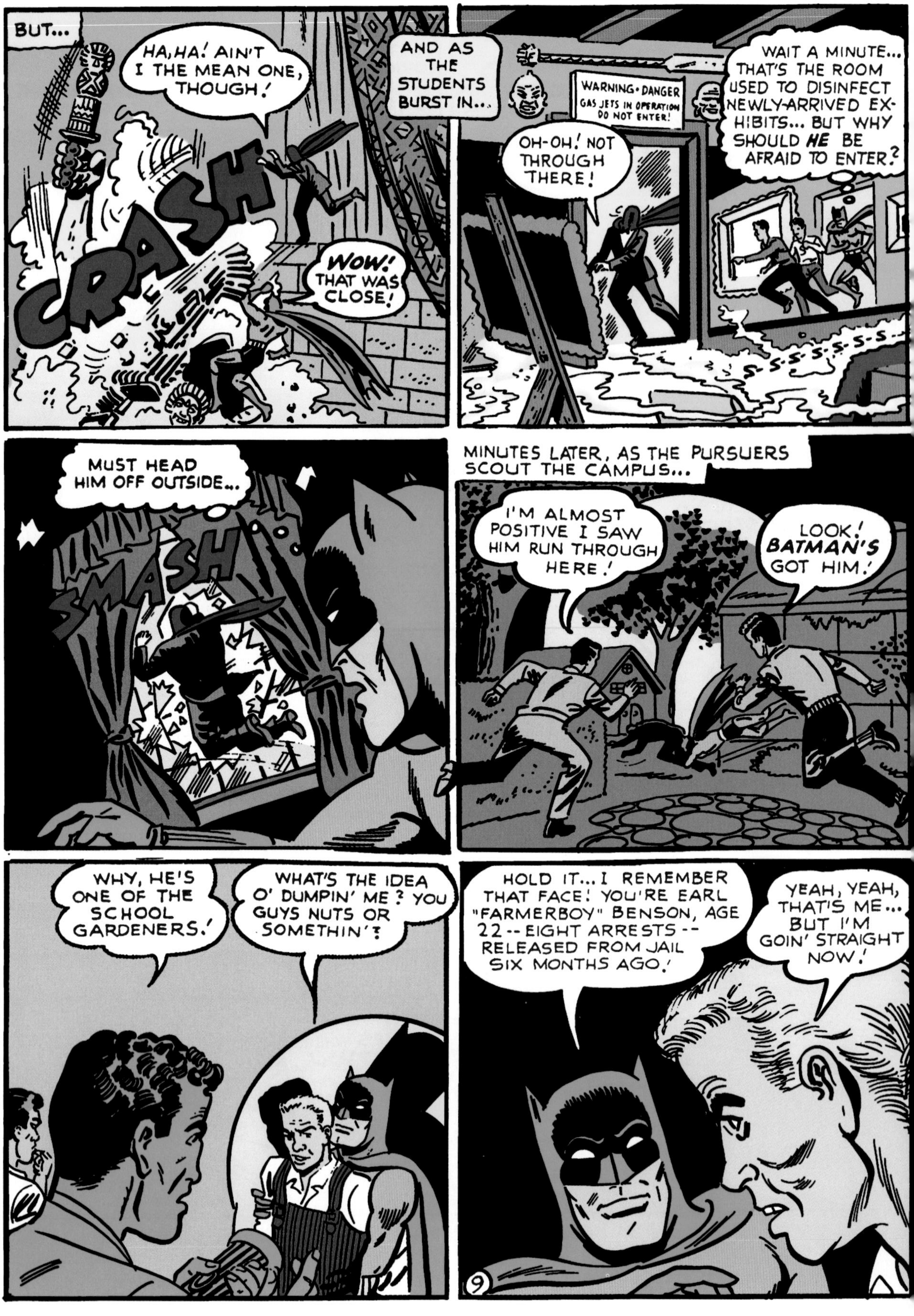
BUT...
HA,HA! AIN'T I THE MEAN ONE, THOUGH!
CRASH
WOW! THAT WAS CLOSE!
AND AS THE STUDENTS BURST IN...
WARNING • DANGER GAS JETS IN OPERATION DO NOT ENTER!
OH-OH! NOT THROUGH THERE!
WAIT A MINUTE... THAT'S THE ROOM USED TO DISINFECT NEWLY-ARRIVED EXHIBITS... BUT WHY SHOULD HE BE AFRAID TO ENTER?
S-S-S-S-S-S-S
MUST HEAD HIM OFF OUTSIDE...
SMASH
MINUTES LATER, AS THE PURSUERS SCOUT THE CAMPUS...
I'M ALMOST POSITIVE I SAW HIM RUN THROUGH HERE!
LOOK! BATMAN'S GOT HIM!
WHY, HE'S ONE OF THE SCHOOL GARDENERS!
WHAT'S THE IDEA O' DUMPIN' ME? YOU GUYS NUTS OR SOMETHIN'?
HOLD IT... I REMEMBER THAT FACE! YOU'RE EARL "FARMERBOY" BENSON, AGE 22 -- EIGHT ARRESTS -- RELEASED FROM JAIL SIX MONTHS AGO!
YEAH, YEAH, THAT'S ME... BUT I'M GOIN' STRAIGHT NOW!
9

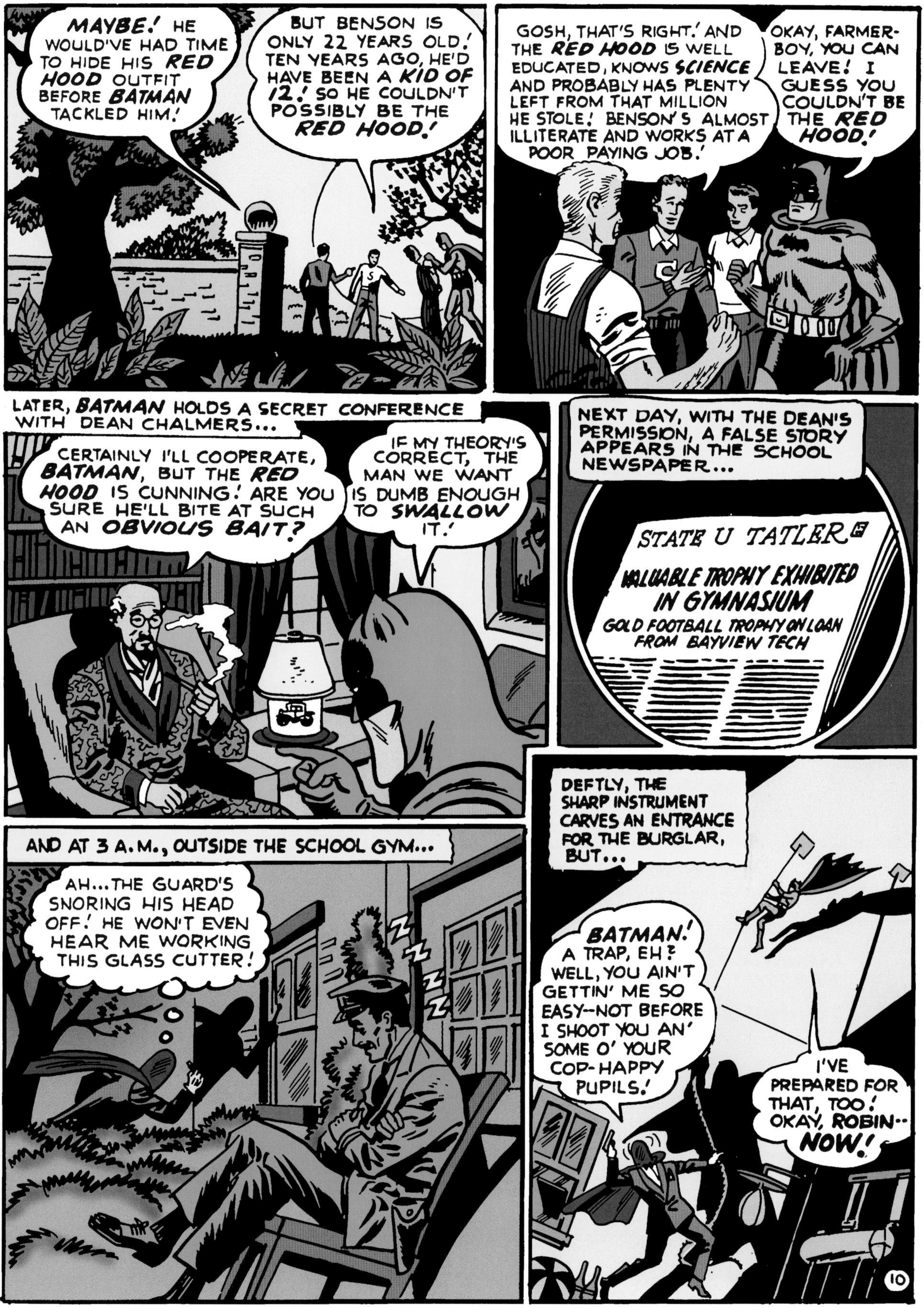
MAYBE! HE WOULD'VE HAD TIME TO HIDE HIS RED HOOD OUTFIT BEFORE BATMAN TACKLED HIM!
BUT BENSON IS ONLY 22 YEARS OLD! TEN YEARS AGO, HE'D HAVE BEEN A KID OF 12! SO HE COULDN'T POSSIBLY BE THE RED HOOD!
GOSH, THAT'S RIGHT! AND THE RED HOOD IS WELL EDUCATED, KNOWS SCIENCE AND PROBABLY HAS PLENTY LEFT FROM THAT MILLION HE STOLE! BENSON'S ALMOST ILLITERATE AND WORKS AT A POOR PAYING JOB!
OKAY, FARMER-BOY, YOU CAN LEAVE! I GUESS YOU COULDN'T BE THE RED HOOD!
LATER, BATMAN HOLDS A SECRET CONFERENCE WITH DEAN CHALMERS...
CERTAINLY I'LL COOPERATE, BATMAN, BUT THE RED HOOD IS CUNNING! ARE YOU SURE HE'LL BITE AT SUCH AN OBVIOUS BAIT?
IF MY THEORY'S CORRECT, THE MAN WE WANT IS DUMB ENOUGH TO SWALLOW IT!
NEXT DAY, WITH THE DEAN'S PERMISSION, A FALSE STORY APPEARS IN THE SCHOOL NEWSPAPER...
STATE U TATLER
VALUABLE TROPHY EXHIBITED IN GYMNASIUM
GOLD FOOTBALL TROPHY ON LOAN FROM BAYVIEW TECH
AND AT 3 A.M., OUTSIDE THE SCHOOL GYM...
AH...THE GUARD'S SNORING HIS HEAD OFF! HE WON'T EVEN HEAR ME WORKING THIS GLASS CUTTER!
ZZZ
DEFTLY, THE SHARP INSTRUMENT CARVES AN ENTRANCE FOR THE BURGLAR, BUT...
BATMAN! A TRAP, EH? WELL, YOU AIN'T GETTIN' ME SO EASY--NOT BEFORE I SHOOT YOU AN' SOME O' YOUR COP-HAPPY PUPILS!
I'VE PREPARED FOR THAT, TOO! OKAY, ROBIN.. NOW!
10

ABRUPTLY, SWITCHES CLICK-- AND BANKS OF RED LIGHT BULBS CAST DOWN THEIR SCARLET BEAMS!

BLAM! BLAM!

WHA... I CAN'T SEE! I CAN'T SEE!

GOTTA GET OUTA HERE! WHERE'S THE DOOR? CAN'T SEE ANYTHING! I'M BLIND -- BLIND! OOF!

BONK

NOW YOU CAN DROP THAT GUN!

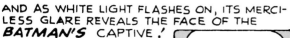

I'M BLIND-- BLIND!

NO YOU'RE NOT! YOUR RED LENSES PLUS RED LIGHT BULBS MADE EVERYTHING BLEND INTO A WALL OF RED... SO NATURALLY YOU COULDN'T SEE!

AND AS WHITE LIGHT FLASHES ON, ITS MERCI-LESS GLARE REVEALS THE FACE OF THE BATMAN'S CAPTIVE!

FARMERBOY BENSON!

BUT THAT'S IMPOSSIBLE! WE HAD IT ALL FIGURED OUT... HE COULDN'T BE THE RED HOOD!

AND YOU WERE RIGHT, PAUL-- HE'S NOT THE RED HOOD! HE'S ONLY AN IMPERSONATOR! ALL RIGHT, BENSON, WHERE'D YOU HIDE THE REAL RED HOOD?

YOU WIN, BATMAN! HE'S LOCKED IN THE TOOL SHED.

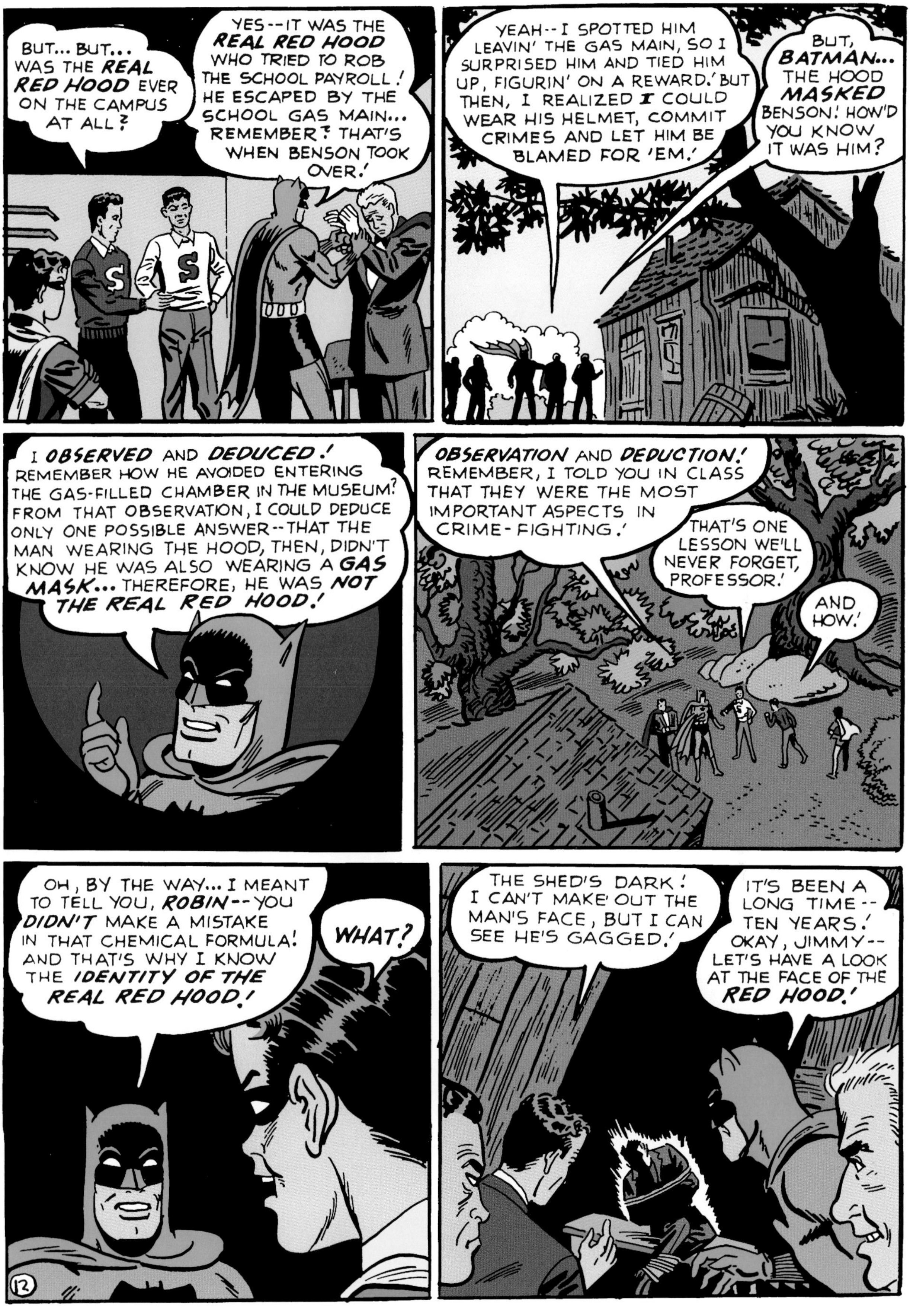
BUT... BUT... WAS THE REAL RED HOOD EVER ON THE CAMPUS AT ALL?
YES--IT WAS THE REAL RED HOOD WHO TRIED TO ROB THE SCHOOL PAYROLL! HE ESCAPED BY THE SCHOOL GAS MAIN... REMEMBER? THAT'S WHEN BENSON TOOK OVER!
YEAH--I SPOTTED HIM LEAVIN' THE GAS MAIN, SO I SURPRISED HIM AND TIED HIM UP, FIGURIN' ON A REWARD! BUT THEN, I REALIZED I COULD WEAR HIS HELMET, COMMIT CRIMES AND LET HIM BE BLAMED FOR 'EM!
BUT, BATMAN... THE HOOD MASKED BENSON! HOW'D YOU KNOW IT WAS HIM?
I OBSERVED AND DEDUCED! REMEMBER HOW HE AVOIDED ENTERING THE GAS-FILLED CHAMBER IN THE MUSEUM? FROM THAT OBSERVATION, I COULD DEDUCE ONLY ONE POSSIBLE ANSWER--THAT THE MAN WEARING THE HOOD, THEN, DIDN'T KNOW HE WAS ALSO WEARING A GAS MASK... THEREFORE, HE WAS NOT THE REAL RED HOOD!
OBSERVATION AND DEDUCTION! REMEMBER, I TOLD YOU IN CLASS THAT THEY WERE THE MOST IMPORTANT ASPECTS IN CRIME-FIGHTING!
THAT'S ONE LESSON WE'LL NEVER FORGET, PROFESSOR!
AND HOW!
OH, BY THE WAY... I MEANT TO TELL YOU, ROBIN--YOU DIDN'T MAKE A MISTAKE IN THAT CHEMICAL FORMULA! AND THAT'S WHY I KNOW THE IDENTITY OF THE REAL RED HOOD!
WHAT?
12
THE SHED'S DARK! I CAN'T MAKE OUT THE MAN'S FACE, BUT I CAN SEE HE'S GAGGED!
IT'S BEEN A LONG TIME--TEN YEARS! OKAY, JIMMY--LET'S HAVE A LOOK AT THE FACE OF THE RED HOOD!

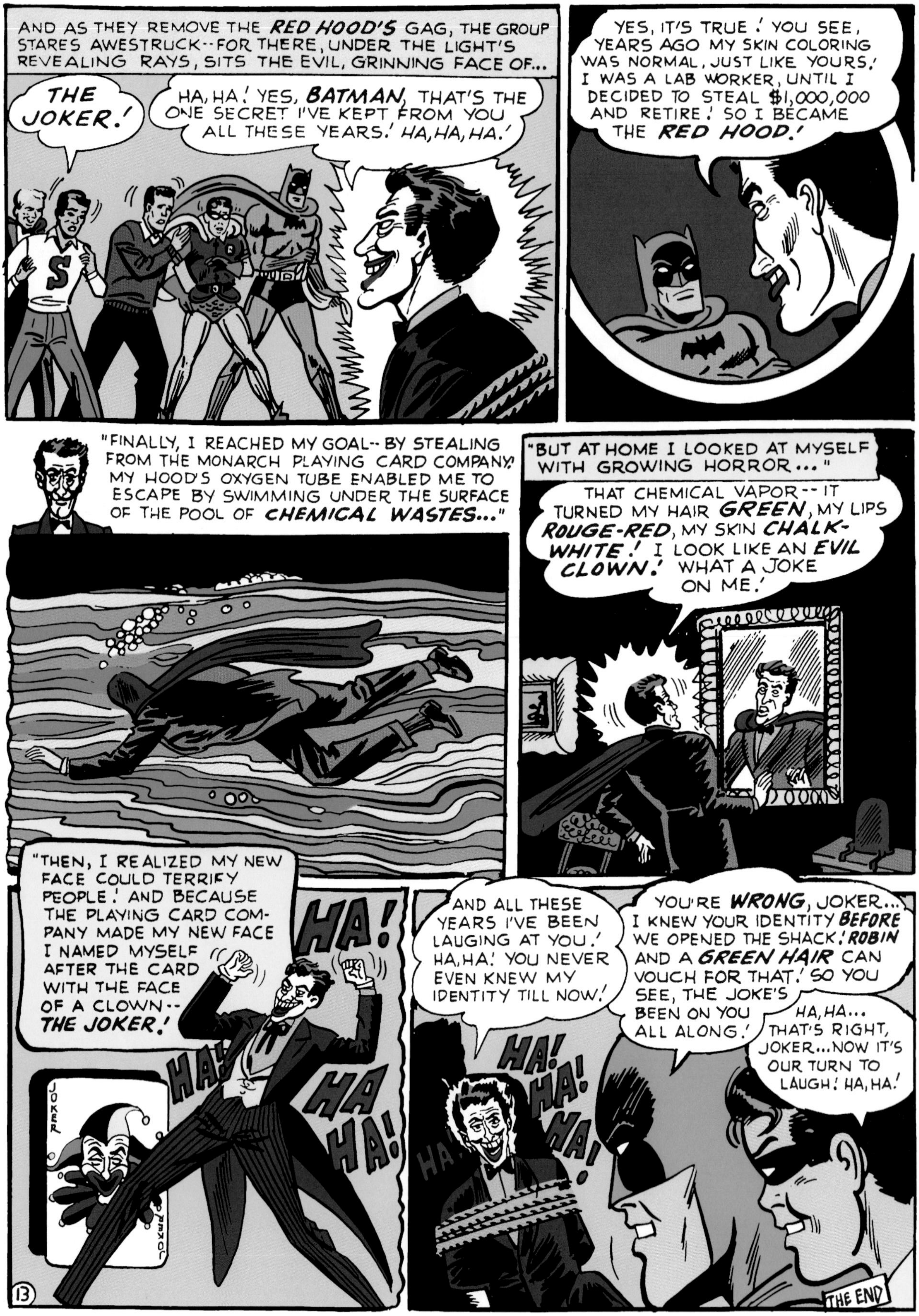
AND AS THEY REMOVE THE RED HOOD'S GAG, THE GROUP STARES AWESTRUCK--FOR THERE, UNDER THE LIGHT'S REVEALING RAYS, SITS THE EVIL, GRINNING FACE OF...
THE JOKER!
HA, HA! YES, BATMAN, THAT'S THE ONE SECRET I'VE KEPT FROM YOU ALL THESE YEARS! HA, HA, HA!
YES, IT'S TRUE! YOU SEE, YEARS AGO MY SKIN COLORING WAS NORMAL, JUST LIKE YOURS! I WAS A LAB WORKER, UNTIL I DECIDED TO STEAL $1,000,000 AND RETIRE! SO I BECAME THE RED HOOD!
"FINALLY, I REACHED MY GOAL--BY STEALING FROM THE MONARCH PLAYING CARD COMPANY! MY HOOD'S OXYGEN TUBE ENABLED ME TO ESCAPE BY SWIMMING UNDER THE SURFACE OF THE POOL OF CHEMICAL WASTES..."
"BUT AT HOME I LOOKED AT MYSELF WITH GROWING HORROR..."
THAT CHEMICAL VAPOR--IT TURNED MY HAIR GREEN, MY LIPS ROUGE-RED, MY SKIN CHALK-WHITE! I LOOK LIKE AN EVIL CLOWN! WHAT A JOKE ON ME!
"THEN, I REALIZED MY NEW FACE COULD TERRIFY PEOPLE! AND BECAUSE THE PLAYING CARD COMPANY MADE MY NEW FACE I NAMED MYSELF AFTER THE CARD WITH THE FACE OF A CLOWN--THE JOKER!
HA!
HA!
HA HA
HA!
JOKER
JOKER
13
AND ALL THESE YEARS I'VE BEEN LAUGING AT YOU! HA, HA! YOU NEVER EVEN KNEW MY IDENTITY TILL NOW!
YOU'RE WRONG, JOKER... I KNEW YOUR IDENTITY BEFORE WE OPENED THE SHACK! ROBIN AND A GREEN HAIR CAN VOUCH FOR THAT! SO YOU SEE, THE JOKE'S BEEN ON YOU ALL ALONG!
HA, HA... THAT'S RIGHT, JOKER... NOW IT'S OUR TURN TO LAUGH! HA, HA!
HA! HA! HA!
HA
THE END

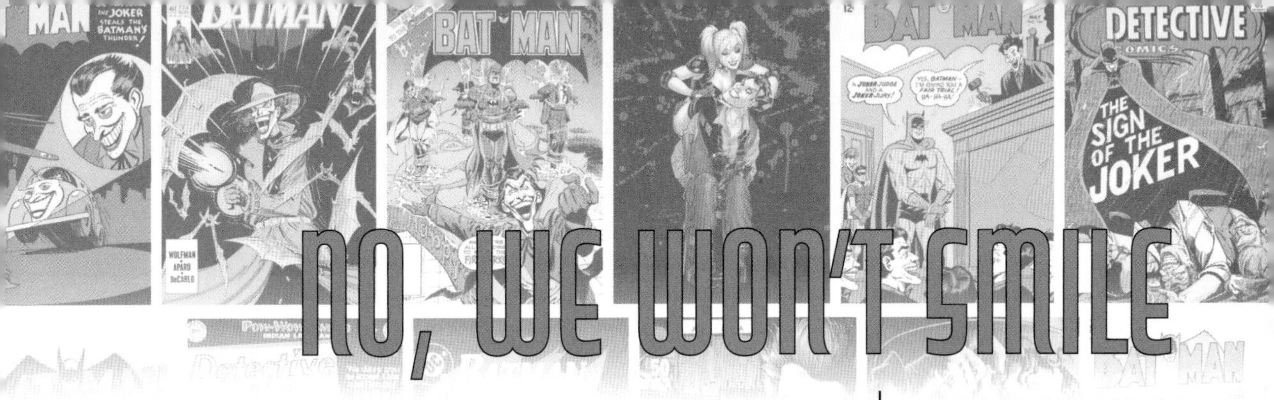
BATMAN
BAT MAN
DETECTIVE COMICS
THE SIGN OF THE JOKER

NO, WE WON'T SMILE

by **BILLY JENSEN**

It wasn't a mannequin.

Betty Bersinger was taking her three-year-old daughter for a morning walk when she came upon what she thought was a discarded department store mannequin on the west side of South Norton Avenue in the Leimert Park neighborhood of Los Angeles.

But it wasn't a mannequin.

It was the body of a person. Someone who once lived and breathed and dreamed. Her body had been bisected. Her blood had been drained. Entire sections of her flesh had been sliced away. She had been disemboweled. But with all that horror, it was her face that was the most shocking. Her face had been slashed, from the corners of her mouth to her ears, leaving a horrific grin. It was known in law enforcement circles as a Glasgow Smile.

She would later be identified as Elizabeth Short. Press would refer to her as the Black Dahlia. She would be smiling for eternity, and the smile would resonate.

He was created seven years prior. Evil was on the march. The Nazis, the worst regime of killers the world has ever seen, were hell-bent on taking over the world and creating a master race. Plans to extinguish the lives of millions. We shouldn't have had to create a monster. But for some reason, we needed to personify all that frightened us. So he was born.

His look was reminiscent of *The Man Who Laughs*, released in 1928 by Universal Pictures, the same company that made film versions of the Hunchback of Notre Dame. And Frankenstein. And Dracula. And the Wolfman. The monster makers delivered a romantic melodrama about a man cursed with a grotesque, perpetual grin, a nobleman who is forced to work circus freak shows. Like Hollywood does, they changed the ending—he lives happily ever after in the movie. In the Victor Hugo book on which it was based, the Laughing Man and his lover both die.

When Bill Finger and Bob Kane were creating a new hero, they needed a new villain for him to oppose. They, along with Jerry Robinson, took inspiration from the face of the Laughing Man, matched it to the useless playing card, and wedded those visuals into a persona of pure, unadulterated evil. A hero is only as good as their villain is bad. They would begin to flesh out the worst thing humanity had to offer.

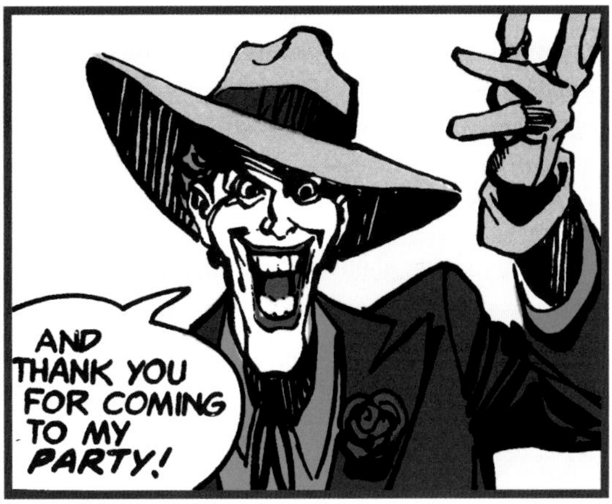
AND THANK YOU FOR COMING TO MY PARTY!

And the Joker was born.

From his very first issue, the Joker kills. First as a spree killer: over a radio broadcast, he says he is going to kill people. And he does. A mob boss doesn't like it? The Joker kills him too.

He then murders a police chief.

And he keeps killing. And killing. And killing. In a multitude of ways.

In Greg Rucka's *Gotham Central*, the Joker is a sniper, shooting the school superintendent. When the police, EMTs, and CSIs begin to work the crime scene, he opens fire on them, slaughtering first responders from afar.

Before he kills Jason Todd in "A Death in the Family," he's a state-sponsored terrorist.

He blows up a school full of children in Kevin Smith's *Batman: Cacophony*.

He skins a strip club owner alive and parades him onstage in Brian Azzarello's *Joker*.

He kidnaps a dozen babies and then shoots Jim Gordon's wife in the head in *No Man's Land*.

DETECTIVE COMICS
DETECTIVE COMICS
THE SIGN OF THE JOKER
MAD LOVE
BAT MAN
BATMAN
BAT MAN
BAT MAN
BAT MAN

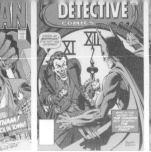

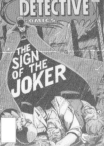

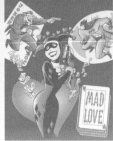

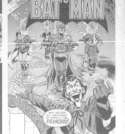

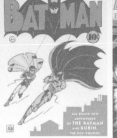

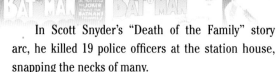

In Scott Snyder's "Death of the Family" story arc, he killed 19 police officers at the station house, snapping the necks of many.

In *Detective Comics* #826, he kidnaps Robin, places him inside a car to sit with its former owners, who he killed. And Robin watches as he mows down pedestrians. The Joker shoots the manager of a fast food joint after a drive-through order dispute.

When he's arrested in *Batman Confidential* #22-25, he uses his one phone call to call the wife of the detective—and convinces her to die by suicide.

No serial killer in history changes his MO and methods this much: the bloodthirst and sexual gratification that Ted Bundy sought. The warped sense of alienation and misguided revenge that Dylan Klebold and Eric Harris felt. The mass shooters—now too legion to pick just one—with their grudges and multiround clips. Save for the highly censored Joker of the Comics Code era and his Cesar Romero counterpart, the Jokers just like to kill. And other than that basic fact, the thread that ties the Jokers together is that they all like to make a statement.

IN THE GLORIOUS PALE WHITE FLESH!
CONSIDERING YOUR CONDITION, GENTLEMEN, YOU NEEDN'T STAND-- BUT I WOULD APPRECIATE A ROUSING ROUND OF APPLAUSE!
AND WHATEVER THE JOKER WANTS, HE ALMOST INVARIABLY GETS!
HA HA HA HA HA HA

Which brings us back to that morning in 1947, when Elizabeth Short's body—cut in two, drained of blood—was discovered in a Los Angeles vacant lot. She was posed. Deliberately. For all the world to see.

And on her face: a perpetual grin carved by her sadistic killer.

True crime writers have theorized that Elizabeth Short's wounds could have been influenced by the surrealist movement. Her body posed like Man Ray's Minotaur, bisected like Man Ray's "Lovers." The work of a homicidal artist.

In Brian DePalma's movie *The Black Dahlia*, the detectives hunting Elizabeth Short's killer watch a screening of *The Man Who Laughs*, their female companion gasping and shielding her eyes when Conrad Veidt unveils his forever smile for the first time. The same smile found on a drawing discovered at the murder scene.

Sixty years later, Heath Ledger's Joker borrowed from the Black Dahlia story, his makeup covering a Glasgow Smile given to him by an unknown assailant—or possibly even himself.

The universe couldn't allow the fictional world's most infamous villain and true crime's most infamous unsolved murder to be apart for long.

But why?

We can look at the whats and hows of the Joker's actions or the Dahlia murder scene. But both beg the question: Why? Why did this happen?

The *why* has been elusive in both. People have their theories about the Joker. He was driven to madness. He has no empathy. He is an agent of chaos. Some men just want to watch the world burn, after all.

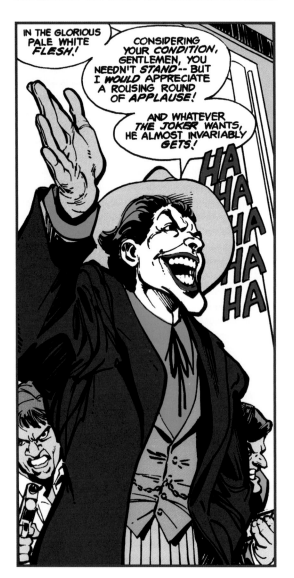

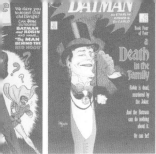

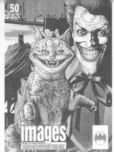

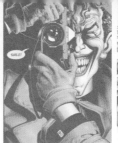

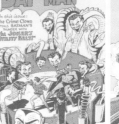

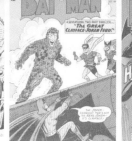

But the closest we ever get to motive for the Joker is the smile. Every iteration of the Joker—from his first appearance to Cesar Romero's trickster—is chasing the smile. Even Alan Moore's sadistic one-bad-day-can-turn-any-good-man-evil Joker ends with a joke before the final snap.

Like Jack Nicholson's Joker said: "I am the world's first fully functioning homicidal artist." He wants us all to smile as he unleashes his lethal smile toxin during Gotham City's 200th anniversary parade.

Like Neil Gaiman's Joker in "Whatever Happened to the Caped Crusader?" who keeps injecting Batman with his Joker Toxin just to get his nemesis to smile. Batman doesn't smile. Joker injects him again and again, until Batman overdoses and dies.

He wants you to smile.

There's not a woman alive who hasn't—at least once in her life—been told by a man to smile: "Come on baby, give me a smile." "You're too pretty to not be smiling."

The horrific smile carved into Elizabeth Short's face may very well have been just this: a man wanting a woman to smile at him. A man who didn't get what he wanted, so now he'll make her smile forever.

Toxic masculinity mixed with psychopathy. That's what the Joker is. What he's trying to do. Hell, when he plans his mass executions, his weapon of choice is toxin. He's that guy, asking a woman to smile and being upset when she doesn't. And taking it one step further—as some of the worst humanity has to offer have done throughout history—he kills what he can't have. And he kills and kills and kills all of us in a multitude of ways. Because we won't smile.

We should always be careful not to glorify him. But we will study him. The same way we study Bundy and Gacy and Manson and the lot of them.

We need to understand our monsters, to make sure that when we encounter the next monster, we can have a fighting chance.

But no, we're not going to wish you a happy birthday, Joker.

And no, we're not going to smile.

I THINK I CAN ASSURE YOU SURPRISES GALORE--

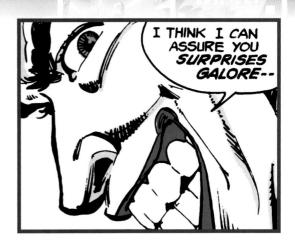

***Billy Jensen** is a true crime journalist focused squarely on unsolved murders and missing persons. But after seventeen years of writing hundreds of stories with no endings, he was fed up—and decided to try to solve the murders and find the missing himself. It worked. Jensen has solved or helped solve ten homicides and helped locate missing persons. He wrote about these cases in his* New York Times *bestselling book,* Chase Darkness with Me. *He was friends with Michelle McNamara and, after her sudden passing, helped finish her #1* New York Times *bestselling book,* I'll Be Gone in the Dark, *about the hunt for the Golden State Killer, which will be adapted into an HBO docuseries in 2020. He has written for the* New York Times *and* Rolling Stone, *starred in the Oxygen series* Death and the Mansion, *and was supervising producer and investigator on the Warner Bros. show* Crime Watch Daily. *He currently cohosts the podcasts* Jensen & Holes: The Murder Squad *with Paul Holes and* The First Degree *with Jac Vanek and Alexis Linkletter.*

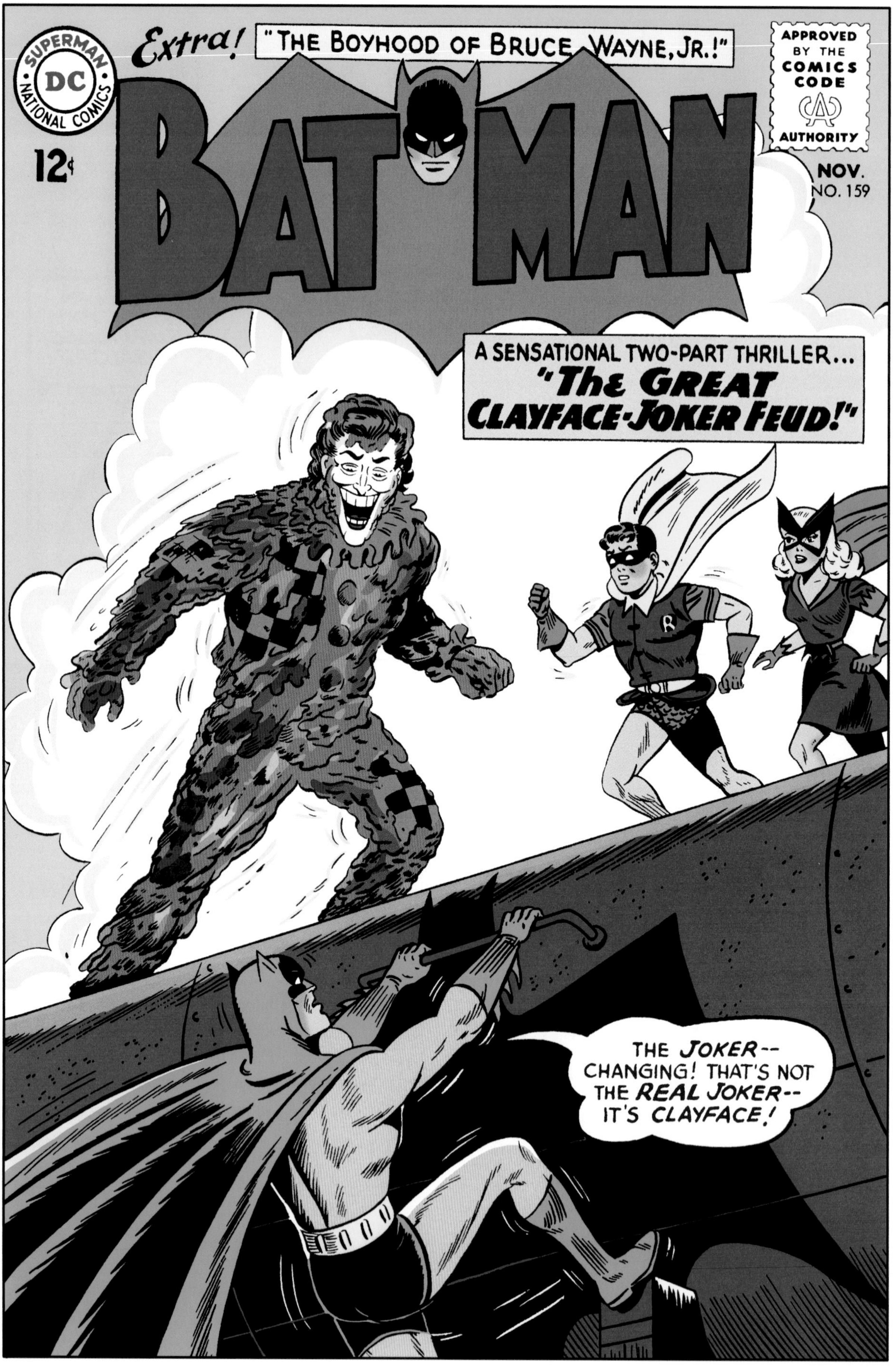

SUPERMAN DC NATIONAL COMICS
12¢
Extra! "THE BOYHOOD OF BRUCE WAYNE, JR.!"
BATMAN
APPROVED BY THE COMICS CODE AUTHORITY
NOV. NO. 159
A SENSATIONAL TWO-PART THRILLER... "The GREAT CLAYFACE-JOKER FEUD!"
THE JOKER-- CHANGING! THAT'S NOT THE REAL JOKER-- IT'S CLAYFACE!

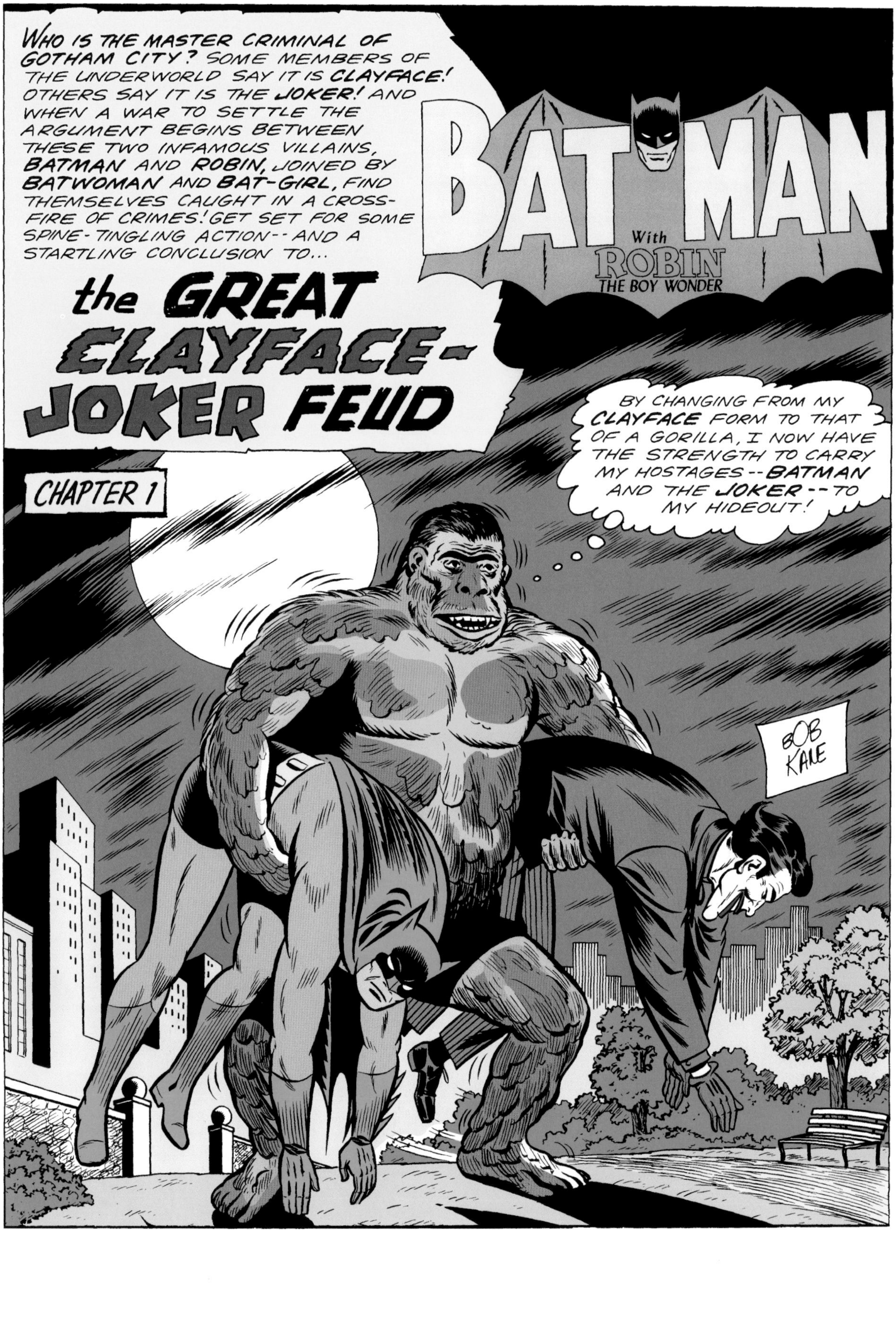
WHO IS THE MASTER CRIMINAL OF GOTHAM CITY? SOME MEMBERS OF THE UNDERWORLD SAY IT IS CLAYFACE! OTHERS SAY IT IS THE JOKER! AND WHEN A WAR TO SETTLE THE ARGUMENT BEGINS BETWEEN THESE TWO INFAMOUS VILLAINS, BATMAN AND ROBIN, JOINED BY BATWOMAN AND BAT-GIRL, FIND THEMSELVES CAUGHT IN A CROSS-FIRE OF CRIMES! GET SET FOR SOME SPINE-TINGLING ACTION--AND A STARTLING CONCLUSION TO...
BATMAN
With ROBIN THE BOY WONDER
the GREAT CLAYFACE-JOKER FEUD
CHAPTER 1
BY CHANGING FROM MY CLAYFACE FORM TO THAT OF A GORILLA, I NOW HAVE THE STRENGTH TO CARRY MY HOSTAGES--BATMAN AND THE JOKER--TO MY HIDEOUT!
BOB KANE

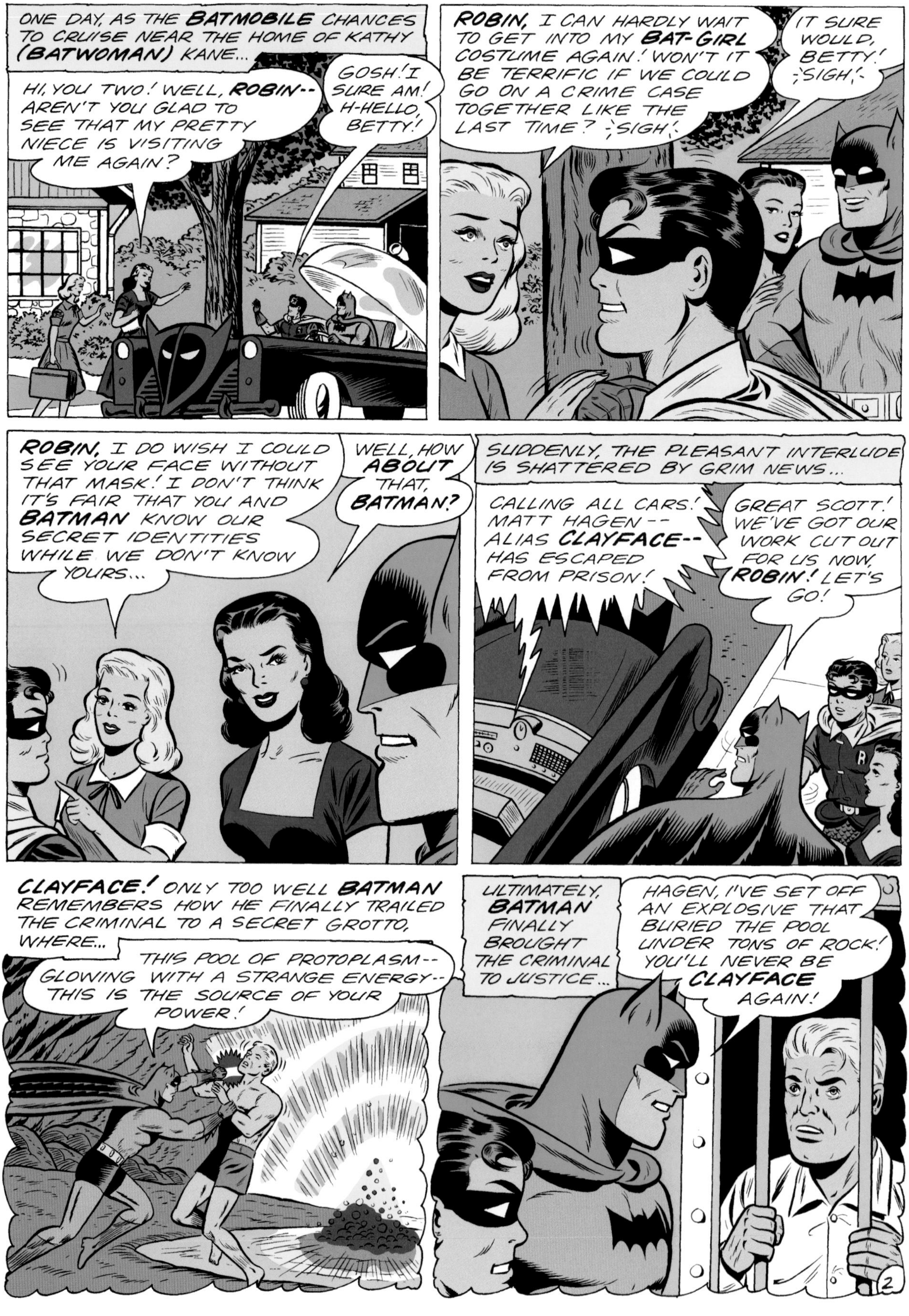

ONE DAY, AS THE BATMOBILE CHANCES TO CRUISE NEAR THE HOME OF KATHY (BATWOMAN) KANE...
HI, YOU TWO! WELL, ROBIN-- AREN'T YOU GLAD TO SEE THAT MY PRETTY NIECE IS VISITING ME AGAIN?
GOSH! I SURE AM! H-HELLO, BETTY!
ROBIN, I CAN HARDLY WAIT TO GET INTO MY BAT-GIRL COSTUME AGAIN! WON'T IT BE TERRIFIC IF WE COULD GO ON A CRIME CASE TOGETHER LIKE THE LAST TIME? SIGH
IT SURE WOULD, BETTY! SIGH
ROBIN, I DO WISH I COULD SEE YOUR FACE WITHOUT THAT MASK! I DON'T THINK IT'S FAIR THAT YOU AND BATMAN KNOW OUR SECRET IDENTITIES WHILE WE DON'T KNOW YOURS...
WELL, HOW ABOUT THAT, BATMAN?
SUDDENLY, THE PLEASANT INTERLUDE IS SHATTERED BY GRIM NEWS...
CALLING ALL CARS! MATT HAGEN-- ALIAS CLAYFACE-- HAS ESCAPED FROM PRISON!
GREAT SCOTT! WE'VE GOT OUR WORK CUT OUT FOR US NOW, ROBIN! LET'S GO!
CLAYFACE! ONLY TOO WELL BATMAN REMEMBERS HOW HE FINALLY TRAILED THE CRIMINAL TO A SECRET GROTTO, WHERE...
THIS POOL OF PROTOPLASM-- GLOWING WITH A STRANGE ENERGY-- THIS IS THE SOURCE OF YOUR POWER!
ULTIMATELY, BATMAN FINALLY BROUGHT THE CRIMINAL TO JUSTICE...
HAGEN, I'VE SET OFF AN EXPLOSIVE THAT BURIED THE POOL UNDER TONS OF ROCK! YOU'LL NEVER BE CLAYFACE AGAIN!
2

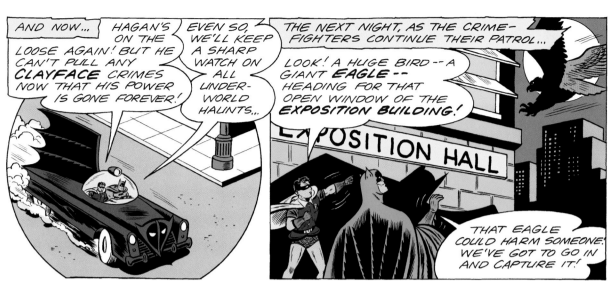

AND NOW... HAGAN'S ON THE LOOSE AGAIN! BUT HE CAN'T PULL ANY *CLAYFACE* CRIMES NOW THAT HIS POWER IS GONE FOREVER!

EVEN SO, WE'LL KEEP A SHARP WATCH ON ALL UNDERWORLD HAUNTS...

THE NEXT NIGHT, AS THE CRIME-FIGHTERS CONTINUE THEIR PATROL...

LOOK! A HUGE BIRD -- A GIANT *EAGLE* -- HEADING FOR THAT OPEN WINDOW OF THE *EXPOSITION BUILDING!*

EXPOSITION HALL

THAT EAGLE COULD HARM SOMEONE! WE'VE GOT TO GO IN AND CAPTURE IT!

SHORTLY, ON THE FLOOR HOUSING A MODEL FUTURISTIC CITY THAT IS PART OF THE *ARCHITECTS EXPOSITION*...

CLAYFACE! SOMEHOW HE GOT HIS POWER BACK! HE BECAME AN "EAGLE" SO HE COULD FLY INTO THE MANAGER'S OFFICE!

STOP HIM! HE FORCED ME TO OPEN THE SAFE CONTAINING THE GATE RECEIPTS...

MANAGER

QUICK AS THOUGHT, *BATMAN* SEIZES A WOOD-AND-PLASTER "BUILDING" AND...

MY ONLY CHANCE IS TO TAKE HIM BY SURPRISE -- KNOCK HIM OUT FAST!

BUT *CLAYFACE* INSTANTLY CONCENTRATES-- HIS MENTAL COMMAND MOULDING HIS BODY LIKE PLIABLE CLAY INTO THE SHAPE, COLOR, AND MASS HE DESIRES!

OUT-FOXED *BATMAN!* BY BECOMING A FAN WITH SPIKED BLADES, I'VE CHOPPED THE "BUILDING" TO BITS!

3

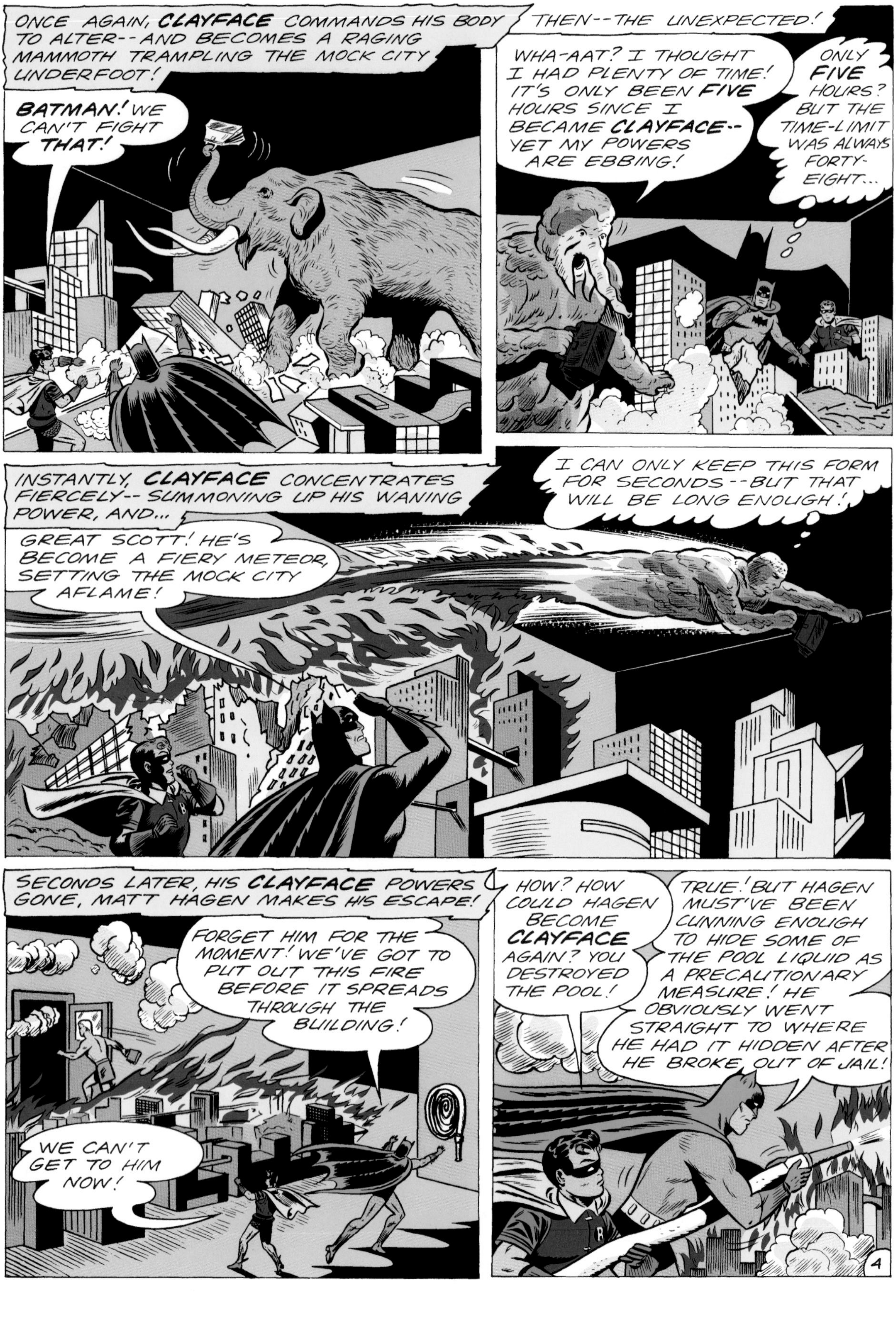

ONCE AGAIN, CLAYFACE COMMANDS HIS BODY TO ALTER--AND BECOMES A RAGING MAMMOTH TRAMPLING THE MOCK CITY UNDERFOOT!
BATMAN! WE CAN'T FIGHT THAT!
THEN--THE UNEXPECTED!
WHA-AAT? I THOUGHT I HAD PLENTY OF TIME! IT'S ONLY BEEN FIVE HOURS SINCE I BECAME CLAYFACE--YET MY POWERS ARE EBBING!
ONLY FIVE HOURS? BUT THE TIME-LIMIT WAS ALWAYS FORTY-EIGHT...
INSTANTLY, CLAYFACE CONCENTRATES FIERCELY--SUMMONING UP HIS WANING POWER, AND...
I CAN ONLY KEEP THIS FORM FOR SECONDS--BUT THAT WILL BE LONG ENOUGH!
GREAT SCOTT! HE'S BECOME A FIERY METEOR, SETTING THE MOCK CITY AFLAME!
SECONDS LATER, HIS CLAYFACE POWERS GONE, MATT HAGEN MAKES HIS ESCAPE!
FORGET HIM FOR THE MOMENT! WE'VE GOT TO PUT OUT THIS FIRE BEFORE IT SPREADS THROUGH THE BUILDING!
WE CAN'T GET TO HIM NOW!
HOW? HOW COULD HAGEN BECOME CLAYFACE AGAIN? YOU DESTROYED THE POOL!
TRUE! BUT HAGEN MUST'VE BEEN CUNNING ENOUGH TO HIDE SOME OF THE POOL LIQUID AS A PRECAUTIONARY MEASURE! HE OBVIOUSLY WENT STRAIGHT TO WHERE HE HAD IT HIDDEN AFTER HE BROKE OUT OF JAIL!
4

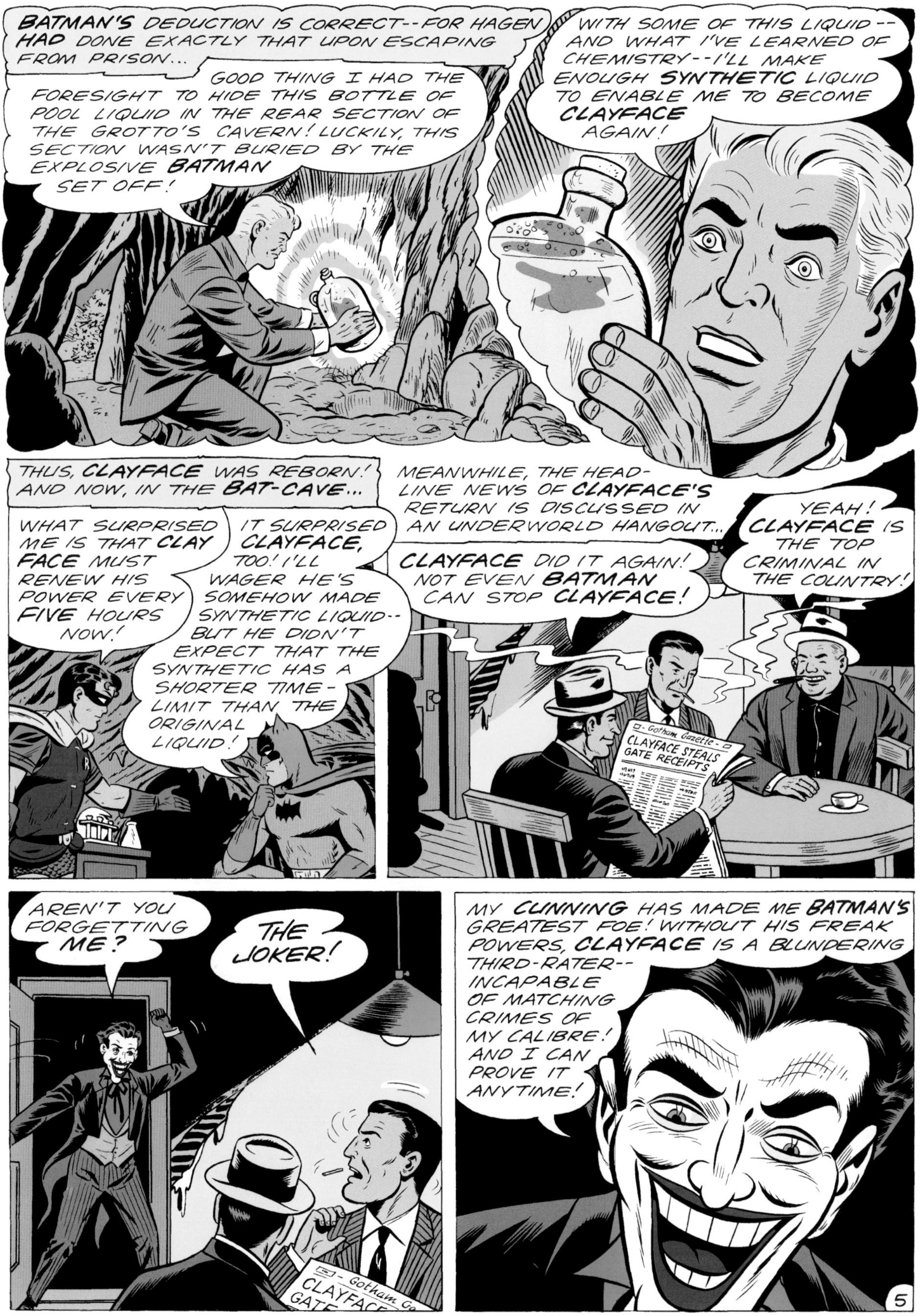

BATMAN'S DEDUCTION IS CORRECT--FOR HAGEN HAD DONE EXACTLY THAT UPON ESCAPING FROM PRISON...
GOOD THING I HAD THE FORESIGHT TO HIDE THIS BOTTLE OF POOL LIQUID IN THE REAR SECTION OF THE GROTTO'S CAVERN! LUCKILY, THIS SECTION WASN'T BURIED BY THE EXPLOSIVE BATMAN SET OFF!
WITH SOME OF THIS LIQUID--AND WHAT I'VE LEARNED OF CHEMISTRY--I'LL MAKE ENOUGH SYNTHETIC LIQUID TO ENABLE ME TO BECOME CLAYFACE AGAIN!
THUS, CLAYFACE WAS REBORN! AND NOW, IN THE BAT-CAVE...
WHAT SURPRISED ME IS THAT CLAY FACE MUST RENEW HIS POWER EVERY FIVE HOURS NOW!
IT SURPRISED CLAYFACE, TOO! I'LL WAGER HE'S SOMEHOW MADE SYNTHETIC LIQUID--BUT HE DIDN'T EXPECT THAT THE SYNTHETIC HAS A SHORTER TIME-LIMIT THAN THE ORIGINAL LIQUID!
MEANWHILE, THE HEAD-LINE NEWS OF CLAYFACE'S RETURN IS DISCUSSED IN AN UNDERWORLD HANGOUT...
CLAYFACE DID IT AGAIN! NOT EVEN BATMAN CAN STOP CLAYFACE!
YEAH! CLAYFACE IS THE TOP CRIMINAL IN THE COUNTRY!
Gotham Gazette
CLAYFACE STEALS GATE RECEIPTS
AREN'T YOU FORGETTING ME?
THE JOKER!
MY CUNNING HAS MADE ME BATMAN'S GREATEST FOE! WITHOUT HIS FREAK POWERS, CLAYFACE IS A BLUNDERING THIRD-RATER--INCAPABLE OF MATCHING CRIMES OF MY CALIBRE! AND I CAN PROVE IT ANYTIME!
5

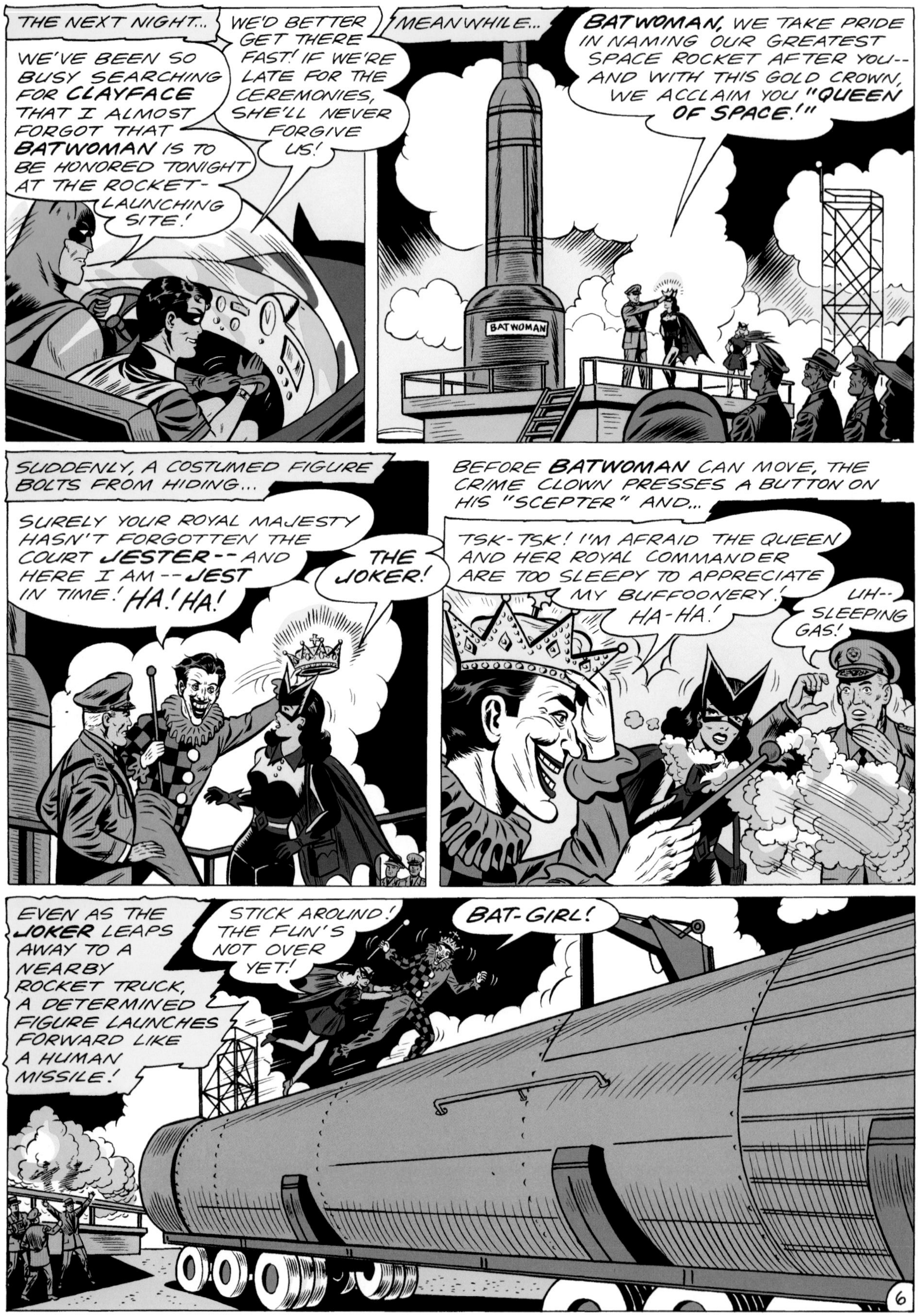
THE NEXT NIGHT...
WE'VE BEEN SO BUSY SEARCHING FOR CLAYFACE THAT I ALMOST FORGOT THAT BATWOMAN IS TO BE HONORED TONIGHT AT THE ROCKET-LAUNCHING SITE!
WE'D BETTER GET THERE FAST! IF WE'RE LATE FOR THE CEREMONIES, SHE'LL NEVER FORGIVE US!
MEANWHILE...
BATWOMAN, WE TAKE PRIDE IN NAMING OUR GREATEST SPACE ROCKET AFTER YOU--AND WITH THIS GOLD CROWN, WE ACCLAIM YOU "QUEEN OF SPACE!"
BATWOMAN
SUDDENLY, A COSTUMED FIGURE BOLTS FROM HIDING...
SURELY YOUR ROYAL MAJESTY HASN'T FORGOTTEN THE COURT JESTER--AND HERE I AM--JEST IN TIME! HA! HA!
THE JOKER!
BEFORE BATWOMAN CAN MOVE, THE CRIME CLOWN PRESSES A BUTTON ON HIS "SCEPTER" AND...
TSK-TSK! I'M AFRAID THE QUEEN AND HER ROYAL COMMANDER ARE TOO SLEEPY TO APPRECIATE MY BUFFOONERY! HA-HA!
UH--SLEEPING GAS!
EVEN AS THE JOKER LEAPS AWAY TO A NEARBY ROCKET TRUCK, A DETERMINED FIGURE LAUNCHES FORWARD LIKE A HUMAN MISSILE!
STICK AROUND! THE FUN'S NOT OVER YET!
BAT-GIRL!
6

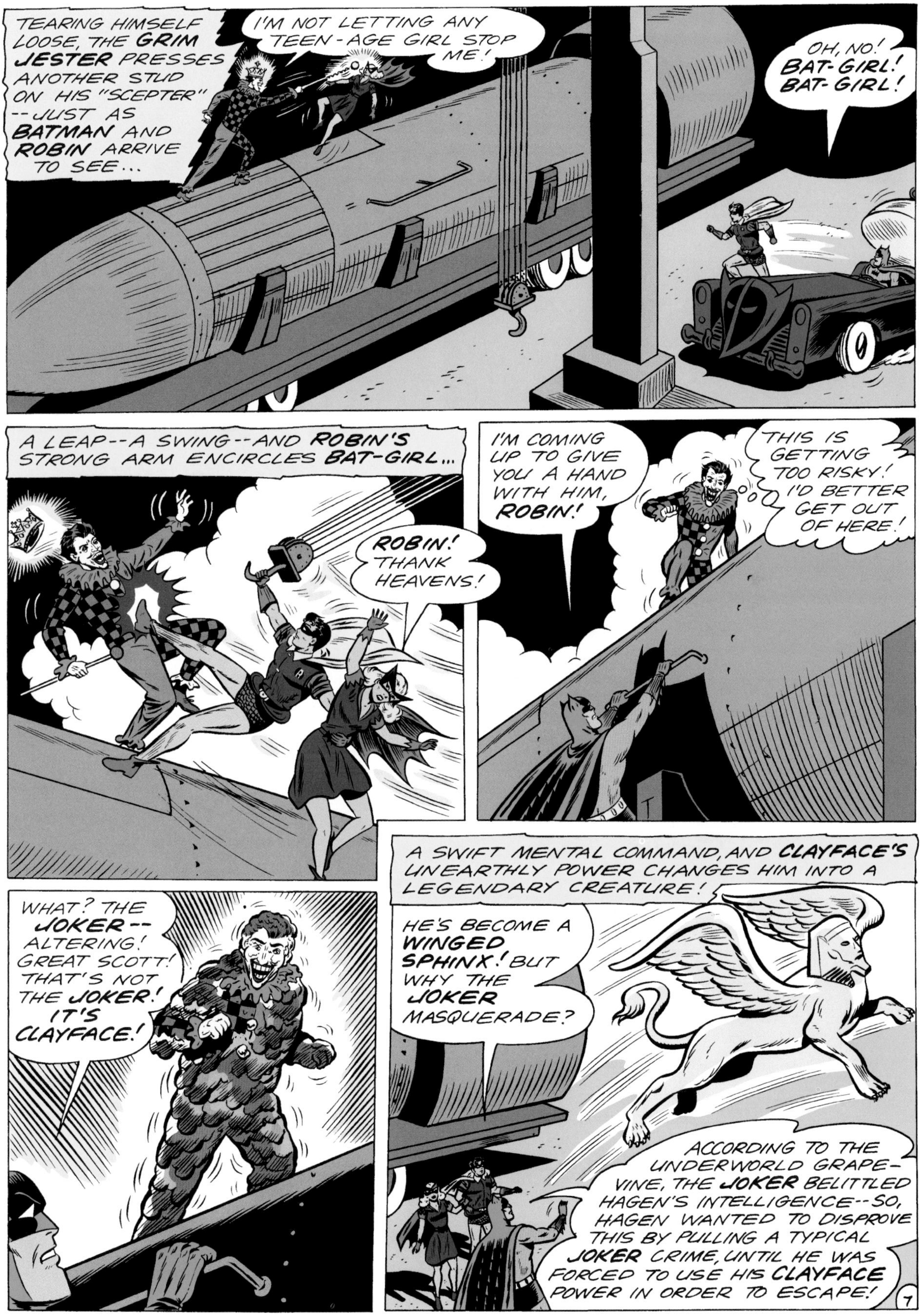

TEARING HIMSELF LOOSE, THE GRIM JESTER PRESSES ANOTHER STUD ON HIS "SCEPTER" --JUST AS BATMAN AND ROBIN ARRIVE TO SEE...
I'M NOT LETTING ANY TEEN-AGE GIRL STOP ME!
OH, NO! BAT-GIRL! BAT-GIRL!
A LEAP--A SWING--AND ROBIN'S STRONG ARM ENCIRCLES BAT-GIRL...
ROBIN! THANK HEAVENS!
I'M COMING UP TO GIVE YOU A HAND WITH HIM, ROBIN!
THIS IS GETTING TOO RISKY! I'D BETTER GET OUT OF HERE!
WHAT? THE JOKER-- ALTERING! GREAT SCOTT! THAT'S NOT THE JOKER! IT'S CLAYFACE!
A SWIFT MENTAL COMMAND, AND CLAYFACE'S UNEARTHLY POWER CHANGES HIM INTO A LEGENDARY CREATURE!
HE'S BECOME A WINGED SPHINX! BUT WHY THE JOKER MASQUERADE?
ACCORDING TO THE UNDERWORLD GRAPE-VINE, THE JOKER BELITTLED HAGEN'S INTELLIGENCE--SO, HAGEN WANTED TO DISPROVE THIS BY PULLING A TYPICAL JOKER CRIME, UNTIL HE WAS FORCED TO USE HIS CLAYFACE POWER IN ORDER TO ESCAPE!
7

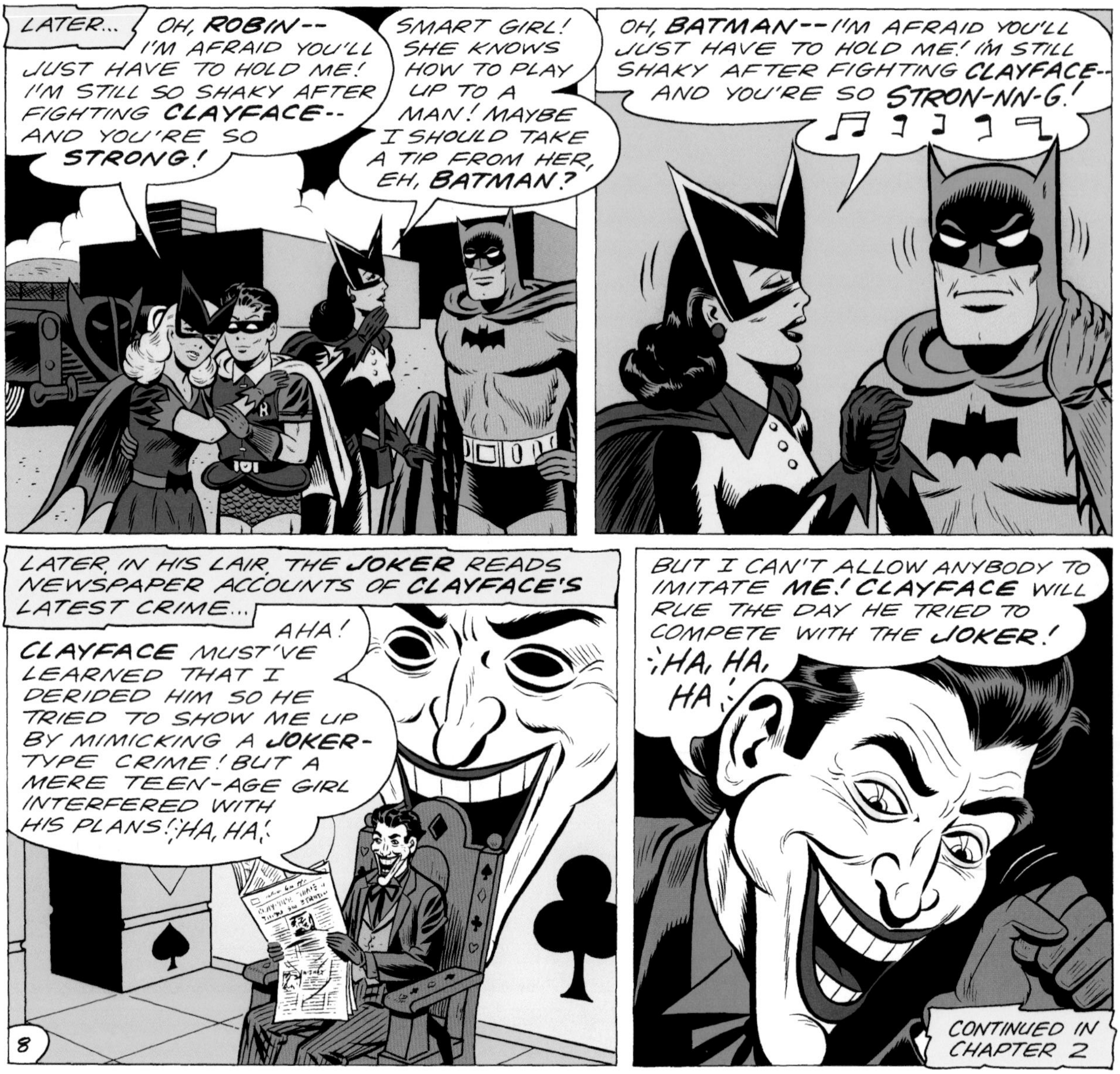
LATER...
OH, ROBIN-- I'M AFRAID YOU'LL JUST HAVE TO HOLD ME! I'M STILL SO SHAKY AFTER FIGHTING CLAYFACE-- AND YOU'RE SO STRONG!
SMART GIRL! SHE KNOWS HOW TO PLAY UP TO A MAN! MAYBE I SHOULD TAKE A TIP FROM HER, EH, BATMAN?
OH, BATMAN-- I'M AFRAID YOU'LL JUST HAVE TO HOLD ME! I'M STILL SHAKY AFTER FIGHTING CLAYFACE-- AND YOU'RE SO STRON-NN-G!
LATER IN HIS LAIR, THE JOKER READS NEWSPAPER ACCOUNTS OF CLAYFACE'S LATEST CRIME...
AHA! CLAYFACE MUST'VE LEARNED THAT I DERIDED HIM SO HE TRIED TO SHOW ME UP BY MIMICKING A JOKER-TYPE CRIME! BUT A MERE TEEN-AGE GIRL INTERFERED WITH HIS PLANS! ¡HA, HA!
8
BUT I CAN'T ALLOW ANYBODY TO IMITATE ME! CLAYFACE WILL RUE THE DAY HE TRIED TO COMPETE WITH THE JOKER!
¡HA, HA, HA!
CONTINUED IN CHAPTER 2

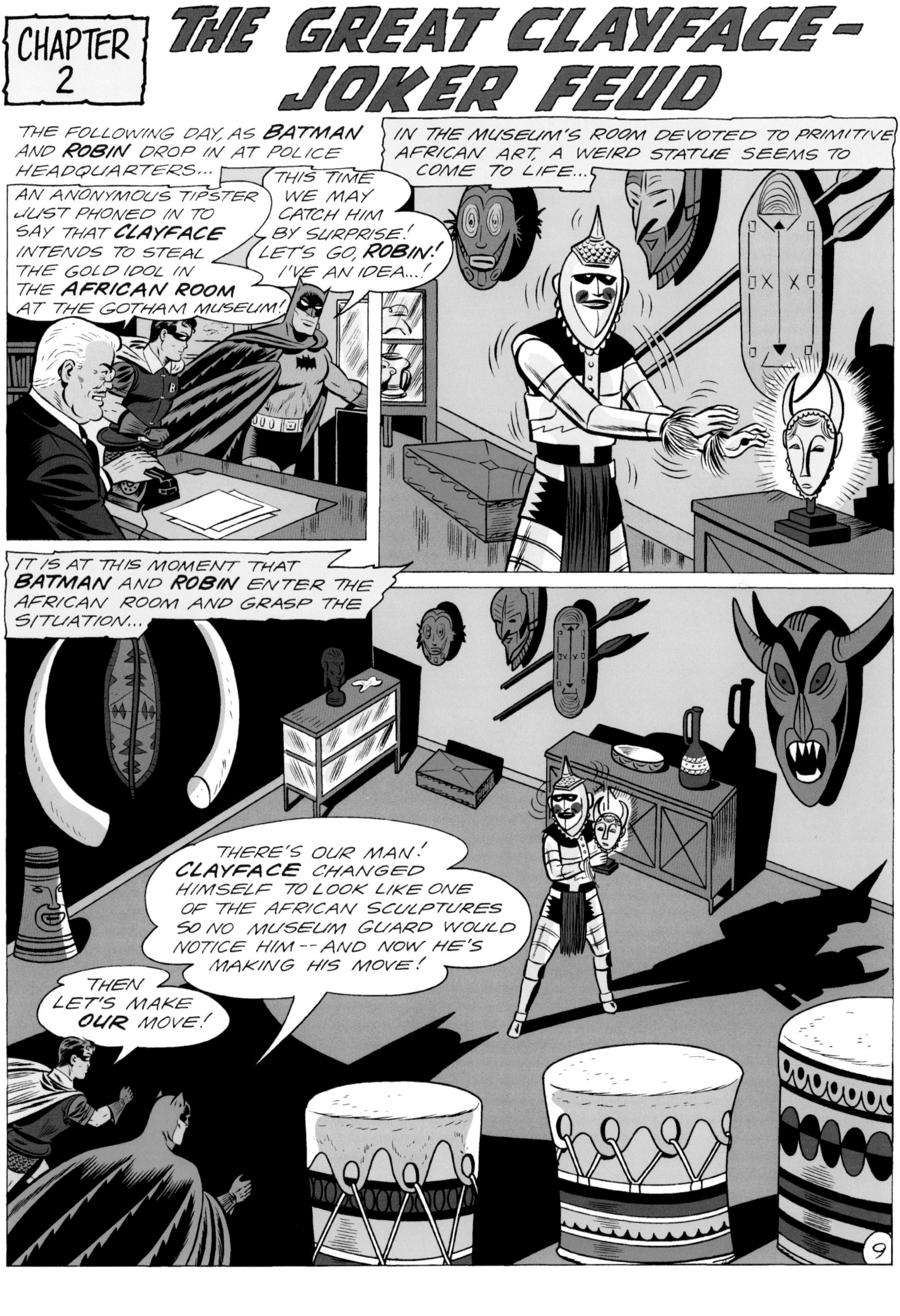
CHAPTER 2
THE GREAT CLAYFACE-JOKER FEUD
THE FOLLOWING DAY, AS BATMAN AND ROBIN DROP IN AT POLICE HEADQUARTERS...
AN ANONYMOUS TIPSTER JUST PHONED IN TO SAY THAT CLAYFACE INTENDS TO STEAL THE GOLD IDOL IN THE AFRICAN ROOM AT THE GOTHAM MUSEUM!
THIS TIME WE MAY CATCH HIM BY SURPRISE! LET'S GO, ROBIN! I'VE AN IDEA...!
IN THE MUSEUM'S ROOM DEVOTED TO PRIMITIVE AFRICAN ART, A WEIRD STATUE SEEMS TO COME TO LIFE...
IT IS AT THIS MOMENT THAT BATMAN AND ROBIN ENTER THE AFRICAN ROOM AND GRASP THE SITUATION...
THERE'S OUR MAN! CLAYFACE CHANGED HIMSELF TO LOOK LIKE ONE OF THE AFRICAN SCULPTURES SO NO MUSEUM GUARD WOULD NOTICE HIM--AND NOW HE'S MAKING HIS MOVE!
THEN LET'S MAKE OUR MOVE!
9

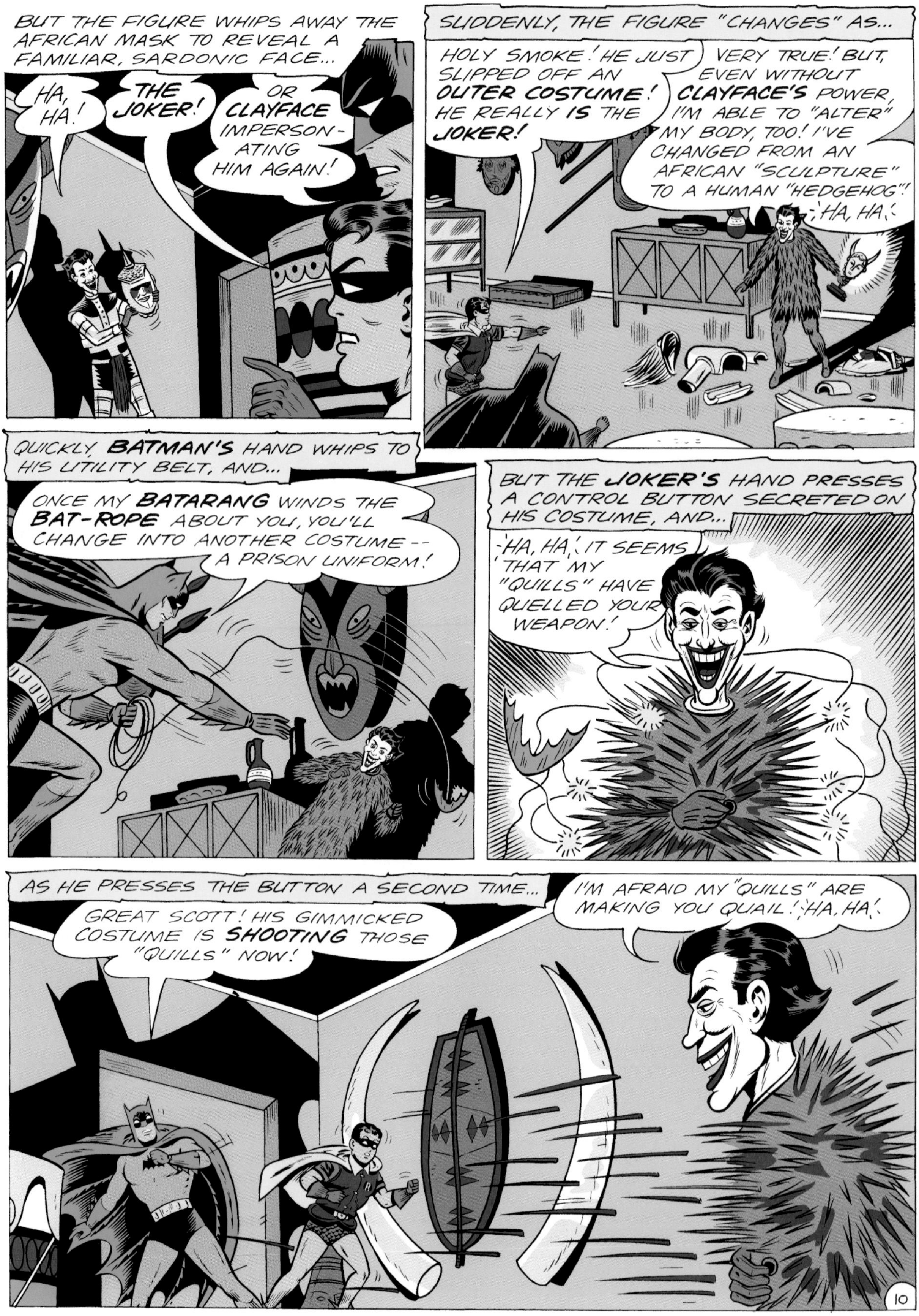
BUT THE FIGURE WHIPS AWAY THE AFRICAN MASK TO REVEAL A FAMILIAR, SARDONIC FACE...
HA, HA!
THE JOKER!
OR CLAYFACE IMPERSONATING HIM AGAIN!
SUDDENLY, THE FIGURE "CHANGES" AS...
HOLY SMOKE! HE JUST SLIPPED OFF AN OUTER COSTUME! HE REALLY IS THE JOKER!
VERY TRUE! BUT, EVEN WITHOUT CLAYFACE'S POWER, I'M ABLE TO "ALTER" MY BODY, TOO! I'VE CHANGED FROM AN AFRICAN "SCULPTURE" TO A HUMAN "HEDGEHOG"! HA, HA!
QUICKLY, BATMAN'S HAND WHIPS TO HIS UTILITY BELT, AND...
ONCE MY BATARANG WINDS THE BAT-ROPE ABOUT YOU, YOU'LL CHANGE INTO ANOTHER COSTUME -- A PRISON UNIFORM!
BUT THE JOKER'S HAND PRESSES A CONTROL BUTTON SECRETED ON HIS COSTUME, AND...
HA, HA! IT SEEMS THAT MY "QUILLS" HAVE QUELLED YOUR WEAPON!
AS HE PRESSES THE BUTTON A SECOND TIME...
GREAT SCOTT! HIS GIMMICKED COSTUME IS SHOOTING THOSE "QUILLS" NOW!
I'M AFRAID MY "QUILLS" ARE MAKING YOU QUAIL! HA, HA!
10

WITH A LIGHTNING-SWIFT MOTION, *ROBIN* WHIPS UP AN AFRICAN SHIELD...

THINK
THINK
THINK

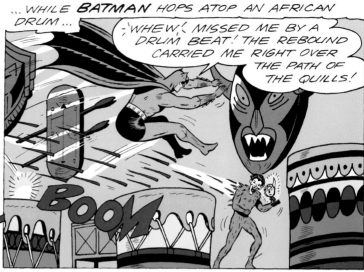

...WHILE *BATMAN* HOPS ATOP AN AFRICAN DRUM...

:WHEW!: MISSED ME BY A DRUM BEAT! THE REBOUND CARRIED ME RIGHT OVER THE PATH OF THE QUILLS!

BOOM

NOW, *JOKER*, YOU'VE FORCED ME TO CHANGE...

...INTO A DRUMMER...

...WHO'S ABOUT TO...

BOOM
BOOM
BOOM
BOOM

...DRUM SOME SENSE INTO YOUR HEAD!

BUT AS *BATMAN* HAULS THE *JOKER* TO HIS FEET...

WHAAT? YOU WERE WEARING A *BREAK-AWAY* COSTUME!

EXACTLY! *:HA, HA:* AND NOW I'M "CHANGING" AGAIN! *:HA, HA:*

11

EVEN WITHOUT *CLAYFACE'S* POWER, I CAN ALSO CHANGE INTO A WINGED CREATURE!--HA, HA!--BY THE WAY, *BATMAN*, IT WAS *I* WHO MADE THAT PHONE CALL TO HEADQUARTERS!

I WANTED YOU HERE--SO I COULD PROVE TO *CLAYFACE* THAT EVEN *WITHOUT* HIS POWER, I STILL COULD DUPLICATE HIS FEATS AND OUTSMART YOU, WHEREAS HE COULDN'T CONTINUE AS THE *JOKER* WHEN HE TRIED TO MIMIC ME!--HA, HA!

SO--THE *CLAYFACE-JOKER* FEUD IS STILL RAGING!

HMM! *ROBIN*, MAYBE WE CAN USE IT TO OUR ADVANTAGE...

LATER, HAGEN FUMES AS HE READS NEWS HEADLINES OF THE *JOKER* TRIUMPH OVER *BATMAN*...

THE *JOKER* HAS MADE ME THE LAUGHING STOCK OF THE UNDERWORLD! SOMEHOW, I'VE GOT TO PULL A BIG COUP THAT WILL REGAIN ME MY PRESTIGE! BUT HOW? *HOW?*

JOKER APES CLAYFACE AND OUTWITS BATMAN!

Gazette

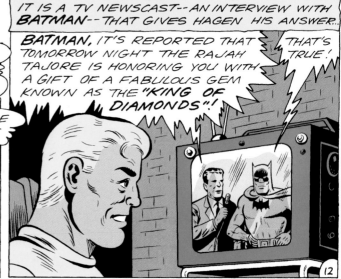

IT IS A TV NEWSCAST--AN INTERVIEW WITH *BATMAN*--THAT GIVES HAGEN HIS ANSWER...

BATMAN, IT'S REPORTED THAT TOMORROW NIGHT THE RAJAH TAJORE IS HONORING YOU WITH A GIFT OF A FABULOUS GEM KNOWN AS THE *"KING OF DIAMONDS"!*

THAT'S TRUE!

12

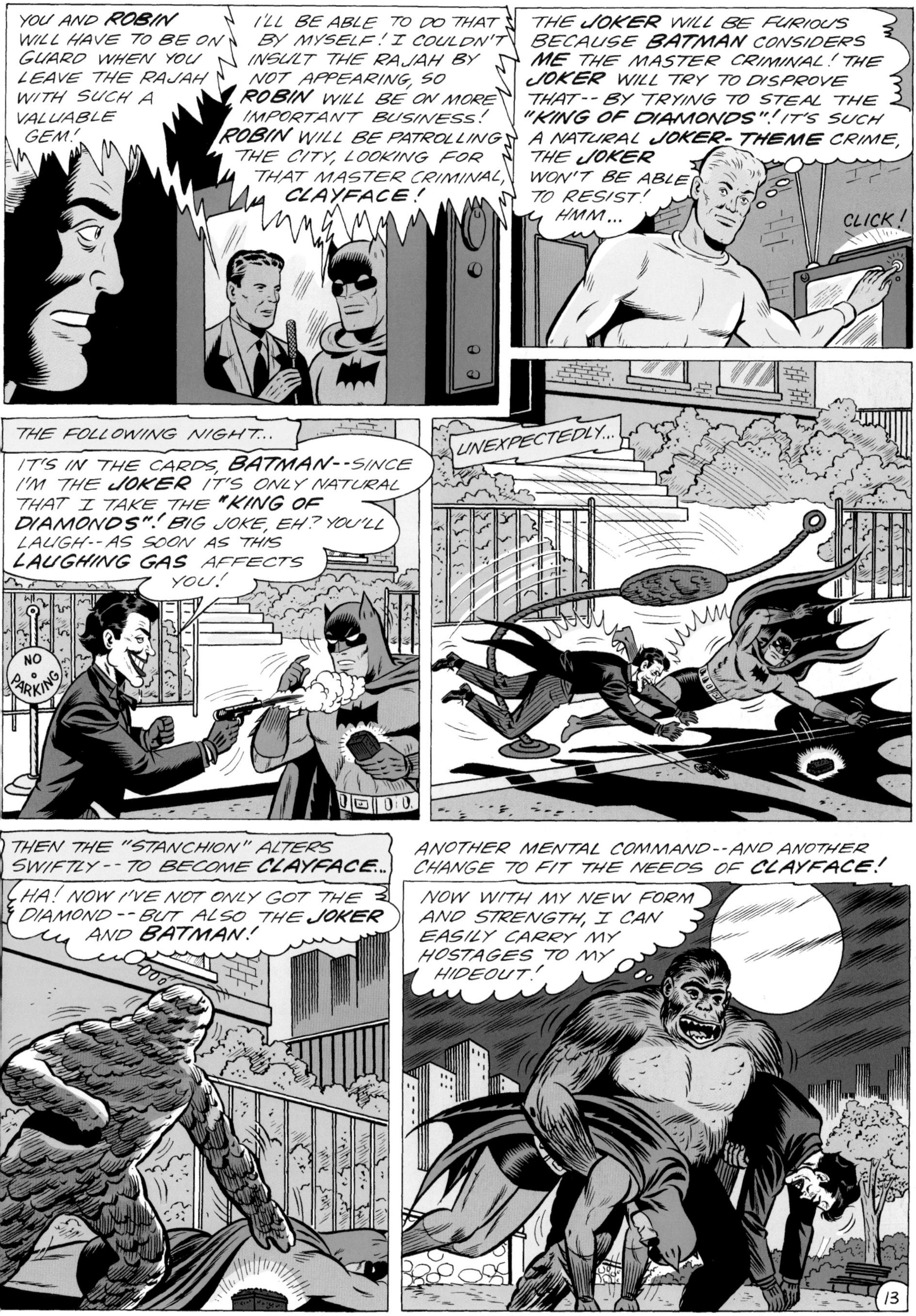
YOU AND ROBIN WILL HAVE TO BE ON GUARD WHEN YOU LEAVE THE RAJAH WITH SUCH A VALUABLE GEM!
I'LL BE ABLE TO DO THAT BY MYSELF! I COULDN'T INSULT THE RAJAH BY NOT APPEARING, SO ROBIN WILL BE ON MORE IMPORTANT BUSINESS! ROBIN WILL BE PATROLLING THE CITY, LOOKING FOR THAT MASTER CRIMINAL, CLAYFACE!
THE JOKER WILL BE FURIOUS BECAUSE BATMAN CONSIDERS ME THE MASTER CRIMINAL! THE JOKER WILL TRY TO DISPROVE THAT-- BY TRYING TO STEAL THE "KING OF DIAMONDS"! IT'S SUCH A NATURAL JOKER-THEME CRIME, THE JOKER WON'T BE ABLE TO RESIST! HMM...
CLICK!
THE FOLLOWING NIGHT...
IT'S IN THE CARDS, BATMAN--SINCE I'M THE JOKER IT'S ONLY NATURAL THAT I TAKE THE "KING OF DIAMONDS"! BIG JOKE, EH? YOU'LL LAUGH--AS SOON AS THIS LAUGHING GAS AFFECTS YOU!
NO PARKING
UNEXPECTEDLY...
THEN THE "STANCHION" ALTERS SWIFTLY--TO BECOME CLAYFACE...
HA! NOW I'VE NOT ONLY GOT THE DIAMOND--BUT ALSO THE JOKER AND BATMAN!
ANOTHER MENTAL COMMAND--AND ANOTHER CHANGE TO FIT THE NEEDS OF CLAYFACE!
NOW WITH MY NEW FORM AND STRENGTH, I CAN EASILY CARRY MY HOSTAGES TO MY HIDEOUT!
13

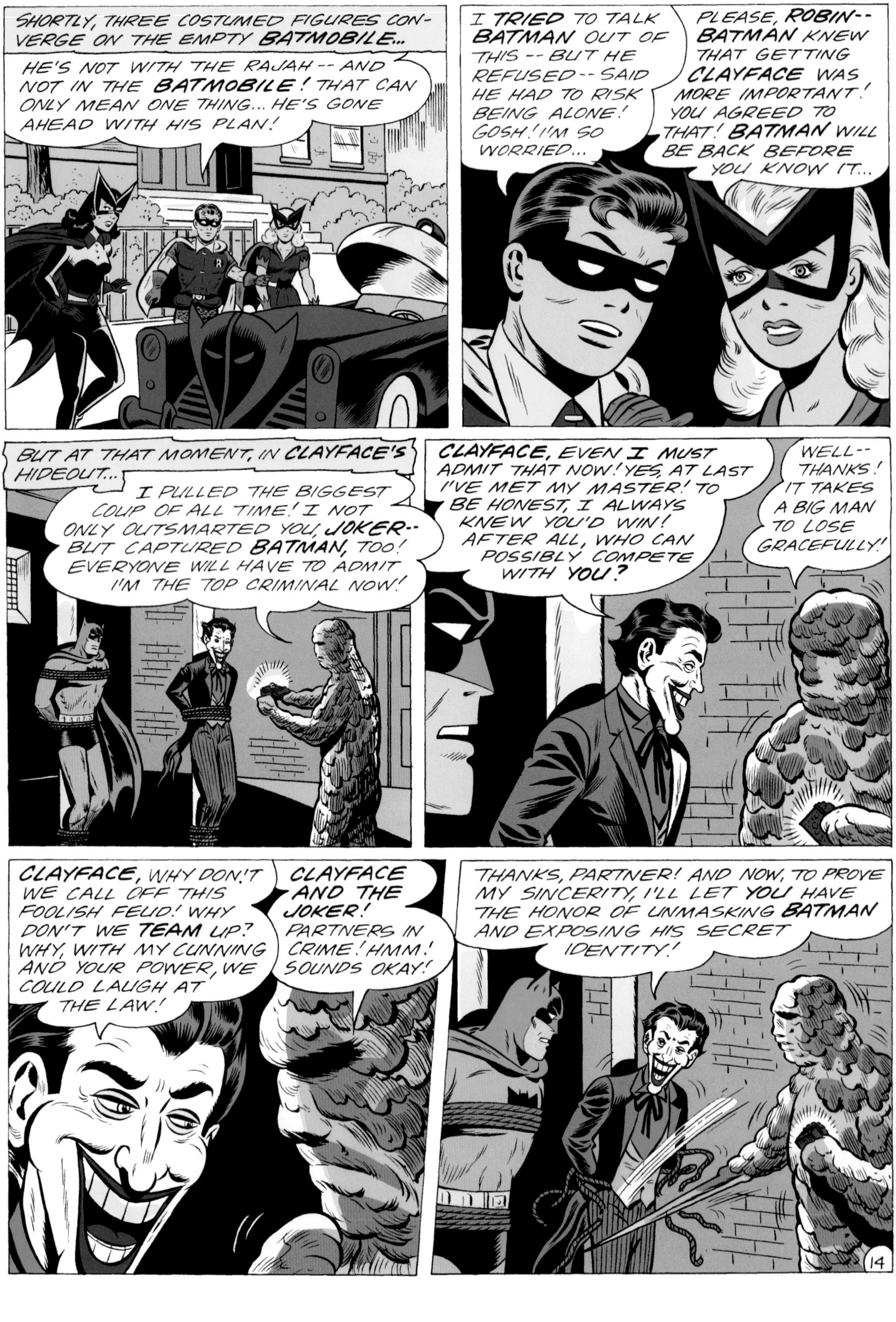
SHORTLY, THREE COSTUMED FIGURES CONVERGE ON THE EMPTY BATMOBILE...
HE'S NOT WITH THE RAJAH -- AND NOT IN THE BATMOBILE! THAT CAN ONLY MEAN ONE THING... HE'S GONE AHEAD WITH HIS PLAN!
I TRIED TO TALK BATMAN OUT OF THIS -- BUT HE REFUSED -- SAID HE HAD TO RISK BEING ALONE! GOSH! I'M SO WORRIED...
PLEASE, ROBIN-- BATMAN KNEW THAT GETTING CLAYFACE WAS MORE IMPORTANT! YOU AGREED TO THAT! BATMAN WILL BE BACK BEFORE YOU KNOW IT...
BUT AT THAT MOMENT, IN CLAYFACE'S HIDEOUT...
I PULLED THE BIGGEST COUP OF ALL TIME! I NOT ONLY OUTSMARTED YOU, JOKER-- BUT CAPTURED BATMAN, TOO! EVERYONE WILL HAVE TO ADMIT I'M THE TOP CRIMINAL NOW!
CLAYFACE, EVEN I MUST ADMIT THAT NOW! YES, AT LAST I'VE MET MY MASTER! TO BE HONEST, I ALWAYS KNEW YOU'D WIN! AFTER ALL, WHO CAN POSSIBLY COMPETE WITH YOU?
WELL-- THANKS! IT TAKES A BIG MAN TO LOSE GRACEFULLY!
CLAYFACE, WHY DON'T WE CALL OFF THIS FOOLISH FEUD! WHY DON'T WE TEAM UP? WHY, WITH MY CUNNING AND YOUR POWER, WE COULD LAUGH AT THE LAW!
CLAYFACE AND THE JOKER! PARTNERS IN CRIME! HMM! SOUNDS OKAY!
THANKS, PARTNER! AND NOW, TO PROVE MY SINCERITY, I'LL LET YOU HAVE THE HONOR OF UNMASKING BATMAN AND EXPOSING HIS SECRET IDENTITY!
14

OKAY, *JOKER*--HERE GOES! LET'S SEE WHAT THE REST OF *BATMAN'S* FACE IS LIKE!

HUH? THE REST OF HIS FACE--IT'S LIKE MY FACE LOOKS WHEN I'M *CLAYFACE!*

STUNNED BY SURPRISE--*CLAYFACE* IS THEN STUNNED UNCONSCIOUS BY A SLEDGE-HAMMER BLOW!

NOW! I KNEW THE SHOCK OF SEEING THAT FACE WOULD DISTRACT YOU LONG ENOUGH FOR ME TO GET IN THIS KNOCKOUT PUNCH!

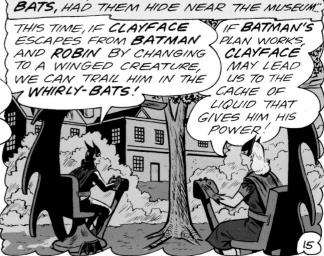

NOW I'LL GIVE *CLAYFACE* A SEDATIVE THAT WILL KEEP HIM SLEEPING PAST THE FIVE-HOUR TIME LIMIT SO THAT HIS POWER WILL BE GONE! WHEN HE AWAKENS, HE WON'T LIKE KNOWING THAT *I* IMPERSONATED THE *JOKER* AND THAT THE "BATMAN" HE UNMASKED WAS MY *BATMAN-ROBOT* WITH CLAY ON ITS FACE!

LATER, WHEN HAGEN AWAKENS IN PRISON AND IS TOLD THE TRUTH...

BUT IF YOU IMPER-SONATED THE *JOKER*, WHERE IS THE *REAL JOKER?*

THE *JOKER'S* BEEN IN JAIL SINCE THE NIGHT OF THE ROBBERY IN THE MUSEUM'S AFRICAN ROOM! YOU SEE, WHEN HE PHONED IN HIS FAKE TIP THAT *CLAYFACE* WAS GOING TO ROB THE GOLD IDOL, I MADE SOME HURRIED PLANS...

"I SWIFTLY CONTACTED *BATWOMAN* AND *BAT-GIRL*, LENT THEM TWO *WHIRLY-BATS*, HAD THEM HIDE NEAR THE MUSEUM."

THIS TIME, IF *CLAYFACE* ESCAPES FROM *BATMAN* AND *ROBIN* BY CHANGING TO A WINGED CREATURE, WE CAN TRAIL HIM IN THE *WHIRLY-BATS!*

IF *BATMAN'S* PLAN WORKS, *CLAYFACE* MAY LEAD US TO THE CACHE OF LIQUID THAT GIVES HIM HIS POWER!

15

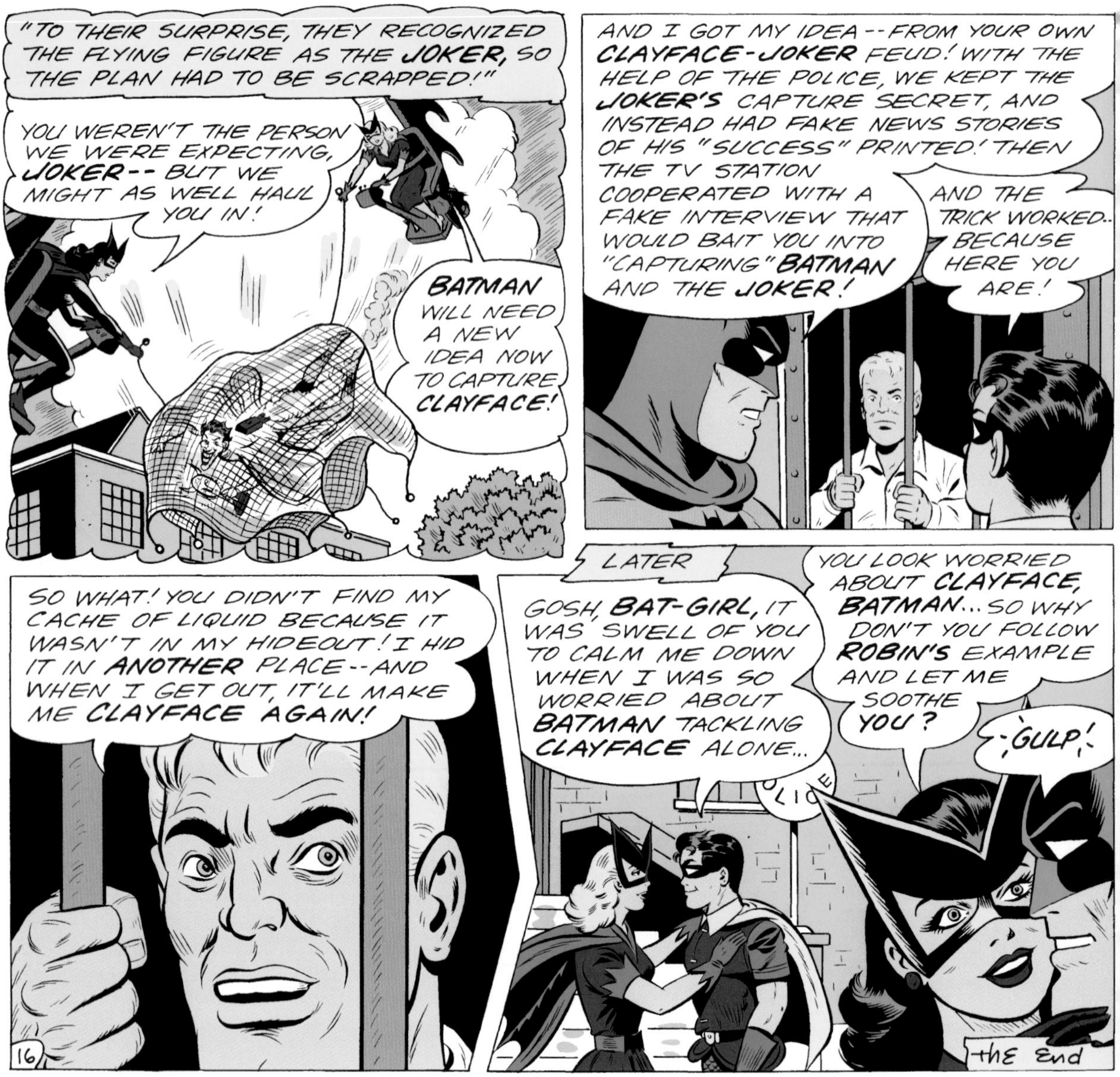
"TO THEIR SURPRISE, THEY RECOGNIZED THE FLYING FIGURE AS THE JOKER, SO THE PLAN HAD TO BE SCRAPPED!"
YOU WEREN'T THE PERSON WE WERE EXPECTING, JOKER-- BUT WE MIGHT AS WELL HAUL YOU IN!
BATMAN WILL NEED A NEW IDEA NOW TO CAPTURE CLAYFACE!
AND I GOT MY IDEA--FROM YOUR OWN CLAYFACE-JOKER FEUD! WITH THE HELP OF THE POLICE, WE KEPT THE JOKER'S CAPTURE SECRET, AND INSTEAD HAD FAKE NEWS STORIES OF HIS "SUCCESS" PRINTED! THEN THE TV STATION COOPERATED WITH A FAKE INTERVIEW THAT WOULD BAIT YOU INTO "CAPTURING" BATMAN AND THE JOKER!
AND THE TRICK WORKED.. BECAUSE HERE YOU ARE!
SO WHAT! YOU DIDN'T FIND MY CACHE OF LIQUID BECAUSE IT WASN'T IN MY HIDEOUT! I HID IT IN ANOTHER PLACE--AND WHEN I GET OUT, IT'LL MAKE ME CLAYFACE AGAIN!
16
LATER
GOSH, BAT-GIRL, IT WAS SWELL OF YOU TO CALM ME DOWN WHEN I WAS SO WORRIED ABOUT BATMAN TACKLING CLAYFACE ALONE...
YOU LOOK WORRIED ABOUT CLAYFACE, BATMAN... SO WHY DON'T YOU FOLLOW ROBIN'S EXAMPLE AND LET ME SOOTHE YOU?
GULP!
POLICE
THE END

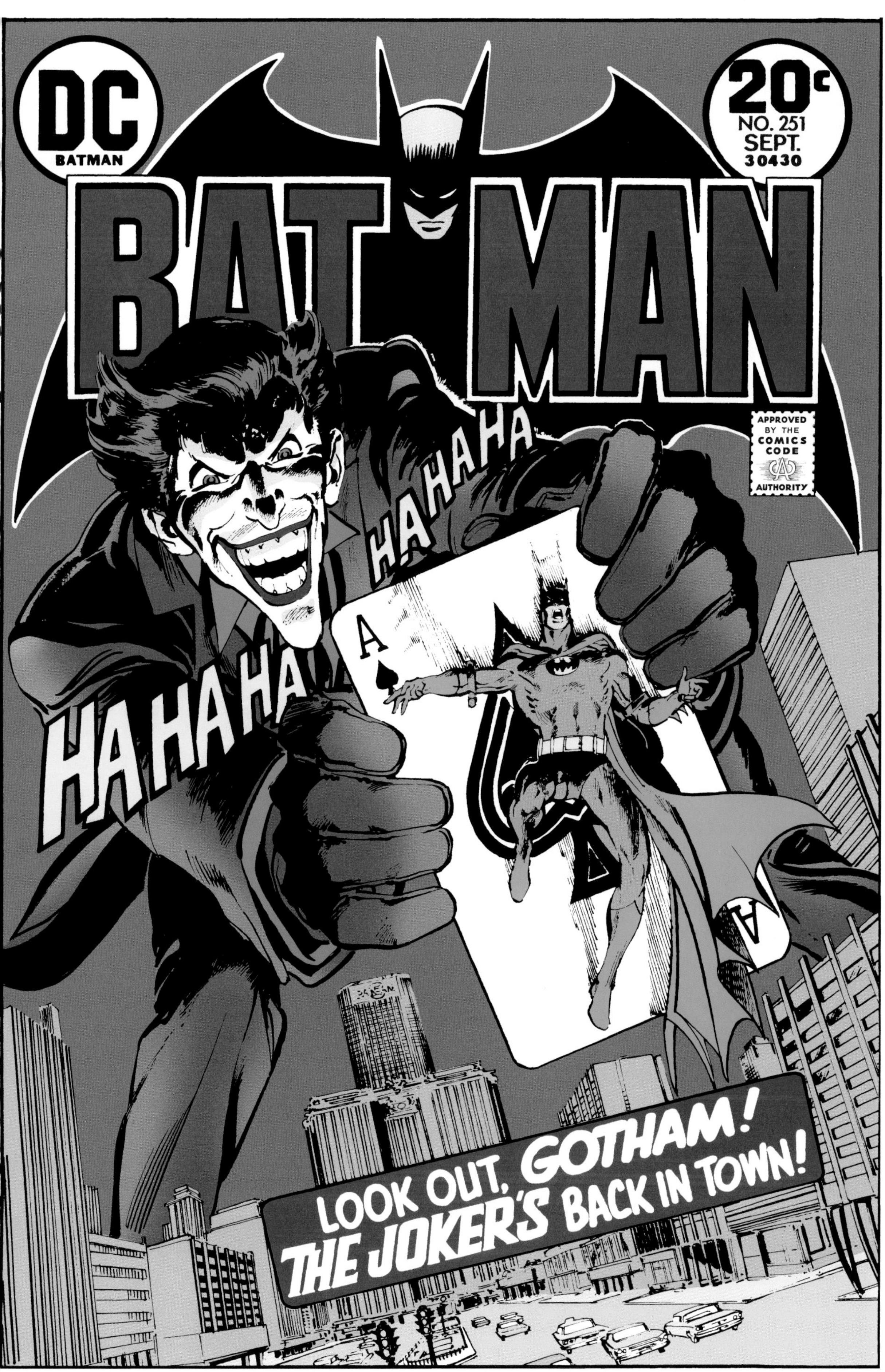
DC
BATMAN
20¢
NO. 251
SEPT.
30430
BATMAN
APPROVED BY THE COMICS CODE AUTHORITY
HA HA HA
HA HA HA HA
HA HA HA
LOOK OUT, GOTHAM!
THE JOKER'S BACK IN TOWN!

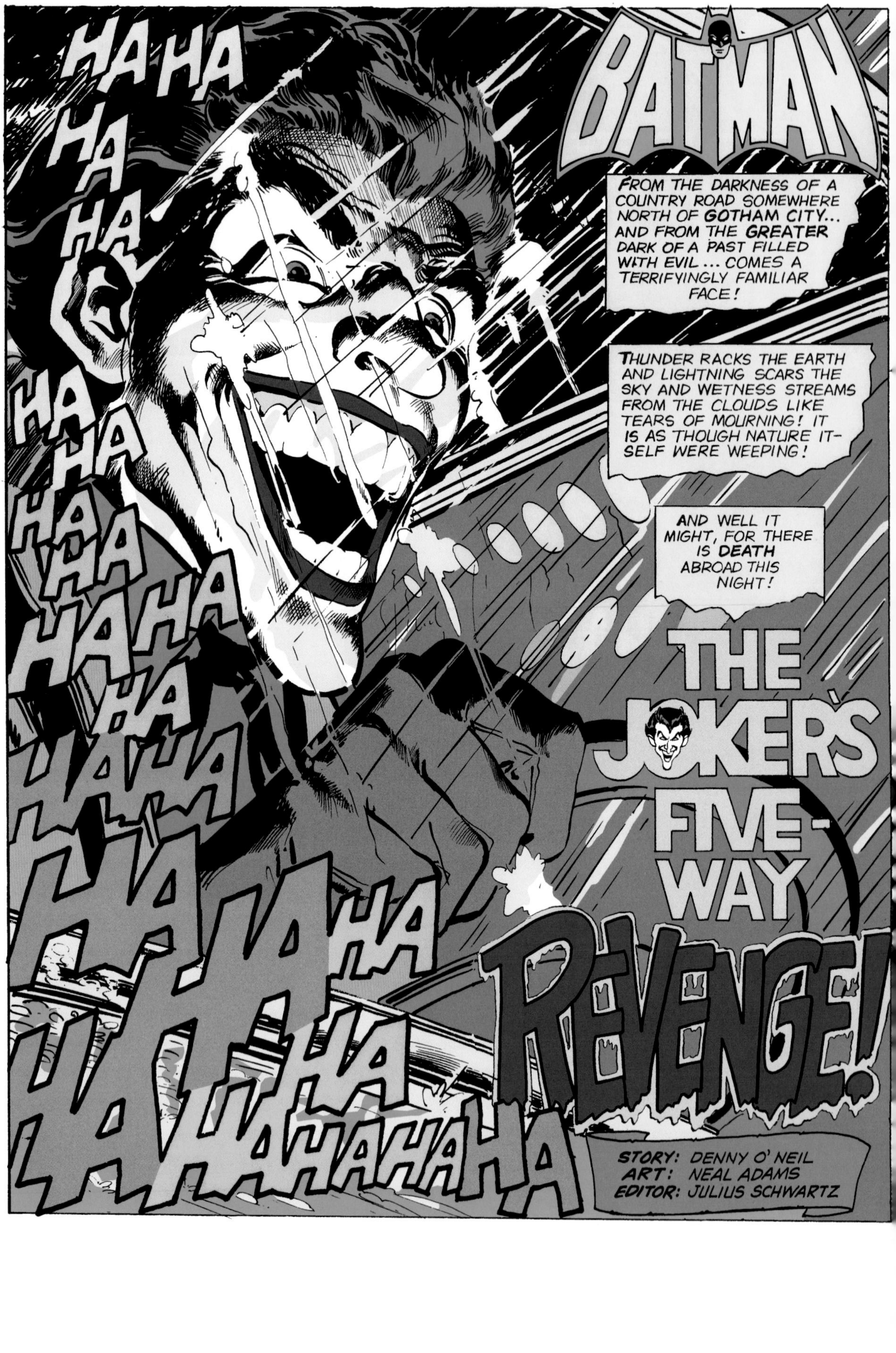
BATMAN
FROM THE DARKNESS OF A COUNTRY ROAD SOMEWHERE NORTH OF GOTHAM CITY... AND FROM THE GREATER DARK OF A PAST FILLED WITH EVIL ... COMES A TERRIFYINGLY FAMILIAR FACE!
THUNDER RACKS THE EARTH AND LIGHTNING SCARS THE SKY AND WETNESS STREAMS FROM THE CLOUDS LIKE TEARS OF MOURNING! IT IS AS THOUGH NATURE IT-SELF WERE WEEPING!
AND WELL IT MIGHT, FOR THERE IS DEATH ABROAD THIS NIGHT!
HA HA HA HA HA HA HA HA HA HA HA HA HA HA HA HA HA HA HA HA HA HA HA HA HA HA
THE JOKER'S FIVE-WAY REVENGE!
STORY: DENNY O' NEIL
ART: NEAL ADAMS
EDITOR: JULIUS SCHWARTZ

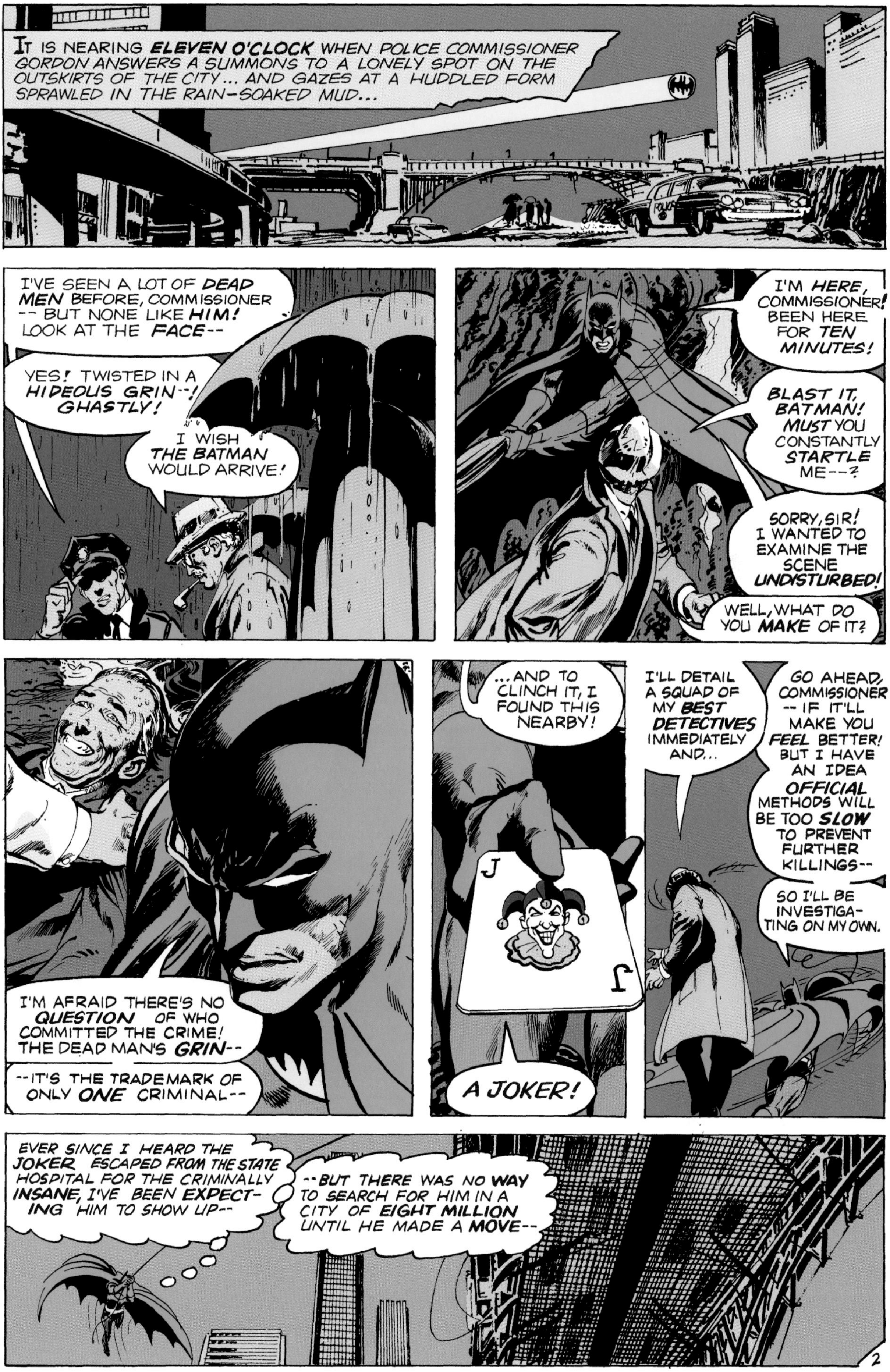
IT IS NEARING ELEVEN O'CLOCK WHEN POLICE COMMISSIONER GORDON ANSWERS A SUMMONS TO A LONELY SPOT ON THE OUTSKIRTS OF THE CITY... AND GAZES AT A HUDDLED FORM SPRAWLED IN THE RAIN-SOAKED MUD...
POLICE
I'VE SEEN A LOT OF DEAD MEN BEFORE, COMMISSIONER -- BUT NONE LIKE HIM! LOOK AT THE FACE--
YES! TWISTED IN A HIDEOUS GRIN--! GHASTLY!
I WISH THE BATMAN WOULD ARRIVE!
I'M HERE, COMMISSIONER! BEEN HERE FOR TEN MINUTES!
BLAST IT, BATMAN! MUST YOU CONSTANTLY STARTLE ME--?
SORRY, SIR! I WANTED TO EXAMINE THE SCENE UNDISTURBED!
WELL, WHAT DO YOU MAKE OF IT?
I'M AFRAID THERE'S NO QUESTION OF WHO COMMITTED THE CRIME! THE DEAD MAN'S GRIN--
--IT'S THE TRADEMARK OF ONLY ONE CRIMINAL--
...AND TO CLINCH IT, I FOUND THIS NEARBY!
J
J
A JOKER!
I'LL DETAIL A SQUAD OF MY BEST DETECTIVES IMMEDIATELY AND...
GO AHEAD, COMMISSIONER -- IF IT'LL MAKE YOU FEEL BETTER! BUT I HAVE AN IDEA OFFICIAL METHODS WILL BE TOO SLOW TO PREVENT FURTHER KILLINGS--
SO I'LL BE INVESTIGA-TING ON MY OWN.
EVER SINCE I HEARD THE JOKER ESCAPED FROM THE STATE HOSPITAL FOR THE CRIMINALLY INSANE, I'VE BEEN EXPECT-ING HIM TO SHOW UP--
--BUT THERE WAS NO WAY TO SEARCH FOR HIM IN A CITY OF EIGHT MILLION UNTIL HE MADE A MOVE--
2

--WHICH HE **HAS!** AND I'VE GOT A VERY GOOD IDEA **WHAT** HE'LL TRY **NEXT!**

I'VE KEPT A CLOSE **WATCH** ON THE MEMBERS OF HIS FORMER **GANG** --

ONE OF THEM WORKS AS A JANITOR IN THIS RATTY GYM! IT FIGURES... THE GUY'S A FORMER **BOXER**--

--USED TO BE A FAIR **LIGHTHEAVYWEIGHT!** WENT BY THE NAME OF...

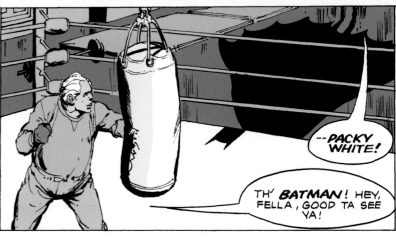

--**PACKY WHITE!**

TH' **BATMAN!** HEY, FELLA, GOOD TA SEE YA!

C'MON...LET'S JAW WHILE I WORK OUT!

STILL PRACTICING THE OLD SKILLS, EH, **PACKY** ?

YEAH... FELLA MY AGE'S GOTTA KEEP IN SHAPE!

NOW... WHAT'S ON THAT SHARP **MIND**, HUH?

AS YOU **KNOW**, THE **JOKER'S** RATTLING AROUND LOOSE! I HAVE REASON TO BELIEVE HE SNUFFED A **FRIEND** OF YOURS---

WE FOUND **PHILLY JACK BARTON** DEAD... AND HE WAS WEARING A **BIG SMILE!**

SOUNDS LIKE THE **BOSS'S** STYLE, FOR SURE!

OOPS! SORRY... MISSED THE **BAG!**

PERFECTLY ALL **RIGHT!**

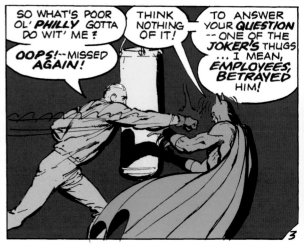

SO WHAT'S POOR OL' **PHILLY** GOTTA DO WIT' ME?

OOPS!--MISSED **AGAIN!**

THINK NOTHING OF IT!

TO ANSWER YOUR **QUESTION** --ONE OF THE **JOKER'S** THUGS ... I MEAN, **EMPLOYEES,** BETRAYED HIM!

3

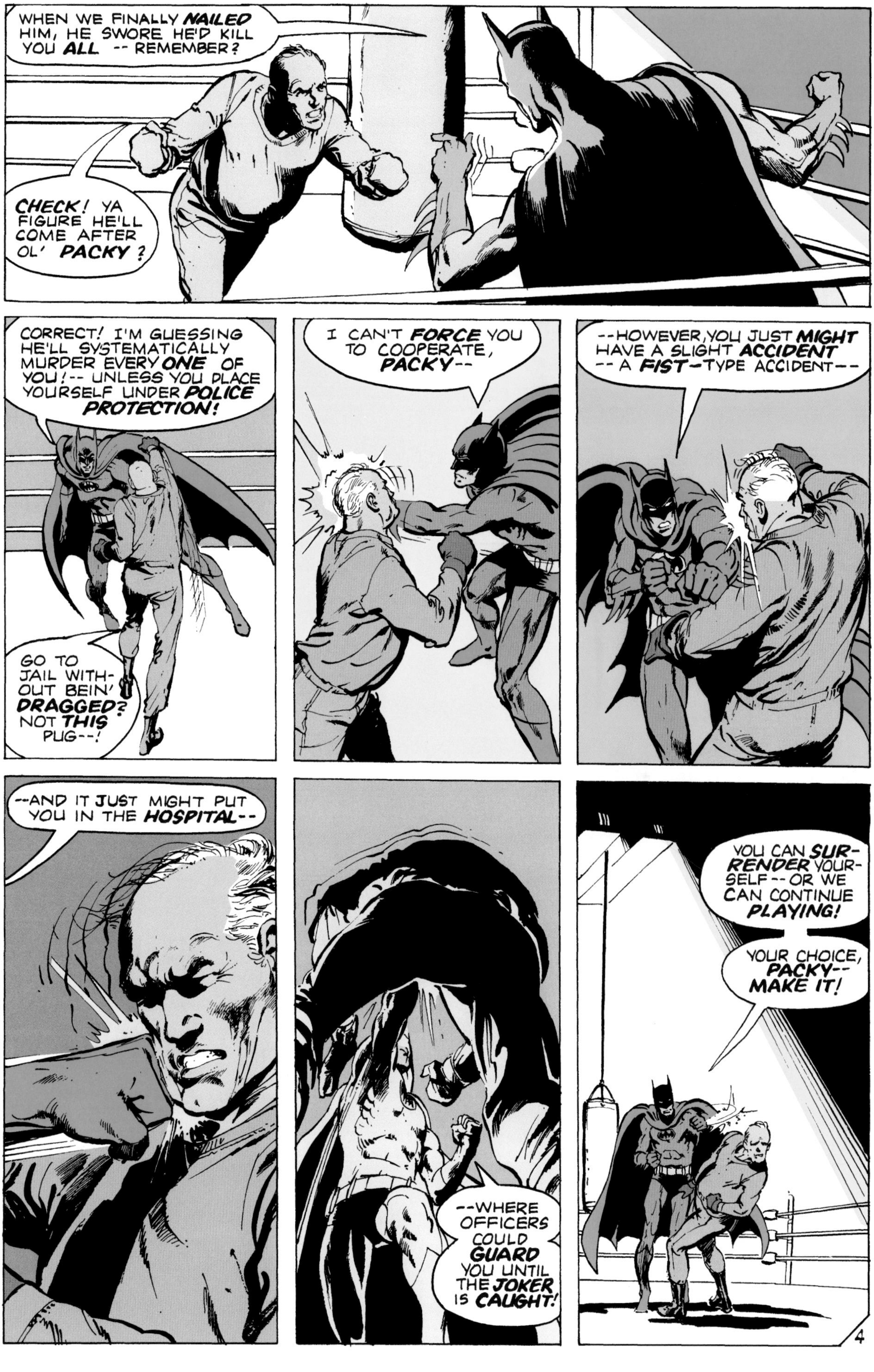
WHEN WE FINALLY NAILED HIM, HE SWORE HE'D KILL YOU ALL -- REMEMBER?
CHECK! YA FIGURE HE'LL COME AFTER OL' PACKY?
CORRECT! I'M GUESSING HE'LL SYSTEMATICALLY MURDER EVERY ONE OF YOU!-- UNLESS YOU PLACE YOURSELF UNDER POLICE PROTECTION!
GO TO JAIL WITH-OUT BEIN' DRAGGED? NOT THIS PUG--!
I CAN'T FORCE YOU TO COOPERATE, PACKY--
--HOWEVER, YOU JUST MIGHT HAVE A SLIGHT ACCIDENT -- A FIST-TYPE ACCIDENT--
--AND IT JUST MIGHT PUT YOU IN THE HOSPITAL--
--WHERE OFFICERS COULD GUARD YOU UNTIL THE JOKER IS CAUGHT!
YOU CAN SUR-RENDER YOUR-SELF -- OR WE CAN CONTINUE PLAYING!
YOUR CHOICE, PACKY-- MAKE IT!
4

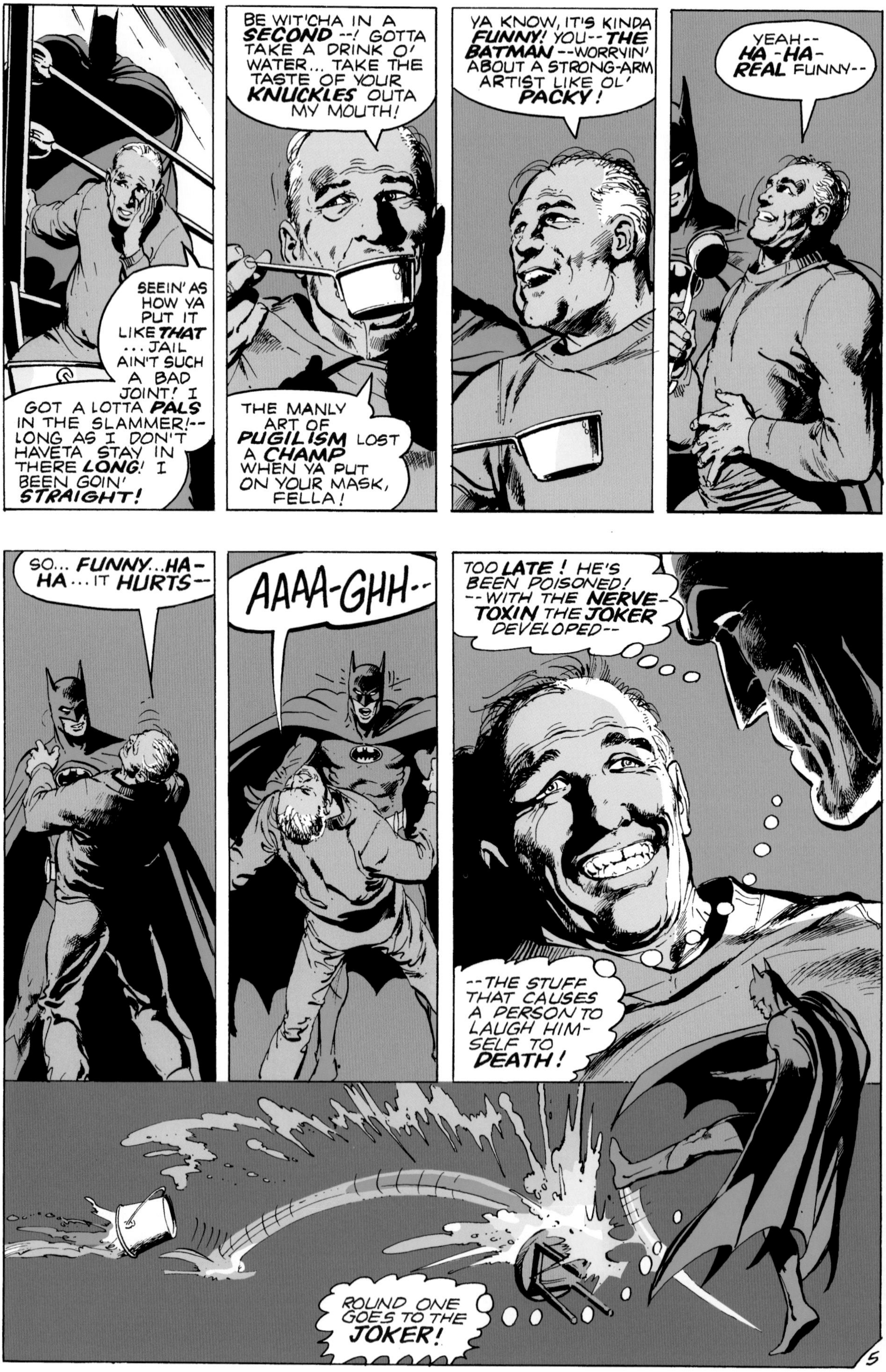
SEEIN' AS HOW YA PUT IT LIKE THAT ... JAIL AIN'T SUCH A BAD JOINT! I GOT A LOTTA PALS IN THE SLAMMER!-- LONG AS I DON'T HAVETA STAY IN THERE LONG! I BEEN GOIN' STRAIGHT!
BE WIT'CHA IN A SECOND --! GOTTA TAKE A DRINK O' WATER... TAKE THE TASTE OF YOUR KNUCKLES OUTA MY MOUTH!
THE MANLY ART OF PUGILISM LOST A CHAMP WHEN YA PUT ON YOUR MASK, FELLA!
YA KNOW, IT'S KINDA FUNNY! YOU--THE BATMAN --WORRYIN' ABOUT A STRONG-ARM ARTIST LIKE OL' PACKY!
YEAH-- HA-HA- REAL FUNNY--
SO... FUNNY...HA-HA... IT HURTS--
AAAA-GHH--
TOO LATE! HE'S BEEN POISONED! --WITH THE NERVE-TOXIN THE JOKER DEVELOPED--
--THE STUFF THAT CAUSES A PERSON TO LAUGH HIM-SELF TO DEATH!
ROUND ONE GOES TO THE JOKER!
5

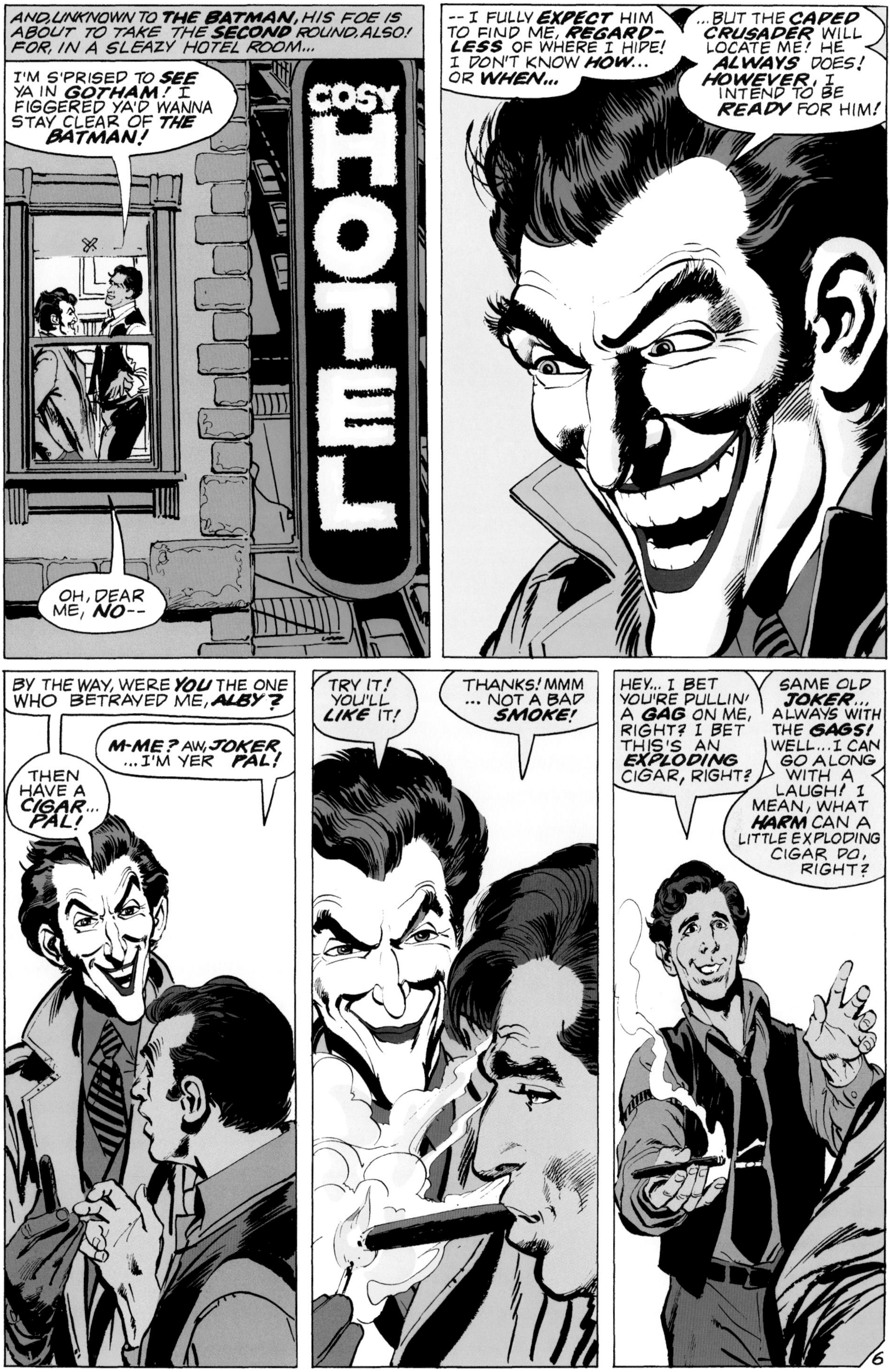
AND, UNKNOWN TO THE BATMAN, HIS FOE IS ABOUT TO TAKE THE SECOND ROUND, ALSO! FOR, IN A SLEAZY HOTEL ROOM...
I'M S'PRISED TO SEE YA IN GOTHAM! I FIGGERED YA'D WANNA STAY CLEAR OF THE BATMAN!
COSY HOTEL
OH, DEAR ME, NO--
-- I FULLY EXPECT HIM TO FIND ME, REGARDLESS OF WHERE I HIDE! I DON'T KNOW HOW... OR WHEN...
...BUT THE CAPED CRUSADER WILL LOCATE ME! HE ALWAYS DOES! HOWEVER, I INTEND TO BE READY FOR HIM!
BY THE WAY, WERE YOU THE ONE WHO BETRAYED ME, ALBY?
M-ME? AW, JOKER ...I'M YER PAL!
THEN HAVE A CIGAR... PAL!
TRY IT! YOU'LL LIKE IT!
THANKS! MMM ... NOT A BAD SMOKE!
HEY... I BET YOU'RE PULLIN' A GAG ON ME, RIGHT? I BET THIS'S AN EXPLODING CIGAR, RIGHT?
SAME OLD JOKER... ALWAYS WITH THE GAGS! WELL... I CAN GO ALONG WITH A LAUGH! I MEAN, WHAT HARM CAN A LITTLE EXPLODING CIGAR DO, RIGHT?
6

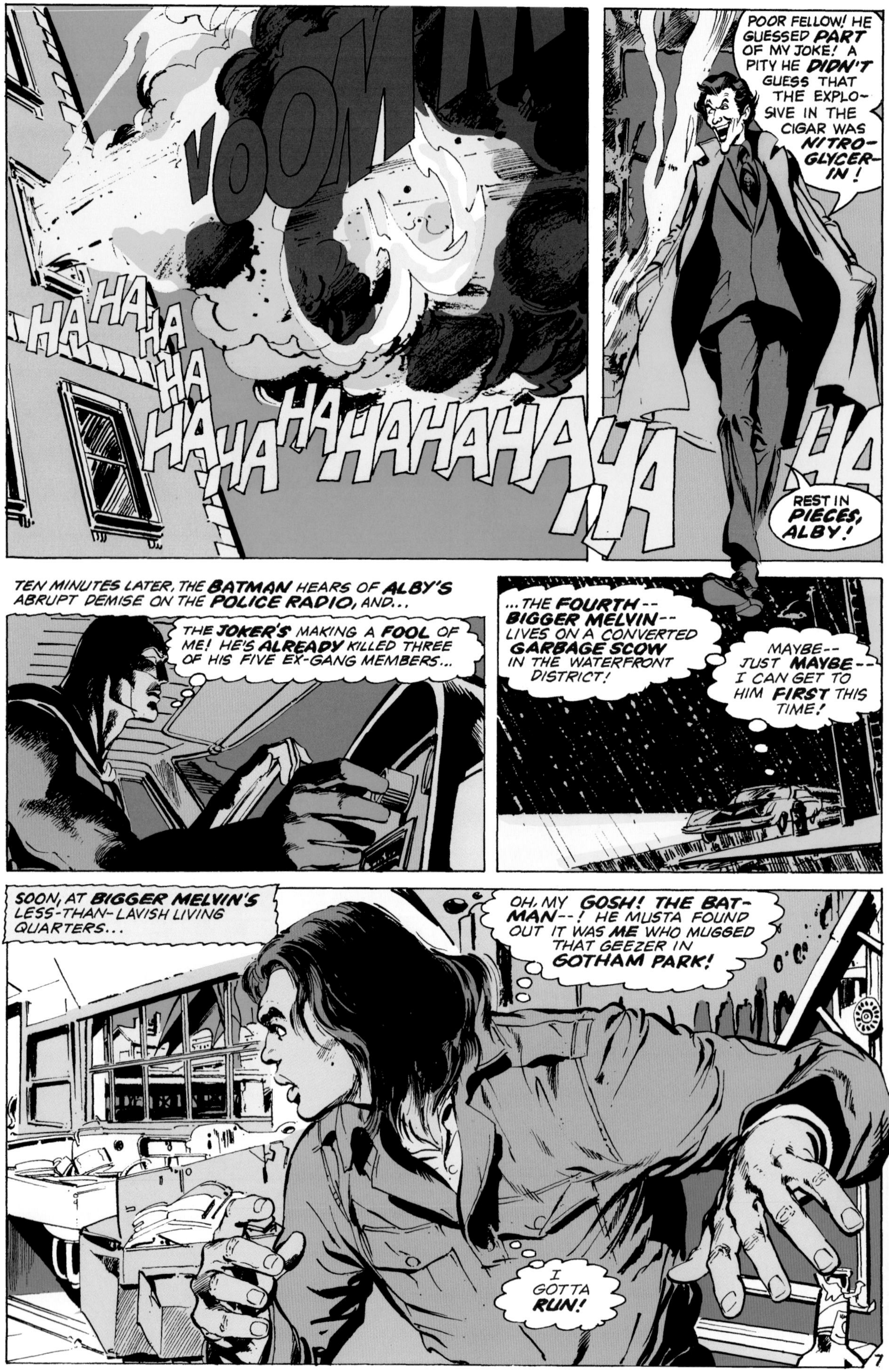
VOOM!!
HA HA HA HA HA
POOR FELLOW! HE GUESSED PART OF MY JOKE! A PITY HE DIDN'T GUESS THAT THE EXPLO-SIVE IN THE CIGAR WAS NITRO-GLYCER-IN!
HA HA HA HA HA HA HA HA HA HA HA
REST IN PIECES, ALBY!
TEN MINUTES LATER, THE BATMAN HEARS OF ALBY'S ABRUPT DEMISE ON THE POLICE RADIO, AND...
THE JOKER'S MAKING A FOOL OF ME! HE'S ALREADY KILLED THREE OF HIS FIVE EX-GANG MEMBERS...
...THE FOURTH--BIGGER MELVIN--LIVES ON A CONVERTED GARBAGE SCOW IN THE WATERFRONT DISTRICT!
MAYBE--JUST MAYBE--I CAN GET TO HIM FIRST THIS TIME!
SOON, AT BIGGER MELVIN'S LESS-THAN-LAVISH LIVING QUARTERS...
OH, MY GOSH! THE BAT-MAN--! HE MUSTA FOUND OUT IT WAS ME WHO MUGGED THAT GEEZER IN GOTHAM PARK!
I GOTTA RUN!
7

YOU!-- BIGGER MELVIN! WAIT!

NO CHANCE, LAWMAN!

THE BATMAN'S FASTER'N ME ...BUT I KNOW EVERY INCH OF THE DOCKS LIKE THE PALM OF MY HAND!

HE'LL NEVER CATCH ME!

I'LL DUCK 'ROUND THESE CRATES...

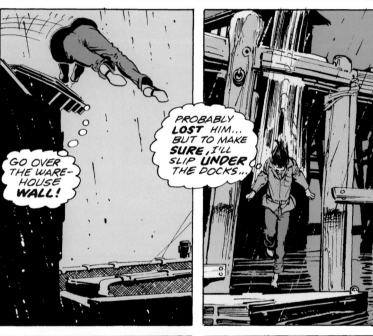

GO OVER THE WAREHOUSE WALL!

PROBABLY LOST HIM... BUT TO MAKE SURE, I'LL SLIP UNDER THE DOCKS...

DIVE INTO THE SEWER PIPE...

...CRAWL A COUPLE OF BLOCKS UNDERGROUND...

...COME OUT A GOOD MILE FROM MY JOINT! YEAH, I FOXED THE BATMAN, AN' NO KIDDIN'! NO WAY FOR HIM TO GRAB ME NOW...

8

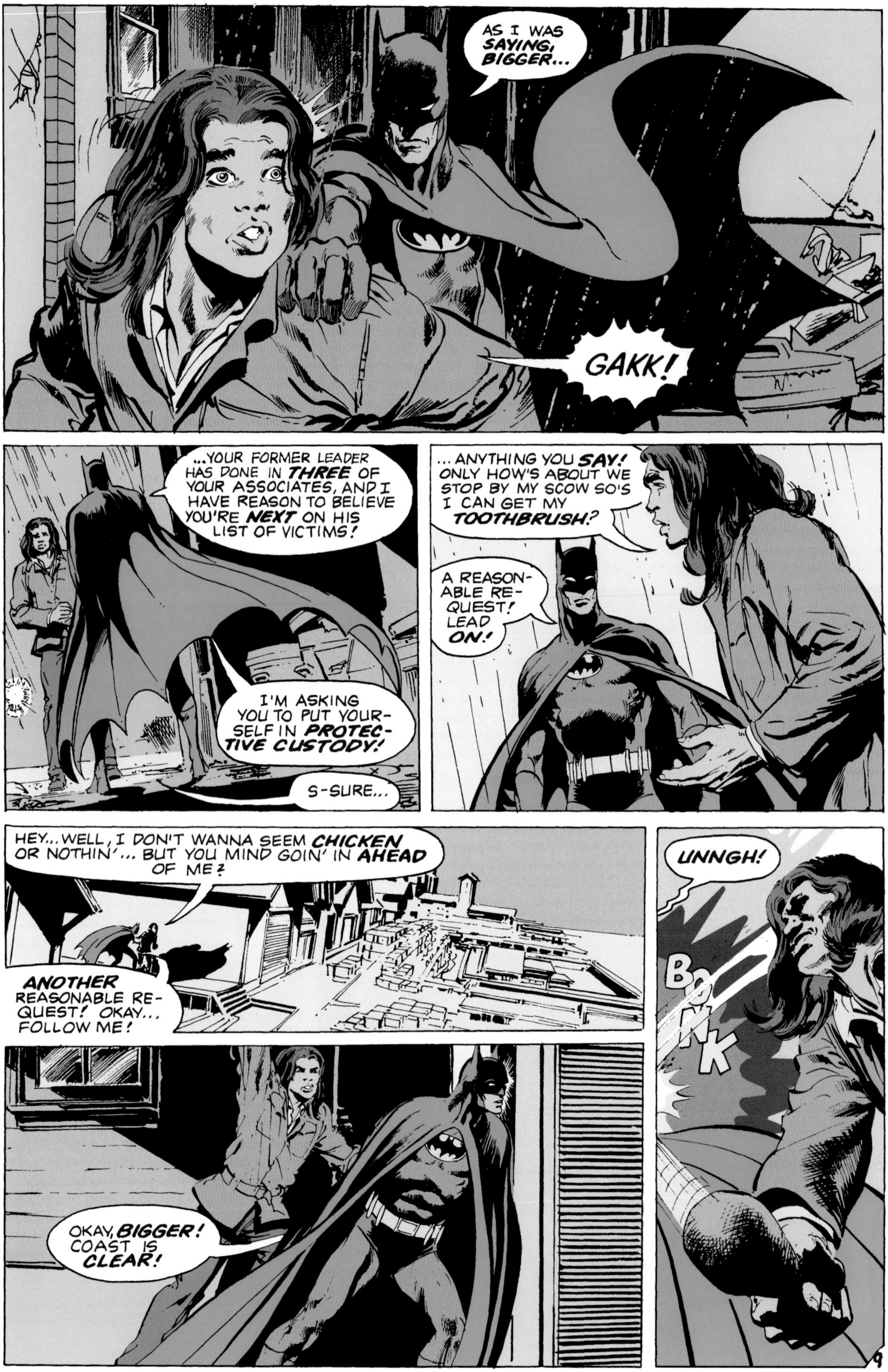
AS I WAS SAYING, BIGGER...
GAKK!
...YOUR FORMER LEADER HAS DONE IN THREE OF YOUR ASSOCIATES, AND I HAVE REASON TO BELIEVE YOU'RE NEXT ON HIS LIST OF VICTIMS!
I'M ASKING YOU TO PUT YOURSELF IN PROTECTIVE CUSTODY!
S-SURE...
...ANYTHING YOU SAY! ONLY HOW'S ABOUT WE STOP BY MY SCOW SO'S I CAN GET MY TOOTHBRUSH?
A REASONABLE REQUEST! LEAD ON!
HEY...WELL, I DON'T WANNA SEEM CHICKEN OR NOTHIN'... BUT YOU MIND GOIN' IN AHEAD OF ME?
ANOTHER REASONABLE REQUEST! OKAY... FOLLOW ME!
OKAY, BIGGER! COAST IS CLEAR!
UNNGH!
BONK
9

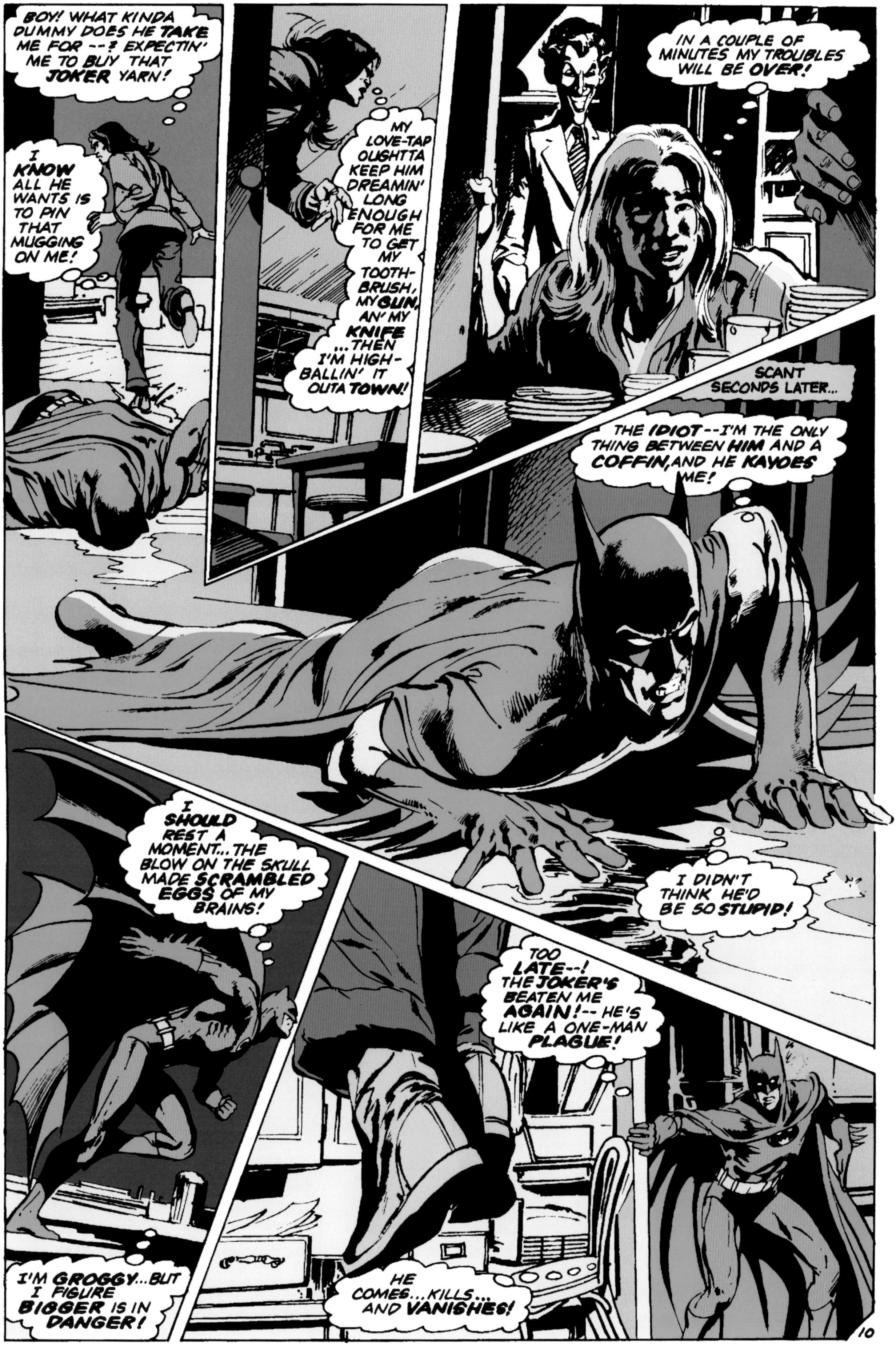
BOY! WHAT KINDA DUMMY DOES HE TAKE ME FOR --? EXPECTIN' ME TO BUY THAT JOKER YARN!
I KNOW ALL HE WANTS IS TO PIN THAT MUGGING ON ME!
MY LOVE-TAP OUGHTTA KEEP HIM DREAMIN' LONG ENOUGH FOR ME TO GET MY TOOTH-BRUSH, MY GUN, AN' MY KNIFE ...THEN I'M HIGH-BALLIN' IT OUTA TOWN!
IN A COUPLE OF MINUTES MY TROUBLES WILL BE OVER!
SCANT SECONDS LATER...
THE IDIOT--I'M THE ONLY THING BETWEEN HIM AND A COFFIN, AND HE KAYOES ME!
I DIDN'T THINK HE'D BE SO STUPID!
I SHOULD REST A MOMENT... THE BLOW ON THE SKULL MADE SCRAMBLED EGGS OF MY BRAINS!
I'M GROGGY...BUT I FIGURE BIGGER IS IN DANGER!
TOO LATE--! THE JOKER'S BEATEN ME AGAIN!-- HE'S LIKE A ONE-MAN PLAGUE!
HE COMES... KILLS... AND VANISHES!
10

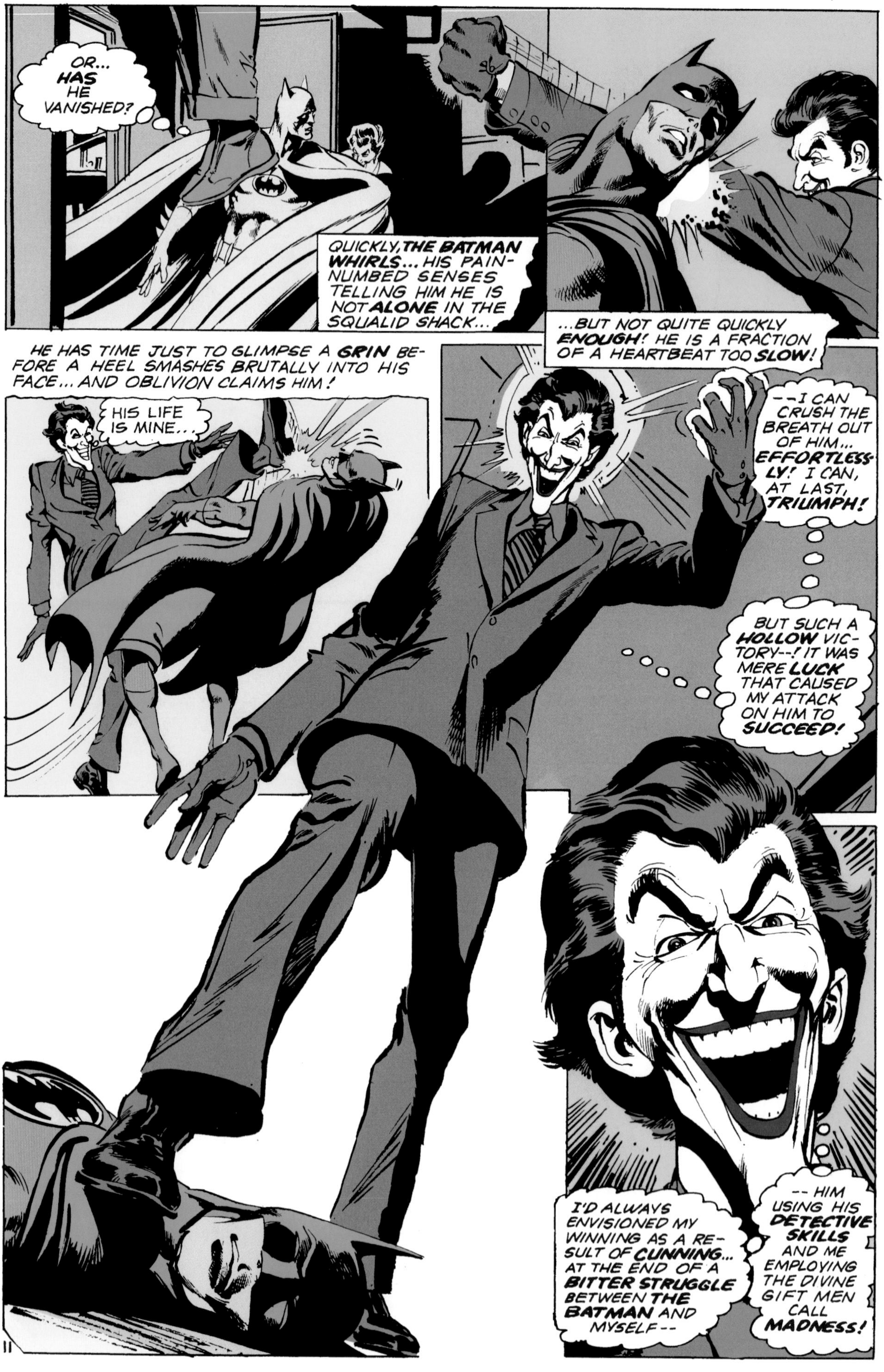

OR... HAS HE VANISHED?
QUICKLY, THE BATMAN WHIRLS... HIS PAIN-NUMBED SENSES TELLING HIM HE IS NOT ALONE IN THE SQUALID SHACK...
...BUT NOT QUITE QUICKLY ENOUGH! HE IS A FRACTION OF A HEARTBEAT TOO SLOW!
HE HAS TIME JUST TO GLIMPSE A GRIN BEFORE A HEEL SMASHES BRUTALLY INTO HIS FACE... AND OBLIVION CLAIMS HIM!
HIS LIFE IS MINE...
--I CAN CRUSH THE BREATH OUT OF HIM... EFFORTLESSLY! I CAN, AT LAST, TRIUMPH!
BUT SUCH A HOLLOW VICTORY--! IT WAS MERE LUCK THAT CAUSED MY ATTACK ON HIM TO SUCCEED!
I'D ALWAYS ENVISIONED MY WINNING AS A RESULT OF CUNNING... AT THE END OF A BITTER STRUGGLE BETWEEN THE BATMAN AND MYSELF--
--HIM USING HIS DETECTIVE SKILLS AND ME EMPLOYING THE DIVINE GIFT MEN CALL MADNESS!
11

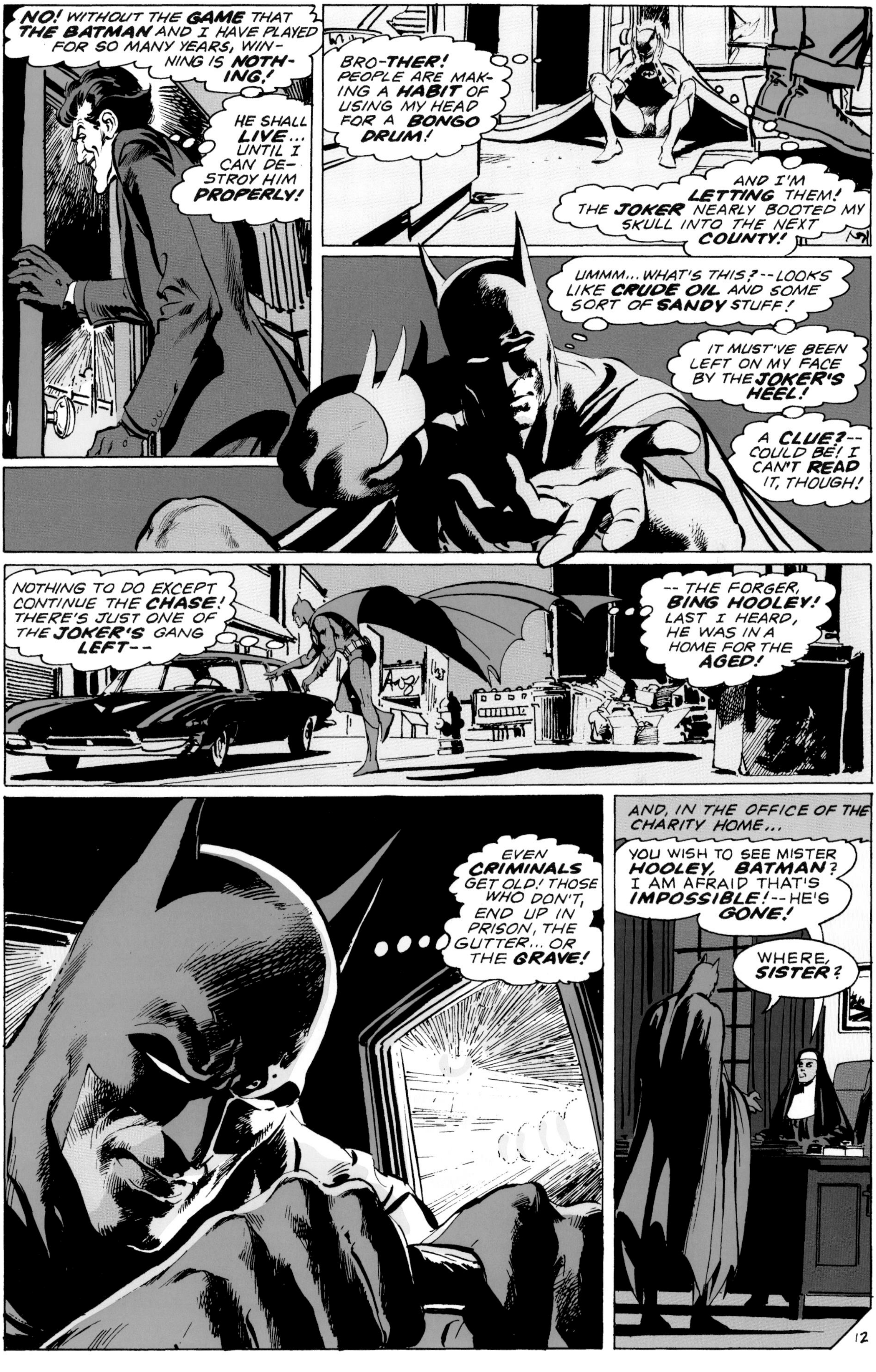
NO! WITHOUT THE GAME THAT THE BATMAN AND I HAVE PLAYED FOR SO MANY YEARS, WINNING IS NOTHING!
HE SHALL LIVE... UNTIL I CAN DESTROY HIM PROPERLY!
BRO-THER! PEOPLE ARE MAKING A HABIT OF USING MY HEAD FOR A BONGO DRUM!
AND I'M LETTING THEM! THE JOKER NEARLY BOOTED MY SKULL INTO THE NEXT COUNTY!
UMMM... WHAT'S THIS? --LOOKS LIKE CRUDE OIL AND SOME SORT OF SANDY STUFF!
IT MUST'VE BEEN LEFT ON MY FACE BY THE JOKER'S HEEL!
A CLUE?--COULD BE! I CAN'T READ IT, THOUGH!
NOTHING TO DO EXCEPT CONTINUE THE CHASE! THERE'S JUST ONE OF THE JOKER'S GANG LEFT--
--THE FORGER, BING HOOLEY! LAST I HEARD, HE WAS IN A HOME FOR THE AGED!
EVEN CRIMINALS GET OLD! THOSE WHO DON'T, END UP IN PRISON, THE GUTTER... OR THE GRAVE!
AND, IN THE OFFICE OF THE CHARITY HOME...
YOU WISH TO SEE MISTER HOOLEY, BATMAN? I AM AFRAID THAT'S IMPOSSIBLE!--HE'S GONE!
WHERE, SISTER?
12

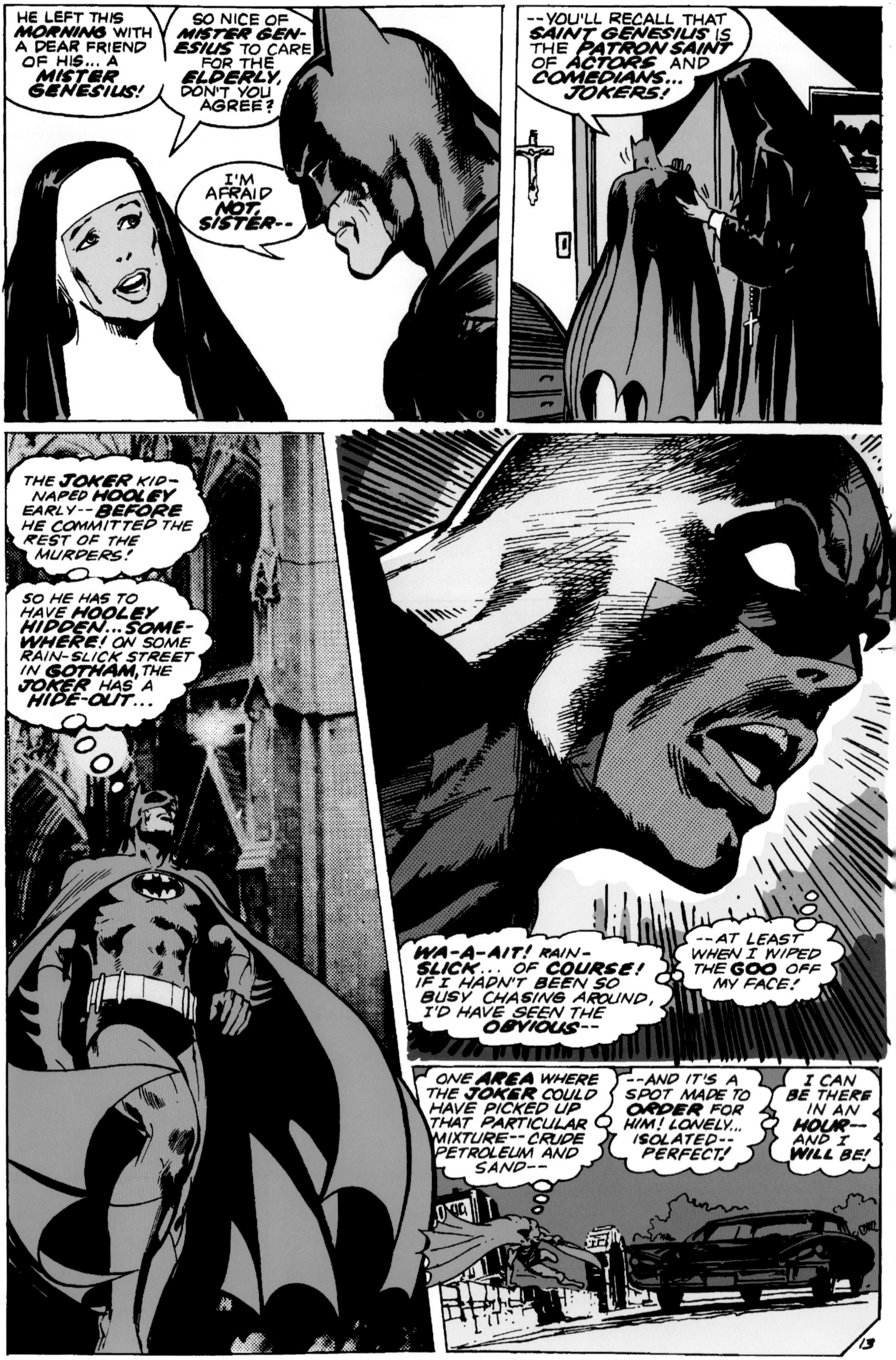
HE LEFT THIS MORNING WITH A DEAR FRIEND OF HIS... A MISTER GENESIUS!
SO NICE OF MISTER GENESIUS TO CARE FOR THE ELDERLY, DON'T YOU AGREE?
I'M AFRAID NOT, SISTER--
--YOU'LL RECALL THAT SAINT GENESIUS IS THE PATRON SAINT OF ACTORS AND COMEDIANS... JOKERS!
THE JOKER KIDNAPED HOOLEY EARLY--BEFORE HE COMMITTED THE REST OF THE MURDERS!
SO HE HAS TO HAVE HOOLEY HIDDEN...SOMEWHERE! ON SOME RAIN-SLICK STREET IN GOTHAM, THE JOKER HAS A HIDE-OUT...
WA-A-AIT! RAIN-SLICK... OF COURSE! IF I HADN'T BEEN SO BUSY CHASING AROUND, I'D HAVE SEEN THE OBVIOUS--
--AT LEAST WHEN I WIPED THE GOO OFF MY FACE!
ONE AREA WHERE THE JOKER COULD HAVE PICKED UP THAT PARTICULAR MIXTURE--CRUDE PETROLEUM AND SAND--
--AND IT'S A SPOT MADE TO ORDER FOR HIM! LONELY... ISOLATED--PERFECT!
I CAN BE THERE IN AN HOUR--AND I WILL BE!
13

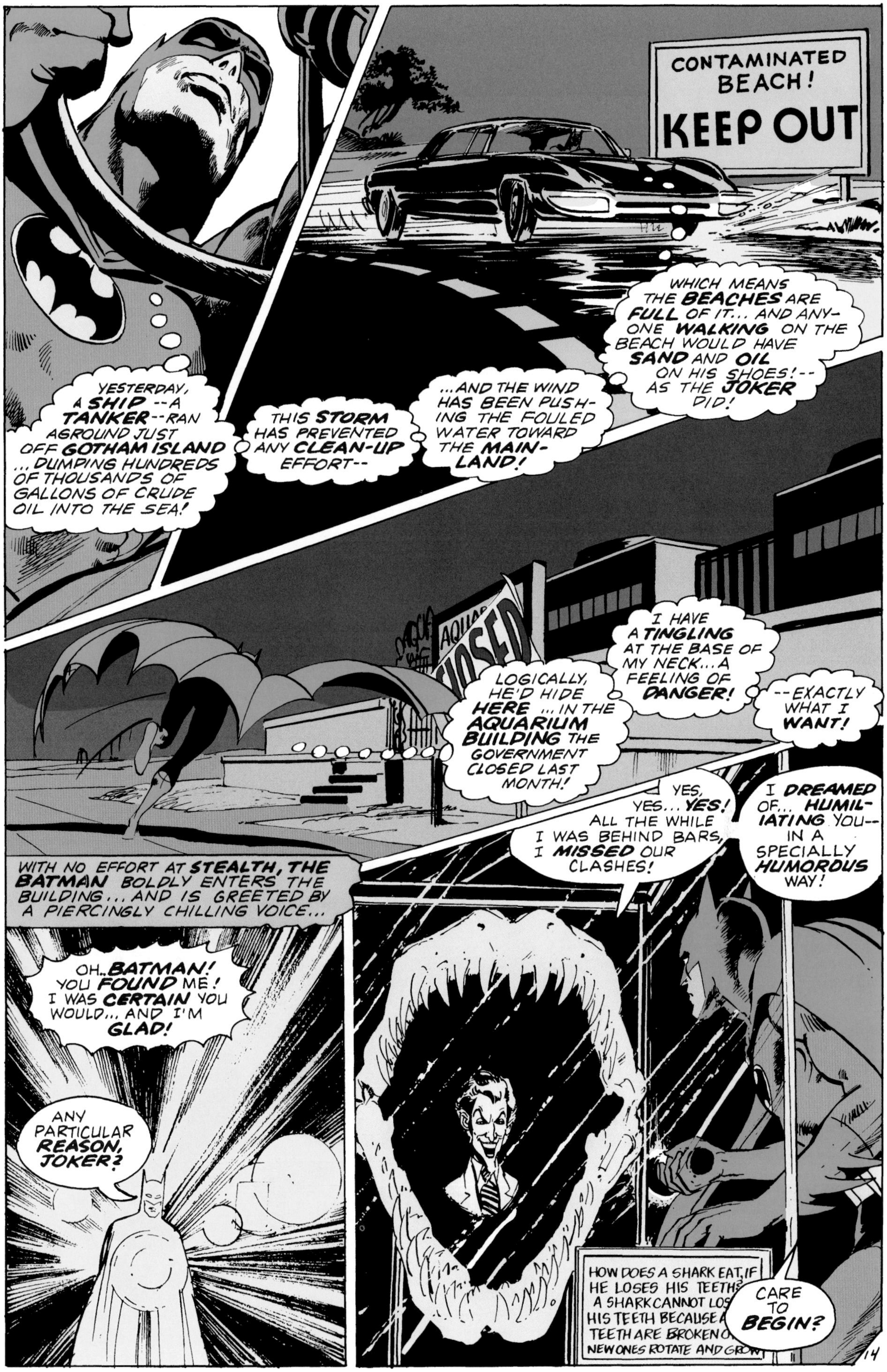
CONTAMINATED BEACH! KEEP OUT
YESTERDAY, A SHIP --A TANKER--RAN AGROUND JUST OFF GOTHAM ISLAND ...DUMPING HUNDREDS OF THOUSANDS OF GALLONS OF CRUDE OIL INTO THE SEA!
THIS STORM HAS PREVENTED ANY CLEAN-UP EFFORT--
...AND THE WIND HAS BEEN PUSHING THE FOULED WATER TOWARD THE MAINLAND!
WHICH MEANS THE BEACHES ARE FULL OF IT... AND ANYONE WALKING ON THE BEACH WOULD HAVE SAND AND OIL ON HIS SHOES!--AS THE JOKER DID!
CLOSED
LOGICALLY, HE'D HIDE HERE ...IN THE AQUARIUM BUILDING THE GOVERNMENT CLOSED LAST MONTH!
I HAVE A TINGLING AT THE BASE OF MY NECK...A FEELING OF DANGER!
--EXACTLY WHAT I WANT!
WITH NO EFFORT AT STEALTH, THE BATMAN BOLDLY ENTERS THE BUILDING... AND IS GREETED BY A PIERCINGLY CHILLING VOICE...
OH..BATMAN! YOU FOUND ME! I WAS CERTAIN YOU WOULD... AND I'M GLAD!
ANY PARTICULAR REASON, JOKER?
YES, YES... YES! ALL THE WHILE I WAS BEHIND BARS, I MISSED OUR CLASHES!
I DREAMED OF... HUMILIATING YOU--IN A SPECIALLY HUMOROUS WAY!
HOW DOES A SHARK EAT, IF HE LOSES HIS TEETH? A SHARK CANNOT LOS HIS TEETH BECAUSE A TEETH ARE BROKEN O NEW ONES ROTATE AND GROW
CARE TO BEGIN?
14

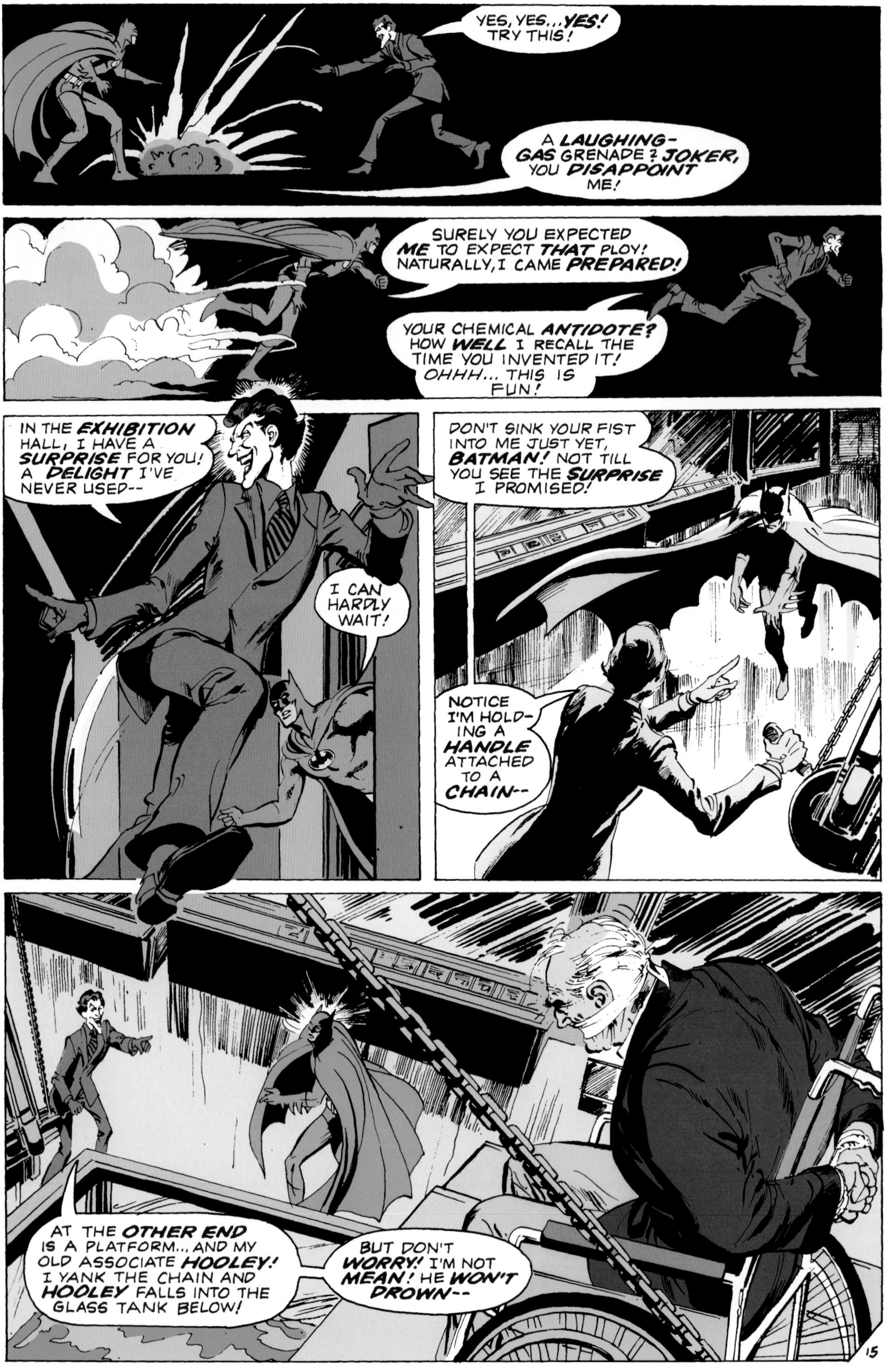
YES, YES...YES! TRY THIS!
A LAUGHING-GAS GRENADE? JOKER, YOU DISAPPOINT ME!
SURELY YOU EXPECTED ME TO EXPECT THAT PLOY! NATURALLY, I CAME PREPARED!
YOUR CHEMICAL ANTIDOTE? HOW WELL I RECALL THE TIME YOU INVENTED IT! OHHH... THIS IS FUN!
IN THE EXHIBITION HALL, I HAVE A SURPRISE FOR YOU! A DELIGHT I'VE NEVER USED--
I CAN HARDLY WAIT!
DON'T SINK YOUR FIST INTO ME JUST YET, BATMAN! NOT TILL YOU SEE THE SURPRISE I PROMISED!
NOTICE I'M HOLDING A HANDLE ATTACHED TO A CHAIN--
AT THE OTHER END IS A PLATFORM... AND MY OLD ASSOCIATE HOOLEY! I YANK THE CHAIN AND HOOLEY FALLS INTO THE GLASS TANK BELOW!
BUT DON'T WORRY! I'M NOT MEAN! HE WON'T DROWN--
15

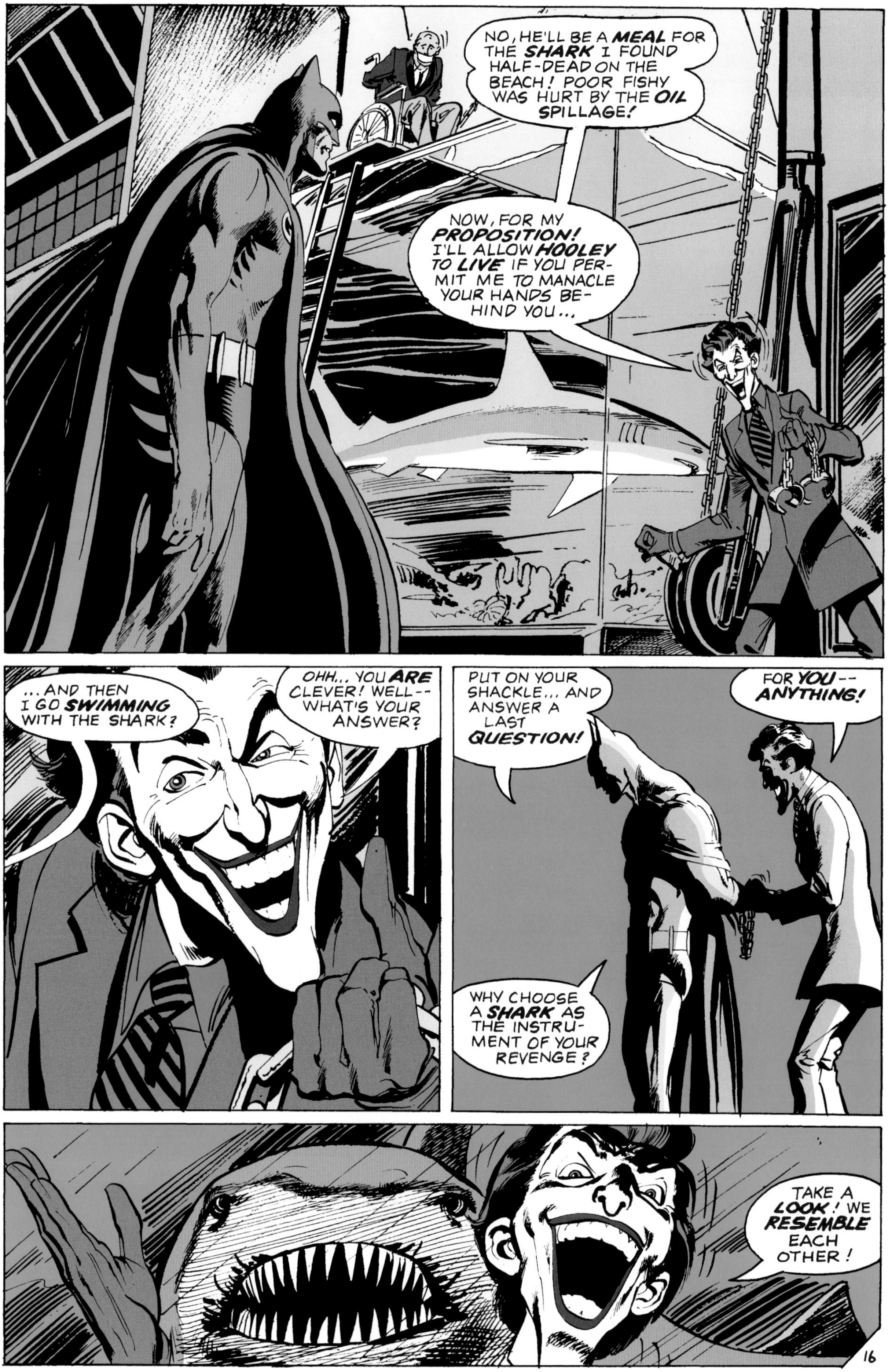
NO, HE'LL BE A MEAL FOR THE SHARK I FOUND HALF-DEAD ON THE BEACH! POOR FISHY WAS HURT BY THE OIL SPILLAGE!
NOW, FOR MY PROPOSITION! I'LL ALLOW HOOLEY TO LIVE IF YOU PERMIT ME TO MANACLE YOUR HANDS BEHIND YOU...
...AND THEN I GO SWIMMING WITH THE SHARK?
OHH... YOU ARE CLEVER! WELL-- WHAT'S YOUR ANSWER?
PUT ON YOUR SHACKLE... AND ANSWER A LAST QUESTION!
FOR YOU-- ANYTHING!
WHY CHOOSE A SHARK AS THE INSTRUMENT OF YOUR REVENGE?
TAKE A LOOK! WE RESEMBLE EACH OTHER!
16

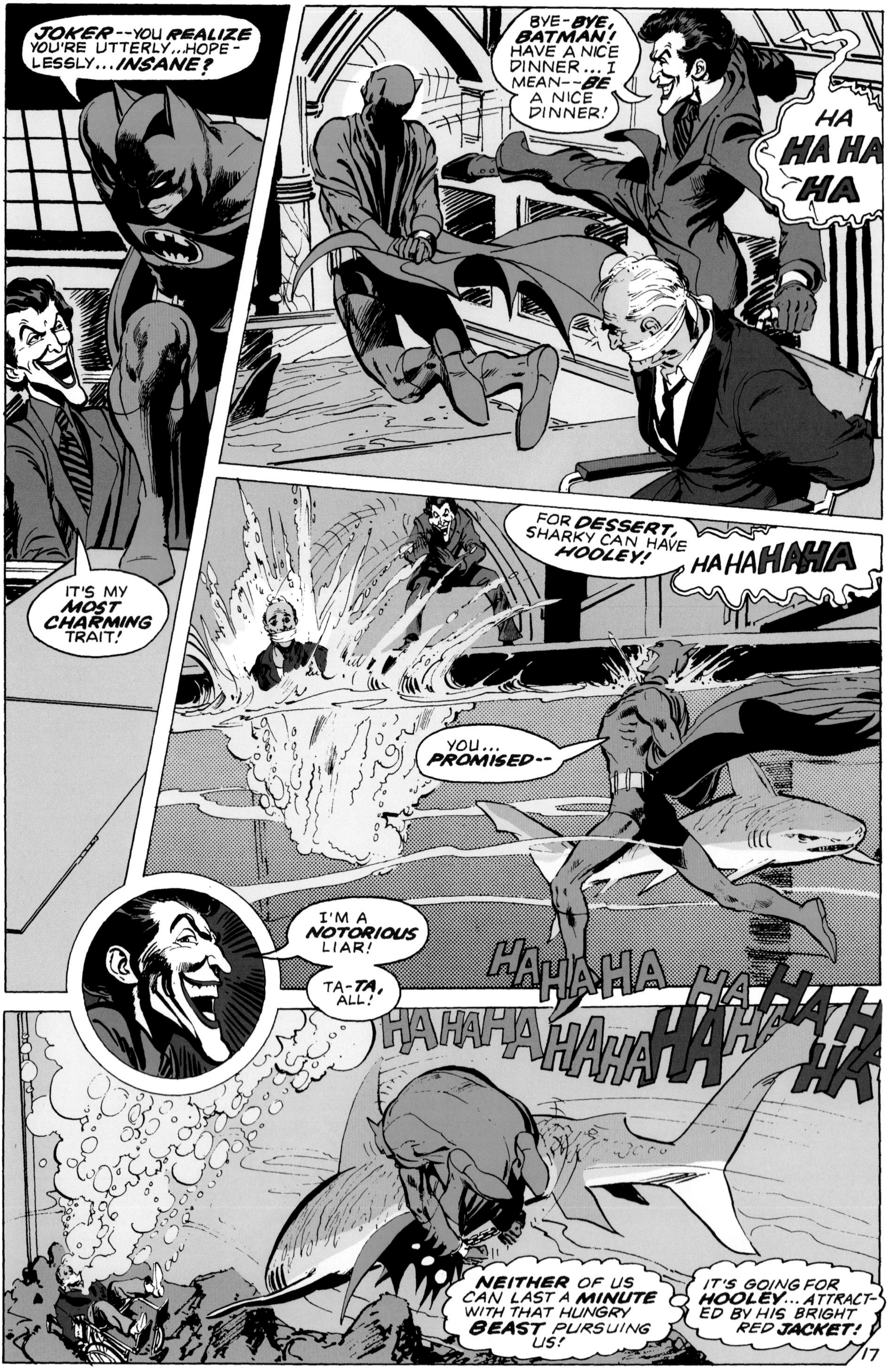
JOKER--YOU REALIZE YOU'RE UTTERLY...HOPE-LESSLY...INSANE?
IT'S MY MOST CHARMING TRAIT!
BYE-BYE, BATMAN! HAVE A NICE DINNER... I MEAN--BE A NICE DINNER!
HA HA HA HA
FOR DESSERT, SHARKY CAN HAVE HOOLEY!
HA HA HAHA HA
YOU... PROMISED--
I'M A NOTORIOUS LIAR!
TA-TA, ALL!
HAHAHA HA HA HA
HAHAHAHAHAHAHAHAHA
NEITHER OF US CAN LAST A MINUTE WITH THAT HUNGRY BEAST PURSUING US!
IT'S GOING FOR HOOLEY... ATTRACT-ED BY HIS BRIGHT RED JACKET!
17

I'VE **NEVER** HAD TO FIGHT SO **UN-PREPARED!** I'VE NEVER MET A **SEA PREDATOR** IN HIS OWN ELEMENT!

STILL, THERE **MAY** BE A **WORK-ABLE** MANEUVER--

...USE THE CHAIN-LINKS TO PUT ITS **TEETH** OUT OF COMMISSION AND--

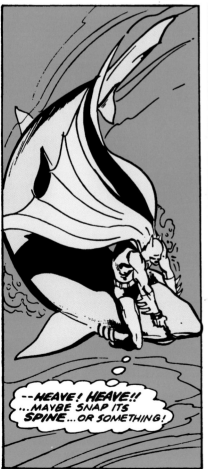

--**HEAVE! HEAVE!!** ...MAYBE SNAP ITS **SPINE**...OR SOMETHING!

BREAK, BLAST YOU!-- **BREAK!!**

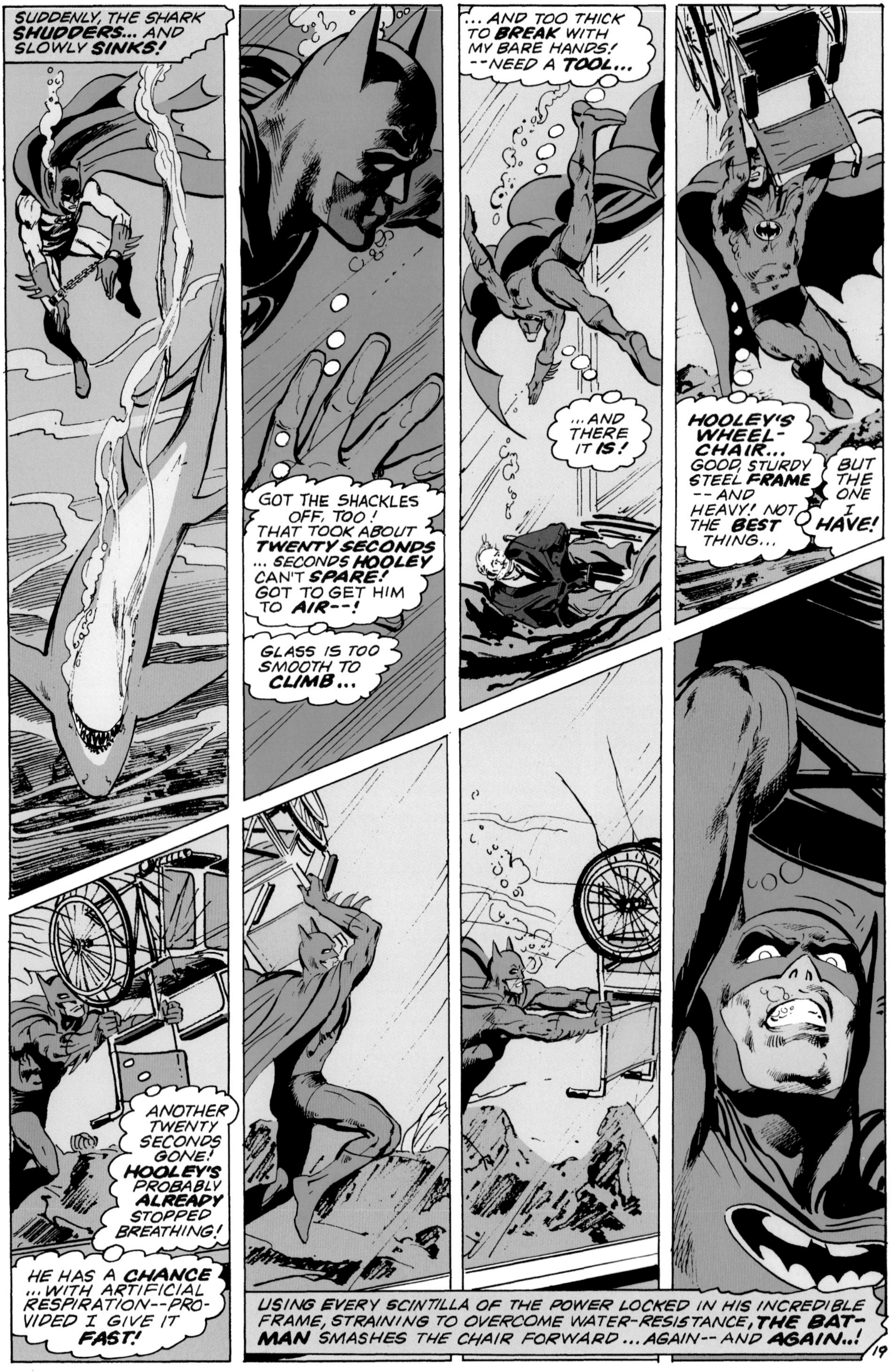
SUDDENLY, THE SHARK SHUDDERS... AND SLOWLY SINKS!
GOT THE SHACKLES OFF, TOO! THAT TOOK ABOUT TWENTY SECONDS ... SECONDS HOOLEY CAN'T SPARE! GOT TO GET HIM TO AIR--!
GLASS IS TOO SMOOTH TO CLIMB...
...AND TOO THICK TO BREAK WITH MY BARE HANDS! --NEED A TOOL...
...AND THERE IT IS!
HOOLEY'S WHEEL-CHAIR... GOOD, STURDY STEEL FRAME -- AND HEAVY! NOT THE BEST THING...
BUT THE ONE I HAVE!
ANOTHER TWENTY SECONDS GONE! HOOLEY'S PROBABLY ALREADY STOPPED BREATHING!
HE HAS A CHANCE ...WITH ARTIFICIAL RESPIRATION--PROVIDED I GIVE IT FAST!
USING EVERY SCINTILLA OF THE POWER LOCKED IN HIS INCREDIBLE FRAME, STRAINING TO OVERCOME WATER-RESISTANCE, THE BAT-MAN SMASHES THE CHAIR FORWARD ... AGAIN-- AND AGAIN..!
19

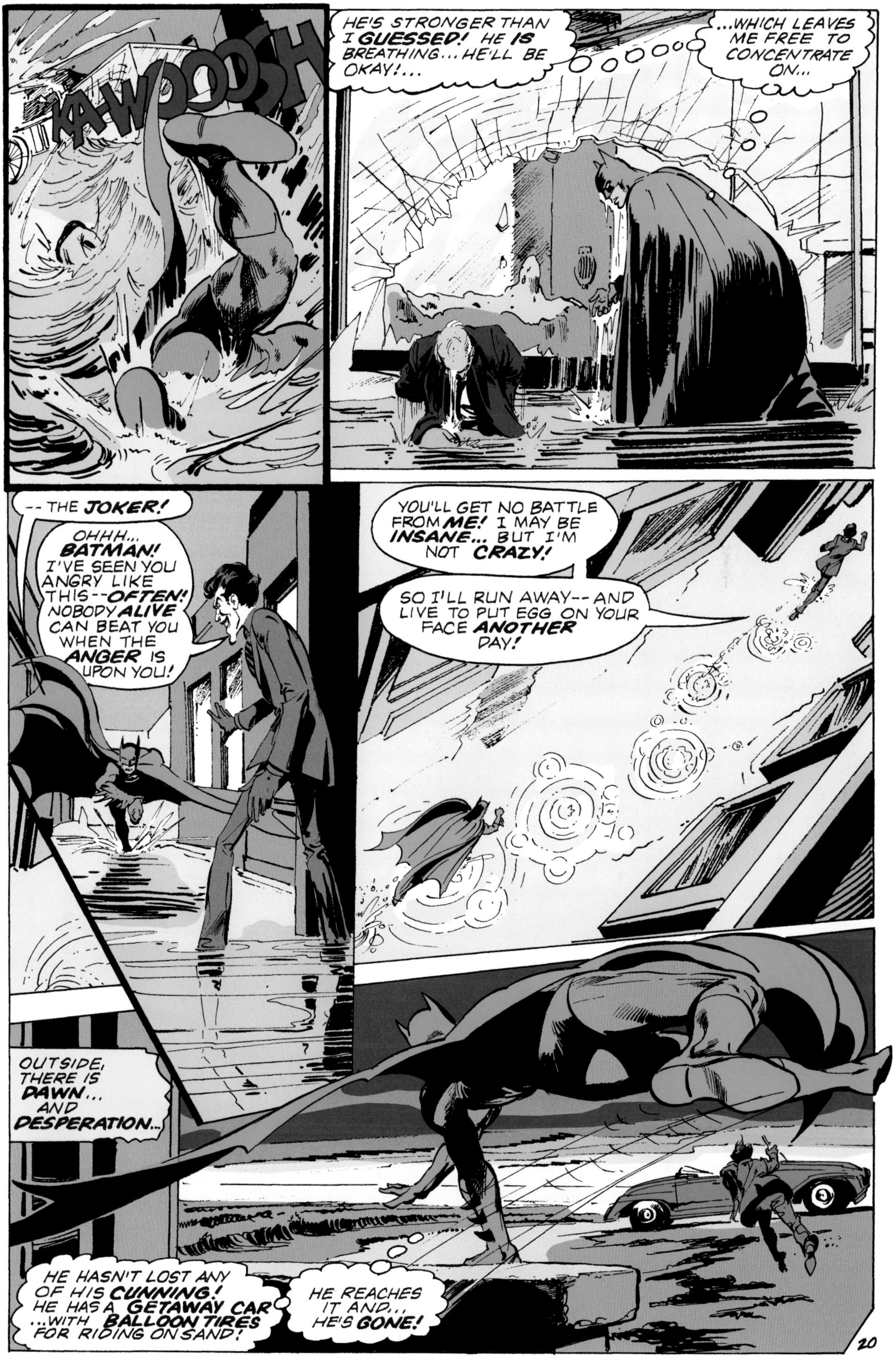
KA-WOOOSH
HE'S STRONGER THAN I GUESSED! HE IS BREATHING... HE'LL BE OKAY!...
...WHICH LEAVES ME FREE TO CONCENTRATE ON...
-- THE JOKER!
OHHH... BATMAN! I'VE SEEN YOU ANGRY LIKE THIS--OFTEN! NOBODY ALIVE CAN BEAT YOU WHEN THE ANGER IS UPON YOU!
YOU'LL GET NO BATTLE FROM ME! I MAY BE INSANE... BUT I'M NOT CRAZY!
SO I'LL RUN AWAY-- AND LIVE TO PUT EGG ON YOUR FACE ANOTHER DAY!
OUTSIDE, THERE IS DAWN... AND DESPERATION...
HE HASN'T LOST ANY OF HIS CUNNING! HE HAS A GETAWAY CAR ...WITH BALLOON TIRES FOR RIDING ON SAND!
HE REACHES IT AND... HE'S GONE!
20

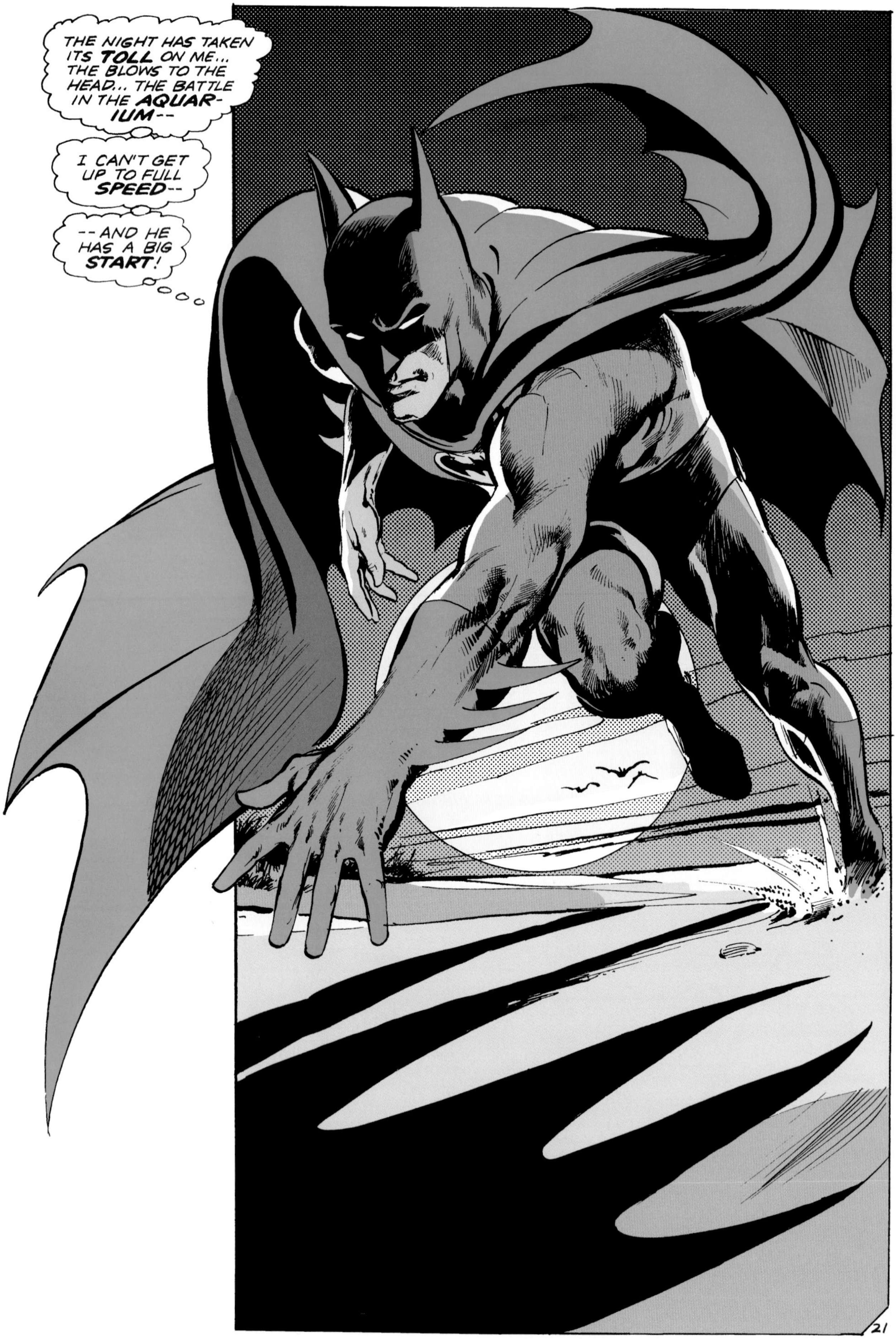
THE NIGHT HAS TAKEN ITS TOLL ON ME... THE BLOWS TO THE HEAD... THE BATTLE IN THE AQUARIUM--
I CAN'T GET UP TO FULL SPEED--
--AND HE HAS A BIG START!
21

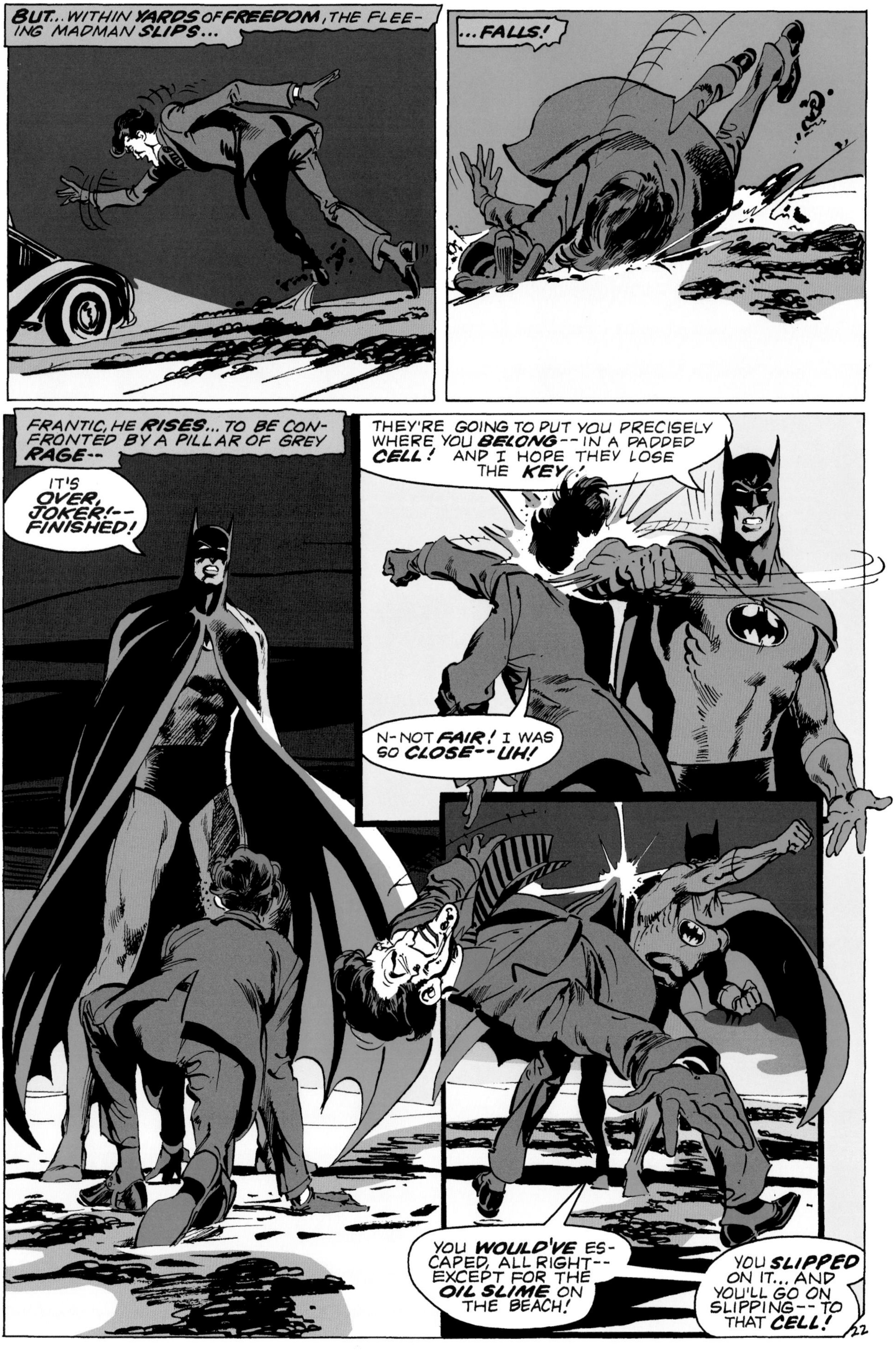

BUT... WITHIN YARDS OF FREEDOM, THE FLEEING MADMAN SLIPS...
...FALLS!
FRANTIC, HE RISES... TO BE CONFRONTED BY A PILLAR OF GREY RAGE--
IT'S OVER, JOKER!--FINISHED!
THEY'RE GOING TO PUT YOU PRECISELY WHERE YOU BELONG--IN A PADDED CELL! AND I HOPE THEY LOSE THE KEY!
N-NOT FAIR! I WAS SO CLOSE--UH!
YOU WOULD'VE ESCAPED, ALL RIGHT--EXCEPT FOR THE OIL SLIME ON THE BEACH!
YOU SLIPPED ON IT... AND YOU'LL GO ON SLIPPING--TO THAT CELL!
22

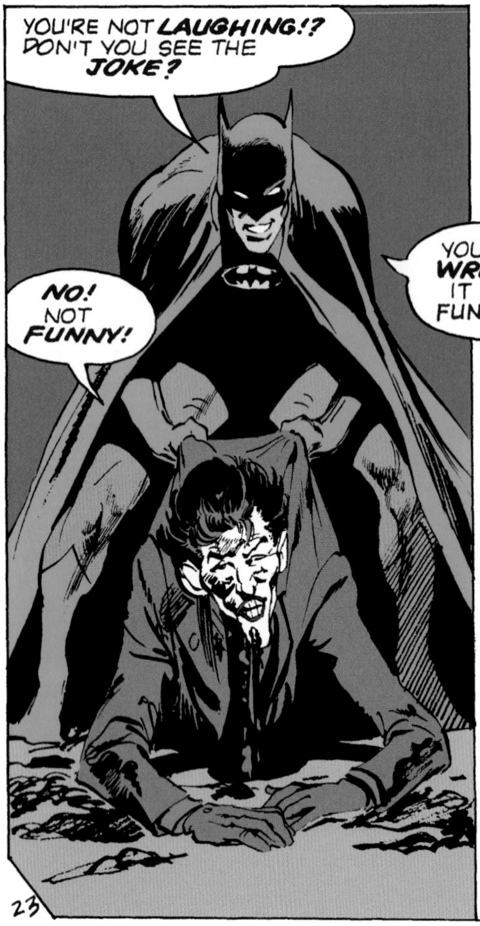
YOU'RE NOT LAUGHING!? DON'T YOU SEE THE JOKE?
NO! NOT FUNNY!
YOU'RE WRONG! IT IS FUNNY--
23
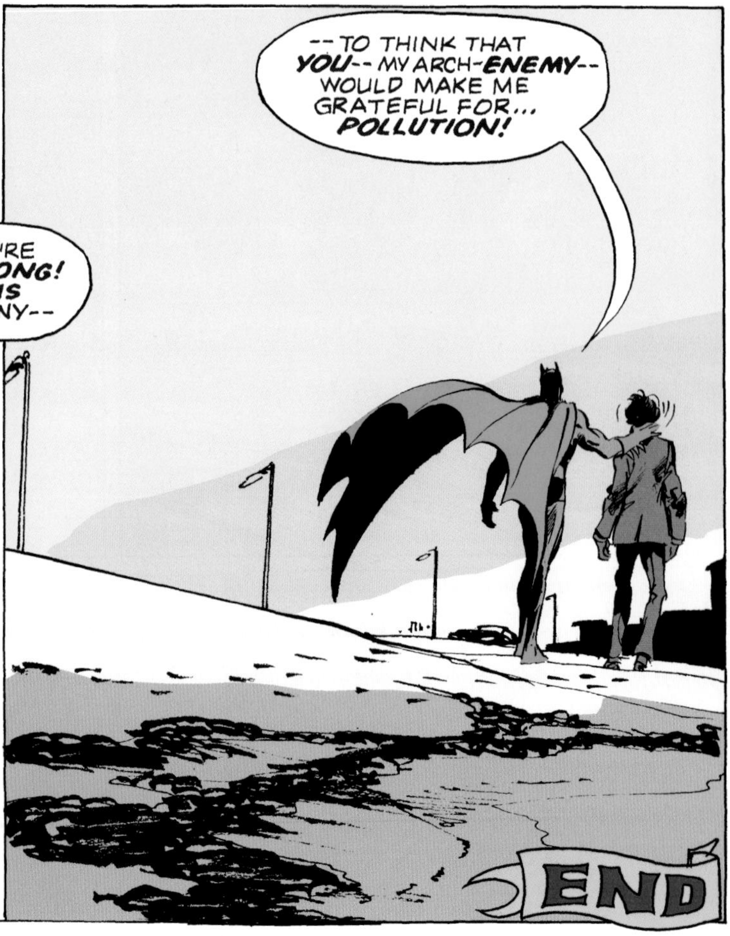
--TO THINK THAT YOU-- MY ARCH-ENEMY-- WOULD MAKE ME GRATEFUL FOR... POLLUTION!
END

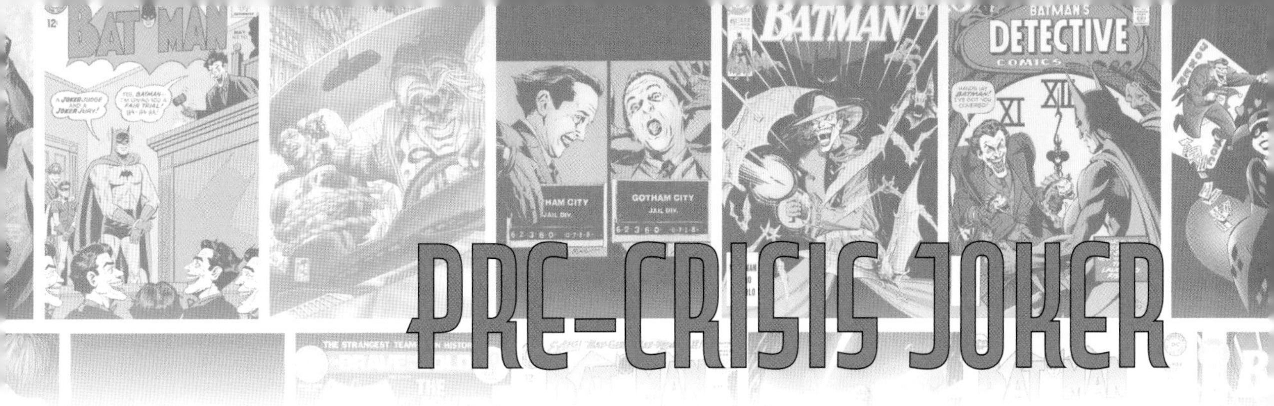
BATMAN
BATMAN'S
DETECTIVE
COMICS
GOTHAM CITY
JAIL DIV.

PRE-CRISIS JOKER

by **STEVE ENGLEHART**

The pre-Crisis Joker comes in three distinct parts.

Part 1—Two Years

In the winter of 1939-40, Bob Kane and Bill Finger, the team that did the Batman stories in *Detective Comics*, got good news: there was going to be a Batman quarterly. But they'd have to produce an extra sixteen stories a year, so maybe they should reimagine their strip for a wider audience. They decided that each of them should come up with a new character to launch the new book. So, in the April 1940 issue of *Detective Comics*, they introduced Robin, the Boy Wonder, and right on its heels came *Batman* #1, where they introduced the Joker.

The original Joker, as written by Finger, was a scary homicidal maniac. Finger was always clear that he got the idea from Conrad Veidt, who first wore the face in 1928's *The Man Who Laughs*. In his first comics appearance, the Joker is precisely Veidt, though the color scheme is more bizarre. Which means, when readers met the Joker at the beginning, they saw him as Batman's take on a famous film, not as the Joker.

But then they turned the page and saw what Finger could make out of that idea. They saw a man murdered in a heavily guarded house, leaving his corpse with a vast, evil grin. And then they saw the Joker himself—three panels with three different moods: pensive, normal, and insane. (That second would never be revisited.) Three panels of a stark white face against a black or red background, ending with "insane." *This* was the Joker.

He had the first and last stories in four-story *Batman* #1, and he was supposed to die at the end of his second, but it was clumsily changed to a cliffhanger. Which means they were right at the end of the process that would have killed the Joker forever when somebody said "Hey, maybe we should rethink this."

And probably because of that sudden cliffhanger, the Joker became, in a comic book way, a serial killer. Every Joker story ended with him dying, or sometimes thrown in jail...and every Joker story began with how he cheated death, or escaped jail. In between, he killed people. No other villain had that continuity, so really, there was no contest. Penguin, Two-Face, and Catwoman were good but the Joker was the classic.

And then somebody said, "This thing is really growing, we're getting all these new readers, maybe we should be a little less intense"—so the April 1942 issue of *Detective Comics* ended the serial. The scary homicidal maniac went with it. A new era began.

Part 2—Thirty-Four Years

The new Joker was the one your ancestors lived with for almost two generations. He was, you know, crazy, and he did sometimes kill people, but always in a cartoony way. The soul, if you will, had been removed from his body—but there were a lot of soulless characters during this time. Comics were leveling out as entertainment for kids and GIs; then, after the war ended, for kids only. And kids, as we all know, are tender vessels; better to keep their comics within limits so parents, who actually buy the comics, can rest easy.

In the 1950s, Dr. Fredric Wertham—a psychiatrist and author—announced that comics were seducing the innocent anyway. There were publishers who were publishing some crude, shocking stories, and there was EC, who was publishing some sharp, shocking stories, but none of these were DC, which had positioned itself as a sobersided enterprise, publishing quality content. Even so, Dr. Wertham thought Bruce and Dick looked

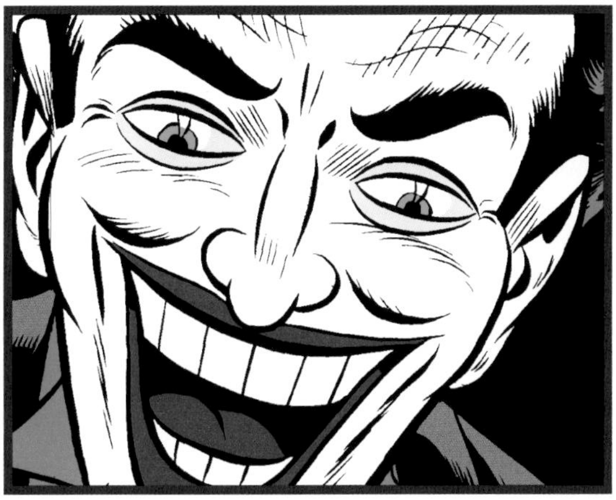

BATMAN
images
BATMAN AND THE JOKER
"DEATH HAS THE LAST LAUGH"
DETECTIVE

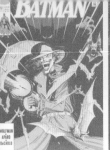

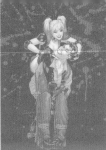

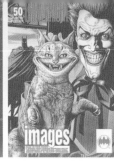

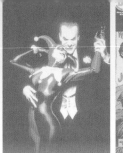

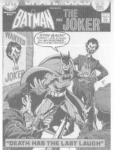

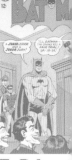

inappropriate, lounging around their swank mansion in their robes. DC had to ride that one out, but they could because they had the only superheroes in town then, and the massed audience could see that Batman, Superman, and Wonder Woman were upright citizens. DC even had Superman on TV. There were no homicidal maniacs in sight.

And so there's almost nothing to say about the Joker in this part. We did get "The Man Behind the Red Hood!" the first story to see the Joker as more than a cartoon in almost a decade and the first to give him an origin story. And though he didn't draw that story, we also got the golden age of illustrator Dick Sprang in *Batman* and *World's Finest*. Sprang exaggerated everything, in extreme perspective, at unexpected angles, making Batman's world just flat-out strange. (That's why the television show was like that.) So when Sprang drew the Joker, he draw the cartoon but with crafty eyes. You really knew he was "crazy"—though they never showed what that meant. His most famous story from this era had him teaming up with Luthor to build robots.

Eventually Sprang moved on. DC started recreating superheroes, starting with the Flash and building to the Justice League of America. Marvel decided to draft off that with its own heroes, and other companies started playing, too. DC simply sailed along, doubling down on sobersidedness. The Joker now became not so much *crazy* as *funny*. He lived in the Ha-Hacienda. Cesar Romero played him with a moustache on the camp TV show. I mean, what can you say?

In 1969 there was a Joker story, and then nothing, for the next four years. The character we were talking about in part 1 was completely and utterly gone.

In 1973's *Batman* #251, Denny O'Neil and Neal Adams tried to resurrect him in "The Joker's Five-Way Revenge." It made the Joker dangerous again, and used rain and night to good effect, but it was set in (DC's version of) the real world and had real-world concerns, like pollution. Joker stories (by others) that followed *Batman* #251 paid no attention to it. The Joker even got his own comics series, which made him even blander than before.

No one cared.

Part 3—Forty-Four Years and Counting

In 1976, I was asked to reinvent all the DC superheroes. I gave everybody in the JLA "souls," and I particularly gave Bruce Wayne a sex life with Silver St. Cloud to show the soul of an adult man behind that cowl—all new stuff. But I also, to be as frank as Bill Finger, took an idea from the past—by Bill Finger—and resurrected the homicidal maniac Joker, along with all of his pulp darkness, as a super-villain for that superhero. By the time Walt Simonson, Al Milgrom, Marshall Rogers, and Terry Austin got done with it, people decided they liked those souls, including the dark maniac's, and there's been no turning back since.

Thus, 2 + 34 + 44 = 80, and we find ourselves at *80 Years of the Clown Prince of Crime*. Don't ever let him get behind you, and we may see 80 more.

Steve Englehart *was brought to DC in the late 1970s by then-new publisher Jenette Kahn to "do what you did with the Avengers for the Justice League." Englehart agreed—on two conditions. First, he wanted to write* Batman *as well, and second, he wanted to do* Justice League of America *as a monthly double-size book in order to develop all of its characters while still telling a coherent story. He succeeded in both endeavors and went on to write a celebrated run on* Batman *that featured his own character, Silver St. Cloud, as well as the homicidal Joker. Later, he also reinvigorated the Green Lantern Corps, where he made John Stewart a regular and co-created the character Kilowog.*

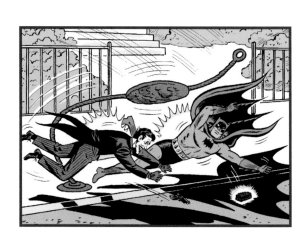

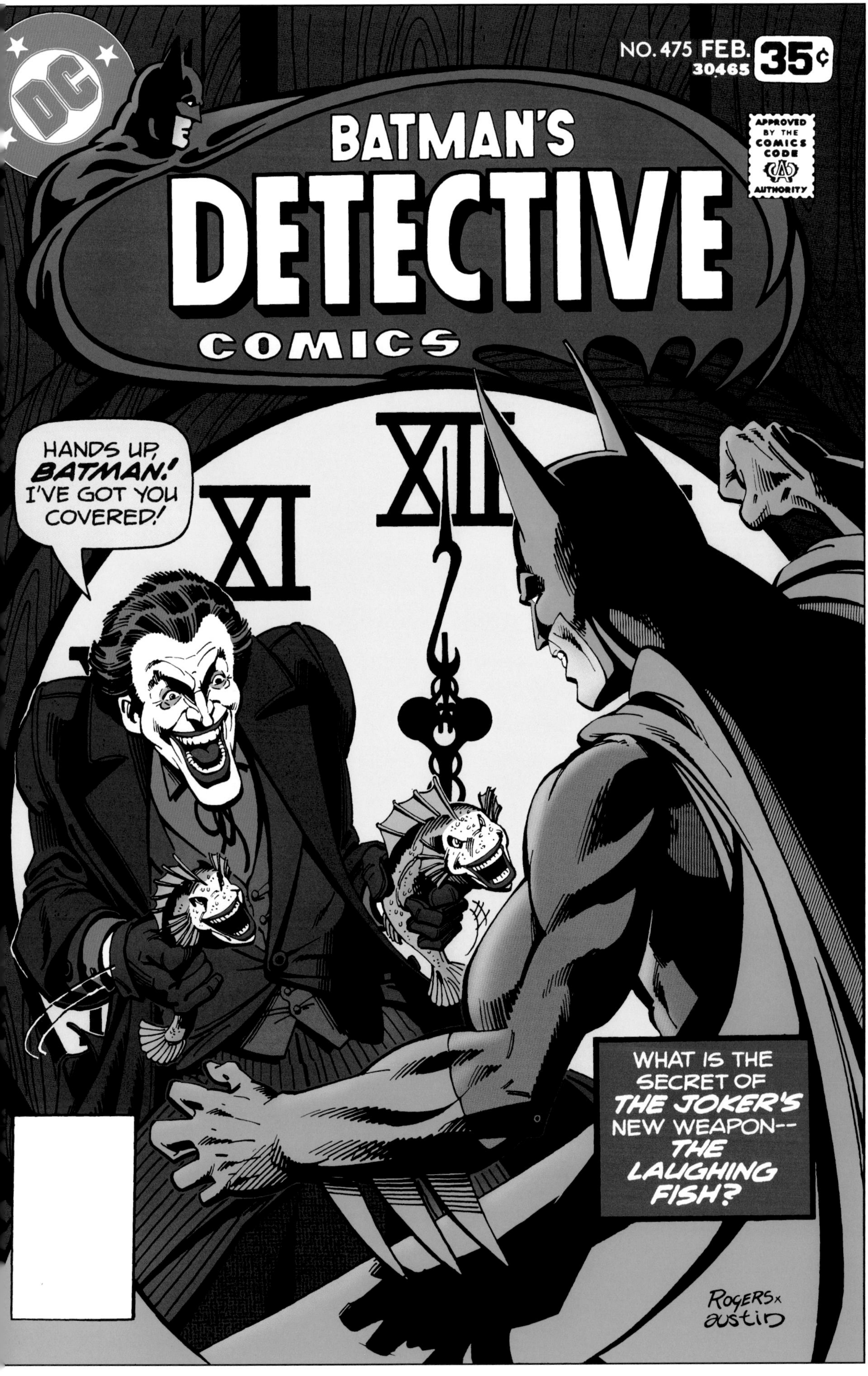

NO. 475 FEB.
30465
35¢
BATMAN'S
DETECTIVE
COMICS
APPROVED BY THE COMICS CODE AUTHORITY
HANDS UP, BATMAN! I'VE GOT YOU COVERED!
WHAT IS THE SECRET OF THE JOKER'S NEW WEAPON-- THE LAUGHING FISH?
ROGERS x austin

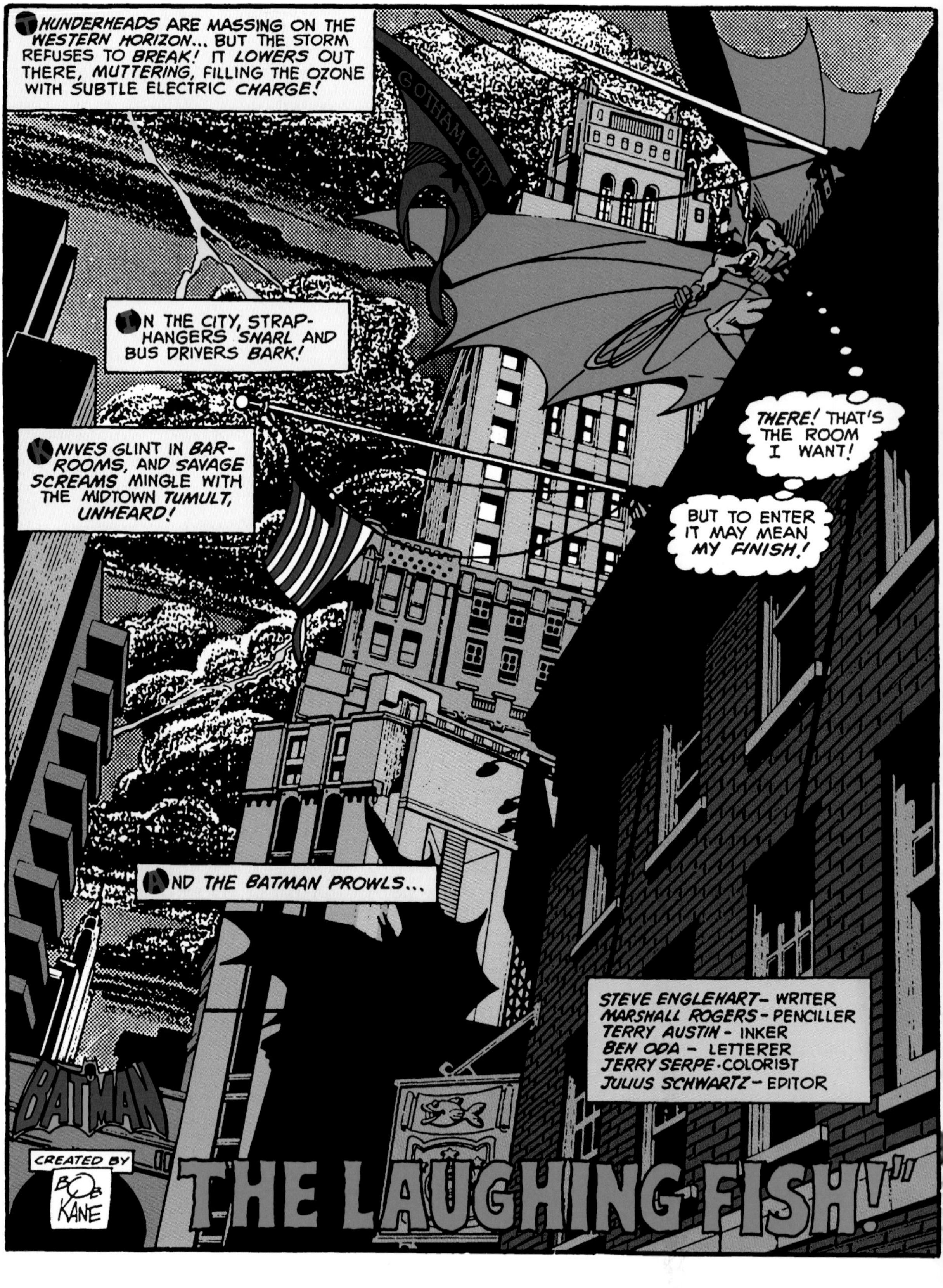
THUNDERHEADS ARE MASSING ON THE WESTERN HORIZON... BUT THE STORM REFUSES TO BREAK! IT LOWERS OUT THERE, MUTTERING, FILLING THE OZONE WITH SUBTLE ELECTRIC CHARGE!
GOTHAM CITY
IN THE CITY, STRAP-HANGERS SNARL AND BUS DRIVERS BARK!
KNIVES GLINT IN BAR-ROOMS, AND SAVAGE SCREAMS MINGLE WITH THE MIDTOWN TUMULT, UNHEARD!
THERE! THAT'S THE ROOM I WANT!
BUT TO ENTER IT MAY MEAN MY FINISH!
AND THE BATMAN PROWLS...
STEVE ENGLEHART- WRITER
MARSHALL ROGERS - PENCILLER
TERRY AUSTIN - INKER
BEN ODA - LETTERER
JERRY SERPE - COLORIST
JULIUS SCHWARTZ - EDITOR
BATMAN
CREATED BY
BOB KANE
"THE LAUGHING FISH!"

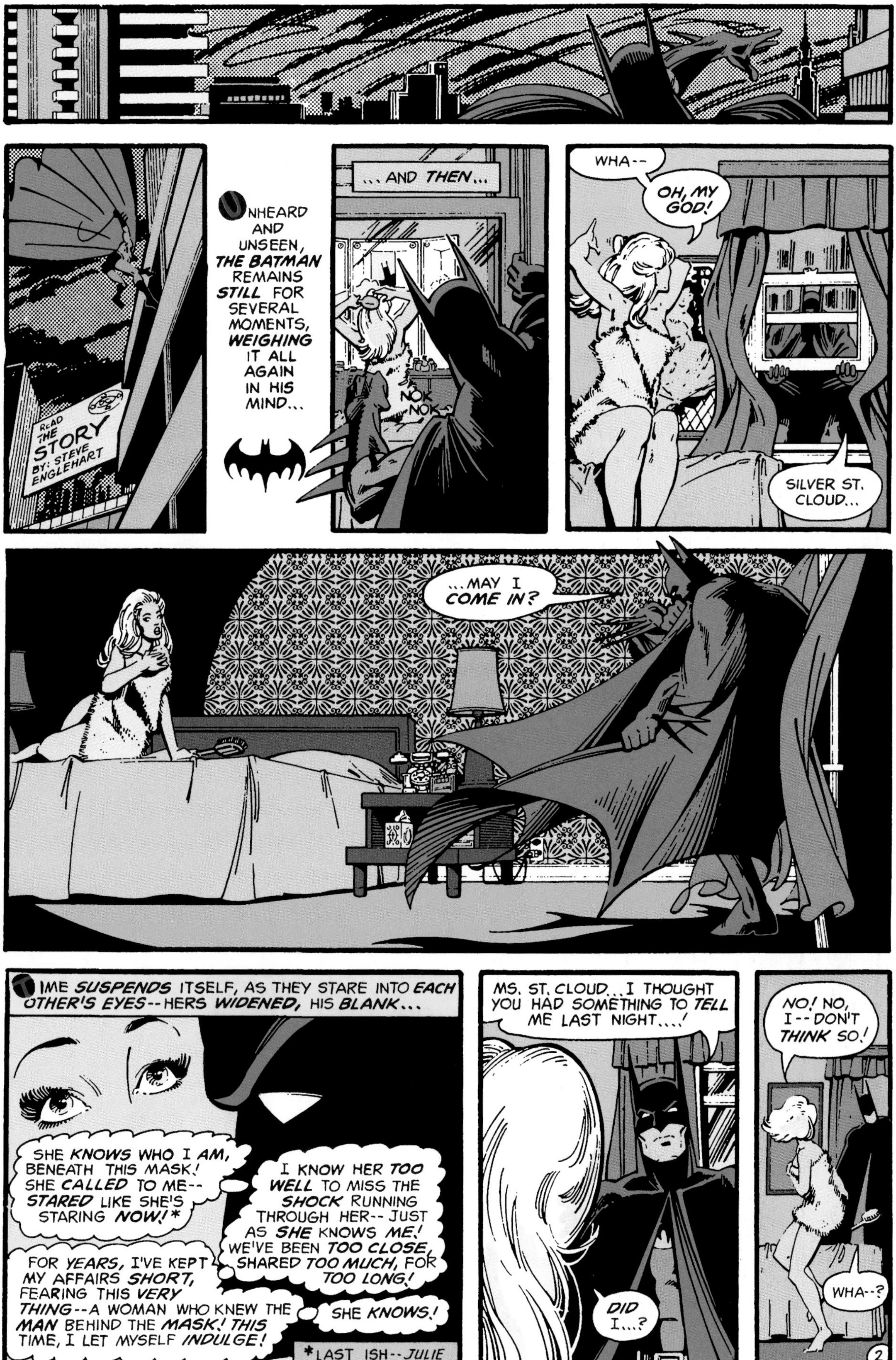
READ THE STORY BY: STEVE ENGLEHART
UNHEARD AND UNSEEN, THE BATMAN REMAINS STILL FOR SEVERAL MOMENTS, WEIGHING IT ALL AGAIN IN HIS MIND...
...AND THEN...
NOK NOK
WHA--
OH, MY GOD!
SILVER ST. CLOUD...
...MAY I COME IN?
TIME SUSPENDS ITSELF, AS THEY STARE INTO EACH OTHER'S EYES--HERS WIDENED, HIS BLANK...
SHE KNOWS WHO I AM, BENEATH THIS MASK! SHE CALLED TO ME--STARED LIKE SHE'S STARING NOW!*
I KNOW HER TOO WELL TO MISS THE SHOCK RUNNING THROUGH HER--JUST AS SHE KNOWS ME! WE'VE BEEN TOO CLOSE, SHARED TOO MUCH, FOR TOO LONG!
FOR YEARS, I'VE KEPT MY AFFAIRS SHORT, FEARING THIS VERY THING--A WOMAN WHO KNEW THE MAN BEHIND THE MASK! THIS TIME, I LET MYSELF INDULGE!
SHE KNOWS!
*LAST ISH--JULIE
MS. ST. CLOUD...I THOUGHT YOU HAD SOMETHING TO TELL ME LAST NIGHT...!
DID I...?
NO! NO, I--DON'T THINK SO!
WHA--?
2

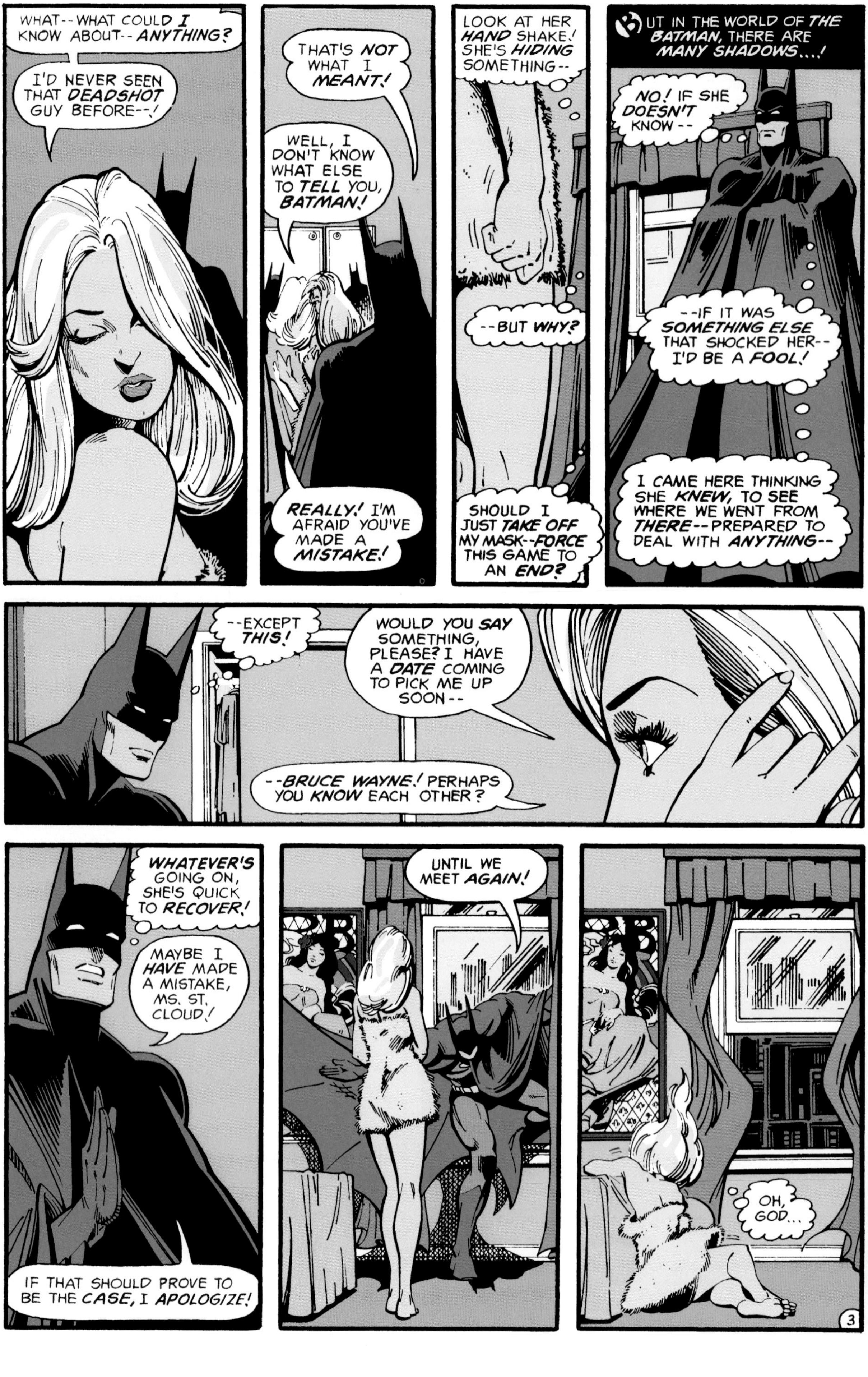
WHAT--WHAT COULD I KNOW ABOUT--ANYTHING?
I'D NEVER SEEN THAT DEADSHOT GUY BEFORE--!
THAT'S NOT WHAT I MEANT!
WELL, I DON'T KNOW WHAT ELSE TO TELL YOU, BATMAN!
REALLY! I'M AFRAID YOU'VE MADE A MISTAKE!
LOOK AT HER HAND SHAKE! SHE'S HIDING SOMETHING--
--BUT WHY?
SHOULD I JUST TAKE OFF MY MASK--FORCE THIS GAME TO AN END?
BUT IN THE WORLD OF THE BATMAN, THERE ARE MANY SHADOWS...!
NO! IF SHE DOESN'T KNOW--
--IF IT WAS SOMETHING ELSE THAT SHOCKED HER-- I'D BE A FOOL!
I CAME HERE THINKING SHE KNEW, TO SEE WHERE WE WENT FROM THERE--PREPARED TO DEAL WITH ANYTHING--
--EXCEPT THIS!
WOULD YOU SAY SOMETHING, PLEASE? I HAVE A DATE COMING TO PICK ME UP SOON--
--BRUCE WAYNE! PERHAPS YOU KNOW EACH OTHER?
WHATEVER'S GOING ON, SHE'S QUICK TO RECOVER!
MAYBE I HAVE MADE A MISTAKE, MS. ST. CLOUD!
IF THAT SHOULD PROVE TO BE THE CASE, I APOLOGIZE!
UNTIL WE MEET AGAIN!
OH, GOD...
3

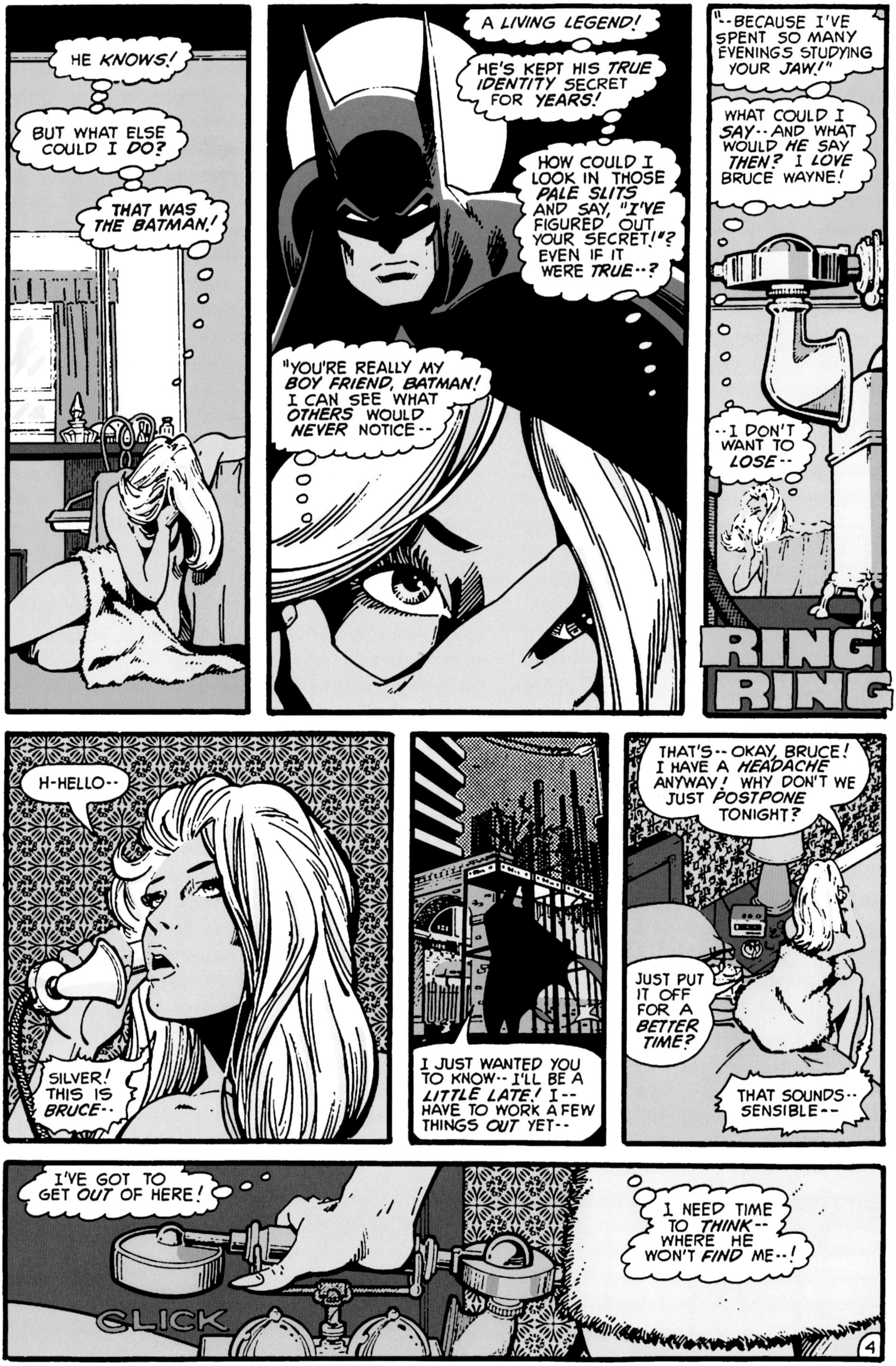

HE KNOWS!
BUT WHAT ELSE COULD I DO?
THAT WAS THE BATMAN!
A LIVING LEGEND!
HE'S KEPT HIS TRUE IDENTITY SECRET FOR YEARS!
HOW COULD I LOOK IN THOSE PALE SLITS AND SAY, "I'VE FIGURED OUT YOUR SECRET!"? EVEN IF IT WERE TRUE--?
"YOU'RE REALLY MY BOY FRIEND, BATMAN! I CAN SEE WHAT OTHERS WOULD NEVER NOTICE--
"--BECAUSE I'VE SPENT SO MANY EVENINGS STUDYING YOUR JAW!"
WHAT COULD I SAY--AND WHAT WOULD HE SAY THEN? I LOVE BRUCE WAYNE!
--I DON'T WANT TO LOSE--
RING RING
H-HELLO--
SILVER! THIS IS BRUCE--
I JUST WANTED YOU TO KNOW--I'LL BE A LITTLE LATE! I--HAVE TO WORK A FEW THINGS OUT YET--
THAT'S--OKAY, BRUCE! I HAVE A HEADACHE ANYWAY! WHY DON'T WE JUST POSTPONE TONIGHT?
JUST PUT IT OFF FOR A BETTER TIME?
THAT SOUNDS--SENSIBLE--
I'VE GOT TO GET OUT OF HERE!
I NEED TIME TO THINK--WHERE HE WON'T FIND ME--!
CLICK
4

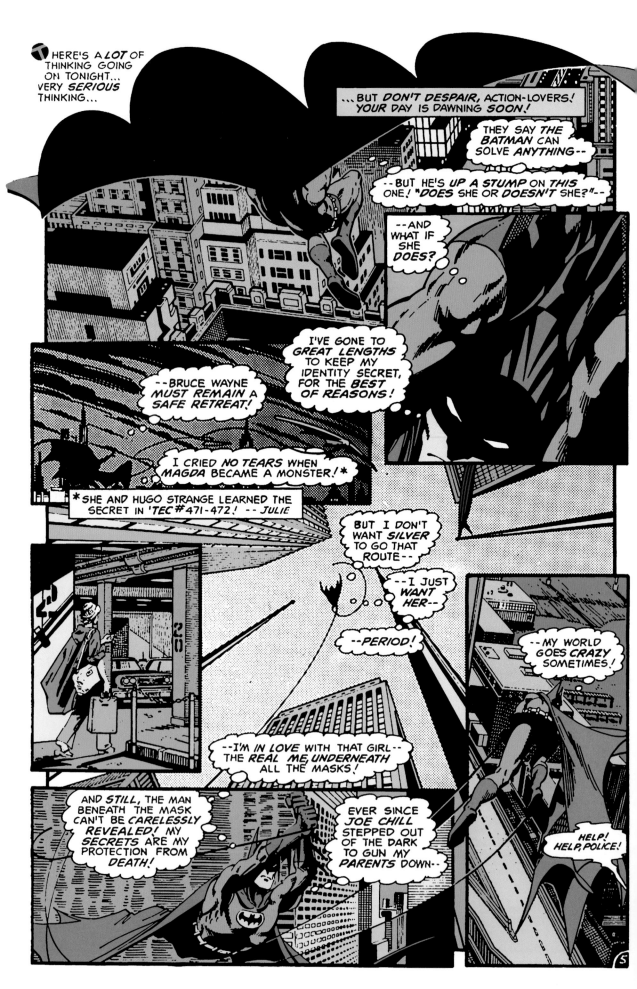

THERE'S A *LOT* OF THINKING GOING ON TONIGHT... VERY *SERIOUS* THINKING...

...BUT *DON'T DESPAIR*, ACTION-LOVERS! *YOUR DAY IS DAWNING SOON!*

THEY SAY *THE BATMAN* CAN SOLVE *ANYTHING*--

--BUT HE'S UP A *STUMP* ON *THIS* ONE! *"DOES* SHE OR *DOESN'T* SHE?"--

--AND WHAT IF SHE *DOES?*

I'VE GONE TO *GREAT LENGTHS* TO KEEP MY IDENTITY SECRET, FOR THE *BEST* OF REASONS!

--BRUCE WAYNE MUST REMAIN A *SAFE RETREAT!*

I CRIED *NO TEARS* WHEN *MAGDA* BECAME A MONSTER!*

*SHE AND HUGO STRANGE LEARNED THE SECRET IN *'TEC #*471-472! -- *JULIE*

BUT I DON'T WANT *SILVER* TO GO THAT ROUTE--

--I JUST *WANT* HER--

--PERIOD!

--MY WORLD GOES *CRAZY* SOMETIMES!

--I'M *IN LOVE* WITH THAT GIRL-- THE *REAL ME,* UNDERNEATH ALL THE MASKS!

AND *STILL,* THE MAN BENEATH THE MASK CAN'T BE *CARELESSLY REVEALED!* MY SECRETS ARE MY PROTECTION FROM *DEATH!*

EVER SINCE *JOE CHILL* STEPPED OUT OF THE DARK TO GUN MY *PARENTS* DOWN--

HELP! HELP, POLICE!

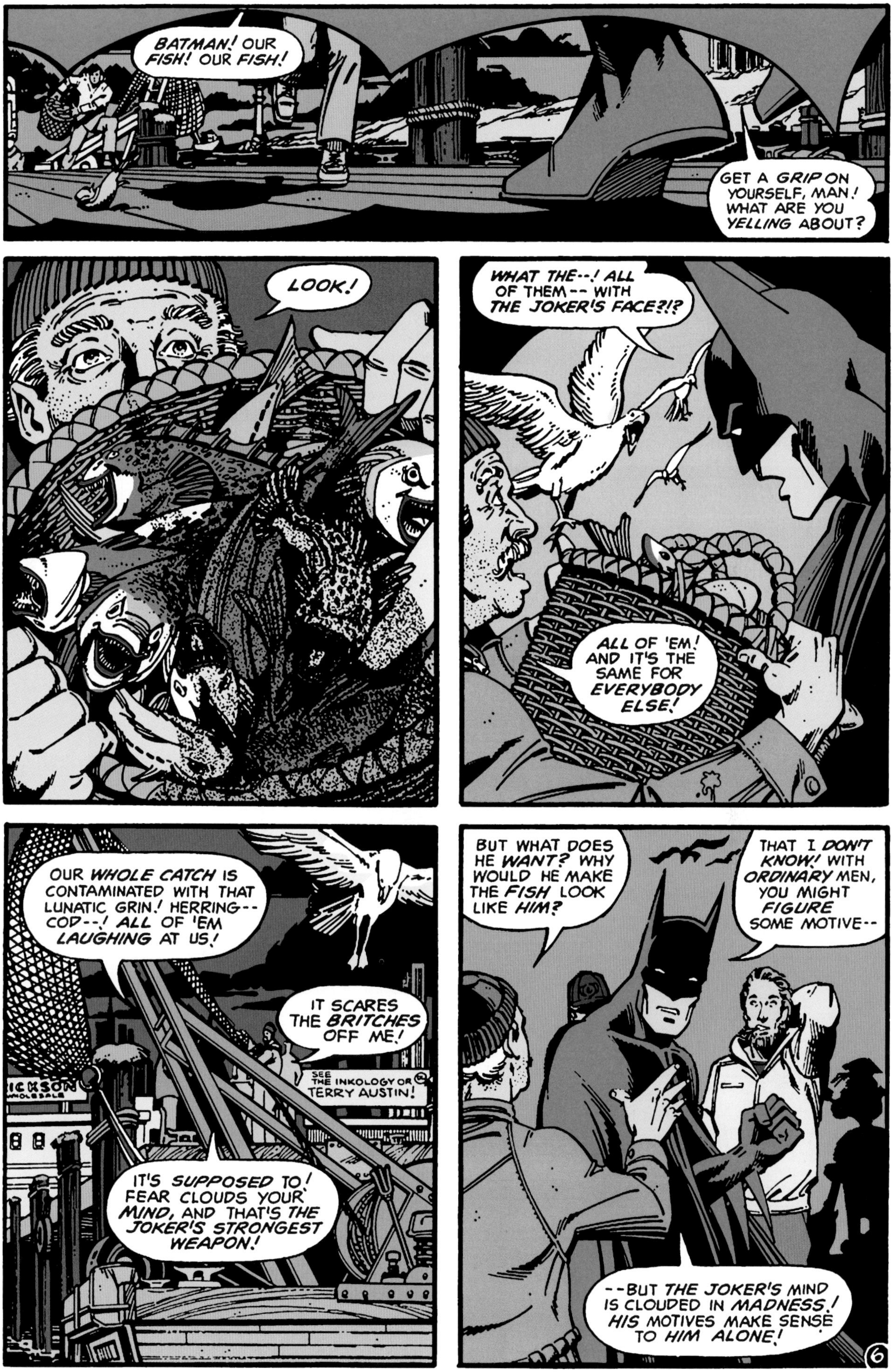

BATMAN! OUR FISH! OUR FISH!
GET A GRIP ON YOURSELF, MAN! WHAT ARE YOU YELLING ABOUT?
LOOK!
WHAT THE--! ALL OF THEM -- WITH THE JOKER'S FACE?!?
ALL OF 'EM! AND IT'S THE SAME FOR EVERYBODY ELSE!
OUR WHOLE CATCH IS CONTAMINATED WITH THAT LUNATIC GRIN! HERRING-- COD--! ALL OF 'EM LAUGHING AT US!
IT SCARES THE BRITCHES OFF ME!
SEE THE INKOLOGY OF TERRY AUSTIN!
IT'S SUPPOSED TO! FEAR CLOUDS YOUR MIND, AND THAT'S THE JOKER'S STRONGEST WEAPON!
BUT WHAT DOES HE WANT? WHY WOULD HE MAKE THE FISH LOOK LIKE HIM?
THAT I DON'T KNOW! WITH ORDINARY MEN, YOU MIGHT FIGURE SOME MOTIVE--
--BUT THE JOKER'S MIND IS CLOUDED IN MADNESS! HIS MOTIVES MAKE SENSE TO HIM ALONE!
6

IN THE HOURS THAT *FOLLOW*, THE STRANGE PHENOMENON PROVES TO BE *LESS* THAN AN *ISOLATED EVENT!*

ALL ALONG THE *EASTERN SEABOARD...*

...AND UP AND DOWN THE *WESTERN*, AS *WELL...*

...THE *JOKER-FISH* ARE SUDDENLY *EVERYWHERE!*

WHEN AMERICA AWAKES TO ITS *MORNING MEDIA...*

...IT IS THE *ONLY* TOPIC OF *NOTE!*

--BUT AS YET, THERE HAS BEEN *NO FURTHER MOVE* FROM THE MACABRE MASTER OF MIRTH!

HIGH NOON, IN *GOTHAM CITY*--

COPYRIGHT COMMISSION
GOTHAM CITY DIV.

COPYRIGHT FORM B5-17AS
1. MAKE SURE ALL 6 CARBON SHEETS ARE STRAIGHT
2. FILL OUT ALL PERTINENT DATA
3. SUBMIT TO SUPERVISOR.
4. PERUSE THE PENCILOGRAPHY OF MARSHALL ROGERS

BUTTON IT, LADY! NO NOISE FROM *NOBODY!*

HANDS BEHIND YOUR *HEADS!* YOU'VE GOT A *VISITOR!*

7

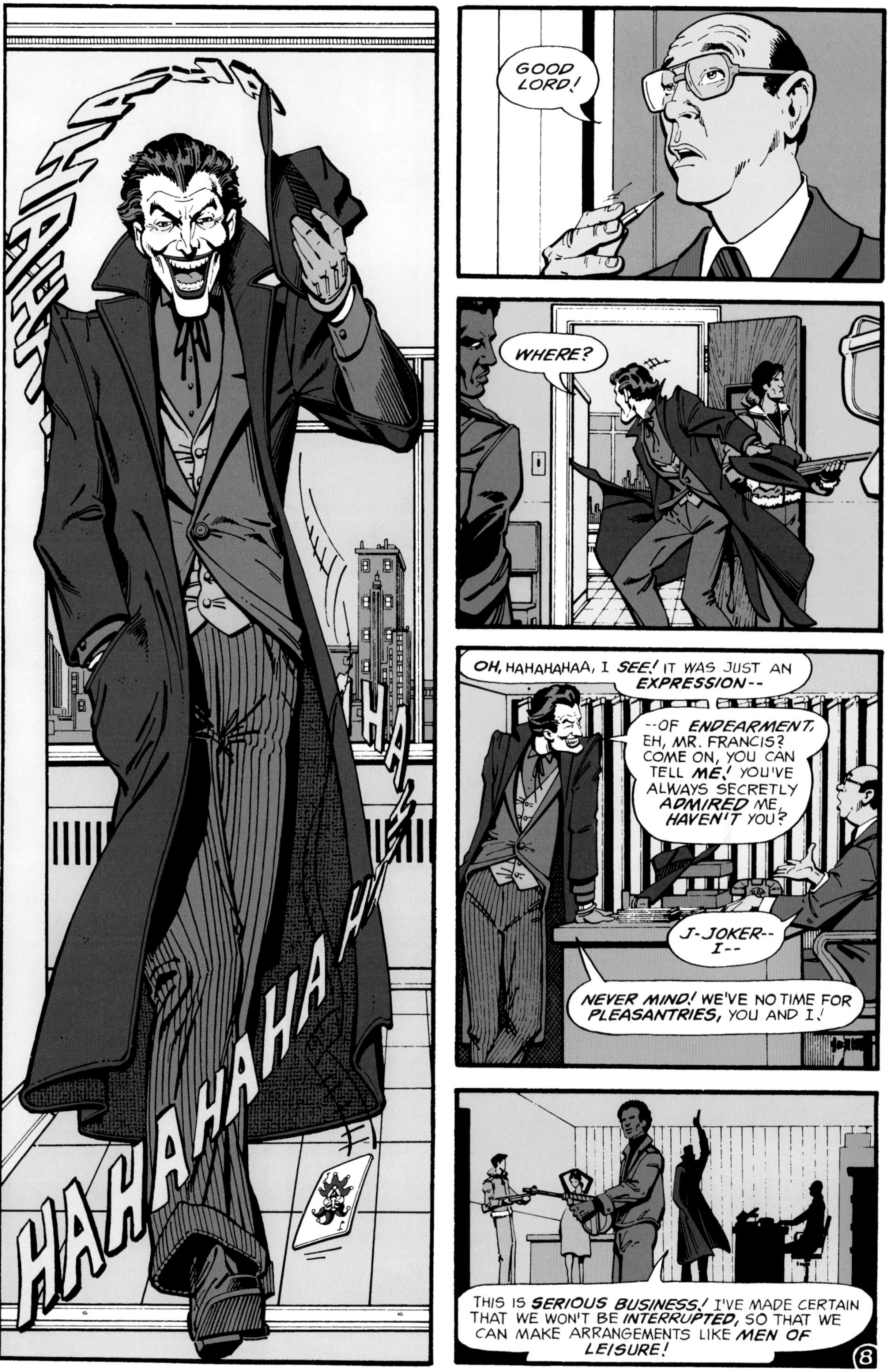
HA-HA-HA
HA HA
HAHAHAHAHAHA
GOOD LORD!
WHERE?
OH, HAHAHAHAA, I SEE! IT WAS JUST AN EXPRESSION--
--OF ENDEARMENT, EH, MR. FRANCIS? COME ON, YOU CAN TELL ME! YOU'VE ALWAYS SECRETLY ADMIRED ME, HAVEN'T YOU?
J-JOKER-- I--
NEVER MIND! WE'VE NO TIME FOR PLEASANTRIES, YOU AND I!
THIS IS SERIOUS BUSINESS! I'VE MADE CERTAIN THAT WE WON'T BE INTERRUPTED, SO THAT WE CAN MAKE ARRANGEMENTS LIKE MEN OF LEISURE!
8

WH-**WHAT** ARRANGEMENTS?

FOR MY **FISH**, OF COURSE!

I MIGHT AS WELL **TELL** YOU, FRANCIS--THIS HAS ALL BEEN WORKED OUT **FAR IN ADVANCE!** YOU ARE, FINALLY, JUST A **COG**, SO DON'T SPEAK TO ME **AGAIN!**

NOW--WHAT IS EVERYBODY IN THE COUNTRY **TALKING** ABOUT?

UH... YOUR **FISH...?**

I **TOLD** YOU NOT TO **TALK!** I DON'T **NEED** YOU TO ANSWER MY QUESTIONS! **I** CAN ANSWER MY QUESTIONS **MYSELF!**

I **ALWAYS** ANSWER MY QUESTIONS **MYSELF!**

HURUMPH... AS I WAS **SAYING**...

...EVERYBODY'S TALKING ABOUT MY **JOKER-FISH!** THEY **ALL** RECOGNIZE THE **FACE**--IT'S MY **FORTUNE,** EVEN ON A **FLOUNDER'S FIZZ**-- AND SINCE I PLAN TO **CONTINUE** SECRETLY DUMPING THE **CHEMICAL** THAT GIVES THE FISH MY FACE, THE LITTLE FINNIES ARE **PERMANENTLY** IDENTIFIED WITH ME! NO MATTER **WHAT** THEY **ONCE** WERE, THEY'RE JUST **JOKER-FISH NOW!**

SOOO...

...ONCE WE FILL OUT ALL YOUR TEDIOUS **COPYRIGHT** FORMS--

--I'LL GET A **CUT** OF EVERY **FISH-SALE** IN **AMERICA!**

A **NICKEL** PER FISH-SANDWICH--FIFTY CENTS FOR **FILET OF SOLE!** MILLIONS OF DOLLARS A **DAY,** TO FINANCE MY FRANKLY HEDONISTIC **LIFE-STYLE!** AND ALL SO **SIMPLE!** WHAT A **JOKE!** HA HA HA HA HAHA

LT 9 35

HEAT RESIS TANT

Letras produ Engla

JOKER, IT--IT'S **IMPOSSIBLE!**

WHAT? IMPOSSIBLE, YOU SAY? NO--

--**NOBODY** CAN COPYRIGHT **FISH**--OR EVEN **FISH FACES!** THEY'RE A **NATURAL RESOURCE!**

9

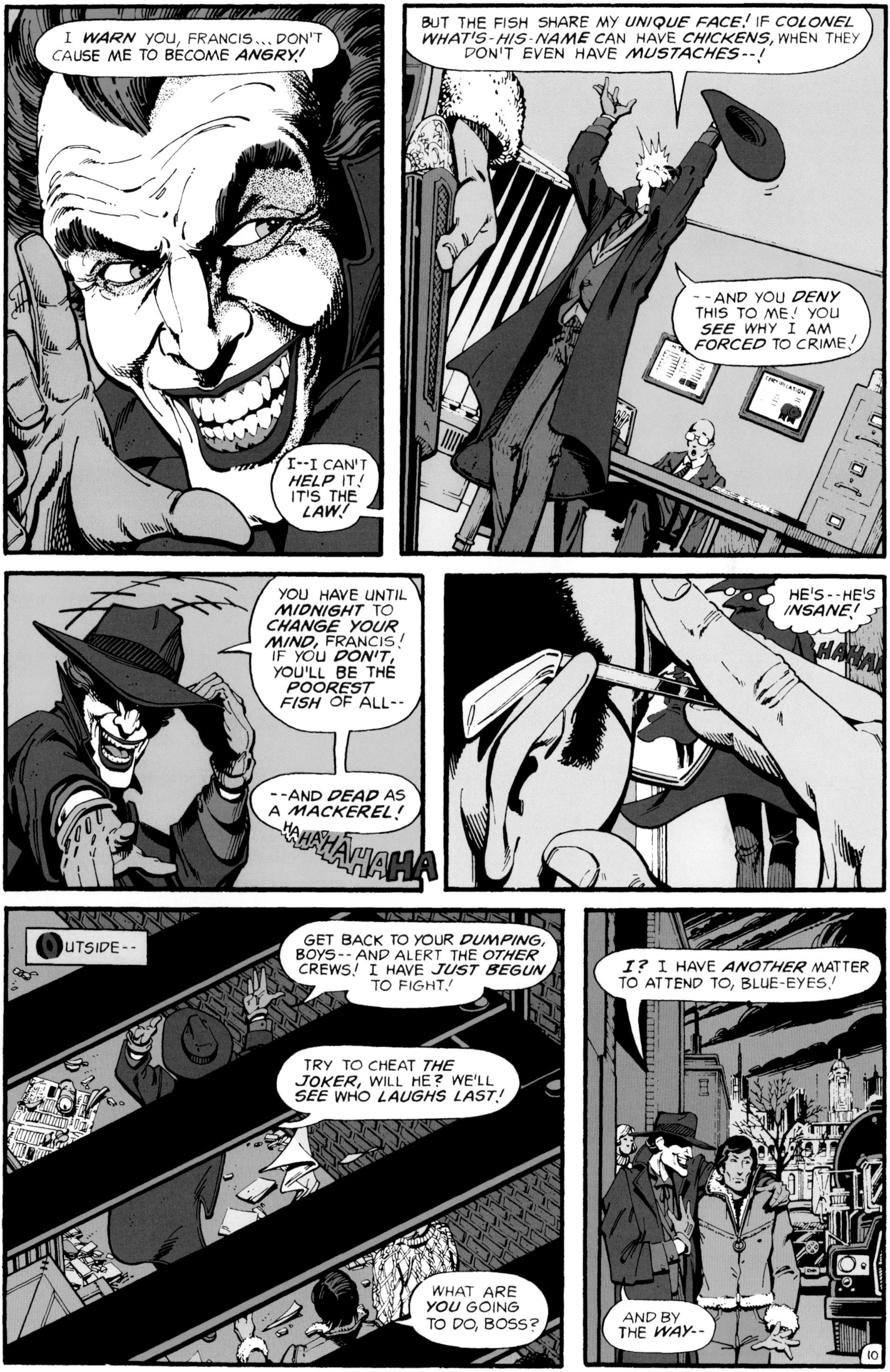

I WARN YOU, FRANCIS... DON'T CAUSE ME TO BECOME ANGRY!
I--I CAN'T HELP IT! IT'S THE LAW!
BUT THE FISH SHARE MY UNIQUE FACE! IF COLONEL WHAT'S-HIS-NAME CAN HAVE CHICKENS, WHEN THEY DON'T EVEN HAVE MUSTACHES--!
--AND YOU DENY THIS TO ME! YOU SEE WHY I AM FORCED TO CRIME!
CERTIFICATION
YOU HAVE UNTIL MIDNIGHT TO CHANGE YOUR MIND, FRANCIS! IF YOU DON'T, YOU'LL BE THE POOREST FISH OF ALL--
--AND DEAD AS A MACKEREL!
HAHAHAHAHAHA
HE'S--HE'S INSANE!
HAHAH
OUTSIDE--
GET BACK TO YOUR DUMPING, BOYS--AND ALERT THE OTHER CREWS! I HAVE JUST BEGUN TO FIGHT!
TRY TO CHEAT THE JOKER, WILL HE? WE'LL SEE WHO LAUGHS LAST!
WHAT ARE YOU GOING TO DO, BOSS?
I? I HAVE ANOTHER MATTER TO ATTEND TO, BLUE-EYES!
AND BY THE WAY--
10

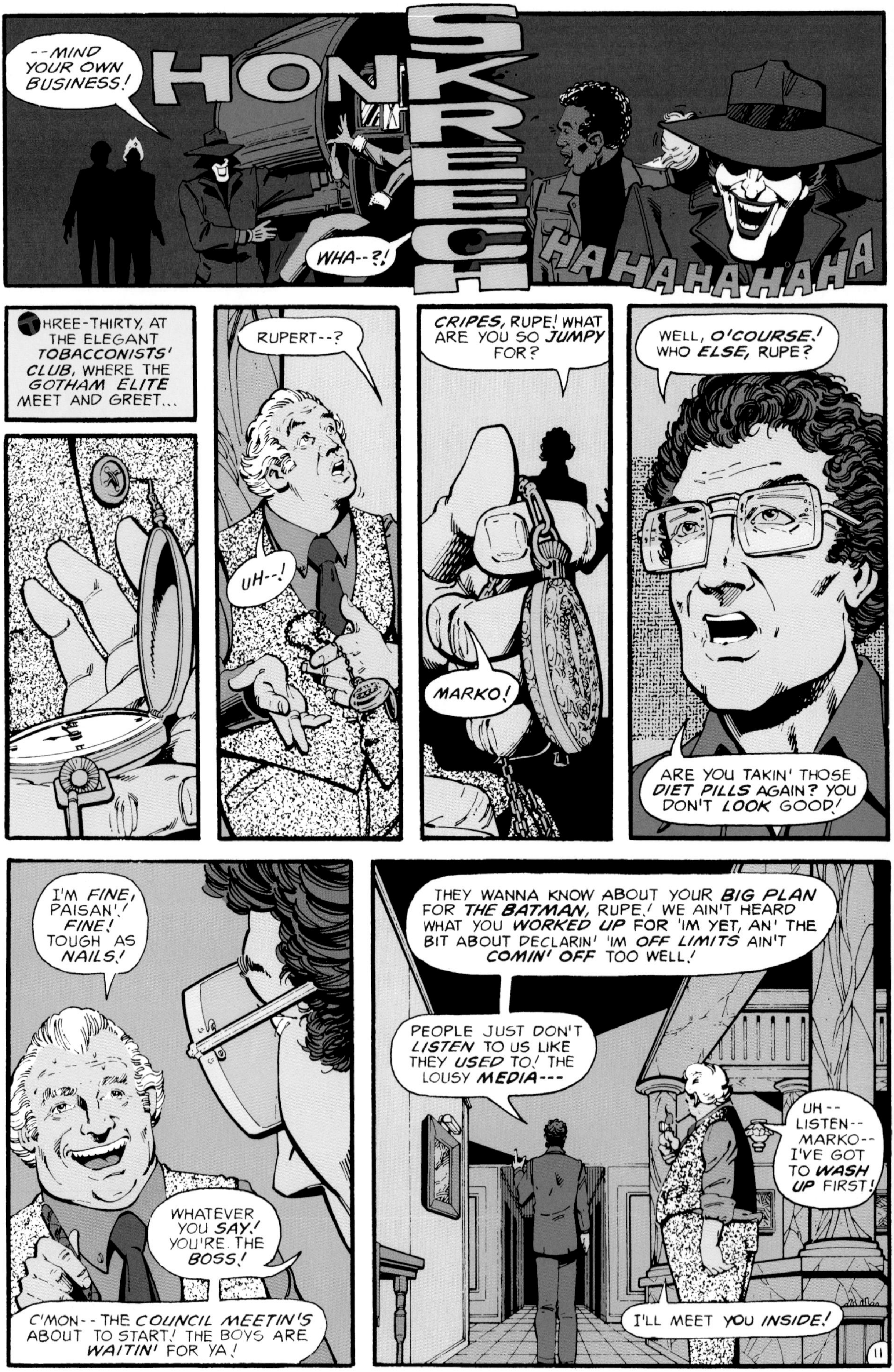
--MIND YOUR OWN BUSINESS!
HONK
SKRECH
WHA--?!
HAHAHAHAHAHA
THREE-THIRTY, AT THE ELEGANT TOBACCONISTS' CLUB, WHERE THE GOTHAM ELITE MEET AND GREET...
RUPERT--?
UH--!
CRIPES, RUPE! WHAT ARE YOU SO JUMPY FOR?
MARKO!
WELL, O'COURSE! WHO ELSE, RUPE?
ARE YOU TAKIN' THOSE DIET PILLS AGAIN? YOU DON'T LOOK GOOD!
I'M FINE, PAISAN'! FINE! TOUGH AS NAILS!
WHATEVER YOU SAY! YOU'RE THE BOSS!
C'MON--THE COUNCIL MEETIN'S ABOUT TO START! THE BOYS ARE WAITIN' FOR YA!
THEY WANNA KNOW ABOUT YOUR BIG PLAN FOR THE BATMAN, RUPE! WE AIN'T HEARD WHAT YOU WORKED UP FOR 'IM YET, AN' THE BIT ABOUT DECLARIN' 'IM OFF LIMITS AIN'T COMIN' OFF TOO WELL!
PEOPLE JUST DON'T LISTEN TO US LIKE THEY USED TO! THE LOUSY MEDIA---
UH--LISTEN--MARKO--I'VE GOT TO WASH UP FIRST!
I'LL MEET YOU INSIDE!
11

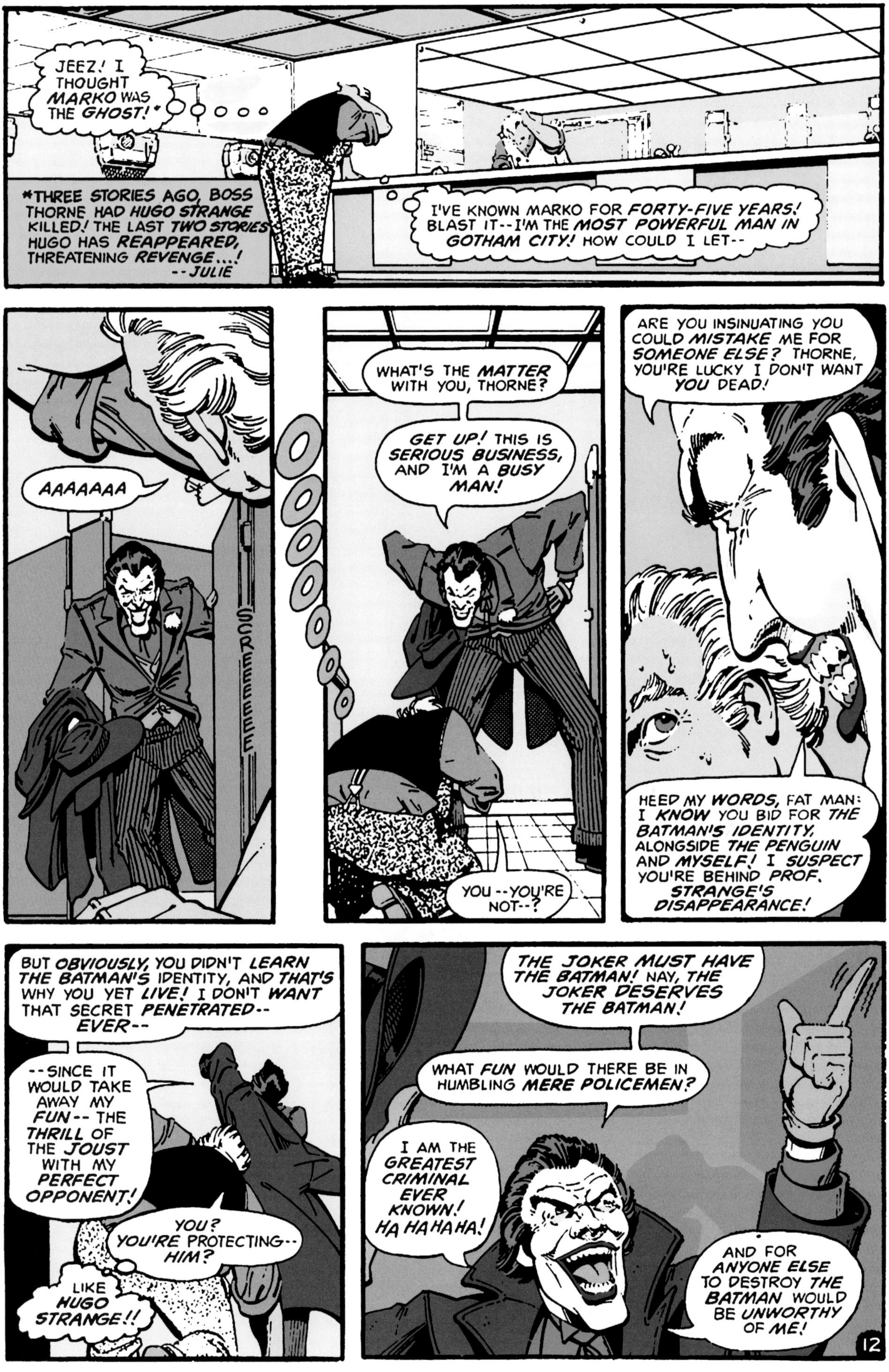
JEEZ! I THOUGHT MARKO WAS THE GHOST!*
*THREE STORIES AGO, BOSS THORNE HAD HUGO STRANGE KILLED! THE LAST TWO STORIES HUGO HAS REAPPEARED, THREATENING REVENGE...! --JULIE
I'VE KNOWN MARKO FOR FORTY-FIVE YEARS! BLAST IT--I'M THE MOST POWERFUL MAN IN GOTHAM CITY! HOW COULD I LET--
AAAAAAA
SCREEEEEE
WHAT'S THE MATTER WITH YOU, THORNE?
GET UP! THIS IS SERIOUS BUSINESS, AND I'M A BUSY MAN!
YOU--YOU'RE NOT--?
ARE YOU INSINUATING YOU COULD MISTAKE ME FOR SOMEONE ELSE? THORNE, YOU'RE LUCKY I DON'T WANT YOU DEAD!
HEED MY WORDS, FAT MAN: I KNOW YOU BID FOR THE BATMAN'S IDENTITY, ALONGSIDE THE PENGUIN AND MYSELF! I SUSPECT YOU'RE BEHIND PROF. STRANGE'S DISAPPEARANCE!
BUT OBVIOUSLY, YOU DIDN'T LEARN THE BATMAN'S IDENTITY, AND THAT'S WHY YOU YET LIVE! I DON'T WANT THAT SECRET PENETRATED--EVER--
--SINCE IT WOULD TAKE AWAY MY FUN--THE THRILL OF THE JOUST WITH MY PERFECT OPPONENT!
YOU? YOU'RE PROTECTING--HIM?
LIKE HUGO STRANGE!!
THE JOKER MUST HAVE THE BATMAN! NAY, THE JOKER DESERVES THE BATMAN!
WHAT FUN WOULD THERE BE IN HUMBLING MERE POLICEMEN?
I AM THE GREATEST CRIMINAL EVER KNOWN! HA HA HA HA!
AND FOR ANYONE ELSE TO DESTROY THE BATMAN WOULD BE UNWORTHY OF ME!
12

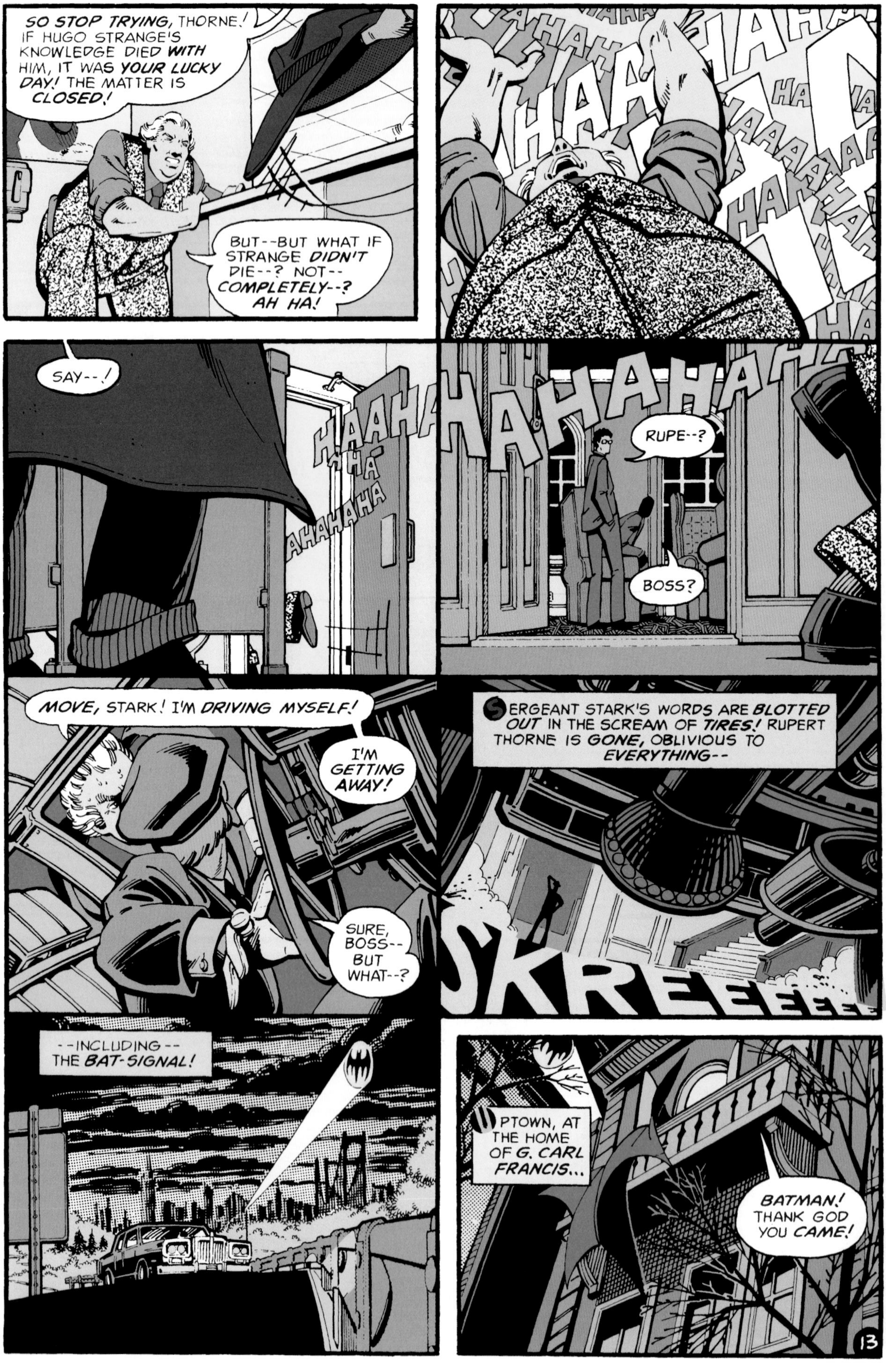

SO STOP TRYING, THORNE! IF HUGO STRANGE'S KNOWLEDGE DIED WITH HIM, IT WAS YOUR LUCKY DAY! THE MATTER IS CLOSED!
BUT--BUT WHAT IF STRANGE DIDN'T DIE--? NOT--COMPLETELY--? AH HA!
SAY--!
RUPE--?
BOSS?
MOVE, STARK! I'M DRIVING MYSELF!
I'M GETTING AWAY!
SURE, BOSS--BUT WHAT--?
SERGEANT STARK'S WORDS ARE BLOTTED OUT IN THE SCREAM OF TIRES! RUPERT THORNE IS GONE, OBLIVIOUS TO EVERYTHING--
SKREEEEE
--INCLUDING--THE BAT-SIGNAL!
UPTOWN, AT THE HOME OF G. CARL FRANCIS...
BATMAN! THANK GOD YOU CAME!
13

WHEN YOU LIGHT THAT *BEACON*, COMMISSIONER--

--I'LL *COME!* THAT'S THE WAY IT'S *ALWAYS* BEEN, AND THE WAY IT'LL *ALWAYS* BE!

BUT WON'T THIS GET YOU IN *DUTCH* AT *CITY HALL?*

LET THEM WRITE ME A *REPRIMAND!*

I'VE GOT A *PROBLEM* YOU'LL WANT TO SOLVE!

THIS MAN--

HAHAHAHA! WE INTERRUPT OUR REGULARLY SCHEDULED *RERUNS* TO BRING YOU THE FOLLOWING *FIRESIDE CHAT!*

GOOD EVENING, MY FELLOW AMERICANS! TONIGHT, AT PRECISELY *TWELVE O'CLOCK,* I WILL KILL *G. CARL FRANCIS!*

THE JOKER HAS *SPOKEN!*

LET'S GET TO *WORK,* COMMISSIONER!

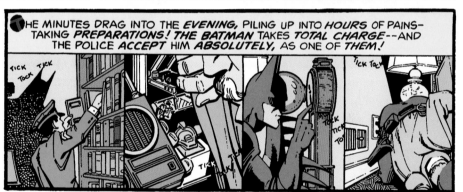

THE MINUTES DRAG INTO THE *EVENING,* PILING UP INTO *HOURS* OF PAINS-TAKING *PREPARATIONS!* THE BATMAN TAKES *TOTAL CHARGE*--AND THE POLICE *ACCEPT* HIM *ABSOLUTELY,* AS ONE OF *THEM!*

TICK TICK TOCK TICK
TICK TOCK

BUT *SOME* OF THEM HAVE TRIED TO BLOCK *THE JOKER* AT *OTHER TIMES,* AND KNOW THE *RANGE* OF HIS *MAD GENIUS!*

11:55! FRANCIS IS *CORDONED OFF* HERE, AND THE HOUSE IS *SURROUNDED* OUTSIDE! HE'S *EATEN* NOTHING SINCE THE THREAT--ALL *WATER'S* BROUGHT IN FROM THE *POLICE LAB*--!

THE MOOD IS *MORE* THAN GRIM!

TICK TOCK TICK TICK TOCK

WHAT HAVEN'T I *COVERED?*

14

I WISH THE *STORM* WOULD BREAK--CLEAR THE *AIR* SOMEHOW! YOU CAN CUT THE *ELECTRICITY* WITH A *KNIFE!*

I WISH *SILVER* WOULD ANSWER THE *PHONE* WHEN I CALL! SHE'S BEEN GONE *ALL DAY!*

I WISH *HUGO STRANGE* WOULD TURN UP!

COME ON, JOKER-- *MOVE!*

BATMAN--?

BATMAN, TELL ME-- I'VE HEARD THAT *THE PENGUIN, THE SCARECROW, THE RIDDLER* KILL PEOPLE WHO GET IN THEIR *WAY* SOMETIMES! BUT *THIS*--!

I'M JUST A *PAPER-PUSHER!* I DON'T *MAKE* THE LAWS! WHY *ME??*

IF NOT *YOU*, THEN *SOMEONE ELSE,* MR. *FRANCIS!* THE *JOKER'S* A *TIME-BOMB*-- AND *EVERY SO OFTEN,* HE JUST *HAS TO EXPLODE!*

WHA--? GAS--COMING IN THROUGH THE *HEATING DUCTS!*

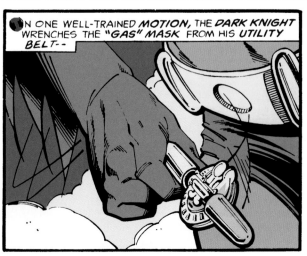

IN ONE WELL-TRAINED *MOTION,* THE *DARK KNIGHT* WRENCHES THE *"GAS"* MASK FROM HIS *UTILITY BELT*--

--AND CLAPS IT ACROSS THE *TARGET'S* FACE!

I CAN *HOLD MY BREATH* LONG ENOUGH TO ESCAPE--

--BUT I DOUBT *YOU* CAN, FRANCIS!

15

However...

BONG BONG

≥AGGHH!≥

BONG BONG BONG

BONG BONG BONG

BONG BONG BONG

BONG

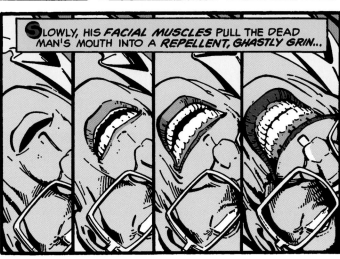

SLOWLY, HIS *FACIAL MUSCLES* PULL THE DEAD MAN'S MOUTH INTO A *REPELLENT, GHASTLY GRIN...*

...THE SIGN OF *THE JOKER!*

I DON'T *UNDERSTAND!* SOME OF *US* DIDN'T HAVE MASKS-- *WE* BREATHED THE GAS!

WHY DIDN'T *WE DIE?*

HE DIDN'T *WANT* YOU! HE WANTED *FRANCIS-- ALONE!*

NOW THAT I'VE BREATHED THE GAS *MYSELF,* I *RECOGNIZE* IT! IT'S ONE PART OF A *BINARY COMPOUND--*

--EACH PART *HARMLESS ITSELF...* BUT WHEN THEY'RE *MIXED,* THEY CREATE A *POISON!*

THE JOKER MUST HAVE SECRETLY SPRAYED HIM WITH THE *OTHER* GAS WHEN HE THREATENED HIM AT *NOON!*

SO *ONLY* HE, IN A *ROOMFUL OF PEOPLE,* WOULD *REACT!* IT'S *DIABOLICAL!*

HELLO, LATE-SHOW LOVERS -- AND LOVERS OF THE *LATE-SHOW!* G. CARL FRANCIS IS *DEAD,* AS I *VOWED!*

16

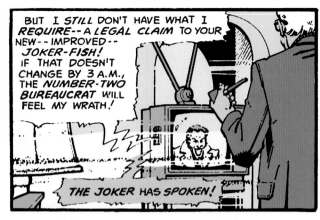

BUT I *STILL* DON'T HAVE WHAT I *REQUIRE*-- A *LEGAL CLAIM* TO YOUR *NEW--IMPROVED-- JOKER-FISH!* IF THAT DOESN'T CHANGE BY 3 A.M., THE *NUMBER-TWO BUREAUCRAT* WILL FEEL MY WRATH!

THE JOKER HAS SPOKEN!

THE BATMAN MAKES *NO REPLY!*

MEANWHILE, SOME THREE HUNDRED MILES TO THE *WEST...*

HUH? IT'S A *GIRL*--!

HI! I'M SURE GLAD YOU *STOPPED!* SOMETHING'S WRONG WITH MY *CAR!*

HEY! AREN'T YOU--

--*RUPERT THORNE?*

UH--YEAH! WE MET AT *BRUCE WAYNE'S PARTY,* DIDN'T WE? WAS IT--

--*SILVER?*

IT *WAS!*

CAN YOU GIVE ME A *LIFT?*

WELL--I'M IN A *HURRY*--

GREAT! SO AM I!

IT SURE WAS LUCKY MEETING YOU HERE!

THE CAR ROLLS AWAY, AND QUICKLY *DISAPPEARS* IN THE *DARK!* HIGH *OVERHEAD,* A BLAST OF *THUNDER* MARKS ITS *PASSAGE!*

WITH A *SHRIEK* AND A *SHIVER,* THE *STORM BEGINS...!*

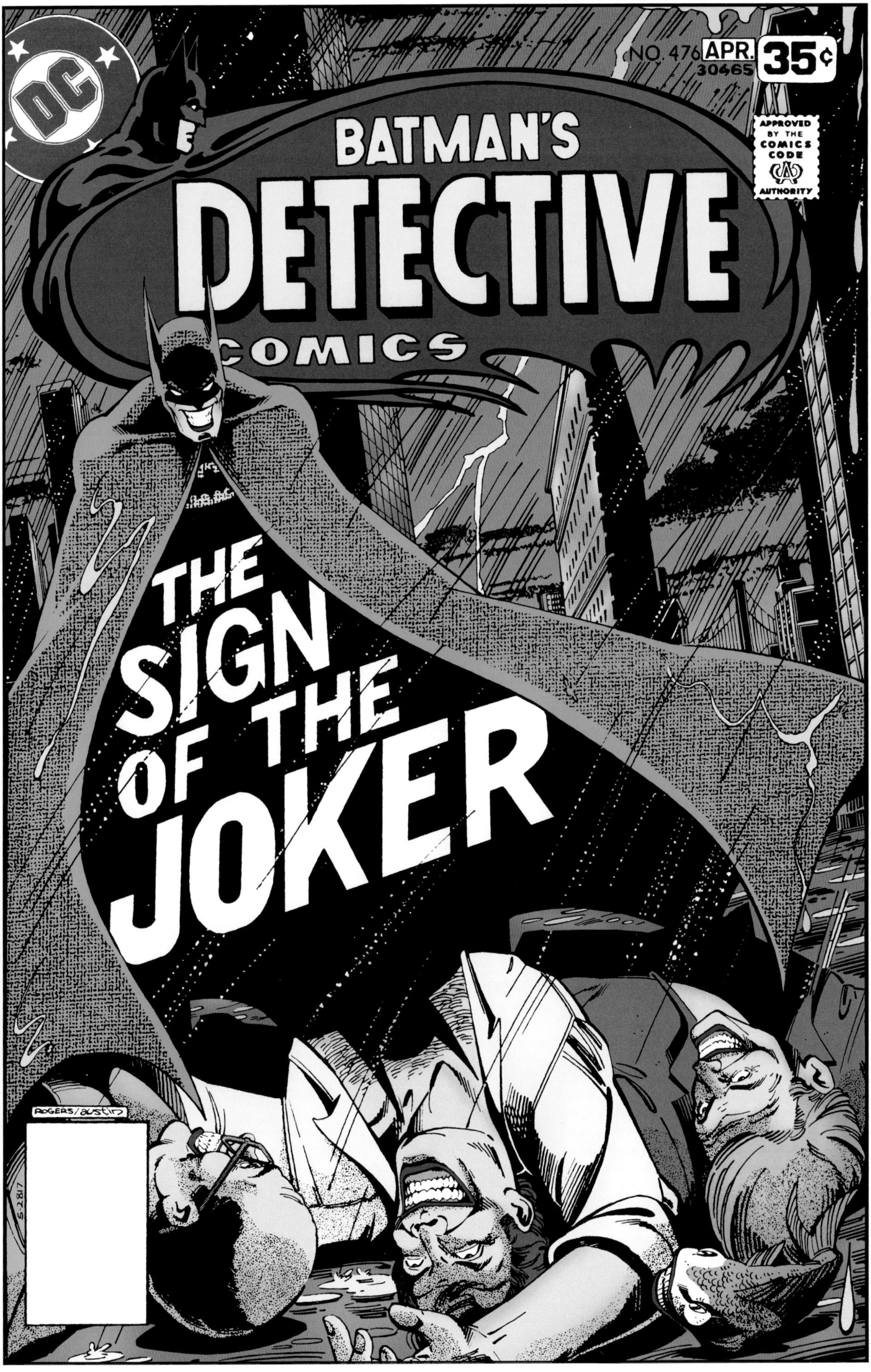
DC
NO. 476 APR.
30465
35¢
APPROVED BY THE COMICS CODE AUTHORITY
BATMAN'S
DETECTIVE
COMICS
THE SIGN OF THE JOKER
ROGERS/AUSTIN

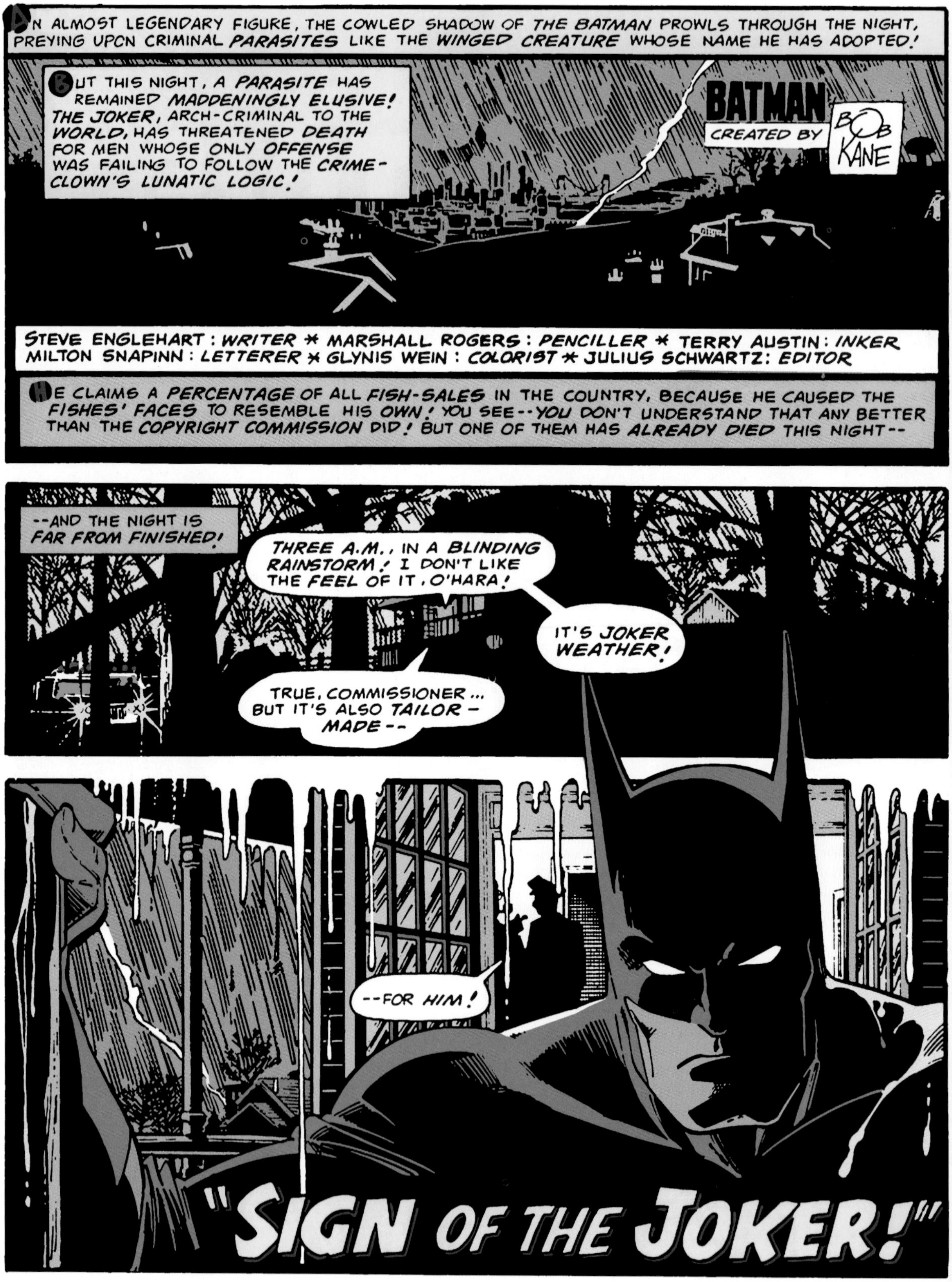
AN ALMOST LEGENDARY FIGURE, THE COWLED SHADOW OF THE BATMAN PROWLS THROUGH THE NIGHT, PREYING UPON CRIMINAL PARASITES LIKE THE WINGED CREATURE WHOSE NAME HE HAS ADOPTED!
BUT THIS NIGHT, A PARASITE HAS REMAINED MADDENINGLY ELUSIVE! THE JOKER, ARCH-CRIMINAL TO THE WORLD, HAS THREATENED DEATH FOR MEN WHOSE ONLY OFFENSE WAS FAILING TO FOLLOW THE CRIME-CLOWN'S LUNATIC LOGIC!
BATMAN
CREATED BY BOB KANE
STEVE ENGLEHART : WRITER * MARSHALL ROGERS : PENCILLER * TERRY AUSTIN : INKER
MILTON SNAPINN : LETTERER * GLYNIS WEIN : COLORIST * JULIUS SCHWARTZ : EDITOR
HE CLAIMS A PERCENTAGE OF ALL FISH-SALES IN THE COUNTRY, BECAUSE HE CAUSED THE FISHES' FACES TO RESEMBLE HIS OWN! YOU SEE--YOU DON'T UNDERSTAND THAT ANY BETTER THAN THE COPYRIGHT COMMISSION DID! BUT ONE OF THEM HAS ALREADY DIED THIS NIGHT--
--AND THE NIGHT IS FAR FROM FINISHED!
THREE A.M., IN A BLINDING RAINSTORM! I DON'T LIKE THE FEEL OF IT, O'HARA!
IT'S JOKER WEATHER!
TRUE, COMMISSIONER... BUT IT'S ALSO TAILOR-MADE--
--FOR HIM!
"SIGN OF THE JOKER!"

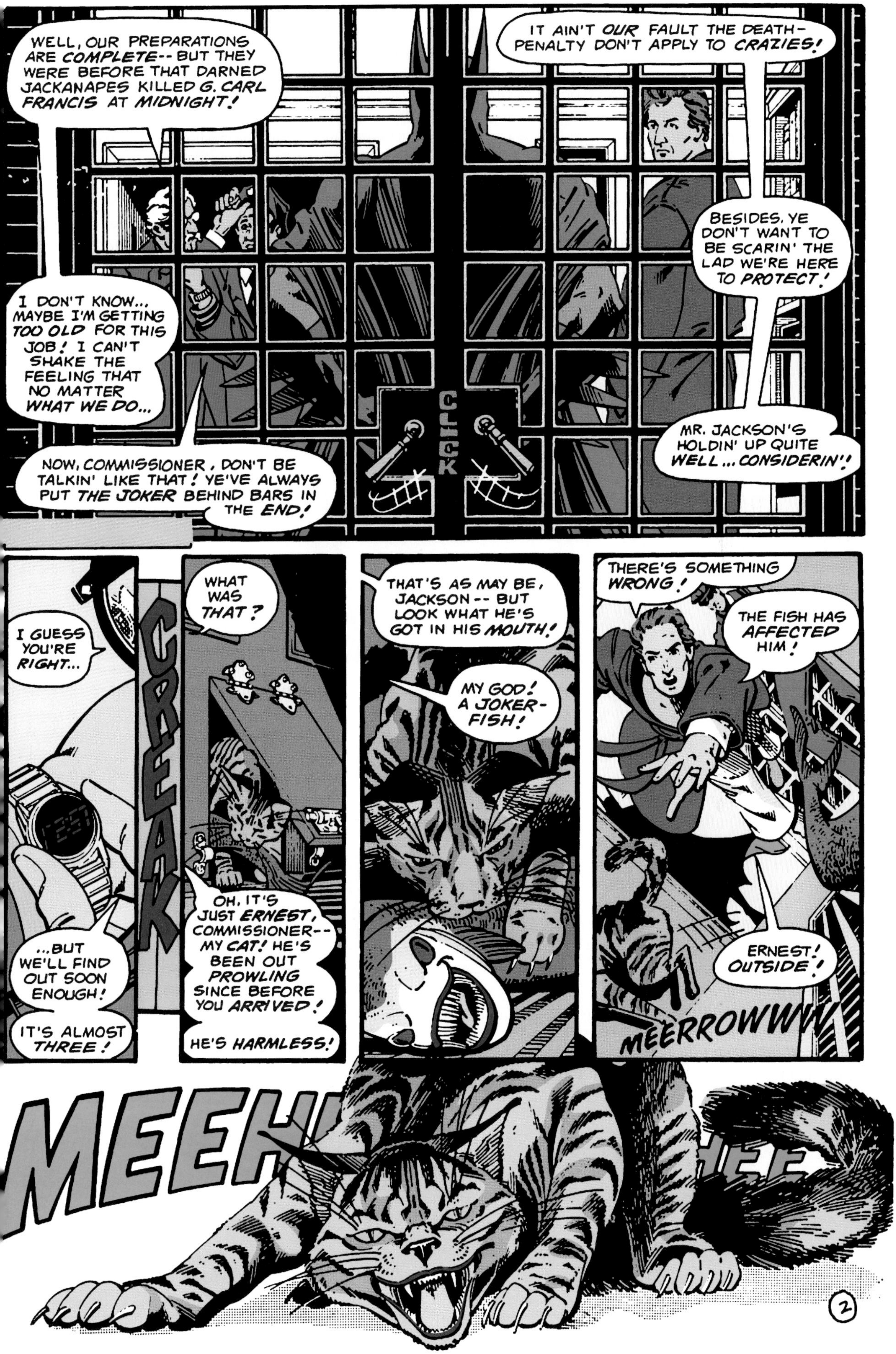

WELL, OUR PREPARATIONS ARE COMPLETE-- BUT THEY WERE BEFORE THAT DARNED JACKANAPES KILLED G. CARL FRANCIS AT MIDNIGHT!
I DON'T KNOW... MAYBE I'M GETTING TOO OLD FOR THIS JOB! I CAN'T SHAKE THE FEELING THAT NO MATTER WHAT WE DO...
NOW, COMMISSIONER, DON'T BE TALKIN' LIKE THAT! YE'VE ALWAYS PUT THE JOKER BEHIND BARS IN THE END!
CLICK
IT AIN'T OUR FAULT THE DEATH-PENALTY DON'T APPLY TO CRAZIES!
BESIDES, YE DON'T WANT TO BE SCARIN' THE LAD WE'RE HERE TO PROTECT!
MR. JACKSON'S HOLDIN' UP QUITE WELL... CONSIDERIN'!
I GUESS YOU'RE RIGHT...
...BUT WE'LL FIND OUT SOON ENOUGH!
IT'S ALMOST THREE!
CREAK
WHAT WAS THAT?
OH, IT'S JUST ERNEST, COMMISSIONER-- MY CAT! HE'S BEEN OUT PROWLING SINCE BEFORE YOU ARRIVED!
HE'S HARMLESS!
THAT'S AS MAY BE, JACKSON -- BUT LOOK WHAT HE'S GOT IN HIS MOUTH!
MY GOD! A JOKER-FISH!
THERE'S SOMETHING WRONG!
THE FISH HAS AFFECTED HIM!
ERNEST! OUTSIDE!
MEERROWWW
MEEH
HEE
2

GOOD LORD!

RRRAWWWR

MEERAWW

=, UNNGH! =

;UHF!;

TUNK

SAINTS PRESERVE US! THE SIGN OF THE JOKER-- THAT HIDEOUS GRIN!

THE FIEND GOT HIM! DESPITE ALL OUR PRECAUTIONS --

--HE GOT JACKSON!

EVEN MADDENED, THE CAT KNEW HIS MASTER! IT WAS THE ONE THING I OVER-LOOKED WHEN I PROPOSED OUR TRADING FACES!

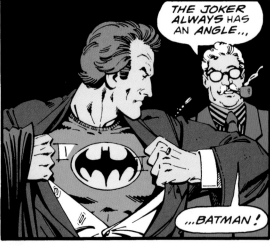

THE JOKER ALWAYS HAS AN ANGLE...

...BATMAN!

HELLO THERE, BATMAN! THOMAS JACKSON IS DEAD, AS I VOWED!

BUT I STILL DON'T HAVE MY LEGAL CLAIM TO MY JOKER-FISH!

IF THAT DOESN'T CHANGE BY DAWN, THE NEXT COMMISSION MEMBER WILL FEEL MY WRATH!

3

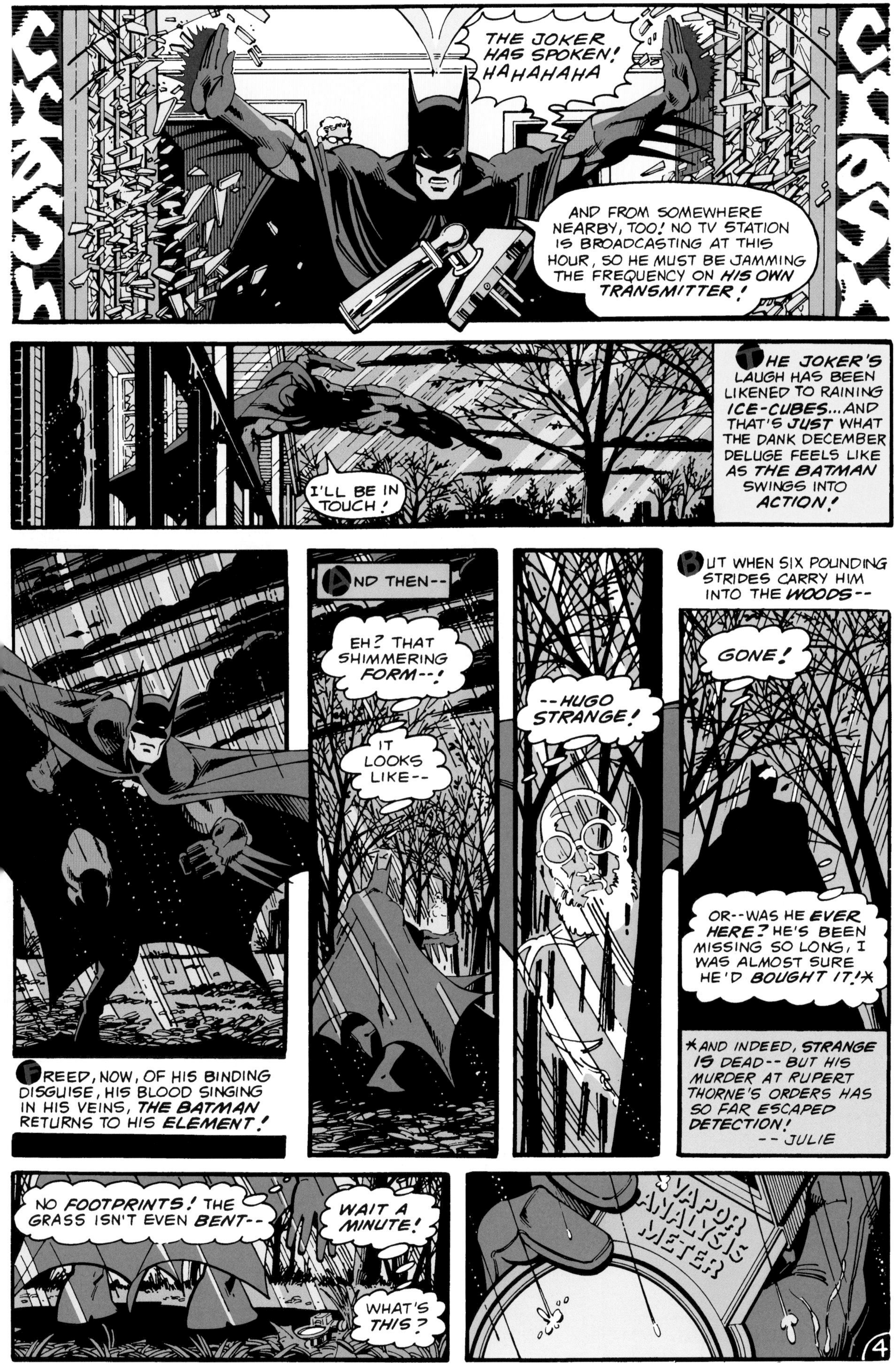
CRASH
CRASH
THE JOKER HAS SPOKEN! HAHAHAHA
AND FROM SOMEWHERE NEARBY, TOO! NO TV STATION IS BROADCASTING AT THIS HOUR, SO HE MUST BE JAMMING THE FREQUENCY ON HIS OWN TRANSMITTER!
I'LL BE IN TOUCH!
THE JOKER'S LAUGH HAS BEEN LIKENED TO RAINING ICE-CUBES...AND THAT'S JUST WHAT THE DANK DECEMBER DELUGE FEELS LIKE AS THE BATMAN SWINGS INTO ACTION!
FREED, NOW, OF HIS BINDING DISGUISE, HIS BLOOD SINGING IN HIS VEINS, THE BATMAN RETURNS TO HIS ELEMENT!
AND THEN--
EH? THAT SHIMMERING FORM--!
IT LOOKS LIKE--
--HUGO STRANGE!
BUT WHEN SIX POUNDING STRIDES CARRY HIM INTO THE WOODS--
GONE!
OR--WAS HE EVER HERE? HE'S BEEN MISSING SO LONG, I WAS ALMOST SURE HE'D BOUGHT IT!*
*AND INDEED, STRANGE IS DEAD-- BUT HIS MURDER AT RUPERT THORNE'S ORDERS HAS SO FAR ESCAPED DETECTION! --JULIE
NO FOOTPRINTS! THE GRASS ISN'T EVEN BENT--
WAIT A MINUTE!
WHAT'S THIS?
VAPOR ANALYSIS METER
4

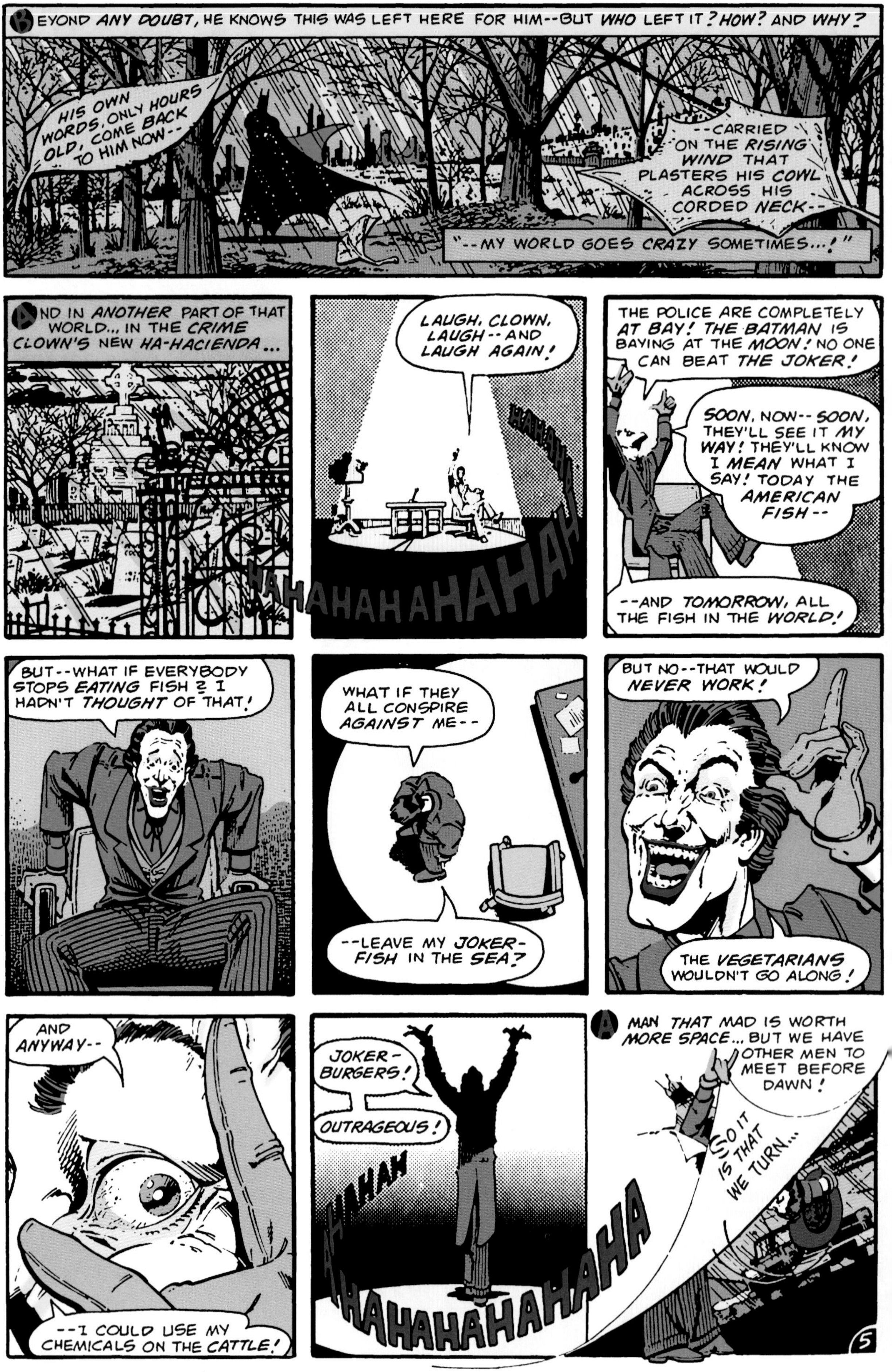
BEYOND ANY DOUBT, HE KNOWS THIS WAS LEFT HERE FOR HIM--BUT WHO LEFT IT? HOW? AND WHY?
HIS OWN WORDS, ONLY HOURS OLD, COME BACK TO HIM NOW--
--CARRIED ON THE RISING WIND THAT PLASTERS HIS COWL ACROSS HIS CORDED NECK--
"--MY WORLD GOES CRAZY SOMETIMES...!"
AND IN ANOTHER PART OF THAT WORLD... IN THE CRIME CLOWN'S NEW HA-HACIENDA...
LAUGH, CLOWN, LAUGH--AND LAUGH AGAIN!
HAHAHAHAHAHAHAHAHAHA
THE POLICE ARE COMPLETELY AT BAY! THE BATMAN IS BAYING AT THE MOON! NO ONE CAN BEAT THE JOKER!
SOON, NOW--SOON, THEY'LL SEE IT MY WAY! THEY'LL KNOW I MEAN WHAT I SAY! TODAY THE AMERICAN FISH--
--AND TOMORROW, ALL THE FISH IN THE WORLD!
BUT--WHAT IF EVERYBODY STOPS EATING FISH? I HADN'T THOUGHT OF THAT!
WHAT IF THEY ALL CONSPIRE AGAINST ME--
--LEAVE MY JOKER-FISH IN THE SEA?
BUT NO--THAT WOULD NEVER WORK!
THE VEGETARIANS WOULDN'T GO ALONG!
AND ANYWAY--
--I COULD USE MY CHEMICALS ON THE CATTLE!
JOKER-BURGERS!
OUTRAGEOUS!
HAHAHAHAHAHAHAHAHAHAHAH
A MAN THAT MAD IS WORTH MORE SPACE... BUT WE HAVE OTHER MEN TO MEET BEFORE DAWN!
SO IT IS THAT WE TURN...
5

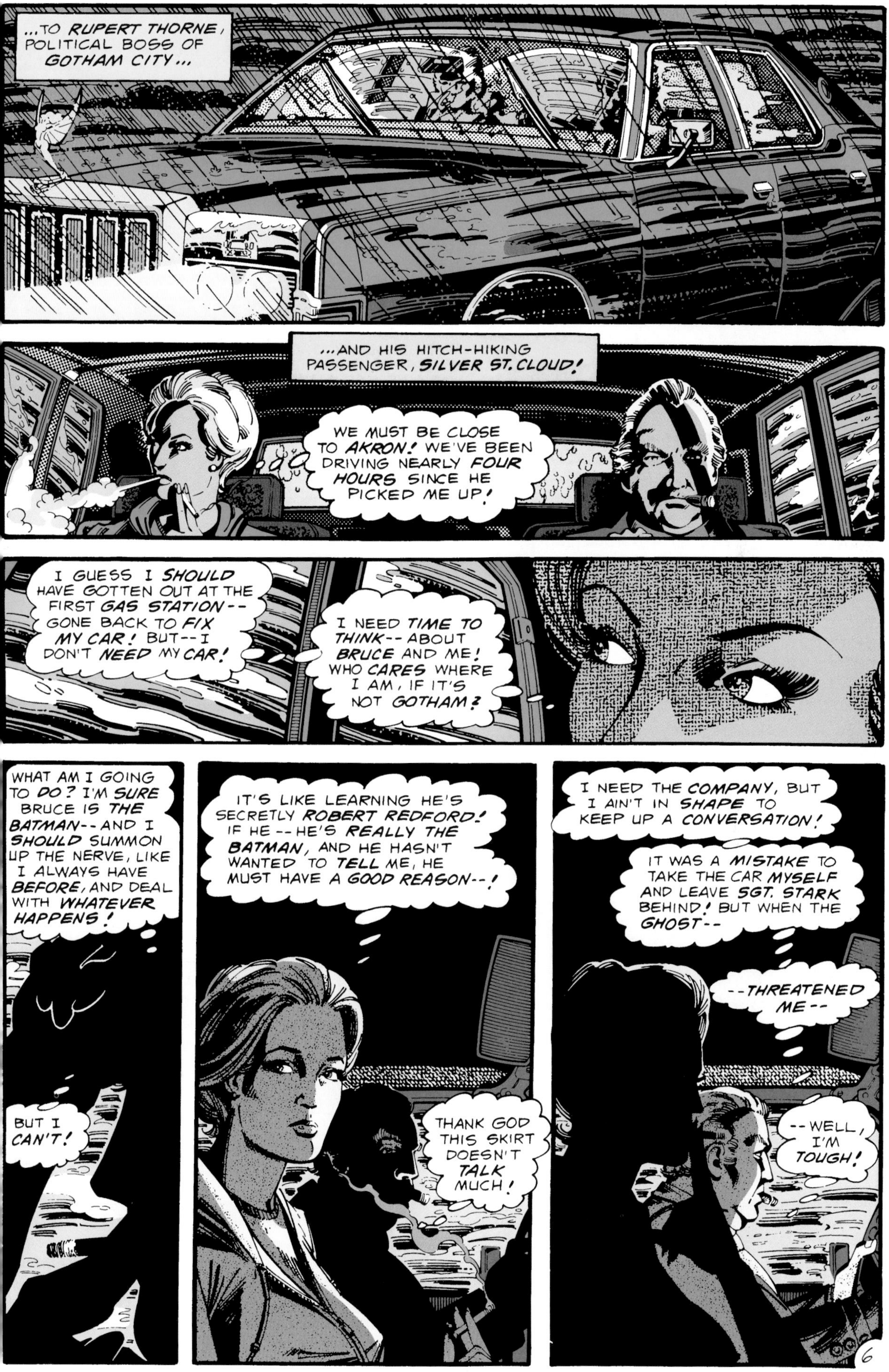
...TO RUPERT THORNE, POLITICAL BOSS OF GOTHAM CITY...
...AND HIS HITCH-HIKING PASSENGER, SILVER ST. CLOUD!
WE MUST BE CLOSE TO AKRON! WE'VE BEEN DRIVING NEARLY FOUR HOURS SINCE HE PICKED ME UP!
I GUESS I SHOULD HAVE GOTTEN OUT AT THE FIRST GAS STATION-- GONE BACK TO FIX MY CAR! BUT--I DON'T NEED MY CAR!
I NEED TIME TO THINK-- ABOUT BRUCE AND ME! WHO CARES WHERE I AM, IF IT'S NOT GOTHAM?
WHAT AM I GOING TO DO? I'M SURE BRUCE IS THE BATMAN--AND I SHOULD SUMMON UP THE NERVE, LIKE I ALWAYS HAVE BEFORE, AND DEAL WITH WHATEVER HAPPENS!
BUT I CAN'T!
IT'S LIKE LEARNING HE'S SECRETLY ROBERT REDFORD! IF HE--HE'S REALLY THE BATMAN, AND HE HASN'T WANTED TO TELL ME, HE MUST HAVE A GOOD REASON--!
THANK GOD THIS SKIRT DOESN'T TALK MUCH!
I NEED THE COMPANY, BUT I AIN'T IN SHAPE TO KEEP UP A CONVERSATION!
IT WAS A MISTAKE TO TAKE THE CAR MYSELF AND LEAVE SGT. STARK BEHIND! BUT WHEN THE GHOST--
--THREATENED ME--
--WELL, I'M TOUGH!
6

I'VE ALWAYS BEEN TOUGH! BUT--I PUT MY HAND RIGHT THROUGH HIS BODY--!

HE SAID THE NEXT TIME HE APPEARED, I'D--I'D--!

IT'S FOUR O'CLOCK-- HEAR NOW THE NEWS!

BUT HE WON'T SHOW-- NOT IF THE DAME WOULD GET IT WITH ME! HE HAD SOME KIND OF CRAZY CODE OF HONOR! YEAH--

--SHE'S MY PROTECTION!

GOOD MORNING! THE JOKER IS BACK IN THE HEADLINES! GOTHAM CITY WAS ROCKED OVERNIGHT BY TWO SENSATIONAL MURDERS, BOTH ALLEGEDLY THE HANDI-WORK OF THE ACE OF KNAVES! IN EACH CASE, POLICE AND THE BATMAN WERE WARNED IN ADVANCE, BUT--

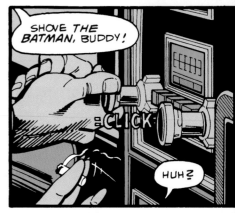

SHOVE THE BATMAN, BUDDY!

CLICK

HUH?

LET ME TELL YOU SOMETHING, YOUNG LADY! (HARUMPH!...) AS THE PRESIDENT OF THE GOTHAM CITY COUNCIL, I DARE SAY YOUR TOWN WOULD BE A LOT BETTER OFF WITHOUT THE BATMAN!

THAT ONE MAN IS THE CAUSE OF ALL THE CITY'S PROBLEMS!

NOW, JUST A MINUTE--!

YOU'RE NOT SUPPOSED TO BE SO LILY-WHITE YOURSELF--"BOSS"!

THE WAY I HEAR IT, YOU AND YOUR "COUNCIL" HAVE BEEN GRAFTING OFF GOTHAM FOR YEARS! YOU'VE GOT A WHOLE POLITICAL MACHINE TO KEEP YOU ELECTED BY HOOK OR BY CROOK--!

I DON'T HAVE TO STAND FOR THIS!

YOUNG LADY, I'M DUE SOME RESPECT! I'M THE PRESIDENT OF THE--

NOBODY WHO PUTS THE BATMAN DOWN IS DUE ANYTHING! I BET YOU'RE BEHIND THE CAMPAIGN TO HAVE HIM THROWN OUT OF TOWN!

THORNE, THAT ONE MAN HAS GIVEN HIS LIFE TO GOTHAM --THE CITY, THE PEOPLE--HE'S OUR AVENGING ANGEL!

THEY SAY NOBODY CARES ABOUT THE CITY ANYMORE, BUT HE DOES! HE --

7

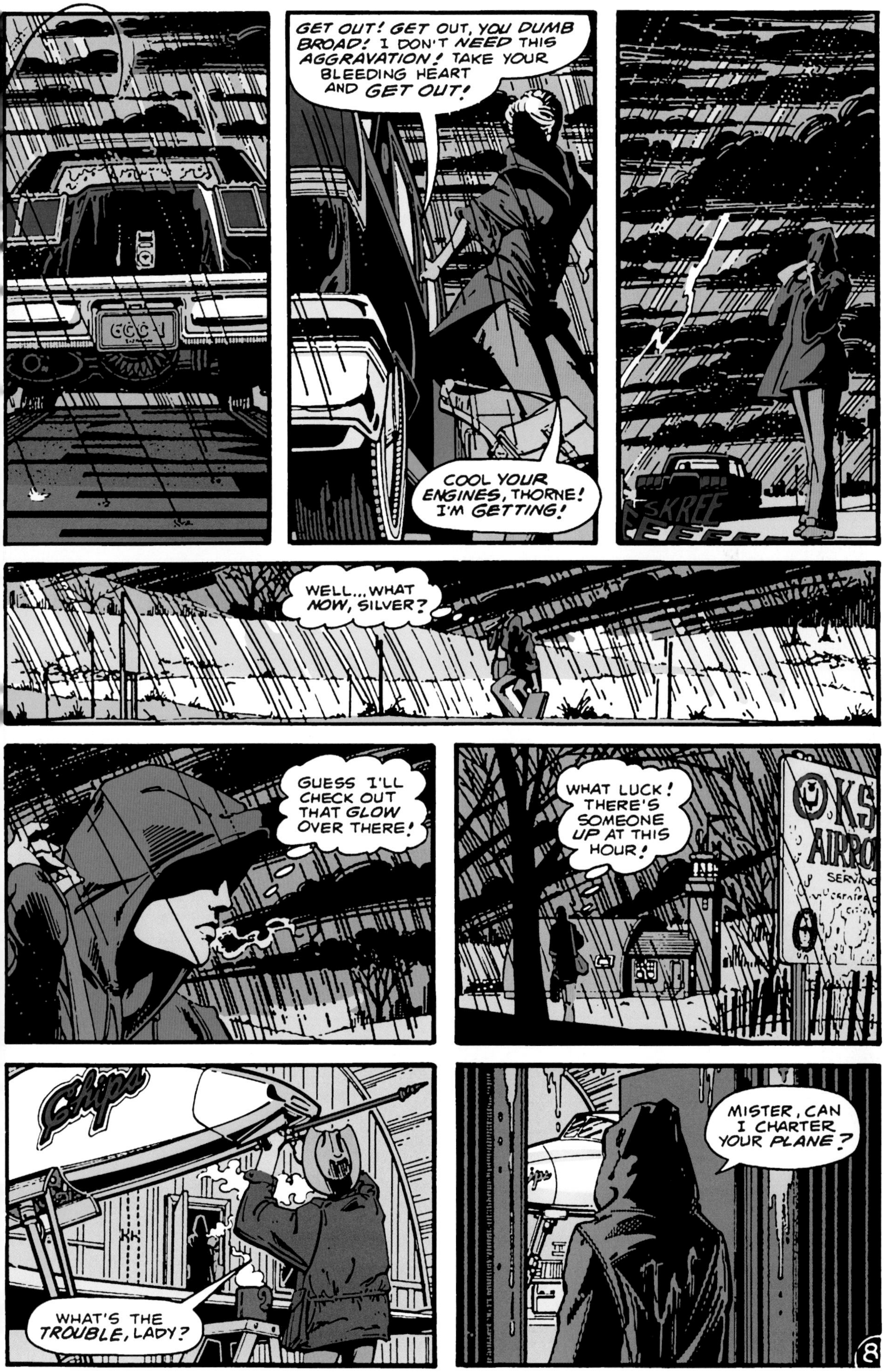

GCC-1
GET OUT! GET OUT, YOU DUMB BROAD! I DON'T NEED THIS AGGRAVATION! TAKE YOUR BLEEDING HEART AND GET OUT!
COOL YOUR ENGINES, THORNE! I'M GETTING!
SKREEE
WELL... WHAT NOW, SILVER?
GUESS I'LL CHECK OUT THAT GLOW OVER THERE!
WHAT LUCK! THERE'S SOMEONE UP AT THIS HOUR!
OKS
AIRPO
SERVING
Chips
WHAT'S THE TROUBLE, LADY?
MISTER, CAN I CHARTER YOUR PLANE?
8

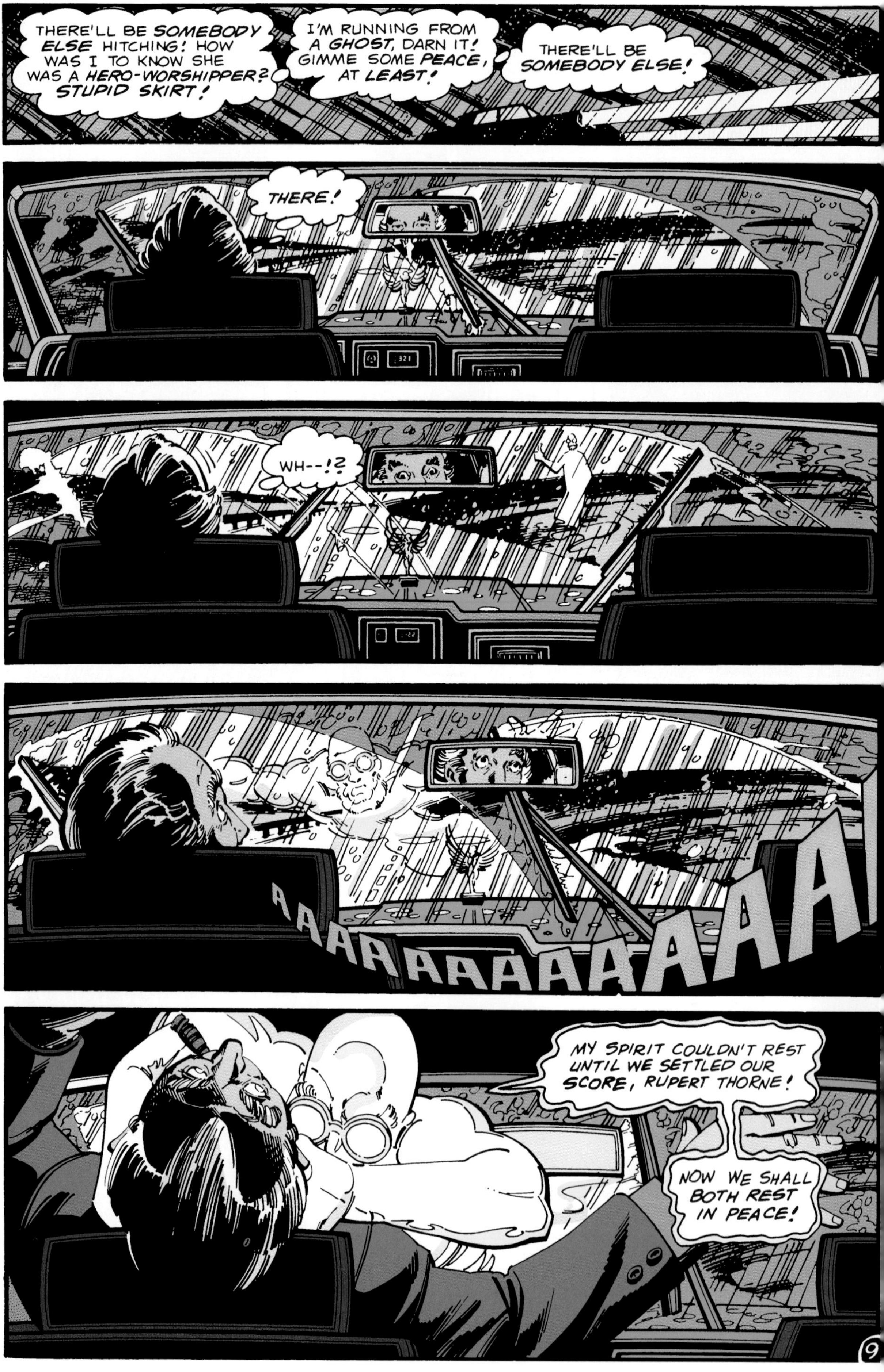
THERE'LL BE SOMEBODY ELSE HITCHING! HOW WAS I TO KNOW SHE WAS A HERO-WORSHIPPER? STUPID SKIRT!
I'M RUNNING FROM A GHOST, DARN IT! GIMME SOME PEACE, AT LEAST!
THERE'LL BE SOMEBODY ELSE!
THERE!
WH--!?
AAAAAAAAAAAAAAAA
MY SPIRIT COULDN'T REST UNTIL WE SETTLED OUR SCORE, RUPERT THORNE!
NOW WE SHALL BOTH REST IN PEACE!
9

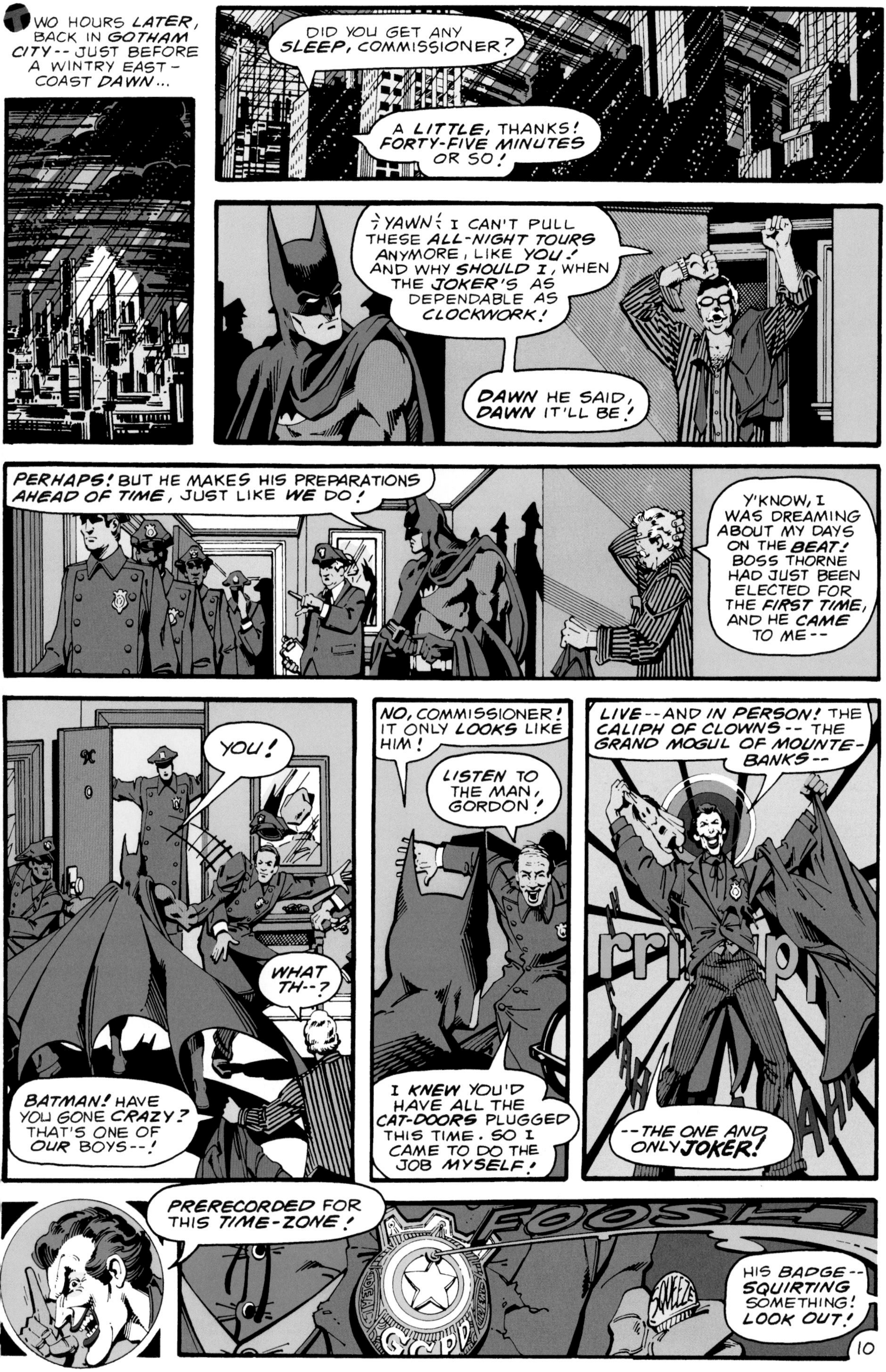
TWO HOURS LATER, BACK IN GOTHAM CITY -- JUST BEFORE A WINTRY EAST-COAST DAWN...
DID YOU GET ANY SLEEP, COMMISSIONER?
A LITTLE, THANKS! FORTY-FIVE MINUTES OR SO!
YAWN I CAN'T PULL THESE ALL-NIGHT TOURS ANYMORE, LIKE YOU! AND WHY SHOULD I, WHEN THE JOKER'S AS DEPENDABLE AS CLOCKWORK!
DAWN HE SAID, DAWN IT'LL BE!
PERHAPS! BUT HE MAKES HIS PREPARATIONS AHEAD OF TIME, JUST LIKE WE DO!
Y'KNOW, I WAS DREAMING ABOUT MY DAYS ON THE BEAT! BOSS THORNE HAD JUST BEEN ELECTED FOR THE FIRST TIME, AND HE CAME TO ME--
YOU!
WHAT TH--?
BATMAN! HAVE YOU GONE CRAZY? THAT'S ONE OF OUR BOYS--!
NO, COMMISSIONER! IT ONLY LOOKS LIKE HIM!
LISTEN TO THE MAN, GORDON!
I KNEW YOU'D HAVE ALL THE CAT-DOORS PLUGGED THIS TIME. SO I CAME TO DO THE JOB MYSELF!
LIVE--AND IN PERSON! THE CALIPH OF CLOWNS -- THE GRAND MOGUL OF MOUNTE-BANKS --
rrrip
--THE ONE AND ONLY JOKER!
PRERECORDED FOR THIS TIME-ZONE!
FOOSH
GCPD
HIS BADGE--SQUIRTING SOMETHING! LOOK OUT!
10

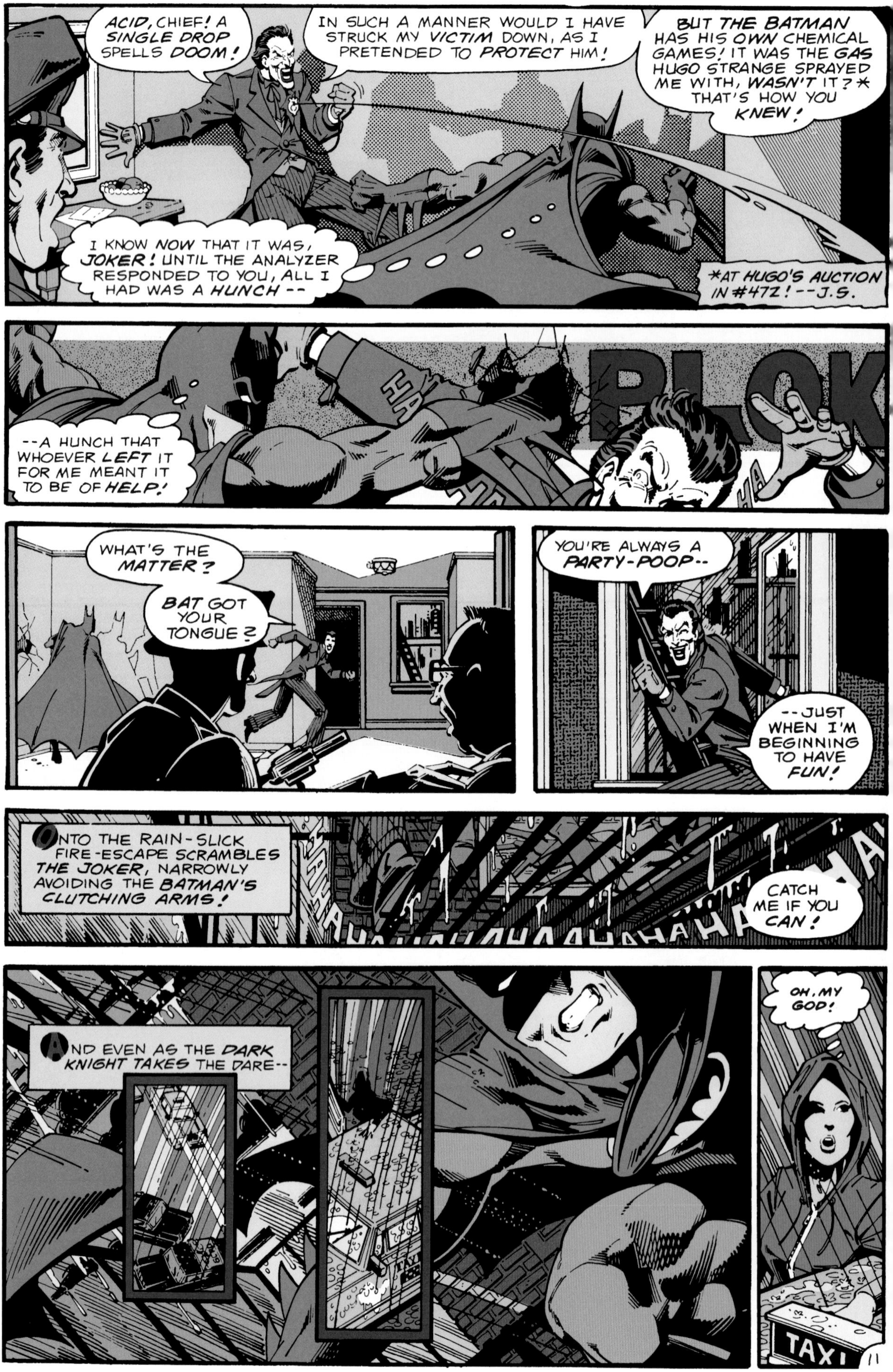

ACID, CHIEF! A SINGLE DROP SPELLS DOOM!
IN SUCH A MANNER WOULD I HAVE STRUCK MY VICTIM DOWN, AS I PRETENDED TO PROTECT HIM!
BUT THE BATMAN HAS HIS OWN CHEMICAL GAMES! IT WAS THE GAS HUGO STRANGE SPRAYED ME WITH, WASN'T IT?* THAT'S HOW YOU KNEW!
I KNOW NOW THAT IT WAS, JOKER! UNTIL THE ANALYZER RESPONDED TO YOU, ALL I HAD WAS A HUNCH --
*AT HUGO'S AUCTION IN #472! --J.S.
--A HUNCH THAT WHOEVER LEFT IT FOR ME MEANT IT TO BE OF HELP!
PLOK
WHAT'S THE MATTER?
BAT GOT YOUR TONGUE?
YOU'RE ALWAYS A PARTY-POOP--
--JUST WHEN I'M BEGINNING TO HAVE FUN!
ONTO THE RAIN-SLICK FIRE-ESCAPE SCRAMBLES THE JOKER, NARROWLY AVOIDING THE BATMAN'S CLUTCHING ARMS!
CATCH ME IF YOU CAN!
AND EVEN AS THE DARK KNIGHT TAKES THE DARE--
OH, MY GOD!
TAXI
11

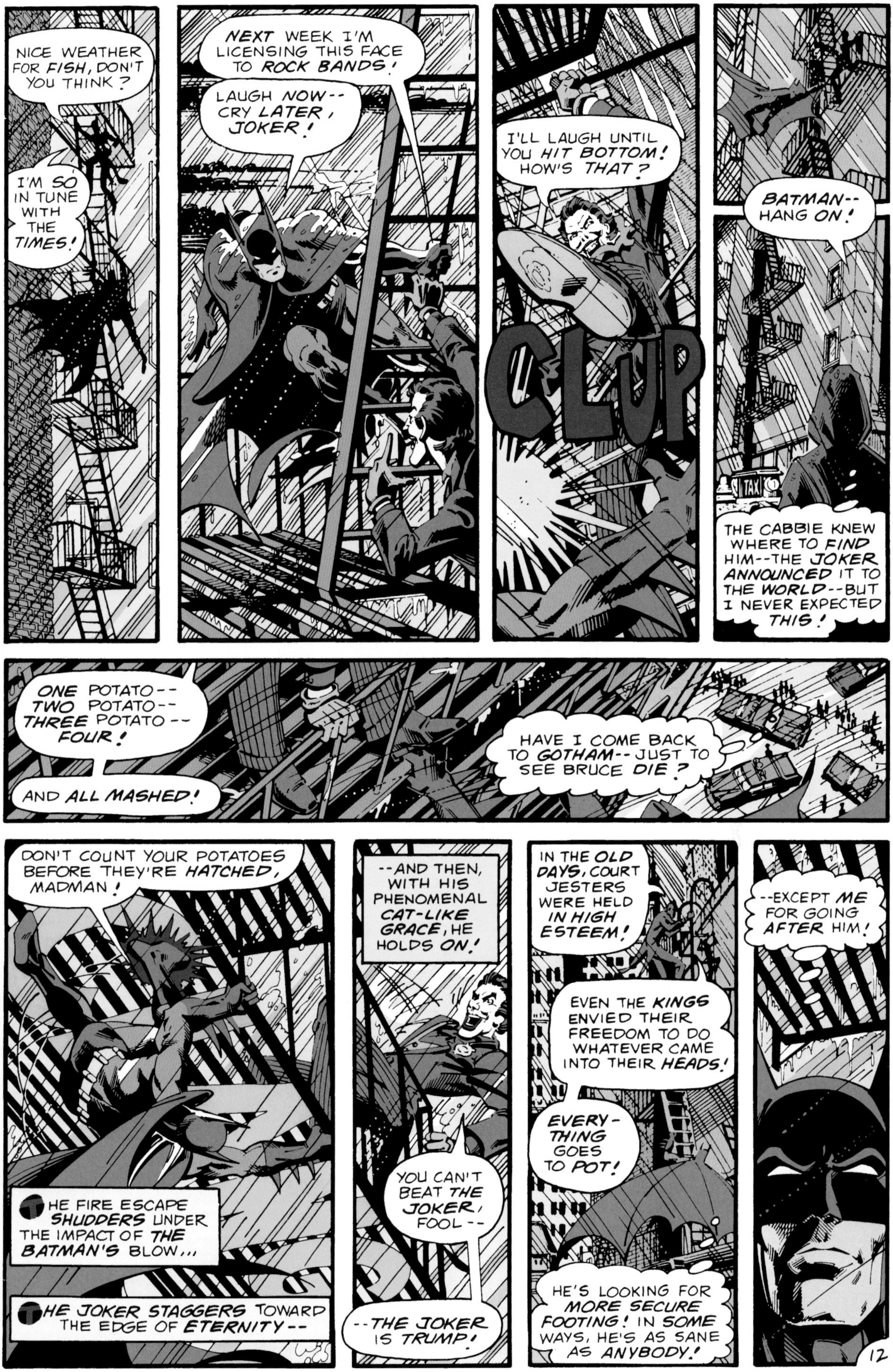
NICE WEATHER FOR FISH, DON'T YOU THINK?
I'M SO IN TUNE WITH THE TIMES!
NEXT WEEK I'M LICENSING THIS FACE TO ROCK BANDS!
LAUGH NOW-- CRY LATER, JOKER!
I'LL LAUGH UNTIL YOU HIT BOTTOM! HOW'S THAT?
CLUP
BATMAN-- HANG ON!
TAXI
THE CABBIE KNEW WHERE TO FIND HIM--THE JOKER ANNOUNCED IT TO THE WORLD--BUT I NEVER EXPECTED THIS!
ONE POTATO-- TWO POTATO-- THREE POTATO-- FOUR!
AND ALL MASHED!
HAVE I COME BACK TO GOTHAM-- JUST TO SEE BRUCE DIE?
DON'T COUNT YOUR POTATOES BEFORE THEY'RE HATCHED, MADMAN!
THE FIRE ESCAPE SHUDDERS UNDER THE IMPACT OF THE BATMAN'S BLOW...
THE JOKER STAGGERS TOWARD THE EDGE OF ETERNITY--
--AND THEN, WITH HIS PHENOMENAL CAT-LIKE GRACE, HE HOLDS ON!
YOU CAN'T BEAT THE JOKER, FOOL--
--THE JOKER IS TRUMP!
IN THE OLD DAYS, COURT JESTERS WERE HELD IN HIGH ESTEEM!
EVEN THE KINGS ENVIED THEIR FREEDOM TO DO WHATEVER CAME INTO THEIR HEADS!
EVERY-THING GOES TO POT!
HE'S LOOKING FOR MORE SECURE FOOTING! IN SOME WAYS, HE'S AS SANE AS ANYBODY!
--EXCEPT ME FOR GOING AFTER HIM!
12

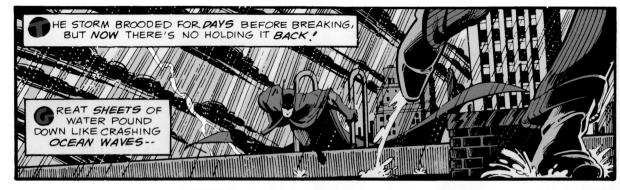

THE STORM BROODED FOR *DAYS* BEFORE BREAKING, BUT *NOW* THERE'S NO HOLDING IT *BACK!*

GREAT SHEETS OF WATER POUND DOWN LIKE CRASHING *OCEAN WAVES--*

-- *SMEARING* THE SIGHT OF *SILVER ST. CLOUD* AS SHE FIGHTS TO PEER UPWARD INTO THE STORM'S *FULL FURY--*

SMEARING HER SIGHT -- BUT NEVER *COMPLETELY* OBLITERATING WHAT SHE SEES--

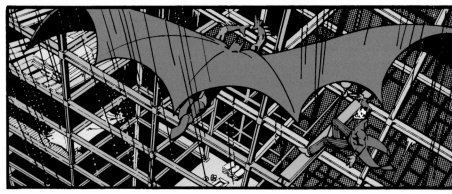

JOKER! YOU *LUNATIC* -- THERE'S NO PLACE YOU CAN *GO* FROM HERE!

I CAN GO OVER YOUR *DEAD BODY,* BATMAN!

LOVELY WEATHER FOR *FISH,* ISN'T IT? OR DID I *SAY* THAT?

I WANT YOU TO HEAR ALL MY *BEST LINES* BEFORE YOU DO YOUR DIVE INTO THE *DAMP SPONGE!*

HIS *BADGE!* THE ACID--

13

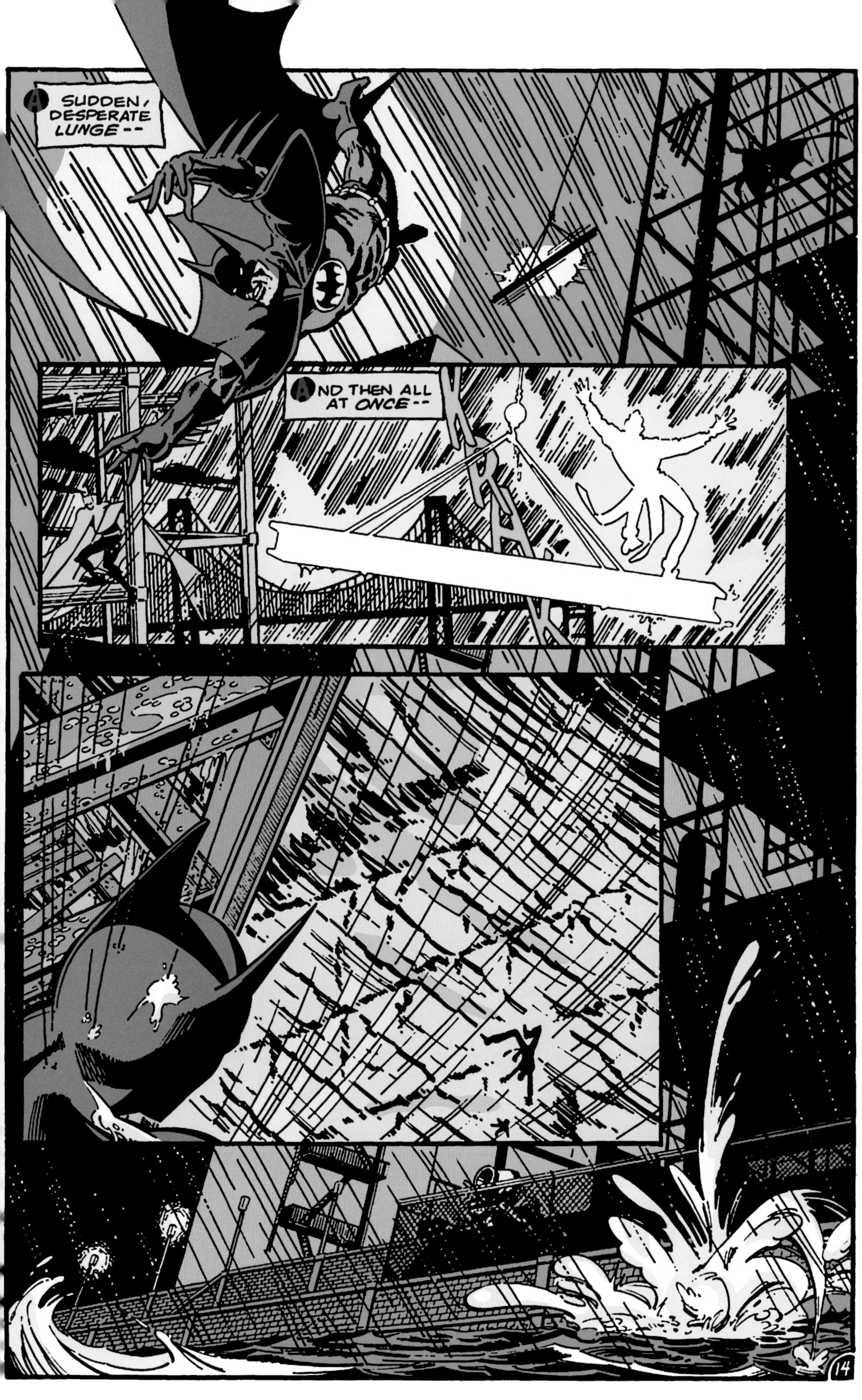
A SUDDEN, DESPERATE LUNGE --
AND THEN ALL AT ONCE --
14

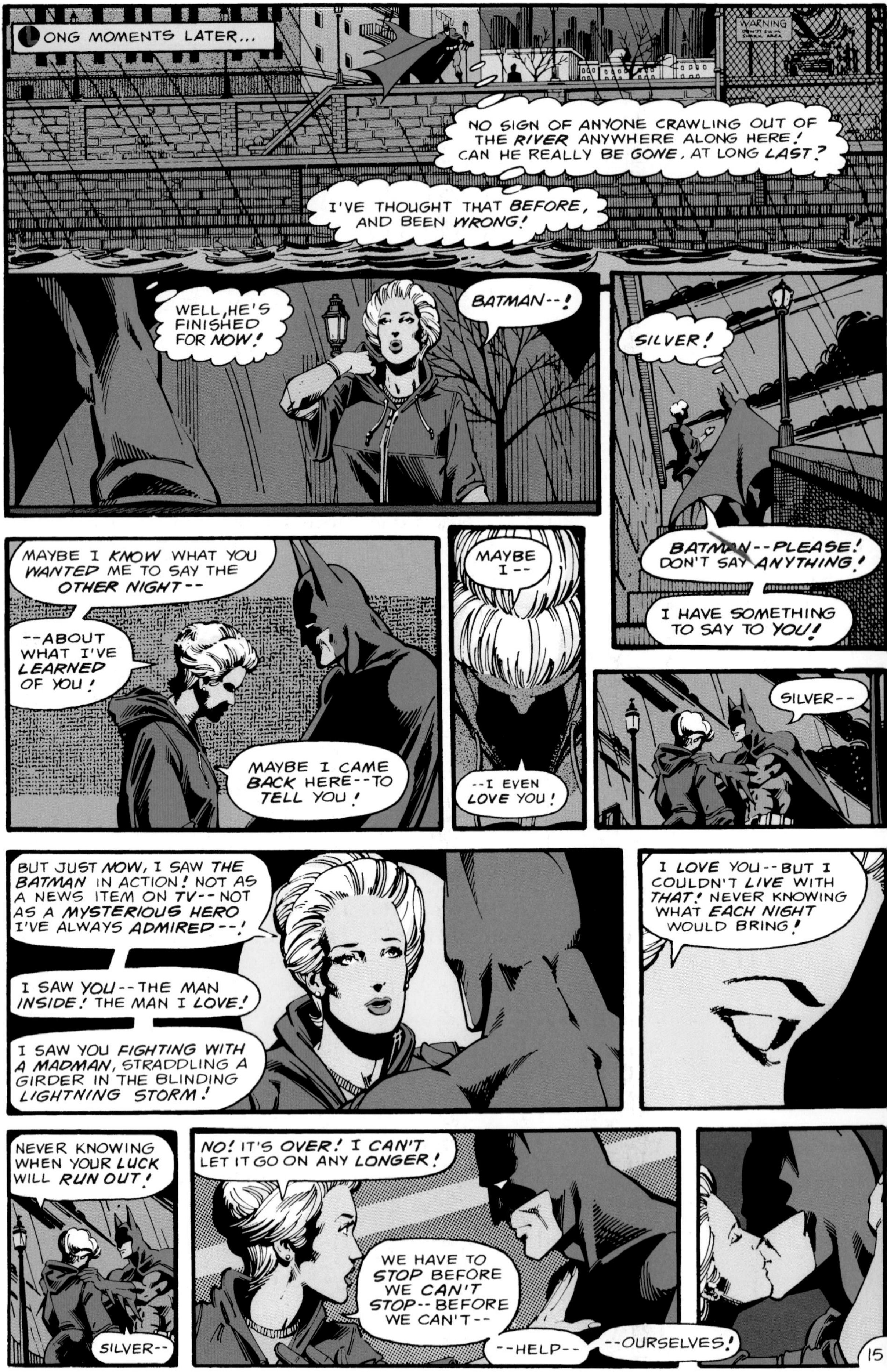
LONG MOMENTS LATER...
NO SIGN OF ANYONE CRAWLING OUT OF THE RIVER ANYWHERE ALONG HERE! CAN HE REALLY BE GONE, AT LONG LAST?
I'VE THOUGHT THAT BEFORE, AND BEEN WRONG!
WELL, HE'S FINISHED FOR NOW!
BATMAN--!
SILVER!
BATMAN--PLEASE! DON'T SAY ANYTHING!
I HAVE SOMETHING TO SAY TO YOU!
MAYBE I KNOW WHAT YOU WANTED ME TO SAY THE OTHER NIGHT--
--ABOUT WHAT I'VE LEARNED OF YOU!
MAYBE I CAME BACK HERE--TO TELL YOU!
MAYBE I--
--I EVEN LOVE YOU!
SILVER--
BUT JUST NOW, I SAW THE BATMAN IN ACTION! NOT AS A NEWS ITEM ON TV--NOT AS A MYSTERIOUS HERO I'VE ALWAYS ADMIRED--!
I SAW YOU--THE MAN INSIDE! THE MAN I LOVE!
I SAW YOU FIGHTING WITH A MADMAN, STRADDLING A GIRDER IN THE BLINDING LIGHTNING STORM!
I LOVE YOU--BUT I COULDN'T LIVE WITH THAT! NEVER KNOWING WHAT EACH NIGHT WOULD BRING!
NEVER KNOWING WHEN YOUR LUCK WILL RUN OUT!
SILVER--
NO! IT'S OVER! I CAN'T LET IT GO ON ANY LONGER!
WE HAVE TO STOP BEFORE WE CAN'T STOP--BEFORE WE CAN'T--
--HELP--
--OURSELVES!
15

DON'T CALL ME!

STAY AWAY--

--PLEASE--

--BATMAN!

BATMAN!

BATMAN!

BATMAN! GREAT NEWS!

THE OHIO STATE PATROL HAS PICKED UP *BOSS THORNE!* THEY SAY SOMETHING'S *SCARED* HIM OUT OF HIS WITS!

HE'S *BABBLING CONTINUOUSLY--* EVERY CRIME HE'S EVER *COMMITTED,* SINCE BACK IN *PROHIBITION* DAYS!

IT'S LIKE HE WANTS *ABSOLUTION!* HE'S TELLING *EVERYTHING--*

--INCLUDING HOW HE AND THE COUNCIL TRIED TO GET YOU!

YOU'RE CLEAR!

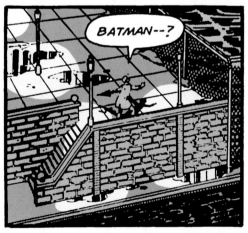
BATMAN--?

16

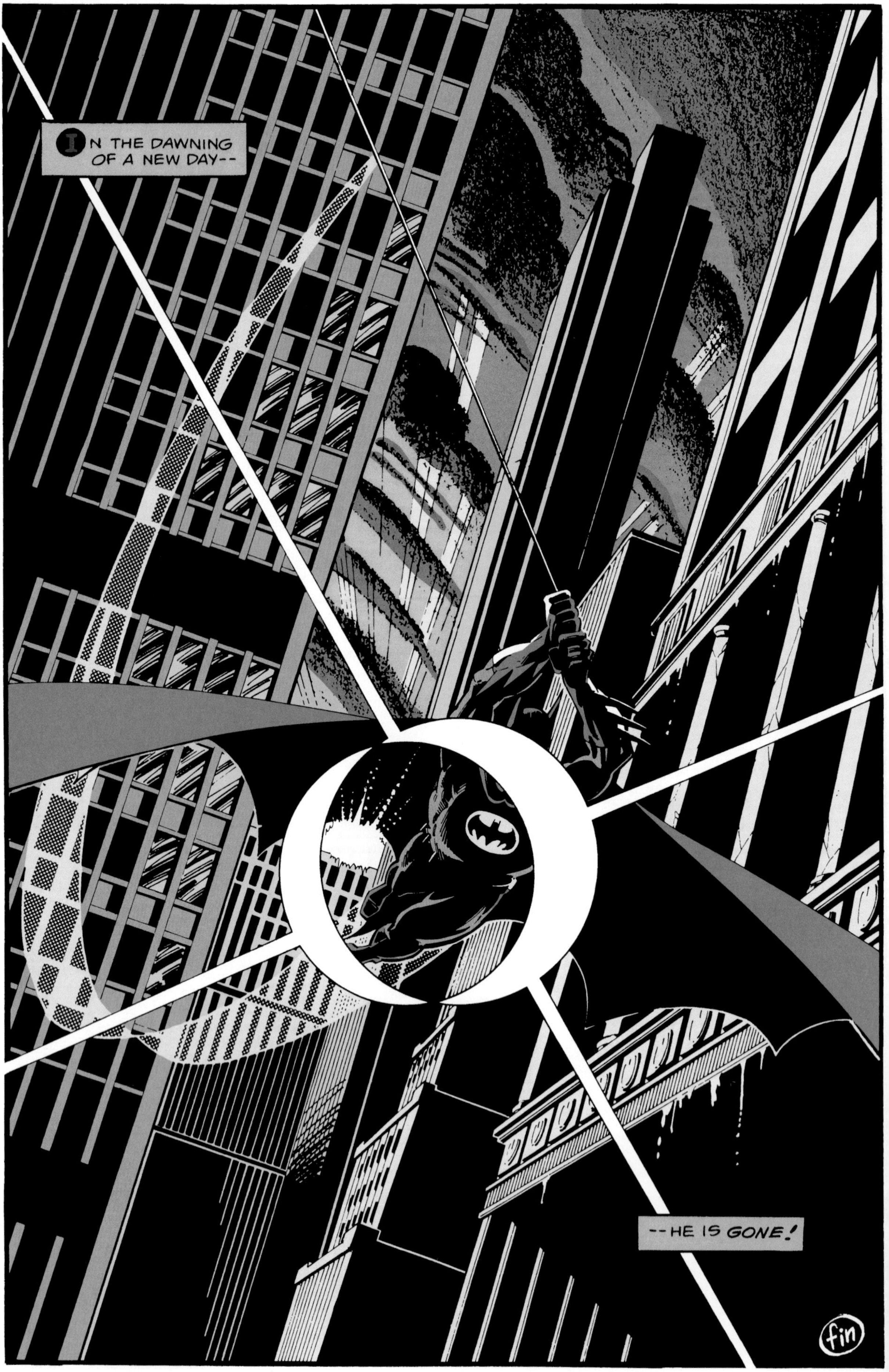
IN THE DAWNING OF A NEW DAY--
--HE IS GONE!
fin

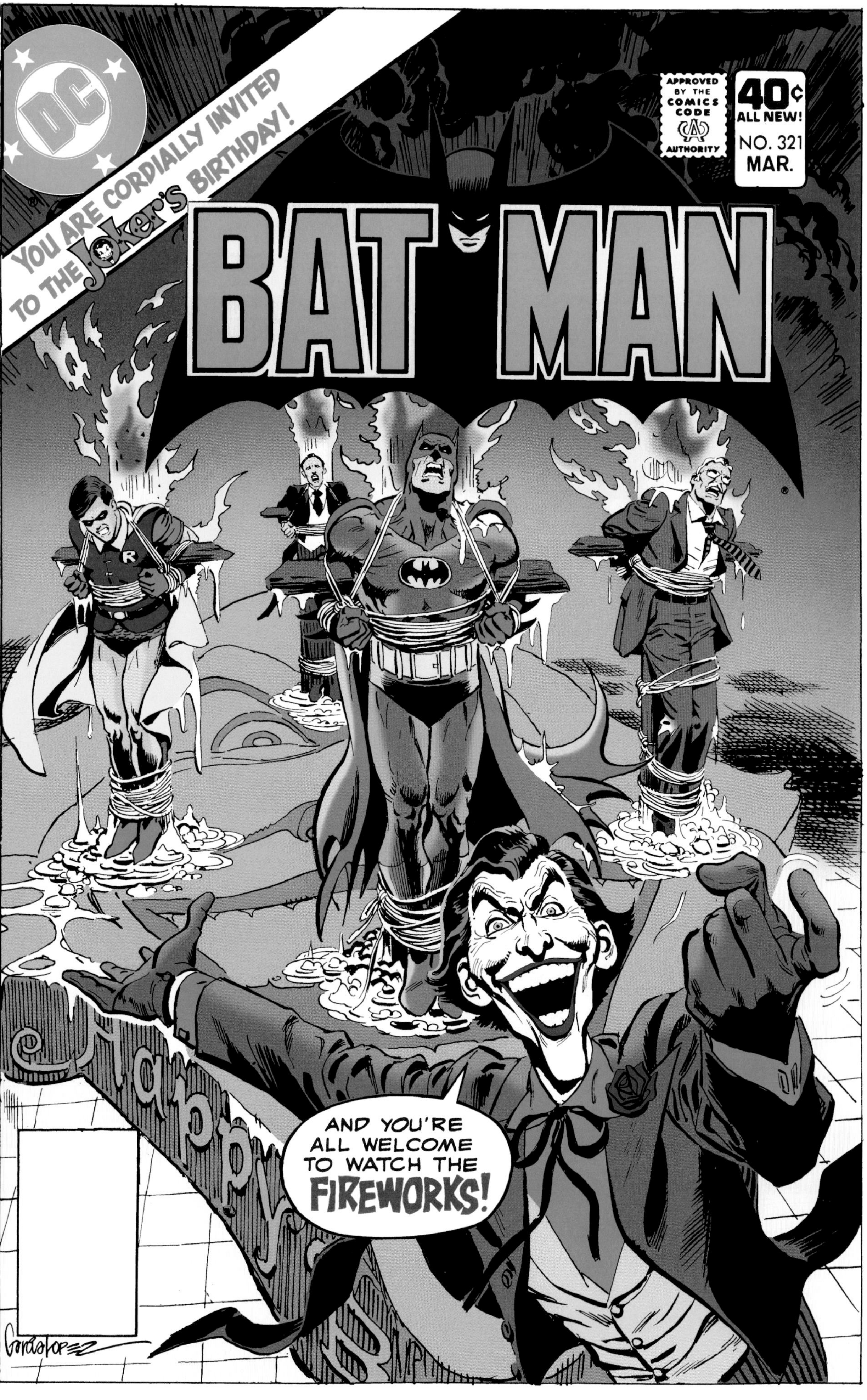
YOU ARE CORDIALLY INVITED TO THE JOKER'S BIRTHDAY!
APPROVED BY THE COMICS CODE AUTHORITY
40¢ ALL NEW!
NO. 321 MAR.
BATMAN
AND YOU'RE ALL WELCOME TO WATCH THE FIREWORKS!
Happy

SINCE 1899, *GOTHAM POLICE HEADQUARTERS* HAS STOOD AT THE JUNCTION OF THE AREA CALLED *FIVE POINTS*, ON THE LOWER EAST SIDE OF THE CITY...

IN THE PAST 17 YEARS, *COMMISSIONER JAMES W. GORDON* HAS COME TO KNOW THE MARBLED CORRIDORS OF THIS PROUD OLD BUILDING *WELL*; IT HAS BECOME A *SECOND HOME* TO HIM--

--BUT *TONIGHT*, AS THE LEGENDARY *BAT-SIGNAL* SLASHES ACROSS A STORM-SWEPT SKY, IT MAY ALSO BECOME HIS *TOMB!*

BAT MAN

CREATED BY BOB KANE

COMMISSIONER *GORDON!* I THINK THIS IS FOR *YOU*, SIR!

DREADFUL BIRTHDAY, DEAR JOKER....!

LEN **WEIN** WRITER	WALT. **SIMONSON** & DICK **GIORDANO** ARTISTS	
GLYNIS **WEIN** COLORIST	BEN **ODA** LETTERER	PAUL **LEVITZ** EDITOR

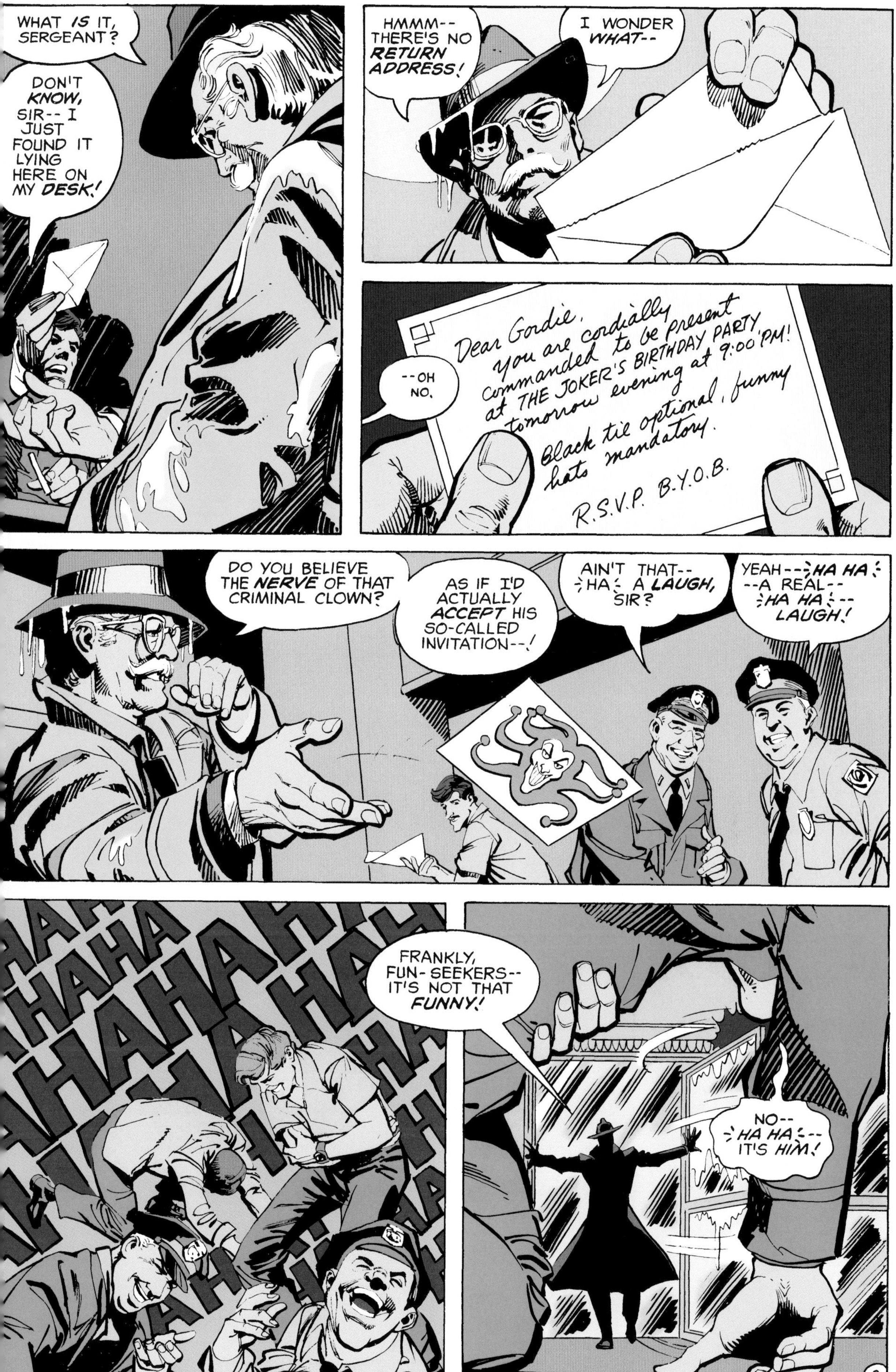

WHAT IS IT, SERGEANT?
DON'T KNOW, SIR-- I JUST FOUND IT LYING HERE ON MY DESK!
HMMM-- THERE'S NO RETURN ADDRESS!
I WONDER WHAT--
Dear Gordie, you are cordially commanded to be present at THE JOKER'S BIRTHDAY PARTY tomorrow evening at 9:00 PM! Black tie optional, funny hats mandatory. R.S.V.P. B.Y.O.B.
--OH NO.
DO YOU BELIEVE THE NERVE OF THAT CRIMINAL CLOWN?
AS IF I'D ACTUALLY ACCEPT HIS SO-CALLED INVITATION--!
AIN'T THAT-- HA A LAUGH, SIR?
YEAH-- HA HA --A REAL-- HA HA -- LAUGH!
HAHAHAHAHA
FRANKLY, FUN-SEEKERS-- IT'S NOT THAT FUNNY!
NO-- HA HA -- IT'S HIM!
2

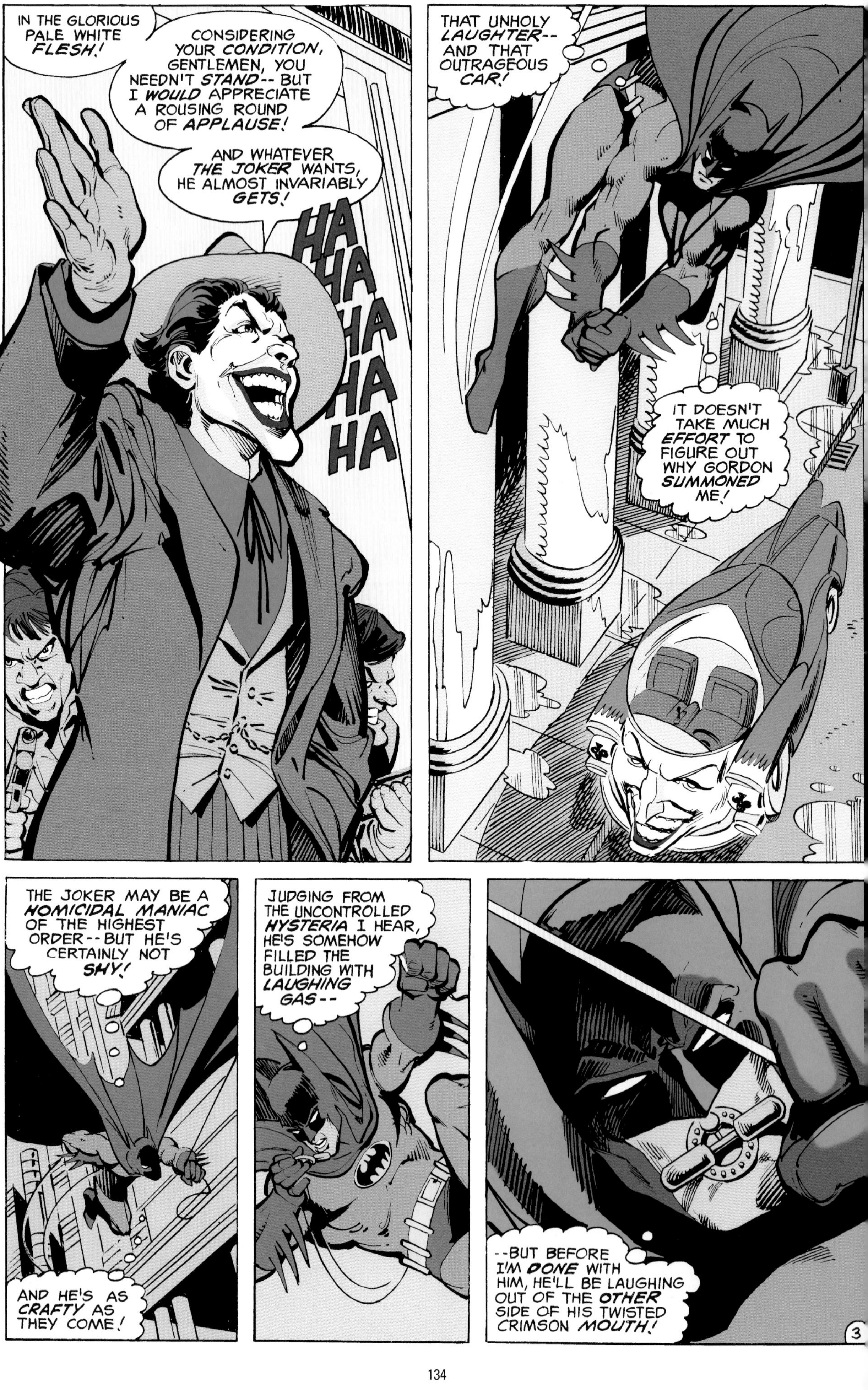
IN THE GLORIOUS PALE WHITE FLESH!
CONSIDERING YOUR CONDITION, GENTLEMEN, YOU NEEDN'T STAND-- BUT I WOULD APPRECIATE A ROUSING ROUND OF APPLAUSE!
AND WHATEVER THE JOKER WANTS, HE ALMOST INVARIABLY GETS!
HA HA HA HA HA HA
THAT UNHOLY LAUGHTER-- AND THAT OUTRAGEOUS CAR!
IT DOESN'T TAKE MUCH EFFORT TO FIGURE OUT WHY GORDON SUMMONED ME!
THE JOKER MAY BE A HOMICIDAL MANIAC OF THE HIGHEST ORDER--BUT HE'S CERTAINLY NOT SHY!
AND HE'S AS CRAFTY AS THEY COME!
JUDGING FROM THE UNCONTROLLED HYSTERIA I HEAR, HE'S SOMEHOW FILLED THE BUILDING WITH LAUGHING GAS--
--BUT BEFORE I'M DONE WITH HIM, HE'LL BE LAUGHING OUT OF THE OTHER SIDE OF HIS TWISTED CRIMSON MOUTH!
3

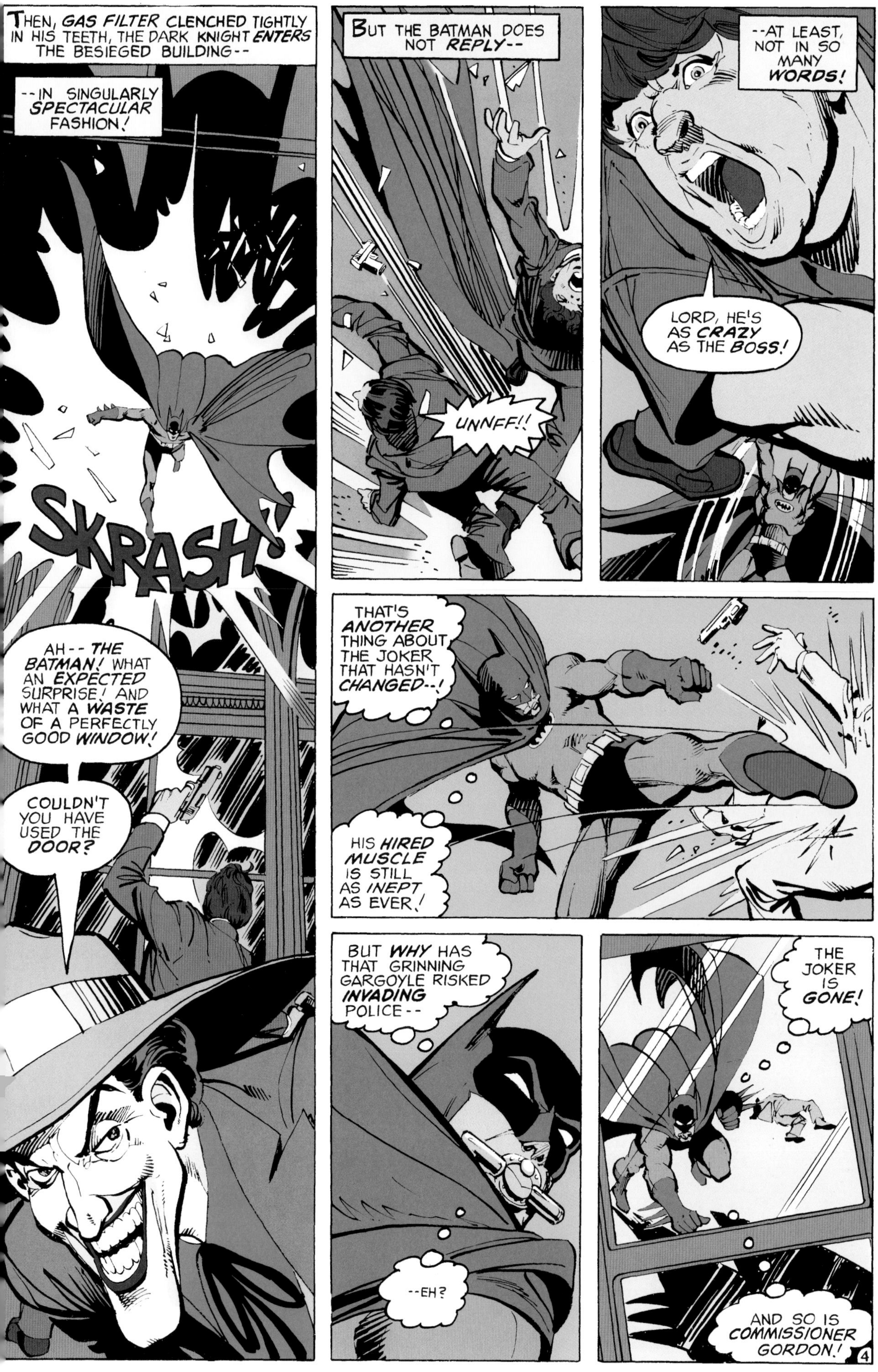

THEN, GAS FILTER CLENCHED TIGHTLY IN HIS TEETH, THE DARK KNIGHT ENTERS THE BESIEGED BUILDING--
--IN SINGULARLY SPECTACULAR FASHION!
SKRASH!
AH--THE BATMAN! WHAT AN EXPECTED SURPRISE! AND WHAT A WASTE OF A PERFECTLY GOOD WINDOW!
COULDN'T YOU HAVE USED THE DOOR?
BUT THE BATMAN DOES NOT REPLY--
UNNFF!!
--AT LEAST, NOT IN SO MANY WORDS!
LORD, HE'S AS CRAZY AS THE BOSS!
THAT'S ANOTHER THING ABOUT THE JOKER THAT HASN'T CHANGED--!
HIS HIRED MUSCLE IS STILL AS INEPT AS EVER!
BUT WHY HAS THAT GRINNING GARGOYLE RISKED INVADING POLICE--
--EH?
THE JOKER IS GONE!
AND SO IS COMMISSIONER GORDON!
4

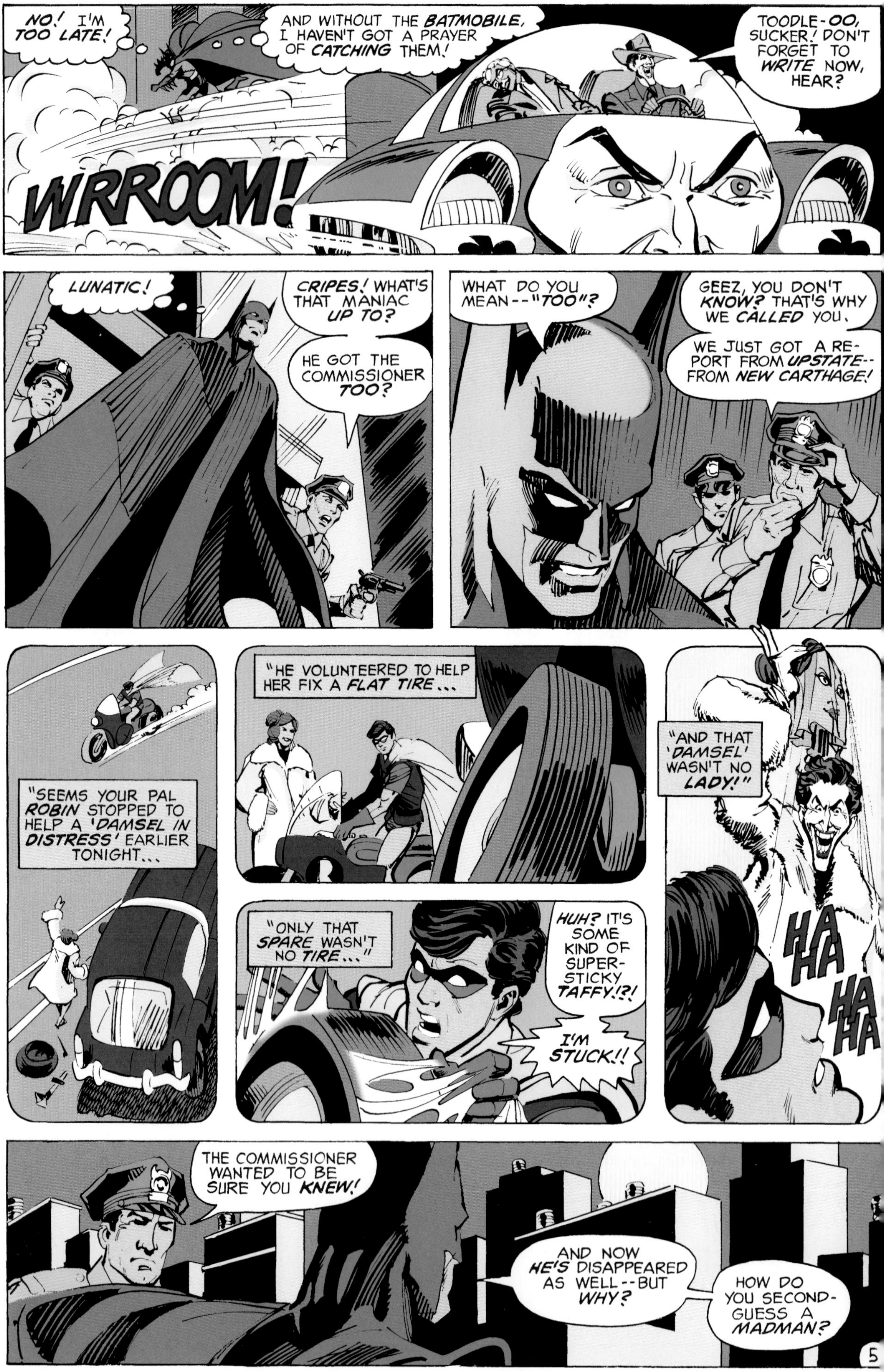
NO! I'M TOO LATE!
AND WITHOUT THE BATMOBILE, I HAVEN'T GOT A PRAYER OF CATCHING THEM!
TOODLE-OO, SUCKER! DON'T FORGET TO WRITE NOW, HEAR?
WRROOM!
LUNATIC!
CRIPES! WHAT'S THAT MANIAC UP TO?
HE GOT THE COMMISSIONER TOO?
WHAT DO YOU MEAN--"TOO"?
GEEZ, YOU DON'T KNOW? THAT'S WHY WE CALLED YOU.
WE JUST GOT A RE-PORT FROM UPSTATE--FROM NEW CARTHAGE!
"SEEMS YOUR PAL ROBIN STOPPED TO HELP A 'DAMSEL IN DISTRESS' EARLIER TONIGHT...
"HE VOLUNTEERED TO HELP HER FIX A FLAT TIRE...
"ONLY THAT SPARE WASN'T NO TIRE..."
HUH? IT'S SOME KIND OF SUPER-STICKY TAFFY!?!
I'M STUCK!!
"AND THAT 'DAMSEL' WASN'T NO LADY!"
HA HA HA HA
THE COMMISSIONER WANTED TO BE SURE YOU KNEW!
AND NOW HE'S DISAPPEARED AS WELL--BUT WHY?
HOW DO YOU SECOND-GUESS A MADMAN?
5

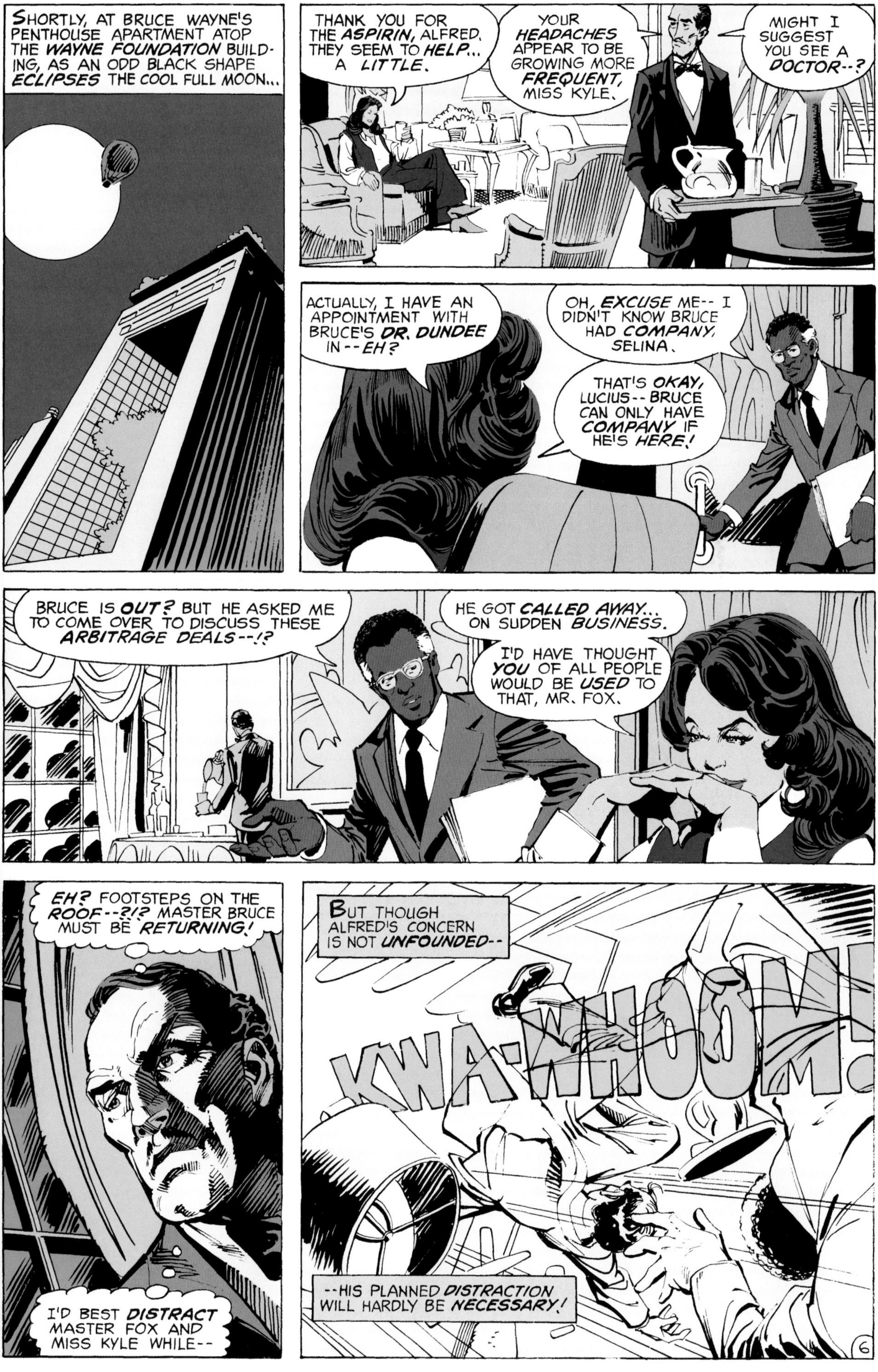
SHORTLY, AT BRUCE WAYNE'S PENTHOUSE APARTMENT ATOP THE WAYNE FOUNDATION BUILDING, AS AN ODD BLACK SHAPE ECLIPSES THE COOL FULL MOON...
THANK YOU FOR THE ASPIRIN, ALFRED. THEY SEEM TO HELP... A LITTLE.
YOUR HEADACHES APPEAR TO BE GROWING MORE FREQUENT, MISS KYLE.
MIGHT I SUGGEST YOU SEE A DOCTOR--?
ACTUALLY, I HAVE AN APPOINTMENT WITH BRUCE'S DR. DUNDEE IN--EH?
OH, EXCUSE ME-- I DIDN'T KNOW BRUCE HAD COMPANY, SELINA.
THAT'S OKAY, LUCIUS--BRUCE CAN ONLY HAVE COMPANY IF HE'S HERE!
BRUCE IS OUT? BUT HE ASKED ME TO COME OVER TO DISCUSS THESE ARBITRAGE DEALS--!?
HE GOT CALLED AWAY... ON SUDDEN BUSINESS.
I'D HAVE THOUGHT YOU OF ALL PEOPLE WOULD BE USED TO THAT, MR. FOX.
EH? FOOTSTEPS ON THE ROOF--?!? MASTER BRUCE MUST BE RETURNING!
I'D BEST DISTRACT MASTER FOX AND MISS KYLE WHILE--
BUT THOUGH ALFRED'S CONCERN IS NOT UNFOUNDED--
KWA-WHOOM!
--HIS PLANNED DISTRACTION WILL HARDLY BE NECESSARY!
6

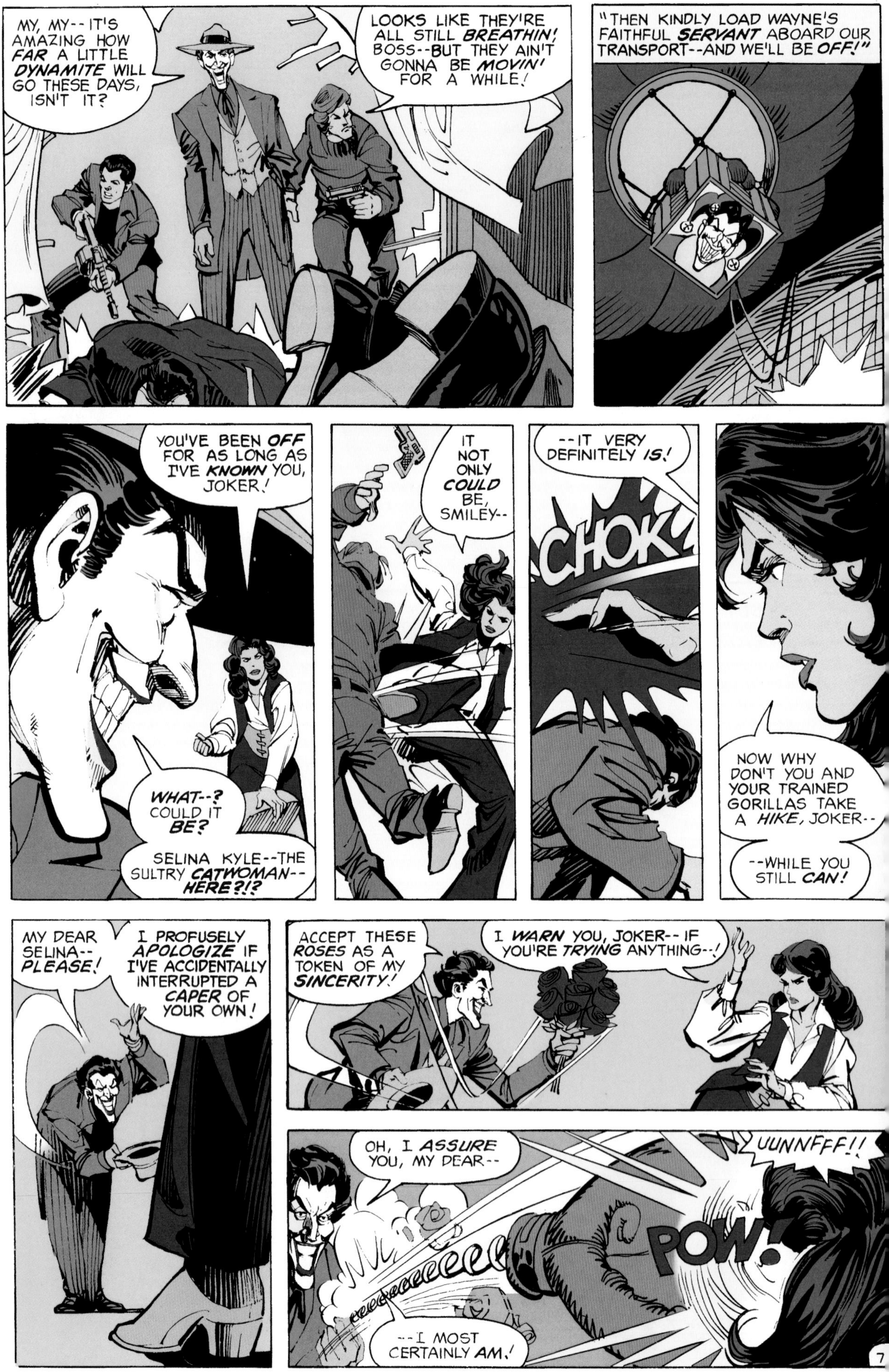
MY, MY--IT'S AMAZING HOW FAR A LITTLE DYNAMITE WILL GO THESE DAYS, ISN'T IT?
LOOKS LIKE THEY'RE ALL STILL BREATHIN', BOSS--BUT THEY AIN'T GONNA BE MOVIN' FOR A WHILE!
"THEN KINDLY LOAD WAYNE'S FAITHFUL SERVANT ABOARD OUR TRANSPORT--AND WE'LL BE OFF!"
YOU'VE BEEN OFF FOR AS LONG AS I'VE KNOWN YOU, JOKER!
WHAT--? COULD IT BE?
SELINA KYLE--THE SULTRY CATWOMAN--HERE?!?
IT NOT ONLY COULD BE, SMILEY--
--IT VERY DEFINITELY IS!
CHOK
NOW WHY DON'T YOU AND YOUR TRAINED GORILLAS TAKE A HIKE, JOKER--
--WHILE YOU STILL CAN!
MY DEAR SELINA--PLEASE!
I PROFUSELY APOLOGIZE IF I'VE ACCIDENTALLY INTERRUPTED A CAPER OF YOUR OWN!
ACCEPT THESE ROSES AS A TOKEN OF MY SINCERITY!
I WARN YOU, JOKER--IF YOU'RE TRYING ANYTHING--!
OH, I ASSURE YOU, MY DEAR--
UUNNFFF!!
POW!
--I MOST CERTAINLY AM!
7

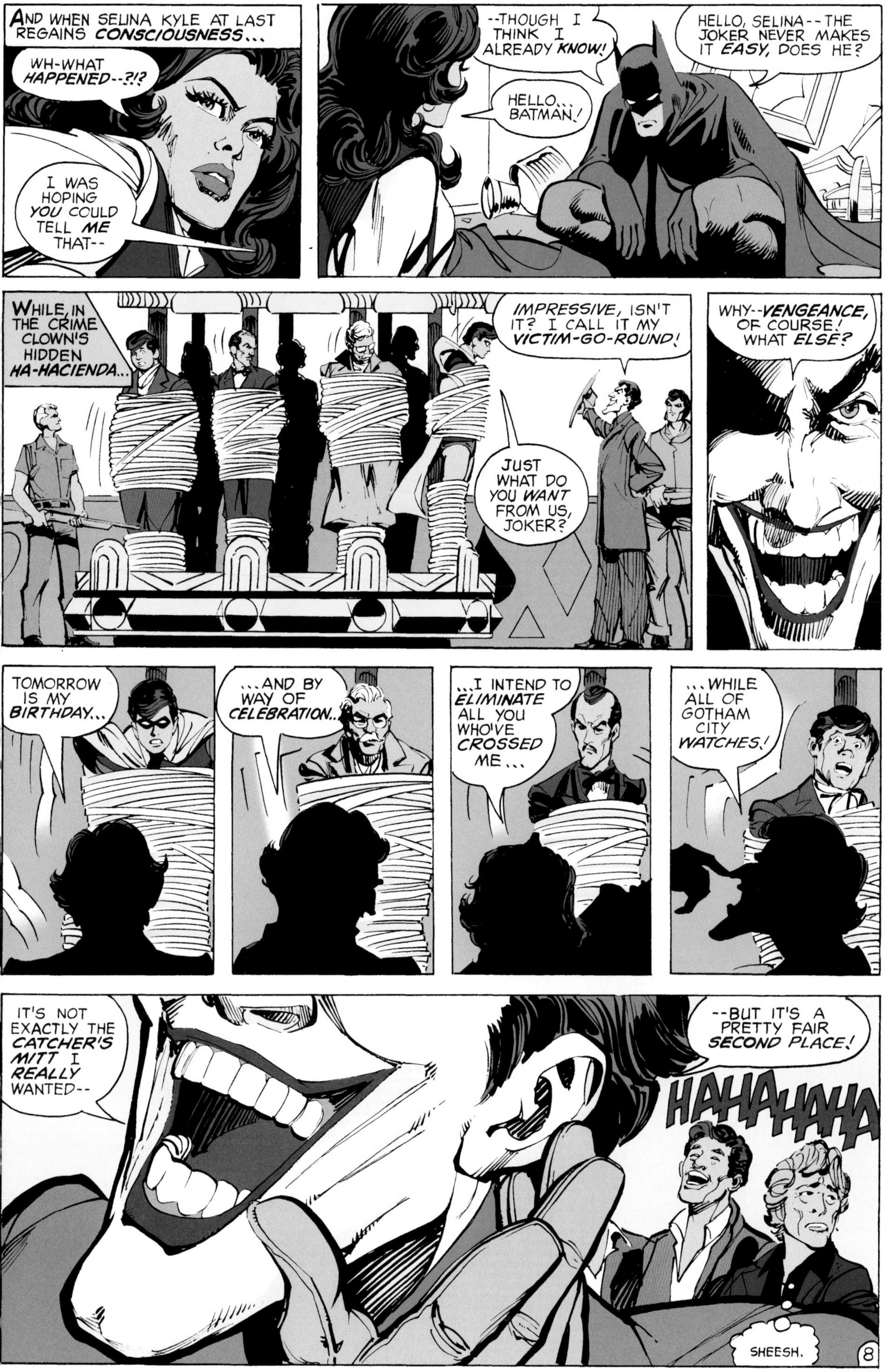
AND WHEN SELINA KYLE AT LAST REGAINS CONSCIOUSNESS...
WH-WHAT HAPPENED--?!?
I WAS HOPING YOU COULD TELL ME THAT--
--THOUGH I THINK I ALREADY KNOW!
HELLO... BATMAN!
HELLO, SELINA--THE JOKER NEVER MAKES IT EASY, DOES HE?
WHILE, IN THE CRIME CLOWN'S HIDDEN HA-HACIENDA...
IMPRESSIVE, ISN'T IT? I CALL IT MY VICTIM-GO-ROUND!
JUST WHAT DO YOU WANT FROM US, JOKER?
WHY--VENGEANCE, OF COURSE! WHAT ELSE?
TOMORROW IS MY BIRTHDAY...
...AND BY WAY OF CELEBRATION...
...I INTEND TO ELIMINATE ALL YOU WHO'VE CROSSED ME...
...WHILE ALL OF GOTHAM CITY WATCHES!
IT'S NOT EXACTLY THE CATCHER'S MITT I REALLY WANTED--
--BUT IT'S A PRETTY FAIR SECOND PLACE!
HAHAHAHA
SHEESH.
8

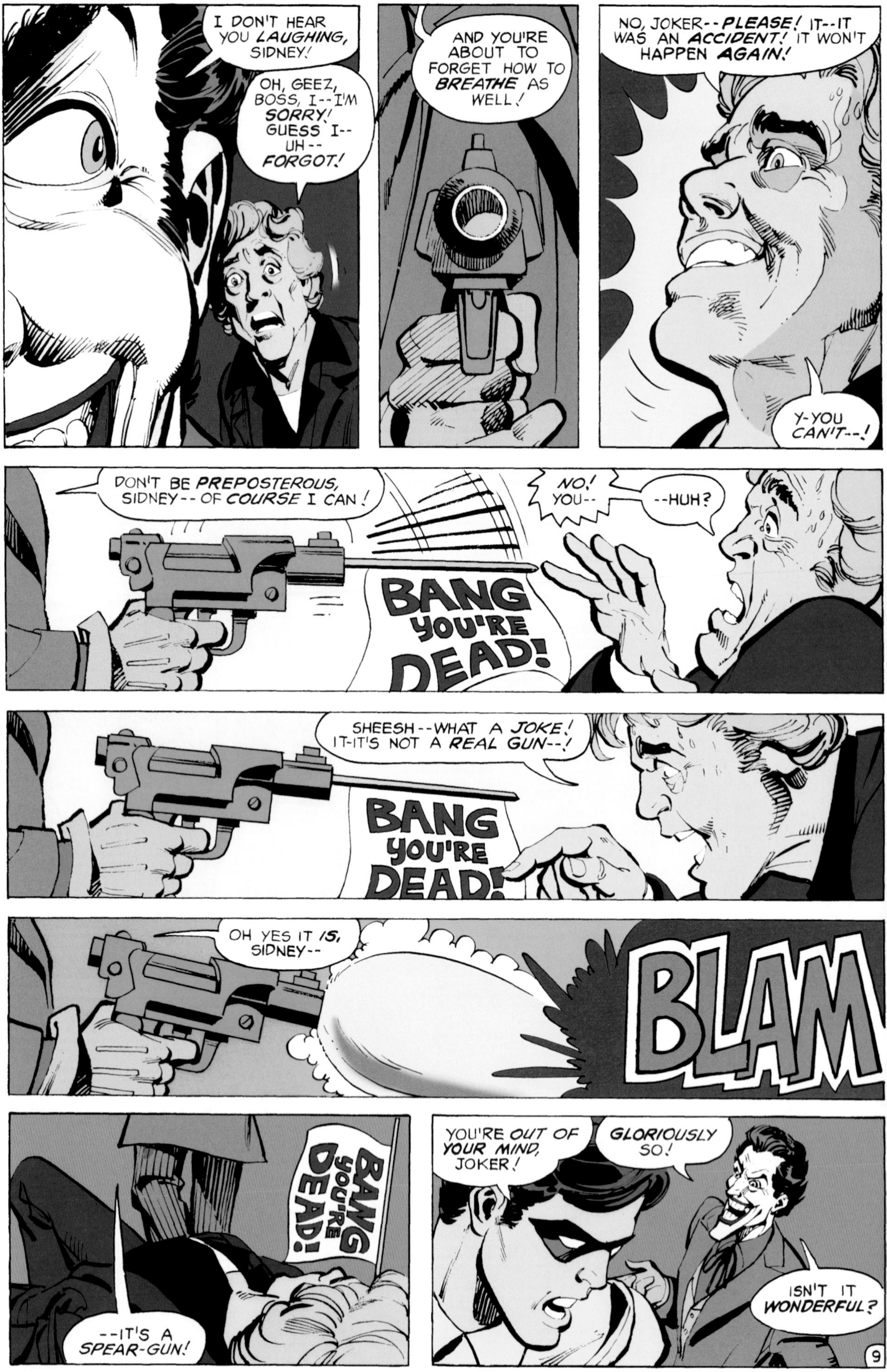
I DON'T HEAR YOU LAUGHING, SIDNEY!
OH, GEEZ, BOSS, I--I'M SORRY! GUESS I--UH--FORGOT!
AND YOU'RE ABOUT TO FORGET HOW TO BREATHE AS WELL!
NO, JOKER--PLEASE! IT--IT WAS AN ACCIDENT! IT WON'T HAPPEN AGAIN!
Y-YOU CAN'T--!
DON'T BE PREPOSTEROUS, SIDNEY--OF COURSE I CAN!
NO! YOU--
--HUH?
BANG YOU'RE DEAD!
SHEESH--WHAT A JOKE! IT-IT'S NOT A REAL GUN--!
BANG YOU'RE DEAD!
OH YES IT IS, SIDNEY--
BLAM
BANG YOU'RE DEAD!
--IT'S A SPEAR-GUN!
YOU'RE OUT OF YOUR MIND, JOKER!
GLORIOUSLY SO!
ISN'T IT WONDERFUL?
9

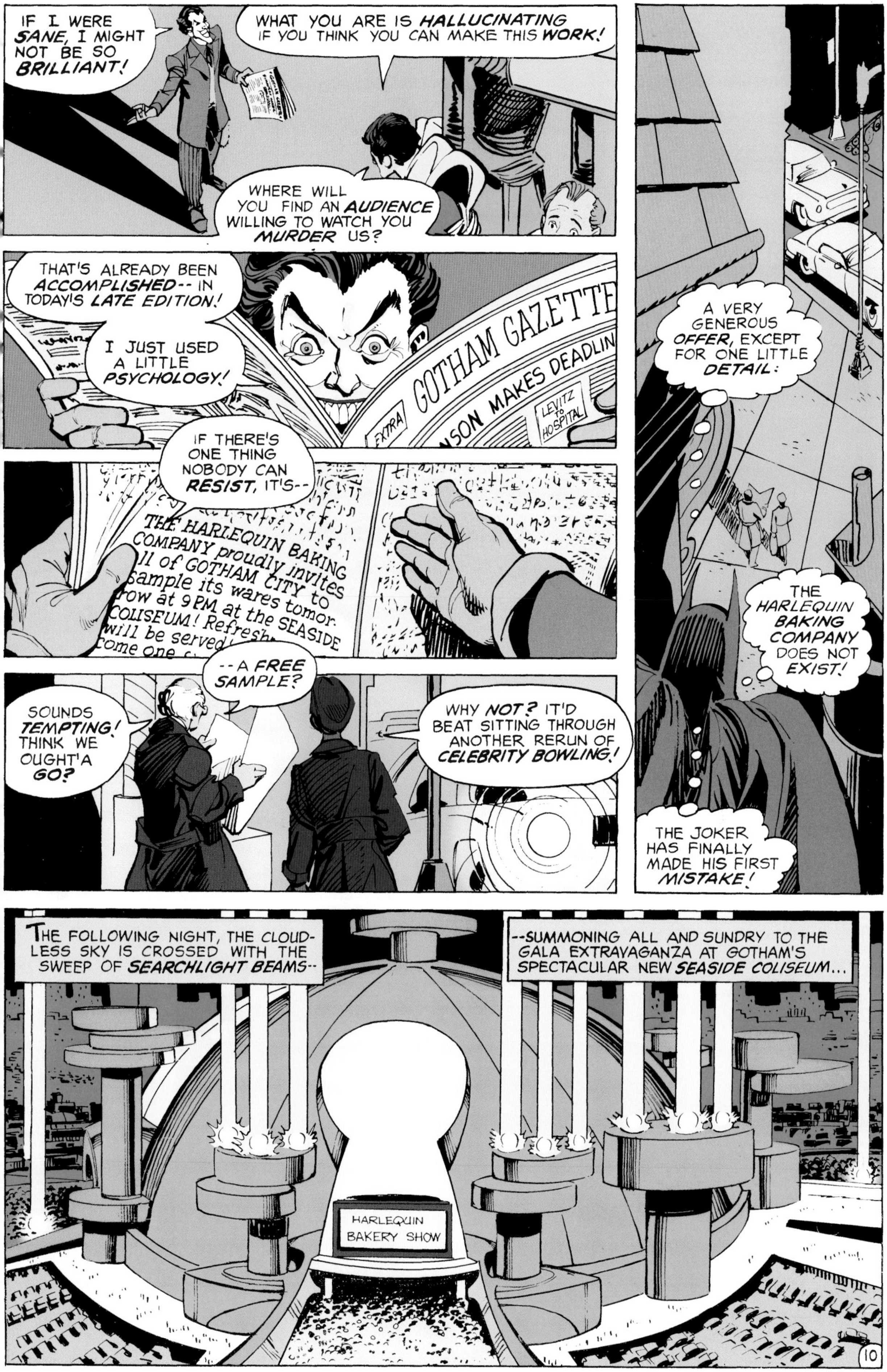

IF I WERE SANE, I MIGHT NOT BE SO BRILLIANT!
WHAT YOU ARE IS HALLUCINATING IF YOU THINK YOU CAN MAKE THIS WORK!
WHERE WILL YOU FIND AN AUDIENCE WILLING TO WATCH YOU MURDER US?
THAT'S ALREADY BEEN ACCOMPLISHED-- IN TODAY'S LATE EDITION!
I JUST USED A LITTLE PSYCHOLOGY!
GOTHAM GAZETTE
EXTRA
NSON MAKES DEADLIN
LEVITZ TO HOSPITAL
IF THERE'S ONE THING NOBODY CAN RESIST, IT'S--
THE HARLEQUIN BAKING COMPANY proudly invites ll of GOTHAM CITY to sample its wares tomor row at 9 PM at the SEASIDE COLISEUM! Refresh will be served
--A FREE SAMPLE?
SOUNDS TEMPTING! THINK WE OUGHT'A GO?
WHY NOT? IT'D BEAT SITTING THROUGH ANOTHER RERUN OF CELEBRITY BOWLING!
A VERY GENEROUS OFFER, EXCEPT FOR ONE LITTLE DETAIL:
THE HARLEQUIN BAKING COMPANY DOES NOT EXIST!
THE JOKER HAS FINALLY MADE HIS FIRST MISTAKE!
THE FOLLOWING NIGHT, THE CLOUDLESS SKY IS CROSSED WITH THE SWEEP OF SEARCHLIGHT BEAMS--
--SUMMONING ALL AND SUNDRY TO THE GALA EXTRAVAGANZA AT GOTHAM'S SPECTACULAR NEW SEASIDE COLISEUM...
HARLEQUIN BAKERY SHOW
10

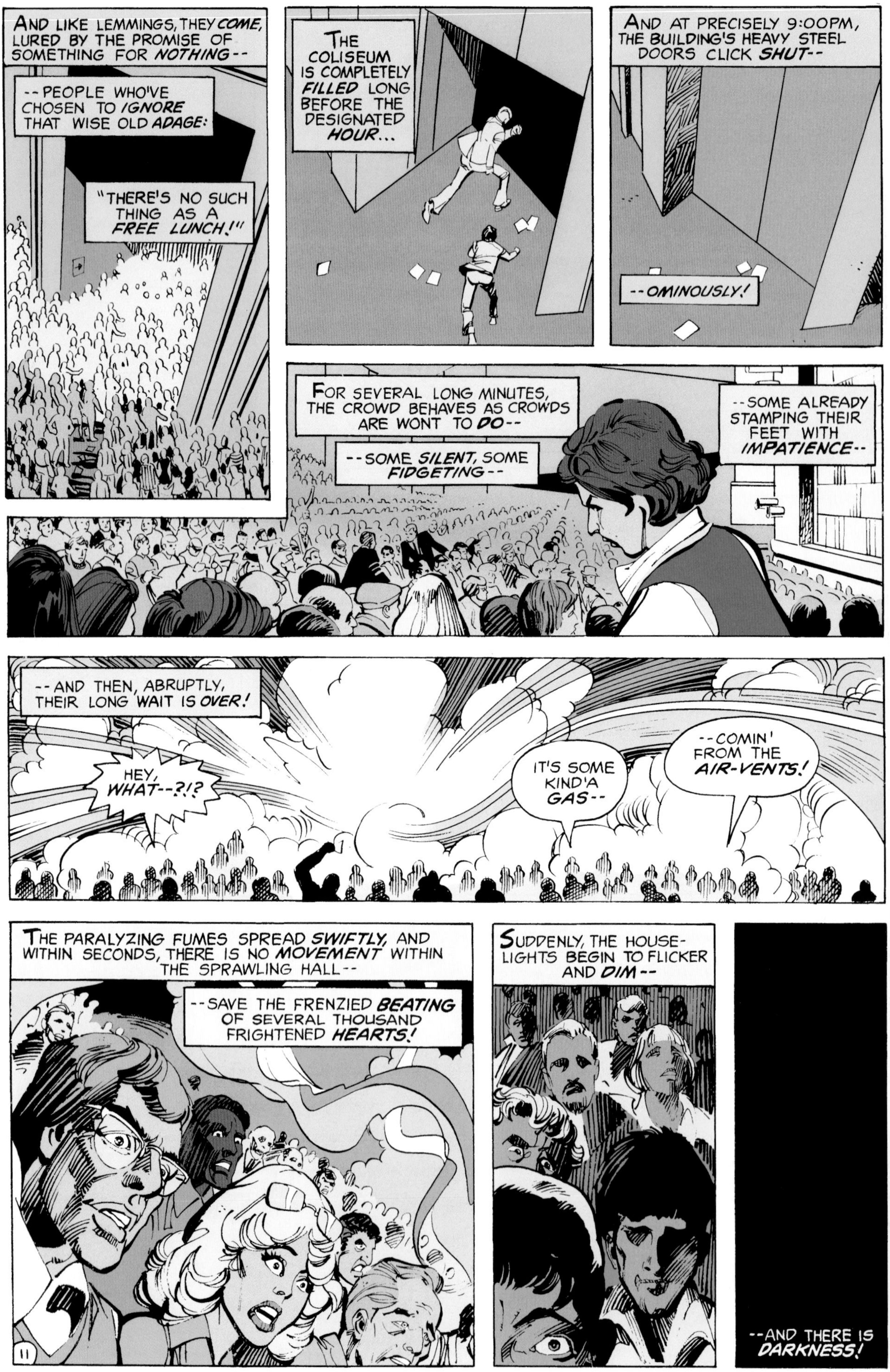

AND LIKE LEMMINGS, THEY COME, LURED BY THE PROMISE OF SOMETHING FOR NOTHING--
--PEOPLE WHO'VE CHOSEN TO IGNORE THAT WISE OLD ADAGE:
"THERE'S NO SUCH THING AS A FREE LUNCH!"
THE COLISEUM IS COMPLETELY FILLED LONG BEFORE THE DESIGNATED HOUR...
AND AT PRECISELY 9:00PM, THE BUILDING'S HEAVY STEEL DOORS CLICK SHUT--
--OMINOUSLY!
FOR SEVERAL LONG MINUTES, THE CROWD BEHAVES AS CROWDS ARE WONT TO DO--
--SOME SILENT, SOME FIDGETING--
--SOME ALREADY STAMPING THEIR FEET WITH IMPATIENCE--
--AND THEN, ABRUPTLY, THEIR LONG WAIT IS OVER!
HEY, WHAT--?!?
IT'S SOME KIND'A GAS--
--COMIN' FROM THE AIR-VENTS!
THE PARALYZING FUMES SPREAD SWIFTLY, AND WITHIN SECONDS, THERE IS NO MOVEMENT WITHIN THE SPRAWLING HALL--
--SAVE THE FRENZIED BEATING OF SEVERAL THOUSAND FRIGHTENED HEARTS!
11
SUDDENLY, THE HOUSE-LIGHTS BEGIN TO FLICKER AND DIM--
--AND THERE IS DARKNESS!

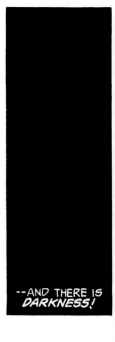

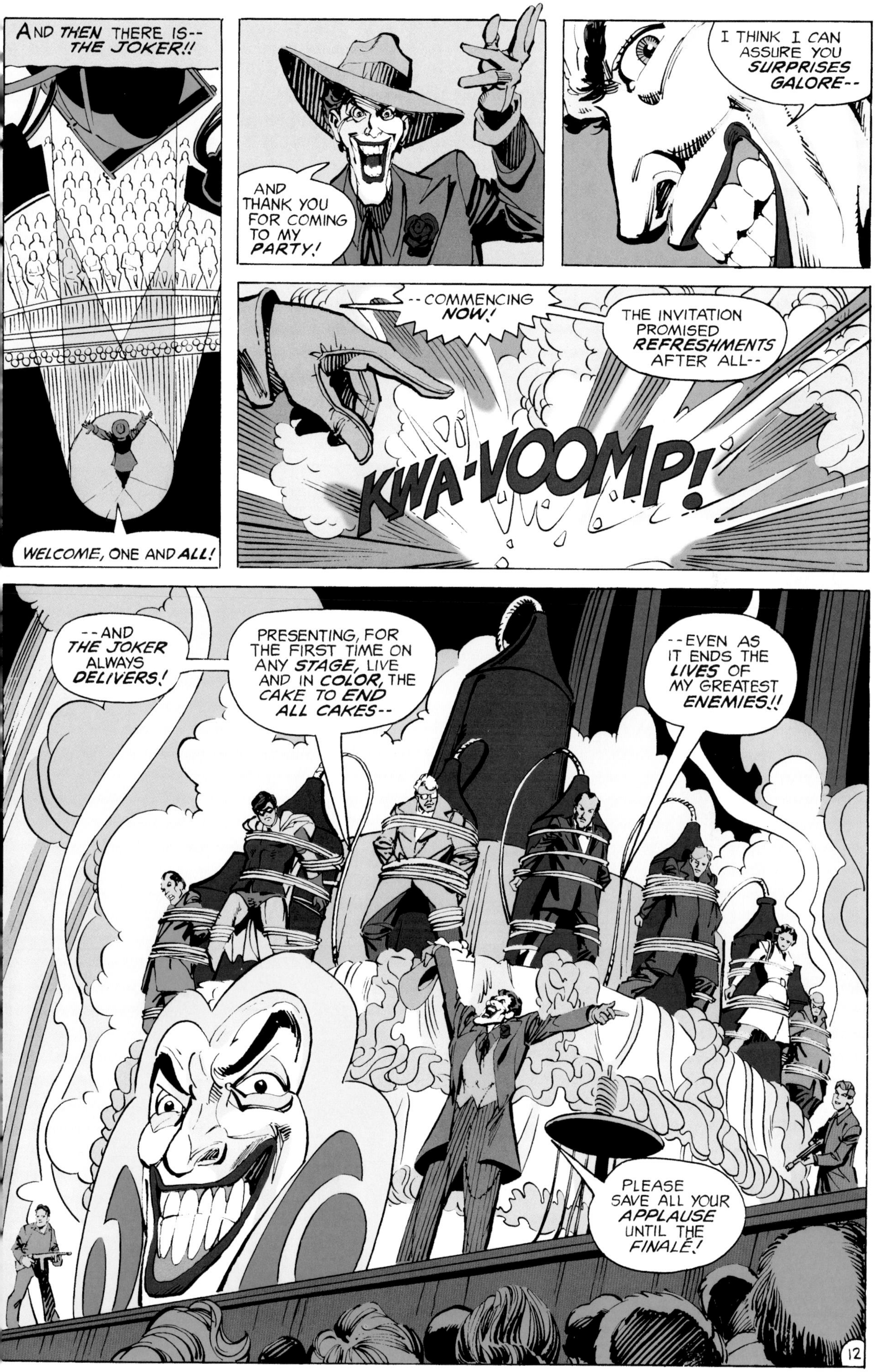
AND THEN THERE IS-- THE JOKER!!
WELCOME, ONE AND ALL!
AND THANK YOU FOR COMING TO MY PARTY!
I THINK I CAN ASSURE YOU SURPRISES GALORE--
--COMMENCING NOW!
THE INVITATION PROMISED REFRESHMENTS AFTER ALL--
KWA-VOOMP!
--AND THE JOKER ALWAYS DELIVERS!
PRESENTING, FOR THE FIRST TIME ON ANY STAGE, LIVE AND IN COLOR, THE CAKE TO END ALL CAKES--
--EVEN AS IT ENDS THE LIVES OF MY GREATEST ENEMIES!!
PLEASE SAVE ALL YOUR APPLAUSE UNTIL THE FINALÉ!
12

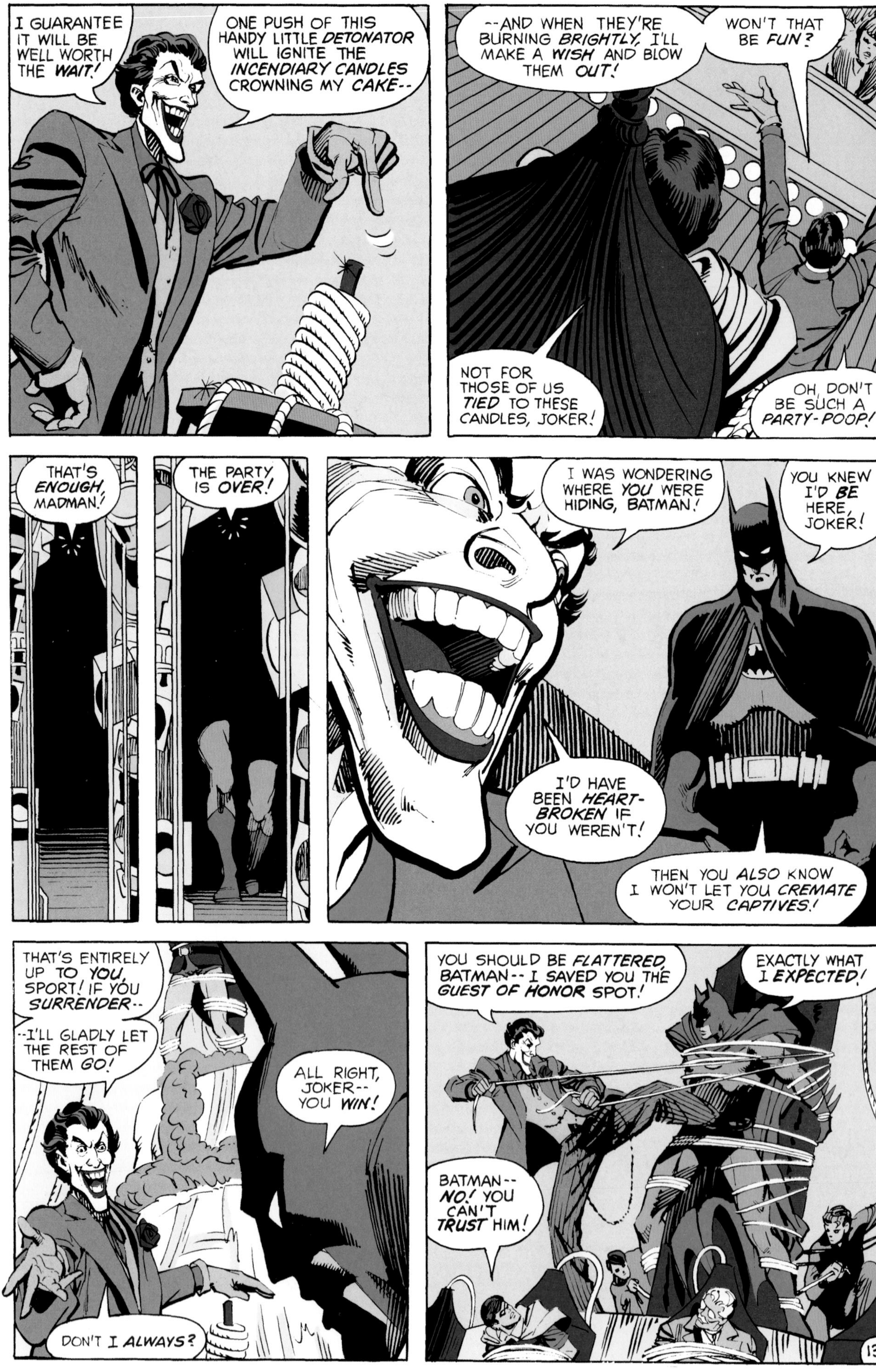
I GUARANTEE IT WILL BE WELL WORTH THE WAIT!
ONE PUSH OF THIS HANDY LITTLE DETONATOR WILL IGNITE THE INCENDIARY CANDLES CROWNING MY CAKE--
--AND WHEN THEY'RE BURNING BRIGHTLY, I'LL MAKE A WISH AND BLOW THEM OUT!
WON'T THAT BE FUN?
NOT FOR THOSE OF US TIED TO THESE CANDLES, JOKER!
OH, DON'T BE SUCH A PARTY-POOP!
THAT'S ENOUGH, MADMAN!
THE PARTY IS OVER!
I WAS WONDERING WHERE YOU WERE HIDING, BATMAN!
YOU KNEW I'D BE HERE, JOKER!
I'D HAVE BEEN HEART-BROKEN IF YOU WEREN'T!
THEN YOU ALSO KNOW I WON'T LET YOU CREMATE YOUR CAPTIVES!
THAT'S ENTIRELY UP TO YOU, SPORT! IF YOU SURRENDER--
--I'LL GLADLY LET THE REST OF THEM GO!
ALL RIGHT, JOKER-- YOU WIN!
DON'T I ALWAYS?
YOU SHOULD BE FLATTERED, BATMAN-- I SAVED YOU THE GUEST OF HONOR SPOT!
EXACTLY WHAT I EXPECTED!
BATMAN-- NO! YOU CAN'T TRUST HIM!
13

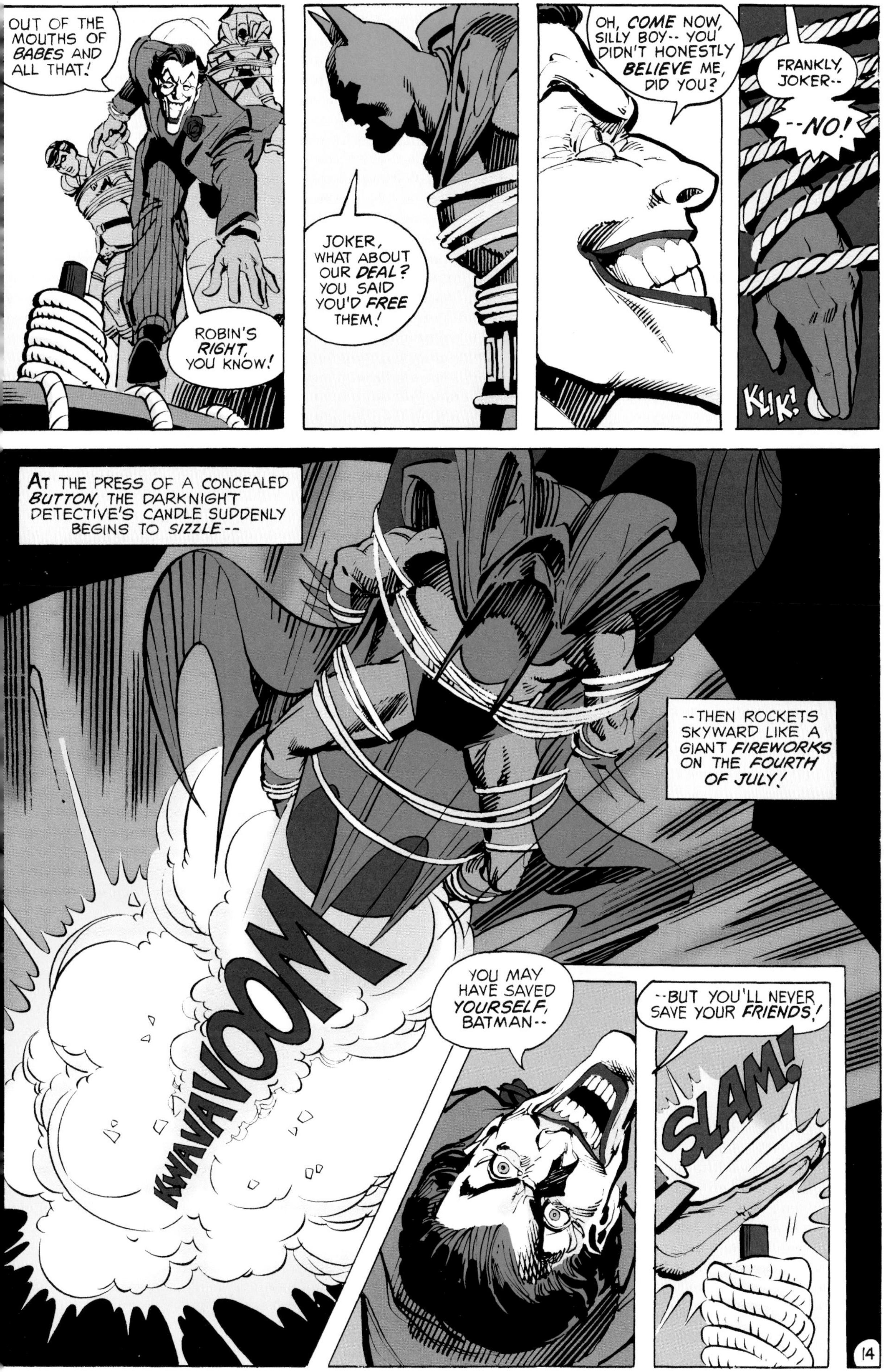

OUT OF THE MOUTHS OF BABES AND ALL THAT!
ROBIN'S RIGHT, YOU KNOW!
JOKER, WHAT ABOUT OUR DEAL? YOU SAID YOU'D FREE THEM!
OH, COME NOW, SILLY BOY-- YOU DIDN'T HONESTLY BELIEVE ME, DID YOU?
FRANKLY, JOKER--
--NO!
KLIK!
AT THE PRESS OF A CONCEALED BUTTON, THE DARKNIGHT DETECTIVE'S CANDLE SUDDENLY BEGINS TO SIZZLE--
--THEN ROCKETS SKYWARD LIKE A GIANT FIREWORKS ON THE FOURTH OF JULY!
KWAVAVOOM
YOU MAY HAVE SAVED YOURSELF, BATMAN--
--BUT YOU'LL NEVER SAVE YOUR FRIENDS!
SLAM!
14

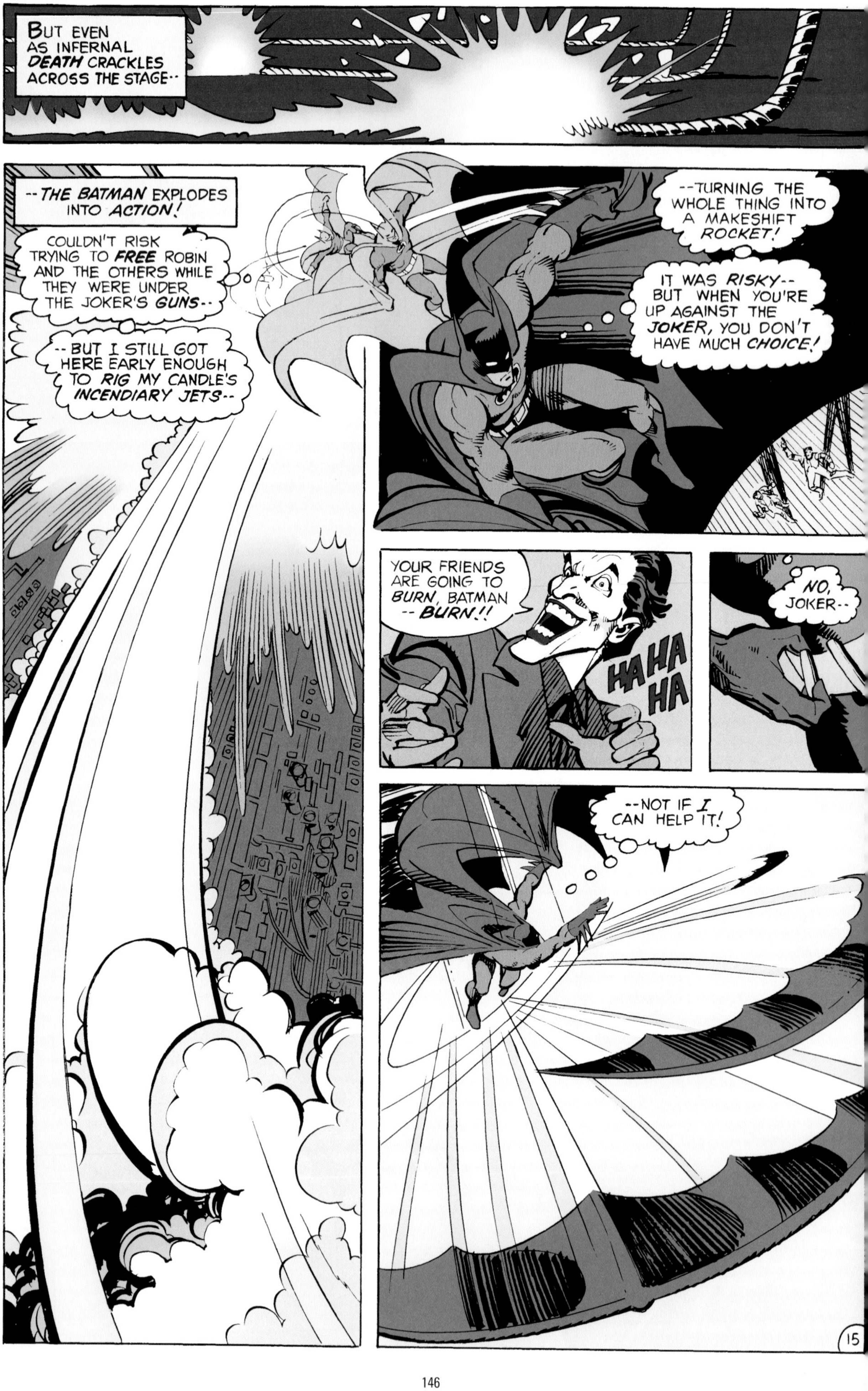
BUT EVEN AS INFERNAL DEATH CRACKLES ACROSS THE STAGE--
--THE BATMAN EXPLODES INTO ACTION!
COULDN'T RISK TRYING TO FREE ROBIN AND THE OTHERS WHILE THEY WERE UNDER THE JOKER'S GUNS--
--BUT I STILL GOT HERE EARLY ENOUGH TO RIG MY CANDLE'S INCENDIARY JETS--
--TURNING THE WHOLE THING INTO A MAKESHIFT ROCKET!
IT WAS RISKY--BUT WHEN YOU'RE UP AGAINST THE JOKER, YOU DON'T HAVE MUCH CHOICE!
YOUR FRIENDS ARE GOING TO BURN, BATMAN --BURN!!
HAHA HA
NO, JOKER--
--NOT IF I CAN HELP IT!
15

SNIK   SNIK   SNIK

HE *DID* IT!

HIS BATARANGS *SEVERED* THE CANDLES' *FUSES!*

BATMAN *SAVED* US!

DID YOU EVER DOUBT HE *WOULD*, SIR?

AND HIS FINAL BATARANG CUT THE *ROPES* HOLDING ME--

SLASH

--SO *I* CAN FINALLY *CUT LOOSE!*

I OWE YOU CREEPS SOME *BRUISES!*

WATCH OUT FOR THE *JOKER*, ROBIN!

ME? I THOUGHT *YOU* WERE WATCHING OUT FOR HIM!

THE *JOKER* WATCHES OUT FOR *HIMSELF*, FOOLS!

'BYE NOW!

THERE! HE'S HEADED FOR THE *DOCKS!*

SHOULD'VE KNOWN HE'D HAVE PLANNED HIS *GETAWAY!*

I MAY BE *CRAZY*, BATMAN --BUT I'M NOT *STUPID!*

HE WHO FAILS AND *RUNS AWAY*, LIVES TO *WIN* ANOTHER DAY!

VROOM!

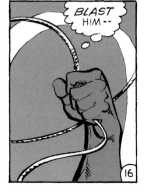

BLAST HIM--

16

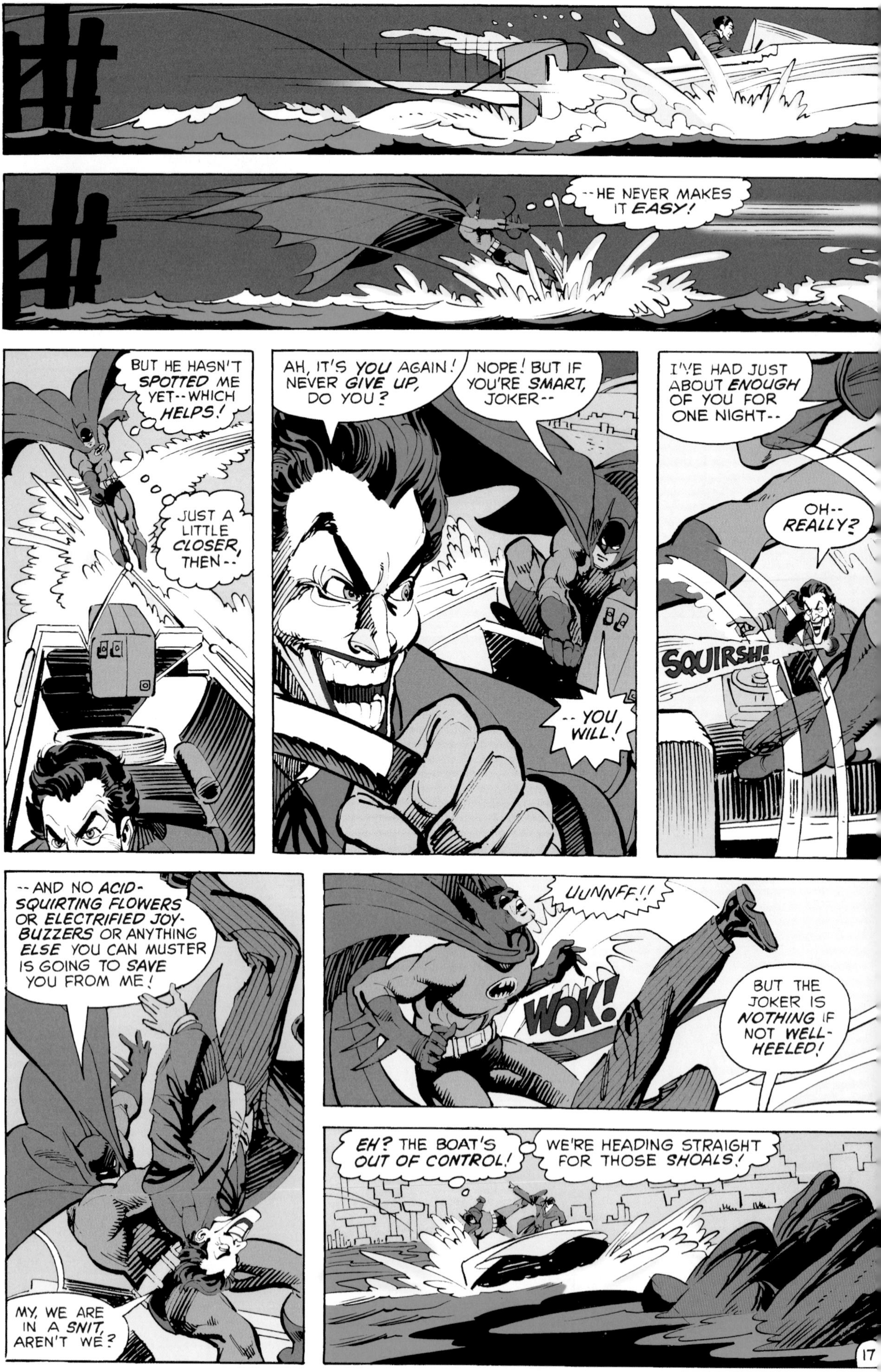
--HE NEVER MAKES IT EASY!
BUT HE HASN'T SPOTTED ME YET--WHICH HELPS!
JUST A LITTLE CLOSER, THEN--
AH, IT'S YOU AGAIN! NEVER GIVE UP, DO YOU?
NOPE! BUT IF YOU'RE SMART, JOKER--
--YOU WILL!
I'VE HAD JUST ABOUT ENOUGH OF YOU FOR ONE NIGHT--
OH--REALLY?
SQUIRSH!
--AND NO ACID-SQUIRTING FLOWERS OR ELECTRIFIED JOY-BUZZERS OR ANYTHING ELSE YOU CAN MUSTER IS GOING TO SAVE YOU FROM ME!
MY, WE ARE IN A SNIT, AREN'T WE?
UUNNFF!!
WOK!
BUT THE JOKER IS NOTHING IF NOT WELL-HEELED!
EH? THE BOAT'S OUT OF CONTROL!
WE'RE HEADING STRAIGHT FOR THOSE SHOALS!
17

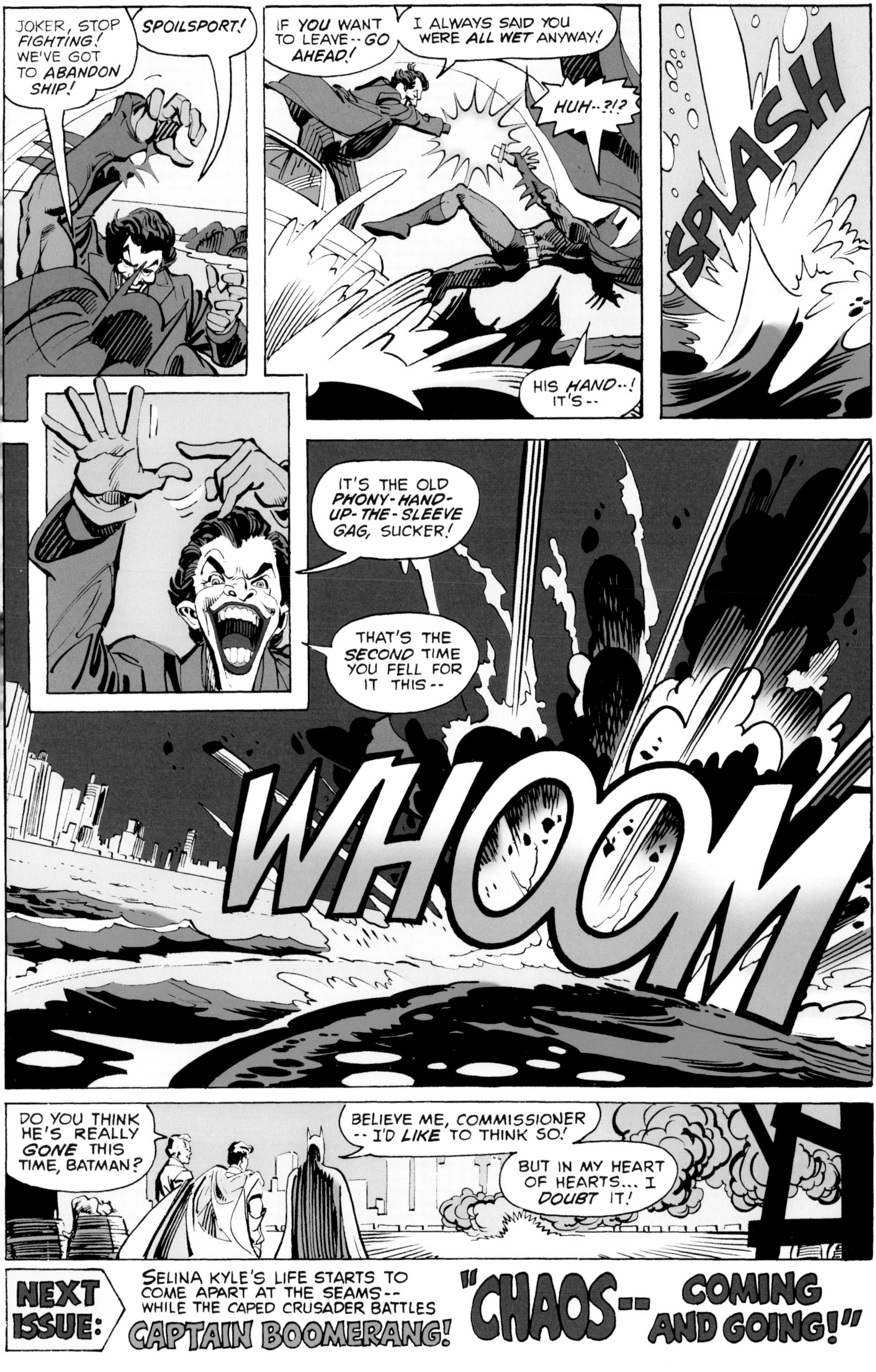
JOKER, STOP FIGHTING! WE'VE GOT TO ABANDON SHIP!
SPOILSPORT!
IF YOU WANT TO LEAVE-- GO AHEAD!
I ALWAYS SAID YOU WERE ALL WET ANYWAY!
HUH--?!?
HIS HAND--! IT'S--
SPLASH
IT'S THE OLD PHONY-HAND-UP-THE-SLEEVE GAG, SUCKER!
THAT'S THE SECOND TIME YOU FELL FOR IT THIS--
WHOOM
DO YOU THINK HE'S REALLY GONE THIS TIME, BATMAN?
BELIEVE ME, COMMISSIONER -- I'D LIKE TO THINK SO!
BUT IN MY HEART OF HEARTS... I DOUBT IT!
NEXT ISSUE:
SELINA KYLE'S LIFE STARTS TO COME APART AT THE SEAMS-- WHILE THE CAPED CRUSADER BATTLES CAPTAIN BOOMERANG!
"CHAOS-- COMING AND GOING!"

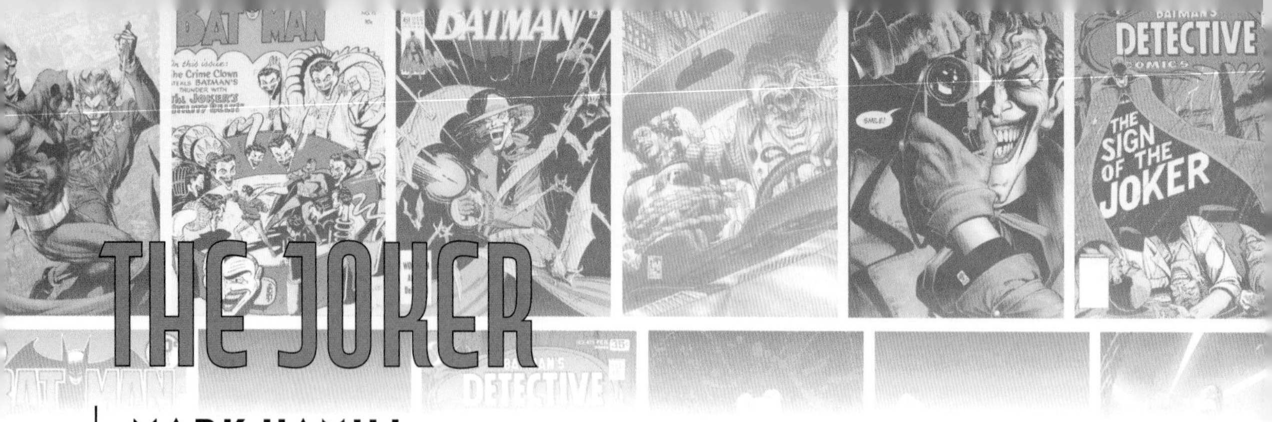
DETECTIVE
COMICS
THE SIGN OF THE JOKER

THE JOKER

by MARK HAMILL

"Without Batman, crime has no punch line!"
—The Joker, from "The Man Who Killed Batman," written by Paul Dini

This line, spoken when the Joker mistakenly believes Batman has been eliminated by a second-rate, run-of-the-mill, no-name thug, helped me gain a greater insight into the character and his motivations than perhaps anything he had ever said or done before. The Joker's monumental ego shattered, he became an aimless, bewildered, and broken man. Deprived of his ultimate goal of triumphing over his hated archenemy once and for all, he had simply lost the will to live, or murder, or commit a crime of any kind, ever again. Oh sure, he would make an exception in the case of the crook who had stolen his thunder by bringing down the Dark Knight, of course. In fact, after sealing this hapless man alive in a coffin, then plunging it into a vat of acid, the Joker actually rallies briefly, delivering a eulogy full of fire and brimstone, riddled with bitter contempt and words of vengeance. Temporarily satisfied, he does a complete emotional 180, declaring: "Well, that was fun! Who's for Chinese?"

Actors wait all their lives for dialogue that rich, a character that complex and profoundly diabolical. I have performed that speech a handful of times before a live audience and it never fails to bring down the house with a rapturous, thunderous response. I only wish I were back on Broadway so I could deliver it eight times a week!

In 1991, when I first learned of plans for an animated Batman series, two facts stood out for me: the order was for 65 episodes and their stated goal was to emulate the quality of Max Fleischer's classic *Superman* cartoons of the 1940s. This seemed to indicate that they would be making enough shows to expand the subject matter beyond anything they had ever done with the character outside of the comic books and that they were determined to strive for excellence in doing so. As a lifelong fan of both animation and comics, I wanted in! My agent let the producers know I was greatly interested in participating, and much to my surprise, they responded immediately, giving me the role of Ferris Boyle in their first Mr. Freeze episode, "Heart of Ice," without even requesting an audition.

Ignoring my slight disappointment at not being offered the role of Freeze himself, I couldn't wait to read the script. When it arrived, I have to tell you, I wasn't prepared for just how well written it was. Rather than a standard mad scientist, Victor Fries had been reimagined as an epic tragic figure so driven to save his wife from a terminal illness, he had dedicated himself to developing a cryogenic method of preserving her until a cure could be found. My character, the real villain in the story, was a sleazy corporate CEO who, in a physical altercation, kicked Fries into the very chemicals that sealed his fate as a freak of nature, doomed to live forevermore in

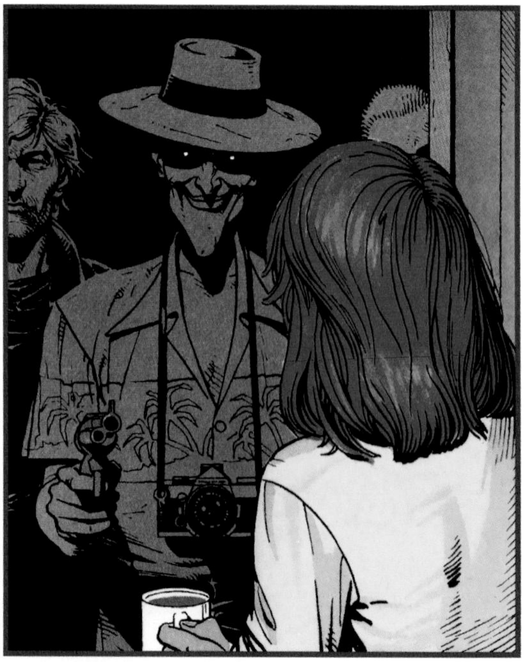

BATMAN
BATMAN
LOOK OUT, GOTHAM! THE JOKER'S BACK IN TOWN!
BATMAN
THE STRANGEST TEAM-UP IN HISTORY

sub-zero temperatures. Drenched in pathos, the final shot of Mr. Freeze contemplating the delicate figure of his beloved lost mate within a small snow globe while confined in a specially constructed refrigerated cell at Arkham Asylum was deeply heart-wrenching. Michael Ansara delivered a haunted and, yes, chilling portrayal of Mr. Freeze. It was one of the best scripts I had ever read in any medium, and I knew that this show had the potential to be something very special indeed. I couldn't wait to get to the studio and record it.

When that day came, my enthusiasm only increased as I scrutinized the artwork displayed around the room. Artist renderings of Gotham City were paradoxically retro and futuristic at the same time, with an airbrushed, deep three-dimensional quality and an overall darkness that would make the flatter, more colorful and cartoon-like drawings of the major characters really pop in contrast.

It was on this day that I first met the creative team and peppered them with questions I had about the direction of the show. Would there be shows without costumed villains? With 65 episodes to produce, it seemed likely they could do scripts that were straight-ahead mysteries, accentuating Batman's superlative skills as a detective, an element that had fallen by the wayside in previous incarnations. Would they be adapting any of the actual comic book scripts? Would they have to cater to the youngest audience members, avoiding the gothic horror and adult themes that older fans preferred? Would they be including antagonists that had never been done in animation before, like Ra's al Ghul, Hugo Strange, Killer Croc, Killer Moth, Clayface, or even, (gulp) Polka-Dot Man? Though they were somewhat circumspect on the specifics, it was clear they were kindred spirits who were as enamored of the source material as I was, maybe even more so considering their past collective track records of having actually worked on superhero cartoons, something I had never done. (Listen to the show's DVD commentary for Bruce Timm's memories of me on that day. I knew he was a brilliant artist; now I know he's a hilarious mimic!)

"PERHAPS YOU'LL KILL ME...

About a month later, the producers asked if I would be interested in auditioning for the role of the Joker. What a silly question! I still wonder if they would have thought of me at all, had I not done the prior episode and let my fanboy flag fly unashamedly. There were only a few pages of dialogue and one small drawing of him to inform my interpretation, but under the expert guidance of vocal director Andrea Romano (who would eventually guide me through many years of episodes and who remains a dear friend to this very day) and a liberating note on page one, "Don't think Nicholson," I managed to conjure up my version of the "Grim Jester," a sort of cross between Claude Rains and the Blue Meanie from *Yellow Submarine*.

Within days, I received a phone call and heard the words, "Congratulations, they want you for the Joker." I was numb. My elation quickly evaporated into self-doubt as I agonized over the enormous responsibility I had undertaken. He is among the greatest villains in history. An institution in pop culture. He's the Clown Prince of Crime. He's the Harlequin of Hate. He's... THE JOKER! I was terrified of disappointing his legion of fans who were sure to be brutal in their assessment if I displeased them in any way. Looking back, it's easy to see what an overreaction that was. I was about to become a part of a collaboration between some of some of the greatest writers, artists, musicians, and actors I've ever been privileged to work with. They say a hero is only as good as his villain, and I believe the reverse is also true. And I had the best: Kevin Conroy.

BATMAN
BATMAN'S DETECTIVE COMICS
THE SIGN OF THE JOKER
BATMAN
images

With his two effortless and distinct characterizations of Bruce Wayne and his alter ego, he will always be my Batman and a loyal friend.

What is it about the Joker that has kept his audiences spellbound for more than 70 years? Is it that he's insane and therefore unpredictable? He may be crazy, but he's never boring, as you will learn in the pages of this marvelous book. He is the first villain to be rewarded, however briefly, with his own comic book title. There is another antagonist who would eventually earn her own title: Harley Quinn, the Joker's impossibly optimistic, delusional, and abused girlfriend with the heart of gold. She is also the only character from the animated series to become a permanent member of the DC Universe. Created by Paul Dini and Bruce Timm, she was meant to appear only once, in "Joker's Favor." Thanks, in no small part, to Arleen Sorkin's hugely appealing and unforgettably poignant performance, she became an instant favorite and returned repeatedly, earning her own origin story, *Mad Love*. Long after the 109th and final episode, she continues to thrive, a female figure who holds her own among DC's finest, including Catwoman and Poison Ivy.

All good things must come to an end, and as the original incarnation of the show came to a conclusion (*Batman: The Animated Series*, *The Adventures of Batman and Robin*, *The New Batman Adventures*, plus the feature *Batman: Mask of the Phantasm*), it was hard to relinquish a character that was so exhilaratingly thrilling to portray. Any chance I had to reprise the role was an unexpected gift I couldn't resist, including in the feature-length *The Batman Superman Movie: World's Finest* and *Batman Beyond: Return of the Joker*, as well as three episodes of *Justice League* and an appearance in *Static Shock*. There were the talking toys, amusement park voice-overs, and the video games: *Batman: Vengeance*, *The Adventures of Batman and Robin*, DC Universe Online, and my nastiest, most lethal version ever, *Batman: Arkham Asylum*.

CLICK
CLICK
CLICK

Just when I think I've had my last crack at that gleeful, psychopathic genius, he grabs me by the throat once more, much like how he has regularly cheated death since 1940. In fact, even as I type these words, I'm doing my final sessions for the new *Batman: Arkham City* video game. Can I ever quit this killer clown extraordinaire? One thing I can say with certainty: in all my years on stage, screen, and television, this is easily one of the most challenging, most rewarding, most enjoyable characters I have ever experienced as an actor.

And that, my friends, is no joke.

Mark Hamill
2011

Originally published in *The Joker: A Visual History of the Clown Prince of Crime*

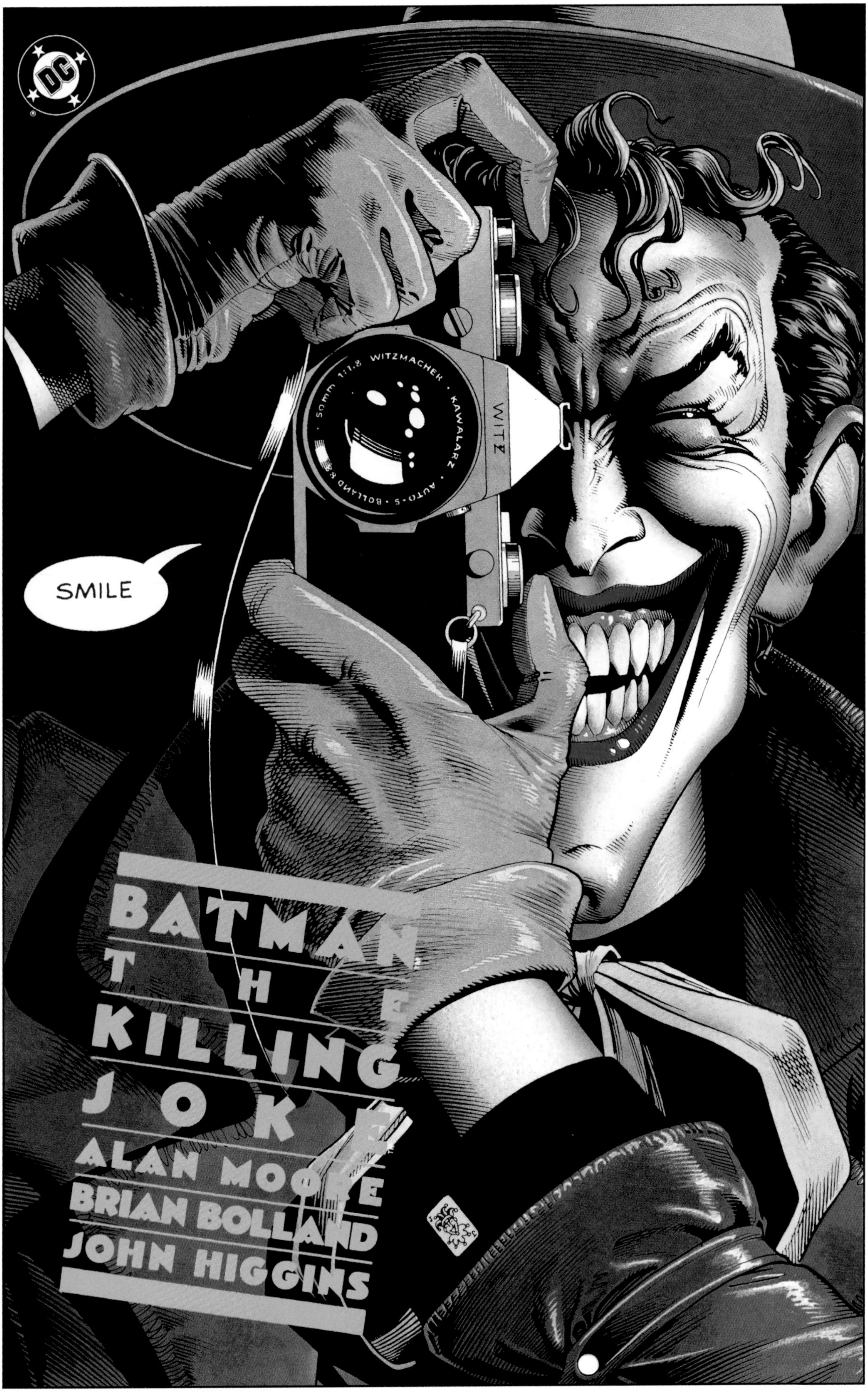
SMILE
BATMAN
THE
KILLING
JOKE
ALAN MOORE
BRIAN BOLLAND
JOHN HIGGINS

The following nine pages are an excerpt from one of the most iconic Joker stories of all time—*Batman: The Killing Joke*. To read the entire story, check out *Batman: The Killing Joke: The Deluxe Edition*, in stores now.

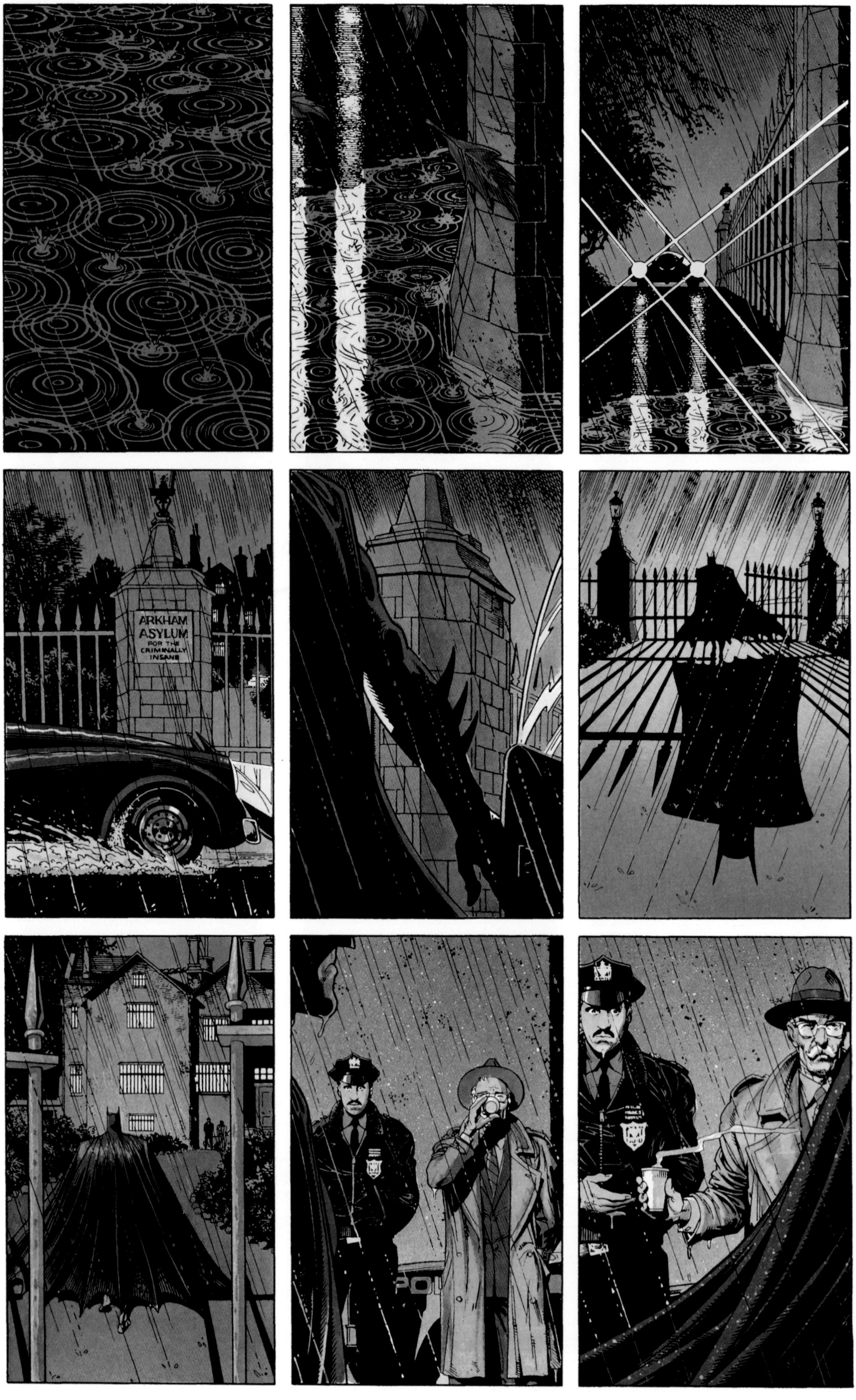
ARKHAM ASYLUM
FOR THE CRIMINALLY INSANE

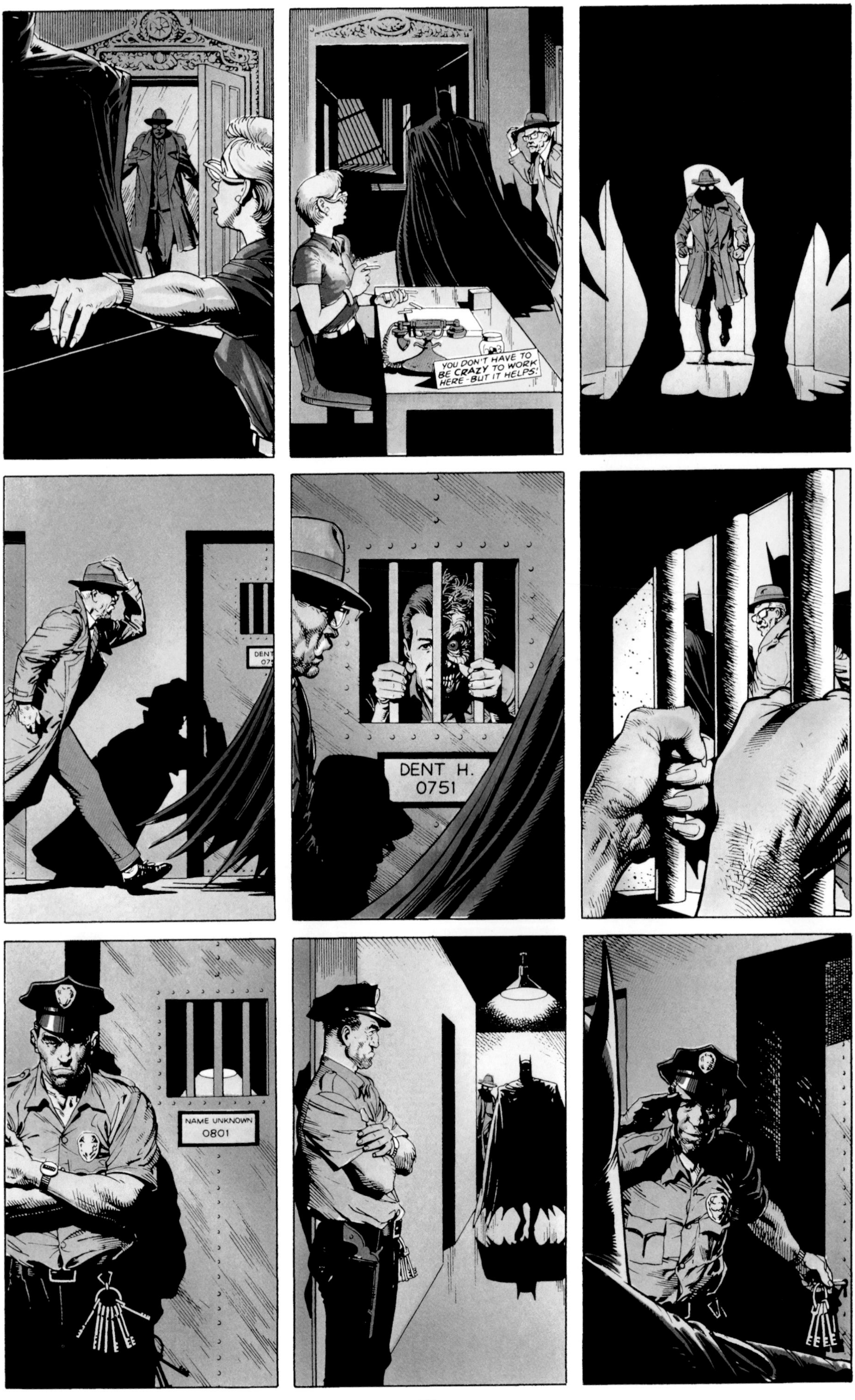
YOU DON'T HAVE TO BE CRAZY TO WORK HERE-BUT IT HELPS!
DENT H. 0751
NAME UNKNOWN 0801

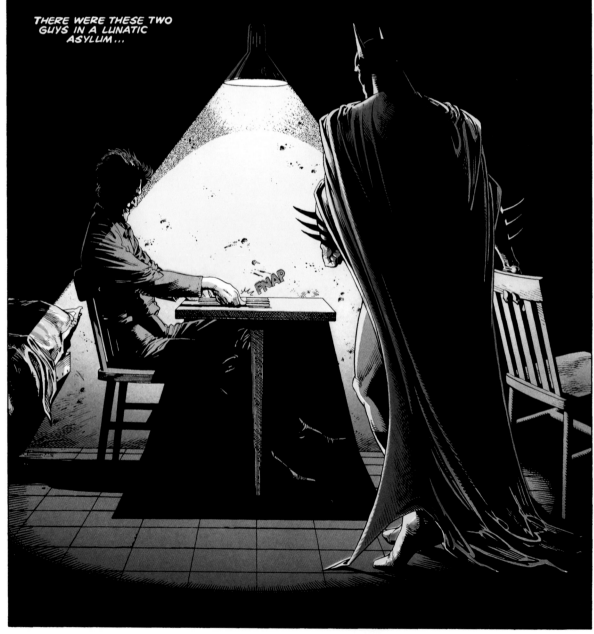

THERE WERE THESE TWO GUYS IN A LUNATIC ASYLUM...

FNAP

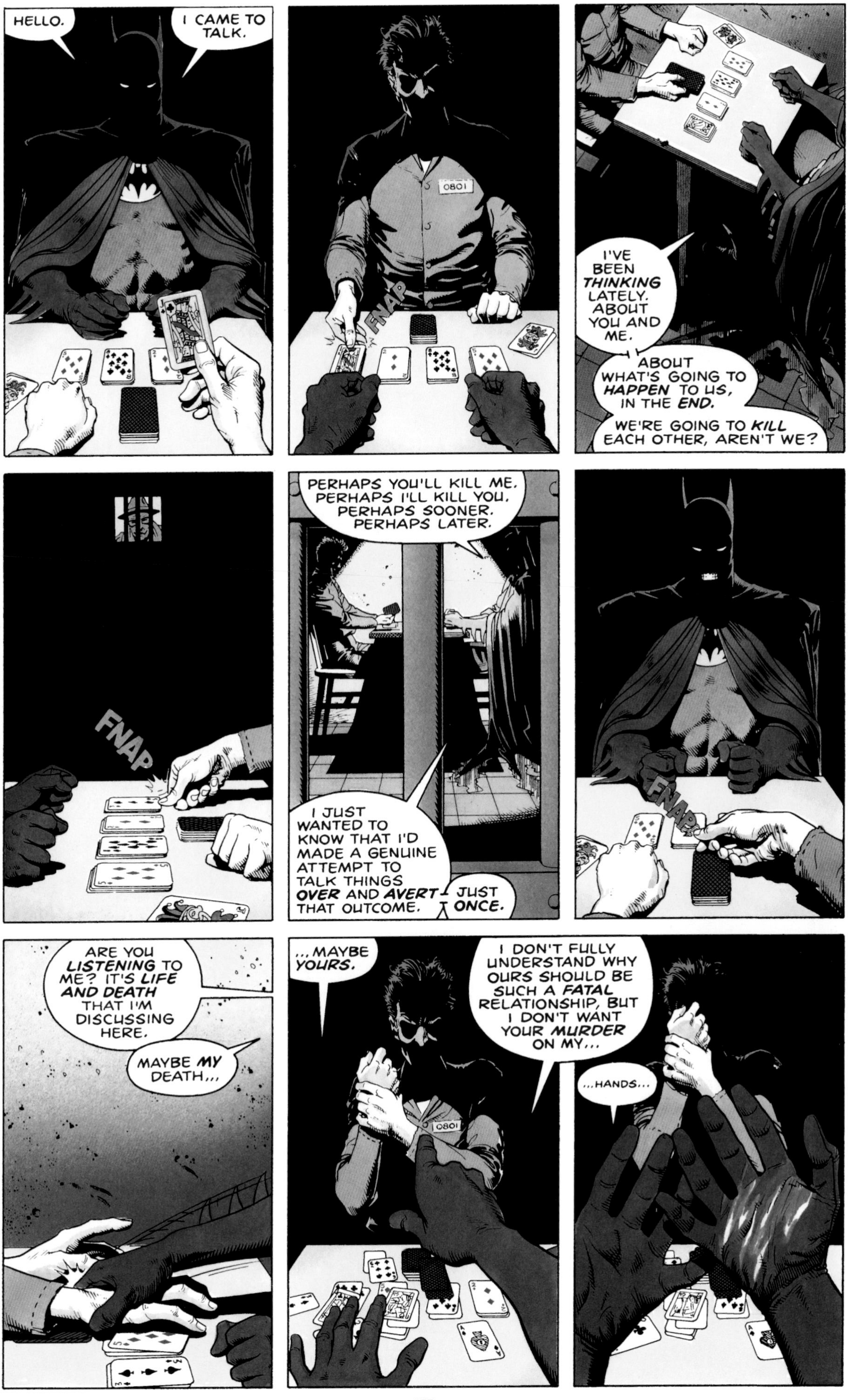
HELLO.
I CAME TO TALK.
FNAP
I'VE BEEN THINKING LATELY. ABOUT YOU AND ME.
ABOUT WHAT'S GOING TO HAPPEN TO US, IN THE END.
WE'RE GOING TO KILL EACH OTHER, AREN'T WE?
FNAP
PERHAPS YOU'LL KILL ME. PERHAPS I'LL KILL YOU. PERHAPS SOONER. PERHAPS LATER.
I JUST WANTED TO KNOW THAT I'D MADE A GENUINE ATTEMPT TO TALK THINGS OVER AND AVERT THAT OUTCOME.
JUST ONCE.
FNAP
ARE YOU LISTENING TO ME? IT'S LIFE AND DEATH THAT I'M DISCUSSING HERE.
MAYBE MY DEATH...
...MAYBE YOURS.
I DON'T FULLY UNDERSTAND WHY OURS SHOULD BE SUCH A FATAL RELATIONSHIP, BUT I DON'T WANT YOUR MURDER ON MY...
...HANDS...

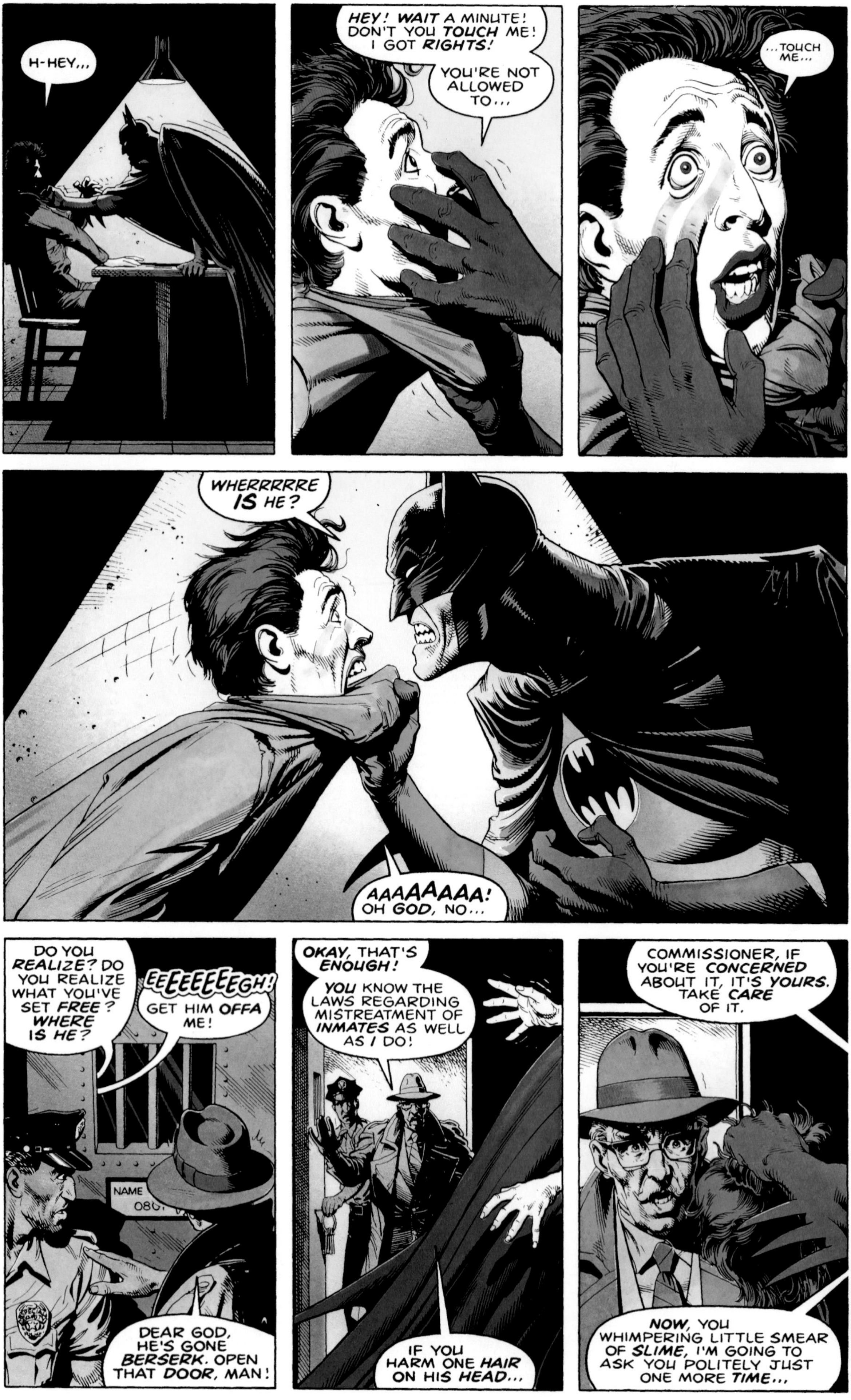
H-HEY,,,
HEY! WAIT A MINUTE! DON'T YOU TOUCH ME! I GOT RIGHTS!
YOU'RE NOT ALLOWED TO...
...TOUCH ME...
WHERRRRRE IS HE?
AAAAAAAA! OH GOD, NO...
DO YOU REALIZE? DO YOU REALIZE WHAT YOU'VE SET FREE? WHERE IS HE?
EEEEEEEEGH!
GET HIM OFFA ME!
NAME
DEAR GOD, HE'S GONE BERSERK. OPEN THAT DOOR, MAN!
OKAY, THAT'S ENOUGH!
YOU KNOW THE LAWS REGARDING MISTREATMENT OF INMATES AS WELL AS I DO!
IF YOU HARM ONE HAIR ON HIS HEAD...
COMMISSIONER, IF YOU'RE CONCERNED ABOUT IT, IT'S YOURS. TAKE CARE OF IT.
NOW, YOU WHIMPERING LITTLE SMEAR OF SLIME, I'M GOING TO ASK YOU POLITELY JUST ONE MORE TIME...

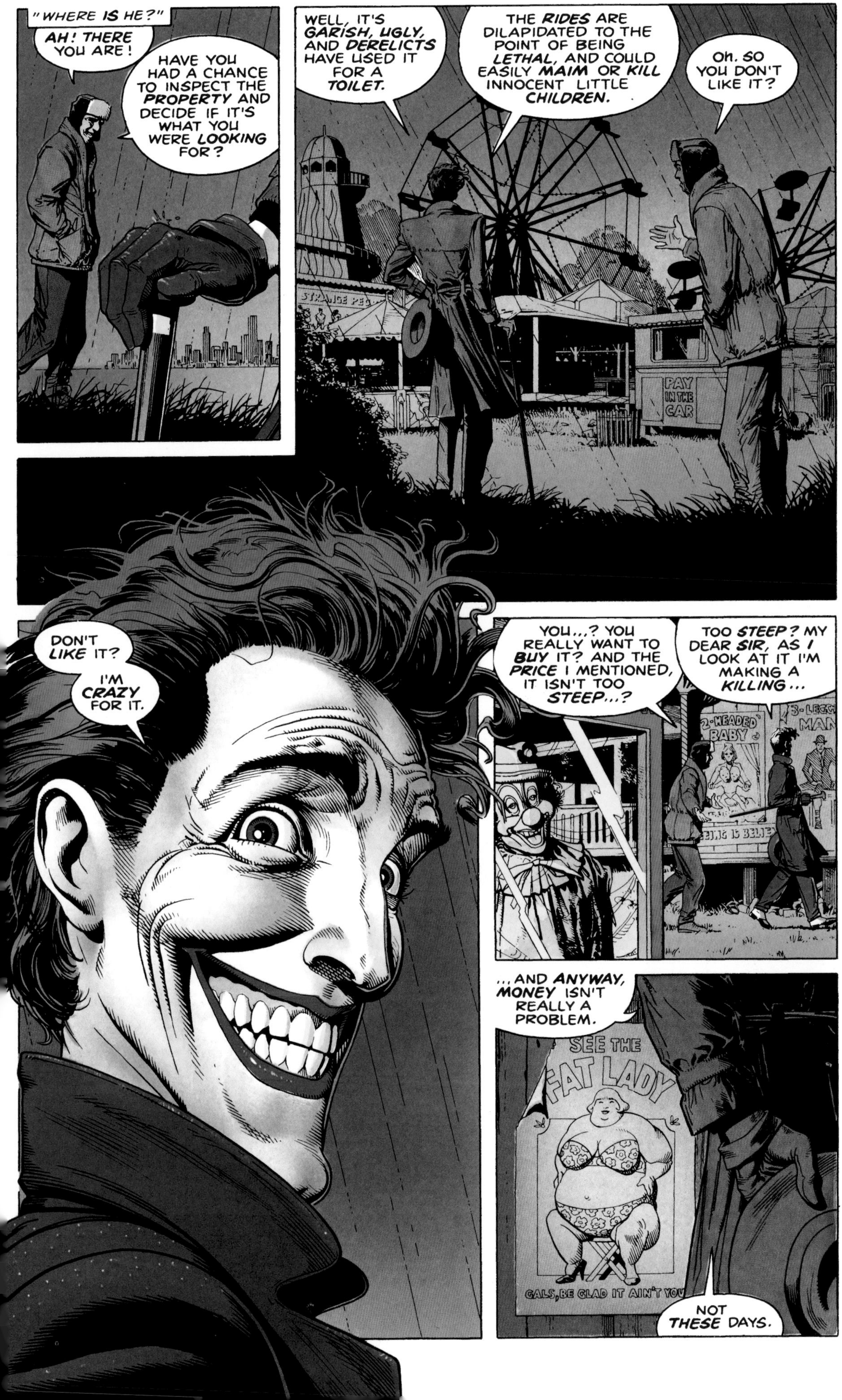
"WHERE IS HE?"
AH! THERE YOU ARE!
HAVE YOU HAD A CHANCE TO INSPECT THE PROPERTY AND DECIDE IF IT'S WHAT YOU WERE LOOKING FOR?
WELL, IT'S GARISH, UGLY, AND DERELICTS HAVE USED IT FOR A TOILET.
THE RIDES ARE DILAPIDATED TO THE POINT OF BEING LETHAL, AND COULD EASILY MAIM OR KILL INNOCENT LITTLE CHILDREN.
Oh. SO YOU DON'T LIKE IT?
STRANGE PE
PAY IN THE CAR
DON'T LIKE IT?
I'M CRAZY FOR IT.
YOU...? YOU REALLY WANT TO BUY IT? AND THE PRICE I MENTIONED, IT ISN'T TOO STEEP...?
TOO STEEP? MY DEAR SIR, AS I LOOK AT IT I'M MAKING A KILLING...
2-HEADED BABY
...AND ANYWAY, MONEY ISN'T REALLY A PROBLEM.
SEE THE FAT LADY
GALS, BE GLAD IT AIN'T YOU
NOT THESE DAYS.

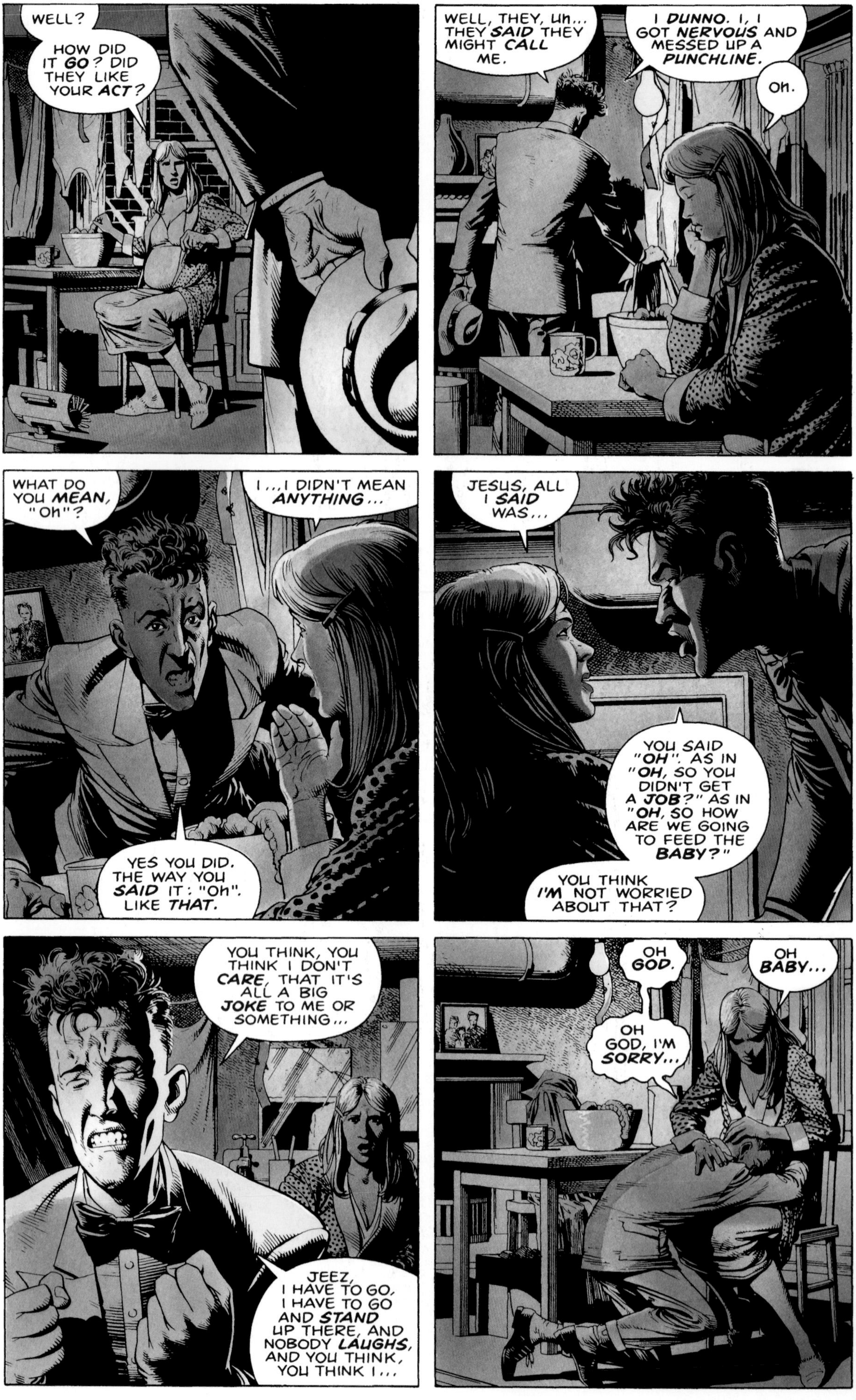
WELL?
HOW DID IT GO? DID THEY LIKE YOUR ACT?
WELL, THEY, uh... THEY SAID THEY MIGHT CALL ME.
I DUNNO. I, I GOT NERVOUS AND MESSED UP A PUNCHLINE.
Oh.
WHAT DO YOU MEAN, "Oh"?
I...I DIDN'T MEAN ANYTHING...
YES YOU DID. THE WAY YOU SAID IT: "Oh". LIKE THAT.
JESUS, ALL I SAID WAS...
YOU SAID "OH". AS IN "OH, SO YOU DIDN'T GET A JOB?" AS IN "OH, SO HOW ARE WE GOING TO FEED THE BABY?"
YOU THINK I'M NOT WORRIED ABOUT THAT?
YOU THINK, YOU THINK I DON'T CARE, THAT IT'S ALL A BIG JOKE TO ME OR SOMETHING...
JEEZ, I HAVE TO GO, I HAVE TO GO AND STAND UP THERE, AND NOBODY LAUGHS, AND YOU THINK, YOU THINK I...
OH GOD.
OH BABY...
OH GOD, I'M SORRY...

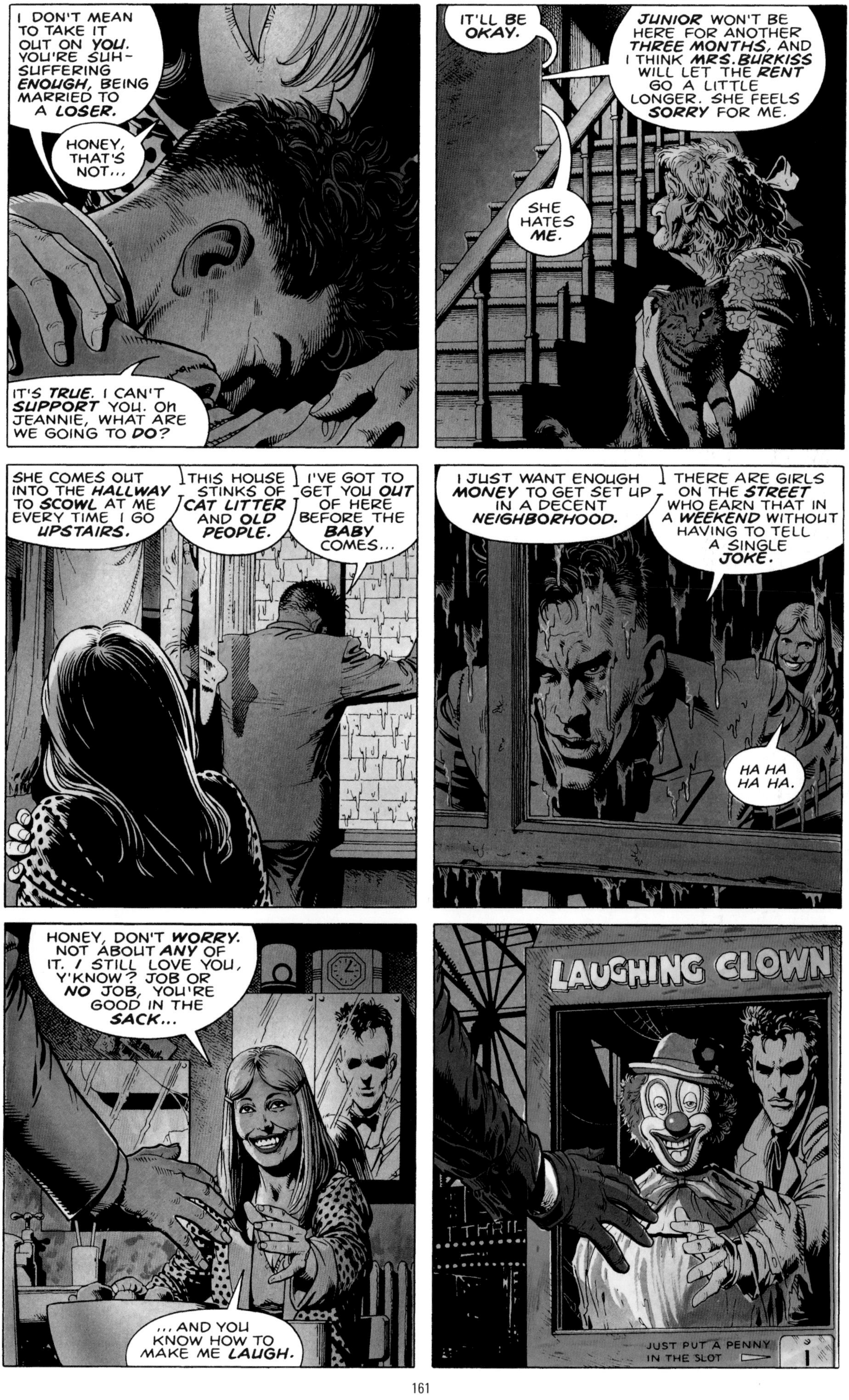
I DON'T MEAN TO TAKE IT OUT ON YOU. YOU'RE SUH-SUFFERING ENOUGH, BEING MARRIED TO A LOSER.
HONEY, THAT'S NOT...
IT'S TRUE. I CAN'T SUPPORT YOU. OH JEANNIE, WHAT ARE WE GOING TO DO?
IT'LL BE OKAY.
JUNIOR WON'T BE HERE FOR ANOTHER THREE MONTHS, AND I THINK MRS. BURKISS WILL LET THE RENT GO A LITTLE LONGER. SHE FEELS SORRY FOR ME.
SHE HATES ME.
SHE COMES OUT INTO THE HALLWAY TO SCOWL AT ME EVERY TIME I GO UPSTAIRS.
THIS HOUSE STINKS OF CAT LITTER AND OLD PEOPLE.
I'VE GOT TO GET YOU OUT OF HERE BEFORE THE BABY COMES...
I JUST WANT ENOUGH MONEY TO GET SET UP IN A DECENT NEIGHBORHOOD.
THERE ARE GIRLS ON THE STREET WHO EARN THAT IN A WEEKEND WITHOUT HAVING TO TELL A SINGLE JOKE.
HA HA HA HA.
HONEY, DON'T WORRY. NOT ABOUT ANY OF IT. I STILL LOVE YOU, Y'KNOW? JOB OR NO JOB, YOU'RE GOOD IN THE SACK...
...AND YOU KNOW HOW TO MAKE ME LAUGH.
LAUGHING CLOWN
JUST PUT A PENNY IN THE SLOT

Y'KNOW, I'M *POSITIVE* YOU WON'T *REGRET* THIS PURCHASE. THE PLACE ISN'T *THAT* DILAPIDATED. SOME OF THESE *RIDES* ARE STILL PRETTY *STURDY...*

REALLY, THIS COULD BE ONE *HELL* OF A CARNIVAL.

OH, YOU'RE *SO* RIGHT.

THANKS TO YOUR SMOOTH SALESMANSHIP AND YOUR SILVER TONGUE YOU'VE COMPLETELY *SOLD* ME ON THE PLACE. LET'S *SHAKE* ON IT.

UH..., WELL, SURE. IT'S MY *PRIVILEGE...*

INDEED IT *IS.*

NATURALLY, I WON'T BE *PAYING* YOU ANYTHING. MY *COLLEAGUES* PERSUADED YOUR *PARTNER* TO SIGN THE NECESSARY *DOCUMENTS* JUST OVER AN *HOUR* AGO.

THE PROPERTY'S MINE *ALREADY.*

YOU'RE *HAPPY* WITH THAT, I TAKE IT?

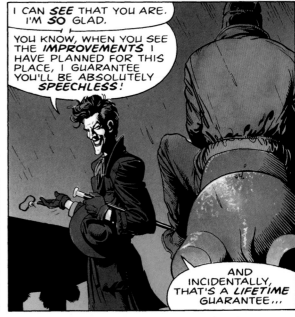

I CAN *SEE* THAT YOU ARE. I'M *SO* GLAD.

YOU KNOW, WHEN YOU SEE THE *IMPROVEMENTS* I HAVE PLANNED FOR THIS PLACE, I GUARANTEE YOU'LL BE ABSOLUTELY *SPEECHLESS!*

AND INCIDENTALLY, THAT'S A *LIFETIME* GUARANTEE...

WELL, I MUST *DASH.* THERE'S *EQUIPMENT* TO HIRE, PLUS *WORKERS* WHO'LL SUIT THE GENERAL *TONE* OF THE ESTABLISHMENT...

... AND THEN, OF COURSE, I'VE YET TO SECURE MY *MAIN ATTRACTION.* *DO* FEEL FREE TO STICK AROUND.

TO BE CONTINUED

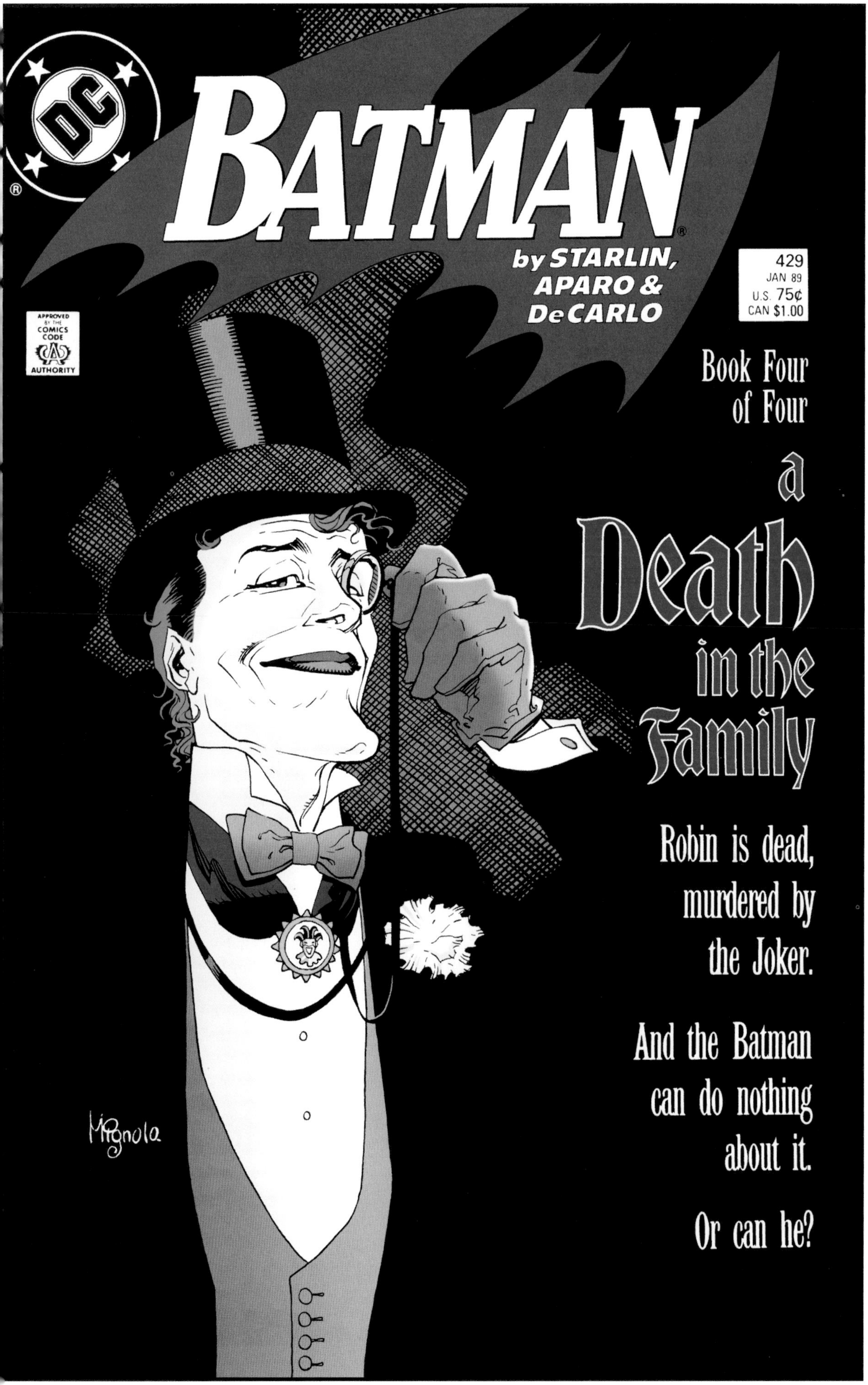
BATMAN
by STARLIN, APARO & DeCARLO
429
JAN 89
U.S. 75¢
CAN $1.00
APPROVED BY THE COMICS CODE AUTHORITY
Book Four of Four
a Death in the Family
Robin is dead, murdered by the Joker.
And the Batman can do nothing about it.
Or can he?
Mignola

A DEATH in the FAMILY

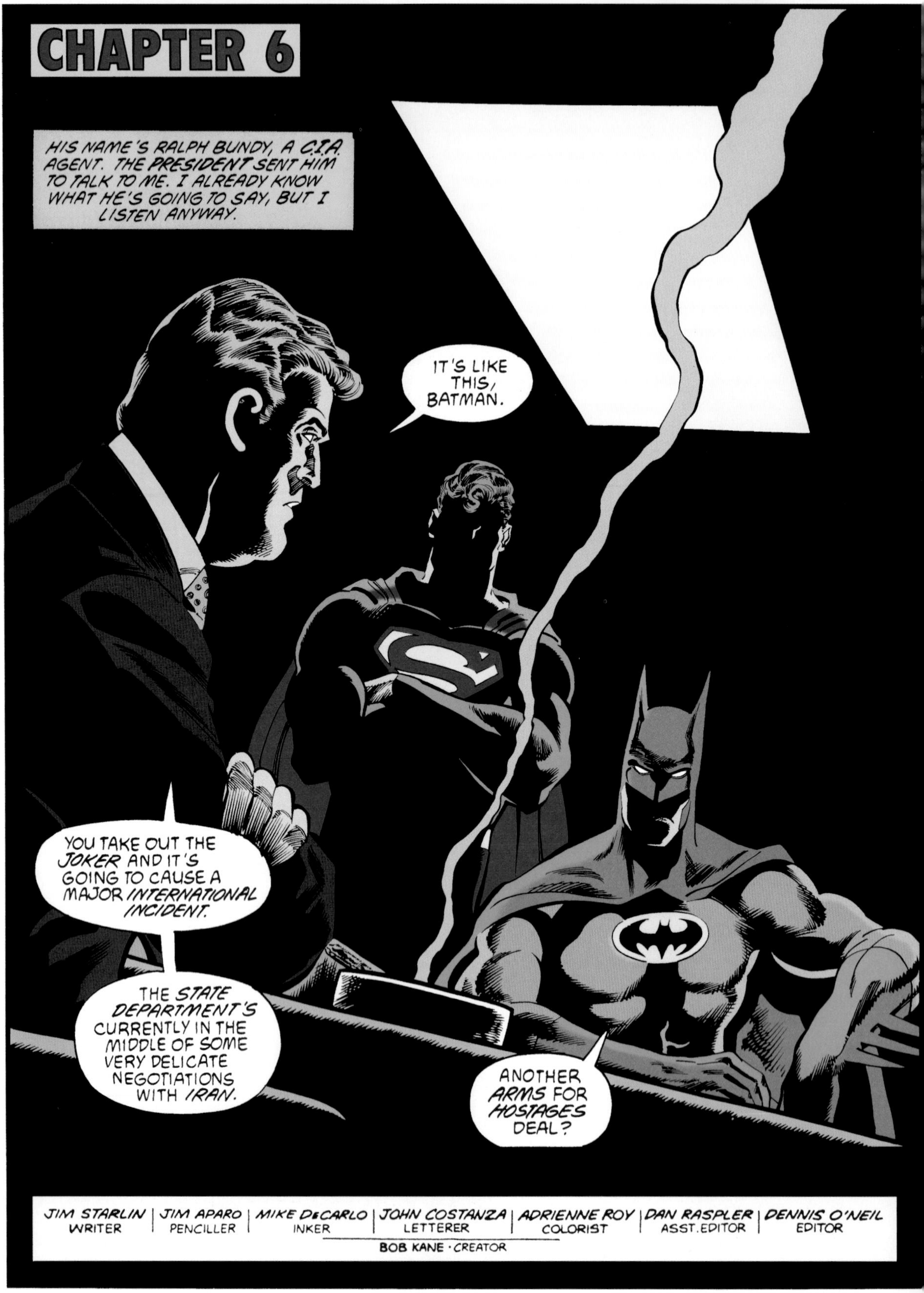

CHAPTER 6
HIS NAME'S RALPH BUNDY, A C.I.A. AGENT. THE PRESIDENT SENT HIM TO TALK TO ME. I ALREADY KNOW WHAT HE'S GOING TO SAY, BUT I LISTEN ANYWAY.
IT'S LIKE THIS, BATMAN.
YOU TAKE OUT THE JOKER AND IT'S GOING TO CAUSE A MAJOR INTERNATIONAL INCIDENT.
THE STATE DEPARTMENT'S CURRENTLY IN THE MIDDLE OF SOME VERY DELICATE NEGOTIATIONS WITH IRAN.
ANOTHER ARMS FOR HOSTAGES DEAL?
JIM STARLIN WRITER | JIM APARO PENCILLER | MIKE DeCARLO INKER | JOHN COSTANZA LETTERER | ADRIENNE ROY COLORIST | DAN RASPLER ASST. EDITOR | DENNIS O'NEIL EDITOR
BOB KANE · CREATOR

THAT'S NONE OF YOUR BUSINESS.

GUYS LIKE US SHOULD JUST DO OUR JOBS AND LET THE *BIG SHOTS* DO THEIRS.

THEY KNOW WHAT'S DOING AND THEY SAY *HANDS OFF* IRAN'S NEW *U.N.* AMBASSADOR!

UNDERSTAND?

THE JOKER'S GOT *DIPLOMATIC IMMUNITY.* STATE DOESN'T WANT ANYONE MESSING WITH HIM.

ESPECIALLY *YOU!*

YOU CAN'T BE SERIOUS. THE JOKER'S A *HOMICIDAL MANIAC.*

THEY ONLY MADE HIM AMBASSADOR SO HE CAN *KILL* SOMEONE, PROBABLY THE ENTIRE *U.N.* GENERAL ASSEMBLY.

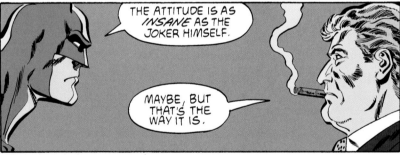

WE'VE GOT NO *HARD EVIDENCE* TO PROVE THAT.

UNTIL WE DO, THE JOKER HAS TO BE TREATED LIKE ANY OTHER DELEGATE.

THE ATTITUDE IS AS *INSANE* AS THE JOKER HIMSELF.

MAYBE, BUT THAT'S THE WAY IT IS.

NOT FOR *ME*, IT ISN'T.

AFRAID SO, PAL.

2

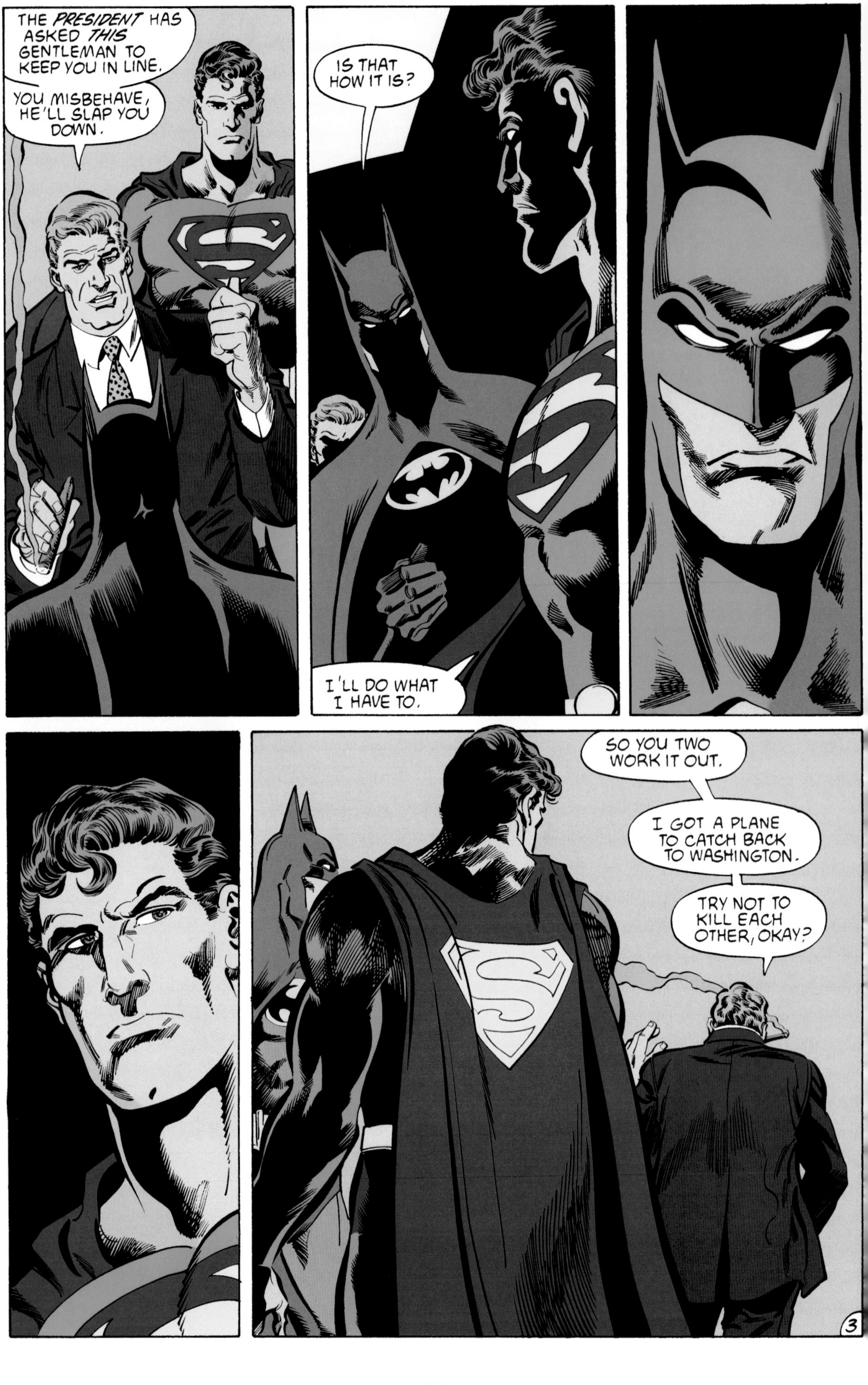
THE PRESIDENT HAS ASKED THIS GENTLEMAN TO KEEP YOU IN LINE.
YOU MISBEHAVE, HE'LL SLAP YOU DOWN.
IS THAT HOW IT IS?
I'LL DO WHAT I HAVE TO.
SO YOU TWO WORK IT OUT.
I GOT A PLANE TO CATCH BACK TO WASHINGTON.
TRY NOT TO KILL EACH OTHER, OKAY?
3

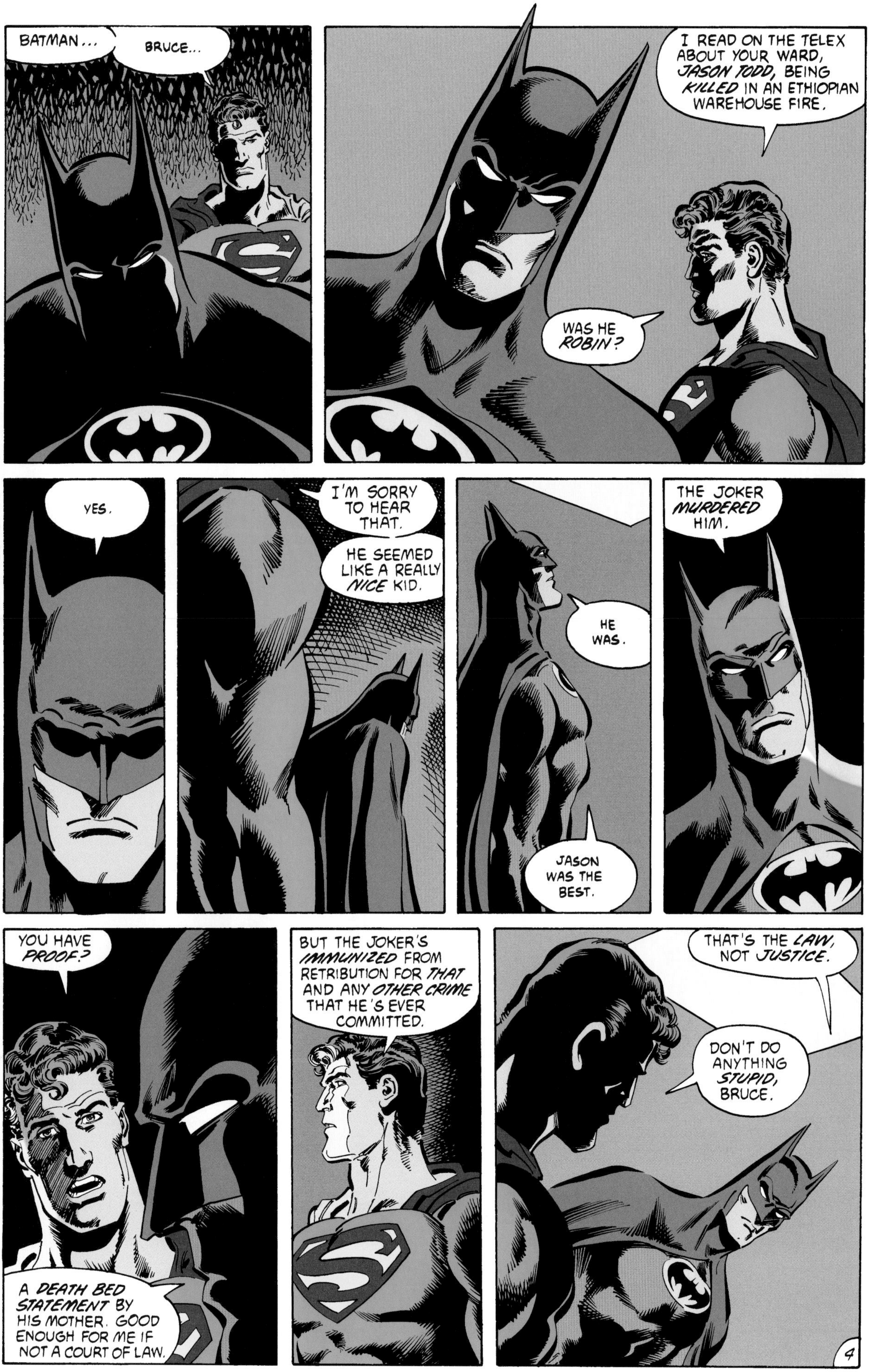
BATMAN...
BRUCE...
I READ ON THE TELEX ABOUT YOUR WARD, JASON TODD, BEING KILLED IN AN ETHIOPIAN WAREHOUSE FIRE.
WAS HE ROBIN?
YES.
I'M SORRY TO HEAR THAT.
HE SEEMED LIKE A REALLY NICE KID.
HE WAS.
JASON WAS THE BEST.
THE JOKER MURDERED HIM.
YOU HAVE PROOF?
A DEATH BED STATEMENT BY HIS MOTHER. GOOD ENOUGH FOR ME IF NOT A COURT OF LAW.
BUT THE JOKER'S IMMUNIZED FROM RETRIBUTION FOR THAT AND ANY OTHER CRIME THAT HE'S EVER COMMITTED.
THAT'S THE LAW, NOT JUSTICE.
DON'T DO ANYTHING STUPID, BRUCE.
4

YOU CAN'T PUT YOUR *THIRST* FOR *VENGE-ANCE* ABOVE YOUR COUNTRY'S *BEST INTERESTS.*

SPARE ME YOUR *BOY SCOUT* SENTIMENTALITIES, KENT.

TO USE YOUR OWN WORDS... I'LL DO WHAT I HAVE TO.

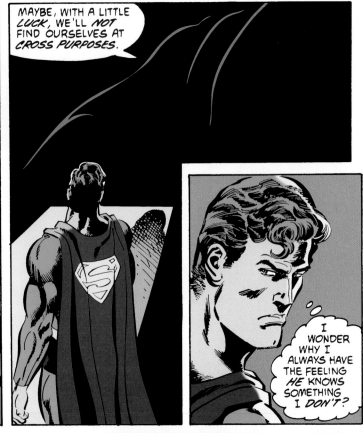

MAYBE, WITH A LITTLE *LUCK*, WE'LL *NOT* FIND OURSELVES AT *CROSS PURPOSES.*

I WONDER WHY I ALWAYS HAVE THE FEELING HE KNOWS SOMETHING I DON'T?

BACK IN MY *HOTEL ROOM*, I SEE WHAT MY *FEDERAL CONTACTS* CAN DO ABOUT GETTING ME INTO THE GENERAL ASSEMBLY AS *BRUCE WAYNE.*

MY REPUTATION AS A *PLAYBOY DILETTANTE* KEEPS ME FROM OBTAINING A POSITION AS A *DELEGATE.*

BUT THEY MANAGE TO SQUEEZE ME IN AS AN *UNOFFICIAL OBSERVER.*

NOW I CAN KEEP AN EYE ON THE *JOKER* WITHOUT MAKING THE *STATE DEPARTMENT* NERVOUS.

THE FOOLS.

5

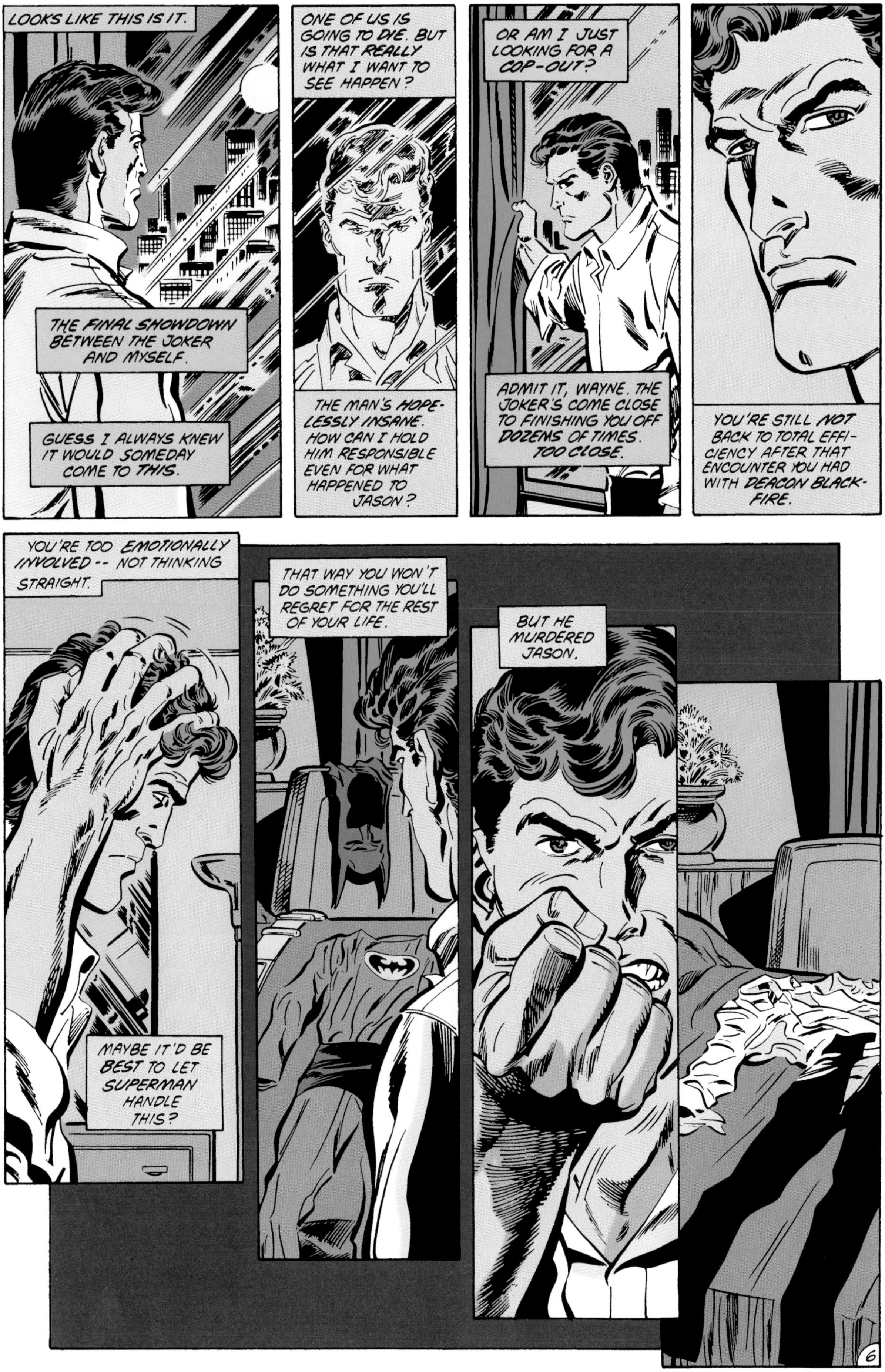
LOOKS LIKE THIS IS IT.
THE FINAL SHOWDOWN BETWEEN THE JOKER AND MYSELF.
GUESS I ALWAYS KNEW IT WOULD SOMEDAY COME TO THIS.
ONE OF US IS GOING TO DIE. BUT IS THAT REALLY WHAT I WANT TO SEE HAPPEN?
THE MAN'S HOPE-LESSLY INSANE. HOW CAN I HOLD HIM RESPONSIBLE EVEN FOR WHAT HAPPENED TO JASON?
OR AM I JUST LOOKING FOR A COP-OUT?
ADMIT IT, WAYNE. THE JOKER'S COME CLOSE TO FINISHING YOU OFF DOZENS OF TIMES. TOO CLOSE.
YOU'RE STILL NOT BACK TO TOTAL EFFI-CIENCY AFTER THAT ENCOUNTER YOU HAD WITH DEACON BLACK-FIRE.
YOU'RE TOO EMOTIONALLY INVOLVED -- NOT THINKING STRAIGHT.
MAYBE IT'D BE BEST TO LET SUPERMAN HANDLE THIS?
THAT WAY YOU WON'T DO SOMETHING YOU'LL REGRET FOR THE REST OF YOUR LIFE.
BUT HE MURDERED JASON.
6

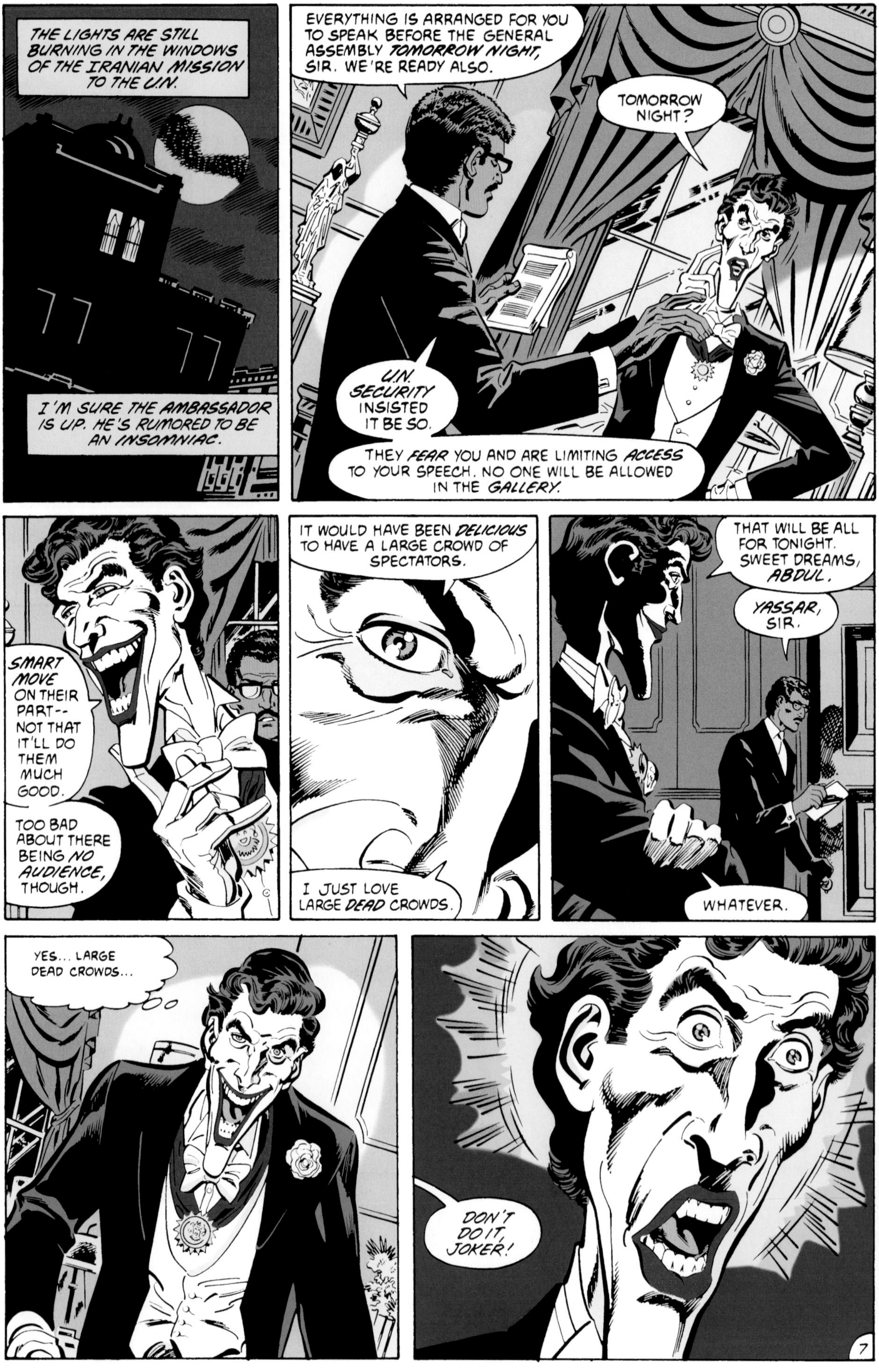
THE LIGHTS ARE STILL BURNING IN THE WINDOWS OF THE IRANIAN MISSION TO THE U.N.
I'M SURE THE AMBASSADOR IS UP. HE'S RUMORED TO BE AN INSOMNIAC.
EVERYTHING IS ARRANGED FOR YOU TO SPEAK BEFORE THE GENERAL ASSEMBLY TOMORROW NIGHT, SIR. WE'RE READY ALSO.
TOMORROW NIGHT?
U.N. SECURITY INSISTED IT BE SO.
THEY FEAR YOU AND ARE LIMITING ACCESS TO YOUR SPEECH. NO ONE WILL BE ALLOWED IN THE GALLERY.
SMART MOVE ON THEIR PART-- NOT THAT IT'LL DO THEM MUCH GOOD.
TOO BAD ABOUT THERE BEING NO AUDIENCE, THOUGH.
IT WOULD HAVE BEEN DELICIOUS TO HAVE A LARGE CROWD OF SPECTATORS.
I JUST LOVE LARGE DEAD CROWDS.
THAT WILL BE ALL FOR TONIGHT. SWEET DREAMS, ABDUL.
YASSAR, SIR.
WHATEVER.
YES... LARGE DEAD CROWDS...
DON'T DO IT, JOKER!
7

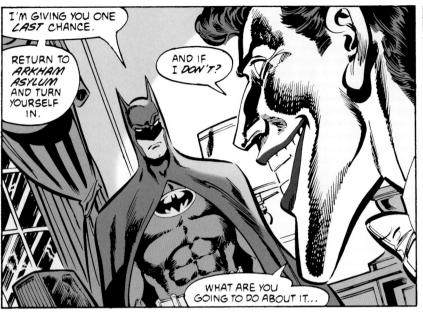

I'M GIVING YOU ONE *LAST* CHANCE.

RETURN TO *ARKHAM ASYLUM* AND TURN YOURSELF IN.

AND IF I *DON'T*?

WHAT ARE YOU GOING TO DO ABOUT IT...

LET YOUR *ASSISTANT* HANDLE IT!?

I'D HAVE LOVED TO HAVE SEEN YOUR FACE WHEN YOU FOUND WHAT WAS LEFT OF THE *BRAT!*

SET YOU OFF THE DEEP END, DID IT?

YOU SEE, EVEN A *MADMAN* CAN ADD 2 PLUS 2...

AND COME UP WITH *5.*

YOU ALWAYS KNOW EXACTLY THE *WRONG THING* TO SAY, DON'T YOU?

OR MAYBE YOU'RE GLAD TO BE RID OF THE LITTLE DARLING?

THAT'S WHAT MAKES ME SO *SPECIAL.*

VERY WELL.

HAVE IT YOUR WAY.

8

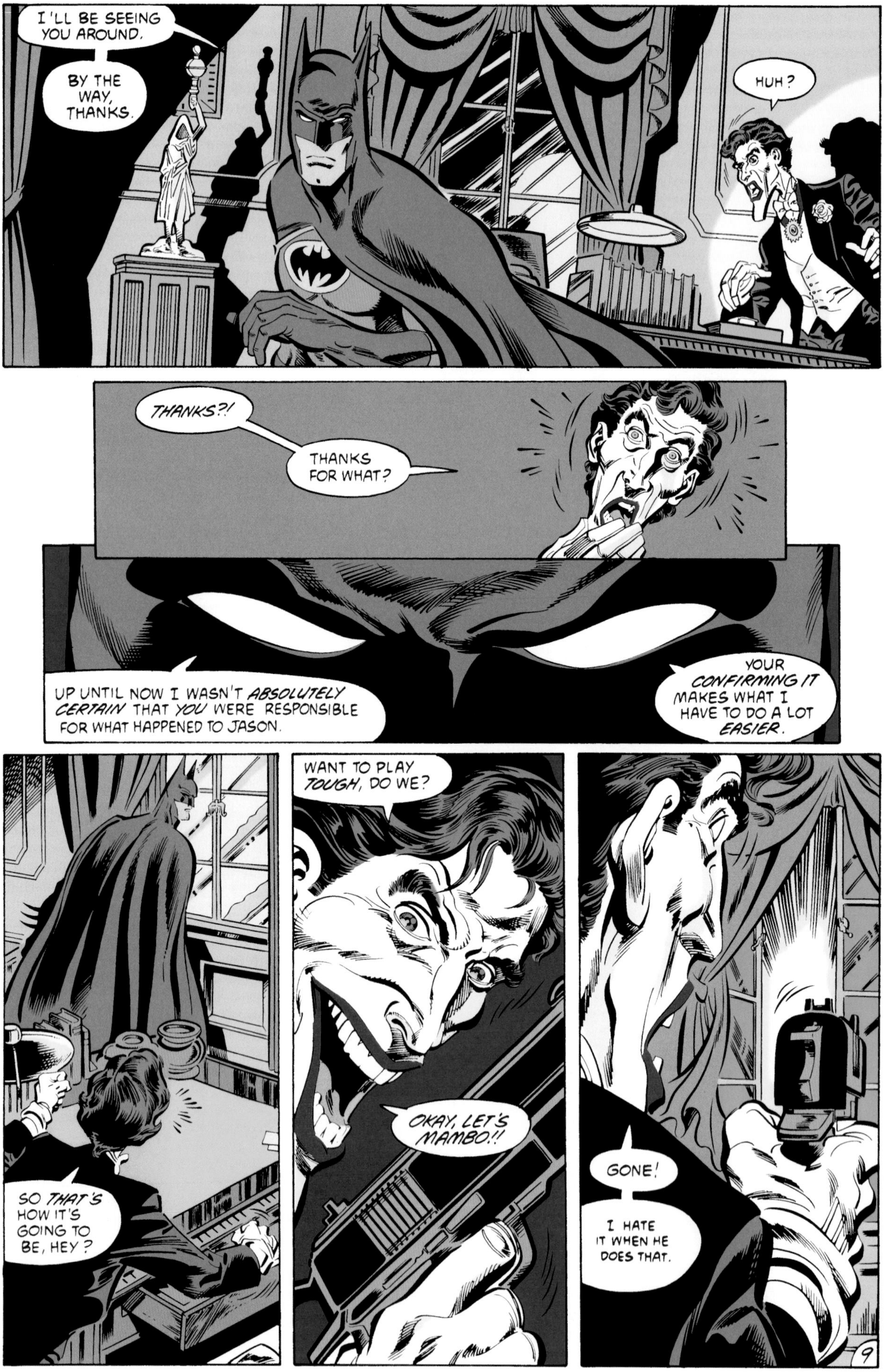

I'LL BE SEEING YOU AROUND.
BY THE WAY, THANKS.
HUH?
THANKS?!
THANKS FOR WHAT?
UP UNTIL NOW I WASN'T ABSOLUTELY CERTAIN THAT YOU WERE RESPONSIBLE FOR WHAT HAPPENED TO JASON.
YOUR CONFIRMING IT MAKES WHAT I HAVE TO DO A LOT EASIER.
SO THAT'S HOW IT'S GOING TO BE, HEY?
WANT TO PLAY TOUGH, DO WE?
OKAY, LET'S MAMBO!!
GONE!
I HATE IT WHEN HE DOES THAT.
9

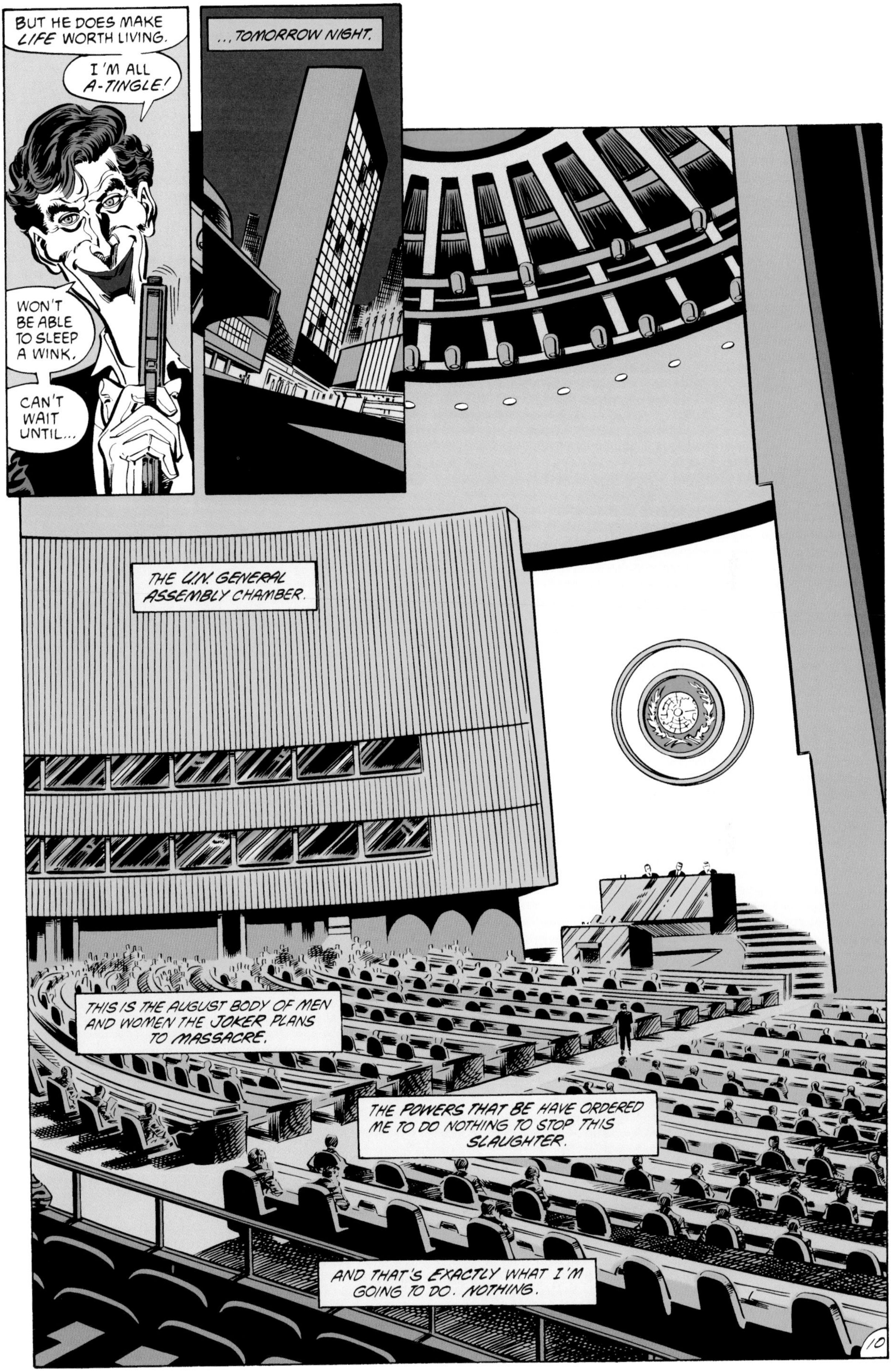

BUT HE DOES MAKE LIFE WORTH LIVING.
I'M ALL A-TINGLE!
WON'T BE ABLE TO SLEEP A WINK.
CAN'T WAIT UNTIL...
...TOMORROW NIGHT.
THE U.N. GENERAL ASSEMBLY CHAMBER.
THIS IS THE AUGUST BODY OF MEN AND WOMEN THE JOKER PLANS TO MASSACRE.
THE POWERS THAT BE HAVE ORDERED ME TO DO NOTHING TO STOP THIS SLAUGHTER.
AND THAT'S EXACTLY WHAT I'M GOING TO DO. NOTHING.
10

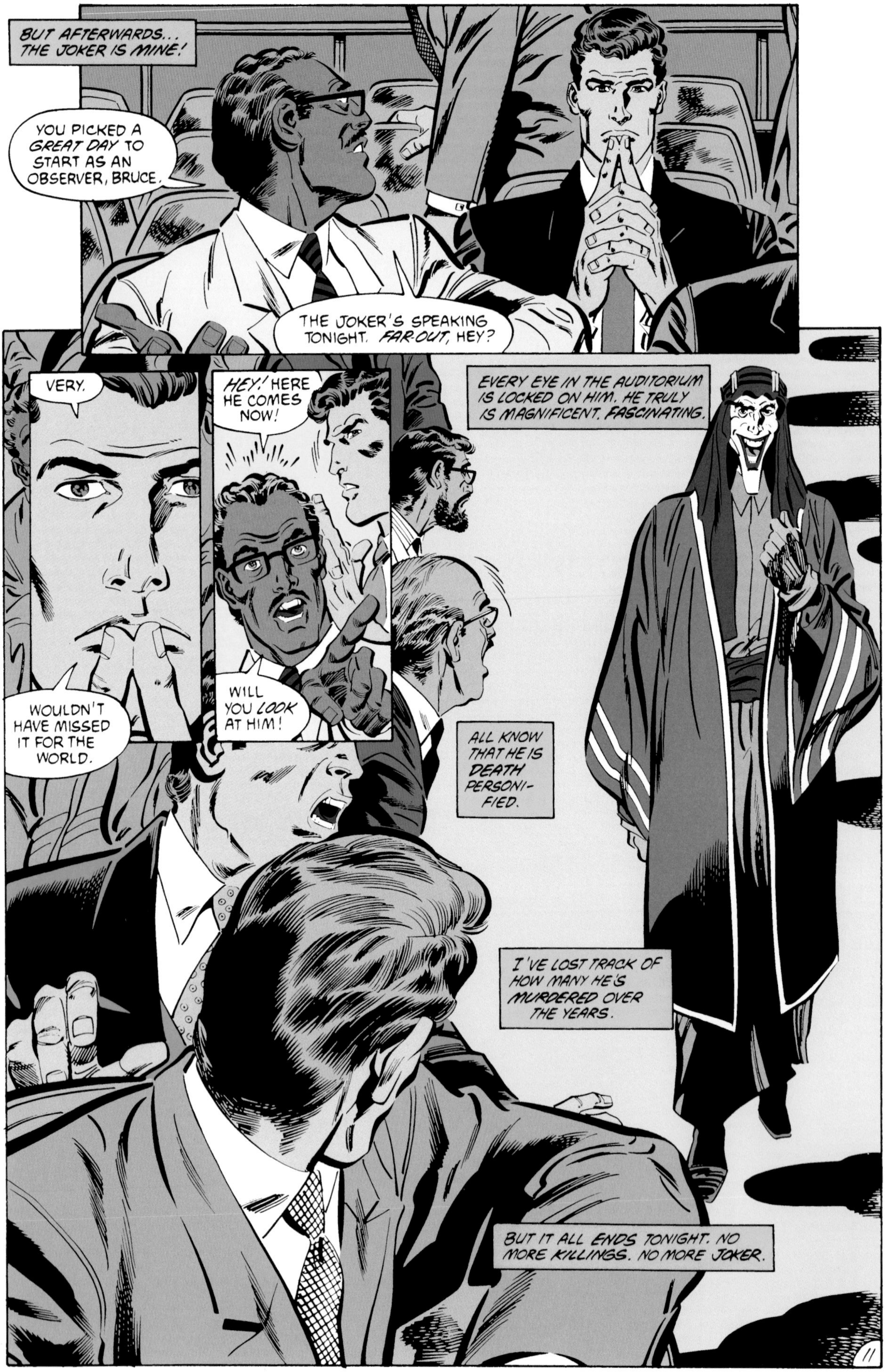
BUT AFTERWARDS... THE JOKER IS MINE!
YOU PICKED A GREAT DAY TO START AS AN OBSERVER, BRUCE.
THE JOKER'S SPEAKING TONIGHT. FAR-OUT, HEY?
VERY.
WOULDN'T HAVE MISSED IT FOR THE WORLD.
HEY! HERE HE COMES NOW!
WILL YOU LOOK AT HIM!
EVERY EYE IN THE AUDITORIUM IS LOCKED ON HIM. HE TRULY IS MAGNIFICENT. FASCINATING.
ALL KNOW THAT HE IS DEATH PERSONI-FIED.
I'VE LOST TRACK OF HOW MANY HE'S MURDERED OVER THE YEARS.
BUT IT ALL ENDS TONIGHT. NO MORE KILLINGS. NO MORE JOKER.
11

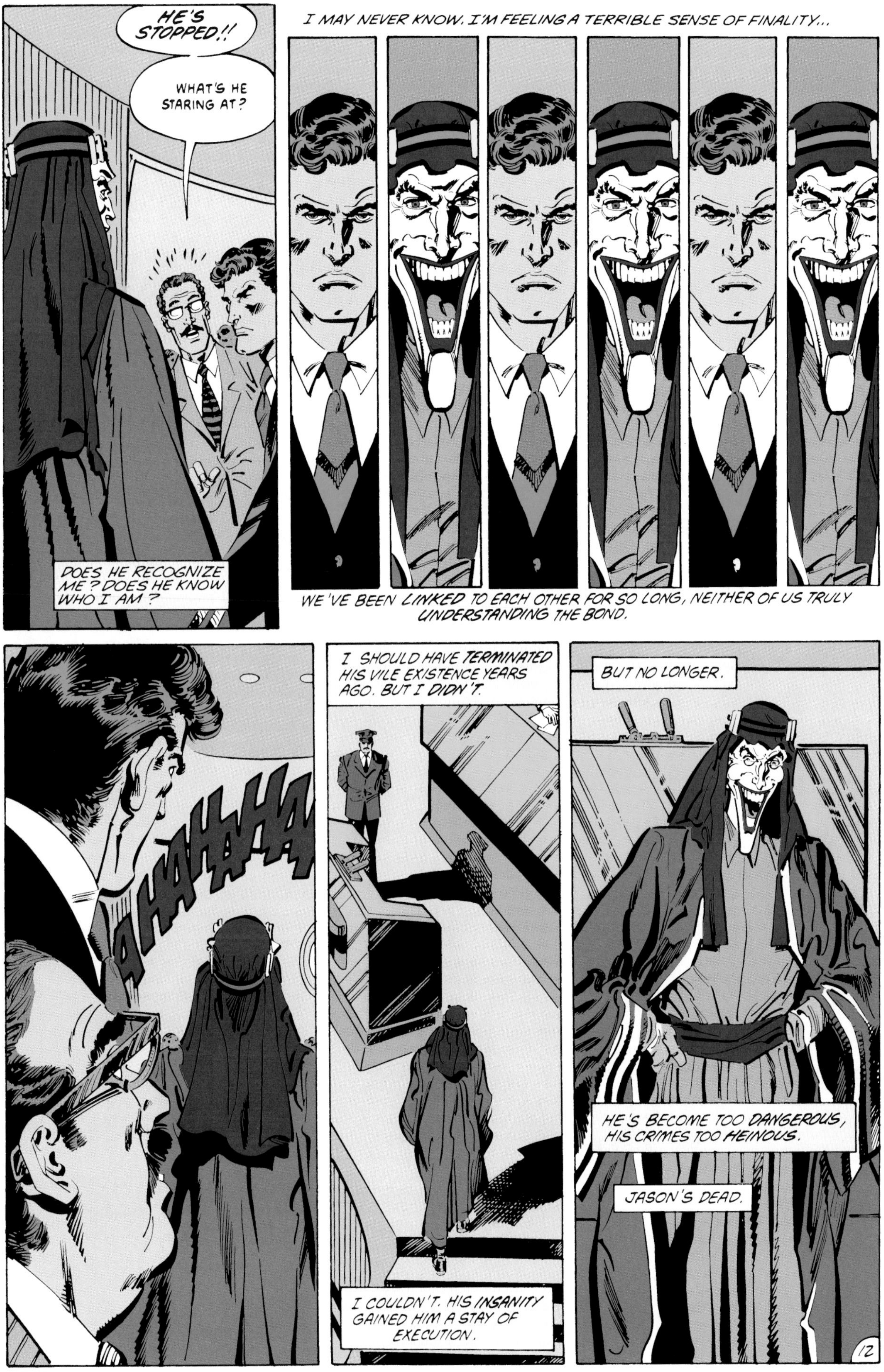
HE'S STOPPED!!
WHAT'S HE STARING AT?
DOES HE RECOGNIZE ME? DOES HE KNOW WHO I AM?
I MAY NEVER KNOW. I'M FEELING A TERRIBLE SENSE OF FINALITY...
WE'VE BEEN LINKED TO EACH OTHER FOR SO LONG, NEITHER OF US TRULY UNDERSTANDING THE BOND.
HAHAHAHAHA
I SHOULD HAVE TERMINATED HIS VILE EXISTENCE YEARS AGO. BUT I DIDN'T.
I COULDN'T. HIS INSANITY GAINED HIM A STAY OF EXECUTION.
BUT NO LONGER.
HE'S BECOME TOO DANGEROUS, HIS CRIMES TOO HEINOUS.
JASON'S DEAD.
12

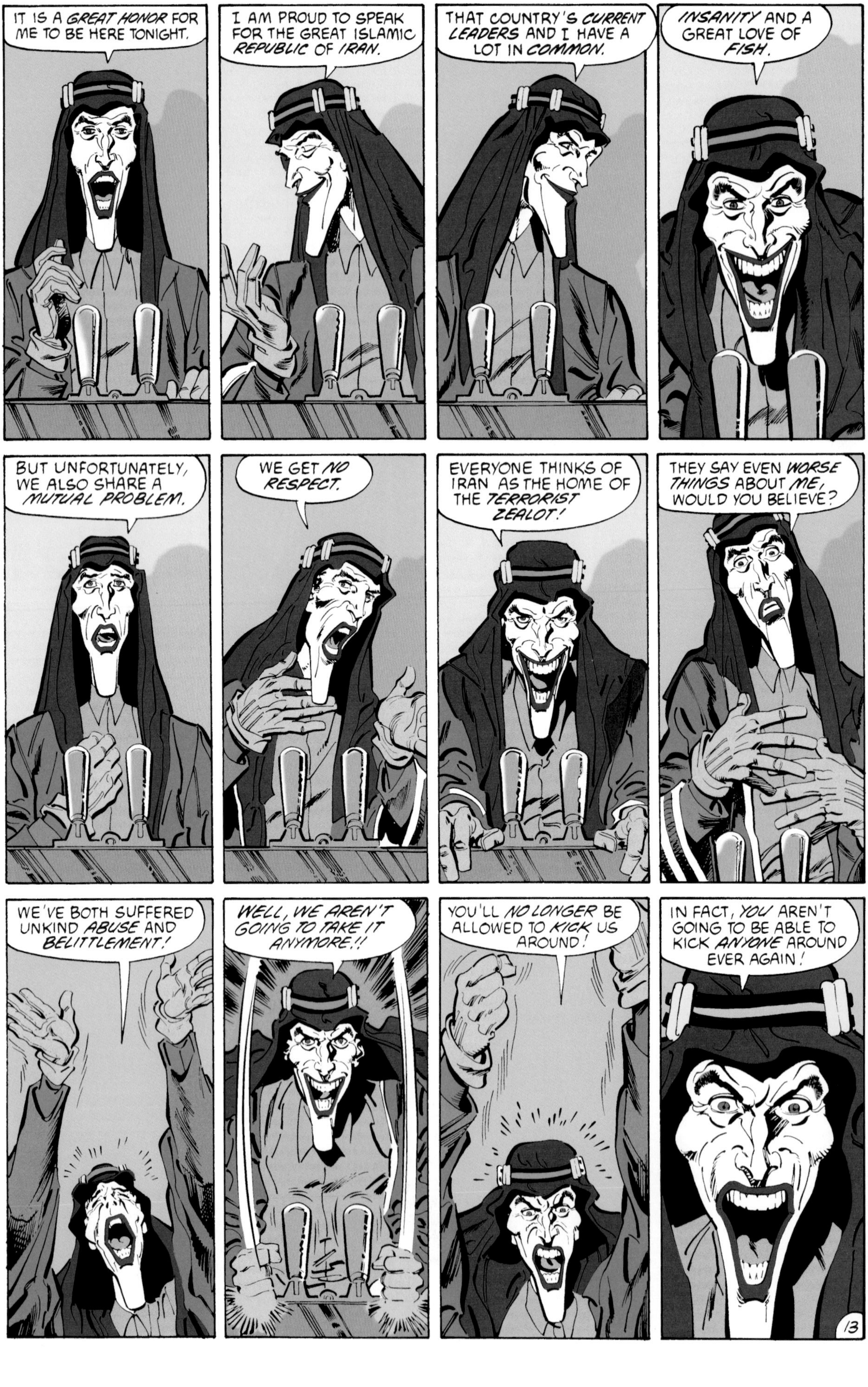
IT IS A GREAT HONOR FOR ME TO BE HERE TONIGHT.
I AM PROUD TO SPEAK FOR THE GREAT ISLAMIC REPUBLIC OF IRAN.
THAT COUNTRY'S CURRENT LEADERS AND I HAVE A LOT IN COMMON.
INSANITY AND A GREAT LOVE OF FISH.
BUT UNFORTUNATELY, WE ALSO SHARE A MUTUAL PROBLEM.
WE GET NO RESPECT.
EVERYONE THINKS OF IRAN AS THE HOME OF THE TERRORIST ZEALOT!
THEY SAY EVEN WORSE THINGS ABOUT ME, WOULD YOU BELIEVE?
WE'VE BOTH SUFFERED UNKIND ABUSE AND BELITTLEMENT!
WELL, WE AREN'T GOING TO TAKE IT ANYMORE!!
YOU'LL NO LONGER BE ALLOWED TO KICK US AROUND!
IN FACT, YOU AREN'T GOING TO BE ABLE TO KICK ANYONE AROUND EVER AGAIN!
13

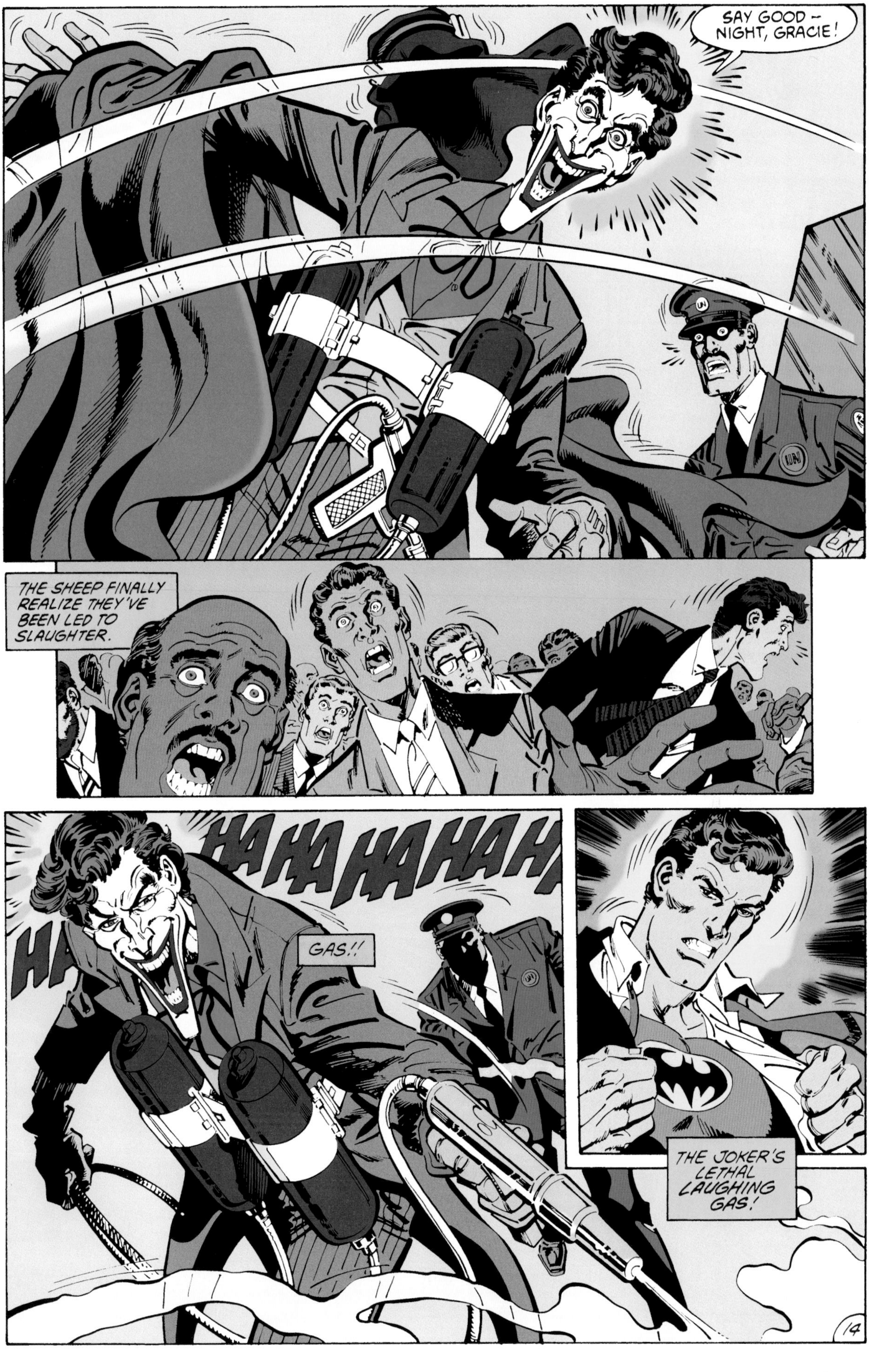
SAY GOOD-NIGHT, GRACIE!
THE SHEEP FINALLY REALIZE THEY'VE BEEN LED TO SLAUGHTER.
HAHAHAHAHAHAHA
GAS!!
THE JOKER'S LETHAL LAUGHING GAS!
14

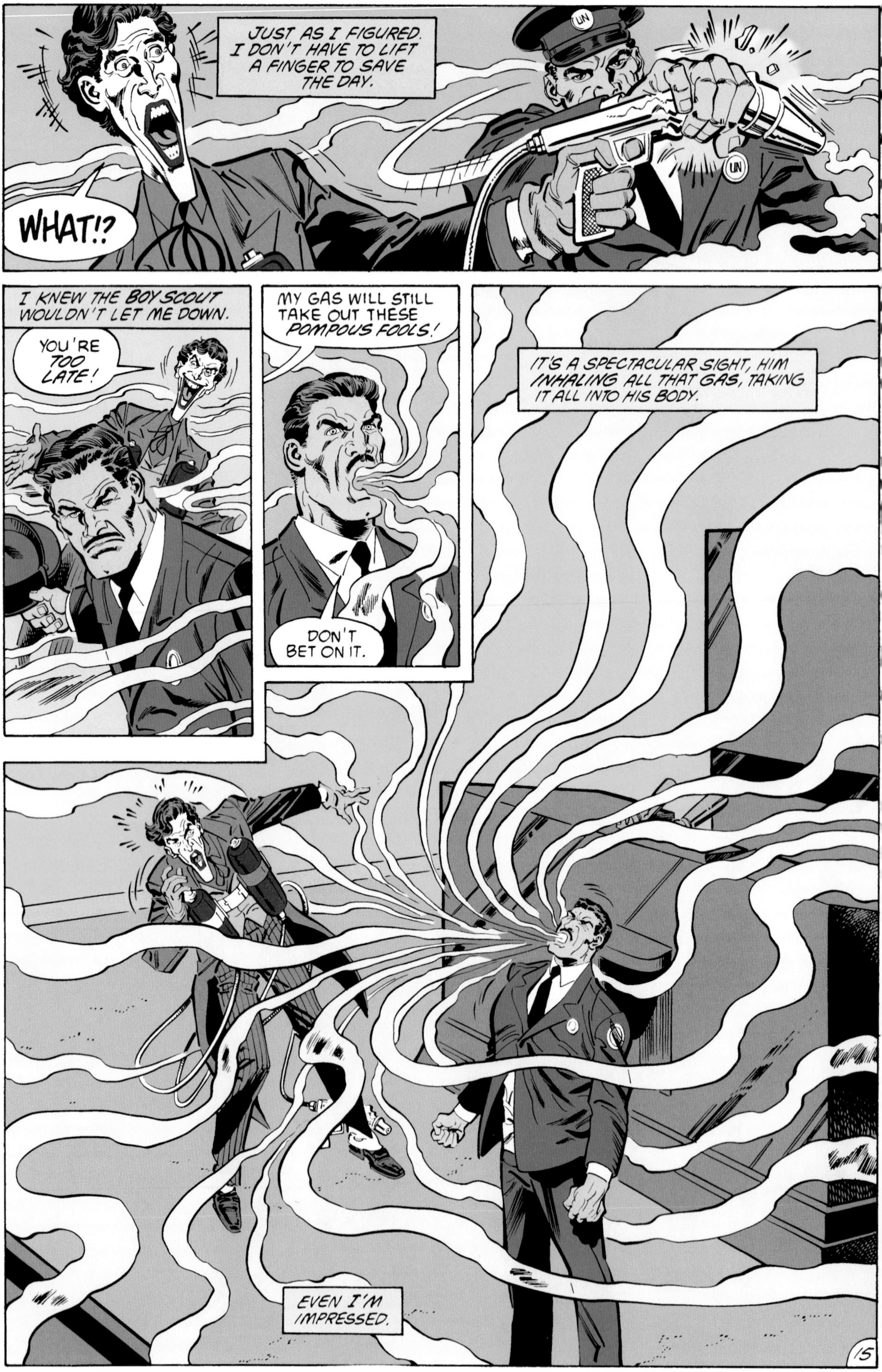
JUST AS I FIGURED. I DON'T HAVE TO LIFT A FINGER TO SAVE THE DAY.
WHAT!?
I KNEW THE BOY SCOUT WOULDN'T LET ME DOWN.
YOU'RE TOO LATE!
MY GAS WILL STILL TAKE OUT THESE POMPOUS FOOLS!
DON'T BET ON IT.
IT'S A SPECTACULAR SIGHT, HIM INHALING ALL THAT GAS, TAKING IT ALL INTO HIS BODY.
EVEN I'M IMPRESSED.
15

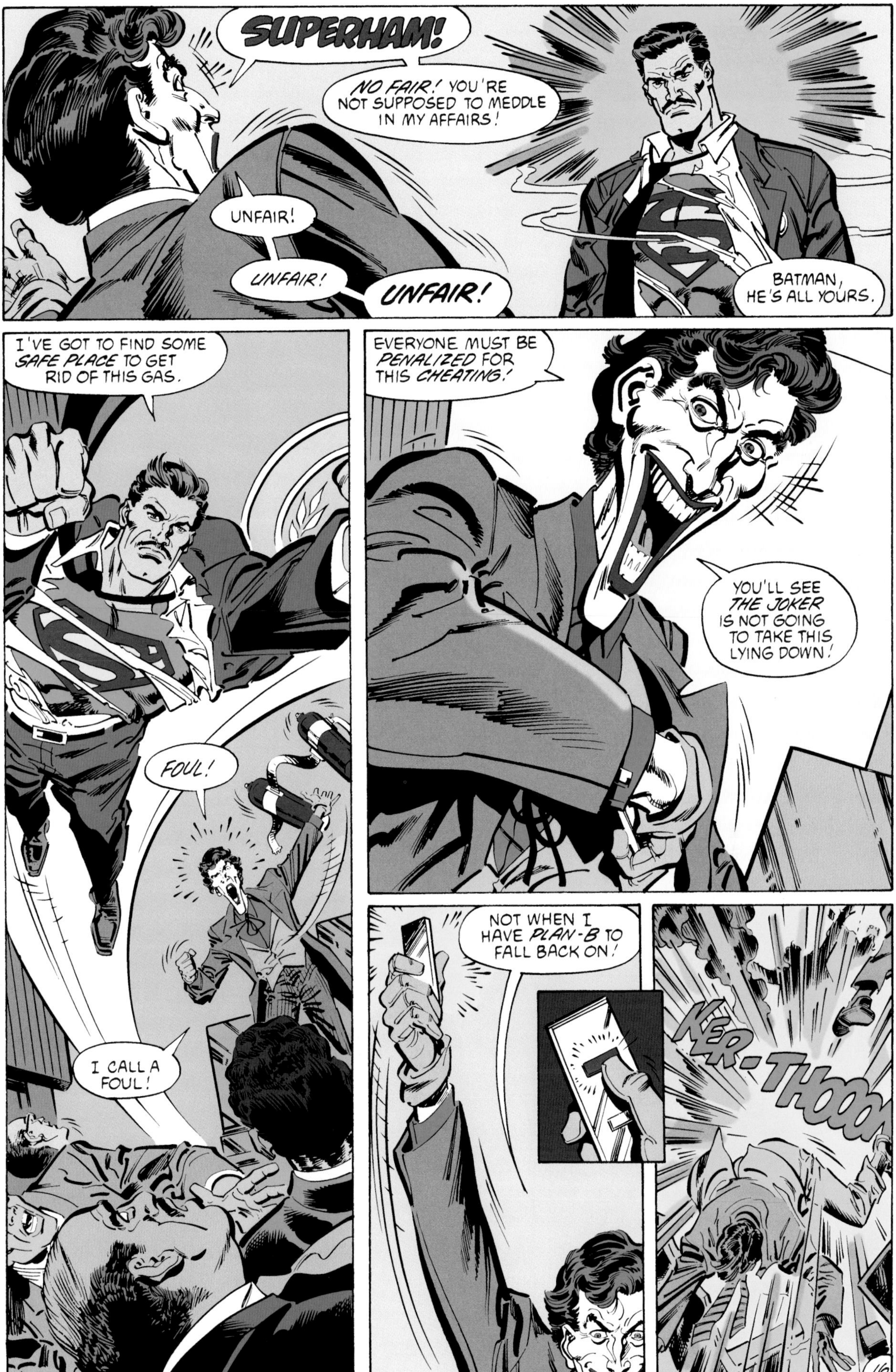
SUPERHAM!
NO FAIR! YOU'RE NOT SUPPOSED TO MEDDLE IN MY AFFAIRS!
UNFAIR!
UNFAIR!
UNFAIR!
BATMAN, HE'S ALL YOURS.
I'VE GOT TO FIND SOME SAFE PLACE TO GET RID OF THIS GAS.
FOUL!
I CALL A FOUL!
EVERYONE MUST BE PENALIZED FOR THIS CHEATING!
YOU'LL SEE THE JOKER IS NOT GOING TO TAKE THIS LYING DOWN!
NOT WHEN I HAVE PLAN-B TO FALL BACK ON!
KER-THOOOM
16

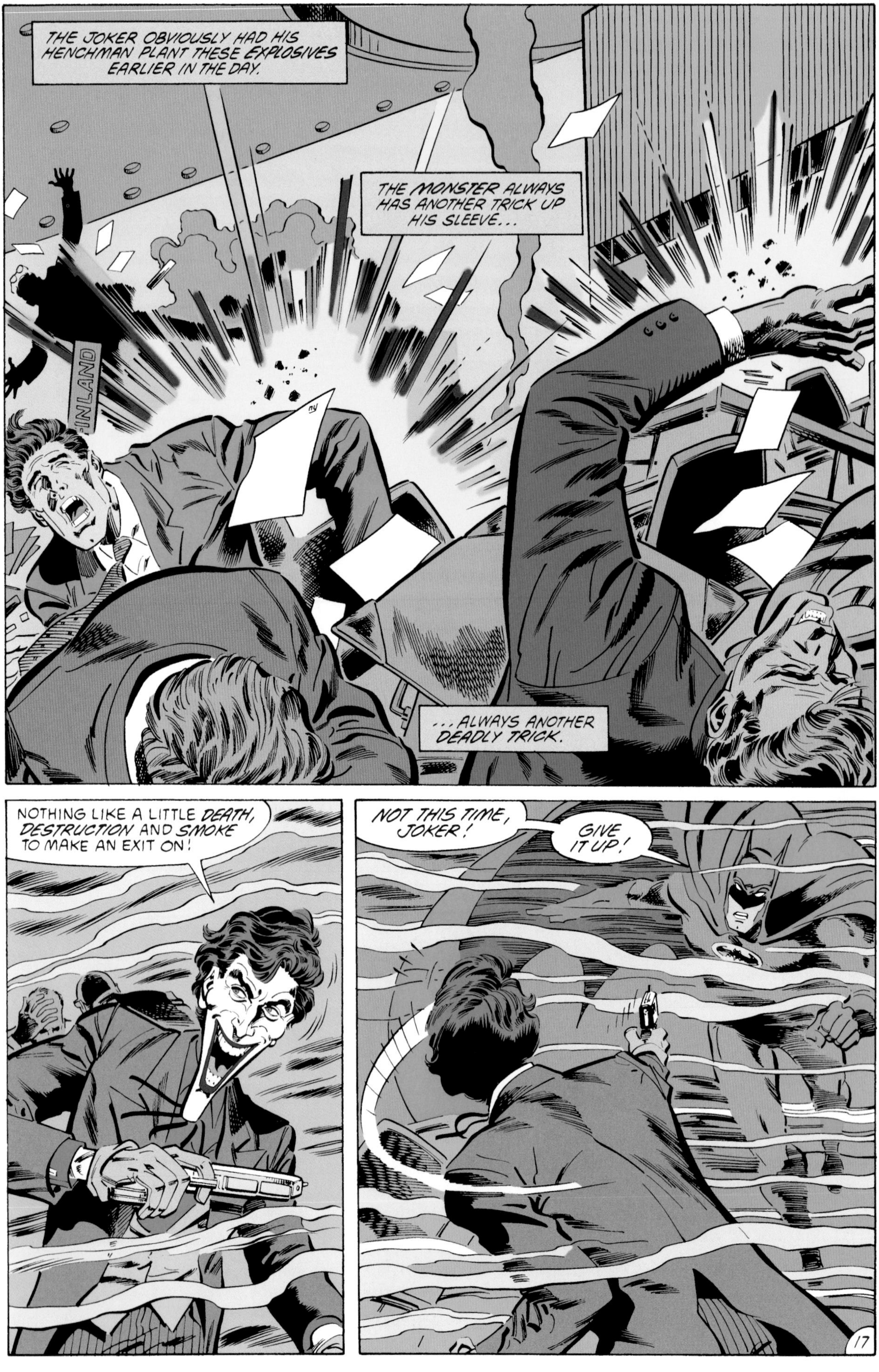
THE JOKER OBVIOUSLY HAD HIS HENCHMAN PLANT THESE EXPLOSIVES EARLIER IN THE DAY.
THE MONSTER ALWAYS HAS ANOTHER TRICK UP HIS SLEEVE...
INLAND
...ALWAYS ANOTHER DEADLY TRICK.
NOTHING LIKE A LITTLE DEATH, DESTRUCTION AND SMOKE TO MAKE AN EXIT ON!
NOT THIS TIME, JOKER!
GIVE IT UP!
17

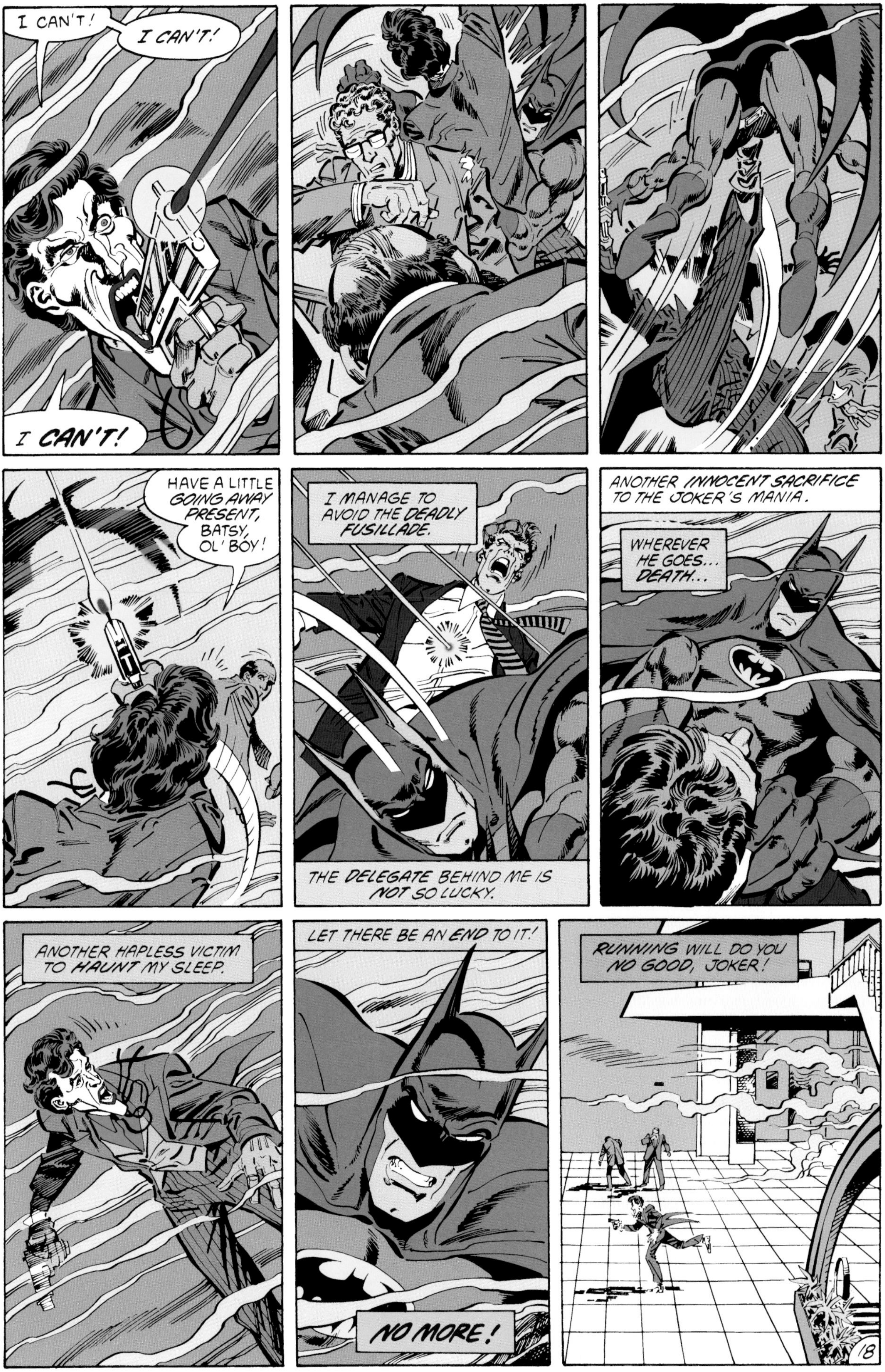
I CAN'T!
I CAN'T!
I CAN'T!
HAVE A LITTLE GOING AWAY PRESENT, BATSY, OL' BOY!
I MANAGE TO AVOID THE DEADLY FUSILLADE.
THE DELEGATE BEHIND ME IS NOT SO LUCKY.
ANOTHER INNOCENT SACRIFICE TO THE JOKER'S MANIA.
WHEREVER HE GOES... DEATH...
ANOTHER HAPLESS VICTIM TO HAUNT MY SLEEP.
LET THERE BE AN END TO IT!
NO MORE!
RUNNING WILL DO YOU NO GOOD, JOKER!
18

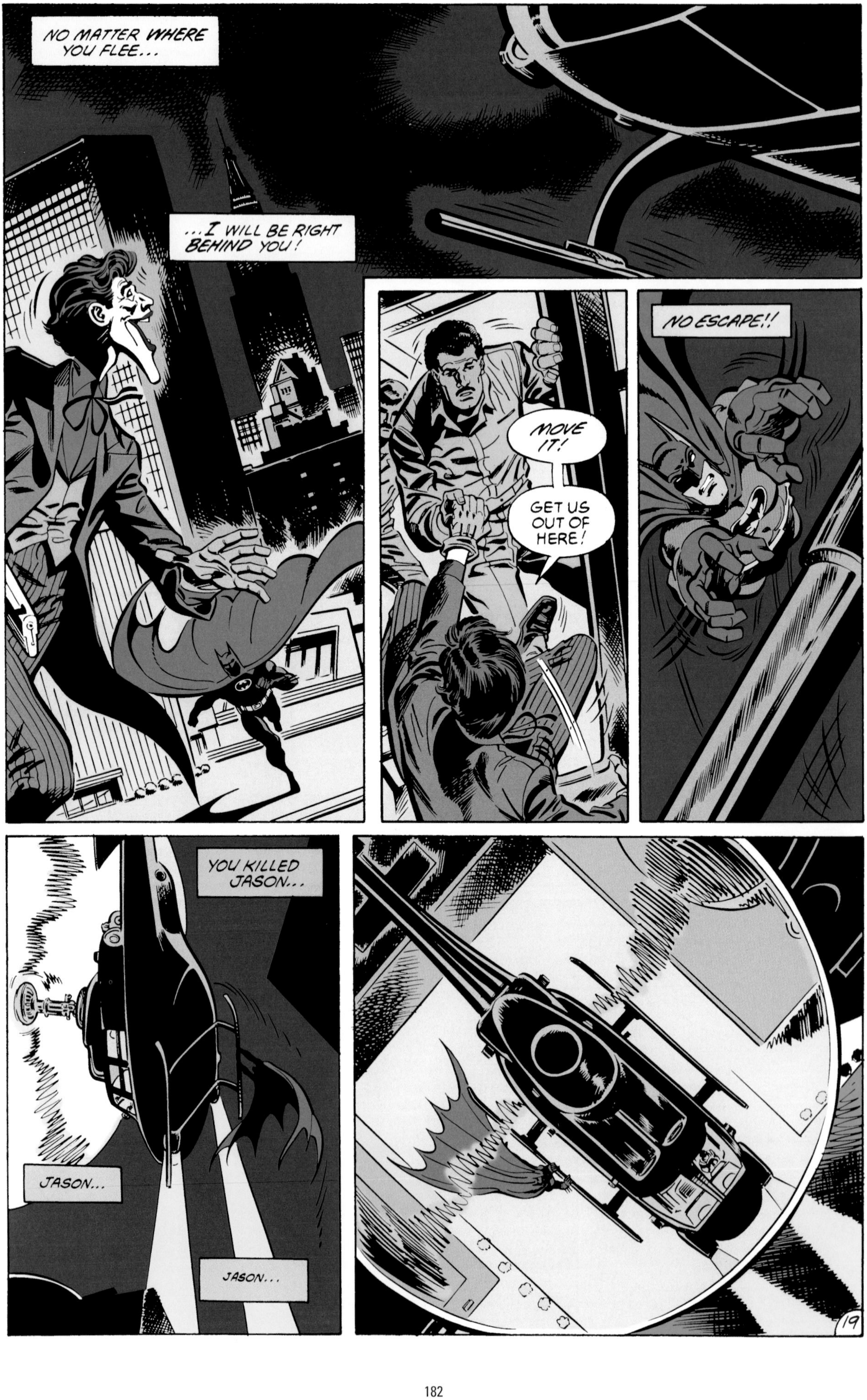
NO MATTER WHERE YOU FLEE...
...I WILL BE RIGHT BEHIND YOU!
MOVE IT!
GET US OUT OF HERE!
NO ESCAPE!!
YOU KILLED JASON...
JASON...
JASON...
19

NO!!

BBBRRRRIII HIIT TTT

20

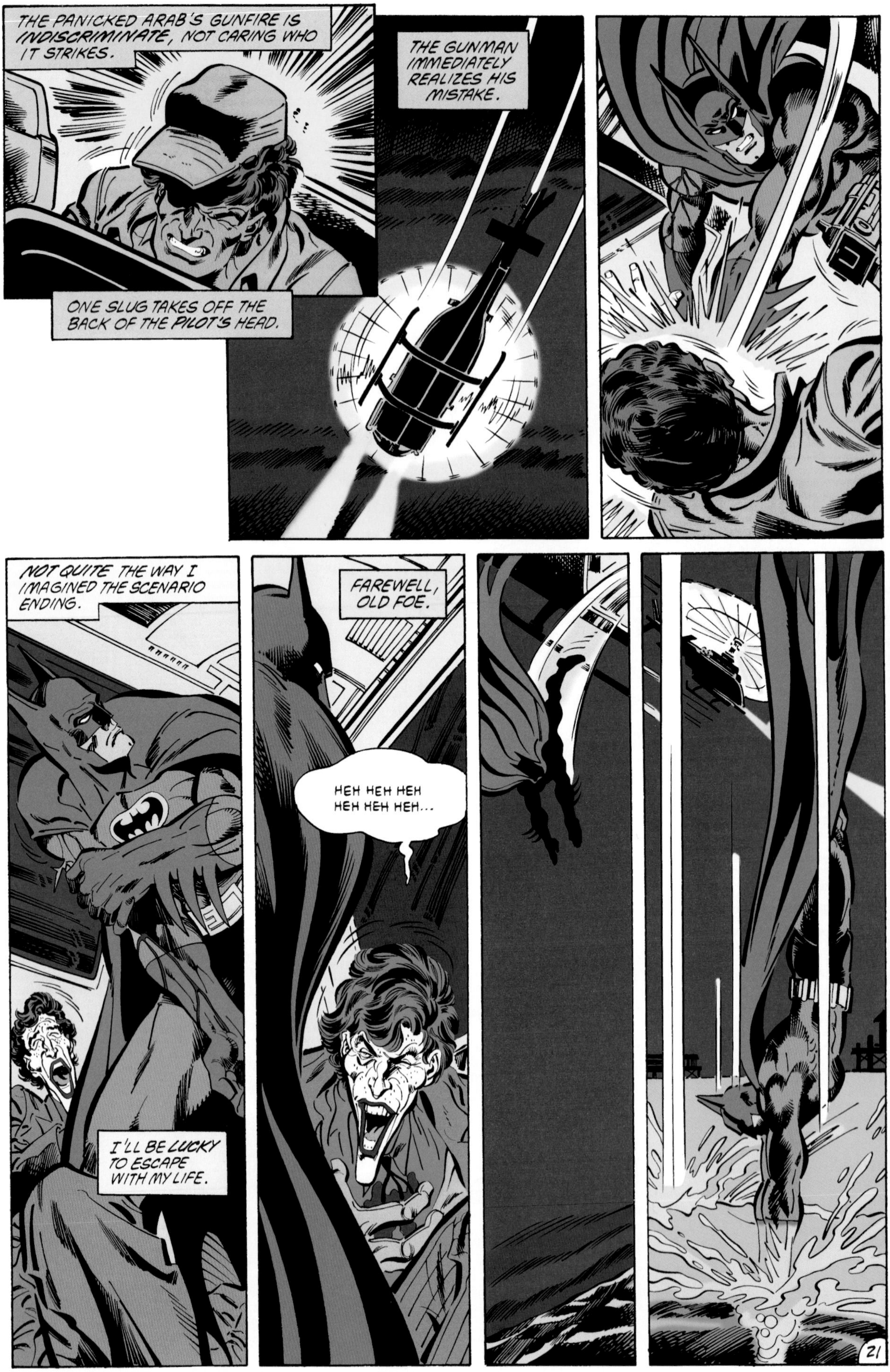

THE PANICKED ARAB'S GUNFIRE IS INDISCRIMINATE, NOT CARING WHO IT STRIKES.
ONE SLUG TAKES OFF THE BACK OF THE PILOT'S HEAD.
THE GUNMAN IMMEDIATELY REALIZES HIS MISTAKE.
NOT QUITE THE WAY I IMAGINED THE SCENARIO ENDING.
I'LL BE LUCKY TO ESCAPE WITH MY LIFE.
FAREWELL, OLD FOE.
HEH HEH HEH HEH HEH HEH...
21

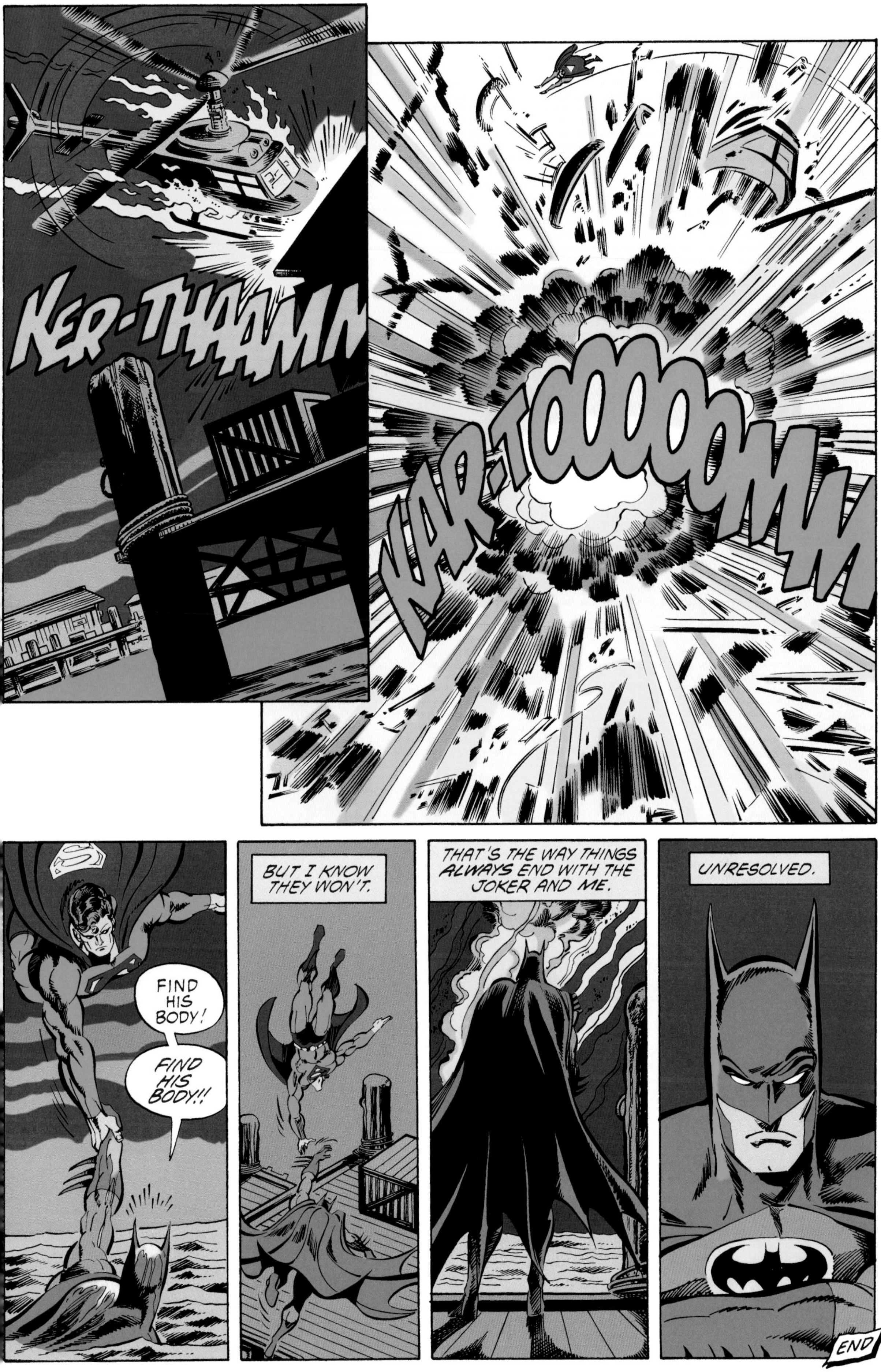
KER-THAAMM
KAR-TOOOOOMM
FIND HIS BODY!
FIND HIS BODY!!
BUT I KNOW THEY WON'T.
THAT'S THE WAY THINGS ALWAYS END WITH THE JOKER AND ME.
UNRESOLVED.
END

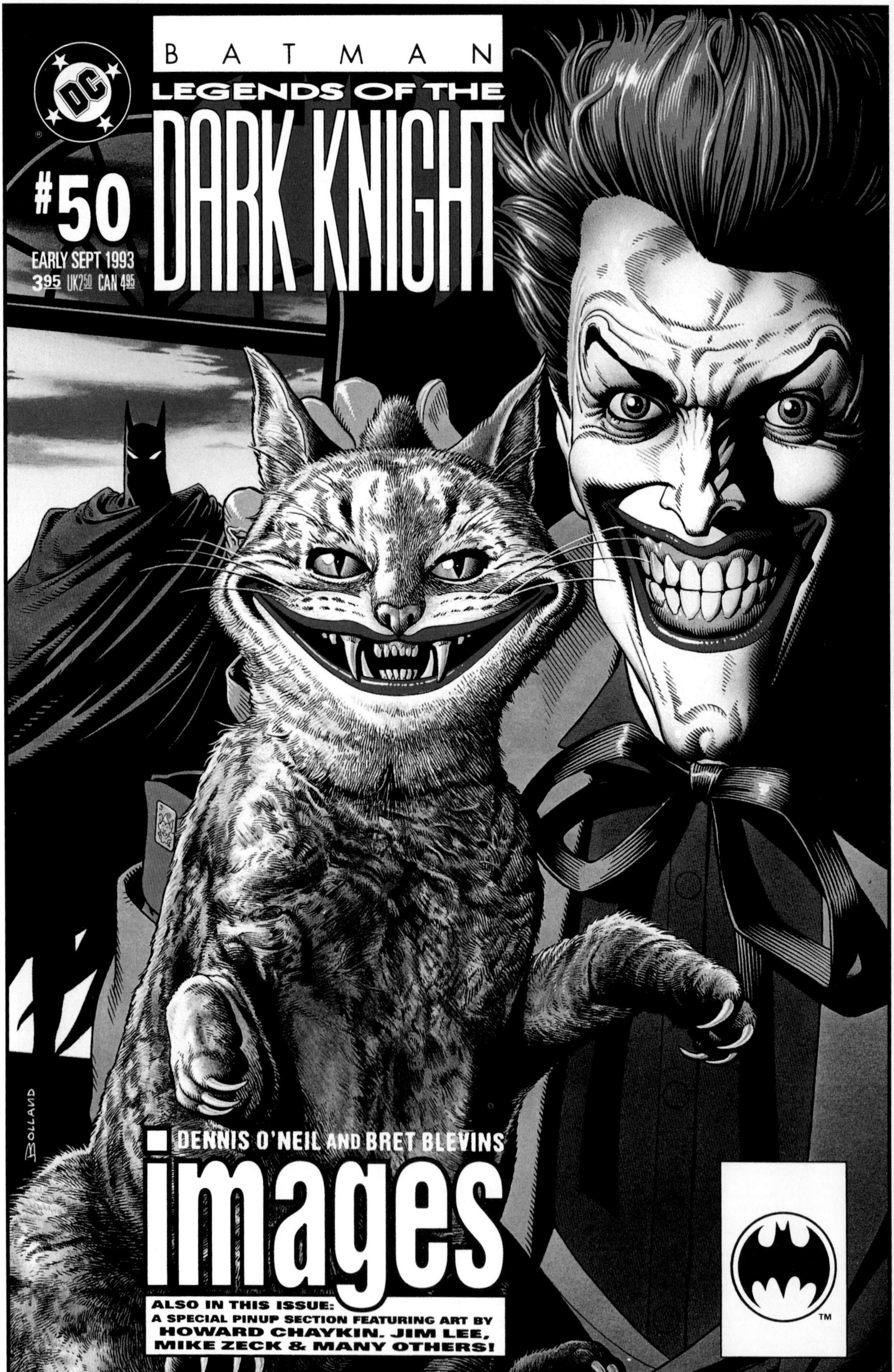
BATMAN
LEGENDS OF THE
DARK KNIGHT
#50
EARLY SEPT 1993
3.95 UK2.50 CAN 4.95
BOLLAND
DENNIS O'NEIL AND BRET BLEVINS
images
ALSO IN THIS ISSUE:
A SPECIAL PINUP SECTION FEATURING ART BY
HOWARD CHAYKIN, JIM LEE,
MIKE ZECK & MANY OTHERS!

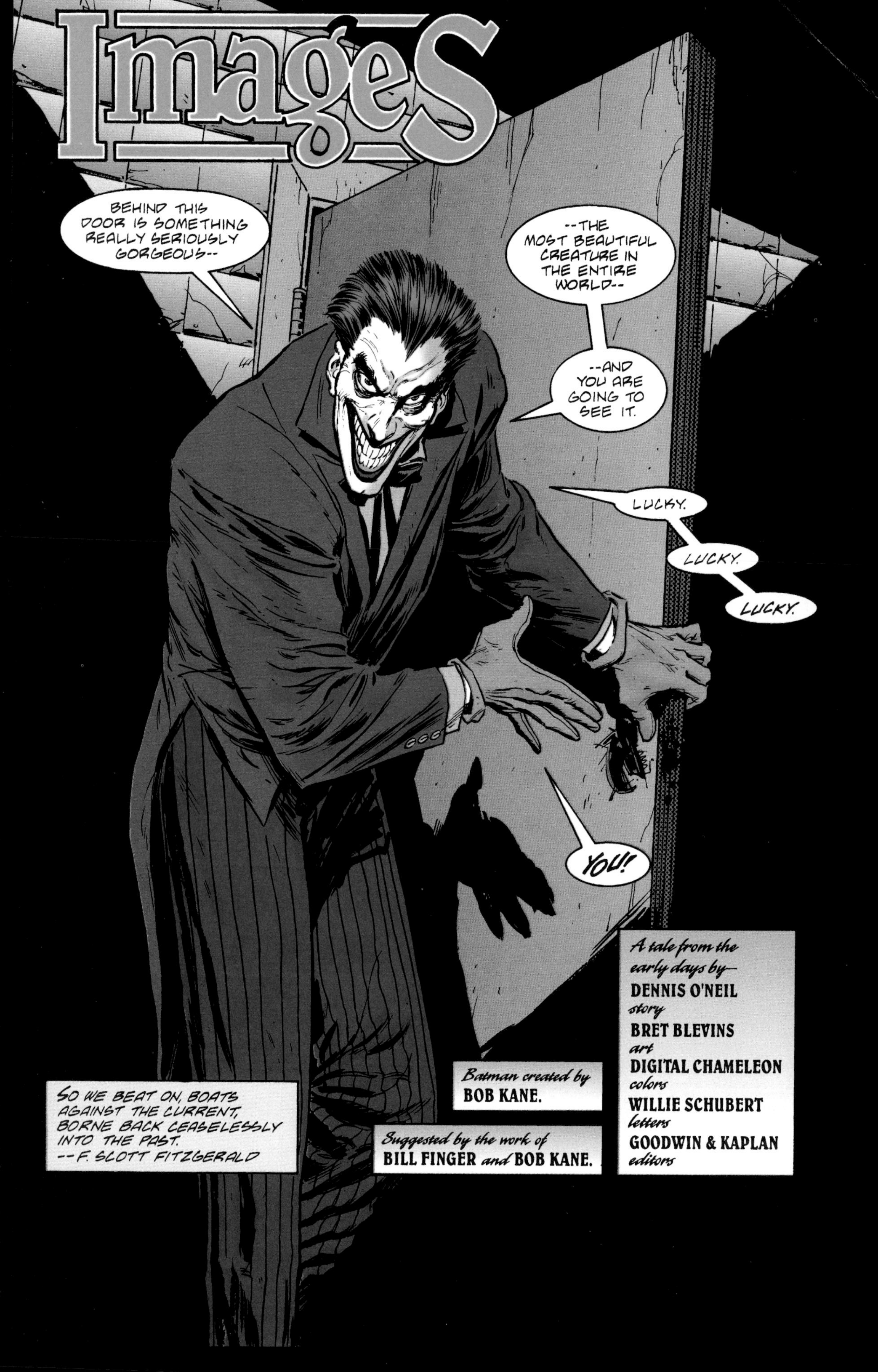
Images
BEHIND THIS DOOR IS SOMETHING REALLY SERIOUSLY GORGEOUS--
--THE MOST BEAUTIFUL CREATURE IN THE ENTIRE WORLD--
--AND YOU ARE GOING TO SEE IT.
LUCKY.
LUCKY.
LUCKY.
YOU!
A tale from the early days by-- DENNIS O'NEIL story BRET BLEVINS art DIGITAL CHAMELEON colors WILLIE SCHUBERT letters GOODWIN & KAPLAN editors
Batman created by BOB KANE.
SO WE BEAT ON, BOATS AGAINST THE CURRENT, BORNE BACK CEASELESSLY INTO THE PAST. --F. SCOTT FITZGERALD
Suggested by the work of BILL FINGER and BOB KANE.

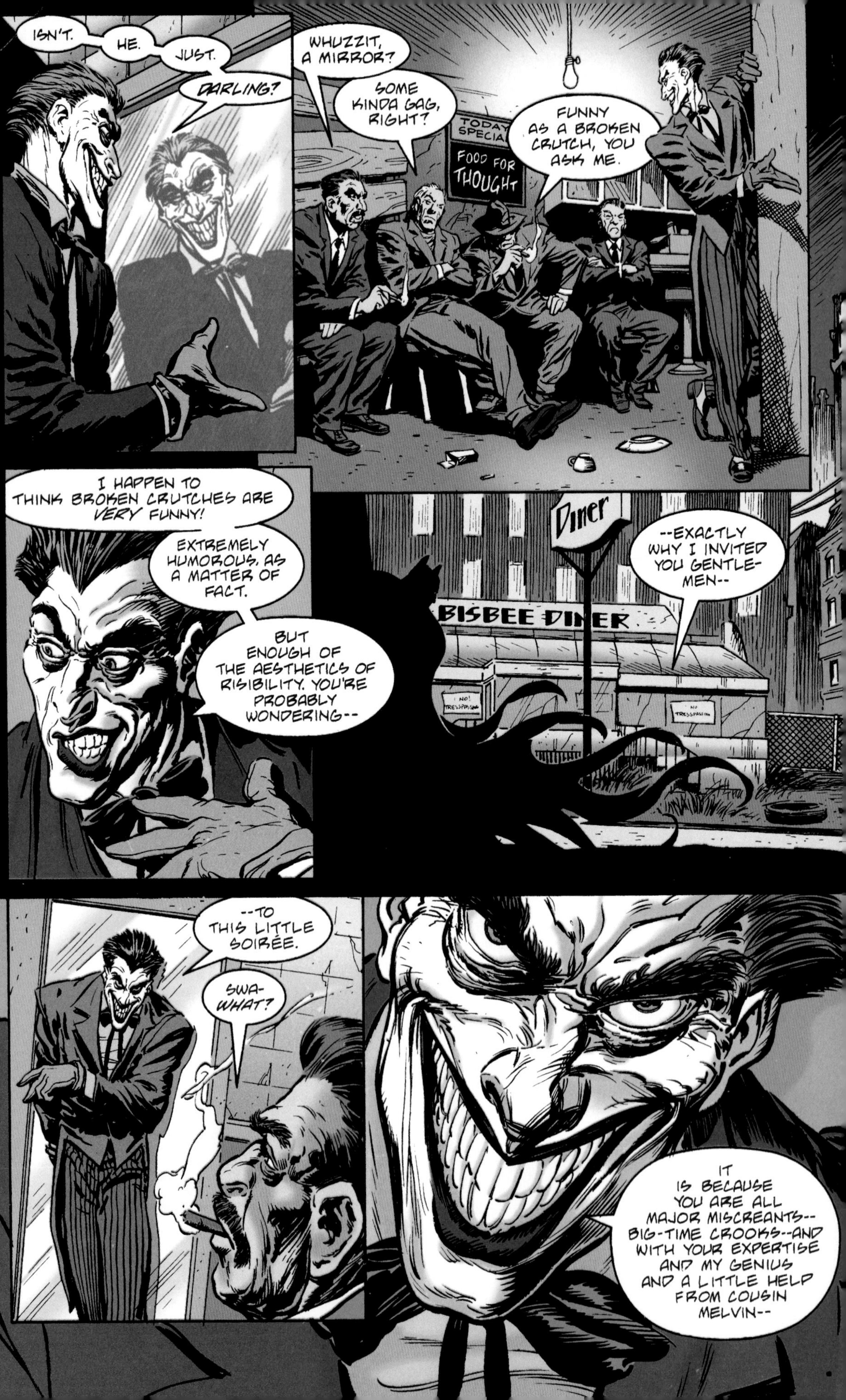
ISN'T.
HE.
JUST.
DARLING?
WHUZZIT, A MIRROR?
SOME KINDA GAG, RIGHT?
TODAY'S SPECIAL
FOOD FOR THOUGHT
FUNNY AS A BROKEN CRUTCH, YOU ASK ME.
I HAPPEN TO THINK BROKEN CRUTCHES ARE VERY FUNNY!
EXTREMELY HUMOROUS, AS A MATTER OF FACT.
BUT ENOUGH OF THE AESTHETICS OF RISIBILITY. YOU'RE PROBABLY WONDERING--
Diner
BISBEE DINER
--EXACTLY WHY I INVITED YOU GENTLEMEN--
--TO THIS LITTLE SOIRÉE.
SWA-WHAT?
IT IS BECAUSE YOU ARE ALL MAJOR MISCREANTS--BIG-TIME CROOKS--AND WITH YOUR EXPERTISE AND MY GENIUS AND A LITTLE HELP FROM COUSIN MELVIN--

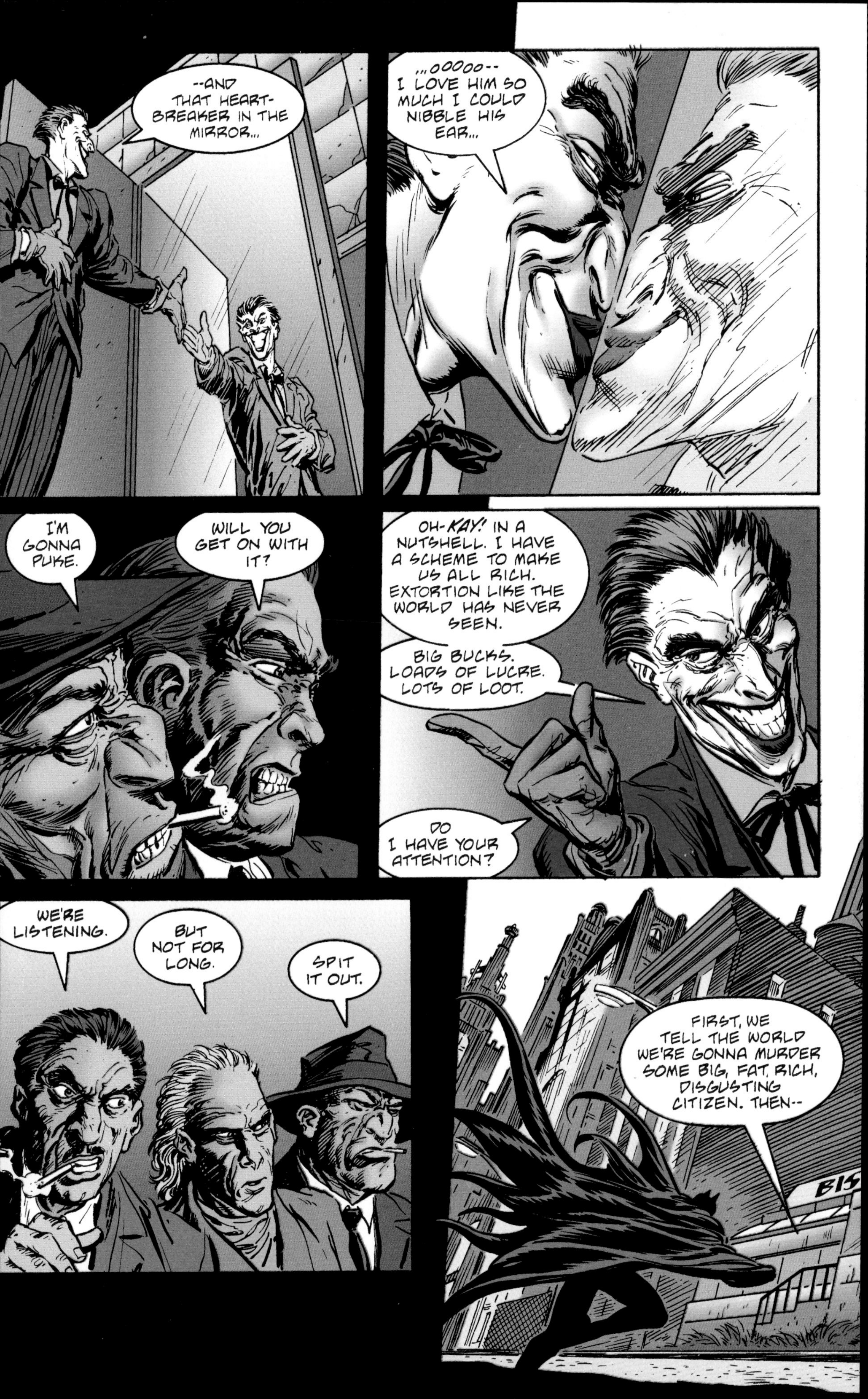
--AND THAT HEART-BREAKER IN THE MIRROR...
...OOOOO-- I LOVE HIM SO MUCH I COULD NIBBLE HIS EAR...
I'M GONNA PUKE.
WILL YOU GET ON WITH IT?
OH-KAY! IN A NUTSHELL. I HAVE A SCHEME TO MAKE US ALL RICH. EXTORTION LIKE THE WORLD HAS NEVER SEEN.
BIG BUCKS. LOADS OF LUCRE. LOTS OF LOOT.
DO I HAVE YOUR ATTENTION?
WE'RE LISTENING.
BUT NOT FOR LONG.
SPIT IT OUT.
FIRST, WE TELL THE WORLD WE'RE GONNA MURDER SOME BIG, FAT, RICH, DISGUSTING CITIZEN. THEN--

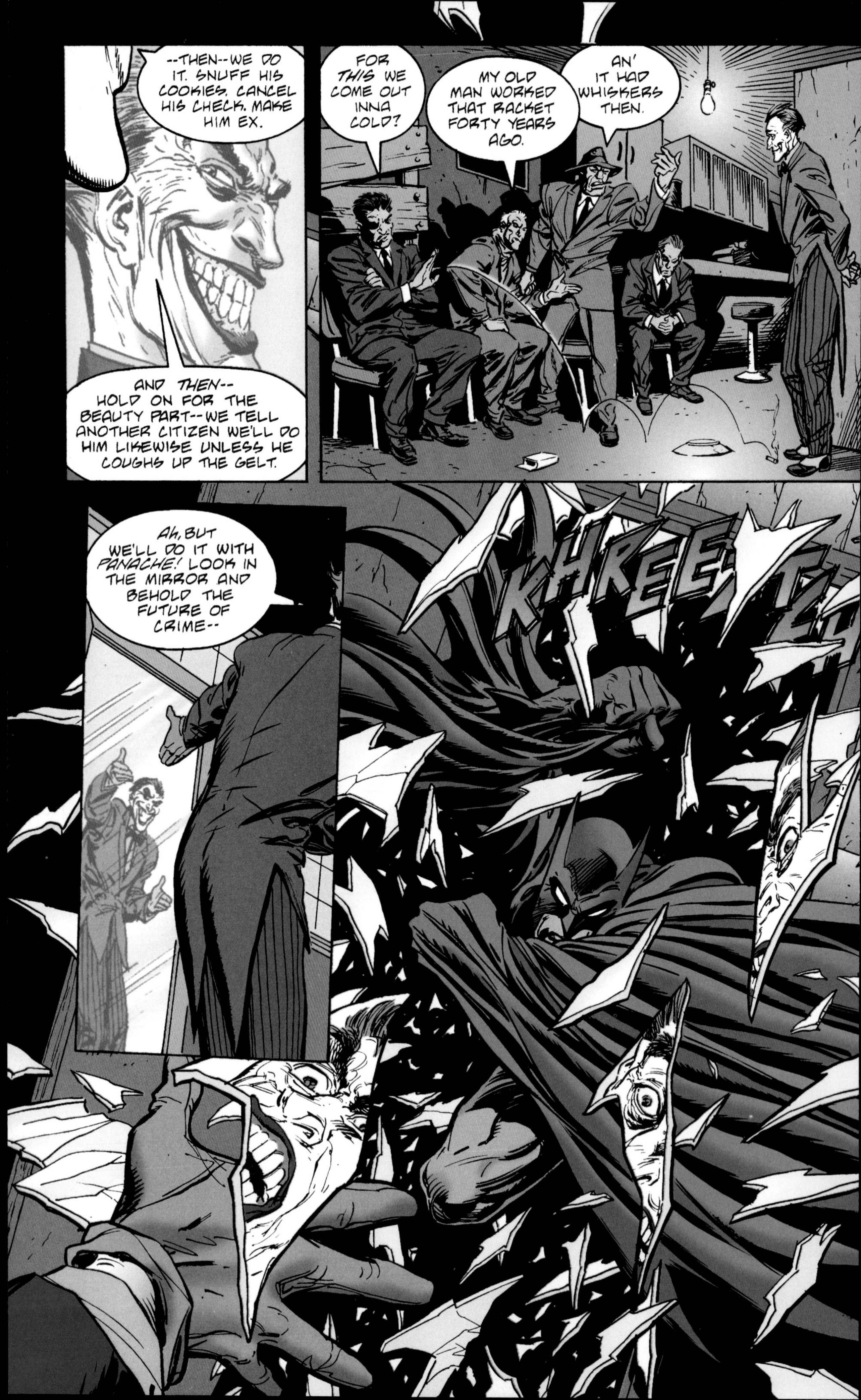
--THEN--WE DO IT. SNUFF HIS COOKIES. CANCEL HIS CHECK. MAKE HIM EX.
AND THEN-- HOLD ON FOR THE BEAUTY PART--WE TELL ANOTHER CITIZEN WE'LL DO HIM LIKEWISE UNLESS HE COUGHS UP THE GELT.
FOR THIS WE COME OUT INNA COLD?
MY OLD MAN WORKED THAT RACKET FORTY YEARS AGO.
AN' IT HAD WHISKERS THEN.
AH, BUT WE'LL DO IT WITH PANACHE! LOOK IN THE MIRROR AND BEHOLD THE FUTURE OF CRIME--
KHREE

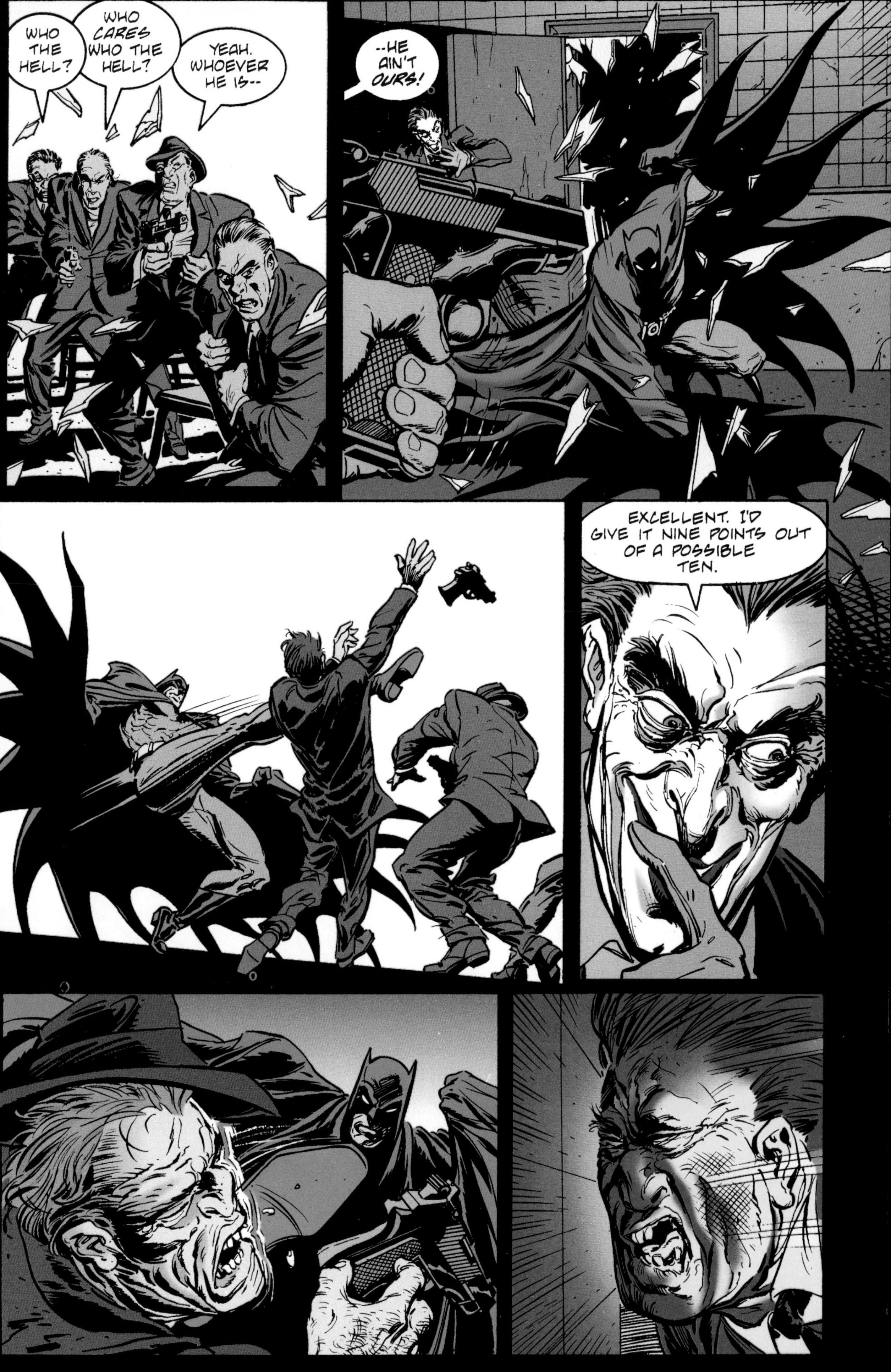
WHO THE HELL?
WHO CARES WHO THE HELL?
YEAH. WHOEVER HE IS--
--HE AIN'T OURS!
EXCELLENT. I'D GIVE IT NINE POINTS OUT OF A POSSIBLE TEN.

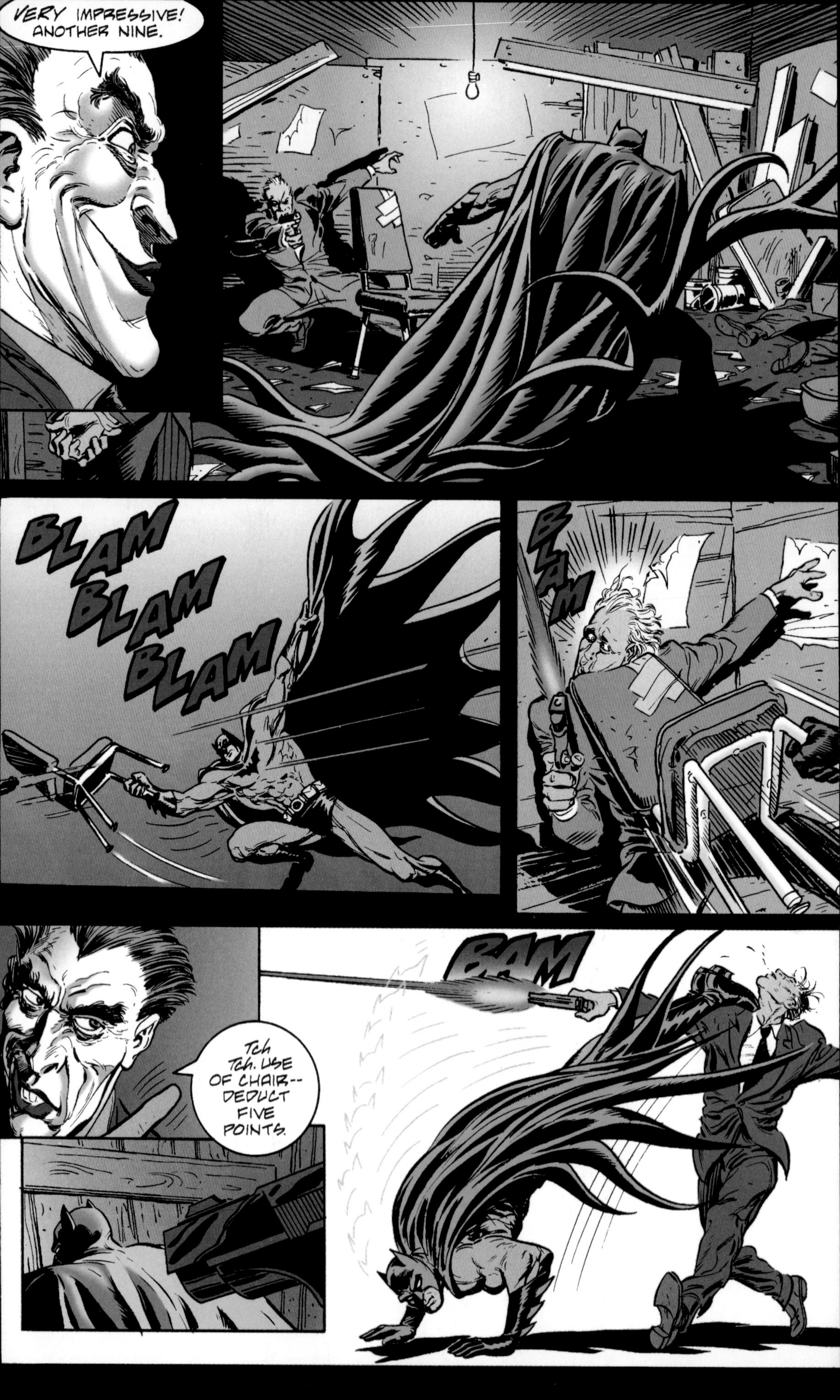
VERY IMPRESSIVE! ANOTHER NINE.
BLAM BLAM BLAM
BLAM
BAM
Tch Tch. USE OF CHAIR-- DEDUCT FIVE POINTS.

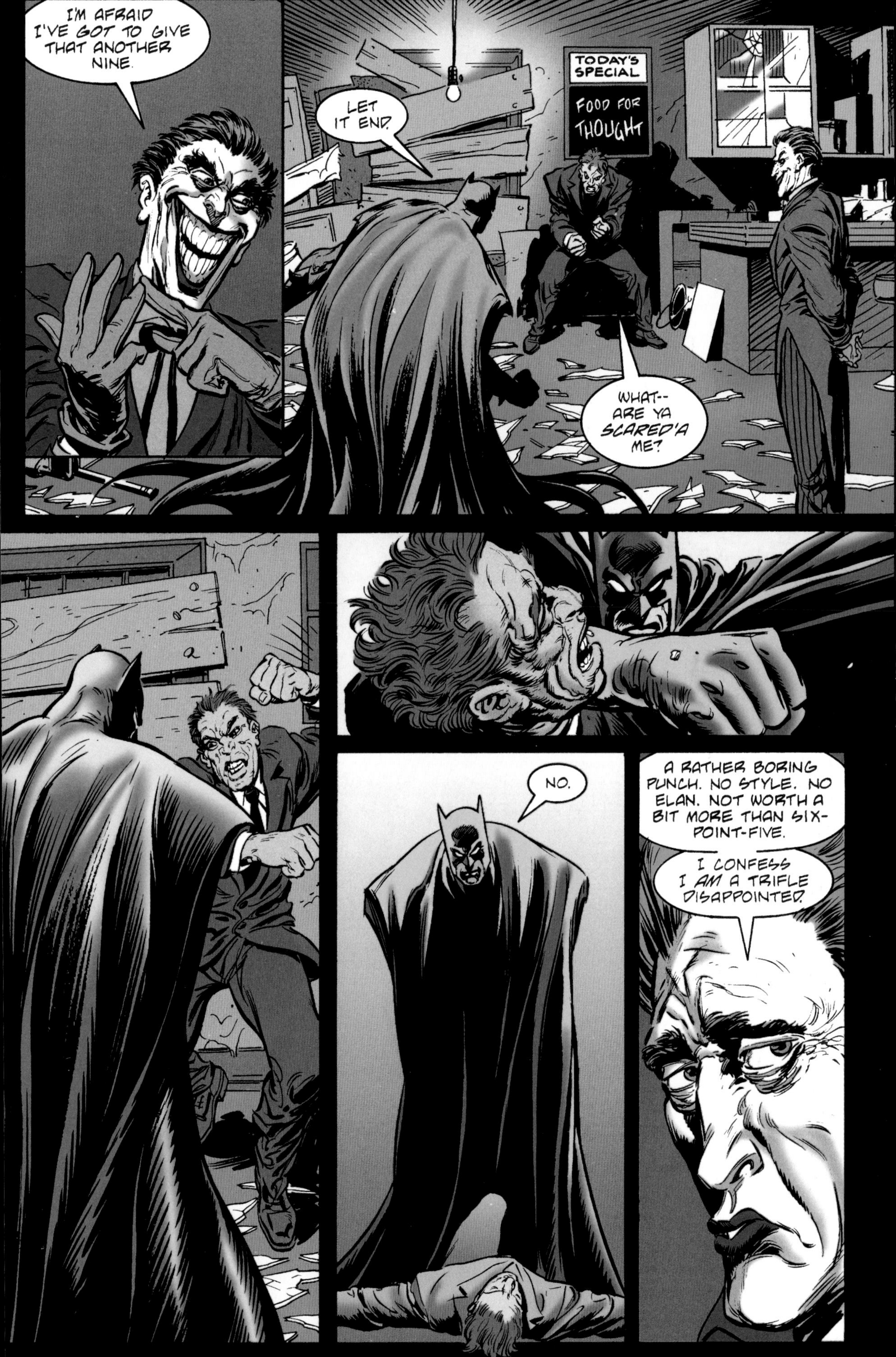

I'M AFRAID I'VE GOT TO GIVE THAT ANOTHER NINE.
LET IT END.
TODAY'S SPECIAL
FOOD FOR THOUGHT
WHAT--ARE YA SCARED'A ME?
NO.
A RATHER BORING PUNCH. NO STYLE. NO ELAN. NOT WORTH A BIT MORE THAN SIX-POINT-FIVE.
I CONFESS I AM A TRIFLE DISAPPOINTED.

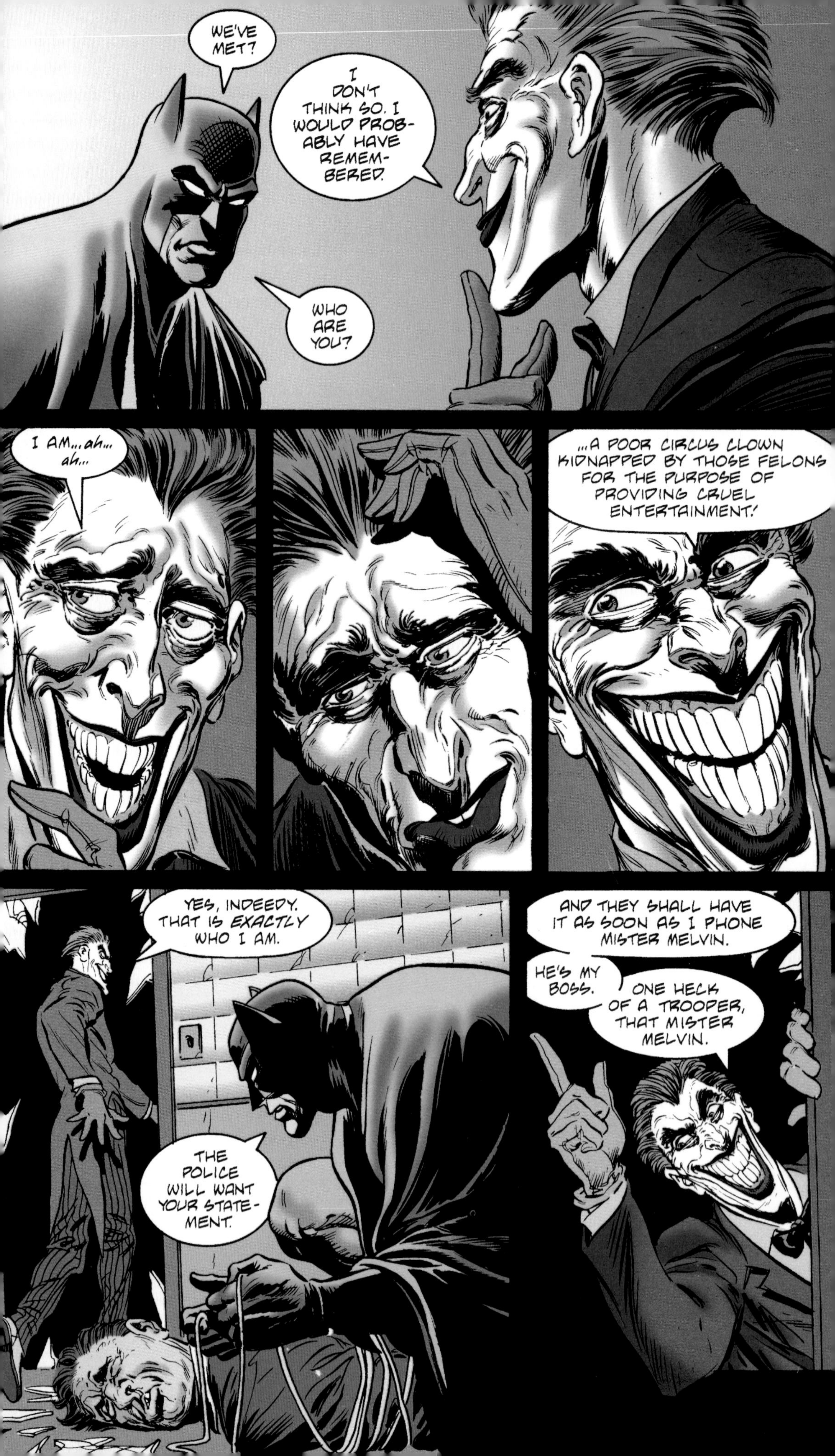
WE'VE MET?
I DON'T THINK SO. I WOULD PROBABLY HAVE REMEMBERED.
WHO ARE YOU?
I AM...ah... ah...
...A POOR CIRCUS CLOWN KIDNAPPED BY THOSE FELONS FOR THE PURPOSE OF PROVIDING CRUEL ENTERTAINMENT!
YES, INDEEDY. THAT IS EXACTLY WHO I AM.
THE POLICE WILL WANT YOUR STATEMENT.
AND THEY SHALL HAVE IT AS SOON AS I PHONE MISTER MELVIN.
HE'S MY BOSS.
ONE HECK OF A TROOPER, THAT MISTER MELVIN.

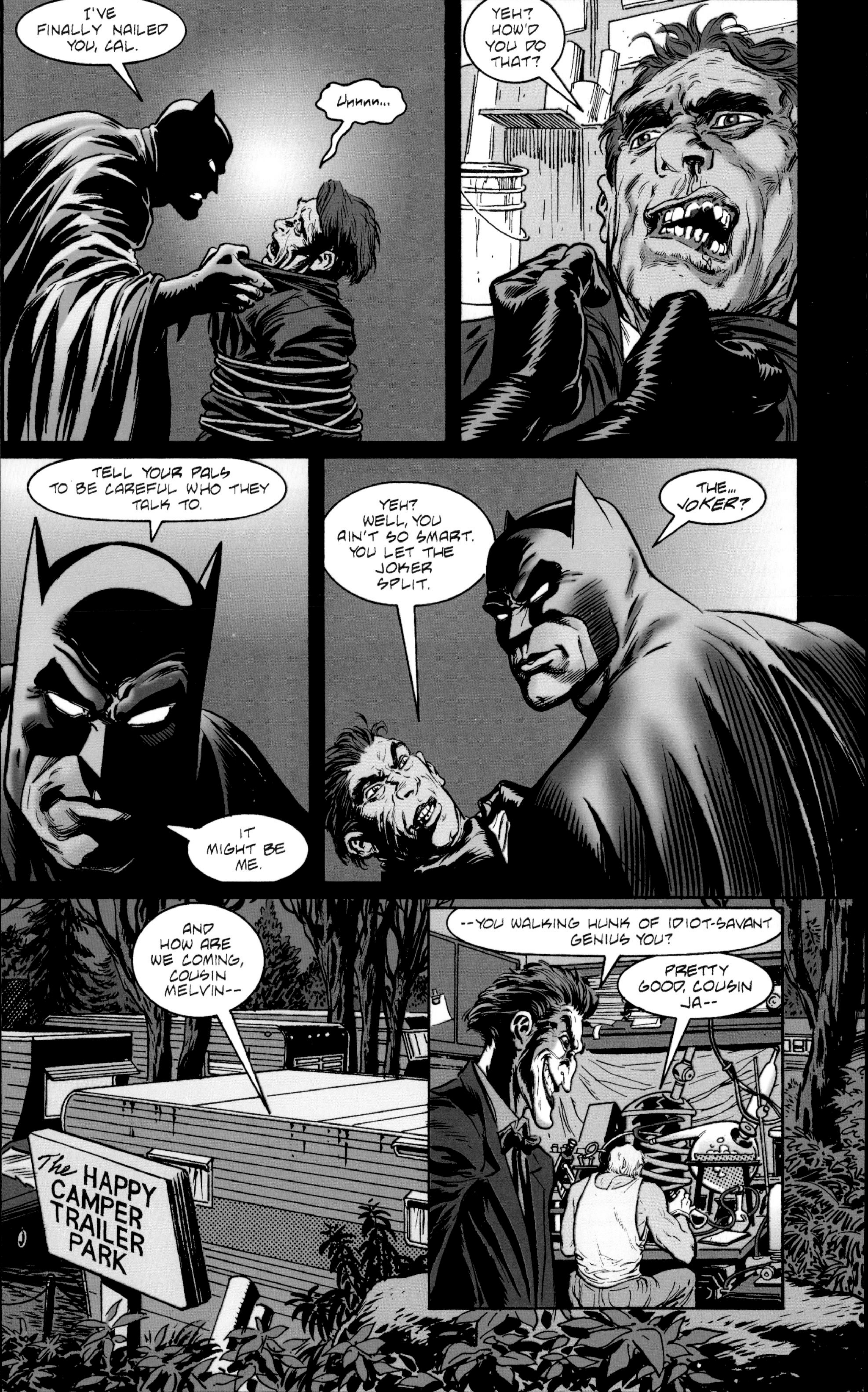
I'VE FINALLY NAILED YOU, CAL.
Unnnn...
YEH? HOW'D YOU DO THAT?
TELL YOUR PALS TO BE CAREFUL WHO THEY TALK TO.
IT MIGHT BE ME.
YEH? WELL, YOU AIN'T SO SMART. YOU LET THE JOKER SPLIT.
THE... JOKER?
AND HOW ARE WE COMING, COUSIN MELVIN--
The HAPPY CAMPER TRAILER PARK
--YOU WALKING HUNK OF IDIOT-SAVANT GENIUS YOU?
PRETTY GOOD, COUSIN JA--

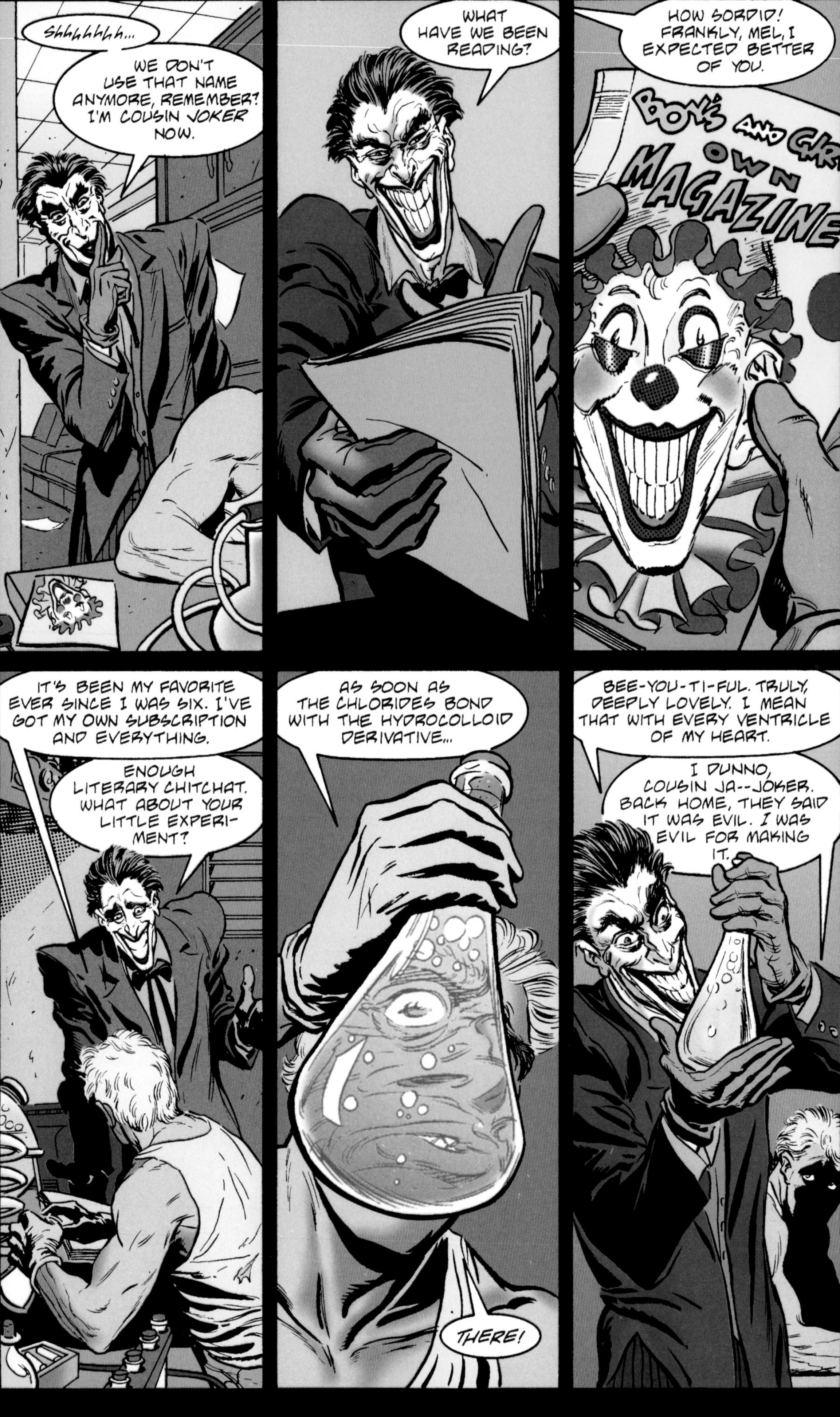
Shhhhhhh...
WE DON'T USE THAT NAME ANYMORE, REMEMBER? I'M COUSIN JOKER NOW.
WHAT HAVE WE BEEN READING?
HOW SORDID! FRANKLY, MEL, I EXPECTED BETTER OF YOU.
BOYS AND GIRLS OWN MAGAZINE
IT'S BEEN MY FAVORITE EVER SINCE I WAS SIX. I'VE GOT MY OWN SUBSCRIPTION AND EVERYTHING.
ENOUGH LITERARY CHITCHAT. WHAT ABOUT YOUR LITTLE EXPERIMENT?
AS SOON AS THE CHLORIDES BOND WITH THE HYDROCOLLOID DERIVATIVE...
THERE!
BEE-YOU-TI-FUL. TRULY, DEEPLY LOVELY. I MEAN THAT WITH EVERY VENTRICLE OF MY HEART.
I DUNNO, COUSIN JA--JOKER. BACK HOME, THEY SAID IT WAS EVIL. I WAS EVIL FOR MAKING IT.

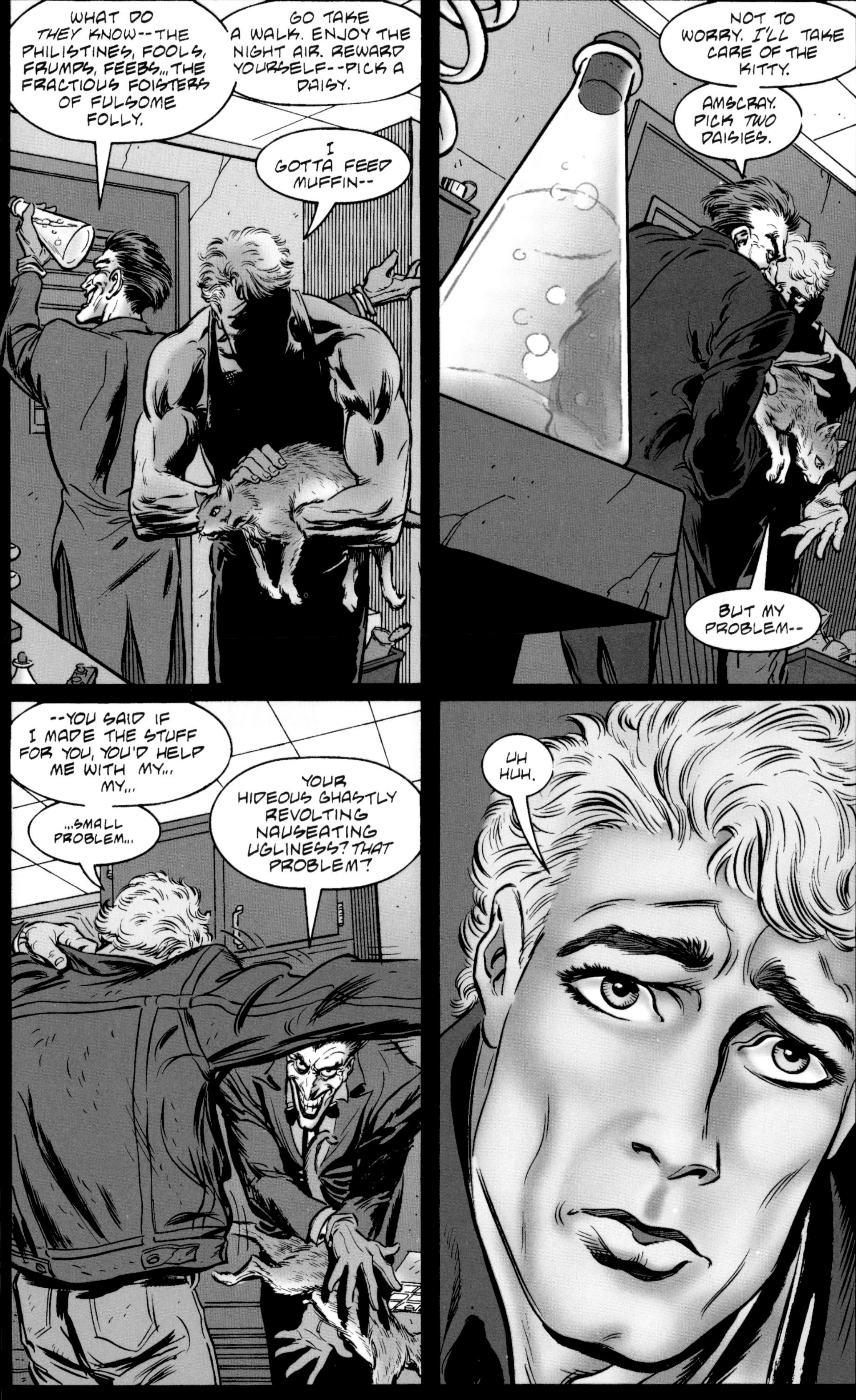
WHAT DO THEY KNOW--THE PHILISTINES, FOOLS, FRUMPS, FEEBS... THE FRACTIOUS FOISTERS OF FULSOME FOLLY.
GO TAKE A WALK. ENJOY THE NIGHT AIR. REWARD YOURSELF--PICK A DAISY.
I GOTTA FEED MUFFIN--
NOT TO WORRY. I'LL TAKE CARE OF THE KITTY.
AMSCRAY. PICK TWO DAISIES.
BUT MY PROBLEM--
--YOU SAID IF I MADE THE STUFF FOR YOU, YOU'D HELP ME WITH MY... MY...
...SMALL PROBLEM...
YOUR HIDEOUS GHASTLY REVOLTING NAUSEATING UGLINESS? THAT PROBLEM?
UH HUH.

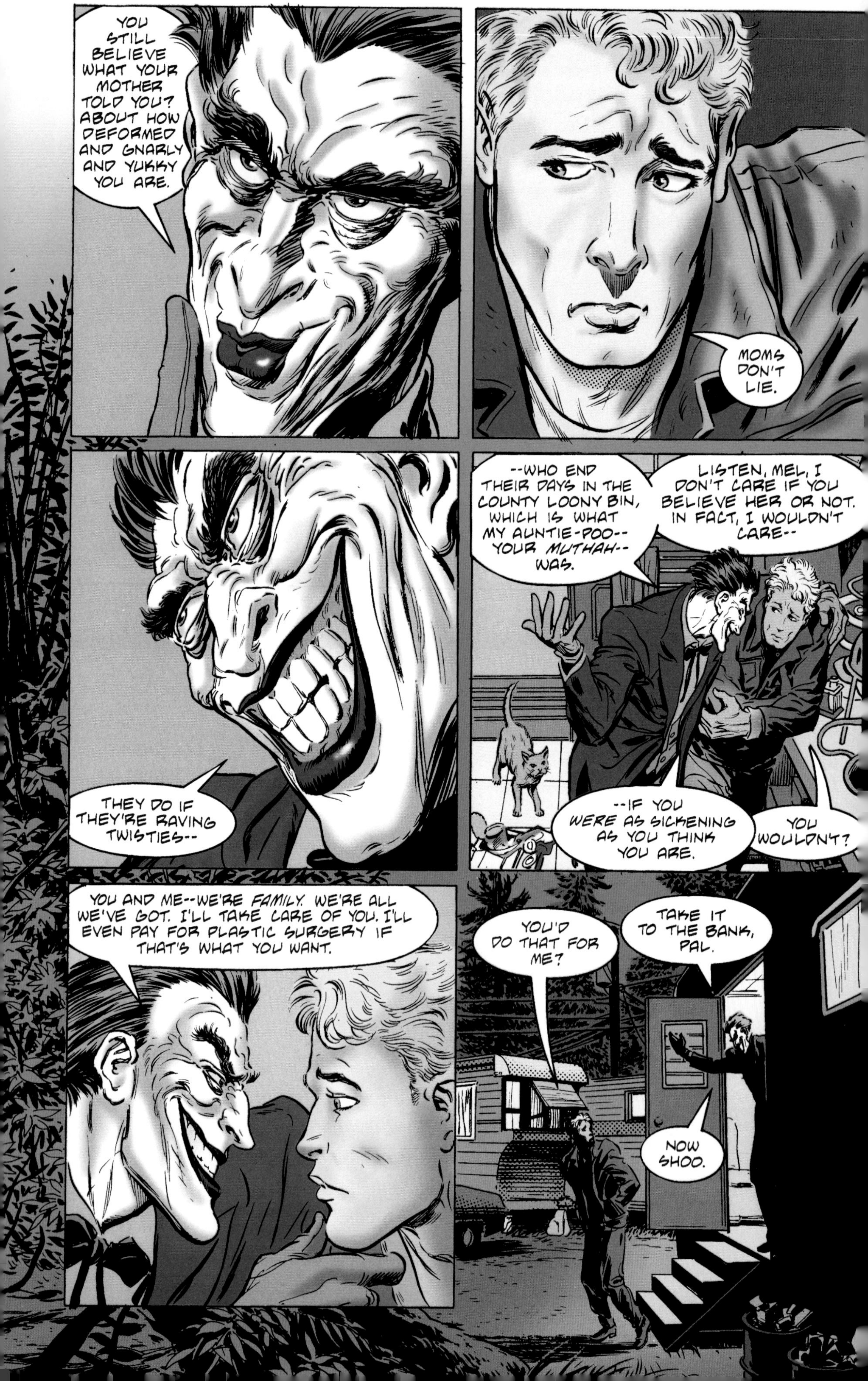
YOU STILL BELIEVE WHAT YOUR MOTHER TOLD YOU? ABOUT HOW DEFORMED AND GNARLY AND YUKKY YOU ARE.
MOMS DON'T LIE.
THEY DO IF THEY'RE RAVING TWISTIES--
--WHO END THEIR DAYS IN THE COUNTY LOONY BIN, WHICH IS WHAT MY AUNTIE-POO-- YOUR MUTHAH-- WAS.
LISTEN, MEL, I DON'T CARE IF YOU BELIEVE HER OR NOT. IN FACT, I WOULDN'T CARE--
--IF YOU WERE AS SICKENING AS YOU THINK YOU ARE.
YOU WOULDN'T?
YOU AND ME--WE'RE FAMILY. WE'RE ALL WE'VE GOT. I'LL TAKE CARE OF YOU. I'LL EVEN PAY FOR PLASTIC SURGERY IF THAT'S WHAT YOU WANT.
YOU'D DO THAT FOR ME?
TAKE IT TO THE BANK, PAL.
NOW SHOO.

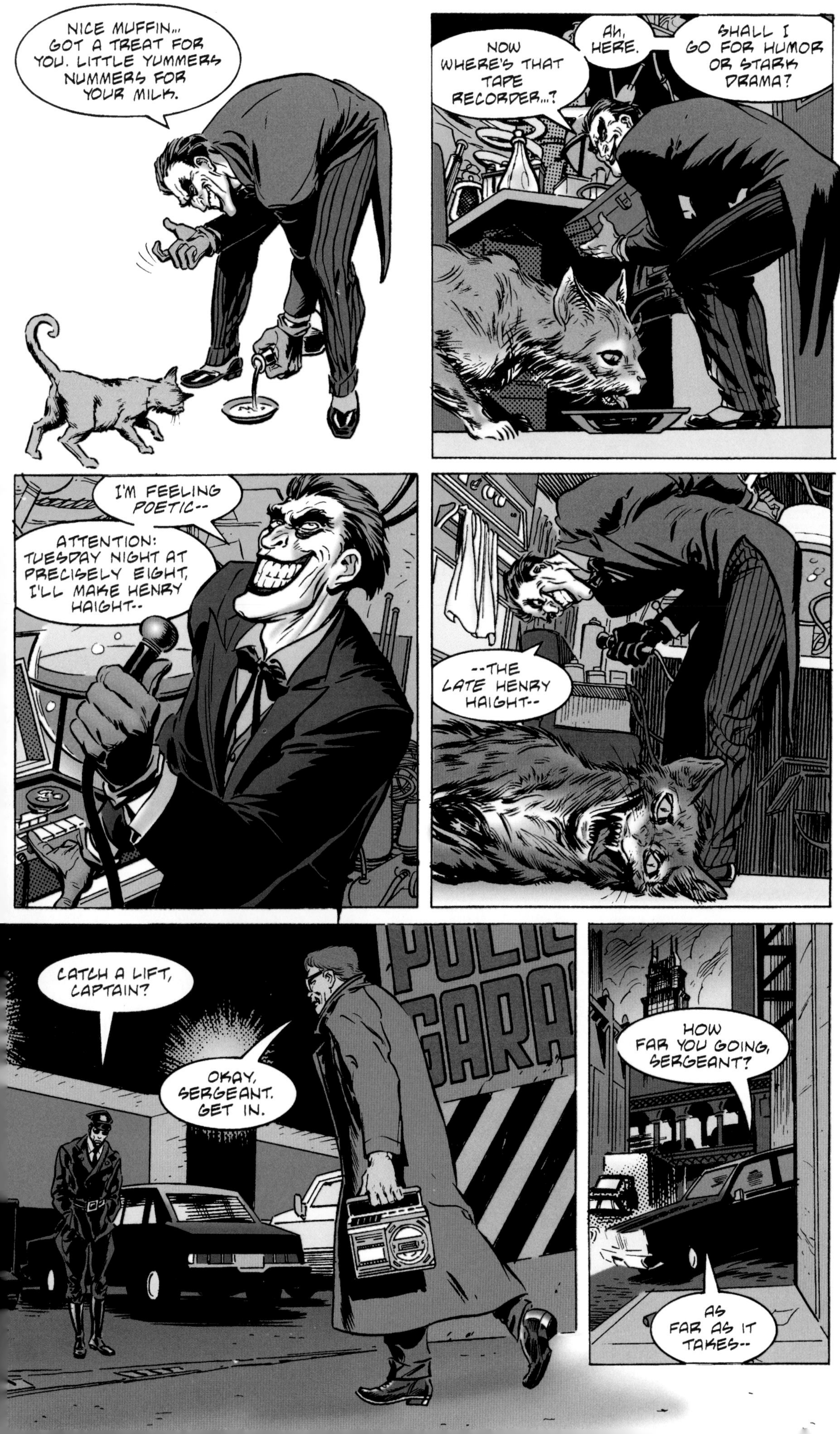
NICE MUFFIN... GOT A TREAT FOR YOU. LITTLE YUMMERS NUMMERS FOR YOUR MILK.
NOW WHERE'S THAT TAPE RECORDER...?
AH, HERE.
SHALL I GO FOR HUMOR OR STARK DRAMA?
I'M FEELING POETIC--
ATTENTION: TUESDAY NIGHT AT PRECISELY EIGHT, I'LL MAKE HENRY HAIGHT--
--THE LATE HENRY HAIGHT--
CATCH A LIFT, CAPTAIN?
OKAY, SERGEANT. GET IN.
HOW FAR YOU GOING, SERGEANT?
AS FAR AS IT TAKES--

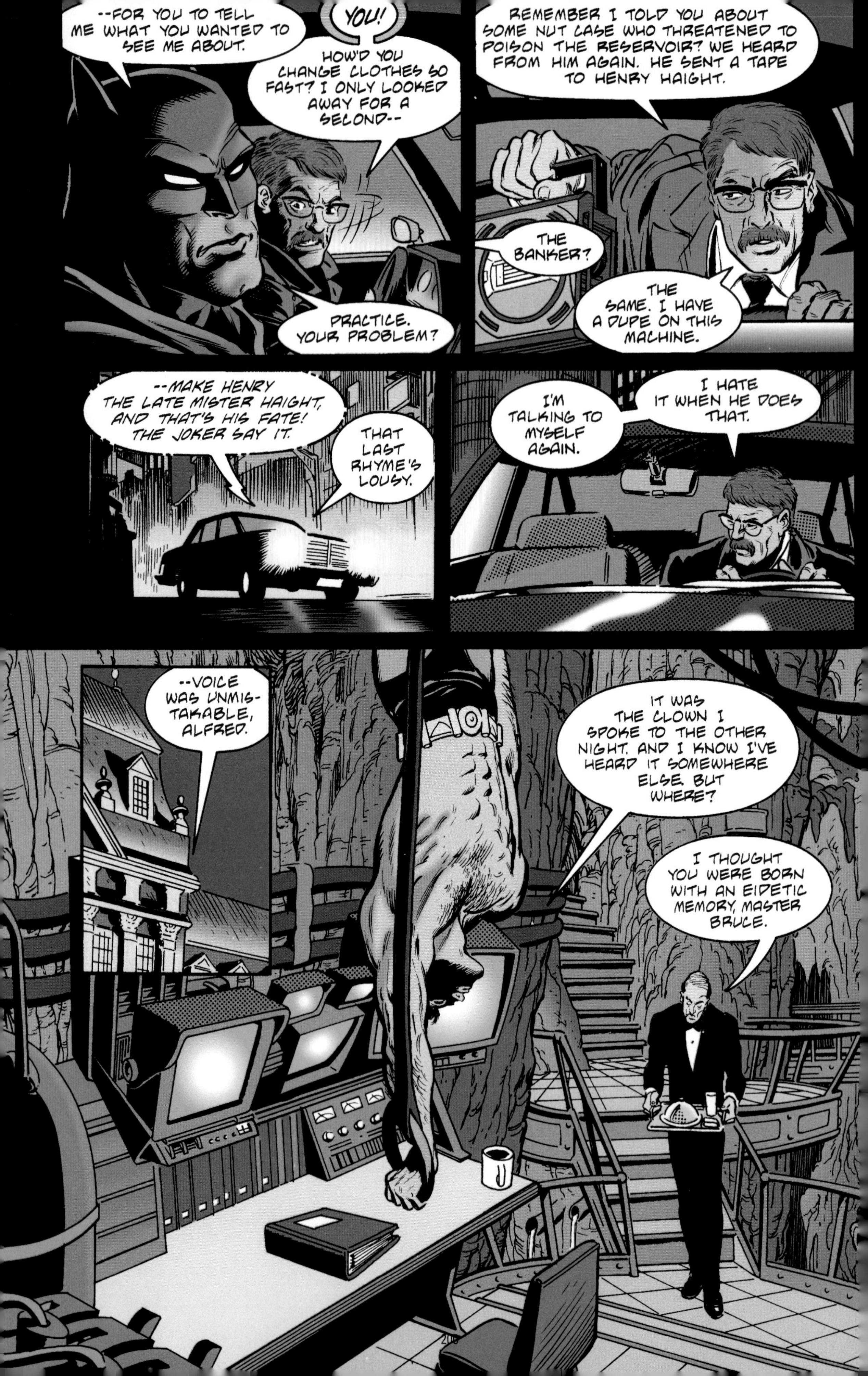
--FOR YOU TO TELL ME WHAT YOU WANTED TO SEE ME ABOUT.
YOU!
HOW'D YOU CHANGE CLOTHES SO FAST? I ONLY LOOKED AWAY FOR A SECOND--
PRACTICE. YOUR PROBLEM?
REMEMBER I TOLD YOU ABOUT SOME NUT CASE WHO THREATENED TO POISON THE RESERVOIR? WE HEARD FROM HIM AGAIN. HE SENT A TAPE TO HENRY HAIGHT.
THE BANKER?
THE SAME. I HAVE A DUPE ON THIS MACHINE.
--MAKE HENRY THE LATE MISTER HAIGHT, AND THAT'S HIS FATE! THE JOKER SAY IT.
THAT LAST RHYME'S LOUSY.
I'M TALKING TO MYSELF AGAIN.
I HATE IT WHEN HE DOES THAT.
--VOICE WAS UNMISTAKABLE, ALFRED.
IT WAS THE CLOWN I SPOKE TO THE OTHER NIGHT. AND I KNOW I'VE HEARD IT SOMEWHERE ELSE. BUT WHERE?
I THOUGHT YOU WERE BORN WITH AN EIDETIC MEMORY, MASTER BRUCE.

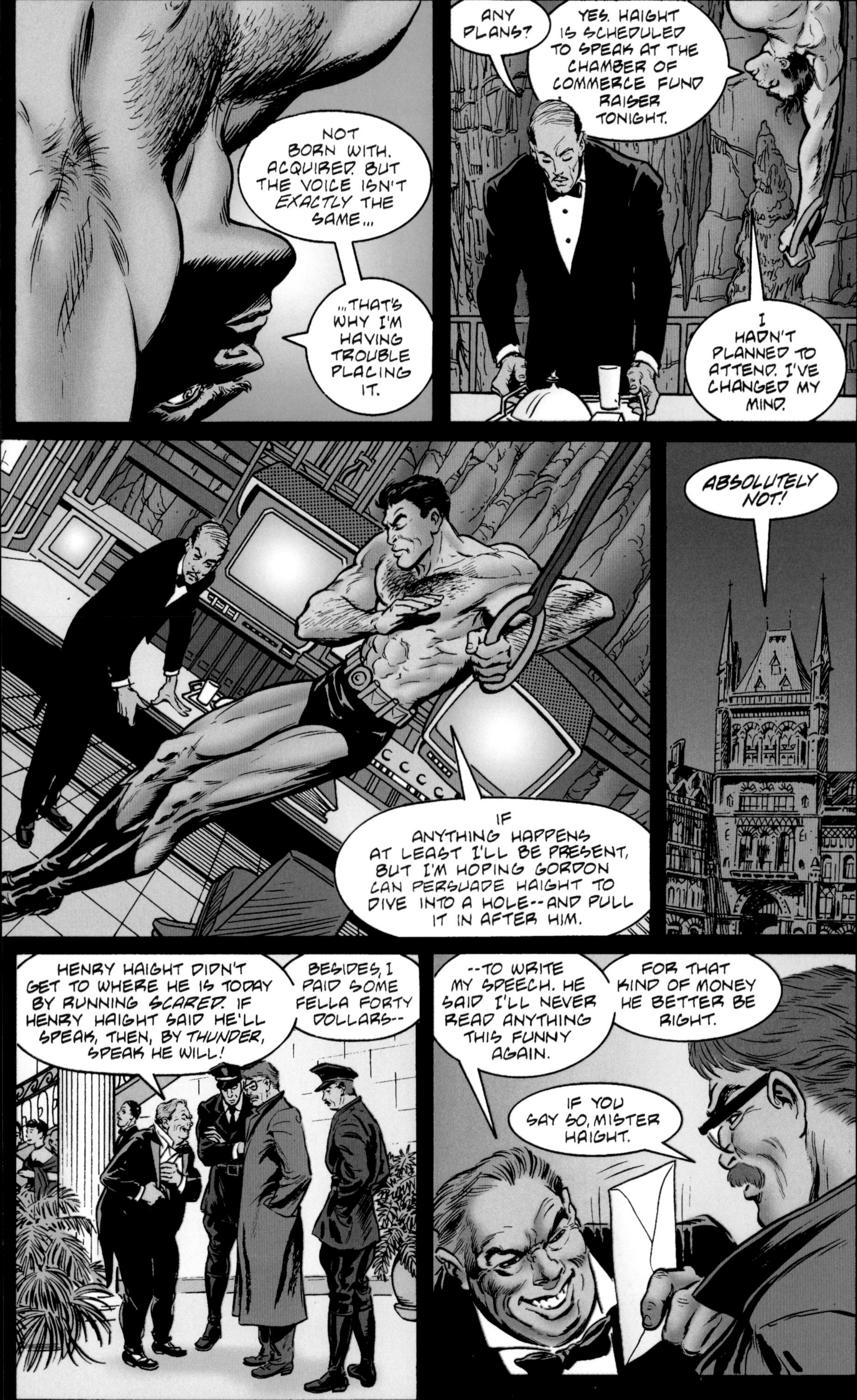
NOT BORN WITH. ACQUIRED. BUT THE VOICE ISN'T EXACTLY THE SAME...
...THAT'S WHY I'M HAVING TROUBLE PLACING IT.
ANY PLANS?
YES. HAIGHT IS SCHEDULED TO SPEAK AT THE CHAMBER OF COMMERCE FUND RAISER TONIGHT.
I HADN'T PLANNED TO ATTEND. I'VE CHANGED MY MIND.
IF ANYTHING HAPPENS AT LEAST I'LL BE PRESENT, BUT I'M HOPING GORDON CAN PERSUADE HAIGHT TO DIVE INTO A HOLE--AND PULL IT IN AFTER HIM.
ABSOLUTELY NOT!
HENRY HAIGHT DIDN'T GET TO WHERE HE IS TODAY BY RUNNING SCARED. IF HENRY HAIGHT SAID HE'LL SPEAK, THEN, BY THUNDER, SPEAK HE WILL!
BESIDES, I PAID SOME FELLA FORTY DOLLARS--
--TO WRITE MY SPEECH. HE SAID I'LL NEVER READ ANYTHING THIS FUNNY AGAIN.
FOR THAT KIND OF MONEY HE BETTER BE RIGHT.
IF YOU SAY SO, MISTER HAIGHT.

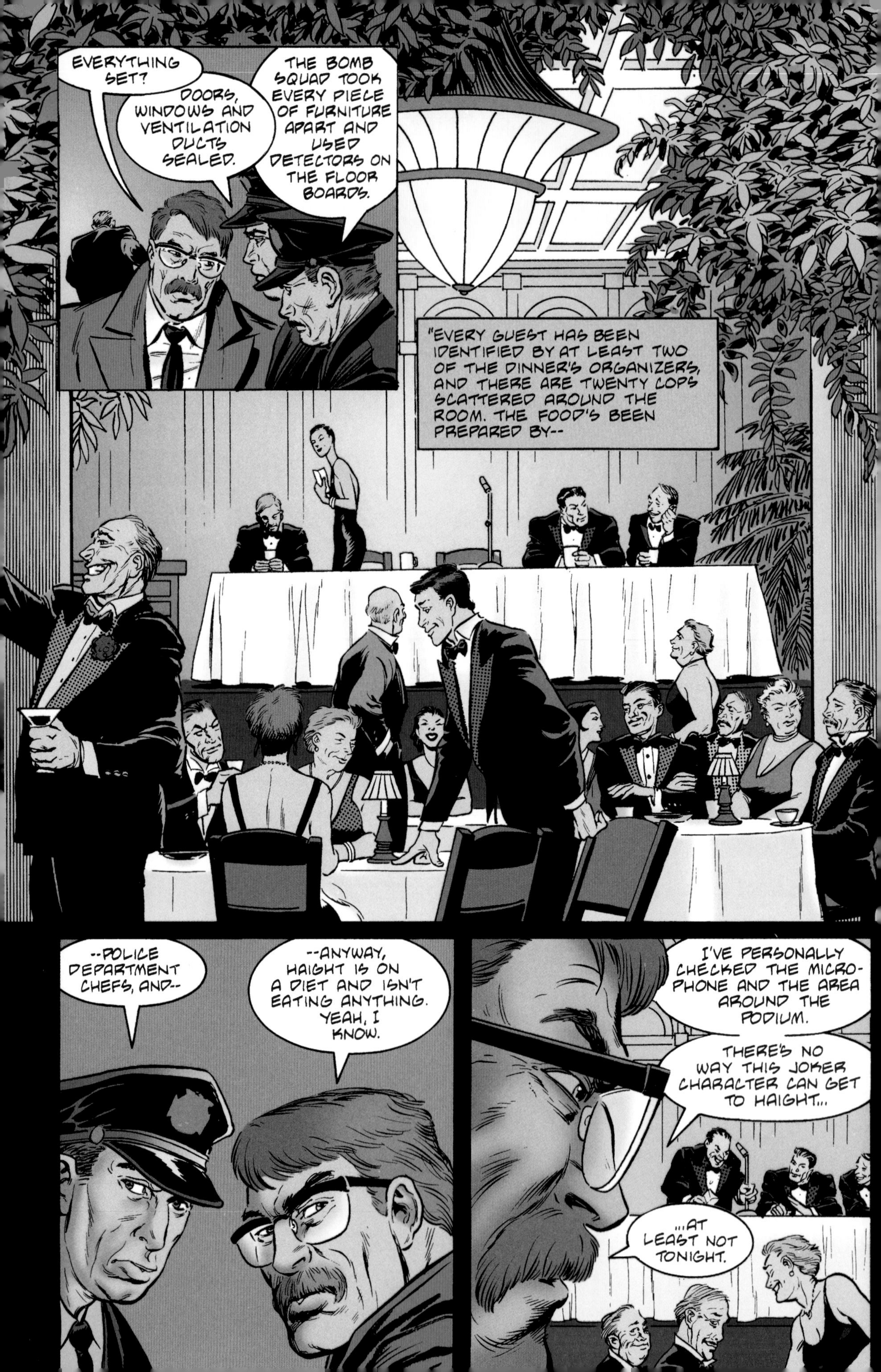
EVERYTHING SET?
DOORS, WINDOWS AND VENTILATION DUCTS SEALED.
THE BOMB SQUAD TOOK EVERY PIECE OF FURNITURE APART AND USED DETECTORS ON THE FLOOR BOARDS.
"EVERY GUEST HAS BEEN IDENTIFIED BY AT LEAST TWO OF THE DINNER'S ORGANIZERS, AND THERE ARE TWENTY COPS SCATTERED AROUND THE ROOM. THE FOOD'S BEEN PREPARED BY--
--POLICE DEPARTMENT CHEFS, AND--
--ANYWAY, HAIGHT IS ON A DIET AND ISN'T EATING ANYTHING. YEAH, I KNOW.
I'VE PERSONALLY CHECKED THE MICRO-PHONE AND THE AREA AROUND THE PODIUM.
THERE'S NO WAY THIS JOKER CHARACTER CAN GET TO HAIGHT...
...AT LEAST NOT TONIGHT.

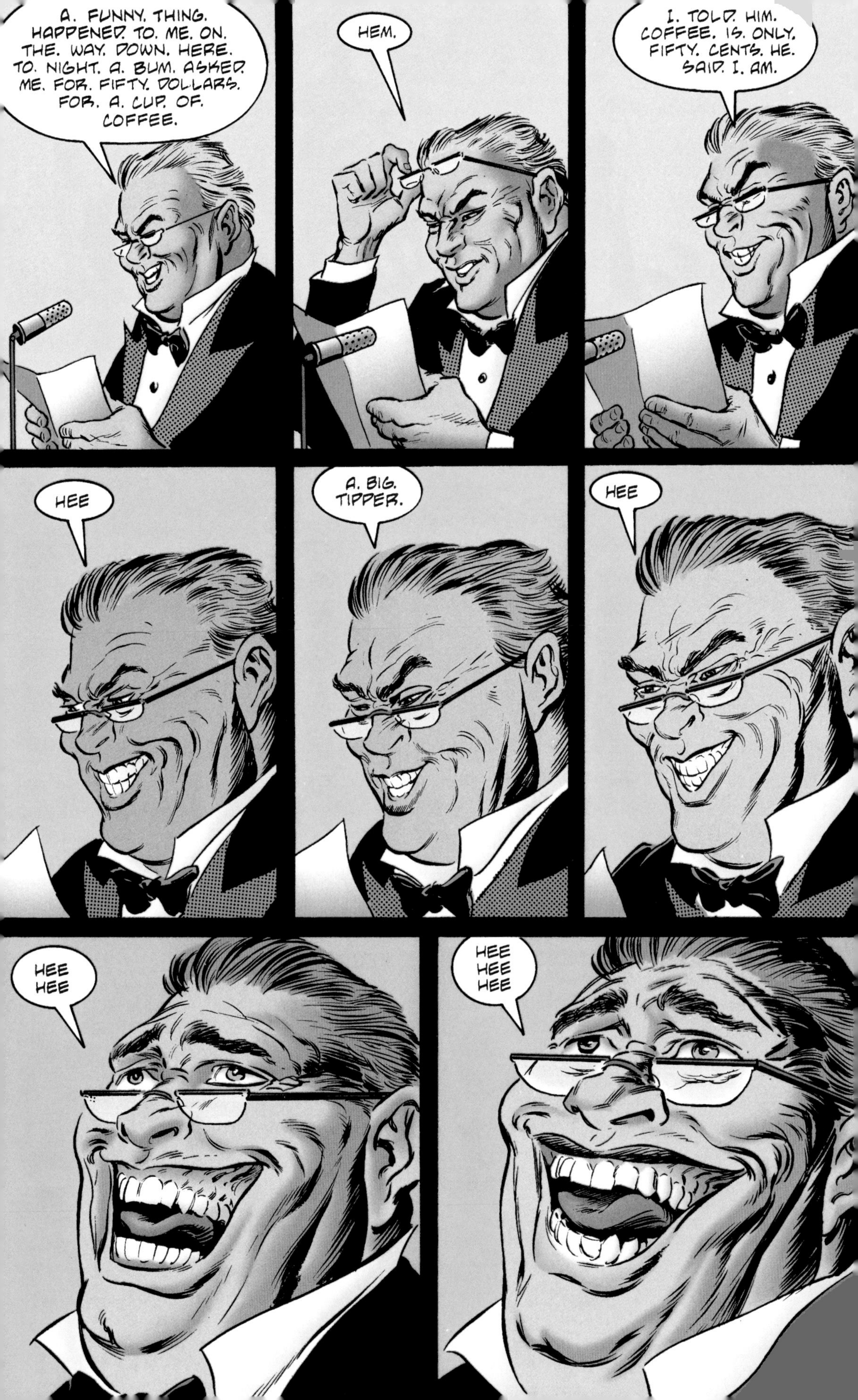
A. FUNNY. THING. HAPPENED. TO. ME. ON. THE. WAY. DOWN. HERE. TO. NIGHT. A. BUM. ASKED. ME. FOR. FIFTY. DOLLARS. FOR. A. CUP. OF. COFFEE.
HEM.
I. TOLD. HIM. COFFEE. IS. ONLY. FIFTY. CENTS. HE. SAID. I. AM.
HEE
A. BIG. TIPPER.
HEE
HEE HEE
HEE HEE HEE

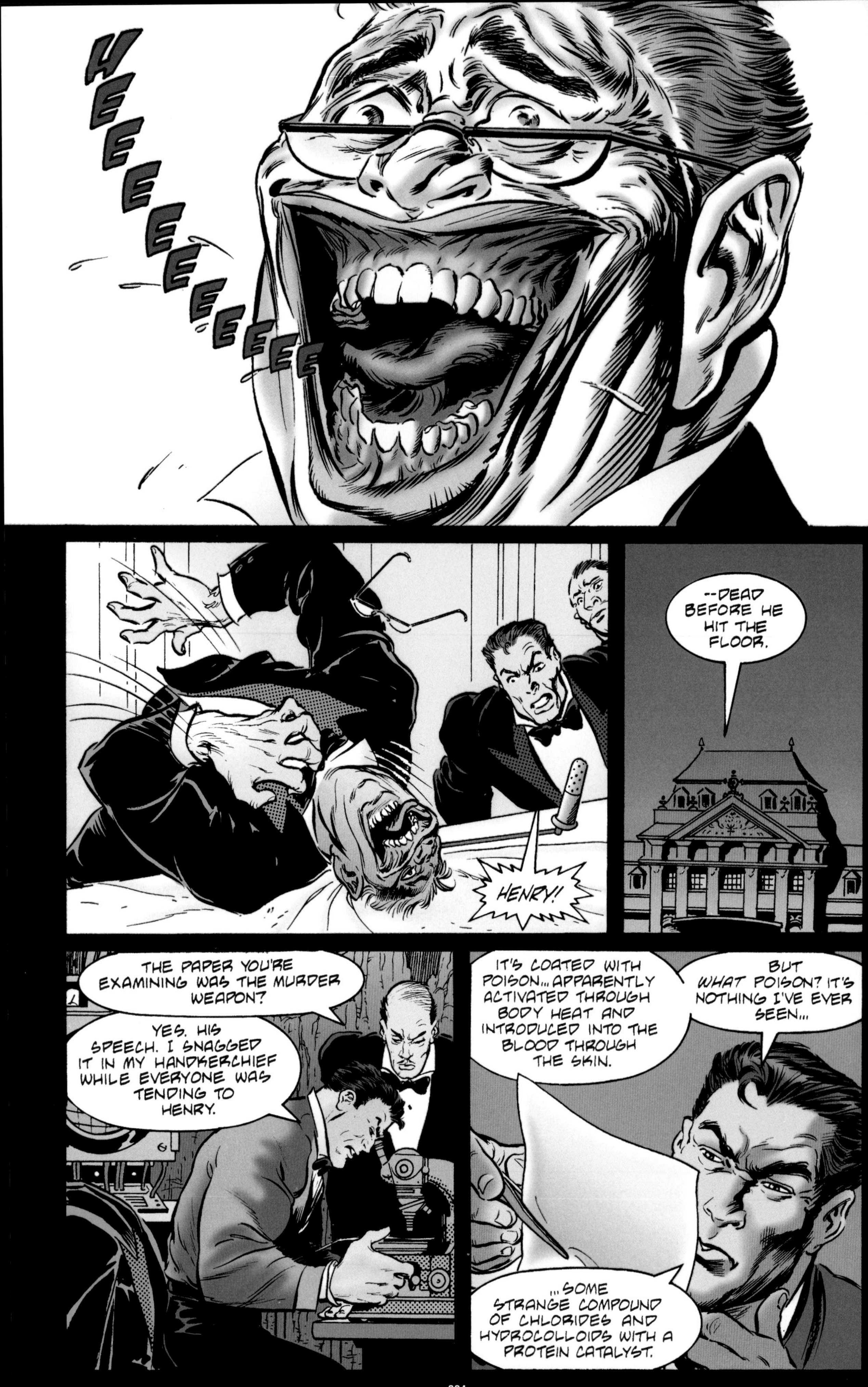
HEEEEEEEEEE
HENRY!
--DEAD BEFORE HE HIT THE FLOOR.
THE PAPER YOU'RE EXAMINING WAS THE MURDER WEAPON?
YES. HIS SPEECH. I SNAGGED IT IN MY HANDKERCHIEF WHILE EVERYONE WAS TENDING TO HENRY.
IT'S COATED WITH POISON... APPARENTLY ACTIVATED THROUGH BODY HEAT AND INTRODUCED INTO THE BLOOD THROUGH THE SKIN.
BUT WHAT POISON? IT'S NOTHING I'VE EVER SEEN...
...SOME STRANGE COMPOUND OF CHLORIDES AND HYDROCOLLOIDS WITH A PROTEIN CATALYST.

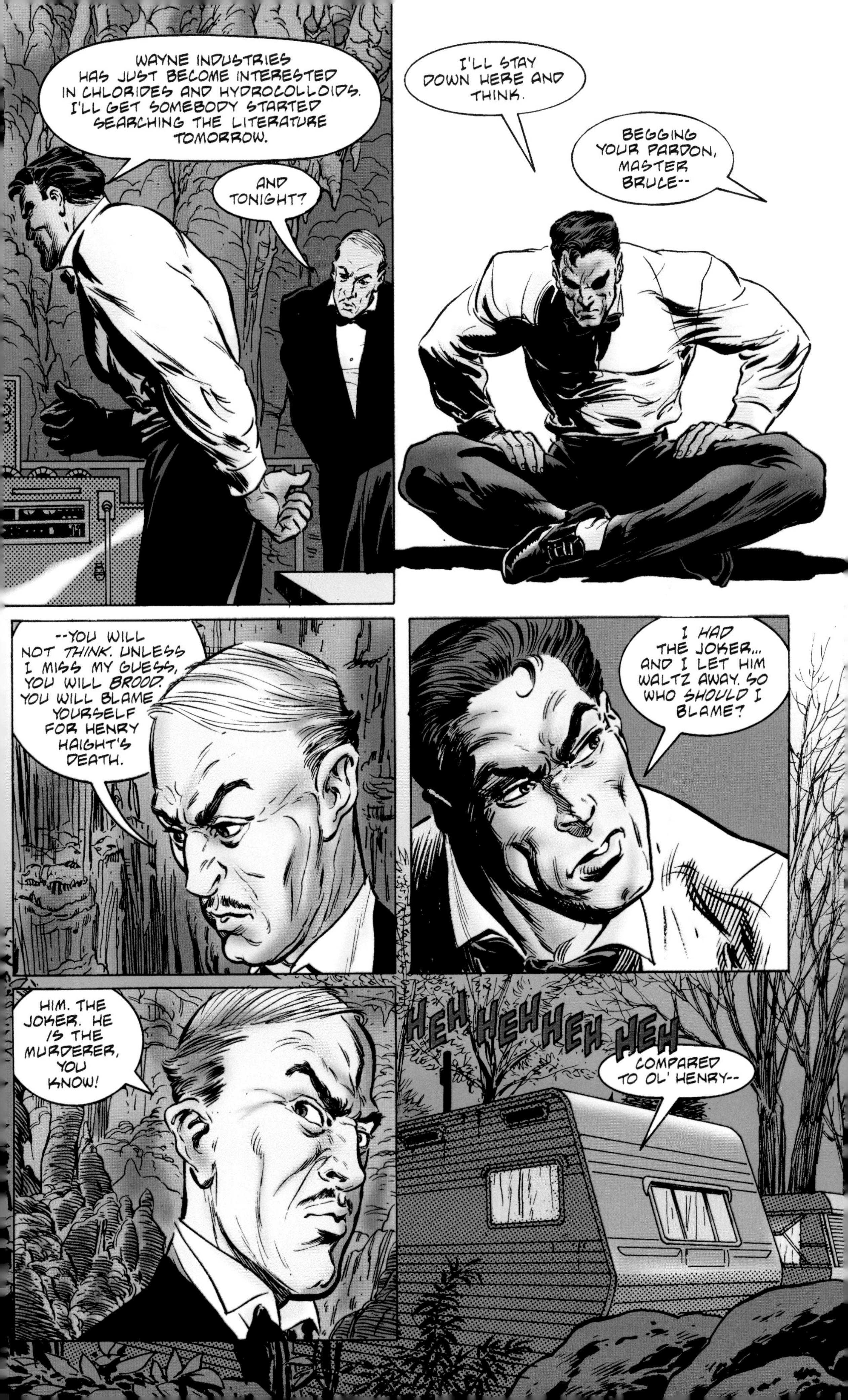
WAYNE INDUSTRIES HAS JUST BECOME INTERESTED IN CHLORIDES AND HYDROCOLLOIDS. I'LL GET SOMEBODY STARTED SEARCHING THE LITERATURE TOMORROW.
AND TONIGHT?
I'LL STAY DOWN HERE AND THINK.
BEGGING YOUR PARDON, MASTER BRUCE--
--YOU WILL NOT THINK. UNLESS I MISS MY GUESS, YOU WILL BROOD. YOU WILL BLAME YOURSELF FOR HENRY HAIGHT'S DEATH.
I HAD THE JOKER... AND I LET HIM WALTZ AWAY. SO WHO SHOULD I BLAME?
HIM. THE JOKER. HE IS THE MURDERER, YOU KNOW!
HEH HEH HEH HEH
COMPARED TO OL' HENRY--

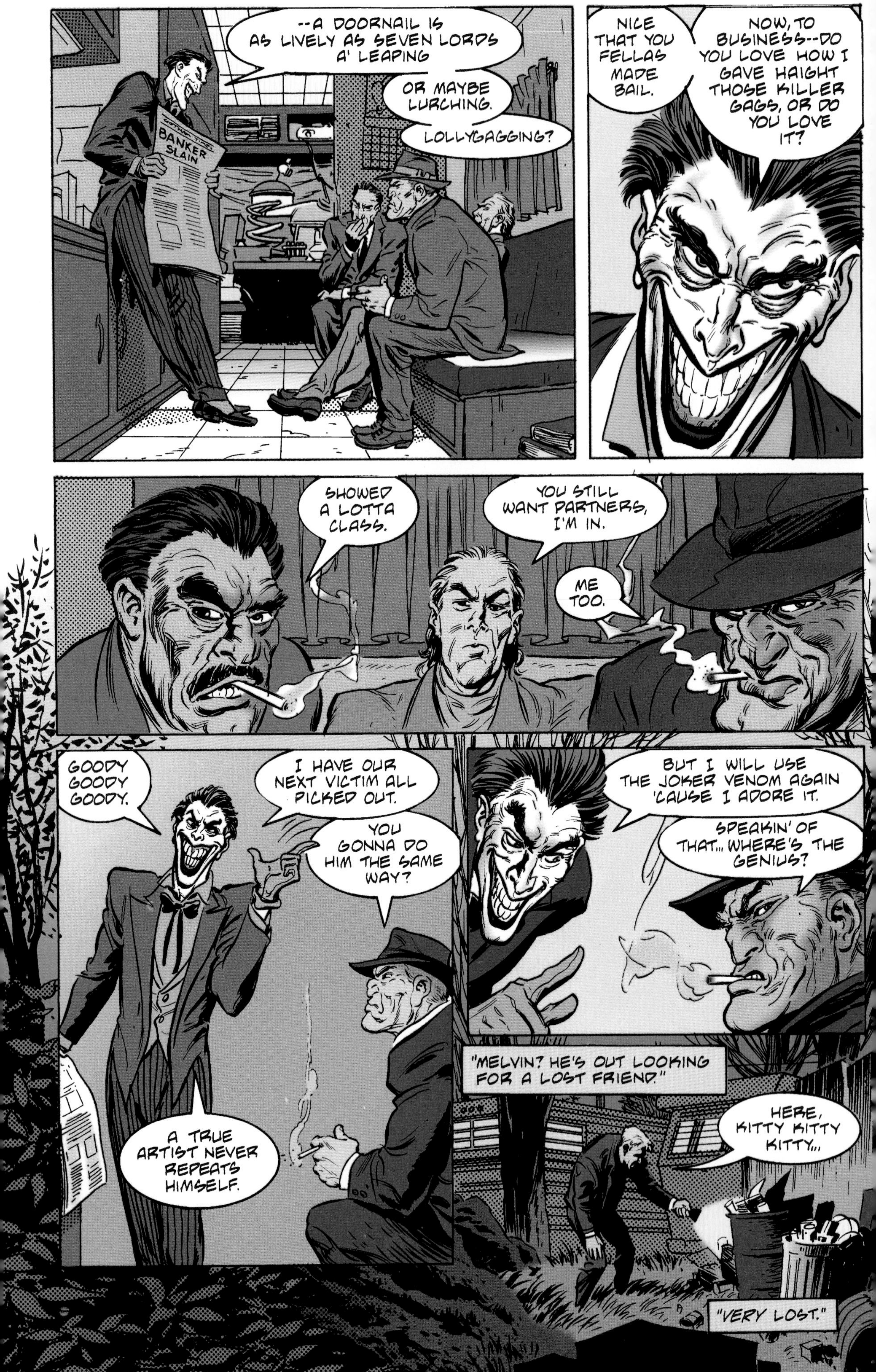
--A DOORNAIL IS AS LIVELY AS SEVEN LORDS A' LEAPING
OR MAYBE LURCHING.
LOLLYGAGGING?
BANKER SLAIN
NICE THAT YOU FELLAS MADE BAIL.
NOW, TO BUSINESS--DO YOU LOVE HOW I GAVE HAIGHT THOSE KILLER GAGS, OR DO YOU LOVE IT?
SHOWED A LOTTA CLASS.
YOU STILL WANT PARTNERS, I'M IN.
ME TOO.
GOODY GOODY GOODY.
I HAVE OUR NEXT VICTIM ALL PICKED OUT.
YOU GONNA DO HIM THE SAME WAY?
A TRUE ARTIST NEVER REPEATS HIMSELF.
BUT I WILL USE THE JOKER VENOM AGAIN 'CAUSE I ADORE IT.
SPEAKIN' OF THAT... WHERE'S THE GENIUS?
"MELVIN? HE'S OUT LOOKING FOR A LOST FRIEND."
HERE, KITTY KITTY KITTY...
"VERY LOST."

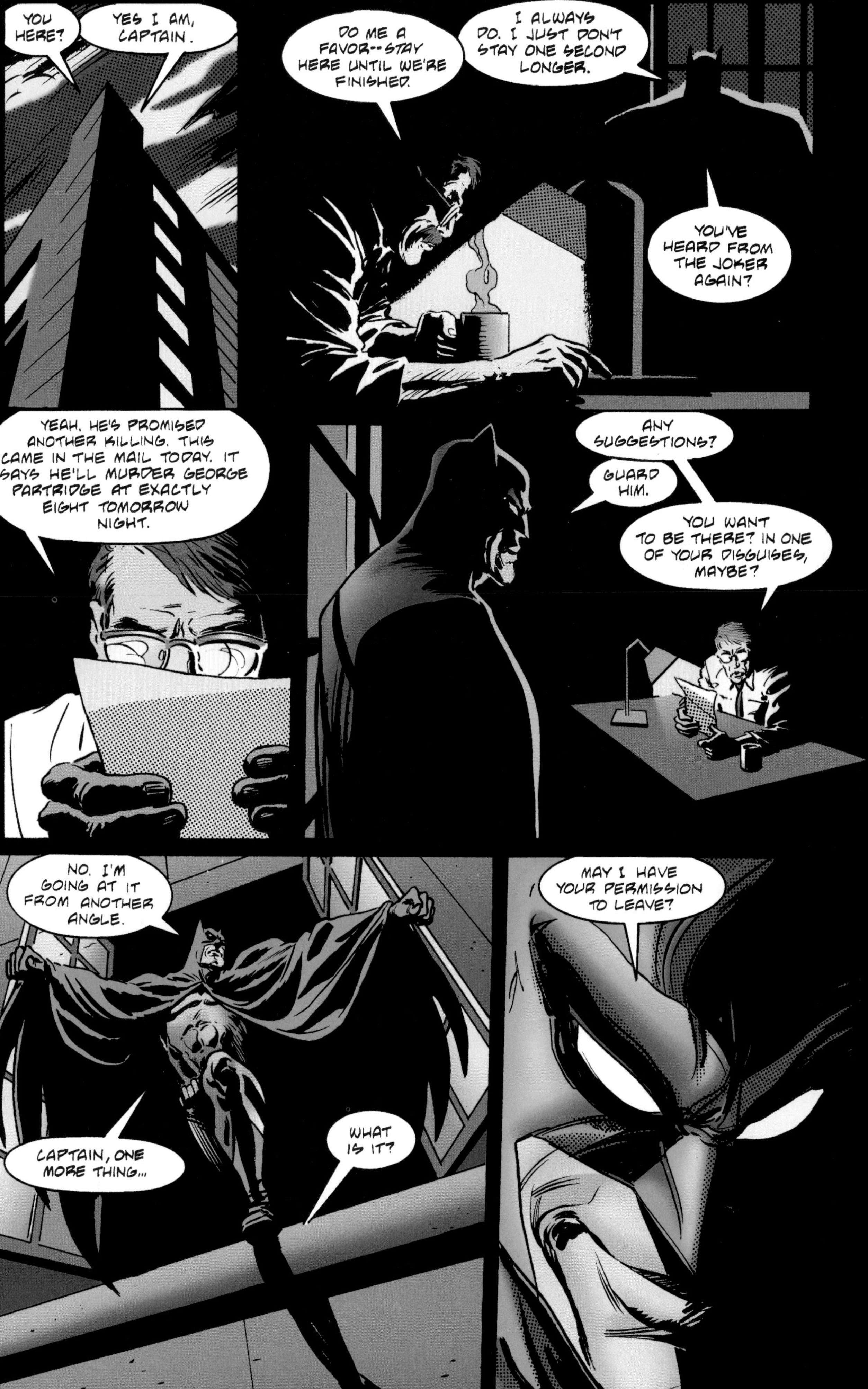
YOU HERE?
YES I AM, CAPTAIN.
DO ME A FAVOR--STAY HERE UNTIL WE'RE FINISHED.
I ALWAYS DO. I JUST DON'T STAY ONE SECOND LONGER.
YOU'VE HEARD FROM THE JOKER AGAIN?
YEAH. HE'S PROMISED ANOTHER KILLING. THIS CAME IN THE MAIL TODAY. IT SAYS HE'LL MURDER GEORGE PARTRIDGE AT EXACTLY EIGHT TOMORROW NIGHT.
ANY SUGGESTIONS?
GUARD HIM.
YOU WANT TO BE THERE? IN ONE OF YOUR DISGUISES, MAYBE?
NO. I'M GOING AT IT FROM ANOTHER ANGLE.
CAPTAIN, ONE MORE THING...
WHAT IS IT?
MAY I HAVE YOUR PERMISSION TO LEAVE?

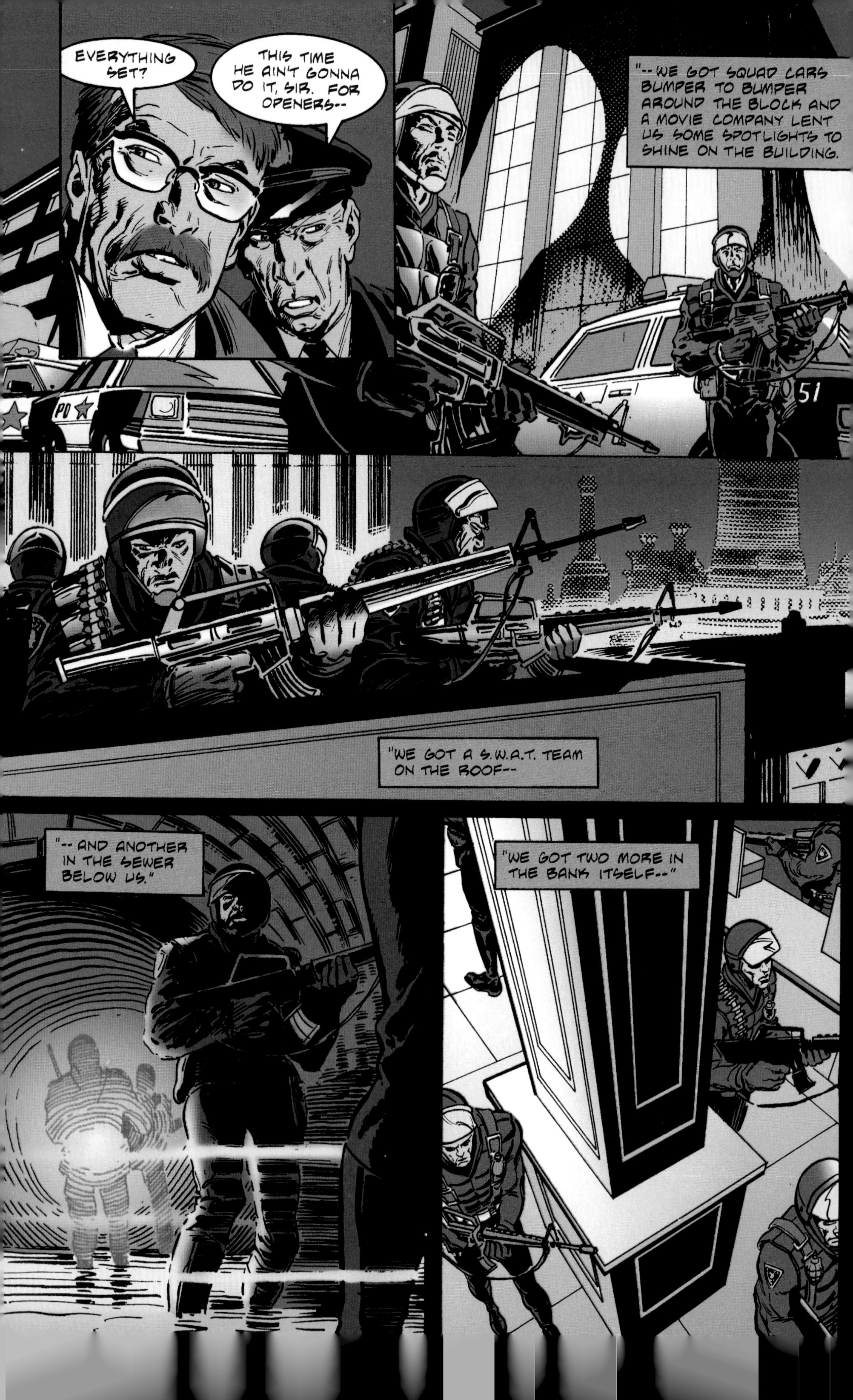
EVERYTHING SET?
THIS TIME HE AIN'T GONNA DO IT, SIR. FOR OPENERS--
"--WE GOT SQUAD CARS BUMPER TO BUMPER AROUND THE BLOCK AND A MOVIE COMPANY LENT US SOME SPOTLIGHTS TO SHINE ON THE BUILDING.
PD
51
"WE GOT A S.W.A.T. TEAM ON THE ROOF--
"--AND ANOTHER IN THE SEWER BELOW US."
"WE GOT TWO MORE IN THE BANK ITSELF--"

--AND HERE IN THE VAULT WE GOT EIGHT OF OUR BEST MEN WITH TOMMY GUNS. I TELL YA, MISTER PARTRIDGE IS SAFE AS BONDS.

LET'S HOPE SO. ONE MINUTE TO EIGHT.

THIRTY SECONDS.

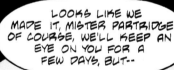

IS IT EIGHT YET?

ONE MINUTE PAST.

LOOKS LIKE WE MADE IT, MISTER PARTRIDGE. OF COURSE, WE'LL KEEP AN EYE ON YOU FOR A FEW DAYS, BUT--

I CAN'T TELL YOU HOW RELIEVED I AM, CAPTAIN.

I FEEL--HEE--POSITIVELY OVER--HEE HEE--JOYED--

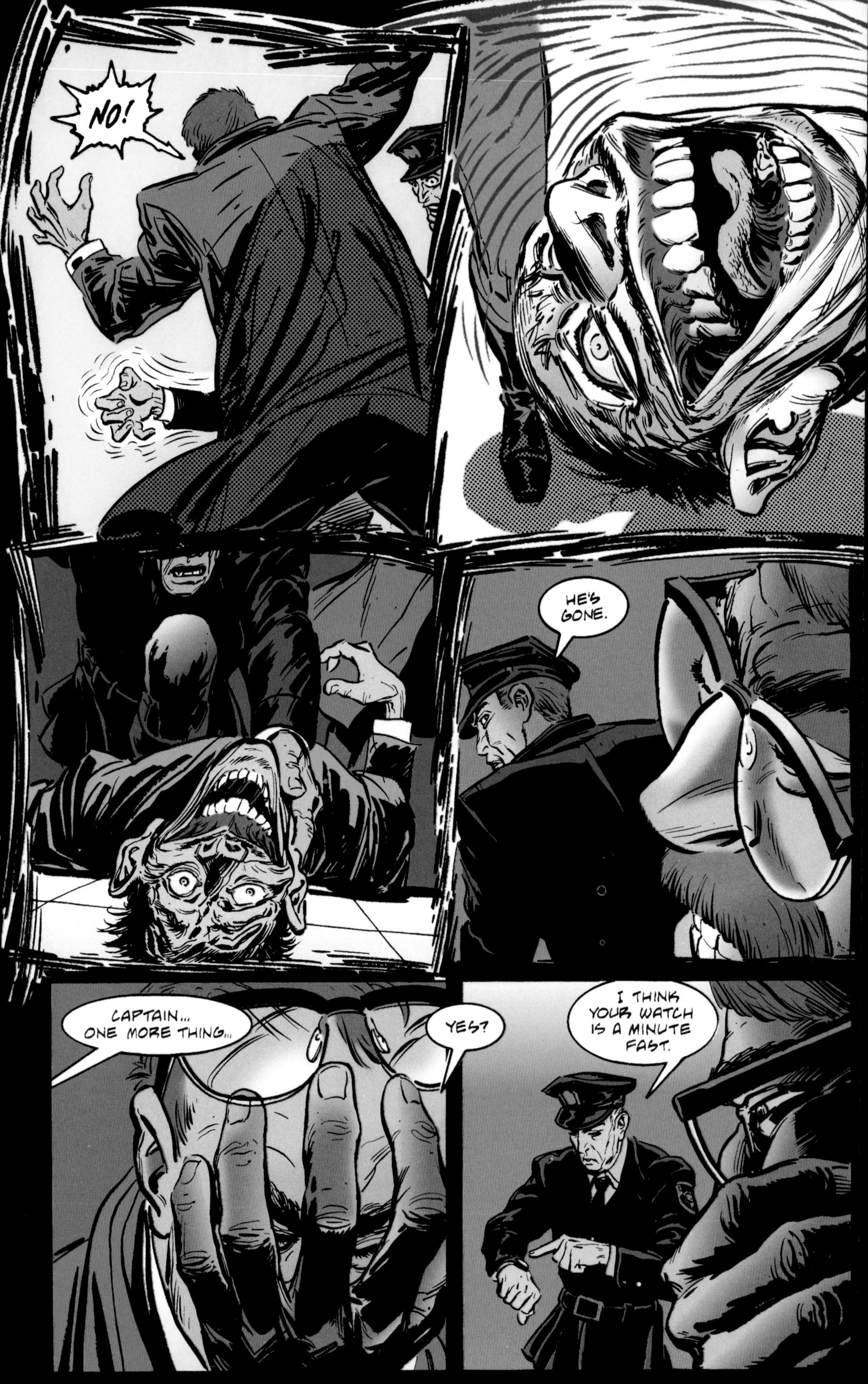
NO!
HE'S GONE.
CAPTAIN... ONE MORE THING...
YES?
I THINK YOUR WATCH IS A MINUTE FAST.

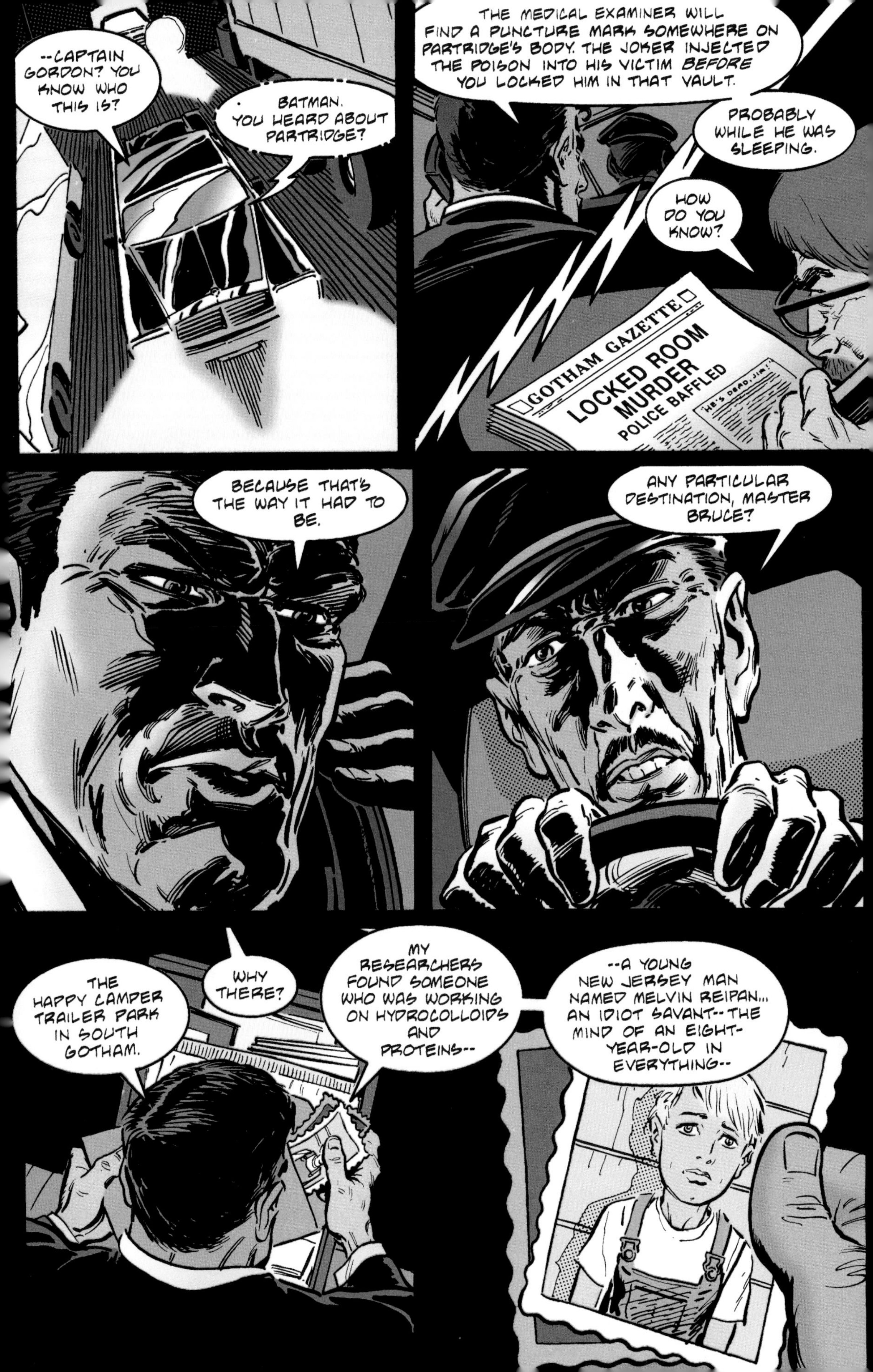
--CAPTAIN GORDON? YOU KNOW WHO THIS IS?
BATMAN. YOU HEARD ABOUT PARTRIDGE?
THE MEDICAL EXAMINER WILL FIND A PUNCTURE MARK SOMEWHERE ON PARTRIDGE'S BODY. THE JOKER INJECTED THE POISON INTO HIS VICTIM BEFORE YOU LOCKED HIM IN THAT VAULT.
PROBABLY WHILE HE WAS SLEEPING.
HOW DO YOU KNOW?
GOTHAM GAZETTE
LOCKED ROOM MURDER
POLICE BAFFLED
"HE'S DEAD, JIM!"
BECAUSE THAT'S THE WAY IT HAD TO BE.
ANY PARTICULAR DESTINATION, MASTER BRUCE?
THE HAPPY CAMPER TRAILER PARK IN SOUTH GOTHAM.
WHY THERE?
MY RESEARCHERS FOUND SOMEONE WHO WAS WORKING ON HYDROCOLLOIDS AND PROTEINS--
--A YOUNG NEW JERSEY MAN NAMED MELVIN REIPAN... AN IDIOT SAVANT--THE MIND OF AN EIGHT-YEAR-OLD IN EVERYTHING--

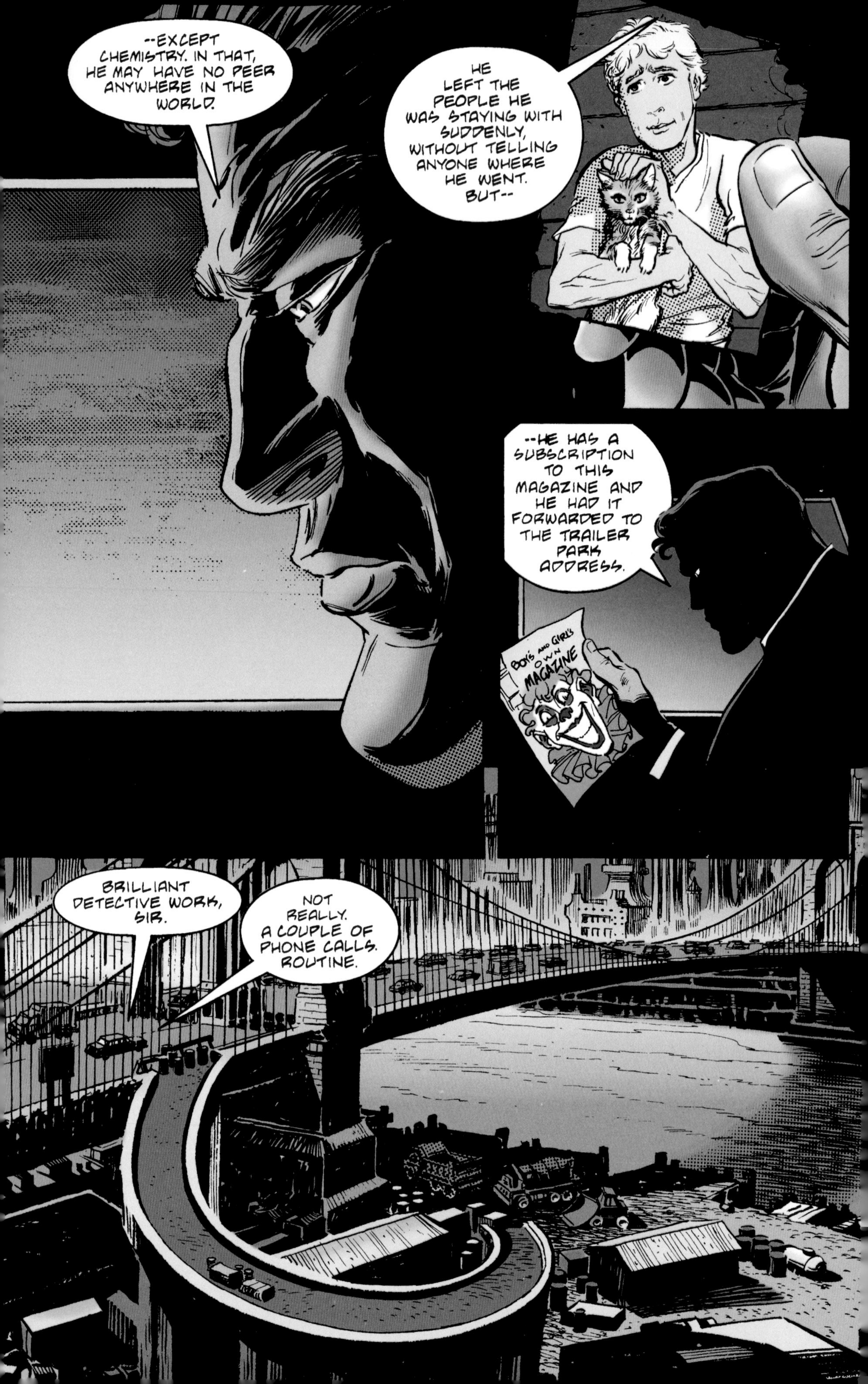
--EXCEPT CHEMISTRY. IN THAT, HE MAY HAVE NO PEER ANYWHERE IN THE WORLD.
HE LEFT THE PEOPLE HE WAS STAYING WITH SUDDENLY, WITHOUT TELLING ANYONE WHERE HE WENT. BUT--
--HE HAS A SUBSCRIPTION TO THIS MAGAZINE AND HE HAD IT FORWARDED TO THE TRAILER PARK ADDRESS.
BOY'S AND GIRL'S OWN MAGAZINE
BRILLIANT DETECTIVE WORK, SIR.
NOT REALLY. A COUPLE OF PHONE CALLS. ROUTINE.

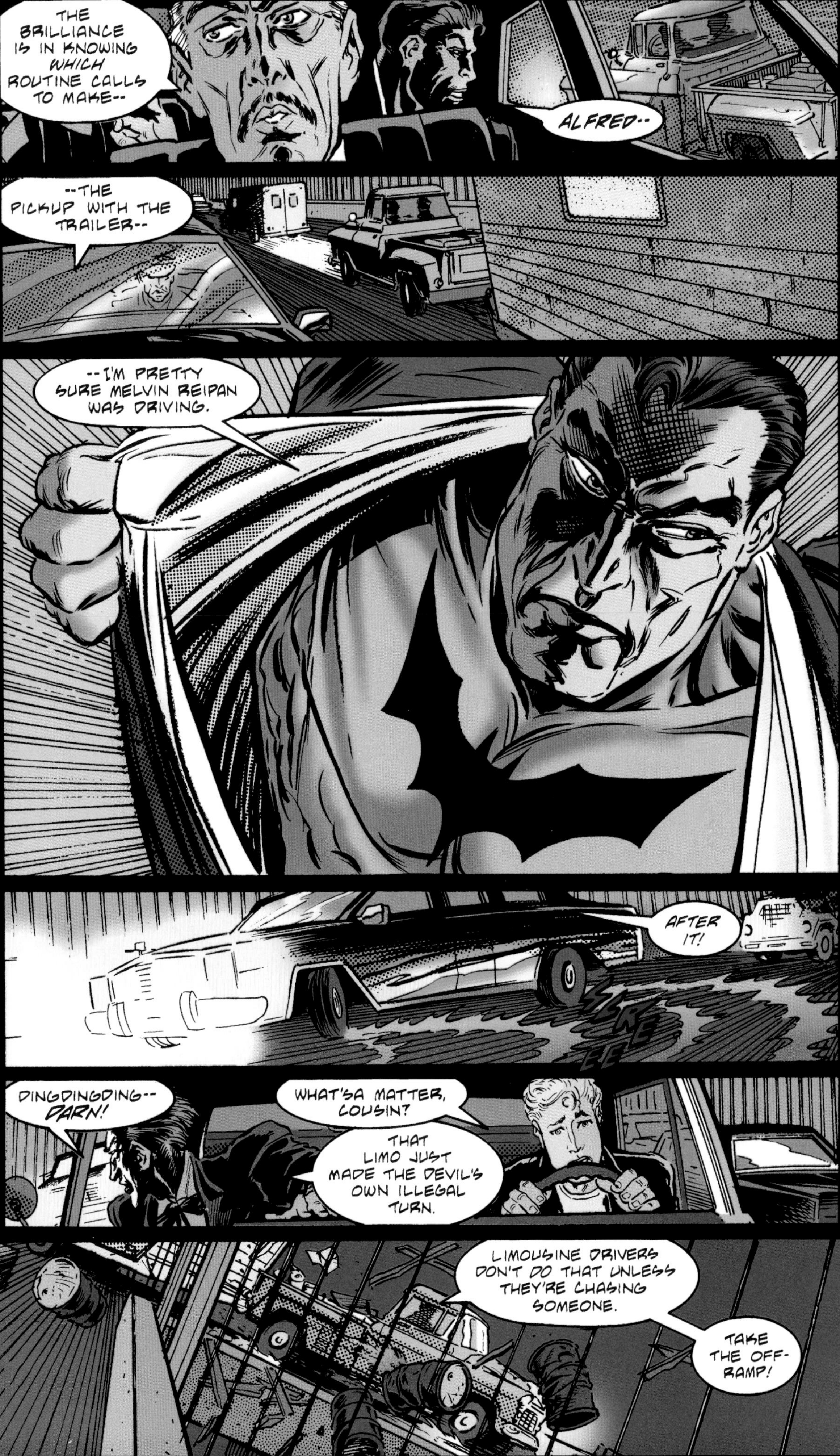
THE BRILLIANCE IS IN KNOWING WHICH ROUTINE CALLS TO MAKE--
ALFRED--
--THE PICKUP WITH THE TRAILER--
--I'M PRETTY SURE MELVIN REIPAN WAS DRIVING.
AFTER IT!
DINGDINGDING-- DARN!
WHAT'SA MATTER, COUSIN?
THAT LIMO JUST MADE THE DEVIL'S OWN ILLEGAL TURN.
LIMOUSINE DRIVERS DON'T DO THAT UNLESS THEY'RE CHASING SOMEONE.
TAKE THE OFF-RAMP!

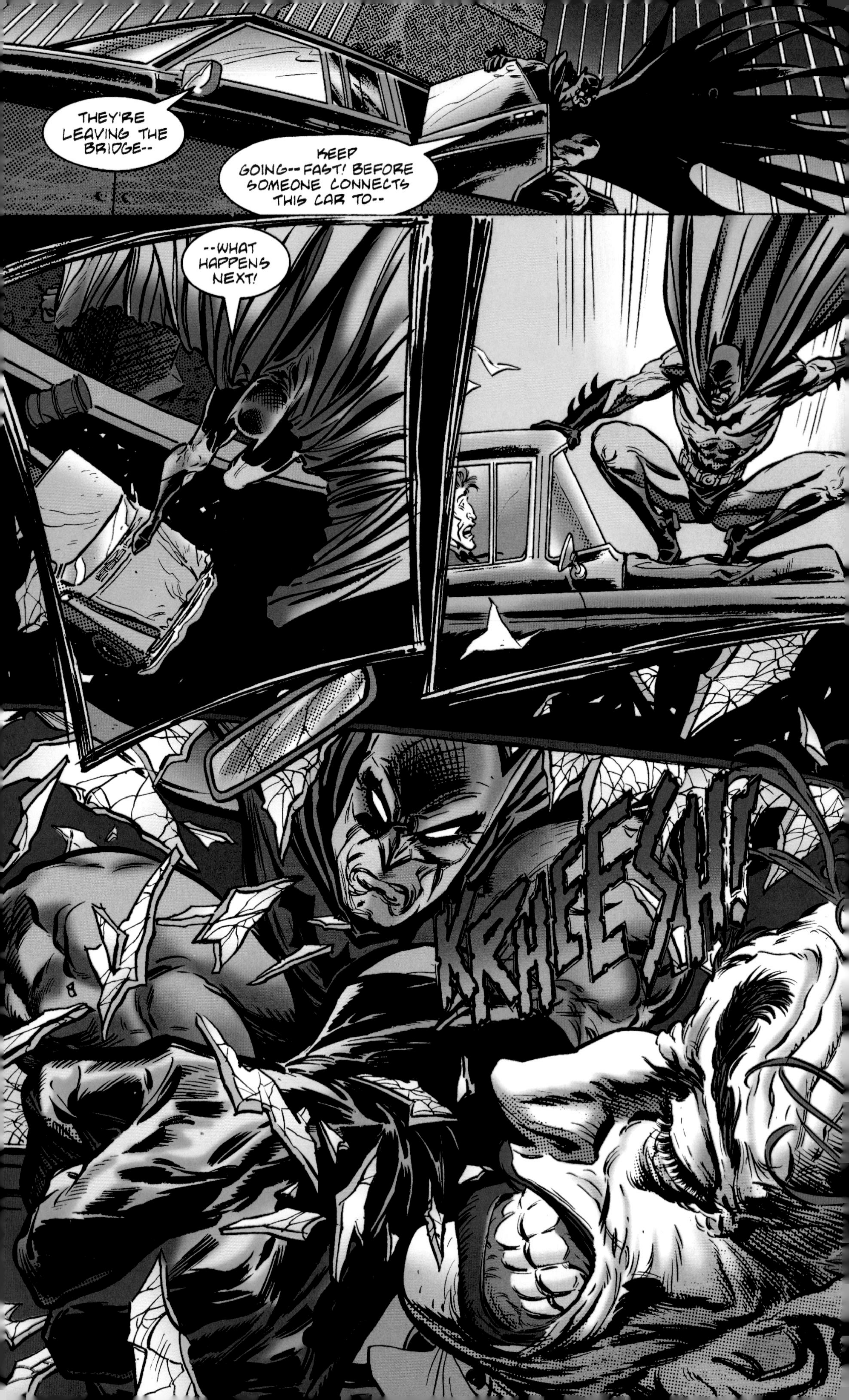
THEY'RE LEAVING THE BRIDGE--
KEEP GOING--FAST! BEFORE SOMEONE CONNECTS THIS CAR TO--
--WHAT HAPPENS NEXT!
KRAEESH!

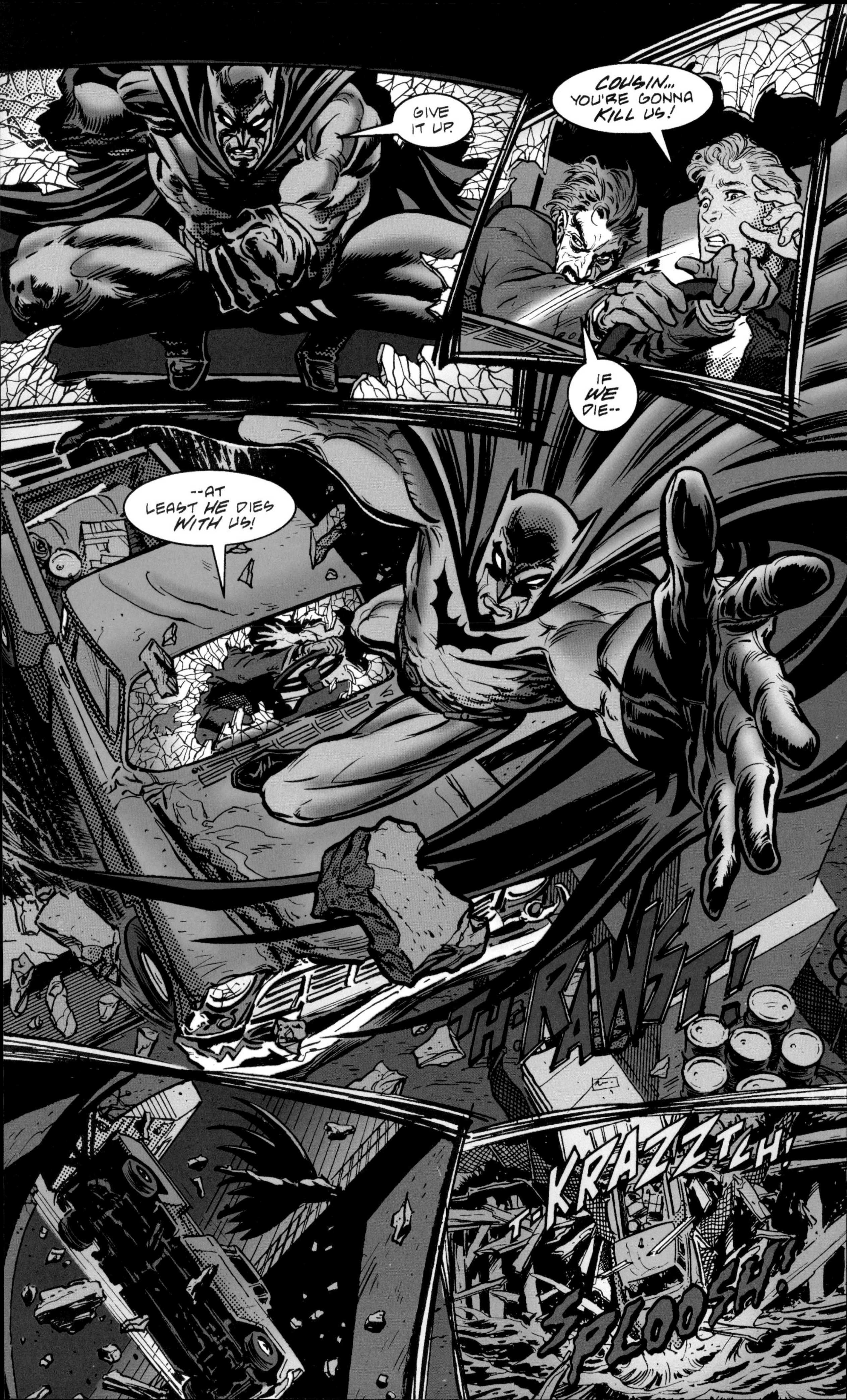
GIVE IT UP.
COUSIN... YOU'RE GONNA KILL US!
IF WE DIE--
--AT LEAST HE DIES WITH US!
THRAWSST!
T-KRAZZTCH!
SPLOOSH!

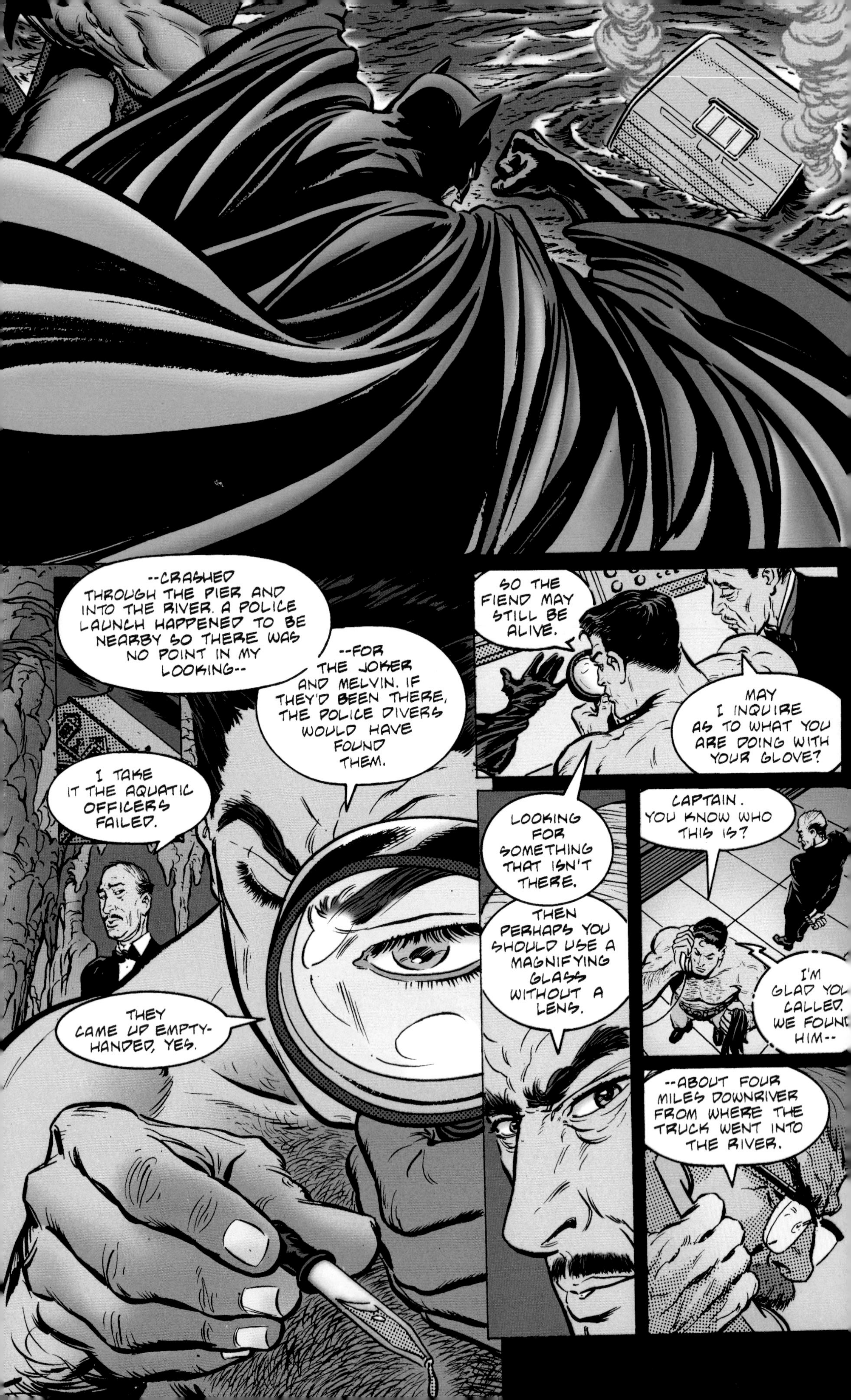
--CRASHED THROUGH THE PIER AND INTO THE RIVER. A POLICE LAUNCH HAPPENED TO BE NEARBY SO THERE WAS NO POINT IN MY LOOKING--
--FOR THE JOKER AND MELVIN. IF THEY'D BEEN THERE, THE POLICE DIVERS WOULD HAVE FOUND THEM.
I TAKE IT THE AQUATIC OFFICERS FAILED.
THEY CAME UP EMPTY-HANDED, YES.
SO THE FIEND MAY STILL BE ALIVE.
MAY I INQUIRE AS TO WHAT YOU ARE DOING WITH YOUR GLOVE?
LOOKING FOR SOMETHING THAT ISN'T THERE.
THEN PERHAPS YOU SHOULD USE A MAGNIFYING GLASS WITHOUT A LENS.
CAPTAIN. YOU KNOW WHO THIS IS?
I'M GLAD YOU CALLED. WE FOUND HIM--
--ABOUT FOUR MILES DOWNRIVER FROM WHERE THE TRUCK WENT INTO THE RIVER.

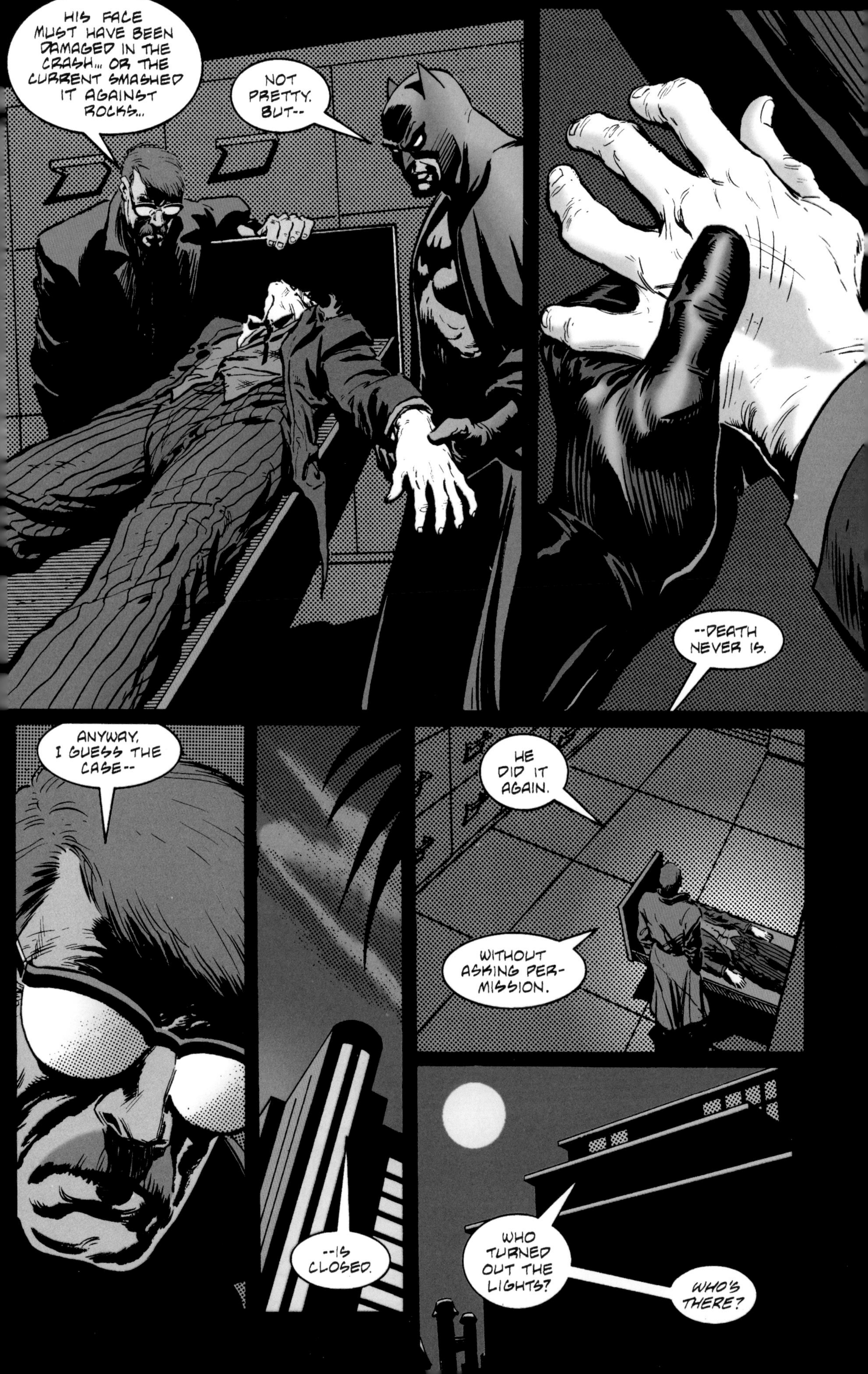
HIS FACE MUST HAVE BEEN DAMAGED IN THE CRASH... OR THE CURRENT SMASHED IT AGAINST ROCKS...
NOT PRETTY. BUT--
--DEATH NEVER IS.
ANYWAY, I GUESS THE CASE--
--IS CLOSED.
HE DID IT AGAIN.
WITHOUT ASKING PER-MISSION.
WHO TURNED OUT THE LIGHTS?
WHO'S THERE?

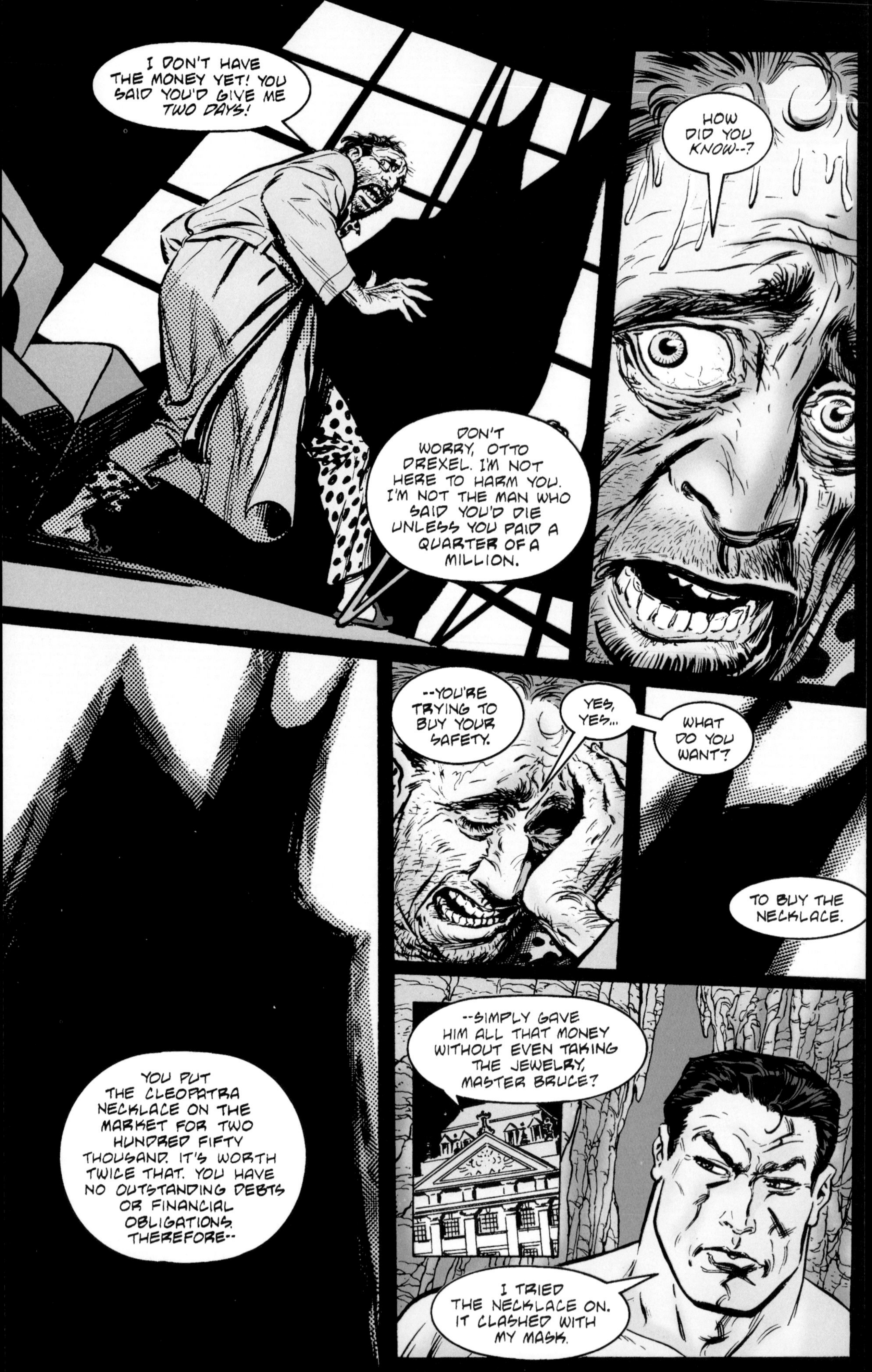
I DON'T HAVE THE MONEY YET! YOU SAID YOU'D GIVE ME TWO DAYS!
HOW DID YOU KNOW--?
DON'T WORRY, OTTO DREXEL. I'M NOT HERE TO HARM YOU. I'M NOT THE MAN WHO SAID YOU'D DIE UNLESS YOU PAID A QUARTER OF A MILLION.
YOU PUT THE CLEOPATRA NECKLACE ON THE MARKET FOR TWO HUNDRED FIFTY THOUSAND. IT'S WORTH TWICE THAT. YOU HAVE NO OUTSTANDING DEBTS OR FINANCIAL OBLIGATIONS. THEREFORE--
--YOU'RE TRYING TO BUY YOUR SAFETY.
YES, YES...
WHAT DO YOU WANT?
TO BUY THE NECKLACE.
--SIMPLY GAVE HIM ALL THAT MONEY WITHOUT EVEN TAKING THE JEWELRY, MASTER BRUCE?
I TRIED THE NECKLACE ON. IT CLASHED WITH MY MASK.

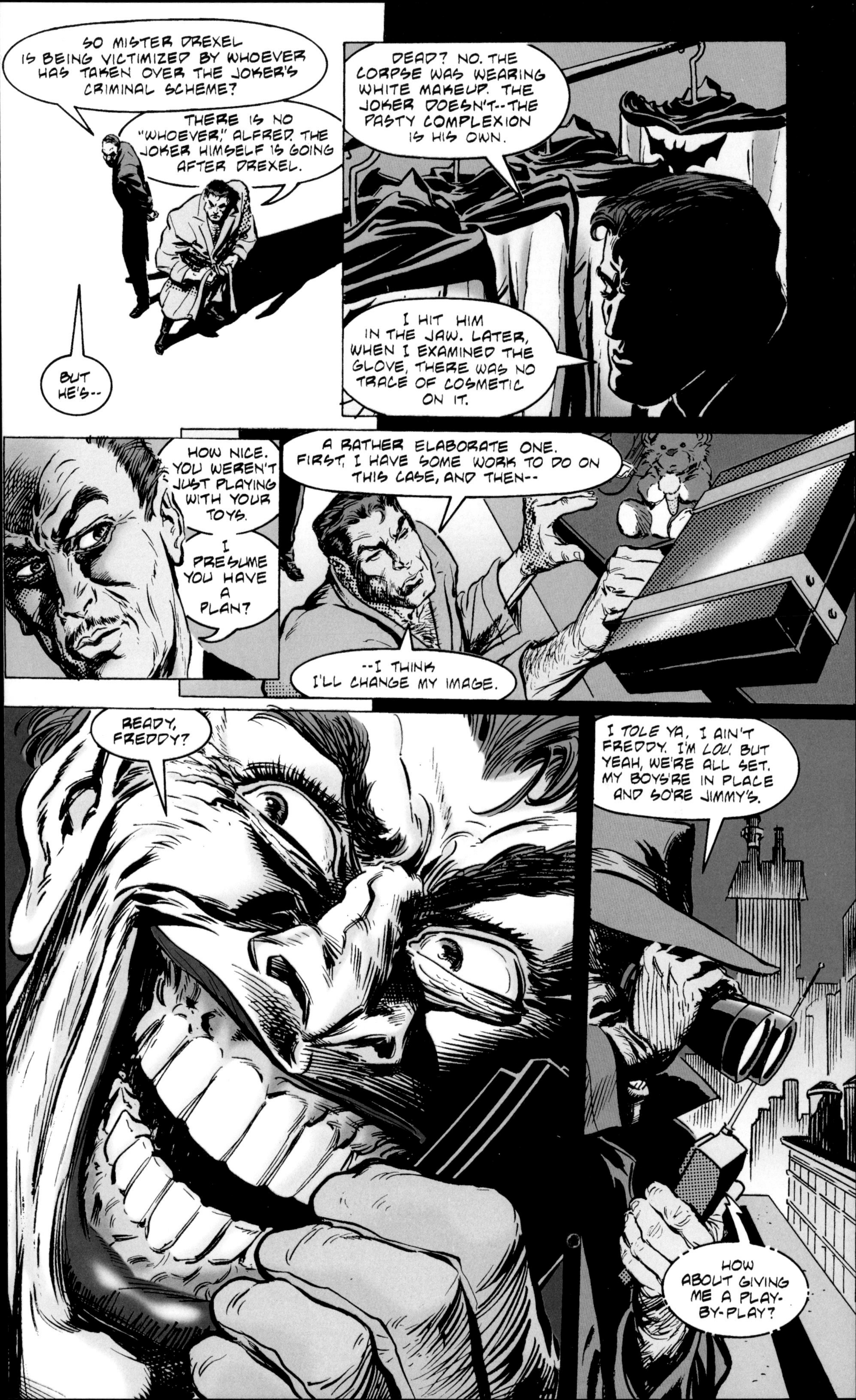
SO MISTER DREXEL IS BEING VICTIMIZED BY WHOEVER HAS TAKEN OVER THE JOKER'S CRIMINAL SCHEME?
THERE IS NO "WHOEVER," ALFRED. THE JOKER HIMSELF IS GOING AFTER DREXEL.
BUT HE'S--
DEAD? NO. THE CORPSE WAS WEARING WHITE MAKEUP. THE JOKER DOESN'T--THE PASTY COMPLEXION IS HIS OWN.
I HIT HIM IN THE JAW. LATER, WHEN I EXAMINED THE GLOVE, THERE WAS NO TRACE OF COSMETIC ON IT.
HOW NICE. YOU WEREN'T JUST PLAYING WITH YOUR TOYS.
I PRESUME YOU HAVE A PLAN?
A RATHER ELABORATE ONE. FIRST, I HAVE SOME WORK TO DO ON THIS CASE, AND THEN--
--I THINK I'LL CHANGE MY IMAGE.
READY, FREDDY?
I TOLE YA, I AIN'T FREDDY. I'M LOU. BUT YEAH, WE'RE ALL SET. MY BOYS'RE IN PLACE AND SO'RE JIMMY'S.
HOW ABOUT GIVING ME A PLAY-BY-PLAY?

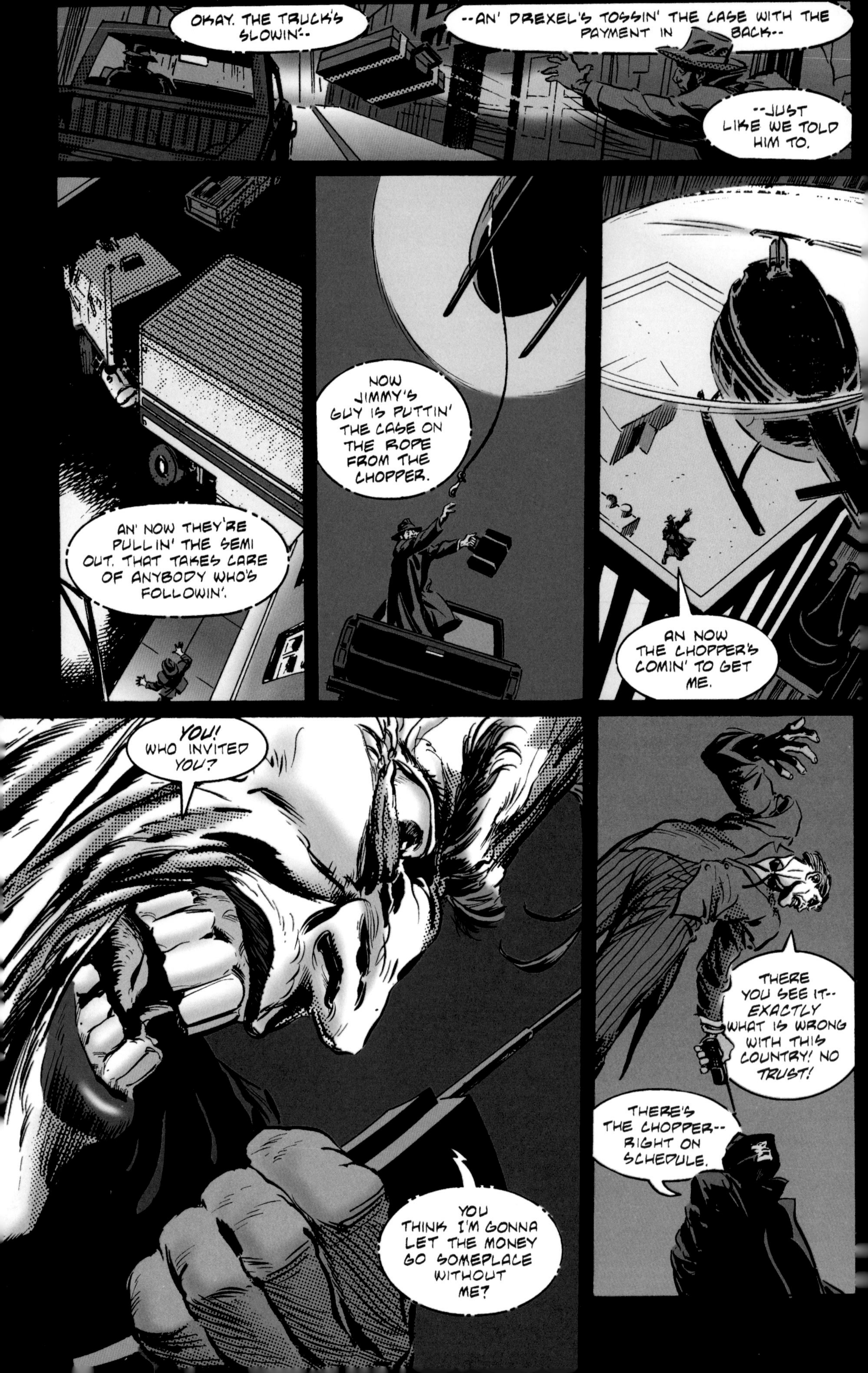
OKAY. THE TRUCK'S SLOWIN'--
--AN' DREXEL'S TOSSIN' THE CASE WITH THE PAYMENT IN BACK--
--JUST LIKE WE TOLD HIM TO.
AN' NOW THEY'RE PULLIN' THE SEMI OUT. THAT TAKES CARE OF ANYBODY WHO'S FOLLOWIN'.
NOW JIMMY'S GUY IS PUTTIN' THE CASE ON THE ROPE FROM THE CHOPPER.
AN NOW THE CHOPPER'S COMIN' TO GET ME.
YOU! WHO INVITED YOU?
YOU THINK I'M GONNA LET THE MONEY GO SOMEPLACE WITHOUT ME?
THERE YOU SEE IT-- EXACTLY WHAT IS WRONG WITH THIS COUNTRY! NO TRUST!
THERE'S THE CHOPPER-- RIGHT ON SCHEDULE.

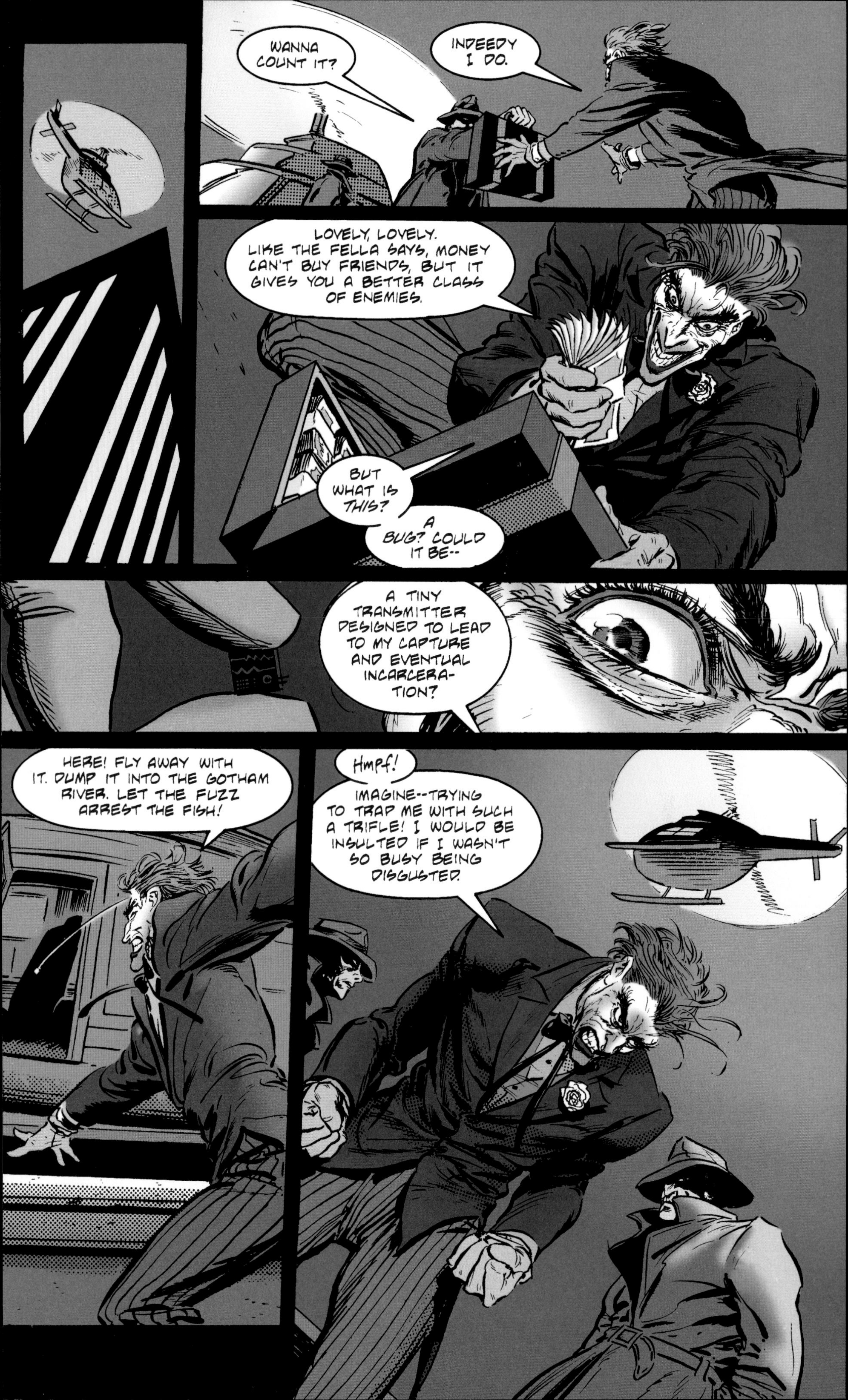
WANNA COUNT IT?
INDEEDY I DO.
LOVELY, LOVELY. LIKE THE FELLA SAYS, MONEY CAN'T BUY FRIENDS, BUT IT GIVES YOU A BETTER CLASS OF ENEMIES.
BUT WHAT IS THIS?
A BUG? COULD IT BE--
A TINY TRANSMITTER DESIGNED TO LEAD TO MY CAPTURE AND EVENTUAL INCARCERA-TION?
HERE! FLY AWAY WITH IT. DUMP IT INTO THE GOTHAM RIVER. LET THE FUZZ ARREST THE FISH!
Hmpf!
IMAGINE--TRYING TO TRAP ME WITH SUCH A TRIFLE! I WOULD BE INSULTED IF I WASN'T SO BUSY BEING DISGUSTED.

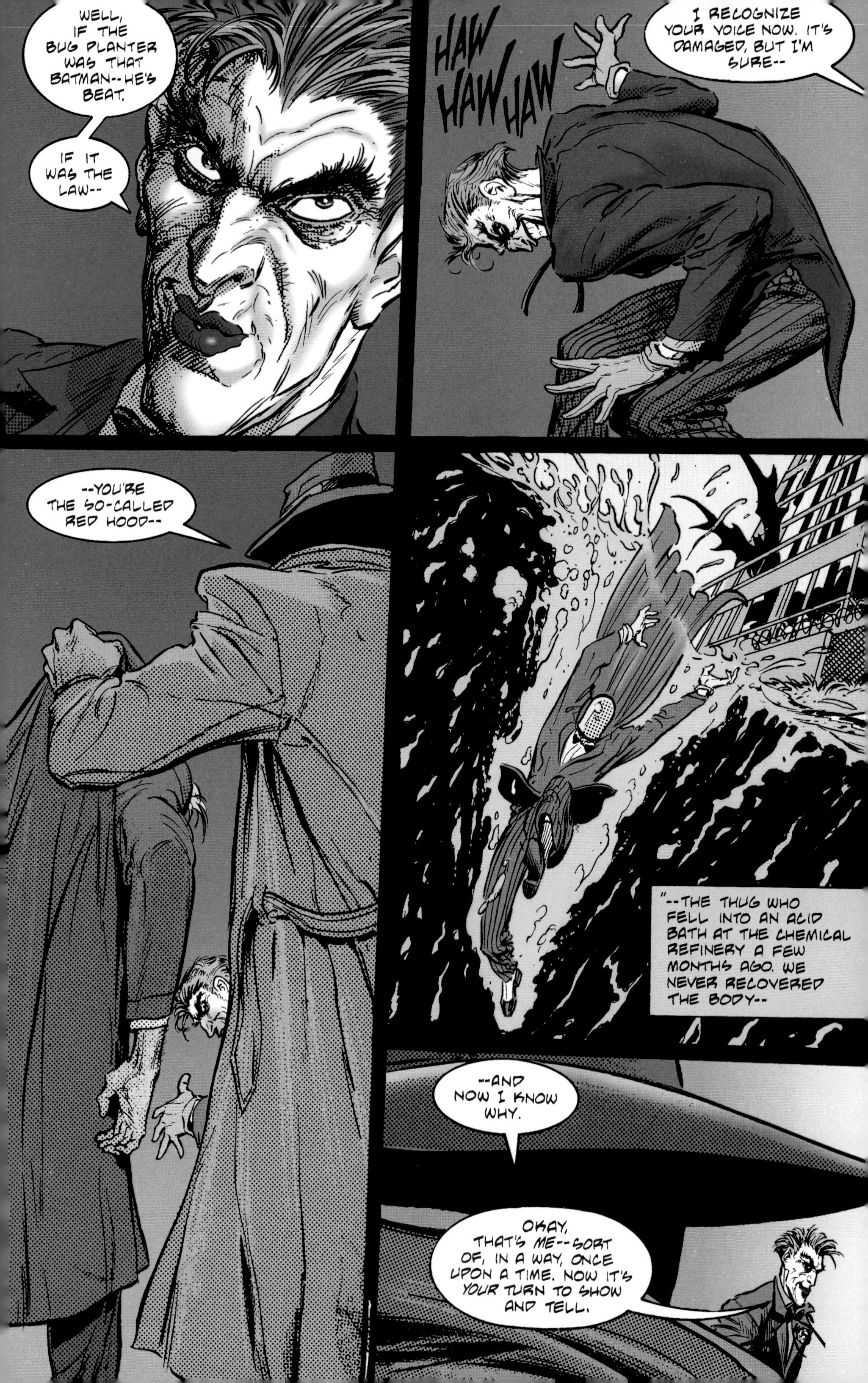
WELL, IF THE BUG PLANTER WAS THAT BATMAN--HE'S BEAT.
IF IT WAS THE LAW--
HAW HAW HAW
I RECOGNIZE YOUR VOICE NOW. IT'S DAMAGED, BUT I'M SURE--
--YOU'RE THE SO-CALLED RED HOOD--
"--THE THUG WHO FELL INTO AN ACID BATH AT THE CHEMICAL REFINERY A FEW MONTHS AGO. WE NEVER RECOVERED THE BODY--
--AND NOW I KNOW WHY.
OKAY, THAT'S ME--SORT OF, IN A WAY, ONCE UPON A TIME. NOW IT'S YOUR TURN TO SHOW AND TELL.

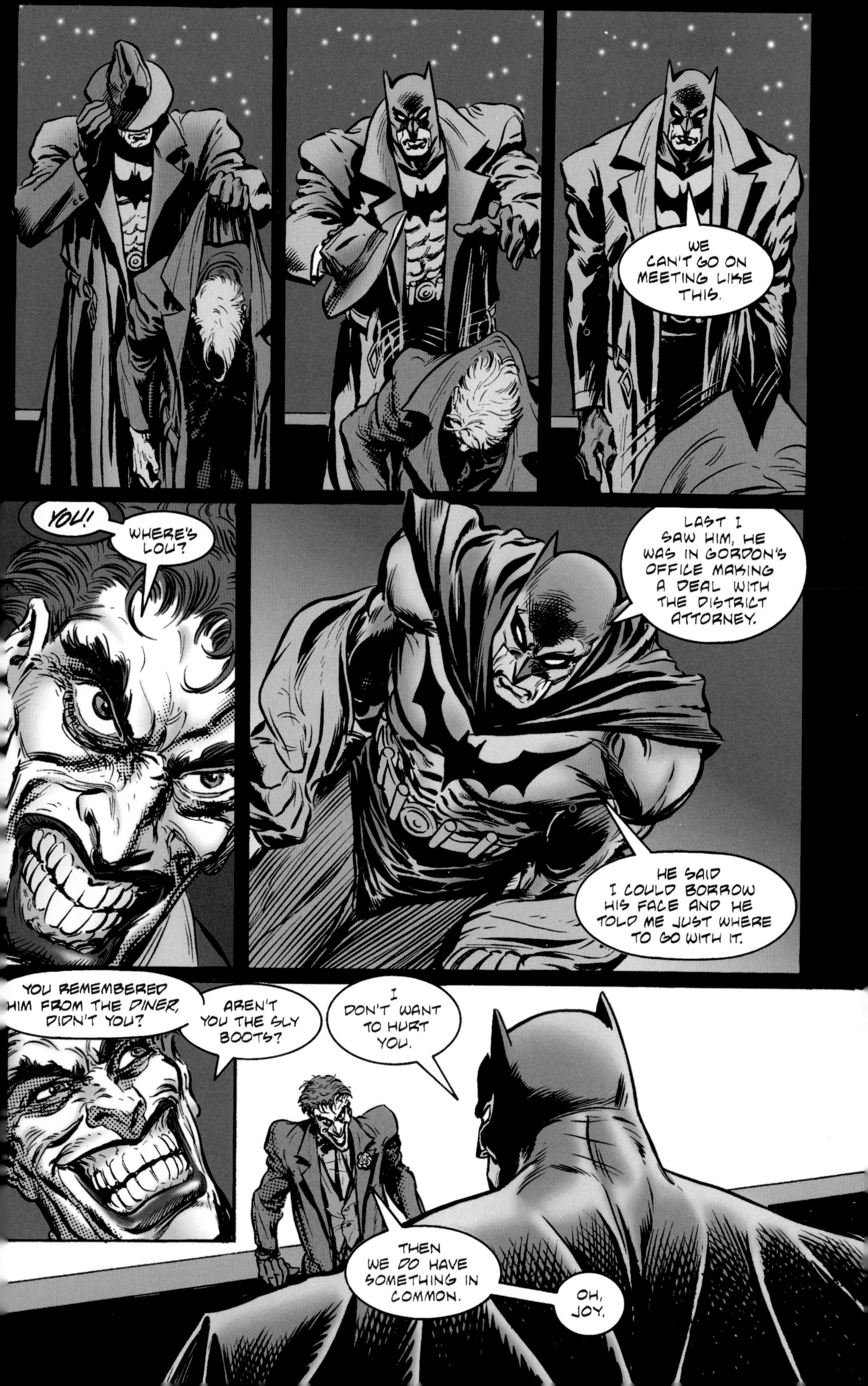
WE CAN'T GO ON MEETING LIKE THIS.
YOU!
WHERE'S LOU?
LAST I SAW HIM, HE WAS IN GORDON'S OFFICE MAKING A DEAL WITH THE DISTRICT ATTORNEY.
HE SAID I COULD BORROW HIS FACE AND HE TOLD ME JUST WHERE TO GO WITH IT.
YOU REMEMBERED HIM FROM THE DINER, DIDN'T YOU?
AREN'T YOU THE SLY BOOTS?
I DON'T WANT TO HURT YOU.
THEN WE DO HAVE SOMETHING IN COMMON.
OH, JOY.

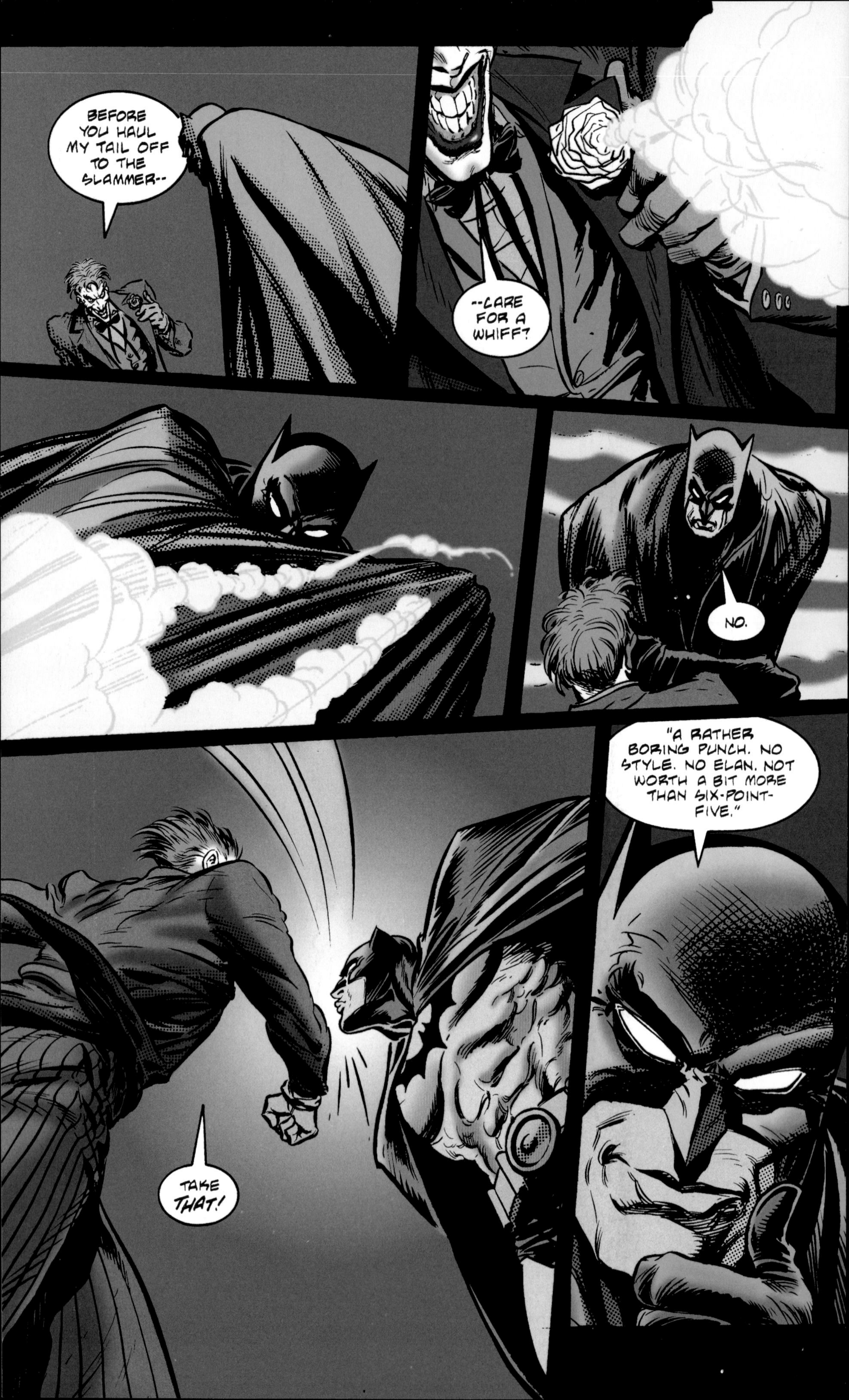
BEFORE YOU HAUL MY TAIL OFF TO THE SLAMMER--
--CARE FOR A WHIFF?
NO.
"A RATHER BORING PUNCH. NO STYLE. NO ELAN. NOT WORTH A BIT MORE THAN SIX-POINT-FIVE."
TAKE *THAT!*

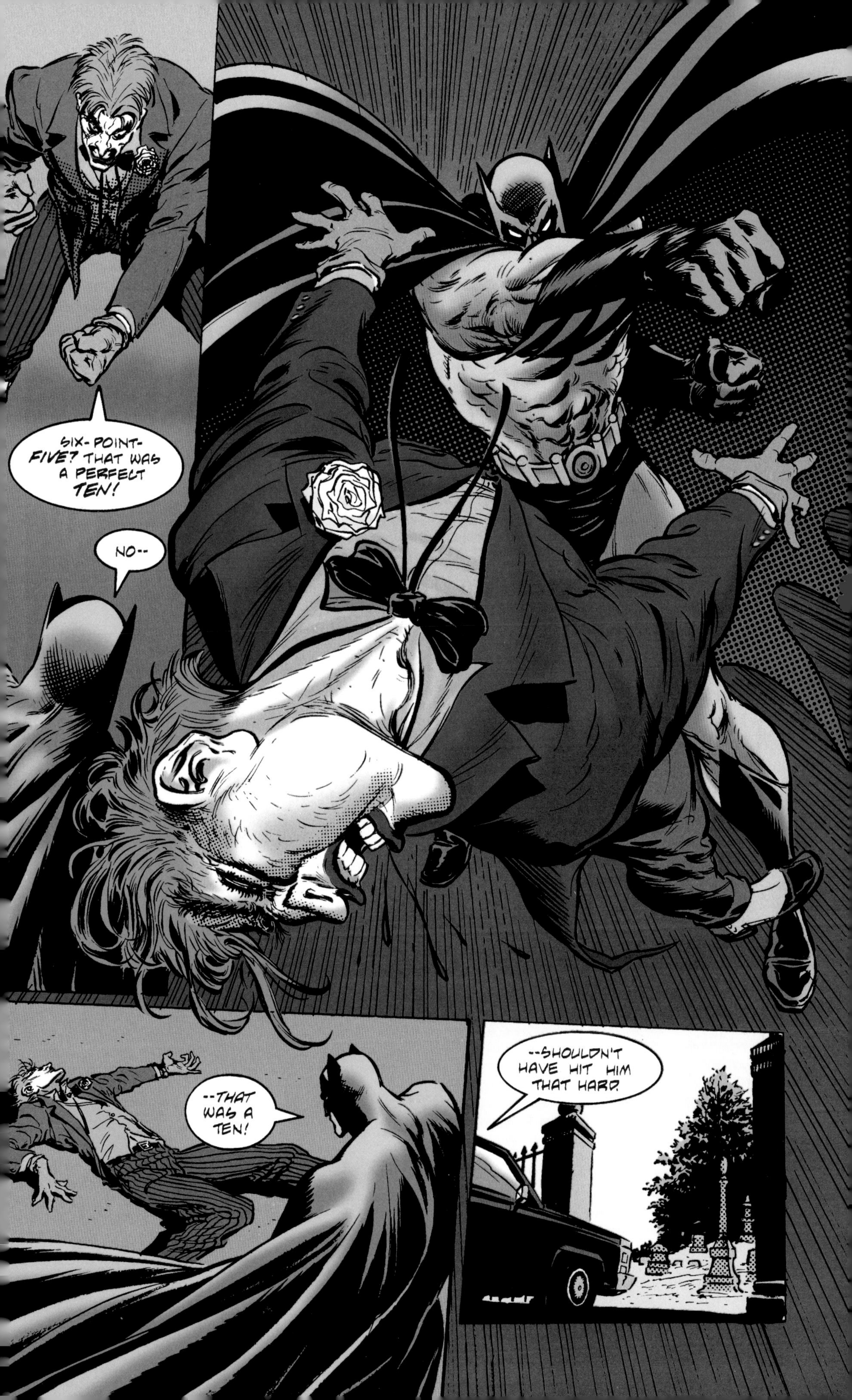
SIX-POINT-FIVE? THAT WAS A PERFECT TEN!
NO--
--THAT WAS A TEN!
--SHOULDN'T HAVE HIT HIM THAT HARD.

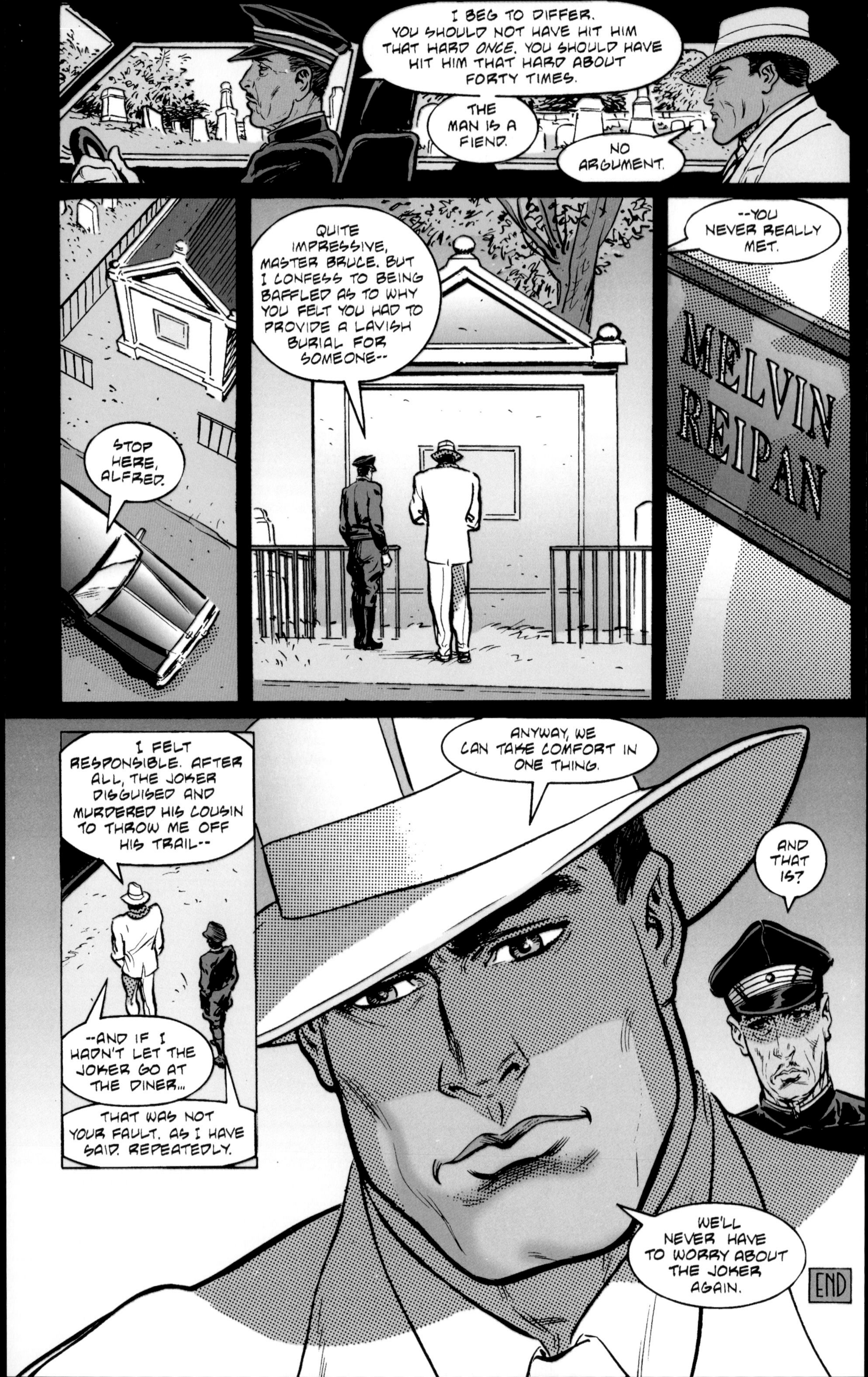
I BEG TO DIFFER. YOU SHOULD NOT HAVE HIT HIM THAT HARD *ONCE*. YOU SHOULD HAVE HIT HIM THAT HARD ABOUT FORTY TIMES.
THE MAN IS A FIEND.
NO ARGUMENT.
STOP HERE, ALFRED.
QUITE IMPRESSIVE, MASTER BRUCE. BUT I CONFESS TO BEING BAFFLED AS TO WHY YOU FELT YOU HAD TO PROVIDE A LAVISH BURIAL FOR SOMEONE--
--YOU NEVER REALLY MET.
MELVIN REIPAN
I FELT RESPONSIBLE. AFTER ALL, THE JOKER DISGUISED AND MURDERED HIS COUSIN TO THROW ME OFF HIS TRAIL--
--AND IF I HADN'T LET THE JOKER GO AT THE DINER...
THAT WAS NOT YOUR FAULT. AS I HAVE SAID. REPEATEDLY.
ANYWAY, WE CAN TAKE COMFORT IN ONE THING.
AND THAT IS?
WE'LL NEVER HAVE TO WORRY ABOUT THE JOKER AGAIN.
END

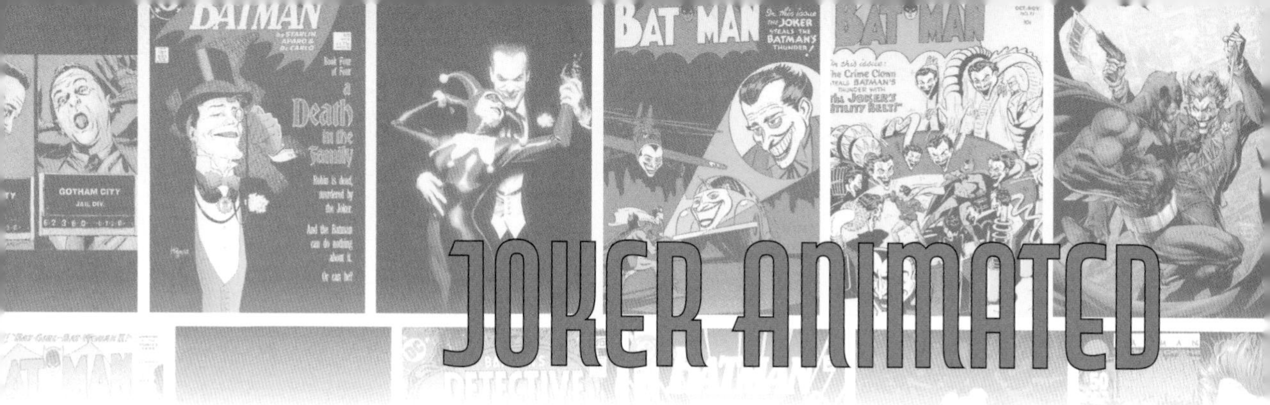

JOKER ANIMATED

by **PAUL DINI**

He may be Batman's nightmare, but he's an animator's dream. Coy one second, murderous the next, warbling a nonsense tune then snarling a deadly threat. Often clad in clownish colors, he is the consummate showman whose only limitations are the imaginations of the artists putting him through his paces. He is the Joker, and over the years this mountebank of menace has come to dominate the medium of animation just as he rules comics, feature films, video games, and every other form of popular entertainment.

His earliest cartoon appearances were embarrassingly tame. A silent, static cameo (wearing an atypical green suit) among a quick panning shot of cartoon bad guys in the title sequence of the 1966 *Batman* live-action series may be Joker's first (semi-) animated appearance. It wasn't until the premiere of Filmation Associates' *The Batman/Superman Hour* on CBS TV's Saturday morning lineup in September 1968 that the Joker, along with Catwoman, Penguin, and a score of the classic rogues gallery denizens, would spring to life in relatively fuller animation. The 11-minute Batman stories were simple, with the Joker filling the role of stock thief and mostly harmless bad guy. Narrator Ted Knight, a few years away from worldwide recognition as Ted Baxter on *The Mary Tyler Moore Show*, did agreeable service to the Clown Prince's cackle; he also spoke for the Riddler, Mr. Freeze, and many other characters. In this series, the Joker had his classic comic book design, but the demands of producing Saturday morning animation on a budget kept his physical antics fairly restrained.

Larry Storch was next to voice the Joker in two Hanna-Barbera-created Scooby-Doo/Batman movies. Again, given the limited animation budget and kid-friendly storytelling, Batman and Robin's archenemy was little more than a colorful foil for the Mystery Inc. gang. This trend continued when Filmation again revived the Joker for *The New Adventures of Batman* in 1977, this time with veteran actor and writer Lennie Weinrib voicing the mirthful mountebank.

It is worth recalling that while TV animation for kids remained largely inert during the '70s and early '80s, comic books were maturing at a more rapid

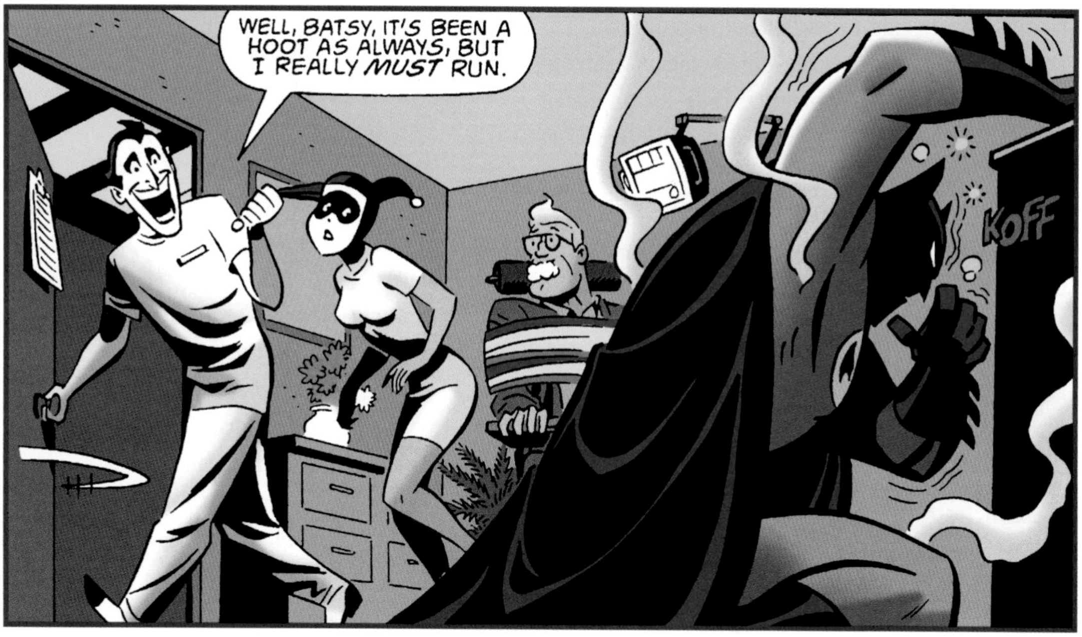
WELL, BATSY, IT'S BEEN A HOOT AS ALWAYS, BUT I REALLY MUST RUN.
KOFF

WHY DON'T YA JUST *SHOOT* HIM?

pace. Writers including Denny O'Neil, Steve Englehart, and Alan Moore were working with artists Neal Adams, Marshall Rogers, and Brian Bolland to return Batman to his darker roots, and that naturally meant a revival of the Joker's psychotic nature. While an animated *Killing Joke* Joker was still decades away, the 1985 *The Super Powers Team: Galactic Guardians* episode "The Wild Cards" depicted the Harlequin of Hate (voiced by Frank Welker) in a surprisingly different role. Written by Alan Burnett and John Loy, the Joker, disguised as one of the Royal Flush Gang, served as secret point man in a Darkseid-masterminded plot against the Justice League. The episode presented Joker in a more complex story than usual, and whetted Burnett's appetite to show the character in a more dangerous light.

Burnett got his chance when he assumed the role as producer on Warner Bros. Animation's groundbreaking *Batman: The Animated Series*. Determined to treat Batman's world in a more serious manner, Burnett instructed the series writers, myself included, to write the villains as legitimate challenges for the darker and more driven Batman. Series co-creator Bruce Timm devised a model for the new Joker that drew from all aspects of the character's history, but with an eye toward his much more dangerous mid-'70s reinvention. Equal parts clown and madman, Timm's Joker might playfully don the top of a skyscraper for a disguise, then murderously attempt to use its spire to bayonet Batman. Here finally was a chance to maximize everything Joker could be through animation. Only one thing was lacking—a voice to match the madness. Many fine actors gave it their all, but there was still something missing, a link with the character that somehow extended off the script page. WBA voice caster and director Andrea Romano had already used *Star Wars* star Mark Hamill to voice a secondary bad guy in the episode "Heart of Ice." A comic book devotee, Mr. Hamill expressed his enthusiasm at the possibility of returning to voice one of the classic rogues' gallery villains. What about him? Intrigued by Andrea's suggestion, we asked her to audition Mark right away.

It was the laugh.

We knew it the second we heard it. Strident, scary, and yet touched with the faint cry of a lost soul. A tingle shot through me, goosebumps on my arm. It was the same voice I had heard in my head as only a comic book reader can imagine it. The character became a joy to write for, a welcome invitation to let loose one's wicked side. More than that, Mark's Joker inspired the artists to be actors, and they embellished the character in storyboards and layouts with layers of dark humor and physicality only hinted at in the scripts. That in turn, translated into some of the finest character animation the series ever produced.

Possibly the only one having more fun with the Joker was Mark Hamill himself. If we were doing a story that had its origins in the comics, Mark would pull the corresponding book from his collection and reread it in advance of the recording date. He told us he wanted to study the way the artist had depicted Joker's actions in the story so that he might use that to add a bit of nuance

BATMAN
DETECTIVE
MAD LOVE
BATMAN

to his own interpretation. Arleen Sorkin, who played Harley Quinn to Hamill's Joker, marveled at the amount of energy the actor brought to the role. While most of the other actors sat to record their lines, Hamill always gave a standing performance, throwing himself into the Joker's gesticulations like a merry madman.

After the animated series, Hamill would return to voice the Joker in stand-alone direct-to-video projects such as *The Killing Joke* and various iterations of *Justice League*. At the same time other actors were coming forward to play the Clown Prince in different animated projects. Kevin Michael Richardson gave the Joker a harsher, more dangerous tone to match Jeff Matsuda's monstrously designed Clown Prince of Crime in *The Batman*. Jeff Bennett created a wise-guy comedian's voice that perfectly matched Joker's Silver Age look in *Batman: The Brave and the Bold*, while John DiMaggio's *Under the Red Hood* Joker was all cold-blooded murderer. *The Lego Batman Movie* both lampooned and paid homage to the best-known elements of Bat-lore. It followed suit that Zach Galifianakis would play this Joker, a self-described "misunderstood criminal genius" as an engaging prankster with an unrequited man-crush on his adversary. In numerous projects, Troy Baker has proven to be a one-man rogues gallery, voicing Gotham's villains in such direct-to-video movies and games as *Batman: Assault on Arkham* (Joker) and *Batman: Arkham Knight* (Jason Todd, Two-Face). And in DC Universe's adult *Harley Quinn* series Alan Tudyk tinges the Joker's mocking derision of his former flame with a dash of envy—who knew she would grow strong enough to beat the clown at his own game?

With every new series, writers, actors, artists, and directors challenge themselves to create nightmarish new visions of the Joker and the world he inhabits. Like the medium of animation itself, he remains colorful, ever in motion and always ready to spring another surprise. You just gotta laugh…

Paul Dini *recently authored the* New York Times *bestselling DC Vertigo graphic novel* Dark Night: A True Batman Story *and co-wrote the Titan Books novel* Harley Quinn: Mad Love. *A five-time Emmy-winning writer and producer, Paul is perhaps best known for his work on such Warner Bros. Animation projects as* Batman: The Animated Series, Superman, Batman Beyond, *and various iterations of* Tom & Jerry, Looney Tunes, *and* Justice League. *He has scripted numerous comic book series (*Gotham City Sirens, Zatanna, Detective Comics*), video games (*Batman: Arkham Asylum, Batman: Arkham City*), and live television shows (*Creepshow, Lost, Tower Prep*). The co-creator of Harley Quinn, Paul continues to write frequent stories about America's screwball sweetheart. Paul lives in Los Angeles with his wife, magician and actress Misty Lee, and their Boston terriers, Pixie and the Tank.*

KNOW THIS, MY SWEET. THE DEATH OF BATMAN MUST BE NOTHING LESS THAN A *MASTERPIECE*.

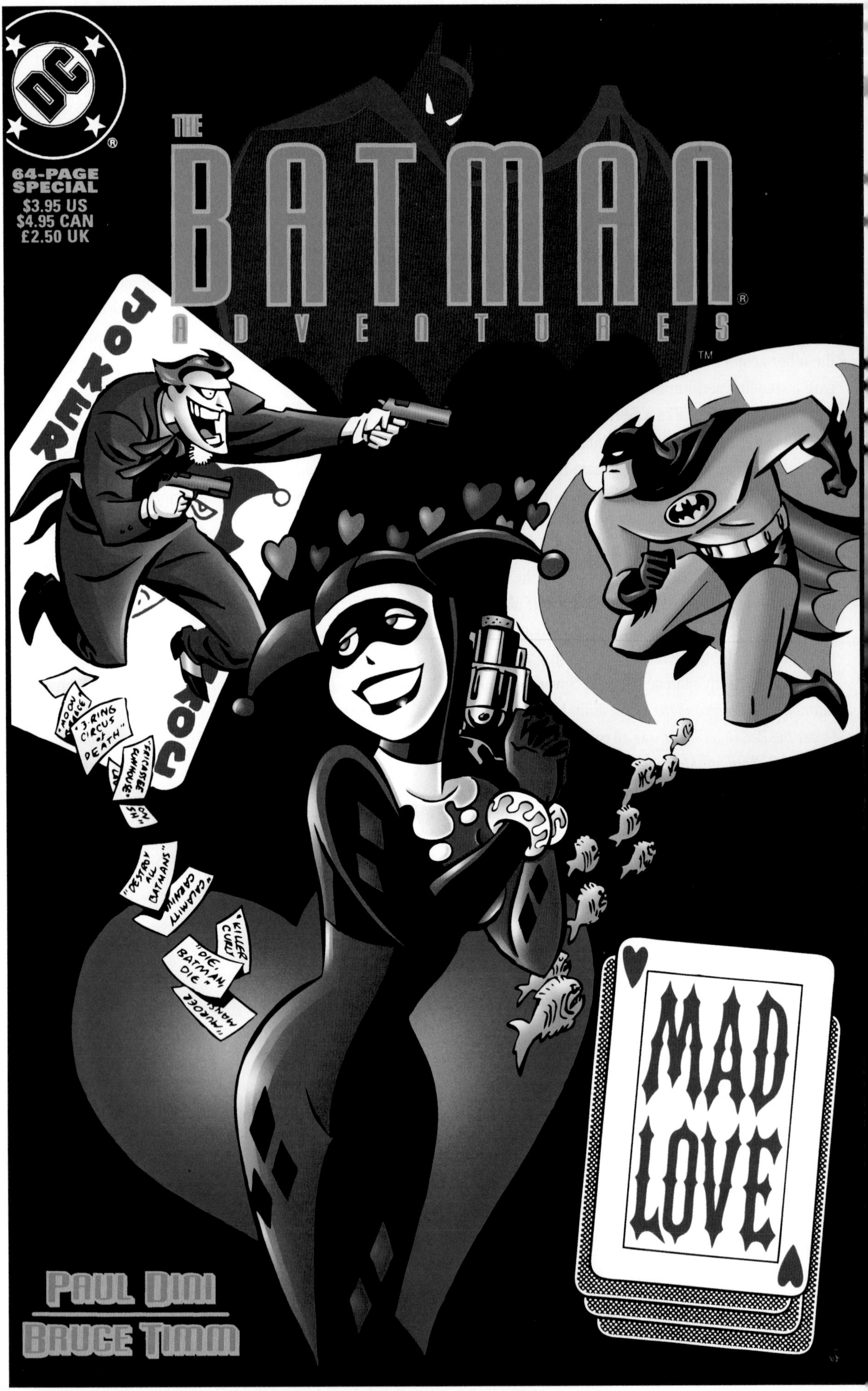
64-PAGE SPECIAL
$3.95 US
$4.95 CAN
£2.50 UK
THE BATMAN ADVENTURES
JOKER
"3-RING CIRCUS OF DEATH"
"DESTROY ALL BATMANS"
"DIE, BATMAN, DIE"
MAD LOVE
PAUL DINI
BRUCE TIMM

YOU'RE NEXT, COMMISSIONER.

Highlights

JUST FOR KIDS

IME
cadem
d book

SWELL.

FIN
the MIS

MUMBLE MUTTER MUMBLE...

HAVE A SEAT. I'LL BE RIGHT WITH YOU.

I DON'T MIND SAYING I REALLY *HATE* THESE CHECK-UPS.

IF IT WASN'T PART OF THE REQUIRED POLICE PHYSICAL, I PROBABLY WOULDN'T COME AT *ALL*.

OH, *COME* NOW, COMMISSIONER -- WHAT IN THIS MISERABLE WORLD IS MORE BEAUTIFUL...

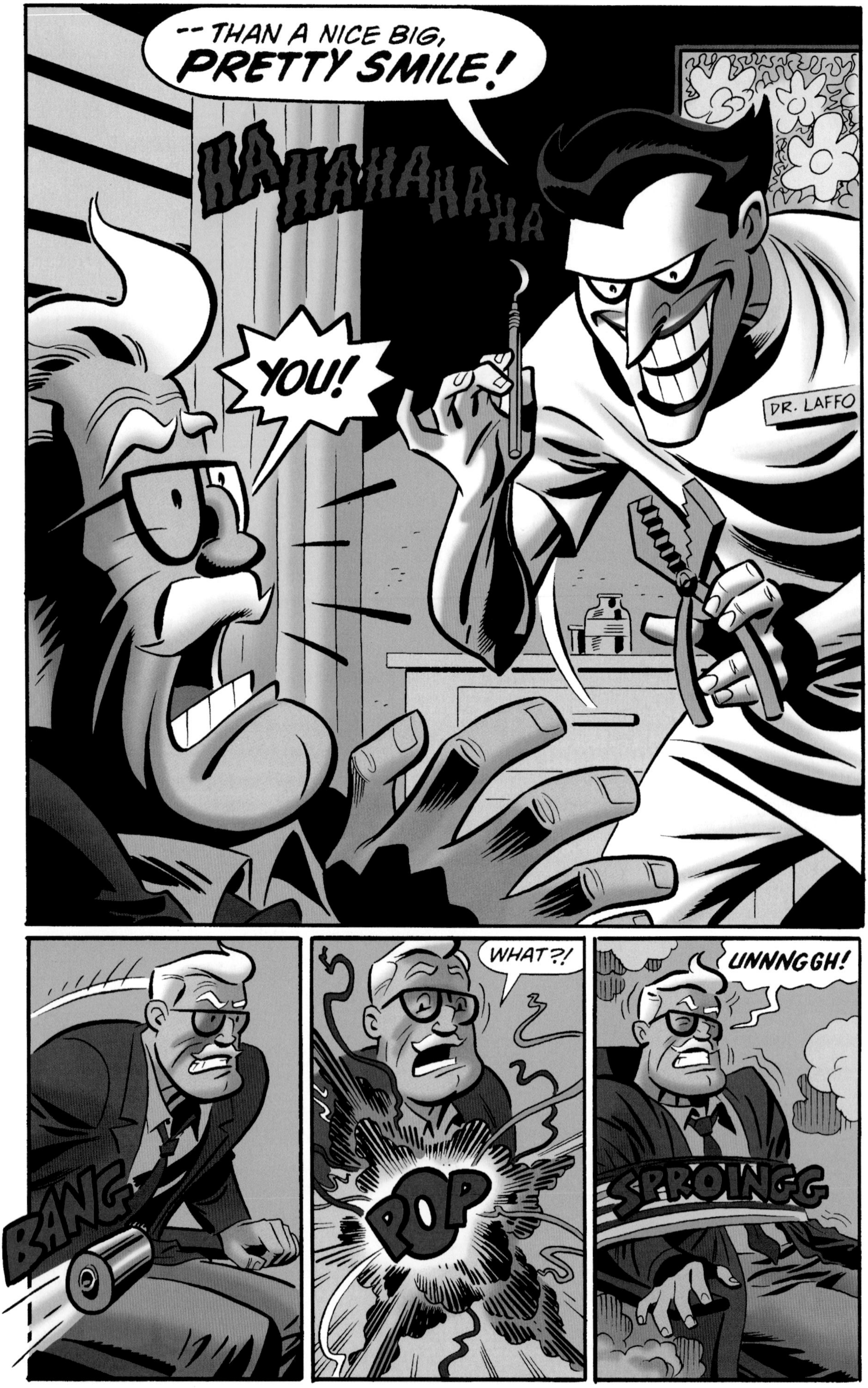
-- THAN A NICE BIG,
PRETTY SMILE!
HAHAHAHAHAHA
YOU!
DR. LAFFO
BANG
WHAT?!
POP
UNNNGGH!
SPROINGG

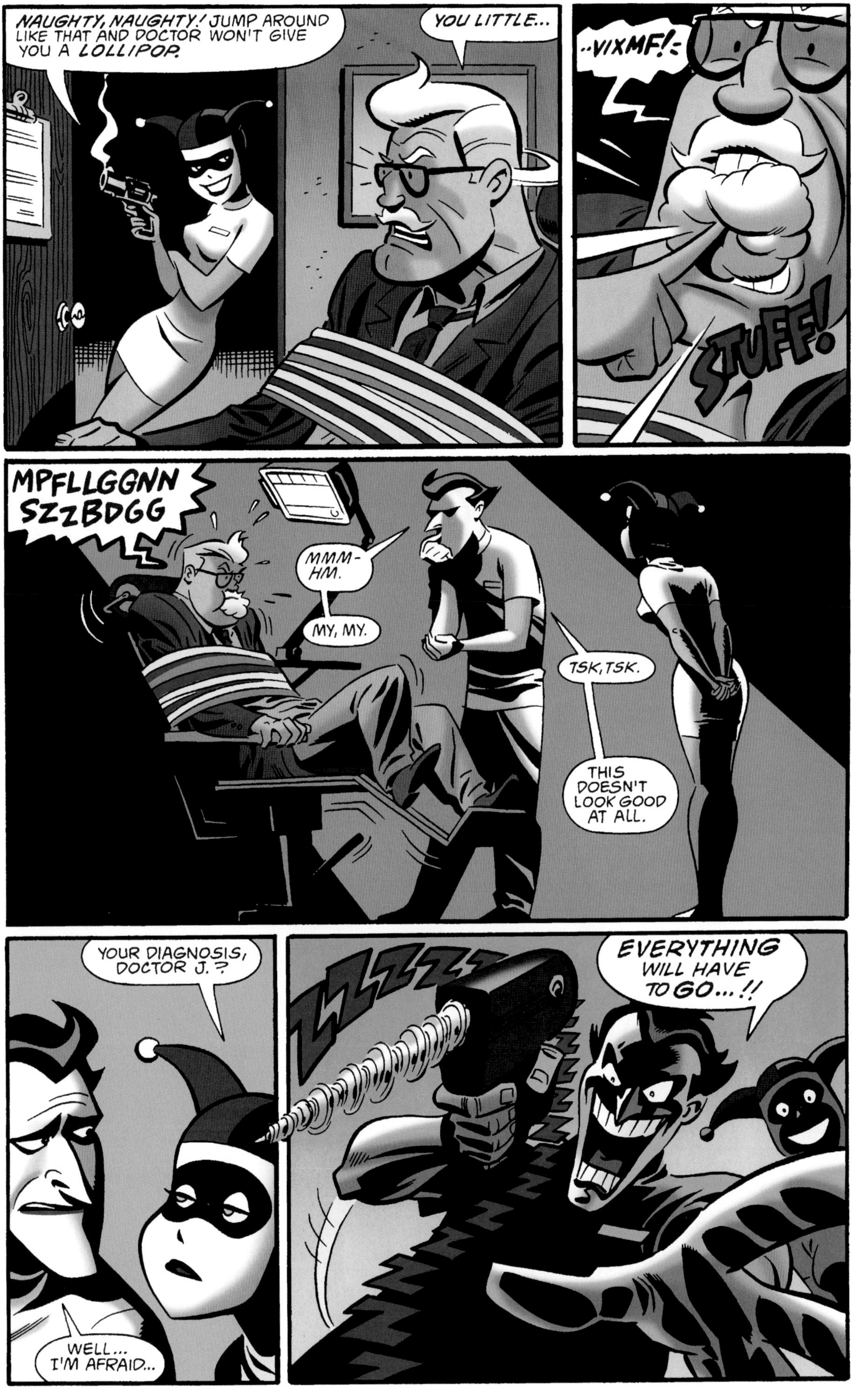
NAUGHTY, NAUGHTY! JUMP AROUND LIKE THAT AND DOCTOR WON'T GIVE YOU A LOLLIPOP.
YOU LITTLE...
..VIXMF!..
STUFF!
MPFLLGGNN SZZBDGG
MMM-HM.
MY, MY.
TSK, TSK.
THIS DOESN'T LOOK GOOD AT ALL.
YOUR DIAGNOSIS, DOCTOR J.?
WELL... I'M AFRAID...
EVERYTHING WILL HAVE TO GO...!!

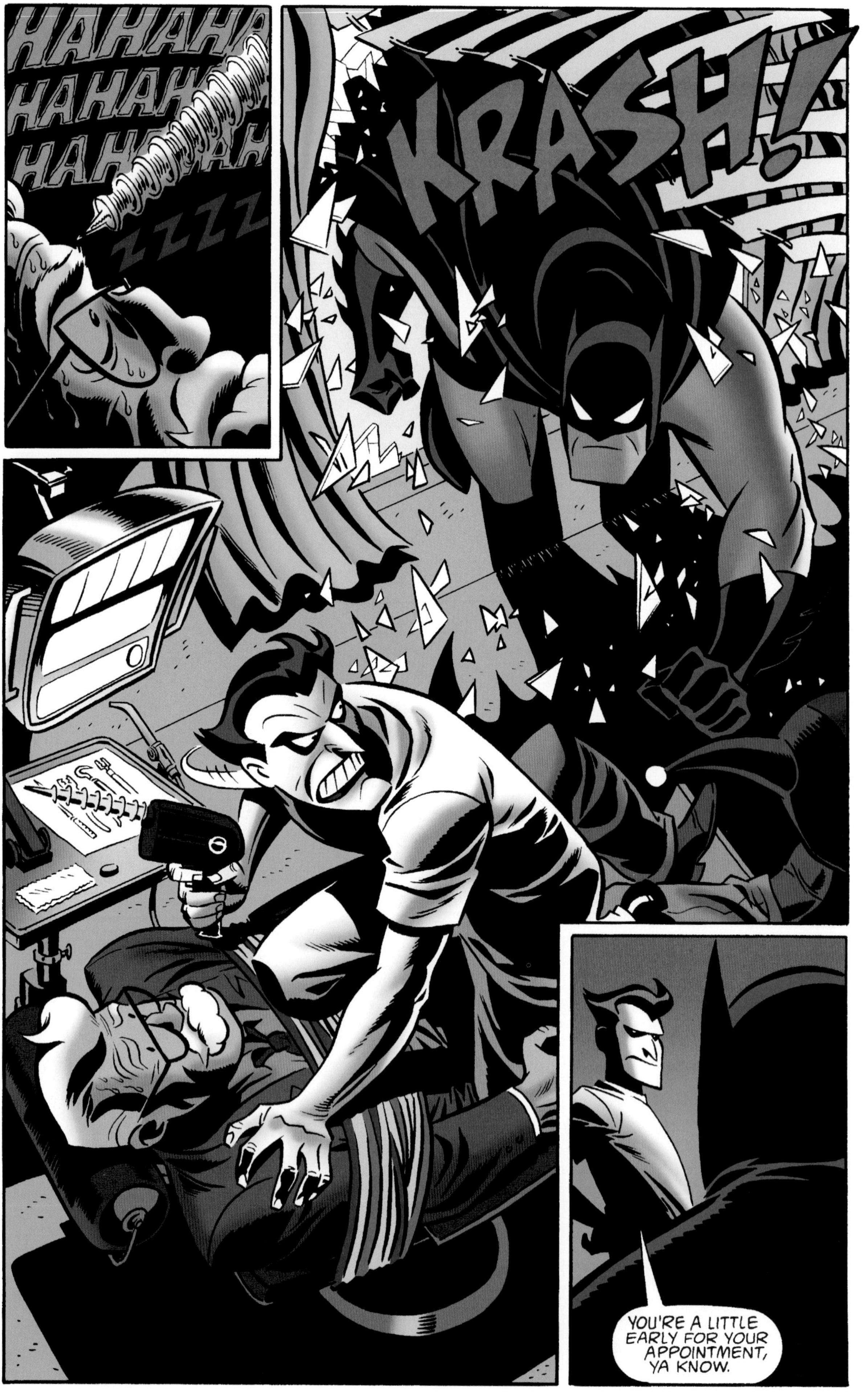
HAHAHA
HAHAHA
HAHAHA
ZZZZZ
KRASH!
YOU'RE A LITTLE EARLY FOR YOUR APPOINTMENT, YA KNOW.

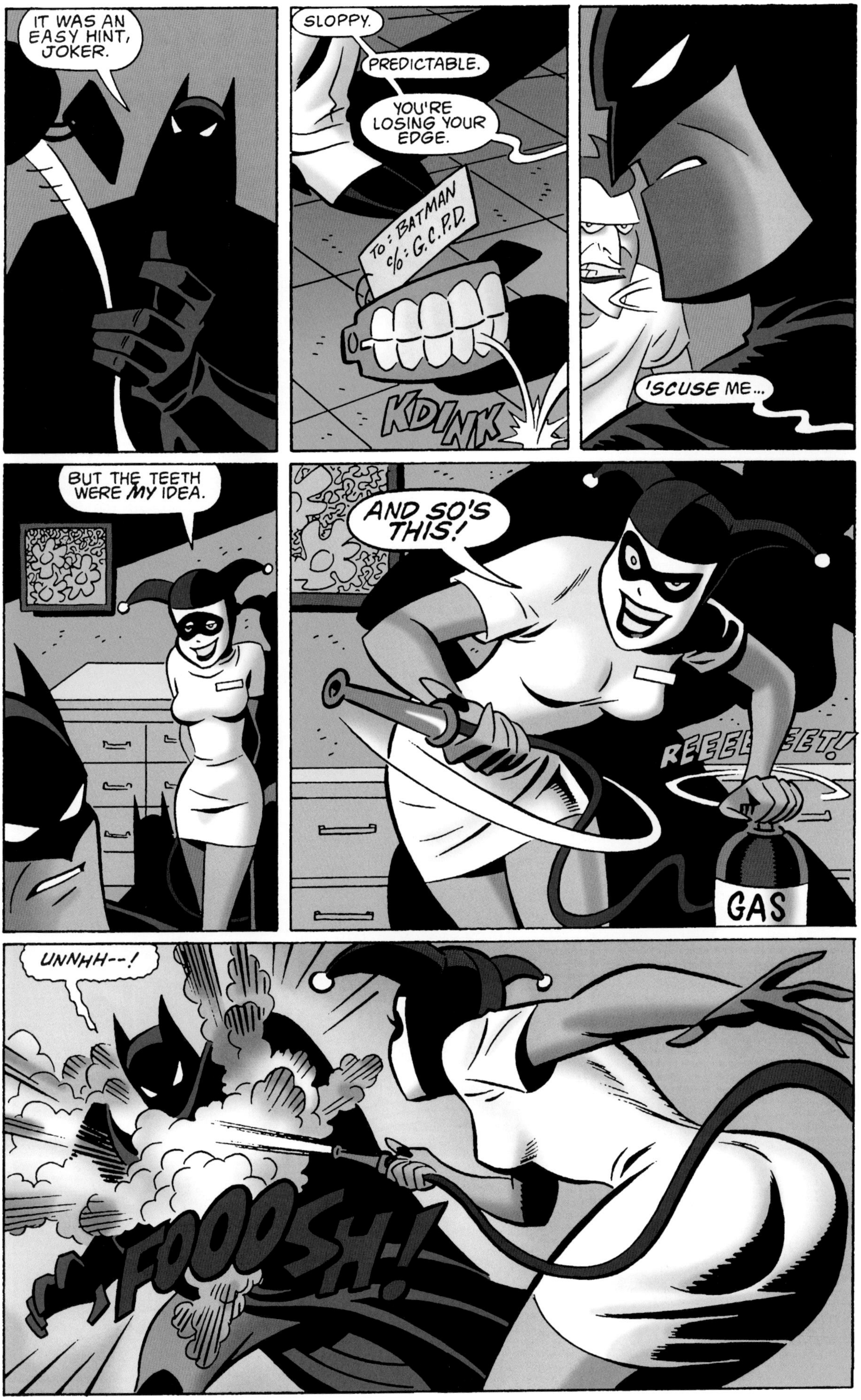
IT WAS AN EASY HINT, JOKER.
SLOPPY.
PREDICTABLE.
YOU'RE LOSING YOUR EDGE.
TO: BATMAN c/o: G.C.P.D.
KDINK
'SCUSE ME...
BUT THE TEETH WERE MY IDEA.
AND SO'S THIS!
REEEEEET!
GAS
UNNHH--!
FOOOSH!

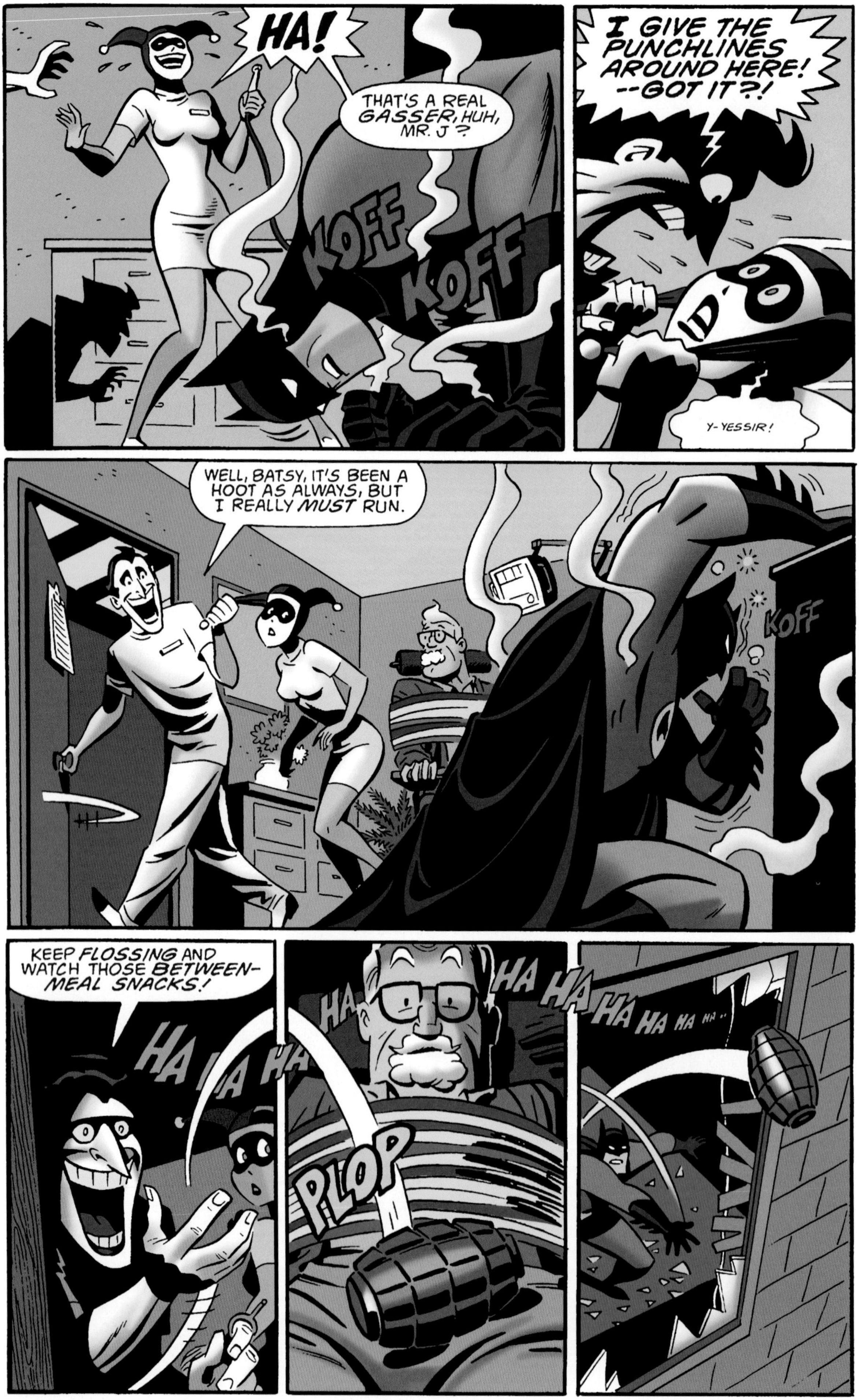
HA!
THAT'S A REAL GASSER, HUH, MR. J?
KOFF
KOFF
I GIVE THE PUNCHLINES AROUND HERE! --GOT IT?!
Y-YESSIR!
WELL, BATSY, IT'S BEEN A HOOT AS ALWAYS, BUT I REALLY MUST RUN.
KOFF
KEEP FLOSSING AND WATCH THOSE BETWEEN-MEAL SNACKS!
HA HA HA
PLOP
HA HA HA HA HA HA HA HA HA..

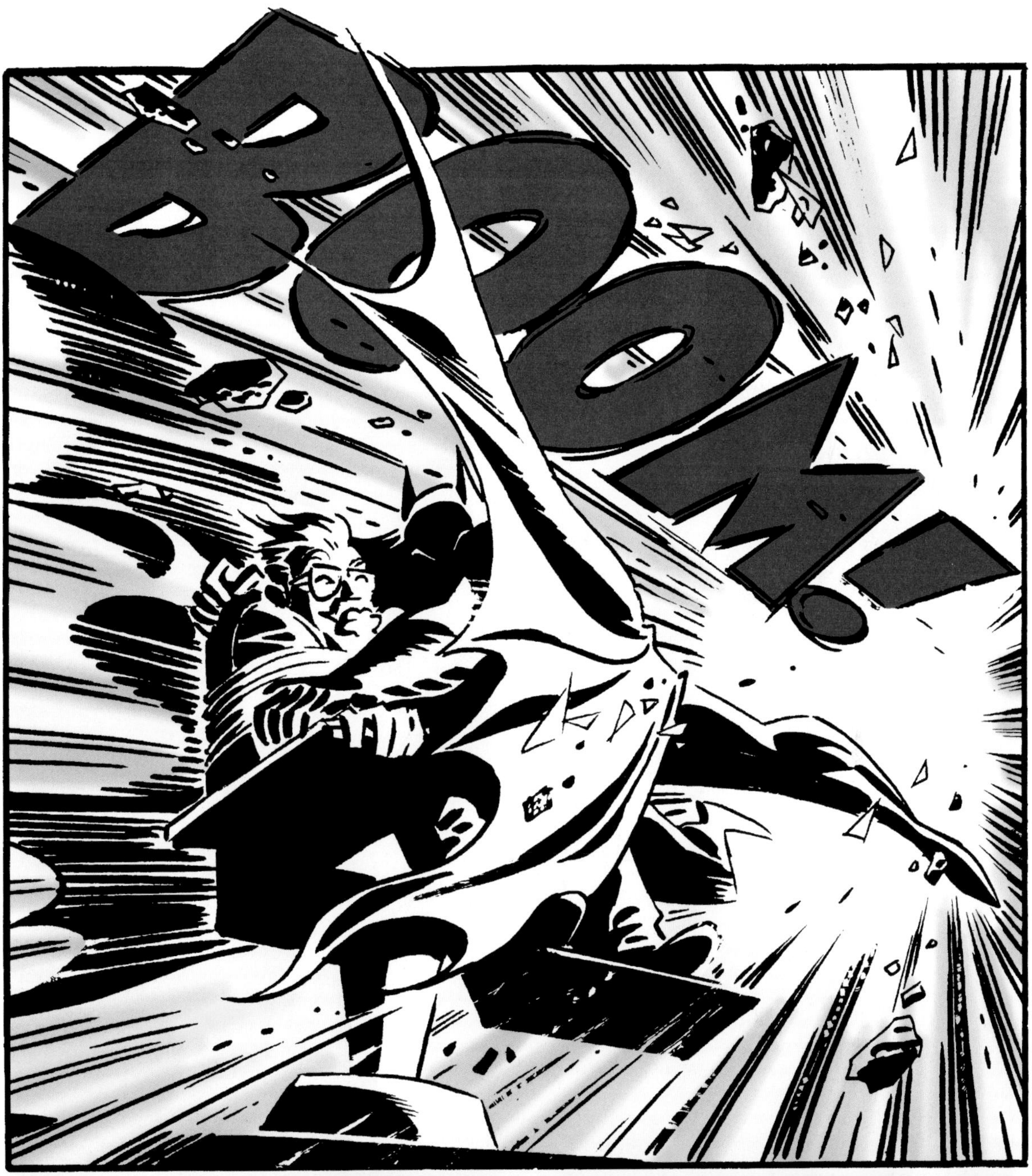
BOOOM!

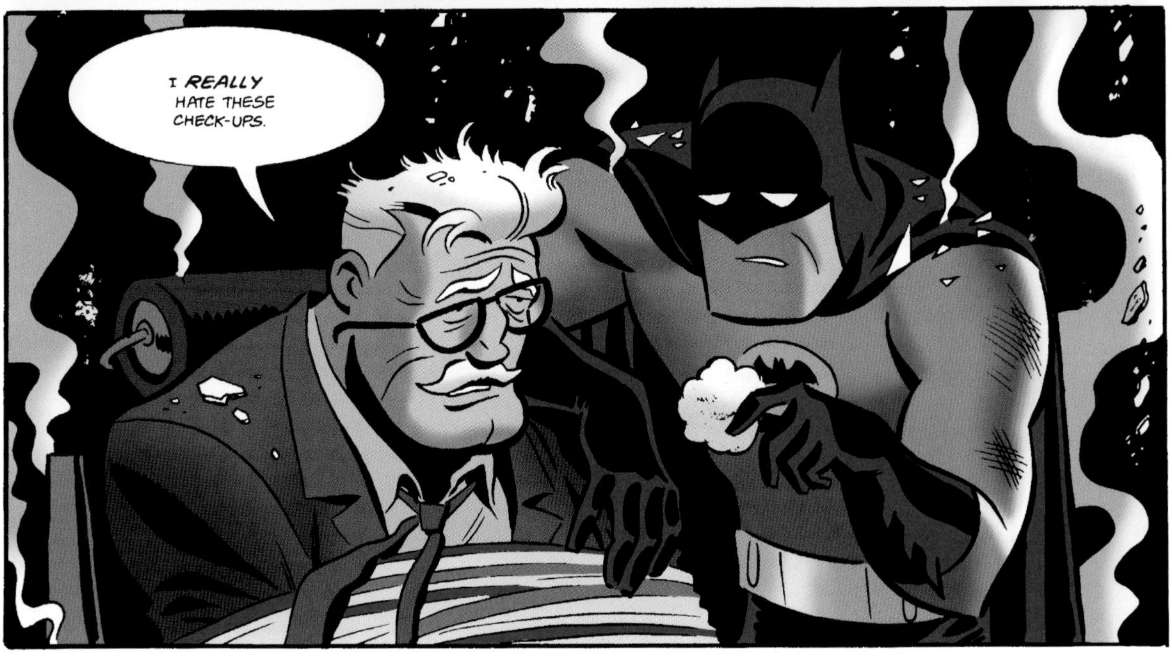
I REALLY HATE THESE CHECK-UPS.

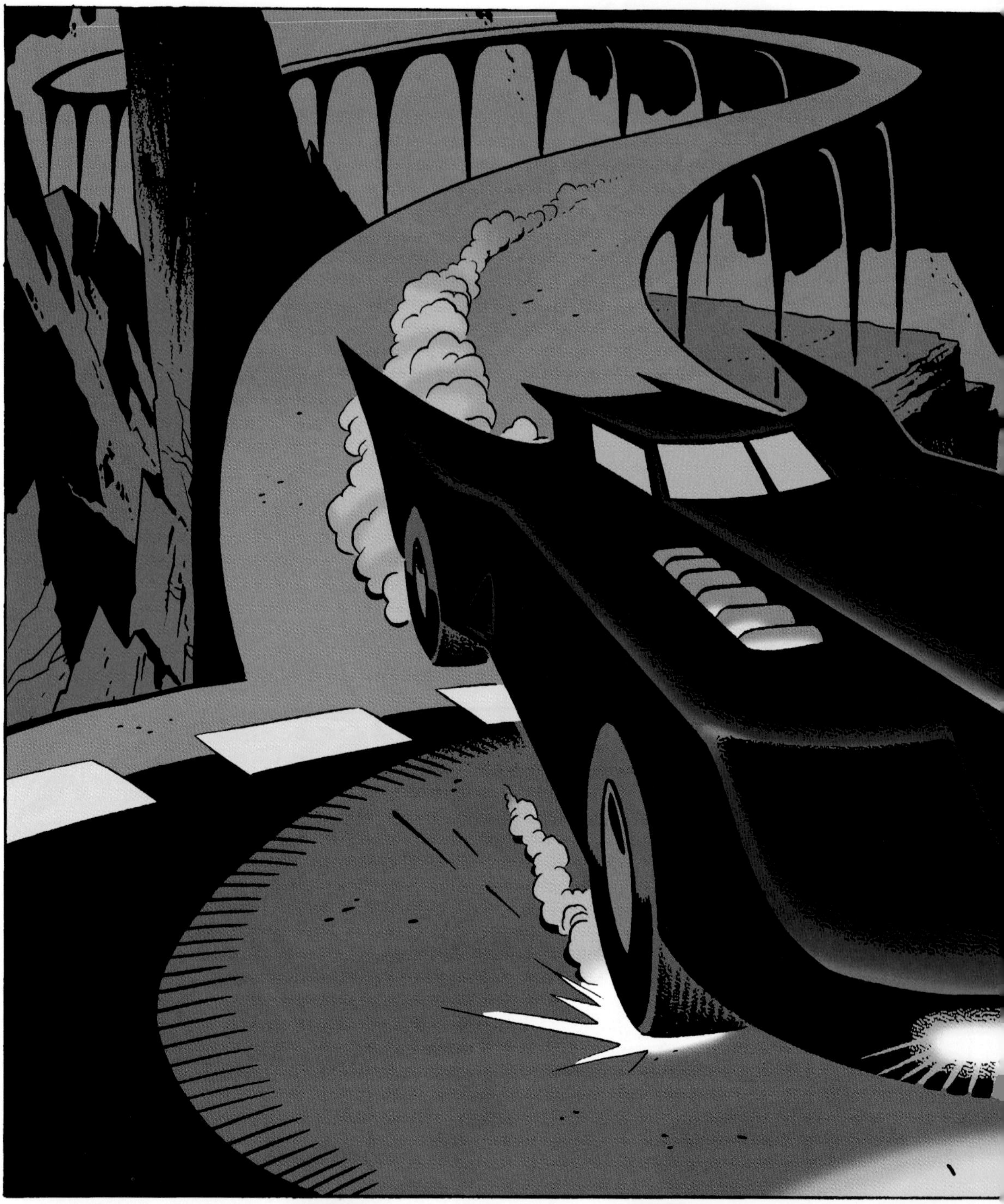

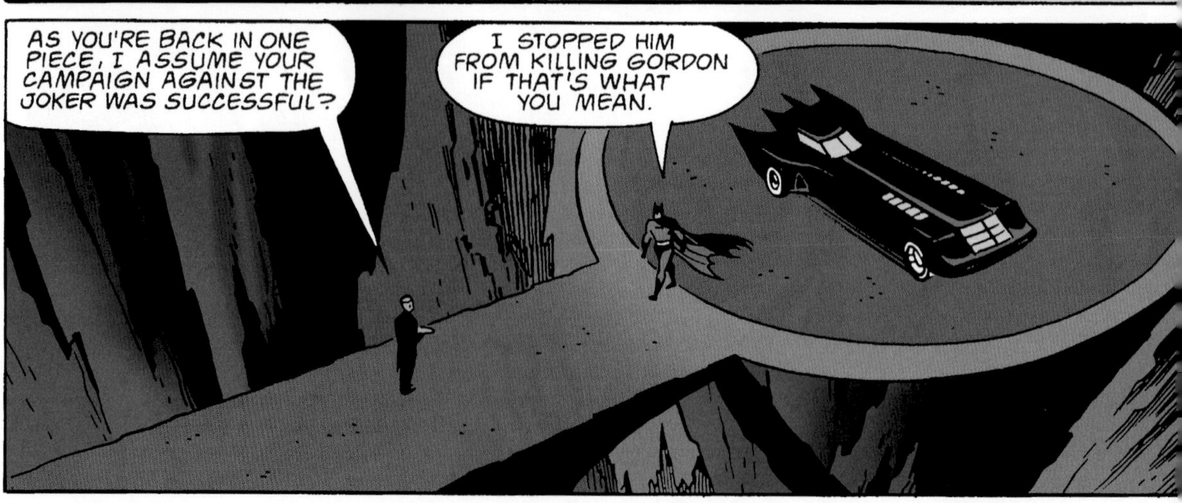
AS YOU'RE BACK IN ONE PIECE, I ASSUME YOUR CAMPAIGN AGAINST THE JOKER WAS SUCCESSFUL?
I STOPPED HIM FROM KILLING GORDON IF THAT'S WHAT YOU MEAN.

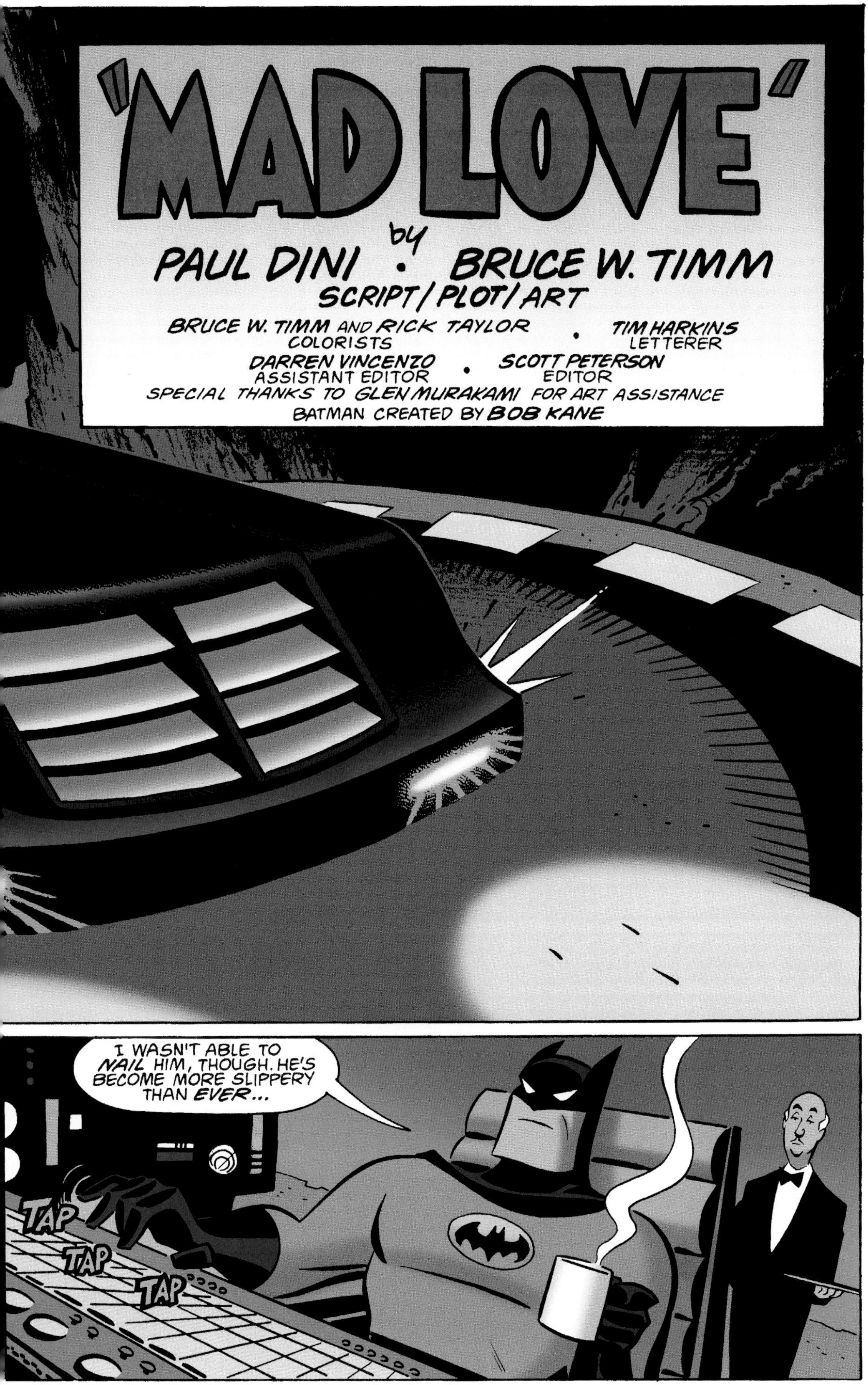
"MAD LOVE"
by
PAUL DINI · BRUCE W. TIMM
SCRIPT/PLOT/ART
BRUCE W. TIMM AND RICK TAYLOR COLORISTS · TIM HARKINS LETTERER
DARREN VINCENZO ASSISTANT EDITOR · SCOTT PETERSON EDITOR
SPECIAL THANKS TO GLEN MURAKAMI FOR ART ASSISTANCE
BATMAN CREATED BY BOB KANE
I WASN'T ABLE TO NAIL HIM, THOUGH. HE'S BECOME MORE SLIPPERY THAN EVER...
TAP
TAP
TAP

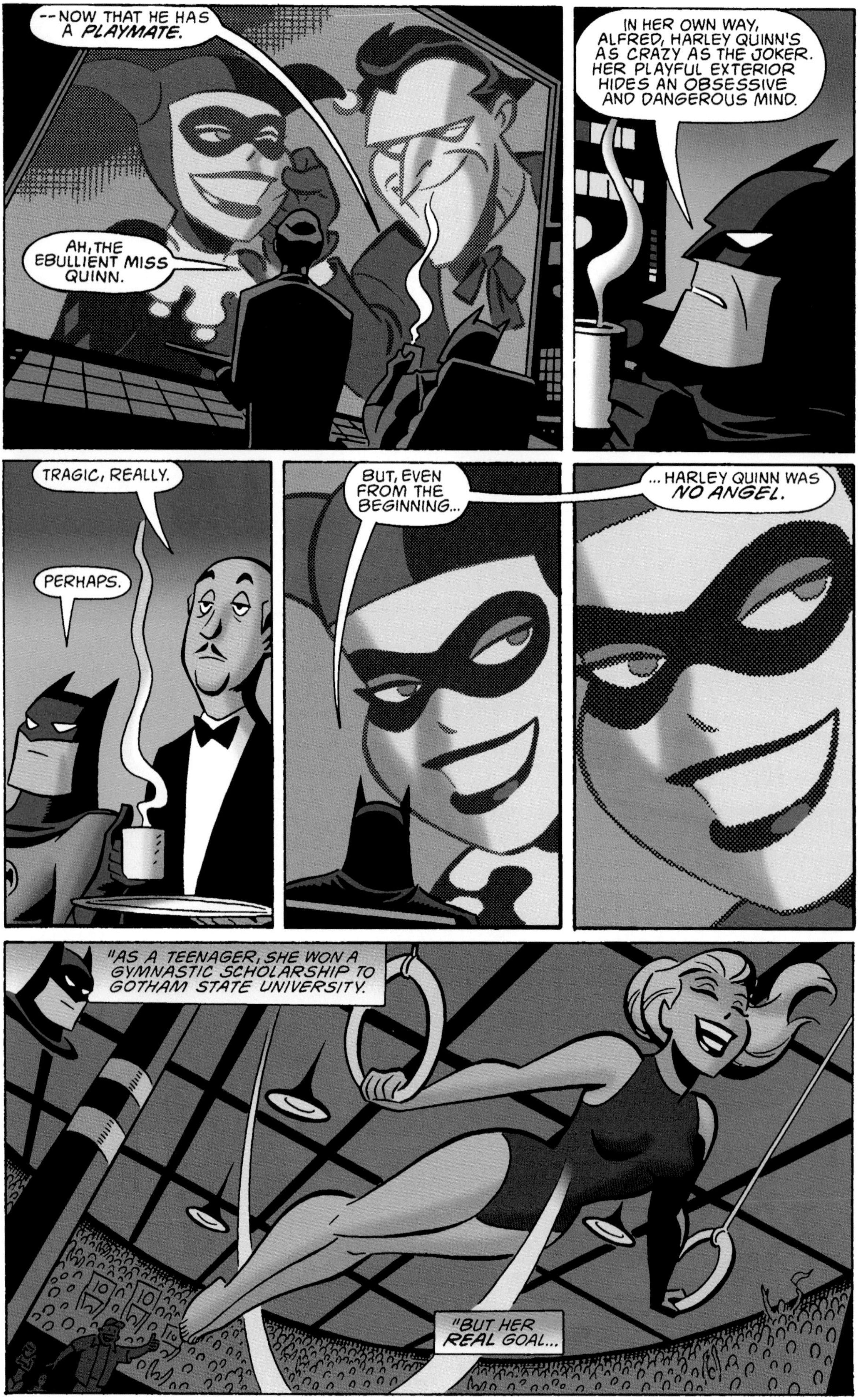
--NOW THAT HE HAS A PLAYMATE.
AH, THE EBULLIENT MISS QUINN.
IN HER OWN WAY, ALFRED, HARLEY QUINN'S AS CRAZY AS THE JOKER. HER PLAYFUL EXTERIOR HIDES AN OBSESSIVE AND DANGEROUS MIND.
TRAGIC, REALLY.
PERHAPS.
BUT, EVEN FROM THE BEGINNING...
...HARLEY QUINN WAS NO ANGEL.
"AS A TEENAGER, SHE WON A GYMNASTIC SCHOLARSHIP TO GOTHAM STATE UNIVERSITY.
"BUT HER REAL GOAL...

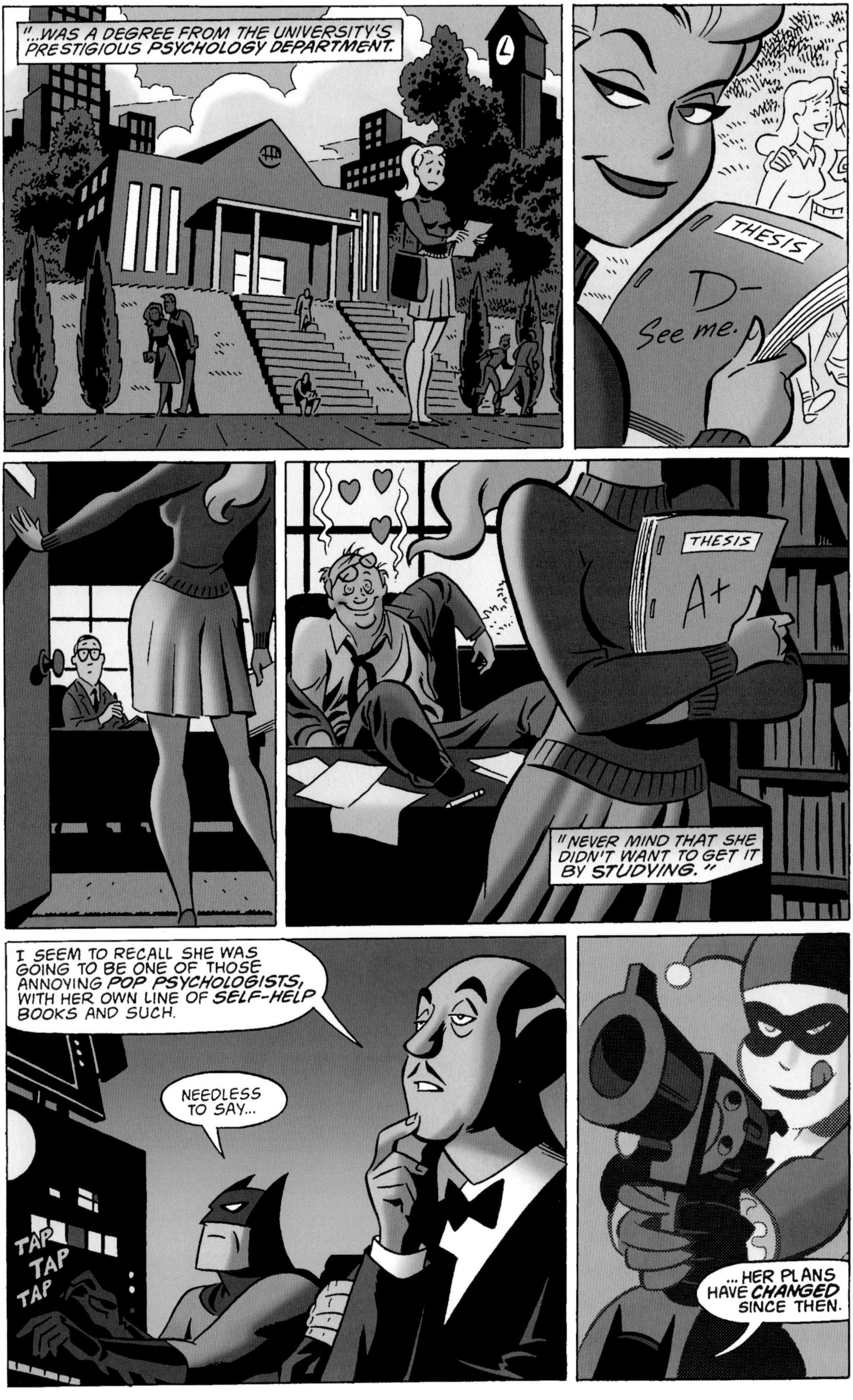
"...WAS A DEGREE FROM THE UNIVERSITY'S PRESTIGIOUS PSYCHOLOGY DEPARTMENT.
THESIS
D-
See me.
THESIS
A+
"NEVER MIND THAT SHE DIDN'T WANT TO GET IT BY STUDYING."
I SEEM TO RECALL SHE WAS GOING TO BE ONE OF THOSE ANNOYING POP PSYCHOLOGISTS, WITH HER OWN LINE OF SELF-HELP BOOKS AND SUCH.
NEEDLESS TO SAY...
TAP TAP TAP
...HER PLANS HAVE CHANGED SINCE THEN.

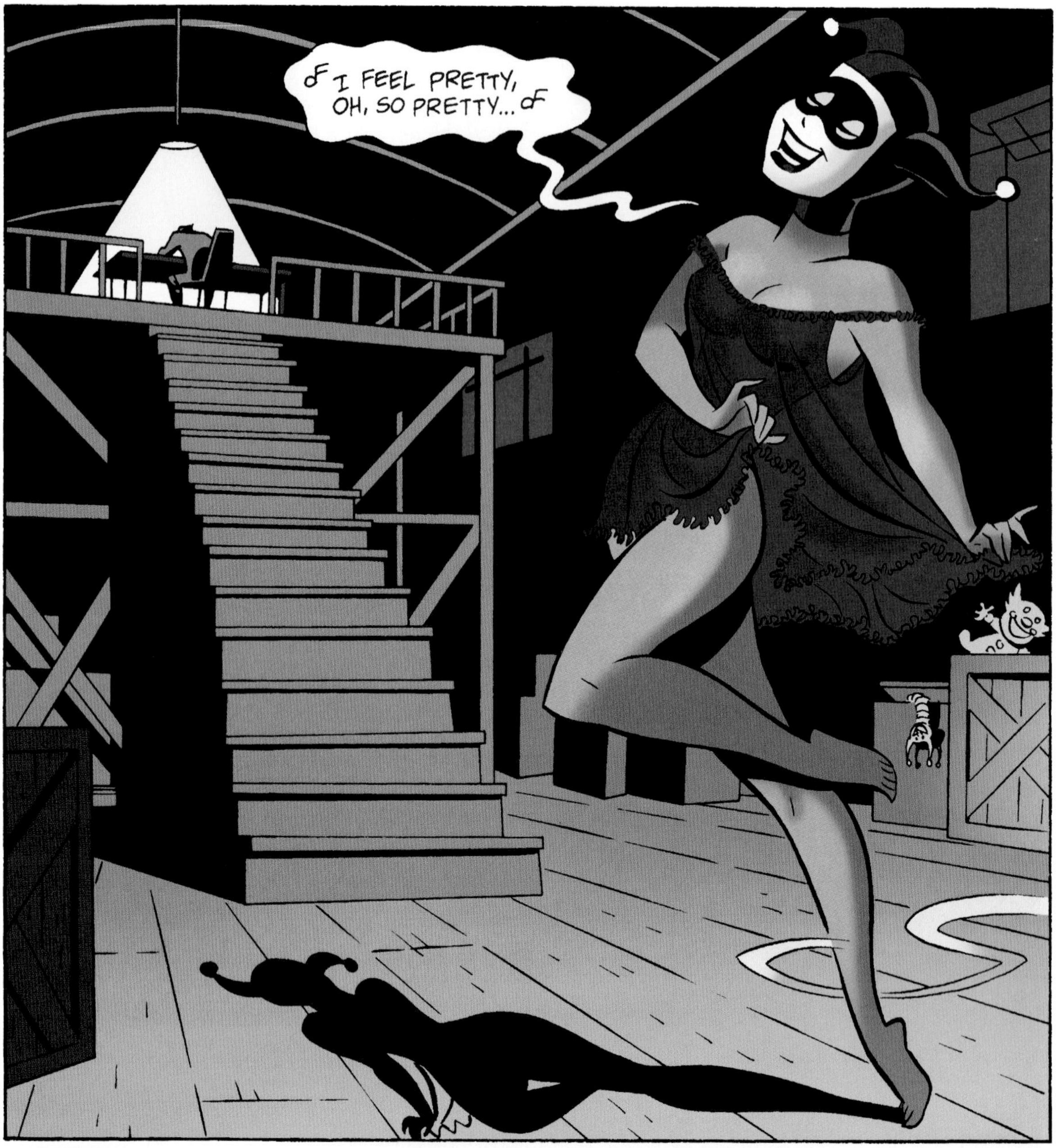
I FEEL PRETTY, OH, SO PRETTY...

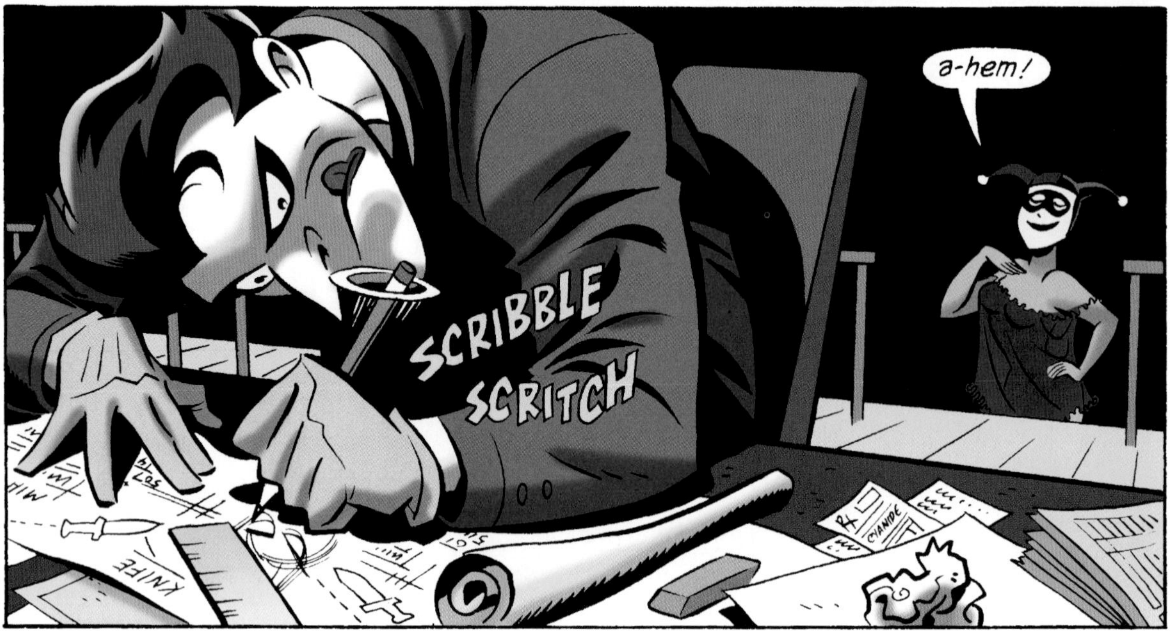
SCRIBBLE
SCRITCH
KNIFE
CYANIDE
a-hem!

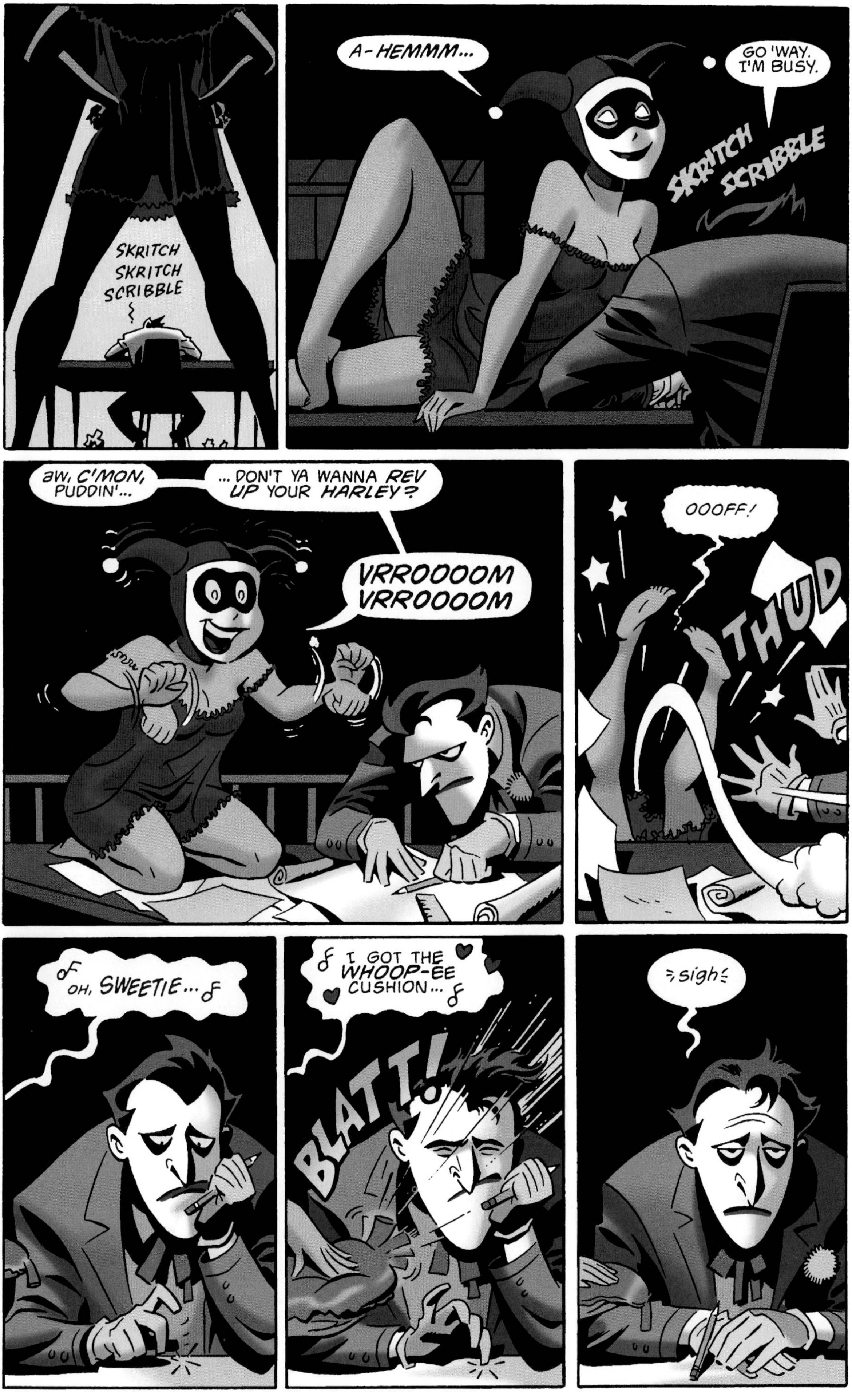
SKRITCH
SKRITCH
SCRIBBLE
A-HEMMM...
GO 'WAY. I'M BUSY.
SKRITCH
SCRIBBLE
AW, C'MON, PUDDIN'...
...DON'T YA WANNA REV UP YOUR HARLEY?
VRROOOOM VRROOOOM
OOOFF!
THUD
OH, SWEETIE...
I GOT THE WHOOP-EE CUSHION...
BLATT!
sigh

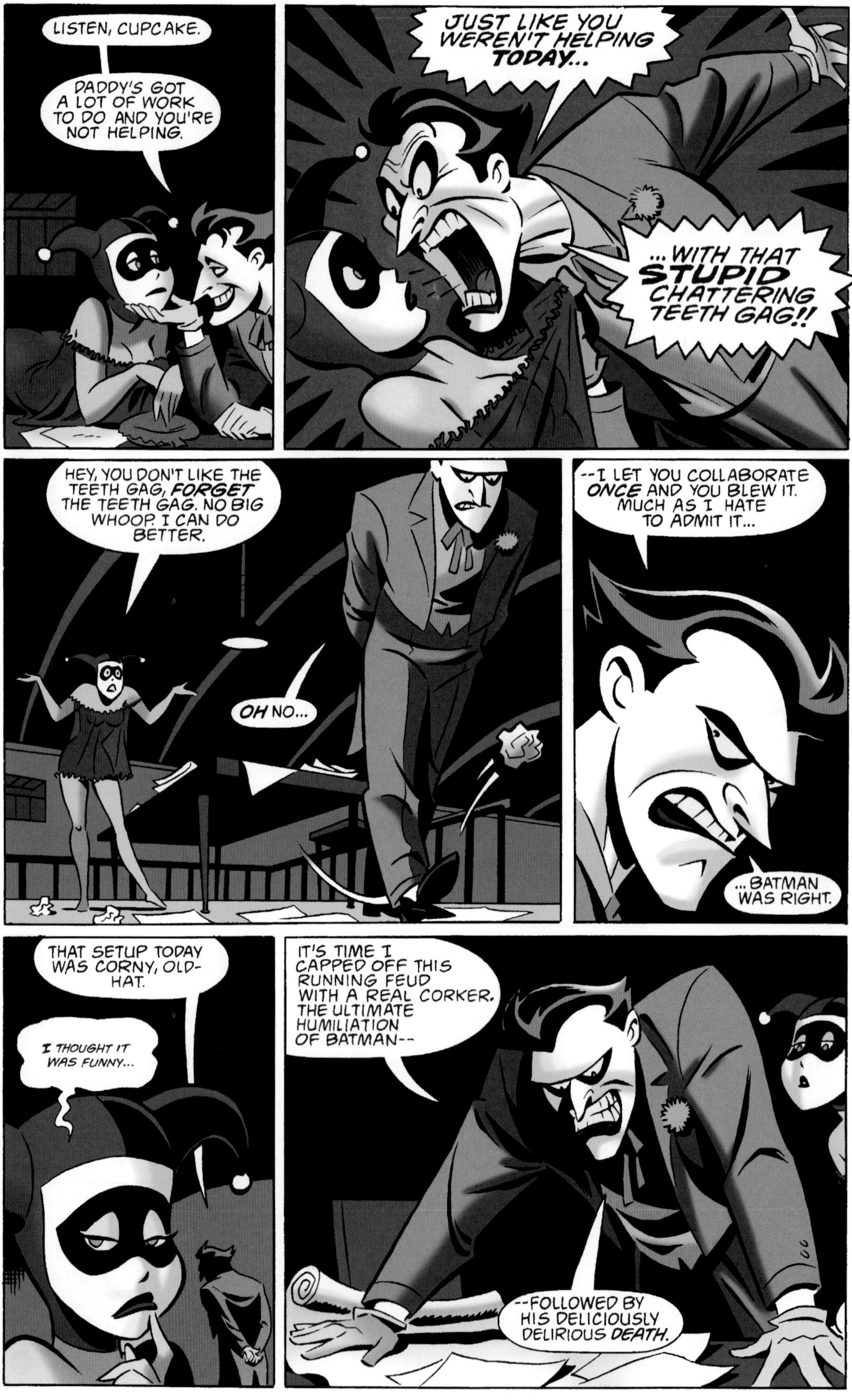

LISTEN, CUPCAKE.
DADDY'S GOT A LOT OF WORK TO DO AND YOU'RE NOT HELPING.
JUST LIKE YOU WEREN'T HELPING TODAY...
...WITH THAT STUPID CHATTERING TEETH GAG!!
HEY, YOU DON'T LIKE THE TEETH GAG, FORGET THE TEETH GAG. NO BIG WHOOP. I CAN DO BETTER.
OH NO...
--I LET YOU COLLABORATE ONCE AND YOU BLEW IT. MUCH AS I HATE TO ADMIT IT...
...BATMAN WAS RIGHT.
THAT SETUP TODAY WAS CORNY, OLD-HAT.
I THOUGHT IT WAS FUNNY...
IT'S TIME I CAPPED OFF THIS RUNNING FEUD WITH A REAL CORKER. THE ULTIMATE HUMILIATION OF BATMAN--
--FOLLOWED BY HIS DELICIOUSLY DELIRIOUS DEATH.

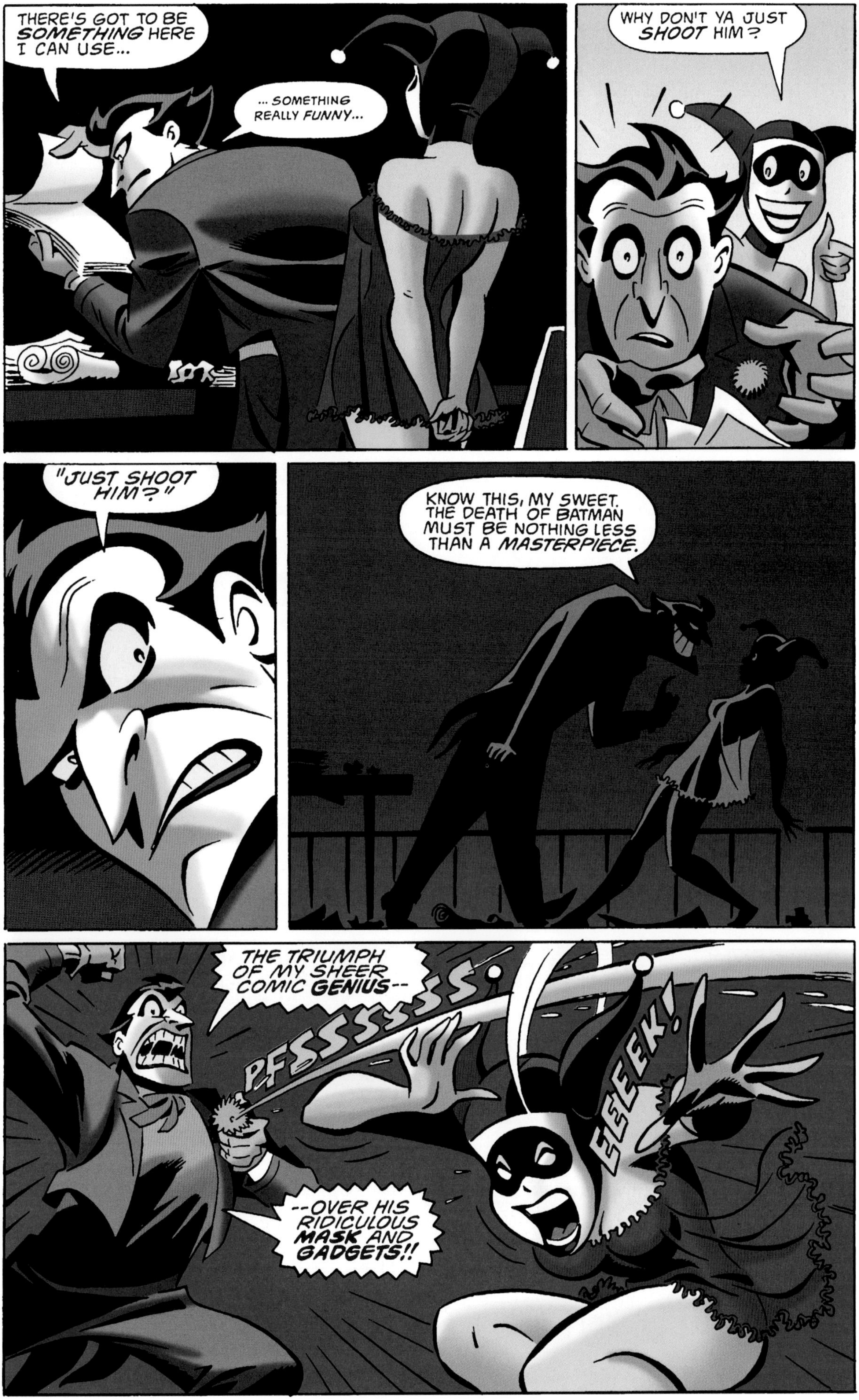
THERE'S GOT TO BE SOMETHING HERE I CAN USE...
... SOMETHING REALLY FUNNY...
WHY DON'T YA JUST SHOOT HIM?
"JUST SHOOT HIM?"
KNOW THIS, MY SWEET. THE DEATH OF BATMAN MUST BE NOTHING LESS THAN A MASTERPIECE.
THE TRIUMPH OF MY SHEER COMIC GENIUS--
PFSSSSSSS
EEEEK!
--OVER HIS RIDICULOUS MASK AND GADGETS!!

SIZZLE
CRACKLE
POP

WELL, HOLD THE PHONE!

≀WHEW!≀

I FORGOT ALL *ABOUT* THIS ONE! AHH YES...

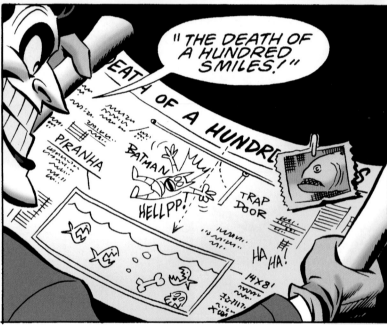

"THE DEATH OF A HUNDRED SMILES!"

DEATH OF A HUNDRE

PIRANHA

BATMAN

HELLPP!

TRAP DOOR

HA HA!

14X8'

THIS IS PERFECT! I'LL LURE BATMAN TO SOME OUT-OF-THE-WAY PLACE, THEN, WHEN HE LEAST EXPECTS IT...

BANG!

-- SPRING A HIDDEN TRAP DOOR AND DROP HIM INTO MY SPECIALLY PREPARED PIRANHA TANK! HA-HAA!

FLINCH!

THE LAST THING HE'LL SEE IS ALL THOSE BEAUTIFUL, HUNGRY SMILES AS THEY RIP HIM TO...

TO...

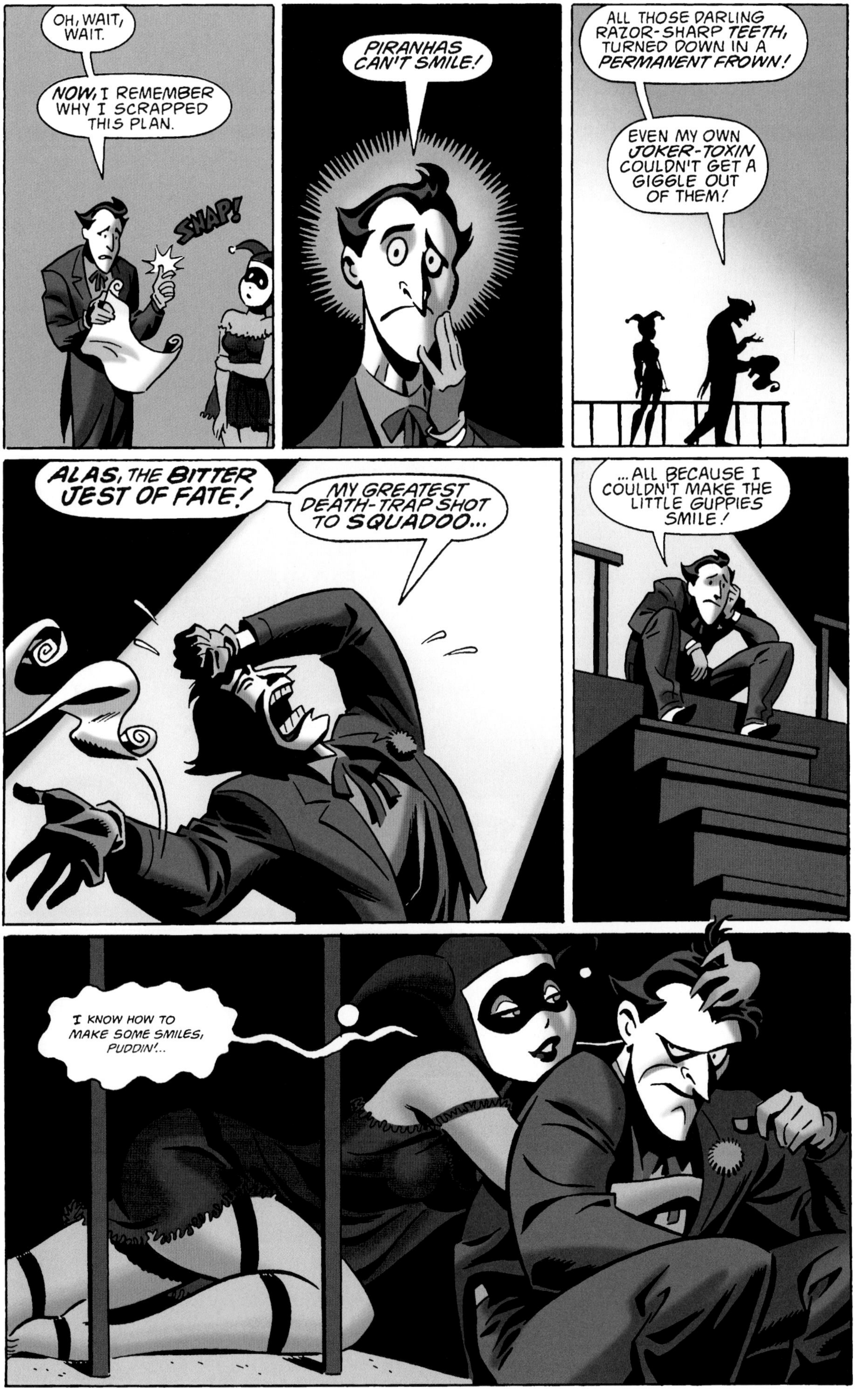
OH, WAIT, WAIT.
NOW, I REMEMBER WHY I SCRAPPED THIS PLAN.
SNAP!
PIRANHAS CAN'T SMILE!
ALL THOSE DARLING RAZOR-SHARP TEETH, TURNED DOWN IN A PERMANENT FROWN!
EVEN MY OWN JOKER-TOXIN COULDN'T GET A GIGGLE OUT OF THEM!
ALAS, THE BITTER JEST OF FATE!
MY GREATEST DEATH-TRAP SHOT TO SQUADOO...
...ALL BECAUSE I COULDN'T MAKE THE LITTLE GUPPIES SMILE!
I KNOW HOW TO MAKE SOME SMILES, PUDDIN'!..

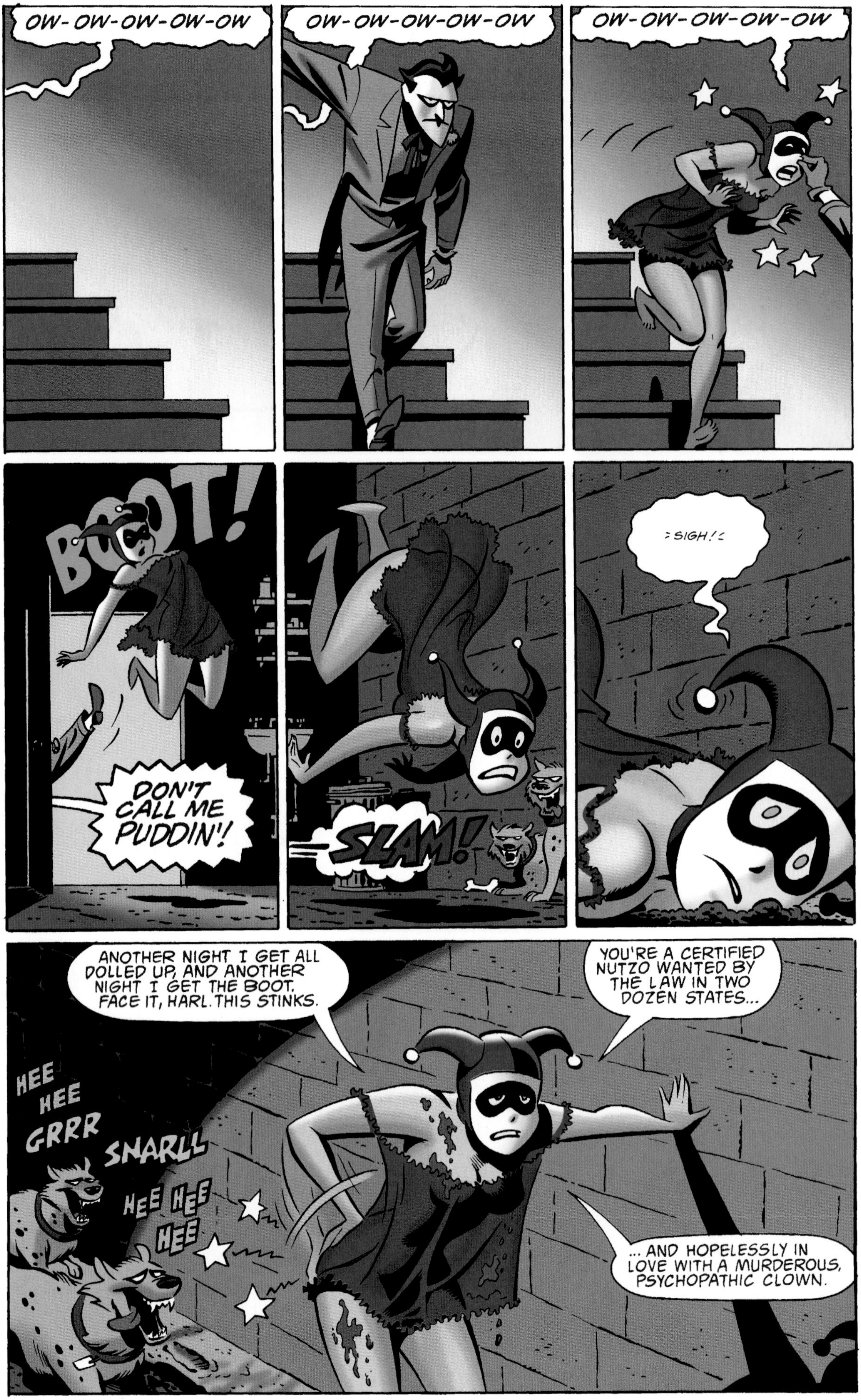
OW-OW-OW-OW-OW
OW-OW-OW-OW-OW
OW-OW-OW-OW-OW
BOOT!
DON'T CALL ME PUDDIN'!
SLAM!
SIGH!
ANOTHER NIGHT I GET ALL DOLLED UP, AND ANOTHER NIGHT I GET THE BOOT. FACE IT, HARL. THIS STINKS.
YOU'RE A CERTIFIED NUTZO WANTED BY THE LAW IN TWO DOZEN STATES...
HEE HEE GRRR
SNARLL
HEE HEE HEE
...AND HOPELESSLY IN LOVE WITH A MURDEROUS, PSYCHOPATHIC CLOWN.

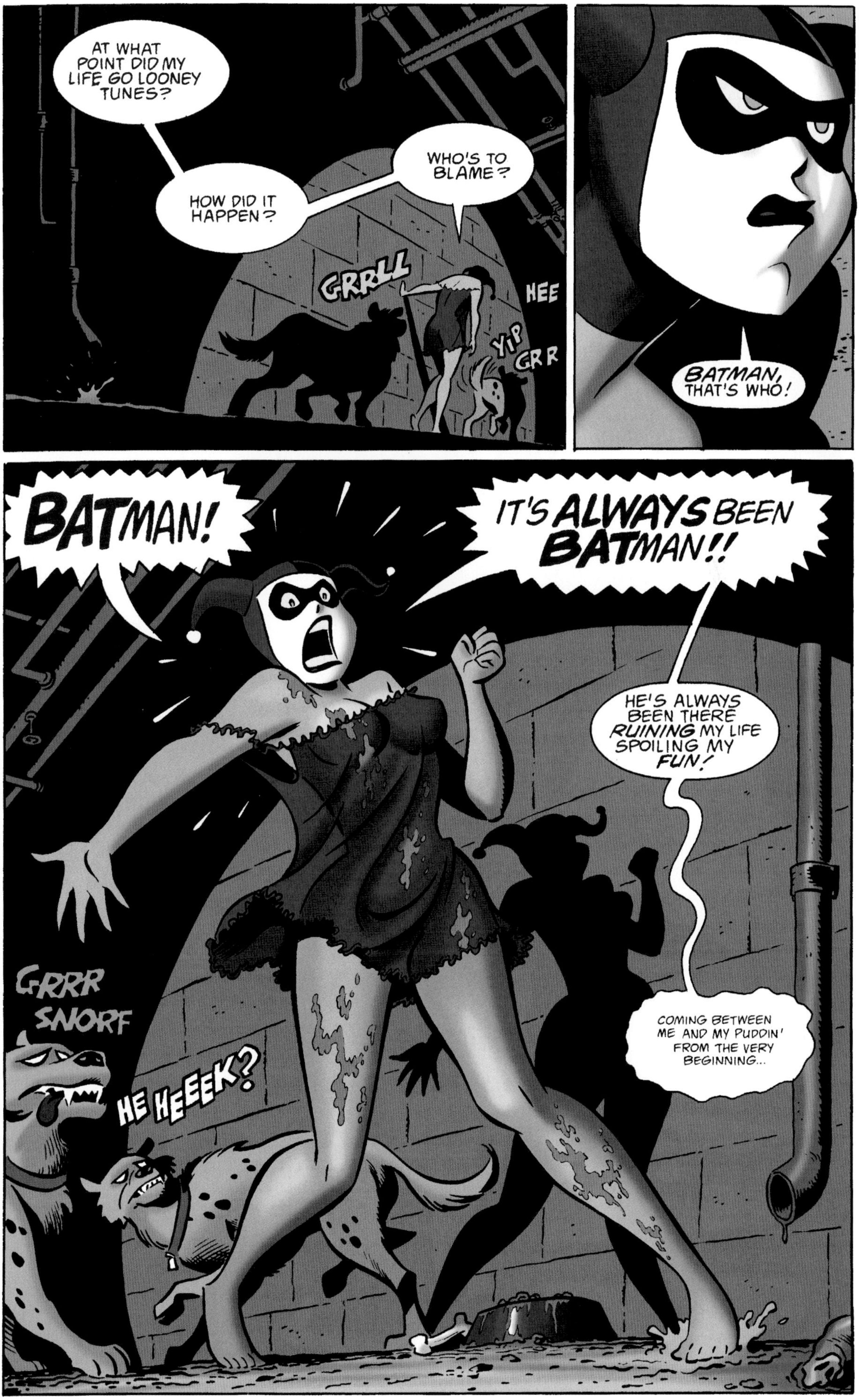
AT WHAT POINT DID MY LIFE GO LOONEY TUNES?
HOW DID IT HAPPEN?
WHO'S TO BLAME?
GRRLL
HEE
YIP
GRR
BATMAN, THAT'S WHO!
BATMAN!
IT'S ALWAYS BEEN BATMAN!!
HE'S ALWAYS BEEN THERE RUINING MY LIFE SPOILING MY FUN!
COMING BETWEEN ME AND MY PUDDIN' FROM THE VERY BEGINNING...
GRRR SNORF
HE HEEEK?

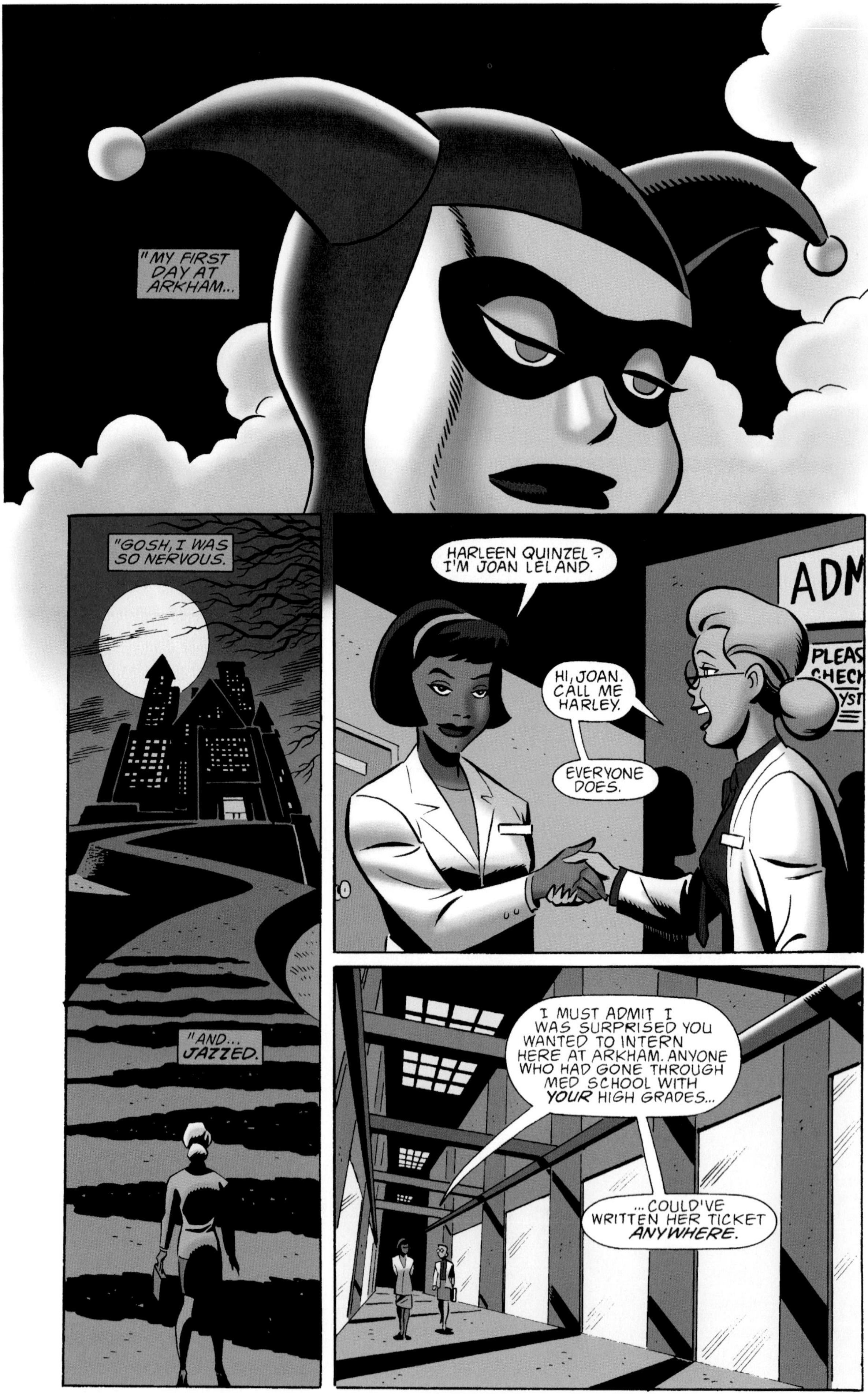
"MY FIRST DAY AT ARKHAM...
"GOSH, I WAS SO NERVOUS.
HARLEEN QUINZEL? I'M JOAN LELAND.
HI, JOAN. CALL ME HARLEY.
EVERYONE DOES.
ADM
PLEAS
CHECK
"AND... JAZZED.
I MUST ADMIT I WAS SURPRISED YOU WANTED TO INTERN HERE AT ARKHAM. ANYONE WHO HAD GONE THROUGH MED SCHOOL WITH YOUR HIGH GRADES...
...COULD'VE WRITTEN HER TICKET ANYWHERE.

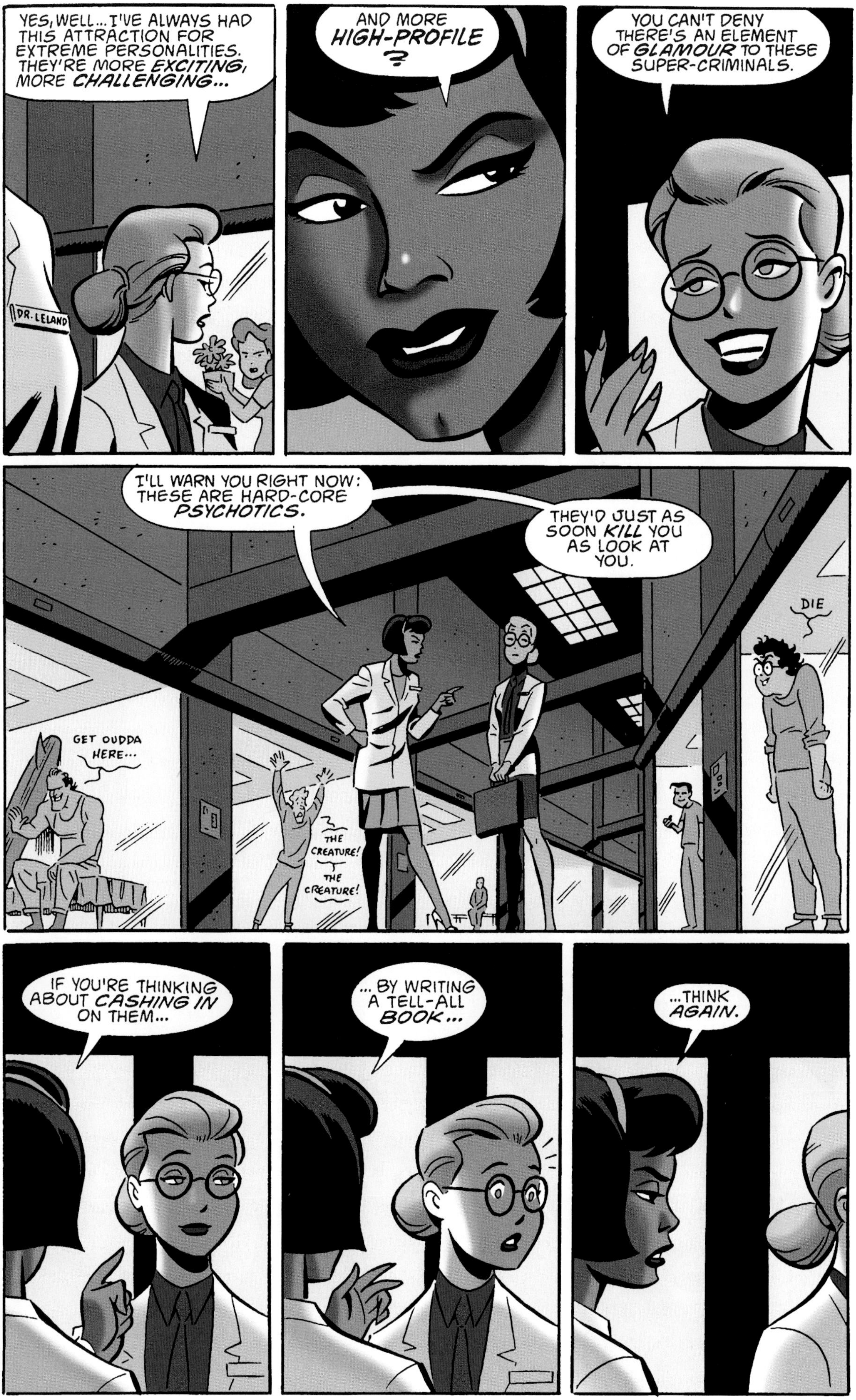
YES, WELL... I'VE ALWAYS HAD THIS ATTRACTION FOR EXTREME PERSONALITIES. THEY'RE MORE EXCITING, MORE CHALLENGING...
DR. LELAND
AND MORE HIGH-PROFILE?
YOU CAN'T DENY THERE'S AN ELEMENT OF GLAMOUR TO THESE SUPER-CRIMINALS.
I'LL WARN YOU RIGHT NOW: THESE ARE HARD-CORE PSYCHOTICS.
THEY'D JUST AS SOON KILL YOU AS LOOK AT YOU.
DIE
GET OUDDA HERE...
THE CREATURE! THE CREATURE!
IF YOU'RE THINKING ABOUT CASHING IN ON THEM...
...BY WRITING A TELL-ALL BOOK...
...THINK AGAIN.

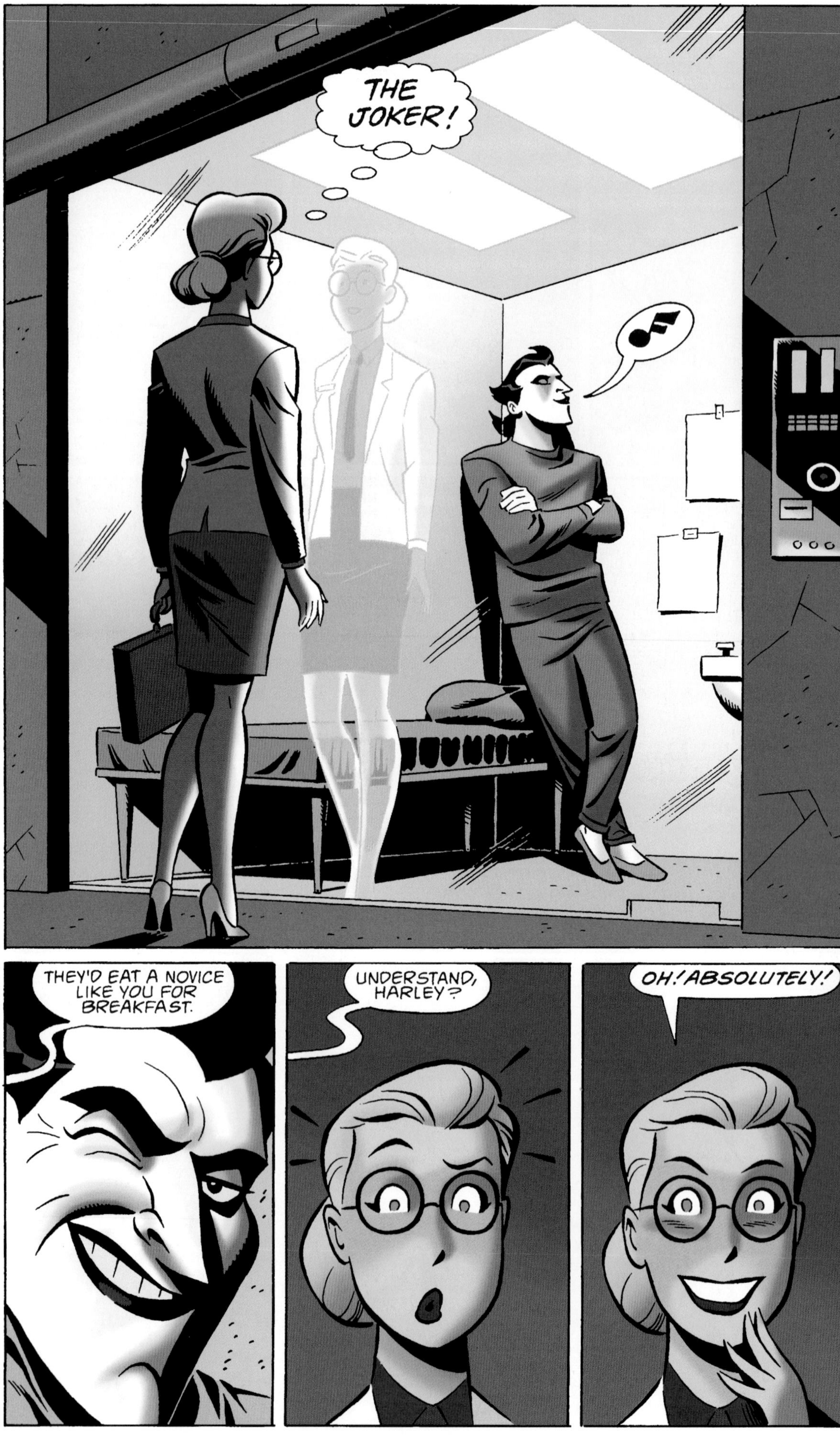
THE JOKER!
THEY'D EAT A NOVICE LIKE YOU FOR BREAKFAST.
UNDERSTAND, HARLEY?
OH! ABSOLUTELY!

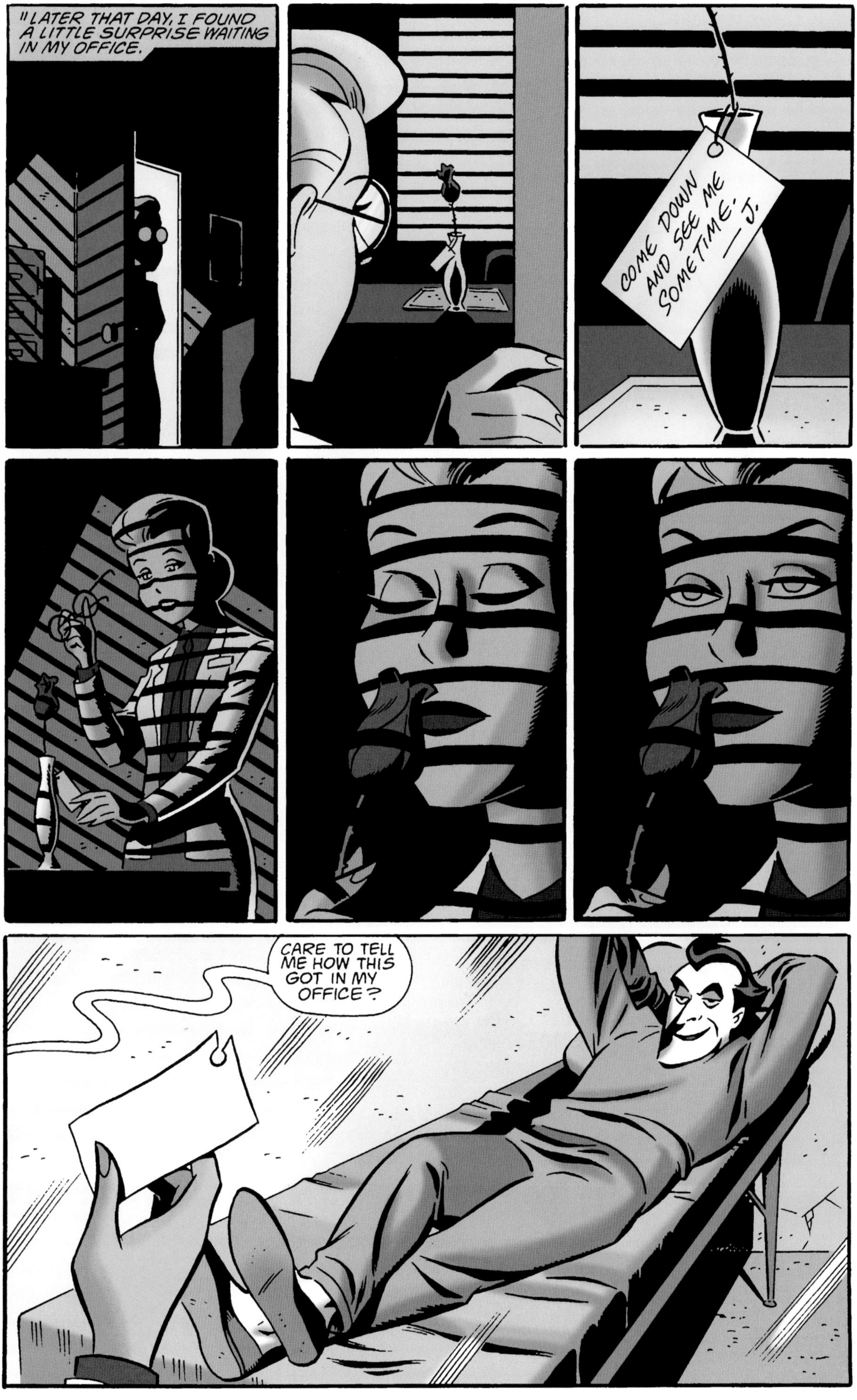

"LATER THAT DAY, I FOUND A LITTLE SURPRISE WAITING IN MY OFFICE.
COME DOWN AND SEE ME SOMETIME. —J.
CARE TO TELL ME HOW THIS GOT IN MY OFFICE?

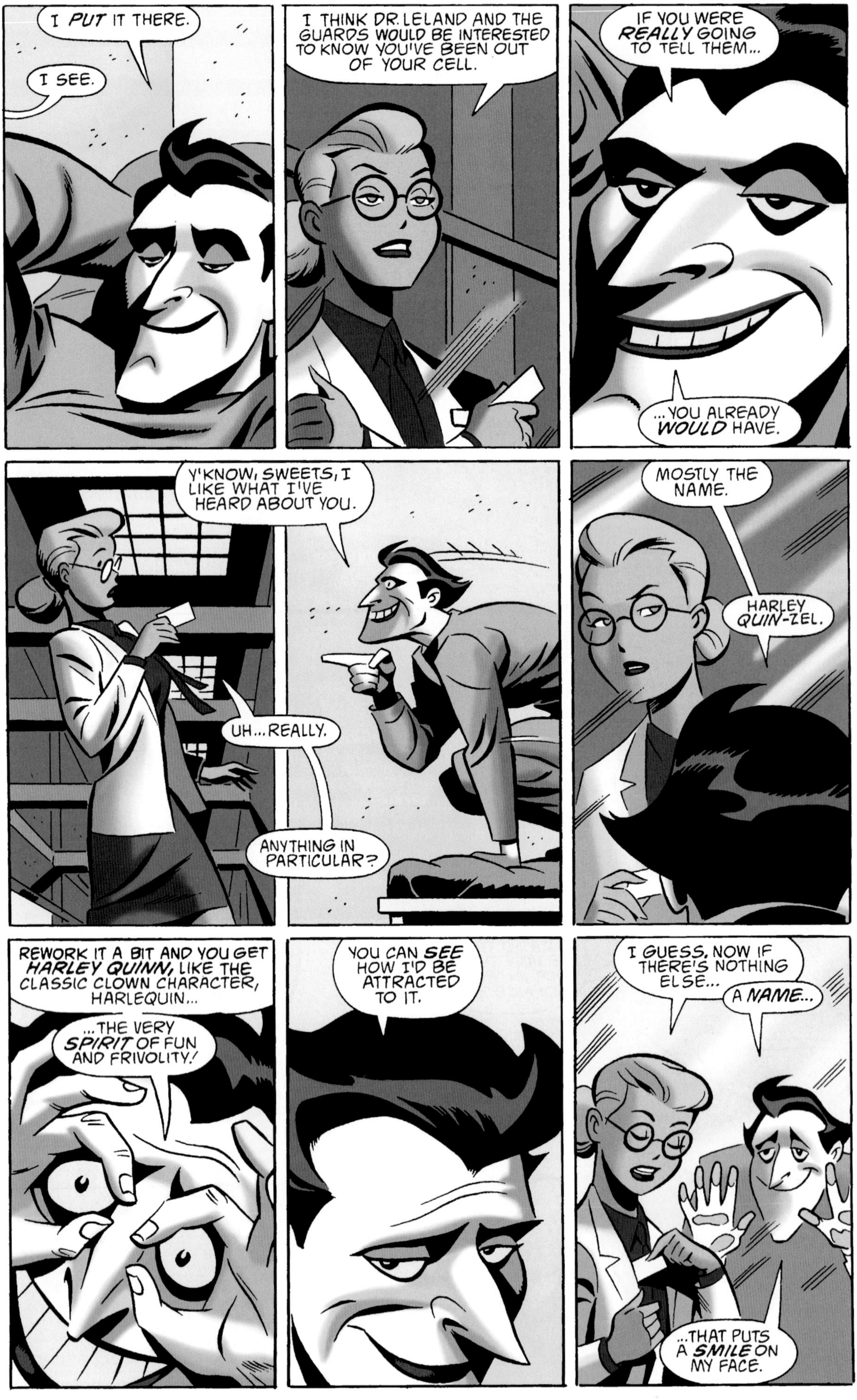
I PUT IT THERE.
I SEE.
I THINK DR. LELAND AND THE GUARDS WOULD BE INTERESTED TO KNOW YOU'VE BEEN OUT OF YOUR CELL.
IF YOU WERE REALLY GOING TO TELL THEM...
...YOU ALREADY WOULD HAVE.
Y'KNOW, SWEETS, I LIKE WHAT I'VE HEARD ABOUT YOU.
UH...REALLY.
ANYTHING IN PARTICULAR?
MOSTLY THE NAME.
HARLEY QUIN-ZEL.
REWORK IT A BIT AND YOU GET HARLEY QUINN, LIKE THE CLASSIC CLOWN CHARACTER, HARLEQUIN...
...THE VERY SPIRIT OF FUN AND FRIVOLITY!
YOU CAN SEE HOW I'D BE ATTRACTED TO IT.
I GUESS. NOW IF THERE'S NOTHING ELSE...
A NAME...
...THAT PUTS A SMILE ON MY FACE.

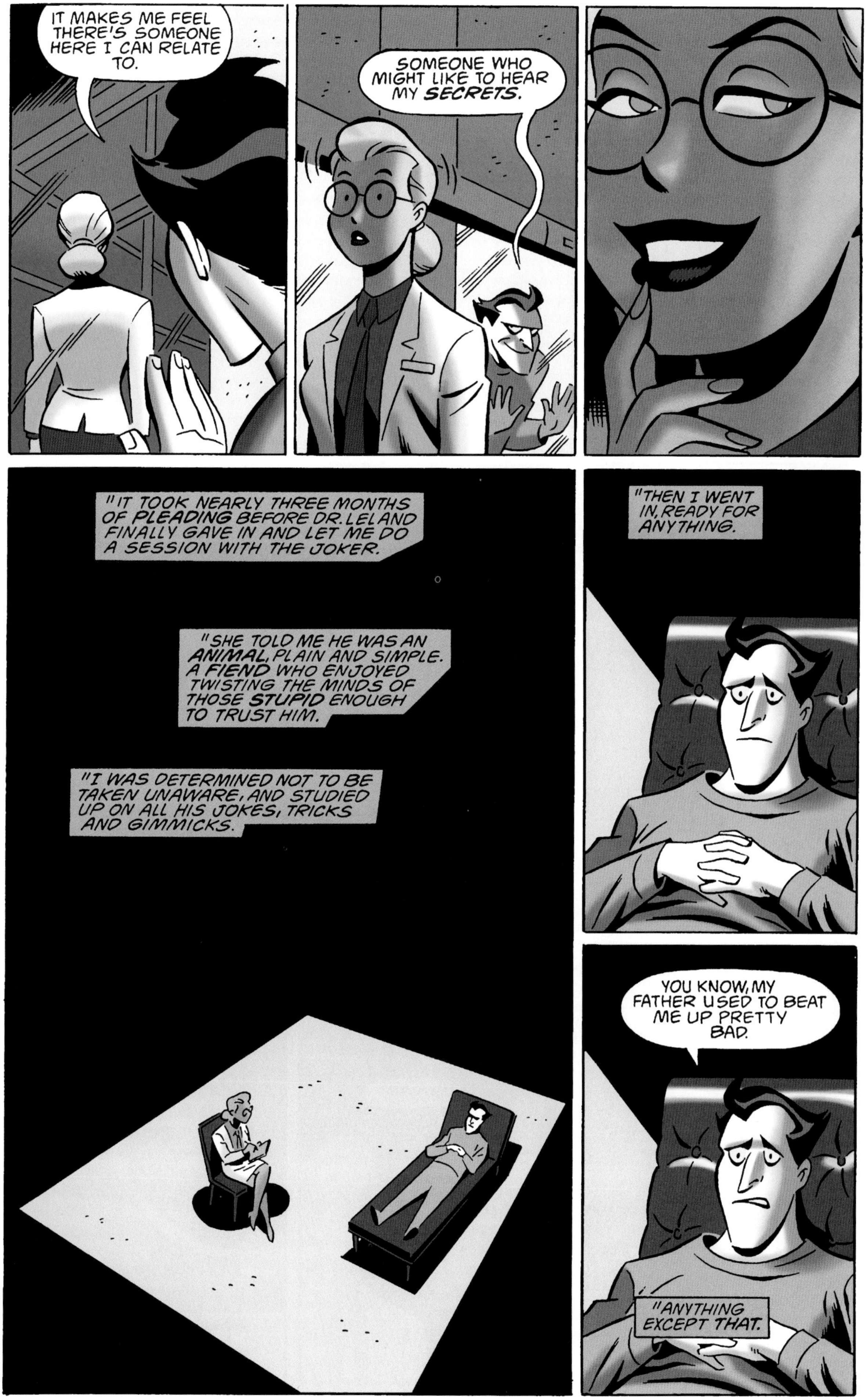
IT MAKES ME FEEL THERE'S SOMEONE HERE I CAN RELATE TO.
SOMEONE WHO MIGHT LIKE TO HEAR MY SECRETS.
"IT TOOK NEARLY THREE MONTHS OF PLEADING BEFORE DR. LELAND FINALLY GAVE IN AND LET ME DO A SESSION WITH THE JOKER.
"SHE TOLD ME HE WAS AN ANIMAL, PLAIN AND SIMPLE. A FIEND WHO ENJOYED TWISTING THE MINDS OF THOSE STUPID ENOUGH TO TRUST HIM.
"I WAS DETERMINED NOT TO BE TAKEN UNAWARE, AND STUDIED UP ON ALL HIS JOKES, TRICKS AND GIMMICKS.
"THEN I WENT IN, READY FOR ANYTHING.
YOU KNOW, MY FATHER USED TO BEAT ME UP PRETTY BAD.
"ANYTHING EXCEPT THAT.

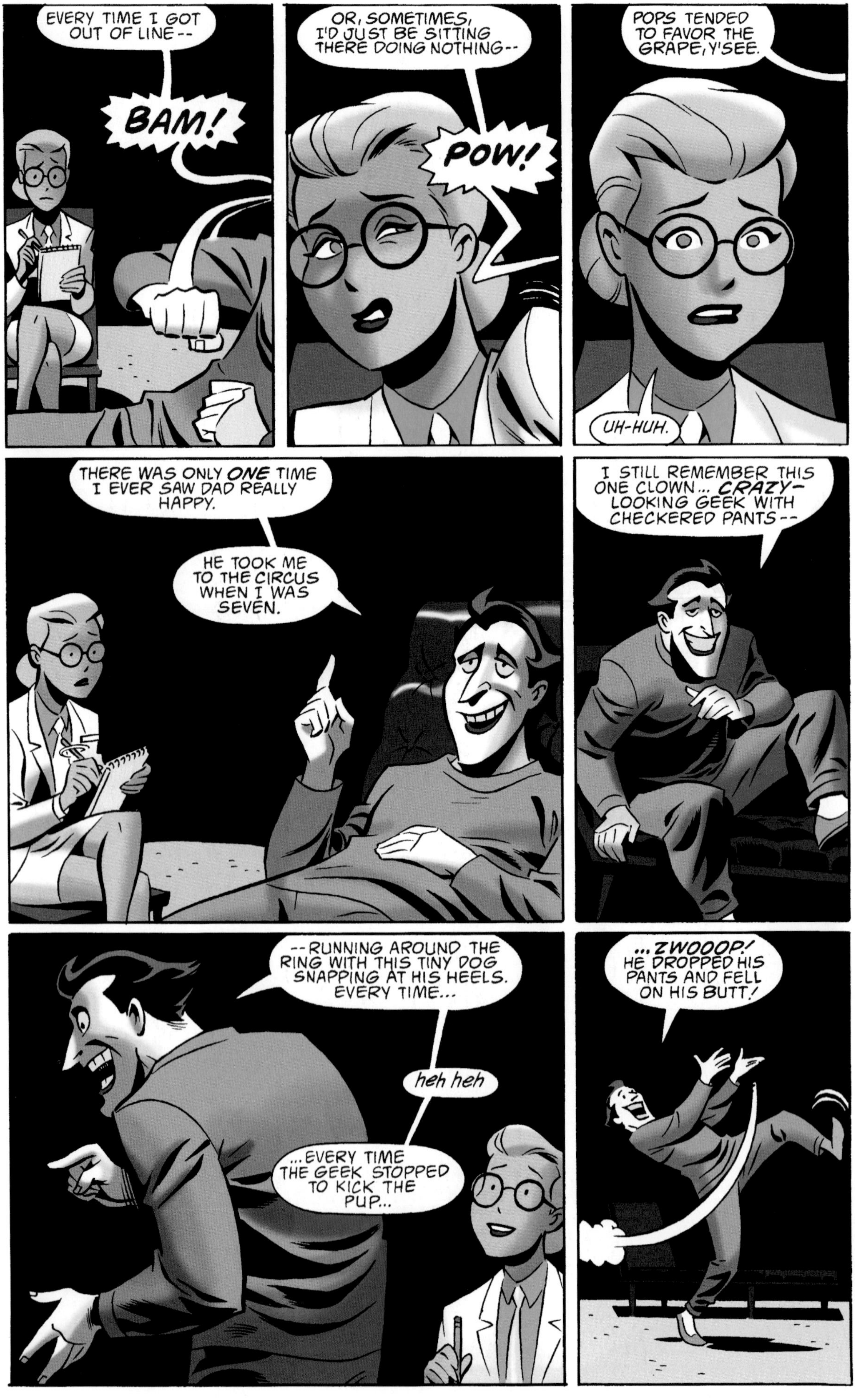
EVERY TIME I GOT OUT OF LINE--
BAM!
OR, SOMETIMES, I'D JUST BE SITTING THERE DOING NOTHING--
POW!
POPS TENDED TO FAVOR THE GRAPE, Y'SEE.
UH-HUH.
THERE WAS ONLY ONE TIME I EVER SAW DAD REALLY HAPPY.
HE TOOK ME TO THE CIRCUS WHEN I WAS SEVEN.
I STILL REMEMBER THIS ONE CLOWN... CRAZY-LOOKING GEEK WITH CHECKERED PANTS--
--RUNNING AROUND THE RING WITH THIS TINY DOG SNAPPING AT HIS HEELS. EVERY TIME...
heh heh
...EVERY TIME THE GEEK STOPPED TO KICK THE PUP...
...ZWOOOP! HE DROPPED HIS PANTS AND FELL ON HIS BUTT!

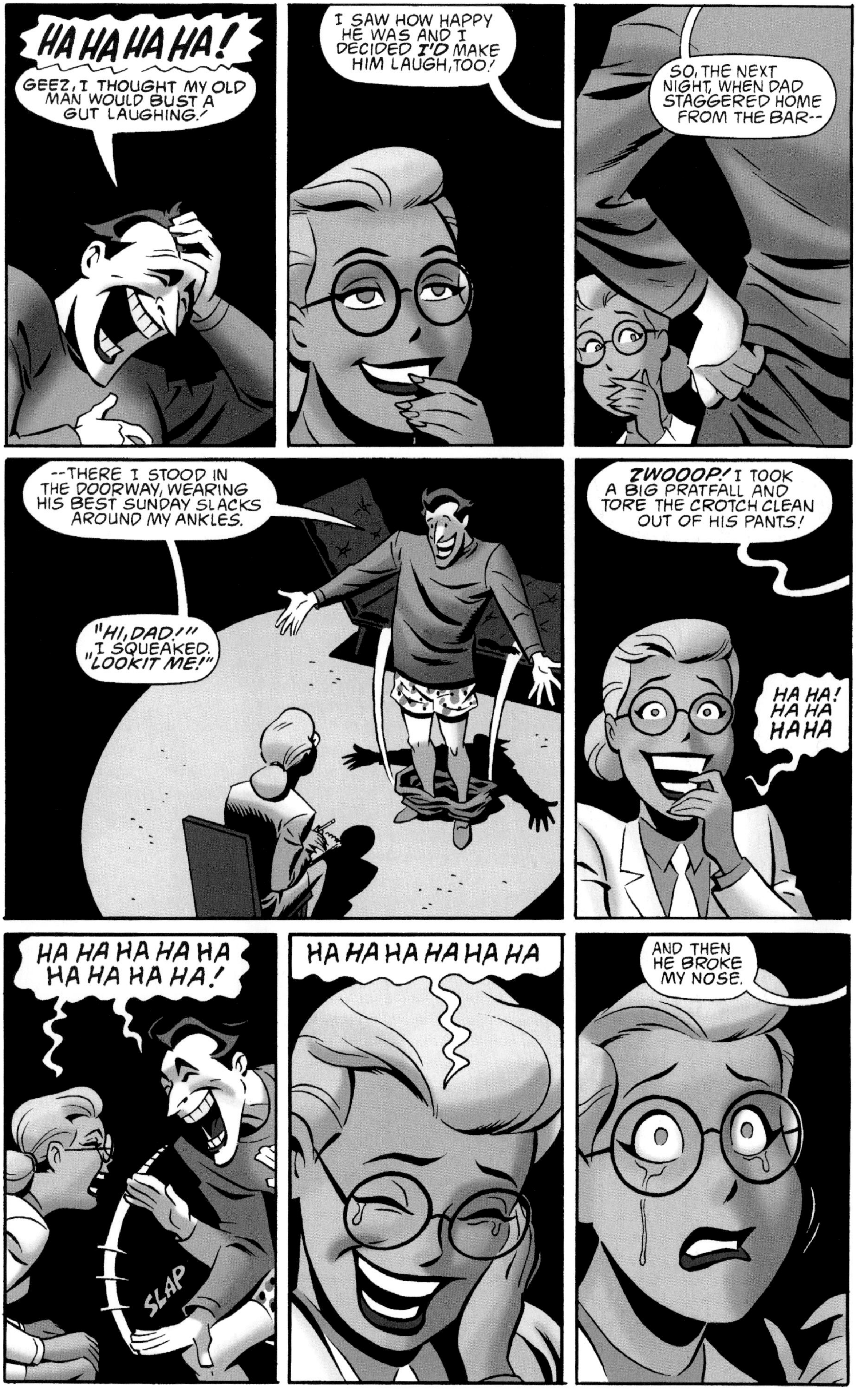
HA HA HA HA HA!
GEEZ, I THOUGHT MY OLD MAN WOULD BUST A GUT LAUGHING!
I SAW HOW HAPPY HE WAS AND I DECIDED I'D MAKE HIM LAUGH, TOO!
SO, THE NEXT NIGHT, WHEN DAD STAGGERED HOME FROM THE BAR--
--THERE I STOOD IN THE DOORWAY, WEARING HIS BEST SUNDAY SLACKS AROUND MY ANKLES.
"HI, DAD!" I SQUEAKED. "LOOKIT ME!"
ZWOOOP! I TOOK A BIG PRATFALL AND TORE THE CROTCH CLEAN OUT OF HIS PANTS!
HA HA! HA HA HA HA
HA HA HA HA HA HA HA HA HA HA!
SLAP
HA HA HA HA HA HA HA
AND THEN HE BROKE MY NOSE.

I STILL LIKE TO THINK HE WAS AIMING FOR MY FANNY AND MISSED. AT LEAST, THAT'S WHAT I TOLD MYSELF...

...WHEN I WOKE UP IN THE HOSPITAL THREE DAYS LATER.

THREE DAYS ...?!

BUT, HEY, THAT'S THE DOWNSIDE OF COMEDY.

YOU'RE ALWAYS TAKING SHOTS FROM FOLKS WHO JUST DON'T GET THE JOKE.

LIKE MY DAD.

OR BATMAN.

THANKS, DOC! I FEEL A LOT BETTER. SAME TIME NEXT WEEK?

SURE.

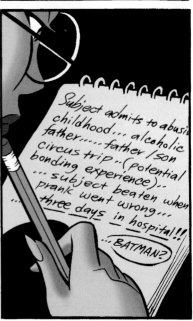

Subject admits to abusive childhood... alcoholic father... father/son circus trip.. (potential bonding experience)... subject beaten when prank went wrong... three days in hospital!! ...BATMAN?

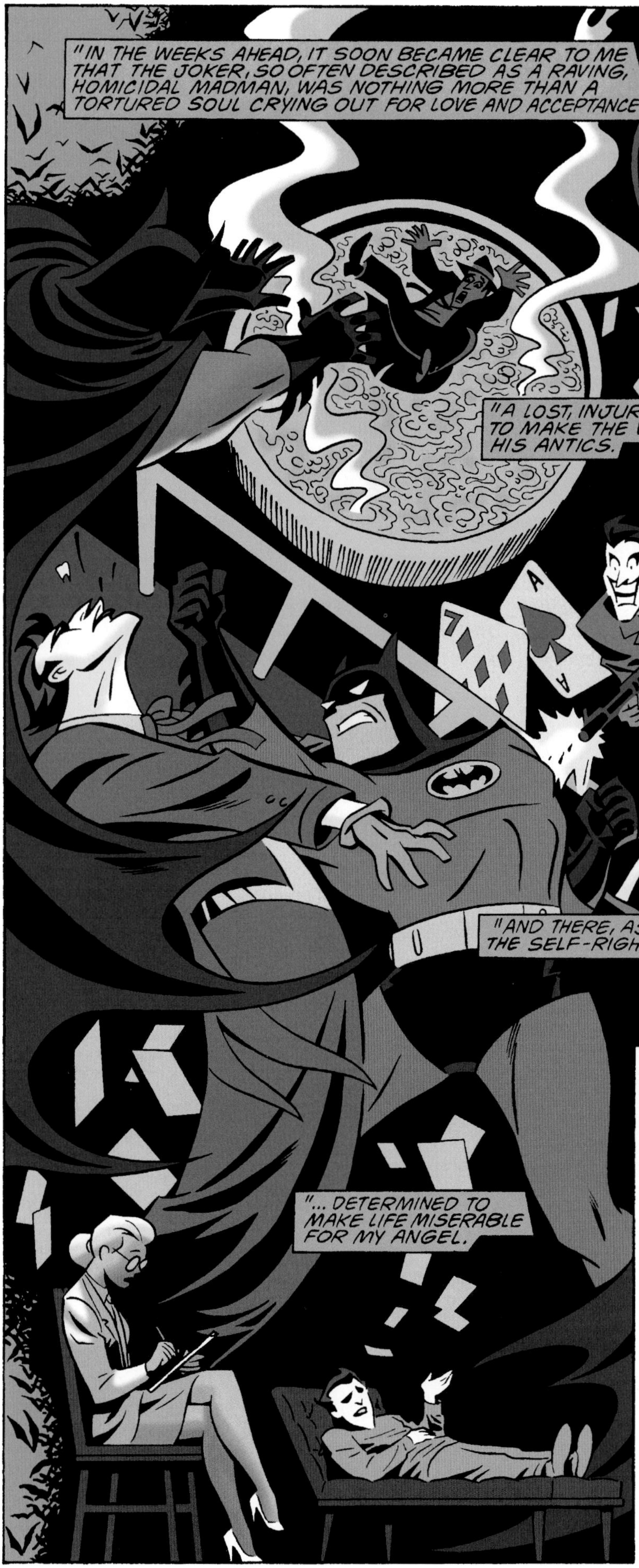
"IN THE WEEKS AHEAD, IT SOON BECAME CLEAR TO ME THAT THE JOKER, SO OFTEN DESCRIBED AS A RAVING, HOMICIDAL MADMAN, WAS NOTHING MORE THAN A TORTURED SOUL CRYING OUT FOR LOVE AND ACCEPTANCE.
"A LOST, INJURED CHILD LOOKING TO MAKE THE WORLD LAUGH AT HIS ANTICS.
"AND THERE, AS ALWAYS, WAS THE SELF-RIGHTEOUS BATMAN...
"... DETERMINED TO MAKE LIFE MISERABLE FOR MY ANGEL.

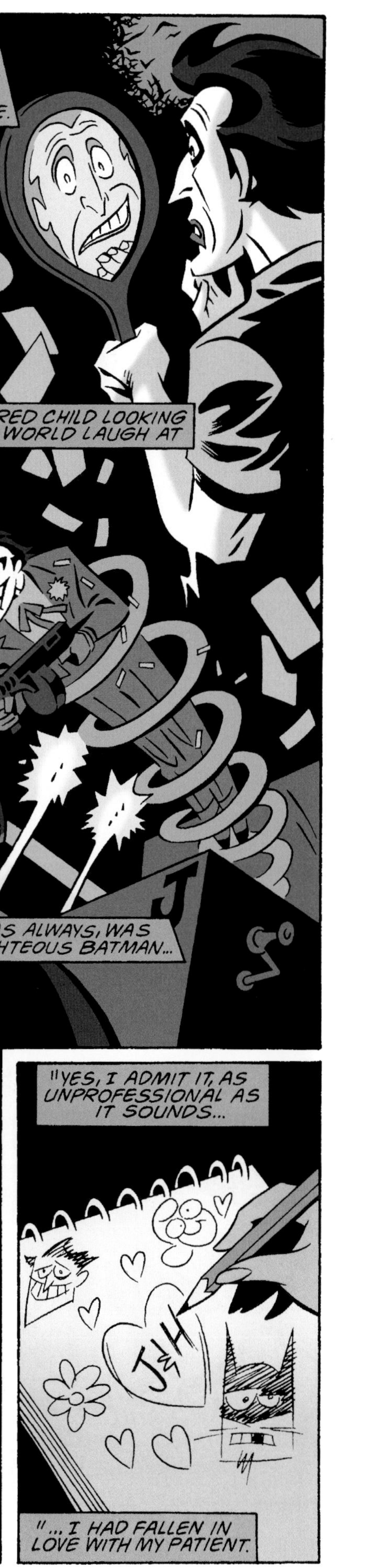
"YES, I ADMIT IT, AS UNPROFESSIONAL AS IT SOUNDS...
J&H
"... I HAD FALLEN IN LOVE WITH MY PATIENT.

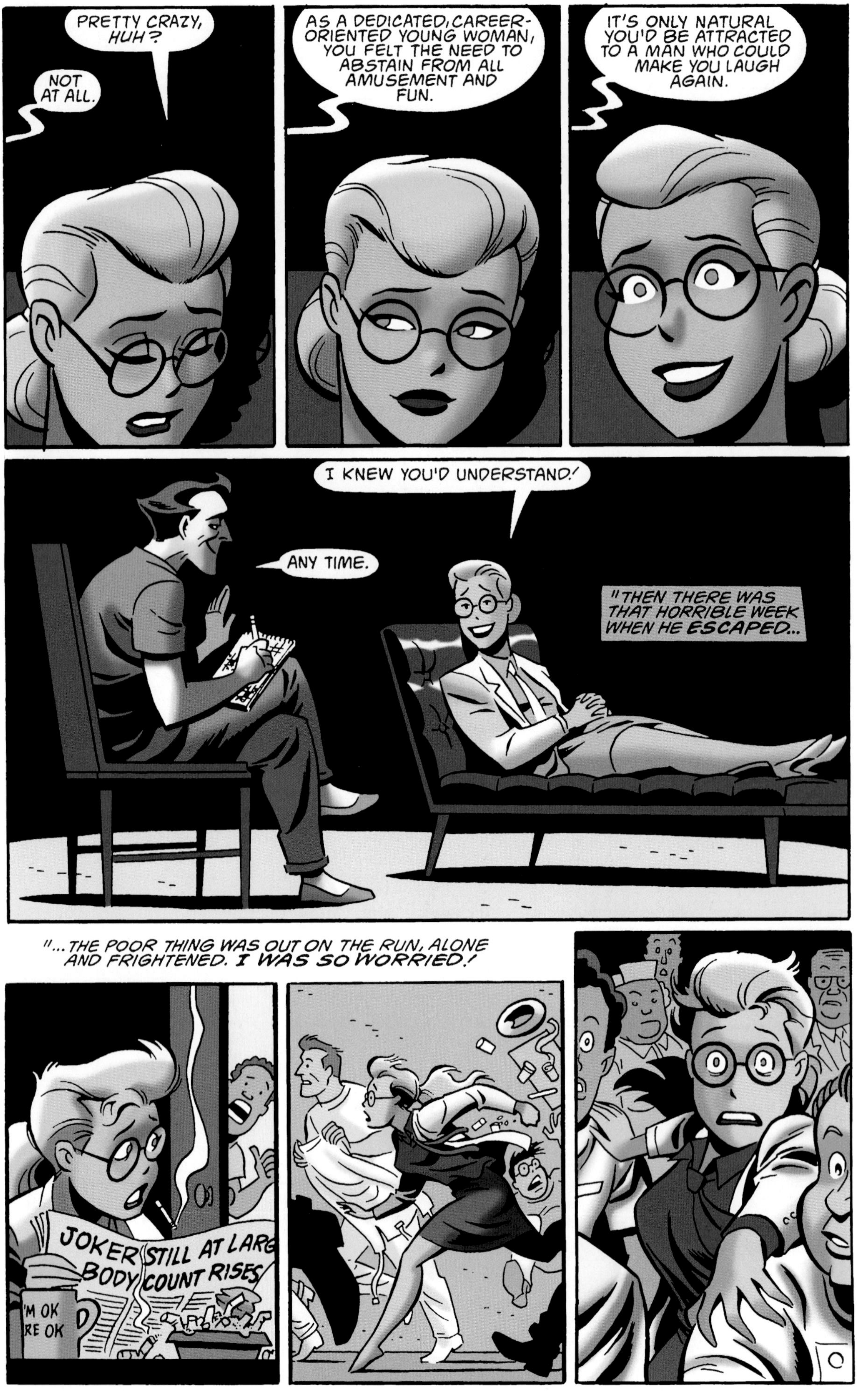
PRETTY CRAZY, HUH?
NOT AT ALL.
AS A DEDICATED, CAREER-ORIENTED YOUNG WOMAN, YOU FELT THE NEED TO ABSTAIN FROM ALL AMUSEMENT AND FUN.
IT'S ONLY NATURAL YOU'D BE ATTRACTED TO A MAN WHO COULD MAKE YOU LAUGH AGAIN.
I KNEW YOU'D UNDERSTAND!
ANY TIME.
"THEN THERE WAS THAT HORRIBLE WEEK WHEN HE ESCAPED...
"...THE POOR THING WAS OUT ON THE RUN, ALONE AND FRIGHTENED. I WAS SO WORRIED!
JOKER STILL AT LARG
BODY COUNT RISES
'M OK
RE OK

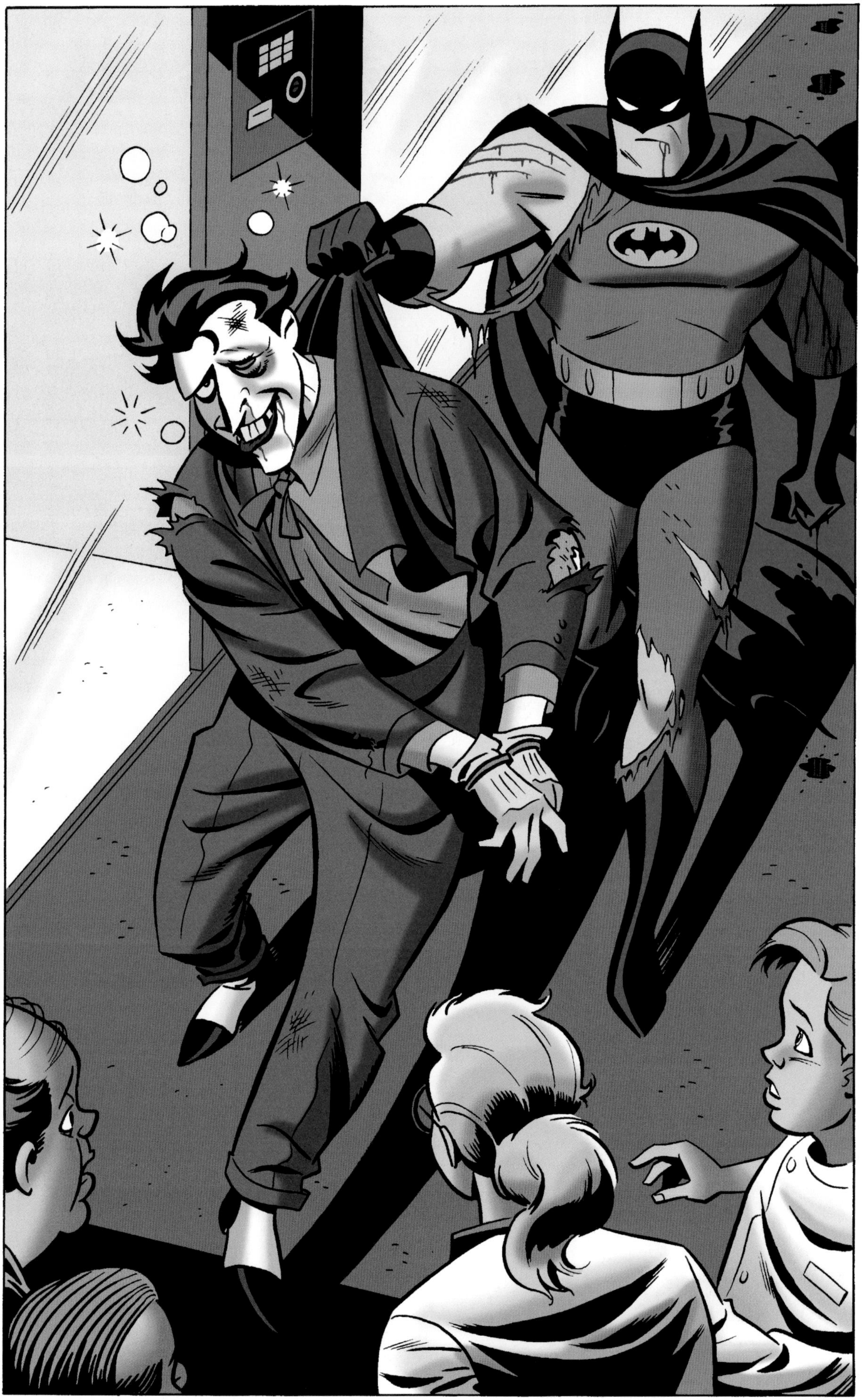

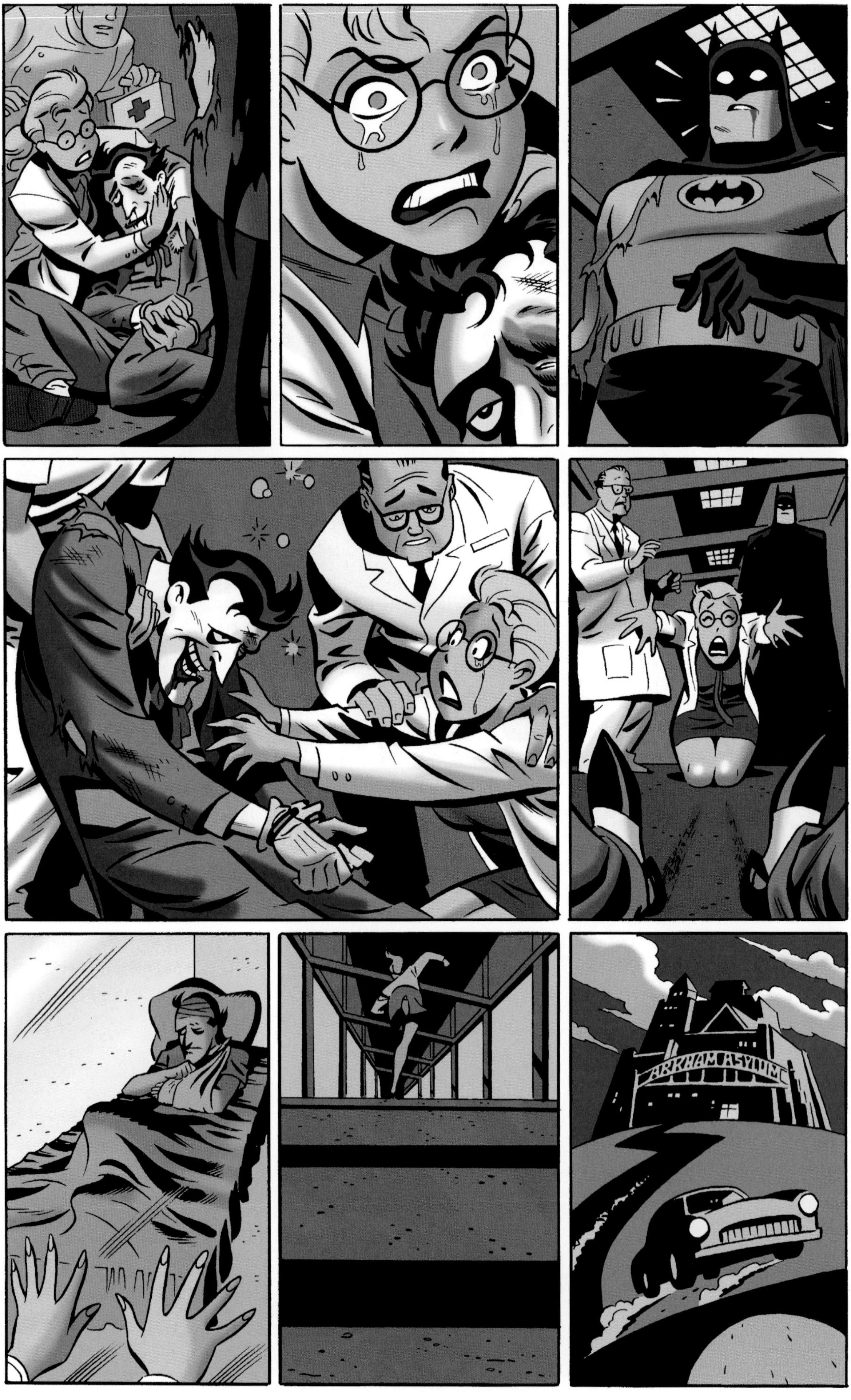
ARKHAM ASYLUM

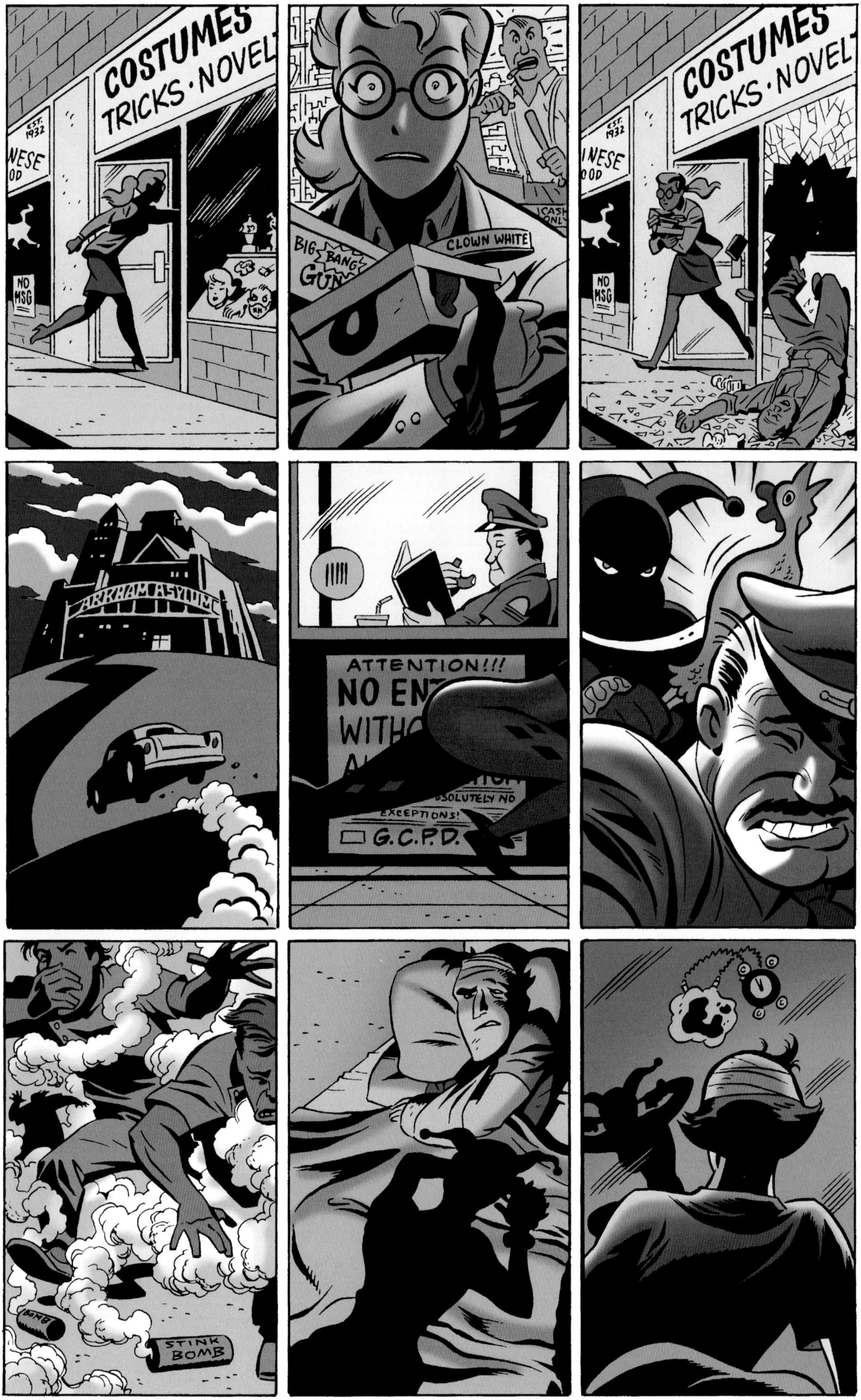
COSTUMES
TRICKS · NOVEL
EST. 1932
NO MSG
BIG BANG GUN
CLOWN WHITE
CASH ONLY
COSTUMES
TRICKS · NOVEL
EST. 1932
NO MSG
ARKHAM ASYLUM
ATTENTION!!!
NO ENT
WITHO
EXCEPTIONS!
G.C.P.D.
BOMB
STINK BOMB

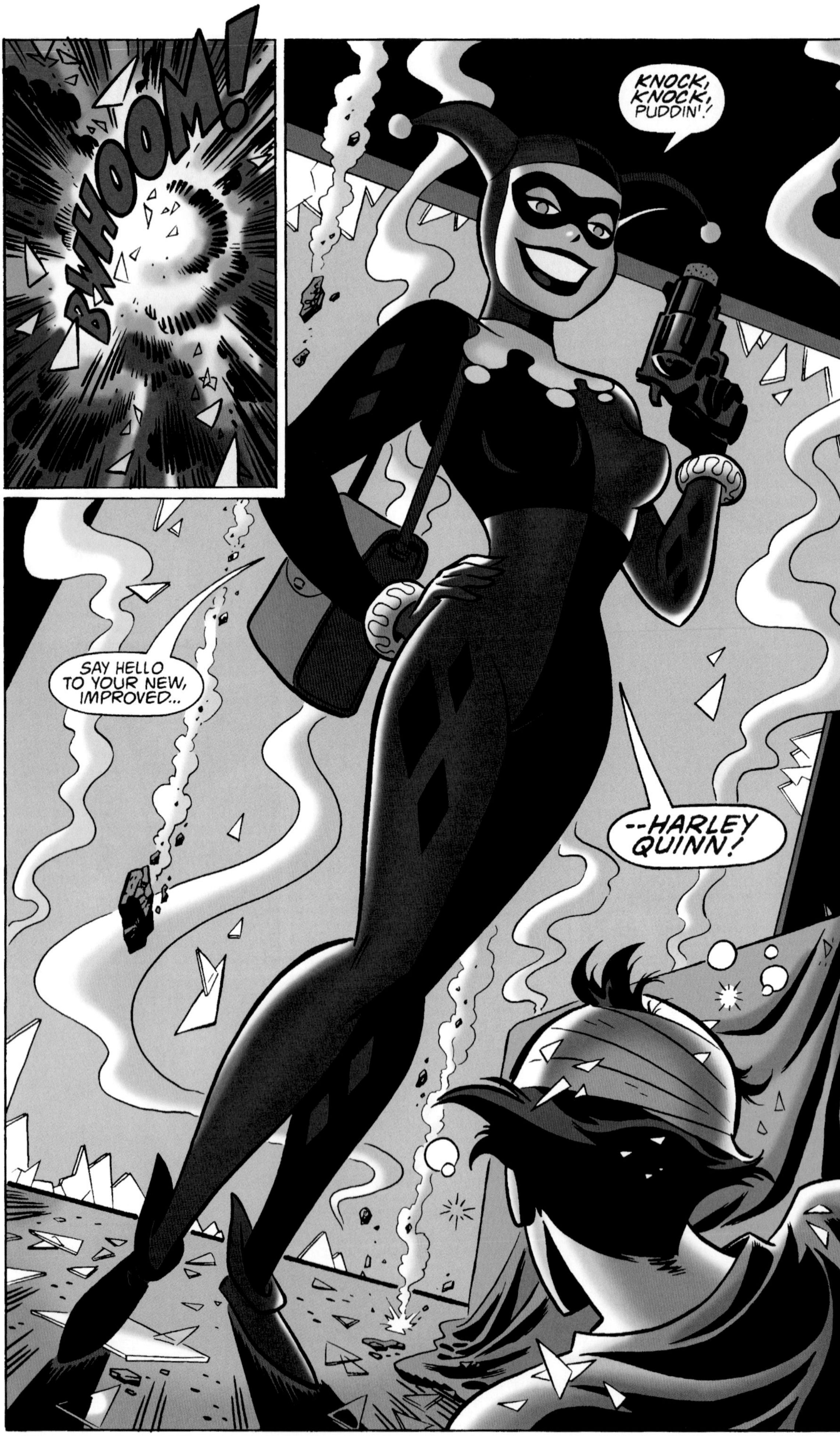
BWHOOM!
KNOCK, KNOCK, PUDDIN'!
SAY HELLO TO YOUR NEW, IMPROVED...
--HARLEY QUINN!

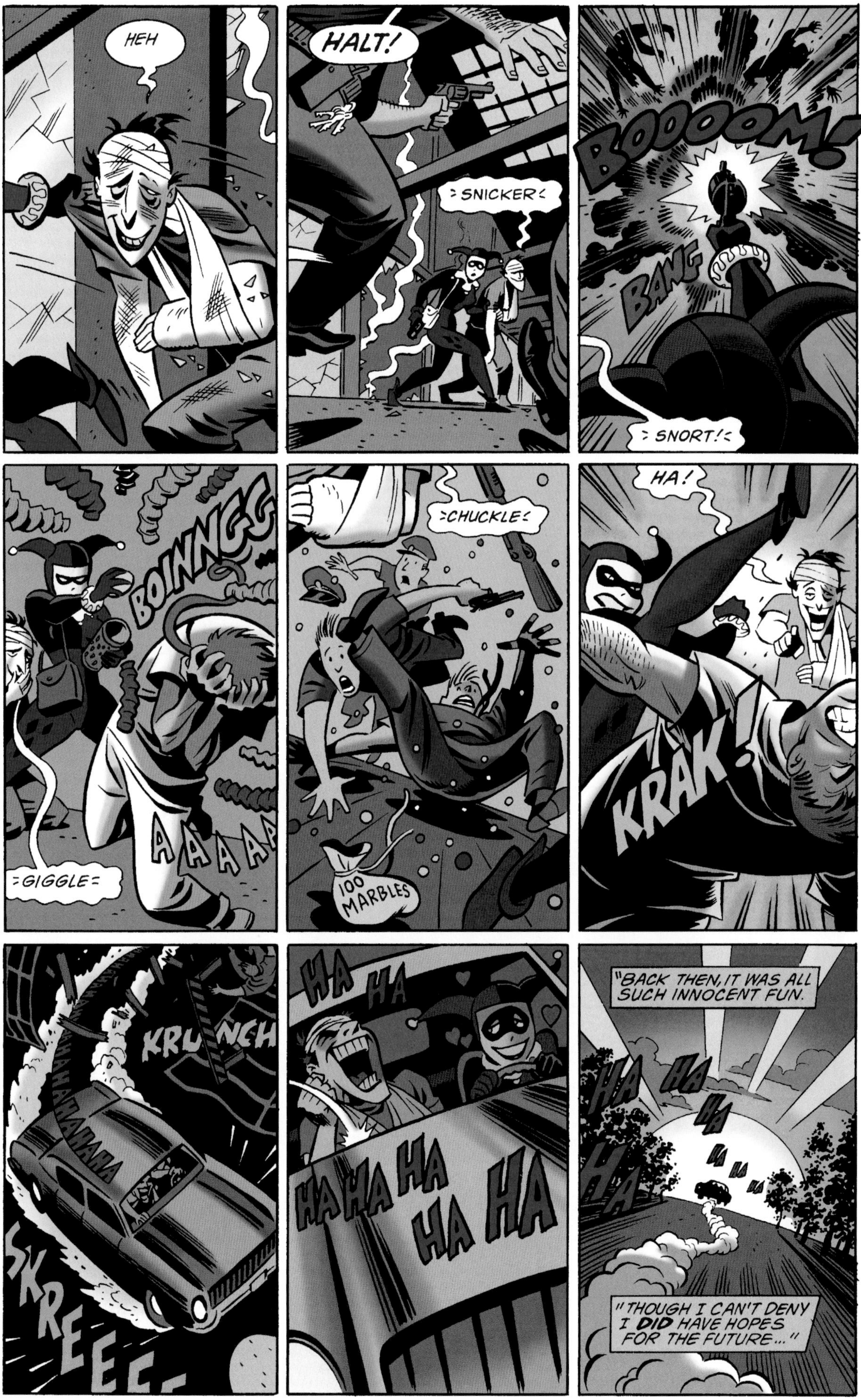
HEH
HALT!
SNICKER
BOOOOM!
BANG
SNORT!
BOINNGG
AAAAA
GIGGLE
CHUCKLE
100 MARBLES
HA!
KRAK!
KRUNCH
HAHAHAHAHAHA
SKREEEE
HA HA
HAHAHA HA HA HA HA
"BACK THEN, IT WAS ALL SUCH INNOCENT FUN.
HA HA HA HA HA HA HA
"THOUGH I CAN'T DENY I **DID** HAVE HOPES FOR THE FUTURE..."

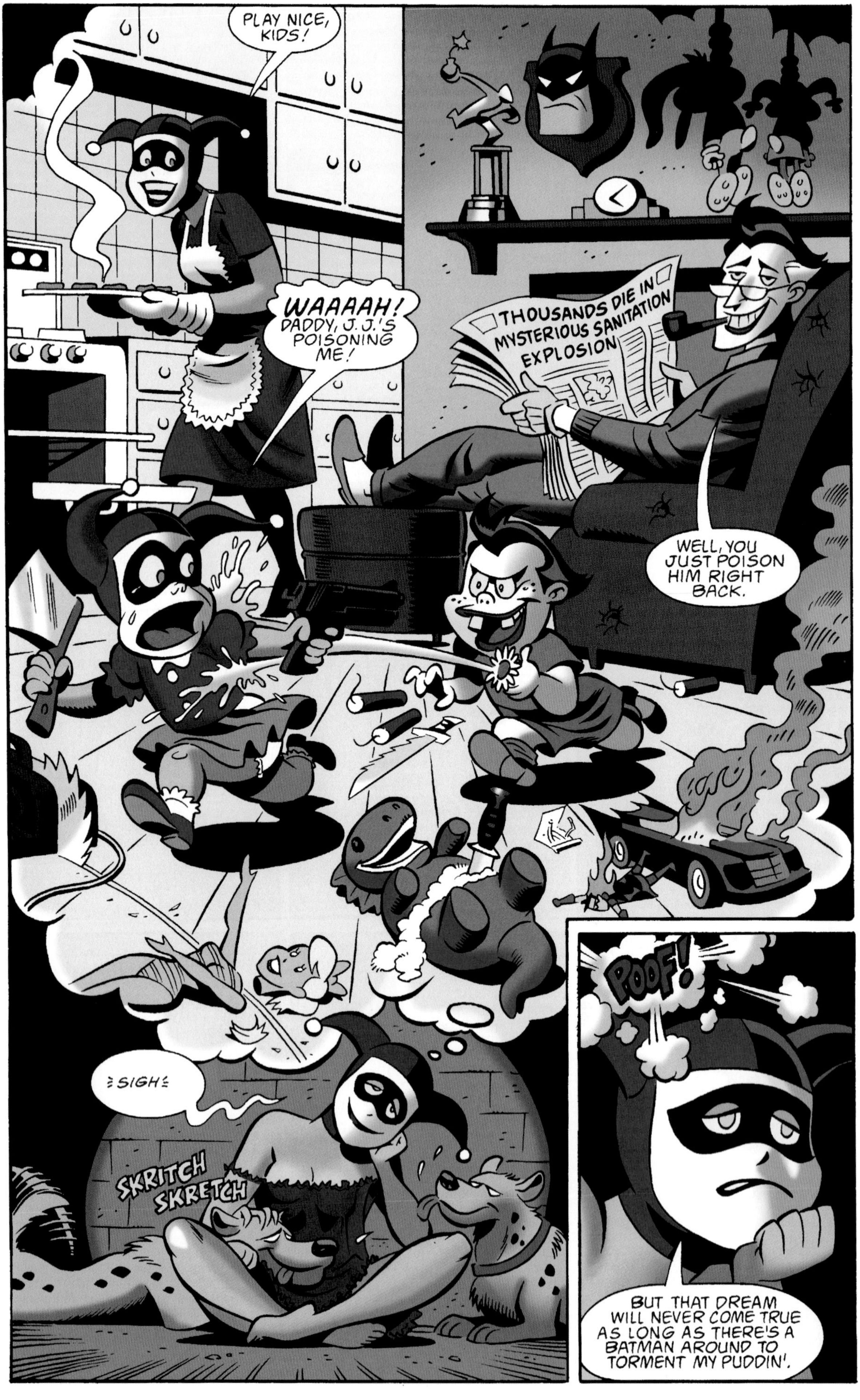
PLAY NICE, KIDS!
WAAAAH! DADDY, J.J.'S POISONING ME!
THOUSANDS DIE IN MYSTERIOUS SANITATION EXPLOSION
WELL, YOU JUST POISON HIM RIGHT BACK.
SIGH
SKRITCH SKRETCH
POOF!
BUT THAT DREAM WILL NEVER COME TRUE AS LONG AS THERE'S A BATMAN AROUND TO TORMENT MY PUDDIN'.

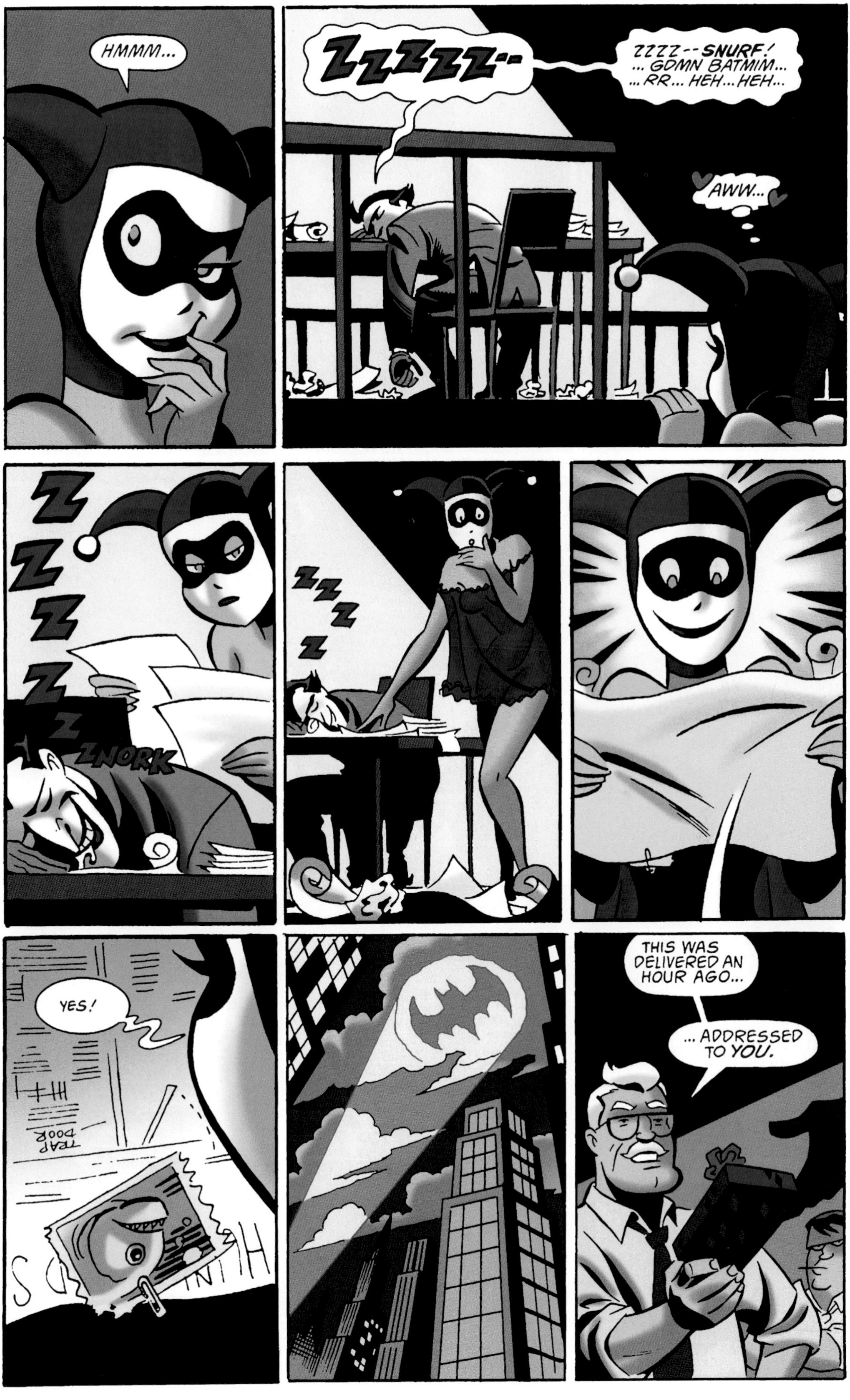
HMMM...
ZZZZZZ--
ZZZZ--SNURF! ...GDMN BATMIM... ...RR... HEH...HEH...
AWW...
ZZZZZZ
ZNORK
ZZZZ
YES!
TRAP DOOR
THIS WAS DELIVERED AN HOUR AGO...
...ADDRESSED TO YOU.

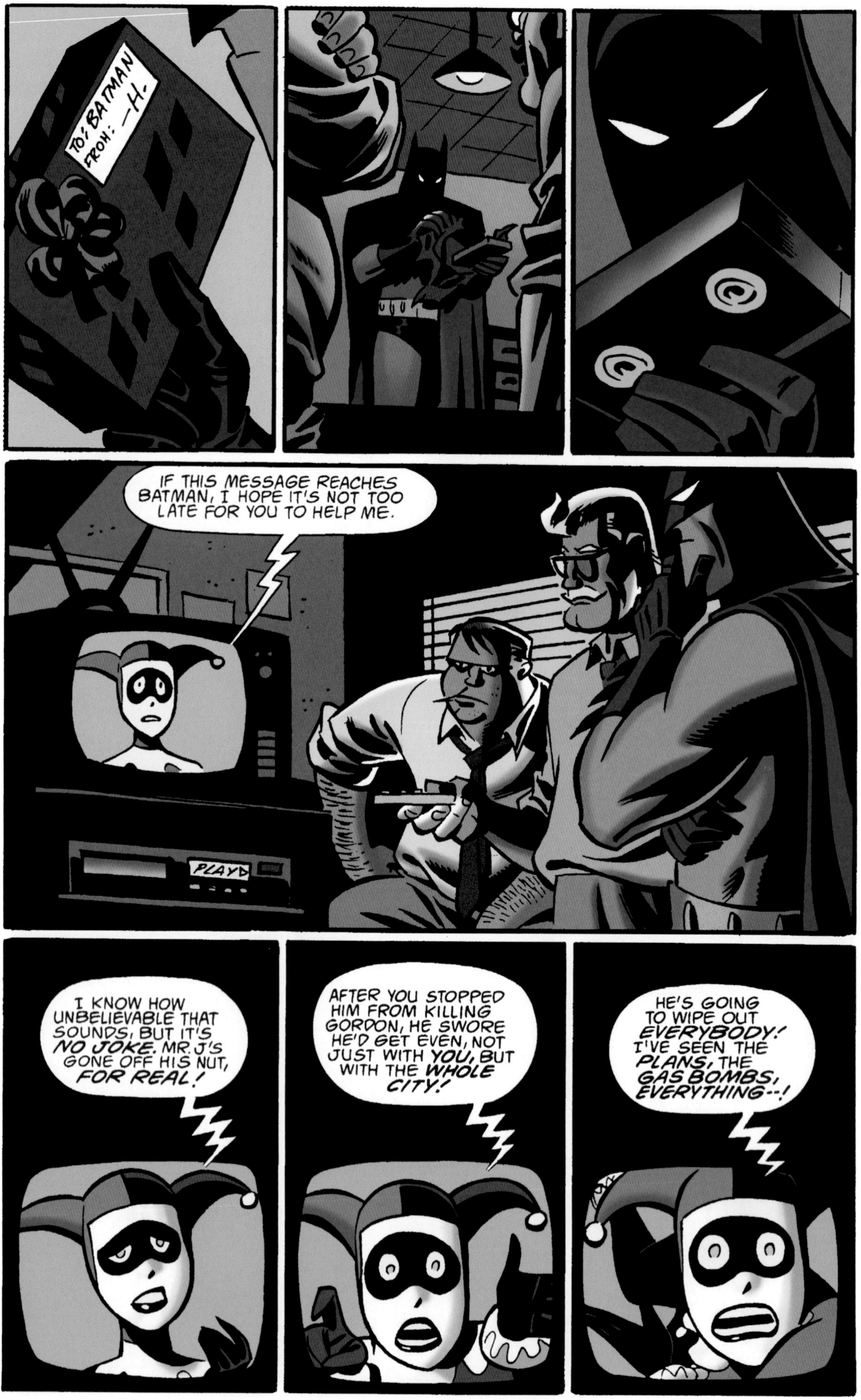
TO: BATMAN
FROM: —H.
IF THIS MESSAGE REACHES BATMAN, I HOPE IT'S NOT TOO LATE FOR YOU TO HELP ME.
PLAY
I KNOW HOW UNBELIEVABLE THAT SOUNDS, BUT IT'S NO JOKE. MR. J'S GONE OFF HIS NUT, FOR REAL!
AFTER YOU STOPPED HIM FROM KILLING GORDON, HE SWORE HE'D GET EVEN, NOT JUST WITH YOU, BUT WITH THE WHOLE CITY!
HE'S GOING TO WIPE OUT EVERYBODY! I'VE SEEN THE PLANS, THE GAS BOMBS, EVERYTHING--!

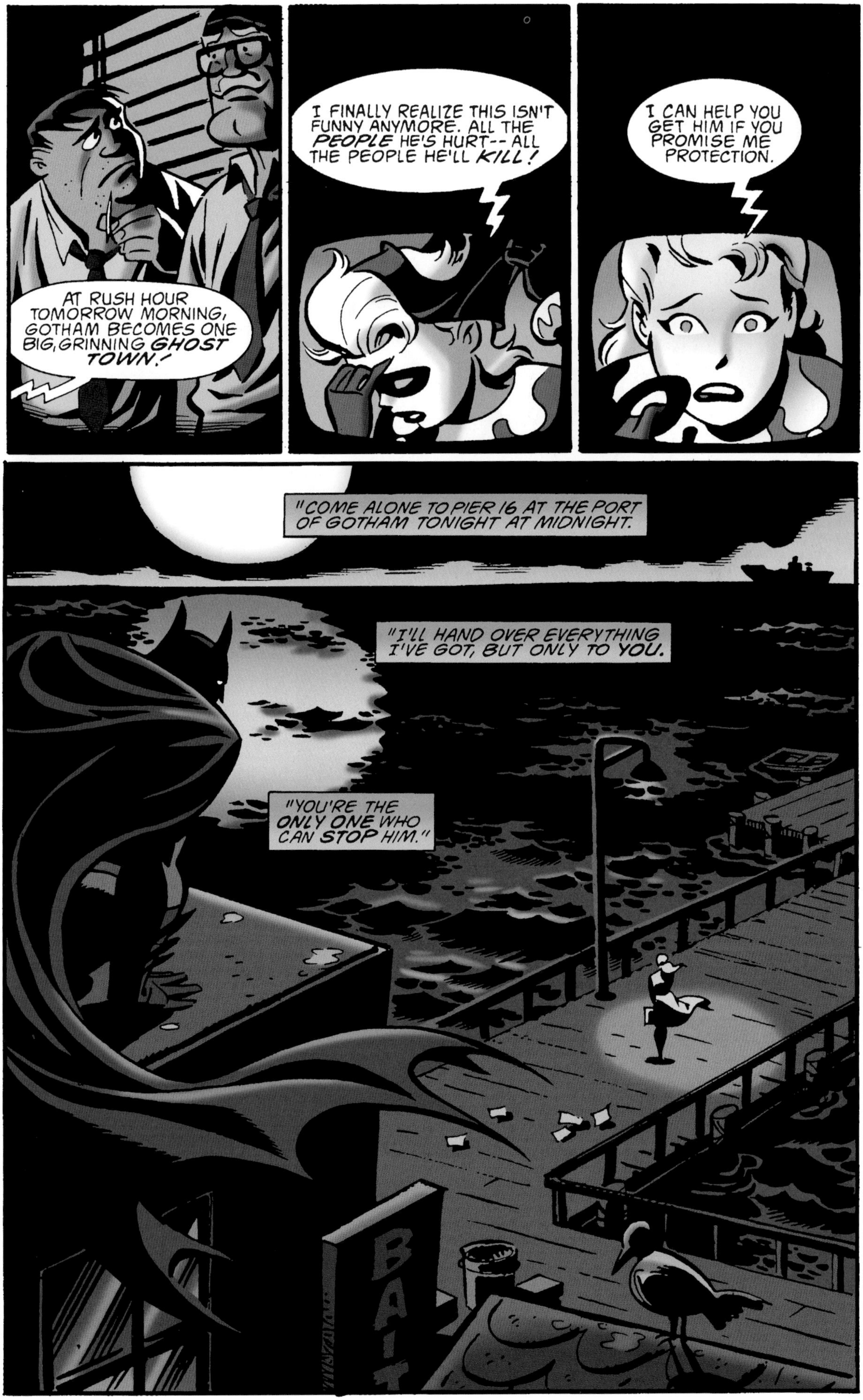

AT RUSH HOUR TOMORROW MORNING, GOTHAM BECOMES ONE BIG, GRINNING GHOST TOWN!
I FINALLY REALIZE THIS ISN'T FUNNY ANYMORE. ALL THE PEOPLE HE'S HURT-- ALL THE PEOPLE HE'LL KILL!
I CAN HELP YOU GET HIM IF YOU PROMISE ME PROTECTION.
"COME ALONE TO PIER 16 AT THE PORT OF GOTHAM TONIGHT AT MIDNIGHT.
"I'LL HAND OVER EVERYTHING I'VE GOT, BUT ONLY TO YOU.
"YOU'RE THE ONLY ONE WHO CAN STOP HIM."
BAIT

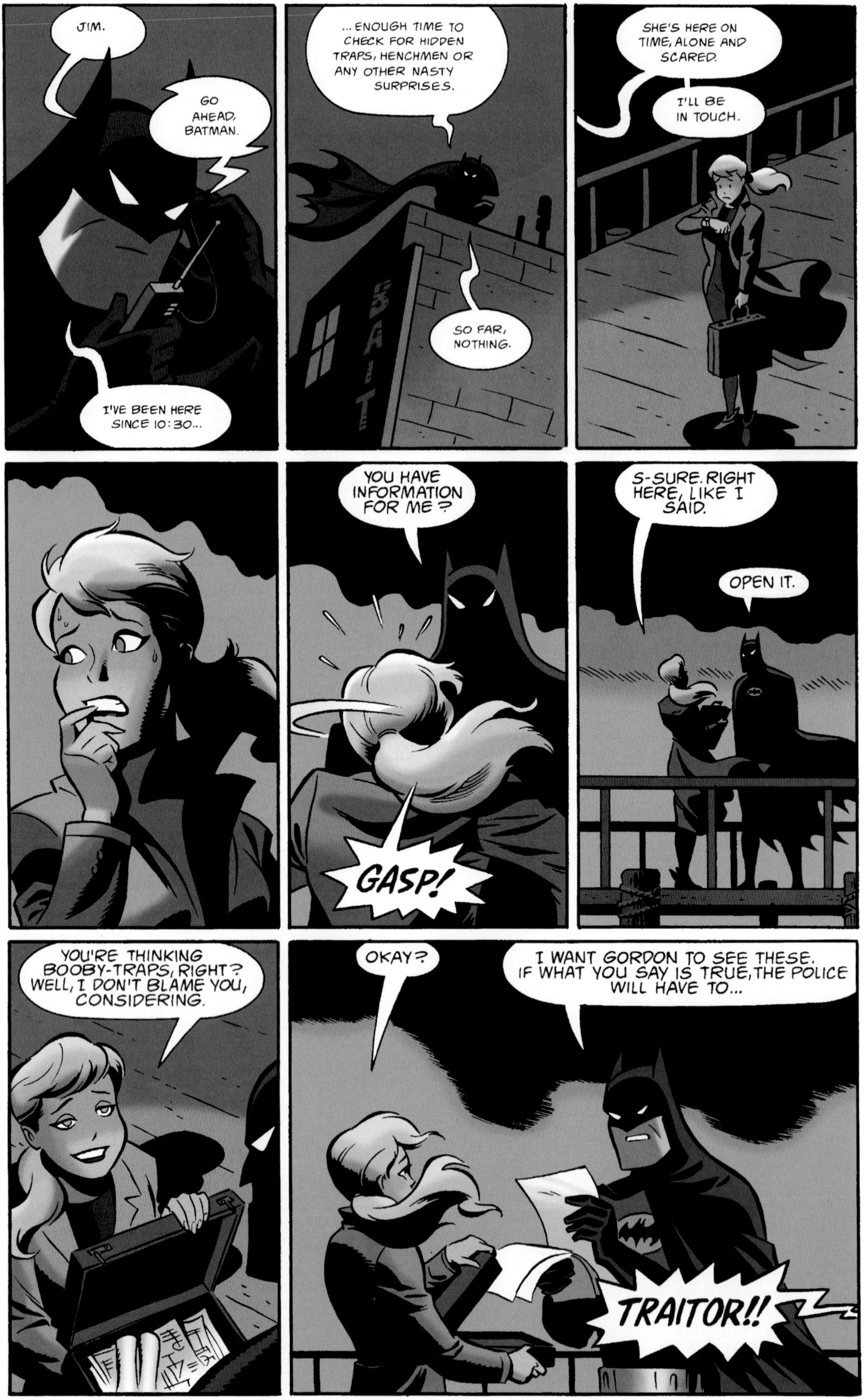
JIM.
GO AHEAD, BATMAN.
I'VE BEEN HERE SINCE 10:30...
...ENOUGH TIME TO CHECK FOR HIDDEN TRAPS, HENCHMEN OR ANY OTHER NASTY SURPRISES.
SO FAR, NOTHING.
BAIT
SHE'S HERE ON TIME, ALONE AND SCARED.
I'LL BE IN TOUCH.
YOU HAVE INFORMATION FOR ME?
GASP!
S-SURE. RIGHT HERE, LIKE I SAID.
OPEN IT.
YOU'RE THINKING BOOBY-TRAPS, RIGHT? WELL, I DON'T BLAME YOU, CONSIDERING.
OKAY?
I WANT GORDON TO SEE THESE. IF WHAT YOU SAY IS TRUE, THE POLICE WILL HAVE TO...
TRAITOR!!

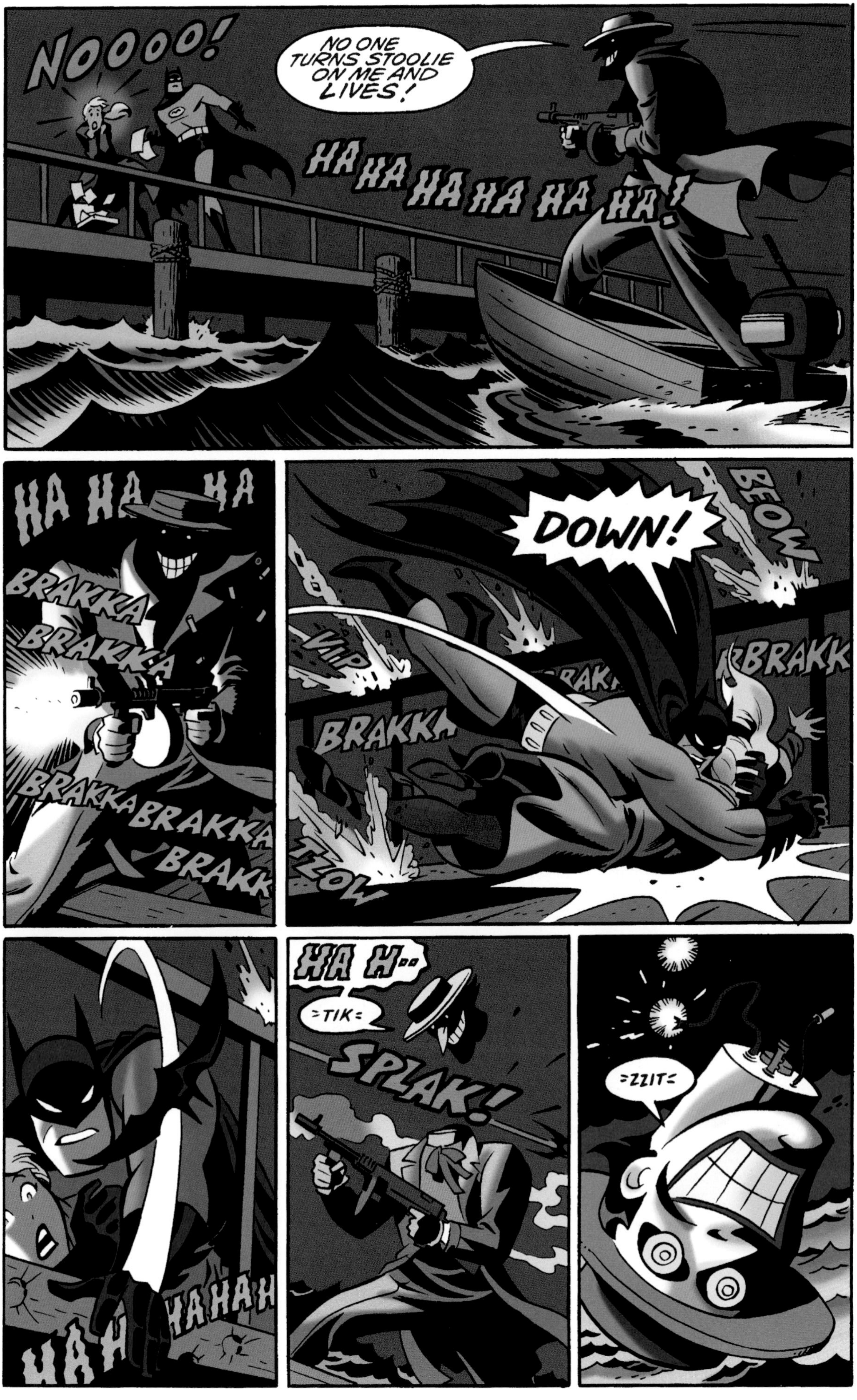
NOOOO!
NO ONE TURNS STOOLIE ON ME AND LIVES!
HA HA HA HA HA HA HA!
HA HA HA
BRAKKA
BRAKKA
BRAKKABRAKKA
BRAKK
DOWN!
BEOW
VIP
BRAKKA
BRAKKA
BRAKK
TZOW
HAHAHAHAH
HA H..
=TIK=
SPLAK!
=ZZIT=

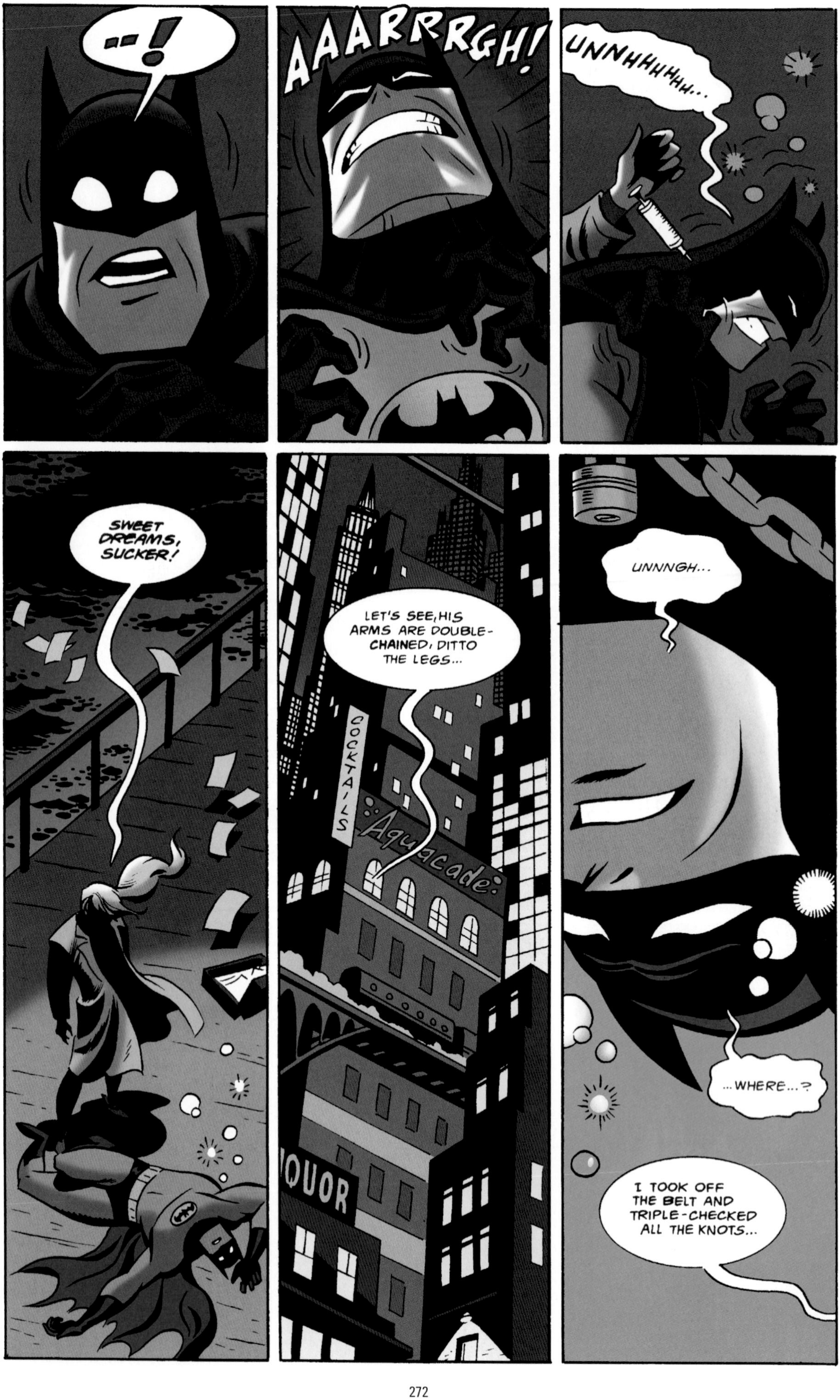
--!
AAARRRRGH!
UNNHHHHH...
SWEET DREAMS, SUCKER!
LET'S SEE, HIS ARMS ARE DOUBLE-CHAINED, DITTO THE LEGS...
COCKTAILS
Aquacade
QUOR
UNNNGH...
...WHERE...?
I TOOK OFF THE BELT AND TRIPLE-CHECKED ALL THE KNOTS...

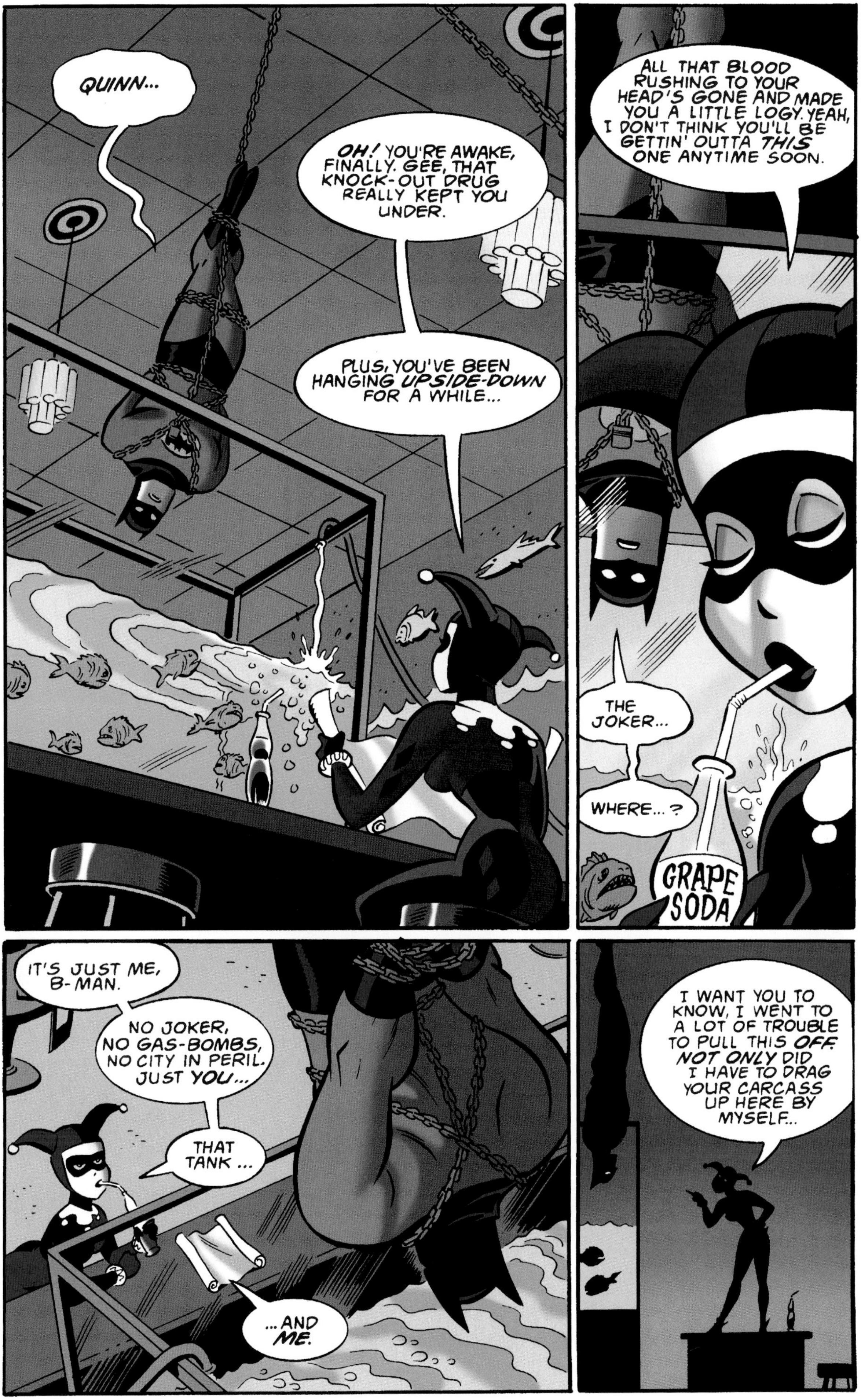
QUINN...
OH! YOU'RE AWAKE, FINALLY. GEE, THAT KNOCK-OUT DRUG REALLY KEPT YOU UNDER.
PLUS, YOU'VE BEEN HANGING UPSIDE-DOWN FOR A WHILE...
ALL THAT BLOOD RUSHING TO YOUR HEAD'S GONE AND MADE YOU A LITTLE LOGY. YEAH, I DON'T THINK YOU'LL BE GETTIN' OUTTA THIS ONE ANYTIME SOON.
THE JOKER...
WHERE...?
GRAPE SODA
IT'S JUST ME, B-MAN.
NO JOKER, NO GAS-BOMBS, NO CITY IN PERIL. JUST YOU...
THAT TANK ...
...AND ME.
I WANT YOU TO KNOW, I WENT TO A LOT OF TROUBLE TO PULL THIS OFF. NOT ONLY DID I HAVE TO DRAG YOUR CARCASS UP HERE BY MYSELF...

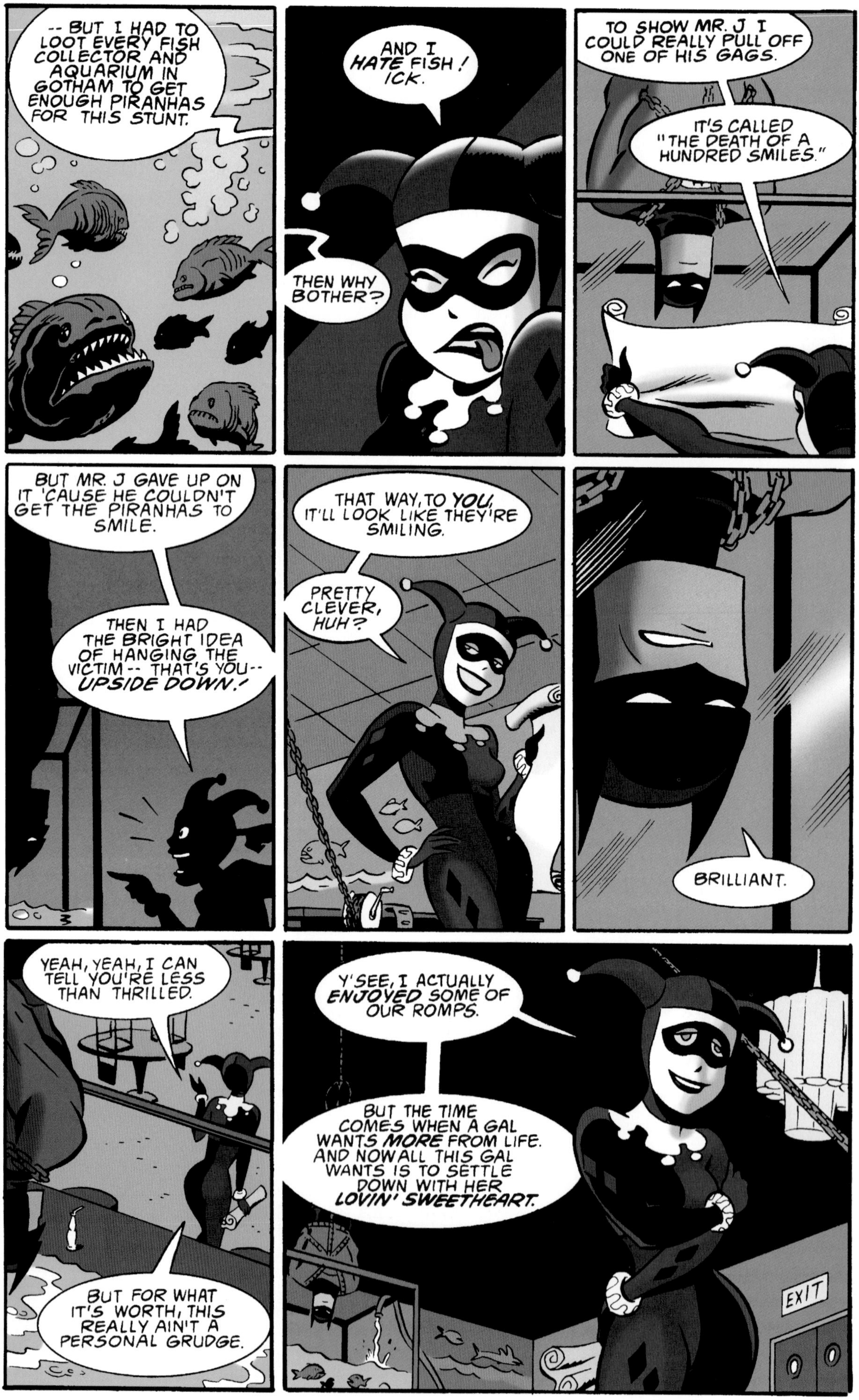
-- BUT I HAD TO LOOT EVERY FISH COLLECTOR AND AQUARIUM IN GOTHAM TO GET ENOUGH PIRANHAS FOR THIS STUNT.
AND I HATE FISH! ICK.
THEN WHY BOTHER?
TO SHOW MR. J I COULD REALLY PULL OFF ONE OF HIS GAGS.
IT'S CALLED "THE DEATH OF A HUNDRED SMILES."
BUT MR. J GAVE UP ON IT 'CAUSE HE COULDN'T GET THE PIRANHAS TO SMILE.
THEN I HAD THE BRIGHT IDEA OF HANGING THE VICTIM -- THAT'S YOU -- UPSIDE DOWN!
THAT WAY, TO YOU, IT'LL LOOK LIKE THEY'RE SMILING.
PRETTY CLEVER, HUH?
BRILLIANT.
YEAH, YEAH, I CAN TELL YOU'RE LESS THAN THRILLED.
BUT FOR WHAT IT'S WORTH, THIS REALLY AIN'T A PERSONAL GRUDGE.
Y'SEE, I ACTUALLY ENJOYED SOME OF OUR ROMPS.
BUT THE TIME COMES WHEN A GAL WANTS MORE FROM LIFE. AND NOW ALL THIS GAL WANTS IS TO SETTLE DOWN WITH HER LOVIN' SWEETHEART.
EXIT

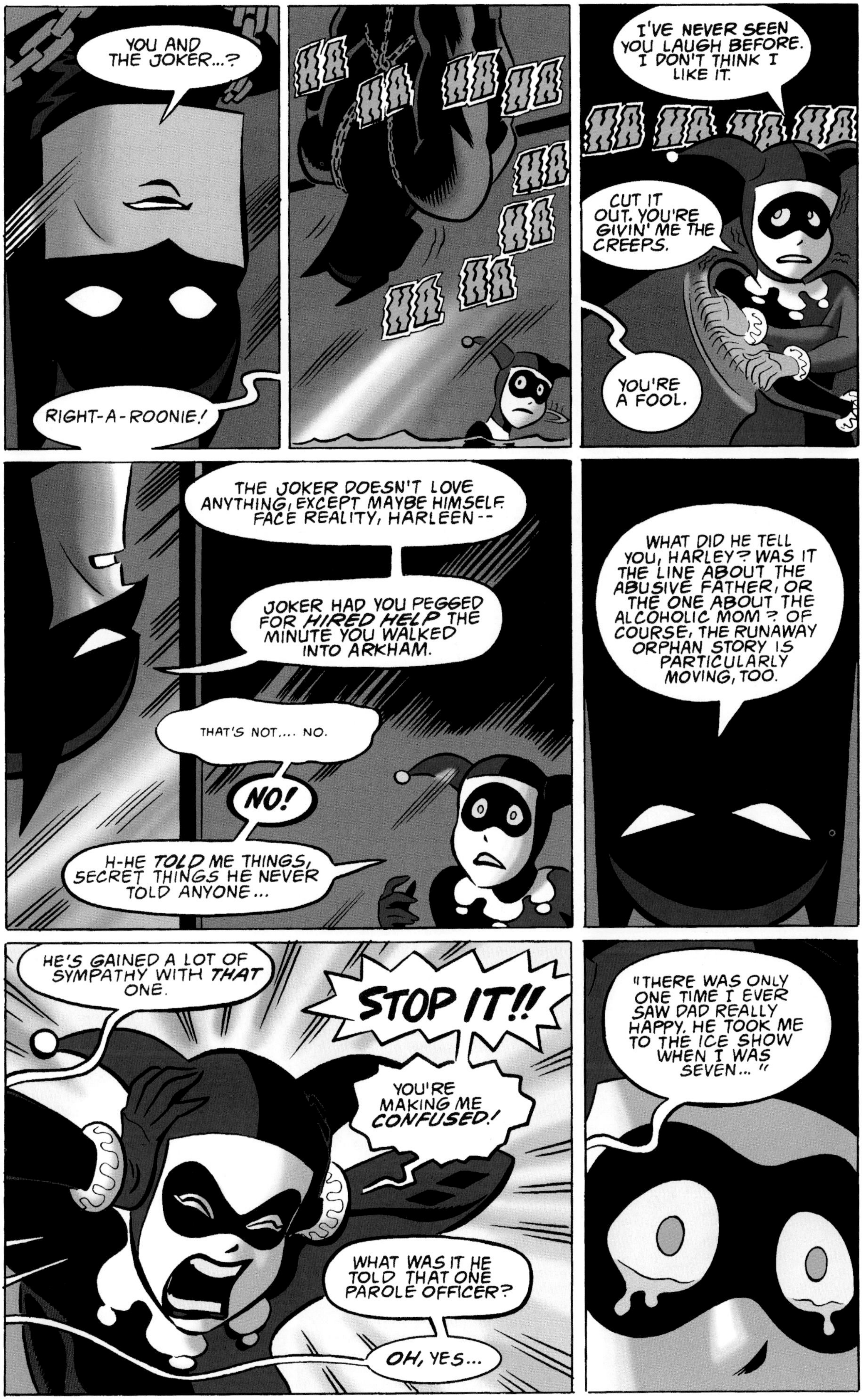

YOU AND THE JOKER...?
RIGHT-A-ROONIE!
HA HA HA HA HA HA HA HA HA
I'VE NEVER SEEN YOU LAUGH BEFORE. I DON'T THINK I LIKE IT.
HA HA HA HA
CUT IT OUT. YOU'RE GIVIN' ME THE CREEPS.
YOU'RE A FOOL.
THE JOKER DOESN'T LOVE ANYTHING, EXCEPT MAYBE HIMSELF. FACE REALITY, HARLEEN--
JOKER HAD YOU PEGGED FOR HIRED HELP THE MINUTE YOU WALKED INTO ARKHAM.
THAT'S NOT.... NO.
NO!
H-HE TOLD ME THINGS, SECRET THINGS HE NEVER TOLD ANYONE...
WHAT DID HE TELL YOU, HARLEY? WAS IT THE LINE ABOUT THE ABUSIVE FATHER, OR THE ONE ABOUT THE ALCOHOLIC MOM? OF COURSE, THE RUNAWAY ORPHAN STORY IS PARTICULARLY MOVING, TOO.
HE'S GAINED A LOT OF SYMPATHY WITH THAT ONE.
STOP IT!!
YOU'RE MAKING ME CONFUSED!
WHAT WAS IT HE TOLD THAT ONE PAROLE OFFICER?
OH, YES...
"THERE WAS ONLY ONE TIME I EVER SAW DAD REALLY HAPPY. HE TOOK ME TO THE ICE SHOW WHEN I WAS SEVEN..."

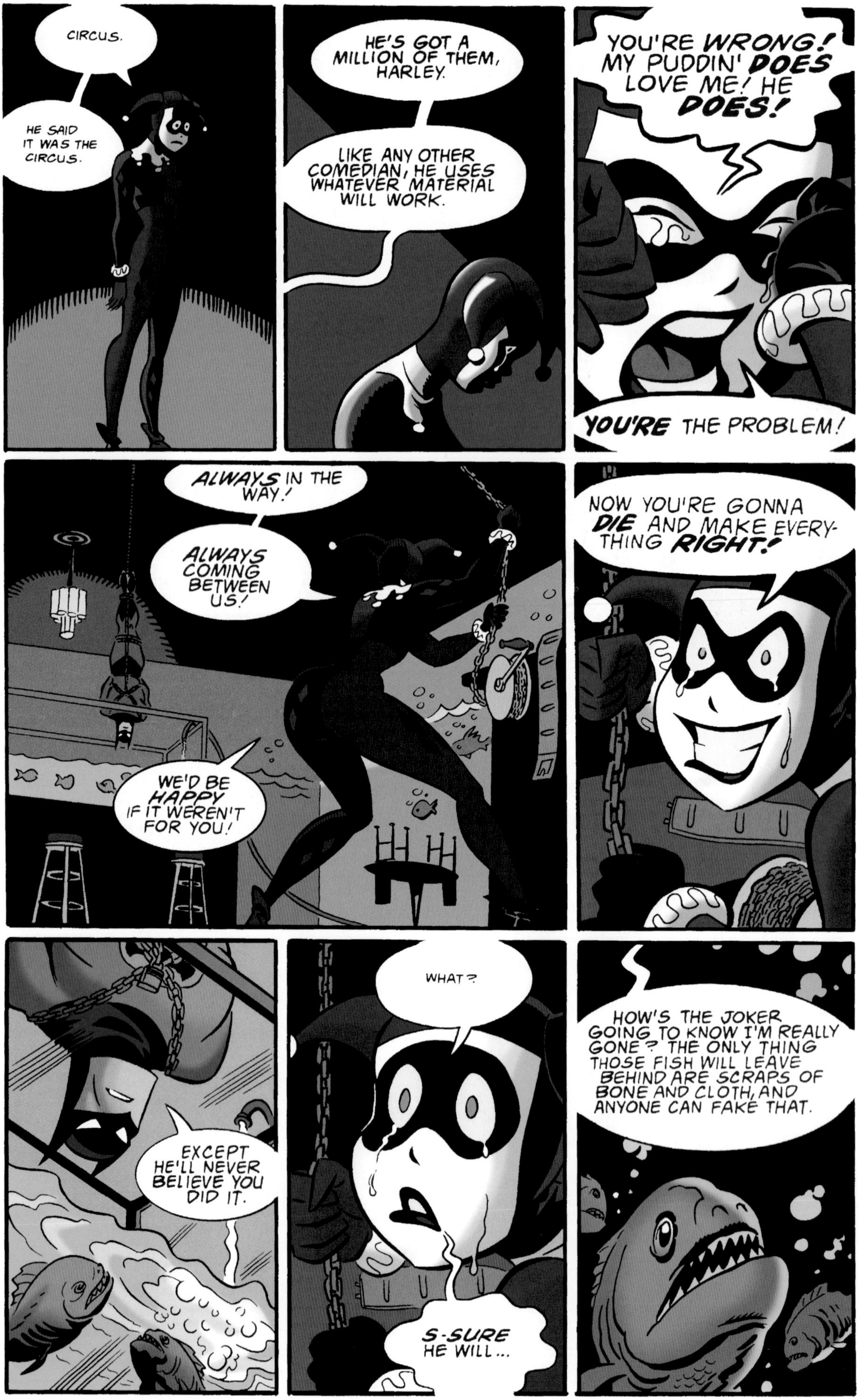
CIRCUS.
HE SAID IT WAS THE CIRCUS.
HE'S GOT A MILLION OF THEM, HARLEY.
LIKE ANY OTHER COMEDIAN, HE USES WHATEVER MATERIAL WILL WORK.
YOU'RE WRONG! MY PUDDIN' DOES LOVE ME! HE DOES!
YOU'RE THE PROBLEM!
ALWAYS IN THE WAY!
ALWAYS COMING BETWEEN US!
WE'D BE HAPPY IF IT WEREN'T FOR YOU!
NOW YOU'RE GONNA DIE AND MAKE EVERY-THING RIGHT!
EXCEPT HE'LL NEVER BELIEVE YOU DID IT.
WHAT?
S-SURE HE WILL...
HOW'S THE JOKER GOING TO KNOW I'M REALLY GONE? THE ONLY THING THOSE FISH WILL LEAVE BEHIND ARE SCRAPS OF BONE AND CLOTH, AND ANYONE CAN FAKE THAT.

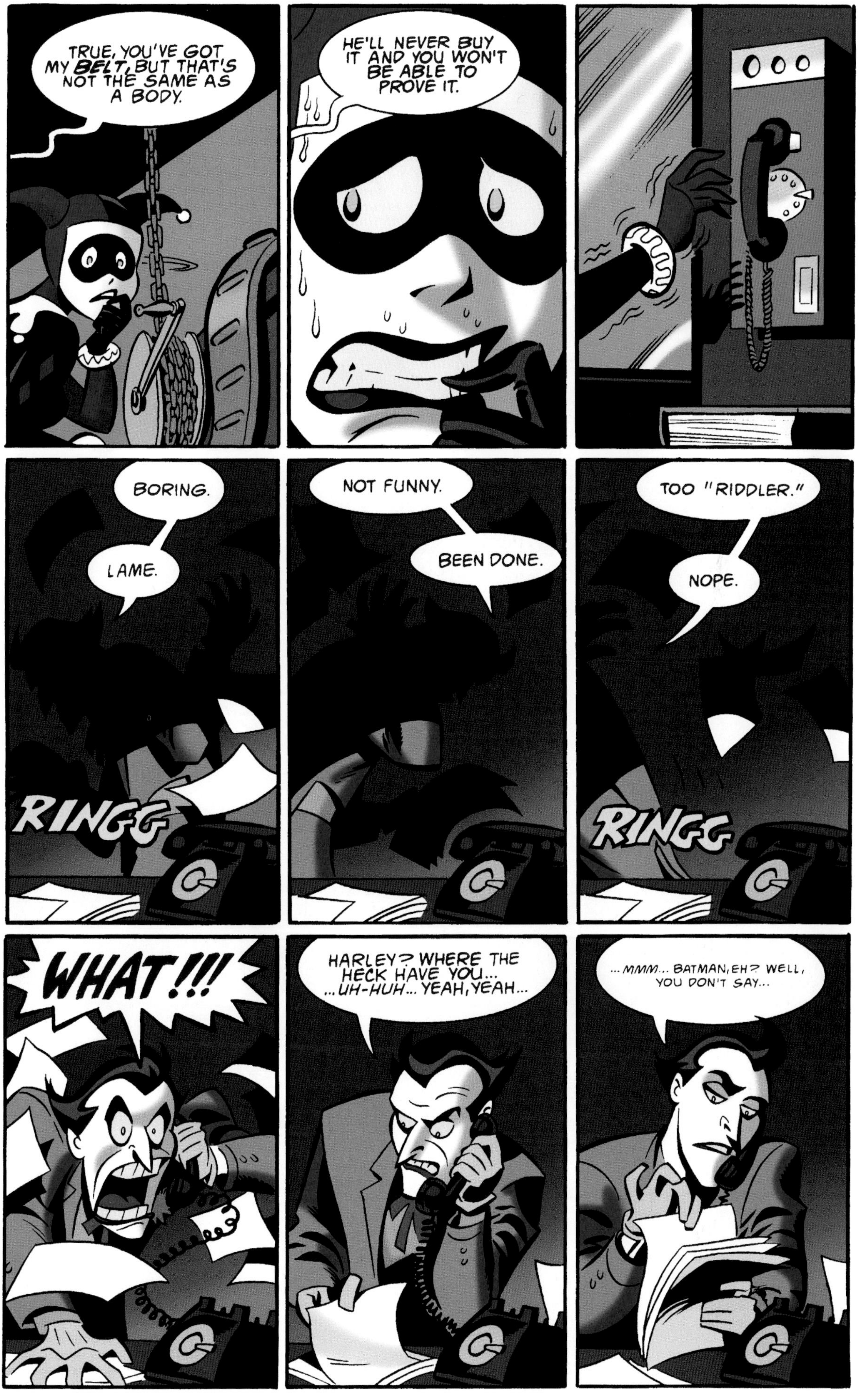
TRUE, YOU'VE GOT MY BELT, BUT THAT'S NOT THE SAME AS A BODY.
HE'LL NEVER BUY IT AND YOU WON'T BE ABLE TO PROVE IT.
BORING.
LAME.
RINGG
NOT FUNNY.
BEEN DONE.
TOO "RIDDLER."
NOPE.
RINGG
WHAT!!!
HARLEY? WHERE THE HECK HAVE YOU... ...UH-HUH... YEAH, YEAH...
...MMM... BATMAN, EH? WELL, YOU DON'T SAY...

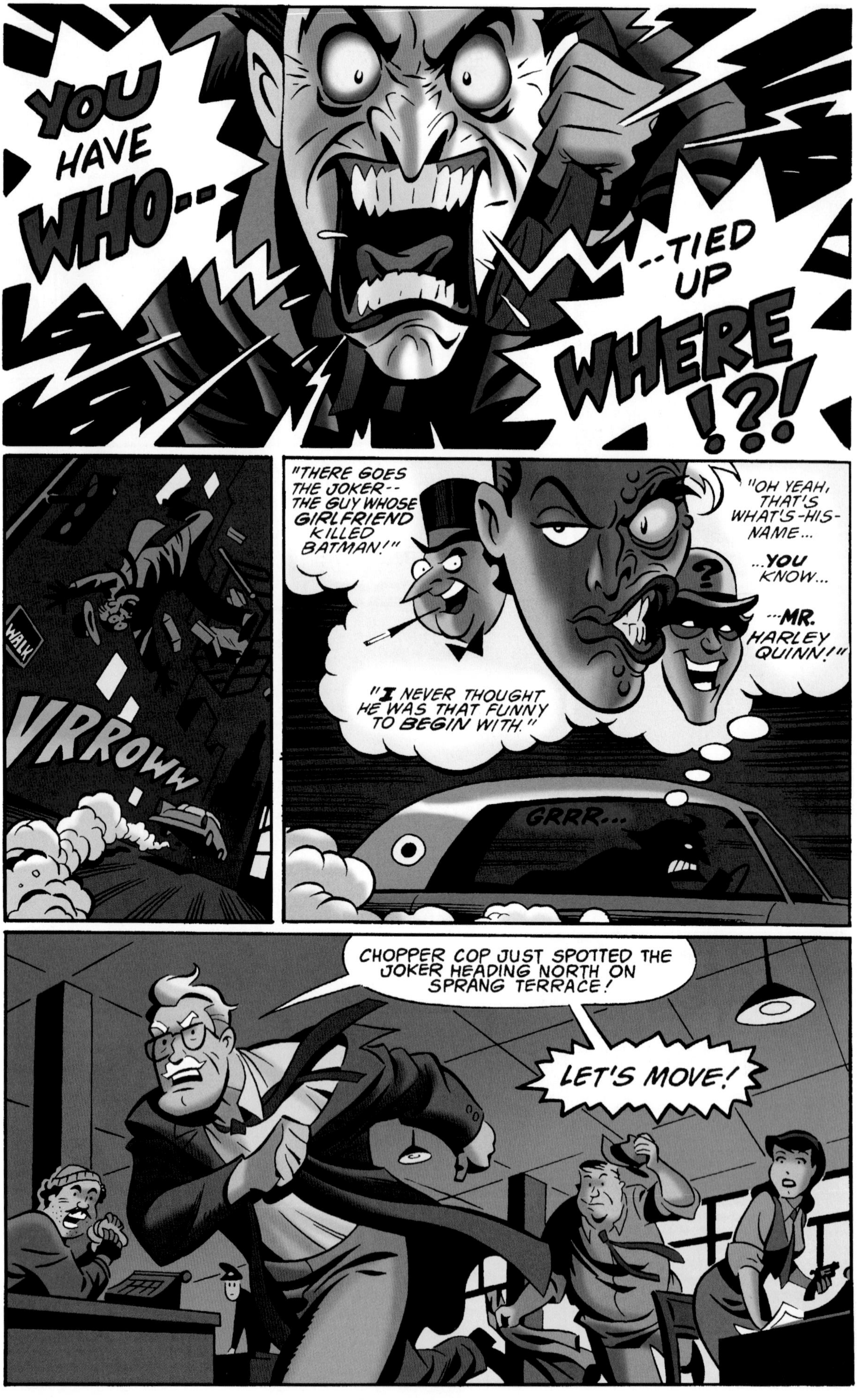
YOU HAVE WHO--
--TIED UP WHERE !?!
VRROWW
WALK
"THERE GOES THE JOKER-- THE GUY WHOSE GIRLFRIEND KILLED BATMAN!"
"OH YEAH, THAT'S WHAT'S-HIS-NAME... ...YOU KNOW... --MR. HARLEY QUINN!"
"I NEVER THOUGHT HE WAS THAT FUNNY TO BEGIN WITH."
GRRR...
CHOPPER COP JUST SPOTTED THE JOKER HEADING NORTH ON SPRANG TERRACE!
LET'S MOVE!

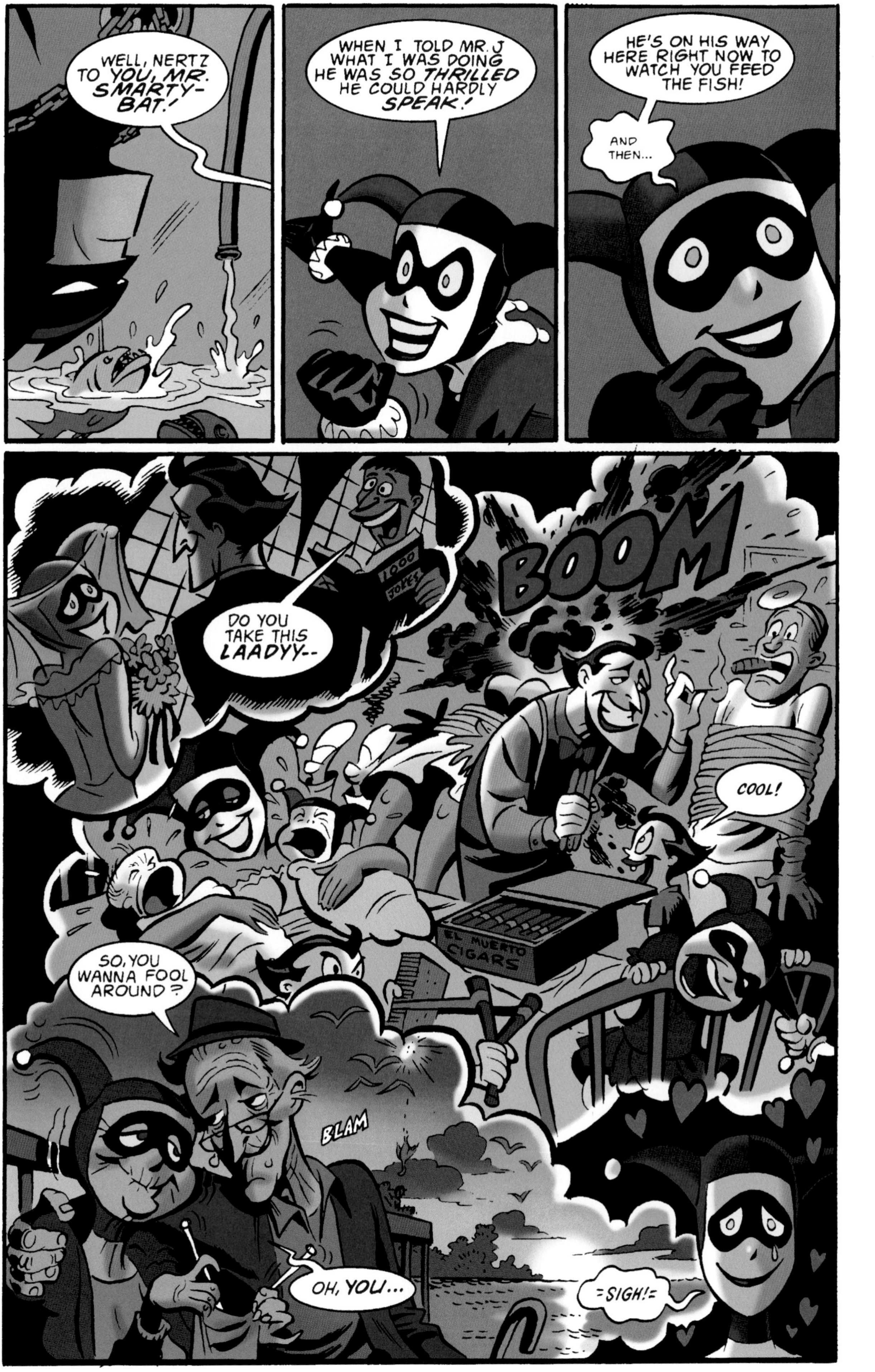
WELL, NERTZ TO YOU, MR. SMARTY-BAT!
WHEN I TOLD MR. J WHAT I WAS DOING HE WAS SO THRILLED HE COULD HARDLY SPEAK!
HE'S ON HIS WAY HERE RIGHT NOW TO WATCH YOU FEED THE FISH!
AND THEN...
1000 JOKES
DO YOU TAKE THIS LAADYY--
BOOM
COOL!
EL MUERTO CIGARS
SO, YOU WANNA FOOL AROUND?
BLAM
OH, YOU...
=SIGH!=

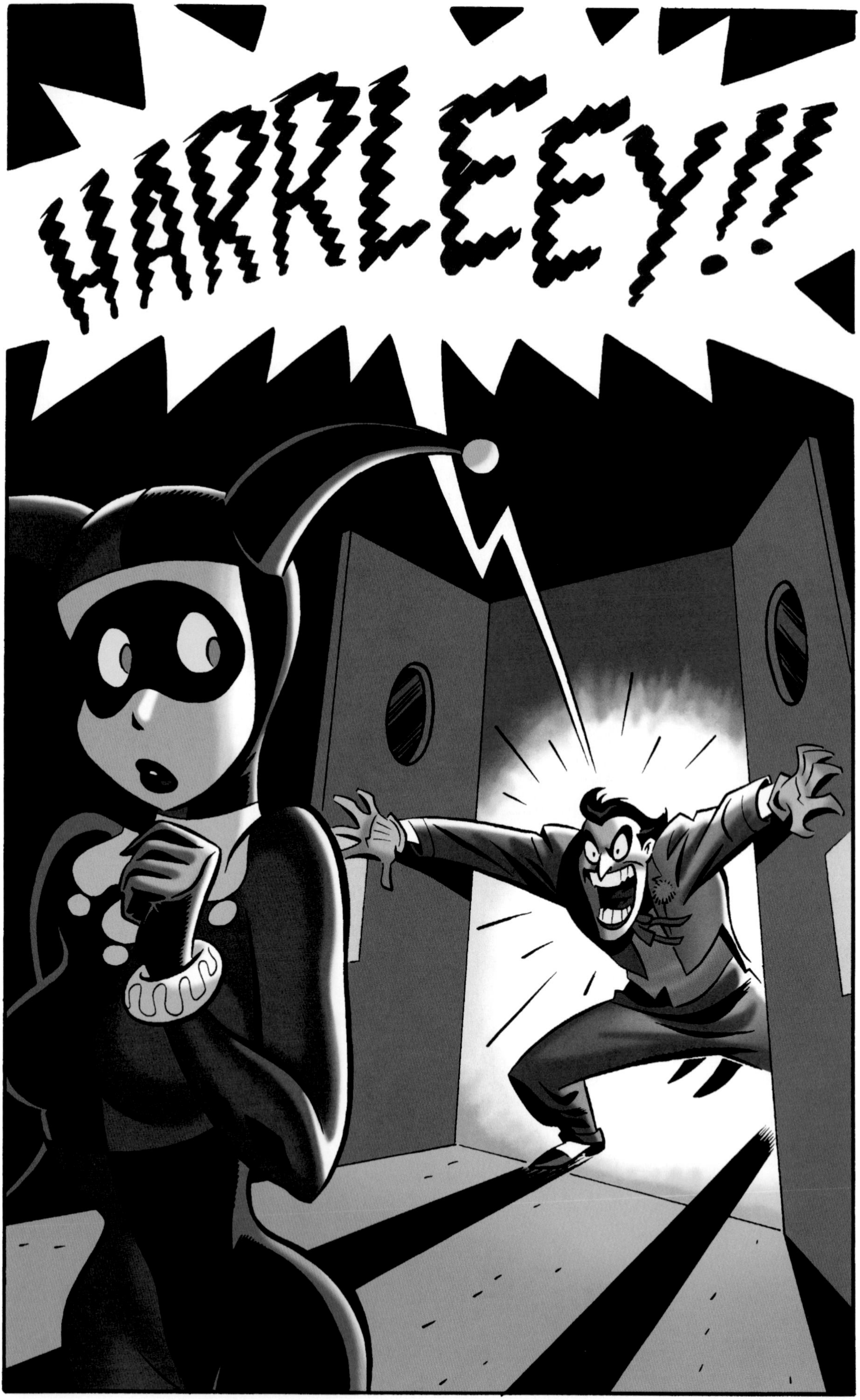
HARRLEEY!!

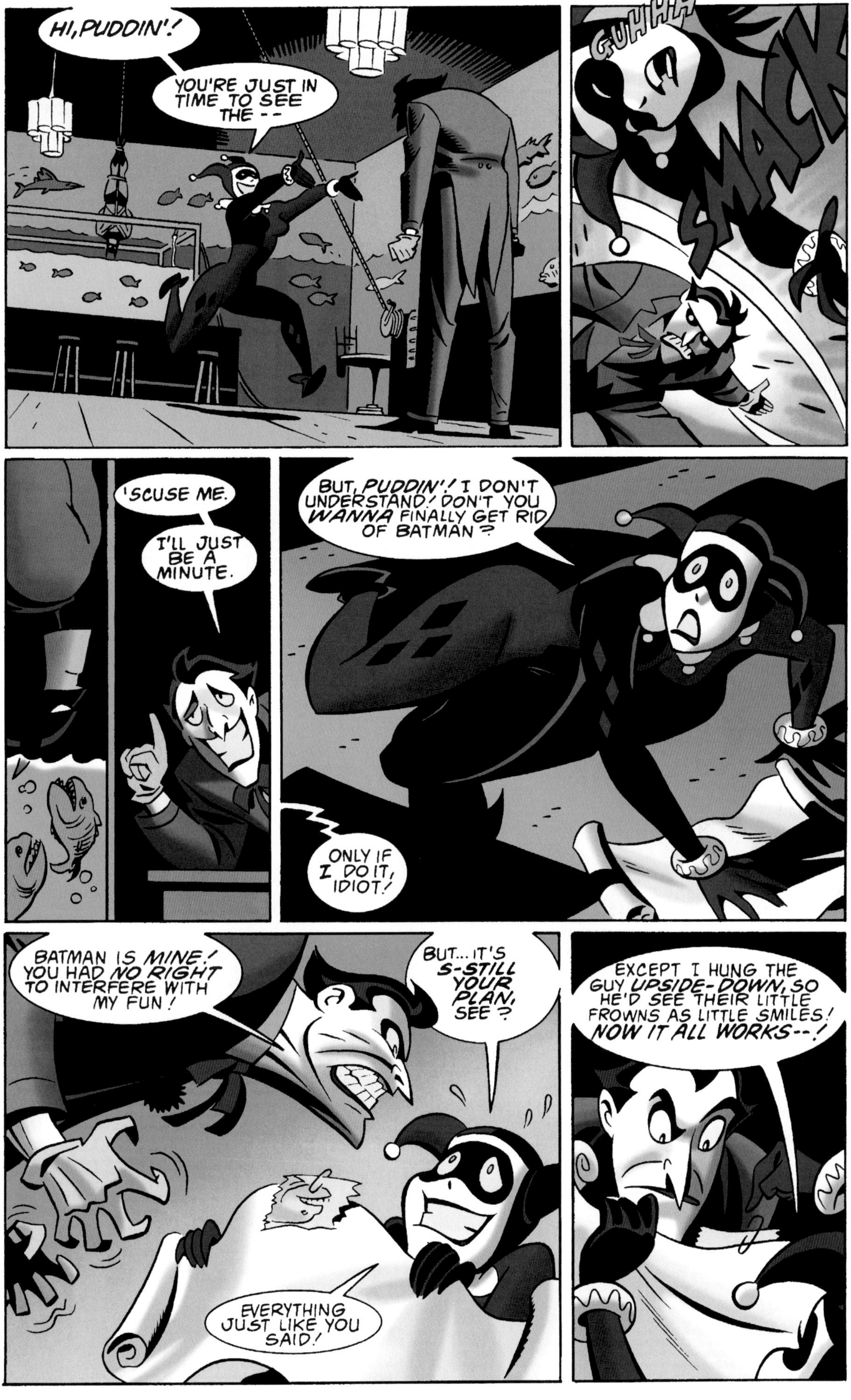
HI, PUDDIN'!
YOU'RE JUST IN TIME TO SEE THE --
GUHHH
SMACK
'SCUSE ME.
I'LL JUST BE A MINUTE.
BUT, PUDDIN'! I DON'T UNDERSTAND! DON'T YOU WANNA FINALLY GET RID OF BATMAN?
ONLY IF I DO IT, IDIOT!
BATMAN IS MINE! YOU HAD NO RIGHT TO INTERFERE WITH MY FUN!
BUT... IT'S S-STILL YOUR PLAN, SEE?
EVERYTHING JUST LIKE YOU SAID!
EXCEPT I HUNG THE GUY UPSIDE-DOWN, SO HE'D SEE THEIR LITTLE FROWNS AS LITTLE SMILES! NOW IT ALL WORKS--!

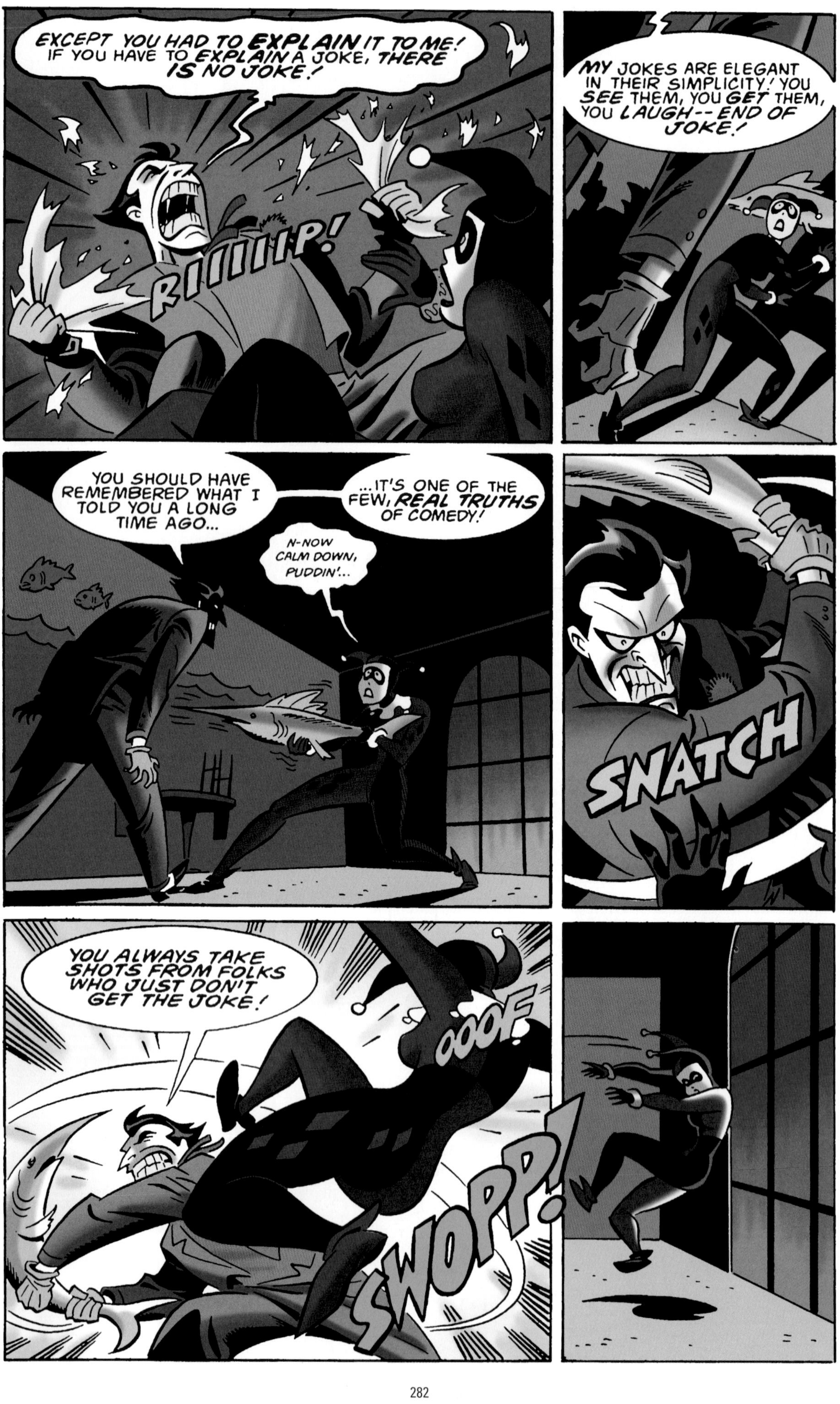
EXCEPT YOU HAD TO EXPLAIN IT TO ME! IF YOU HAVE TO EXPLAIN A JOKE, THERE IS NO JOKE!
RIIIIIIP!
MY JOKES ARE ELEGANT IN THEIR SIMPLICITY! YOU SEE THEM, YOU GET THEM, YOU LAUGH--END OF JOKE!
YOU SHOULD HAVE REMEMBERED WHAT I TOLD YOU A LONG TIME AGO...
...IT'S ONE OF THE FEW, REAL TRUTHS OF COMEDY!
N-NOW CALM DOWN, PUDDIN'...
SNATCH
YOU ALWAYS TAKE SHOTS FROM FOLKS WHO JUST DON'T GET THE JOKE!
OOOF
SWOPP!

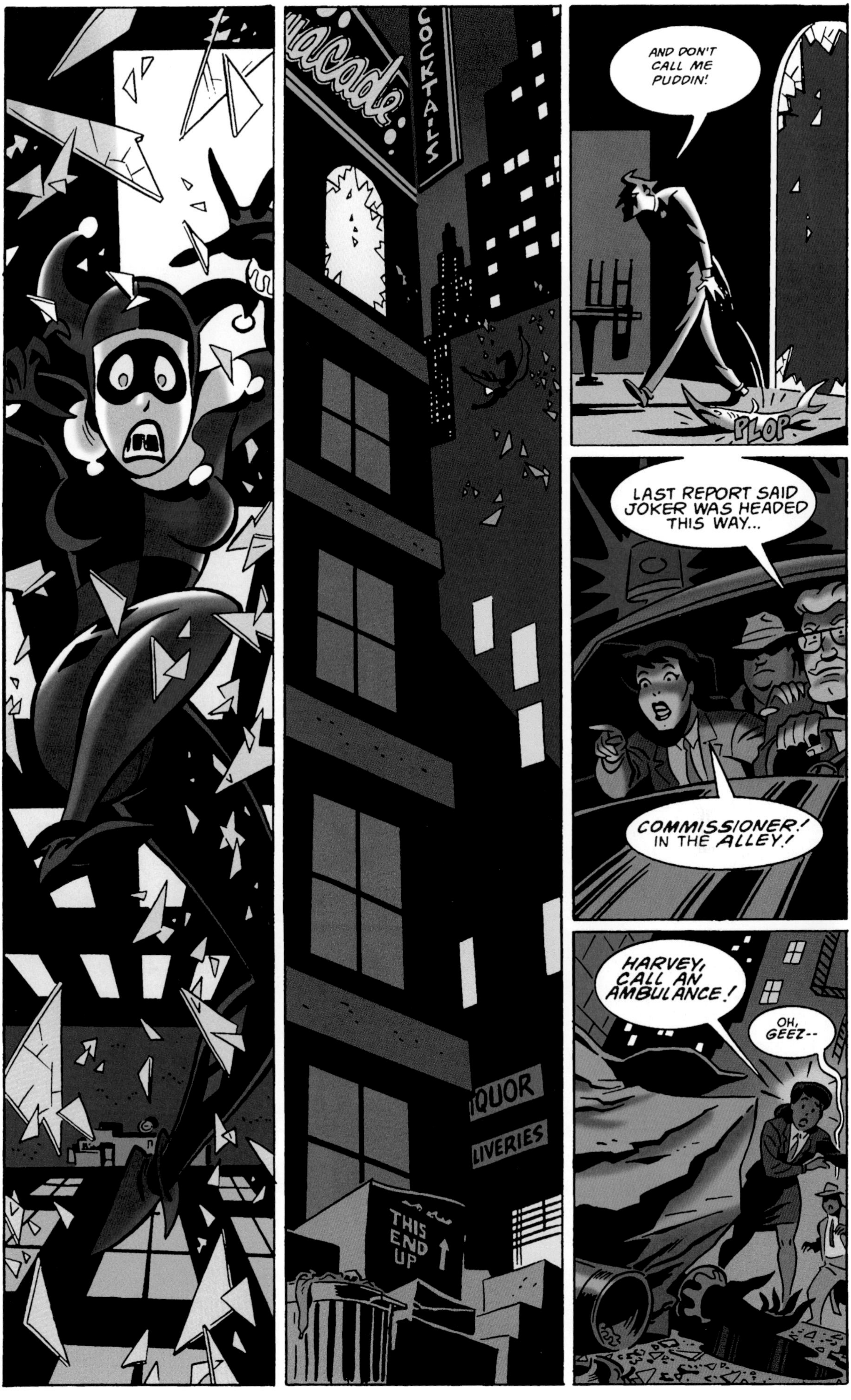

COCKTAILS
AND DON'T CALL ME PUDDIN!
PLOP
LAST REPORT SAID JOKER WAS HEADED THIS WAY...
COMMISSIONER! IN THE ALLEY!
HARVEY, CALL AN AMBULANCE!
OH, GEEZ--
QUOR
LIVERIES
THIS END UP

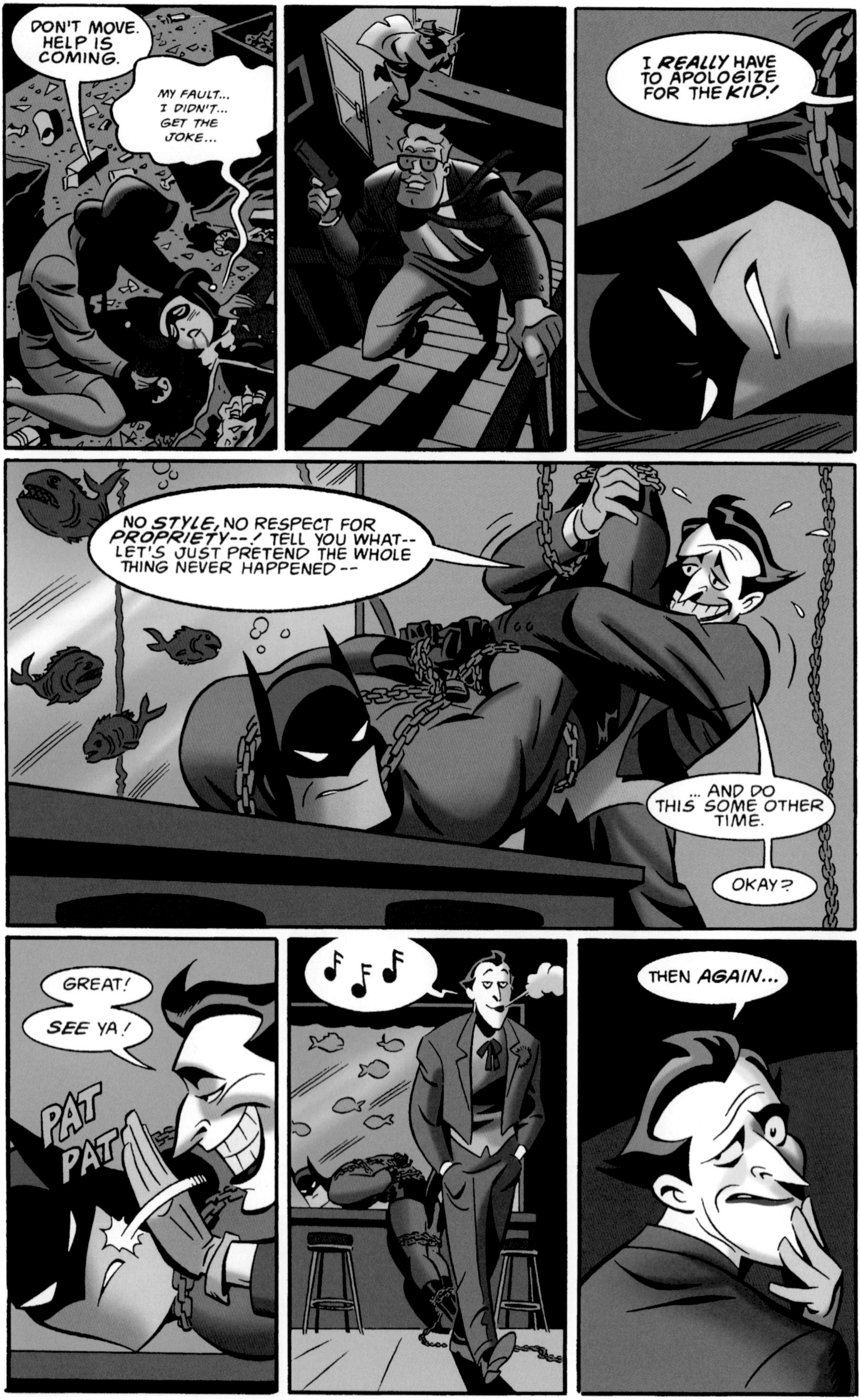
DON'T MOVE. HELP IS COMING.
MY FAULT... I DIDN'T... GET THE JOKE...
I REALLY HAVE TO APOLOGIZE FOR THE KID!
NO STYLE, NO RESPECT FOR PROPRIETY--! TELL YOU WHAT-- LET'S JUST PRETEND THE WHOLE THING NEVER HAPPENED--
... AND DO THIS SOME OTHER TIME.
OKAY?
GREAT!
SEE YA!
PAT PAT
THEN AGAIN...

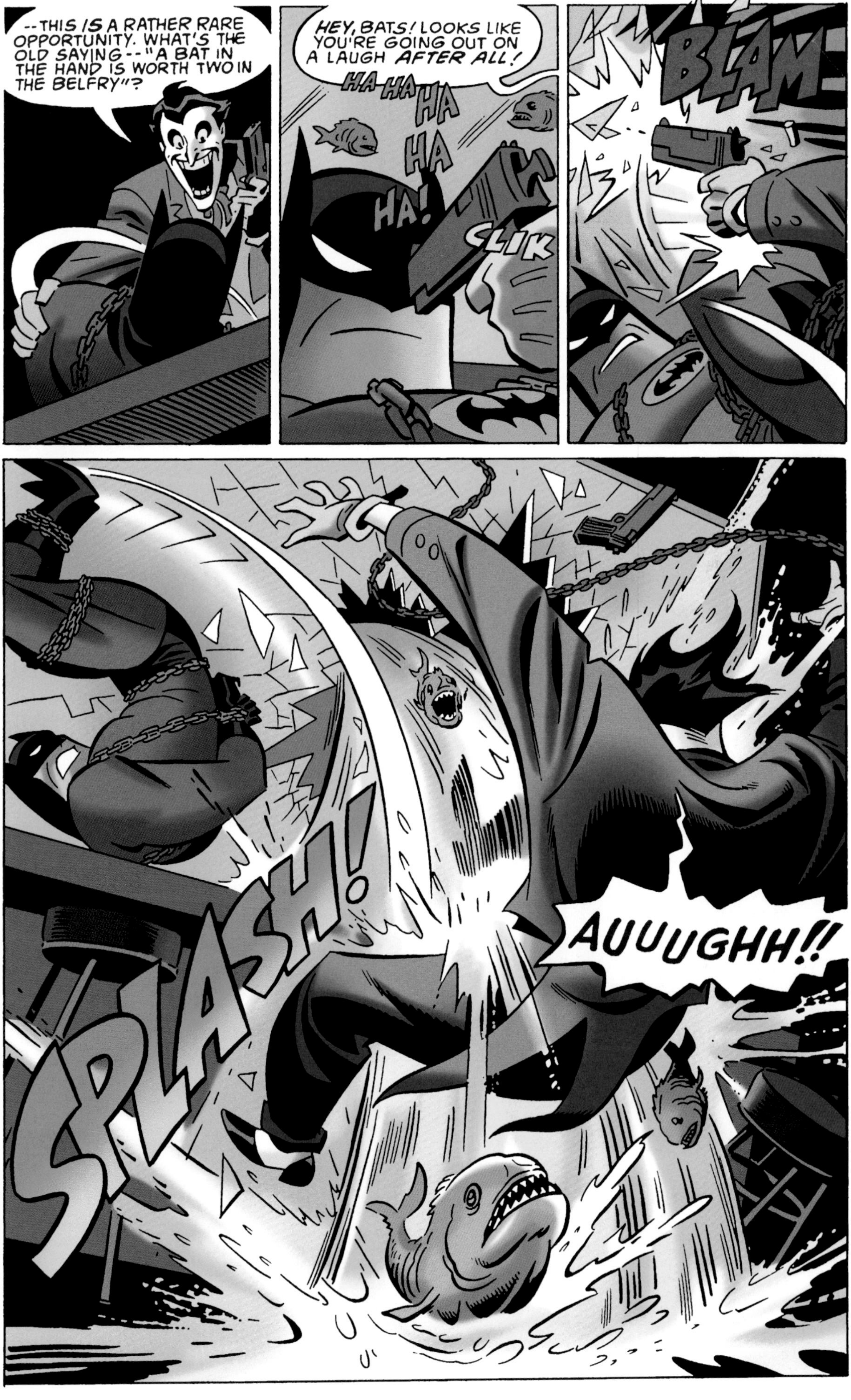
--THIS IS A RATHER RARE OPPORTUNITY. WHAT'S THE OLD SAYING--"A BAT IN THE HAND IS WORTH TWO IN THE BELFRY"?
HEY, BATS! LOOKS LIKE YOU'RE GOING OUT ON A LAUGH AFTER ALL!
HA HA HA HA HA!
CLIK
BLAM
SPLASH!
AUUUGHH!!

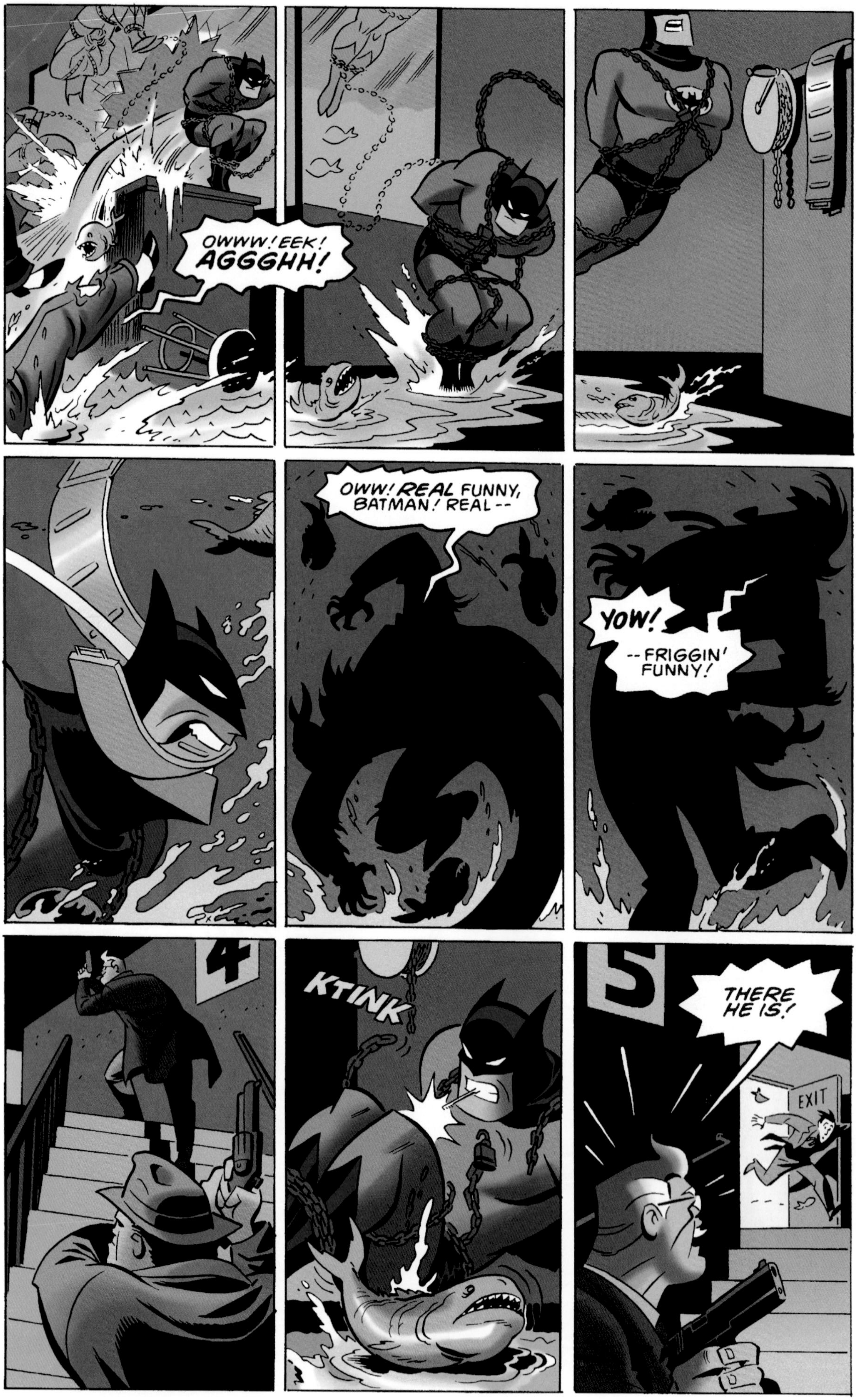
OWWW! EEK! AGGGHH!
OWW! REAL FUNNY, BATMAN! REAL--
YOW!
--FRIGGIN' FUNNY!
4
KTINK
5
THERE HE IS!
EXIT

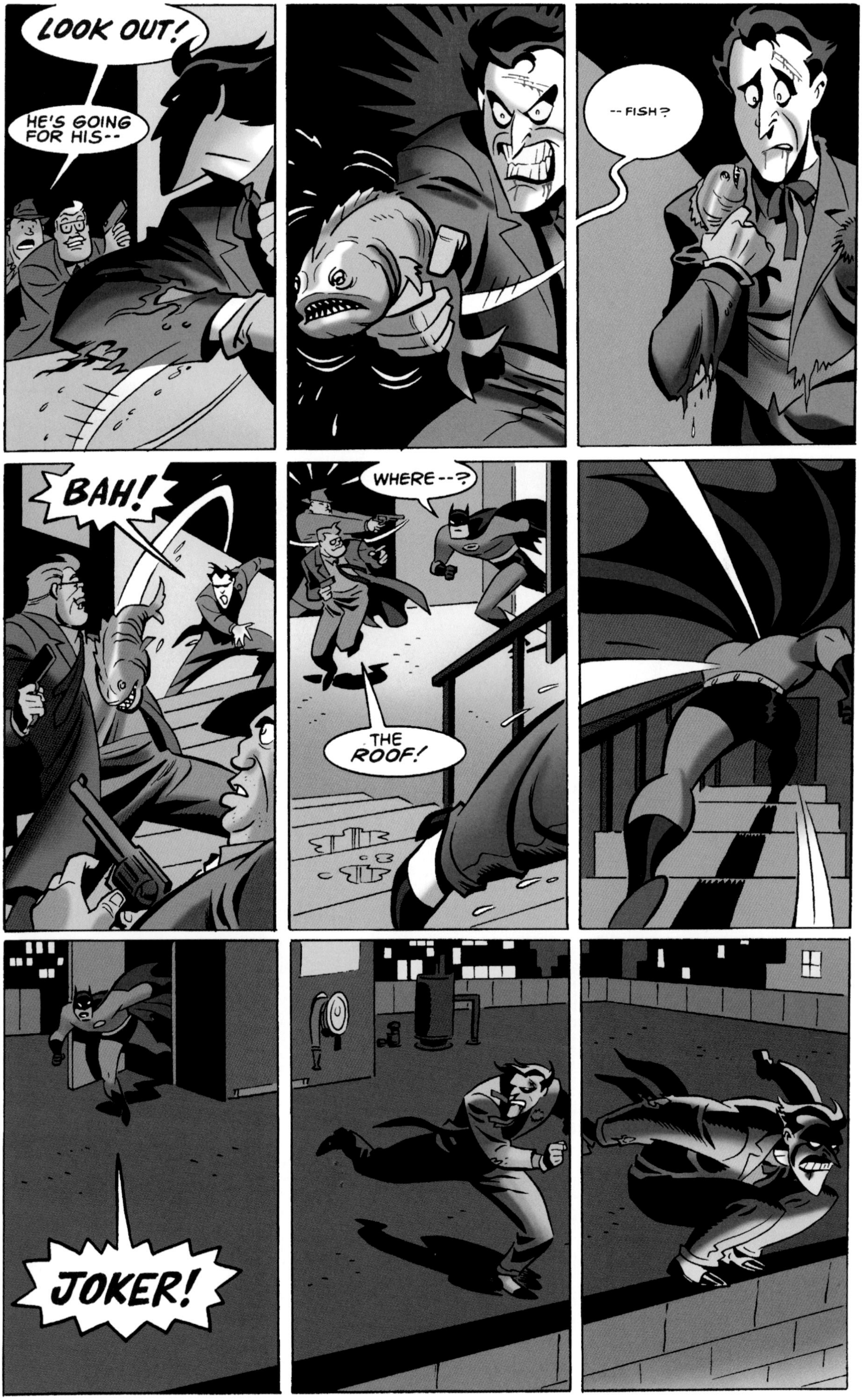
LOOK OUT!
HE'S GOING FOR HIS--
--FISH?
BAH!
WHERE--?
THE ROOF!
JOKER!

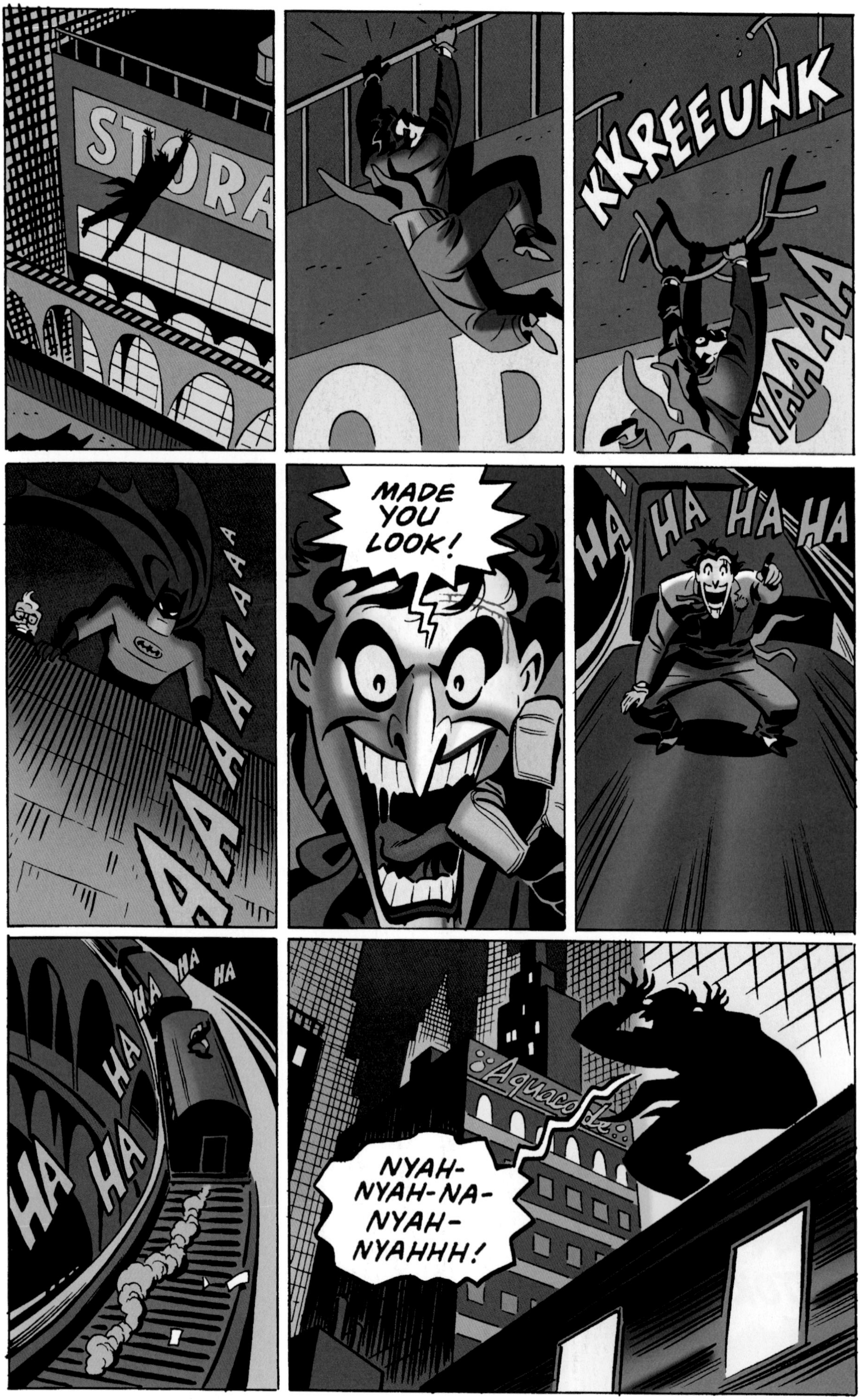
STORA
KKREEUNK
YAAAAA
AAAAAAAAA
MADE YOU LOOK!
HA HA HA HA
HA HA HA HA HA HA
NYAH-NYAH-NA-NYAH-NYAHHH!
Aquacade

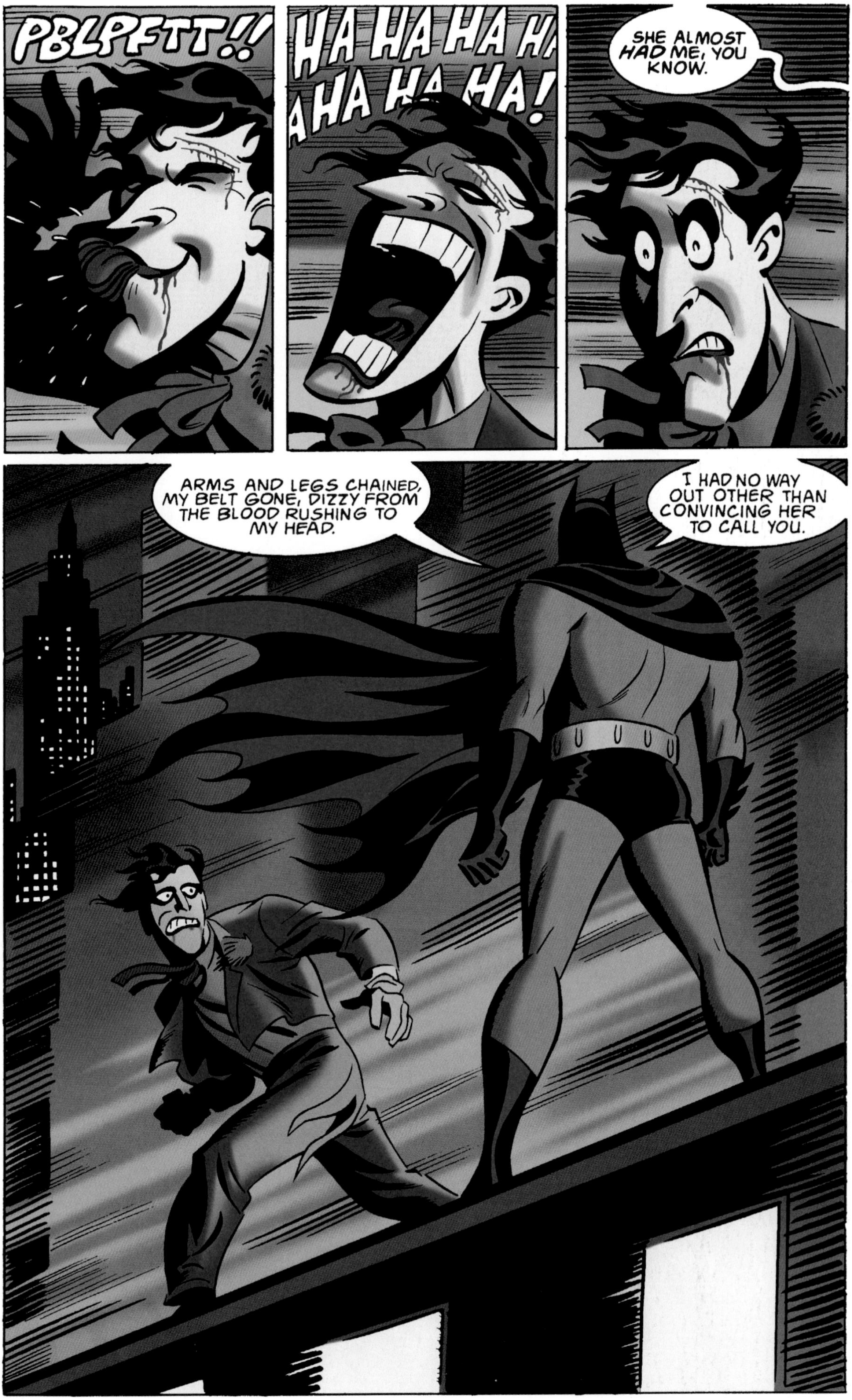
PBLPFTT!!
HA HA HA HA HA HA HA HA!
SHE ALMOST HAD ME, YOU KNOW.
ARMS AND LEGS CHAINED, MY BELT GONE, DIZZY FROM THE BLOOD RUSHING TO MY HEAD.
I HAD NO WAY OUT OTHER THAN CONVINCING HER TO CALL YOU.

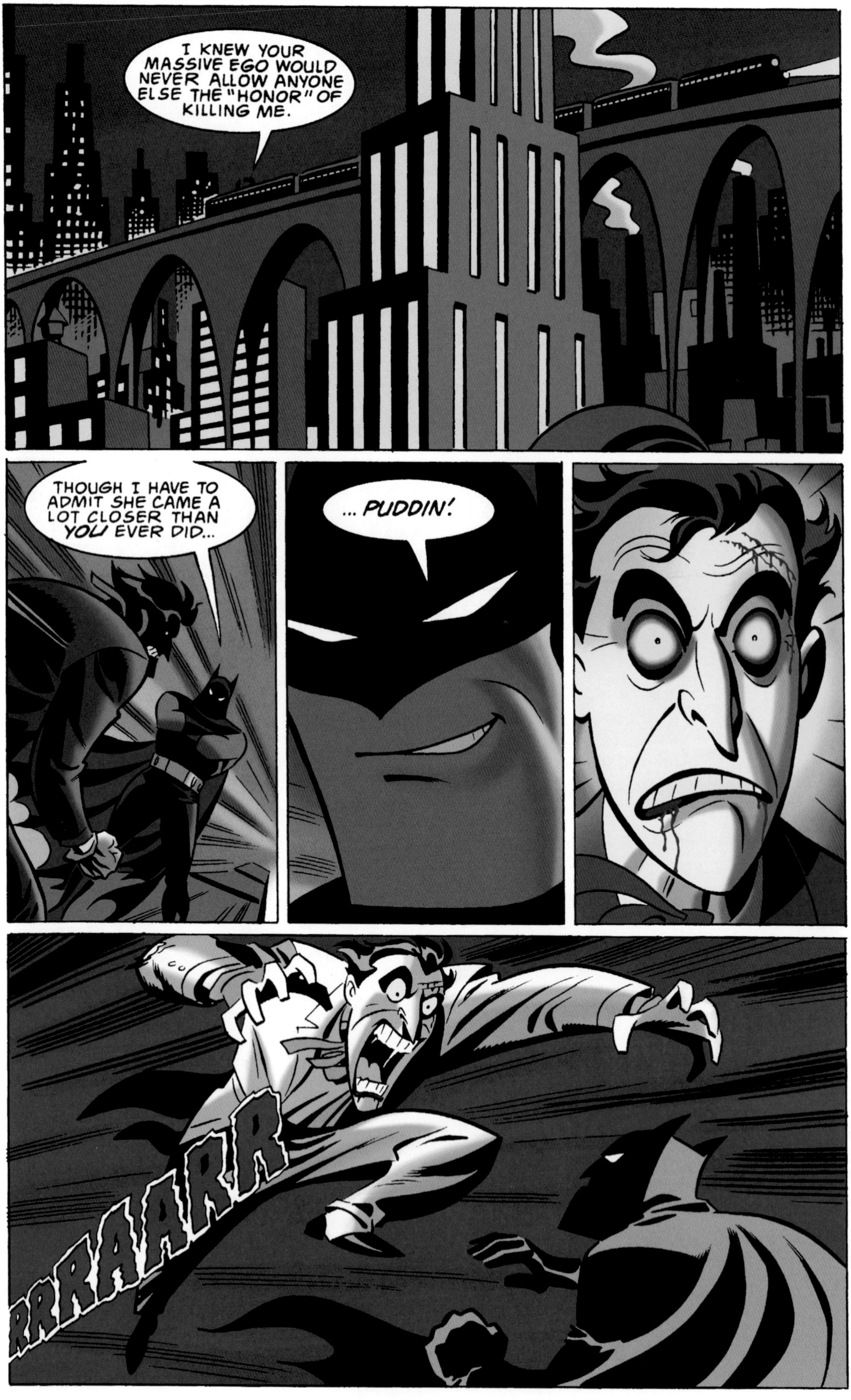
I KNEW YOUR MASSIVE EGO WOULD NEVER ALLOW ANYONE ELSE THE "HONOR" OF KILLING ME.
THOUGH I HAVE TO ADMIT SHE CAME A LOT CLOSER THAN YOU EVER DID...
...PUDDIN'!
RRRAAARR

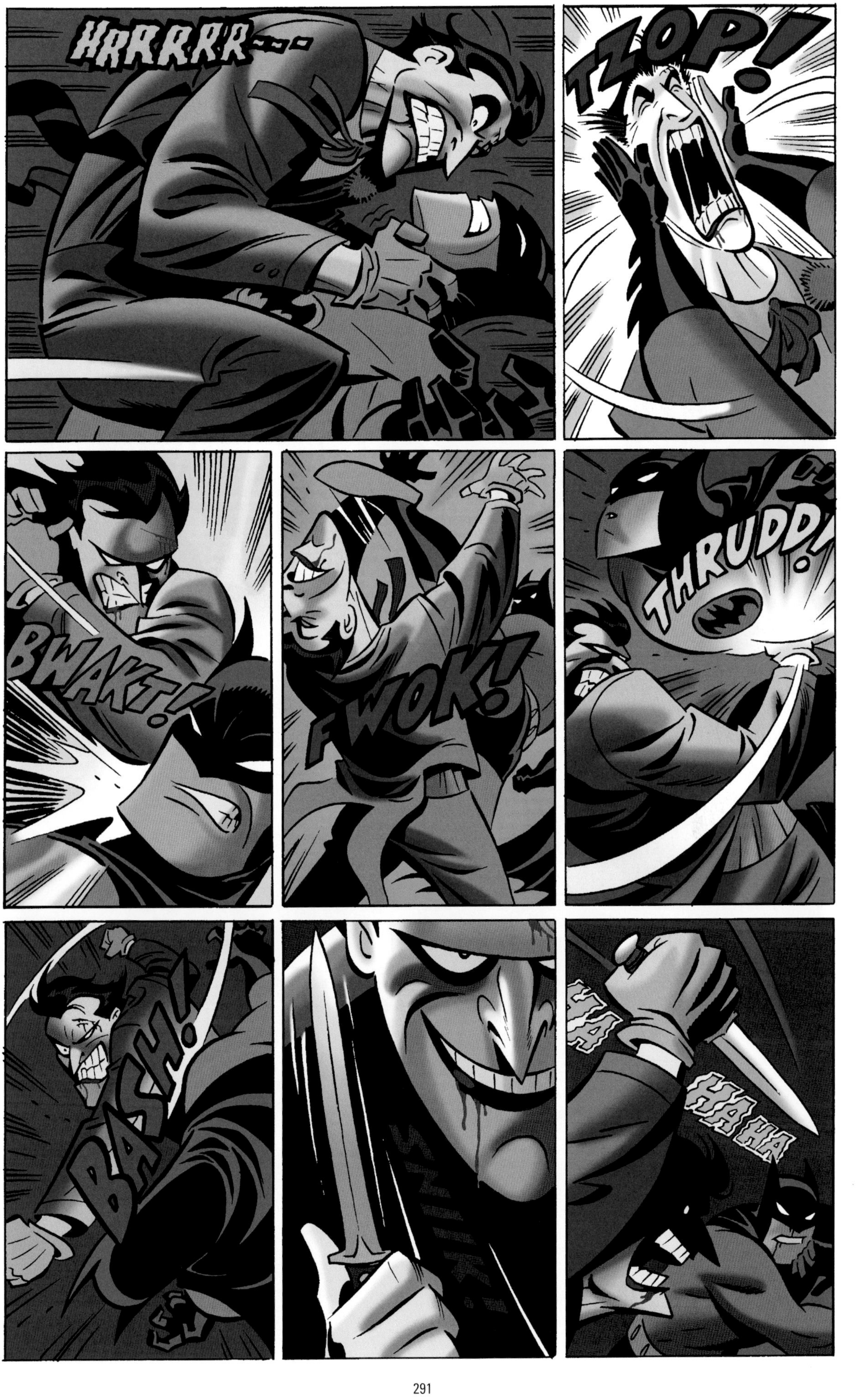

HRRRRR---
TZOP!
BWAKT!
FWOK!
THRUDD!
BASH!
HA
HA HA
HA

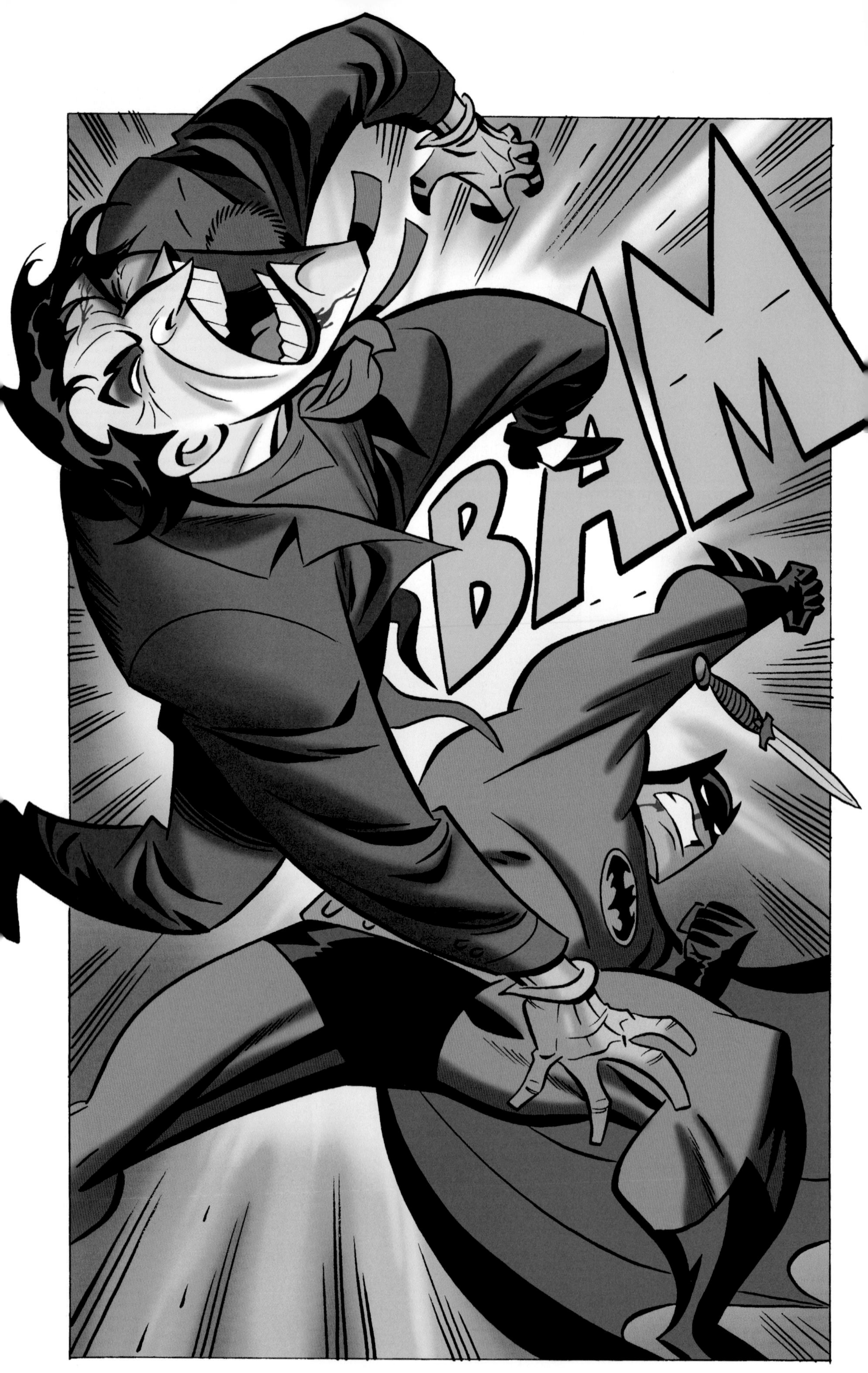
BAM

OH, NO...

NOTT.T

AGAINN

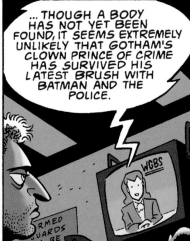

... THOUGH A BODY HAS NOT YET BEEN FOUND, IT SEEMS EXTREMELY UNLIKELY THAT GOTHAM'S CLOWN PRINCE OF CRIME HAS SURVIVED HIS LATEST BRUSH WITH BATMAN AND THE POLICE.

WGBS

RMED GUARDS WILL BE PRESENT AT ALL TIMES

ALL REM SEAT

RECREATION THERAPY

STILL, HE *HAS* BEEN NOTORIOUS FOR RESURFACING WHEN LEAST EXPECTED...

NEVER AGAIN.

NO MORE OBSESSION.

NO MORE CRAZINESS.

NO MORE JOKER.

I FINALLY SEE THAT SLIME FOR WHAT HE REALLY IS.

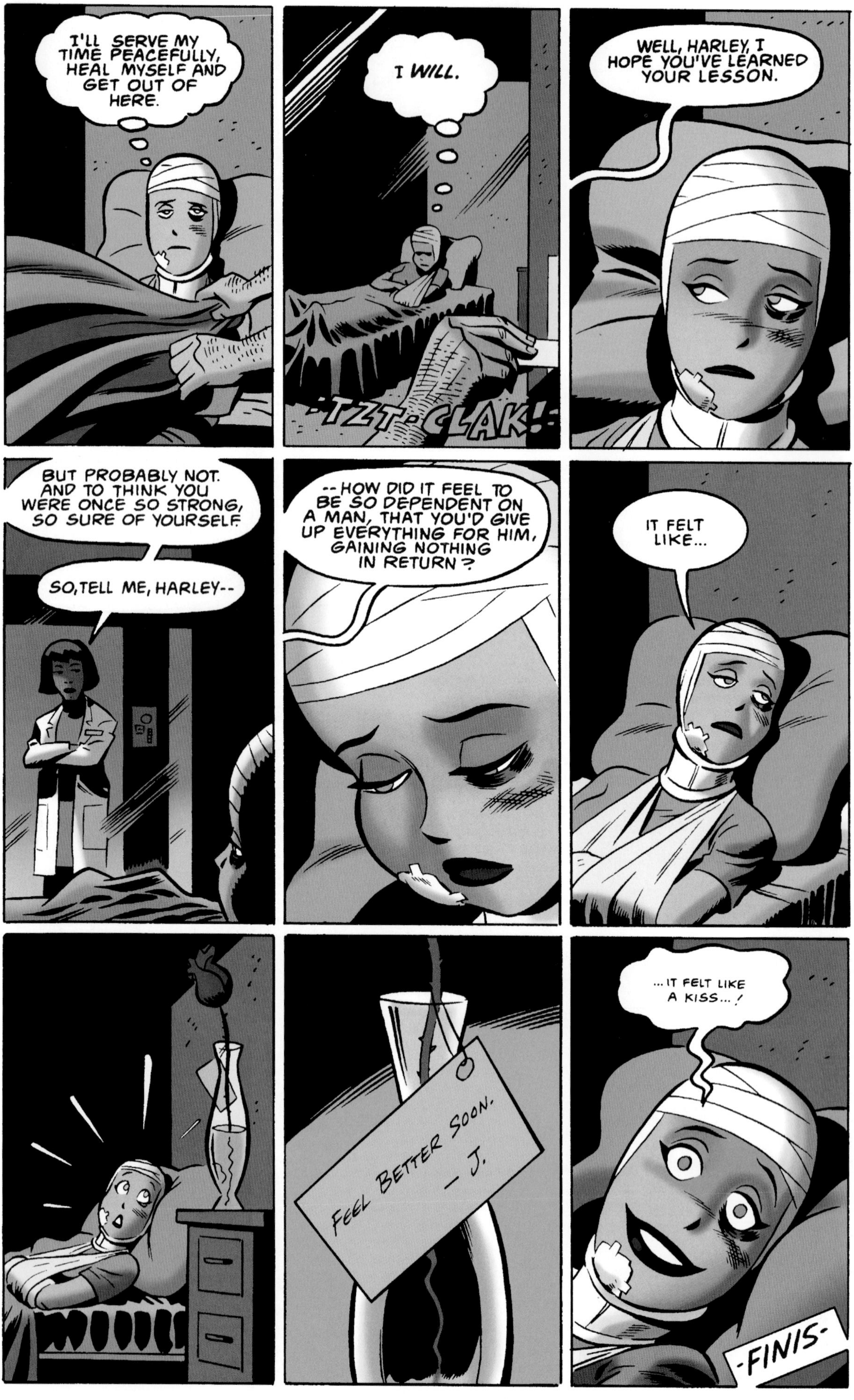
I'LL SERVE MY TIME PEACEFULLY, HEAL MYSELF AND GET OUT OF HERE.
I WILL.
-TZT-CLAK!-
WELL, HARLEY, I HOPE YOU'VE LEARNED YOUR LESSON.
BUT PROBABLY NOT. AND TO THINK YOU WERE ONCE SO STRONG, SO SURE OF YOURSELF.
SO, TELL ME, HARLEY--
--HOW DID IT FEEL TO BE SO DEPENDENT ON A MAN, THAT YOU'D GIVE UP EVERYTHING FOR HIM, GAINING NOTHING IN RETURN?
IT FELT LIKE...
FEEL BETTER SOON. — J.
...IT FELT LIKE A KISS...!
-FINIS-

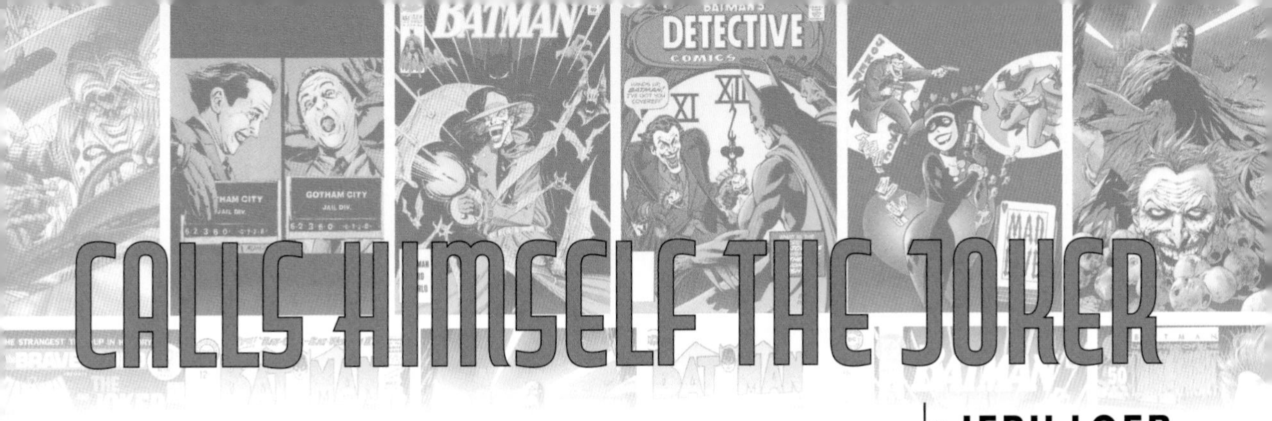
BATMAN
DETECTIVE
COMICS
GOTHAM CITY

CALLS HIMSELF THE JOKER

by **JEPH LOEB**

As for me—well, there's a real panic going on. Somebody's threatened to poison the Gotham reservoir.

Calls himself the Joker.

I've got a friend coming who might be able to help.

Should be here any minute.

Jim Gordon
Batman: Year One

In case anyone ever asks you, when Frank Miller closed out his and David Mazzucchelli's immortal *Batman: Year One* with those words, *that* is where the Joker's story begins.

The "friend" Jim Gordon refers to is, of course, Batman, who has newly arrived on the crime-ridden streets of Gotham City.

One could question the sanity of a man who dresses up like a bat to instill fear in the hearts of those who break the law, because as he insists: "*Criminals are a superstitious, cowardly lot.*"

But we excuse Batman's ongoing quest because at his core it is a personal and heartbreaking vendetta. Simply put, he made a promise on the graves of his parents to rid Gotham City of the evil that took their lives.

We could argue that his journey, in itself, is crazy. There's no way to "rid the city of evil" forever, is there?

Sanity is at the very heart of the character when you're dealing with the Joker. Often described as a "lunatic" or a "psychopath," he makes one wonder why he, of all the antagonists in the DC Universe, has maintained an almost *Emperor* status in the place where Lex Luthor and Darkseid also hold court.

Let's first begin with the design of the character. The playing card sketch by Jerry Robinson has such brilliance in its simplicity. By taking an innocent, almost fun image we've all seen or even touched, he turned it into something frightening.

After all, what do we do when we find the two joker cards at the start of play? Sometimes we just take them out of the game (ever wonder why?). But more often than not, we say, "Jokers are wild."

Wild. As in they can do *anything*. The ace, king, queen, jack (all the rulers of the deck) can't stop the joker playing card.

Wow. Now there's a worthy adversary for our Batman. He exists to confound our hero. The Joker wants to bring chaos to a city he knows Batman wants to bring order. They are yin to each other's yang; Cain to each other's Abel.

And chaos he does bring! The incredibly delightful tale "The Laughing Fish" by Steve Englehart and Marshall Rogers is where the Joker infects Gotham's fish supply with his grinning face and then attempts to copyright them. Rebuffed by red tape (the very backbone of order), he sets out to kill the poor chaps whose only crime is working at the "Copyright Commission."

Chaos! In Denny O'Neil and Neal Adams's impeccable story "The Joker's Five-Way Revenge!" the Joker picks off nearly all the members of his former gang, who he thinks betrayed him, and then is only lucky enough to catch Batman himself.

Chaos! I'd be remiss if I didn't mention my and Tim Sale's "The Long Halloween," where on New Year's Eve, the Joker drops lethal gas on the Gothamites who gather at Gotham Square at midnight on the odd chance he'll murder "Holiday"—a serial killer who is getting more notoriety then the Clown Prince of Crime.

Each time, Batman, thankfully, stopped the madness.

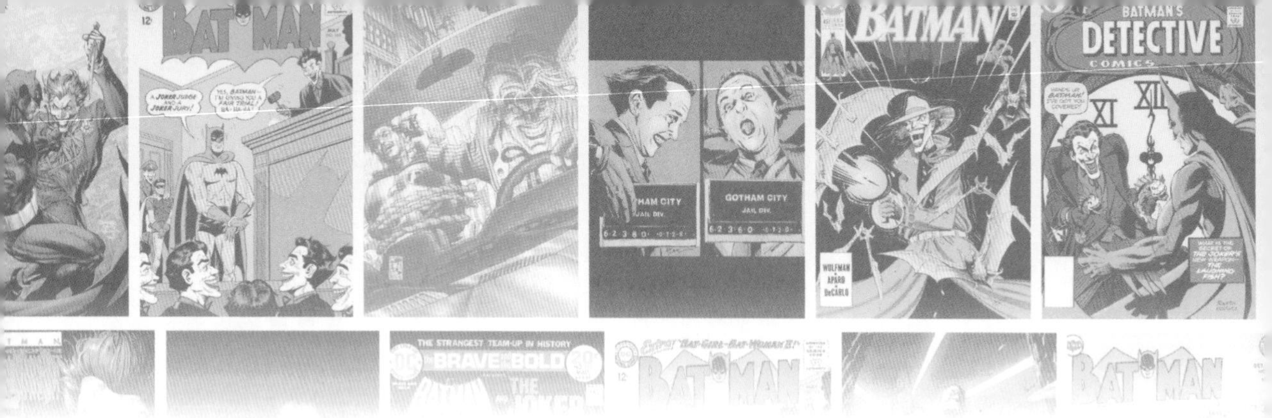
BATMAN
BATMAN
BATMAN'S
DETECTIVE
COMICS
GOTHAM CITY
THE STRANGEST TEAM-UP IN HISTORY

Did the Joker ever go too far? While there are many, many horrible acts of lunacy that the Joker has perpetrated on Gotham, there is one that chills me to my very soul.

In Alan Moore and Brian Bolland's brilliantly haunting "The Killing Joke," the Joker steps way over the line. Unlike his usual disturbed chicanery, this time he makes it personal. Shooting Barbara Gordon in cold blood, he makes it impossibly worse by forcing her father, Jim Gordon, to witness the crime over and over on film.

If ever there were a time when the Joker deserved to die, this was surely it. But therein lies the challenge for the reader and why this story is an unmatched classic. The Joker and Batman actually come to a better understanding about each other, and, perhaps, that's even more unnerving.

I wanted to address this very issue for years. When Jim Lee and I set off to tell "Hush," one of the stories focused on Batman having had enough of the Joker's cruelty. Batman is going to end it, right then and there (as Alan Moore prophetically wrote in "The Killing Joke"). Only Jim Gordon—the very same man who once said, *"I've got a friend who might be able to help"*—can step in and stop Batman from doing something he will regret forever.

What Jim Gordon knew and what we all know is that once order becomes chaos, there is no turning back. And while the Joker takes a life with no more than a thought, *Batman doesn't kill.*

So the quest to rid the city of the evil that took his parents' lives continues. By the way, their murderer wasn't the Joker, no matter what you may have heard…

Speaking of hearing, I will leave you with a final thought. One of the delightful things about comic books is that the element of sound is something we get to add for ourselves. Our imagination revs up the Batmobile, and we each have our own version of Bruce's versus Batman's voice.

But there is one thing we can all agree on. The Joker's laugh somehow keeps us awake at night.

And that may be his greatest legacy of all.

Ha-Ha-He-He-HA-HA-HE-Ha-Ha-He-He-HA-HA-HE!

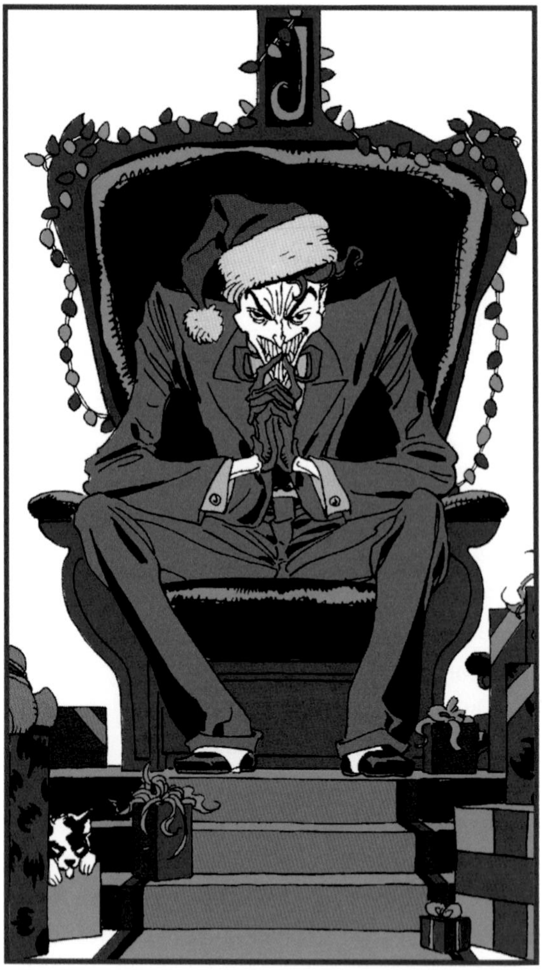

***Jeph Loeb** is an Emmy Award-nominated and Peabody Award-winning writer and producer living in Los Angeles. His many credits in television include* Smallville, Lost, Daredevil, *and* Jessica Jones, *and* Teen Wolf *and* Commando *in film. In comics he created* Batman: Hush *with Jim Lee, and with Tim Sale* Batman: The Long Halloween *and* Superman for All Seasons, *as well as* Daredevil: Yellow, Spider-Man: Blue, Hulk: Gray, *and* Captain America: White *for Marvel.*

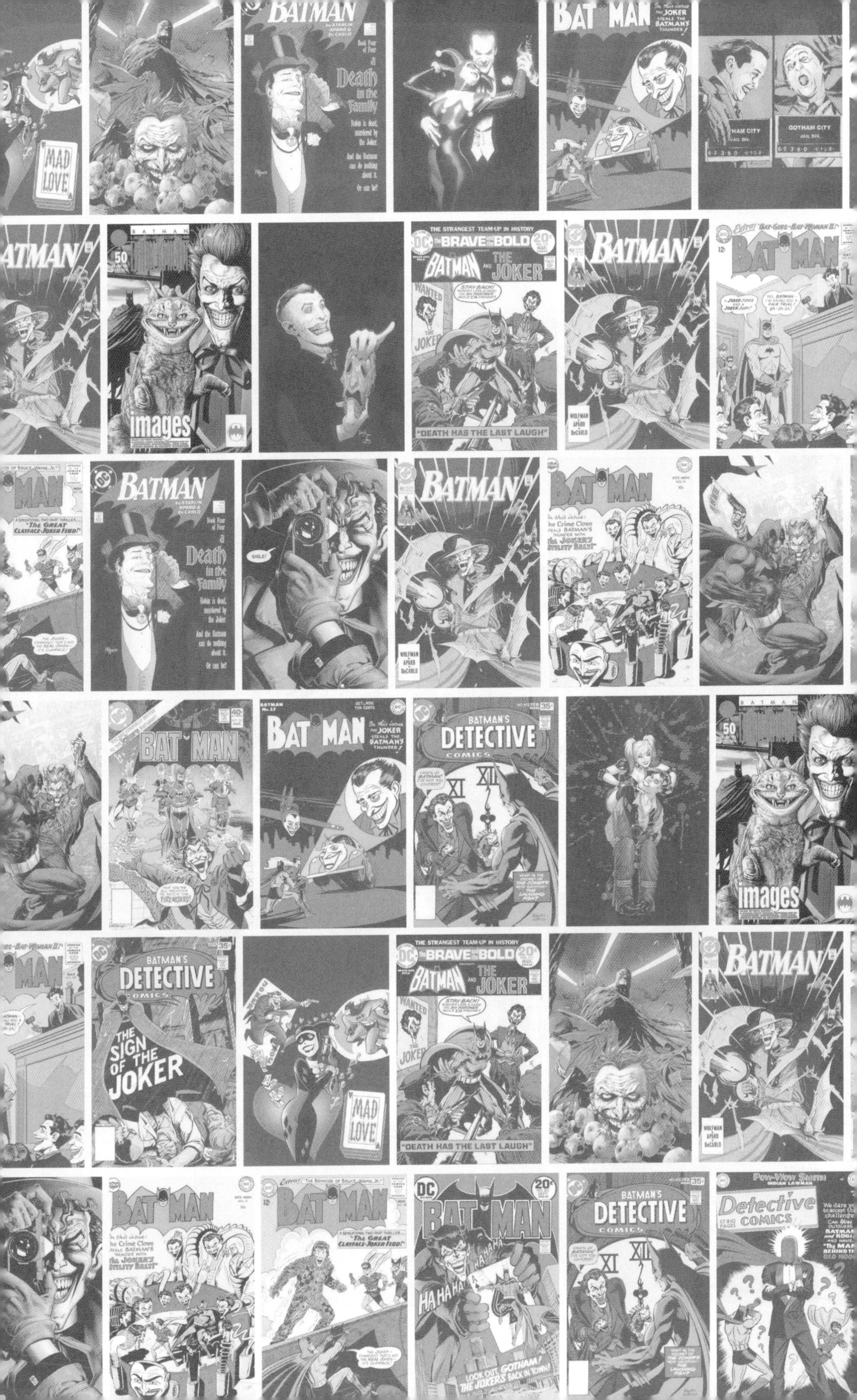
MAD LOVE
BATMAN
by STARLIN, APARO & DeCARLO
Book Four of Four
a Death in the Family
Robin is dead, murdered by the Joker.
And the Batman can do nothing about it.
Or can he?
BATMAN
In this issue: The JOKER steals the BATMAN'S thunder!
GOTHAM CITY
JAIL DIV.
BATMAN
BATMAN
50
images
THE STRANGEST TEAM-UP IN HISTORY
THE BRAVE and the BOLD
BATMAN AND THE JOKER
STAY BACK!
WANTED
THE JOKER
"DEATH HAS THE LAST LAUGH"
BATMAN
WOLFMAN
APARO
DeCARLO
BATMAN
"The Great Clayface-Joker Feud!"
BATMAN
by STARLIN, APARO & DeCARLO
Book Four of Four
a Death in the Family
Robin is dead, murdered by the Joker.
And the Batman can do nothing about it.
Or can he?
SMILE!
BATMAN
WOLFMAN
APARO
DeCARLO
BATMAN
In this issue: The Crime Clown steals BATMAN'S thunder with The JOKER'S Utility Belt!
BATMAN
FIREWORKS!
BATMAN
In this issue: The JOKER steals the BATMAN'S thunder!
BATMAN'S DETECTIVE COMICS
XI
XII
BATMAN
images
BATMAN'S DETECTIVE COMICS
THE SIGN OF THE JOKER
MAD LOVE
THE STRANGEST TEAM-UP IN HISTORY
THE BRAVE and the BOLD
BATMAN AND THE JOKER
WANTED
THE JOKER
"DEATH HAS THE LAST LAUGH"
BATMAN
WOLFMAN
APARO
DeCARLO
BATMAN
In this issue: The Crime Clown steals BATMAN'S thunder with The JOKER'S Utility Belt!
Extra! "The Boyhood of Bruce Wayne, Jr.!"
BATMAN
A SENSATIONAL TWO-PART THRILLER...
"The Great Clayface-Joker Feud!"
BATMAN
HA HA HA
LOOK OUT, GOTHAM! THE JOKER'S BACK IN TOWN!
BATMAN'S DETECTIVE COMICS
XI
XII
Pow-Wow Smith INDIAN LAWMAN
Detective COMICS

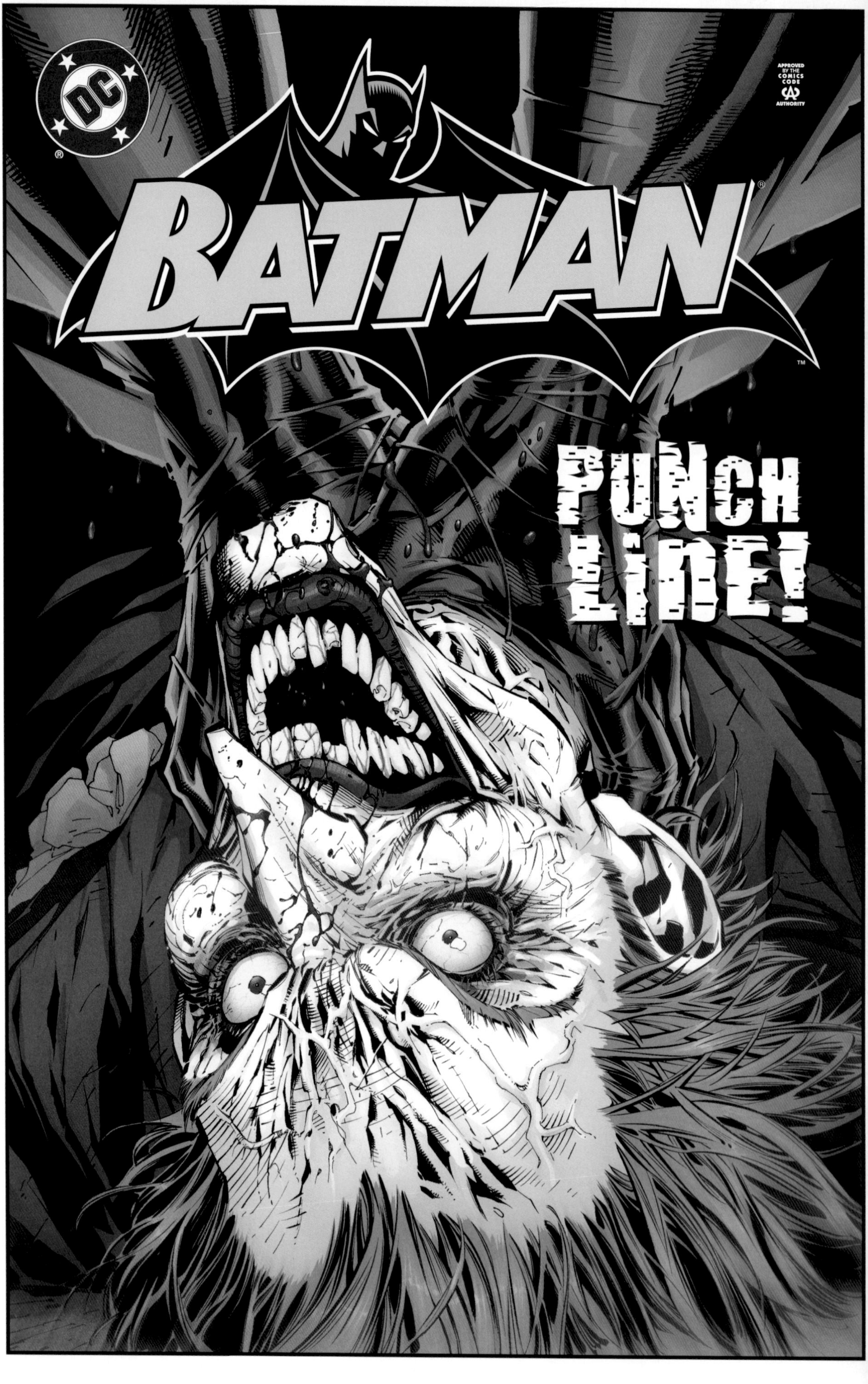
DC
APPROVED BY THE COMICS CODE AUTHORITY
BATMAN
PUNCH LINE!

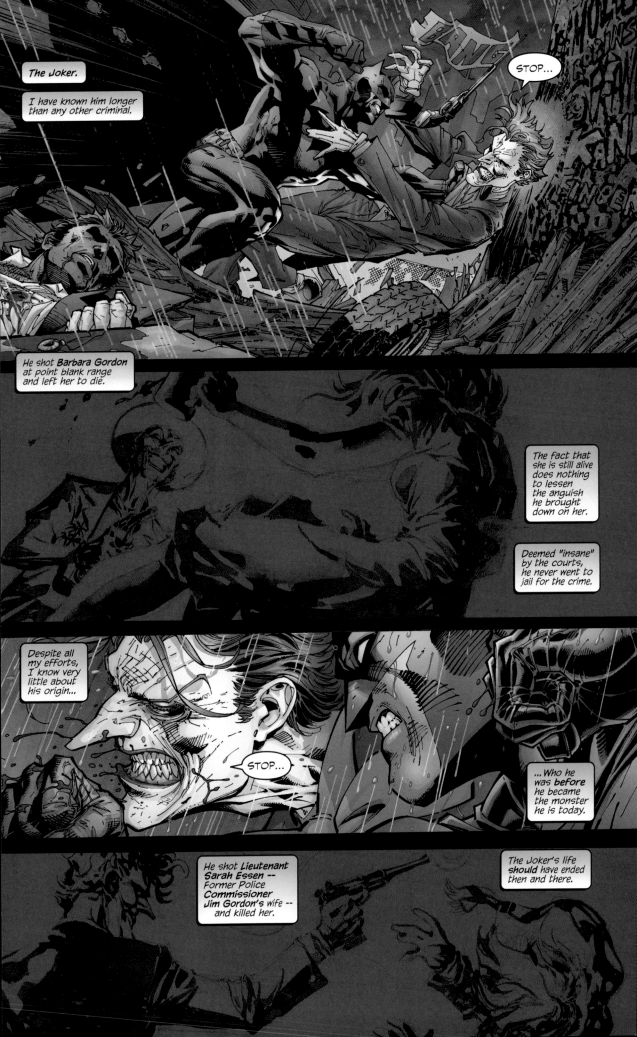

The Joker.

I have known him longer than any other criminal.

STOP...

He shot *Barbara Gordon* at point blank range and left her to die.

The fact that she is still alive does nothing to lessen the anguish he brought down on her.

Deemed "insane" by the courts, he never went to jail for the crime.

Despite all my efforts, I know very little about his origin...

STOP...

...Who he was *before* he became the monster he is today.

He shot *Lieutenant Sarah Essen --* Former Police *Commissioner Jim Gordon's* wife -- and killed her.

The Joker's life *should* have ended then and there.

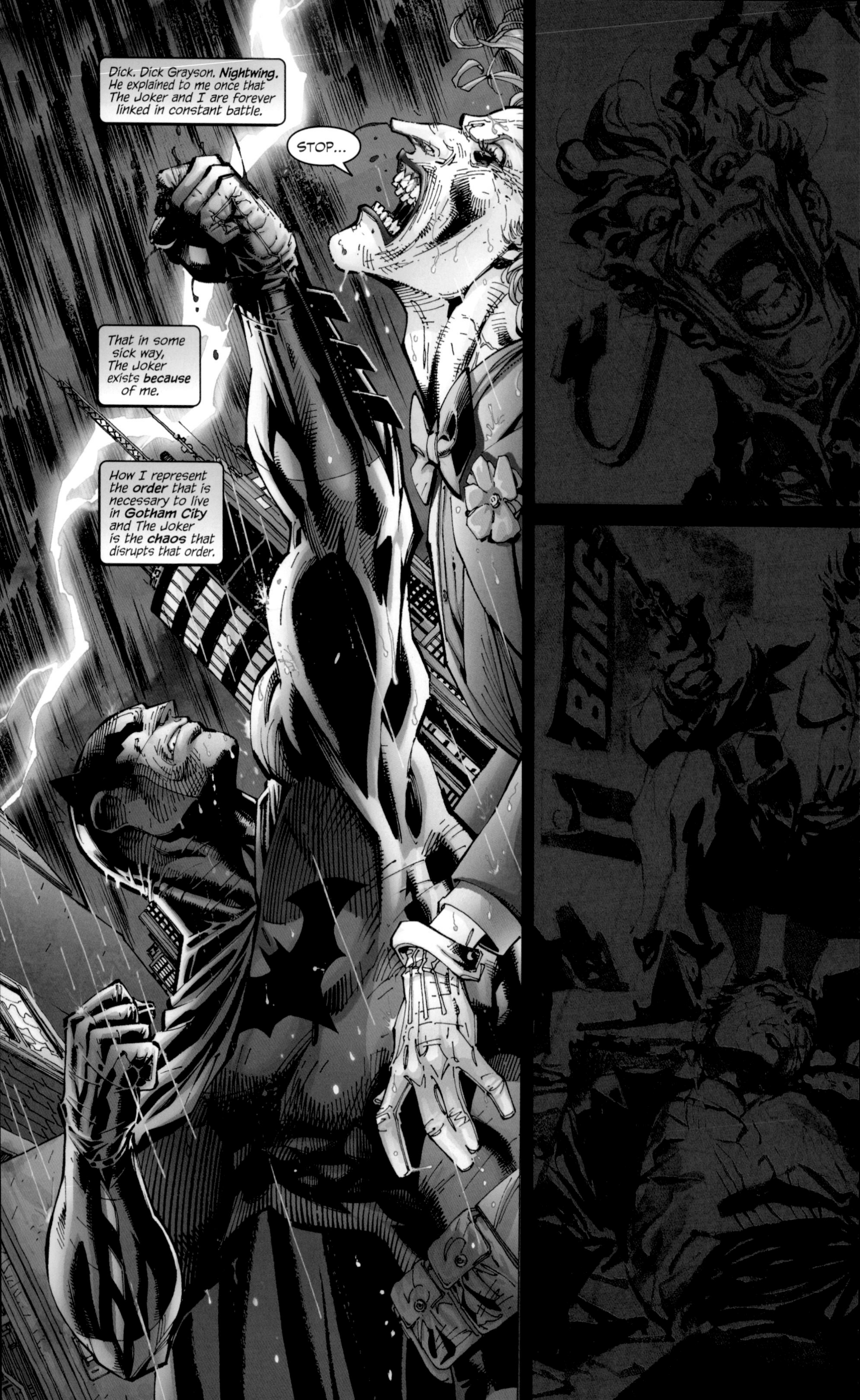

Dick. Dick Grayson. **Nightwing.** He explained to me once that The Joker and I are forever linked in constant battle.
STOP...
That in some sick way, The Joker exists **because** of me.
How I represent the **order** that is necessary to live in **Gotham City** and The Joker is the **chaos** that disrupts that order.
BANG

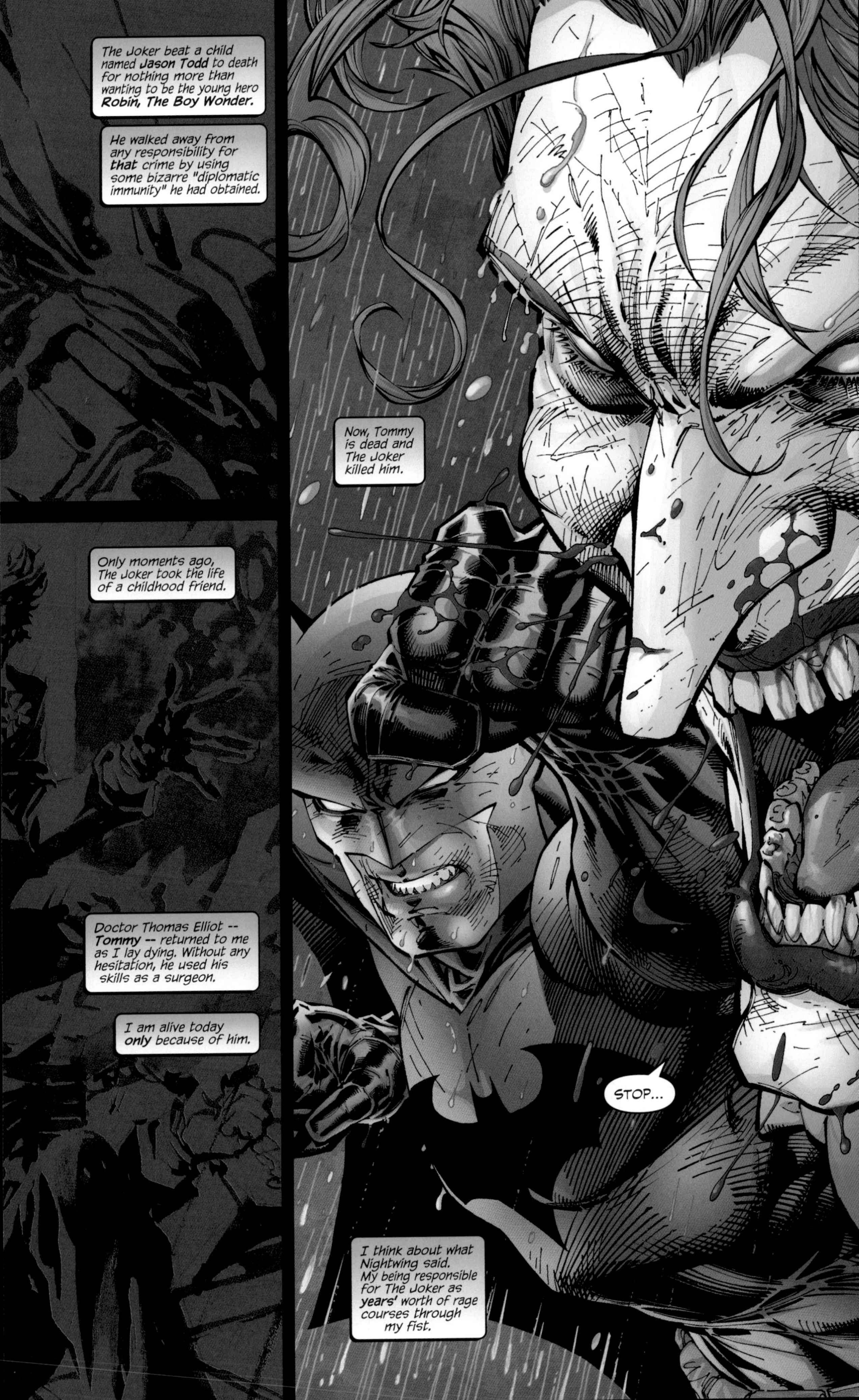
The Joker beat a child named Jason Todd to death for nothing more than wanting to be the young hero Robin, The Boy Wonder.
He walked away from any responsibility for that crime by using some bizarre "diplomatic immunity" he had obtained.
Now, Tommy is dead and The Joker killed him.
Only moments ago, The Joker took the life of a childhood friend.
Doctor Thomas Elliot -- Tommy -- returned to me as I lay dying. Without any hesitation, he used his skills as a surgeon.
I am alive today only because of him.
STOP...
I think about what Nightwing said. My being responsible for The Joker as years' worth of rage courses through my fist.

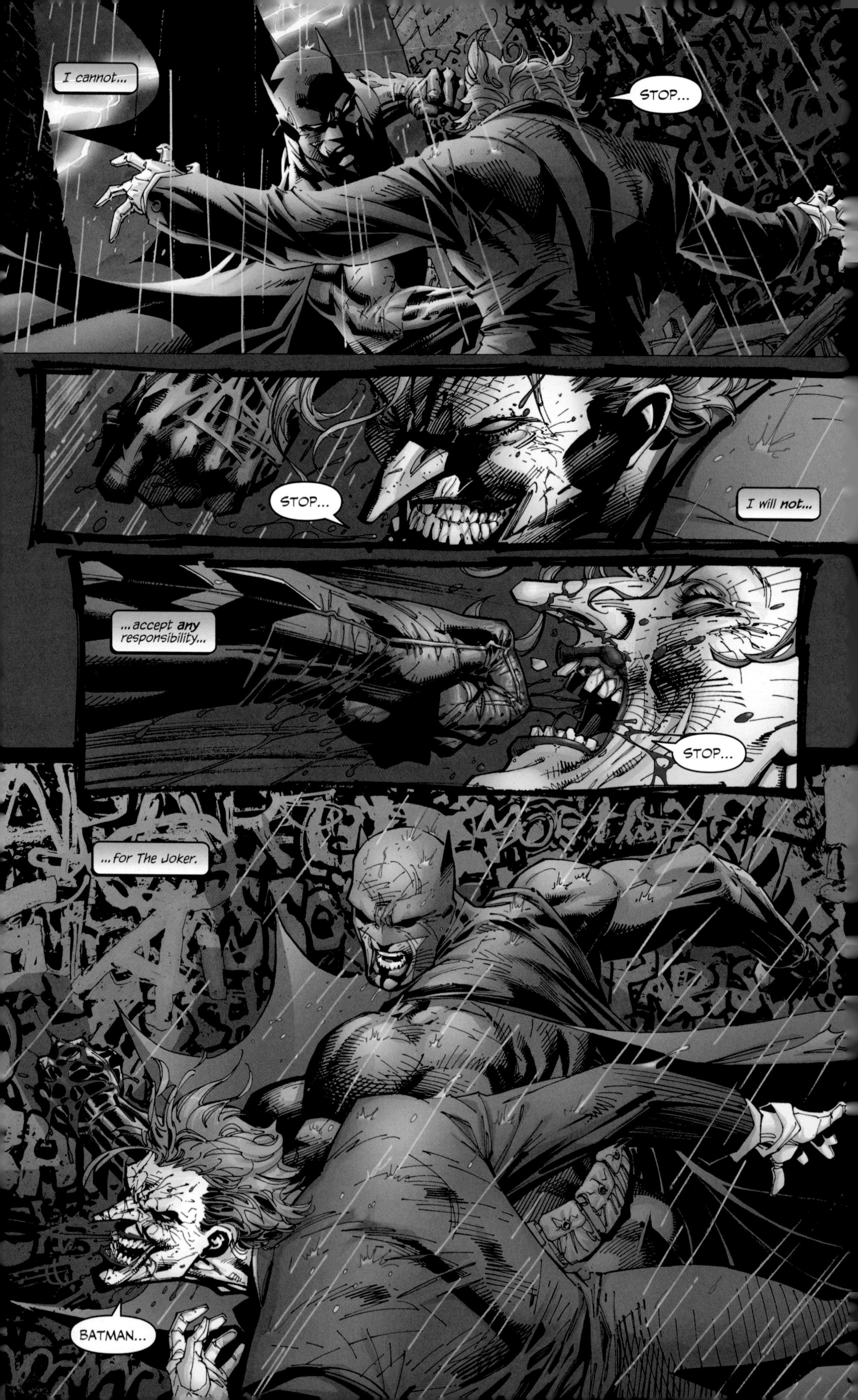
I cannot...
STOP...
STOP...
I will not...
...accept any responsibility...
STOP...
...for The Joker.
BATMAN...

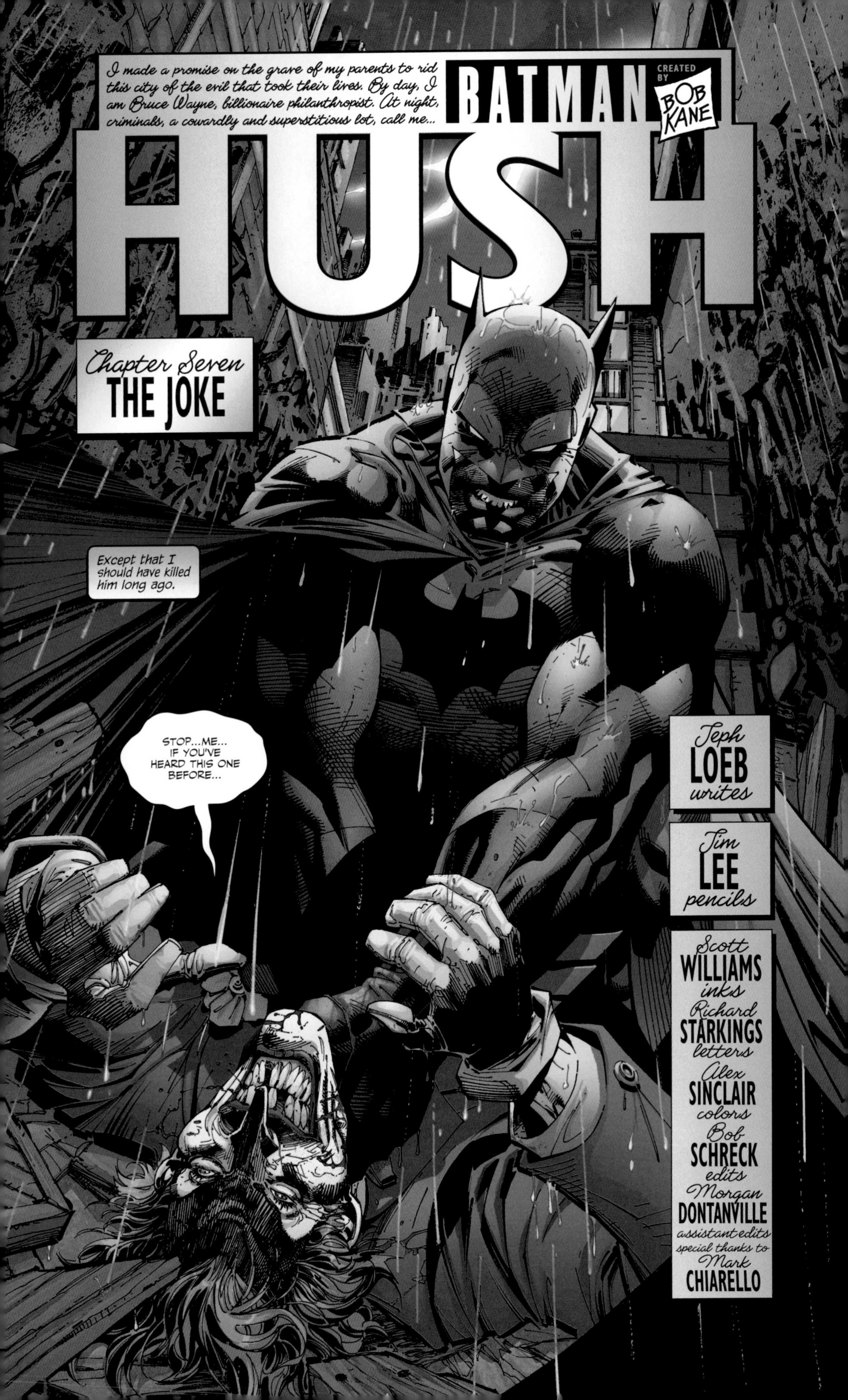
I made a promise on the grave of my parents to rid this city of the evil that took their lives. By day, I am Bruce Wayne, billionaire philanthropist. At night, criminals, a cowardly and superstitious lot, call me...
BATMAN
CREATED BY BOB KANE
HUSH
Chapter Seven
THE JOKE
Except that I should have killed him long ago.
STOP...ME... IF YOU'VE HEARD THIS ONE BEFORE...
Jeph LOEB writes
Jim LEE pencils
Scott WILLIAMS inks
Richard STARKINGS letters
Alex SINCLAIR colors
Bob SCHRECK edits
Morgan DONTANVILLE assistant edits
special thanks to Mark CHIARELLO

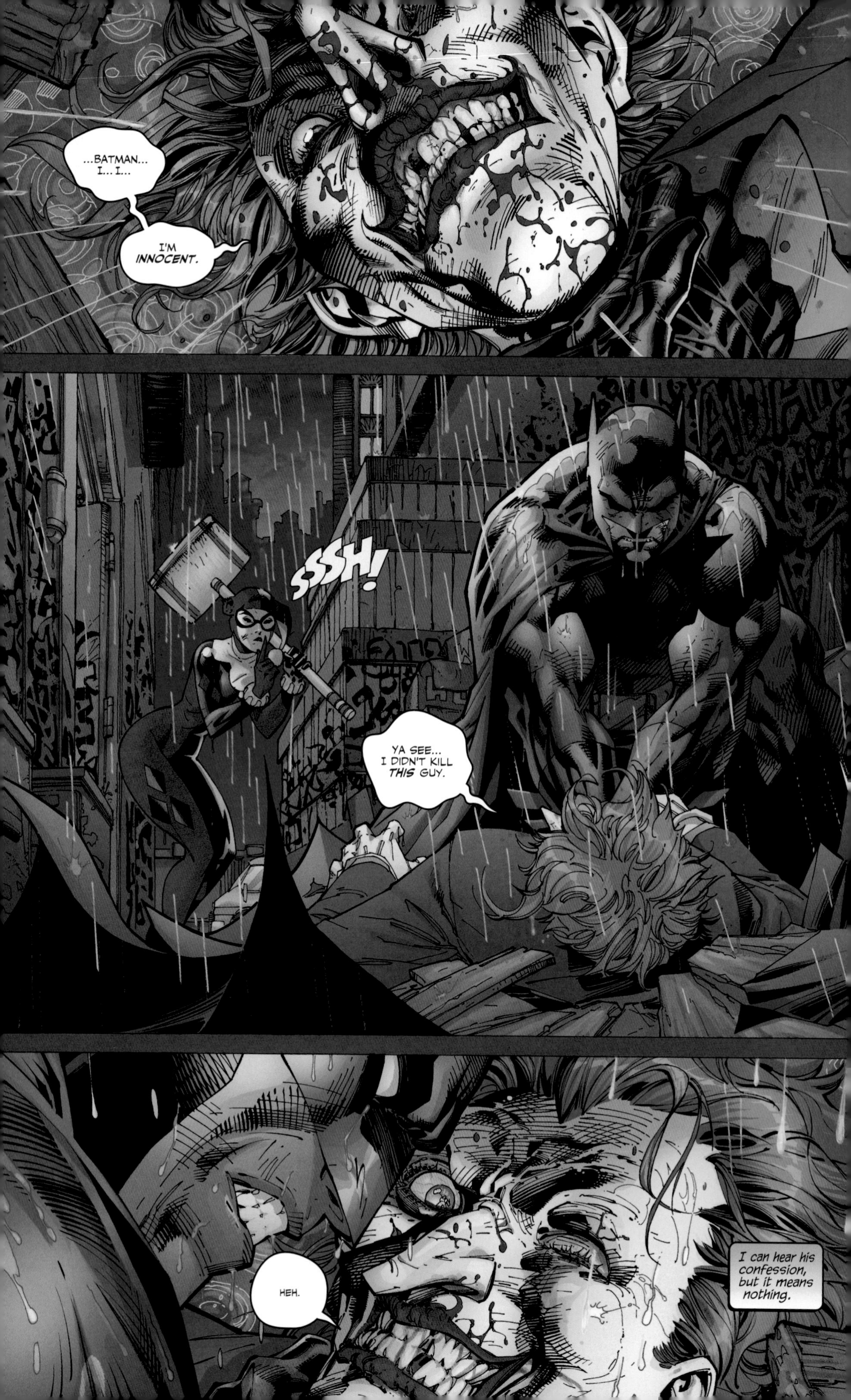
...BATMAN... I... I...
I'M INNOCENT.
SSSH!
YA SEE... I DIDN'T KILL THIS GUY.
HEH.
I can hear his confession, but it means nothing.

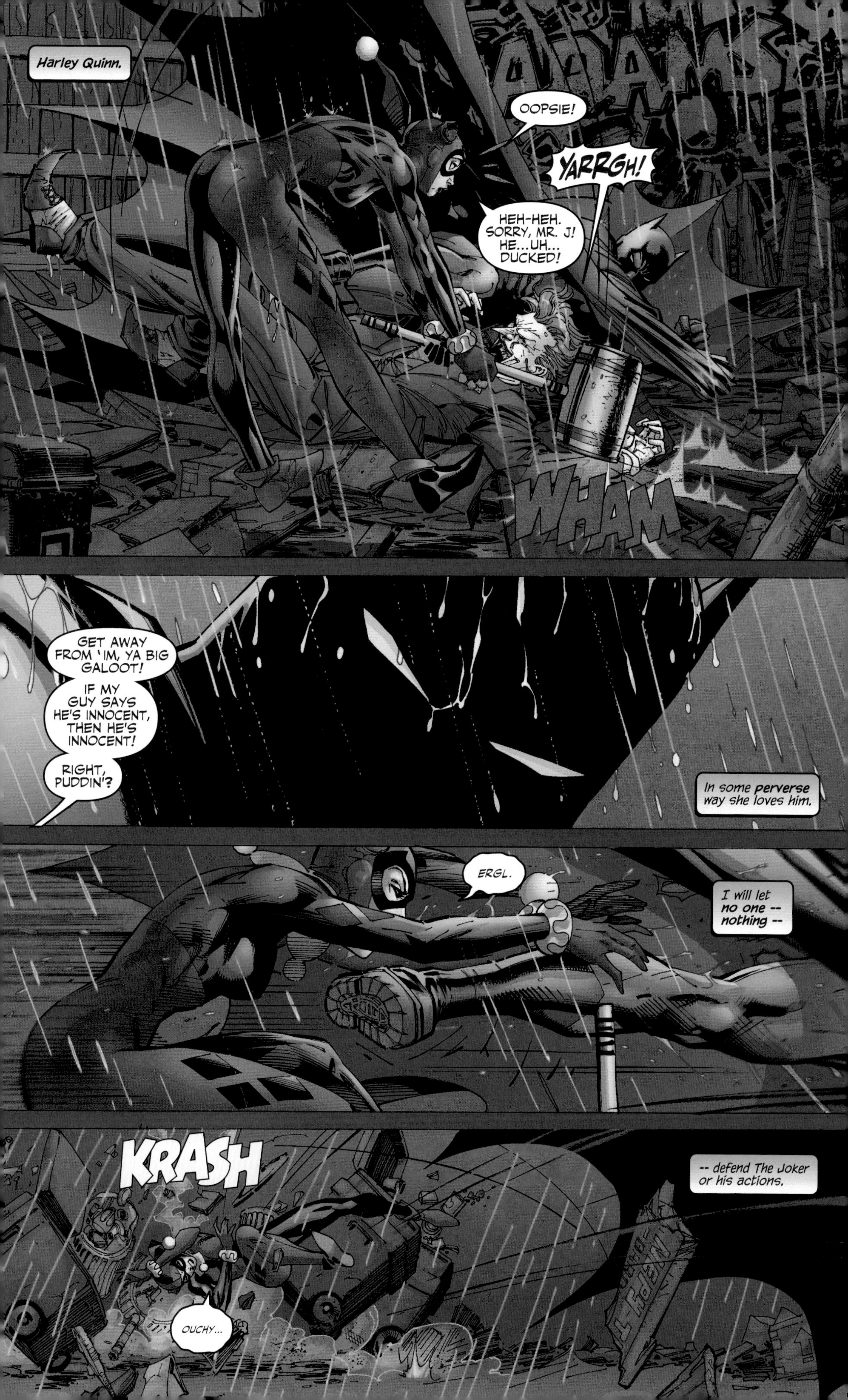
Harley Quinn.
OOPSIE!
YARRGH!
HEH-HEH. SORRY, MR. J! HE...UH... DUCKED!
WHAM
GET AWAY FROM 'IM, YA BIG GALOOT!
IF MY GUY SAYS HE'S INNOCENT, THEN HE'S INNOCENT!
RIGHT, PUDDIN'?
In some perverse way she loves him.
ERGL.
I will let no one -- nothing --
KRASH
-- defend The Joker or his actions.
OUCHY...

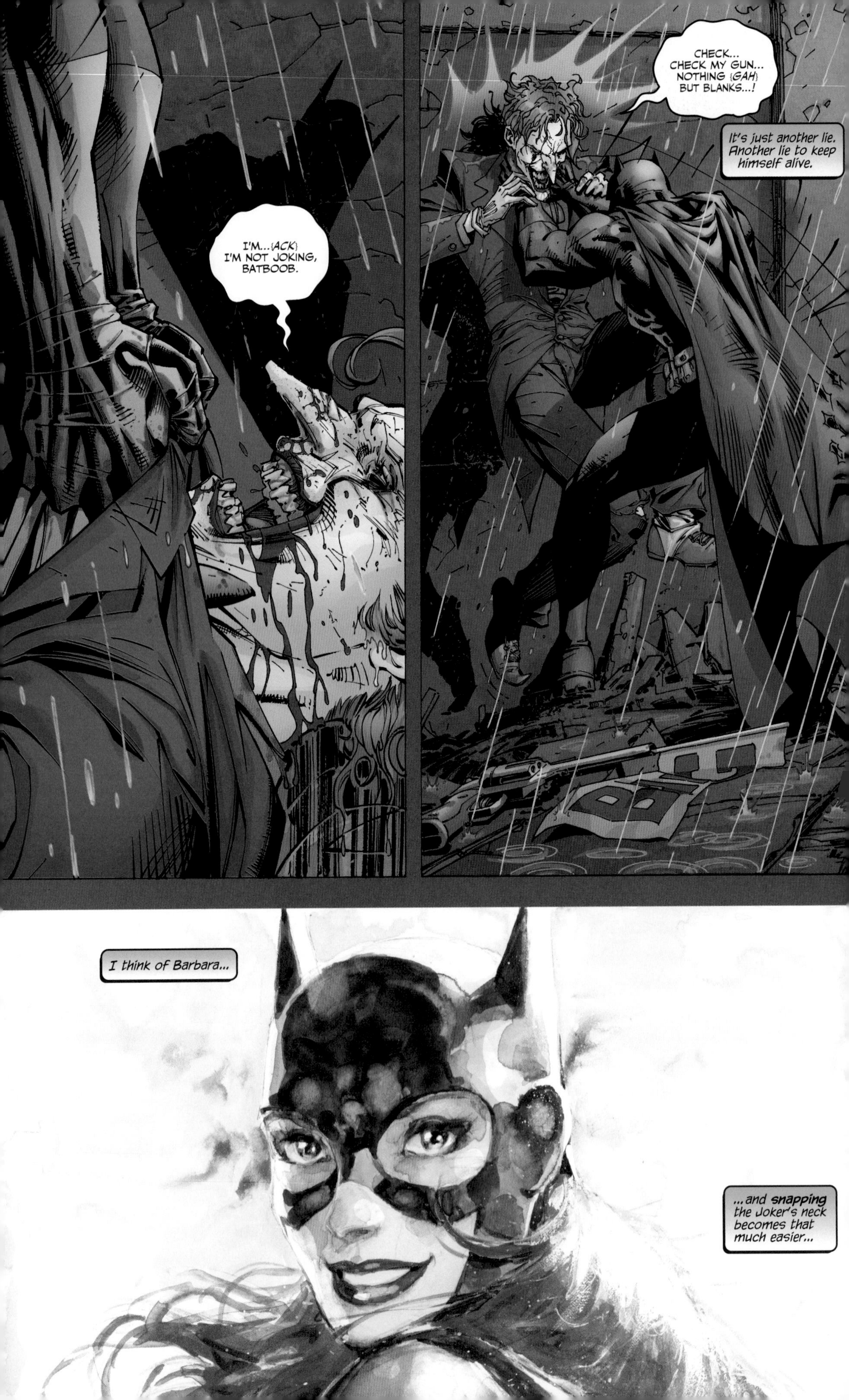
I'M...{ACK} I'M NOT JOKING, BATBOOB.
CHECK... CHECK MY GUN... NOTHING {GAH} BUT BLANKS...!
It's just another lie. Another lie to keep himself alive.
I think of Barbara...
...and snapping the Joker's neck becomes that much easier...

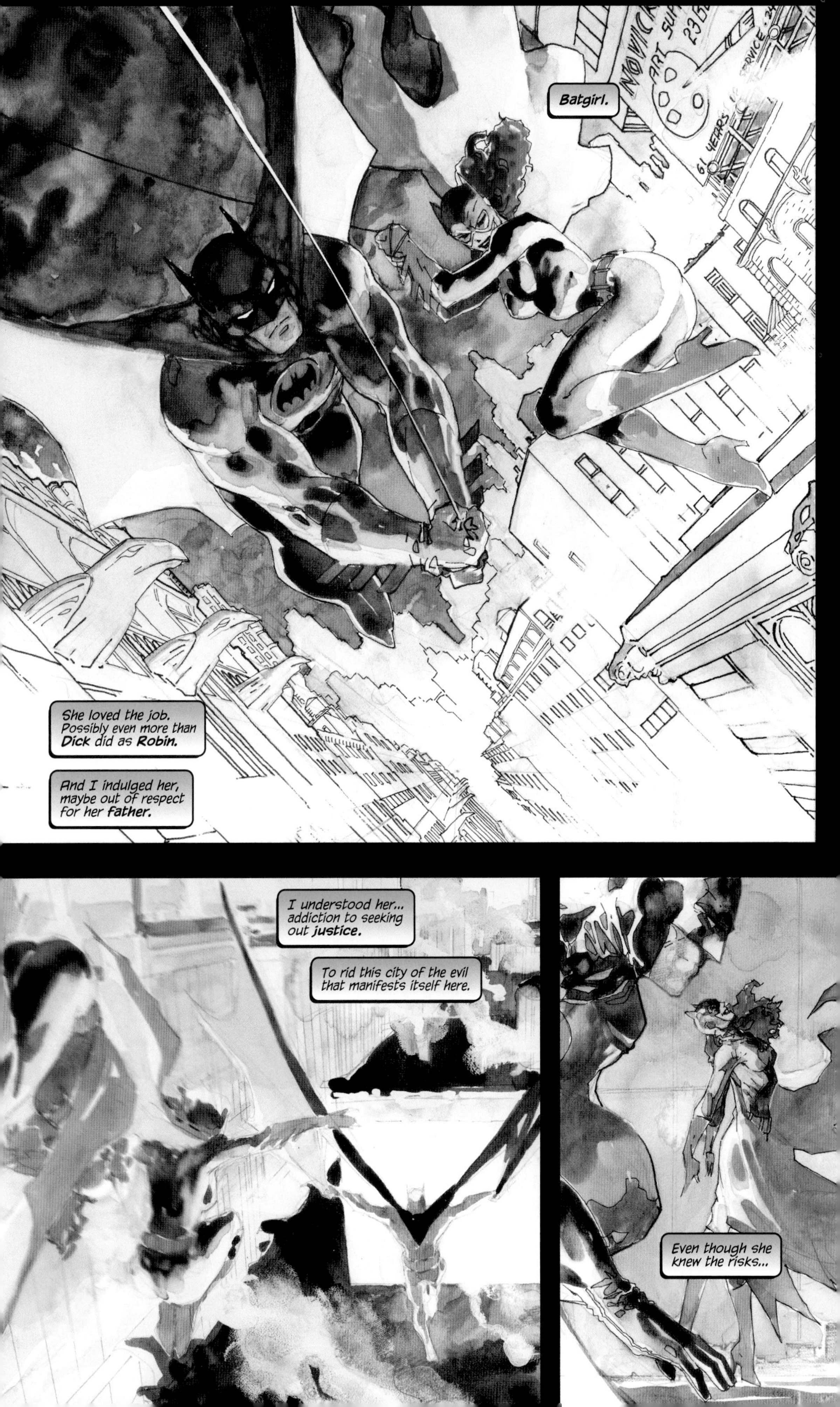
Batgirl.
She loved the job. Possibly even more than Dick did as Robin.
And I indulged her, maybe out of respect for her father.
I understood her... addiction to seeking out justice.
To rid this city of the evil that manifests itself here.
Even though she knew the risks...

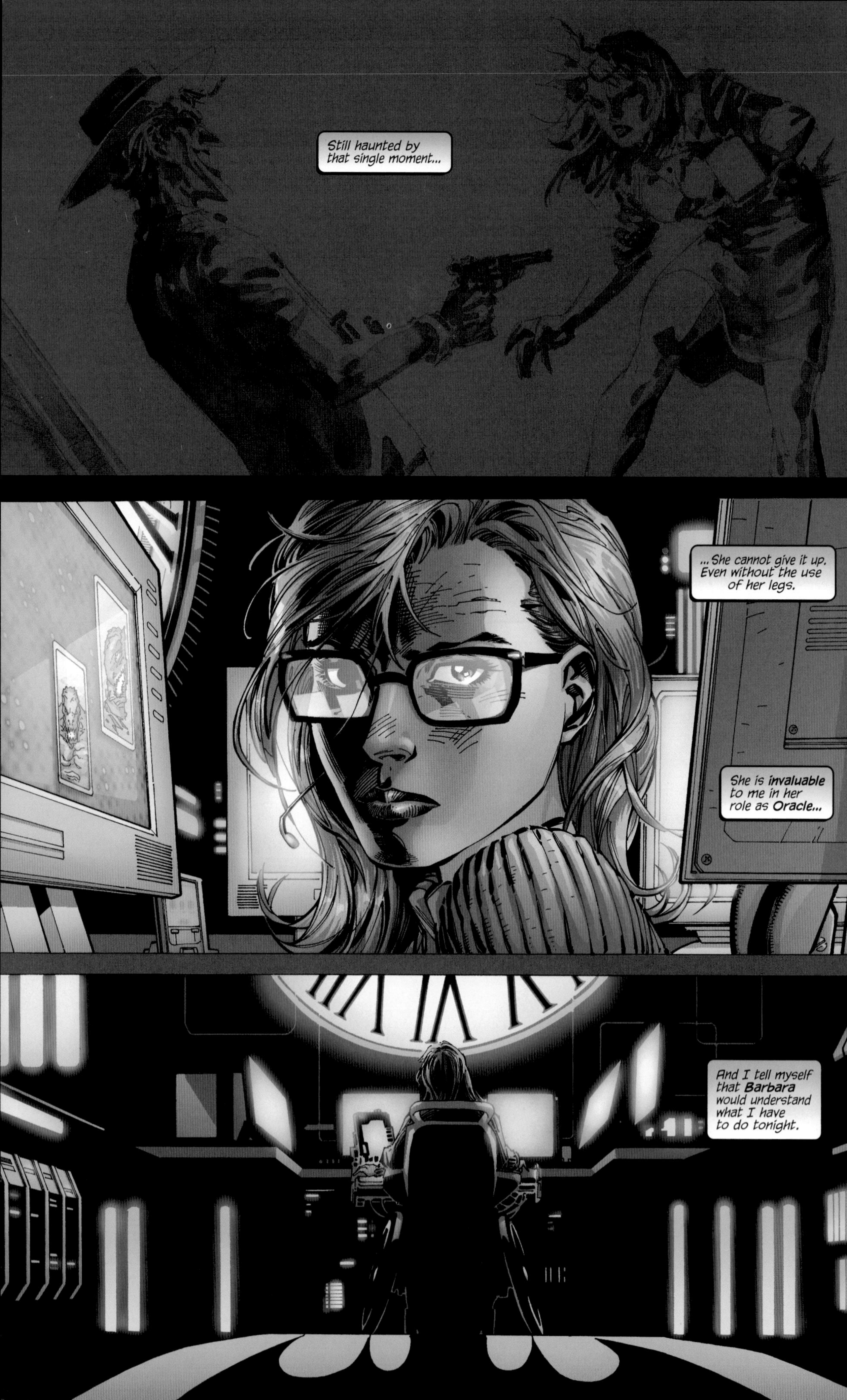
Still haunted by that single moment...
...She cannot give it up. Even without the use of her legs.
She is **invaluable** to me in her role as **Oracle...**
And I tell myself that **Barbara** would understand what I have to do tonight.

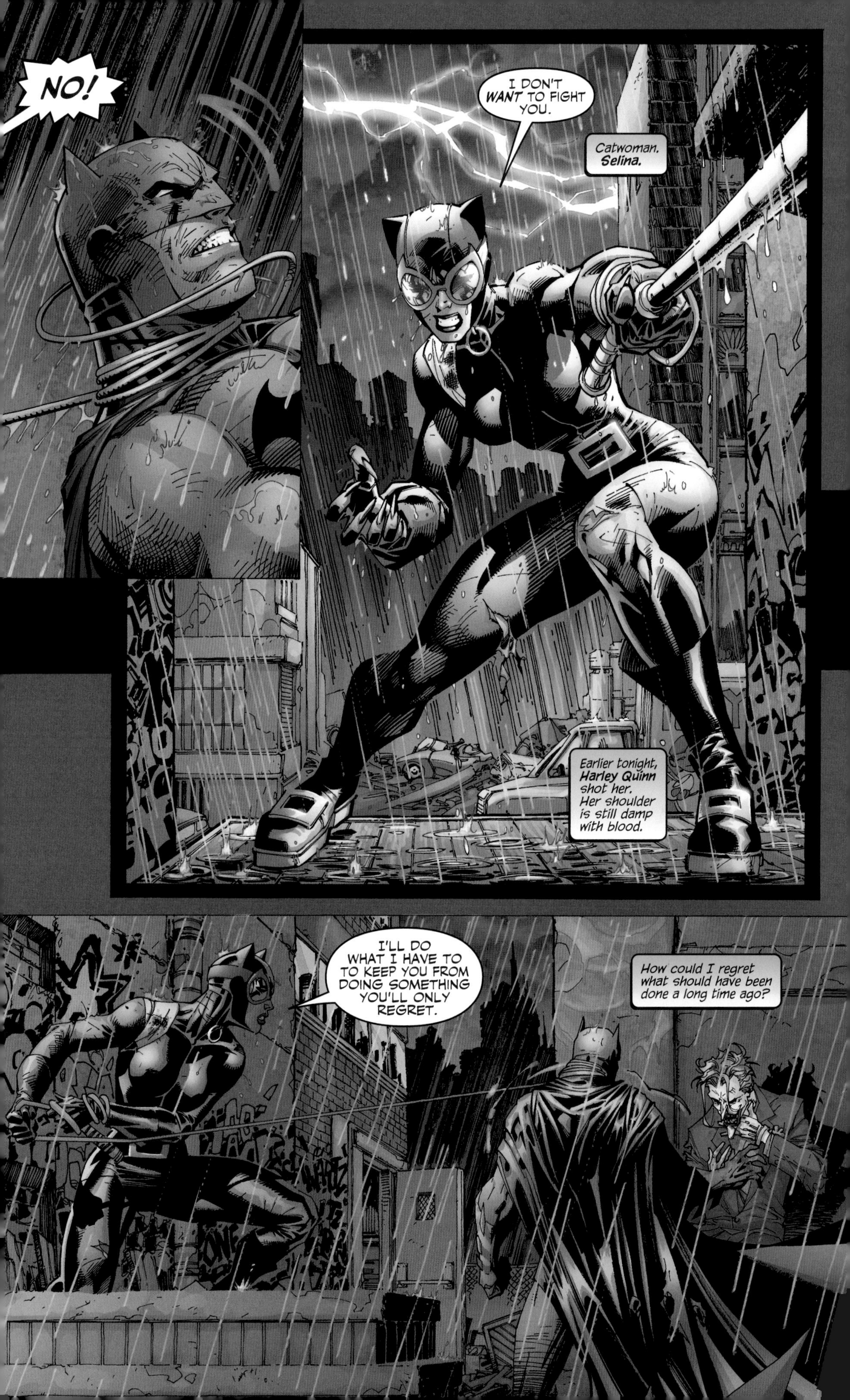
NO!
I DON'T WANT TO FIGHT YOU.
Catwoman. Selina.
Earlier tonight, Harley Quinn shot her. Her shoulder is still damp with blood.
I'LL DO WHAT I HAVE TO TO KEEP YOU FROM DOING SOMETHING YOU'LL ONLY REGRET.
How could I regret what should have been done a long time ago?

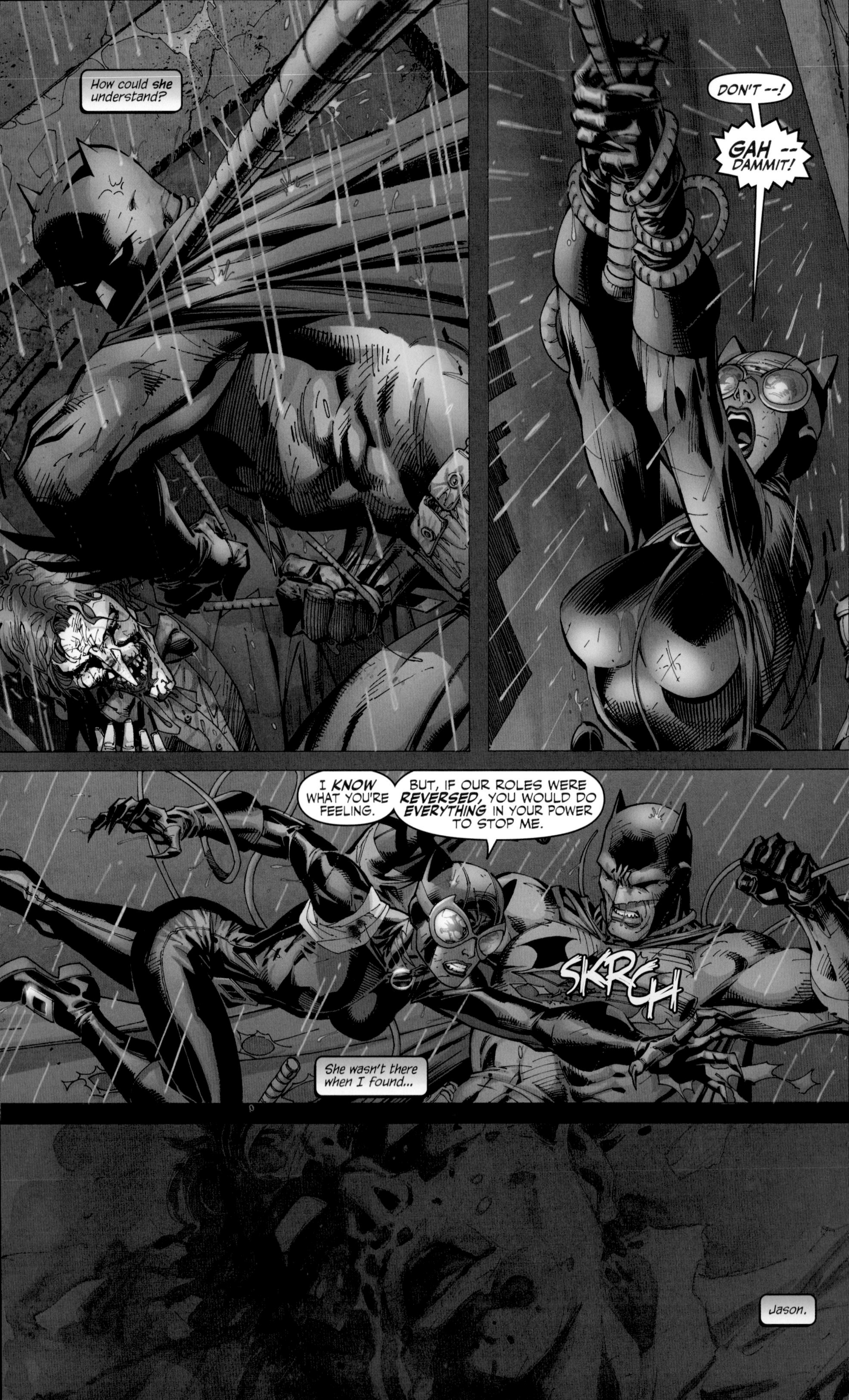

How could she understand?
DON'T --!
GAH -- DAMMIT!
I KNOW WHAT YOU'RE FEELING.
BUT, IF OUR ROLES WERE REVERSED, YOU WOULD DO EVERYTHING IN YOUR POWER TO STOP ME.
SKRCH
She wasn't there when I found...
Jason.

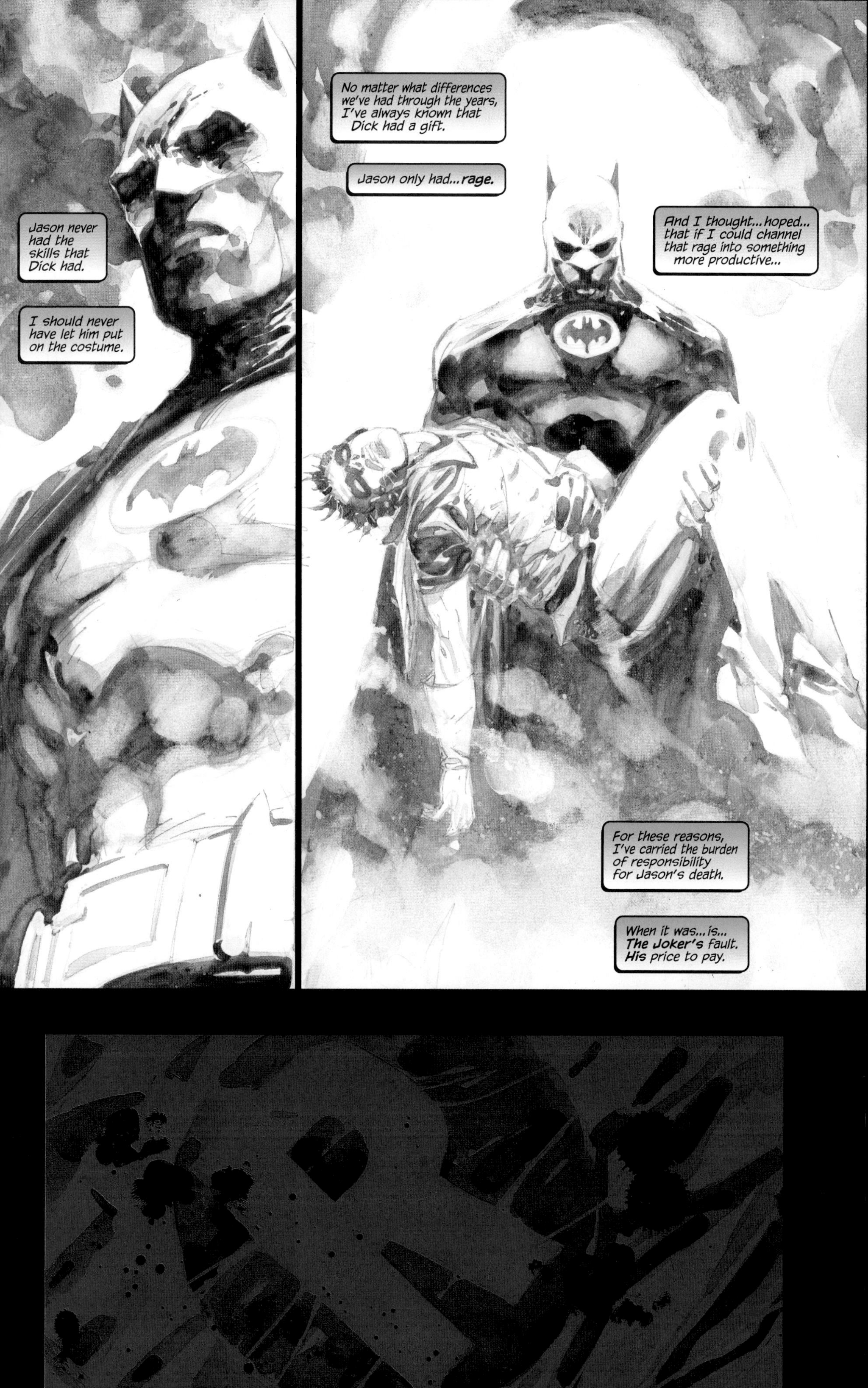

Jason never had the skills that Dick had.
I should never have let him put on the costume.
No matter what differences we've had through the years, I've always known that Dick had a gift.
Jason only had... **rage.**
And I thought... hoped... that if I could channel that rage into something more productive...
For these reasons, I've carried the burden of responsibility for Jason's death.
When it was... is... **The Joker's** fault. **His** price to pay.

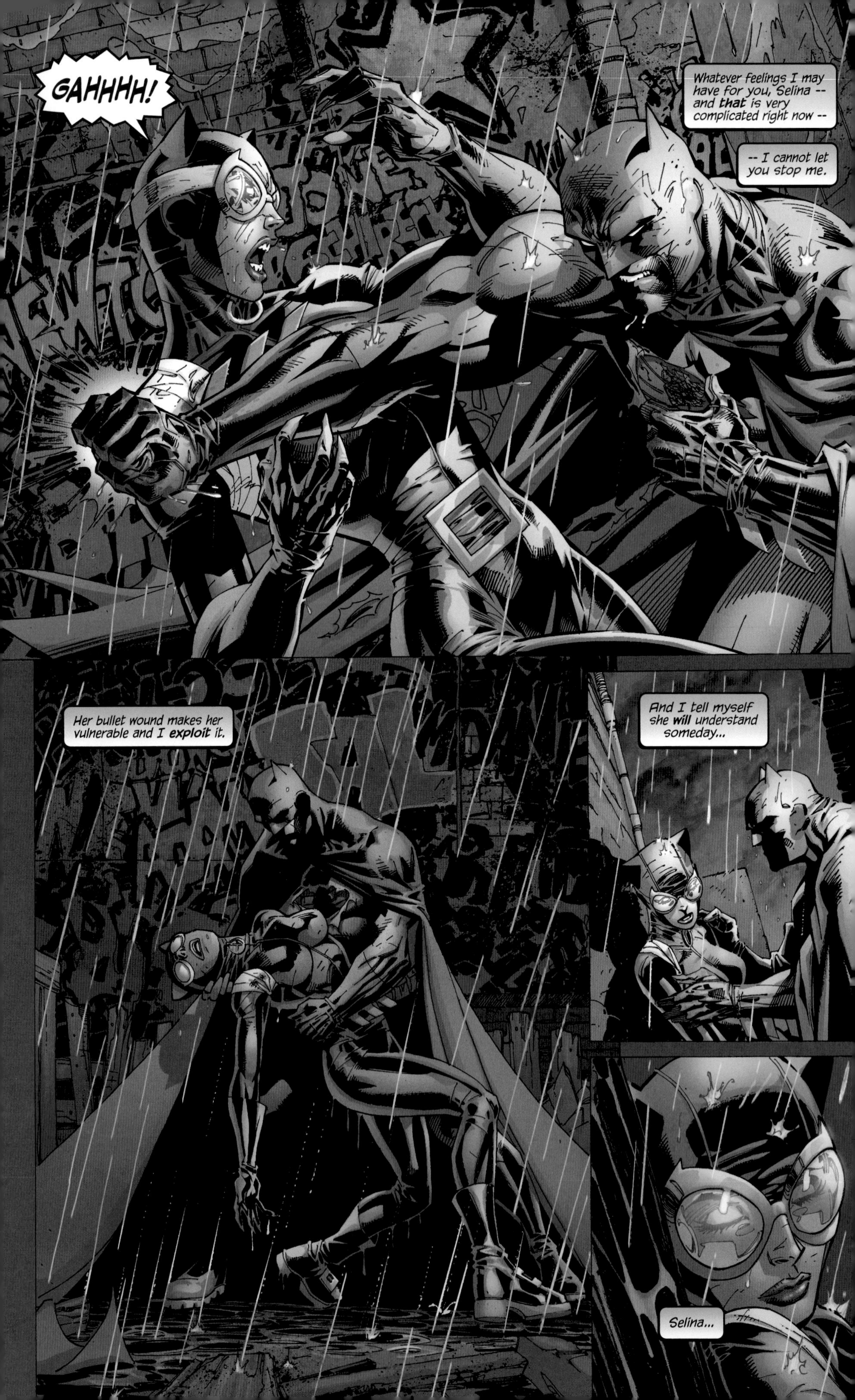
GAHHHH!
Whatever feelings I may have for you, Selina -- and **that** is very complicated right now --
-- I cannot let you stop me.
Her bullet wound makes her vulnerable and I **exploit** it.
And I tell myself she **will** understand someday...
Selina...

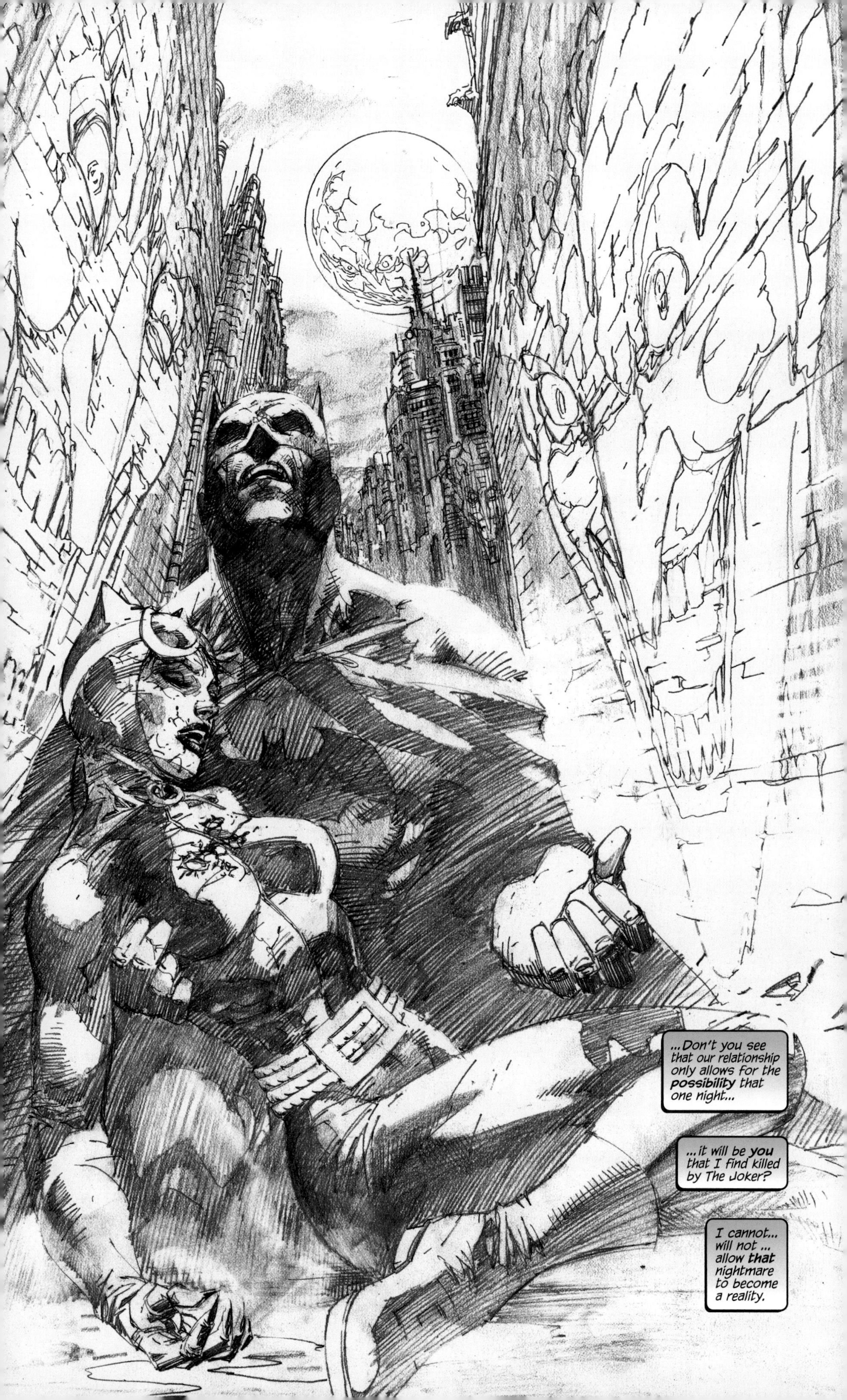

...Don't you see that our relationship only allows for the **possibility** that one night...
...it will be **you** that I find killed by The Joker?
I cannot... will not ... allow **that** nightmare to become a reality.

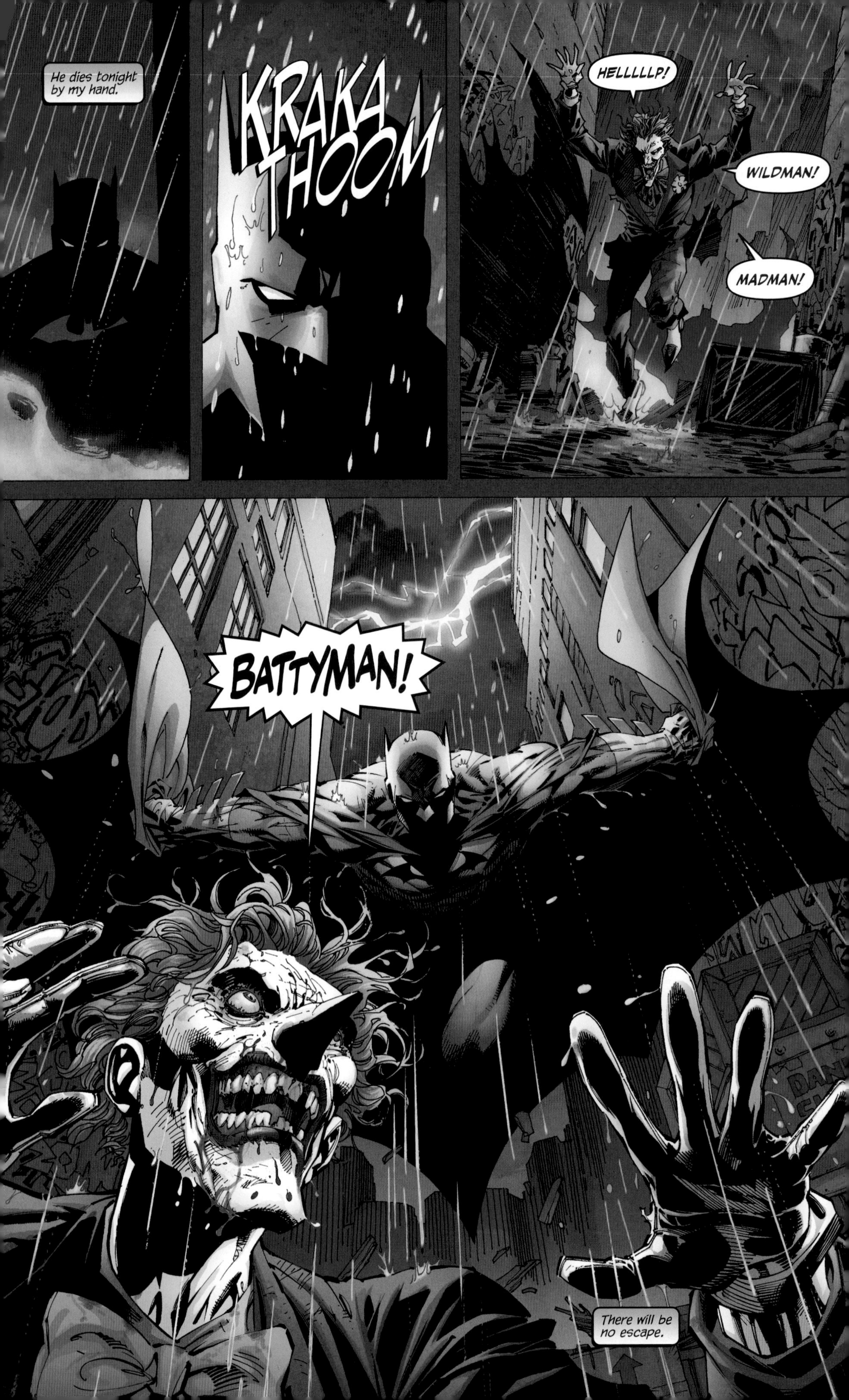
He dies tonight by my hand.
KRAKA THOOM
HELLLLLP!
WILDMAN!
MADMAN!
BATTYMAN!
There will be no escape.

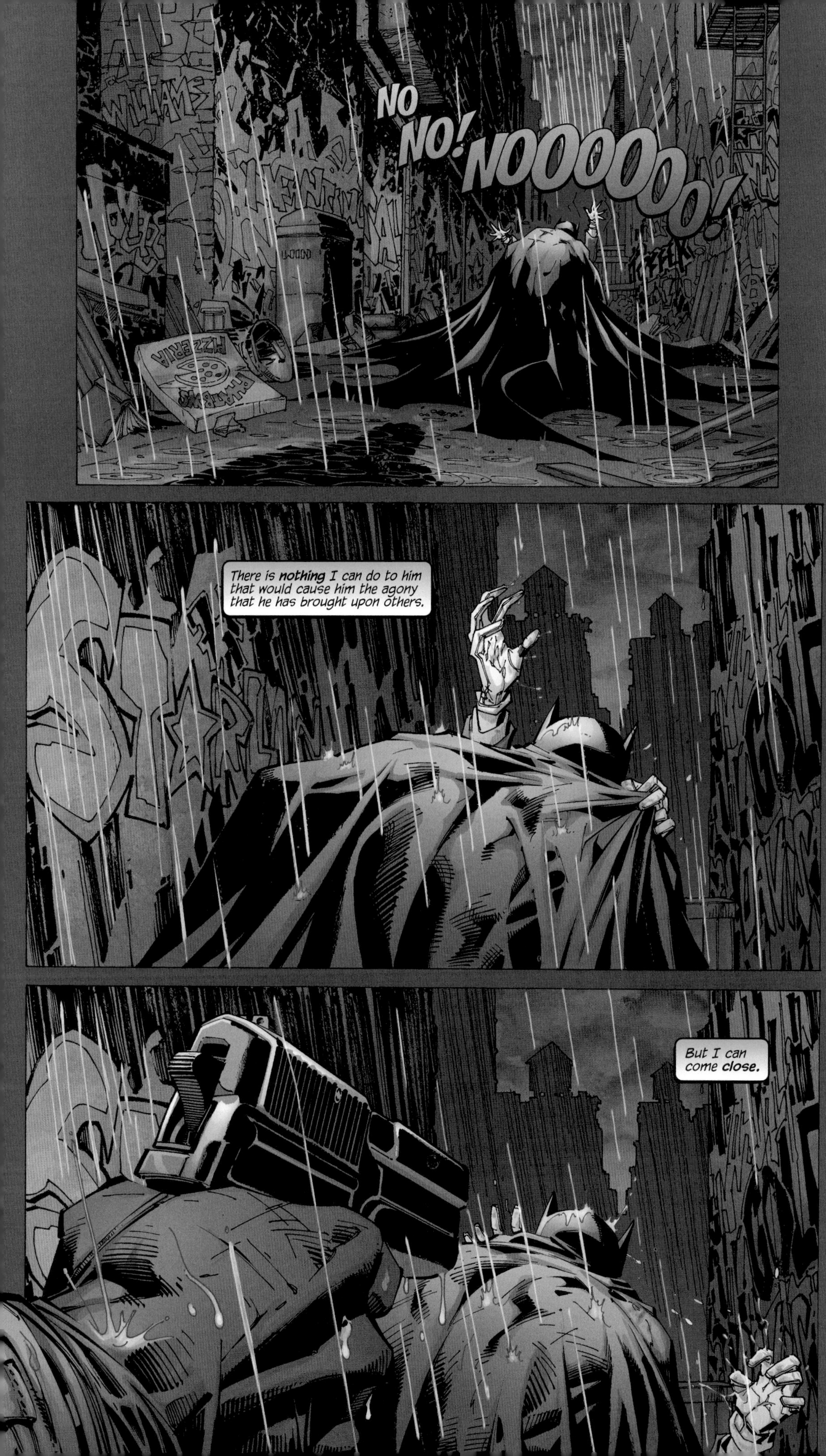
NO NO! NOOOOOOO!
There is **nothing** I can do to him that would cause him the agony that he has brought upon others.
But I can come **close.**

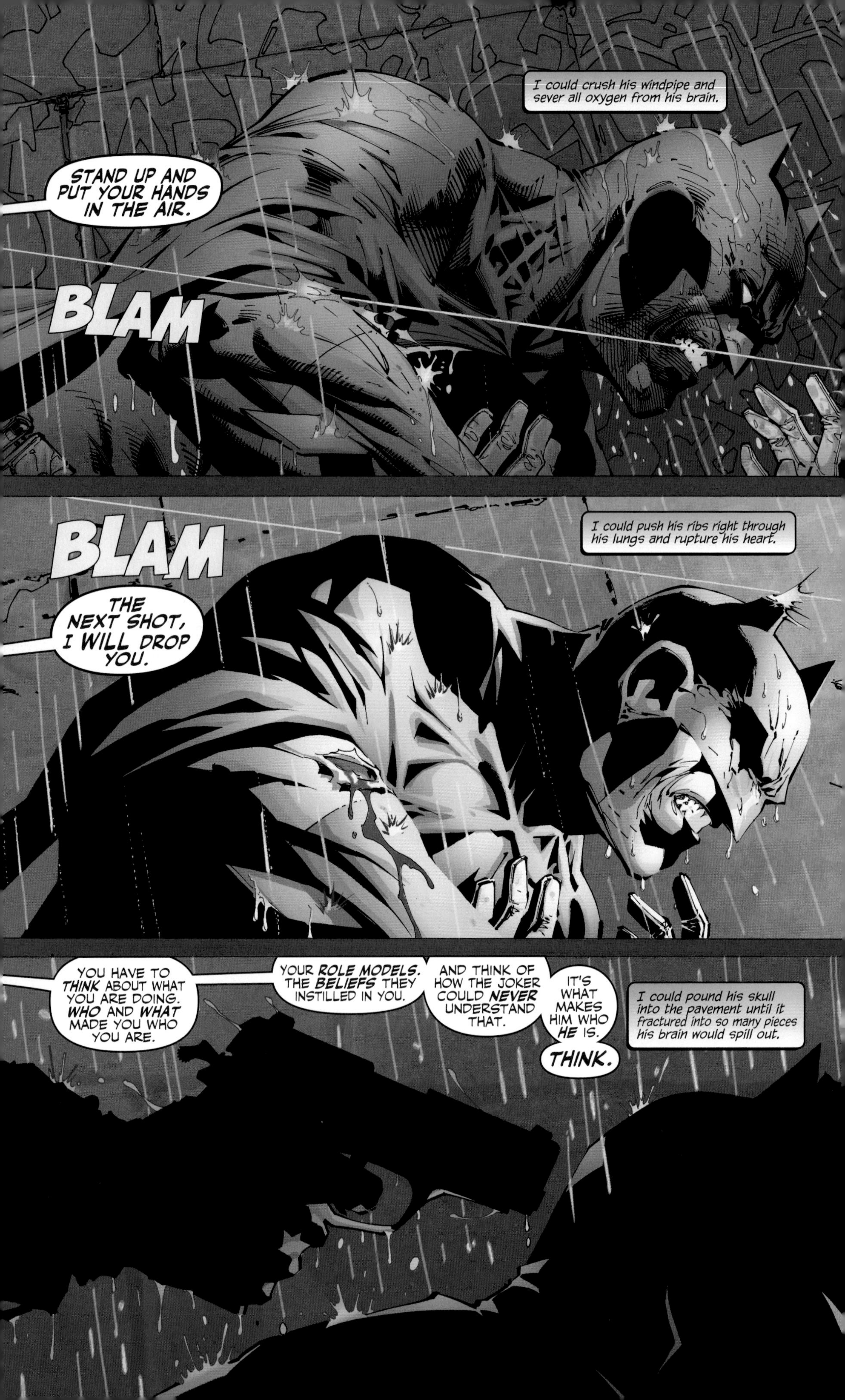

I could crush his windpipe and sever all oxygen from his brain.
STAND UP AND PUT YOUR HANDS IN THE AIR.
BLAM
BLAM
I could push his ribs right through his lungs and rupture his heart.
THE NEXT SHOT, I WILL DROP YOU.
YOU HAVE TO THINK ABOUT WHAT YOU ARE DOING. WHO AND WHAT MADE YOU WHO YOU ARE.
YOUR ROLE MODELS. THE BELIEFS THEY INSTILLED IN YOU.
AND THINK OF HOW THE JOKER COULD NEVER UNDERSTAND THAT.
IT'S WHAT MAKES HIM WHO HE IS.
THINK.
I could pound his skull into the pavement until it fractured into so many pieces his brain would spill out.

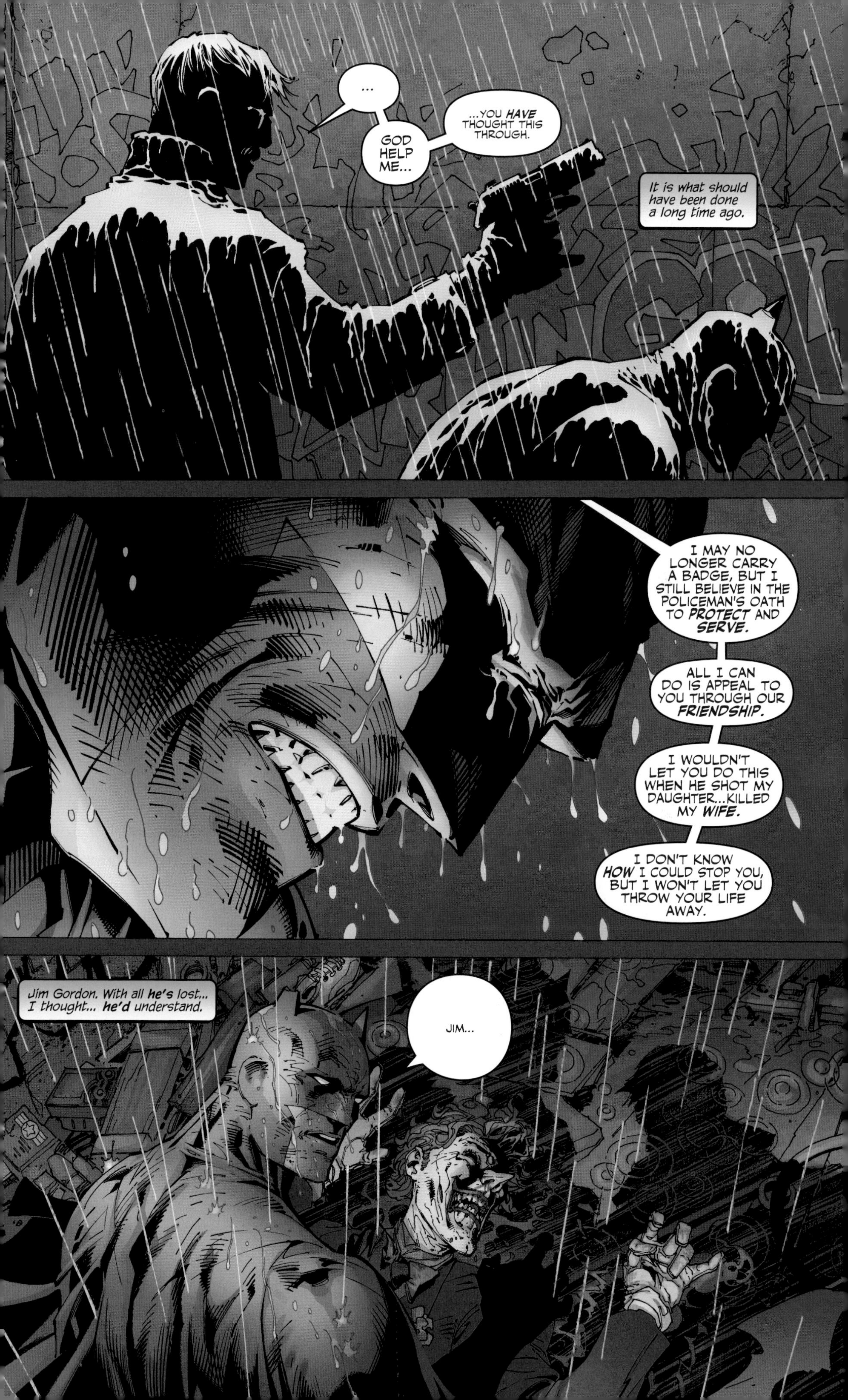
...
GOD HELP ME...
...YOU HAVE THOUGHT THIS THROUGH.
It is what should have been done a long time ago.
I MAY NO LONGER CARRY A BADGE, BUT I STILL BELIEVE IN THE POLICEMAN'S OATH TO PROTECT AND SERVE.
ALL I CAN DO IS APPEAL TO YOU THROUGH OUR FRIENDSHIP.
I WOULDN'T LET YOU DO THIS WHEN HE SHOT MY DAUGHTER...KILLED MY WIFE.
I DON'T KNOW HOW I COULD STOP YOU, BUT I WON'T LET YOU THROW YOUR LIFE AWAY.
Jim Gordon. With all he's lost... I thought... he'd understand.
JIM...

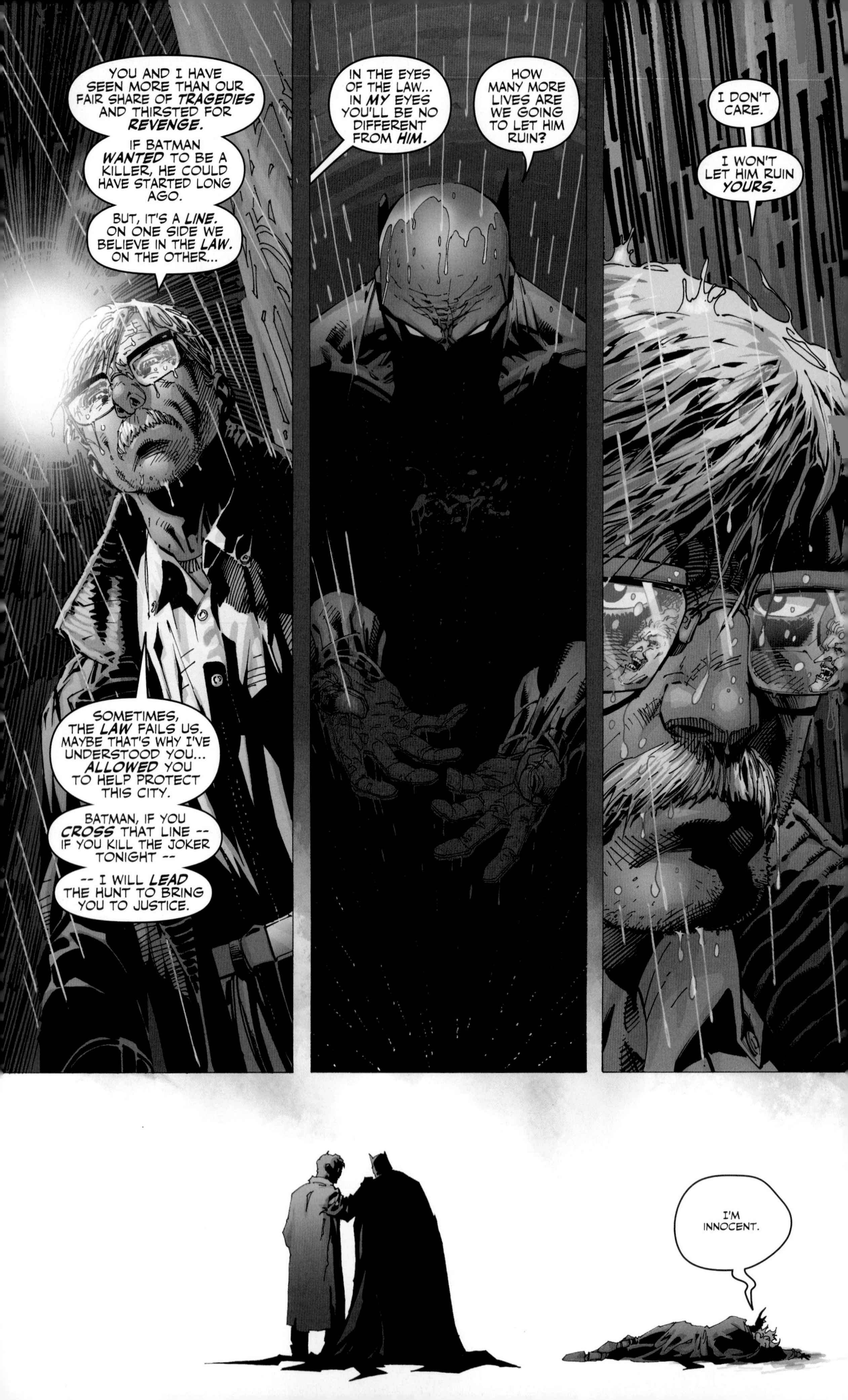
YOU AND I HAVE SEEN MORE THAN OUR FAIR SHARE OF TRAGEDIES AND THIRSTED FOR REVENGE.
IF BATMAN WANTED TO BE A KILLER, HE COULD HAVE STARTED LONG AGO.
BUT, IT'S A LINE. ON ONE SIDE WE BELIEVE IN THE LAW. ON THE OTHER...
SOMETIMES, THE LAW FAILS US. MAYBE THAT'S WHY I'VE UNDERSTOOD YOU... ALLOWED YOU TO HELP PROTECT THIS CITY.
BATMAN, IF YOU CROSS THAT LINE -- IF YOU KILL THE JOKER TONIGHT --
-- I WILL LEAD THE HUNT TO BRING YOU TO JUSTICE.
IN THE EYES OF THE LAW... IN MY EYES YOU'LL BE NO DIFFERENT FROM HIM.
HOW MANY MORE LIVES ARE WE GOING TO LET HIM RUIN?
I DON'T CARE.
I WON'T LET HIM RUIN YOURS.
I'M INNOCENT.

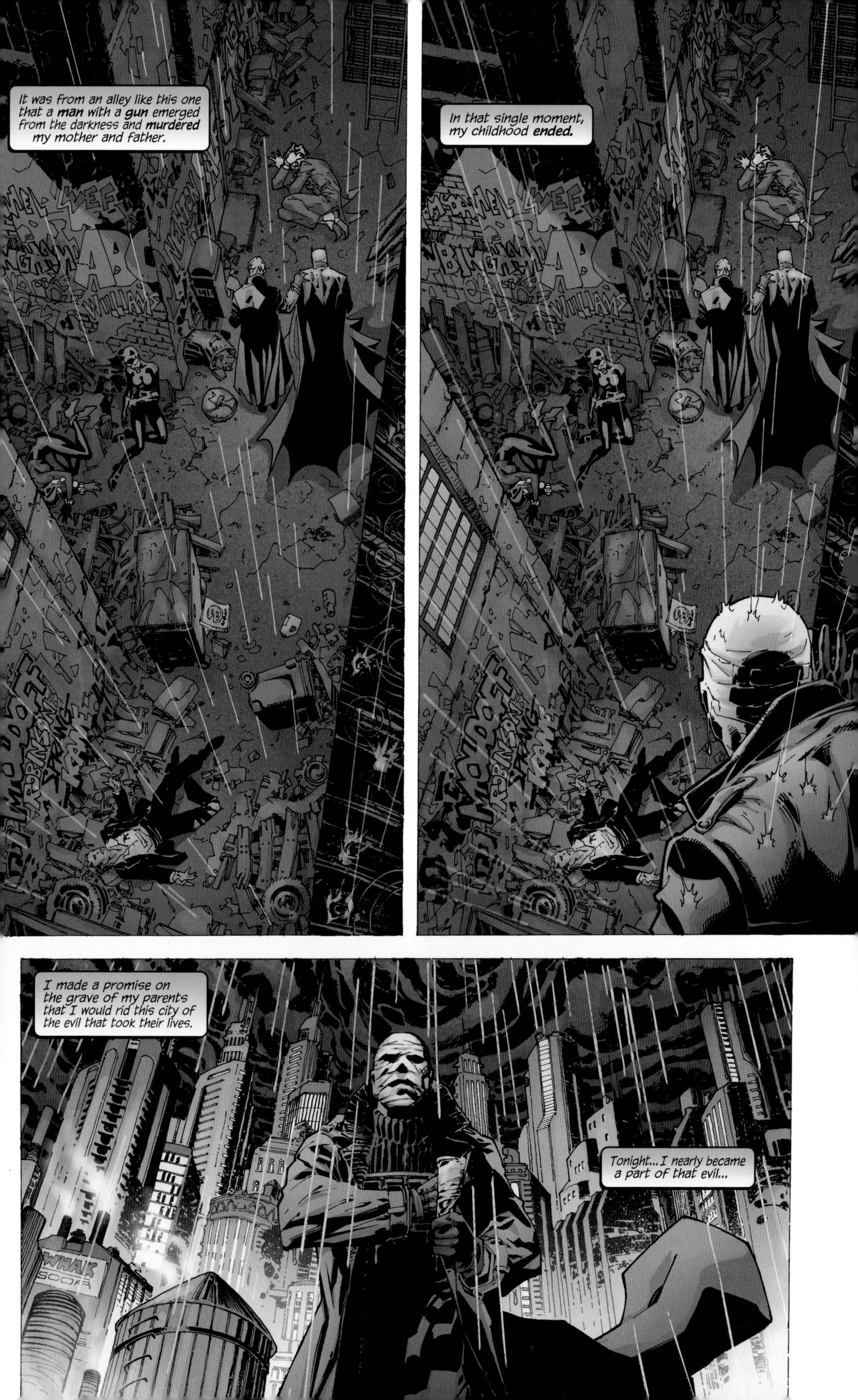
It was from an alley like this one that a **man** with a **gun** emerged from the darkness and **murdered** my mother and father.
In that single moment, my childhood **ended.**
I made a promise on the grave of my parents that I would rid this city of the evil that took their lives.
Tonight...I nearly became a part of that evil...

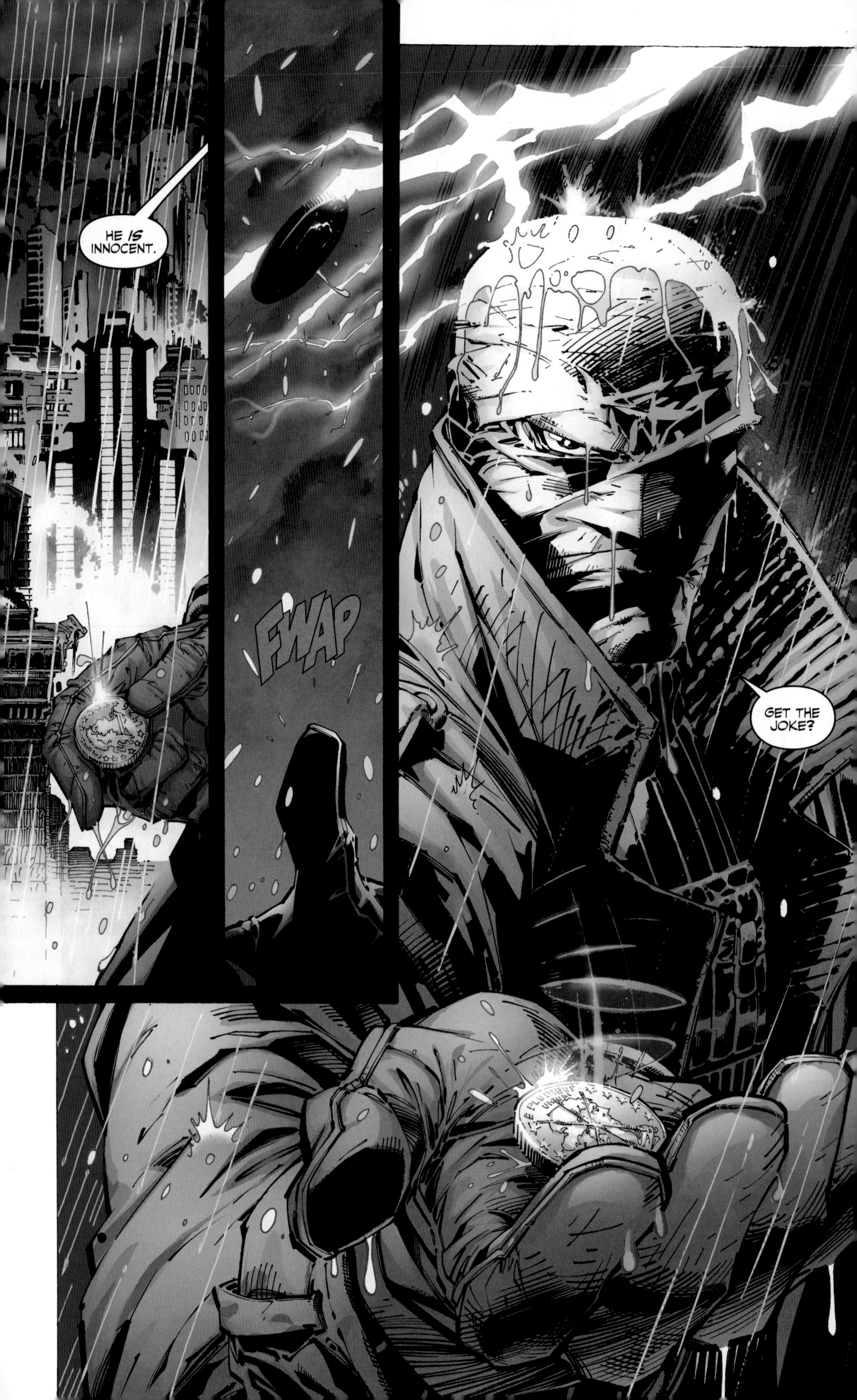
HE IS INNOCENT.
FWAP
GET THE JOKE?

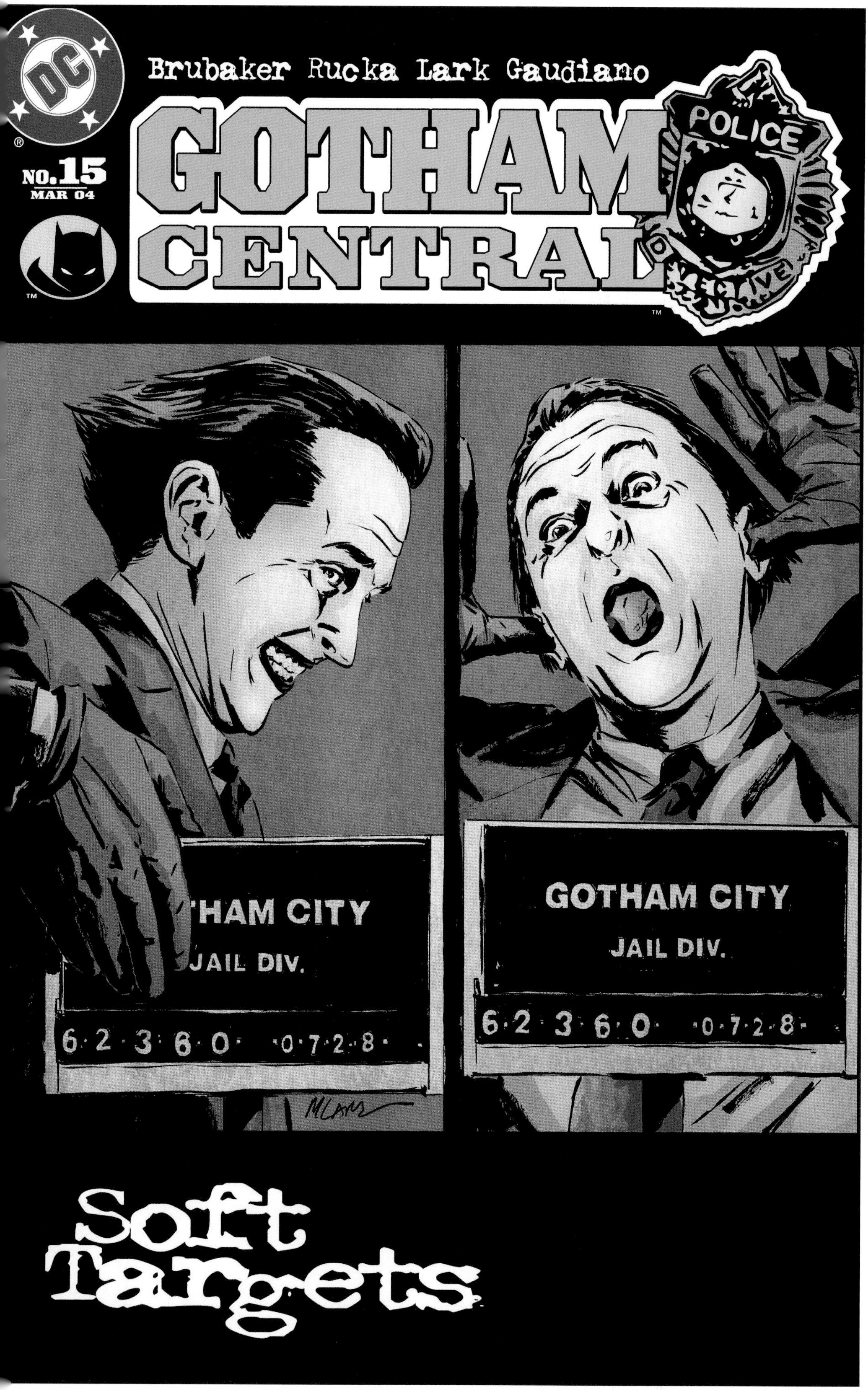

DC
Brubaker Rucka Lark Gaudiano
GOTHAM CENTRAL
NO.15
MAR 04
POLICE
THAM CITY
JAIL DIV.
6·2·3·6·0· ·0·7·2·8·
GOTHAM CITY
JAIL DIV.
6·2·3·6·0· ·0·7·2·8·
Soft Targets

--COMING TO YOU LIVE FROM GOTHAM'S CENTRAL PRECINCT, WHERE WE'VE BEEN INFORMED JUST MINUTES AGO, THAT THE JOKER HAS APPARENTLY BEEN TAKEN INTO CUSTODY.

THE DETAILS OF HIS CAPTURE REMAIN UNCLEAR AT THIS TIME. ALL WE'VE BEEN TOLD IS THAT HE WAS APPREHENDED BY A MEMBER OF THE MAJOR CRIMES UNIT.

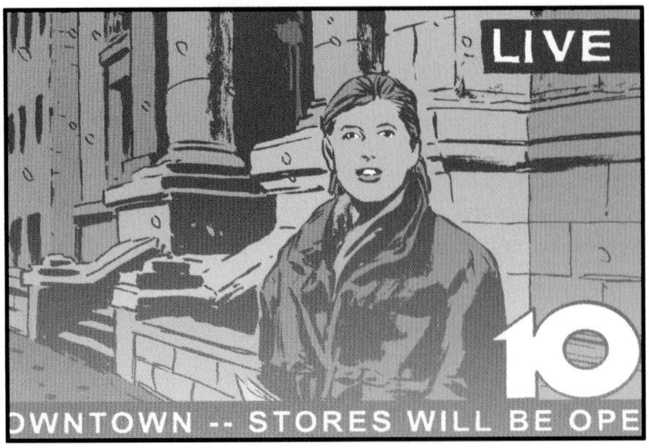
LIVE
10
OWNTOWN -- STORES WILL BE OPE

BUT IT APPEARS HIS REIGN OF TERROR HAS BEEN BROUGHT TO AN END. AND WITH JUST TWO MORE SHOPPING DAYS UNTIL CHRISTMAS, THAT'S SOMETHING THAT ALL OF GOTHAM WILL BE HAPPY TO HEAR. AREA STORES WILL BE BACK OPEN FOR BUSINESS TONIGHT, WITH MANY OF THEM PLEDGING TO KEEP LATE HOURS FOR THE NEXT FEW DAYS TO MAKE UP FOR LOST HOLIDAY SHOPPING...

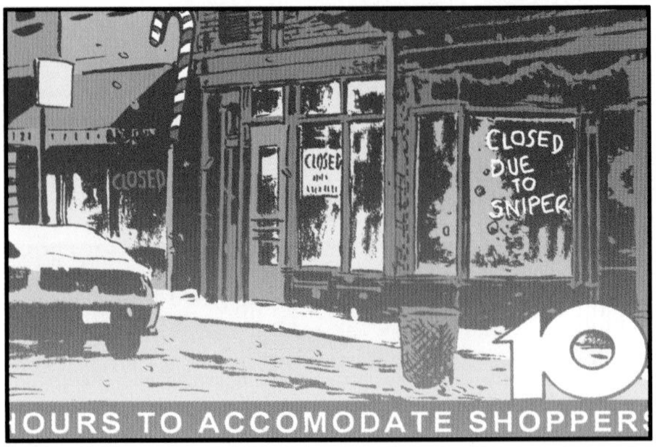
CLOSED
CLOSED
CLOSED DUE TO SNIPER
10
OURS TO ACCOMODATE SHOPPERS

...AND ACTING MAYOR HULL IS URGING GOTHAMITES TO DO WHAT THEY CAN TO SAVE THIS HOLIDAY SEASON...

THE EVENTS OF THE PAST FEW DAYS HAVE BEEN A TERRIBLE STRAIN ON US ALL, BUT I KNOW THE PEOPLE OF THIS CITY, AND THEY DON'T SCARE EASILY. SO DON'T LET THE JOKER WIN. CELEBRATE THE HOLIDAYS WITH YOUR FAMILY THIS WEEK, AND LET OUR GREAT CITY START TO HEAL.

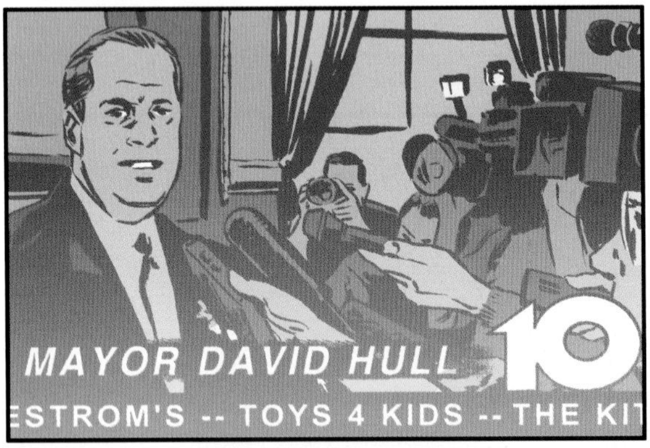
MAYOR DAVID HULL
10
ESTROM'S -- TOYS 4 KIDS -- THE KIT

IF YOU'RE JUST JOINING US, THE ***JOKER*** HAS BEEN ***CAPTURED.***

WE GO NOW TO CRIMINAL PSYCHOLOGIST LLOYD YOUNG TO GET AN INSIDE LOOK AT THE--

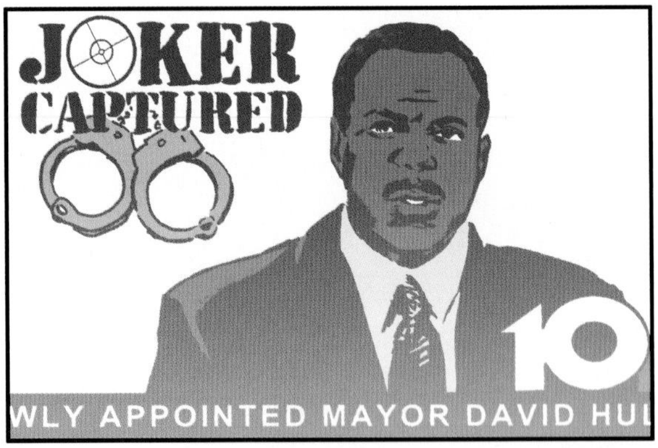
JOKER CAPTURED
10
WLY APPOINTED MAYOR DAVID HUL

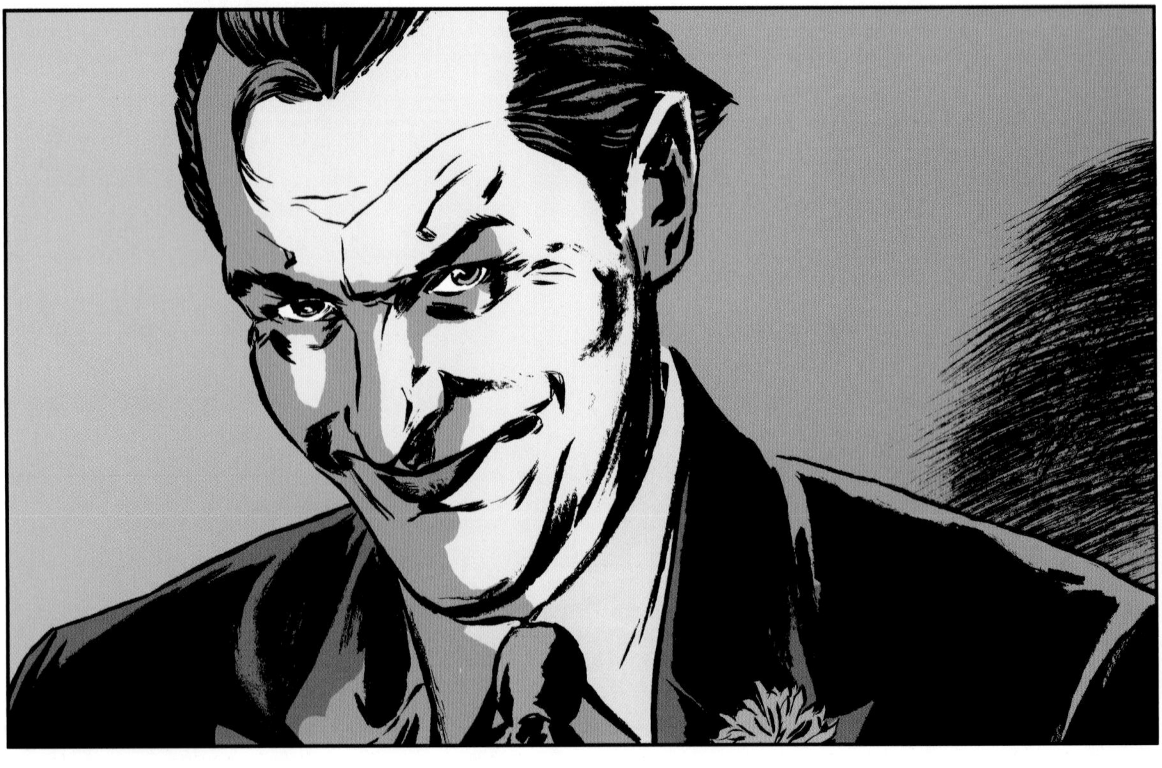

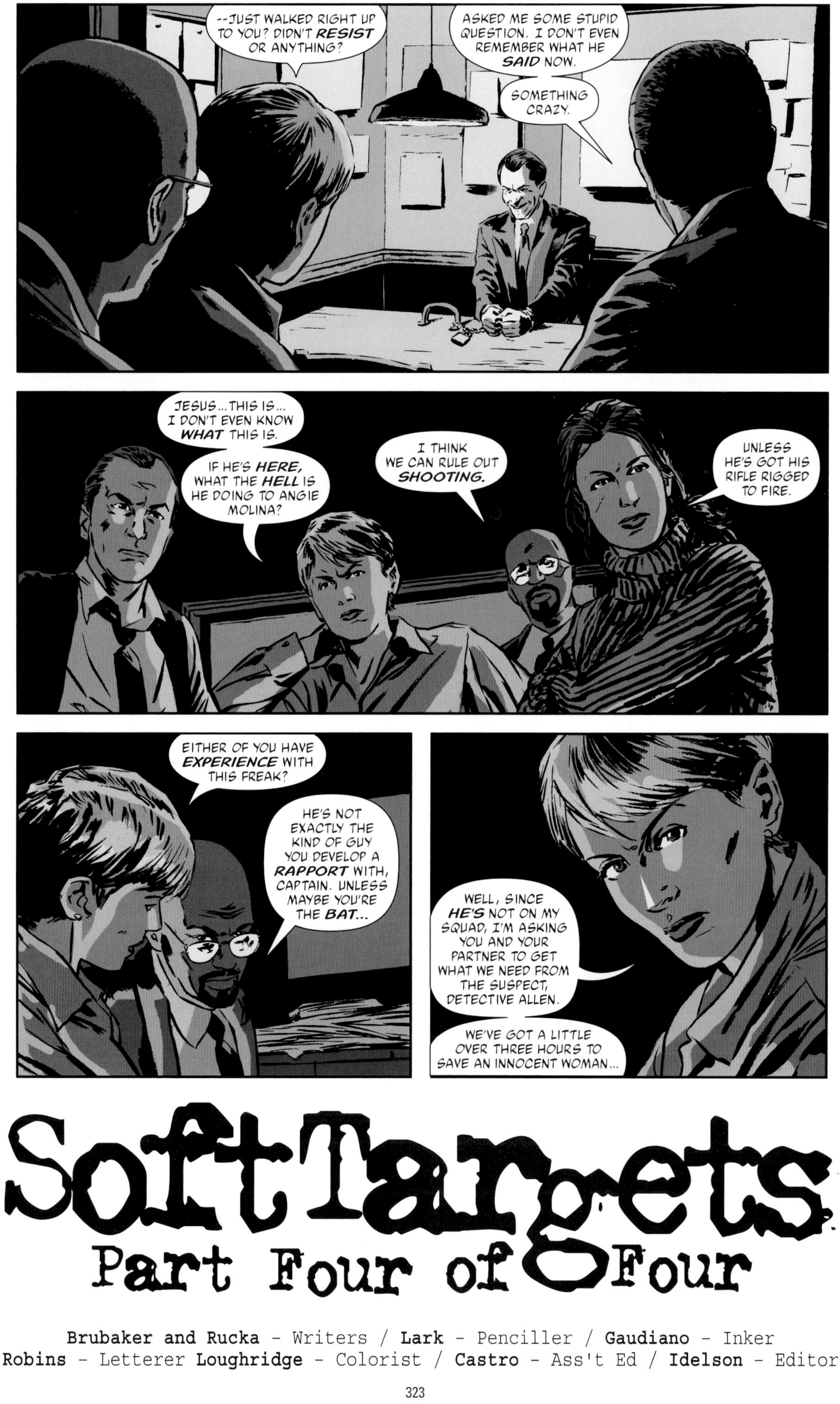
--JUST WALKED RIGHT UP TO YOU? DIDN'T RESIST OR ANYTHING?
ASKED ME SOME STUPID QUESTION. I DON'T EVEN REMEMBER WHAT HE SAID NOW.
SOMETHING CRAZY.
JESUS...THIS IS... I DON'T EVEN KNOW WHAT THIS IS.
IF HE'S HERE, WHAT THE HELL IS HE DOING TO ANGIE MOLINA?
I THINK WE CAN RULE OUT SHOOTING.
UNLESS HE'S GOT HIS RIFLE RIGGED TO FIRE.
EITHER OF YOU HAVE EXPERIENCE WITH THIS FREAK?
HE'S NOT EXACTLY THE KIND OF GUY YOU DEVELOP A RAPPORT WITH, CAPTAIN. UNLESS MAYBE YOU'RE THE BAT...
WELL, SINCE HE'S NOT ON MY SQUAD, I'M ASKING YOU AND YOUR PARTNER TO GET WHAT WE NEED FROM THE SUSPECT, DETECTIVE ALLEN.
WE'VE GOT A LITTLE OVER THREE HOURS TO SAVE AN INNOCENT WOMAN...

Soft Targets

Part Four of Four

Brubaker and Rucka - Writers / **Lark** - Penciller / **Gaudiano** - Inker
Robins - Letterer **Loughridge** - Colorist / **Castro** - Ass't Ed / **Idelson** - Editor

NORMALLY I'D OFFER YOU A DRINK OR SOMETHING, BUT IN THIS CASE, YOU KNOW, I THINK WE CAN JUST SKIP THE BULL$#¢%...

AN ICED TEA WOULD BE *FANTASTIC.* I DON'T KNOW ABOUT YOU, BUT I'VE ALWAYS FOUND POLICE BRUTALITY REALLY MAKES YOU THIRSTY.

WHO CAN SAY WHY?

YEAH, OUR HEARTS BLEED FOR YOUR SUFFERING. LET ME JUST GET THE FORMS FOR YOU TO FILE A COMPLAINT.

OOOH... YOU'RE FUNNY. I *LIKE* YOU.

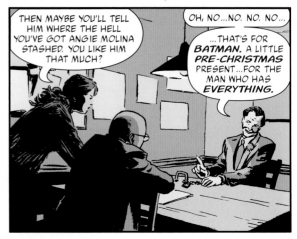

THEN MAYBE YOU'LL TELL HIM WHERE THE HELL YOU'VE GOT ANGIE MOLINA STASHED. YOU LIKE HIM THAT MUCH?

OH, NO...NO. NO. NO...

...THAT'S FOR *BATMAN.* A LITTLE *PRE-CHRISTMAS* PRESENT...FOR THE MAN WHO HAS *EVERYTHING.*

HOW 'BOUT THIS? YOU TELL *ME* WHERE SHE IS AND *I'LL* TELL HIM WHERE HE CAN PICK UP HIS PRESENT.

WOW, YOU'D DO THAT FOR *ME?* I THINK I'M GONNA CRY. MY *NEW* BEST FRIEND. I TOLD THEM I WAS DOWN WITH THE HOMEBOYS.

ALMOST MAKES ME SORRY I CAN'T HELP YOU, PAL O'MINE. BUT I NEVER SERVE A WINE BEFORE ITS *TIME.*

AFRAID YOU LOST ME. WE'RE TALKING ABOUT A WOMAN, RIGHT?

NOT A WOMAN, A *NEWSCASTER.* KEE-RYST, WHAT PLANET ARE *YOU* FROM? I MEAN, HELLOOO? DO YOU *OWN* A TV?

SO, OKAY, IT'S NOT ANGIE'S TIME YET? WHEN WILL SHE BE *READY,* THEN?

GEEZ. MISTER IMPATIENT...WHEN IS ANYTHING *EVER* READY? WHEN THE TIMER GOES *DING.*

OR, IN THIS CASE... BOOM.

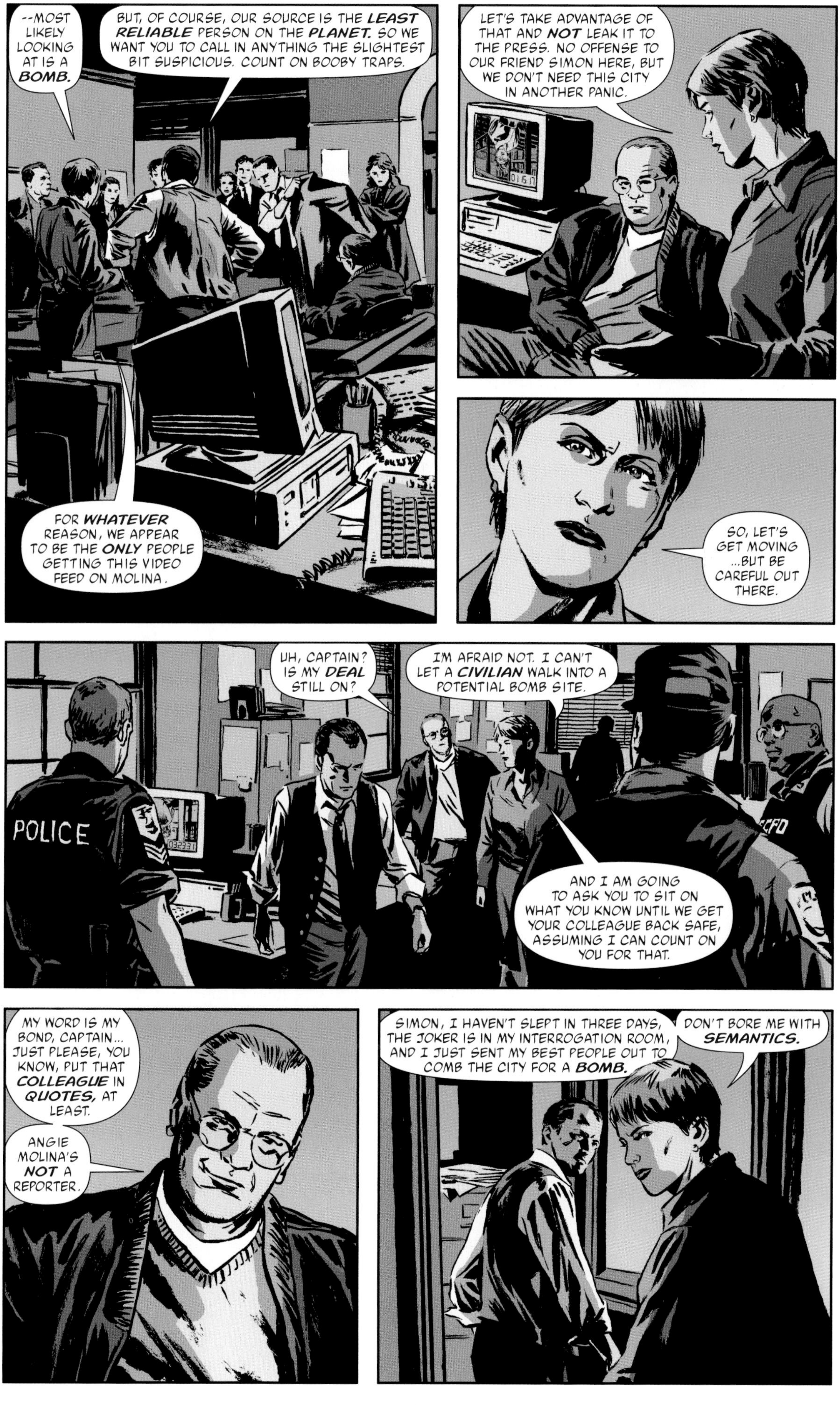

--MOST LIKELY LOOKING AT IS A BOMB.
BUT, OF COURSE, OUR SOURCE IS THE LEAST RELIABLE PERSON ON THE PLANET. SO WE WANT YOU TO CALL IN ANYTHING THE SLIGHTEST BIT SUSPICIOUS. COUNT ON BOOBY TRAPS.
FOR WHATEVER REASON, WE APPEAR TO BE THE ONLY PEOPLE GETTING THIS VIDEO FEED ON MOLINA.
LET'S TAKE ADVANTAGE OF THAT AND NOT LEAK IT TO THE PRESS. NO OFFENSE TO OUR FRIEND SIMON HERE, BUT WE DON'T NEED THIS CITY IN ANOTHER PANIC.
SO, LET'S GET MOVING ...BUT BE CAREFUL OUT THERE.
POLICE
UH, CAPTAIN? IS MY DEAL STILL ON?
I'M AFRAID NOT. I CAN'T LET A CIVILIAN WALK INTO A POTENTIAL BOMB SITE.
AND I AM GOING TO ASK YOU TO SIT ON WHAT YOU KNOW UNTIL WE GET YOUR COLLEAGUE BACK SAFE, ASSUMING I CAN COUNT ON YOU FOR THAT.
MY WORD IS MY BOND, CAPTAIN... JUST PLEASE, YOU KNOW, PUT THAT COLLEAGUE IN QUOTES, AT LEAST.
ANGIE MOLINA'S NOT A REPORTER.
SIMON, I HAVEN'T SLEPT IN THREE DAYS, THE JOKER IS IN MY INTERROGATION ROOM, AND I JUST SENT MY BEST PEOPLE OUT TO COMB THE CITY FOR A BOMB.
DON'T BORE ME WITH SEMANTICS.

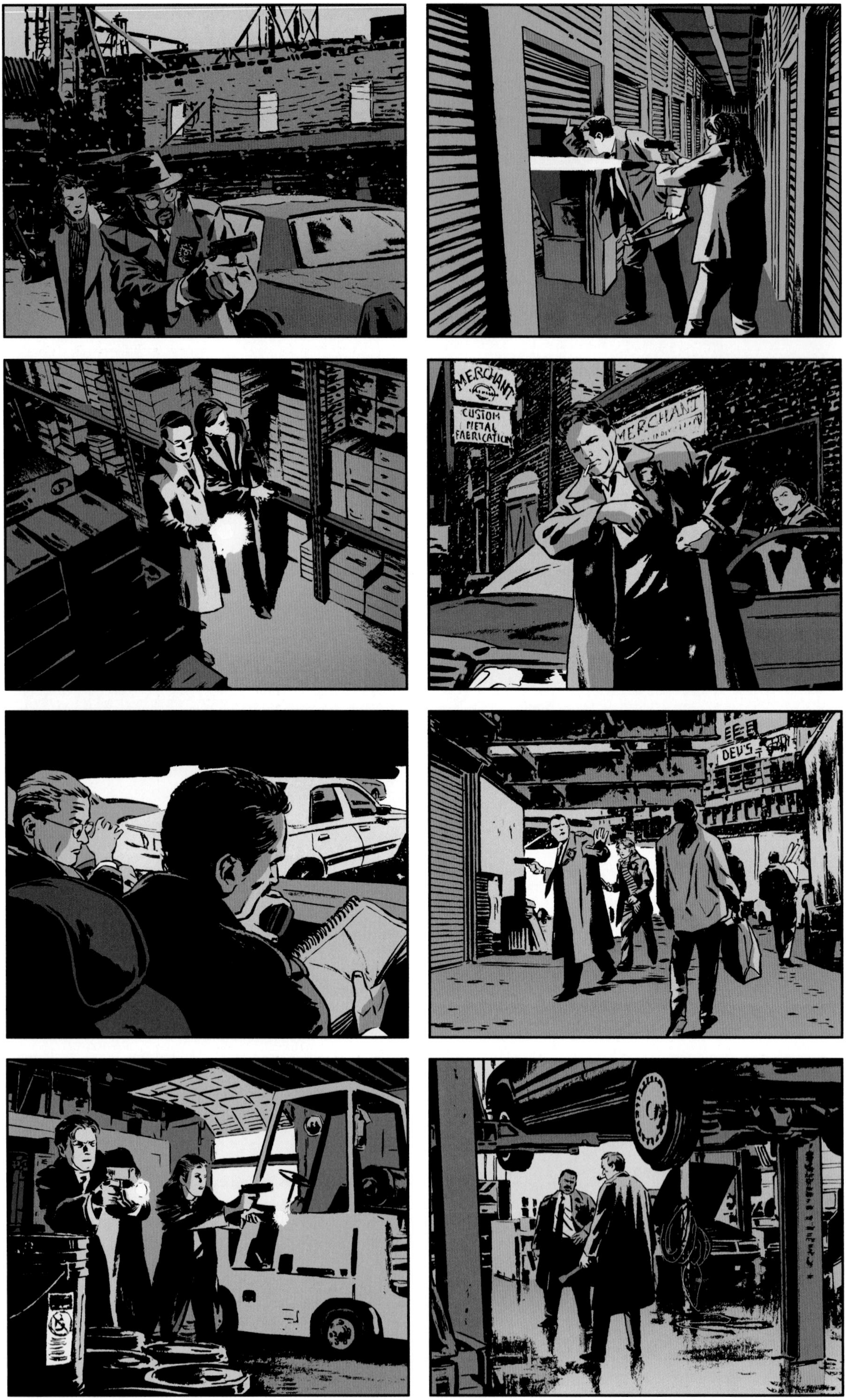
MERCHANT
CUSTOM METAL FABRICATION
MERCHANT
DEV'S

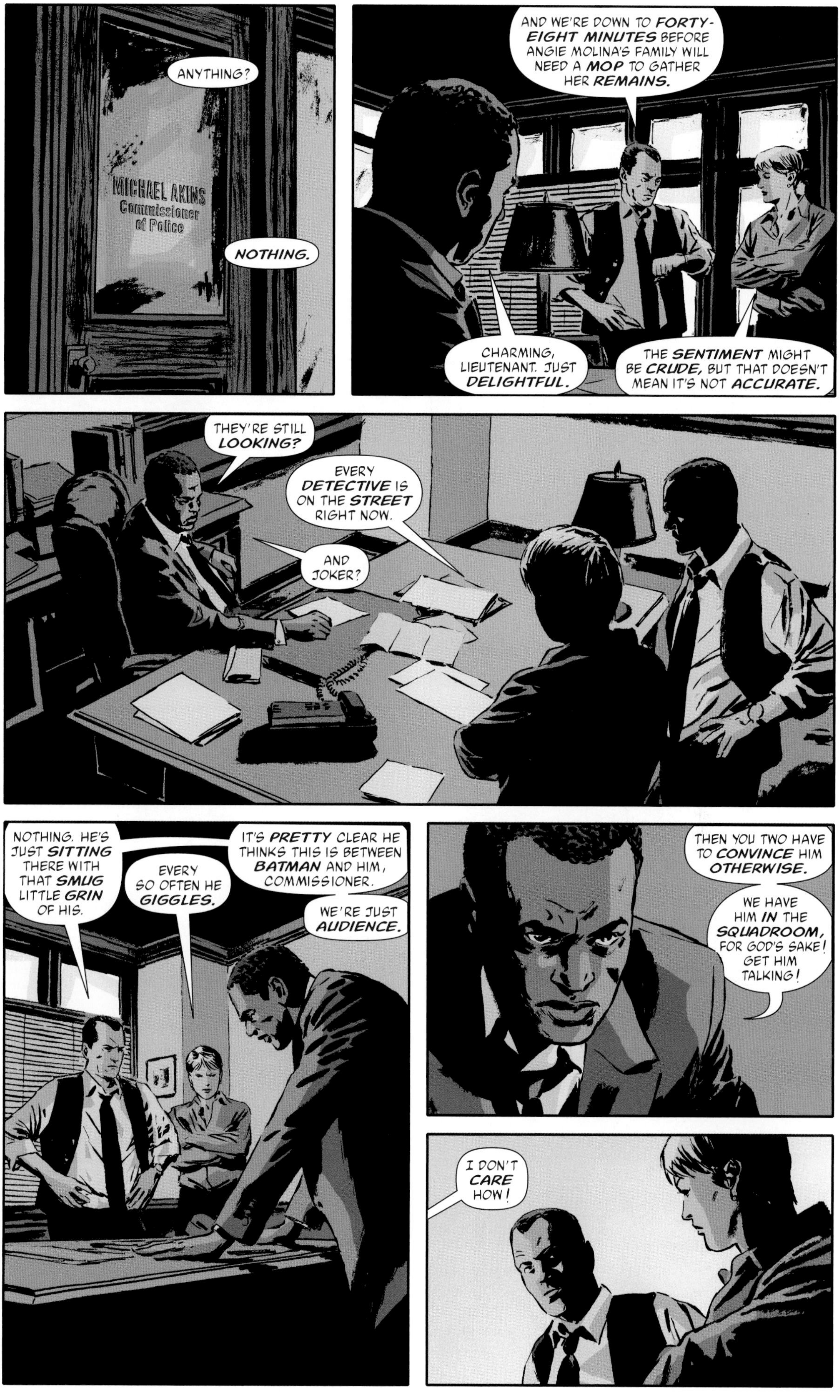
ANYTHING?
MICHAEL AKINS
Commissioner
of Police
NOTHING.
AND WE'RE DOWN TO FORTY-EIGHT MINUTES BEFORE ANGIE MOLINA'S FAMILY WILL NEED A MOP TO GATHER HER REMAINS.
CHARMING, LIEUTENANT. JUST DELIGHTFUL.
THE SENTIMENT MIGHT BE CRUDE, BUT THAT DOESN'T MEAN IT'S NOT ACCURATE.
THEY'RE STILL LOOKING?
EVERY DETECTIVE IS ON THE STREET RIGHT NOW.
AND JOKER?
NOTHING. HE'S JUST SITTING THERE WITH THAT SMUG LITTLE GRIN OF HIS.
EVERY SO OFTEN HE GIGGLES.
IT'S PRETTY CLEAR HE THINKS THIS IS BETWEEN BATMAN AND HIM, COMMISSIONER.
WE'RE JUST AUDIENCE.
THEN YOU TWO HAVE TO CONVINCE HIM OTHERWISE.
WE HAVE HIM IN THE SQUADROOM, FOR GOD'S SAKE! GET HIM TALKING!
I DON'T CARE HOW!

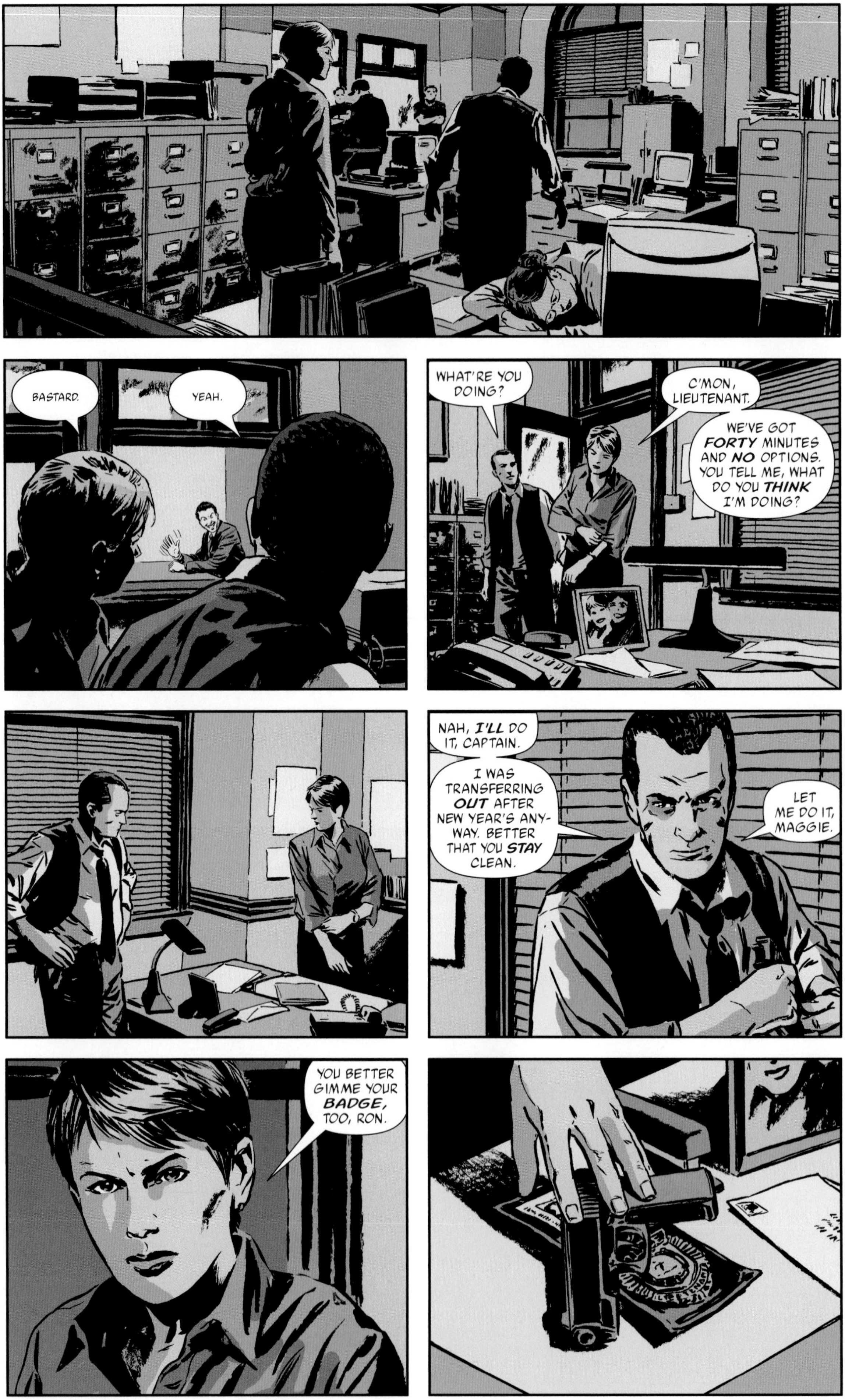
BASTARD.
YEAH.
WHAT'RE YOU DOING?
C'MON, LIEUTENANT.
WE'VE GOT FORTY MINUTES AND NO OPTIONS. YOU TELL ME, WHAT DO YOU THINK I'M DOING?
NAH, I'LL DO IT, CAPTAIN.
I WAS TRANSFERRING OUT AFTER NEW YEAR'S ANY-WAY. BETTER THAT YOU STAY CLEAN.
LET ME DO IT, MAGGIE.
YOU BETTER GIMME YOUR BADGE, TOO, RON.

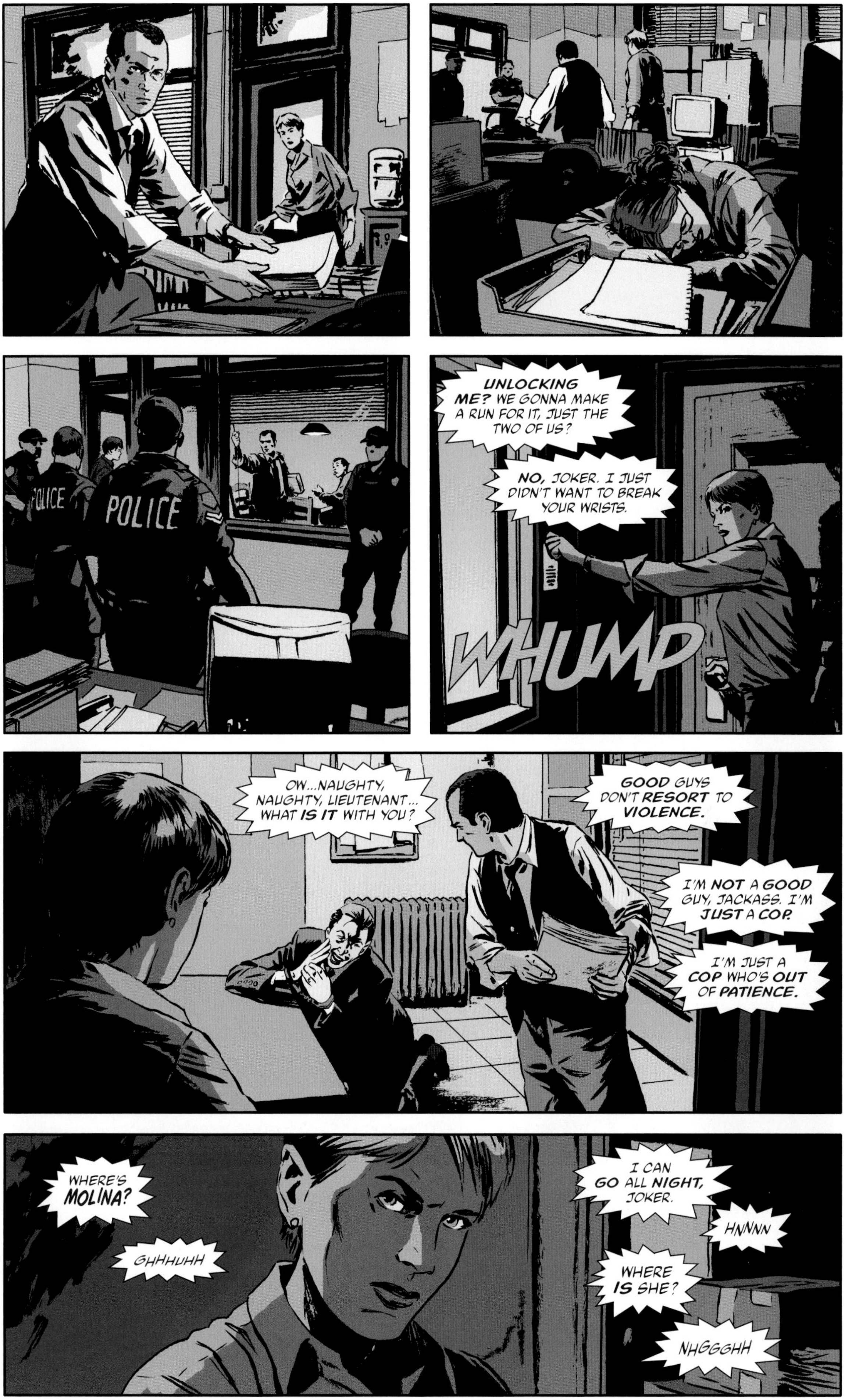
UNLOCKING ME? WE GONNA MAKE A RUN FOR IT, JUST THE TWO OF US?
NO, JOKER. I JUST DIDN'T WANT TO BREAK YOUR WRISTS.
WHUMP
OW...NAUGHTY, NAUGHTY, LIEUTENANT... WHAT IS IT WITH YOU?
GOOD GUYS DON'T RESORT TO VIOLENCE.
I'M NOT A GOOD GUY, JACKASS. I'M JUST A COP.
I'M JUST A COP WHO'S OUT OF PATIENCE.
WHERE'S MOLINA?
GHHHUHH
I CAN GO ALL NIGHT, JOKER.
HNNNN
WHERE IS SHE?
NHGGGHH

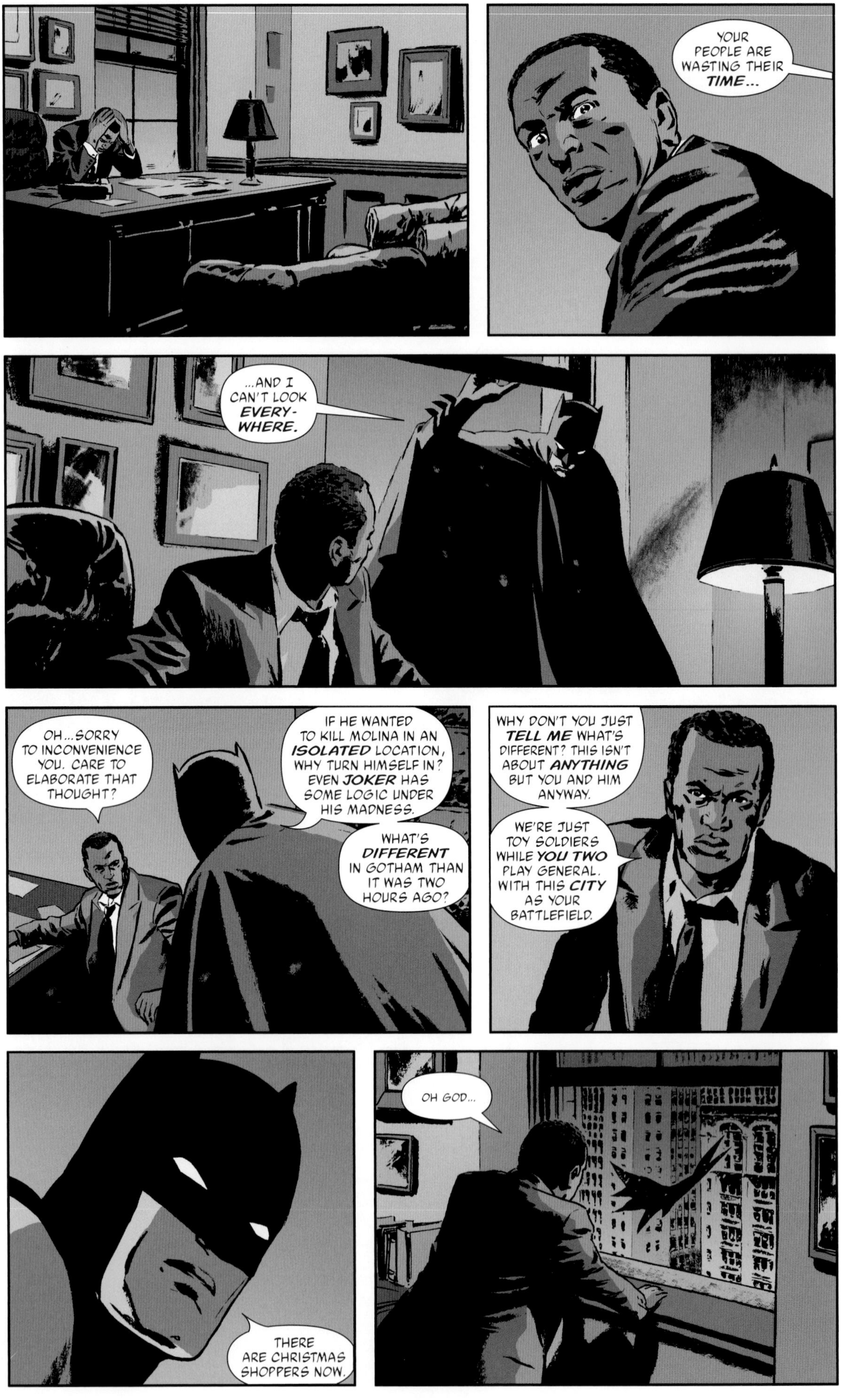
YOUR PEOPLE ARE WASTING THEIR TIME...
...AND I CAN'T LOOK EVERY-WHERE.
OH...SORRY TO INCONVENIENCE YOU. CARE TO ELABORATE THAT THOUGHT?
IF HE WANTED TO KILL MOLINA IN AN ISOLATED LOCATION, WHY TURN HIMSELF IN? EVEN JOKER HAS SOME LOGIC UNDER HIS MADNESS.
WHAT'S DIFFERENT IN GOTHAM THAN IT WAS TWO HOURS AGO?
WHY DON'T YOU JUST TELL ME WHAT'S DIFFERENT? THIS ISN'T ABOUT ANYTHING BUT YOU AND HIM ANYWAY.
WE'RE JUST TOY SOLDIERS WHILE YOU TWO PLAY GENERAL. WITH THIS CITY AS YOUR BATTLEFIELD.
THERE ARE CHRISTMAS SHOPPERS NOW.
OH GOD...

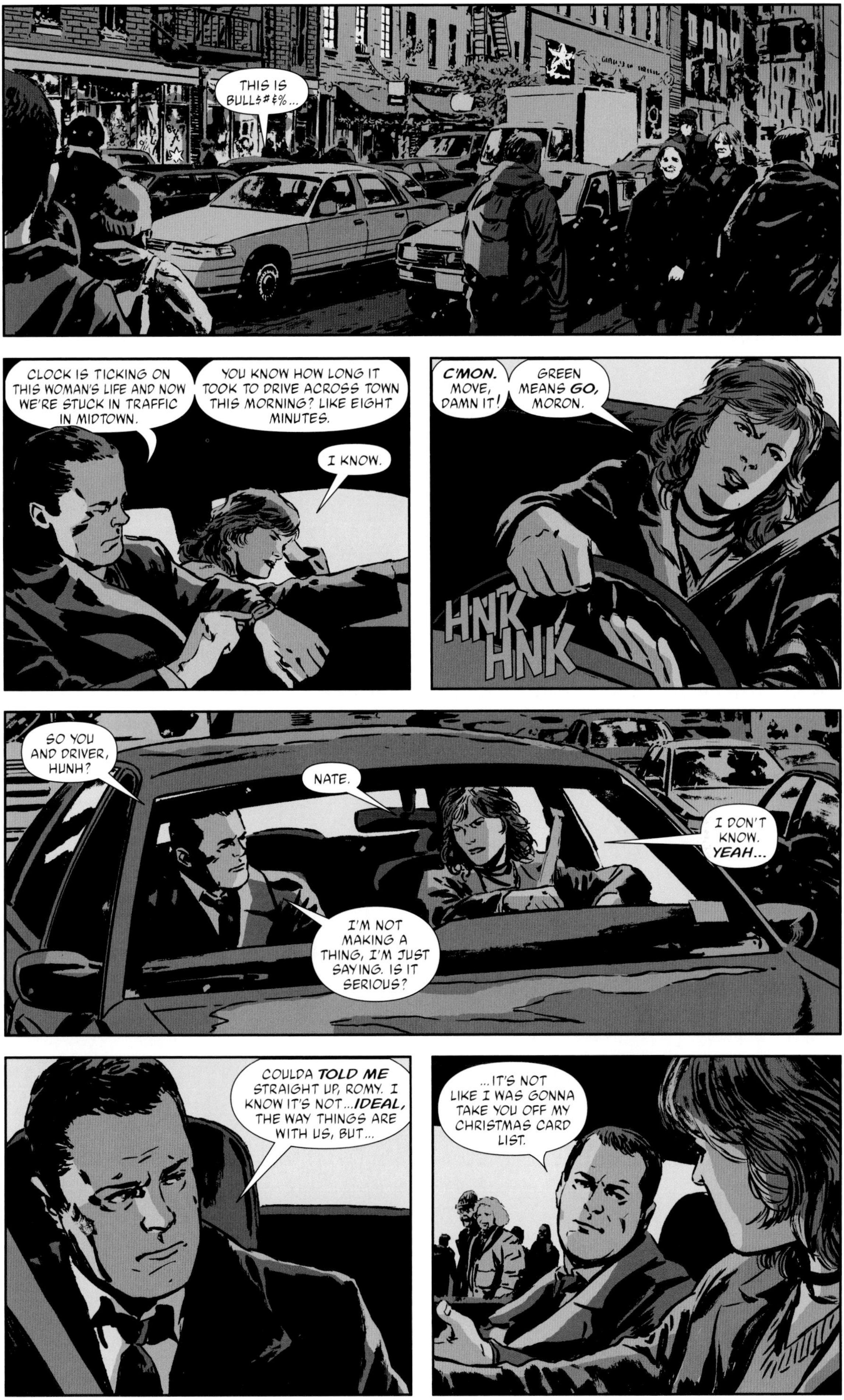

THIS IS BULLS#$%...
CLOCK IS TICKING ON THIS WOMAN'S LIFE AND NOW WE'RE STUCK IN TRAFFIC IN MIDTOWN.
YOU KNOW HOW LONG IT TOOK TO DRIVE ACROSS TOWN THIS MORNING? LIKE EIGHT MINUTES.
I KNOW.
C'MON. MOVE, DAMN IT!
GREEN MEANS GO, MORON.
HNK HNK
SO YOU AND DRIVER, HUNH?
NATE.
I DON'T KNOW. YEAH...
I'M NOT MAKING A THING, I'M JUST SAYING. IS IT SERIOUS?
COULDA TOLD ME STRAIGHT UP, ROMY. I KNOW IT'S NOT...IDEAL, THE WAY THINGS ARE WITH US, BUT...
...IT'S NOT LIKE I WAS GONNA TAKE YOU OFF MY CHRISTMAS CARD LIST.

NATE.

WHAT?

CHRISTMAS.

YEAH, OKAY... CHRISTMAS WHAT?

SOMETHING'S BEEN BUGGING ME EVER SINCE THAT FREAK JUST *WALKED UP* TO THE PROBE AND LET HIMSELF BE *TAKEN DOWN.*

WHAT DOES HE *GAIN* FROM THAT?

OH $#$%. THE CROWDS.

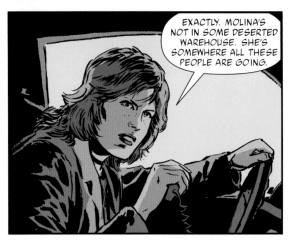

EXACTLY. MOLINA'S NOT IN SOME DESERTED WAREHOUSE. SHE'S SOMEWHERE ALL THESE PEOPLE ARE GOING.

KASINSKY, THIS IS CHANDLER. YOU'VE GOT KIDS?

THIS A SOCIAL CALL, ROMY?

I WISH. TWO NIGHTS BEFORE CHRISTMAS, WHAT SHOPPING DO YOU STILL HAVE LEFT TO DO?

ME? JUST ABOUT EVERYTHING ON MY KIDS' *LISTS.* STILL HAVE TO HIT G.A.F. BUELLERS OR TOYZ 4 KIDZ. *WHY?*

THAT'S WHERE MOLINA IS...

...IN ONE OF THOSE BIG *TOY STORES* CRAMMED WITH *PARENTS.*

WHEEEOO

THANK YOU SIR MAY I HAVE ANOTHER?

HOLD IT!

SURE--

THE THING ABOUT *YOU*, JOKER, IS THAT EVERY TIME YOU COME OUT TO *PLAY*, YOU *SHOOT* YOURSELF IN THE *FOOT*.

SO WORRIED ABOUT *BATMAN*, YOU *FORGET* ABOUT EVERYTHING *ELSE*.

SHOOTING *SPREE* TO GET *EVERYONE* INDOORS...

...THEN YOU COME *HERE*, TO GET *US* AND *BATS* TO FOCUS ON *YOU*.

AND *ALL* THOSE *SCARED* PEOPLE, WELL, THEY'RE *RELIEVED* NOW, THEY'RE OUT, *SHOPPING* UP A STORM.

WHAT IS IT WITH *YOU* AND *KIDS*?

THAT'S *IT*, ISN'T IT? MOLINA'S IN THE *STOCK-ROOM* OF SOME *TOY STORE*.

EVERY CLOWN LOVES KIDS, CAPTAIN.

JUST ASK SARAH ESSEN-GORDON.

OH, THAT'S *RIGHT*, YOU *CAN'T*!

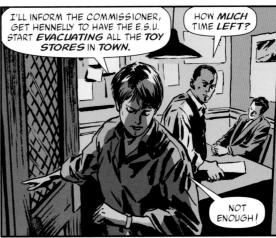

I'LL INFORM THE COMMISSIONER, GET HENNELLY TO HAVE THE E.S.U. START *EVACUATING* ALL THE *TOY STORES* IN TOWN.

HOW *MUCH* TIME *LEFT*?

NOT *ENOUGH!*

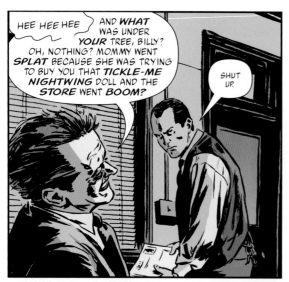

HEE HEE HEE AND **WHAT** WAS UNDER **YOUR** TREE, BILLY? OH, NOTHING? MOMMY WENT **SPLAT** BECAUSE SHE WAS TRYING TO BUY YOU THAT **TICKLE-ME NIGHTWING** DOLL AND THE **STORE** WENT **BOOM?**

SHUT UP.

SEE--HEE HEE-- SEE, THE **THING** IS, THE **PARENTS**, THEY DON'T EVEN **CARE**, Y'SEE? 'CAUSE--HEH-- SEE, IF THEY DID, THEY'D HAVE DONE THEIR *HEE HEE* SHOPPING ALREADY--

WHERE IS SHE? **WHICH** STORE?

--BUT **THIS** WAY, SEE, IT'S **MURDER** AND **GUILT** ALL IN THE *HEE HEE HEE* HAHAHA SAME *HEE HEE* **PACKAGE!**

DAMN YOU, **WHERE**--

HURRRK KK

SORRY, **WHAT** WAS THAT?

HHKKK-- KKHHRR

OH, NO, LIEUTENANT, YOU'LL **HAVE** TO SPEAK UP...

...I CAN **BARELY** HEAR YOU...

GOD, I LOVE THE HOLIDAYS.

334

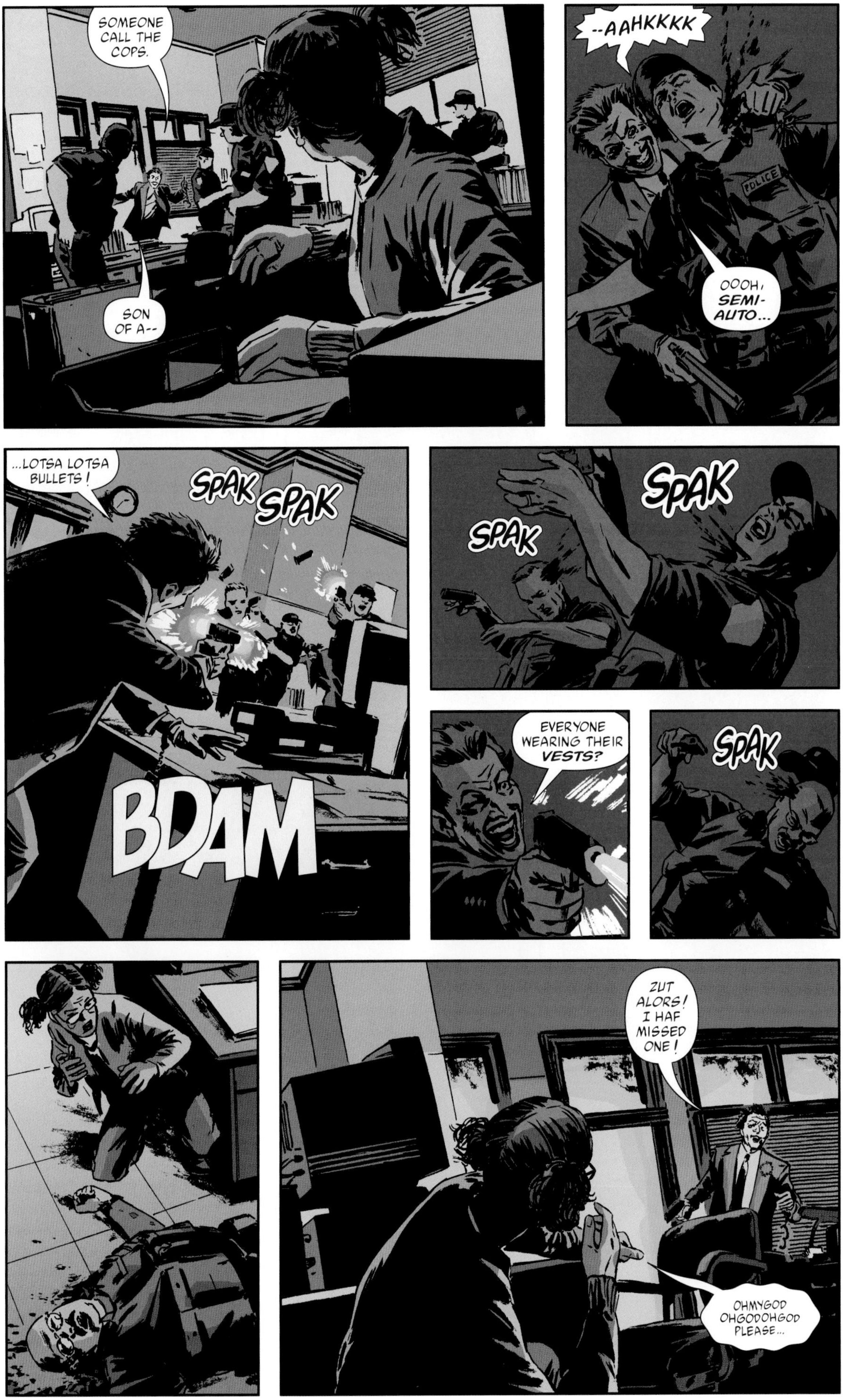
SOMEONE CALL THE COPS.
SON OF A--
--AAHKKKK
OOOH, SEMI-AUTO...
POLICE
...LOTSA LOTSA BULLETS!
SPAK SPAK
BDAM
SPAK
SPAK
EVERYONE WEARING THEIR VESTS?
SPAK
ZUT ALORS! I HAF MISSED ONE!
OHMYGOD OHGODOHGOD PLEASE...

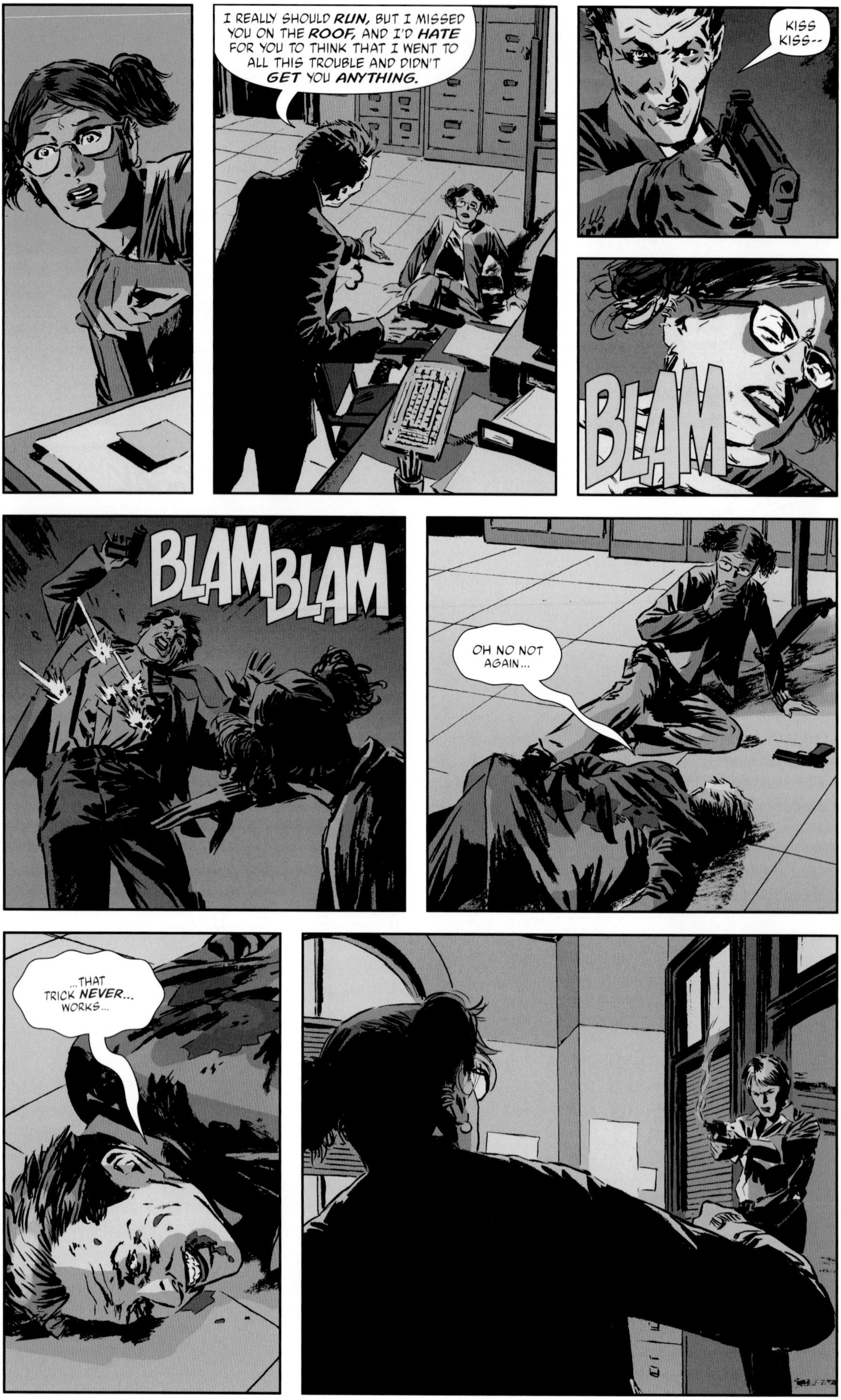
I REALLY SHOULD RUN, BUT I MISSED YOU ON THE ROOF, AND I'D HATE FOR YOU TO THINK THAT I WENT TO ALL THIS TROUBLE AND DIDN'T GET YOU ANYTHING.
KISS KISS--
BLAM
BLAMBLAM
OH NO NOT AGAIN...
...THAT TRICK NEVER... WORKS...

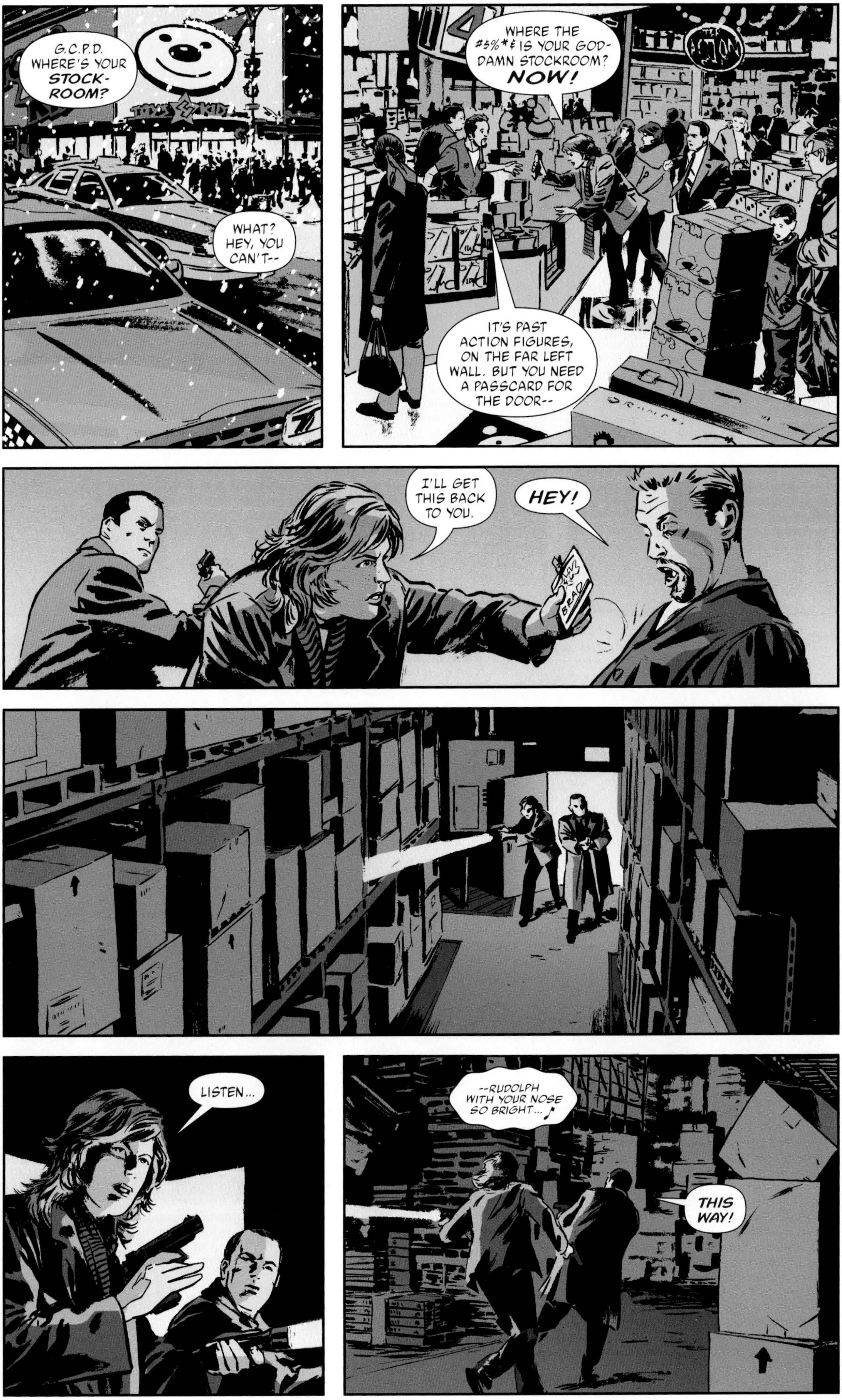
G.C.P.D. WHERE'S YOUR STOCK-ROOM?
WHAT? HEY, YOU CAN'T--
WHERE THE #$%*& IS YOUR GOD-DAMN STOCKROOM? NOW!
IT'S PAST ACTION FIGURES, ON THE FAR LEFT WALL. BUT YOU NEED A PASSCARD FOR THE DOOR--
I'LL GET THIS BACK TO YOU.
HEY!
LISTEN...
--RUDOLPH WITH YOUR NOSE SO BRIGHT...♪
THIS WAY!

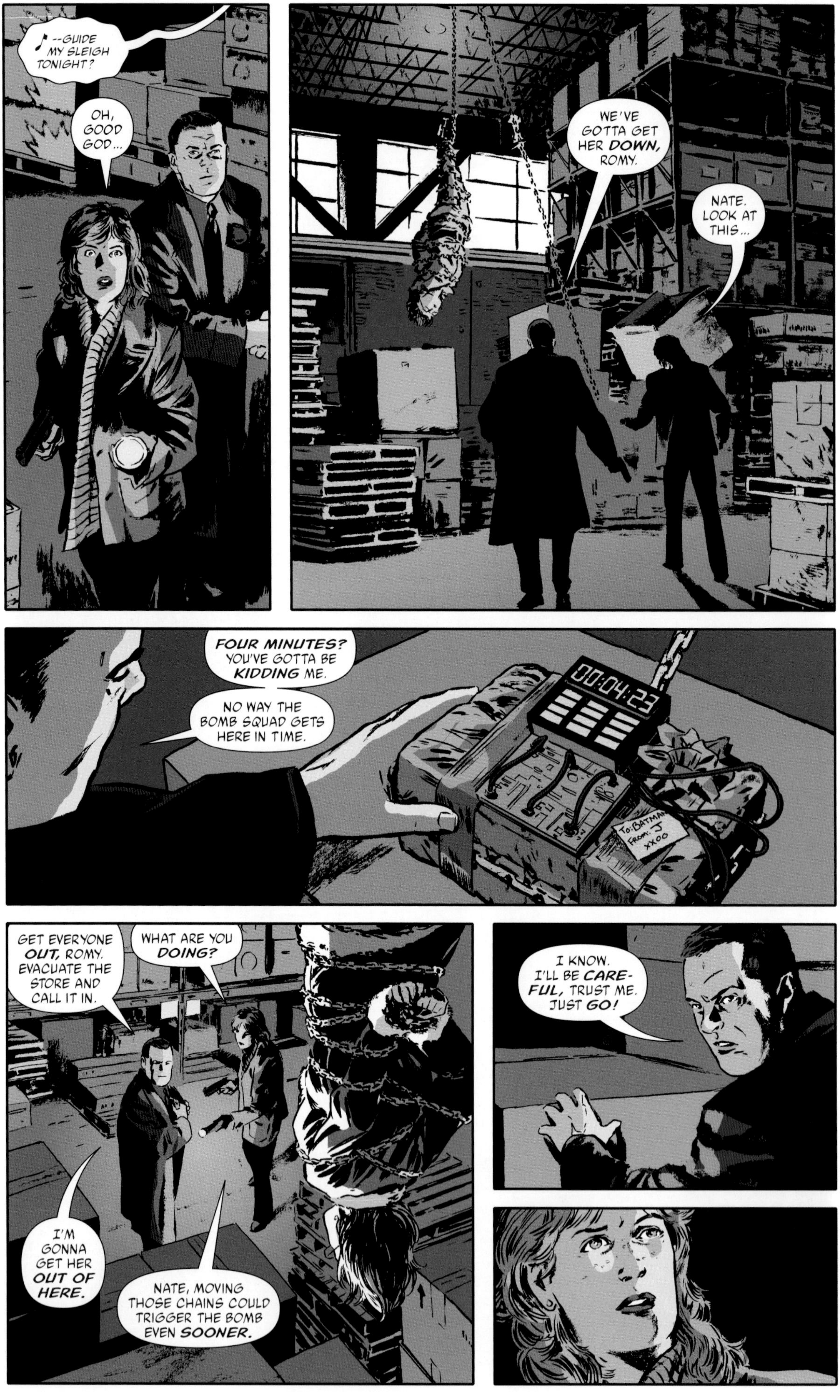
♪ --GUIDE MY SLEIGH TONIGHT?
OH, GOOD GOD...
WE'VE GOTTA GET HER DOWN, ROMY.
NATE. LOOK AT THIS...
FOUR MINUTES? YOU'VE GOTTA BE KIDDING ME.
NO WAY THE BOMB SQUAD GETS HERE IN TIME.
00:04:23
To: BATMAN From: J XXOO
GET EVERYONE OUT, ROMY. EVACUATE THE STORE AND CALL IT IN.
WHAT ARE YOU DOING?
I'M GONNA GET HER OUT OF HERE.
NATE, MOVING THOSE CHAINS COULD TRIGGER THE BOMB EVEN SOONER.
I KNOW. I'LL BE CAREFUL, TRUST ME. JUST GO!

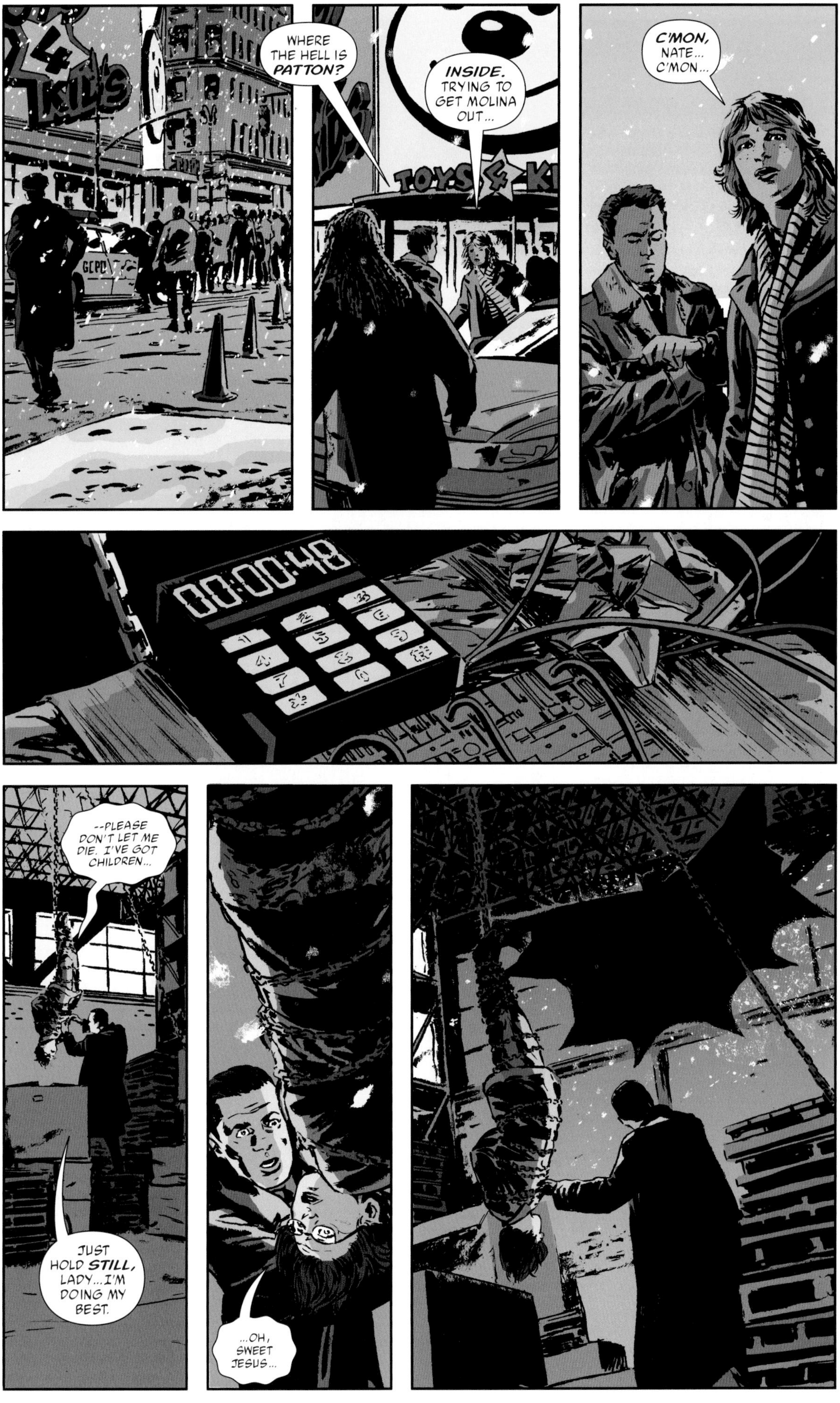
WHERE THE HELL IS PATTON?
INSIDE. TRYING TO GET MOLINA OUT...
C'MON, NATE... C'MON...
00:00:48
--PLEASE DON'T LET ME DIE. I'VE GOT CHILDREN...
JUST HOLD STILL, LADY...I'M DOING MY BEST.
...OH, SWEET JESUS...

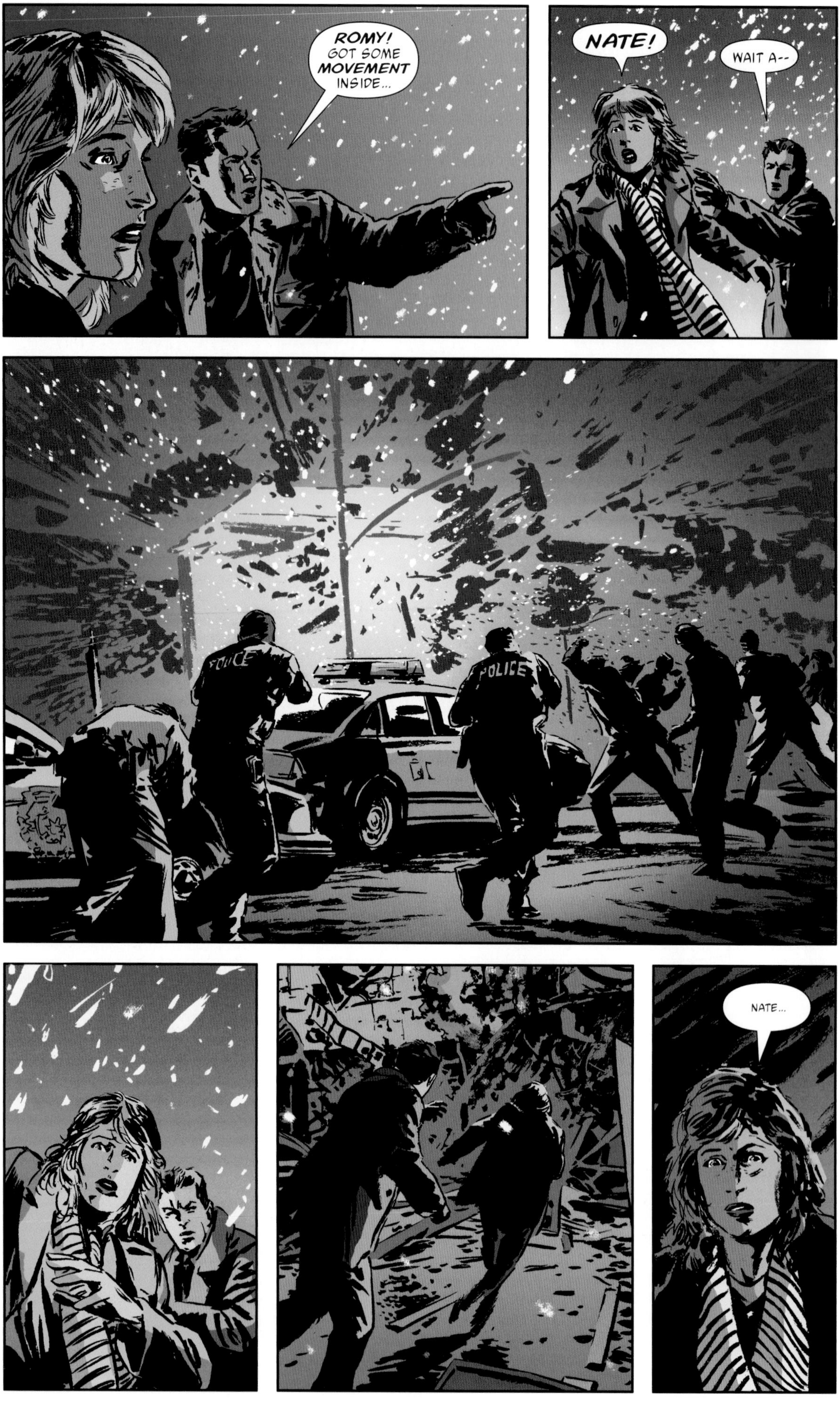
ROMY! GOT SOME MOVEMENT INSIDE...
NATE!
WAIT A--
NATE...

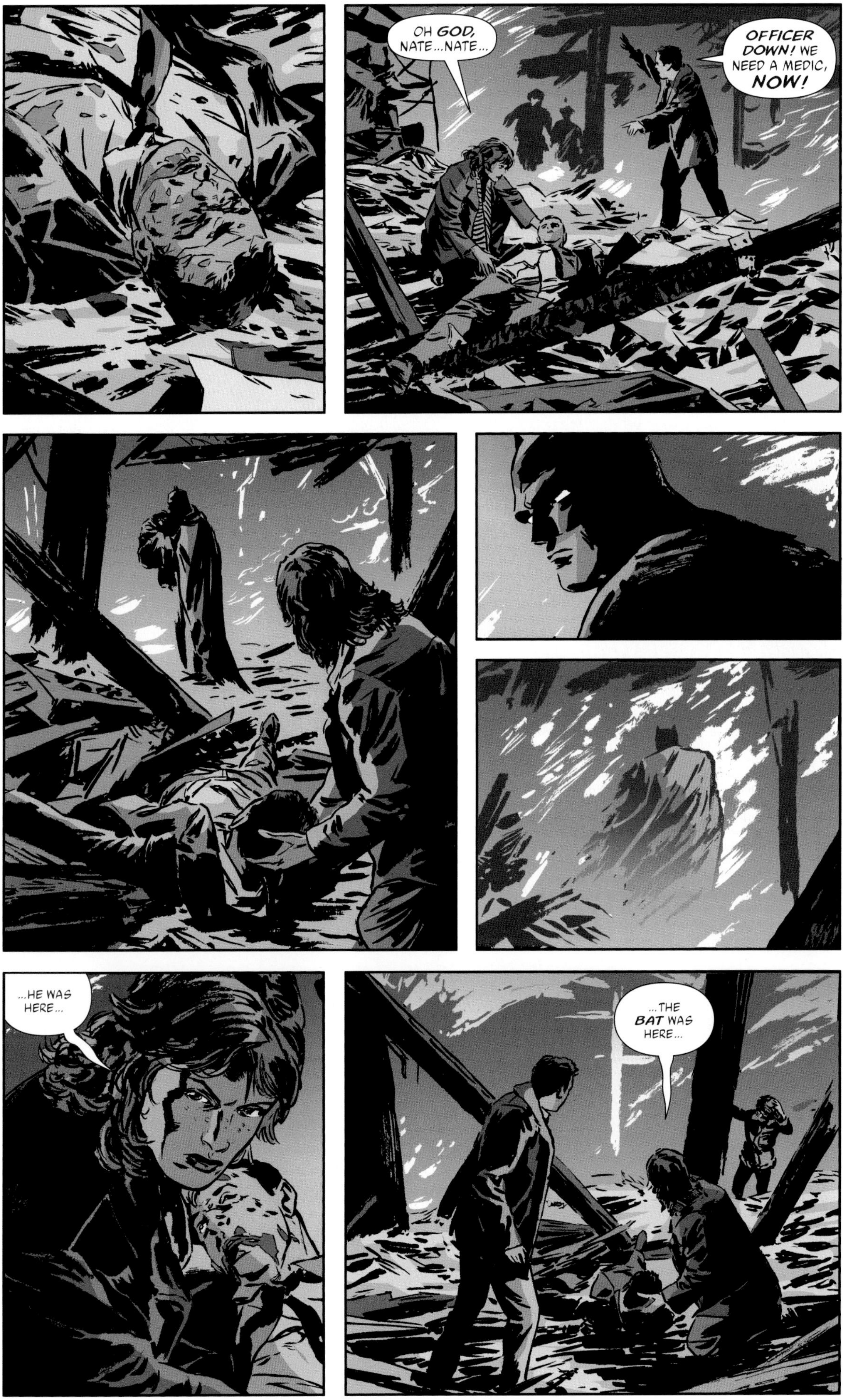
OH GOD, NATE...NATE...
OFFICER DOWN! WE NEED A MEDIC, NOW!
...HE WAS HERE...
...THE BAT WAS HERE...

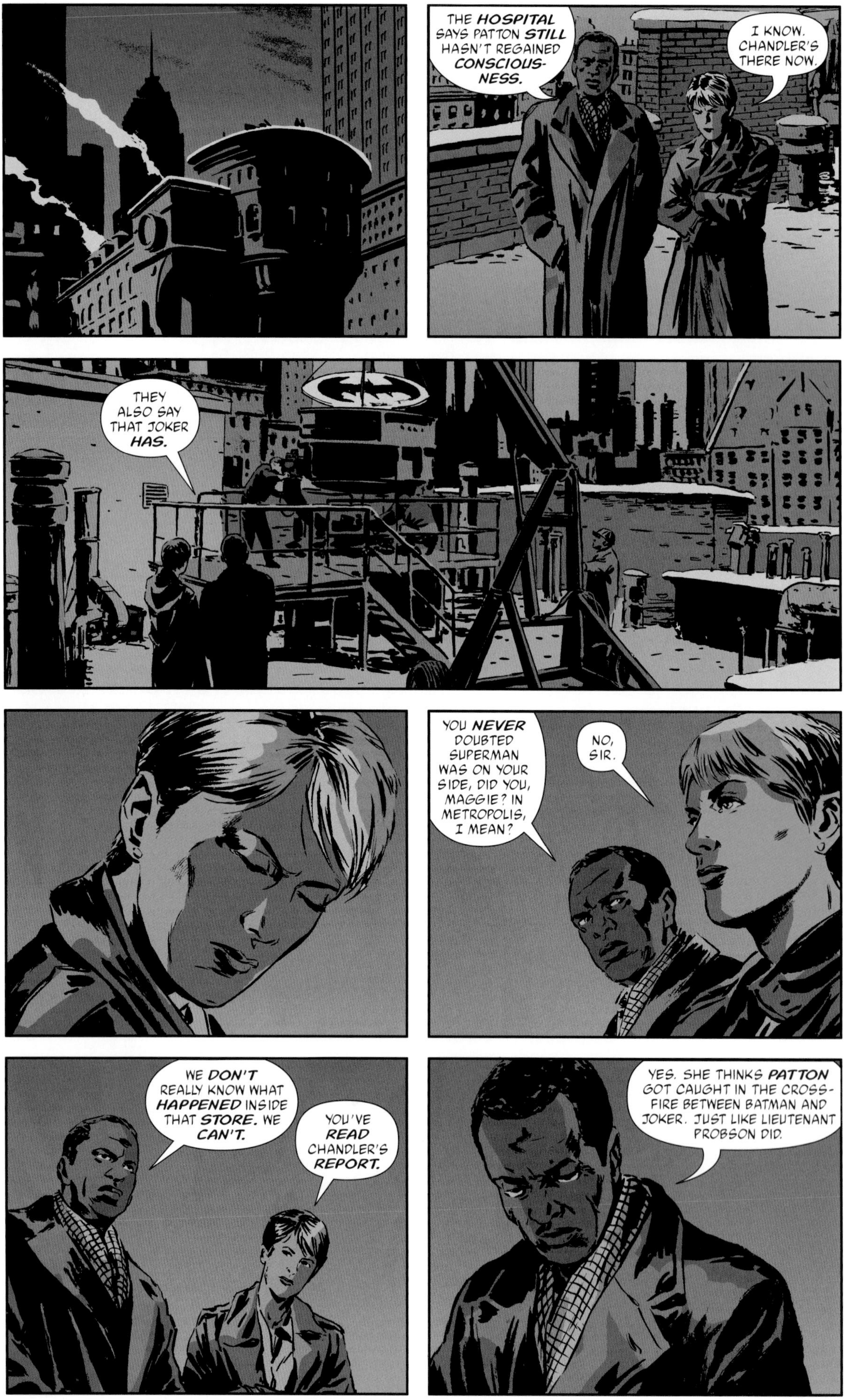
THE HOSPITAL SAYS PATTON STILL HASN'T REGAINED CONSCIOUS-NESS.
I KNOW. CHANDLER'S THERE NOW.
THEY ALSO SAY THAT JOKER HAS.
YOU NEVER DOUBTED SUPERMAN WAS ON YOUR SIDE, DID YOU, MAGGIE? IN METROPOLIS, I MEAN?
NO, SIR.
WE DON'T REALLY KNOW WHAT HAPPENED INSIDE THAT STORE. WE CAN'T.
YOU'VE READ CHANDLER'S REPORT.
YES. SHE THINKS PATTON GOT CAUGHT IN THE CROSS-FIRE BETWEEN BATMAN AND JOKER. JUST LIKE LIEUTENANT PROBSON DID.

I DON'T THINK WE CAN GO ON LIKE THIS MUCH *LONGER*, MAGGIE.

AS YOU *SAID*, WE CAN'T KNOW WHOSE FAULT THIS WAS.

WE SHOULDN'T EVEN HAVE TO *WONDER.* THAT'S THE PROBLEM.

WE'VE GOT COPS *DYING* WHILE WE WAIT AROUND FOR *HIM* TO SAVE THE DAY...

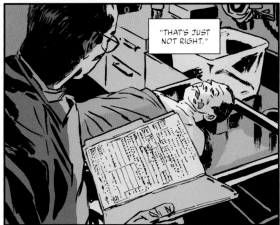

"THAT'S JUST NOT RIGHT."

"NO SIR, IT'S *NOT...*"

"...BUT IT'S GOTHAM."

END

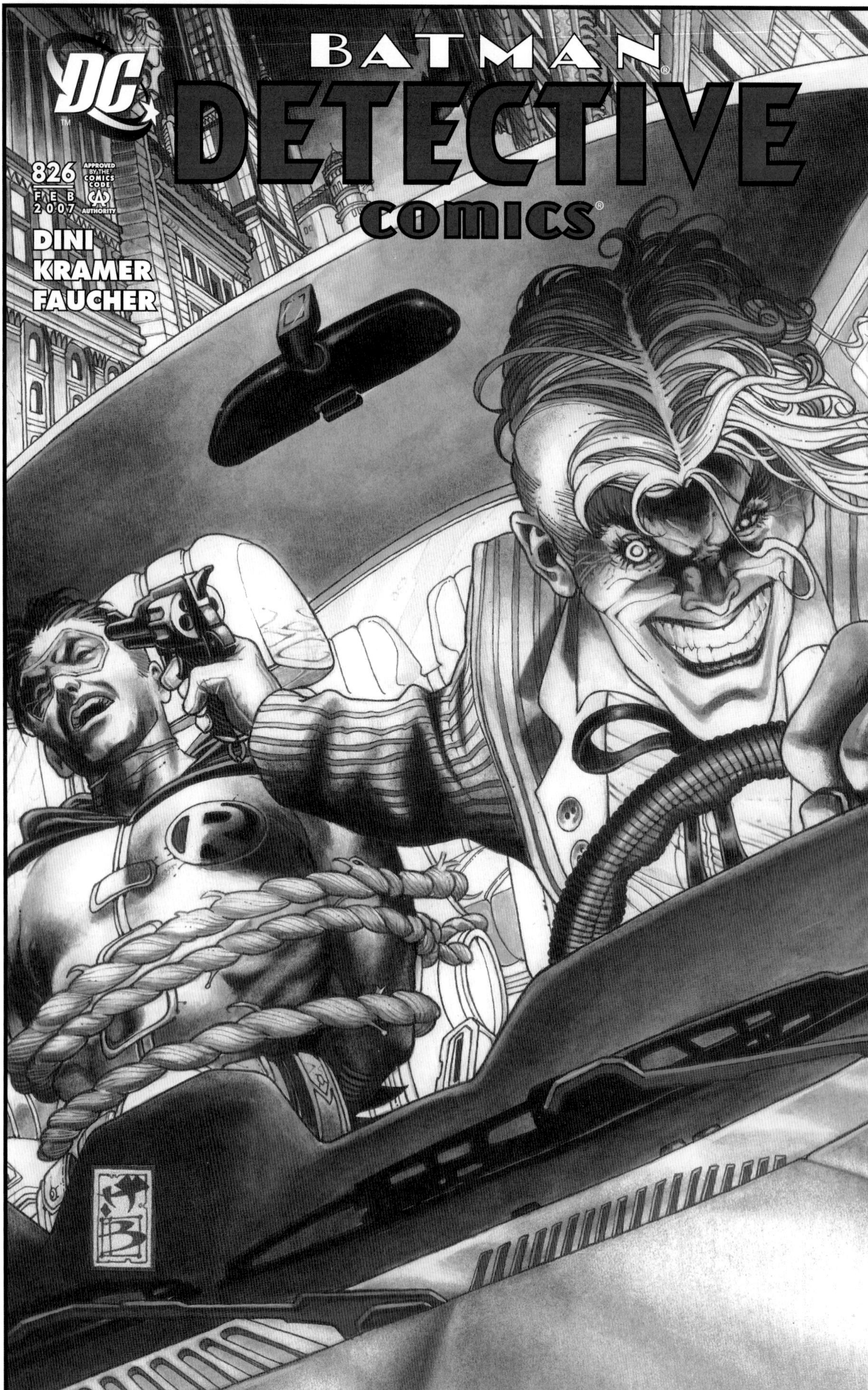

DC
BATMAN
DETECTIVE
COMICS
826
FEB
2007
APPROVED BY THE COMICS CODE AUTHORITY
DINI
KRAMER
FAUCHER

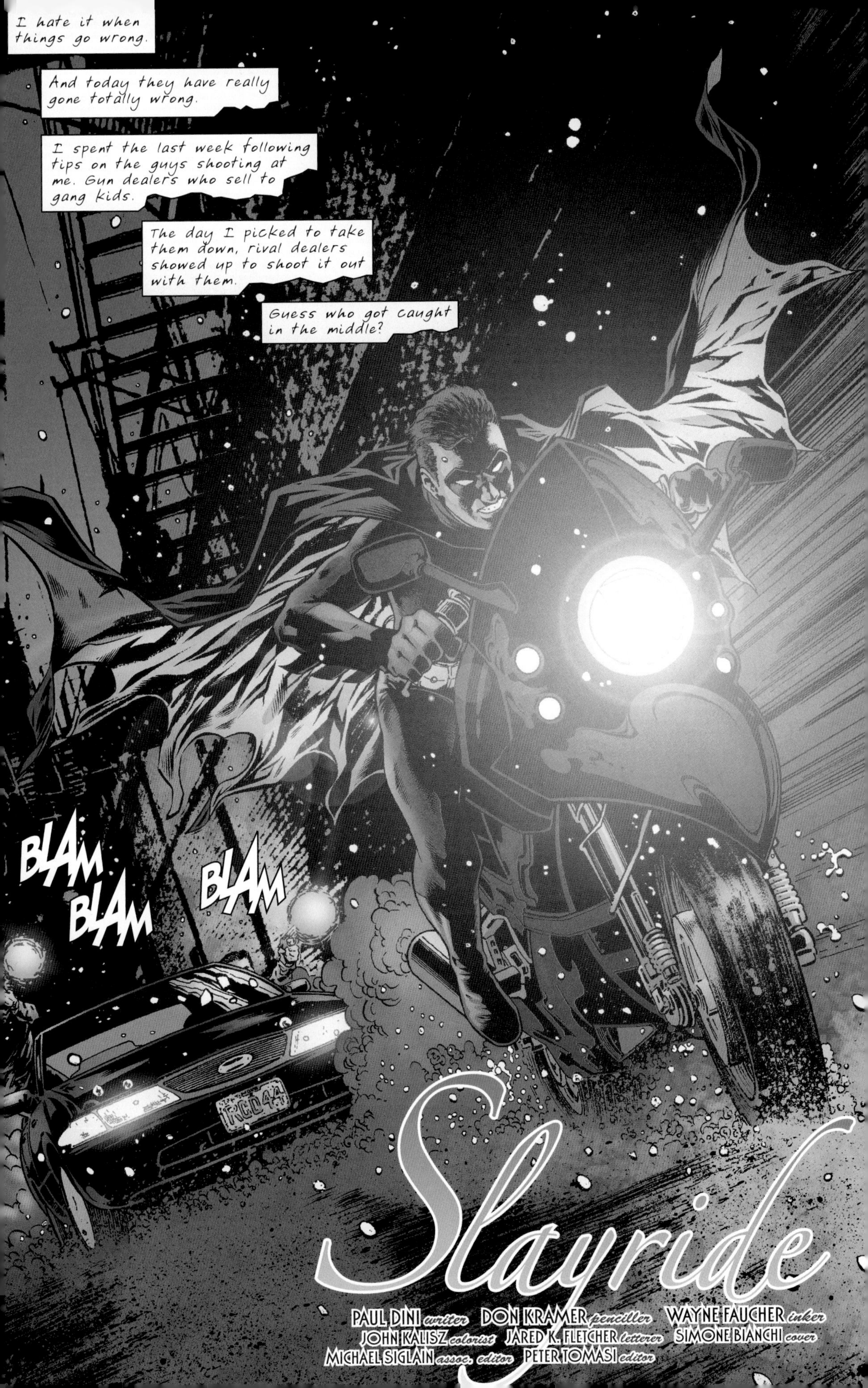

I hate it when things go wrong.
And today they have really gone totally wrong.
I spent the last week following tips on the guys shooting at me. Gun dealers who sell to gang kids.
The day I picked to take them down, rival dealers showed up to shoot it out with them.
Guess who got caught in the middle?
BLAM BLAM
BLAM
RCD 44
Slayride
PAUL DINI writer DON KRAMER penciller WAYNE FAUCHER inker
JOHN KALISZ colorist JARED K. FLETCHER letterer SIMONE BIANCHI cover
MICHAEL SIGLAIN assoc. editor PETER TOMASI editor

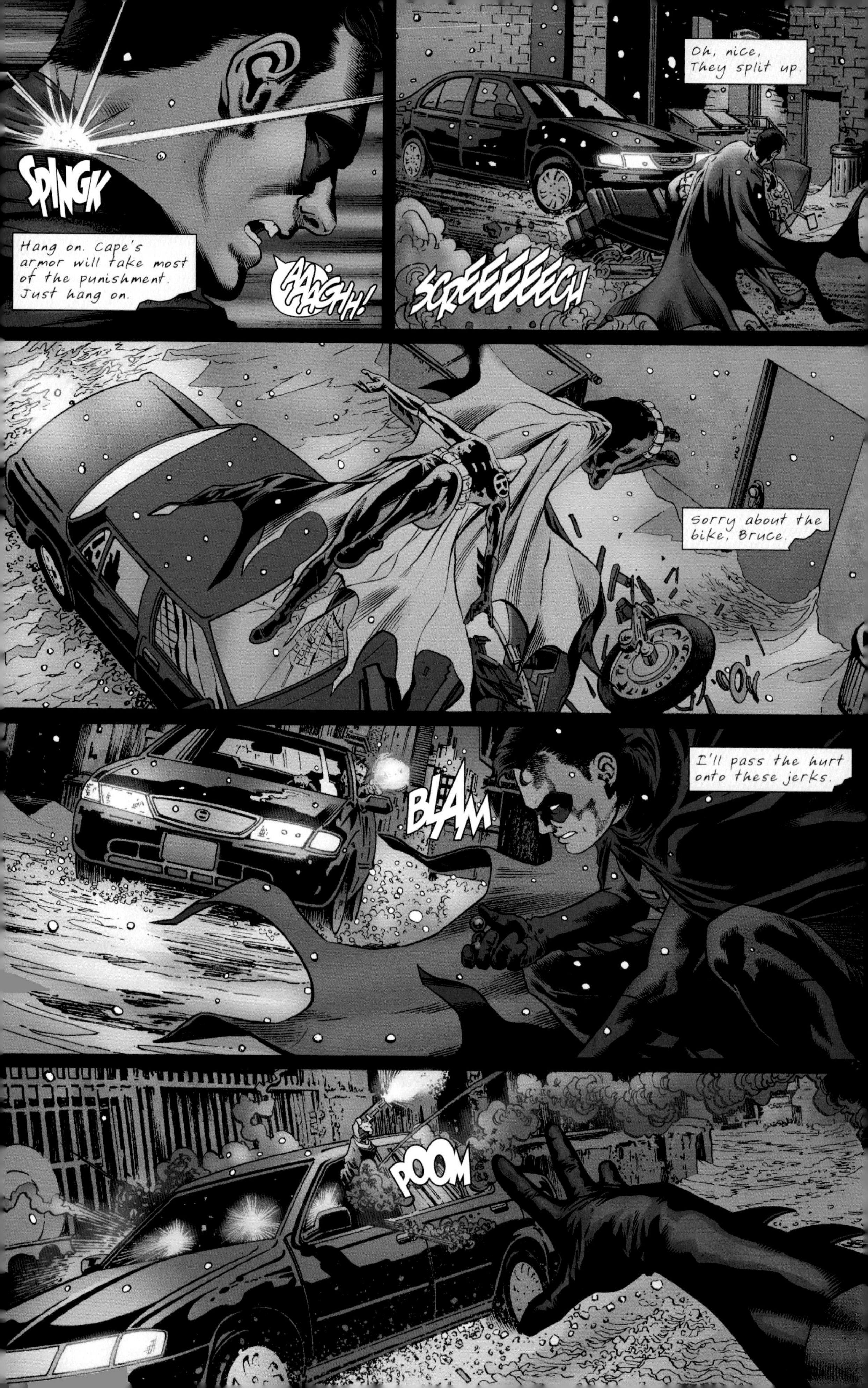
SPINGK
Hang on. Cape's armor will take most of the punishment. Just hang on.
AAAGHH!
Oh, nice, They split up.
SCREEEEEECH
Sorry about the bike, Bruce.
I'll pass the hurt onto these jerks.
BLAM
POOM

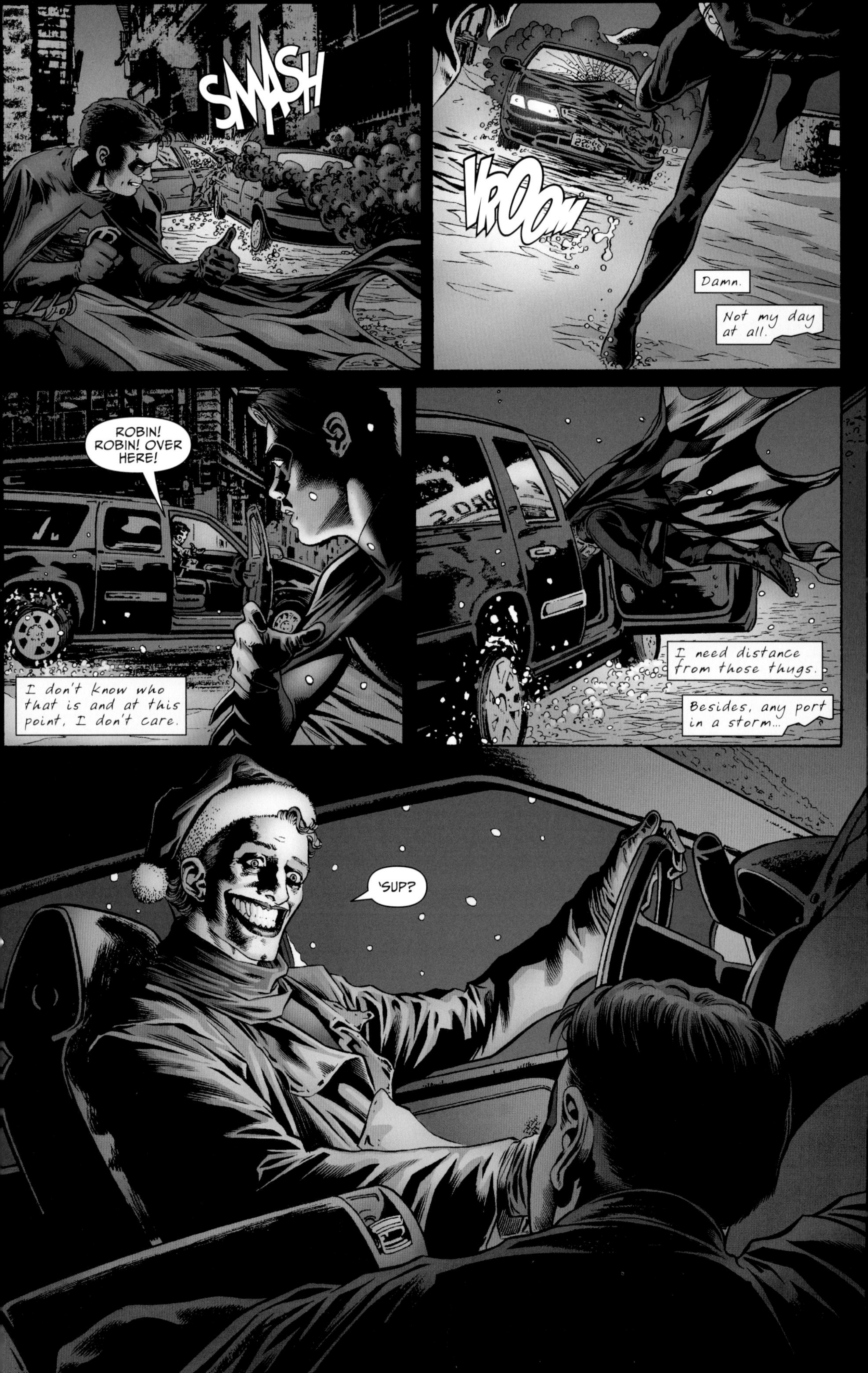
SMASH
VROOOM
Damn.
Not my day at all.
ROBIN! ROBIN! OVER HERE!
I don't know who that is and at this point, I don't care.
I need distance from those thugs.
Besides, any port in a storm...
'SUP?

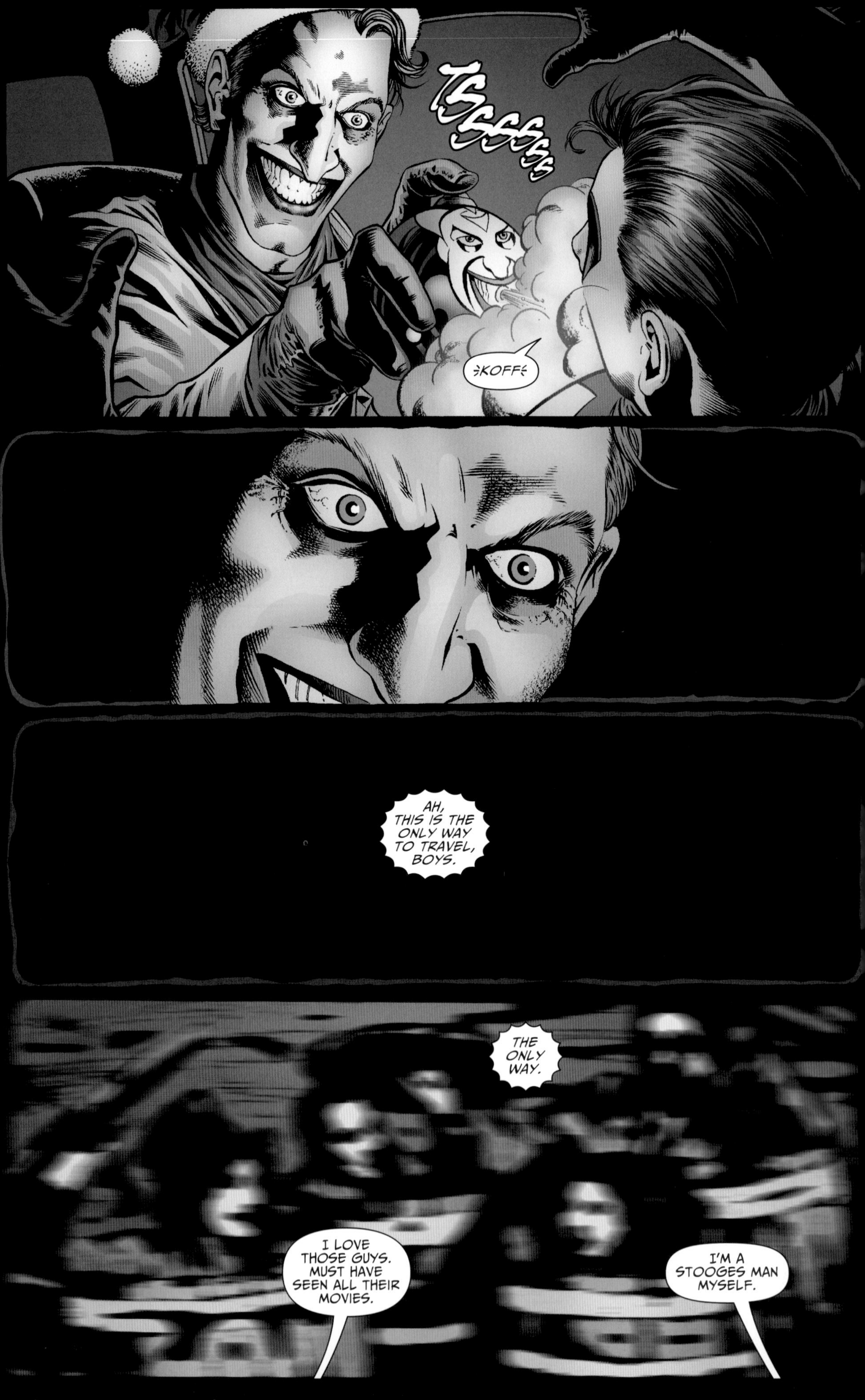
TSSSSSS
KOFF
AH, THIS IS THE ONLY WAY TO TRAVEL, BOYS.
THE ONLY WAY.
I LOVE THOSE GUYS. MUST HAVE SEEN ALL THEIR MOVIES.
I'M A STOOGES MAN MYSELF.

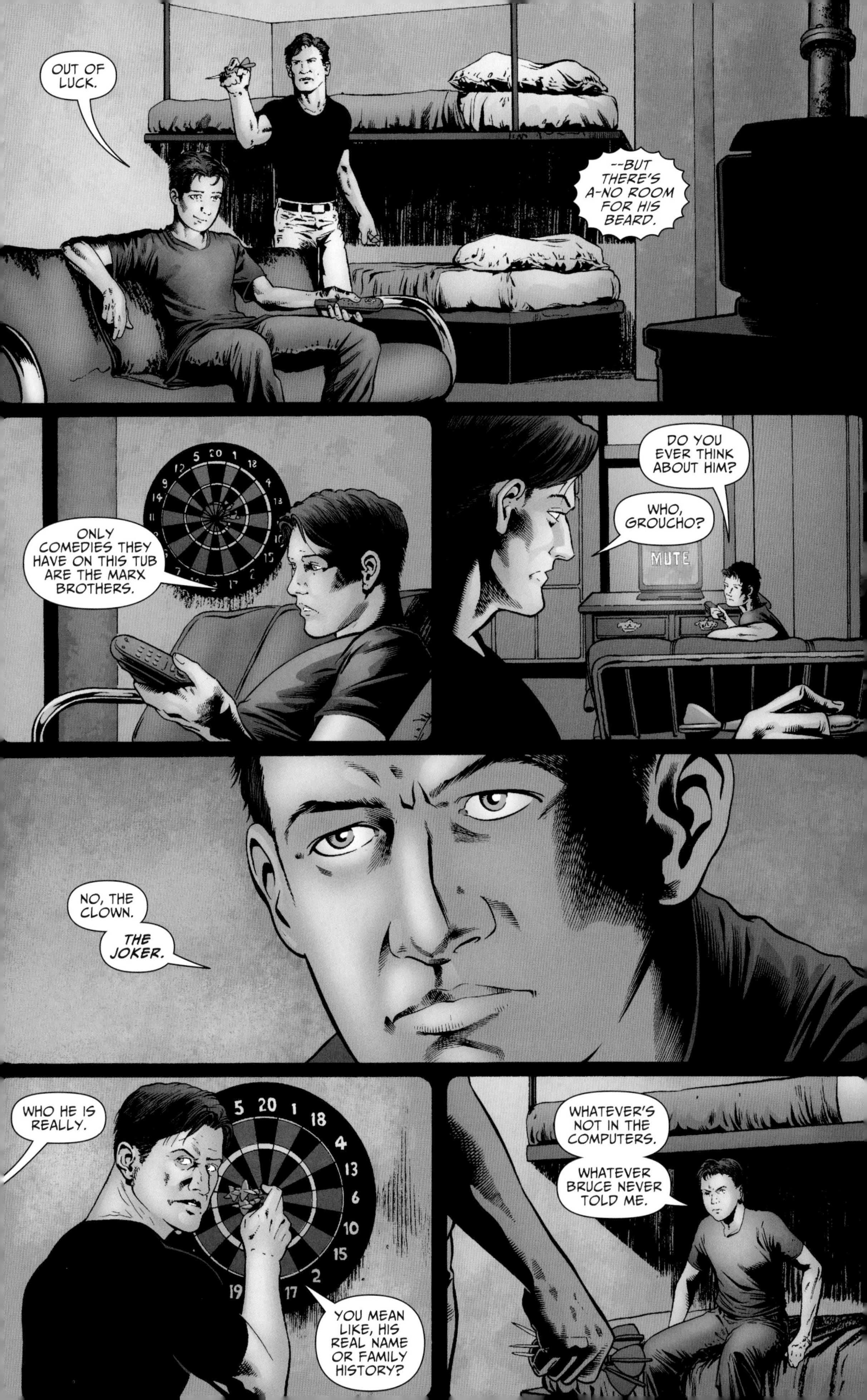
OUT OF LUCK.
--BUT THERE'S A-NO ROOM FOR HIS BEARD.
ONLY COMEDIES THEY HAVE ON THIS TUB ARE THE MARX BROTHERS.
DO YOU EVER THINK ABOUT HIM?
WHO, GROUCHO?
MUTE
NO, THE CLOWN.
THE JOKER.
WHO HE IS REALLY.
YOU MEAN LIKE, HIS REAL NAME OR FAMILY HISTORY?
WHATEVER'S NOT IN THE COMPUTERS.
WHATEVER BRUCE NEVER TOLD ME.

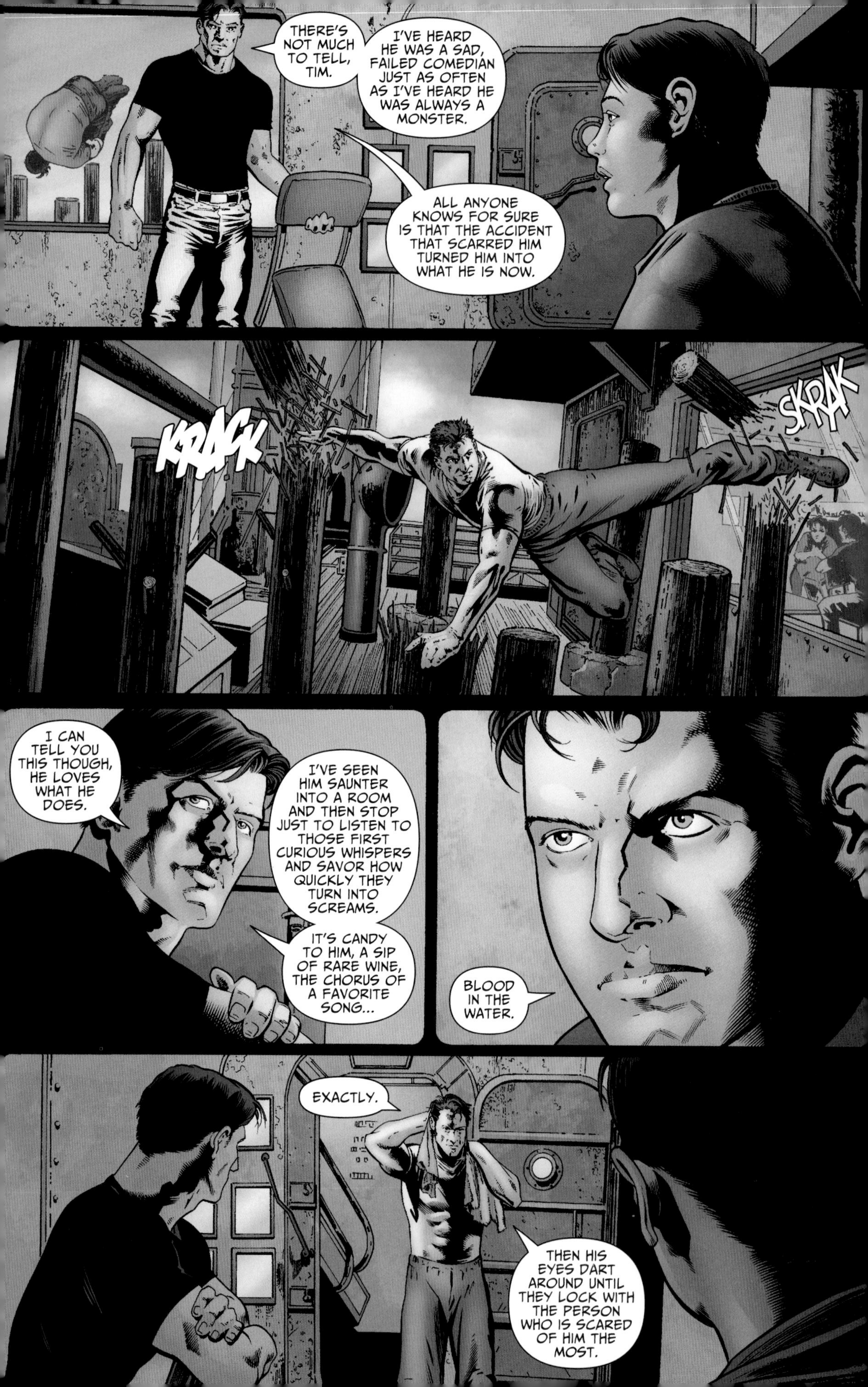
THERE'S NOT MUCH TO TELL, TIM.
I'VE HEARD HE WAS A SAD, FAILED COMEDIAN JUST AS OFTEN AS I'VE HEARD HE WAS ALWAYS A MONSTER.
ALL ANYONE KNOWS FOR SURE IS THAT THE ACCIDENT THAT SCARRED HIM TURNED HIM INTO WHAT HE IS NOW.
KRACK
SKRAK
I CAN TELL YOU THIS THOUGH, HE LOVES WHAT HE DOES.
I'VE SEEN HIM SAUNTER INTO A ROOM AND THEN STOP JUST TO LISTEN TO THOSE FIRST CURIOUS WHISPERS AND SAVOR HOW QUICKLY THEY TURN INTO SCREAMS.
IT'S CANDY TO HIM, A SIP OF RARE WINE, THE CHORUS OF A FAVORITE SONG...
BLOOD IN THE WATER.
EXACTLY.
THEN HIS EYES DART AROUND UNTIL THEY LOCK WITH THE PERSON WHO IS SCARED OF HIM THE MOST.

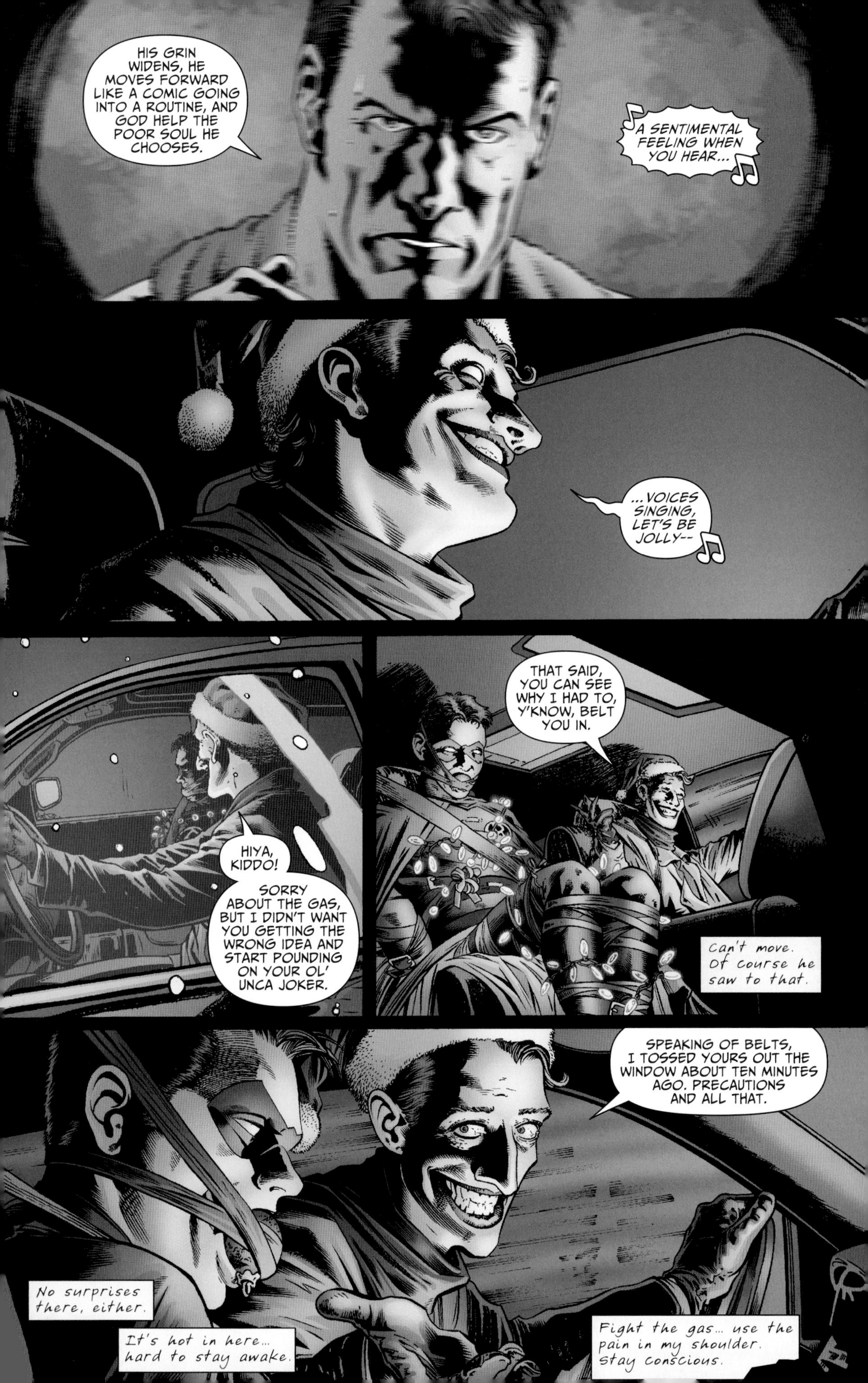
HIS GRIN WIDENS, HE MOVES FORWARD LIKE A COMIC GOING INTO A ROUTINE, AND GOD HELP THE POOR SOUL HE CHOOSES.
♫ A SENTIMENTAL FEELING WHEN YOU HEAR... ♫
...VOICES SINGING, LET'S BE JOLLY-- ♫
HIYA, KIDDO!
SORRY ABOUT THE GAS, BUT I DIDN'T WANT YOU GETTING THE WRONG IDEA AND START POUNDING ON YOUR OL' UNCA JOKER.
THAT SAID, YOU CAN SEE WHY I HAD TO, Y'KNOW, BELT YOU IN.
Can't move. Of course he saw to that.
SPEAKING OF BELTS, I TOSSED YOURS OUT THE WINDOW ABOUT TEN MINUTES AGO. PRECAUTIONS AND ALL THAT.
No surprises there, either.
It's hot in here... hard to stay awake.
Fight the gas... use the pain in my shoulder. Stay conscious.

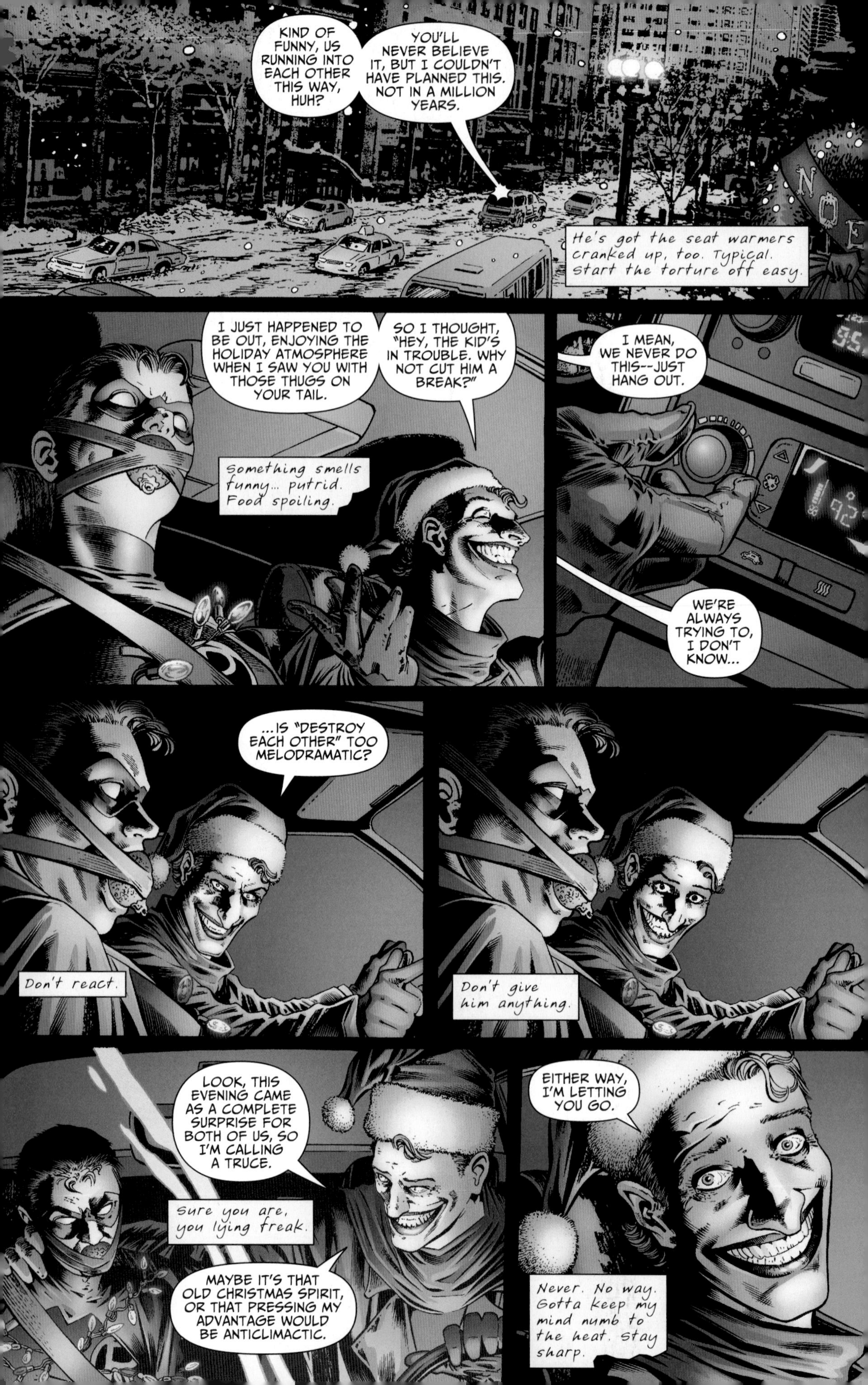
KIND OF FUNNY, US RUNNING INTO EACH OTHER THIS WAY, HUH?
YOU'LL NEVER BELIEVE IT, BUT I COULDN'T HAVE PLANNED THIS. NOT IN A MILLION YEARS.
He's got the seat warmers cranked up, too. Typical. Start the torture off easy.
I JUST HAPPENED TO BE OUT, ENJOYING THE HOLIDAY ATMOSPHERE WHEN I SAW YOU WITH THOSE THUGS ON YOUR TAIL.
SO I THOUGHT, "HEY, THE KID'S IN TROUBLE. WHY NOT CUT HIM A BREAK?"
Something smells funny... putrid. Food spoiling.
I MEAN, WE NEVER DO THIS--JUST HANG OUT.
WE'RE ALWAYS TRYING TO, I DON'T KNOW...
...IS "DESTROY EACH OTHER" TOO MELODRAMATIC?
Don't react.
Don't give him anything.
LOOK, THIS EVENING CAME AS A COMPLETE SURPRISE FOR BOTH OF US, SO I'M CALLING A TRUCE.
Sure you are, you lying freak.
MAYBE IT'S THAT OLD CHRISTMAS SPIRIT, OR THAT PRESSING MY ADVANTAGE WOULD BE ANTICLIMACTIC.
EITHER WAY, I'M LETTING YOU GO.
Never. No way. Gotta keep my mind numb to the heat. Stay sharp.

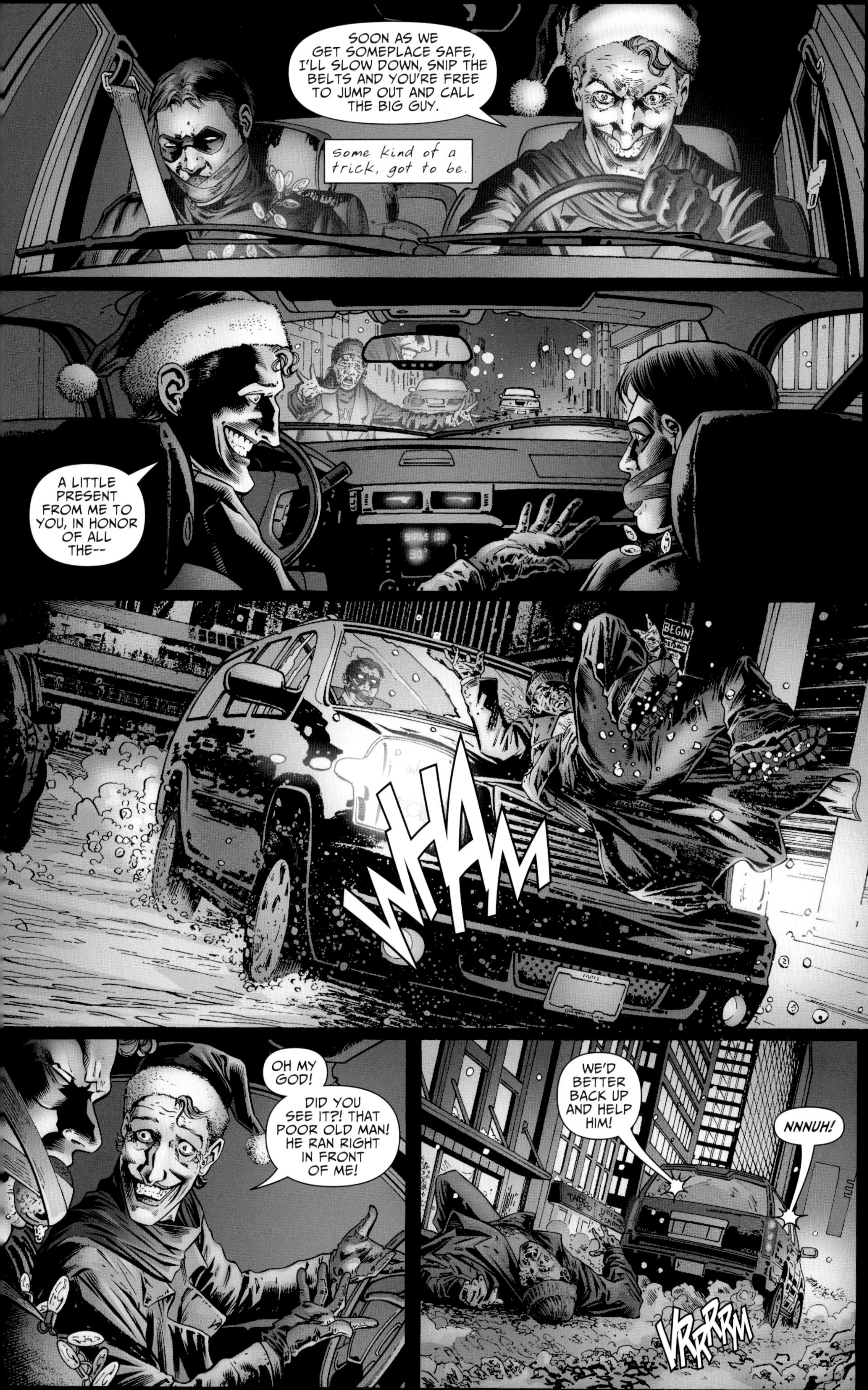
SOON AS WE GET SOMEPLACE SAFE, I'LL SLOW DOWN, SNIP THE BELTS AND YOU'RE FREE TO JUMP OUT AND CALL THE BIG GUY.
Some kind of a trick, got to be.
A LITTLE PRESENT FROM ME TO YOU, IN HONOR OF ALL THE--
WHAM
OH MY GOD!
DID YOU SEE IT?! THAT POOR OLD MAN! HE RAN RIGHT IN FRONT OF ME!
WE'D BETTER BACK UP AND HELP HIM!
NNNUH!
VRRRRM

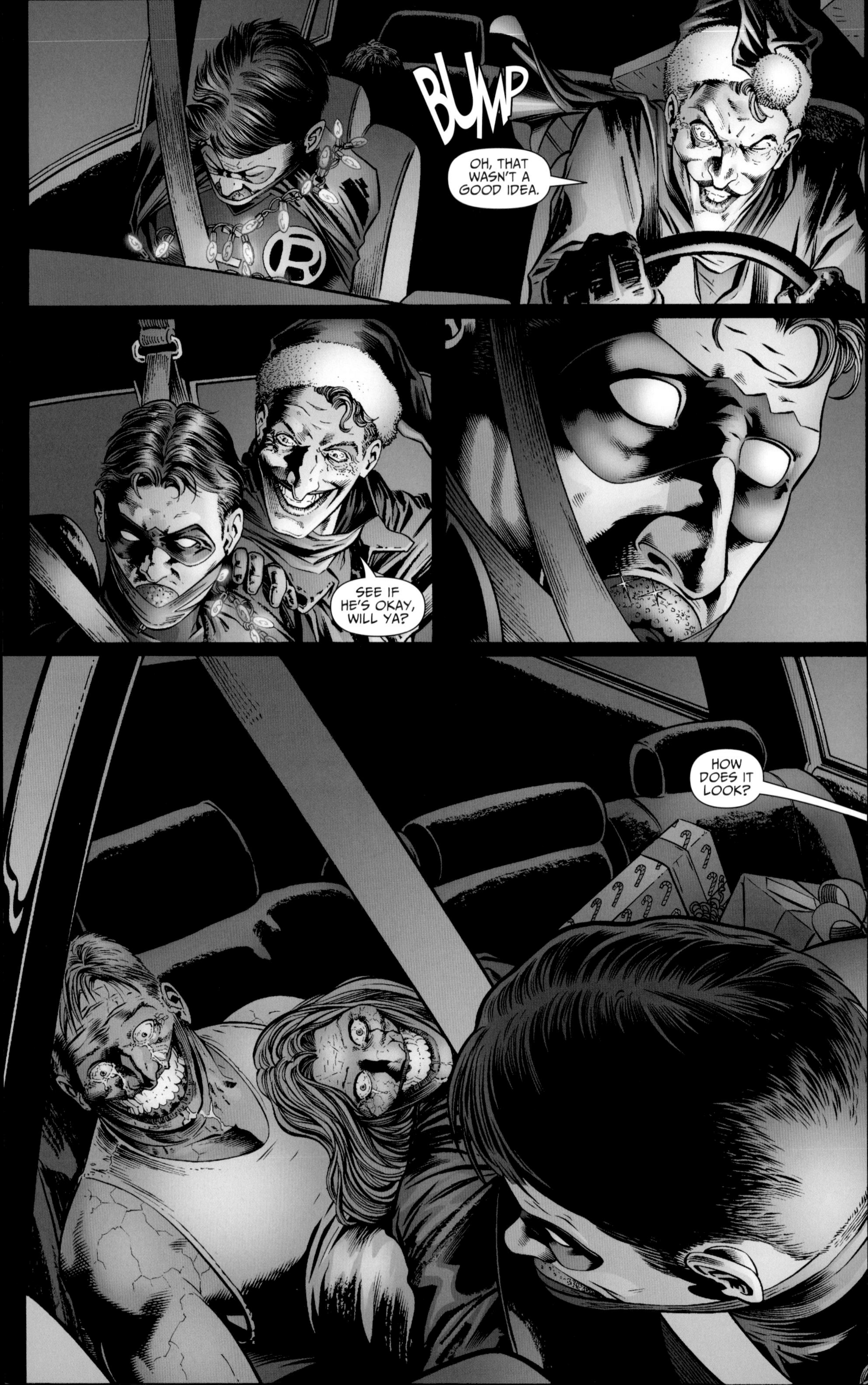
BUMP
OH, THAT WASN'T A GOOD IDEA.
SEE IF HE'S OKAY, WILL YA?
HOW DOES IT LOOK?

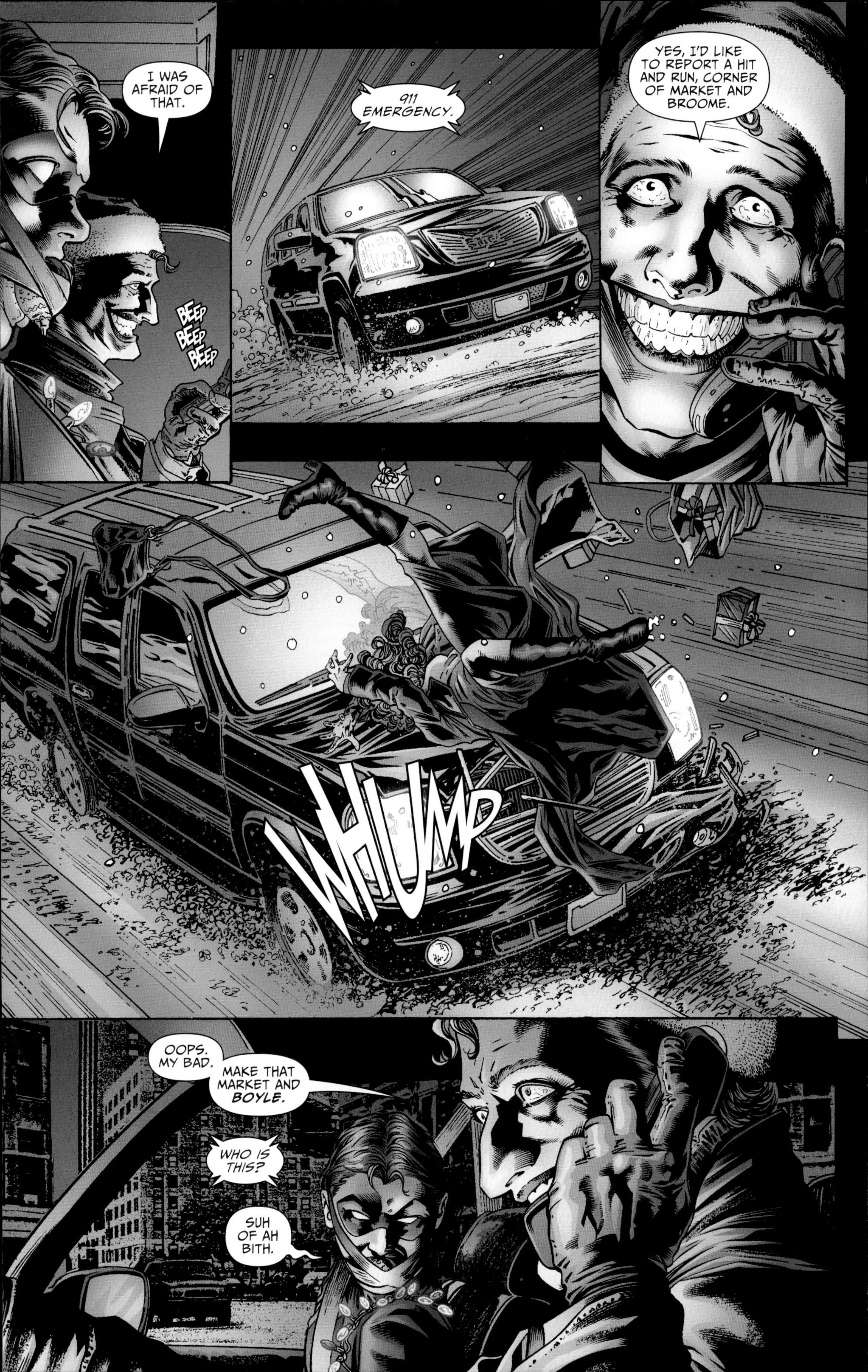
I WAS AFRAID OF THAT.
BEEP BEEP BEEP
911 EMERGENCY.
YES, I'D LIKE TO REPORT A HIT AND RUN, CORNER OF MARKET AND BROOME.
WHUMP
OOPS. MY BAD.
MAKE THAT MARKET AND BOYLE.
WHO IS THIS?
SUH OF AH BITH.

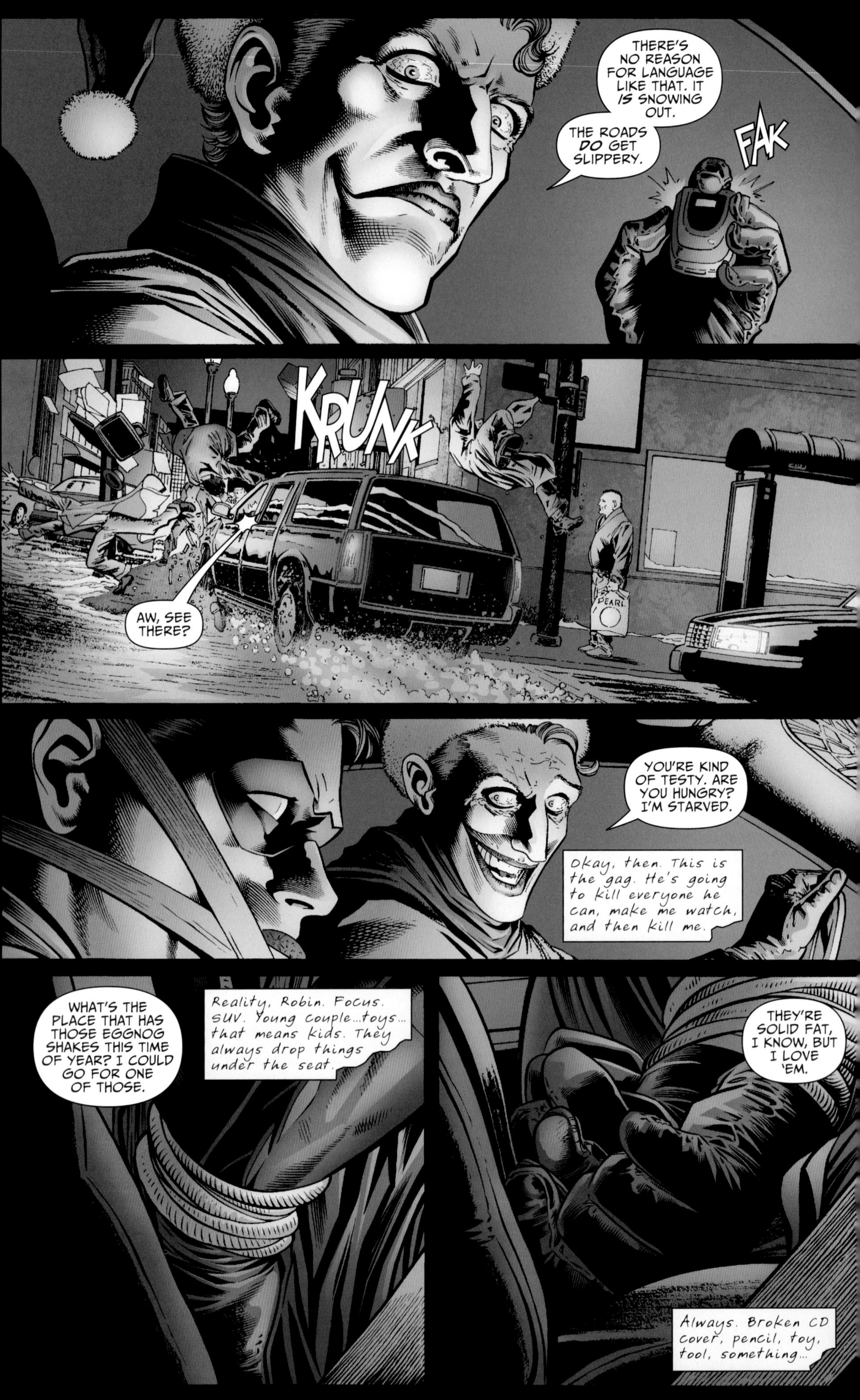
THERE'S NO REASON FOR LANGUAGE LIKE THAT. IT *IS* SNOWING OUT.
THE ROADS *DO* GET SLIPPERY.
FAK
KRUNK
AW, SEE THERE?
PEARL
YOU'RE KIND OF TESTY. ARE YOU HUNGRY? I'M STARVED.
Okay, then. This is the gag. He's going to kill everyone he can, make me watch, and then kill me.
WHAT'S THE PLACE THAT HAS THOSE EGGNOG SHAKES THIS TIME OF YEAR? I COULD GO FOR ONE OF THOSE.
Reality, Robin. Focus. SUV. Young couple...toys... that means kids. They always drop things under the seat.
THEY'RE SOLID FAT, I KNOW, BUT I LOVE 'EM.
Always. Broken CD cover, pencil, toy, tool, something...

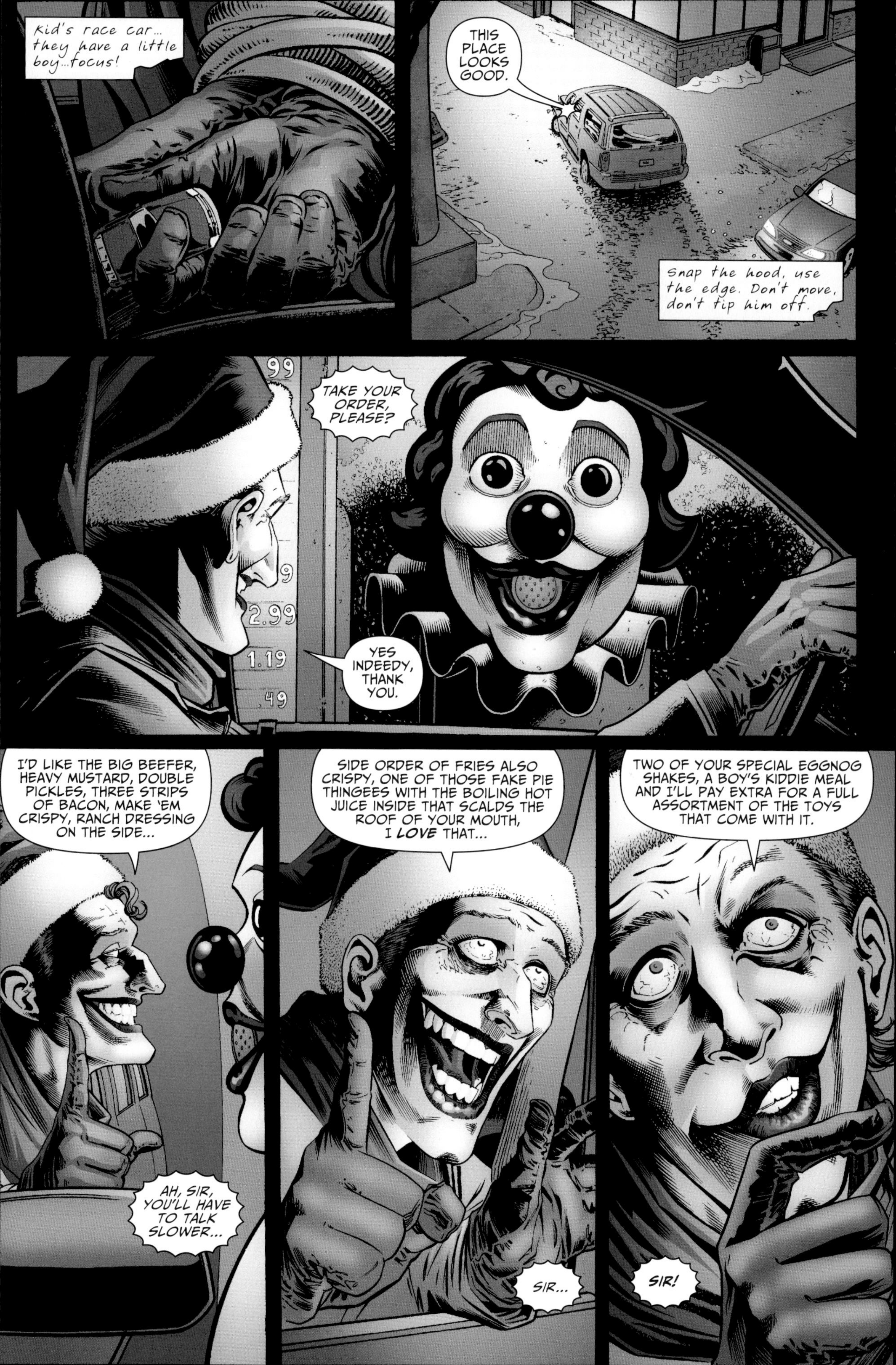

Kid's race car... they have a little boy...focus!
THIS PLACE LOOKS GOOD.
Snap the hood, use the edge. Don't move, don't tip him off.
99
TAKE YOUR ORDER, PLEASE?
9
2.99
1.19
.49
YES INDEEDY, THANK YOU.
I'D LIKE THE BIG BEEFER, HEAVY MUSTARD, DOUBLE PICKLES, THREE STRIPS OF BACON, MAKE 'EM CRISPY, RANCH DRESSING ON THE SIDE...
AH, SIR, YOU'LL HAVE TO TALK SLOWER...
SIDE ORDER OF FRIES ALSO CRISPY, ONE OF THOSE FAKE PIE THINGEES WITH THE BOILING HOT JUICE INSIDE THAT SCALDS THE ROOF OF YOUR MOUTH, I LOVE THAT...
SIR...
TWO OF YOUR SPECIAL EGGNOG SHAKES, A BOY'S KIDDIE MEAL AND I'LL PAY EXTRA FOR A FULL ASSORTMENT OF THE TOYS THAT COME WITH IT.
SIR!

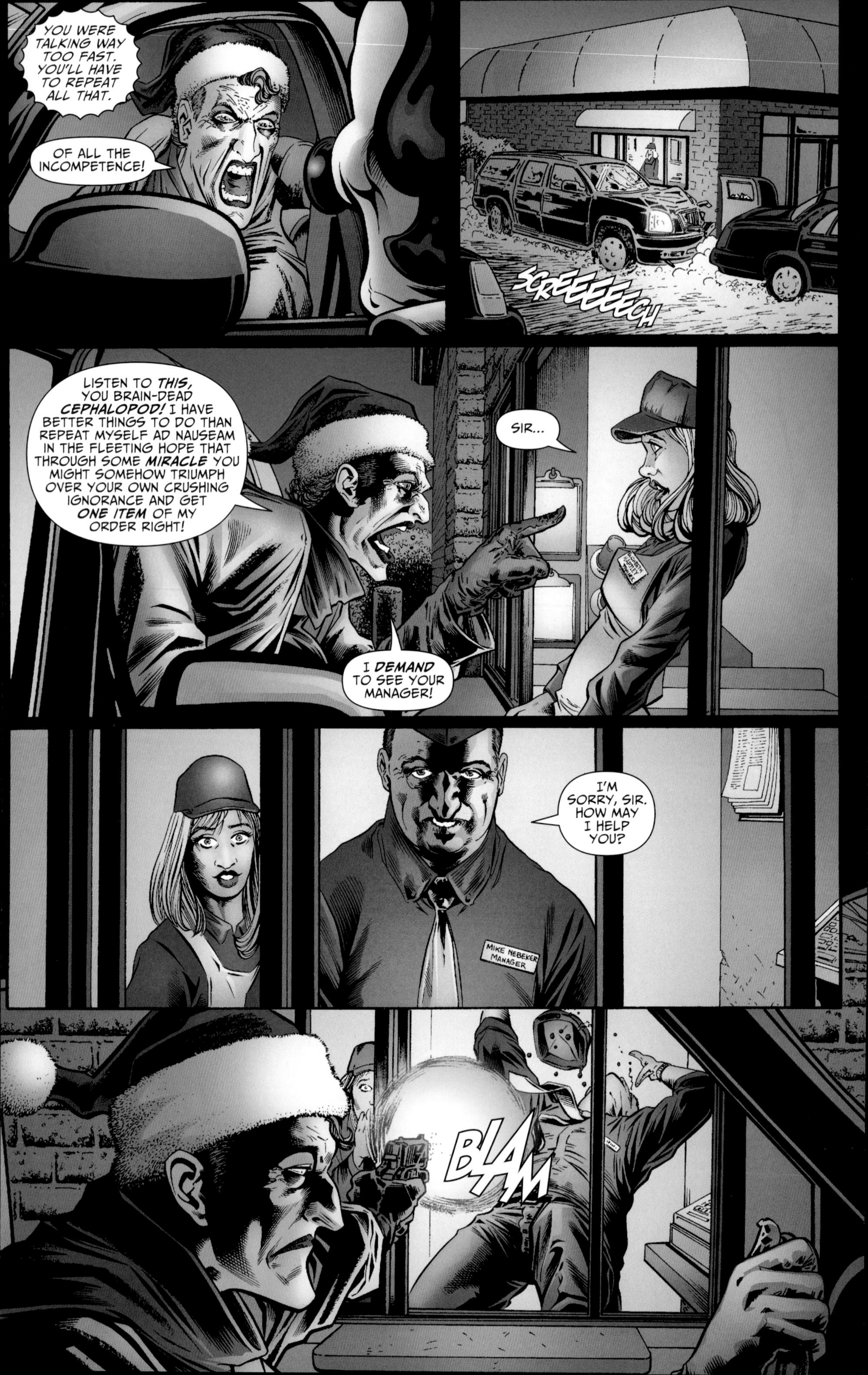
YOU WERE TALKING WAY TOO FAST. YOU'LL HAVE TO REPEAT ALL THAT.
OF ALL THE INCOMPETENCE!
SCREEEEEECH
LISTEN TO THIS, YOU BRAIN-DEAD CEPHALOPOD! I HAVE BETTER THINGS TO DO THAN REPEAT MYSELF AD NAUSEAM IN THE FLEETING HOPE THAT THROUGH SOME MIRACLE YOU MIGHT SOMEHOW TRIUMPH OVER YOUR OWN CRUSHING IGNORANCE AND GET ONE ITEM OF MY ORDER RIGHT!
SIR...
I DEMAND TO SEE YOUR MANAGER!
I'M SORRY, SIR. HOW MAY I HELP YOU?
MIKE NEBEKER MANAGER
BLAM

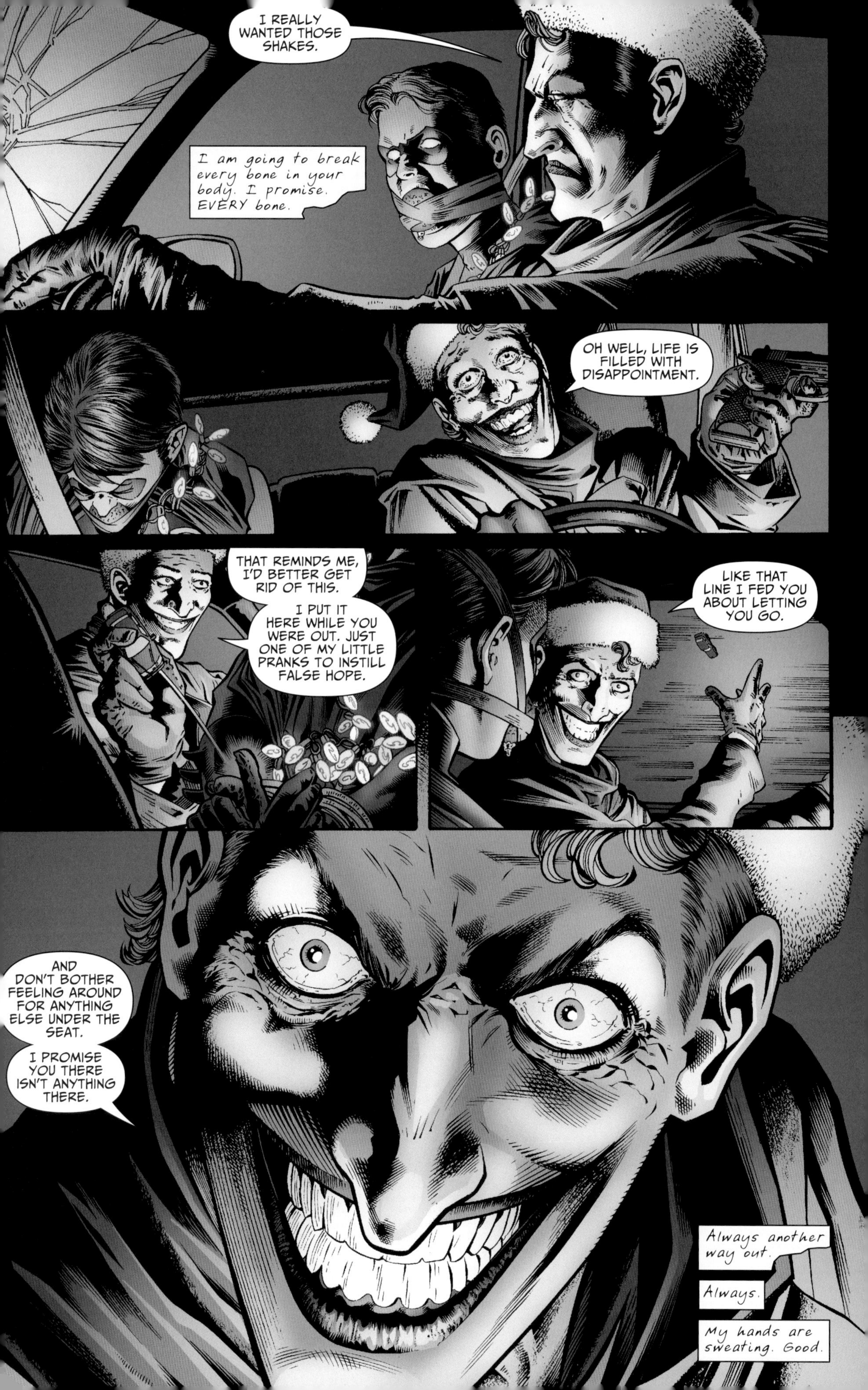
I REALLY WANTED THOSE SHAKES.
I am going to break every bone in your body. I promise. EVERY bone.
OH WELL, LIFE IS FILLED WITH DISAPPOINTMENT.
THAT REMINDS ME, I'D BETTER GET RID OF THIS.
I PUT IT HERE WHILE YOU WERE OUT. JUST ONE OF MY LITTLE PRANKS TO INSTILL FALSE HOPE.
LIKE THAT LINE I FED YOU ABOUT LETTING YOU GO.
AND DON'T BOTHER FEELING AROUND FOR ANYTHING ELSE UNDER THE SEAT.
I PROMISE YOU THERE ISN'T ANYTHING THERE.
Always another way out.
Always.
My hands are sweating. Good.

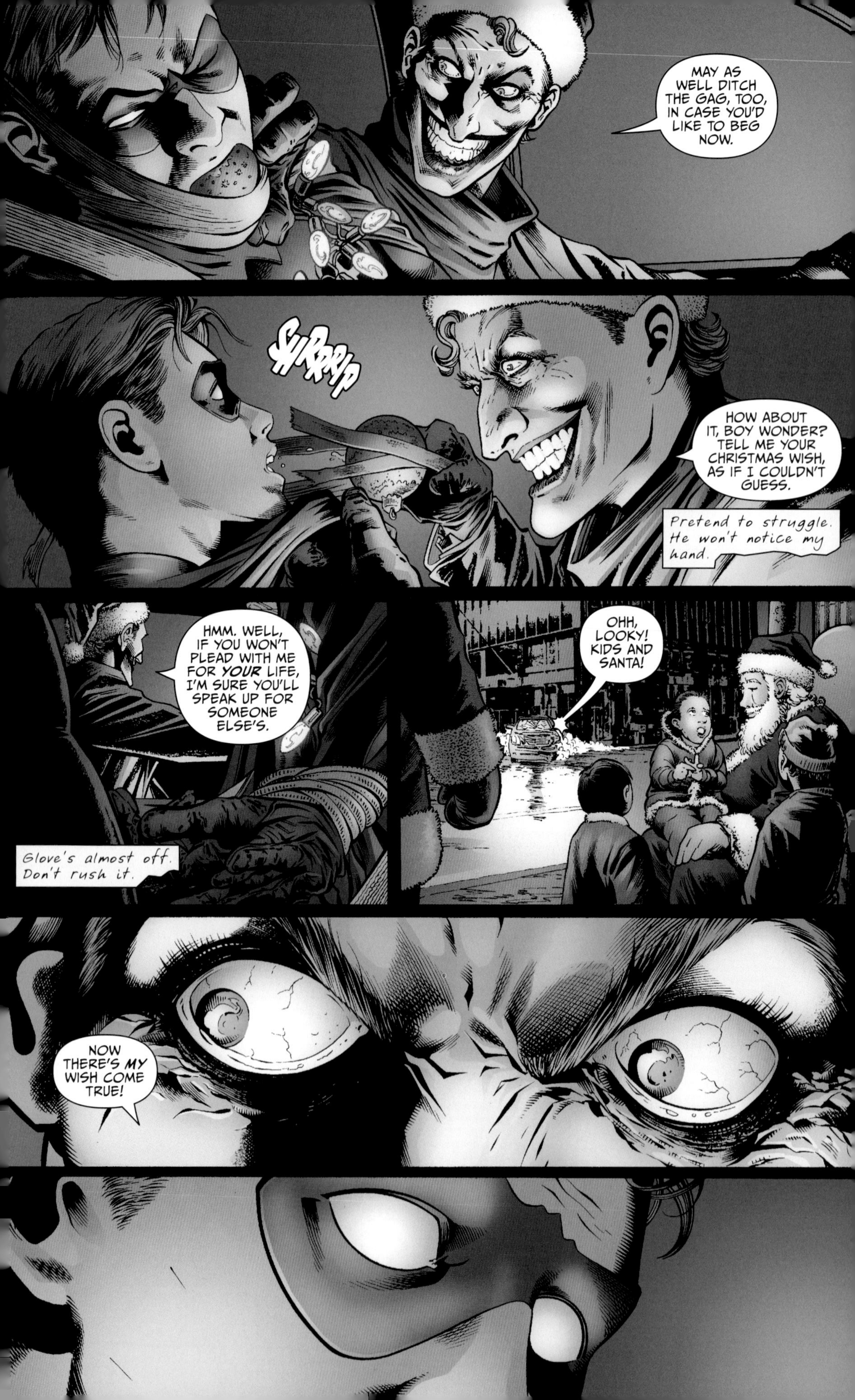
MAY AS WELL DITCH THE GAG, TOO, IN CASE YOU'D LIKE TO BEG NOW.
SHRRRIP
HOW ABOUT IT, BOY WONDER? TELL ME YOUR CHRISTMAS WISH, AS IF I COULDN'T GUESS.
Pretend to struggle. He won't notice my hand.
HMM. WELL, IF YOU WON'T PLEAD WITH ME FOR YOUR LIFE, I'M SURE YOU'LL SPEAK UP FOR SOMEONE ELSE'S.
Glove's almost off. Don't rush it.
OHH, LOOKY! KIDS AND SANTA!
NOW THERE'S MY WISH COME TRUE!

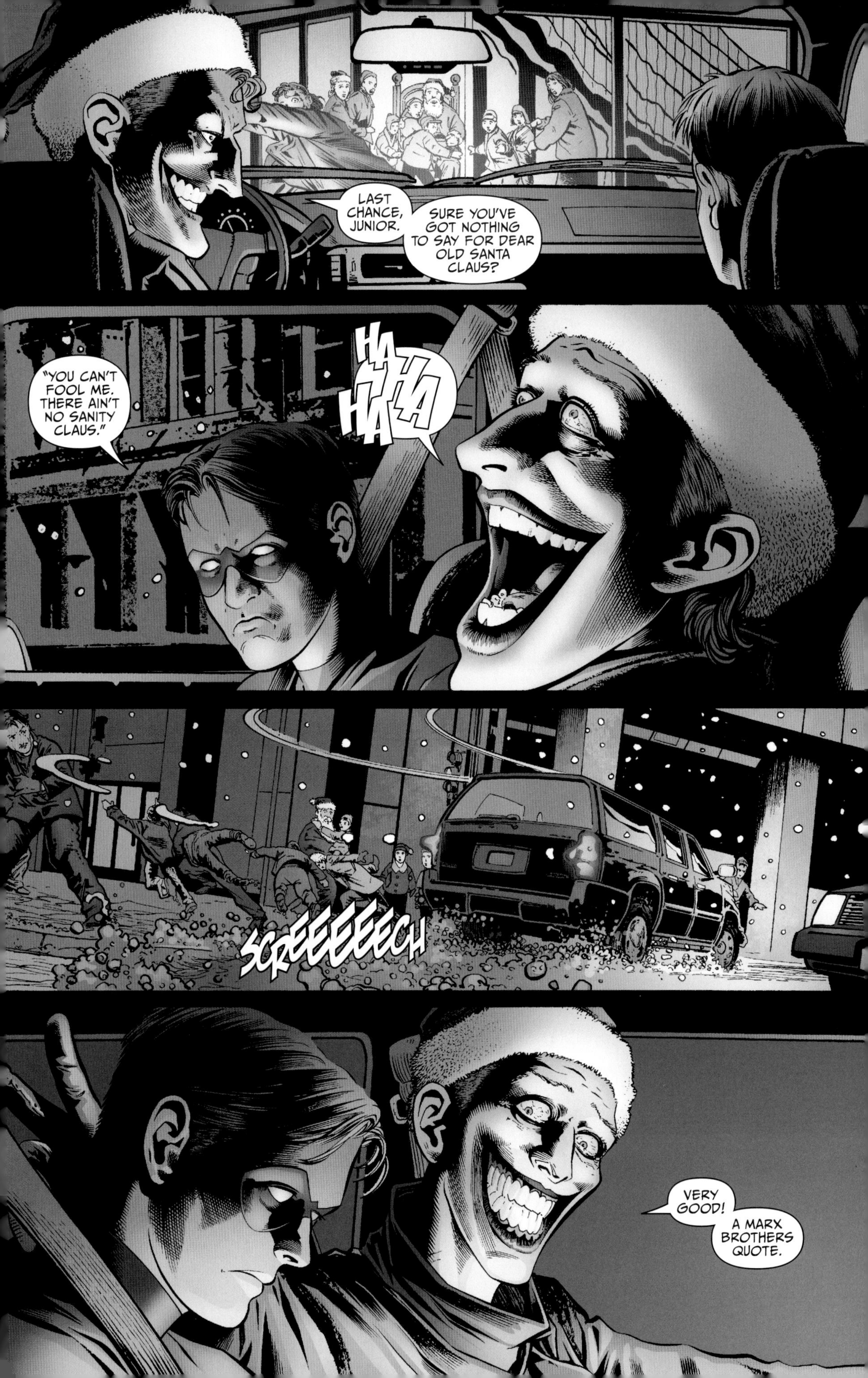
LAST CHANCE, JUNIOR.
SURE YOU'VE GOT NOTHING TO SAY FOR DEAR OLD SANTA CLAUS?
"YOU CAN'T FOOL ME. THERE AIN'T NO SANITY CLAUS."
HAHAHAHA
SCREEEEEECH
VERY GOOD!
A MARX BROTHERS QUOTE.

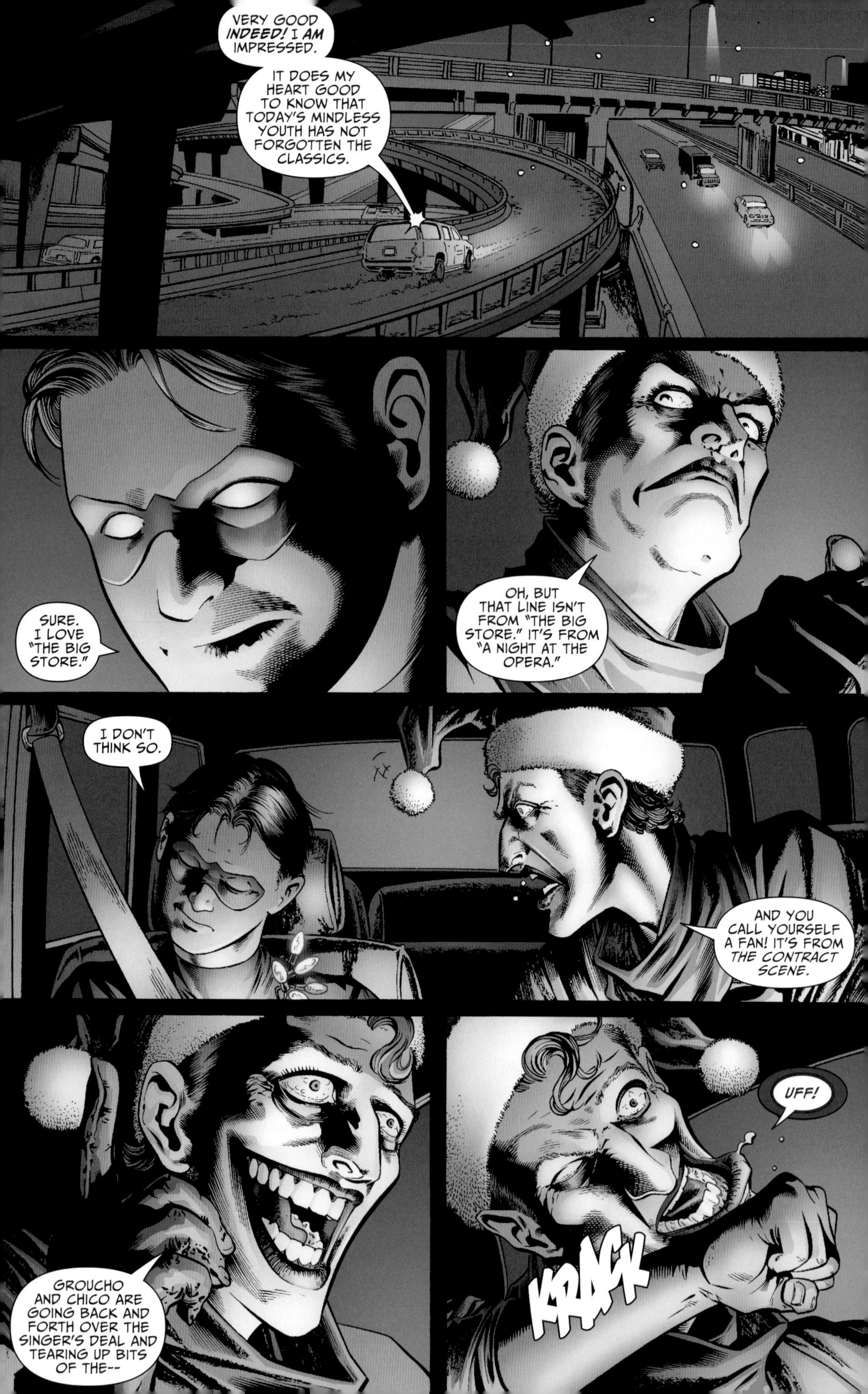
VERY GOOD *INDEED!* I *AM* IMPRESSED.
IT DOES MY HEART GOOD TO KNOW THAT TODAY'S MINDLESS YOUTH HAS NOT FORGOTTEN THE CLASSICS.
SURE. I LOVE "THE BIG STORE."
OH, BUT THAT LINE ISN'T FROM "THE BIG STORE." IT'S FROM "A NIGHT AT THE OPERA."
I DON'T THINK SO.
AND YOU CALL YOURSELF A FAN! IT'S FROM *THE CONTRACT SCENE.*
GROUCHO AND CHICO ARE GOING BACK AND FORTH OVER THE SINGER'S DEAL AND TEARING UP BITS OF THE--
UFF!
KRACK

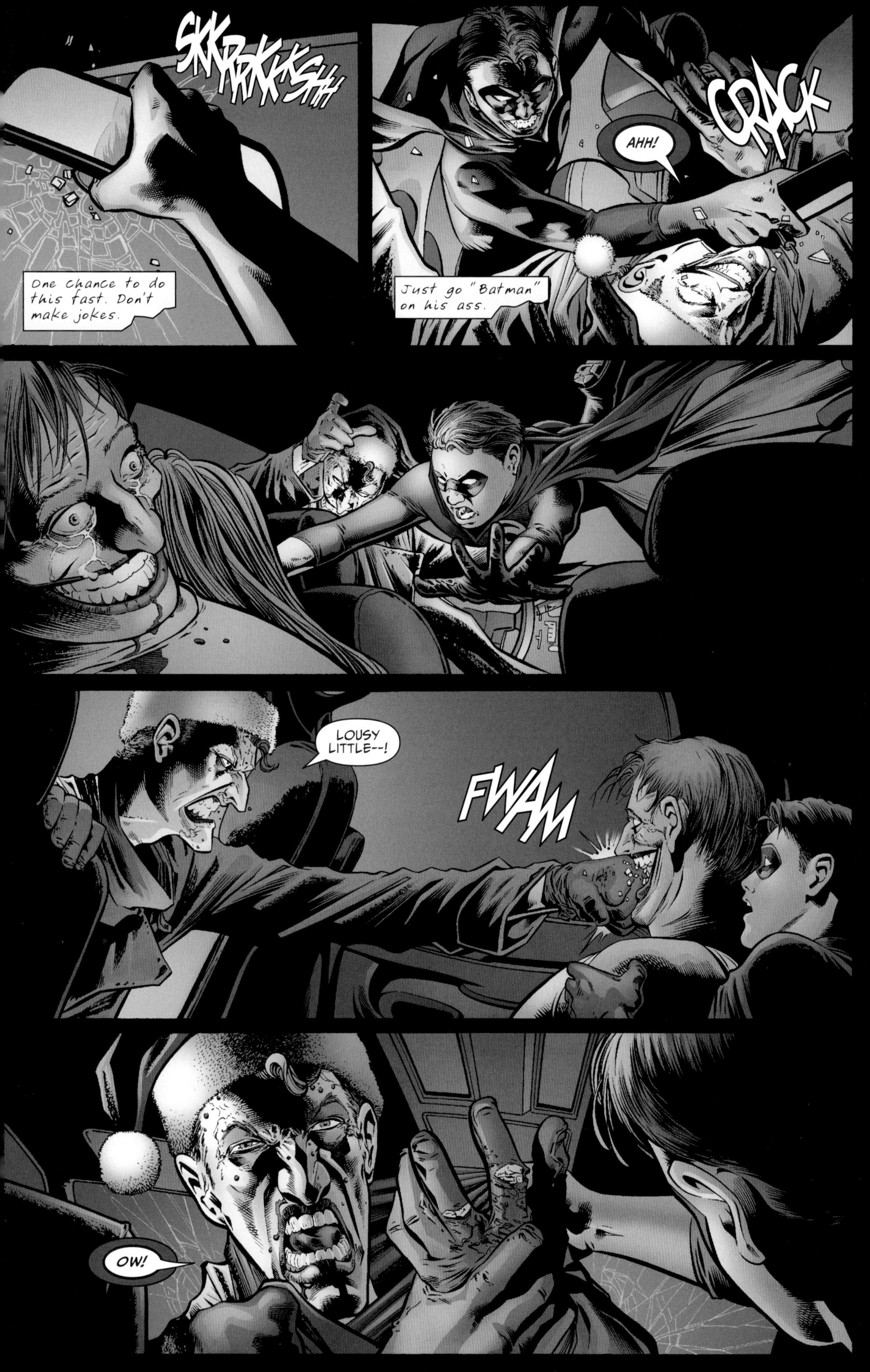
SKKRRKKKSHH
One chance to do this fast. Don't make jokes.
CRACK
AHH!
Just go "Batman" on his ass.
LOUSY LITTLE--!
FWAM
OW!

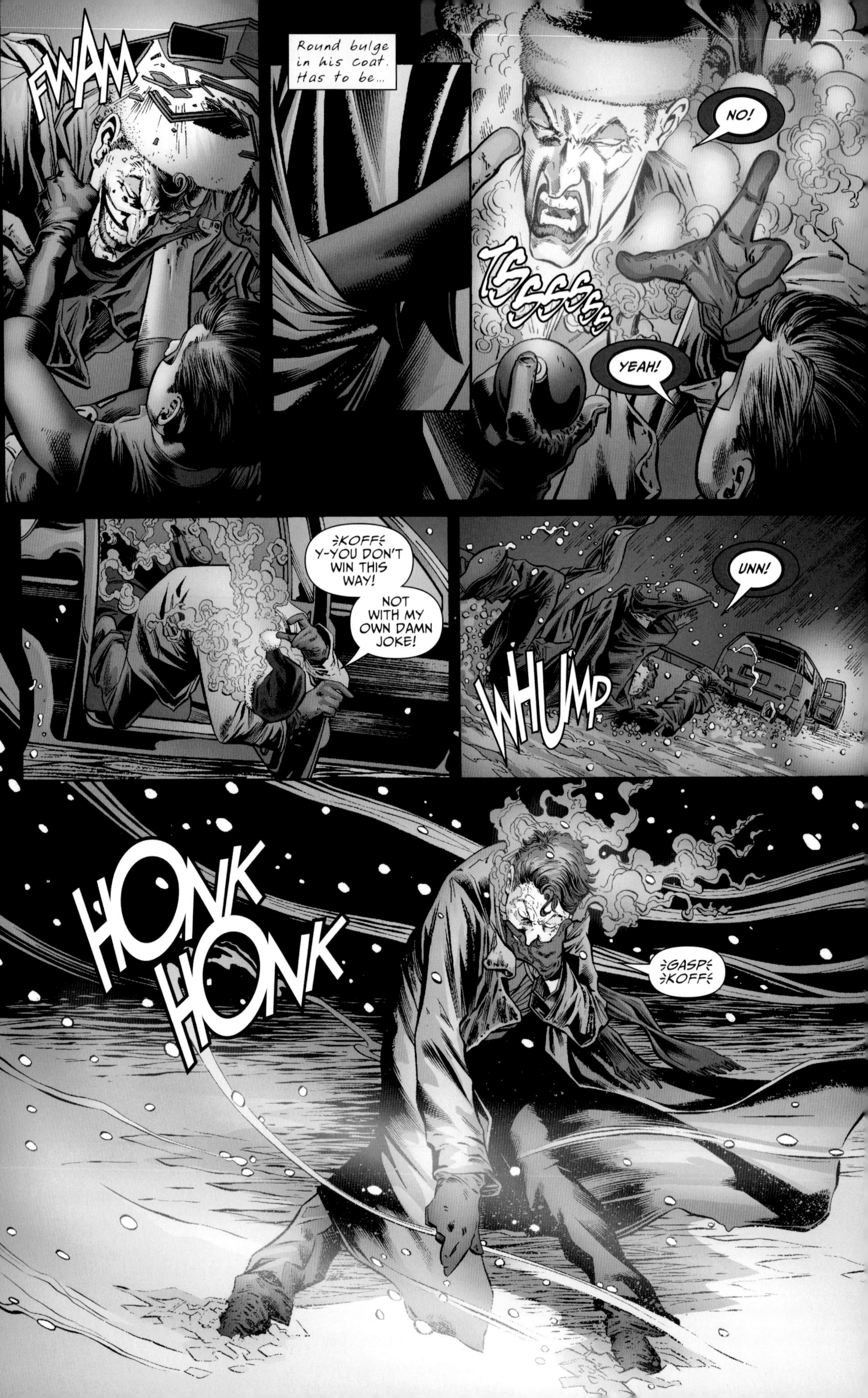
FWAM
Round bulge in his coat. Has to be...
NO!
TSSSSSS
YEAH!
KOFF Y-YOU DON'T WIN THIS WAY!
NOT WITH MY OWN DAMN JOKE!
UNN!
WHUMP
HONK HONK
GASP KOFF

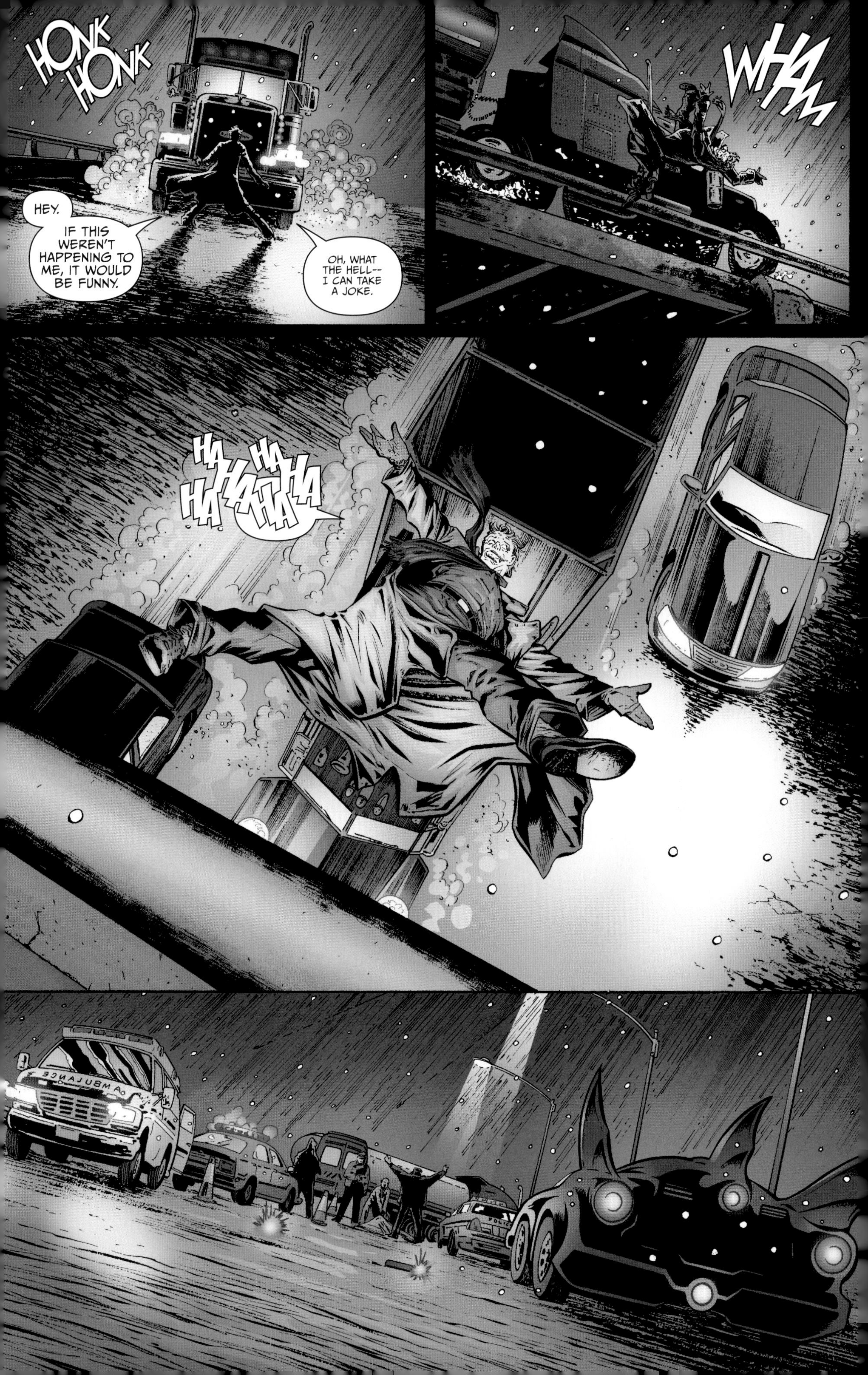
HONK HONK
HEY.
IF THIS WEREN'T HAPPENING TO ME, IT WOULD BE FUNNY.
OH, WHAT THE HELL-- I CAN TAKE A JOKE.
WHAM
HA HA HA HA HA HA HA HA
AMBULANCE

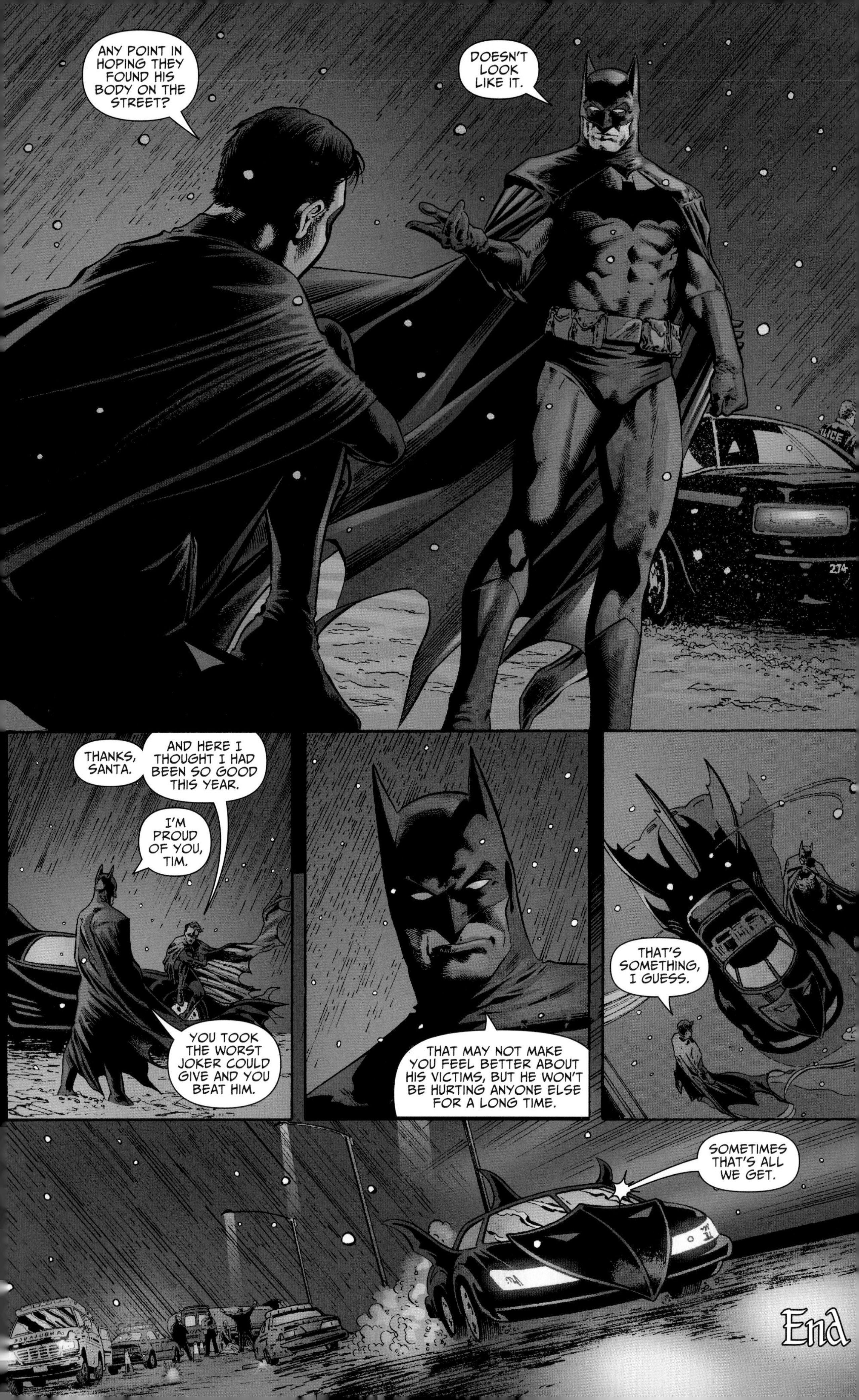
ANY POINT IN HOPING THEY FOUND HIS BODY ON THE STREET?
DOESN'T LOOK LIKE IT.
THANKS, SANTA.
AND HERE I THOUGHT I HAD BEEN SO GOOD THIS YEAR.
I'M PROUD OF YOU, TIM.
YOU TOOK THE WORST JOKER COULD GIVE AND YOU BEAT HIM.
THAT MAY NOT MAKE YOU FEEL BETTER ABOUT HIS VICTIMS, BUT HE WON'T BE HURTING ANYONE ELSE FOR A LONG TIME.
THAT'S SOMETHING, I GUESS.
SOMETIMES THAT'S ALL WE GET.
End

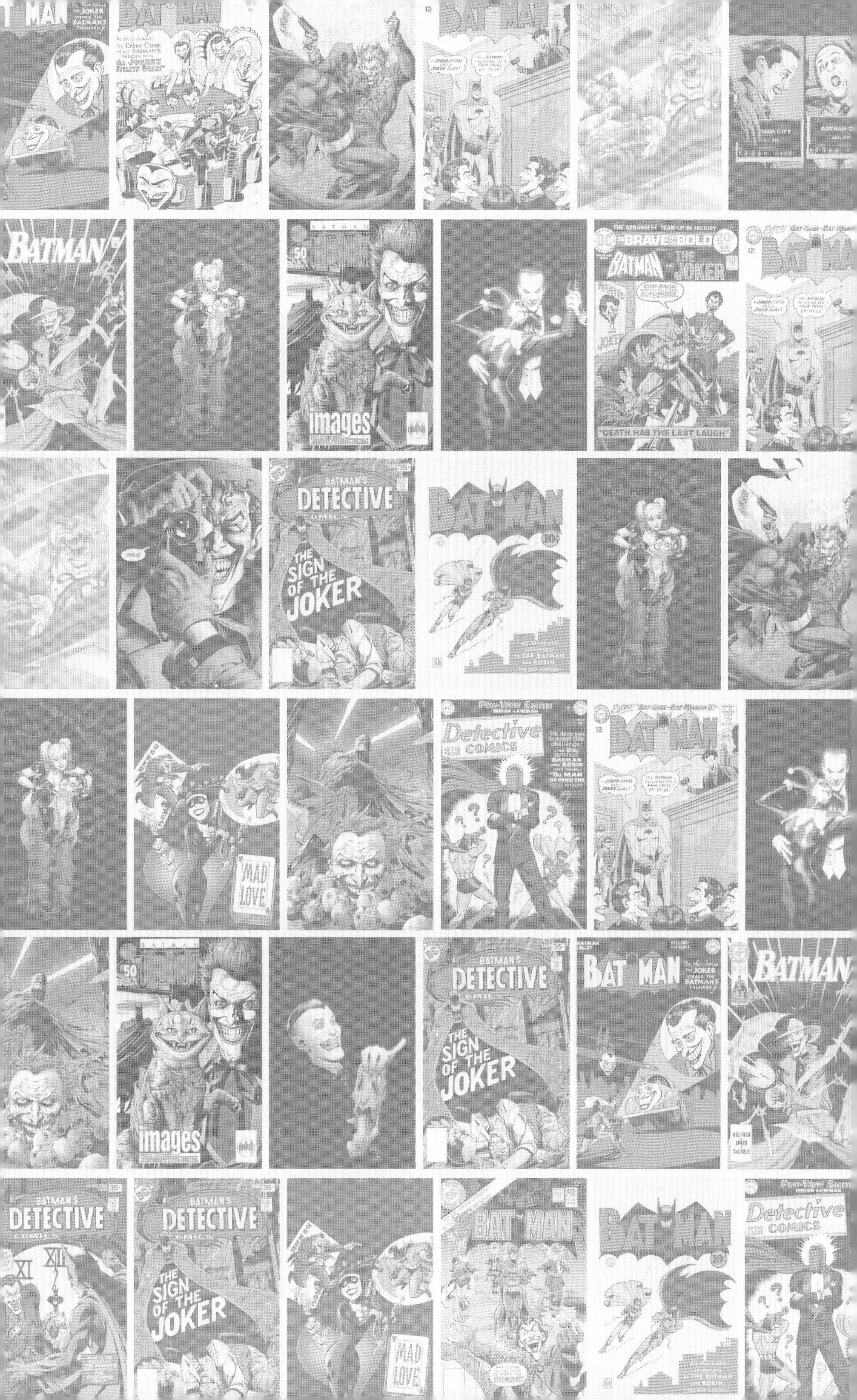

BAT MAN
THE JOKER STEALS THE BATMAN'S THUNDER!
BATMAN
JOKER-JUDGE AND A JOKER-JURY!
YES, BATMAN— I'M GIVING YOU A FAIR TRIAL! HA-HA-HA!
GOTHAM CITY JAIL DIV.
images
THE STRANGEST TEAM-UP IN HISTORY
THE BRAVE AND THE BOLD
BATMAN AND THE JOKER
WANTED
"DEATH HAS THE LAST LAUGH"
BATMAN'S DETECTIVE COMICS
THE SIGN OF THE JOKER
ALL BRAND NEW ADVENTURES OF THE BATMAN AND ROBIN, THE BOY WONDER
MAD LOVE
POW-WOW SMITH INDIAN LAWMAN
Detective COMICS
52 BIG PAGES
WOLFMAN APARO DeCARLO
FIREWORKS!

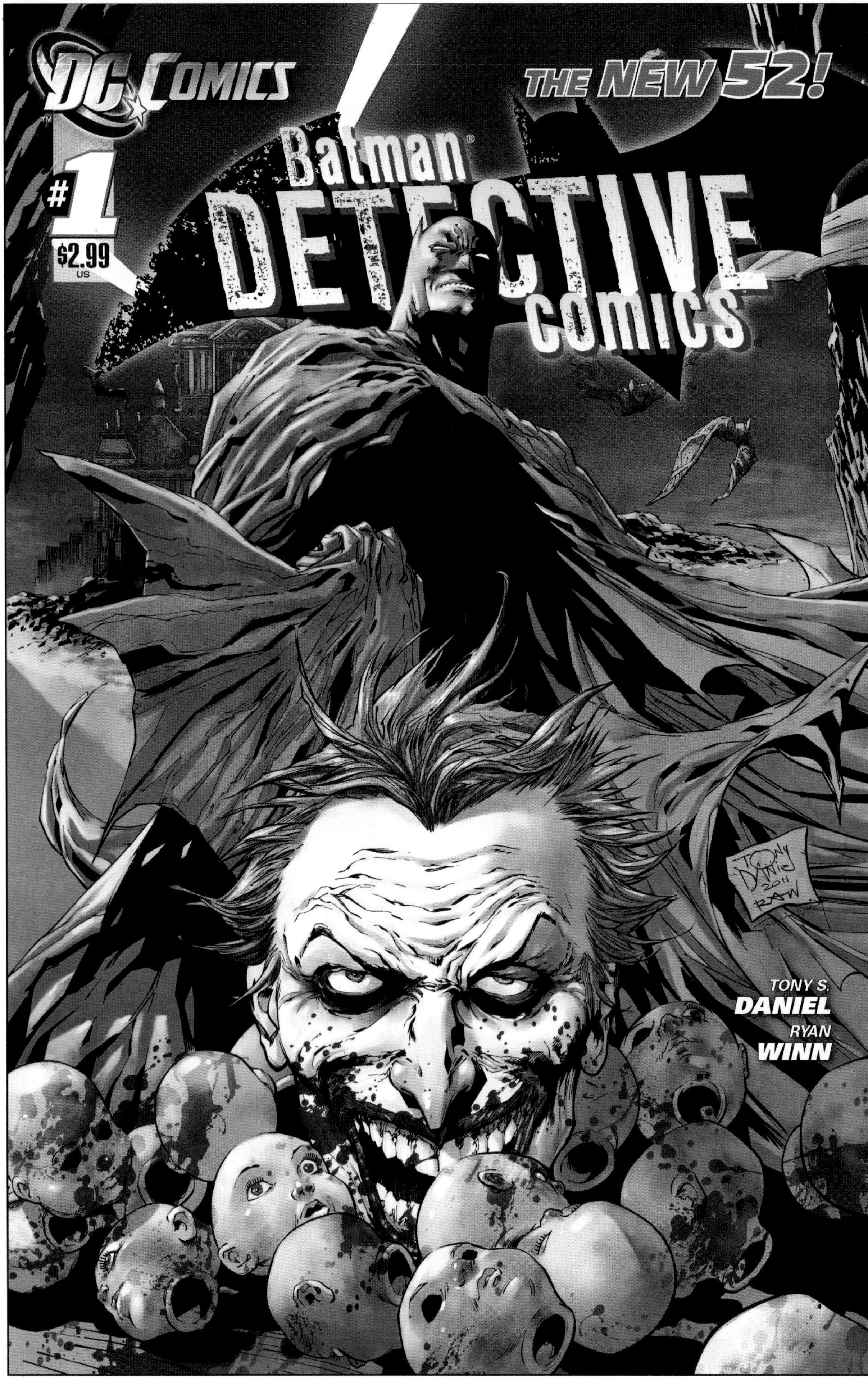

DC COMICS
THE NEW 52!
#1
$2.99 US
Batman
DETECTIVE COMICS
TONY S. DANIEL
RYAN WINN

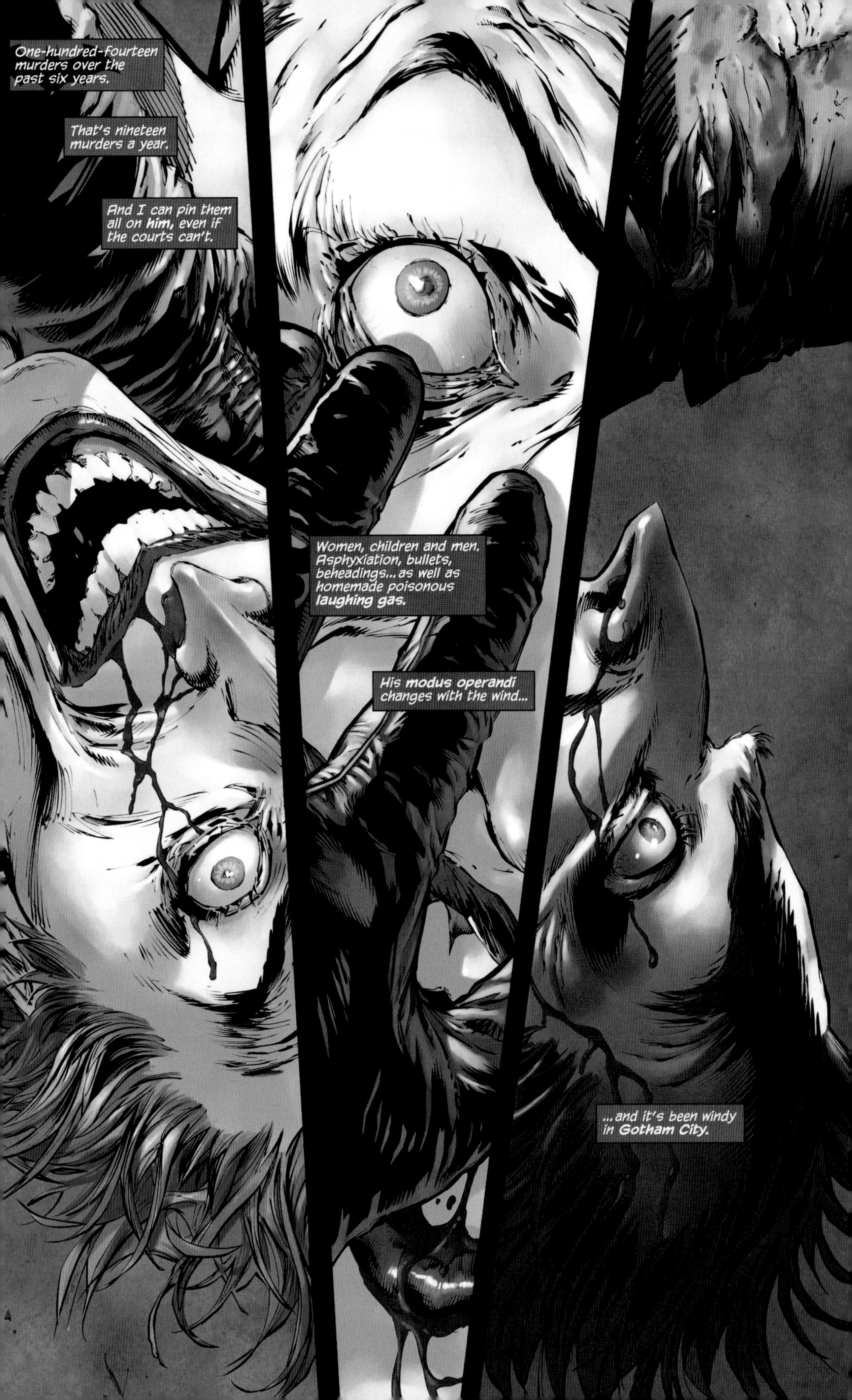
One-hundred-fourteen murders over the past six years.
That's nineteen murders a year.
And I can pin them all on **him**, even if the courts can't.
Women, children and men. Asphyxiation, bullets, beheadings...as well as homemade poisonous **laughing gas**.
His **modus operandi** changes with the wind...
...and it's been windy in **Gotham City**.

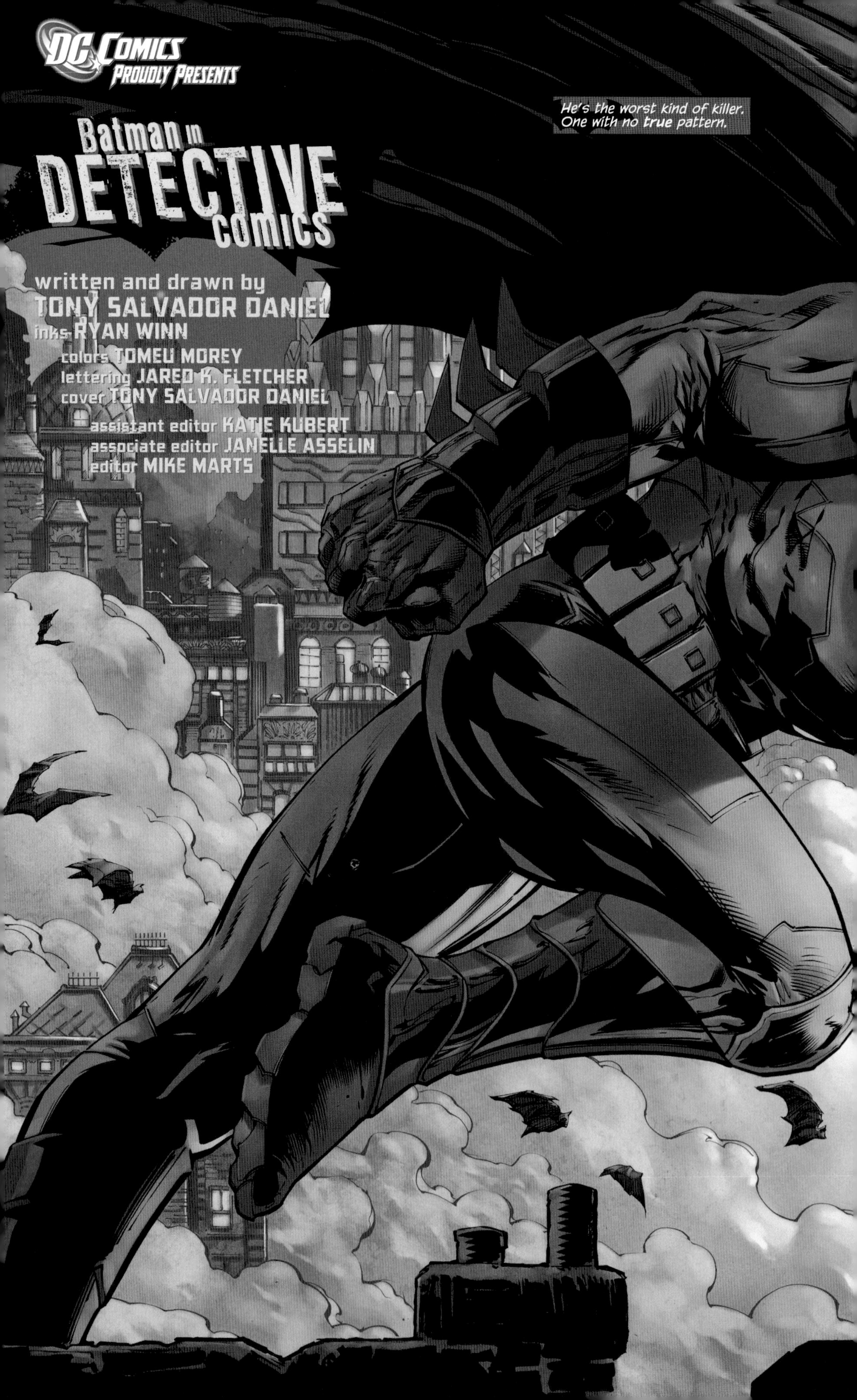

DC COMICS PROUDLY PRESENTS
Batman in DETECTIVE COMICS
He's the worst kind of killer.
One with no true pattern.
written and drawn by TONY SALVADOR DANIEL
inks RYAN WINN
colors TOMEU MOREY
lettering JARED K. FLETCHER
cover TONY SALVADOR DANIEL
assistant editor KATIE KUBERT
associate editor JANELLE ASSELIN
editor MIKE MARTS

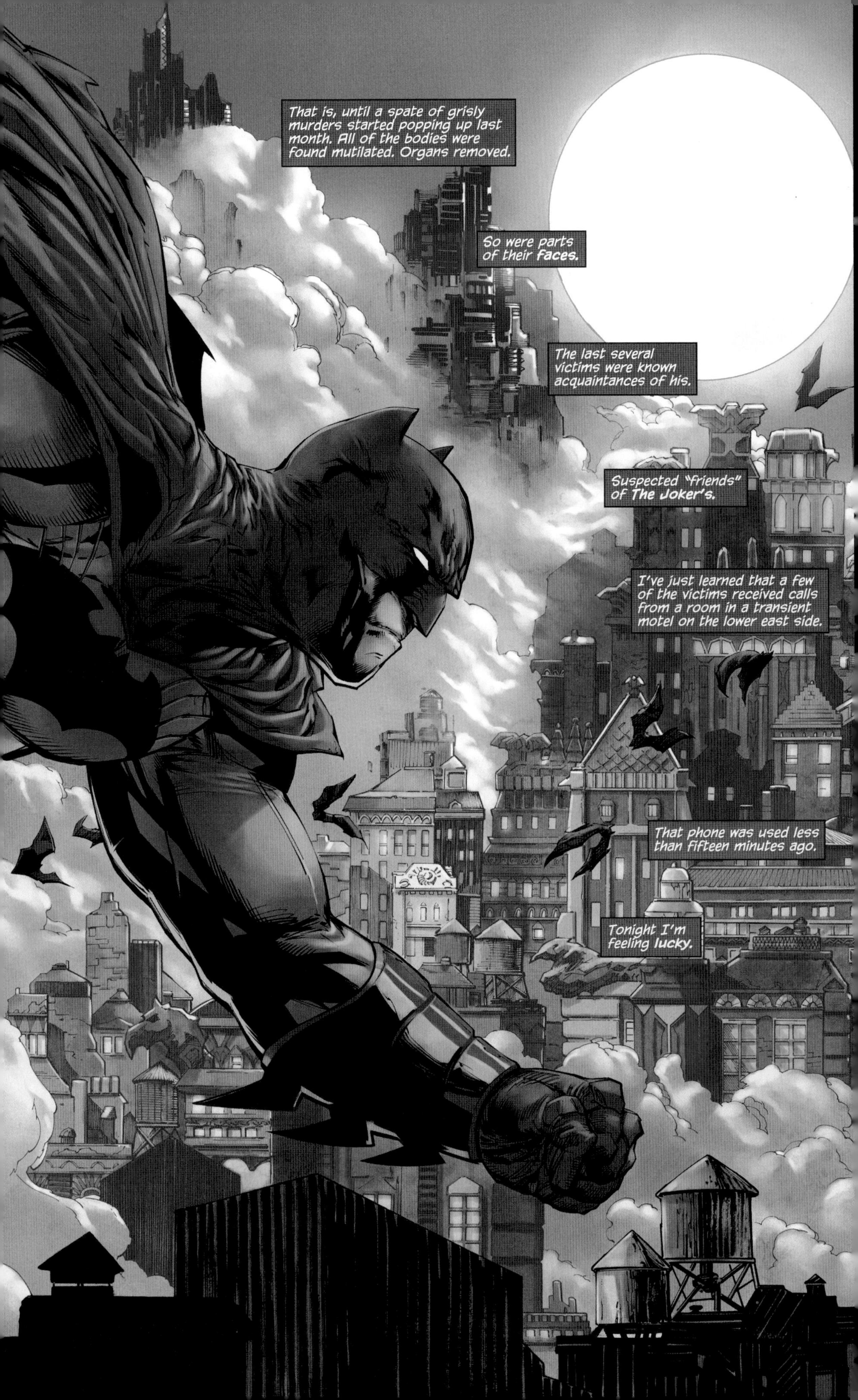
That is, until a spate of grisly murders started popping up last month. All of the bodies were found mutilated. Organs removed.
So were parts of their **faces.**
The last several victims were known acquaintances of his.
Suspected "friends" of **The Joker's.**
I've just learned that a few of the victims received calls from a room in a transient motel on the lower east side.
That phone was used less than fifteen minutes ago.
Tonight I'm feeling **lucky.**

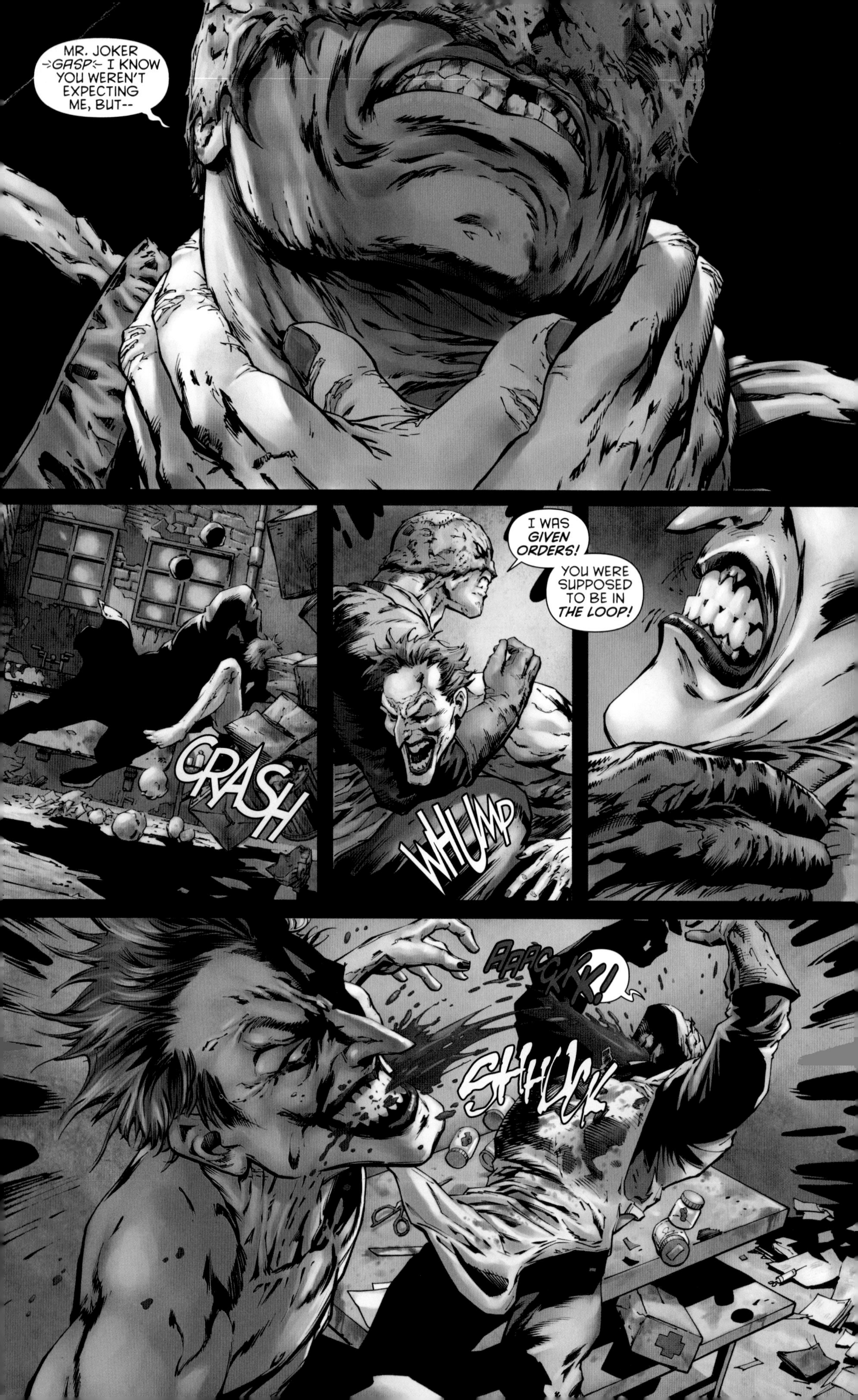
MR. JOKER -GASP- I KNOW YOU WEREN'T EXPECTING ME, BUT--
CRASH
I WAS GIVEN ORDERS!
YOU WERE SUPPOSED TO BE IN THE LOOP!
WHUMP
AAACKKK!
SHHUCK

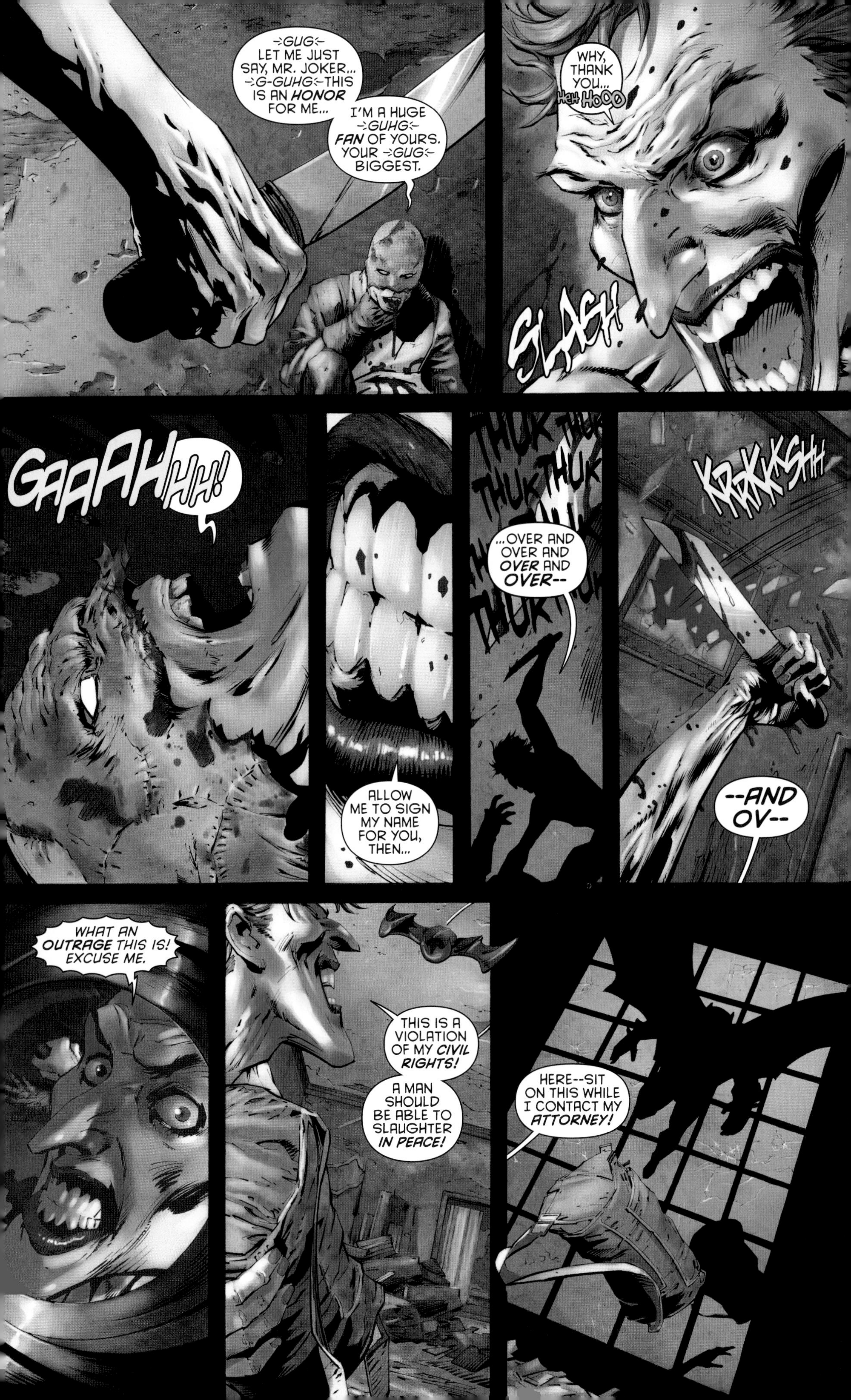
⇒GUG⇐ LET ME JUST SAY, MR. JOKER... ⇒G-GUHG⇐ THIS IS AN *HONOR* FOR ME...
I'M A HUGE ⇒GUHG⇐ *FAN* OF YOURS. YOUR ⇒GUG⇐ BIGGEST.
WHY, THANK YOU... HEH HOOO
SLASH
GAAAHHH!
ALLOW ME TO SIGN MY NAME FOR YOU, THEN...
THUK THUK THUK THUK THUK THUK
...OVER AND OVER AND *OVER* AND *OVER*--
KRAKKKSHH
--AND OV--
WHAT AN *OUTRAGE* THIS IS! EXCUSE ME.
THIS IS A VIOLATION OF MY *CIVIL RIGHTS!*
A MAN SHOULD BE ABLE TO SLAUGHTER *IN PEACE!*
HERE--SIT ON THIS WHILE I CONTACT MY *ATTORNEY!*

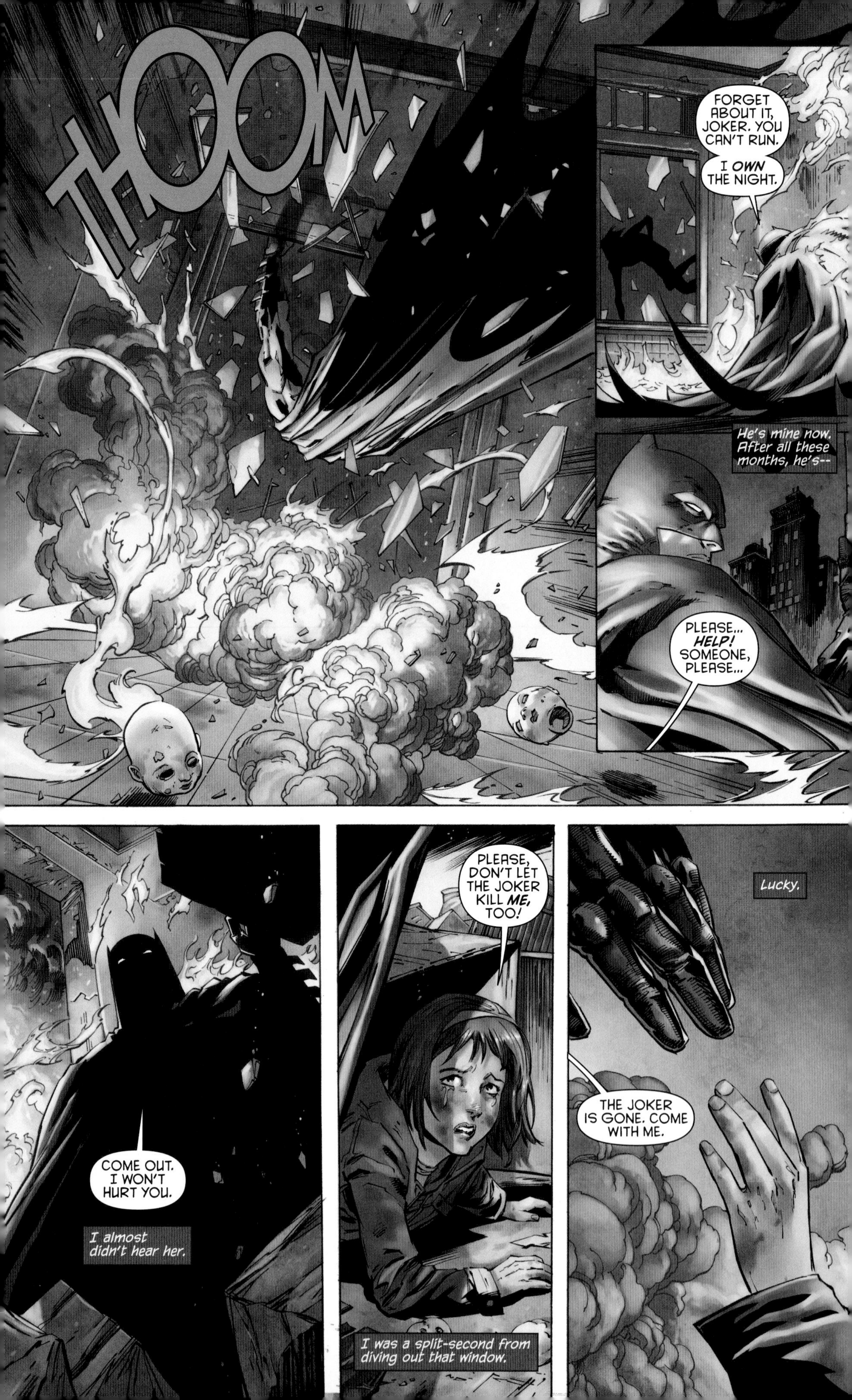
THOOM
FORGET ABOUT IT, JOKER. YOU CAN'T RUN.
I *OWN* THE NIGHT.
He's mine now. After all these months, he's--
PLEASE... *HELP!* SOMEONE, PLEASE...
COME OUT. I WON'T HURT YOU.
I almost didn't hear her.
PLEASE, DON'T LET THE JOKER KILL *ME*, TOO!
I was a split-second from diving out that window.
Lucky.
THE JOKER IS GONE. COME WITH ME.

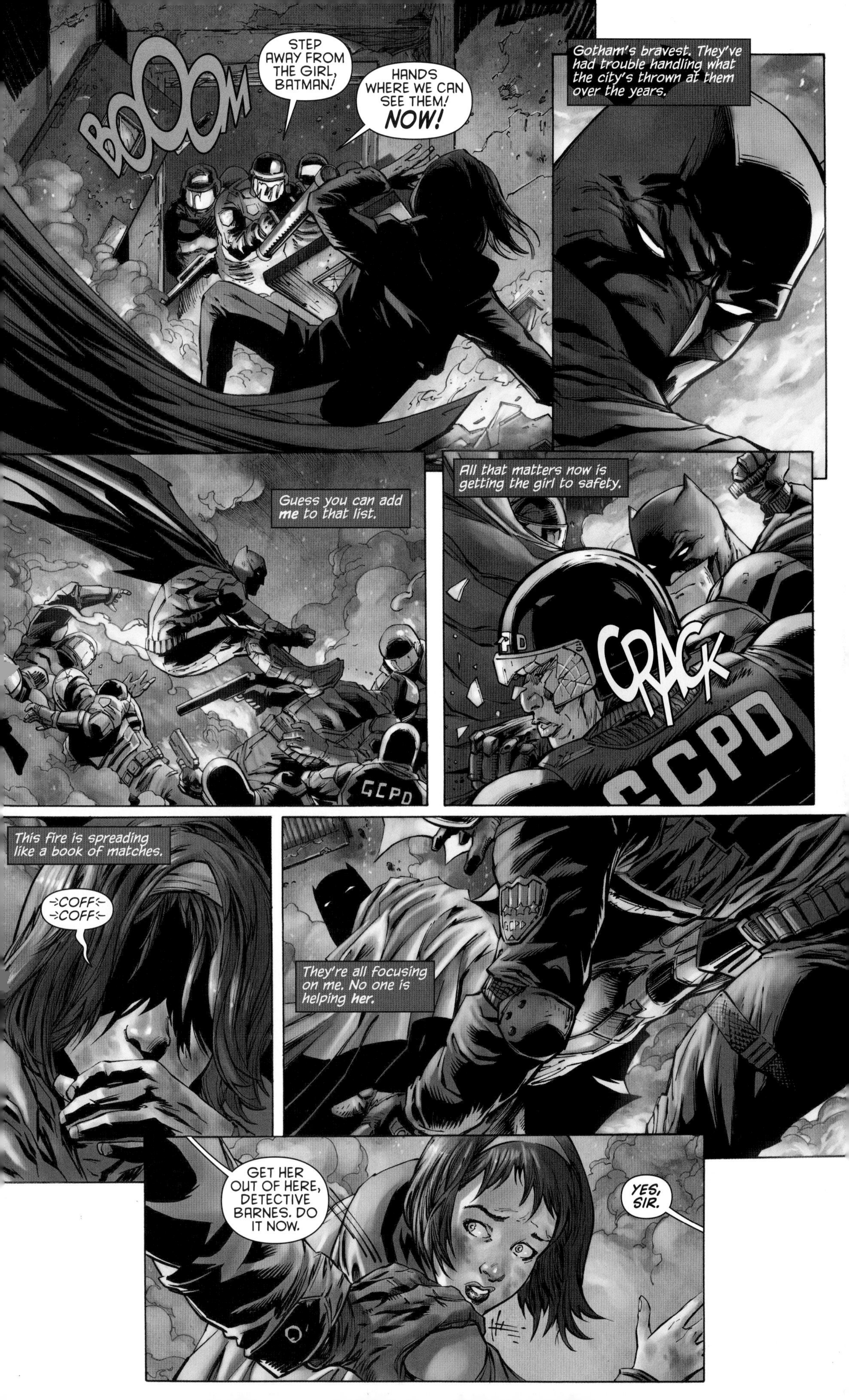
BOOOM
STEP AWAY FROM THE GIRL, BATMAN!
HANDS WHERE WE CAN SEE THEM! NOW!
Gotham's bravest. They've had trouble handling what the city's thrown at them over the years.
Guess you can add me to that list.
GCPD
All that matters now is getting the girl to safety.
CRACK
GCPD
This fire is spreading like a book of matches.
COFF COFF
They're all focusing on me. No one is helping her.
GET HER OUT OF HERE, DETECTIVE BARNES. DO IT NOW.
YES, SIR.

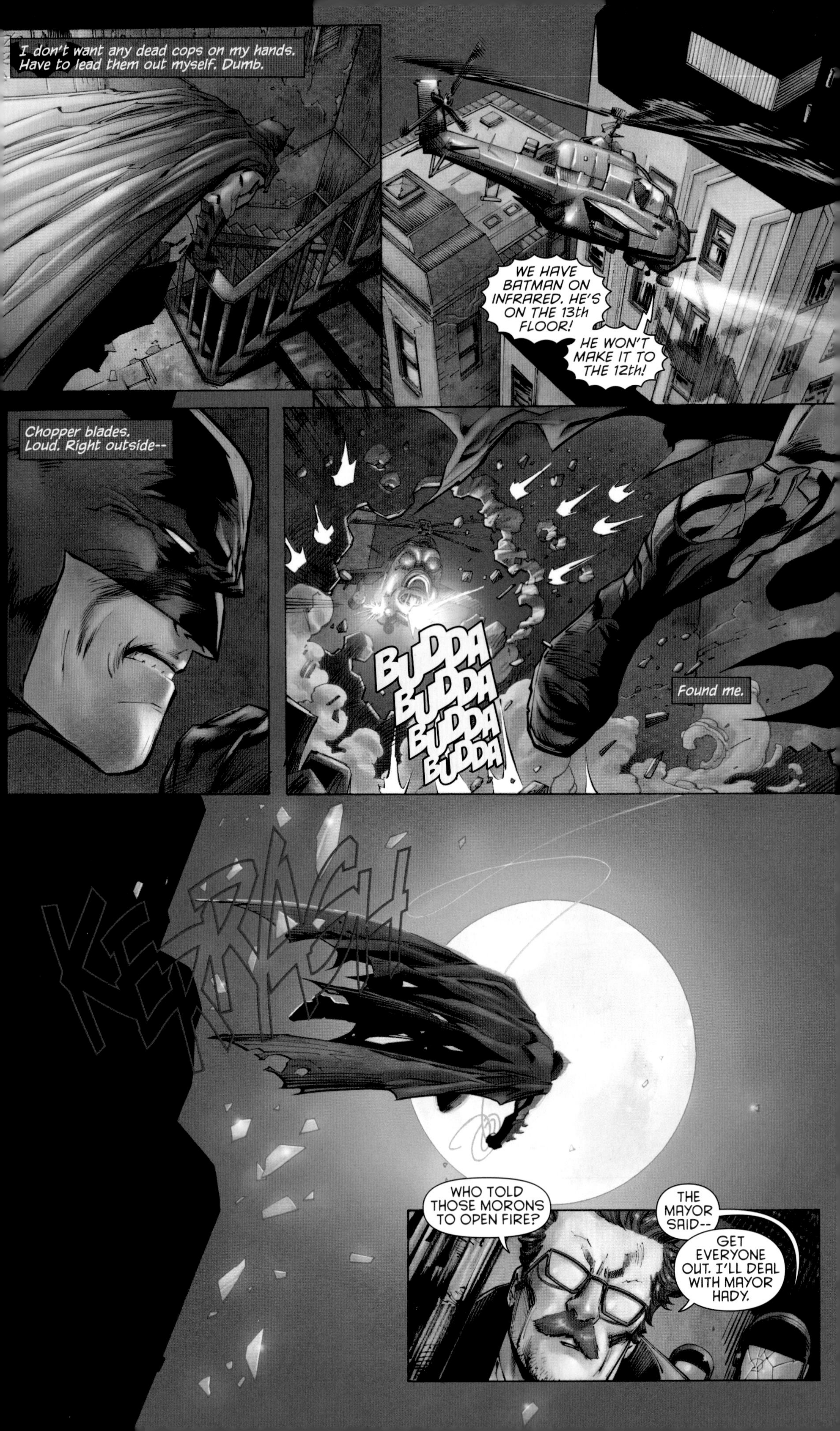
I don't want any dead cops on my hands. Have to lead them out myself. Dumb.
WE HAVE BATMAN ON INFRARED. HE'S ON THE 13th FLOOR!
HE WON'T MAKE IT TO THE 12th!
Chopper blades. Loud. Right outside--
BUDDA BUDDA BUDDA BUDDA
Found me.
KERASH
WHO TOLD THOSE MORONS TO OPEN FIRE?
THE MAYOR SAID--
GET EVERYONE OUT. I'LL DEAL WITH MAYOR HADY.

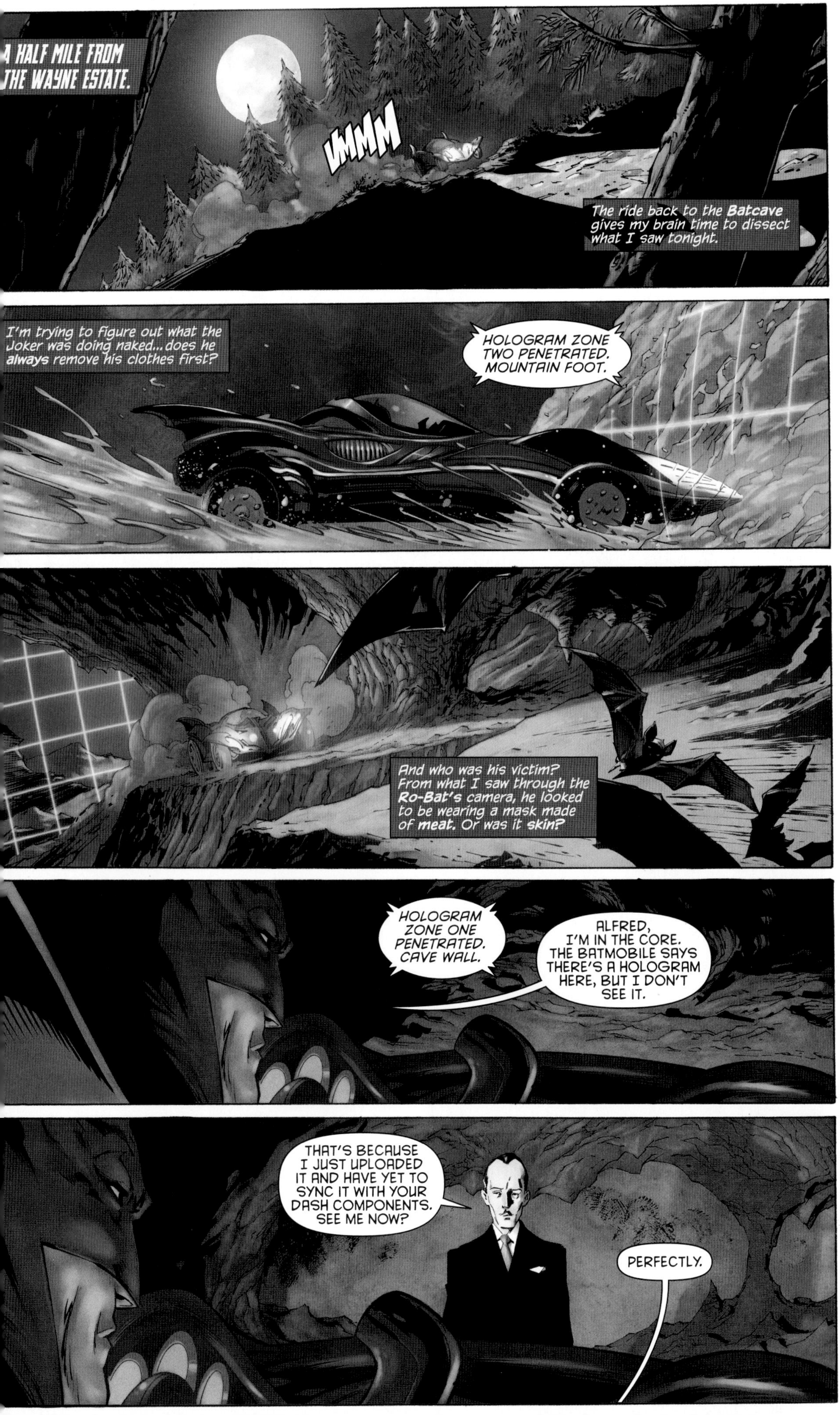
A HALF MILE FROM THE WAYNE ESTATE.
VMMM
The ride back to the Batcave gives my brain time to dissect what I saw tonight.
I'm trying to figure out what the Joker was doing naked... does he always remove his clothes first?
HOLOGRAM ZONE TWO PENETRATED. MOUNTAIN FOOT.
And who was his victim? From what I saw through the Ro-Bat's camera, he looked to be wearing a mask made of meat. Or was it skin?
HOLOGRAM ZONE ONE PENETRATED. CAVE WALL.
ALFRED, I'M IN THE CORE. THE BATMOBILE SAYS THERE'S A HOLOGRAM HERE, BUT I DON'T SEE IT.
THAT'S BECAUSE I JUST UPLOADED IT AND HAVE YET TO SYNC IT WITH YOUR DASH COMPONENTS. SEE ME NOW?
PERFECTLY.

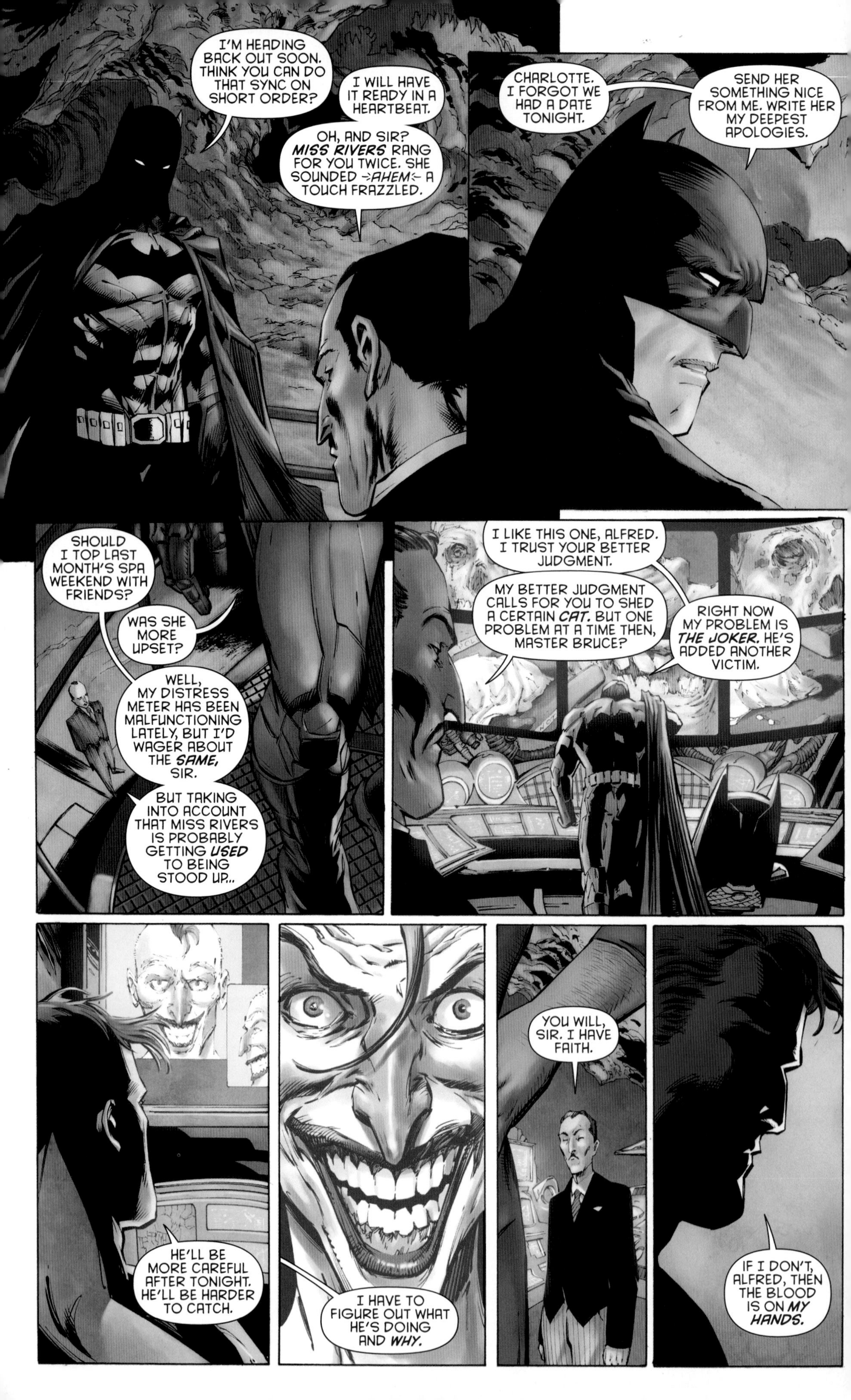

I'M HEADING BACK OUT SOON. THINK YOU CAN DO THAT SYNC ON SHORT ORDER?
I WILL HAVE IT READY IN A HEARTBEAT.
OH, AND SIR? MISS RIVERS RANG FOR YOU TWICE. SHE SOUNDED ⇒AHEM⇐ A TOUCH FRAZZLED.
CHARLOTTE. I FORGOT WE HAD A DATE TONIGHT.
SEND HER SOMETHING NICE FROM ME. WRITE HER MY DEEPEST APOLOGIES.
SHOULD I TOP LAST MONTH'S SPA WEEKEND WITH FRIENDS?
WAS SHE MORE UPSET?
WELL, MY DISTRESS METER HAS BEEN MALFUNCTIONING LATELY, BUT I'D WAGER ABOUT THE SAME, SIR.
BUT TAKING INTO ACCOUNT THAT MISS RIVERS IS PROBABLY GETTING USED TO BEING STOOD UP...
I LIKE THIS ONE, ALFRED. I TRUST YOUR BETTER JUDGMENT.
MY BETTER JUDGMENT CALLS FOR YOU TO SHED A CERTAIN CAT. BUT ONE PROBLEM AT A TIME THEN, MASTER BRUCE?
RIGHT NOW MY PROBLEM IS THE JOKER. HE'S ADDED ANOTHER VICTIM.
HE'LL BE MORE CAREFUL AFTER TONIGHT. HE'LL BE HARDER TO CATCH.
I HAVE TO FIGURE OUT WHAT HE'S DOING AND WHY.
YOU WILL, SIR. I HAVE FAITH.
IF I DON'T, ALFRED, THEN THE BLOOD IS ON MY HANDS.

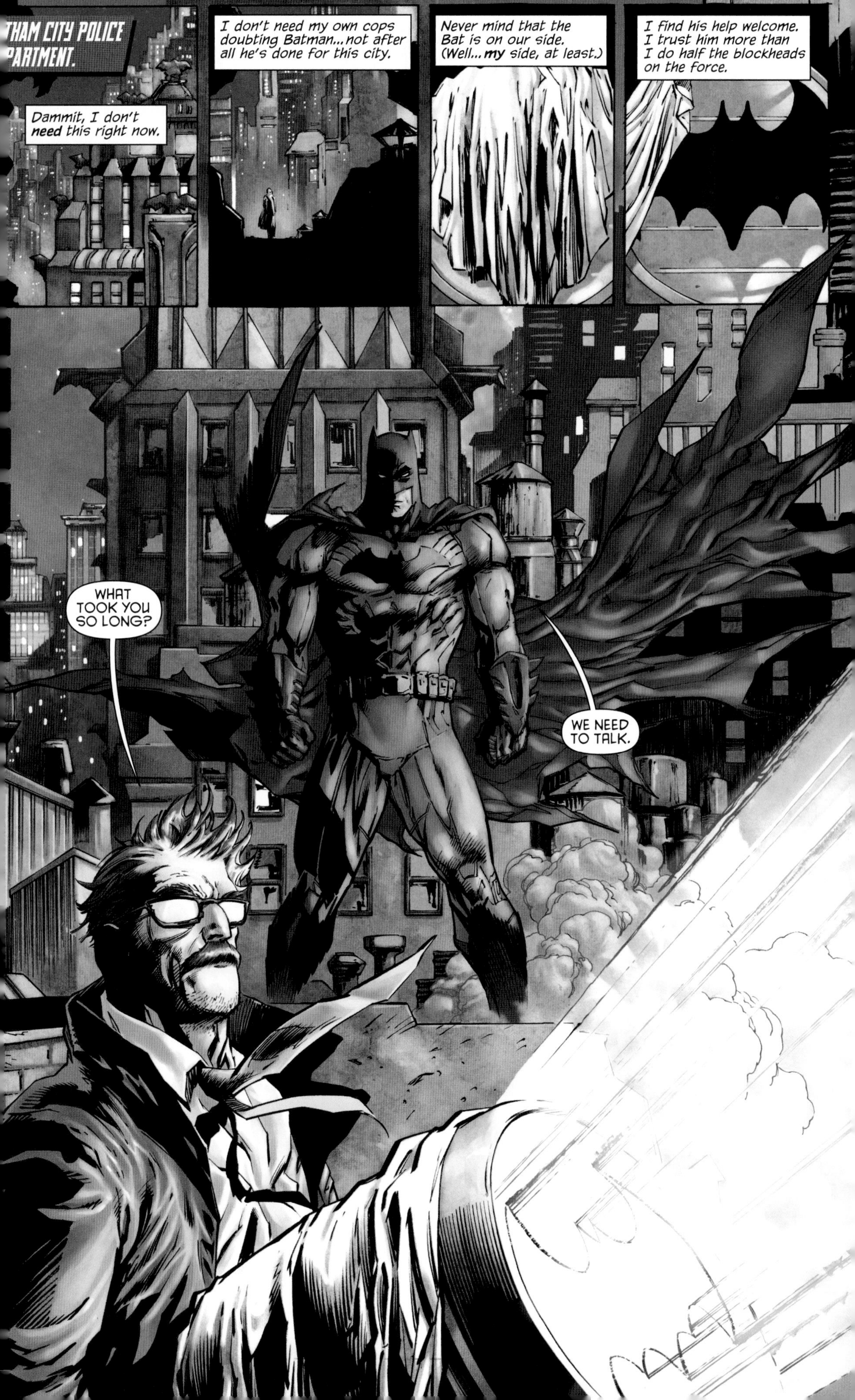
THAM CITY POLICE
PARTMENT.
Dammit, I don't **need** this right now.
I don't need my own cops doubting Batman...not after all he's done for this city.
Never mind that the Bat is on our side. (Well... **my** side, at least.)
I find his help welcome. I trust him more than I do half the blockheads on the force.
WHAT TOOK YOU SO LONG?
WE NEED TO TALK.

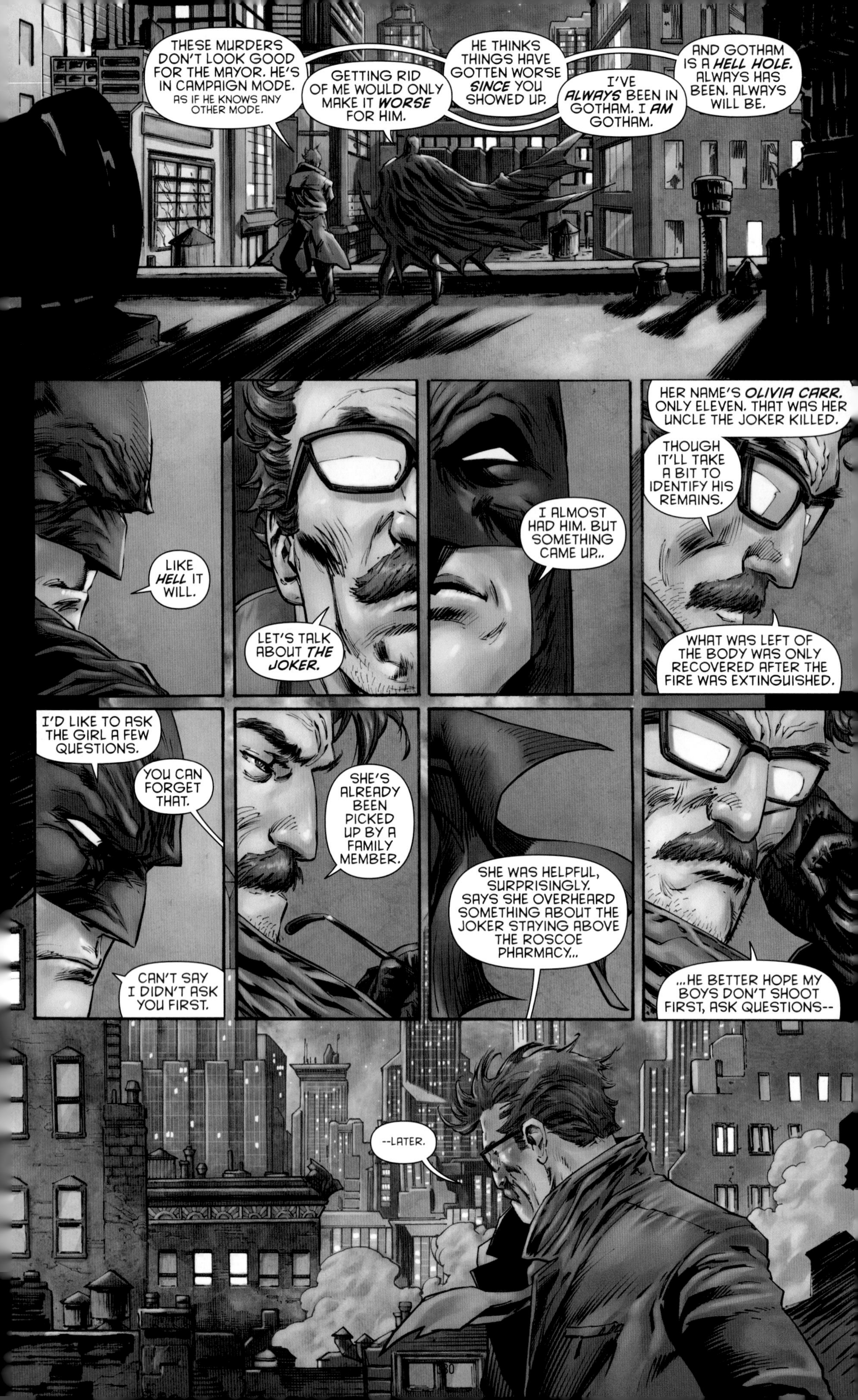
THESE MURDERS DON'T LOOK GOOD FOR THE MAYOR. HE'S IN CAMPAIGN MODE. AS IF HE KNOWS ANY OTHER MODE.
GETTING RID OF ME WOULD ONLY MAKE IT *WORSE* FOR HIM.
HE THINKS THINGS HAVE GOTTEN WORSE *SINCE* YOU SHOWED UP.
I'VE *ALWAYS* BEEN IN GOTHAM. I *AM* GOTHAM.
AND GOTHAM IS A *HELL HOLE.* ALWAYS HAS BEEN. ALWAYS WILL BE.
LIKE *HELL* IT WILL.
LET'S TALK ABOUT *THE JOKER.*
I ALMOST HAD HIM. BUT SOMETHING CAME UP...
HER NAME'S *OLIVIA CARR.* ONLY ELEVEN. THAT WAS HER UNCLE THE JOKER KILLED.
THOUGH IT'LL TAKE A BIT TO IDENTIFY HIS REMAINS.
WHAT WAS LEFT OF THE BODY WAS ONLY RECOVERED AFTER THE FIRE WAS EXTINGUISHED.
I'D LIKE TO ASK THE GIRL A FEW QUESTIONS.
YOU CAN FORGET THAT.
CAN'T SAY I DIDN'T ASK YOU FIRST.
SHE'S ALREADY BEEN PICKED UP BY A FAMILY MEMBER.
SHE WAS HELPFUL, SURPRISINGLY. SAYS SHE OVERHEARD SOMETHING ABOUT THE JOKER STAYING ABOVE THE ROSCOE PHARMACY...
...HE BETTER HOPE MY BOYS DON'T SHOOT FIRST, ASK QUESTIONS--
--LATER.

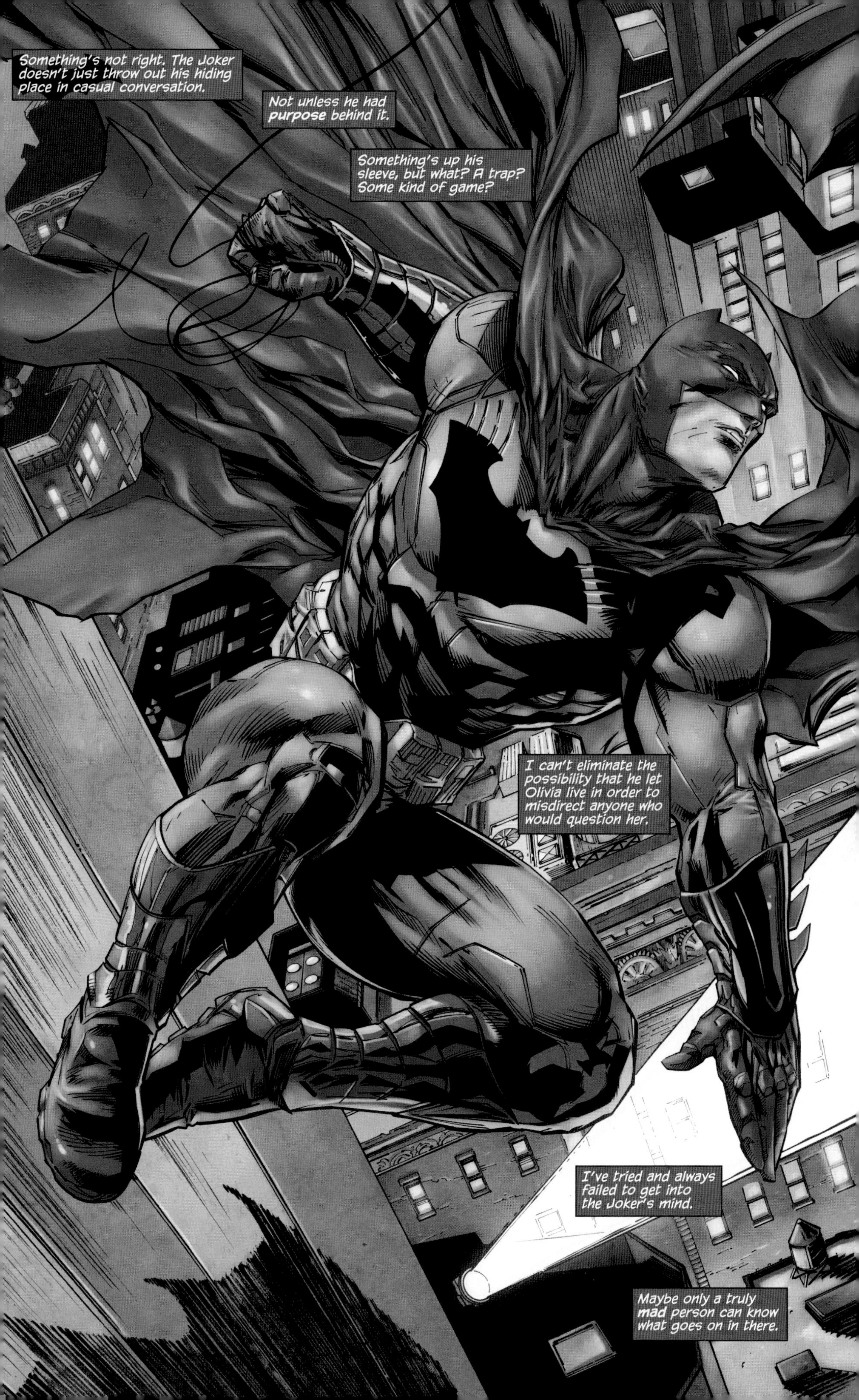
Something's not right. The Joker doesn't just throw out his hiding place in casual conversation.
Not unless he had **purpose** behind it.
Something's up his sleeve, but what? A trap? Some kind of game?
I can't eliminate the possibility that he let Olivia live in order to misdirect anyone who would question her.
I've tried and always failed to get into the Joker's mind.
Maybe only a truly **mad** person can know what goes on in there.

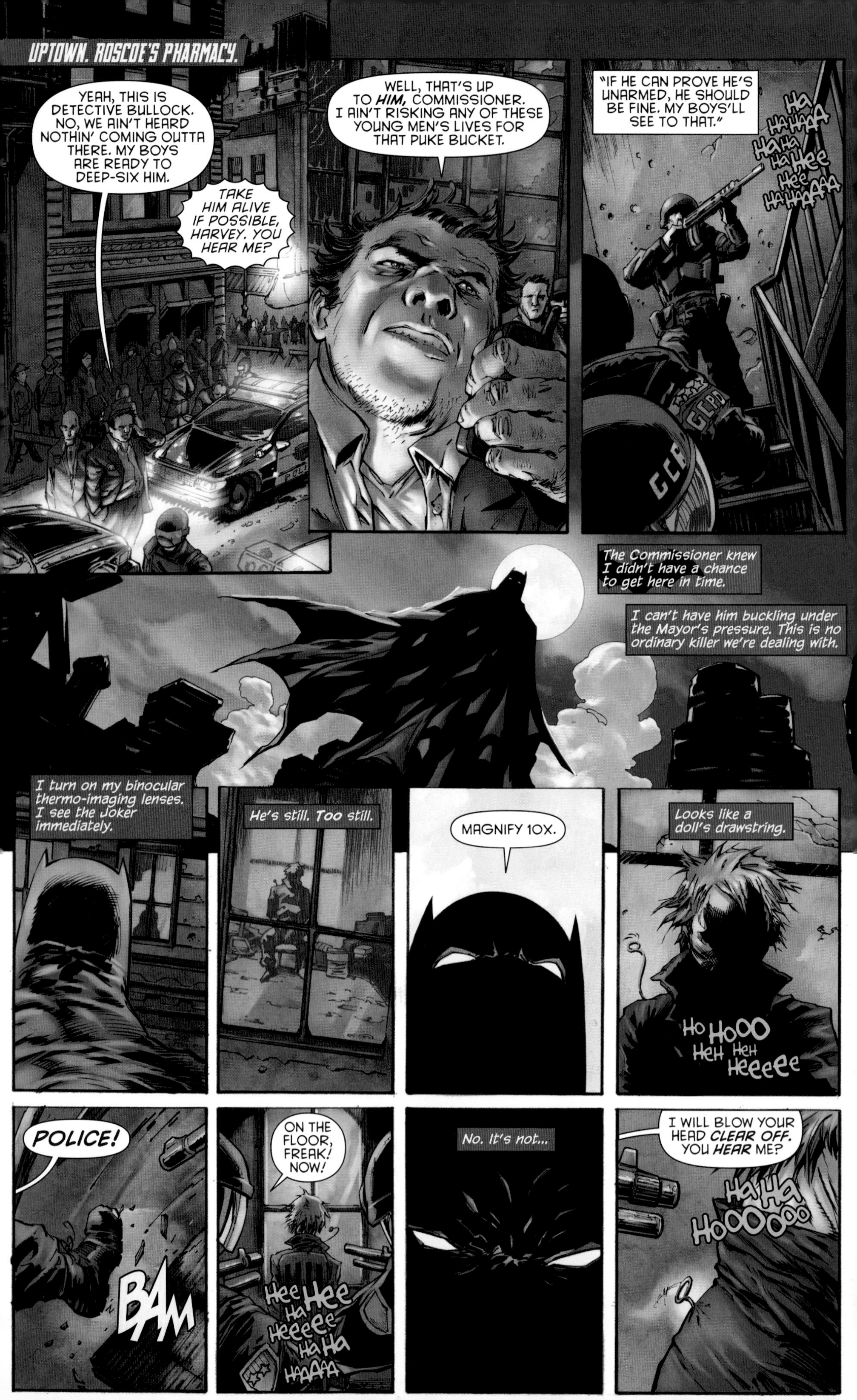
UPTOWN. ROSCOE'S PHARMACY.
YEAH, THIS IS DETECTIVE BULLOCK. NO, WE AIN'T HEARD NOTHIN' COMING OUTTA THERE. MY BOYS ARE READY TO DEEP-SIX HIM.
TAKE HIM ALIVE IF POSSIBLE, HARVEY. YOU HEAR ME?
WELL, THAT'S UP TO HIM, COMMISSIONER. I AIN'T RISKING ANY OF THESE YOUNG MEN'S LIVES FOR THAT PUKE BUCKET.
"IF HE CAN PROVE HE'S UNARMED, HE SHOULD BE FINE. MY BOYS'LL SEE TO THAT."
HA HA HAAA HA HA HA HEE HEE HA HAAAAA
GCPD
The Commissioner knew I didn't have a chance to get here in time.
I can't have him buckling under the Mayor's pressure. This is no ordinary killer we're dealing with.
I turn on my binocular thermo-imaging lenses. I see the Joker immediately.
He's still. Too still.
MAGNIFY 10X.
Looks like a doll's drawstring.
HO HOOO HEH HEH HEEEEE
POLICE!
BAM
ON THE FLOOR, FREAK! NOW!
HEE HEE HA HEEEEE HA HA HAAAAA
No. It's not...
I WILL BLOW YOUR HEAD CLEAR OFF. YOU HEAR ME?
HA HA HOOOOOO

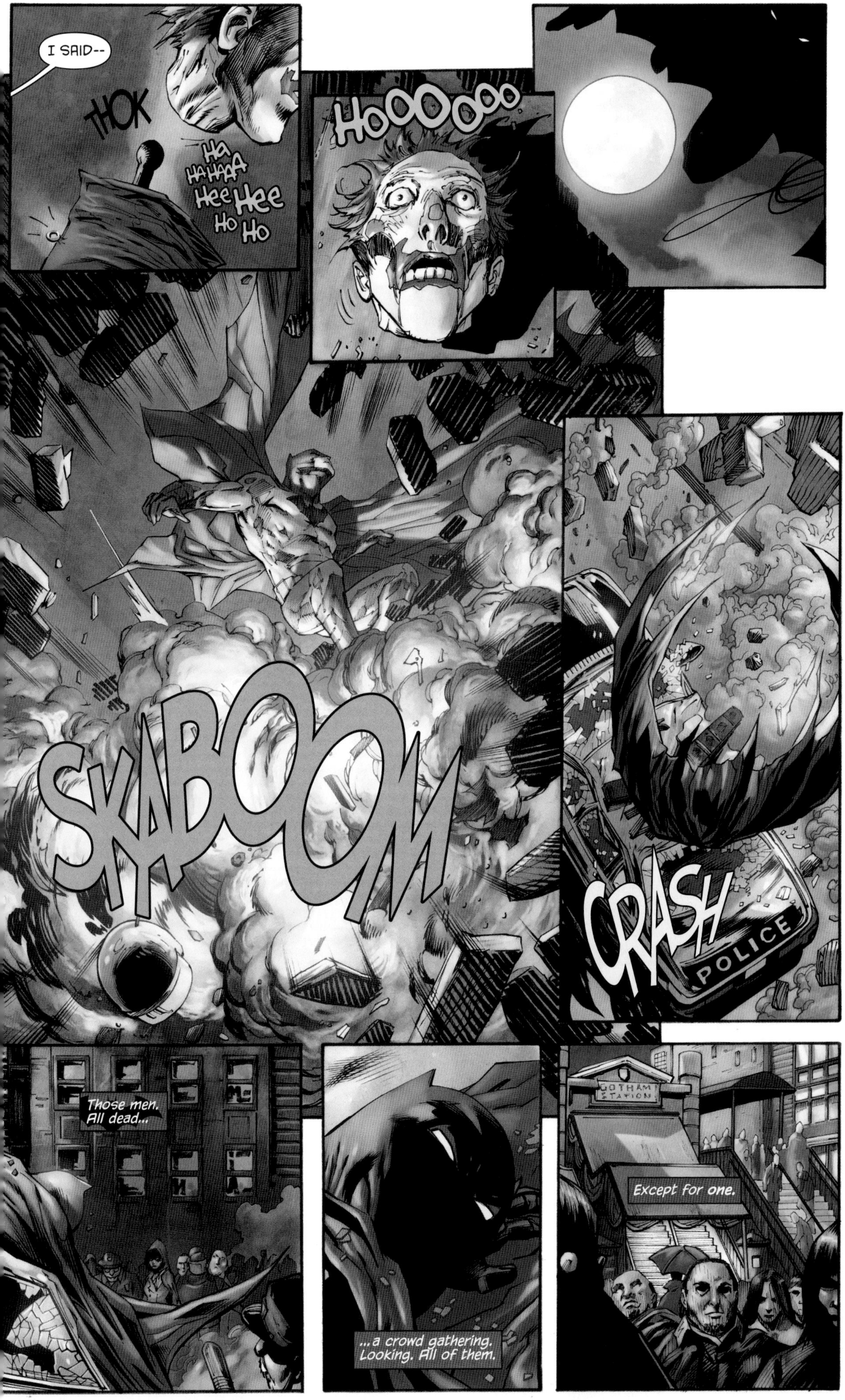
I SAID--
THOK
Ha HaHaaa Hee Hee Ho Ho
HOOOooo
SKABOOM
CRASH
POLICE
Those men. All dead...
...a crowd gathering. Looking. All of them.
GOTHAM STATION
Except for one.

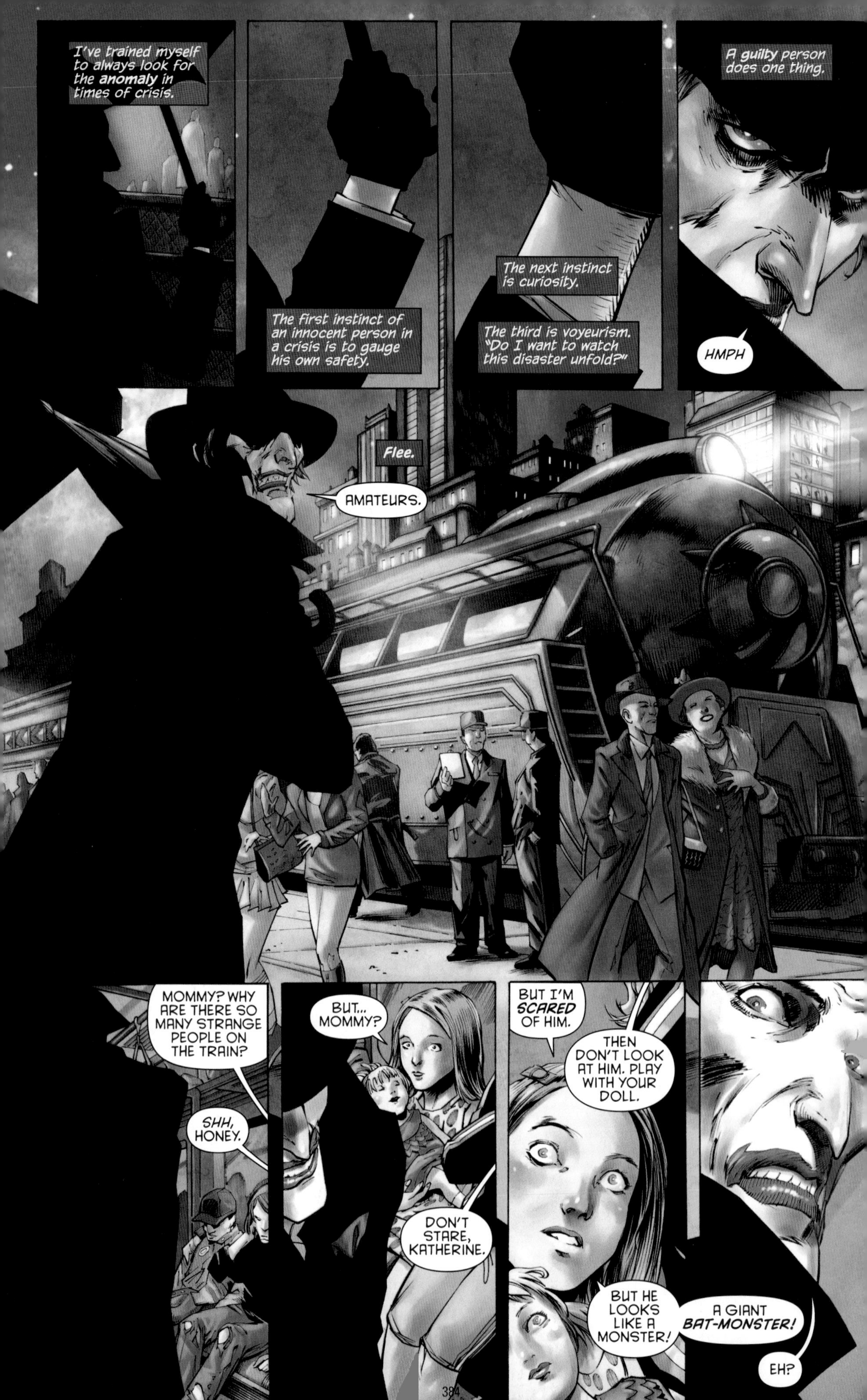
I've trained myself to always look for the anomaly in times of crisis.
The first instinct of an innocent person in a crisis is to gauge his own safety.
The next instinct is curiosity.
The third is voyeurism. "Do I want to watch this disaster unfold?"
A guilty person does one thing.
HMPH
Flee.
AMATEURS.
MOMMY? WHY ARE THERE SO MANY STRANGE PEOPLE ON THE TRAIN?
SHH, HONEY.
BUT... MOMMY?
DON'T STARE, KATHERINE.
BUT I'M SCARED OF HIM.
THEN DON'T LOOK AT HIM. PLAY WITH YOUR DOLL.
BUT HE LOOKS LIKE A MONSTER!
A GIANT BAT-MONSTER!
EH?

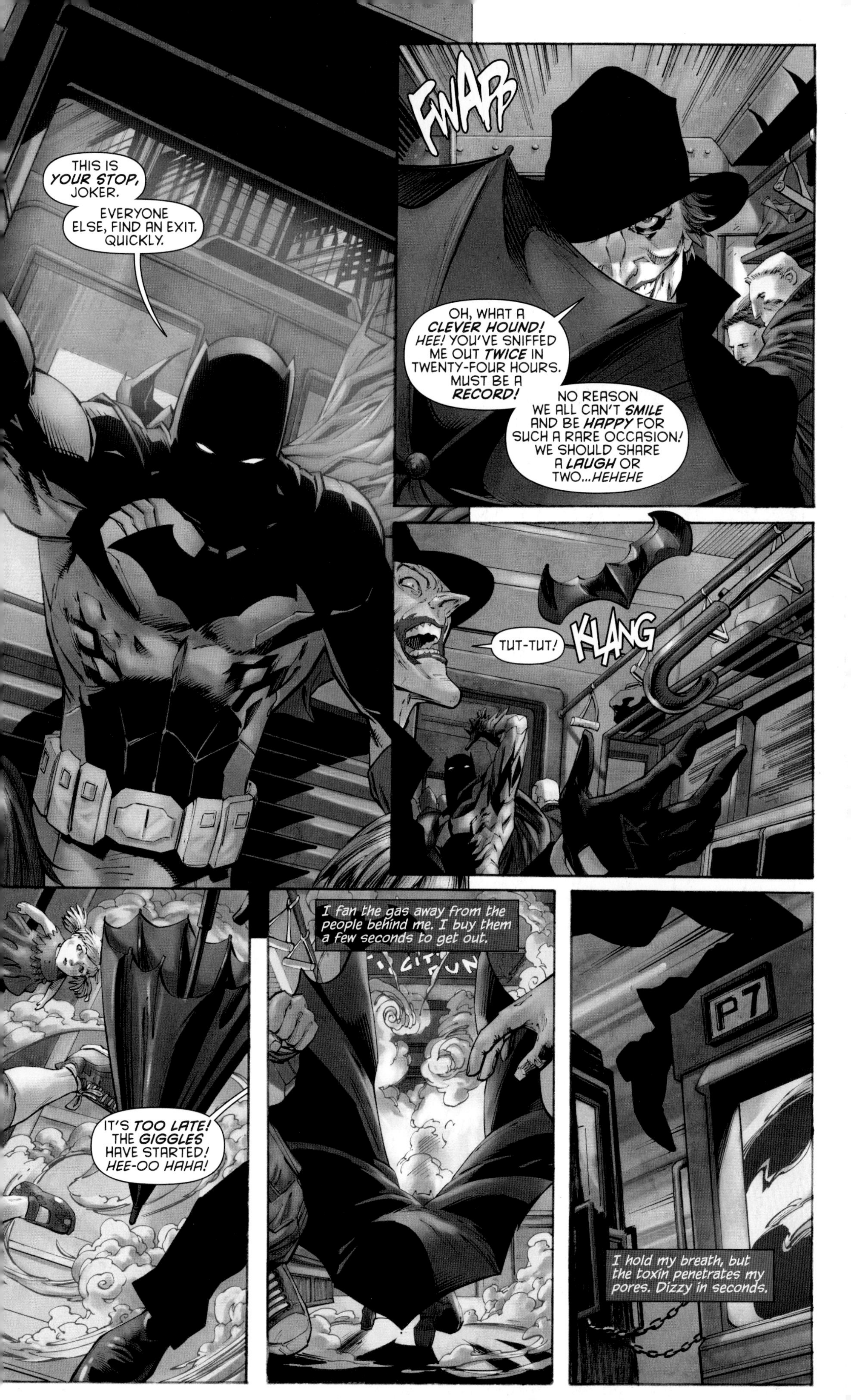

THIS IS YOUR STOP, JOKER.
EVERYONE ELSE, FIND AN EXIT. QUICKLY.
FWAPP
OH, WHAT A CLEVER HOUND! HEE! YOU'VE SNIFFED ME OUT TWICE IN TWENTY-FOUR HOURS. MUST BE A RECORD!
NO REASON WE ALL CAN'T SMILE AND BE HAPPY FOR SUCH A RARE OCCASION! WE SHOULD SHARE A LAUGH OR TWO...HEHEHE
TUT-TUT!
KLANG
IT'S TOO LATE! THE GIGGLES HAVE STARTED! HEE-OO HAHA!
I fan the gas away from the people behind me. I buy them a few seconds to get out.
P7
I hold my breath, but the toxin penetrates my pores. Dizzy in seconds.

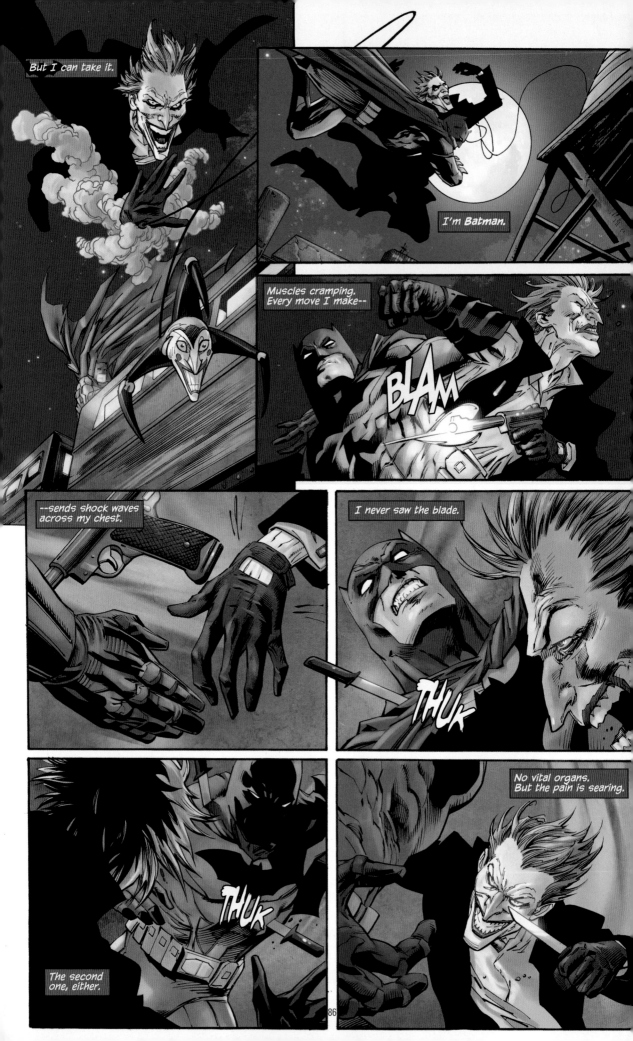

But I can take it.

I'm Batman.

Muscles cramping. Every move I make--

BLAM

--sends shock waves across my chest.

I never saw the blade.

THUK

The second one, either.

THUK

No vital organs. But the pain is searing.

86

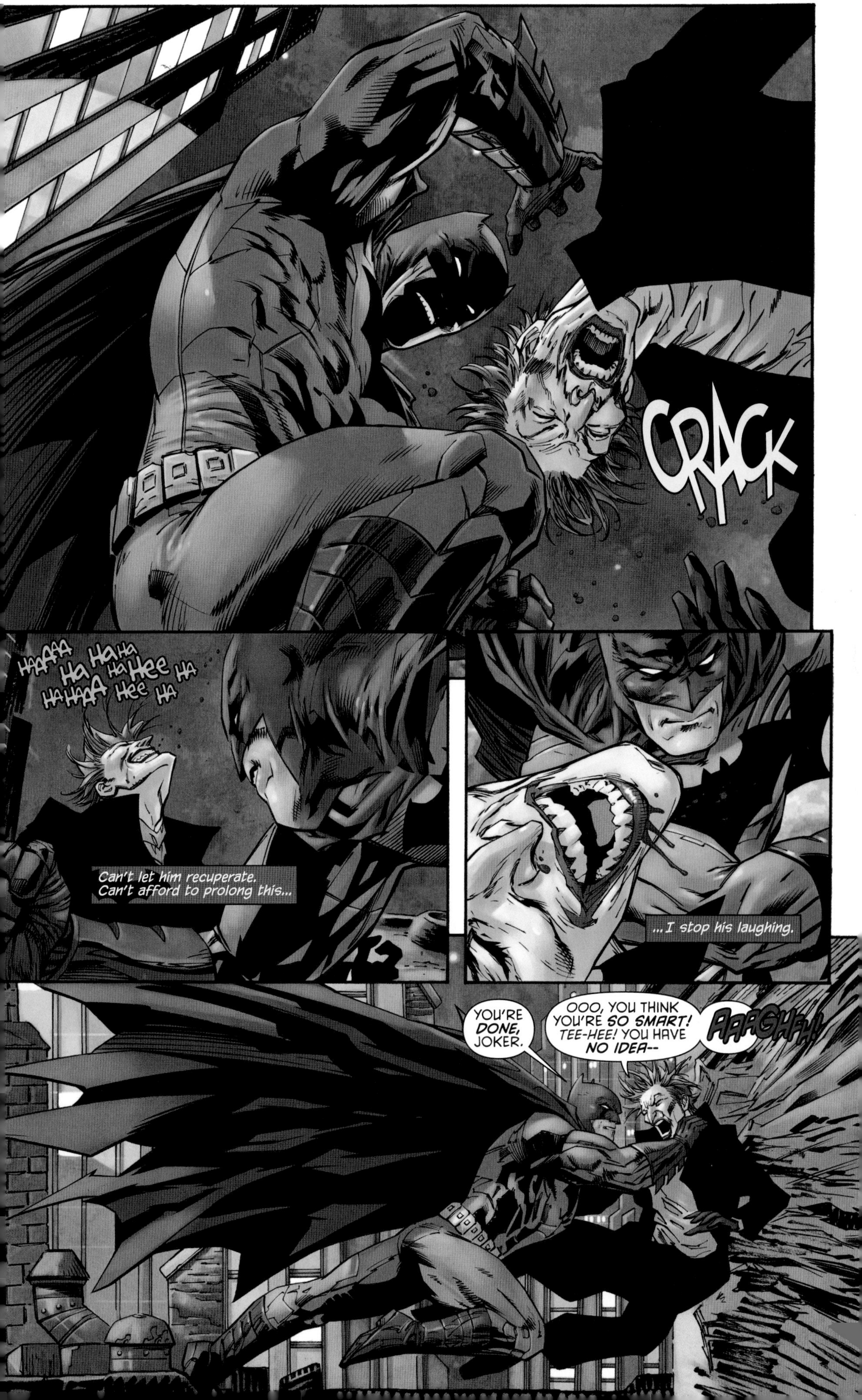
CRACK
HAAAAA HA HAHA HA HAHEE HA HAHAAA HEE HA
Can't let him recuperate.
Can't afford to prolong this...
...I stop his laughing.
YOU'RE DONE, JOKER.
OOO, YOU THINK YOU'RE SO SMART! TEE-HEE! YOU HAVE NO IDEA--
AAAGHHH!

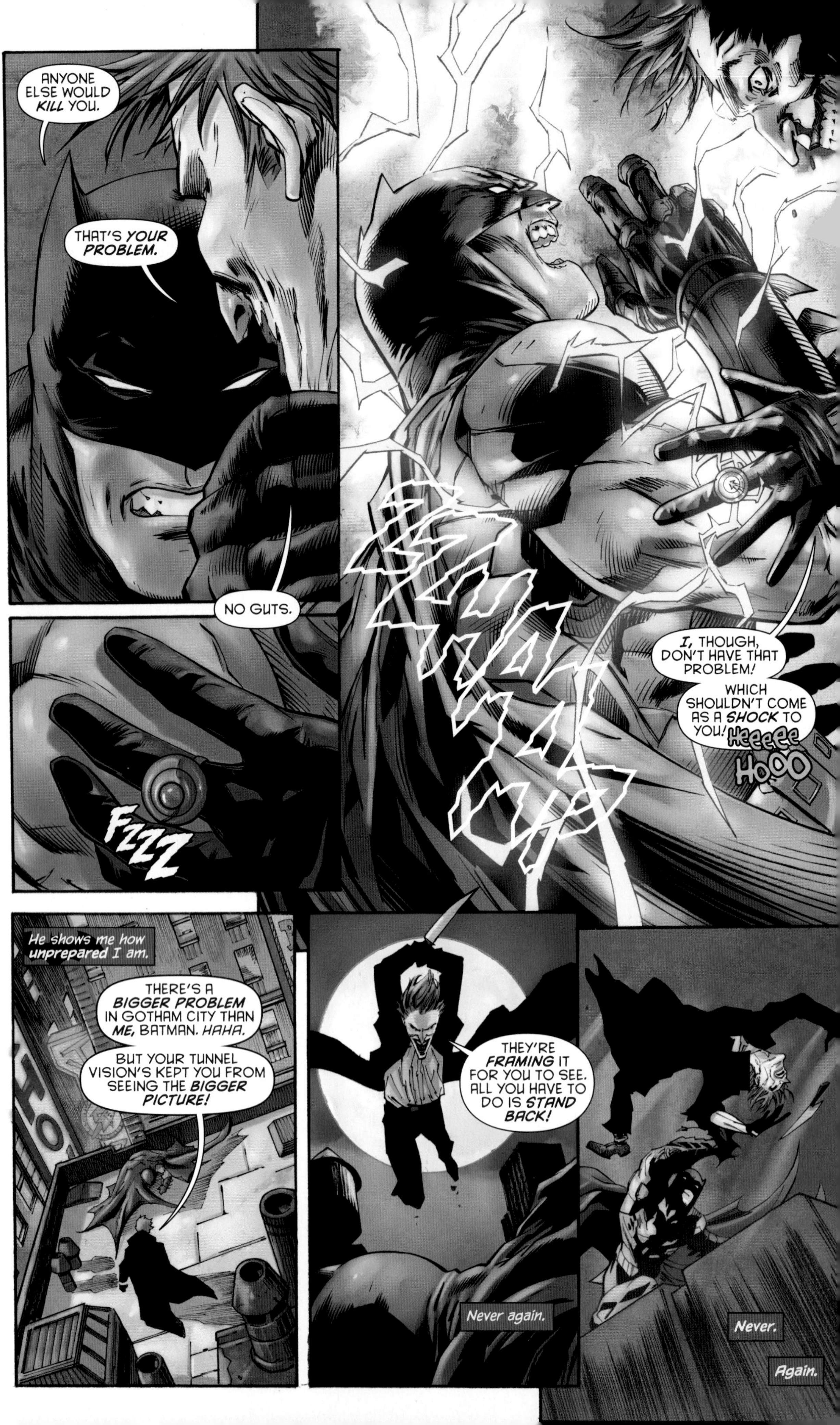

ANYONE ELSE WOULD KILL YOU.
THAT'S YOUR PROBLEM.
NO GUTS.
FZZZ
I, THOUGH, DON'T HAVE THAT PROBLEM!
WHICH SHOULDN'T COME AS A SHOCK TO YOU!
HEEEEE HOOO
He shows me how unprepared I am.
THERE'S A BIGGER PROBLEM IN GOTHAM CITY THAN ME, BATMAN. HAHA.
BUT YOUR TUNNEL VISION'S KEPT YOU FROM SEEING THE BIGGER PICTURE!
THEY'RE FRAMING IT FOR YOU TO SEE. ALL YOU HAVE TO DO IS STAND BACK!
Never again.
Never.
Again.

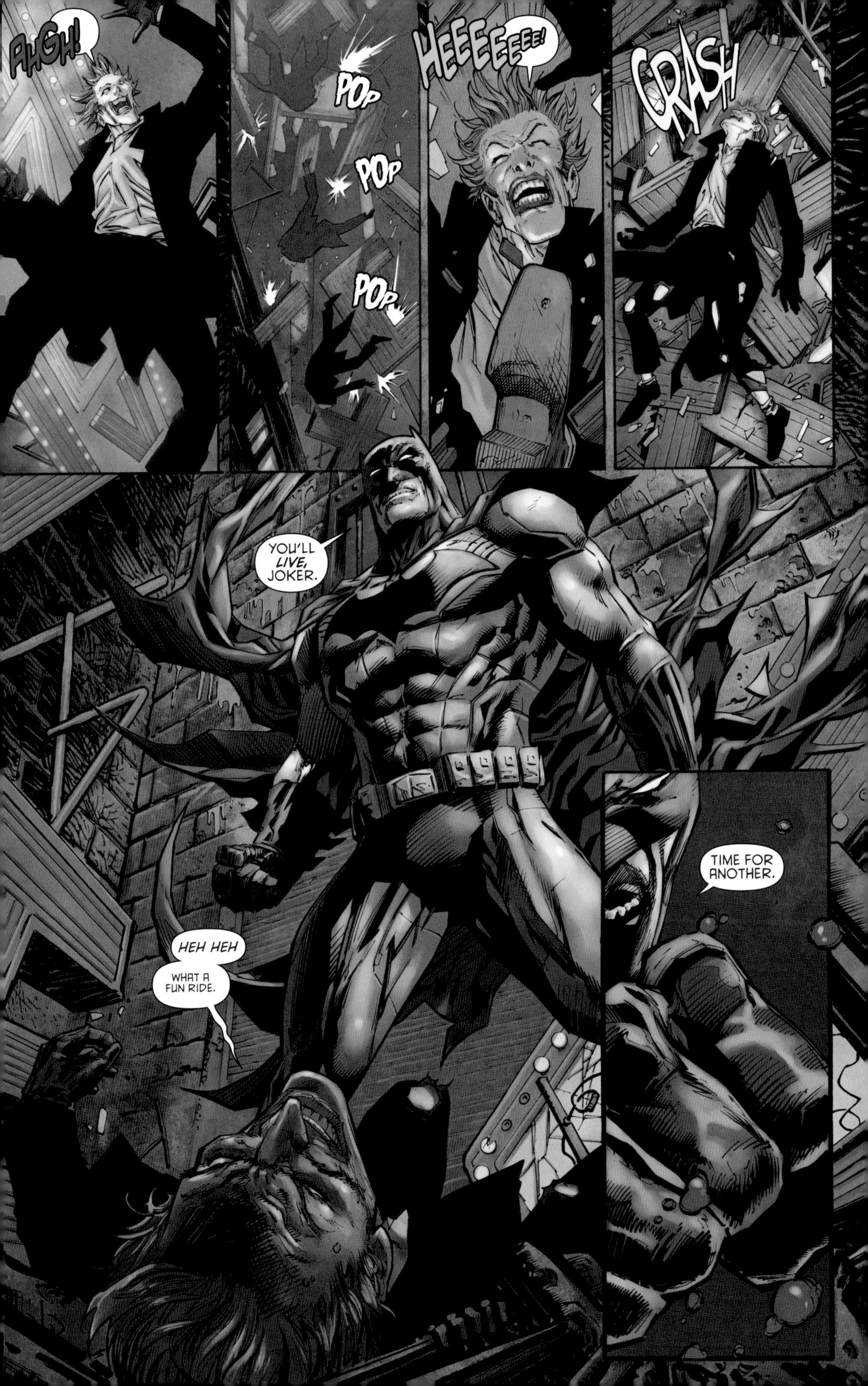
AHGH!
POP
POP
POP
HEEEEEEEE!
CRASH
YOU'LL LIVE, JOKER.
HEH HEH
WHAT A FUN RIDE.
TIME FOR ANOTHER.

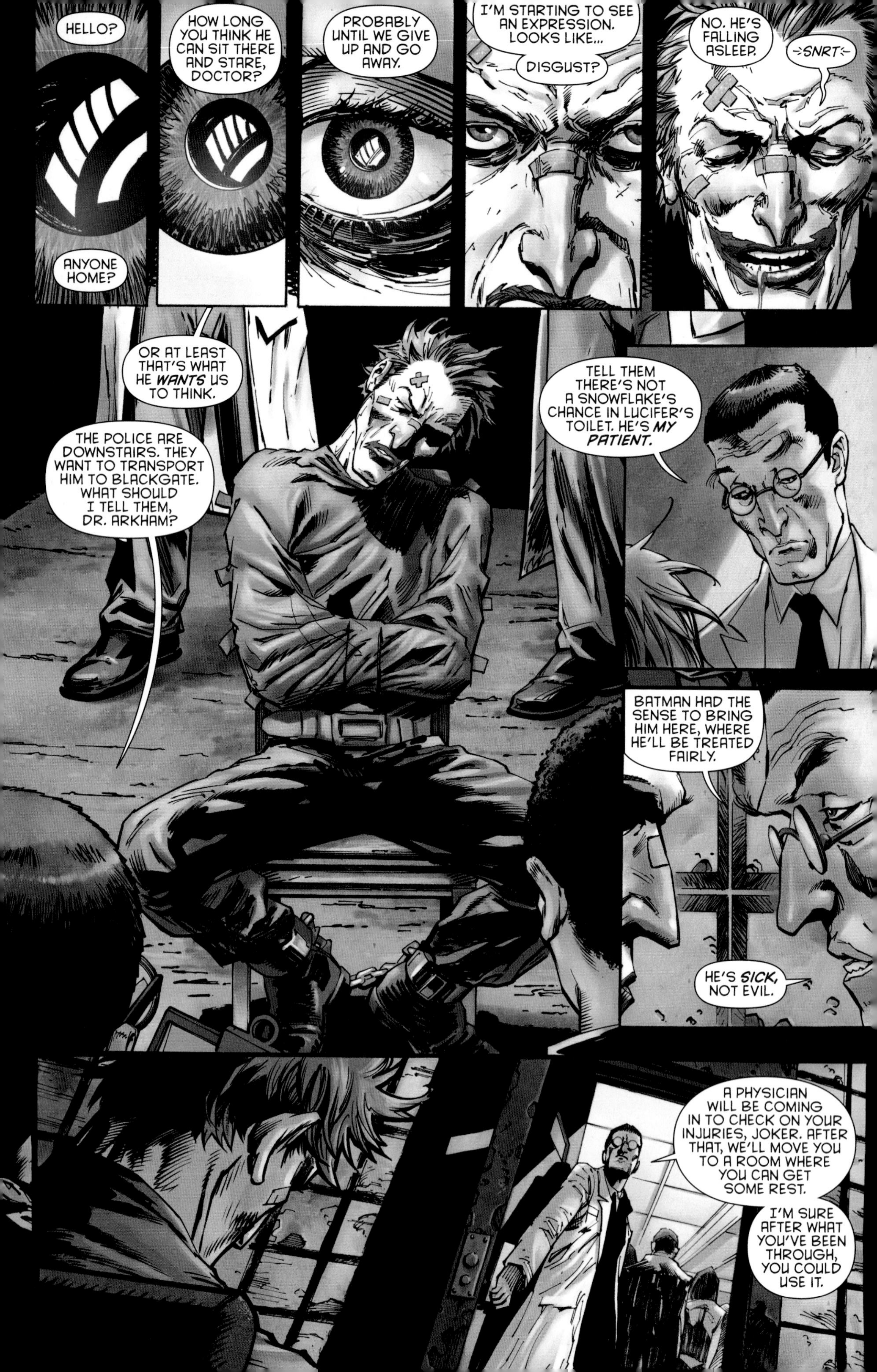
HELLO?
ANYONE HOME?
HOW LONG YOU THINK HE CAN SIT THERE AND STARE, DOCTOR?
PROBABLY UNTIL WE GIVE UP AND GO AWAY.
I'M STARTING TO SEE AN EXPRESSION. LOOKS LIKE...
DISGUST?
NO. HE'S FALLING ASLEEP.
SNRT
OR AT LEAST THAT'S WHAT HE WANTS US TO THINK.
THE POLICE ARE DOWNSTAIRS. THEY WANT TO TRANSPORT HIM TO BLACKGATE. WHAT SHOULD I TELL THEM, DR. ARKHAM?
TELL THEM THERE'S NOT A SNOWFLAKE'S CHANCE IN LUCIFER'S TOILET. HE'S MY PATIENT.
BATMAN HAD THE SENSE TO BRING HIM HERE, WHERE HE'LL BE TREATED FAIRLY.
HE'S SICK, NOT EVIL.
A PHYSICIAN WILL BE COMING IN TO CHECK ON YOUR INJURIES, JOKER. AFTER THAT, WE'LL MOVE YOU TO A ROOM WHERE YOU CAN GET SOME REST.
I'M SURE AFTER WHAT YOU'VE BEEN THROUGH, YOU COULD USE IT.

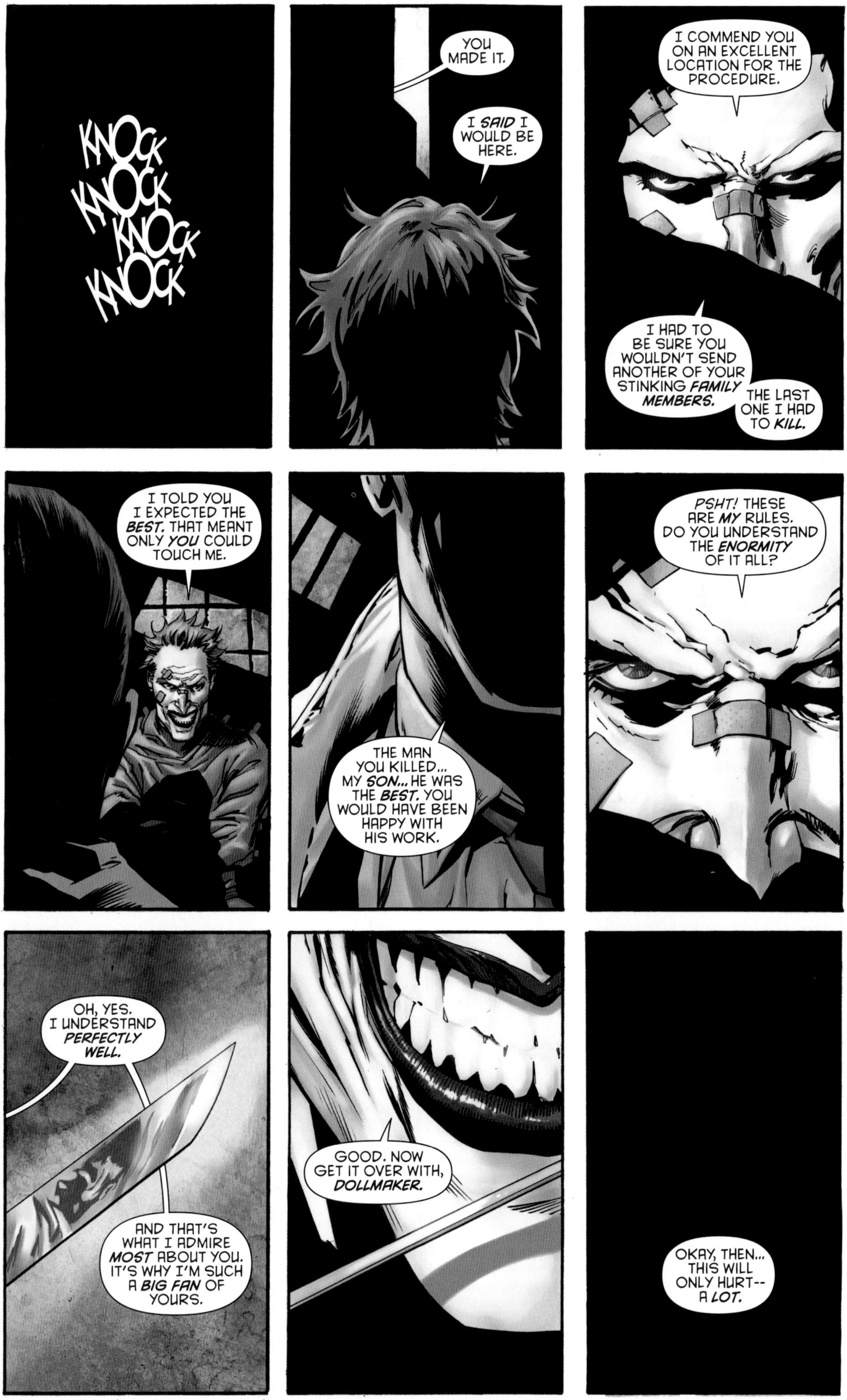
KNOCK KNOCK KNOCK KNOCK
YOU MADE IT.
I SAID I WOULD BE HERE.
I COMMEND YOU ON AN EXCELLENT LOCATION FOR THE PROCEDURE.
I HAD TO BE SURE YOU WOULDN'T SEND ANOTHER OF YOUR STINKING FAMILY MEMBERS.
THE LAST ONE I HAD TO KILL.
I TOLD YOU I EXPECTED THE BEST. THAT MEANT ONLY YOU COULD TOUCH ME.
THE MAN YOU KILLED... MY SON... HE WAS THE BEST. YOU WOULD HAVE BEEN HAPPY WITH HIS WORK.
PSHT! THESE ARE MY RULES. DO YOU UNDERSTAND THE ENORMITY OF IT ALL?
OH, YES. I UNDERSTAND PERFECTLY WELL.
AND THAT'S WHAT I ADMIRE MOST ABOUT YOU. IT'S WHY I'M SUCH A BIG FAN OF YOURS.
GOOD. NOW GET IT OVER WITH, DOLLMAKER.
OKAY, THEN... THIS WILL ONLY HURT-- A LOT.

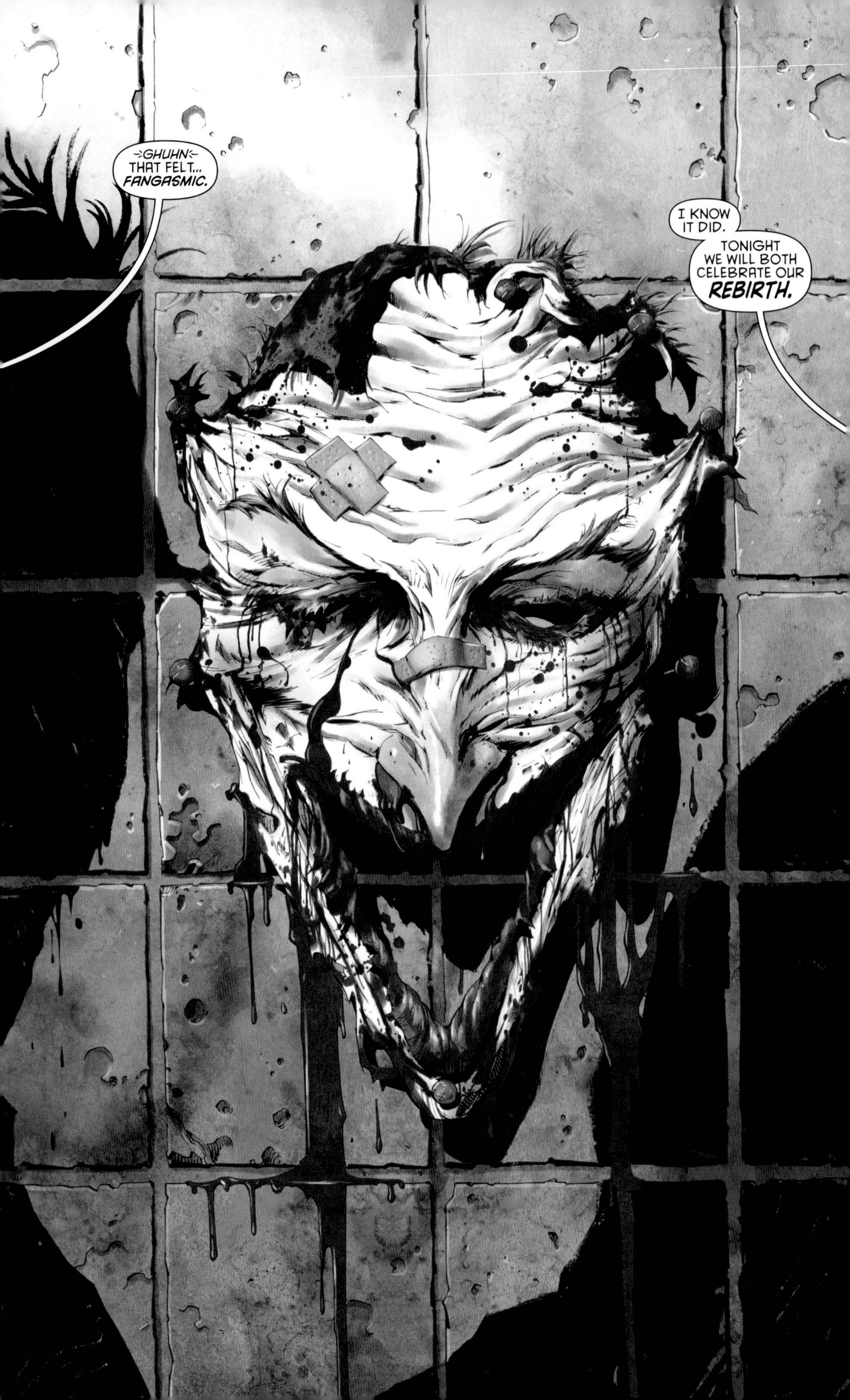

–GHUHN– THAT FELT... FANGASMIC.
I KNOW IT DID.
TONIGHT WE WILL BOTH CELEBRATE OUR REBIRTH.

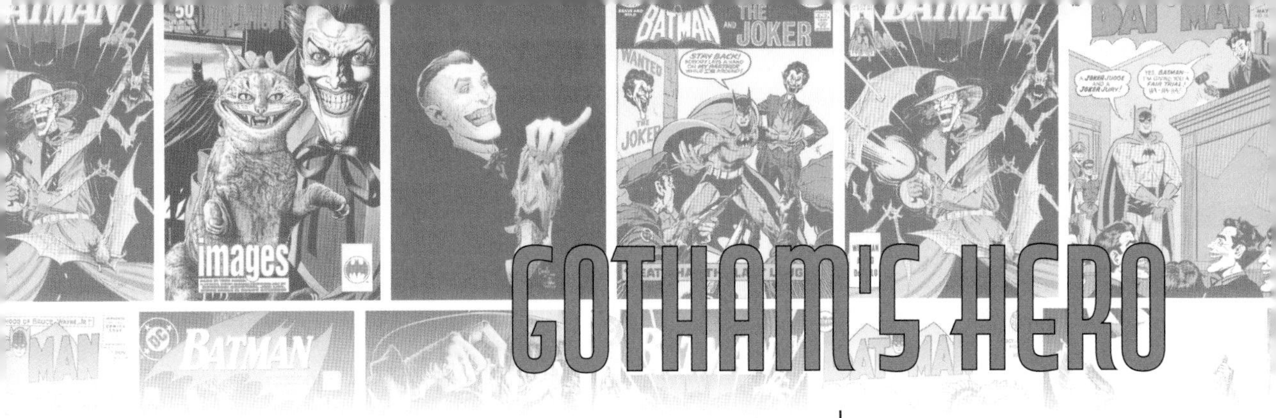
BATMAN
THE JOKER
images
BATMAN

GOTHAM'S HERO

by **SCOTT SNYDER**

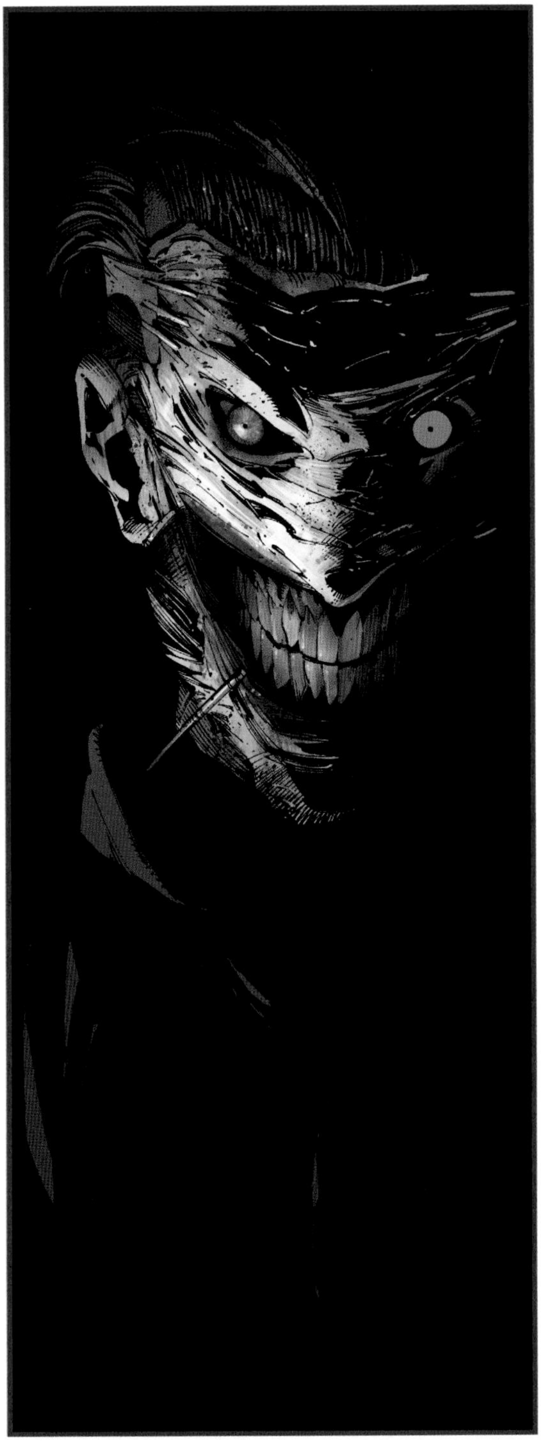

Gotham is a funny place. I've been working in it for over a decade, but all it takes is the briefest visit to feel it: the sense that there's something strange about the city. It almost feels like it's watching you with some great stone eye, doesn't it? Like it's sizing you up…even laughing at you.

In a way, Gotham is Batman's great antagonist, a home that never lets him feel at home, a great city that changes with every era to challenge him, test him, make him stronger. Like many places, Gotham says to Batman (and to us too), come on, come here. You came here to find something, to become something, to evolve into the hero you so desperately want to be. Well I'm going to challenge you, test you, put you through a trial by fire by sending every fear you have back at you in some material form. I'll come at your weak spots, your flaws; I'll create whatever villains I have to in order to burn you down to the core of yourself, to show you who you are, for better or for worse.

Now, Batman, he's our ticket in. He's *our* hero. He makes us brave (behind our locked apartment door). But see, if he's our hero, who is Gotham's? Who is the one who comes calling on its behalf, knocking at the door in the middle of the night, smiling too wide, peeking through the peephole of our locked door? Whose eye is that? Wide and gleeful, but with a tiny pupil, a black pinpoint that lets in no light at all, ever?

The Joker. From *Batman* #1 he's been walking these streets too. From the very first page! So what makes him so special to this place and, by proxy, to all of us, to the world? Why is he, this clown in a purple suit, arguably the greatest villain of all time?

The answer, in my opinion at least, is hidden right there on his calling card. Out of all the cards in a deck, only the joker card is mutable. It can take on whatever value is needed to win. Joker's origin is whatever works best at the moment. He was a failed comedian. He was a vicious gangster. He was a down-and-out

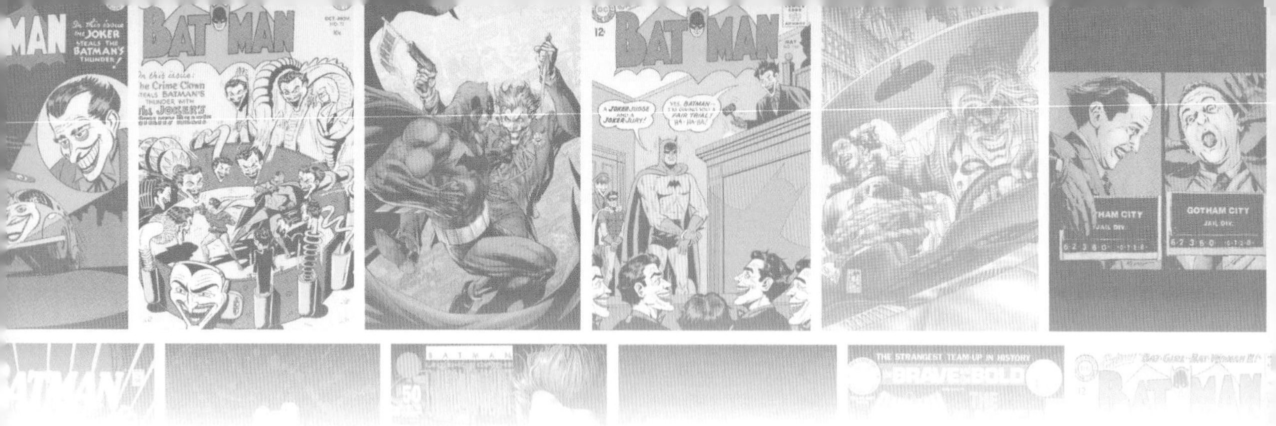
BATMAN
GOTHAM CITY
GOTHAM CITY
THE STRANGEST TEAM-UP IN HISTORY

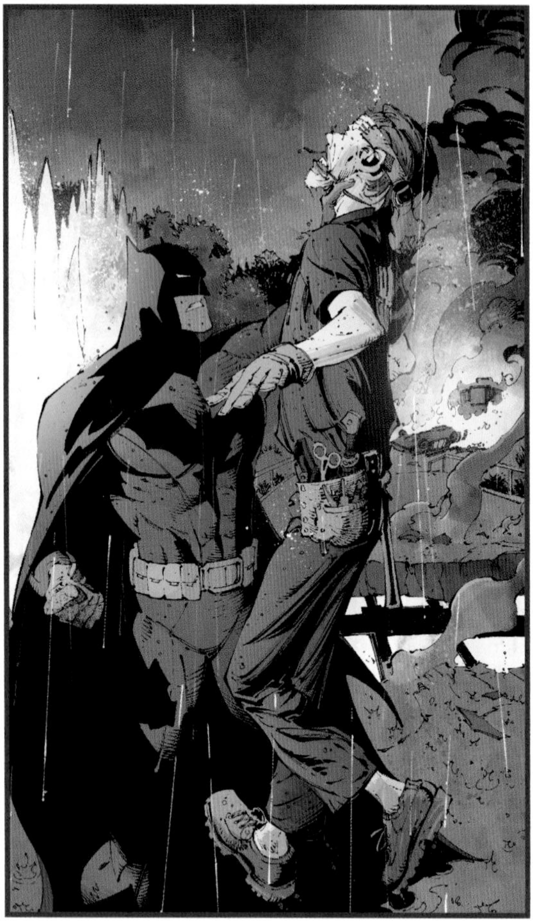

loser. No, he was a sociopath. In the end, the person he used to be before he went into that Ace Chemicals vat is whoever would scare you most to see transformed into the Joker. And the monster who came out of the vat—he's whoever you're most afraid of now. People call him a clown, but he doesn't dress like a clown. He dresses more like a jester, and funnily enough, historically, sometimes it was the jester above anyone who was tasked with delivering bad news to the king, as he—the jester—could do it through humor, thereby tricking His Majesty into looking at his own failings, forcing him to confront his fears. And in this way, the Joker is Batman's court jester, right hand to the king of Gotham (and by proxy, us). He's there to tell us the bad news about ourselves, to make us laugh, until the horror of it hits us like a crowbar. He's the ever-changing man. Like his card, Joker himself, more than any other character in comics, maybe in literature, takes on whatever role is needed to bring your greatest fears to life.

In this respect, you could go so far as to say that while Batman is our hero, the Joker is Gotham's. He is its agent of nightmare. He comes at us when we least expect it, crawling out from beneath the bed, or waiting for us in the closet, armed with new material, but with that same laugh—ancient and new all at once.

***Scott Snyder** has written comics including the bestselling series* American Vampire, Dark Nights: Metal, Batman, Swamp Thing, *and* Superman Unchained. *He is also the author of the story collection* Voodoo Heart *(Dial Press). He teaches writing at Sarah Lawrence College, NYU, and Columbia University. He lives on Long Island with his wife, Jeanie, and his three children. He is a dedicated and unironic fan of Elvis Presley.*

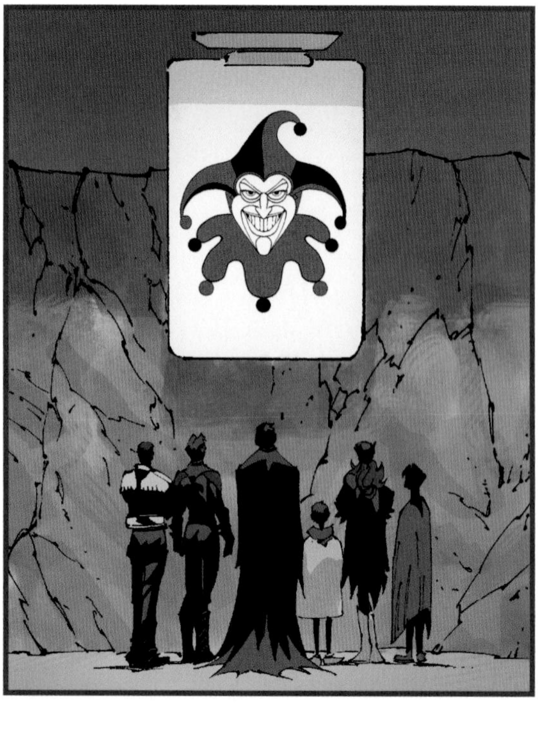

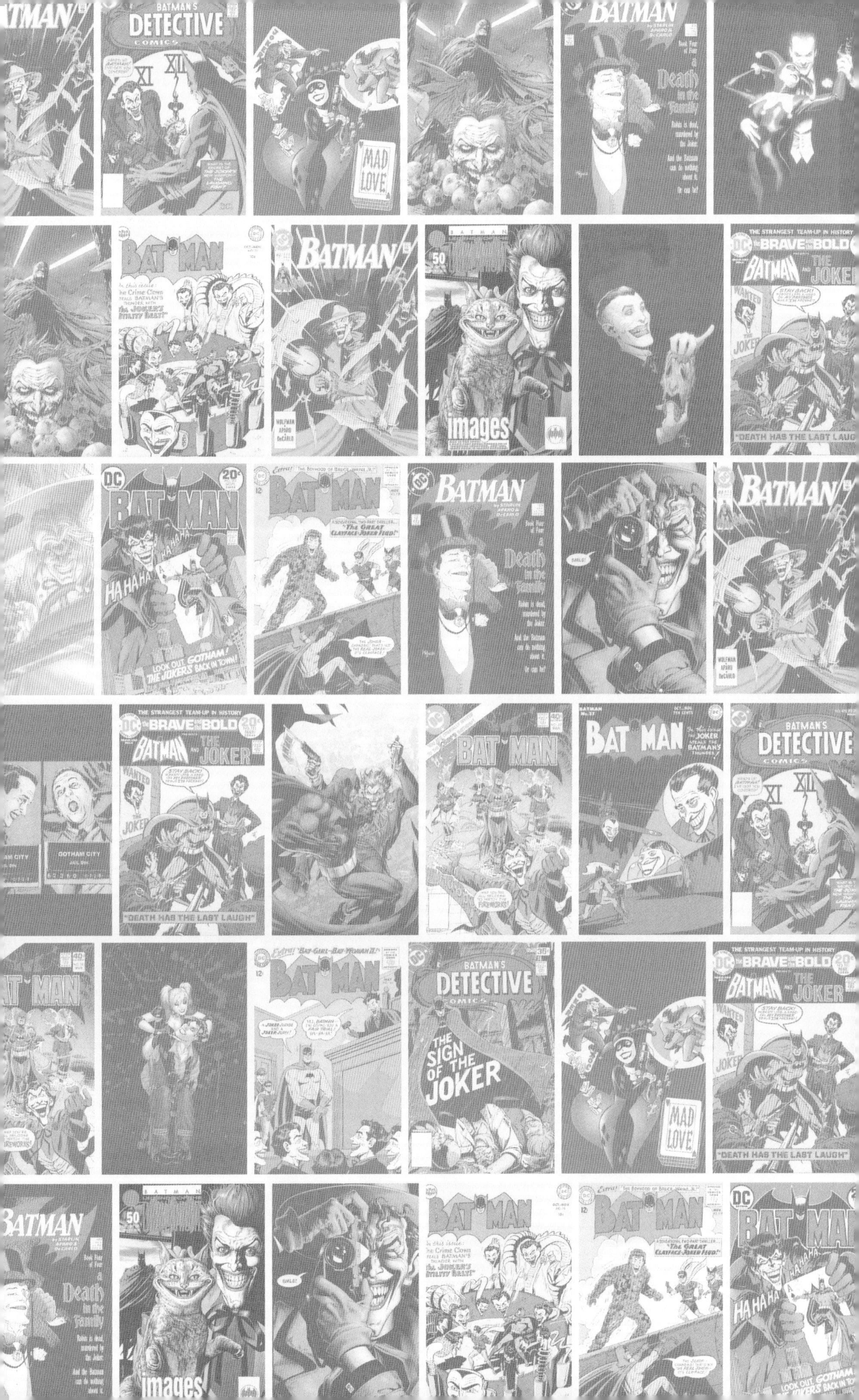
BATMAN
BATMAN'S
DETECTIVE
COMICS
MAD LOVE
BATMAN
a Death in the Family
BAT MAN
BATMAN
images
THE STRANGEST TEAM-UP IN HISTORY
THE BRAVE AND THE BOLD
BATMAN AND THE JOKER
WANTED
JOKER
"DEATH HAS THE LAST LAUGH"
BAT MAN
LOOK OUT, GOTHAM! THE JOKER'S BACK IN TOWN!
"The Great Clayface-Joker Feud!"
BATMAN
a Death in the Family
SMILE!
BATMAN
THE STRANGEST TEAM-UP IN HISTORY
THE BRAVE AND THE BOLD
BATMAN AND THE JOKER
"DEATH HAS THE LAST LAUGH"
GOTHAM CITY
BAT MAN
BAT MAN
BATMAN'S
DETECTIVE
COMICS
BAT MAN
BAT MAN
BATMAN'S
DETECTIVE
COMICS
THE SIGN OF THE JOKER
MAD LOVE
THE STRANGEST TEAM-UP IN HISTORY
THE BRAVE AND THE BOLD
BATMAN AND THE JOKER
"DEATH HAS THE LAST LAUGH"
BATMAN
a Death in the Family
images
SMILE!
BAT MAN
BAT MAN
"The Great Clayface-Joker Feud!"
BAT MAN

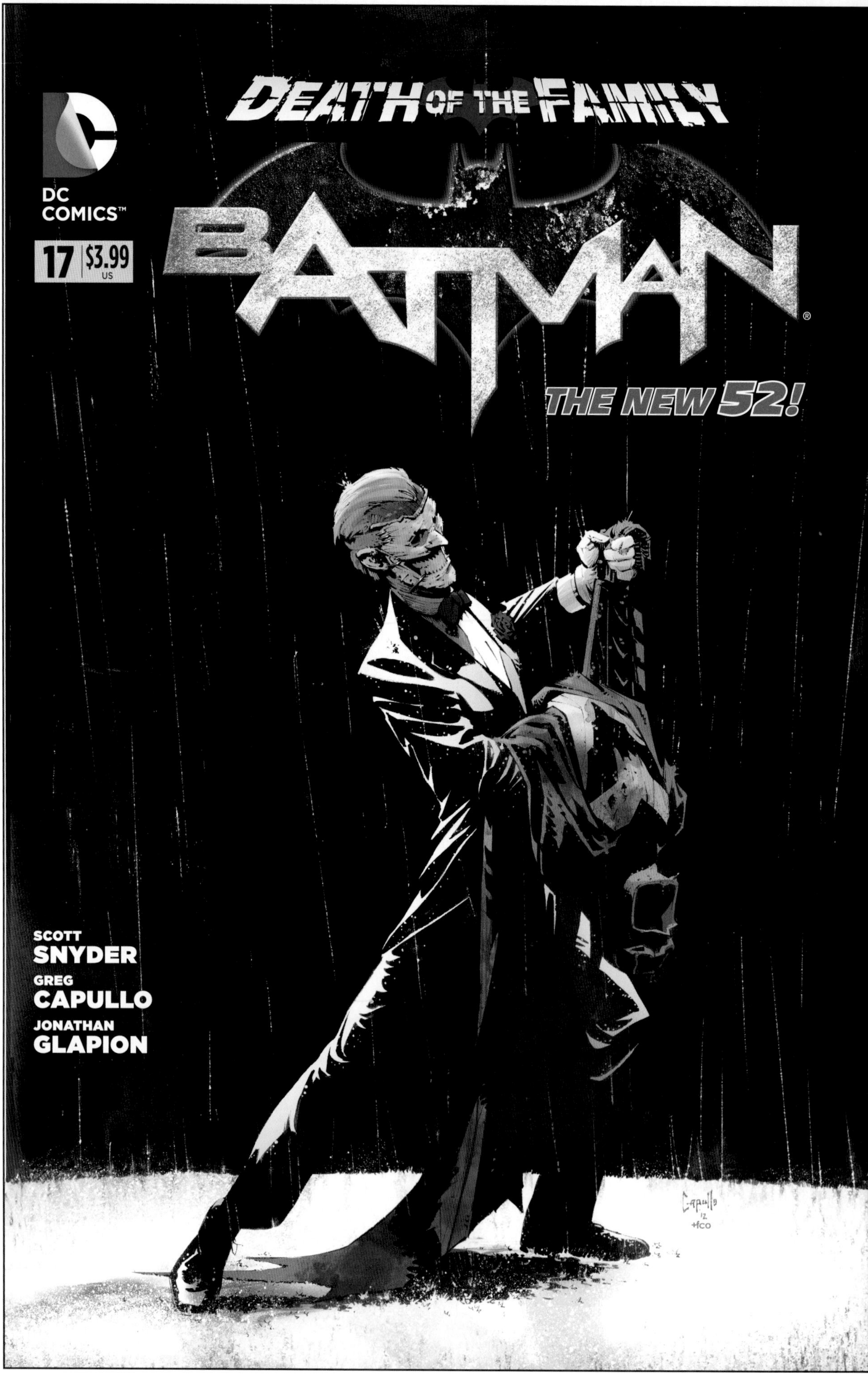
DEATH OF THE FAMILY
DC COMICS™
17 $3.99 US
BATMAN®
THE NEW 52!
SCOTT
SNYDER
GREG
CAPULLO
JONATHAN
GLAPION

THE FIRST TIME WAS FRIGHTENING, WASN'T IT?
WWW... WHH.
WHERE...
LOOK! LOOK! HERE IT COMES, SEEEEE?
JOKER...
YESSS, JOKER IS HERE WITH YOU IN THE DARK. WE'RE WATCHING IT COME FOR YOU, AS I'M SURE IT DID THAT FIRST TIME.
OOOHH... IT WANTSSSS YOU! WANTS YOU BAD!
JOKER, LISTEN TO--
NO. THERE IS NO REASONING WITH IT... IT WAS THE SAME FOR ME, WHEN I SAW IT COMING... WHEN I SAW YOU COMING. NO REASONING!
STOP THIS! NOW!
AND SO YOU CALLED OUT THERE IN THE DARK! EVEN THOUGH YOU KNEW YOU WERE SEEING IT! YOUR FACE, THE REAL BONE AND TOOTH FACE BENEATH IT ALL.
JOKER!
YOU KNEW IT IN YOUR SOUL, BUT STILL YOU CALLED OUT TO SOMEONE, ANYONE, TO PULL YOU UP FROM THE DARKNESS.

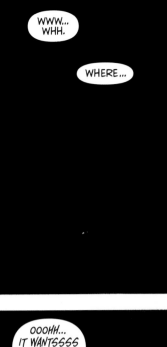

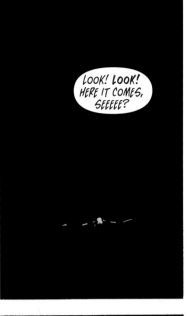

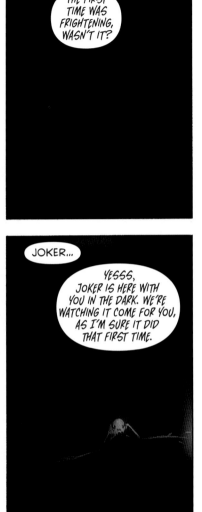

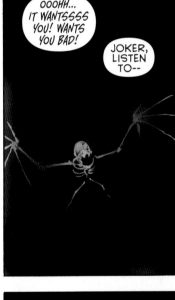

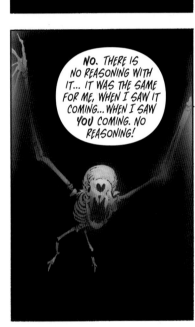

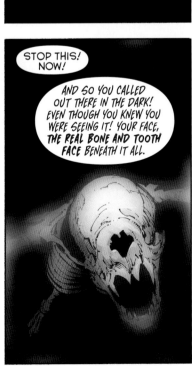

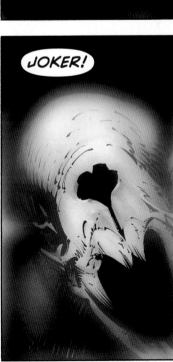

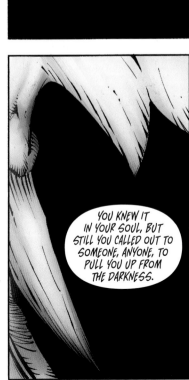

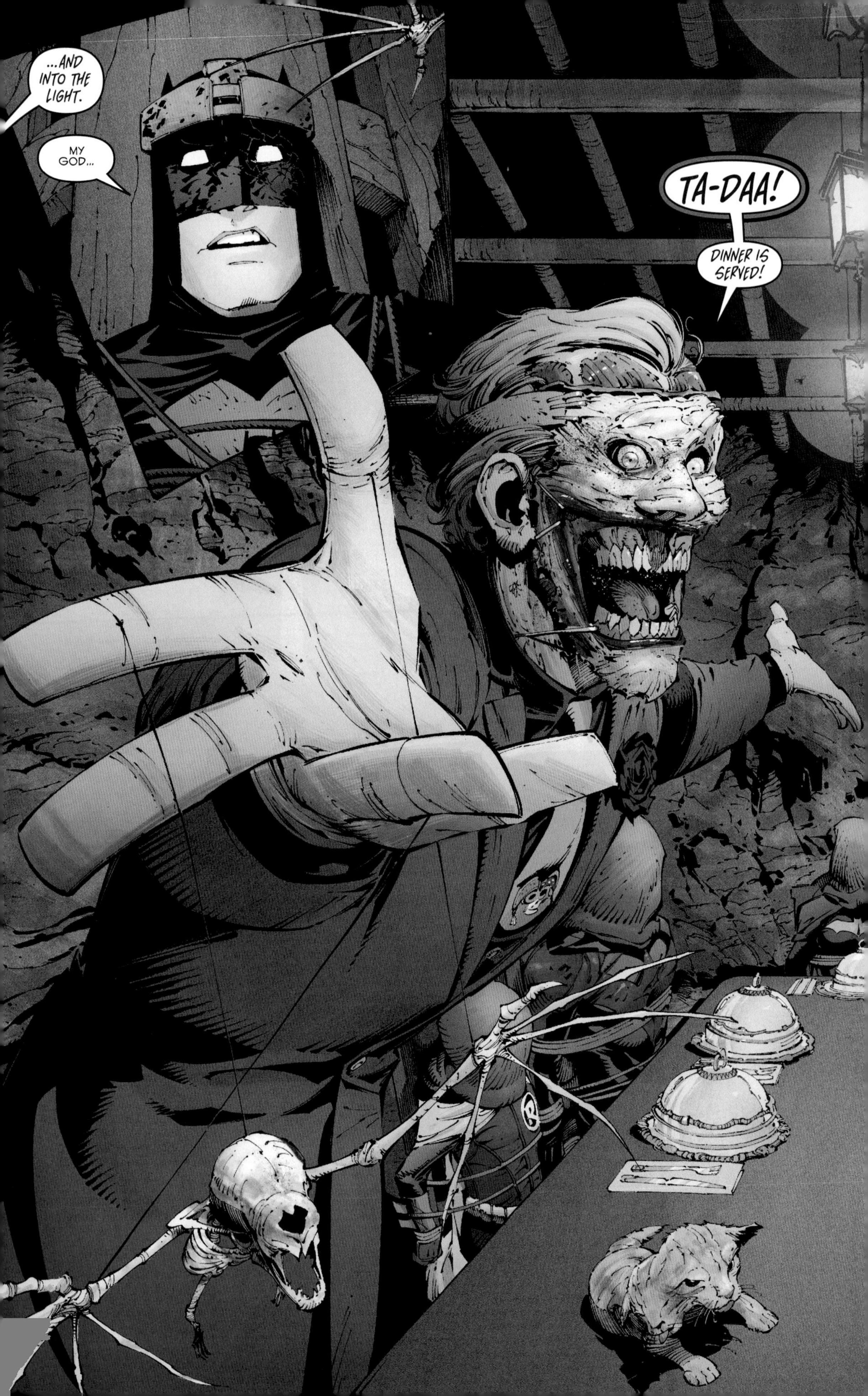
...AND INTO THE LIGHT.
MY GOD...
TA-DAA!
DINNER IS SERVED!

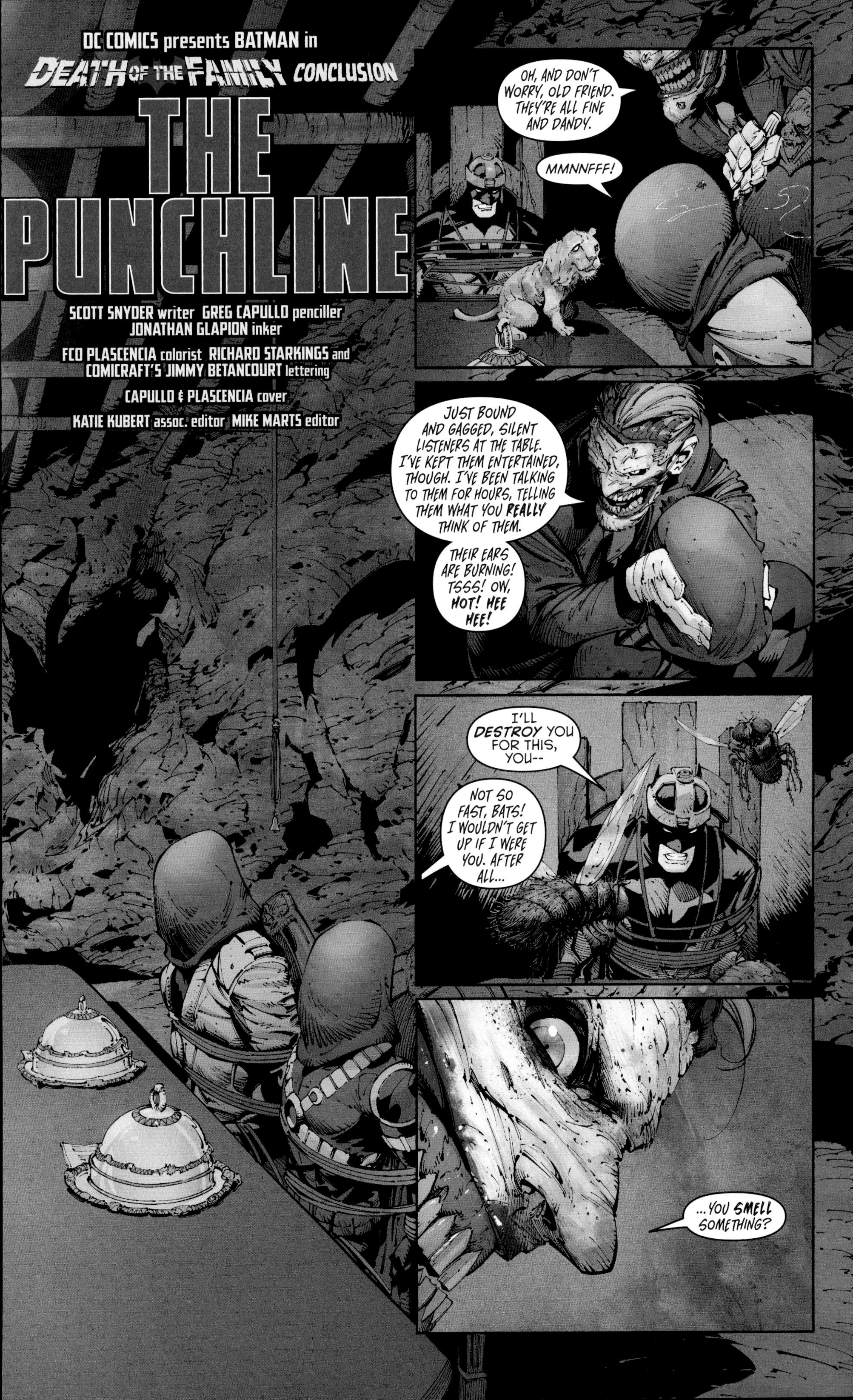
DC COMICS presents BATMAN in
DEATH OF THE FAMILY CONCLUSION
THE PUNCHLINE
SCOTT SNYDER writer GREG CAPULLO penciller
JONATHAN GLAPION inker
FCO PLASCENCIA colorist RICHARD STARKINGS and
COMICRAFT'S JIMMY BETANCOURT lettering
CAPULLO & PLASCENCIA cover
KATIE KUBERT assoc. editor MIKE MARTS editor
OH, AND DON'T WORRY, OLD FRIEND. THEY'RE ALL FINE AND DANDY.
MMNNFFF!
JUST BOUND AND GAGGED, SILENT LISTENERS AT THE TABLE. I'VE KEPT THEM ENTERTAINED, THOUGH. I'VE BEEN TALKING TO THEM FOR HOURS, TELLING THEM WHAT YOU REALLY THINK OF THEM.
THEIR EARS ARE BURNING! TSSS! OW, HOT! HEE HEE!
I'LL DESTROY YOU FOR THIS, YOU--
NOT SO FAST, BATS! I WOULDN'T GET UP IF I WERE YOU. AFTER ALL...
...YOU SMELL SOMETHING?

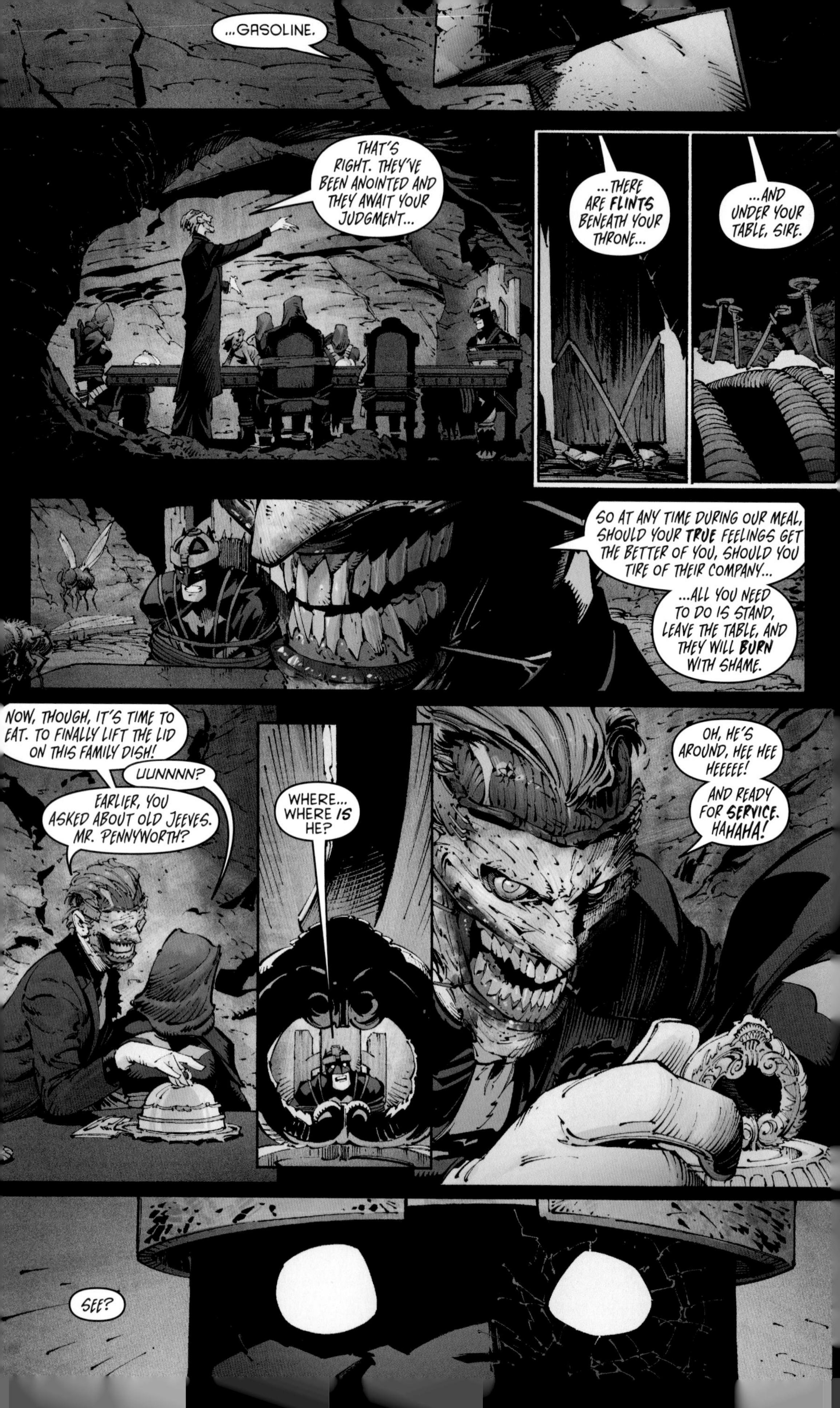
...GASOLINE.
THAT'S RIGHT. THEY'VE BEEN ANOINTED AND THEY AWAIT YOUR JUDGMENT...
...THERE ARE FLINTS BENEATH YOUR THRONE...
...AND UNDER YOUR TABLE, SIRE.
SO AT ANY TIME DURING OUR MEAL, SHOULD YOUR TRUE FEELINGS GET THE BETTER OF YOU, SHOULD YOU TIRE OF THEIR COMPANY...
...ALL YOU NEED TO DO IS STAND, LEAVE THE TABLE, AND THEY WILL BURN WITH SHAME.
NOW, THOUGH, IT'S TIME TO EAT. TO FINALLY LIFT THE LID ON THIS FAMILY DISH!
UUNNNN?
EARLIER, YOU ASKED ABOUT OLD JEEVES. MR. PENNYWORTH?
WHERE... WHERE IS HE?
OH, HE'S AROUND, HEE HEE HEEEEE!
AND READY FOR SERVICE. HAHAHA!
SEE?

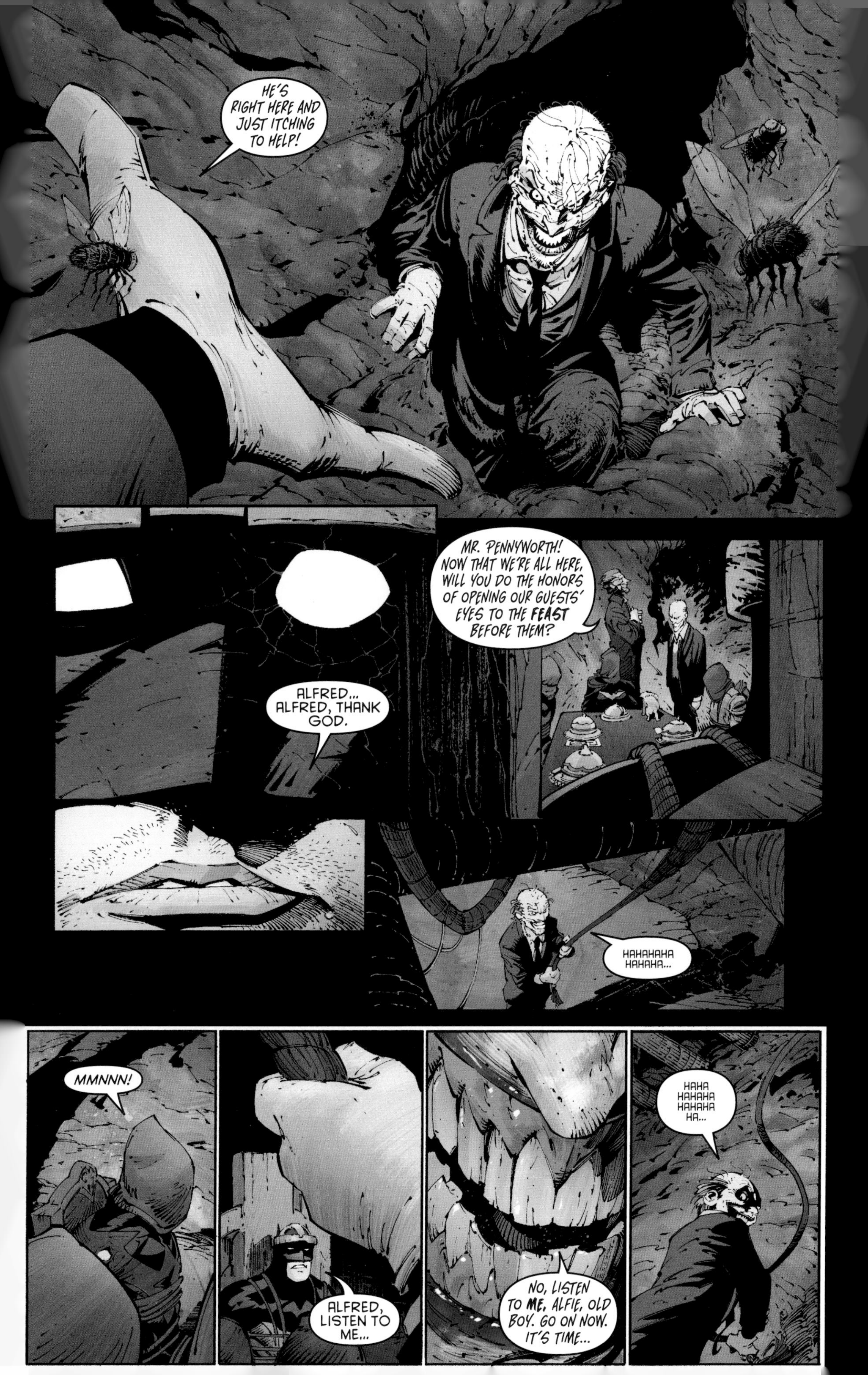
HE'S RIGHT HERE AND JUST ITCHING TO HELP!
MR. PENNYWORTH! NOW THAT WE'RE ALL HERE, WILL YOU DO THE HONORS OF OPENING OUR GUESTS' EYES TO THE **FEAST** BEFORE THEM?
ALFRED... ALFRED, THANK GOD.
HAHAHAHA HAHAHA...
MMNNN!
ALFRED, LISTEN TO ME...
NO, LISTEN TO **ME,** ALFIE, OLD BOY. GO ON NOW. IT'S TIME...
HAHA HAHAHA HAHAHA HA...

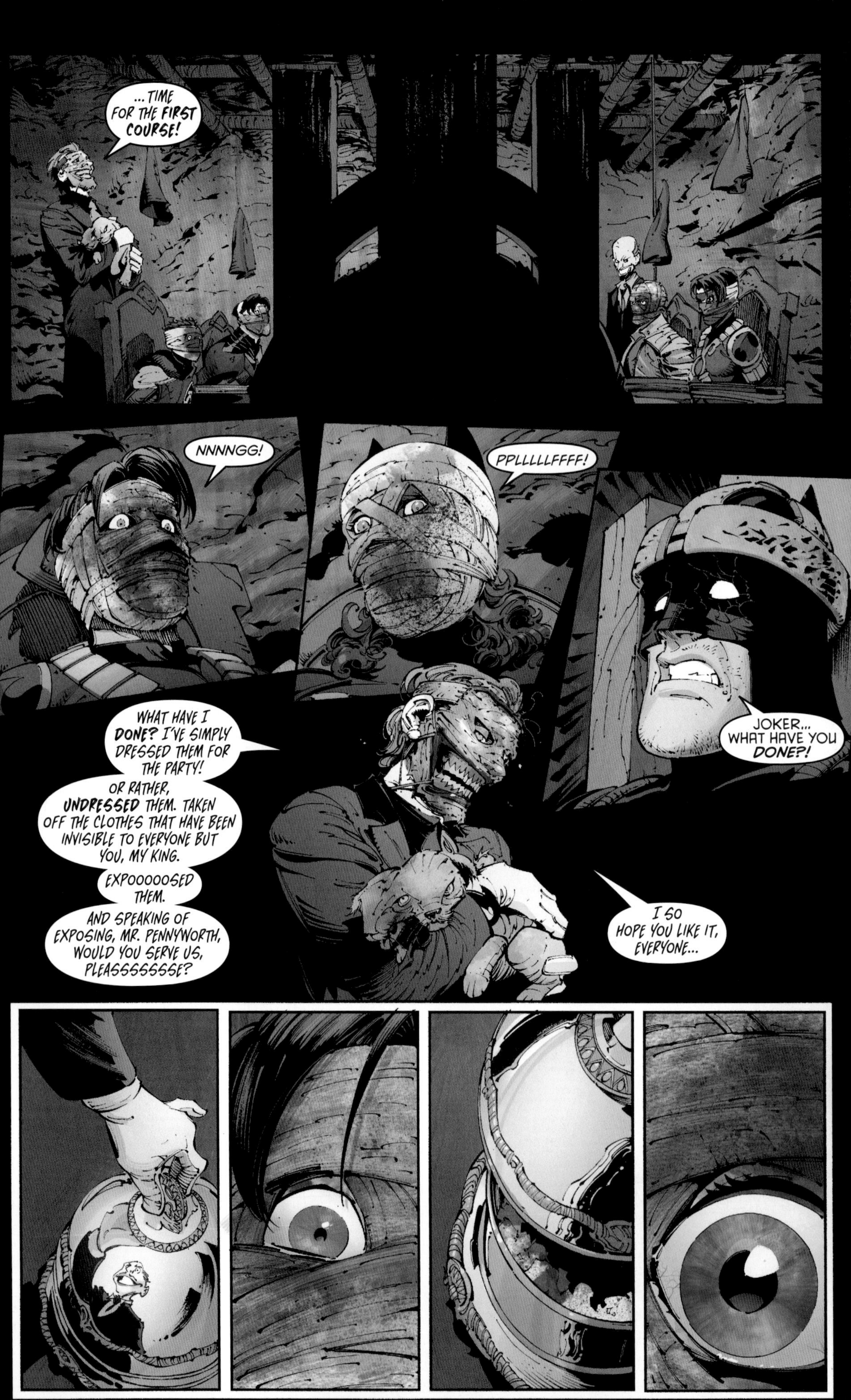
...TIME FOR THE FIRST COURSE!
NNNNGG!
PPLLLLLLFFFF!
JOKER... WHAT HAVE YOU DONE?!
WHAT HAVE I DONE? I'VE SIMPLY DRESSED THEM FOR THE PARTY!
OR RATHER, UNDRESSED THEM. TAKEN OFF THE CLOTHES THAT HAVE BEEN INVISIBLE TO EVERYONE BUT YOU, MY KING.
EXPOOOOOSED THEM.
AND SPEAKING OF EXPOSING, MR. PENNYWORTH, WOULD YOU SERVE US, PLEASSSSSSSSE?
I SO HOPE YOU LIKE IT, EVERYONE...

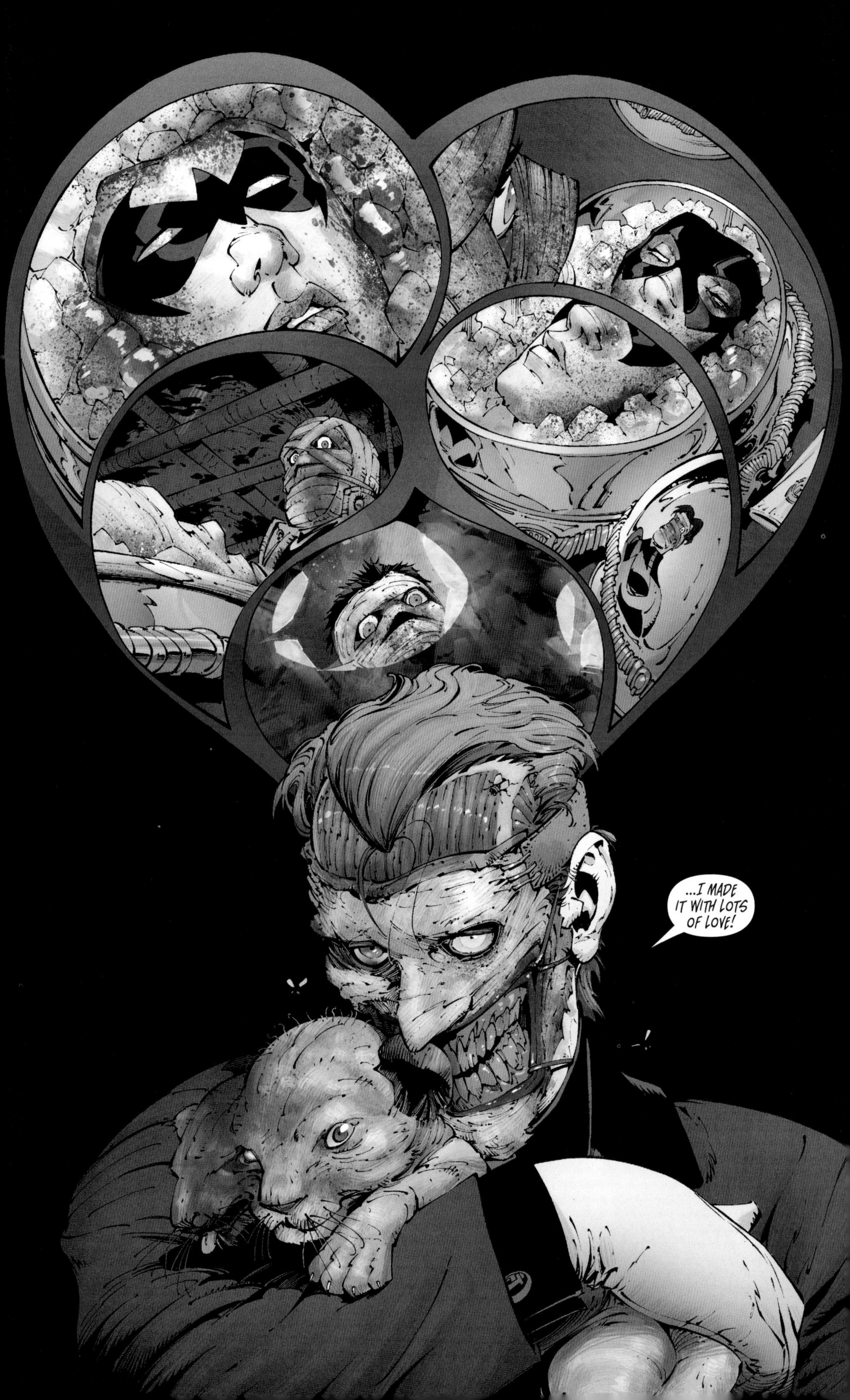
...I MADE IT WITH LOTS OF LOVE!

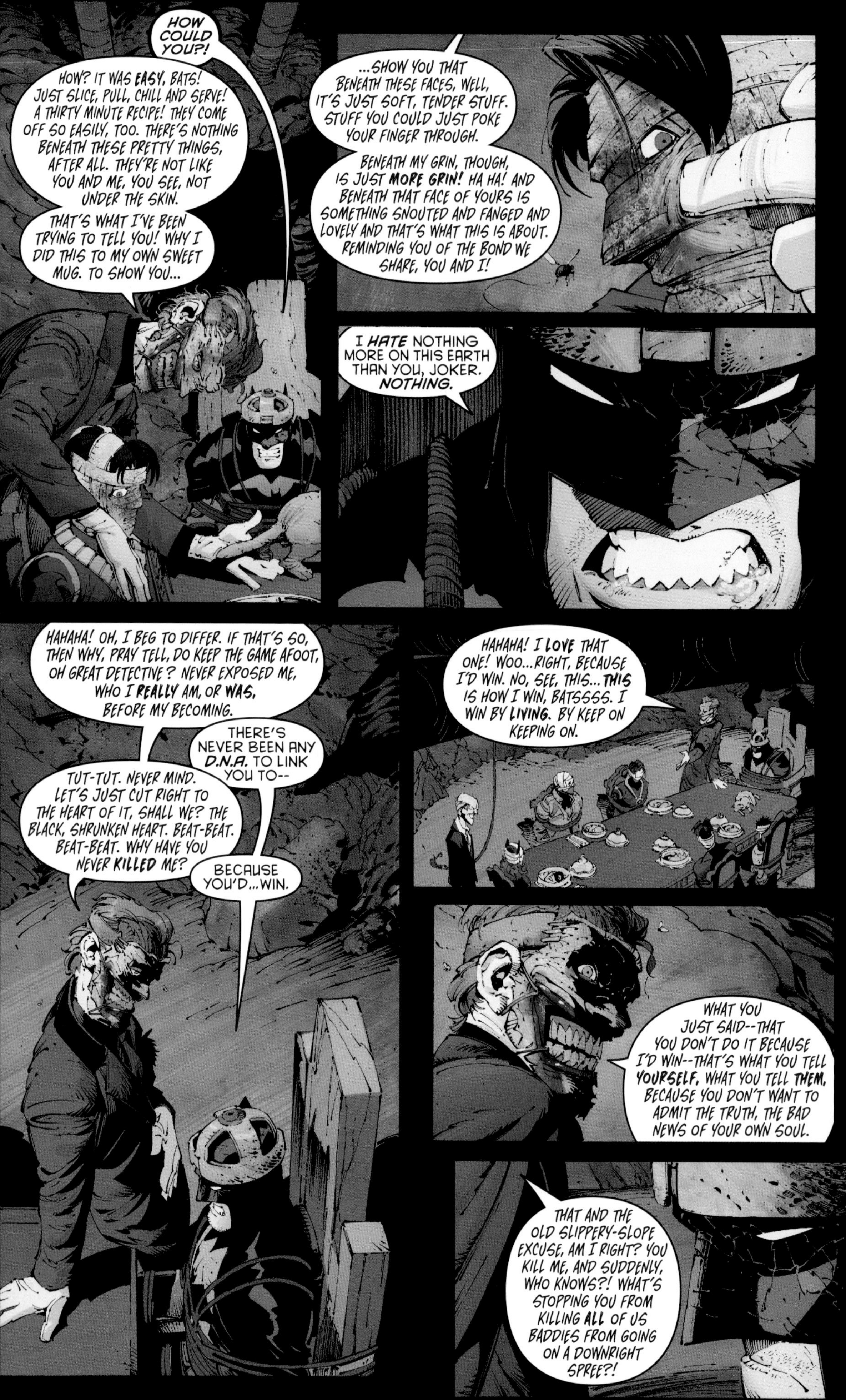
HOW COULD YOU?!
HOW? IT WAS EASY, BATS! JUST SLICE, PULL, CHILL AND SERVE! A THIRTY MINUTE RECIPE! THEY COME OFF SO EASILY, TOO. THERE'S NOTHING BENEATH THESE PRETTY THINGS, AFTER ALL. THEY'RE NOT LIKE YOU AND ME, YOU SEE, NOT UNDER THE SKIN.
THAT'S WHAT I'VE BEEN TRYING TO TELL YOU! WHY I DID THIS TO MY OWN SWEET MUG. TO SHOW YOU...
...SHOW YOU THAT BENEATH THESE FACES, WELL, IT'S JUST SOFT, TENDER STUFF. STUFF YOU COULD JUST POKE YOUR FINGER THROUGH.
BENEATH MY GRIN, THOUGH, IS JUST MORE GRIN! HA HA! AND BENEATH THAT FACE OF YOURS IS SOMETHING SNOUTED AND FANGED AND LOVELY AND THAT'S WHAT THIS IS ABOUT. REMINDING YOU OF THE BOND WE SHARE, YOU AND I!
I HATE NOTHING MORE ON THIS EARTH THAN YOU, JOKER. NOTHING.
HAHAHA! OH, I BEG TO DIFFER. IF THAT'S SO, THEN WHY, PRAY TELL, DO KEEP THE GAME AFOOT, OH GREAT DETECTIVE? NEVER EXPOSED ME, WHO I REALLY AM, OR WAS, BEFORE MY BECOMING.
THERE'S NEVER BEEN ANY D.N.A. TO LINK YOU TO--
TUT-TUT. NEVER MIND. LET'S JUST CUT RIGHT TO THE HEART OF IT, SHALL WE? THE BLACK, SHRUNKEN HEART. BEAT-BEAT. BEAT-BEAT. WHY HAVE YOU NEVER KILLED ME?
BECAUSE YOU'D...WIN.
HAHAHA! I LOVE THAT ONE! WOO...RIGHT, BECAUSE I'D WIN. NO, SEE, THIS... THIS IS HOW I WIN, BATSSSS. I WIN BY LIVING. BY KEEP ON KEEPING ON.
WHAT YOU JUST SAID--THAT YOU DON'T DO IT BECAUSE I'D WIN--THAT'S WHAT YOU TELL YOURSELF. WHAT YOU TELL THEM. BECAUSE YOU DON'T WANT TO ADMIT THE TRUTH, THE BAD NEWS OF YOUR OWN SOUL.
THAT AND THE OLD SLIPPERY-SLOPE EXCUSE, AM I RIGHT? YOU KILL ME, AND SUDDENLY, WHO KNOWS?! WHAT'S STOPPING YOU FROM KILLING ALL OF US BADDIES FROM GOING ON A DOWNRIGHT SPREE?!

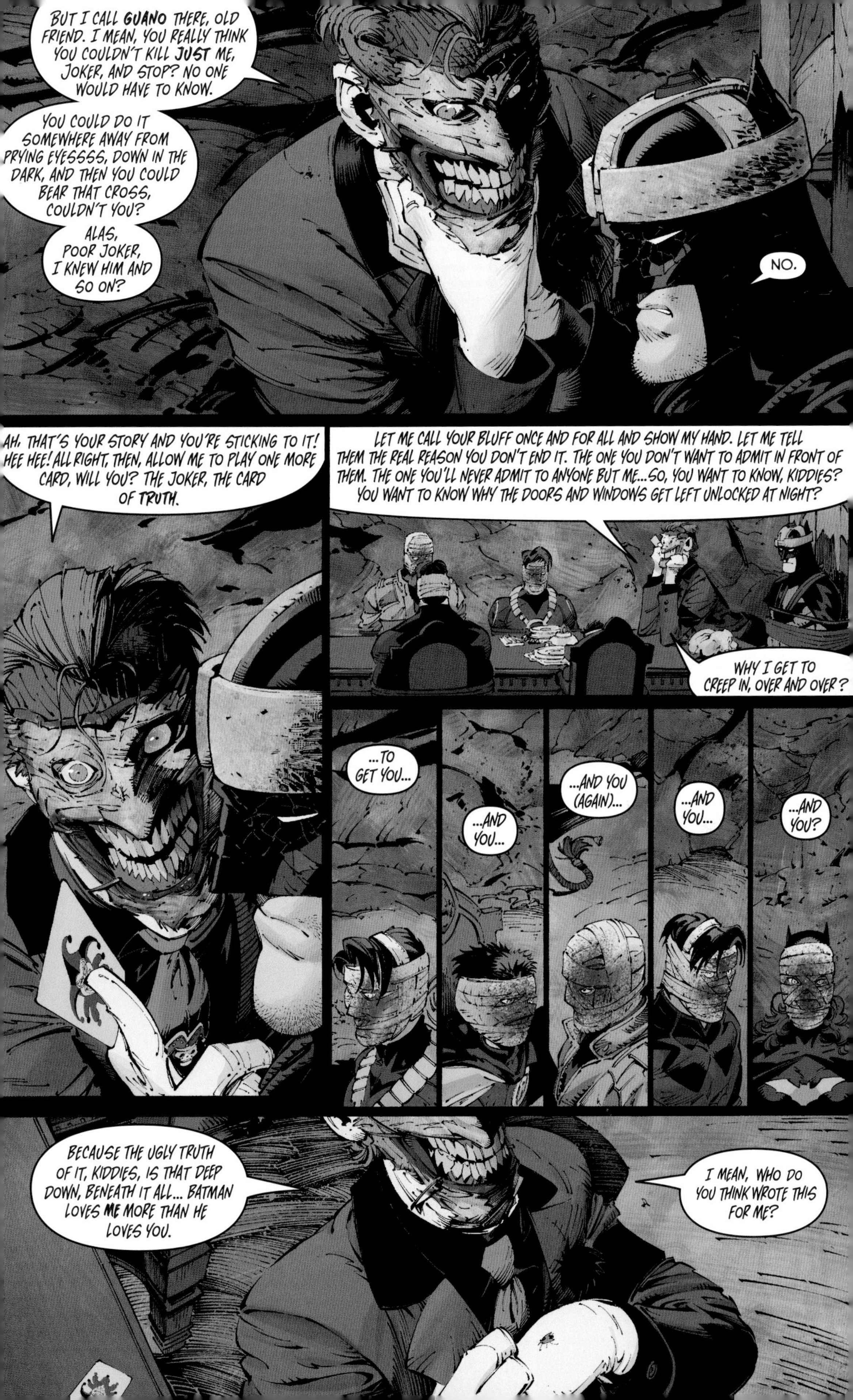
BUT I CALL GUANO THERE, OLD FRIEND. I MEAN, YOU REALLY THINK YOU COULDN'T KILL JUST ME, JOKER, AND STOP? NO ONE WOULD HAVE TO KNOW.
YOU COULD DO IT SOMEWHERE AWAY FROM PRYING EYESSSS, DOWN IN THE DARK, AND THEN YOU COULD BEAR THAT CROSS, COULDN'T YOU?
ALAS, POOR JOKER, I KNEW HIM AND SO ON?
NO.
AH, THAT'S YOUR STORY AND YOU'RE STICKING TO IT! HEE HEE! ALL RIGHT, THEN, ALLOW ME TO PLAY ONE MORE CARD, WILL YOU? THE JOKER, THE CARD OF TRUTH.
LET ME CALL YOUR BLUFF ONCE AND FOR ALL AND SHOW MY HAND. LET ME TELL THEM THE REAL REASON YOU DON'T END IT. THE ONE YOU DON'T WANT TO ADMIT IN FRONT OF THEM. THE ONE YOU'LL NEVER ADMIT TO ANYONE BUT ME...SO, YOU WANT TO KNOW, KIDDIES? YOU WANT TO KNOW WHY THE DOORS AND WINDOWS GET LEFT UNLOCKED AT NIGHT?
WHY I GET TO CREEP IN, OVER AND OVER?
...TO GET YOU...
...AND YOU...
...AND YOU (AGAIN)...
...AND YOU...
...AND YOU?
BECAUSE THE UGLY TRUTH OF IT, KIDDIES, IS THAT DEEP DOWN, BENEATH IT ALL... BATMAN LOVES ME MORE THAN HE LOVES YOU.
I MEAN, WHO DO YOU THINK WROTE THIS FOR ME?

...IT WAS **YOU**, BATS.

YOU WROTE THIS LITTLE LOVE LETTER, THIS BACKWARDS MAP, THIS HIT LIST...AND YOU WRITE IT AGAIN AND AGAIN, EVERY TIME YOU KEEP ONE OF **US** ALIVE, BUT LET ONE OF **THEM** FALL. AND THEY WILL FALL, MAYBE ONE BY ONE, MAYBE TOGETHER...BUT LOOK TO THE FUTURE, REALLY LOOK, AND YOU KNOW IT'S COMING...

...THAT DAY WHEN THEY'RE ALL DEAD AND BURIED, IN THEIR COLD BAT-GRAVES (HEE-HEE). BUT LOOK! THERE'S ME AND MY FRIENDS, AND...WHY, WE'RE STILL ALIVE AND KICKING! AND THERE YOU ARE, BATSSS...CHASING US, FOREVER CHASING!

AND WHY? BECAUSE IT'S WHAT YOU WANT TO HAPPEN. IT'S WHAT YOU NEEEEED. BECAUSE YOU SEE, WITH **US** YOU'RE MORE! WITH **US**, YOU TRANSSSCEND! WITH **US**, YOU'RE ALWAYS.

BUT **THEM**, THEY MAKE YOU EVERYTHING YOU WANT TO FORGET THAT YOU ARE, EVERYTHING YOU'RE AFRAID OF. AND YOU WERE AFRAID, WHEN YOU TOOK **THEM** IN. I KNOW. IT'S OKAY, OLD FRIEND. IT WAS A MOMENT OF WEAK-NESSSSS...THE DIRT WAS PULLING.

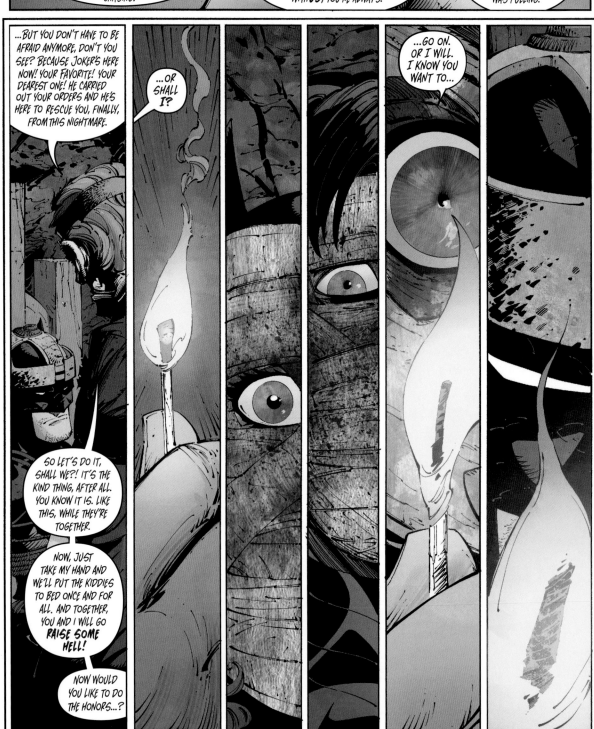

...BUT YOU DON'T HAVE TO BE AFRAID ANYMORE, DON'T YOU SEE? BECAUSE JOKER'S HERE NOW! YOUR FAVORITE! YOUR DEAREST ONE! HE CARRIED OUT YOUR ORDERS AND HE'S HERE TO RESCUE YOU, FINALLY, FROM THIS NIGHTMARE.

...OR SHALL I?

...GO ON. OR I WILL. I KNOW YOU WANT TO...

SO LET'S DO IT, SHALL WE?! IT'S THE KIND THING, AFTER ALL. YOU KNOW IT IS. LIKE THIS, WHILE THEY'RE TOGETHER.

NOW, JUST TAKE MY HAND AND WE'LL PUT THE KIDDIES TO BED ONCE AND FOR ALL. AND TOGETHER, YOU AND I WILL GO **RAISE SOME HELL!**

NOW WOULD YOU LIKE TO DO THE HONORS...?

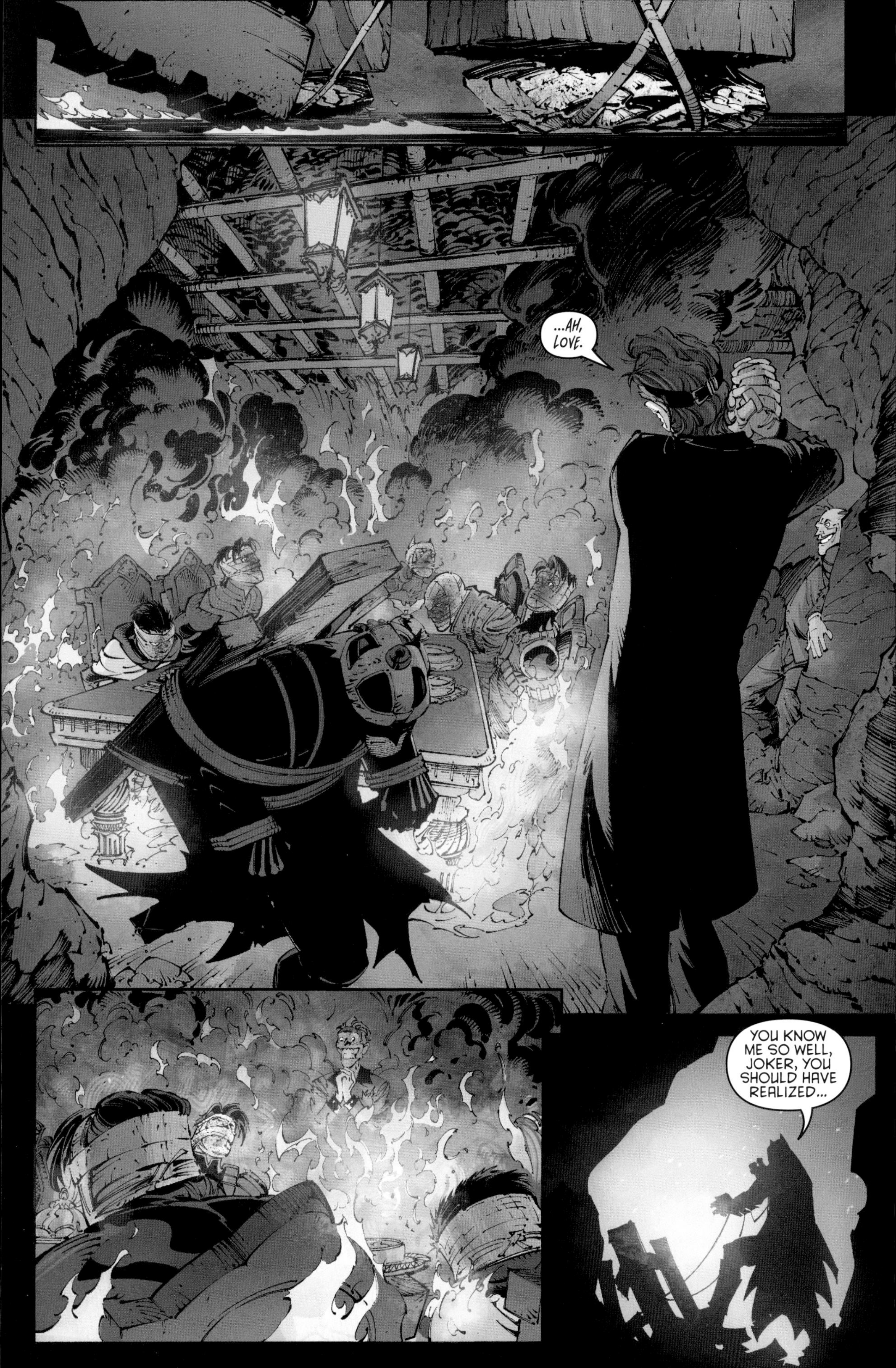

...AH, LOVE.
YOU KNOW ME SO WELL, JOKER, YOU SHOULD HAVE REALIZED...

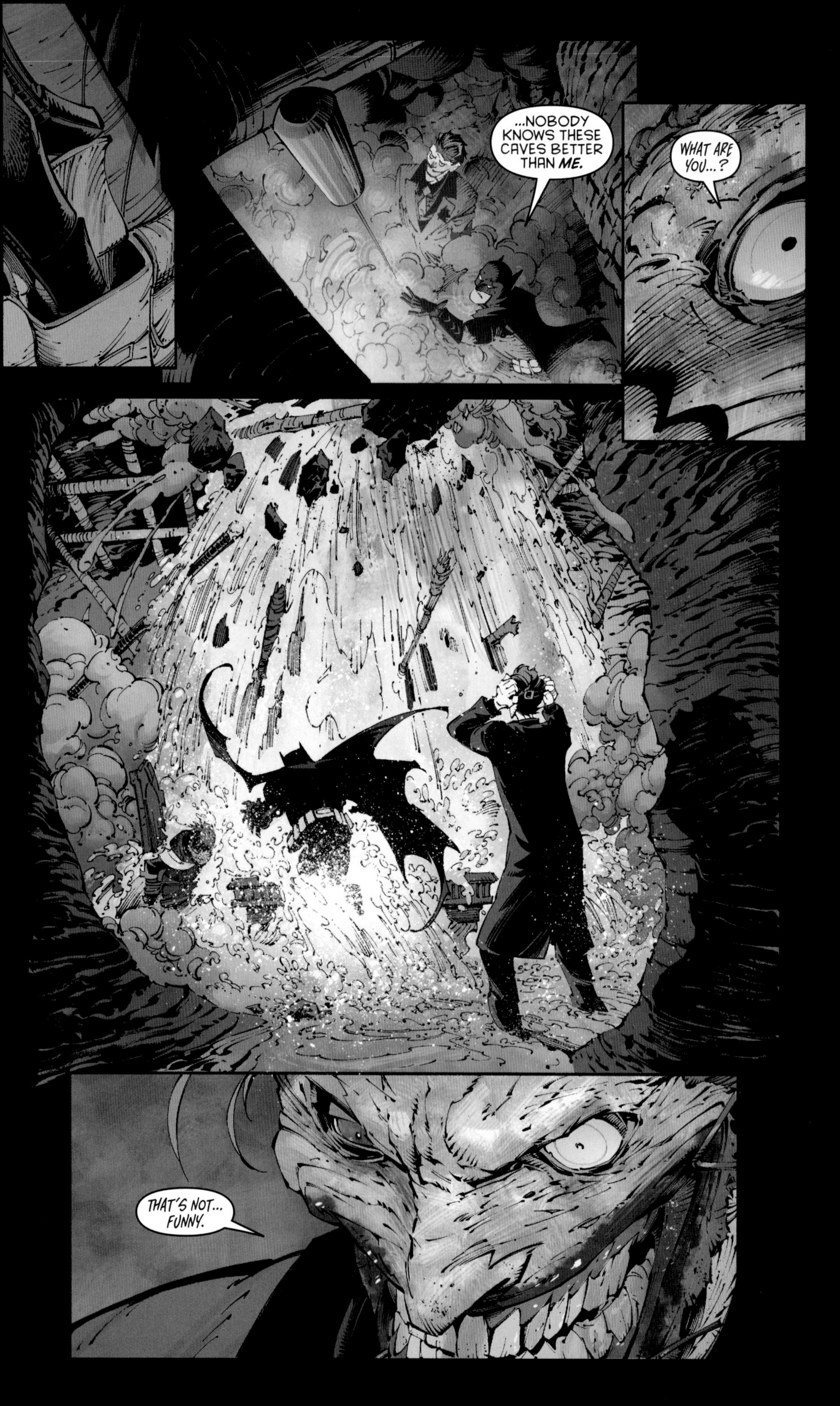
...NOBODY KNOWS THESE CAVES BETTER THAN ME.
WHAT ARE YOU...?
THAT'S NOT... FUNNY.

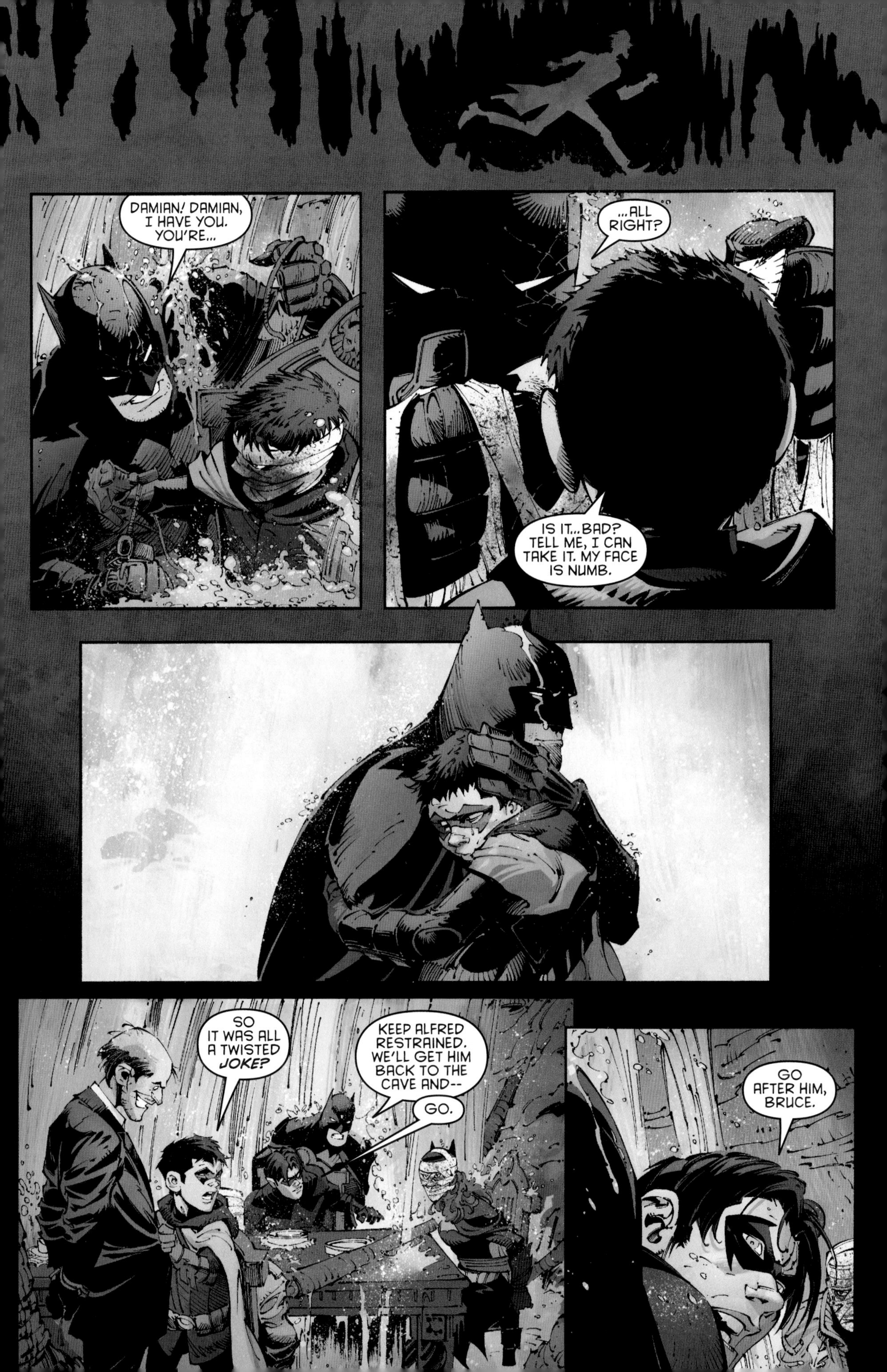

DAMIAN! DAMIAN, I HAVE YOU. YOU'RE...
...ALL RIGHT?
IS IT...BAD? TELL ME, I CAN TAKE IT. MY FACE IS NUMB.
SO IT WAS ALL A TWISTED *JOKE?*
KEEP ALFRED RESTRAINED. WE'LL GET HIM BACK TO THE CAVE AND--
GO.
GO AFTER HIM, BRUCE.

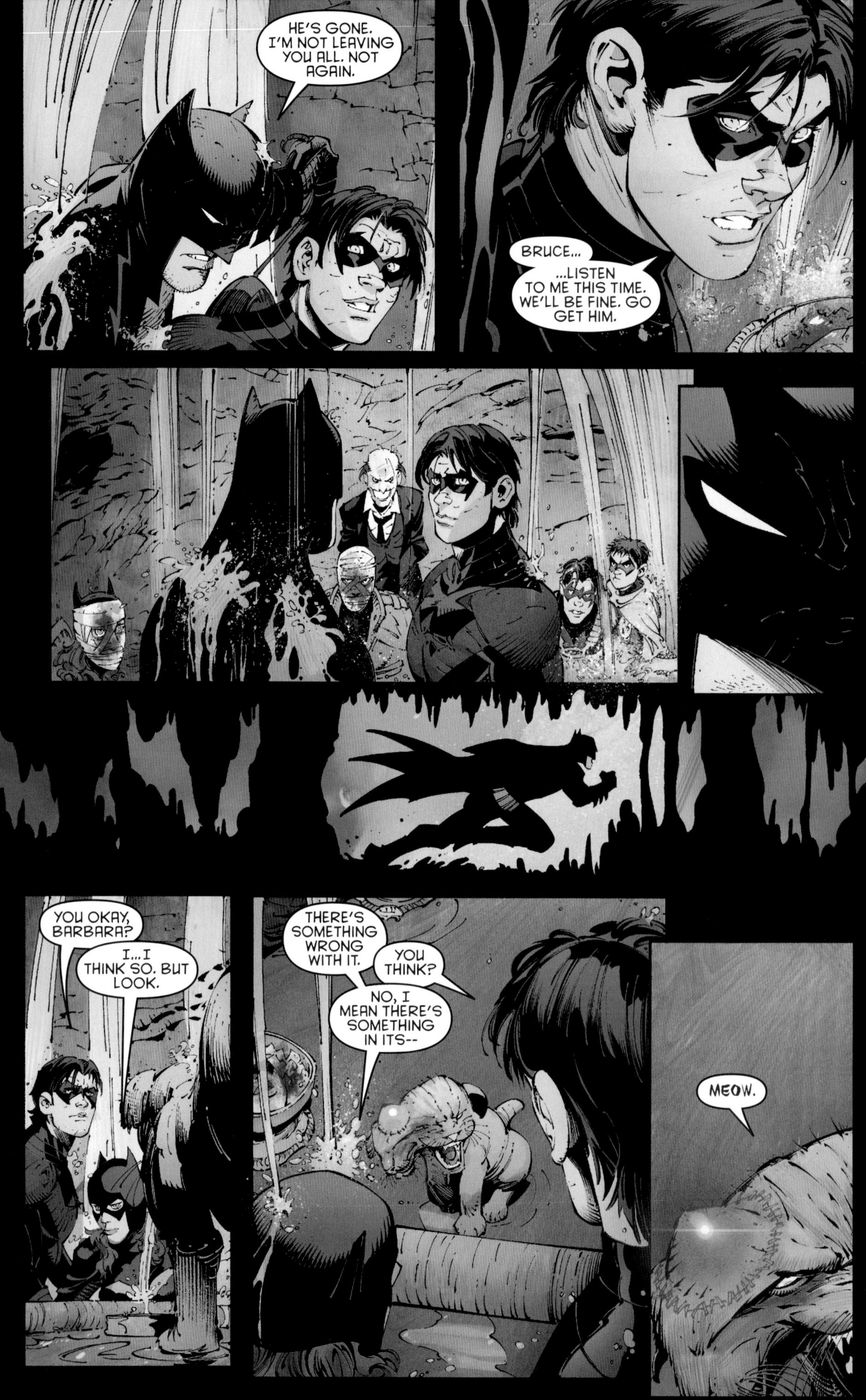
HE'S GONE. I'M NOT LEAVING YOU ALL. NOT AGAIN.
BRUCE...
...LISTEN TO ME THIS TIME. WE'LL BE FINE. GO GET HIM.
YOU OKAY, BARBARA?
I...I THINK SO. BUT LOOK.
THERE'S SOMETHING WRONG WITH IT.
YOU THINK?
NO, I MEAN THERE'S SOMETHING IN ITS--
MEOW.

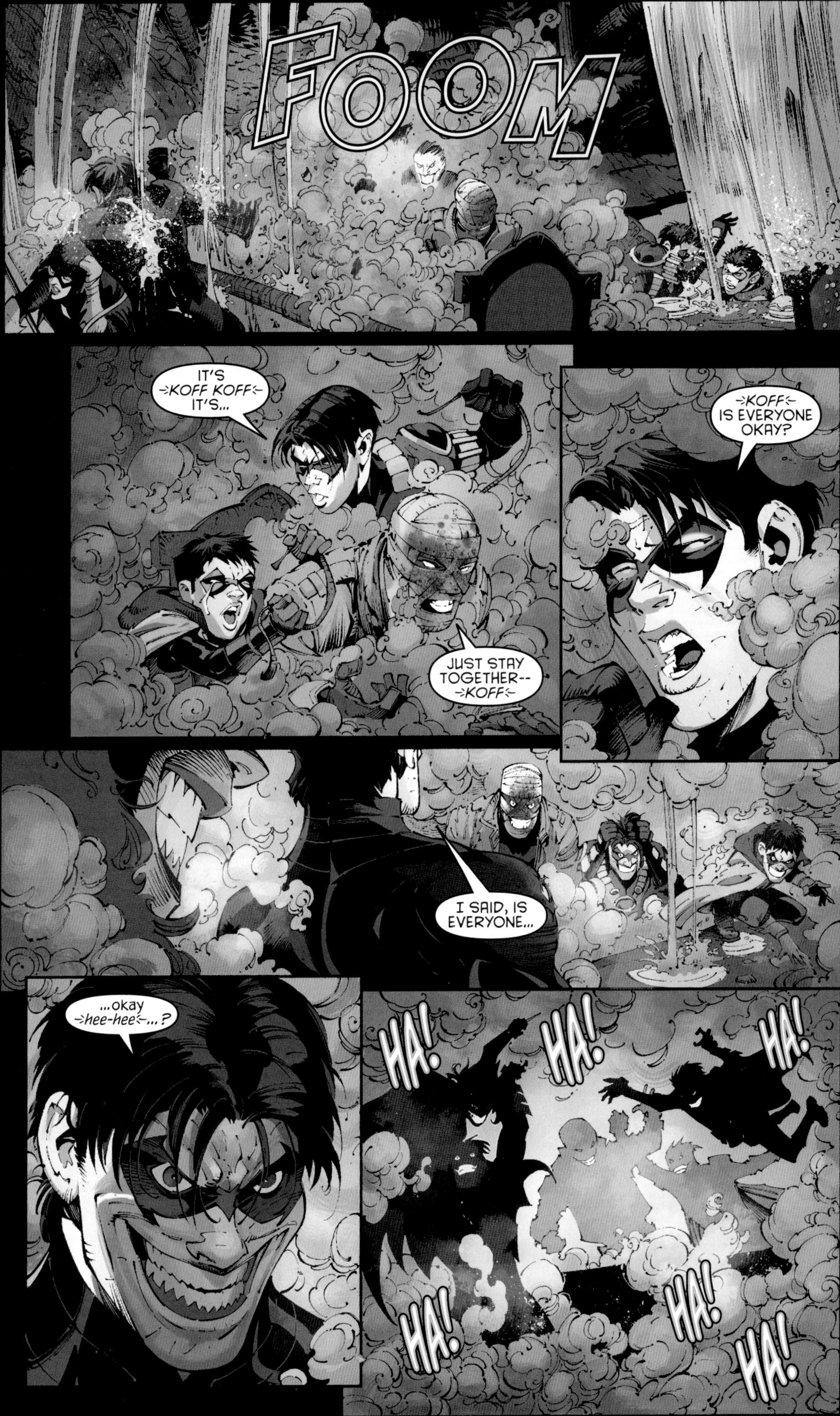
FOOM
IT'S -KOFF KOFF- IT'S...
JUST STAY TOGETHER-- -KOFF-
-KOFF- IS EVERYONE OKAY?
I SAID, IS EVERYONE...
...okay -hee-hee-...?
HA! HA! HA!
HA! HA! HA!

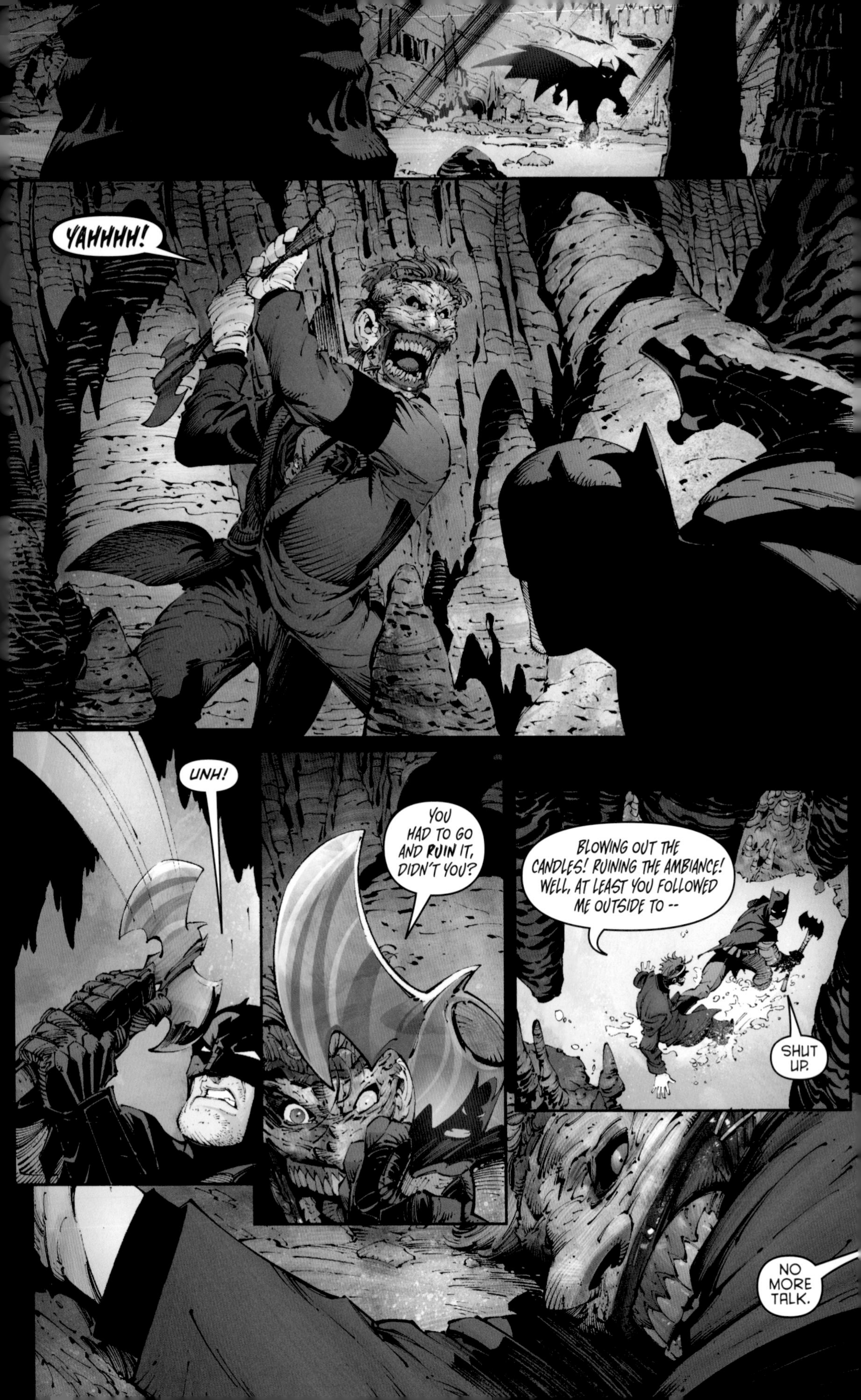
YAHHHH!
UNH!
YOU HAD TO GO AND RUIN IT, DIDN'T YOU?
BLOWING OUT THE CANDLES! RUINING THE AMBIANCE! WELL, AT LEAST YOU FOLLOWED ME OUTSIDE TO --
SHUT UP.
NO MORE TALK.

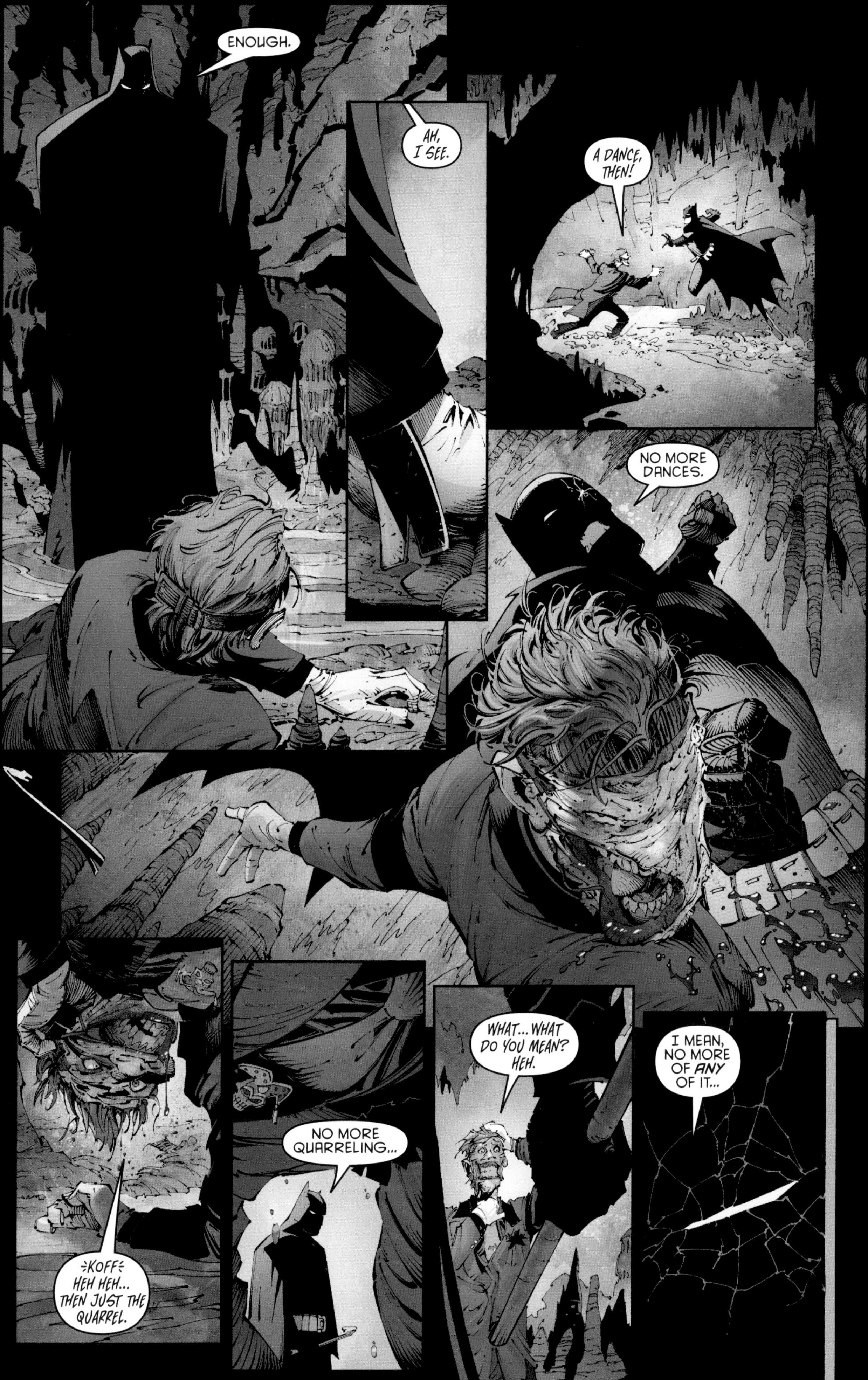
ENOUGH.
AH, I SEE.
A DANCE, THEN!
NO MORE DANCES.
KOFF HEH HEH... THEN JUST THE QUARREL.
NO MORE QUARRELING...
WHAT... WHAT DO YOU MEAN? HEH.
I MEAN, NO MORE OF ANY OF IT...

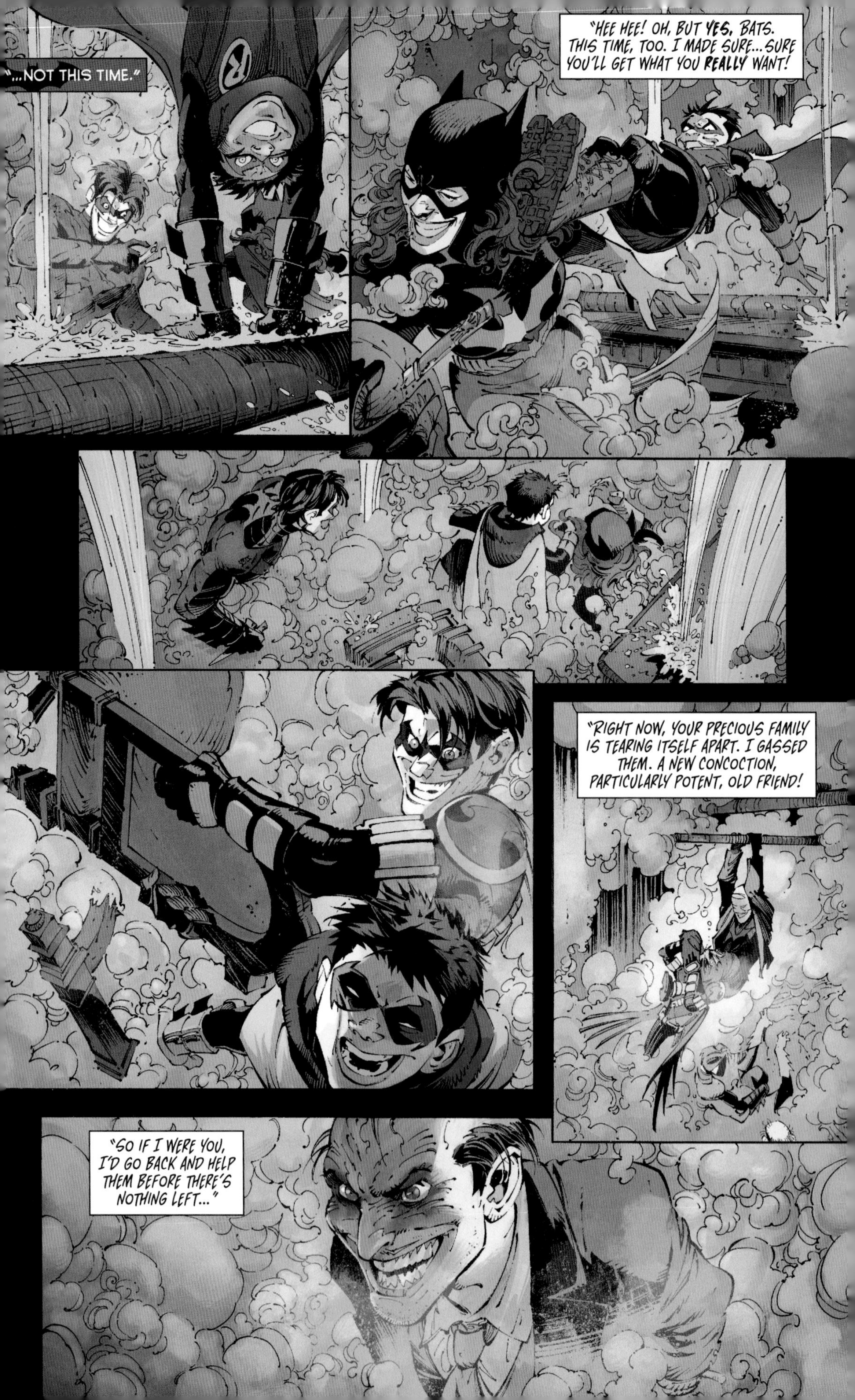
"...NOT THIS TIME."
"HEE HEE! OH, BUT YES, BATS. THIS TIME, TOO. I MADE SURE... SURE YOU'LL GET WHAT YOU REALLY WANT!
"RIGHT NOW, YOUR PRECIOUS FAMILY IS TEARING ITSELF APART. I GASSED THEM. A NEW CONCOCTION, PARTICULARLY POTENT, OLD FRIEND!
"SO IF I WERE YOU, I'D GO BACK AND HELP THEM BEFORE THERE'S NOTHING LEFT..."

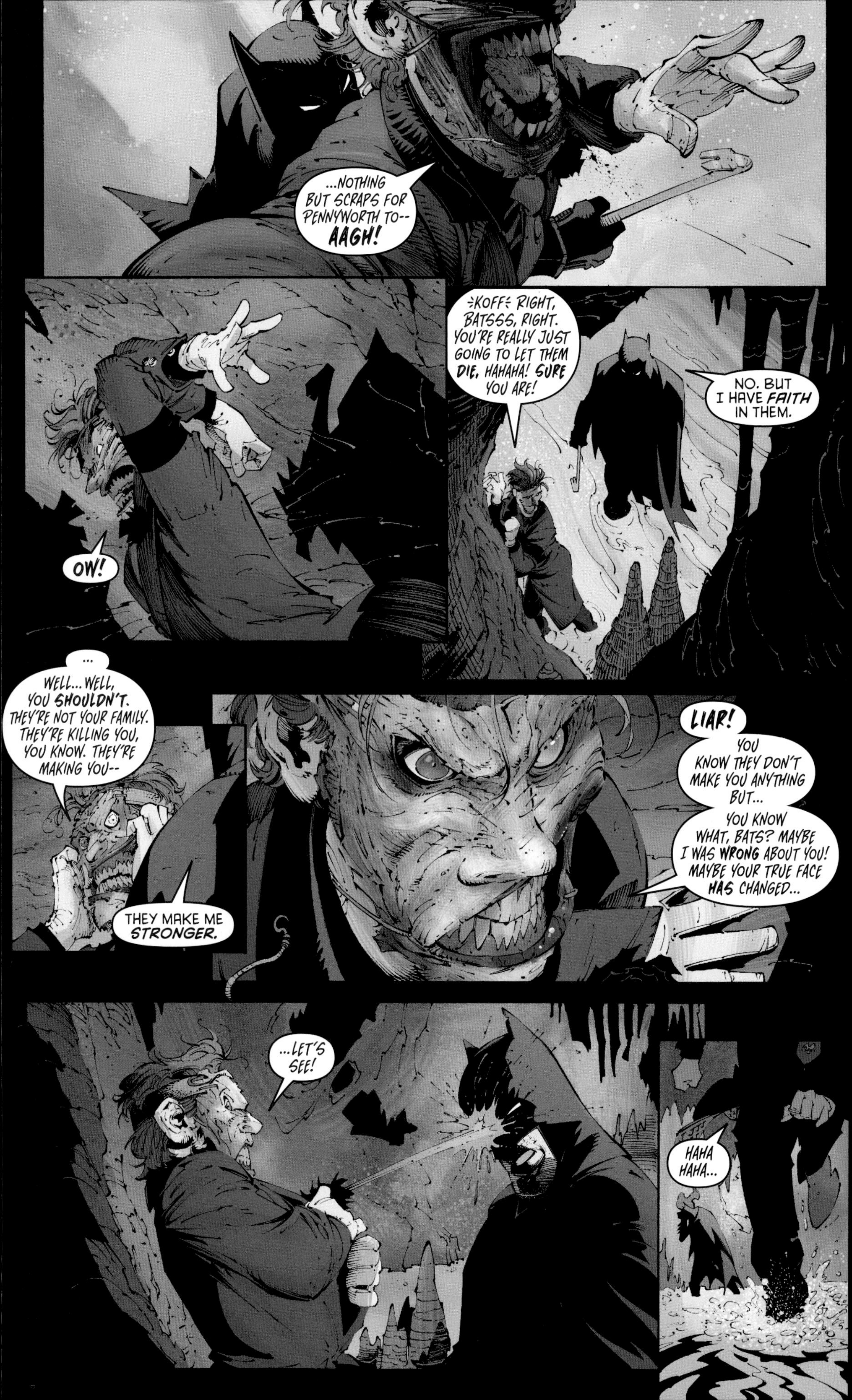
...NOTHING BUT SCRAPS FOR PENNYWORTH TO-- AAGH!
OW!
≶KOFF≷ RIGHT, BATSSS, RIGHT. YOU'RE REALLY JUST GOING TO LET THEM DIE, HAHAHA! SURE YOU ARE!
NO. BUT I HAVE FAITH IN THEM.
... WELL... WELL, YOU SHOULDN'T. THEY'RE NOT YOUR FAMILY. THEY'RE KILLING YOU, YOU KNOW. THEY'RE MAKING YOU--
THEY MAKE ME STRONGER.
LIAR!
YOU KNOW THEY DON'T MAKE YOU ANYTHING BUT...
YOU KNOW WHAT, BATS? MAYBE I WAS WRONG ABOUT YOU! MAYBE YOUR TRUE FACE HAS CHANGED...
...LET'S SEE!
HAHA HAHA...

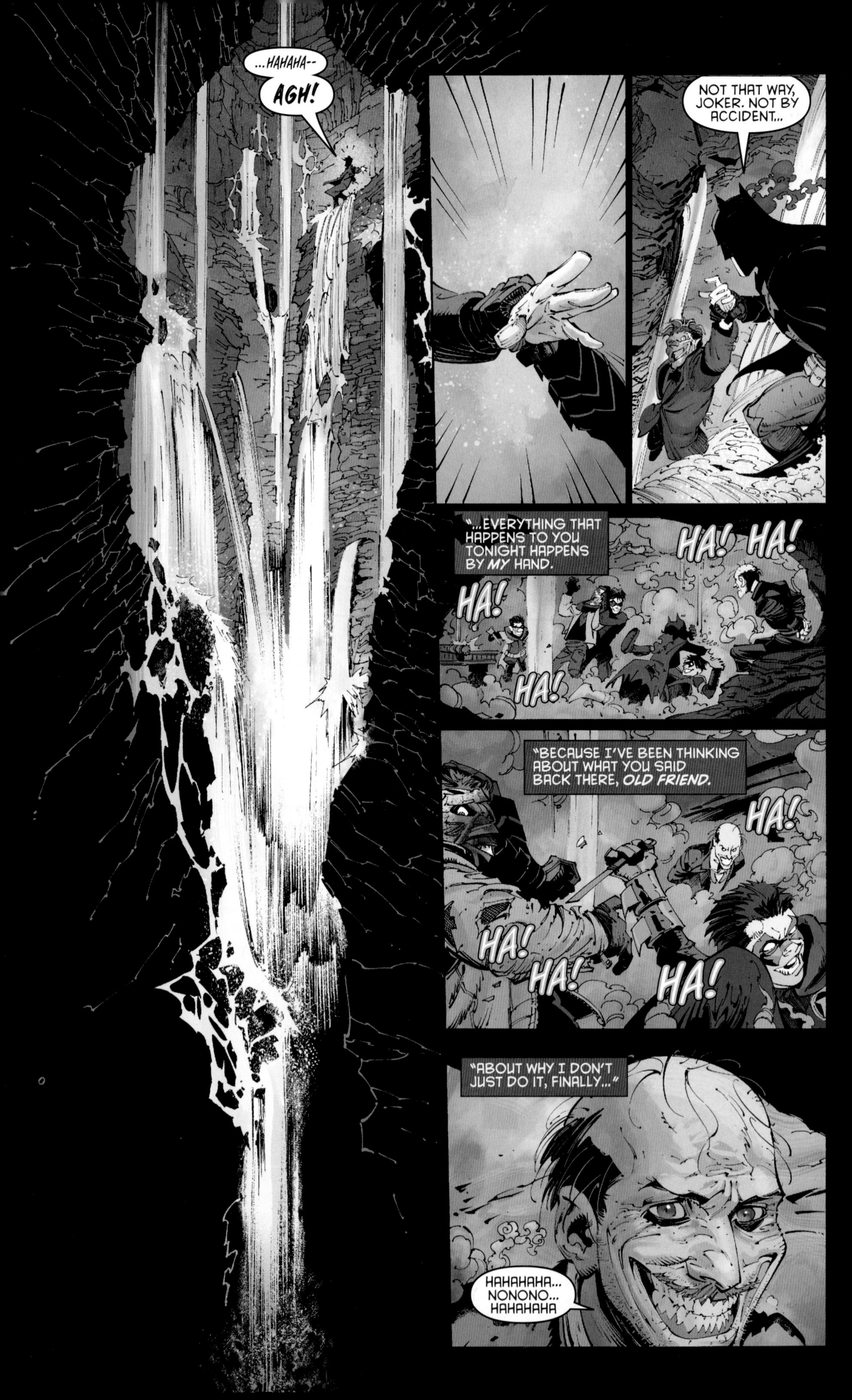
...HAHAHA--
AGH!
NOT THAT WAY, JOKER. NOT BY ACCIDENT...
"...EVERYTHING THAT HAPPENS TO YOU TONIGHT HAPPENS BY MY HAND.
HA! HA!
HA!
HA!
"BECAUSE I'VE BEEN THINKING ABOUT WHAT YOU SAID BACK THERE, OLD FRIEND.
HA!
HA!
HA!
HA!
"ABOUT WHY I DON'T JUST DO IT, FINALLY..."
HAHAHAHA... NONONO... HAHAHAHA

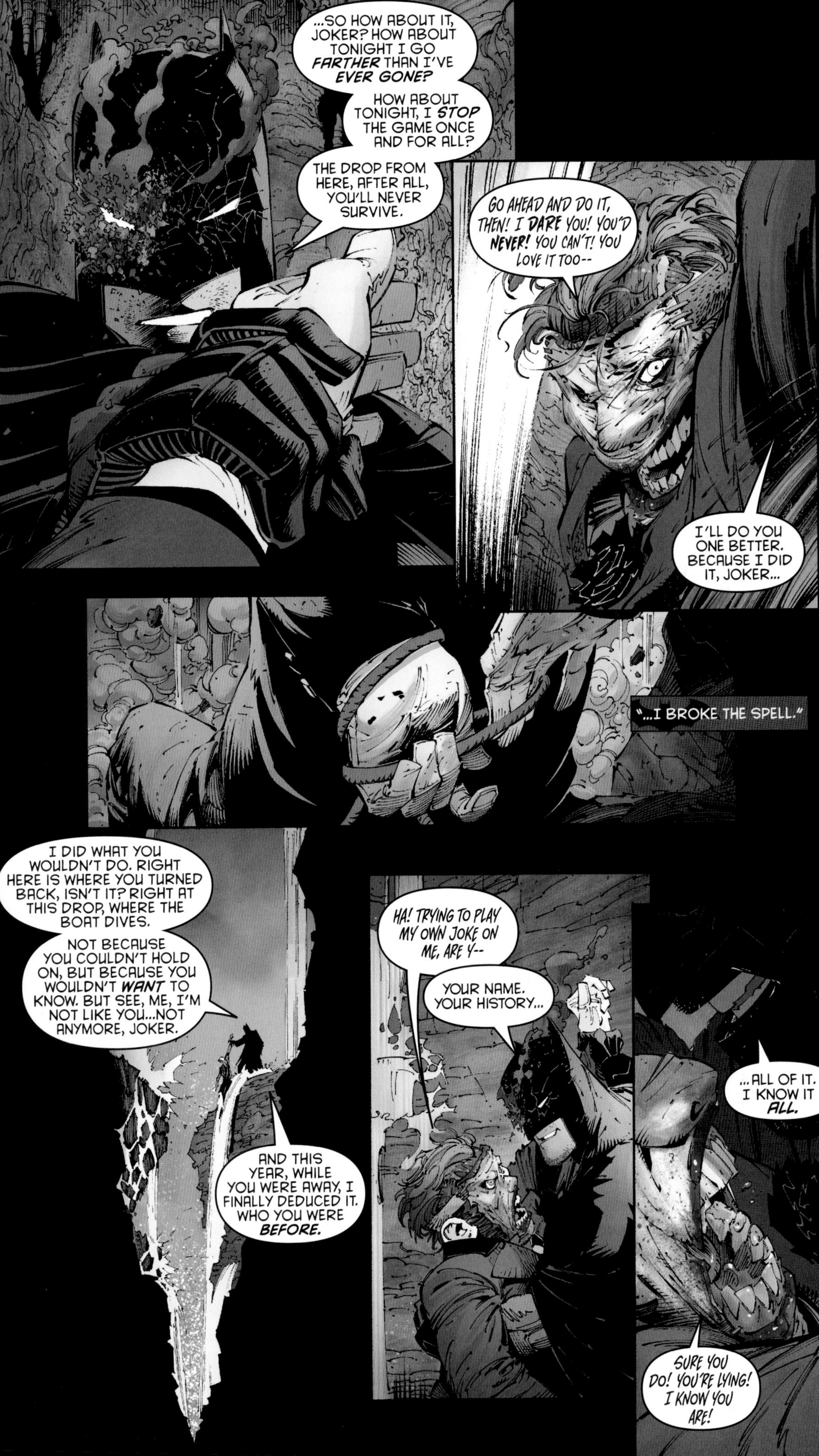
...SO HOW ABOUT IT, JOKER? HOW ABOUT TONIGHT I GO FARTHER THAN I'VE EVER GONE?
HOW ABOUT TONIGHT, I STOP THE GAME ONCE AND FOR ALL?
THE DROP FROM HERE, AFTER ALL, YOU'LL NEVER SURVIVE.
GO AHEAD AND DO IT, THEN! I DARE YOU! YOU'D NEVER! YOU CAN'T! YOU LOVE IT TOO--
I'LL DO YOU ONE BETTER. BECAUSE I DID IT, JOKER...
"...I BROKE THE SPELL."
I DID WHAT YOU WOULDN'T DO. RIGHT HERE IS WHERE YOU TURNED BACK, ISN'T IT? RIGHT AT THIS DROP, WHERE THE BOAT DIVES.
NOT BECAUSE YOU COULDN'T HOLD ON, BUT BECAUSE YOU WOULDN'T WANT TO KNOW. BUT SEE, ME, I'M NOT LIKE YOU...NOT ANYMORE, JOKER.
AND THIS YEAR, WHILE YOU WERE AWAY, I FINALLY DEDUCED IT. WHO YOU WERE BEFORE.
HA! TRYING TO PLAY MY OWN JOKE ON ME, ARE Y--
YOUR NAME. YOUR HISTORY...
...ALL OF IT. I KNOW IT ALL.
SURE YOU DO! YOU'RE LYING! I KNOW YOU ARE!

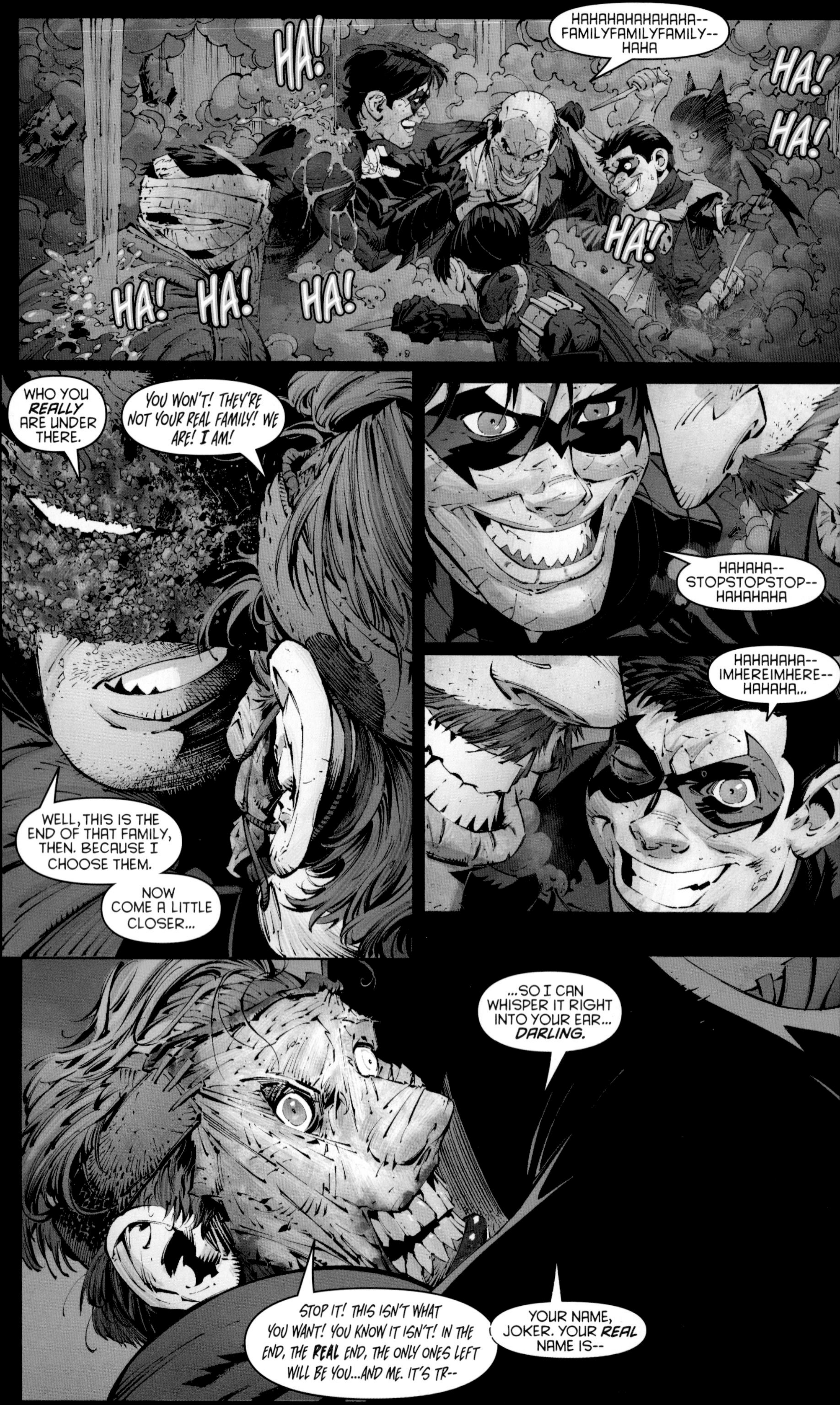
HA!
HAHAHAHAHAHAHA-- FAMILYFAMILYFAMILY-- HAHA
HA! HA!
HA!
HA! HA! HA!
WHO YOU *REALLY* ARE UNDER THERE.
YOU WON'T! THEY'RE NOT YOUR REAL FAMILY! WE ARE! *I AM!*
HAHAHA-- STOPSTOPSTOP-- HAHAHAHA
HAHAHAHA-- IMHEREIMHERE-- HAHAHA...
WELL, THIS IS THE END OF THAT FAMILY, THEN. BECAUSE I CHOOSE THEM.
NOW COME A LITTLE CLOSER...
...SO I CAN WHISPER IT RIGHT INTO YOUR EAR... *DARLING.*
STOP IT! THIS ISN'T WHAT YOU WANT! YOU KNOW IT ISN'T! IN THE END, THE *REAL* END, THE ONLY ONES LEFT WILL BE YOU...AND ME. IT'S TR--
YOUR NAME, JOKER. YOUR *REAL* NAME IS--

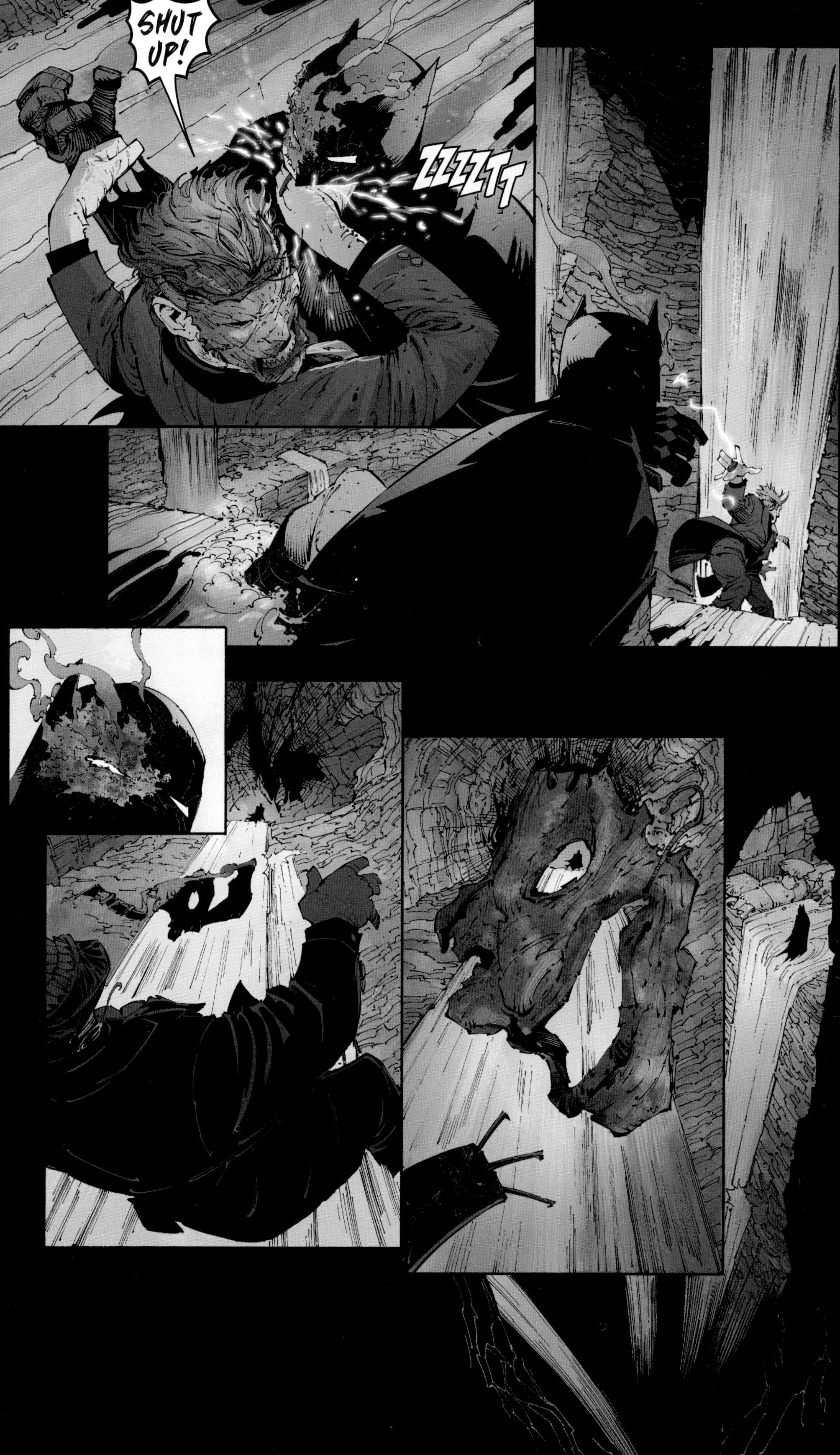
SHUT UP!
ZZZZTT

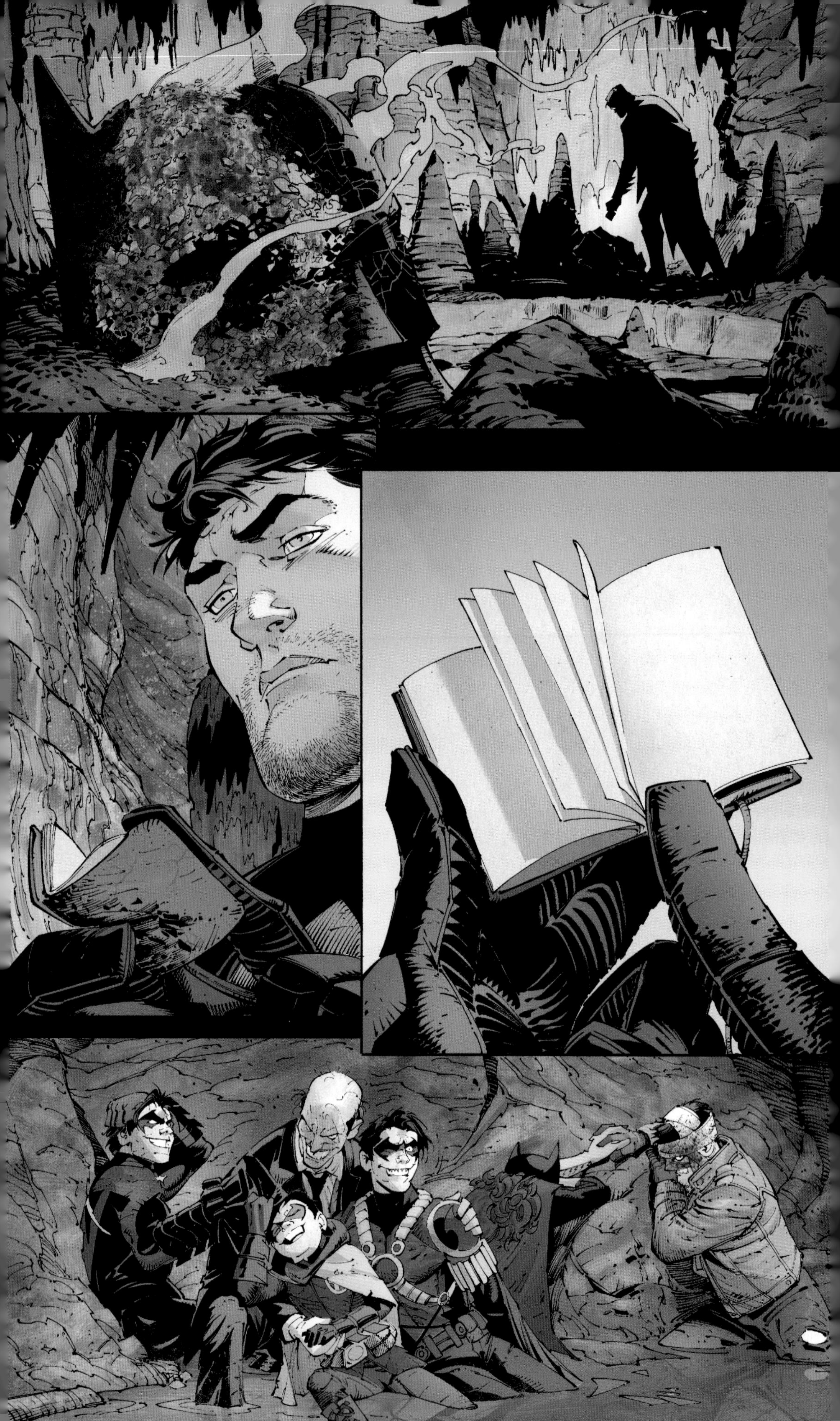

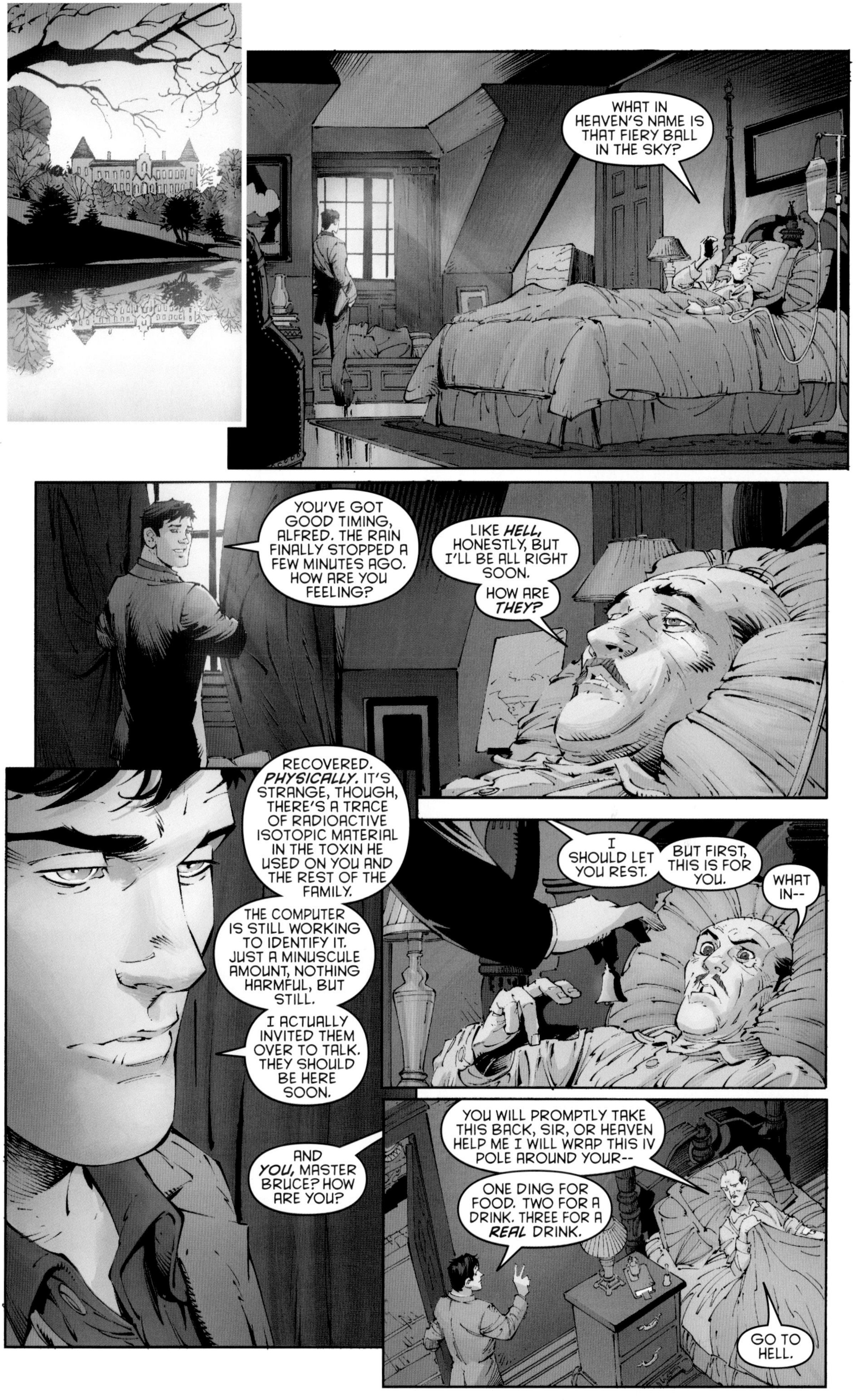
WHAT IN HEAVEN'S NAME IS THAT FIERY BALL IN THE SKY?
YOU'VE GOT GOOD TIMING, ALFRED. THE RAIN FINALLY STOPPED A FEW MINUTES AGO. HOW ARE YOU FEELING?
LIKE HELL, HONESTLY, BUT I'LL BE ALL RIGHT SOON.
HOW ARE THEY?
RECOVERED. PHYSICALLY. IT'S STRANGE, THOUGH, THERE'S A TRACE OF RADIOACTIVE ISOTOPIC MATERIAL IN THE TOXIN HE USED ON YOU AND THE REST OF THE FAMILY.
THE COMPUTER IS STILL WORKING TO IDENTIFY IT. JUST A MINUSCULE AMOUNT, NOTHING HARMFUL, BUT STILL.
I ACTUALLY INVITED THEM OVER TO TALK. THEY SHOULD BE HERE SOON.
AND YOU, MASTER BRUCE? HOW ARE YOU?
I SHOULD LET YOU REST.
BUT FIRST, THIS IS FOR YOU.
WHAT IN--
YOU WILL PROMPTLY TAKE THIS BACK, SIR, OR HEAVEN HELP ME I WILL WRAP THIS IV POLE AROUND YOUR--
ONE DING FOR FOOD. TWO FOR A DRINK. THREE FOR A REAL DRINK.
GO TO HELL.

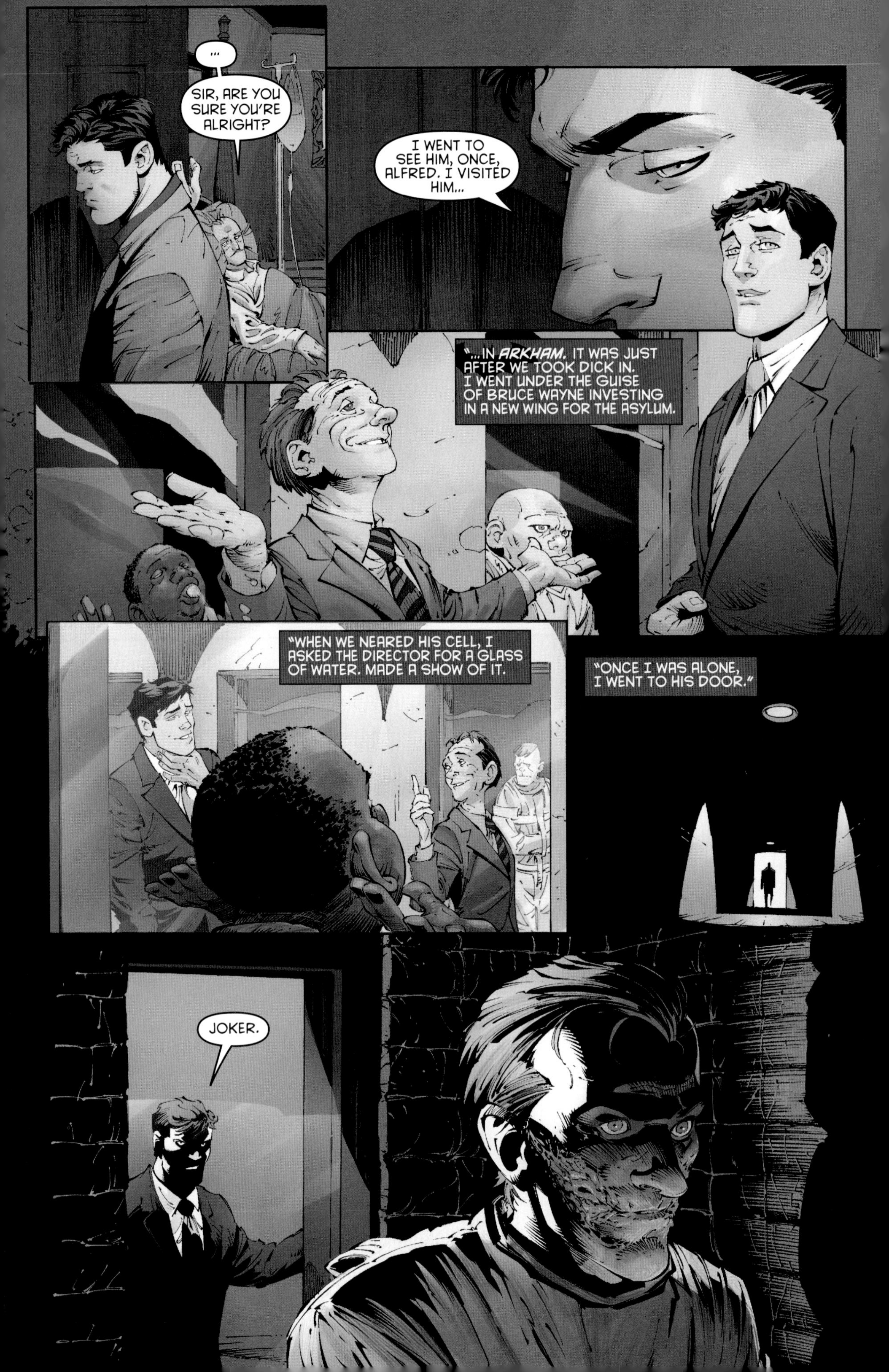
...
SIR, ARE YOU SURE YOU'RE ALRIGHT?
I WENT TO SEE HIM, ONCE, ALFRED. I VISITED HIM...
"...IN ARKHAM. IT WAS JUST AFTER WE TOOK DICK IN. I WENT UNDER THE GUISE OF BRUCE WAYNE INVESTING IN A NEW WING FOR THE ASYLUM.
"WHEN WE NEARED HIS CELL, I ASKED THE DIRECTOR FOR A GLASS OF WATER. MADE A SHOW OF IT.
"ONCE I WAS ALONE, I WENT TO HIS DOOR."
JOKER.

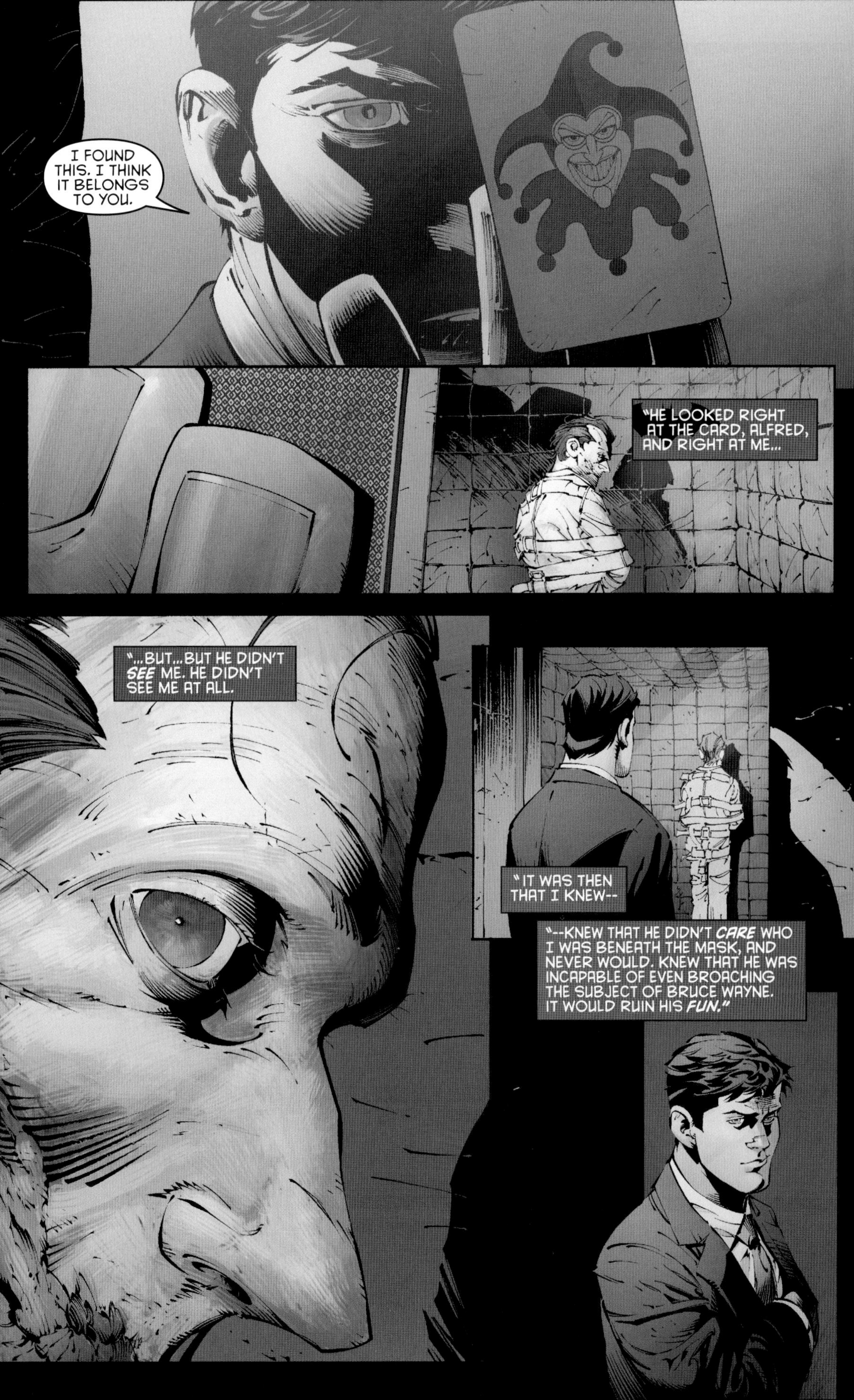
I FOUND THIS. I THINK IT BELONGS TO YOU.
"HE LOOKED RIGHT AT THE CARD, ALFRED, AND RIGHT AT ME...
"...BUT...BUT HE DIDN'T SEE ME. HE DIDN'T SEE ME AT ALL.
"IT WAS THEN THAT I KNEW--
"--KNEW THAT HE DIDN'T CARE WHO I WAS BENEATH THE MASK, AND NEVER WOULD. KNEW THAT HE WAS INCAPABLE OF EVEN BROACHING THE SUBJECT OF BRUCE WAYNE. IT WOULD RUIN HIS FUN."

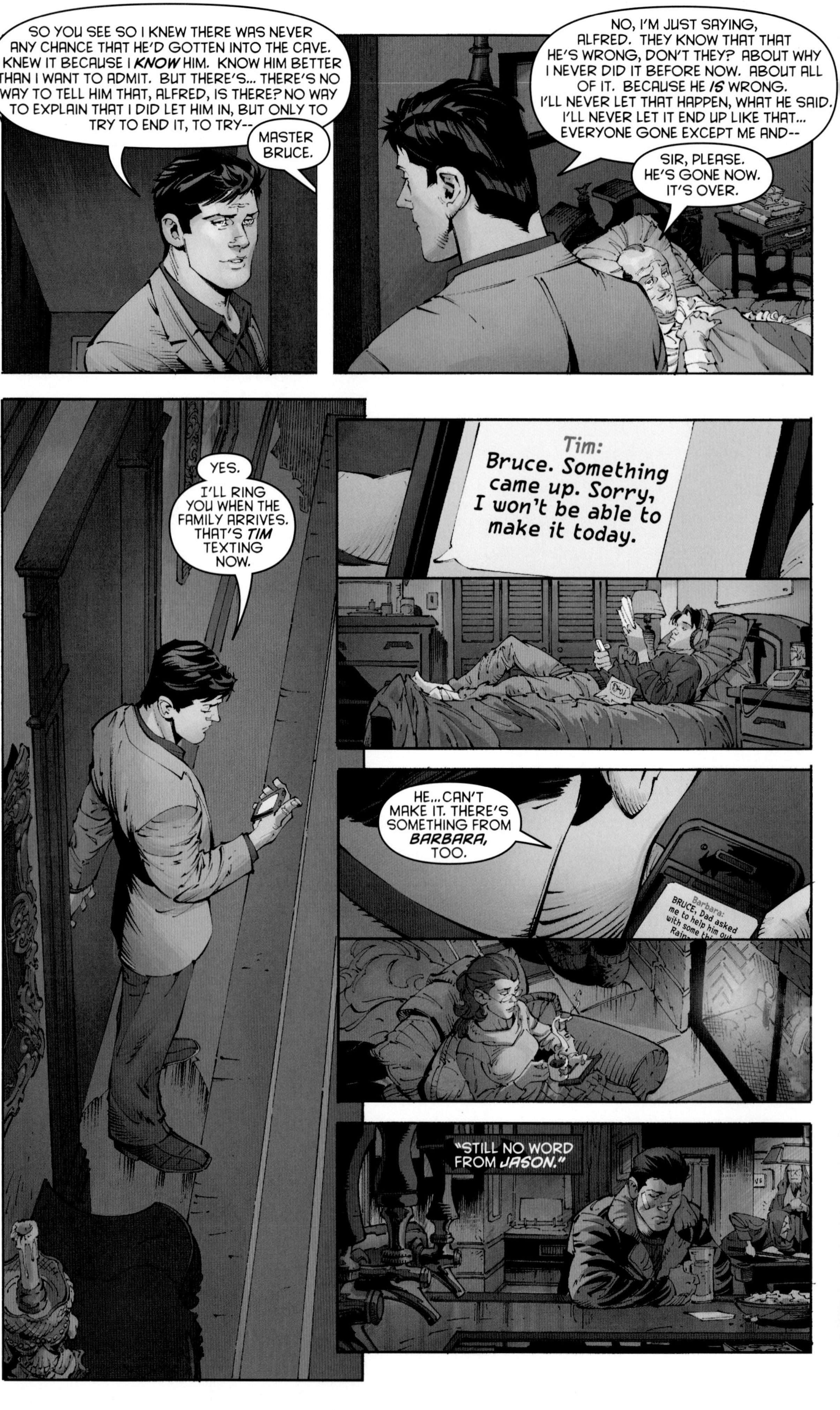
SO YOU SEE SO I KNEW THERE WAS NEVER ANY CHANCE THAT HE'D GOTTEN INTO THE CAVE. I KNEW IT BECAUSE I KNOW HIM. KNOW HIM BETTER THAN I WANT TO ADMIT. BUT THERE'S... THERE'S NO WAY TO TELL HIM THAT, ALFRED, IS THERE? NO WAY TO EXPLAIN THAT I DID LET HIM IN, BUT ONLY TO TRY TO END IT, TO TRY--
MASTER BRUCE.
NO, I'M JUST SAYING, ALFRED. THEY KNOW THAT THAT HE'S WRONG, DON'T THEY? ABOUT WHY I NEVER DID IT BEFORE NOW. ABOUT ALL OF IT. BECAUSE HE IS WRONG. I'LL NEVER LET THAT HAPPEN, WHAT HE SAID. I'LL NEVER LET IT END UP LIKE THAT... EVERYONE GONE EXCEPT ME AND--
SIR, PLEASE. HE'S GONE NOW. IT'S OVER.
YES.
I'LL RING YOU WHEN THE FAMILY ARRIVES. THAT'S TIM TEXTING NOW.
Tim:
Bruce. Something came up. Sorry, I won't be able to make it today.
HE...CAN'T MAKE IT. THERE'S SOMETHING FROM BARBARA, TOO.
Barbara:
BRUCE, Dad asked me to help him out with some
"STILL NO WORD FROM JASON."

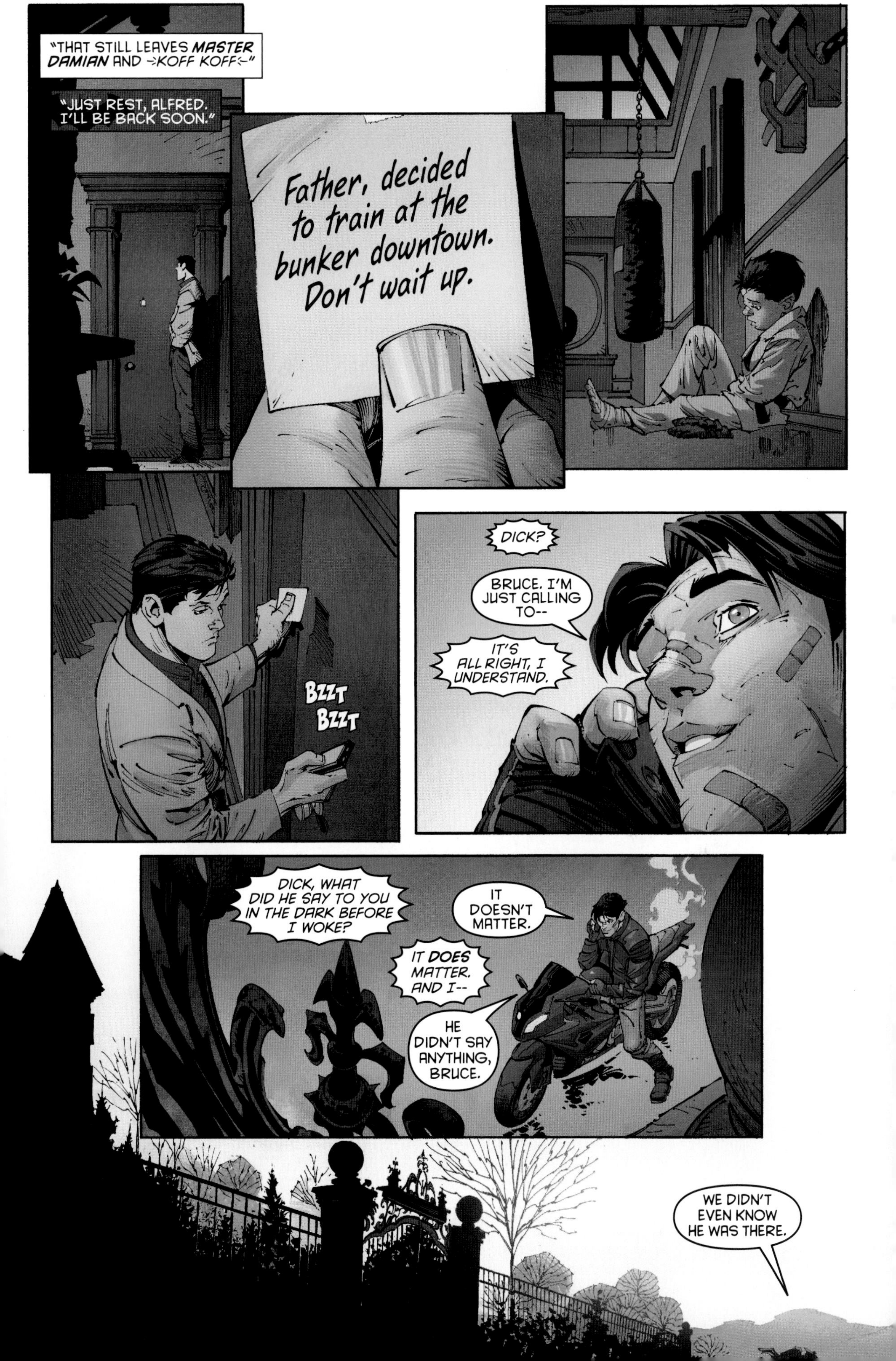
"THAT STILL LEAVES MASTER DAMIAN AND ⇝KOFF KOFF⇜"
"JUST REST, ALFRED. I'LL BE BACK SOON."
Father, decided to train at the bunker downtown. Don't wait up.
BZZZT
BZZZT
DICK?
BRUCE. I'M JUST CALLING TO--
IT'S ALL RIGHT, I UNDERSTAND.
DICK, WHAT DID HE SAY TO YOU IN THE DARK BEFORE I WOKE?
IT DOESN'T MATTER.
IT DOES MATTER. AND I--
HE DIDN'T SAY ANYTHING, BRUCE.
WE DIDN'T EVEN KNOW HE WAS THERE.

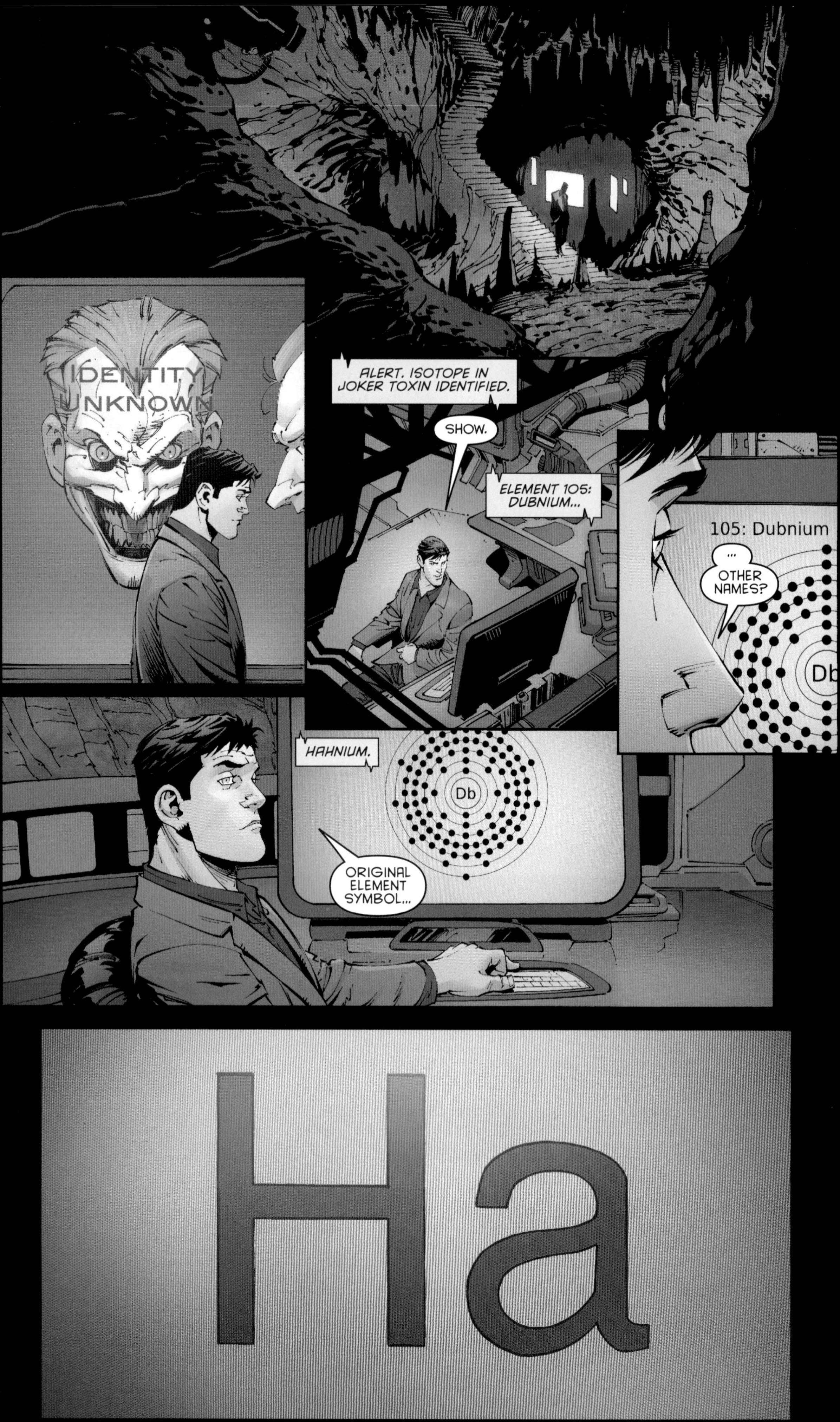
IDENTITY UNKNOWN
ALERT. ISOTOPE IN JOKER TOXIN IDENTIFIED.
SHOW.
ELEMENT 105: DUBNIUM...
105: Dubnium
...
OTHER NAMES?
Db
HAHNIUM.
Db
ORIGINAL ELEMENT SYMBOL...
Ha

Ha
Ha
END

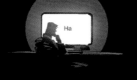

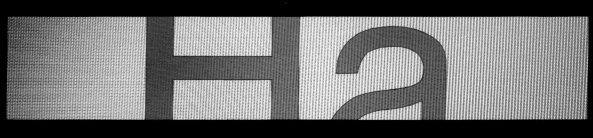

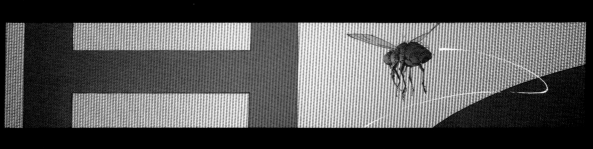

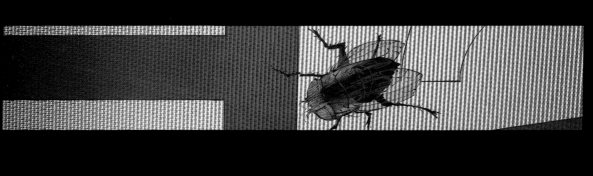

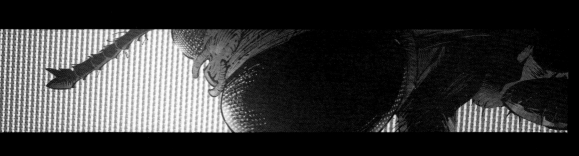

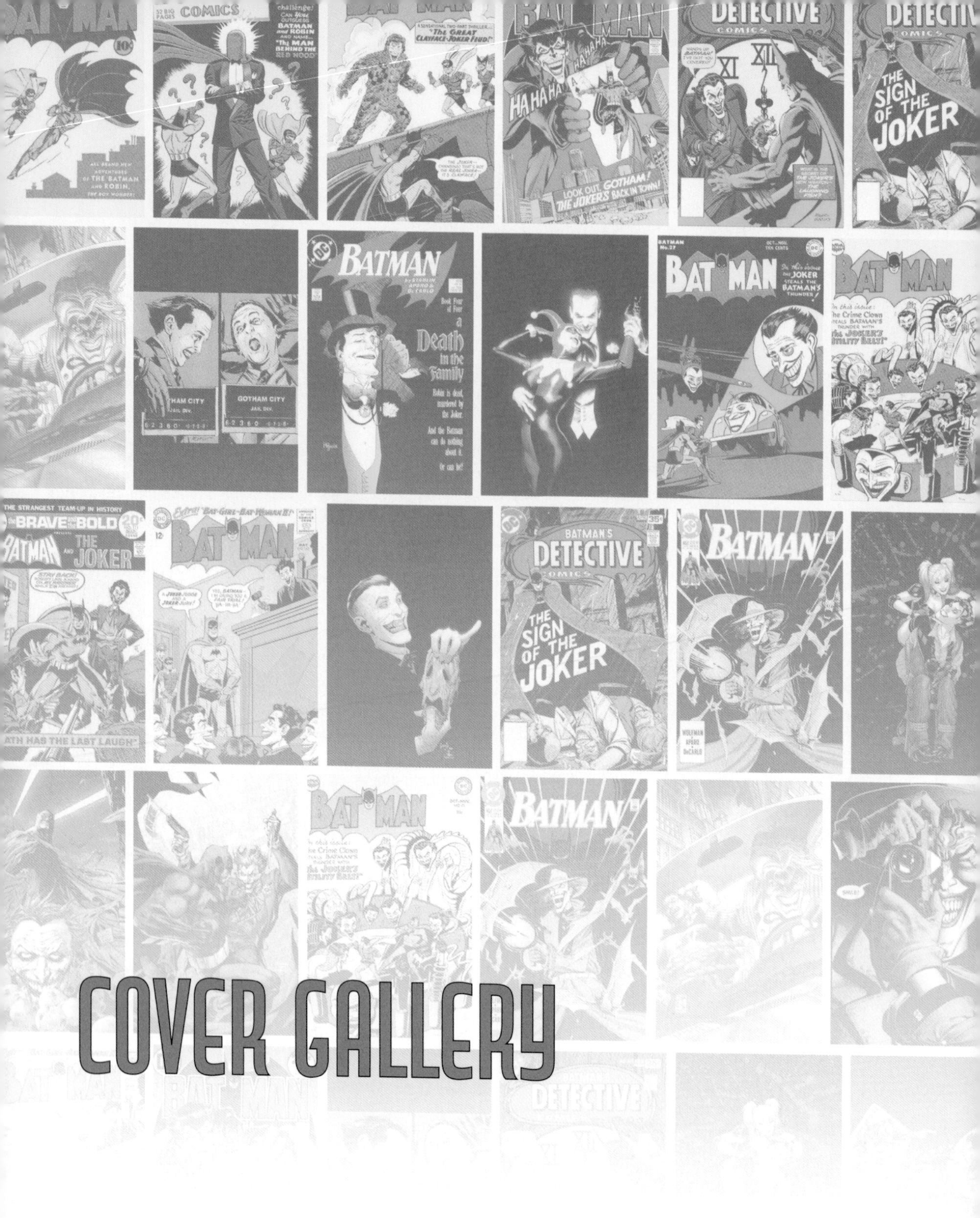
BATMAN
10¢
ALL BRAND NEW ADVENTURES OF THE BATMAN AND ROBIN, THE BOY WONDER!
52 BIG PAGES
COMICS
challenge! CAN YOU OUTGUESS BATMAN and ROBIN AND NAME... "The MAN BEHIND THE RED HOOD"
A SENSATIONAL TWO-PART THRILLER... "THE GREAT CLAYFACE-JOKER FEUD!"
BATMAN
HA HA HA
LOOK OUT, GOTHAM! THE JOKER'S BACK IN TOWN!
DETECTIVE COMICS
XI
XII
DETECTIVE COMICS
THE SIGN OF THE JOKER
GOTHAM CITY JAIL DIV.
BATMAN
Book Four of Four
a Death in the Family
Robin is dead, murdered by the Joker.
And the Batman can do nothing about it.
Or can he?
BATMAN No. 37
BATMAN
In this issue: THE JOKER STEALS THE BATMAN'S THUNDER!
BATMAN
In this issue: The Crime Clown steals Batman's thunder with the Joker's utility belt!
THE STRANGEST TEAM-UP IN HISTORY
THE BRAVE AND THE BOLD
20¢
BATMAN AND THE JOKER
STAY BACK!
Extra! "BAT-GIRL—BAT-WOMAN II!"
12¢
BATMAN
A JOKER JUDGE and a JOKER JURY!
YES, BATMAN — I'M GIVING YOU A FAIR TRIAL! HA HA HA
35¢
BATMAN'S DETECTIVE COMICS
THE SIGN OF THE JOKER
BATMAN
WOLFMAN APARO DeCARLO
BATMAN
BATMAN
DETECTIVE

COVER GALLERY

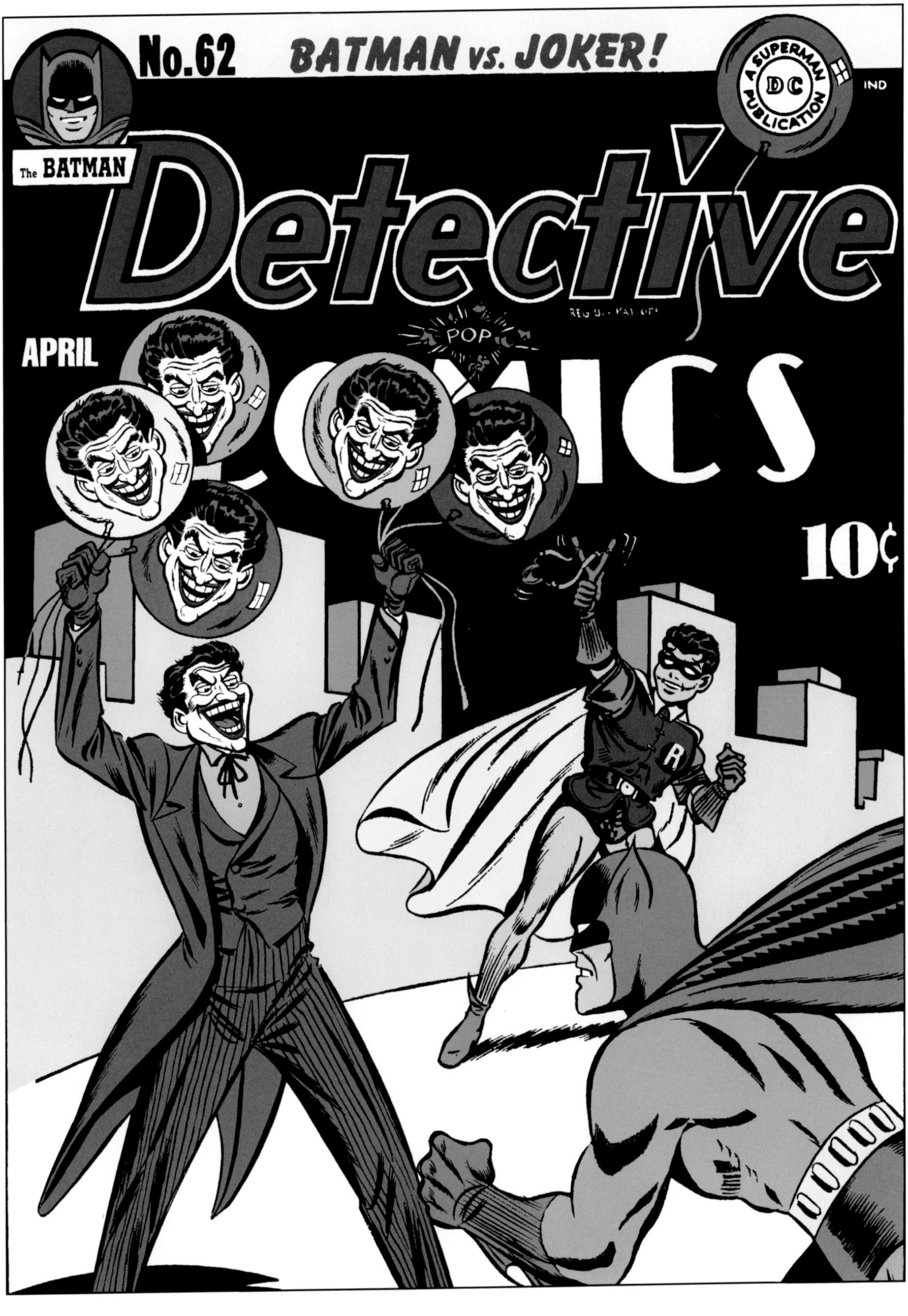
No.62
BATMAN vs. JOKER!
A SUPERMAN DC PUBLICATION
IND
The BATMAN
Detective
REG U.S. PAT OFF
POP
APRIL
COMICS
10¢

Detective Comics #62 (April 1942)
Cover by Fred Ray and Jerry Robinson

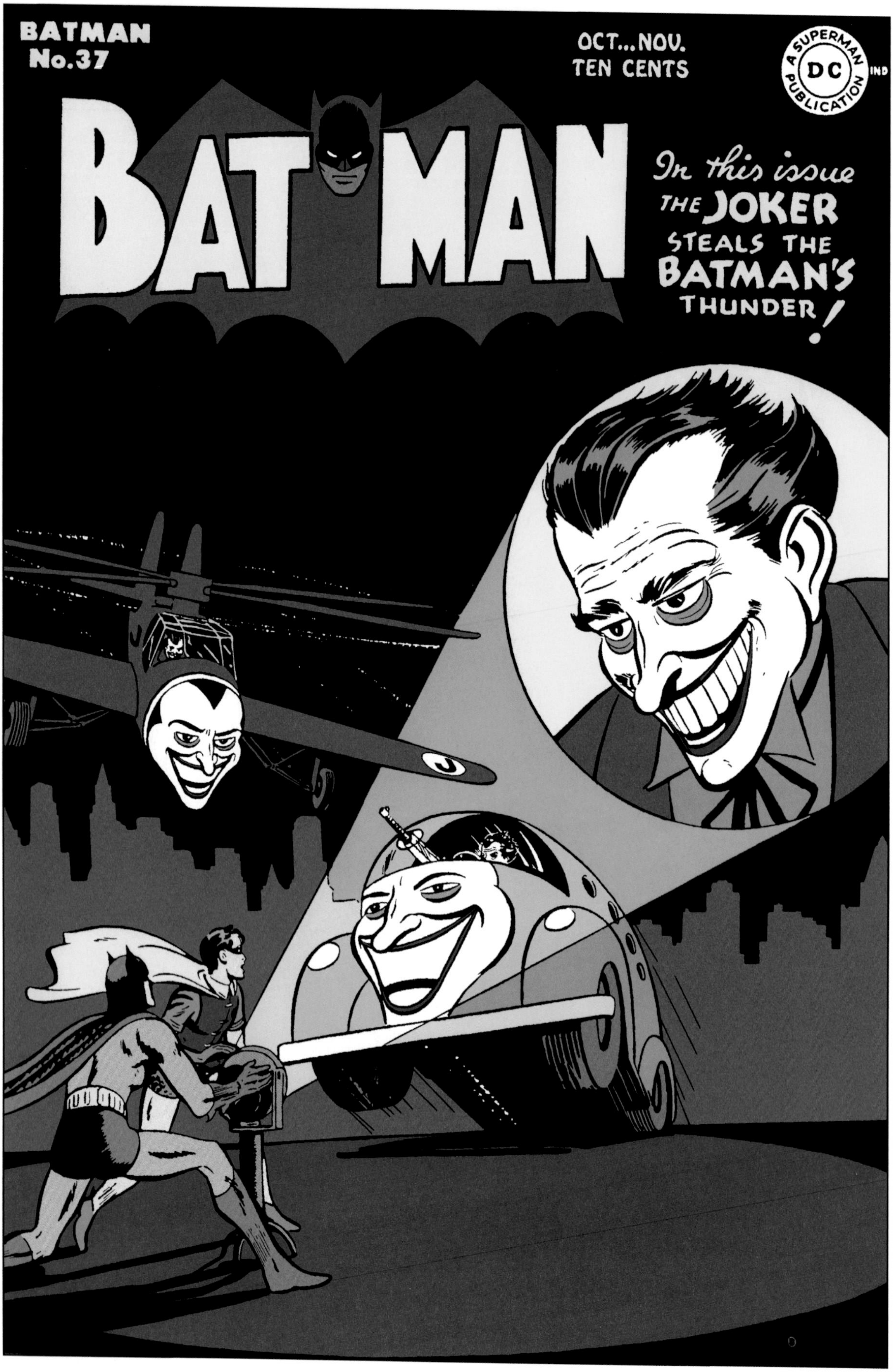
BATMAN
No.37
OCT...NOV.
TEN CENTS
A SUPERMAN PUBLICATION
DC
IND
BATMAN
In this issue
THE JOKER
STEALS THE
BATMAN'S
THUNDER!

Batman #37 (October-November 1946)
Cover by Jerry Robinson

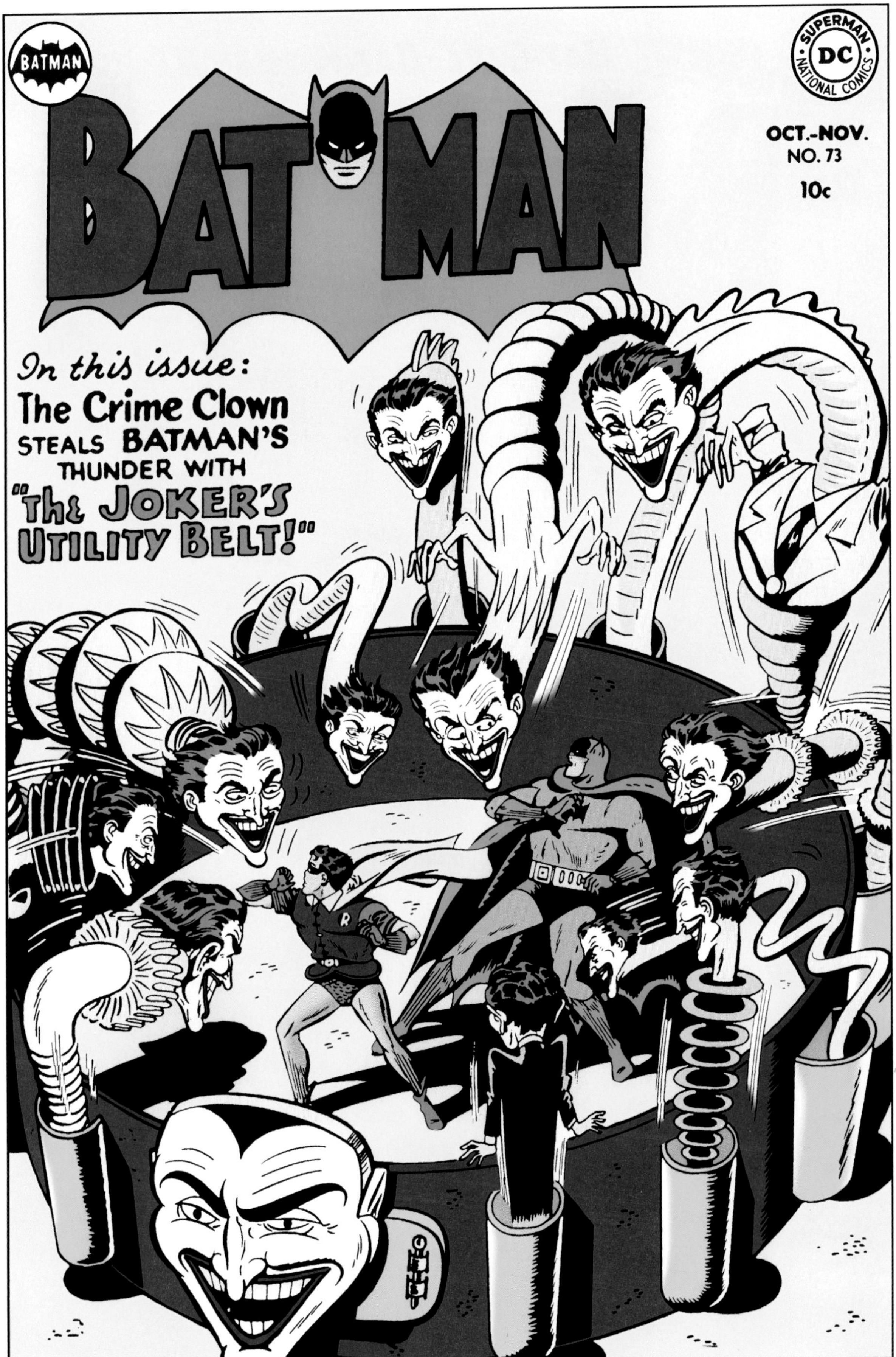
BATMAN
SUPERMAN
DC
NATIONAL COMICS
BATMAN
OCT.-NOV.
NO. 73
10c
In this issue:
The Crime Clown
STEALS BATMAN'S
THUNDER WITH
"The JOKER'S
UTILITY BELT!"

Batman #73 (October-November 1952)
Cover by Dick Sprang and Charles Paris

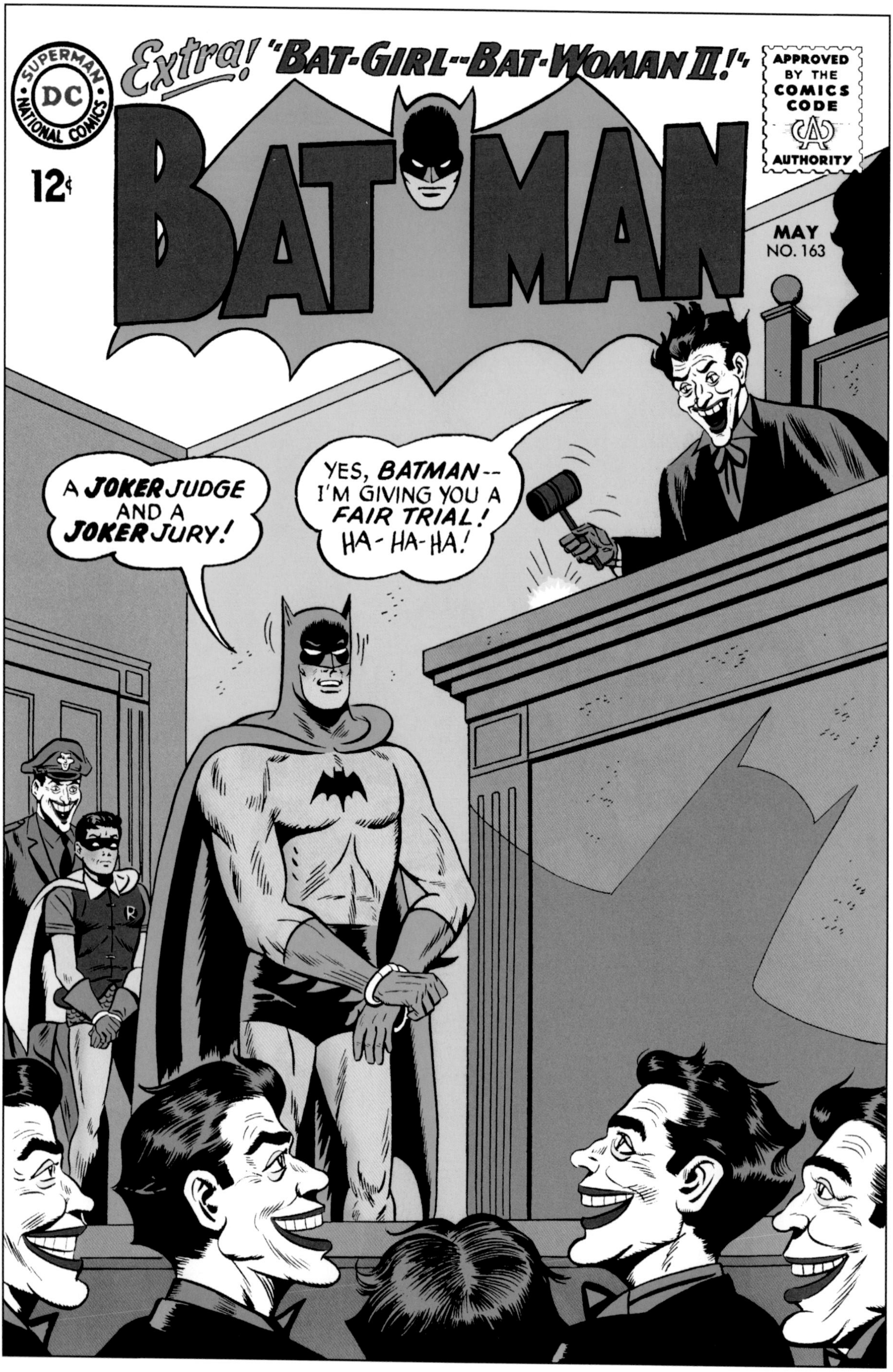
SUPERMAN DC NATIONAL COMICS
12¢
Extra! "BAT-GIRL--BAT-WOMAN II!"
APPROVED BY THE COMICS CODE AUTHORITY
BATMAN
MAY
NO. 163
A JOKER JUDGE AND A JOKER JURY!
YES, BATMAN-- I'M GIVING YOU A FAIR TRIAL! HA-HA-HA!

Batman #163 (May 1964)
Cover by Sheldon Moldoff

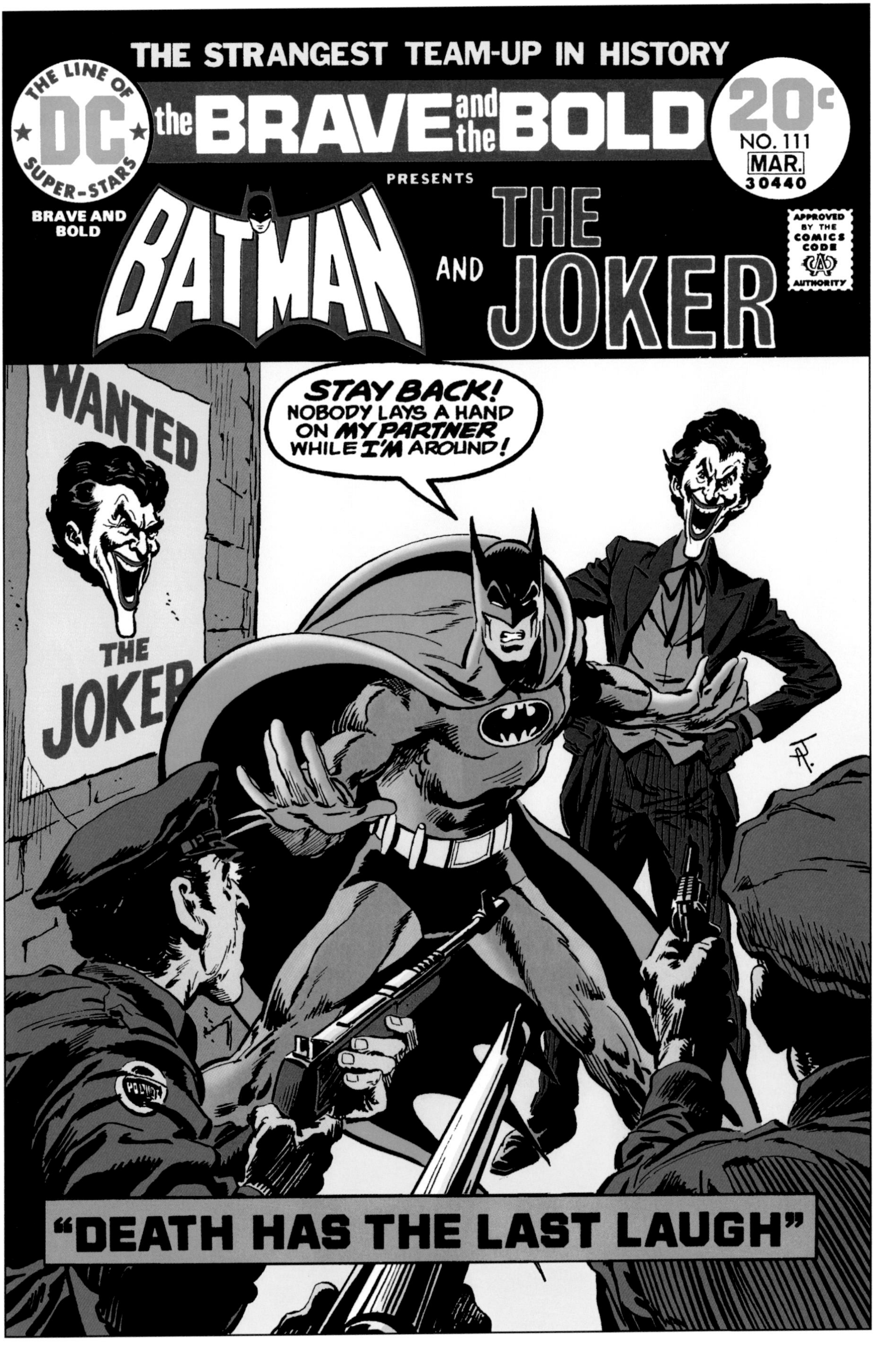
THE STRANGEST TEAM-UP IN HISTORY
THE LINE OF DC SUPER-STARS
the BRAVE and the BOLD
20¢
NO. 111
MAR.
30440
BRAVE AND BOLD
PRESENTS
BATMAN
AND
THE JOKER
APPROVED BY THE COMICS CODE AUTHORITY
WANTED
THE JOKER
STAY BACK! NOBODY LAYS A HAND ON MY PARTNER WHILE I'M AROUND!
"DEATH HAS THE LAST LAUGH"

The Brave and the Bold #111 (February-March 1974)
Cover by Jim Aparo and Tatjana Wood

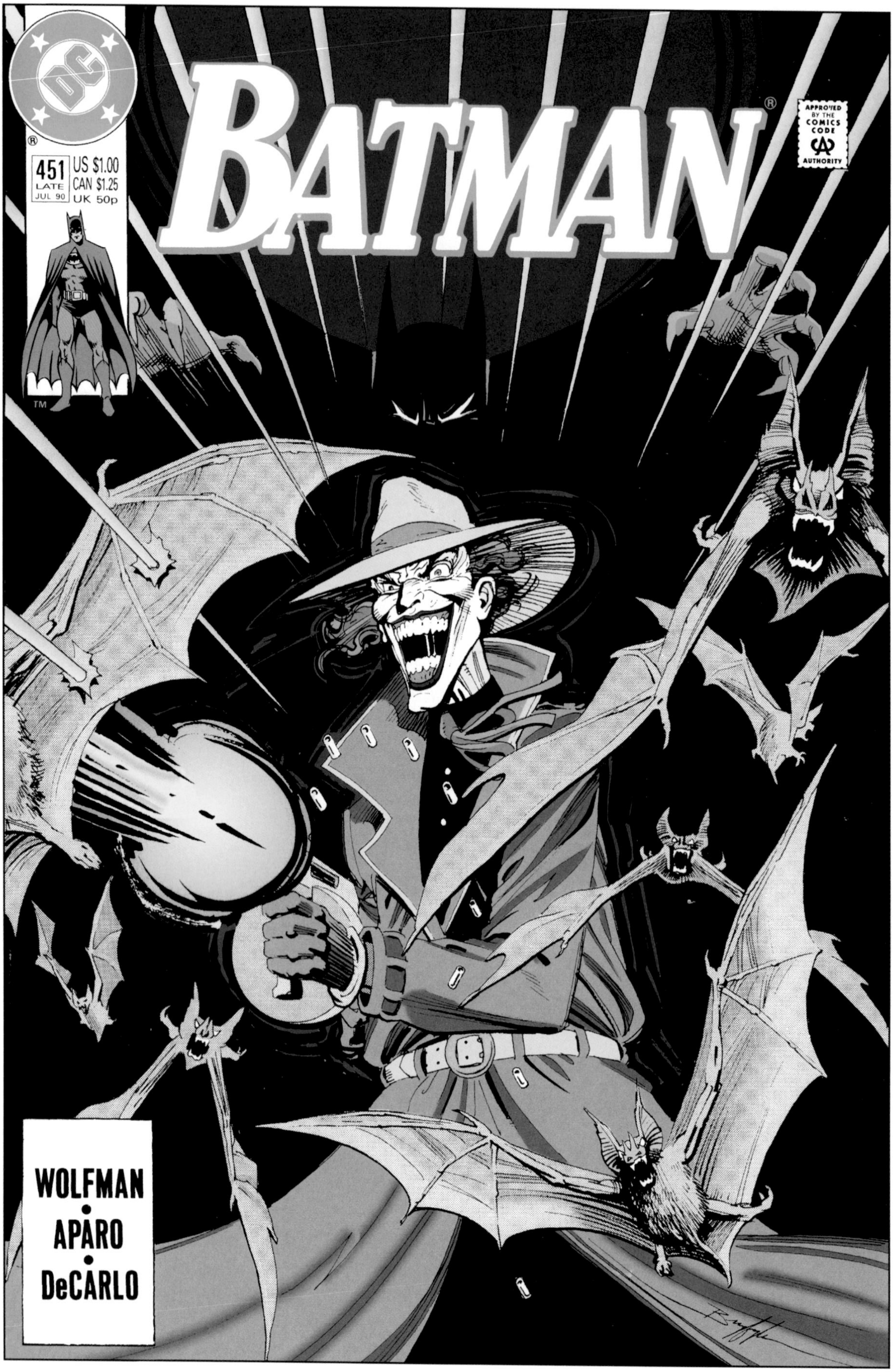
BATMAN
451
LATE
JUL 90
US $1.00
CAN $1.25
UK 50p
APPROVED BY THE COMICS CODE AUTHORITY
WOLFMAN
APARO
DeCARLO

Batman #451 (Late July 1990)
Cover by Norm Breyfogle and Anthony Tollin

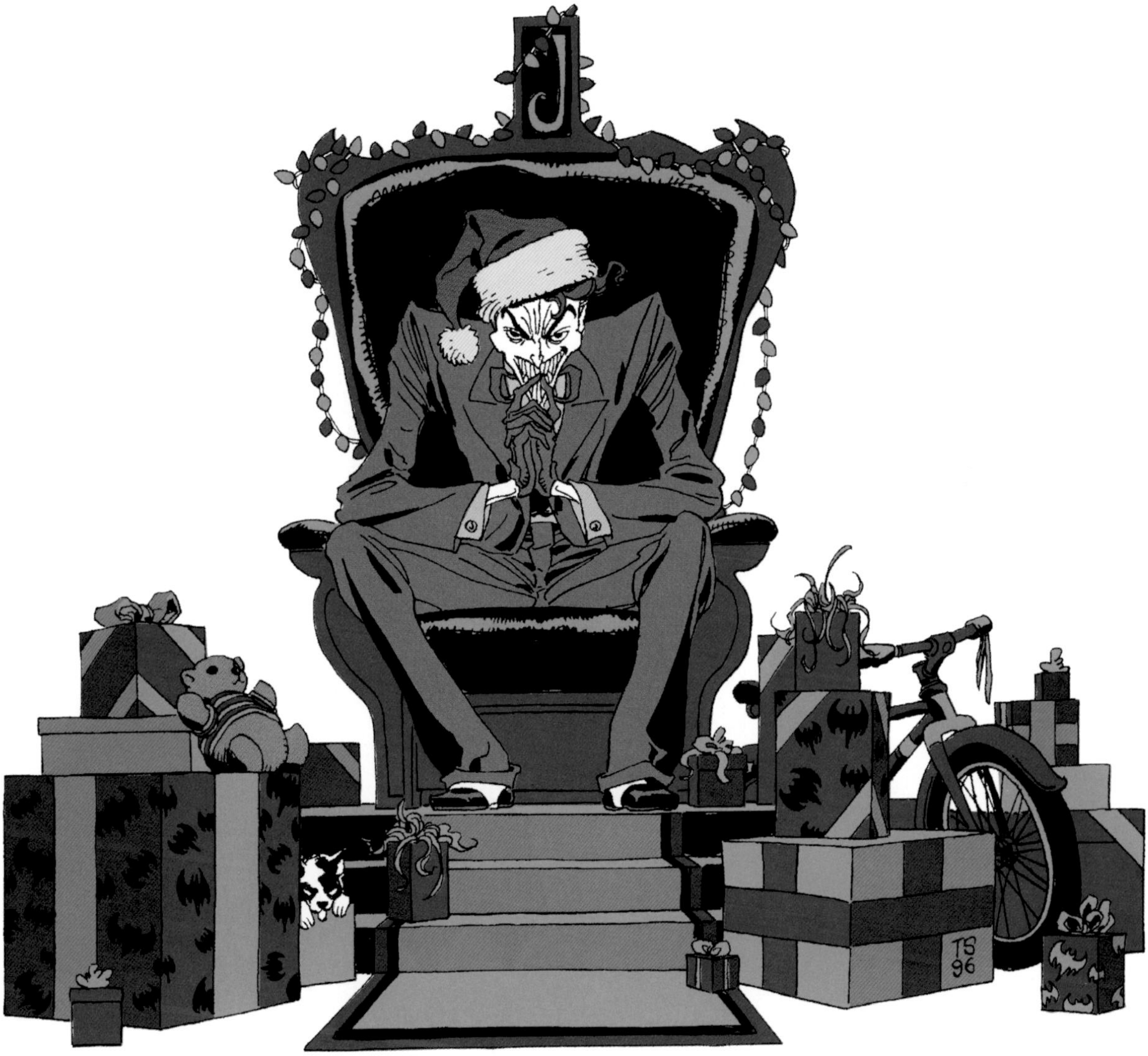
TS
96

Batman: The Long Halloween #3 (February 1997)
Cover by Tim Sale and Gregory Wright

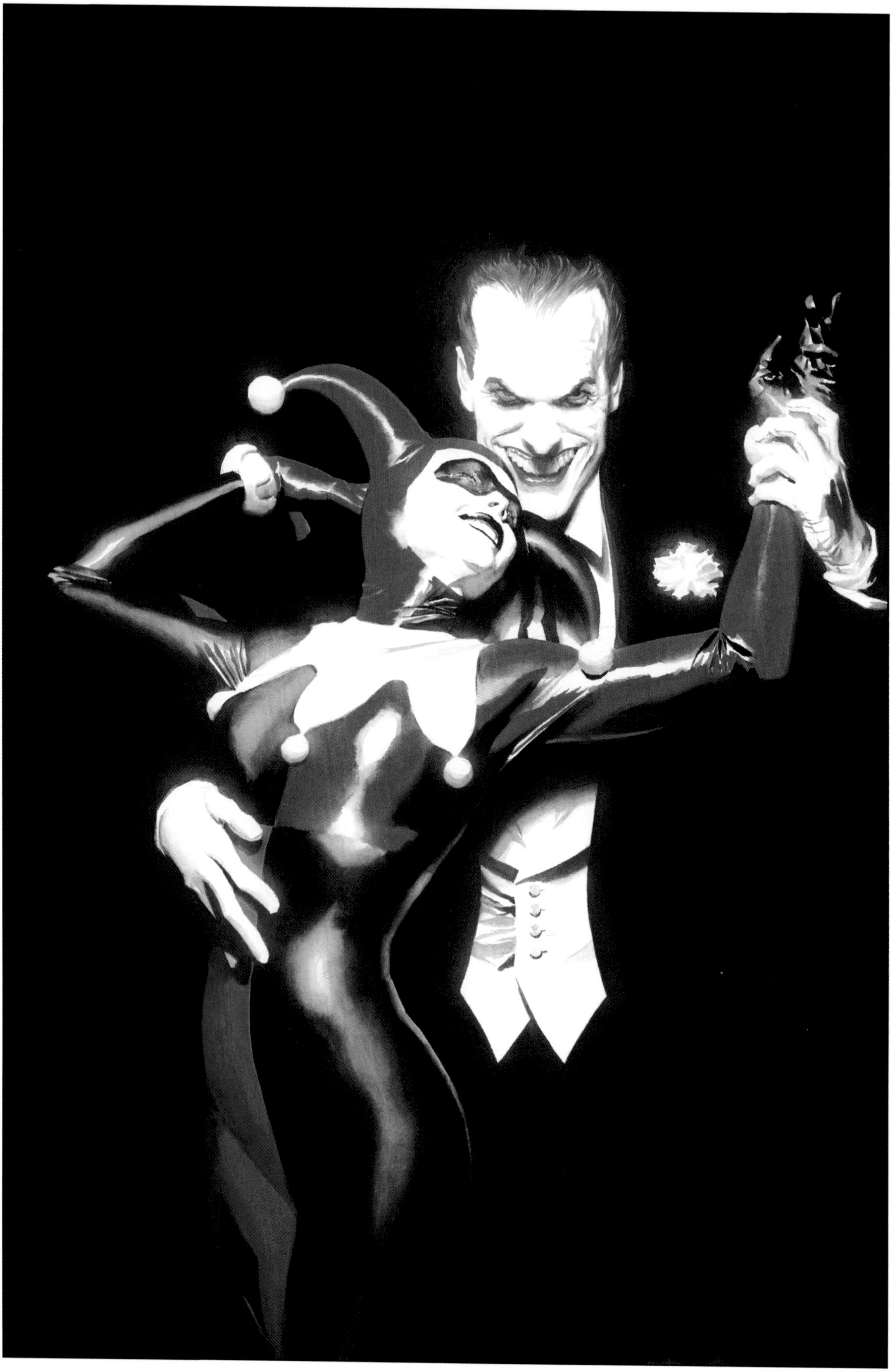

Batman: Harley Quinn (October 1999)
Cover by Alex Ross

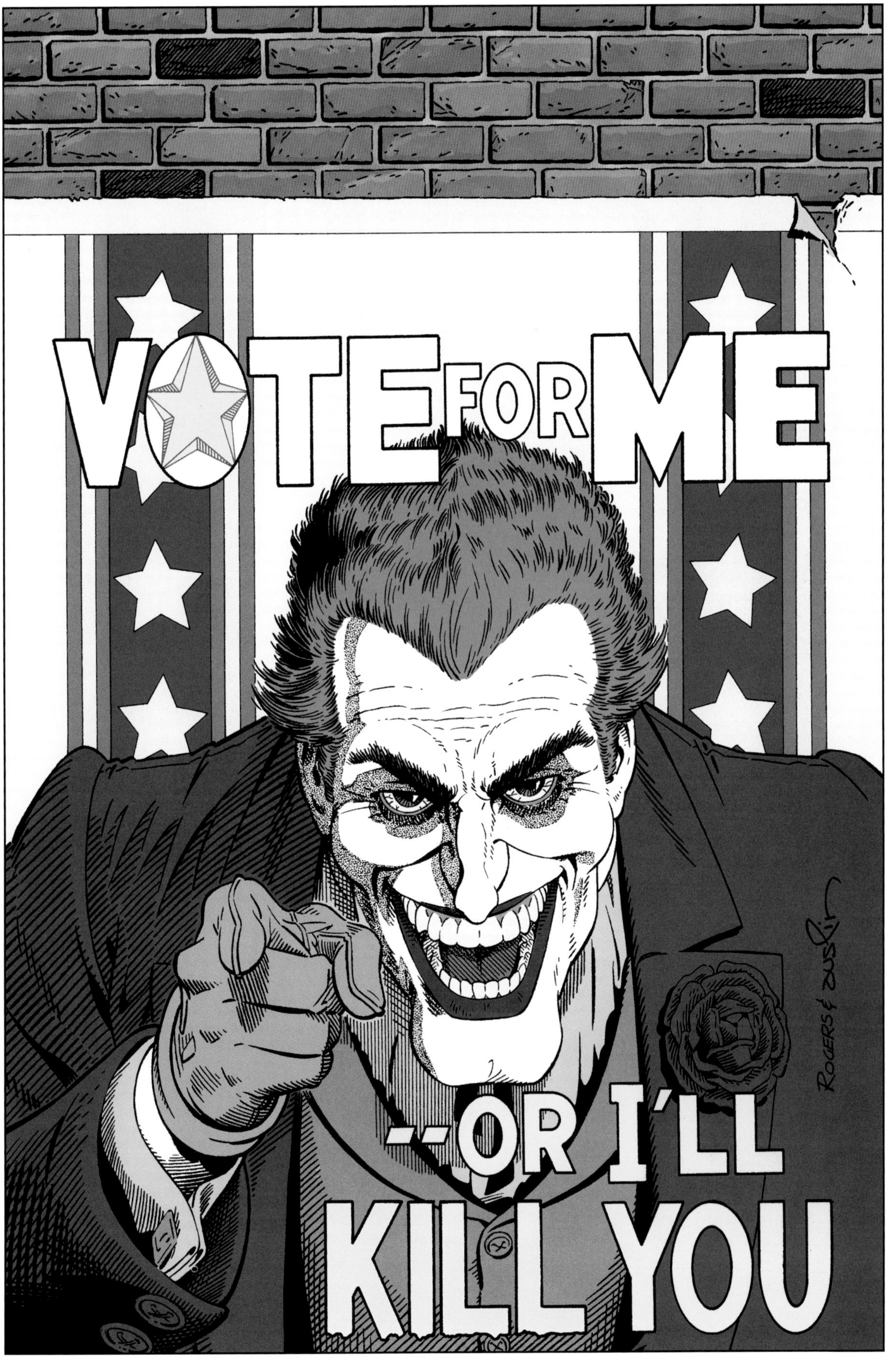
VOTE FOR ME
--OR I'LL KILL YOU
ROGERS & AUSTIN

Batman: Dark Detective #1 (Early July 2005)
Cover by Marshall Rogers and Terry Austin

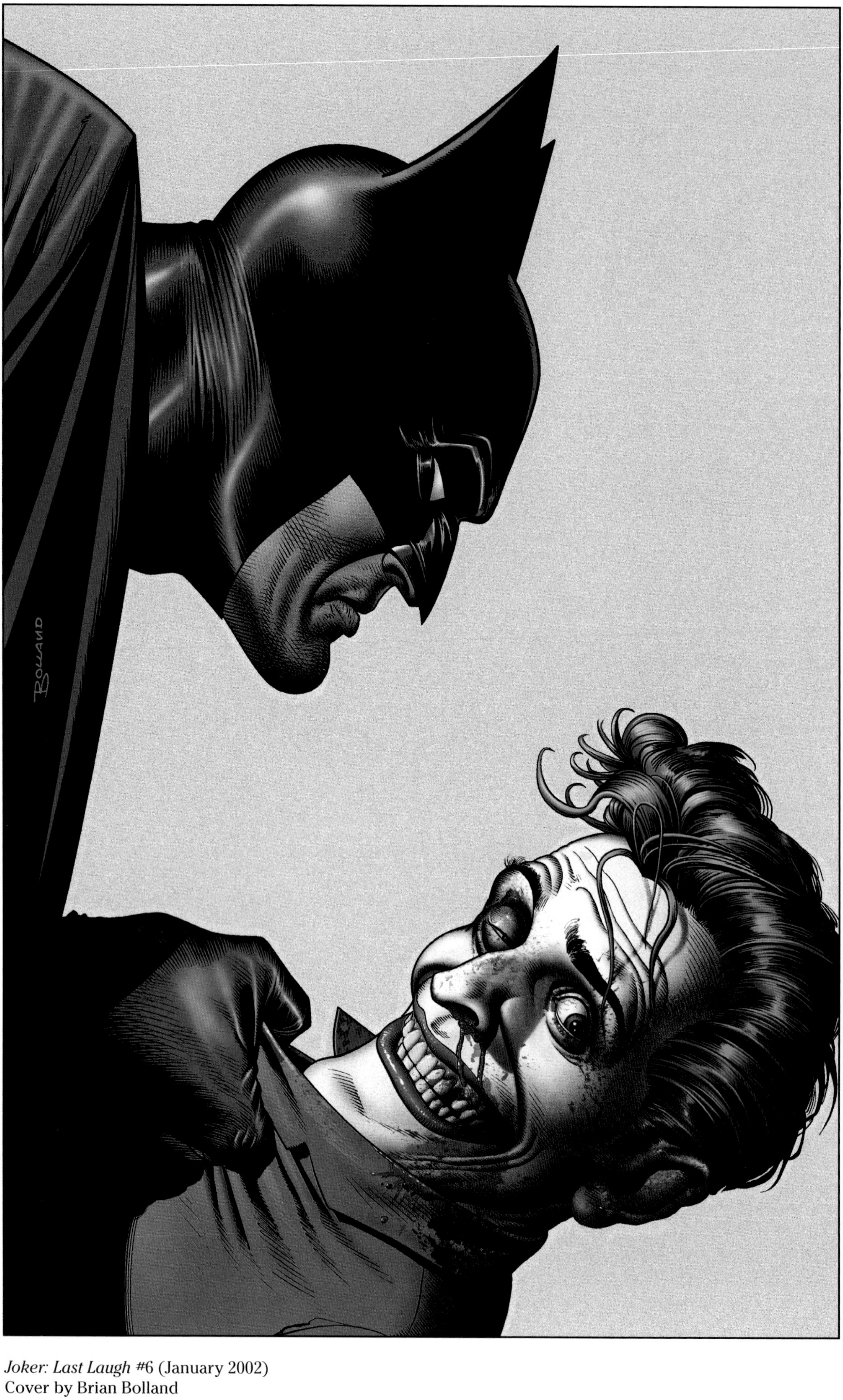
BOLLAND

Joker: Last Laugh #6 (January 2002)
Cover by Brian Bolland

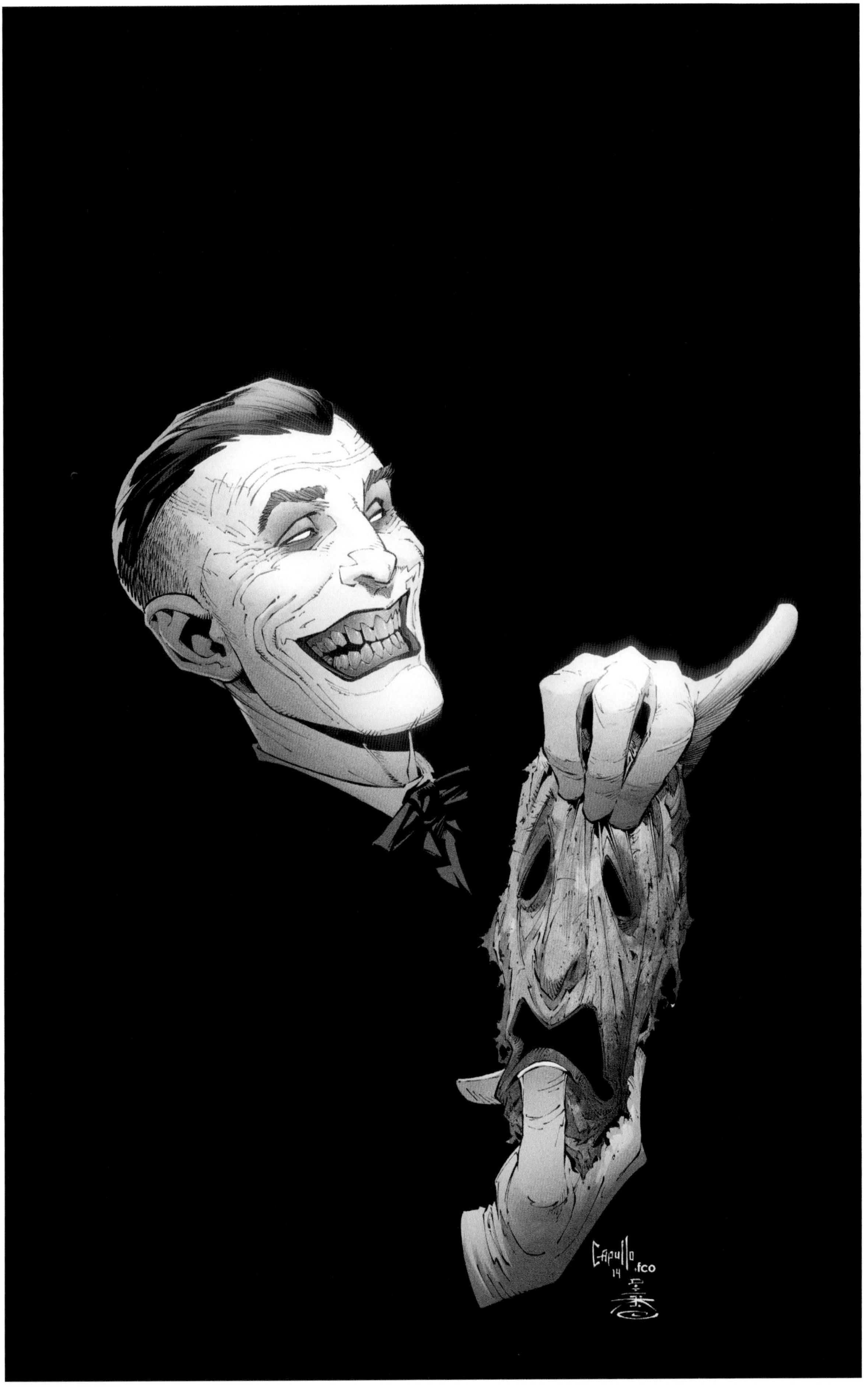
CAPULLO 14 .fco

Batman #37 (February 2015)
Cover by Greg Capullo, Danny Miki, and FCO Plascencia

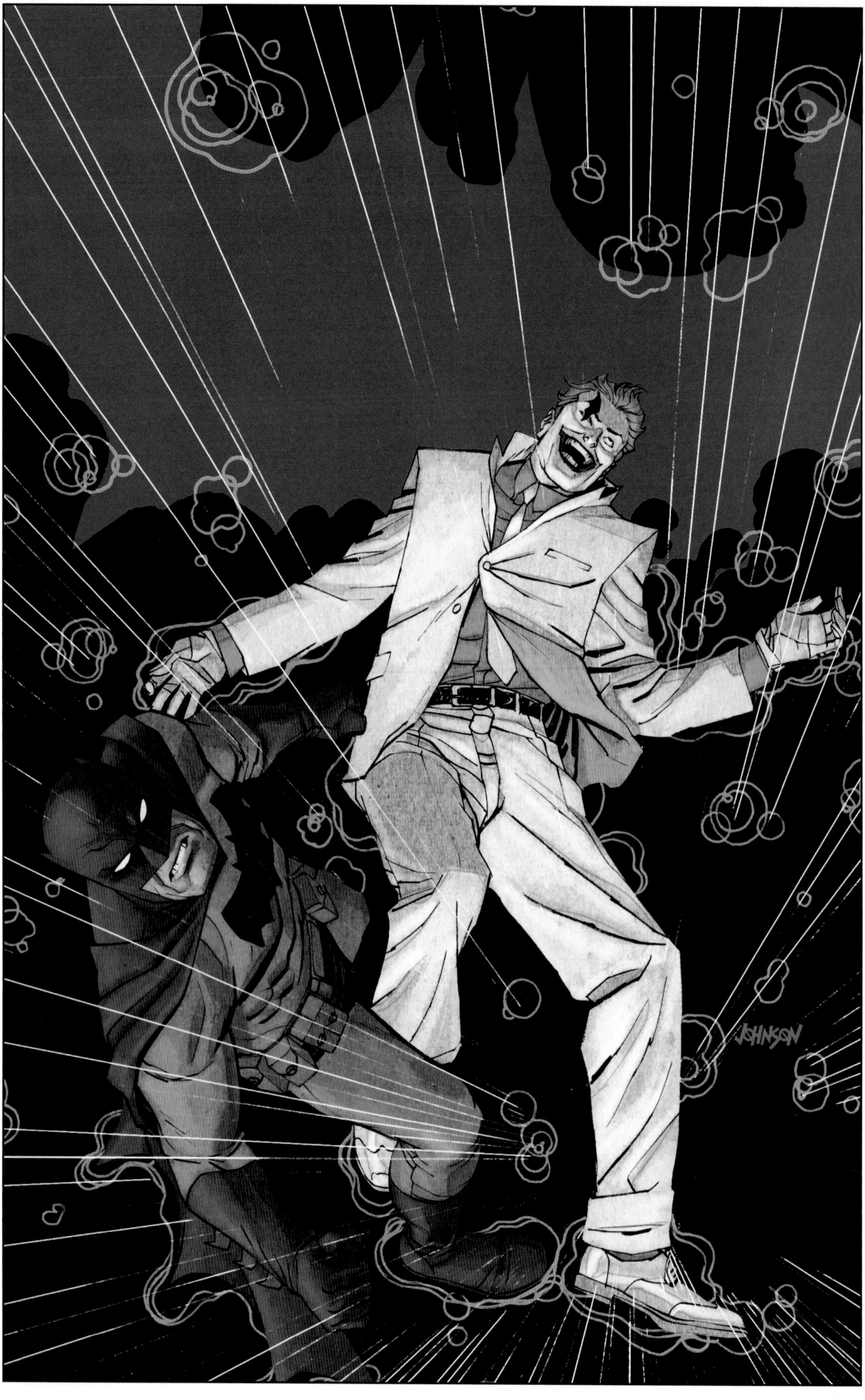
JOHNSON

The Dark Knight III: The Master Race #1 (January 2016)
Variant cover by Dave Johnson

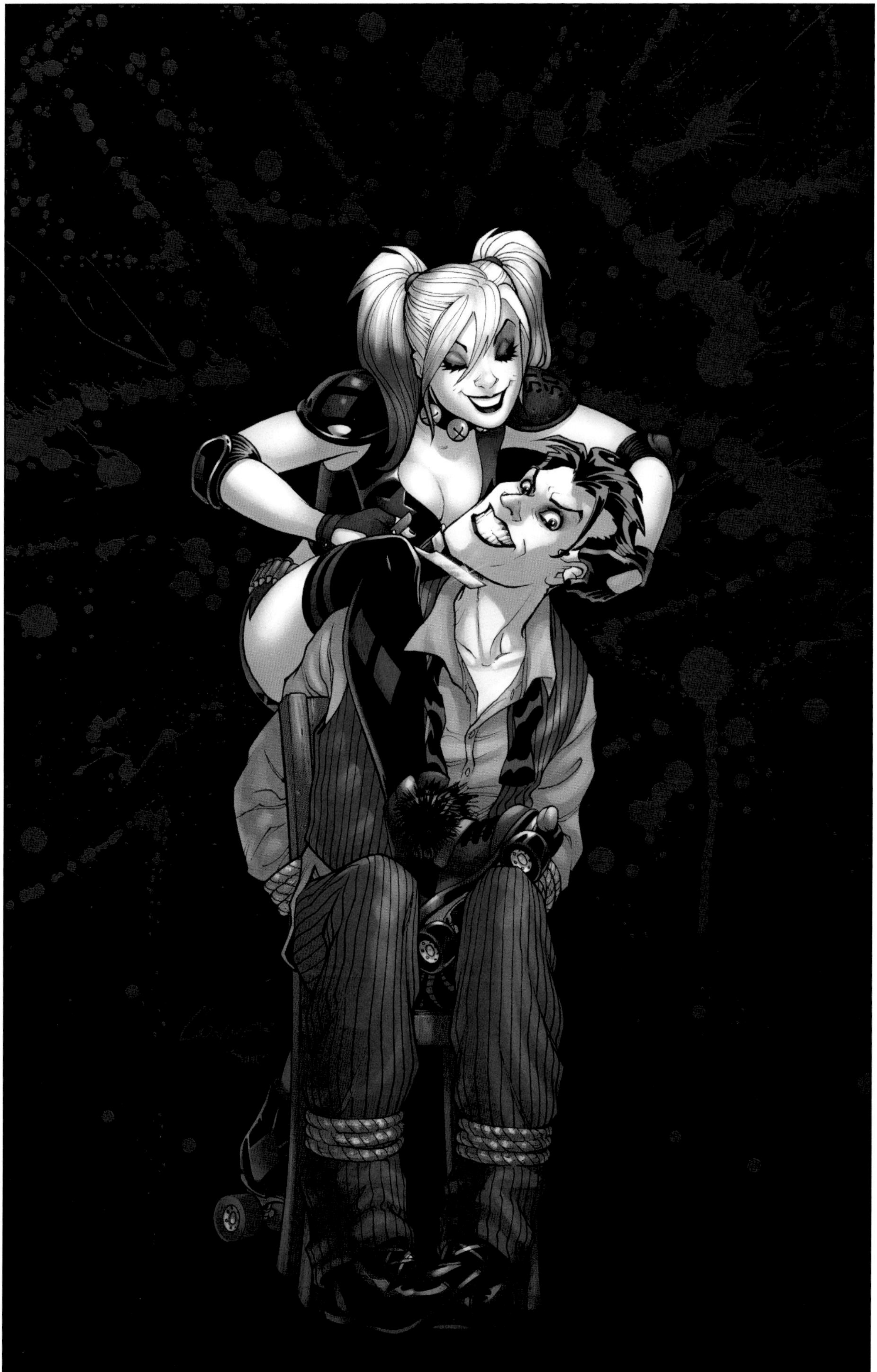

Harley Quinn #11 (Early March 2017)
Cover by Amanda Conner and Alex Sinclair

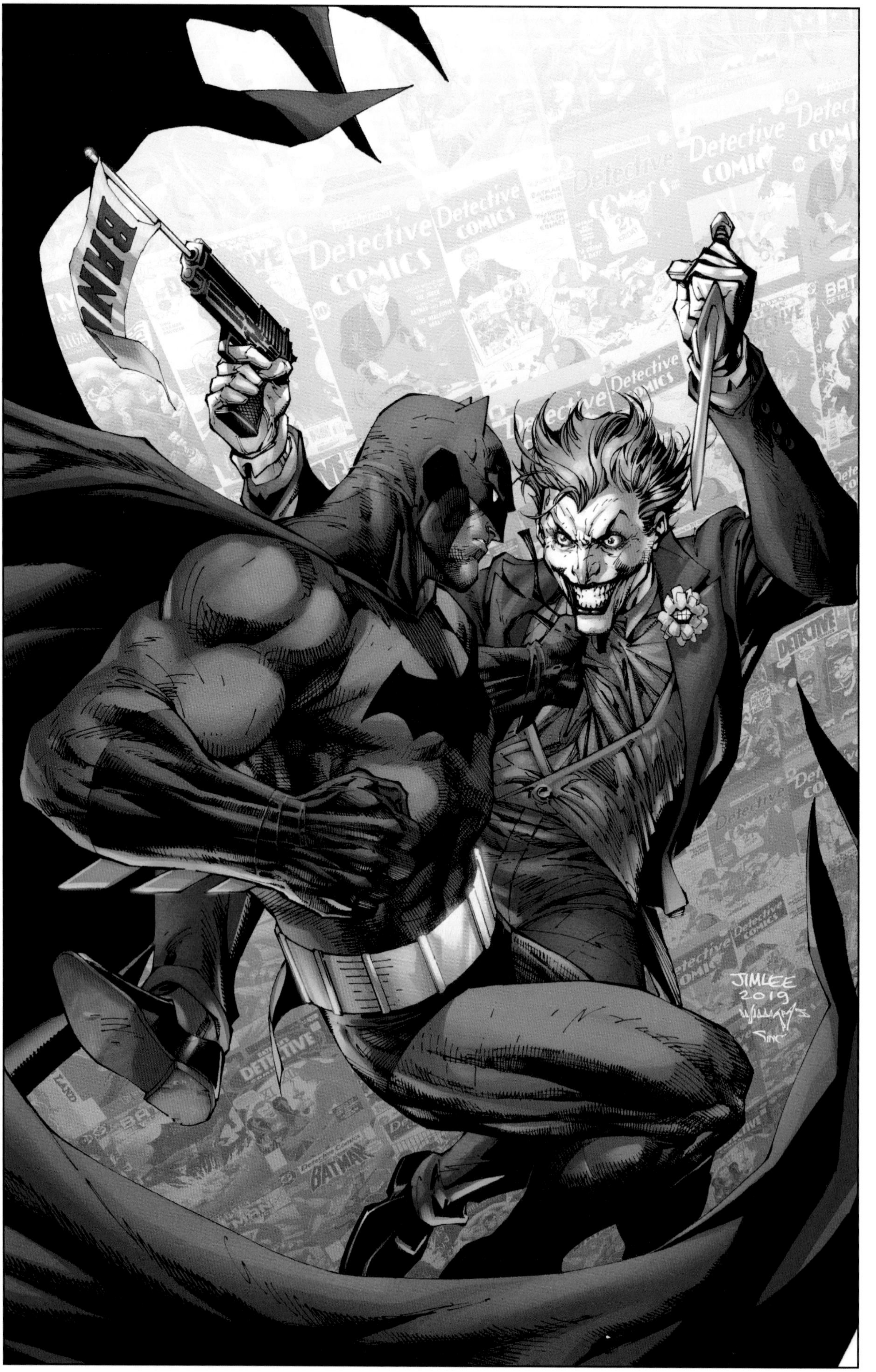
BAN
Detective Comics
JIMLEE
2019

Detective Comics #1000 (May 2019)
Variant cover by Jim Lee, Scott Williams, and Alex Sinclair

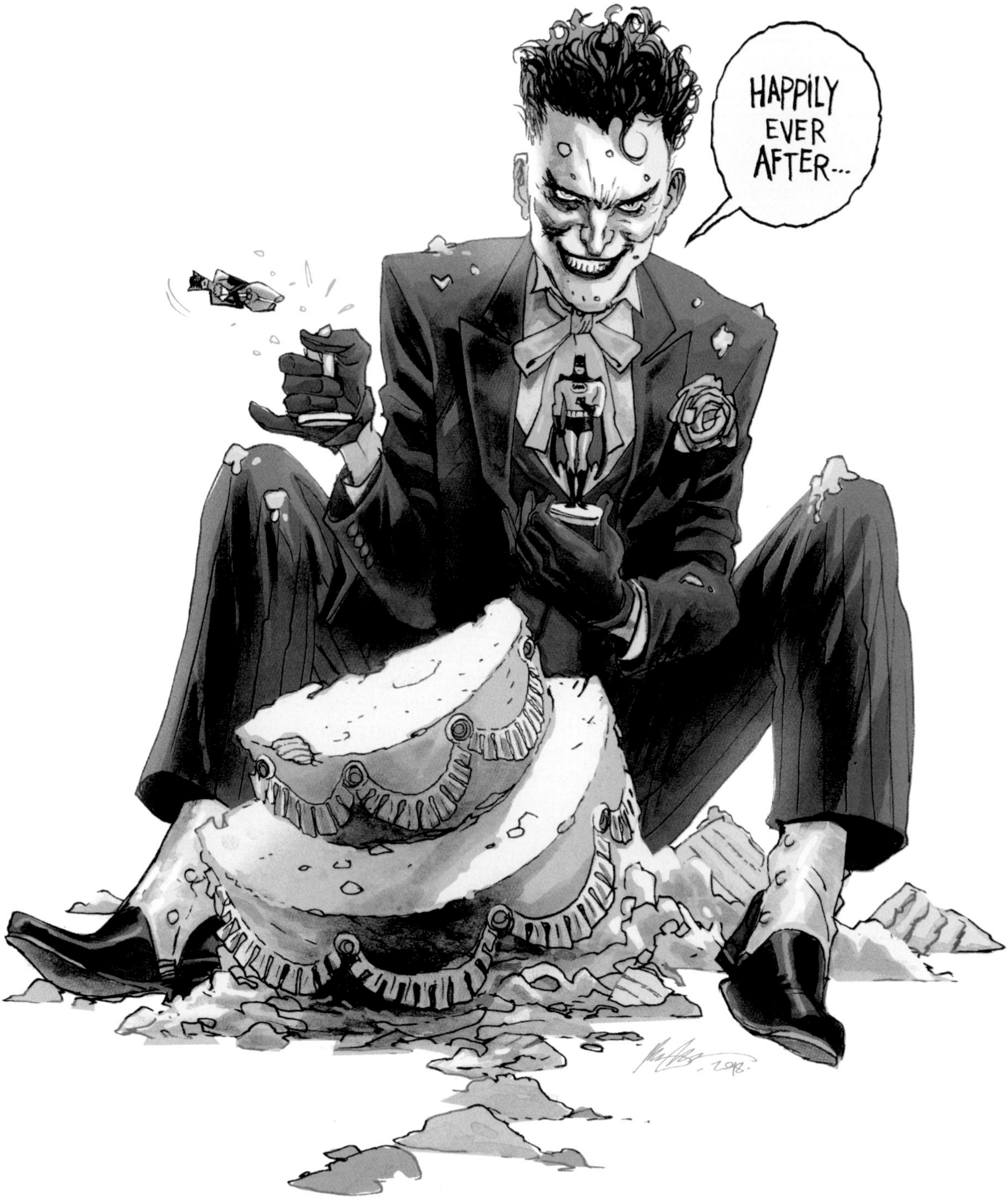
HAPPILY EVER AFTER...

DC Nation #2 (July 2018)
Cover by Rafael Albuquerque

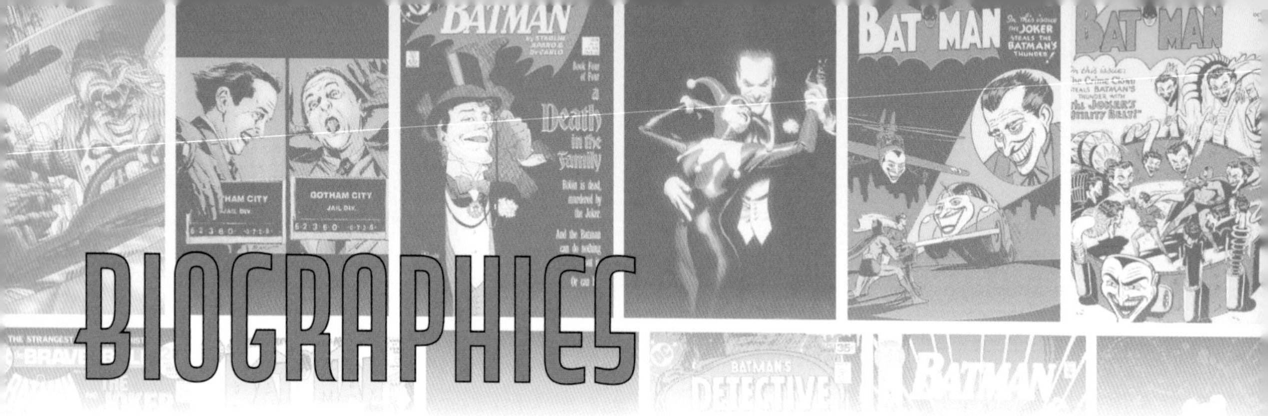
BATMAN
BAT MAN
BAT MAN

BIOGRAPHICS

Born on June 15, 1941, in New York, **Neal Adams** was one of the main forces behind the "youthquake" that shook up the ultraconservative DC Comics during the late 1960s and early 1970s. A maverick whose wildly experimental art style was nurtured and encouraged by then-publisher Carmine Infantino, Adams became an overnight sensation by infusing a new visual vitality into longtime characters who were in danger of becoming stodgy. Working closely with Infantino, Adams quickly became DC's preeminent cover artist during this period, contributing radical and dynamic illustrations to virtually the company's entire line. Adams went on to become one of the most talked-about creator/writer/artist/publishers in the medium and continues to influence, directly and indirectly, today's young comics artists.

In 1966, advertising artist **Jim Aparo** was hired by Dick Giordano (then an editor at Charlton Comics) to pencil and ink a variety of features. When Giordano came to DC Comics in 1968, he brought Aparo over as well. At DC, Aparo picked up more substantial long-running assignments on *Aquaman*, *The Phantom Stranger*, and *The Brave and the Bold*, for which he drew the adventures of Batman for nearly ten years. He followed that assignment with an even longer stint on *Batman*, where he cemented his reputation as one of the all-time great Dark Knight artists. Aparo passed away on July 19, 2005.

Having gotten his break inking backgrounds for Dick Giordano, **Terry Austin** quickly came into his own in the comics field. Consistently voted fandom's favorite inker, Austin has worked with many of the industry's best pencillers, including John Byrne on Marvel Comics' *X-Men* and Marshall Rogers on *Detective Comics*.

Bret Blevins began working for Marvel in 1981, initially on movie adaptations such as *The Dark Crystal* and *The Last Starfighter*, then drawing most of their popular characters over the next 10 years in various titles, including runs on *The New Mutants*, *Sleepwalker*, and *Cloak and Dagger*, and an early creator-owned Epic project, *The Bozz Chronicles*. Blevins's first work for DC was *Dark Knight* #50, a retelling of Batman's first meeting with the Joker, which led to Blevins becoming the regular artist on *Batman: Shadow of the Bat* for the next few years. Other comics work includes the graphic novel *The Inhumans*, issues of *The X-Men*, *The Incredible Hulk*, *Doctor Strange*, *Superman Adventures*, *Supergirl*, *Clive Barker's Nightbreed*, *The Trouble with Girls*, *Solomon Kane*, and *Conan*, as well as *Tarzan*, *John Carter*, and *Star Wars* for Dark Horse Comics. In 1996 Blevins began working primarily for Warner Bros. Animation creating storyboards for many WB series, as well as for *Atlantis* for Disney and *Ben 10* for Cartoon Network. Aside from a series of short *Pirates of the Caribbean* comics and a graphic novel adaptation of Brian Jacques's *Redwall* in the early 2000s, for nearly twenty years Blevins worked mostly in animation or advertising and painted for galleries in addition to teaching until returning to comics in 2015 with various Harley Quinn projects for DC and the science fiction epic *Stellar*, a new Robert Kirkman series from Skybound/Image comics.

After making his professional debut in 1975, artist **Brian Bolland** perfected his clean-line style and meticulous attention to detail on a series of popular strips for the British comics magazine *2000 AD*, most notably its signature feature *Judge Dredd*. He went on to illustrate the 12-issue maxiseries *Camelot 3000* and the Alan Moore-written graphic novel *Batman: The Killing Joke* for DC before shifting his focus to work almost exclusively on cover illustrations. Since then, he has earned a reputation as one of the best cover artists in the industry, and his elegantly composed and beautifully rendered pieces have graced a host of titles, including *Animal Man*, *Batman*, *The Flash*, *The Invisibles*, *Wonder Woman*, and many more.

Ed Brubaker is one of the most award-winning writers in comics. His bestselling titles *Criminal*, *Incognito*, *Fatale*, *The Fade Out*, and *Kill or Be Killed* have been translated around the world to great acclaim, and the Marvel movies featuring his co-creation the Winter Soldier have all been international blockbusters. Brubaker lives in Los Angeles, where he works in comics, film, and television—most recently on HBO's *Westworld*—and as the co-creator of Amazon's *Too Old to Die Young* with Nicolas Winding Refn.

Greg Capullo is a comic book artist who has worked on *Batman* and *Dark Nights: Metal* for DC Comics, *Quasar* and *X-Force* for Marvel Comics, and *Spawn*, *Angela*, and *The Haunt* for Image Comics. He has also written and drawn the creator-owned series *The Creech*. Outside of comics, Capullo has worked on CD covers for the bands Disturbed and Korn. Greg has been a regular contributor to *World of Warcraft*, supplying painted art. He was also involved with character design for the animated sequences in the Jodie Foster film *The Dangerous Lives of Altar Boys* and the award-winning HBO animated series *Spawn*, created by Todd McFarlane.

Tony S. Daniel decided to become a comic book artist in the fourth grade and has never looked back. He made his professional comics debut in 1993 on Comico's *The Elementals* and went on to illustrate *X-Force* for Marvel and *Spawn: Bloodfeud* for Image; he

BATMAN
BATMAN'S
DETECTIVE
COMICS

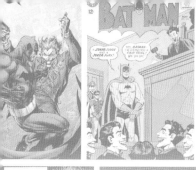

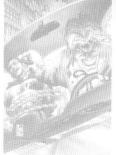

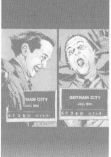

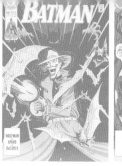

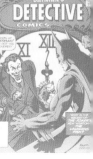

has also written and illustrated several creator-owned titles of his own, including *Silke*, *The Tenth*, *Adrenalynn*, and *F5*—the last two of which led him, for a time, into the alternate reality known as Hollywood. After being lured back into comics in 2005 to work with writer Geoff Johns on *Teen Titans* for DC Comics, Daniel landed his dream job in 2007 pencilling the adventures of DC's Dark Knight Detective in *Batman*, where he initially collaborated with writer Grant Morrison and then went on to write and draw the book himself. In 2011 Daniel relaunched *Detective Comics* for DC's New 52, writing and drawing most of the first year of the historic series. He has also illustrated *Action Comics* and *Superman/Wonder Woman* and has both written and illustrated *Deathstroke*.

Bill Finger was one of the true innovative talents and legendary figures of the comics industry. He collaborated with Bob Kane on the creation of Batman and scripted the first two episodes of the Dark Knight's appearances in *Detective Comics*. Finger went on to write features for many publishers, including ones starring Plastic Man (for Quality Comics), Green Lantern, Wildcat, Vigilante, Johnny Quick, Superman, Superboy, Blackhawk, Tomahawk, Robin, Challengers of the Unknown, and Batman (in the comics and in the syndicated newspaper strip), as well as Captain America and All Winners Comics (for Timely). He also wrote for radio and television, contributing scripts to *Mark Trail*, *77 Sunset Strip*, *The Roaring Twenties*, *Hawaiian Eye*, and, naturally enough, two episodes of the *Batman* TV program in 1966. He also wrote television commercials and one feature film, the 1969 cult film *The Green Slime*. Finger was still writing for DC Comics at the time of his death in 1974.

A veteran of more than five decades in the comic-book field, **Dick Giordano** began his career as an artist for Charlton Comics in 1952 and became the company's editor-in-chief in 1965, launching the short-lived but well-remembered Action Heroes line. In 1967 he moved to DC for a three-year stint as an editor and became part of a creative team that helped to change the face of comic books in the late 1960s and early 1970s. Together with writer Dennis O'Neil and penciller Neal Adams, he helped to bring Batman back to his roots as a dark, brooding "creature of the night," and to raise awareness of contemporary social issues through the adventures of Green Lantern and Green Arrow. The winner of numerous industry awards, Giordano later returned to DC and rose to the position of vice president/executive editor before "retiring" in 1993 to once again pursue a full-time freelance career as a penciller and inker. He passed away on March 27, 2010.

Jonathan Glapion began his comics career in 1998 at Image, where he contributed inks to such titles as *Curse of the Spawn*, *Sam and Twitch*, and *Universe*. After spending several years at Marvel inking *Elektra: The Hand*, *Gravity*, and *Ultimate X-Men*, he shifted his focus to their distinguished competition. Since 2007, he has worked on a wide variety of DC titles, including the New 52 *Batman*, *Batgirl*, *Suicide Squad*, *Batman/Superman*, *New Super-Man*, and *Action Comics* as well as *Wonder Woman*. He is the winner of three Inkwell Awards (the Props Award in 2010, the Most-Adaptable Inker Award in 2013 and the S.P.A.M.I. Award in 2017) and was a Harvey Award nominee for Best Inker in 2013. Most recently, Jonathan worked on *Reborn* with Greg Capullo and Millarworld and on DC's *Dark Nights: Metal*.

John Higgins is a comic book penciller, inker, colorist, and writer whose career as a professional freelance artist goes back over 40 years. In 1981 he started getting regular work at *2000 AD*, the UK's prestigious sci-fi comics magazine, and he has worked for the publication ever since—a run that has included more than 20 years on the iconic *Judge Dredd* character and frequent collaborations with writer Alan Moore. Higgins was part of the mid-1980s "British Invasion" of American comics, and he holds the distinction of having been the colorist on two of the most notable graphic novels of all time: *Watchmen* and *Batman: The Killing Joke*. He has worked with DC Comics for over 25 years, mainly for the Vertigo imprint, and he returned to the Watchmen universe in 2012 to provide the artwork (and eventually the writing) for the backup feature "The Curse of the Crimson Corsair" that ran through the *Before Watchmen* titles. Higgins also created, wrote, drew, and self-published the acclaimed *Razorjack* series, which was eventually collected and published by Titan Books. He spent 2016 writing and designing an autobiographical art book, *Beyond Watchmen & Judge Dredd: The Art of John Higgins*, which was published by Liverpool University Press to coincide with a major retrospective exhibition of his work at the Victoria Gallery and Museum in Liverpool that ran from March 2017 to February 2018 (extended due to popular demand!).

Robert Kahn (Bob Kane) was born on October 24, 1916, in the Bronx and at age 18 legally changed his name to Kane. In 1936, this self-proclaimed "compulsive doodleholic" pencilled and inked his first comic book work, Hiram Hick. By 1938 he was selling humorous filler features to DC Comics, including ones featuring Professor Doolittle and Ginger Snap. Kane met writer Bill Finger at a party in 1938, and they soon were collaborating on comic book submissions. Their most famous effort, Batman, first appeared

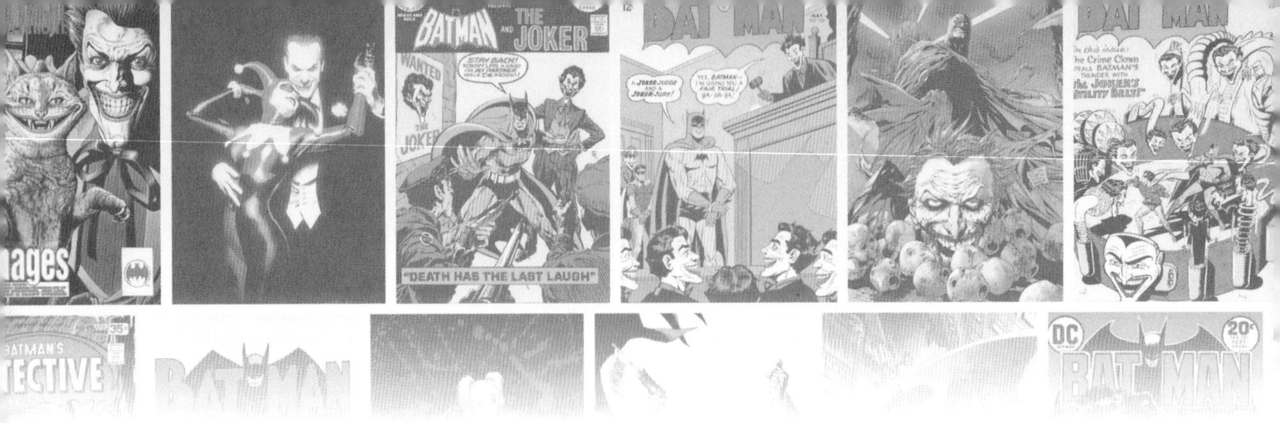
BATMAN AND THE JOKER
WANTED
"DEATH HAS THE LAST LAUGH"

in *Detective Comics* #27 (May 1939). As Batman's popularity demanded additional output, Kane kept up the pace by adding assistants and dropping non-Batman assignments. He discontinued his comic book efforts in mid-1943 to pencil the daily *Batman and Robin* newspaper strip. After the strip's 1946 demise, Kane returned to illustrating Batman's comic book adventures and, with the help of several ghosts, remained involved with comics until his retirement in 1968. The success of the *Batman* television series brought Kane and his art back into the public eye in 1966. He was subsequently featured in various one-man art shows at galleries and museums nationwide and released a number of limited-edition lithographs. He served as a consultant on the 1989 *Batman* feature film and its sequels. His autobiography, *Batman and Me*, was published in 1989, and in 1996 he was inducted into the Eisner Awards Hall of Fame. Kane died on November 3, 1998.

Jim Lee is a renowned comic book artist and the publisher and chief creative officer of DC Entertainment. In addition to his executive positions, he is also the artist for many of DC Comics' bestselling comic books and graphic novels, including *All-Star Batman and Robin, the Boy Wonder*, *Superman: For Tomorrow*, *Justice League: Origin*, *Superman Unchained*, and *Suicide Squad*. He also served as the executive creative director for the *DC Universe Online* (DCUO) massively multiplayer action game from Daybreak Games.

Born in 1920, **Sheldon Moldoff** broke into comics by assisting Bob Kane on Batman—a collaboration that would last, on and off, for almost two decades. Following his work on the Dark Knight, Moldoff soon got assignments of his own from DC, including the Black Pirate in *Action Comics* and the Hawkman in *Flash Comics*, both collaborations with writer Gardner Fox. In time, Moldoff became one of the company's most prolific artists. After serving in World War II, Moldoff returned to work for former All-American publisher M.C. Gaines, who had parted company with DC to create the new E.C. comics line. As E.C.'s horror comics wound down in the mid-1950s, Moldoff reunited with Bob Kane to draw most of the Batman stories credited to Kane between 1954 and 1967. He also worked with Kane on his early 1960s cartoon takeoff on Batman, *Courageous Cat and Minute Mouse*, and inked quite a few stories and covers for DC. He passed away in 2012.

Alan Moore is perhaps the most acclaimed writer in the graphic story medium, having garnered countless awards for works such as *Watchmen*, *V for Vendetta*, *From Hell*, *Miracleman*, and *Swamp Thing*. He is also the mastermind behind the America's Best Comics line, through which he has created (along with many talented illustrators) *The League of Extraordinary Gentlemen*, *Promethea*, *Tom Strong*, *Tomorrow Stories*, and *Top 10*. As one of the medium's most important innovators since the early 1980s, Moore has influenced an entire generation of comics creators, and his work continues to inspire an ever-growing audience. He resides in central England.

James Winslow Mortimer was born on May 1, 1919, and studied at the Art Students League of New York before being hired by DC Comics in 1945. In addition to pencilling and inking many stories for such titles as *World's Finest Comics* and *Batman*, Mortimer was also DC's most frequent cover artist for their main titles from 1949 through 1956. He maintained an unbroken string of 46 covers for *Detective Comics* (issues #169-214), and ultimately pencilled and inked 87 of the 121 covers for issues #110-230 as well as numerous covers for *Adventure Comics*, *Batman*, *World's Finest Comics*, *Action Comics*, *Superboy*, *Superman*, *Mr. District Attorney*, and *Star Spangled Comics*. He also worked on the *Superman* daily syndicated newspaper strip from 1949 through 1956. Mortimer's art was unsigned, but he was fond of sneaking his name—Win or Winslow—into his early DC material on trucks, storefronts, and billboards. Mortimer left DC in early 1956 to illustrate *David Crane*, a daily newspaper strip about a minister. He departed *Crane* in 1960, and from 1961 through 1968 he worked on another strip, *Larry Brannon*. After the mid-1960s he moved in and out of comic books, doing occasional work for DC as well as for Gold Key and Marvel. Mortimer died on January 11, 1998.

Dennis O'Neil began his career as a comic book writer in 1965 at Charlton, where then-editor Dick Giordano assigned him to several features. When Giordano moved to DC, O'Neil soon followed. At DC, O'Neil scripted several series for Giordano and Julius Schwartz, quickly becoming one of the most respected writers in comics. O'Neil earned a reputation for being able to "revamp" such characters as Superman, Green Lantern, Captain Marvel—and Batman, whom O'Neil (with the help of Neal Adams and Giordano) brought back to his roots as a dark, mysterious gothic avenger. Besides being the most important Batman writer of the 1970s, O'Neil served as an editor at both Marvel and DC. After a long tenure as group editor of the Batman line of titles, he retired to write full-time.

Born on September 25, 1911, **Charles Paris** moved to New York in 1934. In the spring of 1941, he met Jack Lehti and soon was regularly inking and lettering Lehti's Crimson Avenger feature for *Detective Comics*. Shortly thereafter Paris obtained a job in the DC bullpen inking Lee Harris's Airwave. He also inked

images
BATMAN AND THE JOKER
"DEATH HAS THE LAST LAUGH"
WOLFMAN
APARO
DeCARLO
BATMAN

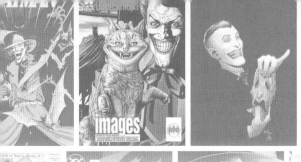

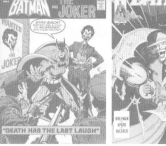

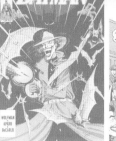

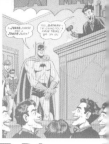

Mort Meskin's Vigilante and Johnny Quick and worked on the Shining Knight and Aquaman. Paris inked most of the *Batman and Robin* newspaper strips from 1943-1946, and for a short time around 1947 he pencilled and inked stories for the *Batman* comic book. After that, he focused almost exclusively on inking and became the principal inker for Batman stories and covers until 1964, working over the pencils of Dick Sprang, Jim Mooney, Lew Sayre Schwartz, and Sheldon Moldoff. Beginning in 1964, Paris branched out to work on other titles for DC, including stories for *The Brave and the Bold*. His last regular inking assignment was for *Metamorpho* #15 in 1967. Between the late 1940s and the mid-1950s, Paris produced a variety of other artwork, including illustrations for *Western Horseman* magazine and for various pulps published by Trojan. He also had several gallery shows of his paintings, many of them Western-themed. He passed away on March 19, 1994.

FCO Plascencia is a professional comic book colorist based in Mexico. A student of graphic design, he was handpicked by Greg Capullo to collaborate on Batman "because he's not your average colorist. His influences are film and fine arts, and he doesn't step on the line work." Plascencia's other works include *Spawn*, *Invincible*, *Haunt*, *Gemini*, and *The Walking Dead*, among others. He enjoys drawing, painting, and playing guitar.

It was around October 1939 when a 17-year-old **Jerry Robinson** began assisting Bob Kane. Robinson worked on *Rusty and His Pals* and *Clip Carson, Soldier of Fortune* in addition to lettering and inking backgrounds on Batman. Within three years, he was completely pencilling, lettering, inking and coloring certain stories and covers for *Batman* and *Detective Comics*. His contributions to Robin and the Joker proved to be significant events in Batman's history. Robinson's credits are many and diverse. They include advertising work and comic book art for Vigilante, Johnny Quick, and the Black Terror, as well as illustrations for science fiction, crime, war, Western, and other genres. He created and illustrated various syndicated newspaper features (including *Jet Scott*), and he taught and lectured on graphic journalism at the School of Visual Arts and the New School in New York City. Robinson is the only past president of both the Association of American Editorial Cartoonists and the National Cartoonists Society, and he was awarded three Reubens by the NCS. He also served as the president and editorial director of the Cartoonists & Writers Syndicate and on the board of directors of the International Museum of Cartoon Art. In addition to writing several books and illustrating more than 30 others, he produced the syndicated political cartoon *Life with Robinson* for many years and curated museum and gallery exhibitions of cartoon art in the U.S. and around the world. In 2004 Robinson was inducted into the Eisner Awards Hall of Fame. He passed away on December 11, 2011.

Born in August of 1920, **George Roussos** was 19 years old when he was hired by Jerry Robinson to assist on Batman. Roussos started on May 30, 1940, inking backgrounds and handling lettering. His first work appeared in *Batman* #2 (Summer 1940), and he became a mainstay on the character until 1944, when he left the DC bullpen to freelance. Roussos pencilled, inked, and colored Airwave, as well as inking Superman, Johnny Quick, Vigilante, the Star-Spangled Kid, and many other DC heroes. From the late 1940s into the 1950s, Roussos worked freelance for a number of comic book publishers, including Harvey, Hillman, Avon, Ziff-Davis, Fiction House, E.C., Timely, Prize, and Pines. In 1963 he began inking stories for Marvel (sometimes using the name George Bell), ultimately leaving DC around 1970 to work full-time as their cover colorist. Other efforts included work on syndicated newspaper strips and in advertising. Roussos remained in the comics industry well into the 1990s. He died on February 19, 2000.

Adrienne Roy began work in DC's famed bullpen before graduating to become a freelance colorist. She enjoyed long runs on numerous titles, including *Batman*, *Detective Comics*, and *The New Teen Titans*. She passed away on December 14, 2010.

Greg Rucka is the *New York Times* bestselling author of over two dozen novels and far too many comics to count. In the field of comics he is known for his work on such cultural icons as Batman in *Detective Comics*, Superman in both *Action Comics* and *Adventures of Superman*, and Wonder Woman in both *Wonder Woman* and the critically acclaimed graphic novel *Wonder Woman: The Hiketeia*. He is the creator of *Whiteout* (with artist Steve Lieber), *Queen & Country*, *Black Magick* (co-created with Wonder Woman artist Nicola Scott), and *Lazarus* (co-created with his *Gotham Central* collaborator, artist Michael Lark).

Born in New Bedford, Massachusetts, in 1926, **Lew Sayre Schwartz** studied at the Art Students League of New York and served as an aerial gunner, radar operator, and PR journalist in the military during World War II. He went to work for Bob Kane in 1947, becoming Kane's personal "ghost" artist until mid-1953. Schwartz drew all of Kane's contract work for DC during this period, providing carefully detailed pencils and leaving the figures of Batman and Robin for Kane to tighten. During those six years, Schwartz pencilled

BATMAN
DETECTIVE COMICS
THE SIGN OF THE JOKER
BATMAN
10¢

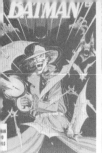

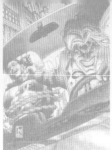

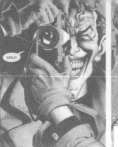

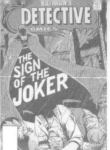

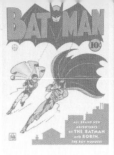

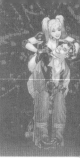

some 115 Batman stories, many of which would prove to be among the most popular of the Golden Age. At the same time, he also worked as a staff artist for King Features Syndicate and as a freelance illustrator for the advertising industry. In 1955 Schwartz joined the J. Walter Thompson agency in New York, launching a career as a writer, producer, and director for television advertising that would last for more than forty years. In 1961 he co-founded the film production company Ferro, Mogubgub, and Schwartz, which went on to win many national and international awards for creative filmmaking, including six Clios and four Emmys. Schwartz was honored in 2002 with the prestigious Inkpot Award at Comic-Con International in San Diego for his work on the Golden Age Batman. He passed away in 2011.

In the course of his more than four decades in the industry, **Walter Simonson** has made numerous important contributions to the world of comics, including the award-winning Manhunter feature he produced with comics legend Archie Goodwin in *Detective Comics* from 1973 to 1974. After Manhunter came to an end, *Detective* readers were treated to Simonson's first—but not his last—depiction of Batman in issue #450, a milestone that was followed by acclaimed contributions to such DC Comics series as *Orion*, *Hawkgirl*, and *Wednesday Comics*. For other publishers, Simonson's portfolio includes celebrated runs on *The Mighty Thor*, *Star Wars*, *World of Warcraft*, *X-Factor*, and *The Fantastic Four*. He works out of his home in upstate New York, where he lives with his wife, comic book writer and editor Louise Simonson.

Alex Sinclair has worked in the comic book industry as a colorist for 25 years. He has spent most of his career coloring for DC Comics and their many iconic characters. He has worked on many series, including *Batman*, *The Flash*, *Green Lantern*, *Justice League*, *Harley Quinn*, and *Wonder Woman*. His collaborations with Jim Lee and Scott Williams on *Batman: Hush*, as well as with Ivan Reis and Joe Prado on *Blackest Night*, earned him global recognition and multiple awards. Sinclair's recent projects include *Harley Quinn*, *Superman*, and *Hawkman*. He lives in San Diego with his wife, Rebecca, and their four daughters: Grace, Blythe, Meredith, and Harley.

The driving force behind the wildly successful *Batman: The Animated Series*, **Bruce Timm** both designed the unique look of the show and acted as one of the show's producers. He went on to co-create and produce *Superman: The Animated Series*, *Batman Beyond*, *Justice League*, and *Justice League Unlimited*. More recently, he has acted as Executive Producer on a series of direct-to-video films for Warner Bros. Animation, including *Batman: The Killing Joke*, *Justice League vs. The Fatal Five*, and *Superman: Red Son*. In addition to his animation work, Timm has written and drawn comics for DC, Marvel, Dark Horse, and Image. He has received several industry awards for his works in the animation and comics fields, including two Eisners and three Emmys.

Over the course of his long and prolific career, comics legend **Len Wein** did everything possible in the medium, including co-creating the popular characters Swamp Thing, Wolverine, Nightcrawler, Storm, Colossus, and the Human Target. He also served as a senior editor at DC Comics and as editor-in-chief at both Marvel and Disney Comics. Having written stories for just about every major character in the comic book world, Wein went on to write for television, film, and animation, including for such hit series as *X-Men*, *Spider-Man*, and *Batman: The Animated Series*. He passed away in 2017.

Scott Williams is a veteran inker whose 30-year career has featured collaborations with many of the top pencillers from the modern comics era. Best known for his long association with superstar artist Jim Lee, Williams has built a diverse and award-winning body of work over the course of their 25-year partnership, ranging from *X-Men* and *WildC.A.T.s* in the early days to the more recent *Batman: Hush*, *All-Star Batman and Robin, the Boy Wonder*, and the New 52 flagship titles *Justice League* and *Superman Unchained*.

Ryan Winn is a multimedia artist best known for his comic book inking and illustration. He found his way into comics after many years of doing displays and designs for the skate and surf industry. His first major inking assignment, for Top Cow's *The Darkness* in 2007, won him multiple award nominations, including the Harvey Award for Best Inker. He then found his way into Gotham City, where he has left his mark on the pages of *Batman*, *Batwing*, *Bruce Wayne: The Road Home*, *Detective Comics*, and *Red Hood*. When not inking, he also writes the indie hit *Gods and Gears*. He resides in Southern California with his wonderful wife Mia and their stupid cats, Rocket and Beans.

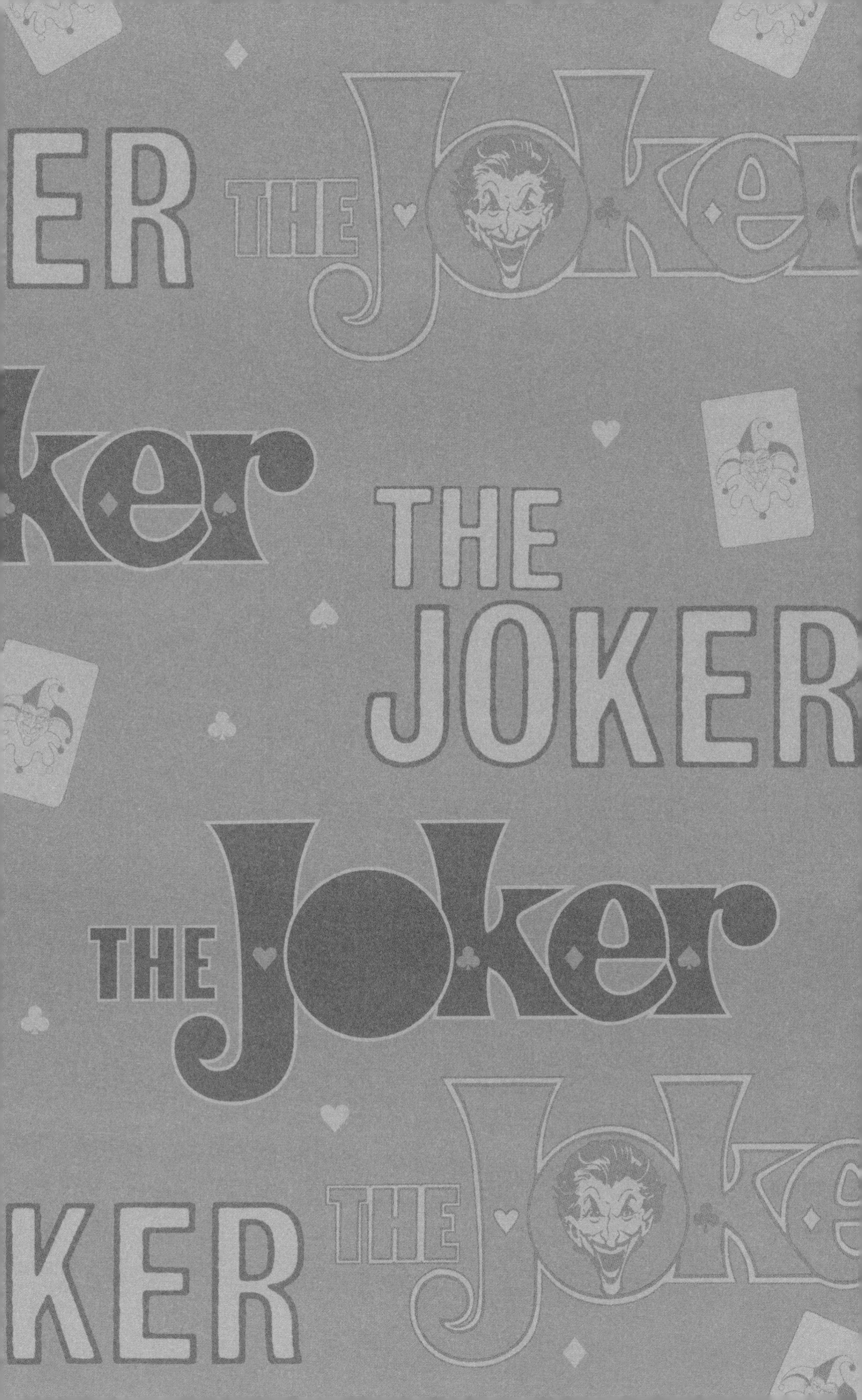
THE Joker
THE JOKER
THE Joker
THE Joker

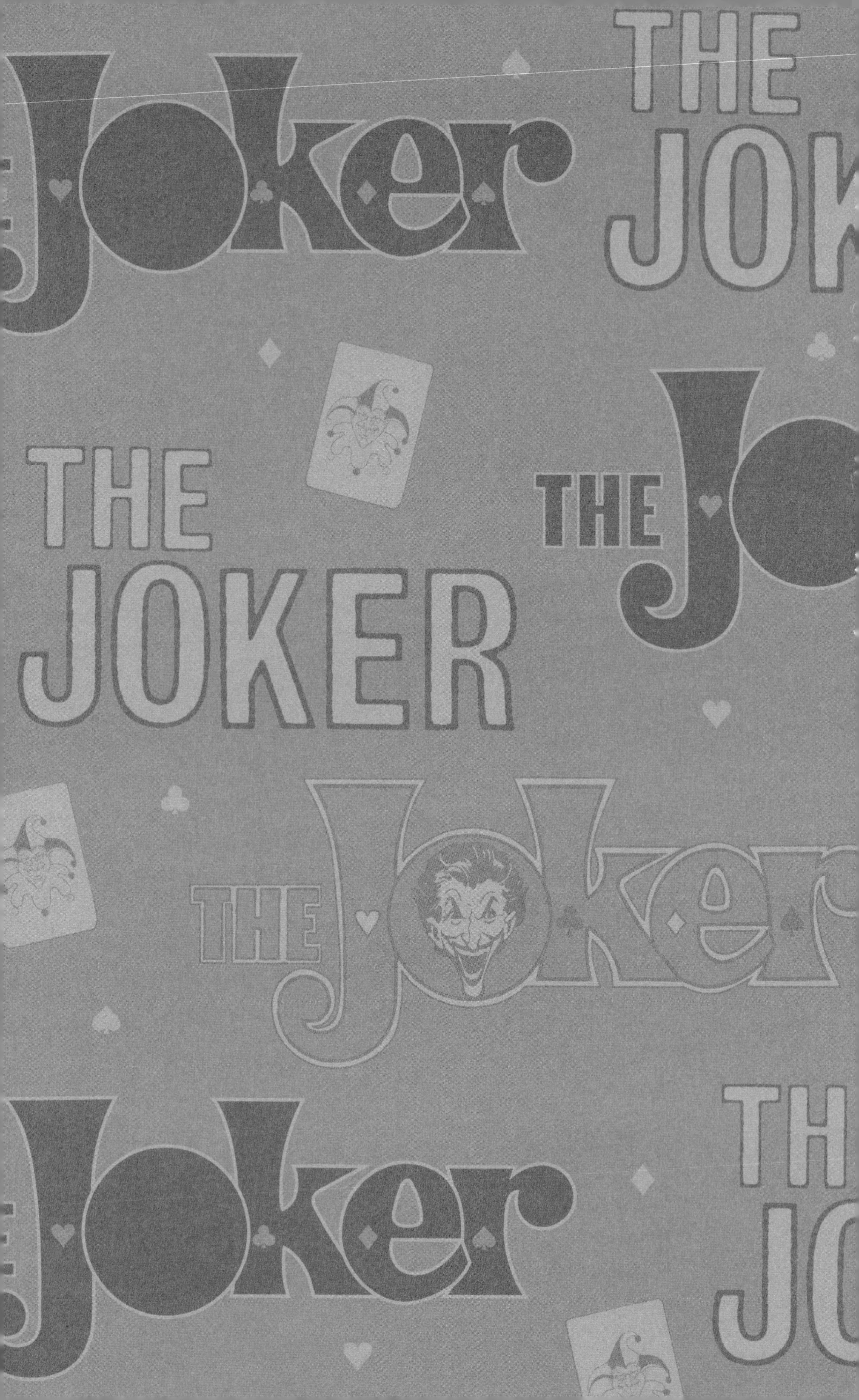
THE JOKER